8/24/05 28-54
8/30 54-66
66-71
9/6/05 227-238
9/13/05: 249-255 & 24[illegible]
9/15/05: assignment for 9[illegible]
~~9/~~ 9/20/05: Assignment for [illegible]
9/22/05: Assignment for 9/~~13~~ (revival) 310-316
Plus finish discussion of canon law (9/15)
9/27/05: 298 & 310-339
9/29/05: 316-350
~~T~~ 10/4/05: 435-458
10/6/05: 476-507
~~Tuesday~~: Tuesday: Prep for 25[illegible] - 795
11/1/05: 902-918 & 928-937
11/3/05 937-954 & 968-975

Paper Outline & Bibliography: Due 10/5

THE CIVIL LAW TRADITION: Europe, Latin America, and East Asia

Kevin C. Frank

The Civil Law Tradition:

Europe, Latin America, and East Asia

JOHN HENRY MERRYMAN
Nelson Bowman Sweitzer and Marie B. Sweitzer Professor of Law Emeritus
Stanford University

DAVID S. CLARK
Professor of Law
Director, Comparative and International Law Center
University of Tulsa

JOHN O. HALEY
Garvey, Schubert & Barer Professor of Law
Director, Asian Law Program
University of Washington

THE MICHIE COMPANY
Law Publishers
CHARLOTTESVILLE, VIRGINIA

Library of Congress Catalog Card No. 94-78455
ISBN 1-55834-180-3

Printed in the United States of America

1231010

To Nancy

— J.H.M.

For Marilee and
Lee, Susanna, Eliina, Liisa, and David

— D.S.C.

To Karin and Jorin, Star and Brook

— J.O.H.

Preface

This book, intended for use in introductory courses in comparative law or civil law systems, is the successor edition to John Henry Merryman and David S. Clark, *Comparative Law: Western European and Latin American Legal Systems* (1978). It is a successor edition rather than a second edition because, although it continues to instruct in the basics of the civil law tradition, it reflects also the truly fundamental changes that have occurred in the relationships among the world's major legal systems during the past 16 years.

First, it is time to recognize and deal with the contribution of the civil law tradition to contemporary national systems in East Asia. The civil law world is no longer confined to Europe and Latin America. Japan, whose legal system clearly displays the influence of French and German law, is the principal example. It is a major economic power exercising substantial *de facto* authority in world affairs. Japanese cultural influence is particularly strong in Taiwan and South Korea, while other East Asian nations have received the civil law through a variety of sources. For Americans engaged in business and governmental affairs, familiarity with the legal systems of East Asia has acquired increasing practical value as East Asian nations have achieved greater economic and political power.

Second, an enlarged 16-member-nation European Union (including Austria, and Finland, Norway, and Sweden, if approved by their electorates, beginning in 1995), serving 375 million persons, continues to integrate politically and to prosper economically. With this success the European Union, along with Japan and the new industrial nations of East Asia and the United States, have become the principal players in world affairs. The original six member states to the core European Community within the European Union, like the other continental countries of western Europe, are civil law nations. These six designed the supranational laws and institutions according to their own ideas about law. Although the United Kingdom and Ireland are today common law members, a thorough background in the civil law tradition is necessary to understand Community and Union law.

Third, with the decline of Soviet socialism has come a decline in the significance of socialist law. In most of the socialist nations, socialist law was little more than a superstructure of socialist concepts imposed on a civil law foundation. With the end of the Soviet empire the superstructure is being rapidly dismantled, and nations once considered "lost" to the European civil law are returning to it. The civil law world once again includes both eastern and western Europe.

Fourth, with the economic and political rise of the European Union and Japan, accompanied by the relative decline of the former Soviet Union and the United States, one cannot ignore the increased presence of Latin America, with a population of 484 million, in our new multipolar world. Brazil now has the tenth largest economy in the world, while Mexico is ranked fifteenth.

The aim of this book is to introduce the student to the family of legal systems common to Europe, Latin America, and East Asia. Throughout we provide readings that explain what binds together countries that participate in the world's oldest, most widely distributed, and most influential legal tradition. At the same time, we use materials from or about specific countries to illustrate the many fascinating variations that exist within the civil law tradition. The principal countries utilized for this purpose are France, Germany, Italy, and Spain within Europe; Argentina, Brazil, Colombia, and Mexico within Latin America; and Indonesia, Japan, South Korea, Taiwan, and Thailand in East Asia.

A distinguishing feature of this book is its relative deemphasis of rules and related doctrine and greater attention to the intellectual history (Chapters 3-5), structure (Chapters 6-7), professional actors (Chapter 8), and processes (Chapters 9-10) that are characteristic of civil law systems. Only in Chapter 11 (entitled "Substantive Rules and the Private Law Codes"), and then only briefly, do we direct our attention to the content of rules of law themselves (although in Chapter 2, "Litigating Cases with Foreign Parties or Foreign Law Issues in American Courts," a different kind of doctrinal emphasis prevails). Elsewhere throughout the book the emphasis is quite deliberately put on other matters. This emphasis expresses our view that it is seldom the rules of law that are truly significant or interesting about a foreign legal system; it is the social and intellectual climate, the institutional structures, the roles played by legal professionals, and the procedures characteristic of the legal system that are instructive. Often the rules of law look very much like our own — indeed, this is more and more true among the Western, capitalist nations, whether common law or civil law, that dominate the legal landscape of Europe, Latin America, and East Asia. As in our own law, finding the rule is often less of a problem than knowing what to do with it, and it is the difficult business of understanding the legal system within which the rules exist and operate that we have tried to illuminate.

We do not expect that many teachers will want to cover or will expect their students to study everything that is in this book. The inclusion of materials on Latin America and East Asia and the depth of treatment given to some topics provide both the opportunity, and the practical necessity, of choice. As with all casebooks, different users will for their own good reasons wish to omit some parts of this one. Where time is short, whole chapters may have to be skipped. With this common problem in mind we offer the following suggestions. The heart of the book is found in Chapters 3 to 11. It is in these chapters that the civil law systems of Europe, Latin America, and East Asia are described in a coherent and cumulative way. Each chapter, nevertheless, has a general treatment of its theme along with some illustrative statutes, cases, or secondary materials. Accordingly, while it is advisable to cover the general materials for all these chapters, it is possible to either narrow the focus by concentrating on Europe, Latin America, or East Asia (especially in Chapters 3 to 6) or by omitting particular materials that are intended for specific country illustration.

Chapters 1, 2, and 12 are more easily severable since they do not build on each other in the same way. Thus Chapter 1, which is an introduction to the civil law tradition and a survey of the principal objectives and methods of comparative law, may be merely assigned for reading without class discussion or omitted entirely in favor of the teacher's own treatment of these topics. Chapter 2, on litigating cases with foreign parties or foreign law issues in United States courts, is in one sense equally dispensable, but we would urge that it be retained. It may be used in two ways. Some have found that it should be taught early in the course so that students will be impressed with the practical nature of comparative law study. Others have found that this material provides a stimulating finale to the course because it clearly relates the study of foreign law to problems arising in domestic practice. The topic is of increasing practical importance, and the cases are interesting. This material also provides a number of opportunities to illustrate and summarize concepts that were introduced in other chapters and is thus a convenient context in which to do such summing up as the teacher may wish to offer. Lastly, Chapter 12 is an epilogue that raises several interesting recent developments within the civil law tradition.

Only selected footnotes have been reprinted. To aid anyone referring to the original source of a judicial opinion or excerpted article, we cite footnotes, when retained, by the numbers of the original. Our footnotes are lettered rather than numbered.

We are all products of the intellectual history of our discipline. It is accordingly proper to begin by acknowledging our indebtedness to the generations of scholars throughout the world whose wisdom and industry are embodied in the literature of comparative law. That literature provides the theoretical and informational base on which we build. We also owe a major undifferentiated debt to our often forbearing colleagues and students for ideas and criticism.

For their contributions to this book Professor Merryman is deeply indebted to Professor Lance Dickson and his staff in the Stanford Law Library for invaluable research and reference support and to Professors Sabino Cassese, Mauro Cappelletti, Giovanni Pugliese, Stefano Rodotà, and the late Gino Gorla for decades of stimulating, instructive conversation about the civil law tradition.

In any endeavor of this diversity, an immeasurable debt is owed to the librarians who assist one in the search for interesting materials. Professor Clark expresses deep appreciation to his friend, Dr. Jürgen Gödan, Director of the Library of the Max Planck Institute for Foreign and International Private Law in Hamburg, for the years of assistance in carrying out the work necessary to compile this volume. He also thanks his colleague at the University of Tulsa, Law Library Director Richard E. Ducey, and the library staffs in both Tulsa and Hamburg for facilitating this project. In addition, Professor Clark is grateful to Professors Ulrich Drobnig and Hein Kötz, directors at the Max Planck Institute, for their kind permission and support over the years to work at their superb institute. Finally, a debt of gratitude is owed to the University of Tulsa secretarial staff — Sharon Miller, Cyndee Jones, and Anna Hail — for typing the manuscript, and to Frances Warren and Don Whitenack at The Michie Company for coordinating the final production of the book.

Professor Haley owes a special thanks to many colleagues and students who have directly or indirectly contributed to these materials. Foremost among them is Dan Fenno Henderson, Professor Emeritus of the University of Washington and several University of Washington colleagues, Professors Don

Clarke, Jack Dull, Dan Foote, and Dan Lev. William McCloy, Comparative Law Librarian, and his assistants Rob Britt and David Ma, have provided invaluable bibliographical research assistance. For typing the manuscript and deciphering a hardly legible hand, Mary Jane Young and Jeri Miles deserve more than passing praise. Finally, acknowledgment is due the consistent support of Dean Wallace D. Loh and the many contributors to the Washington Law School Foundation.

John Henry Merryman
David S. Clark
John O. Haley

Acknowledgments

We acknowledge with thanks permission to reprint the following materials:

Luis Arechederra, The Death of a Bullfighter: Spanish Law on Privacy and the Right to Name and Likeness. This article is reproduced from 1991 Vol. 40 International and Comparative Law Quarterly 442-45 with permission from the publishers, The British Institute of International and Comparative Law, 17 Russell Square, London WC1B 5DR.

Peter Arens, Recent Trends in German Jurisdiction: The Transfer of Political and Administrative Duties to the Courts, in The Role of Courts in Society 97, 111-14, 117-22 (Shimon Shetreet ed. 1988). Reprinted by permission of Kluwer Academic Publishers.

Richard D. Baker, Judicial Review in Mexico: A Study of the Amparo Suit 252-54. Copyright © 1971. Reprinted by permission of the University of Texas Press.

David R. Barnhizer, Prophets, Priests, and Power Blockers: Three Fundamental Roles of Judges and Legal Scholars in America, 50 University of Pittsburgh Law Review 127 (1988). Reprinted by permission of the University of Pittsburgh Law Review and Professor David R. Barnhizer.

Burkhard Bastuck, Regional Developments: Germany, 27 International Lawyer 218, 224-25 (1993). Reprinted with permission of the author and the American Bar Association.

Fritz Baur, Einführung in das deutsche Recht, in Gesellschaft für Rechtsvergleichung, Bibliography of German Law in English and German: A Selection 12, 14 (Courtland H. Peterson trans. 1964). Reprinted with permission of Professor Courtland H. Peterson.

James Beardsley, Proof of Fact in French Civil Procedure, 34 American Journal of Comparative Law 459, 466-69, 475, 485-86 (1986). Reprinted with permission.

Lawrence W. Beer, Japan's Constitutional System and Its Judicial Interpretation, 17 Law in Japan 7, 20-21 (1984). Reprinted with permission.

Lenard R. Berlanstein, The Barristers of Toulouse in the Eighteenth Century (1740-1793), The Johns Hopkins University Press, Baltimore/London, 1975, pp. 1-4, 104-05. Reprinted by permission of Johns Hopkins University Press.

Harold J. Berman, Law and Revolution: The Formation of the Western Legal Tradition 52-59, 76, 81, 208-09, 212, 222-23, 226-34, 237-41, 245-48, 250-53, 297-98, 333-35, 339-41, 346-50 (1983). Reprinted by permission of the publishers from Law and Revolution by Harold J. Berman, Cambridge, Mass.: Harvard University Press, Copyright © 1983 by the President and Fellows of Harvard College. For permission to photocopy this selection, please contact Harvard University Press.

Harold J. Berman & Colin Kaufman, The Law of International Commercial Transactions (Lex Mercatoria), 19 Harvard International Law Journal 221, 226-27. Copyright © 1978 by the President and Fellows of Harvard College. Permission granted by the Harvard International Law Journal.

David Blachman, English translation, Case Comment, 19 Law in Japan 188-90 (1986). Reprinted with permission.

Erhard Blankenburg & Ulrike Schultz, German Advocates: A Highly Regulated Profession, in Lawyers in Society: Vol. 2, The Civil Law World 124, 131-38, 140-41 (Richard L. Abel & Philip S.C. Lewis eds.). Copyright © 1988 The Regents of the University of California. Reprinted with permission of the publisher, the University of California Press.

Anne Boigeol, The French Bar: The Difficulties of Unifying a Divided Profession, in Lawyers in Society: Vol. 2, The Civil Law World 258, 259-60, 262-68 (Richard L. Abel & Philip S.C. Lewis eds.). Copyright © 1988 The Regents of the University of California. Reprinted with permission of the publisher, the University of California Press.

Daniel J. Boorstin, The Mysterious Science of the Law 40, 42, 44, 47, 56, copyright © 1941 by Harvard University Press. Reprinted with permission of the publisher, Harvard University Press.

Woodrow Borah, Justice by Insurance: The General Indian Court of Colonial Mexico and the Legal Aides of the Half-Real 25, 27-32, 34-35, 38-40, 44-51, 53-54, 79, 120-21, 125-30, 144-47, 187, 189-90. Copyright © 1983 The Regents of the University of California. Reprinted with permission of the publisher, the University of California Press.

Gary B. Born & Scott Hoing, Comity and the Lower Courts: Post-*Aérospatiale* Applications of the Hague Evidence Convention, 24 International Lawyer 393-96 (1990). Reprinted with permission of the authors and the American Bar Assocation.

L. Neville Brown, The Sources of Spanish Civil Law. This article is reproduced from 1956 Vol. 5 International and Comparative Law Quarterly 364-70 with permission from the publishers, The British Institute of International and Comparative Law, 17 Russell Square, London WC1B 5DR.

L. Neville Brown & J.F. Garner, French Administrative Law 172-75 (3d ed. 1983). Reprinted by permission of Oxford University Press. Published by Oxford University Press in fourth edition by L. Neville Brown and John S. Bell (1993).

Woodfin L. Butte, Stare Decisis, Doctrine, and Jurisprudence in Mexico and Elsewhere, in The Role of Judicial Decisions & Doctrine in Civil Law & in Mixed Jurisdictions 311, 323-38 (J. Dainow ed. 1974). Reprinted by permission of Louisiana State University Press.

Mauro Cappelletti, John Henry Merryman & Joseph M. Perillo, The Italian Legal System: An Introduction 31-33, 35-38, 40-46, 52-54, 56-58, 60-70, 72-83, 98-99, 126-27, 229-39. Excerpted with permission of the publishers, Stanford University Press. © 1965, 1966 and 1967 by the Board of Trustees of the Leland Stanford Junior University.

Mauro Cappelletti, Monica Seccombe & Joseph H.H. Weiler, Integration Through Law: Europe and the American Federal Experience, A General Introduction, in Integration Through Law I, bk. 1, pp. 3, 5-6, 9-10 (Cappelletti et al. eds. 1986). Reprinted by permission of Walter de Gruyter & Co.

Thomas E. Carbonneau, The French Legal Studies Curriculum: Its History and Relevance as a Model for Reform, 25 McGill Law Journal 445, 463-74 (1980). Reprinted by permission of McGill Law Journal.

Oscar G. Chase, Civil Litigation Delay in Italy and the United States, 36 American Journal of Comparative Law 41, 70-74, 76-77 (1988). Reprinted with permission.

Edward I-to Chen, The Attempt to Integrate the Empire: Legal Perspectives, in The Japanese Colonial Empire, 1895-1945, at 268-74 (Ramon H. Myers & Mark R. Peattie eds. 1984). Copyright © 1984 by Princeton University Press. Reprinted with permission of Princeton University Press.

David S. Clark, The American Legal System and Legal Culture, in Introduction to the Law of the United States 1, 10-11 (Clark & Tuğrul Ansay eds. 1992). Reprinted with permission of Kluwer Law & Taxation Publishers.

David S. Clark, The Idea of the Civil Law Tradition, in Comparative and Private International Law: Essays in Honor of John Henry Merryman on His Seventieth Birthday 11, 12-16, 21-22 (David S. Clark ed. 1990). Reprinted with permission of Duncker & Humblot, Publishers, Berlin.

David S. Clark, Judicial Protection of the Constitution in Latin America, 2 Hastings Constitutional Law Quarterly 405, 416-22, 425-28, 431-42 (1975). Reprinted with permission.

David S. Clark, The Legal Profession in Comparative Perspective: Growth and Specialization, 30 American Journal of Comparative Law 163, 166-69 (Supp. 1982). Reprinted with permission.

David S. Clark, The Medieval Origins of Modern Legal Education: Between Church and State, 35 American Journal of Comparative Law 653, 661-67, 671-700, 717 (1987). Reprinted by permission of David S. Clark.

David S. Clark, The Organization and Social Status of Lawyers, in IXth World Conference on Procedural Law: General Reports 254, 275, 277-79 (1991). Reprinted by permission of David S. Clark.

David S. Clark, The Selection and Accountability of Judges in West Germany: Implementation of a *Rechtsstaat,* 61 Southern California Law Review 1795, 1802-06, 1808-14, 1829-32 (1988). Reprinted with permission of the Southern California Law Review.

David S. Clark, Witchcraft and Legal Pluralism: The Case of Célimo Miquirucamà, 15 Tulsa Law Journal 679, 679-83, 692-98 (1980). Reprinted by permission of The University of Tulsa.

Code of Canon Law, Latin-English Edition xvii-xix, xxviii, 387, 399, 401 (Canon Law Society of America trans. 1983). Copyright © 1983 Canon Law Society of America. Reprinted with permission.

E.J. Cohn, 1 Manual of German Law 56-57, 62-63, 94-96, 170-71, 221-22, 257-60, 282-83 (2d ed. 1968). This excerpt is reproduced with permission from the publishers, The British Institute of International and Comparative Law, 17 Russell Square, London WC1B 5DR.

Michael L. Conniff, Brazil: From Independence to 1964, in Latin America, Its Problems and Its Promise: A Multidisciplinary Introduction 475-79 (Jan Knippers Black ed. 1984). Reprinted by permission of Westview Press, Boulder, Colorado.

P.E.B. Coy, Justice for the Indian in Eighteenth Century Mexico, 12 American Journal of Legal History 41-46, 49 (1968). Reprinted with permission of the American Journal of Legal History.

Bernardo M. Cremades & Eduardo G. Cabiedes, Litigating in Spain 39, 41-46, 71 (1989). Reprinted with permission from Kluwer Law & Taxation Publishers.

Enrique Dahl & Alejandro M. Garro, Argentina: National Appeals Court (Criminal Division) Judgment on Human Rights Violations by Former Military Leaders. Reproduced with permission from 26 International Legal Materials 317, 317-19, 321-27 (1987), published by the American Society of International Law.

Mirjan Damaška, Atomistic and Holistic Evaluation of Evidence: A Comparative View, in Comparative and Private International Law: Essays in Honor of John Henry Merryman on His Seventieth Birthday 91-92 (David S. Clark ed. 1990). Reprinted with permission of Duncker & Humblot, Publishers, Berlin.

Mirjan Damaška, A Continental Lawyer in an American Law School: Trials and Tribulations of Adjustment, 116 University of Pennsylvania Law Review 1363, 1364-70, 1372-75. Copyright © 1968 by the University of Pennsylvania Law Review. Reprinted with permission.

Mirjan Damaška. The Faces of Justice and State Authority: A Comparative Approach to the Legal Process 16-18, copyright © 1986 by Yale University Press. Reprinted by permission of the publisher, Yale University Press.

Frank C. Darling, American Influence on the Evolution of Constitutional Government in Thailand 29-35 (Ph.D. dissertation, American University, 1961). Reprinted with permission of Frank C. Darling.

René David, French Law: Its Structure, Sources and Methodology 19-33, 35-36, 38-39, 41-45, 95-97, 108-22, 127-30, 132-35, 137-42, 144-46, 179-83 (Michael Kindred trans. 1972). Reprinted by permission of Louisiana State University Press.

René David & John E.C. Brierley, Major Legal Systems in the World Today: An Introduction to the Comparative Study of Law 1-3 (3d ed. 1985). Reprinted by permission of the publisher, Sweet & Maxwell Limited.

John P. Dawson, Gifts and Promises: Continental and American Laws Compared 41-42, copyright © 1980 by Yale University Press. Reprinted by permission of the publisher, Yale University Press.

John P. Dawson, The Oracles of the Law 101-03, 109-11, 196, 198-201, 203, 206-07, 227-28, 231, 240-41, 369-71, 375-76, 379-81, 391-94, 397-405, 409-10, 413-16, 425-31, 450-52, 454-60, 475-77 (1968). Reprinted by permission of the University of Michigan.

Louis F. Del Duca, An Historic Convergence of Civil and Common Law Systems — Italy's New "Adversarial" Criminal Procedure System, 10 Dickenson Journal of International Law 73, 87-88 (1991). Permission to reprint granted by the Dickenson Journal of International Law.

Peter J. Donaghy & Michael T. Newton, Spain: A Guide to Political and Economic Institutions 10-13, 19-21, 98, 100, 103-04, 112-13, 117-18 (1987). Reprinted with permission of Cambridge University Press.

Charles Donahue, Jr., On Translating the Digest, 39 Stanford Law Review 1057, 1058-59. Copyright © 1987 by the Board of Trustees of the Leland Stanford Junior University. Reprinted by permission of Stanford Law Review and Fred B. Rothman & Co.

Albert Ehrenzweig, Foreign Rules as "Sources of Law," in Legal Thought in the United States of America Under Contemporary Pressures 71, 77 (John N. Hazard & Wenceslas J. Wagner eds. 1970). Reprinted with permission of the American Journal of Comparative Law.

David M. Engel, Code and Custom in a Thai Provincial Court: The Interaction of Formal and Informal Systems of Justice 46-52 (1978). Reprinted with permission of David M. Engel.

David M. Engel, Law and Kingship in Thailand During the Reign of King Chulalongkorn, 9 Michigan Papers on South and Southeast Asia 16-17, 63-65, 69-70, 74-76 (1975). Reprinted with permission of David M. Engel and the Center for South and Southeast Asian Studies, The University of Michigan, Ann Arbor, Michigan.

Joaquim Falcão, Lawyers in Brazil, in Lawyers in Society: Vol. 2, The Civil Law World 400-01, 403-11, 417-22, 427-30 (Richard L. Abel & Philip S.C. Lewis eds.). Copyright © 1988 by The Regents of the University of California. Reprinted with permission of the publisher, the University of California Press.

William B. Fisch, Recent Developments in West German Civil Procedure, 6 Hastings International and Comparative Law 221, 254-57, 279-82 (1983). Reprinted with permission.

Bruce W. Frier, A Casebook on the Roman Law of Delict 3, 227 (1989). Reprinted by permission of the American Philological Association.

Bruce W. Frier, Autonomy of Law and the Origins of the Legal Profession, 11 Cardozo Law Review 259, 262-66 (1989). Reprinted by permission of Cardozo Law Review.

The Institutes of Gaius 19, 21, 23 (trans. by W.M. Gordon & O.F. Robinson 1988). Reprinted by permission of W.M. Gordon & O.F. Robinson.

Alejandro M. Garro, Nine Years of Transition to Democracy in Argentina: Partial Failure or Qualified Success?, 31 Columbia Journal of Transnational Law 1, 29-34, 37-46 (1993). Reprinted with permission.

Jane C. Ginsburg & Pierre Sirinelli, Authors and Exploitations in International Private Law: The French Supreme Court and the Huston Film Colorization Controversy, 15 Columbia-VLA Journal of Law & the Arts 135, 135-38, 159 (1991). Reprinted with permission.

Mary Ann Glendon, Abortion and Divorce in Western Law 5-8, 16-18, 31-32 (1987). Reprinted by permission of the publishers from Abortion and Divorce in Western Law by Mary Ann Glendon, Cambridge, Mass.: Harvard University Press, copyright © 1987 by the President and Fellows of Harvard College. For permission to photocopy this selection, please contact Harvard University Press.

Mary Ann Glendon, The Sources of Law in a Changing Legal Order, 17 Creighton Law Review 663, 682-84 (1984). Reprinted with permission. Copyright © 1984 by Creighton Law Review.

Mary Ann Glendon, The Transformation of Family Law: State, Law, and Family in the United States and Western Europe 97-99, copyright © 1989 by the University of Chicago Press. Reprinted with permission.

Roger J. Goebel, Professional Qualification and Educational Requirements for Law Practice in a Foreign Country: Bridging the Cultural Gap, 63 Tulane Law Review 443, 444-51, 453-54 (1989). Reprinted with permission of the Tulane Law Review Association.

Abraham S. Goldstein & Martin Marcus, The Myth of Judicial Supervision in Three "Inquisitorial" Systems: France, Italy and Germany, 87 Yale Law Journal 240 (1977). Reprinted by permission of Abraham S. Goldstein.

Gino Gorla, Civilian Judicial Decisions — An Historical Account of Italian Style, 44 Tulane Law Review 740, 748-49 (1970). Reprinted with permission of the Tulane Law Review Association.

Gino Gorla, A Decision of the Rota Fiorentina of 1780 on Liability for Damages Caused by the "Ball Game," 49 Tulane Law Review 346, 346-55 (1975). Reprinted with permission of the Tulane Law Review Association.

Julian Gresser, English translation, Koichiro Fujikura & Akio Morishima, Environmental Law in Japan 86, 91-96 (1981). Reprinted with permission of The MIT Press, Cambridge, Mass., Publisher. Copyright © 1981 by The MIT Press.

John Owen Haley, Authority Without Power: Law and the Japanese Paradox 38-40, 58-62, 70-72, 78-80, 125-33, 135-38 (1991). Copyright © 1991 by Oxford University Press. Reprinted with permission.

John O. Haley, Japanese Administrative Law: Introduction, 19 Law in Japan 1, 4-14 (1986). Reprinted with permission.

John O. Haley, The Myth of the Reluctant Litigant, originally published in The Journal of Japanese Studies, Vol. 4, No. 2, pp. 359-62, 365-71, 378-80 (Summer 1978). Reprinted by permission of the Society for Japanese Studies.

John O. Haley, Redefining the Scope of Practice Under Japan's New Regime for Regulating Foreign Lawyers, 21 Law in Japan 18, 19-21 (1988). Reprinted with permission.

John O. Haley & Dan Fenno Henderson, Law and the Legal Process in Japan 814-16, 897-902 (1988 ed.). Reprinted by permission of the Asian Law Program at the University of Washington.

Fred R. Harris, Mexico: Historical Foundations, in Latin America, Its Problems and Its Promise: A Multidisciplinary Introduction 261, 262-67 (Jan Knippers Black ed. 1984). Reprinted by permission of Westview Press, Boulder, Colorado.

Hiroyuki Hata, Malapportionment of Representation in the National Diet, 53 Law and Contemporary Problems, 157-60, 170 (No. 2, 1990). Copyright 1990, Duke University School of Law. Reprinted with permission.

Hiroyuki Hattori, Stephan M. Salzberg, Winston P. Kiang, Tatsuya Fujimiya, Yutaka Tejima & Junji Furuno, The Patient's Right to Information in Japan: Legal Rules and Doctors' Opinions, 32 Social Science & Medicine (No. 9) 1007-1010 (1991). Reprinted with permission of Pergamon Press Ltd., Oxford, England.

Dan Fenno Henderson, Foreign Enterprise in Japan: Laws and Policies 177-85 (1973). Copyright © 1973 by The University of North Carolina Press. Used by permission of the publisher.

Dan Fenno Henderson, The Japanese Law in English: Some Thoughts on Scope and Method, 16 Vanderbilt Journal of Transnational Law 601, 606-12. Copyright © 1983 by the Vanderbilt Journal of Transnational Law. Reprinted with permission.

Joachim Herrmann, Bargaining Justice — A Bargain for German Criminal Justice?, 53 University of Pittsburgh Law Review 755, 755-56 (1992). Reprinted by permission of the University of Pittsburgh Law Review.

Yoshirō Hiramatsu, Tokugawa Law, 14 Law in Japan 1, 27-28, 31-38 (Dan Fenno Henderson trans. 1981). Reprinted with permission.

Norbert Horn, Hein Kötz & Hans G. Leser, German Private and Commercial Law: An Introduction 16-23 (Tony Weir trans. 1982). Reprinted with permission.

R.A. Humphreys & John Lynch, Introduction, in The Origins of the Latin American Revolutions: 1808-1826, at 3-5, 10-14, 24, 26-27 (R.A. Humphreys & John Lynch eds. 1965). Copyright © 1965 by Alfred A. Knopf, Inc. Reprinted by permission of the publisher.

David Johnston, The Roman Law of Trusts 2-4 (1988). Reprinted by permission of Oxford University Press.

H.F. Jolowicz & Barry Nicholas, Historical Introduction to the Study of Roman Law 118-20 (3d ed. 1972). Reprinted with permission of Cambridge University Press.

Matti Joutsen, Listening to the Victim: The Victim's Role in European Criminal Justice Systems, 34 Wayne Law Review 95, 115-16 (1987). Reprinted with permission of the Wayne Law Review.

1 Digest of Justinian 2, 19-24, 174-75, 179-80, 277, 292-93; 4 Digest of Justinian 819 (Theodor Mommsen, Paul Krueger & Alan Watson eds., Watson trans. 1985). Reprinted by permission of the University of Pennsylvania Press.

Richard L. Kagan, Lawyers and Litigation in Castile, 1500-1750, in Lawyers in Early Modern Europe and America 181, 184-87, edited by Wilfrid Prest (New York: Holmes & Meier, 1981). Copyright © 1981 by Wilfrid Prest. Reprinted by permission of the publisher.

Shoji Kawakami, Precontractual Liability: Japan, in Precontractual Liability: Reports to the XIIIth Congress of the International Academy of Comparative Law 205-21 (E.H. Hondius ed. 1990). Reprinted with permission from Kluwer Law & Taxation Publishers.

Takeyoshi Kawashima, The Concept of Judicial Precedent in Japanese Law, in 1 Ius Privatum Gentium: Festschrift für Max Rheinstein zum 70. Geburtstag am 5. Juli 1969, at 85, 87-88, 91-95, 98-99 (Ernst von Caemmerer, Soia Mentschikoff & Konrad Zweigert eds. 1969). Reprinted with permission of J.C.B. Mohr (Paul Siebeck), Tubingen.

Chin Kim & Eliseo Z. Sisneros, Comparative Overview of Service of Process: United States, Japan, and Attempts at International Unity, 23 Vanderbilt Journal of Transnational Law 299, 306-09. Copyright © 1990 by the Vanderbilt Journal of Transnational Law. Reprinted with permission.

Zentaro Kitagawa, Theory Reception: One Aspect of the Development of Japanese Civil Law, in John O. Haley & Dan Fenno Henderson, Law and the Legal Process in Japan 270-72 (1988 ed.). Reprinted by permission of the Asian Law Program at the University of Washington.

Harvey F. Kline, Colombia: The Struggle Between Traditional "Stability" and New Visions, in Latin American Politics and Development 231, 251-52 (H. Wiarda & H. Kline eds., 3d ed. 1990). Reprinted by permission of Westview Press, Boulder, Colorado.

Takeshi Kojima, Civil Procedure Reform in Japan, 11 Michigan Journal of International Law 1218-19 (1990). Reprinted with permission of the author and the Michigan Journal of International Law.

Donald P. Kommers, The Constitutional Jurisprudence of the Federal Republic of Germany 67-68, 85-88, 366, 368-75, 388. Copyright Duke University Press, 1989. Reprinted with permission of the publisher.

Donald P. Kommers, German Constitutionalism: A Prolegomenon, 40 Emory Law Journal 837-38, 840-52, 855-56, 858-61, 864-73 (1991). Reprinted with permission.

Donald P. Kommers, Judicial Politics in West Germany: A Study of the Federal Constitutional Court 211-12 (1976). Reprinted with permission of Sage Publications.

Hein Kötz, Civil Litigation and the Public Interest, 1 Civil Justice Quarterly 237, 241-43 (1982). Reprinted with permission of Sweet & Maxwell Ltd.

Hein Kötz, Scholarship and the Courts: A Comparative Survey, in Comparative and Private International Law: Essays in Honor of John Henry Merryman on His Seventieth Birthday 183, 184-86, 190-91, 193-94 (David S. Clark ed. 1990). Reprinted with permission of Duncker & Humblot, Publishers, Berlin.

John A. Langbein, Mixed Court and Jury Court: Could the Continental Alternative Fill the American Need?, 1981 American Bar Foundation Research Journal 195, 197-205 (1981). Copyright © 1981 by the American Bar Foundation. Reprinted with permission of the author and of Law and Social Inquiry, Journal of the American Bar Foundation.

Edward P. Lanning, Peru Before the Incas 171-72, copyright © 1967. Reprinted by permission of the publisher, Prentice Hall, a division of Simon & Schuster, Englewood Cliffs, N.J.

F.H. Lawson, A Common Lawyer Looks at the Civil Law 3-4 (1955). Reprinted by permission of the University of Michigan Press.

Daniel S. Lev, Judicial Institutions and Legal Culture in Indonesia, in Culture and Politics in Indonesia 283, 285-87, edited by Claire Holt with the assistance of Benedict R. Anderson & James Siegel. Copyright © 1972 by Cornell University. Used by permission of the publisher, Cornell University Press.

Alain Levasseur, On the Structure of a Civil Code, 44 Tulane Law Review 693, 694-97, 699-703 (1970). Reprinted with permission of the Tulane Law Review Association.

Herbert H.B. Ma, The Sources and Structure of Modern Chinese Law and The Chinese Judicial System, in Trade and Investment in Taiwan 3-5, 27-33,

52-53 (2d ed. 1985). Reprinted by permission of the Institute of European and American Studies, Academia Sinica.

Colin M. MacLachlan, Criminal Justice in Eighteenth-Century Mexico: A Study of the Tribunal of the Acordada 1-2, 15-16, 21-28, 31-32. Copyright © 1974 by The Regents of the University of California. Reprinted with permission of the publisher, the University of California Press.

Juan G. Matus Valencia, The Centenary of the Chilean Civil Code, 7 American Journal of Comparative Law 71-77 (1958). Reprinted with permission.

James R. Maxeiner, Book Review of Procedure in the United States: A Practical Guide for German Businesses, 23 International Lawyer 321, 323 (1989). Reprinted by permission of the American Bar Association.

Robert C. Means, Codification in Latin America: The Colombian Commercial Code of 1853. Published originally in 52 Texas Law Review 18, 20-24 (1973). Copyright © 1973 by the Texas Law Review Association. Reprinted with permission of the author and the Texas Law Review Association.

John Henry Merryman, The Civil Law Tradition: An Introduction to the Legal Systems of Western Europe and Latin America 1-18, 30-32, 40-41, 48-55, 57, 59-67, 69-79, 87-88, 90-108, 111-15, 117-32, 136-40 (2d ed. 1985). Excerpted with permission of the publishers, Stanford University Press. © 1969, 1985 by the Board of Trustees of the Leland Stanford Junior University.

John Henry Merryman, Comparative Law and Scientific Explanation, in Law in the United States of America in Social and Technological Revolution 81, 82-86 (John N. Hazard & Wenceslas J. Wagner eds. 1974). Reprinted by permission of Establissements Emile Bruyland.

John Henry Merryman, Foreign Law as a Problem, 19 Stanford Journal of International Law 151, 154-55, 172-73 (1983). Reprinted with permission.

John Henry Merryman, The Italian Style III: Interpretation, 18 Stanford Law Review 583, 585-96. Copyright © 1966 by the Board of Trustees, Leland Stanford Junior University. Reprinted by permission of Stanford Law Review and Fred B. Rothman & Co.

John Henry Merryman, Legal Education There and Here: A Comparison, 27 Stanford Law Review 859, 861-66, 868-71, 874-76 (1975). Copyright © 1975 by the Board of Trustees of the Leland Stanford Junior University. Reprinted with permission of Stanford Law Review.

John Henry Merryman, On the Convergence (and Divergence) of the Civil Law and the Common Law, 17 Stanford Journal of International Law 357, 359-73, 387-88. Copyright © 1981 by the Board of Trustees, Leland Stanford Junior University. Reprinted by permission of Stanford Journal of International Law.

John Henry Merryman, Ownership and Estate (Variations on a Theme by Lawson), 48 Tulane Law Review 916, 924-45 (1974). Reprinted with permission of the Tulane Law Review Association.

Setsuo Miyazawa, Taking Kawashima Seriously: A Review of Japanese Research on Japanese Legal Consciousness and Disputing Behavior, 21 Law & Society Review 219, 231, 234-35 (1987). Reprinted by permission of the Law and Society Association.

Sally F. Moore, Power and Property in Inca Peru 74-84, 100, 102-03, 111-13, 115-21. Copyright © 1958 by Columbia University Press. Reprinted with permission of the publisher.

F.L. Morton, Judicial Review in France: A Comparative Analysis, 36 American Journal of Comparative Law 89-92, 94-96, 98-100 (1988). Reprinted with permission.

Laura Nader, Harmony Ideology: Justice and Control in a Zapotec Mountain Village 6-8, 10, 15-16, 29-31, 109, 120-22, 125, 127, 146-48, 162-63, 165-67, 169-71, 181 (1990). Excerpted with permission of the publishers, Stanford University Press. © 1990 by the Board of Trustees of the Leland Stanford Junior University.

Mutsuo Nakamura, Freedom of Economic Activities and the Right to Property, 53 Law and Contemporary Problems 1, 4-9 (No. 2, 1990). Copyright 1990, Duke University School of Law. Reprinted with permission.

Martin C. Needler, Mexican Politics: The Containment of Conflict 87-90, 94-96 (2d ed. 1990). Reprinted by permission of Martin C. Needler, Dean, School of International Studies, University of the Pacific, Stockton, CA 95211.

Barry Nicholas, The French Law of Contract 14-16 (1982). Reprinted by permission of Oxford University Press. Published by Oxford University Press in second edition (1992).

Barry Nicholas, An Introduction to Roman Law 3-25, 27-34, 36-42 (1969). Reprinted by permission of Oxford University Press.

Yoshio Ohara, Judicial Assistance to Be Afforded by Japan for Proceedings in the United States, 23 International Lawyer 10-11, 18-22, 25-27 (1989). Reprinted with permission of the author and the American Bar Association.

Vittorio Olgiati & Valerio Pocar, The Italian Legal Profession: An Institutional Dilemma, in Lawyers in Society: Vol. 2, The Civil Law World 336, 344-46 (Richard L. Abel & Philip S.C. Lewis eds.). Copyright © 1988 The Regents of the University of California. Reprinted with permission of the publisher, the University of California Press.

Oliver Passavant & Gerhard Nösser, The German Reunification — Legal Implications for Investment in East Germany, 25 International Lawyer 875-76, 878-79 (1991). Copyright © 1991 American Bar Association. Reprinted with permission.

Rogelio Pérez Perdomo, La justicia penal en la investigación socio-jurídica de América Latina, in Comparative and Private International Law: Essays in Honor of John Henry Merryman on His Seventieth Birthday 257, 272-74 (1990). Reprinted with permission of Duncker & Humblot, Publishers, Berlin.

William T. Pizzi & Luca Marafioti, The New Italian Code of Criminal Procedure: The Difficulties of Building an Adversarial Trial System on a Civil Law Foundation, 17 Yale Journal of International Law 1, 10-15, 17, 19-26, 33-35 (1992). Reprinted with permission.

Alessandro Pizzorusso, The Italian Constitution: Implementation and Reform, 34 Jahrbuch des öffentlichen Rechts der Gegenwart 105, 114-16 (Peter Häberle ed. 1985). Reprinted with permission of J.C.B. Mohr (Paul Siebeck), Tubingen.

André Pouille, Le pouvoir judiciare et les tribunaux 11, 20 (1985). Reprinted by permission of Masson S.A., 120, Boulevard St. Germain, 75280 Paris Cedex 06.

Darrell Prescott & Edwin R. Alley, Effective Evidence-Taking Under the Hague Convention, 22 International Lawyer 939, 964-80 (1988). Reprinted with permission of the authors and the American Bar Association.

Peter E. Quint, Free Speech and Private Law in German Constitutional Theory, 48 Maryland Law Review 247, 339-42, 344-45, 347 (1989). Reprinted by permission of Peter E. Quint.

Dallis Radamaker, The Courts in France, in The Political Role of Law Courts in Modern Democracies 129, 143 (1988). Reprinted by permission of the editors, Jerold L. Waltman and Kenneth M. Holland.

J. Mark Ramseyer, Legal Rules in Repeated Deals: Banking in the Shadow of Defection in Japan, 20 Journal of Legal Studies 91, 110-11, copyright © 1991 by the University of Chicago Press. Reprinted with permission.

J. Mark Ramseyer & Minoru Nakazato, The Rational Litigant: Settlement Amounts and Verdict Rates in Japan, 18 Journal of Legal Studies (No. 2) 263, 266-72, 289-90, copyright © 1989 by the University of Chicago Press. Reprinted with permission.

Recent Developments, 9 Law in Japan 151-52 (1976). Reprinted with permission.

Ruth Redmond-Cooper, The Relevance of Fault in Determining Liability for Road Accidents: The French Experience, 38 International and Comparative Law Quarterly 502-09 (1989). This article is reproduced with permission from the publishers The British Institute of International and Comparative Law, 17 Russell Square, London WC1B 5DR.

Mathias Reimann, The Historical School Against Codification: Savigny, Carter, and the Defeat of the New York Civil Code, 37 American Journal of Comparative Law 95, 97-98 (1989). Reprinted with permission.

John C. Reitz, Why We Probably Cannot Adopt the German Advantage in Civil Procedure, 74 Iowa Law Review 987 (1990). Reprinted by permission of Iowa Law Review.

Max Rheinstein, Comparative Law — Its Functions, Methods and Usages, 22 Arkansas Law Review and Bar Association Journal 415, 418-19 (1968). Reprinted by permission of Arkansas Law Review and Bar Association Journal.

O.F. Robinson, T.D. Fergus & W.M. Gordon, An Introduction to European Legal History 151, 172-73, 176-77, 354-55, 357-58, 360-61 (1985). Reprinted by permission of O.F. Robinson, T.D. Fergus & W.M. Gordon.

Keith S. Rosenn, Brazil's Legal Culture: The Jeito Revisited, 1 Florida International Law Journal 1, 2-5, 14-15, 17-25, 29-30 (1984). Reprinted with permission of the Florida International Law Journal, copyright © 1984.

Keith S. Rosenn, Civil Procedure in Brazil, 34 American Journal of Comparative Law 487-90, 523-25 (1986). Reprinted with permission.

Keith S. Rosenn, A Comparison of the Protection of Individual Rights in the New Constitutions of Colombia and Brazil, 23 University of Miami Inter-American Law Review 659, 680-86 (1992). Reprinted with permission.

Keith S. Rosenn, The Protection of Judicial Independence in Latin America, 19 University of Miami Inter-American Law Review 1, 8, 12, 32 (1987). Reprinted with permission of the University of Miami.

K.W. Ryan, An Introduction to the Civil Law 15-22, 279 (1962). Reprinted by permission of The Law Book Company Limited.

Rudolf B. Schlesinger, Comparing Criminal Procedure: A Plea for Utilizing Foreign Experience, 26 Buffalo Law Review 361, 364-72, 373-81 (1977). Copyright © 1977 by Buffalo Law Review. Reprinted with permission.

Rudolf B. Schlesinger, A Recurrent Problem in Transnational Litigation: The Effect of Failure to Invoke or Prove the Applicable Foreign Law, 59 Cornell Law Review 1, 2-5, 16-23 (1973). Copyright © 1973 by Cornell University. All Rights Reserved. Reprinted with permission of Cornell Law Review and Fred B. Rothman & Co.

Stuart B. Schwartz, Sovereignty and Society in Colonial Brazil: The High Court of Bahia and Its Judges, 1609-1751, xiv-xv, 173-74, 185-86, 293-94, 304-05. Copyright © 1973 by The Regents of the University of California. Reprinted with permission of the publisher, the University of California Press.

Samuel P. Scott, Las Siete Partidas 960-63 (1931). Reproduced with permission from Las Sietas Partidas by Commerce Clearing House, Inc., 4025 W. Peterson Avenue, Chicago, Illinois 60646, © 1993.

William Shaw, Social and Intellectual Aspects of Traditional Korean Law, in Traditional Korean Attitudes 15, 25-32 (Bong Duck Chun, William Shaw & Dai-kwon Choi eds.) (Berkeley: Institute of East Asian Studies, University of California, 1980). Copyright 1980 by The Regents of the University of California. Reprinted by permission.

Shuzo Shiga, Some Remarks on the Judicial System in China: Historical Development and Characteristics, in Traditional and Modern Legal Institutions in Asia and Africa (David C. Buxbaum ed.) 46-51 (1967). Reprinted with permission of E.J. Brill, Ltd., Leiden.

Peter G. Snow & Gary W. Wynia, Argentina: Politics in a Conflict Society, in Latin American Politics and Development 129, 159-61 (H. Wiarda & H. Kline eds., 3d ed. 1990). Reprinted by permission of Westview Press, Boulder, Colorado.

Kazuaki Sono & Yasuhiro Fujioka, The Role of the Abuse of Right Doctrine in Japan. Originally published in 35 Louisiana Law Review 1037, 1038-46. Copyright 1975, The Louisiana Law Review. All rights reserved.

Frederic Spotts & Theodor Weiser, Italy: A Difficult Democracy 158-61, 283, 290-92 (1986). Reprinted with permission of Cambridge University Press.

John G. Sprankling & George R. Lanyi, Pleading and Proof of Foreign Law in American Courts, 19 Stanford Journal of International Law 3, 89 (1983). Reprinted with permission.

Peter G. Stein, "Equitable" Remedies for the Protection of Property, in New Perspectives in the Roman Law of Property: Essays for Barry Nicholas 185, 185-86 (Peter Birks ed. 1989). Reprinted by permission of Oxford University Press.

Thomas B. Stephens, Order and Discipline in China: The Shanghai Mixed Court, 1911-27, at 3-5, 7-9, 11-12 (1992). Reprinted with permission of the University of Washington Press.

Steve Stern, The Social Significance of Judicial Institutions in an Exploitative Society: Huamanga, Peru, 1570-1640, in The Inca and Aztec States, 1400-1800: Anthropology and History 289, 293-94, 307-08, 310-11 (George A. Collier, Renato I. Rosaldo & John D. Wirth eds. 1982). Reprinted by permission of the author and Academic Press.

Richard Stith, New Constitutional and Penal Theory in Spanish Abortion Law, 35 American Journal of Comparative Law 513, 515-19 (1987). Reprinted with permission.

Bailey Stone, The French Parlements and the Crisis of the Old Regime 18-20 (1986). Copyright © 1986 by The University of North Carolina Press. Used by permission of the publisher.

Ferdinand F. Stone, The End to Be Served by Comparative Law, 25 Tulane Law Review 325, 325 (1951). Reprinted with permission of the Tulane Law Review Association.

Kazayuki Takahashi, Comment, 53 Law and Contemporary Problems 189, 190-92 (No. 2, 1990). Copyright 1990, Duke University School of Law. Reprinted with permission.

Denis Tallon, Reforming the Codes in a Civil Law Country, 15 Journal of the Society of Public Teachers of Law 33-41 (1980). Reproduced by permission of Butterworth & Co. (Publishers) Ltd. and Professor P.B.H. Birks, Oxford University.

Hideo Tanaka, The Constitutional System of Japan and the Judicial System, in Law and Business in Japan 1-7, 18-21 (Akira Kawamura ed. 1982). Reprinted with permission.

Hideo Tanaka, The Role of Law in Japanese Society, Comparisons with the West, 19 University of British Columbia Law Review (No. 2) 375-76 (1985). Reprinted by permission of the University of British Columbia Law Review.

Yasuhei Taniguchi, Shihō Kenshū Sho ni okeru hōsō kyōiku (Legal Education at the Legal Training and Research Institute), 25 Jiyū to seigi (Liberty and Justice) 7-12 (1974). Translated and reprinted with permission of Yasuhei Taniguchi.

Edward A. Tomlinson, The Saga of Wiretapping in France: What It Tells Us About the French Criminal Justice System, 53 Louisiana Law Review 1091, 1103-09 (1993). Reprinted with permission of the Louisiana Law Review.

André Tunc, English translation, Traffic Accidents: Fault or Risk?, 15 Seton Hall Law Review 831, 838-39 (1985). Reprinted with permission of the Seton Hall Law Review.

R.C. van Caenegem, Judges, Legislators and Professors: Chapters in European Legal History 114-15, 117-22 (1987). Reprinted with permission of Cambridge University Press.

Paul Veyne, The Roman Empire, in 1 A History of Private Life: From Pagan Rome to Byzantium 166-68 (Veyne ed., Arthur Goldhammer trans. 1987). Reprinted by permission of the publishers from A History of Private Life: From Pagan Rome to Byzantium, Volume I, edited by Paul Veyne, translated by Arthur Goldhammer, Cambridge, Mass.: The Belknap Press of

Harvard University Press, Copyright © 1987 by the President and Fellows of Harvard College.

Carlos Viladás Jene, The Legal Profession in Spain: An Understudied but Booming Occupation, in Lawyers in Society: Vol. 2, The Civil Law World 369-73, 375-76 (Richard L. Abel & Philip S.C. Lewis eds.). Copyright © 1988 by The Regents of the University of California. Reprinted with permission of the publisher, the University of California Press.

Sarasin Viraphol, Law in Traditional Siam and China: A Comparative Study, 65 Journal of the Siam Society 109-15, 124 (1977). Reprinted with permission of the Siam Society.

Cynthia Vroom, Constitutional Protection of Individual Liberties in France: The Conseil Constitutionnel since 1971, 63 Tulane Law Review 265, 266, 279-82, 295-97, 314-15 (1988). Reprinted with permission of the Tulane Law Review Association.

Alan Watson, Failures of the Legal Imagination 11-12 (1988). Reprinted by permission of the University of Pennsylvania Press.

Alan Watson, Society and Legal Change 1-4, 7-8, 23-29, 98-99, 102-05, 140-41 (1977). Reprinted by permission of the Scottish Academic Press.

Alan Watson, The Making of the Civil Law, 168-78 (1981). Reprinted with permission of the publishers from The Making of the Civil Law by Alan Watson, Cambridge, Mass.: Harvard University Press, Copyright © 1981 by the President and Fellows of Harvard College.

James M. West & Dae-Kyu Yoon, The Constitutional Court of the Republic of Korea: Transforming the Jurisprudence of the Vortex, 40 American Journal of Comparative Law 73-77, 88-90, 92-94, 103-06, 111-15 (1992). Reprinted with permission.

Howard J. Wiarda & Harvey F. Kline, The Latin American Tradition and Process of Development, in Latin American Politics and Development 1, 81-94 (H. Wiarda & H. Kline eds., 3d ed. 1990). Reprinted by permission of Westview Press, Boulder, Colorado.

Iêda Siqueira Wiarda, Brazil: The Politics of Order and Progress, in Latin American Politics and Development 167, 190-93 (H. Wiarda & H. Kline eds., 3d ed. 1990). Reprinted by permission of Westview Press, Boulder, Colorado.

Franz Wieacker, The Importance of Roman Law for Western Civilization and Western Legal Thought, 4 Boston College International and Comparative Law Review 257, 267-68 (1981). Reprinted by permission of Boston College International and Comparative Law Review.

Richard J. Wilson, The New Legal Education in North and South America, 25 Stanford Journal of International Law 375, 380-86, 402-03, 411 (1989). Reprinted by permission of Richard J. Wilson, Washington College of Law, American University.

George Winterton, Comparative Law Teaching, 23 American Journal of Comparative Law 69, 99-106, 109, 111-12 (1975). Reprinted with permission.

Frank Wooldridge, The German Rules Governing the Professional Conduct of Rechtsanwälte. This article is reproduced from 1990 Vol. 39 International and Comparative Law Quarterly 683-88 with permission from the publishers, The British Institute of International and Comparative Law, 17 Russell Square, London WC1B 5DR.

Hector Fix Zamudio, A Brief Introduction to the Mexican Writ of Amparo, 9 California Western International Law Journal 306, 316-18, 323-27 (1979). Reprinted by permission of California Western School of Law.

Enrique Zuleta-Puceiro, Statutory Interpretation in Argentina, in Interpreting Statutes: A Comparative Study 29, 33, 60-62, 65, 69-71 (D. Neil MacCormick & Robert S. Summers eds. 1991). Reprinted with permission of Dartmouth Publishing Co., Ltd.

Konrad Zweigert & Hein Kötz, Introduction to Comparative Law I, 4-5, 31, 82-85, 366-69 (Tony Weir trans., 2d ed. 1987). Reprinted by permission of Oxford University Press.

Summary Table of Contents

	Page
Preface	vii
Acknowledgments	xi
Table of Contents	xxix

CHAPTER 1. INTRODUCTION TO COMPARATIVE LAW 1
Note on Comparative Law 1
A. Major Legal Traditions in the Contemporary World 3
B. Comparison of the Common Law and the Civil Law 14
C. Origins, Objectives, and Methods of Comparative Law 28
D. A First Look at the Civil Law Tradition 54
E. Research in Foreign and Comparative Law 66

CHAPTER 2. LITIGATING CASES WITH FOREIGN PARTIES OR FOREIGN LAW ISSUES IN AMERICAN COURTS 71
Note on International Litigation 71
A. Service of Process on Foreign Defendants 73
B. Pleading or Judicial Notice of Foreign Law: Approaches to Recognition of Foreign Law Issues 103
C. Discovery Within Civil Law Countries 125
D. Proving Foreign Law: Expert Witnesses and Other Sources 162
E. Resolution of Foreign Law Issues on Appeal 188
F. Domestic Enforcement of Foreign Country Judgments 191

CHAPTER 3. THE CIVIL LAW TRADITION IN EUROPE BEFORE THE REVOLUTION 213
A. The Roman Civil Law, Canon Law, and Commercial Law Subtraditions 213
B. The Roman Civil Law Legacy 220
C. Law and Government in Medieval Europe 265
D. Revival of Roman Law 281
E. Canon Law 294
F. Commercial Law 316
G. Reception of the *Jus Commune* in Europe 325

CHAPTER 4. THE LEGAL TRADITIONS OF LATIN AMERICA AND EAST ASIA 351
A. Law in Precolonial Latin America 351
B. The Development of Law in Colonial Latin America 364
C. The Legal Traditions of East Asia 399

CHAPTER 5. THE INTELLECTUAL REVOLUTION AND LEGAL SCIENCE 435
A. The Intellectual Revolution 436
B. German Legal Science 476
C. Reception of European Law in East Asia 507

Page

CHAPTER 6. THE STRUCTURE OF LEGAL SYSTEMS 535
Note on Population and Economic Data 535
A. Europe 537
B. Latin America 602
C. East Asia 635
D. Legal Culture and Legal Penetration in Latin America 656
E. Legal Culture and Legal Penetration in East Asia 686

CHAPTER 7. JUDICIAL REVIEW 705
Note on the Division of Jurisdiction 705
A. Judicial Review of Judicial Acts 708
B. Judicial Review of Executive and Administrative Acts 729
C. Judicial Review of Legislative Acts 757

CHAPTER 8. LEGAL EDUCATION AND THE LEGAL PROFESSIONS 841
A. Legal Education 841
B. The Legal Professions 892

CHAPTER 9. THE JUDICIAL PROCESS 937
A. The Sources of Law, Judicial Decisions, and Scholarly Doctrine 937
B. The Interpretation of the Law 975

CHAPTER 10. PROCEDURE 1013
A. Civil Procedure 1013
B. Criminal Procedure 1060

CHAPTER 11. SUBSTANTIVE RULES AND THE PRIVATE LAW CODES 1127
A. How the Law Is Divided 1128
B. Codification and the Codes 1149
C. A Brief Look at Substantive Law: Property 1191
D. The Use of Civil Law General Principles: Tort and Contract in Japan 1227

CHAPTER 12. THE FUTURE OF THE CIVIL LAW TRADITION 1241

Table of Cases 1249
List of Foreign Abbreviations 1253
Table of Tables 1255
Table of Figures 1257
Index 1259

Table of Contents

Page

Preface vii
Acknowledgments xi
Summary Table of Contents xxvii

CHAPTER 1. INTRODUCTION TO COMPARATIVE LAW 1
Note on Comparative Law 1
A. Major Legal Traditions in the Contemporary World 3
1. Legal Traditions 3
John Henry Merryman, The Civil Law Tradition: An Introduction to the Legal Systems of Western Europe and Latin America 1-4 (2d ed. 1985) 3
2. Origins of the Idea of the Civil Law Tradition 5
David S. Clark, The Idea of the Civil Law Tradition, in Comparative and Private International Law: Essays in Honor of John Henry Merryman on His Seventieth Birthday 11, 12-16 (David S. Clark ed. 1990) 5
Note on the Civil Law Tradition in East Asia 6
Note on the Major Religious Legal Traditions 7
Notes and Questions 9
Note on Further Reading About the Major Religious and Non-Western Legal Traditions 11
Note 13
B. Comparison of the Common Law and the Civil Law 14
1. The Comparative Studies of Sir William Blackstone 14
Daniel J. Boorstin, The Mysterious Science of the Law 40, 42, 44, 47, 56 (1941) 14
2. Comparative Study of Law in the United States 15
Roscoe Pound, What May We Expect from Comparative Law?, 22 American Bar Association Journal 56, 57-58 (1936) 15
3. Convergence and Divergence of the Civil Law and the Common Law 16
John Henry Merryman, On the Convergence (and Divergence) of the Civil Law and the Common Law, 17 Stanford Journal of International Law 357, 359-73, 387-88 (1981) 16
4. The Western Legal Tradition 25
David S. Clark, The Idea of the Civil Law Tradition, in Comparative and Private International Law: Essays in Honor of John Henry Merryman on His Seventieth Birthday 11, 21-22 (Clark ed. 1990) 25
Notes and Questions 26
C. Origins, Objectives, and Methods of Comparative Law 28
1. The Origins of Comparative Law 28

Page

René David & John E.C. Brierley, Major Legal Systems in the World Today: An Introduction to the Comparative Study of Law 1-3 (3d ed. 1985) 28
2. Objectives of Comparative Law 29
George Winterton, Comparative Law Teaching, 23 American Journal of Comparative Law 69, 99-106, 109, 111-12 (1975) 29
3. The Practice of Transnational Law 32
Roger J. Goebel, Professional Qualification and Educational Requirements for Law Practice in a Foreign Country: Bridging the Cultural Gap, 63 Tulane Law Review 443, 444-51, 453-54 (1989) 32
4. Scientific Explanation in Comparative Law 34
John Henry Merryman, Comparative Law and Scientific Explanation, in Law in the United States of America in Social and Technological Revolution 81, 82-84 (John N. Hazard & Wenceslas J. Wagner eds. 1974) 34
Note on Law and Development 36
5. The Comparison of Japanese Law 37
Dan Fenno Henderson, The Japanese Law in English: Some Thoughts on Scope and Method, 16 Vanderbilt Journal of Transnational Law 601, 607-12 (1983) 37
Notes and Questions 40
6. Functionalism in Comparative Law 44
Konrad Zweigert & Hein Kötz, 1 Introduction to Comparative Law 31 (Tony Weir trans., 2d ed. 1987) 44
7. The Laboratories of Comparative Analysis 44
Mauro Cappelletti, Monica Seccombe & Joseph H.H. Weiler, Integration Through Law: Europe and the American Federal Experience, A General Introduction, in 1 Integration Through Law bk. 1 at 3, 5-6, 9-10 (Cappelletti et al. eds. 1986) 44
8. Legal Transplants 46
Alan Watson, Society and Legal Change 98-99, 102-05, 140-41 (1977) 46
9. Hortatory Comparative Law 48
Mary Ann Glendon, Abortion and Divorce in Western Law 5-8 (1987) 48
10. Law as Legal Systems 50
Note on "Law" as Legal Rules and as Legal Systems 50
Notes and Questions 53
D. A First Look at the Civil Law Tradition 54
Williams v. Employers Liability Assurance Corp., Ltd. 54
Notes and Questions 65
E. Research in Foreign and Comparative Law 66
Notes on Research in Foreign and Comparative Law 66

Page

CHAPTER 2. LITIGATING CASES WITH FOREIGN PARTIES OR FOREIGN LAW ISSUES IN AMERICAN COURTS 71
Note on International Litigation 71
A. Service of Process on Foreign Defendants 73
1. The Interplay of Service of Process and Jurisdiction 73
Federal Rules of Civil Procedure, Rule 4 73
Advisory Committee Notes, Rule 4 74
Avianca, Inc. v. Corriea 75
Notes and Questions 79
2. The Hague Service Convention 81
Convention on the Service Abroad of Judicial and Extrajudicial Documents in Civil or Commercial Matters 81
Volkswagenwerk Aktiengesellschaft v. Schlunk 85
Notes and Questions 91
3. Service of Process in Japan 93
Bankston v. Toyota Motor Corp. 93
Chin Kim & Eliseo Z. Sisneros, Comparative Overview of Service of Process: United States, Japan, and Attempts at International Unity, 23 Vanderbilt Journal of Transnational Law 299, 306-09 (1990) 95
Notes and Questions 96
4. Service of Process in Germany 97
X Company v. Bavaria 97
Notes and Questions 100
B. Pleading or Judicial Notice of Foreign Law: Approaches to Recognition of Foreign Law Issues 103
Note on the Common Law Fact Approach 103
1. The Fact Approach in Practice 103
Albert Ehrenzweig, Foreign Rules as "Sources of Law," in Legal Thought in the United States of America Under Contemporary Pressures 71, 77 (John N. Hazard & Wenceslas J. Wagner eds. 1970) 103
Philp v. Macri 104
Franklin v. Smalldridge 105
2. Failure to Plead Foreign Law 107
Rudolf B. Schlesinger, A Recurrent Problem in Transnational Litigation: The Effect of Failure to Invoke or Prove the Applicable Foreign Law, 59 Cornell Law Review 1, 2-3 (1973) 107
Notes and Questions 107
3. Theories in Dealing with Foreign Law Problems and Judicial Notice Statutes 108
Rudolf B. Schlesinger, A Recurrent Problem in Transnational Litigation: The Effect of Failure to Invoke or Prove the Applicable Foreign Law, 59 Cornell Law Review 1, 3-5, 16-20 (1973) 108
Federal Rules of Civil Procedure, Rule 44.1 112
Advisory Committee's Note, Rule 44.1 112

Page

California Evidence Code, §§ 310, 311, 452-455, 459, 460 114
New York Civil Practice Law and Rules, Rules 3016, 4511 116
Oklahoma Statutes, tit. 12, §§ 2201, 2203 116
Notes and Questions 117
4. The Summary Judgment Hearing 119
Walpex Trading Co. v. Yacimientos Petroliferos Fiscales Bolivianos 119
Notes and Questions 123
C. Discovery Within Civil Law Countries 125
1. Extraterritorial Discovery and Civil Law Sensibilities 125
Gary B. Born & Scott Hoing, Comity and the Lower Courts: Post-*Aérospatiale* Applications of the Hague Evidence Convention, 24 International Lawyer 393-96 (1990) 125
Federal Rules of Civil Procedure, Rule 28 127
United States Code, tit. 28, § 1783 127
Roberts v. Heim 127
2. Discovery in Japan for Use in the United States 132
Yoshio Ohara, Judicial Assistance to Be Afforded by Japan for Proceedings in the United States, 23 International Lawyer 10-11, 18-22, 25-27 (1989) 132
Notes and Questions 135
3. The Hague Evidence Convention 137
Convention on the Taking of Evidence Abroad in Civil or Commercial Matters 137
4. The Hague Convention in Germany 141
Siemens Aktiengesellschaft v. Bavaria 141
Darrell Prescott & Edwin R. Alley, Effective Evidence-Taking Under the Hague Convention, 22 International Lawyer 939, 975-80 (1988) 146
Notes and Questions 148
5. The Hague Convention in France 149
Société Nationale Industrielle Aérospatiale v. United States District Court 149
Darrell Prescott & Edwin R. Alley, Effective Evidence-Taking Under the Hague Convention, 22 International Lawyer 939, 964-70 (1988) 158
Notes and Questions 160
D. Proving Foreign Law: Expert Witnesses and Other Sources 162
Note 162
1. The Use of Experts and Documents 162
John G. Sprankling & George R. Lanyi, Pleading and Proof of Foreign Law in American Courts, 19 Stanford Journal of International Law 3, 43-45, 58-60 (1983) 162
Diaz v. Southeastern Drilling Co. of Argentina, S.A. 164
Notes and Questions 170
2. *Lesión Corporelle* in French Law 171
Eastern Airlines, Inc. v. Floyd 171

Page

3. *Shubun* in Japanese Law 179
Dan Fenno Henderson, The Japanese Law in English: Some Thoughts on Scope and Method, 16 Vanderbilt Journal of Transnational Law 601, 616-20 (1983) 179
Notes and Questions 181
4. The Court Appointed Expert or Special Master 182
Federal Rules of Evidence, Rule 706 182
Federal Rules of Civil Procedure, Rule 53 182
John Henry Merryman, Foreign Law as a Problem, 19 Stanford Journal of International Law 151, 154-55, 172-73 (1983) 183
Corporacion Salvadorena de Calzado (Corsal), S.A. v. Injection Footwear Corp. 184
Notes and Questions 188
E. Resolution of Foreign Law Issues on Appeal 188
Note 188
1. Foreign Law on Appeal 189
Rudolf B. Schlesinger, A Recurrent Problem in Transnational Litigation: The Effect of Failure to Invoke or Prove the Applicable Foreign Law, 59 Cornell Law Review 1, 21-23 (1973) 189
2. Standards of Review 190
John G. Sprankling & George R. Lanyi, Pleading and Proof of Foreign Law in American Courts, 19 Stanford Journal of International Law 3, 89 (1983) 190
Questions 191
F. Domestic Enforcement of Foreign Country Judgments 191
Note 191
1. The Uniform Recognition Act 192
Uniform Foreign Money-Judgments Recognition Act 192
Nippon Emo-Trans Co. v. Emo-Trans, Inc. 193
Notes and Questions 197
2. The Public Policy Defense and Other Defenses 199
Ackermann v. Levine 199
Questions 205
Panama Processes, S.A. v. Cities Service Co. 206
Notes and Questions 211

CHAPTER 3. THE CIVIL LAW TRADITION IN EUROPE BEFORE THE REVOLUTION 213
A. The Roman Civil Law, Canon Law, and Commercial Law Subtraditions 213
John Henry Merryman, The Civil Law Tradition: An Introduction to the Legal Systems of Western Europe and Latin America 6-13 (2d ed. 1985) 213
Notes and Questions 219
B. The Roman Civil Law Legacy 220

Page
Note on Dates in Roman Legal History ... 220
1. Constitutional History ... 221
Barry Nicholas, An Introduction to Roman Law 3-14 (1969) .. 221
Notes and Questions ... 226
2. Sources of Law: Statutes, Edicts, and Juristic Interpretation ... 227
The Institutes of Gaius 19, 21, 23 (W.M. Gordon & O.F. Robinson trans. 1988) ... 227
1 The Digest of Justinian 2 (Theodor Mommsen, Paul Krueger & Alan Watson eds., Watson trans. 1985) ... 228
Barry Nicholas, An Introduction to Roman Law 14-25, 27-34, 36-38 (1969) ... 228
Notes and Questions ... 237
3. Family Law: *Patria Potestas* ... 238
Samuel P. Scott, 1 The Civil Law iii-iv, 64-65 (1932) ... 238
H.F. Jolowicz & Barry Nicholas, Historical Introduction to the Study of Roman Law 118-120 (3d ed. 1972) ... 239
Notes and Questions ... 240
4. A Roman Law Case ... 242
Caecina v. Aebutius ... 242
Bruce W. Frier, Autonomy of Law and the Origins of the Legal Profession, 11 Cardozo Law Review 259, 262-66 (1989) ... 242
5. The Haves Come Out Ahead ... 245
Paul Veyne, The Roman Empire, in 1 A History of Private Life: From Pagan Rome to Byzantium 5, 166-68 (Veyne ed., Arthur Goldhammer trans. 1987) ... 245
Notes and Questions ... 246
6. Justinian and the *Corpus Juris Civilis* ... 246
Barry Nicholas, An Introduction to Roman Law 39-42 (1969) 246
Charles Donahue, Jr., Book Review, On Translating the Digest, 39 Stanford Law Review 1057, 1058-59 (1987) (reviewing *The Digest of Justinian,* Mommsen, Krueger & Watson eds. 1985) ... 248
Note ... 249
7. Torts: *Lex Aquilia* ... 249
1 The Digest of Justinian 277, 292-93 (Theodor Mommsen, Paul Krueger & Alan Watson eds., Watson trans. 1985) 249
Bruce W. Frier, A Casebook on the Roman Law of Delict 3 (1989) ... 250
8. Inheritance Law: *Legitim* ... 251
Justinian's Institutes 79 (Paul Krueger ed., Peter Birks & Grant McLeod trans. 1987) ... 251
1 The Digest of Justinian 174-75, 179-80 (Theodor Mommsen, Paul Krueger & Alan Watson eds., Watson trans. 1985) 252
David Johnson, The Roman Law of Trusts 2-4 (1988) ... 254
9. *Patria Potestas* Revisited I ... 255
Justinian's Institutes 43, 45, 47, 67, 71 (Paul Krueger ed., Peter Birks & Grant McLeod trans. 1987) ... 255

Page

Samuel P. Scott, 14 The Civil Law 318-19 (1932) 257
1 The Digest of Justinian 19-24 (Theodor Mommsen, Paul Krueger & Alan Watson eds., Watson trans. 1985); 4 ibid. 819 259
10. *Patria Potestas, Emancipatio,* and *Peculium* 261
Alan Watson, Society and Legal Change 23-29 (1977) 261
Notes and Questions 264
C. Law and Government in Medieval Europe 265
1. The Decay of Roman Law 265
Paul Vinogradoff, Roman Law in Medieval Europe 13, 15-18, 24-29 (2d ed. 1929) 265
2. Customary Local Law 268
Harold J. Berman, Law and Revolution: The Formation of the Western Legal Tradition 52-59, 76, 81, 297-98 (1983) 268
3. The Germanic Roman Empire and the Roman Church 273
David S. Clark, The Medieval Origins of Modern Legal Education: Between Church and State: 35 American Journal of Comparative Law 653, 661-67 (1987) 273
4. Feudalism 277
Munroe Smith, The Development of European Law 166-73 (1928) 277
Notes and Questions 280
D. Revival of Roman Law 281
1. The University as the Center for the Revival of Roman Law 281
David S. Clark, The Medieval Origins of Modern Legal Education: Between Church and State, 35 American Journal of Comparative Law 653, 671-75, 681-93, 696-700 (1987) 281
2. Legal Humanism 291
Mauro Cappelletti, John Henry Merryman & Joseph M. Perillo, The Italian Legal System: An Introduction 36-38 (1967) 291
Notes and Questions 292
E. Canon Law 294
1. The Church, Universities, and Canon Law 294
David S. Clark, The Medieval Origins of Modern Legal Education: Between Church and State, 35 American Journal of Comparative Law 653, 675-78, 693-96 (1987) 294
2. Jurisdiction Over Persons and Over Subject Matter 298
Harold J. Berman, Law and Revolution: The Formation of the Western Legal Tradition 222-23, 226-34, 237-41, 245-48, 250-53 (1983) 298
Notes and Questions 307
3. Papal Government 308
Harold J. Berman, Law and Revolution: The Formation of the Western Legal Tradition 208-09, 212 (1983) 308
Note 310
4. *Codex Iuris Canonici* 310

Page

Code of Canon Law: Latin-English Edition xvii-xix, xxviii, 387, 399, 401 (Canon Law Society of America trans. 1983) .. 310
5. A Canon Law Case 313
M v. E 313
Notes and Questions 316
F. Commercial Law 316
1. The Law Merchant 316
Harold J. Berman, Law and Revolution: The Formation of the Western Legal Tradition 333-35, 339-41, 346-50 (1983) 316
Note 322
2. Partnerships and Contracts 322
O.F. Robinson, T.D. Fergus & W.M. Gordon, An Introduction to European Legal History 172-73, 176-77 (1985) 322
Notes and Questions 324
G. Reception of the *Jus Commune* in Europe 325
Note on Italy and the *Jus Commune* 325
1. The Demand for Academic Lawyers 326
David S. Clark, The Medieval Origins of Modern Legal Education: Between Church and State, 35 American Journal of Comparative Law 653, 678-81, 717 (1987) 326
2. A *Jus Commune* Case 327
Fabronis v. Marradi Ball Players 327
Gino Gorla, A Decision of the Rota Fiorentina of 1780 on Liability for Damages Caused by the "Ball Game," 49 Tulane Law Review 346-55 (1975) 327
Notes and Questions 332
3. The Reception in France and Germany 333
K.W. Ryan, An Introduction to the Civil Law 15-22 (1962) 333
John P. Dawson, Gifts and Promises: Continental and American Laws Compared 41-42 (1980) 338
Notes and Questions 338
4. The Reception in Spain, Portugal, and Elsewhere in Europe 340
Mauro Cappelletti, John Henry Merryman & Joseph M. Perillo, The Italian Legal System: An Introduction 31-33, 35-36 (1967) 340
5. Learned Lawyers in Castile 342
Richard L. Kagan, Lawyers and Litigation in Castile, 1500-1750, in Lawyers in Early Modern Europe and America 181, 184-87 (Wilfrid Prest ed. 1981) 342
6. *Patria Potestas* Revisited II 343
Note on the *Siete Partidas* 343
Samuel P. Scott, Las Siete Partidas 960-63 (1931) 343
Notes and Questions 346
7. Resistance to Roman Law in England 347
R.C. van Caenegem, Judges, Legislators and Professors: Chapters in European Legal History 114-15, 118-22 (1987) 347
Notes and Questions 349

Page
Note on Complexity Within the Civil Law Tradition 350

CHAPTER 4. THE LEGAL TRADITIONS OF LATIN AMERICA AND EAST ASIA .. 351
A. Law in Precolonial Latin America 351
Note on the Original American Inhabitants 351
1. The Incas and Their Legal System 352
Note on the Inca Legal System 352
Sally F. Moore, Power and Property in Inca Peru 74-81, 83-84, 100, 102, 111-13, 115-20 (1958) 353
2. The Aztecs and Their Legal System 360
Note on the Aztec Legal System 360
Notes and Questions 362
B. The Development of Law in Colonial Latin America 364
1. The Spanish Conquest of Mexico 364
Fred R. Harris, Mexico: Historical Foundations, in Latin America, Its Problems and Its Promise: A Multidisciplinary Introduction 261, 262-63 (Jan Knippers Black ed. 1984) 364
2. The Spanish Conquest of Peru 365
Edward P. Lanning, Peru Before the Incas 171-72 (1967) 365
Note on the Portuguese Settlement and Legal System in Brazil ... 366
Note on the Spanish Legal System in America 366
3. The *Encomienda* in America 369
P.E.B. Coy, Justice for the Indian in Eighteenth Century Mexico, 12 American Journal of Legal History 41-42 (1968) 369
4. The Spread of Iberian Law to Latin America 370
David S. Clark, Judicial Protection of the Constitution in Latin America, 2 Hastings Constitutional Law Quarterly 405, 407-13 (1975) 370
5. The Judiciary in Mexico 374
Colin M. MacLachlan, Criminal Justice in Eighteenth Century Mexico: A Study of the Tribunal of the *Acordada* 21-28, 31 (1974) 374
6. The Judiciary in Peru 377
Steve Stern, The Social Significance of Judicial Institutions in an Exploitative Society: Huamanga, Peru, 1570-1640, in The Inca and Aztec States, 1400-1800: Anthropology and History 289, 293-94, 307-08, 310-11 (George A. Collier, Renato I. Rosaldo & John D. Wirth eds. 1982) 377
7. The Judiciary in Brazil 379
Stuart B. Schwartz, Sovereignty and Society in Colonial Brazil: The High Court of Bahia and Its Judges, 1609-1751, at xiv-xv, 173-74, 185-86, 293-94, 304-05 (1973) 379
Notes and Questions 381
8. The Accommodation of Spanish and Indian Law 382
Woodrow Borah, Justice by Insurance: The General Indian Court of Colonial Mexico and the Legal Aides of the Half-*Real* 27-32, 34-35, 38-40 (1983) 382

Page

9. Indian Cases in the Royal Courts of Mexico 386
   Woodrow Borah, Justice by Insurance: The General Indian Court of Colonial Mexico and the Legal Aides of the Half-*Real* 44-51, 53-54 (1983) 386
   Texcocan Villages v. Hacienda La Blanca 390
   P.E.B. Coy, Justice for the Indian in Eighteenth Century Mexico, 12 American Journal of Legal History 41, 43-46, 49 (1968) 390
10. The General Indian Court 393
   Woodrow Borah, Justice by Insurance: The General Indian Court of Colonial Mexico and the Legal Aides of the Half-*Real* 79, 120-21, 125-30, 144-47, 187, 189-90 (1983) 393
Note on Justice for the Indians 398
Notes and Questions 398

C. The Legal Traditions of East Asia 399
1. The Hindu-Buddhist Tradition and Law in the Kingdom of Siam 399
   Note on the Hindu-Buddhist Tradition 399
   Sarasin Viraphol, Law in Traditional Siam and China: A Comparative Study, 65 Journal of the Siam Society 109-15, 124 (1977) 400
   Questions 405
2. The Imperial Chinese Tradition: Order Without Law 405
   Note on the Imperial Chinese Tradition 405
   Thomas B. Stephens, Order and Discipline in China: The Shanghai Mixed Court, 1911-27, at 3-5, 7-9, 11-12 (1992) ... 407
   Shuzo Shiga, Some Remarks on the Judicial System in China: Historical Development and Characteristics, in Traditional and Modern Legal Institutions in Asia and Africa (David C. Buxbaum ed.) 46-51 (1967) 411
   Notes and Questions 415
3. The Confucianist Tradition in Yi Korea 416
   William Shaw, Social and Intellectual Aspects of Traditional Korean Law, in Traditional Korean Attitudes 15, 25-32 (Bong Duck Chun, William Shaw & Dai-kwon Choi eds. 1980) 416
   Questions 418
4. Japan's Ambivalent Legal Tradition 418
   Note on Japanese Institutional History 418
   John Owen Haley, Authority Without Power: Law and the Japanese Paradox 38-40 (1991) 420
   Yoshirō Hiramatsu, Tokugawa Law, 14 Law in Japan 1, 27-28, 31-38 (Dan Fenno Henderson trans. 1981) 422
   Questions 429
   John Owen Haley, Authority Without Power: Law and the Japanese Paradox 58-62 (1991) 429
   Notes and Questions 433

Page

CHAPTER 5. THE INTELLECTUAL REVOLUTION AND LEGAL SCIENCE 435
A. The Intellectual Revolution 436
1. The French *Parlements* 436
Bailey Stone, The French *Parlements* and the Crisis of the Old Regime 18-20 (1986) 436
Lenard R. Berlanstein, The Barristers of Toulouse in the Eighteenth Century (1740-1793) 1-4, 104-05 (1975) 437
John P. Dawson, The Oracles of the Law 369-71 (1968) 439
Notes and Questions 440
2. Elements of the Intellectual Revolution 441
John Henry Merryman, The Civil Law Tradition: An Introduction to the Legal Systems of Western Europe and Latin America 14-18 (2d ed. 1985) 441
Note 444
3. Natural Law 444
O.F. Robinson, T.D. Fergus & W.M. Gordon, An Introduction to European Legal History 354-55, 357-58, 360-61 (1985) ... 444
Hugo Grotius, De Jure Belli et Pacis I, Prolegomena §§ 6, 8 (William Whewell trans. & ed. 1853) 446
Constitution of France of 1791 446
Questions 446
4. Intermediate Law and Drafting the French Civil Code 447
Konrad Zweigert & Hein Kötz, Introduction to Comparative Law: The Framework I, 82-85 (Tony Weir trans., 2d ed. 1987) 447
5. Ideology of the French Civil Code 449
John Henry Merryman, The Civil Law Tradition: An Introduction to the Legal Systems of Western Europe and Latin America 27-30 (2d ed. 1985) 449
Civil Code of France, Articles 4, 5, 7, 544, 545, 1123, 1134 452
Notes and Questions 452
Note on the Influence of the French Codes 453
6. The Revolution in Italy 454
Mauro Cappelletti, John Henry Merryman & Joseph M. Perillo, The Italian Legal System: An Introduction 40-46, 52 (1967) 454
Note on the Revolution in Spain 457
Notes and Questions 458
7. The Revolution in Latin America 458
R.A. Humphreys & John Lynch, Introduction, in The Origins of the Latin American Revolutions: 1808-1826, at 3-5, 10-14, 24, 26-27 (R.A. Humphreys & John Lynch eds. 1965) 458
Note on the Latin American Variation 462
8. The Revolution in Mexico 463
Fred R. Harris, Mexico: Historical Foundations, in Latin America, Its Problems and Its Promise: A Multidisciplinary Introduction 261, 264-67 (Jan Knippers Black ed. 1984) 463

Page
Note on Codification in Mexico 467
9. The Revolution in Brazil 467
Michael L. Conniff, Brazil: From Independence to 1964, in Latin America, Its Problems and Its Promise: A Multidisciplinary Introduction 475-79 (Jan Knippers Black ed. 1984) 467
Note 470
10. Codification in Chile 470
Juan G. Matus Valencia, The Centenary of the Chilean Civil Code, 7 American Journal of Comparative Law 71-77 (1958) 470
11. Codification in Colombia 473
Robert C. Means, Codification in Latin America: The Colombian Commercial Code of 1853, 52 Texas Law Review 18, 20-24 (1973) 473
Notes and Questions 475
B. German Legal Science 476
1. The Thibaut-Savigny Debate 476
Mathias Reimann, The Historical School Against Codification: Savigny, Carter, and the Defeat of the New York Civil Code, 37 American Journal of Comparative Law 95, 97-98 (1989) 476
Note on German Romanticism 477
2. Ideology of the German Civil Code 477
John Henry Merryman, The Civil Law Tradition: An Introduction to the Legal Systems of Western Europe and Latin America 30-32 (2d ed. 1985) 477
Note on German Codification 479
Notes and Questions 479
3. Legal Scholars and the Elements of Legal Science 480
John Henry Merryman, The Civil Law Tradition: An Introduction to the Legal Systems of Western Europe and Latin America 57, 59-67 (2d ed. 1985) 480
4. The Scholarly Origins of German Legal Science 485
John P. Dawson, The Oracles of the Law 196, 198-201, 203, 206-07, 227-28, 231, 240-41, 450-52, 454-60 (1968) 485
Notes and Questions 493
Note on the Influence of German Legal Science 493
5. Legal Science in Introduction to Law Courses 494
John Henry Merryman, The Civil Law Tradition: An Introduction to the Legal Systems of Western Europe and Latin America 69-79 (2d ed. 1985) 494
Civil Code of Germany, §§ 116-122 502
Note on the Influence of German Law in the United States 503
Notes and Questions 504
6. *Patria Potestas* Redefined 505
Mary Ann Glendon, The Transformation of Family Law: State, Law, and Family in the United States and Western Europe 97-99 (1989) 505

Page

Question 507

C. Reception of European Law in East Asia 507

Note on the Civil Law Tradition and the Typicality of Civil Law Systems 507

Note on Japan as a Model in East Asia 509

1. Codification and Legal Science in Meiji Japan 509

Note on Codification 509

Richard W. Rabinowitz, Law and the Social Process in Japan, 10 Transactions of the Asiatic Society of Japan 36-37 (Third Series 1968) 511

Notes and Questions 512

Zentaro Kitagawa, Theory Reception: One Aspect of the Development of Japanese Civil Law, in 1 Law and the Legal Process in Japan 270-72 (John Owen Haley & Dan Fenno Henderson eds. 1988) 513

Notes and Questions 515

2. The Meiji Constitution 515

Note 515

John Owen Haley, Authority Without Power: Law and the Japanese Paradox 78-80 (1991) 516

3. Adaptability of Western Law in Japan 518

John Owen Haley, Authority Without Power: Law and the Japanese Paradox 70-72 (1991) 518

Notes and Questions 520

4. Taiwan and Korea Under Japanese Colonial Rule 520

Edward I-to Chen, The Attempt to Integrate the Empire: Legal Perspectives, in The Japanese Colonial Empire, 1895-1945 at 268-74 (Ramon H. Myers & Mark R. Peattie eds. 1984) 520

5. Westernization and Judicial Reform in Siam (Thailand) 522

Frank C. Darling, American Influence on the Evolution of Constitutional Government in Thailand 29-35 (Ph.D. dissertation, American University, 1961) 522

David M. Engel, Law and Kingship in Thailand During the Reign of King Chulalongkorn, 9 Michigan Papers on South and Southeast Asia 16-17, 63-65, 69-70, 74-76 (1975) 524

Notes and Questions 528

6. Indonesia Under Dutch Colonial Rule 528

Daniel S. Lev, Judicial Institutions and Legal Culture in Indonesia, in Culture and Politics in Indonesia 248-57 (Claire Holt ed. 1972) 528

Notes and Questions 533

CHAPTER 6. THE STRUCTURE OF LEGAL SYSTEMS 535

Note on Population and Economic Data 535

A. Europe 537

1. France 537

Page

René David, French Law: Its Structure, Sources, and Methodology 19-33, 35-36, 38-39, 41-45 (Michael Kindred trans. 1972) 537
Note on the Structure of the French Court System 549
Constitution of France, Articles 34, 37, 38 551
Notes and Questions 552

2. Germany 553
Oliver Passavant & Gerhard Nösser, The German Reunification — Legal Implications for Investment in East Germany, 25 International Lawyer 875-76, 878-79 (1991) 553
Donald P. Kommers, German Constitutionalism: A Prolegomenon, 40 Emory Law Journal 837-38, 845-47 (1991) 554
Norbert Horn, Hein Kötz & Hans G. Leser, German Private and Commercial Law: An Introduction 16-23 (Tony Weir trans. 1982) 556
Donald P. Kommers, The Constitutional Jurisprudence of the Federal Republic of Germany 67-68, 85-86 (1989) 561
The Atomic Weapons Referenda Case (English translation published in Kommers, The Constitutional Jurisprudence of the Federal Republic of Germany 86-88 (1989)) 562
David S. Clark, The Selection and Accountability of Judges in West Germany: Implementation of a *Rechtsstaat,* 61 Southern California Law Review 1795, 1808-14 (1988) 564
Notes and Questions 568

3. Italy 569
Mauro Cappelletti, John Henry Merryman & Joseph M. Perillo, The Italian Legal System: An Introduction 53-54, 56-58, 60-70, 72-83 (1967) 569
Frederic Spotts & Theodor Wieser, Italy: A Difficult Democracy 158-161 (1986) 578
Note on Litigation in Italian Courts 581
Frederic Spotts & Theodor Wieser, Italy: A Difficult Democracy 283, 290-92 (1986) 582
Notes and Questions 584

4. Spain 585
Peter J. Donaghy & Michael T. Newton, Spain: A Guide to Political and Economic Institutions 10-13, 19-21, 98, 100, 103-04, 112-13, 117-18 (1987) 585
Bernardo M. Cremades & Eduardo G. Cabiedes, Litigating in Spain 39, 41-46, 71 (1989) 592
Constitution of Spain: Articles 3, 14, 23 597
Vizcaya v. Diputación Foral de Vizcaya 597
Notes and Questions 598

5. Comparative Litigation Rates 599
Note on the Comparison of Civil Litigation Rates Among Nations 599

Page

David S. Clark, Civil Litigation Trends in Europe and Latin America Since 1945: The Advantage of Intracountry Comparisons, 24 Law & Society Review 549, 563-65 (1990) 599
Note on the Comparison of Criminal Litigation Rates Among Nations 601
David S. Clark, The American Legal System and Legal Culture, in Introduction to the Law of the United States 1, 10-11 (Clark & Tuğrul Ansay eds. 1992) 602

B. Latin America 602
1. Independence and the First Latin American Constitutions 602
David S. Clark, Judicial Protection of the Constitution in Latin America, 2 Hastings Constitutional Law Quarterly 405, 413-16 (1975) 602
2. Latin America: Executive Dominance 604
Howard J. Wiarda & Harvey F. Kline, The Latin American Tradition and Process of Development, in Latin American Politics and Development 1, 81-94 (H. Wiarda & H. Kline eds., 3d ed. 1990) 604
3. Argentina 614
Peter G. Snow & Gary W. Wynia, Argentina: Politics in a Conflict Society, in Latin American Politics and Development 129, 159-61 (H. Wiarda & H. Kline eds., 3d ed. 1990) 614
4. Brazil 615
Iêda Siqueira Wiarda, Brazil: The Politics of Order and Progress, in Latin American Politics and Development 167, 190-93 (H. Wiarda & H. Kline eds., 3d ed. 1990) 615
5. Colombia 617
Harvey F. Kline, Colombia: The Struggle between Traditional "Stability" and New Visions, in Latin American Politics and Development 231, 251-52 (H. Wiarda & H. Kline eds., 3d ed. 1990) 617
6. Mexico 618
Martin C. Needler, Mexican Politics: The Containment of Conflict 87-90, 94-96 (2d ed. 1990) 618
Note on the Structure of the Mexican Court System 622
Notes and Questions 623
7. Separation of Powers 625
Bustamante, Natalio 625
Notes and Questions 626
8. The Judiciary and the Military 626
Caicedo Valencia, Arturo 626
The Argentine Military Leaders Case 629
Enrique Dahl & Alejandro M. Garro, Argentina: National Appeals Court (Criminal Division) Judgment on Human Rights Violations by Former Military Leaders, 26 International Legal Materials 317-19, 321-27 (1987) 630
Notes and Questions 634

Page

C. East Asia 635
1. Japan 635
Hideo Tanaka, The Constitutional System of Japan and the Judicial System, in Law and Business in Japan 1-7, 18-21 (Akira Kawamura ed. 1982) 635
Notes and Questions 642
Note on Litigation in Japanese Courts 642
Note on Political and Institutional Change in East Asia 644
2. South Korea 645
James M. West & Dae-Kyu Yoon, The Constitutional Court of the Republic of Korea: Transforming the Jurisprudence of the Vortex, 40 American Journal of Comparative Law 73-77, 88-90, 92-94 (1992) 645
3. Taiwan 649
Herbert H.P. Ma, The Sources and Structure of Modern Chinese Law and the Chinese Judicial System, in Trade and Investment in Taiwan: The Legal and Economic Environment in the Republic of China 3-6, 27-34 (Herbert H.P. Ma ed., 2d ed. 1985) 649
Notes and Questions 655
D. Legal Culture and Legal Penetration in Latin America 656
1. Legal Pluralism and Witchcraft 656
David S. Clark, Witchcraft and Legal Pluralism: The Case of Célimo Miquirucama, 15 Tulsa Law Journal 679-83 (1980) 656
Constitution of Colombia of 1886, Articles 26, 58 658
Miquirucama, Célimo 658
David S. Clark, Witchcraft and Legal Pluralism: The Case of Célimo Miquirucama, 15 Tulsa Law Journal 679, 692-98 (1980) 664
Notes and Questions 667
2. Indian Courts in Rural Mexico 668
Laura Nader, Harmony Ideology: Justice and Control in a Zapotec Mountain Village 6-8, 10, 15-16, 29-31, 109, 120-122, 125, 127, 146-48, 162-63, 165-67, 169-71, 181 (1990) 668
Notes and Questions 677
3. The Legal Culture of Brazil 677
Keith S. Rosenn, Brazil's Legal Culture: The *Jeito* Revisited, 1 Fla. Int'l L.J. 1, 2-5, 14-15, 17-25, 29-30 (1984) 677
Notes and Questions 684
4. The Legal Culture of Mexico 684
Beltran Collantes, Martha 684
Notes and Questions 685
E. Legal Culture and Legal Penetration in East Asia 686
1. The Legal Culture of Indonesia 686

Page

Daniel S. Lev, Judicial Institutions and Legal Culture in Indonesia, in Culture and Politics in Indonesia 283-87 (Claire Holt ed. 1972) 686
Questions 688
2. Litigation in Thailand 688
David M. Engel, Code and Custom in a Thai Provincial Court: The Interaction of Formal and Informal Systems of Justice 46-52 (1978) 688
Question 692
3. Japanese Attitudes Toward Litigation 692
John O. Haley, The Myth of the Reluctant Litigant, 4 Journal of Japanese Studies 359-70, 378-80 (1978) 692
Hideo Tanaka, The Role of Law in Japanese Society, Comparisons with the West, 19 University of British Columbia Law Review 375-76 (1985) 697
Setsuo Miyazawa, Taking Kawashima Seriously: A Review of Japanese Research on Japanese Legal Consciousness and Disputing Behavior, 21 Law & Society Review 219, 231-35 (1987) 698
J. Mark Ramseyer & Minoru Nakazato, The Rational Litigant: Settlement Amounts and Verdict Rates in Japan, 18 Journal of Legal Studies 266-72, 285-90 (1989) 699
Notes and Questions 702

CHAPTER 7. JUDICIAL REVIEW 705
Note on the Division of Jurisdiction 705
A. Judicial Review of Judicial Acts 708
Note 708
1. Ordinary Courts 708
John Henry Merryman, The Civil Law Tradition: An Introduction to the Legal Systems of Western Europe and Latin America 40-41 (2d ed. 1985) 708
2. The German System of Multiple Courts 709
David S. Clark, The Selection and Accountability of Judges in West Germany: Implementation of a *Rechtsstaat*, 61 Southern California Law Review 1797, 1837-40 (1988) 709
Notes and Questions 712
3. The Accountability of Judges 712
The Civil Liability of Judges Case 712
Notes and Questions 717
Japan v. Onda 719
Notes and Questions 720
4. Maintaining the Uniform Interpretation of Law 720
Huston v. Société d'Exploitation de la Cinquième Chaine 720
Jane C. Ginsburg & Pierre Sirinelli, Authors and Exploitations in International Private Law: The French Supreme

Page

Court and the Huston Film Colorization Controversy, 15 Columbia-VLA Journal of Law & the Arts 135-38 (1991) ... 721
Questions ... 723
Constitution of Spain, Articles 18, 20 ... 723
Pantoja v. Prographic Co. ... 723
Luis Arechederra, The Death of a Bullfighter: Spanish Law on Privacy and the Right to Name and Likeness, 40 International and Comparative Law Quarterly 442-45 (1991) ... 724
Notes and Questions ... 727
5. The Mexican "Cassation" *Amparo* ... 727
Hector Fix Zamudio, A Brief Introduction to the Mexican Writ of *Amparo*, 9 California Western International Law Journal 306, 316, 323-25 (1979) ... 727
Notes and Questions ... 728
B. Judicial Review of Executive and Administrative Acts ... 729
1. Administrative Courts ... 729
John Henry Merryman, The Civil Law Tradition: An Introduction to the Legal Systems of Western Europe and Latin America 87-88 (2d ed. 1985) ... 729
2. The French Council of State and Conflicts of Jurisdiction ... 730
L. Neville Brown & J.F. Garner, French Administrative Law 172-75 (3d. 1983) ... 730
Note on the French Conflicts Tribunal ... 732
Prefect of Loire v. Commerce Tribunal of Saint-Etienne ... 733
Notes and Questions ... 734
3. Complex Administrative Law Adjudication in Germany: The Wyhl Atomic Energy Plant Case ... 735
Peter Arens, Recent Trends in German Jurisdiction: The Transfer of Political and Administrative Duties to the Courts, in The Role of Courts in Society 97, 111-14, 117-22 (Shimon Shetreet ed. 1988) ... 735
Notes and Questions ... 739
4. The Mexican *Amparo* ... 740
Hector Fix Zamudio, A Brief Introduction to the Mexican Writ of *Amparo*, 9 California Western International Law Journal 306, 316-18, 325-27 (1979) ... 740
5. Judicial Protection in Brazil and Colombia ... 742
Keith S. Rosenn, A Comparison of the Protection of Individual Rights in the New Constitutions of Colombia and Brazil, 23 University of Miami Inter-American Law Review 659, 680-86 (1992) ... 742
Notes and Questions ... 745
6. Limits on Judicial Protection in Japan ... 745
John O. Haley, Japanese Administrative Law: Introduction, 19 Law in Japan 1, 4-14 (1986) ... 745
7. Judicial Protection Through Compensation Laws in East Asia 752
National Compensation Law of Japan, Articles 1, 2 ... 752

Page

Yamagata Prefecture v. Y.K. Taira Shōji (Turkish Bath Case) 753
National Compensation Law of South Korea, Articles 1, 2 755
State Compensation Law of Taiwan, Articles 2, 3 756
Notes and Questions 757
C. Judicial Review of Legislative Acts 757
1. Constitutionalism 757
John Henry Merryman, The Civil Law Tradition: An Introduction to the Legal Systems of Western Europe and Latin America 136-40 (2d ed. 1985) 757
2. The French Constitutional Council 760
Constitution of France, Articles 61, 62 760
F.L. Morton, Judicial Review in France: A Comparative Analysis, 36 American Journal of Comparative Law 89-92, 94-96, 98-100 (1988) 760
The Freedom of Association Case (English translation published in Mauro Cappelletti & William Cohen, Comparative Constitutional Law: Cases and Materials 50-51 (1979)) 764
Cynthia Vroom, Constitutional Protection of Individual Liberties in France: The *Conseil Constitutionnel* since 1971, 63 Tulane Law Review 265, 266, 279-82, 295-97, 314-15 (1988) 765
Mary Ann Glendon, Abortion and Divorce in Western Law 16-18 (1987) 768
Notes and Questions 770
3. The German Federal Constitutional Court 771
Basic Law of Germany, Articles 93, 94, 100 771
Donald P. Kommers, German Constitutionalism: A Prolegomenon, 40 Emory Law Journal 837, 840-45, 848-52, 855-56, 858-61, 864-73 (1991) 773
The Lüth Boycott Case (English translation published in Kommers, The Constitutional Jurisprudence of the Federal Republic of Germany 366, 368-75 (1989)) 783
Peter E. Quint, Free Speech and Private Law in German Constitutional Theory, 48 Maryland Law Review 247, 339-42, 344-45, 347 (1989) 789
Notes and Questions 791
4. The Italian Constitutional Court 795
Constitution of Italy, Articles 134, 136, 137 795
Alessandro Pizzorusso, The Italian Constitution: Implementation and Reform, 34 Jahrbuch des öffentlichen Rechts der Gegenwart 105, 114-16 (Peter Häberle ed. 1985) 795
Bertett v. Italy (English translation published in Mauro Cappelletti & William Cohen, Comparative Constitutional Law: Cases and Materials 394-97 (1979)) 798
Notes and Questions 801
5. The Spanish Constitutional Court 802
The Spanish Abortion Decision 802

Page

Richard Stith, New Constitutional and Penal Theory in Spanish Abortion Law, 35 American Journal of Comparative Law 513, 515-19 (1987) 802
Notes and Questions 804
6. Judicial Review and Its Independence in Latin America 805
David S. Clark, Judicial Protection of the Constitution in Latin America, 2 Hastings Constitutional Law Quarterly 405, 416-22, 425-28, 431-42 (1975) 805
Keith S. Rosenn, The Protection of Judicial Independence in Latin America, 19 University of Miami Inter-American Law Review 1, 8, 12, 32 (1987) 817
Keith S. Rosenn, A Comparison of the Protection of Individual Rights in the New Constitutions of Colombia and Brazil, 23 University of Miami Inter-American Law Review 659, 685 (1992) 818
Notes and Questions 818
7. The Japanese Supreme Court 819
Lawrence W. Beer, Japan's Constitutional System and Its Judicial Interpretation, 17 Law in Japan 7, 20-21 (1984) 819
Constitution of Japan, Articles 14, 15, 22, 29, 41, 44, 76, 81 ... 820
Notes and Questions 821
Mutsuo Nakamura, Freedom of Economic Activities and the Right to Property, 53 Law and Contemporary Problems 1, 4-9 (No. 2, 1990) 822
Kurokawa v. Chiba Prefecture Election Commission 827
Recent Developments, 9 Law in Japan 151-52 (1976) 827
Hiroyuki Hata, Malapportionment of Representation in the National Diet, 53 Law and Contemporary Problems, 157-60, 170 (No. 2, 1990) 828
Kazuyuki Takahashi, Comment, 53 Law and Contemporary Problems 189, 190-92 (No. 2, 1990) 831
Notes and Questions 833
8. The Korean Constitutional Court 834
James M. West & Dae-Kyu Yoon, The Constitutional Court of the Republic of Korea: Transforming the Jurisprudence of the Vortex?, 40 American Journal of Comparative Law 73, 103-06, 111-15 (1992) 834
Notes and Questions 837
Note on Judicial Review in Taiwan 838

CHAPTER 8. LEGAL EDUCATION AND THE LEGAL PROFESSIONS 841
A. Legal Education 841
1. The Education of a Continental Lawyer 841
Mirjan Damaška, A Continental Lawyer in an American Law School: Trials and Tribulations of Adjustment, 116 University of Pennsylvania Law Review 1363, 1364-70, 1372-75 (1968) 841

Page

2. Legal Education There and Here 847
John Henry Merryman, Legal Education There and Here: A Comparison, 27 Stanford Law Review 859, 861-66, 868-71, 874-76 (1975) 847
Notes and Questions 853
3. France 854
Thomas E. Carbonneau, The French Legal Studies Curriculum: Its History and Relevance as a Model for Reform, 25 McGill Law Journal 445, 463-74 (1980) 854
Notes and Questions 862
4. Germany 863
David S. Clark, The Selection and Accountability of Judges in West Germany: Implementation of a *Rechtsstaat*, 61 Southern California Law Review 1795, 1802-06 (1988) 863
Erhard Blankenburg & Ulrike Schultz, German Advocates: A Highly Regulated Profession, in 2 Lawyers in Society: The Civil Law World 124, 131-32 (Richard L. Abel & Philip S.C. Lewis eds. 1988) 865
Notes and Questions 866
5. Italy 867
Vittorio Olgiati & Valerio Pocar, The Italian Legal Profession: An Institutional Dilemma, in 2 Lawyers in Society: The Civil Law World 336, 344-46 (Richard L. Abel & Philip S.C. Lewis eds. 1988) 867
Note on the University of Rome Law Faculty's Required Courses 868
Notes and Questions 869
6. Spain 869
Carlos Viladás Jene, The Legal Profession in Spain: An Understudied but Booming Occupation, in 2 Lawyers in Society: The Civil Law World 369, 371-73 (Richard L. Abel & Philip S.C. Lewis eds. 1988) 869
Note on European Legal Education 870
Questions 872
7. Colombia 872
Richard J. Wilson, The New Legal Education in North and South America, 25 Stanford Journal of International Law 375, 380-87, 402-03, 411 (1989) 872
8. Brazil 876
Joaquim Falcão, Lawyers in Brazil, in 2 Lawyers in Society: The Civil Law World 400-01, 403-11 (Richard L. Abel & Philip S.C. Lewis eds. 1988) 876
Note on Latin American Legal Education 883
Notes and Questions 883
9. East Asia 884
Note on East Asian Legal Education 884

Page

Yasuhei Taniguchi, Shihō Kenshū Sho ni okeru hōsō kyōiku (Legal Education at the Legal Training and Research Institute), 25 Jiyū to seigi (Liberty and Justice) 7-12 (1974) 888
Notes and Questions 891
B. The Legal Professions 892
1. Multiple Professions 892
John Henry Merryman, The Civil Law Tradition: An Introduction to the Legal Systems of Western Europe and Latin America 101-08 (2d ed. 1985) 892
2. An Initial Comparison 897
David S. Clark, The Legal Profession in Comparative Perspective: Growth and Specialization, 30 American Journal of Comparative Law 163, 166-69 (Supp. 1982) 897
3. A Current Comparison 899
David S. Clark, The Organization and Social Status of Lawyers, in IXth World Conference on Procedural Law: General Reports 254, 275, 277-79 (1991) 899
Notes and Questions 901
4. France 902
Anne Boigeol, The French Bar: The Difficulties of Unifying a Divided Profession, in 2 Lawyers in Society: The Civil Law World 258, 259-60, 262-68 (Richard L. Abel & Philip S.C. Lewis eds. 1988) 902
Note on the New French *Avocat* 906
Notes and Questions 907
5. Germany 908
Erhard Blankenburg & Ulrike Schultz, German Advocates: A Highly Regulated Profession, in 2 Lawyers in Society: The Civil Law World 124, 132-38, 140-41 (Richard L. Abel & Philip S.C. Lewis eds. 1988) 908
David S. Clark, The Selection and Accountability of Judges in West Germany: Implementation of a *Rechtsstaat,* 61 Southern California Law Review 1795, 1806-08 (1988) 912
Frank Wooldridge, The German Rules Governing the Professional Conduct of *Rechtsanwälte*, 39 International and Comparative Law Quarterly 683-88 (1990) 913
Notes and Questions 916
Note on the Italian Legal Profession 917
6. Spain 918
Carlos Viladás Jene, The Legal Profession in Spain: An Understudied but Booming Occupation, in 2 Lawyers in Society: The Civil Law World 369-71, 375-76 (Richard L. Abel & Philip S.C. Lewis eds. 1988) 918
7. Brazil 920
Joaquim Falcão, Lawyers in Brazil, in 2 Lawyers in Society: The Civil Law World 400, 417-22, 427-30 (Richard L. Abel & Philip S.C. Lewis eds. 1988) 920

Page

8. Government Lawyers 925
Mauro Cappelletti, John Henry Merryman & Joseph M. Perillo, The Italian Legal System: An Introduction 98-99 (1967) 925
Note on the Government Lawyer 926
Notes and Questions 926
9. Japan 928
John O. Haley, Redefining the Scope of Practice Under Japan's New Regime for Regulating Foreign Lawyers, 21 Law in Japan 18, 19-21 (1988) 928
Note on the Distribution of Japanese Jurists 930
Dan Fenno Henderson, Foreign Enterprise in Japan: Laws and Policies 177-85 (1973) 930
Notes and Questions 935

CHAPTER 9. THE JUDICIAL PROCESS 937
A. The Sources of Law, Judicial Decisions, and Scholarly Doctrine 937
Note 937
1. The Interplay of Sources of Law 938
Alan Watson, The Making of the Civil Law 168-78 (1981) 938
Note on Sources of Law 943
Notes and Questions 944
2. The Role of Scholarly Doctrine 945
Hein Kötz, Scholarship and the Courts: A Comparative Survey, in Comparative and Private International Law: Essays in Honor of John Henry Merryman on His Seventieth Birthday 183, 184-86, 190-91, 193-94 (David S. Clark ed. 1990) 945
3. Montesquieu and *Stare Decisis* 947
Note 947
André Pouille, Le pouvoir judiciare et les tribunaux 11, 20 (1984) 948
4. The Style and Authority of French Judicial Decisions 948
Gino Gorla, Civilian Judicial Decisions — An Historical Account of Italian Style, 44 Tulane Law Review 740, 748-49 (1970) 948
Barry Nicholas, French Law of Contract 14-16 (1982) 949
5. The Authority of German Judicial Decisions 951
Fritz Baur, Einführung in das deutsche Recht, in Gesellschaft für Rechtsvergleichung, Bibliography of German Law in English and German: A Selection 12, 14 (Courtland H. Peterson trans. 1964) 951
Norbert Horn, Hein Kötz & Hans G. Leser, German Private and Commercial Law: An Introduction 63-64 (Tony Weir trans. 1982) 952
Notes and Questions 952
6. Judicial Lawmaking in Spain 954
Note 954

Page

Civil Code of Spain, Article 1 954
L. Neville Brown, The Sources of Spanish Civil Law, 5 International and Comparative Law Quarterly 364, 366-69 (1956) 954
CIC Co. v. Spain 956
Notes and Questions 958
7. Mexican *Jurisprudencia* 959
Richard D. Baker, Judicial Review in Mexico: A Study of the *Amparo* Suit 252-54, 256, 259-60, 263 (1971) 959
Note 962
Ramírez Méndez, Enrique 962
Woodfin L. Butte, *Stare Decisis,* Doctrine, and Jurisprudence in Mexico and Elsewhere, in The Role of Judicial Decisions & Doctrine in Civil Law & in Mixed Jurisdictions 311, 323-28 (Joseph Dainow ed. 1974) 962
Notes and Questions 966
Note on Sources of Law in East Asia 967
8. The Authority of Japanese Judicial Decisions 968
Takeyoshi Kawashima, The Concept of Judicial Precedent in Japanese Law, in 1 Ius Privatum Gentium: Festschrift für Max Rheinstein zum 70. Geburtstag am 5. Juli 1969, at 85, 87-88, 91-95, 98-99 (Ernst von Caemmerer, Soia Mentschikoff & Konrad Zweigert eds. 1969) 968
Suzuki v. City of Tokyo 971
Note on Public Registries in East Asia 971
Notes and Questions 972
9. The Impact of the Regulatory State 974
Mary Ann Glendon, The Sources of Law in a Changing Legal Order, 17 Creighton Law Review 663, 682-84 (1984) 974
B. The Interpretation of the Law 975
1. Italy: Folklore and Practice 975
John Henry Merryman, The Italian Style III: Interpretation, 18 Stanford Law Review 583, 585-96 (1966) 975
Notes and Questions 979
2. Spain 980
Note 980
The Order of Jesuits v. Spain 980
3. France: Response to the Folklore 983
Note 983
John P. Dawson, The Oracles of the Law 375-76, 379-81, 392, 397-405, 414-16, 431 (1968) 983
Questions 989
Scotch Whisky Association v. S.A. Suprex 989
Notes and Questions 990
Charles v. Desmares (English translation published in André Tunc, Traffic Accidents: Fault or Risk?, 15 Seton Hall Law Review 831, 838-39 (1985)) 991

Page

Ruth Redmond-Cooper, The Relevance of Fault in Determining Liability for Road Accidents: The French Experience, 38 International and Comparative Law Quarterly 502-09 (1989) 992
Notes and Questions 998
4. Certainty and Equity 998
Note 998
John Henry Merryman, The Civil Law Tradition: An Introduction to the Legal Systems of Western Europe and Latin America 48-55 (2d ed. 1985) 998
5. Germany and the Flight into the General Clauses 1001
Note 1001
John P. Dawson, The Oracles of the Law 475-77 (1968) 1002
Notes and Questions 1003
6. The Latin American Variant: Argentina 1004
Enrique Zuleta-Puceiro, Statutory Interpretation in Argentina, in Interpreting Statutes: A Comparative Study 29, 33, 60-62, 65, 69-71 (D. Neil MacCormick & Robert S. Summers eds. 1991) 1004
Question 1008
7. The Abuse of Right Doctrine in Japan 1008
Kazuaki Sono & Yasuhiro Fujioka, The Role of the Abuse of Right Doctrine in Japan, 35 Louisiana Law Review 1037-40, 1043-46 (1975) 1008
Notes and Questions 1011

CHAPTER 10. PROCEDURE 1013
A. Civil Procedure 1013
1. An Overview of Civil Procedure 1013
John Henry Merryman, The Civil Law Tradition: An Introduction to the Legal Systems of Western Europe and Latin America 111-23 (2d ed. 1985) 1013
Notes and Questions 1022
Note on Attorney Fees and Court Costs 1026
Notes and Questions 1028
2. Characteristics of German Civil Procedure and Its "Advantage" 1029
Note 1029
Civil Procedure Code of Germany, Section 139 1029
Hein Kötz, Civil Litigation and the Public Interest, 1 Civil Justice Quarterly 237, 241-43 (1982) 1029
William B. Fisch, Recent Developments in West German Civil Procedure, 6 Hastings International and Comparative Law Review 221, 254-57, 279-82 (1983) 1031
John C. Reitz, Why We Probably Cannot Adopt the German Advantage in Civil Procedure, 75 Iowa Law Review 987-90, 1001-03, 1007-09 (1990) 1035

Page
Notes and Questions ... 1039
3. France and the New Code of Civil Procedure ... 1041
James Beardsley, Proof of Fact in French Civil Procedure, 34 American Journal of Comparative Law 459, 466-69, 475, 485-86 (1986) ... 1041
Note on Types of Civil Proceedings ... 1044
4. Italy: Summary Proceedings and Other Mechanisms to Reduce Delay ... 1045
Oscar G. Chase, Civil Litigation Delay in Italy and the United States, 36 American Journal of Comparative Law 41, 70-74, 76-77 (1988) ... 1045
Notes and Questions ... 1047
5. Brazil: Between Tradition and Reform ... 1049
Note ... 1049
Keith S. Rosenn, Civil Procedure in Brazil, 34 American Journal of Comparative Law 487-90, 523-25 (1986) ... 1049
Notes and Questions ... 1053
6. Japan: Ordinary Litigation and Other Types of Proceedings ... 1054
John O. Haley & Dan F. Henderson, Law and the Legal Process in Japan 814-16, 897-902 (1988) ... 1054
Abe v. Chiba (English translation published in Henderson & Haley, Law and the Legal Process in Japan 647-48 (1979)) 1058
Notes and Questions ... 1059
B. Criminal Procedure ... 1060
1. An Overview of Criminal Procedure ... 1060
John Henry Merryman, The Civil Law Tradition: An Introduction to the Legal Systems of Western Europe and Latin America 124-32 (2d ed. 1985) ... 1060
2. The Course of a Criminal Proceeding from Arrest to Appeal, and the Search for Truth ... 1066
Rudolf B. Schlesinger, Comparing Criminal Procedure: A Plea for Utilizing Foreign Experience, 26 Buffalo Law Review 361, 364-72, 337-81 (1977) ... 1066
Notes and Questions ... 1072
Note on the Joinder of a Civil Plaintiff ... 1073
3. France: The Investigation of Offenses ... 1075
Edward A. Tomlinson, The Saga of Wiretapping in France: What It Tells Us About the French Criminal Justice System, 53 Louisiana Law Review 1091, 1103-09 (1993) ... 1075
Notes and Questions ... 1079
Note on the Guilty Plea, Prosecutorial Discretion, and Plea Bargaining ... 1080
4. Germany: Bargaining Justice ... 1082
Note ... 1082
Joachim Herrmann, Bargaining Justice — A Bargain for German Criminal Justice?, 53 University of Pittsburgh Law Review 755-65, 767-69 (1992) ... 1082

Page
Germany v. D and Y 1087
Notes and Questions 1090
5. Juries and Lay Judges 1091
Note 1091
David S. Clark, The Selection and Accountability of Judges in West Germany: Implementation of a *Rechtsstaat*, 61 Southern California Law Review 1795, 1829-32 (1988) 1091
John H. Langbein, Mixed Court and Jury Court: Could the Continental Alternative Fill the American Need?, 1981 American Bar Foundation Research Journal 195, 197-205 (1981) 1093
Notes and Questions 1098
6. Italy: The 1989 Code of Criminal Procedure 1099
Note on the Italian Revolution in Criminal Procedure 1099
William T. Pizzi & Luca Marafioti, The New Italian Code of Criminal Procedure: The Difficulties of Building an Adversarial Trial System on a Civil Law Foundation, 17 Yale Journal of International Law 1, 10-15, 17, 19-26, 33-35 (1992) 1100
Notes and Questions 1107
7. Latin America: Delay, Social Inequality, and Political Repression 1109
Note 1109
Rogelio Pérez Perdomo, La Justicia Penal en la Investigación Socio-Jurídica de América Latina, in Comparative and Private International Law: Essays in Honor of John Henry Merryman on His Seventieth Birthday 257, 272-74 (1990) 1109
8. Argentina: The Need for Procedural Fairness 1111
Alejandro M. Garro, Nine Years of Transition to Democracy in Argentina: Partial Failure or Qualified Success?, 31 Columbia Journal of Transnational Law 1, 29-34, 37-46 (1993) ... 1111
Notes and Questions 1118
9. Japan: Efficient Leniency 1119
John Owen Haley, Authority Without Power: Law and the Japanese Paradox 125-33, 135-38 (1991) 1119
Notes and Questions 1125

CHAPTER 11. SUBSTANTIVE RULES AND THE PRIVATE LAW CODES 1127
A. How the Law Is Divided 1128
1. Legal Categories 1128
John Henry Merryman, The Civil Law Tradition: An Introduction to the Legal Systems of Western Europe and Latin America 90-100 (2d ed. 1985) 1128
Notes and Questions 1135
2. French Legal Categories 1136

Page

René David, French Law: Its Structure, Sources and Methodology 95-97, 108-22, 127-30, 132-35, 137-42, 144-46 (Michael Kindred trans. 1972) 1136
Notes and Questions 1147
Bibliographic Note 1148
B. Codification and the Codes 1149
1. Codification as a Continuing Process 1149
Denis Tallon, Reforming the Codes in a Civil Law Country, 15 Journal of the Society of Public Teachers of Law 33-41 (1980) 1149
2. The Structure of a Civil Code 1156
Alain Levasseur, On the Structure of a Civil Code, 44 Tulane Law Review 693, 694-97, 699-703 (1970) 1156
3. The French Civil Code 1161
French Civil Code: Principal Headings 1161
Notes and Questions 1162
4. The German Civil Code 1163
E.J. Cohn, I Manual of German Law 56-57, 62-63, 94-96, 170-71, 221-22, 257-60, 282-83 (2d ed. 1968) 1163
German Civil Code: Principal Headings 1173
Notes and Questions 1175
5. The Italian Civil Code 1175
Mauro Cappelletti, John Henry Merryman & Joseph M. Perillo, The Italian Legal System: An Introduction 229-39 (1967) 1175
Italian Civil Code: Principal Headings 1181
Notes and Questions 1183
6. The Mexican Civil Code 1184
Helen L. Clagett & David M. Valderrama, A Revised Guide to the Law & Legal Literature of Mexico 69-70 (1973) 1184
Mexican Civil Code: Principal Headings 1185
Notes and Questions 1186
7. The Japanese Civil Code 1187
Note 1187
Japanese Civil Code: Principal Headings 1187
Notes and Questions 1190
C. A Brief Look at Substantive Law: Property 1191
1. Italian Property Law 1191
John Henry Merryman, Ownership and Estate (Variations on a Theme by Lawson), 48 Tulane Law Review 916, 924-45 (1974) 1191
Notes and Questions 1204
2. An Italian Case: Piercy v. E.T.F.A.S. 1205
Note 1205
Italian Civil Code, Articles 692, 698 1205
Vera Norina Mameli née Piercy v. E.T.F.A.S. 1206
Notes and Questions 1225

Page

Note on the Registration of Rights 1226

D. The Use of Civil Law General Principles: Tort and Contract in Japan 1227

1. Precontractual Liability 1227

Shoji Kawakami, Precontractual Liability: Japan, in Precontractual Liability: Reports to the XIIIth Congress of the International Academy of Comparative Law 205-21 (E.H. Hondius ed. 1990) 1227

2. Informed Consent 1230

Civil Code of Japan, Articles 1, 415, 643-645, 656, 709 1230

Hiroyuki Hattori et al., The Patient's Right to Information in Japan: Legal Rules and Doctors' Opinions, 32 Social Science & Medicine 1007-10 (1991) 1231

3. Negligence 1234

Watanabe v. Chisso K.K. 1234

Notes and Questions 1239

CHAPTER 12. THE FUTURE OF THE CIVIL LAW TRADITION 1241

John Henry Merryman, The Civil Law Tradition: An Introduction to the Legal Systems of Western Europe and Latin America 151-58 (2d ed. 1985) 1241

Questions 1247

Table of Cases 1249

List of Foreign Abbreviations 1253

Table of Tables 1255

Table of Figures 1257

Index 1259

Chapter 1
INTRODUCTION TO COMPARATIVE LAW

NOTE ON COMPARATIVE LAW

Most law schools in Europe, North America, Latin America, East Asia, and in other parts of the world offer courses and support scholarship in something called "comparative law." What is comparative law and why is it studied and taught?

What is comparative law? Most comparative law teaching and scholarship could more accurately be called "foreign law," since its principal aim is to describe foreign legal systems. In the United States comparative law courses usually describe European civil law systems to common law lawyers. The titles of other commonly taught courses, such as French law, Latin American law, or European Union law, more accurately indicate their primarily descriptive, rather than comparative, nature. Some comparison does go on in such courses, but it usually has a descriptive purpose. For example, the statement that French public prosecutors are career civil servants means more when we contrast them with our publicly elected and highly political prosecutors, who have similar functions. In short, most comparative law is only incidentally comparative. True comparative law does exist, but it is relatively rare. When you read the excerpts in this chapter you may find it interesting to ask yourself whether the author is talking about comparative law or something else.

Why study foreign and comparative law? There are several reasons. One is to deprovincialize students, broaden their perspectives, and show them that other people can do things differently and yet survive and prosper. If a nation's legal system reflects its history, culture, and values, foreign and comparative law is part of a liberal legal education; a cultivated American lawyer should be familiar with the principal features of other major legal systems and have some idea of how lawyers in other major nations think, and why they think that way. Another reason is practical: to prepare students to deal effectively with foreign law, lawyers, and legal institutions in an interdependent, highly interactive world. The internationalization of economies and the growing ease and frequency of international travel and communications make it increasingly difficult to practice law parochially; even the most tranquil small-town practitioner in the Heartland will unexpectedly confront foreign problems — a resident traveling in Mexico has an automobile accident; a local manufacturer begins selling to a Japanese buyer; a client inherits property in Italy. Third, foreign legal systems are a source of ideas, of examples of different ways of defining and dealing with common social problems. Just as Solon and Aristotle studied the laws of other city-states in developing their own ideas about laws and constitutions, so today's lawmakers examine and borrow from foreign legal experience. For instance, the condominium, widely employed in the United States since World War II, was directly borrowed from

Mediterranean Europe. A number of civil law nations have adopted aspects of the common law trust. Nations throughout the world live under American-style constitutions, and since World War II many nations have instituted forms of judicial review derived from American experience. Examples of this kind of legal "transplantation" could easily be multiplied. Fourth, since the late 19th century, scholars and politicians have advocated the international unification of private law, an enterprise that necessarily calls for the description and evaluation of different private law systems. The ideal of international unification inspired the first International Congress of Comparative Law held in Paris in 1900 and remains on the agenda of subsequent congresses of comparative law that are now held every fourth year. That ideal also led to establishment of the International Institute for the Unification of Private Law in Rome, which is supported by a large number of nations, including the United States. Fifth, since the growth of interest in the sociology of law, the study of the relations between law and society has naturally encouraged comparative studies. One can learn only so much from the study of law in one society; extending the inquiry to others expands one's database and suggests more generally valid conclusions.

These are the main justifications commonly given today for studying and teaching foreign and comparative law, but comparative law actually emerged as an important field of scholarship out of a specific set of circumstances and ideas in the 19th century. Early in the 1800s, as nations (many of them, like the United States, former colonies) influenced by the American (1776) and French (1789) Revolutions joined the modern, democratic world, their legal systems underwent fundamental change. Much of that change was accomplished through legislation. In France and other European and Latin American nations such legislation took the form of systematic codes intended to replace all prior law. In others, like the United States, much of the old law was retained but extensively amended, and it was interpreted and applied under new democratic constitutions that imposed limits on governmental power. Whichever form it took, it was an "age of legislation," and legislators routinely examined foreign laws as a step in drafting their own new legislative schemes. This intense legislative activity went on in an intellectual atmosphere strongly affected by a scholarly interest in "comparative legislation" as a form of "legal science."

Legal science, an invention of German legal scholars, was an attempt to make law a science in the way that chemistry and physics are sciences. Scholars sought to do this by studying rules of law and, since in Europe at that time rules were preferably put into legislatively enacted form, the study was called comparative legislation. The first scholarly organization of comparative lawyers was the French Societé de Législation Comparée, established in Paris in 1869; its *Bulletin* began publication in 1870. The German *Zeitschrift für vergleichende Rechtswissenschaft* began publication in 1878. Interest in comparative legislation was not confined to continental Europe: the English Society of Comparative Legislation was established in 1898. The legal science movement declined in the 20th century, but by then the other attractions of comparative law were sufficiently evident to support its independent existence.

A. MAJOR LEGAL TRADITIONS IN THE CONTEMPORARY WORLD

1. LEGAL TRADITIONS

JOHN HENRY MERRYMAN, THE CIVIL LAW TRADITION: AN INTRODUCTION TO THE LEGAL SYSTEMS OF WESTERN EUROPE AND LATIN AMERICA 1-4 (2d ed. 1985)

There are [two] highly influential legal traditions in the contemporary world: [the] civil law [and the] common law ....

The reader will observe that the term used is "legal tradition," not "legal system." The purpose is to distinguish between two quite different ideas. A legal system, as that term is here used, is an operating set of legal institutions, procedures, and rules. In this sense there are one federal and fifty state legal systems in the United States, separate legal systems in each of the other nations, and still other distinct legal systems in such organizations as the European Economic Community and the United Nations. In a world organized into sovereign states and organizations of states, there are as many legal systems as there are such states and organizations.

National legal systems are frequently classified into groups or families. Thus the legal systems of England, New Zealand, California, and New York are called "common law" systems, and there are good reasons to group them together in this way. But it is inaccurate to suggest that they have identical legal institutions, processes, and rules. On the contrary, there is great diversity among them, not only in their substantive rules of law, but also in their institutions and processes.

Similarly, France, Germany, Italy, and Switzerland have their own legal systems, as do Argentina, Brazil, and Chile. It is true that they are all frequently spoken of as "civil law" nations.... But it is important to recognize that there are great differences between the operating legal systems in these countries. They have quite different legal rules, legal procedures, and legal institutions....

Such differences in legal systems are reflections of the fact that for several centuries the world has been divided up into individual states, under intellectual conditions that have emphasized the importance of state sovereignty and encouraged a nationalistic emphasis on national characteristics and traditions. In this sense, there is no such thing as *the* civil law system [or] *the* common law system .... Rather, there are many different legal systems within each of these ... groups or families of legal systems. But the fact that different legal systems are grouped together under such a rubric as "civil law," for example, indicates that they have something in common, something that distinguishes them from legal systems classified as "common law." ... It is this uniquely shared something that is here spoken of as a legal tradition and that makes it possible to speak of the French and German (and many other) legal systems as civil law systems.

A legal tradition, as the term implies, is not a set of rules of law about contracts, corporations, and crimes, although such rules will almost always be in some sense a reflection of that tradition. Rather it is a set of deeply rooted, historically conditioned attitudes about the nature of law, about the role of law in the society and the polity, about the proper organization and operation of a legal system, and about the way law is or should be made, applied, studied, perfected, and taught. The legal tradition relates the legal system to the culture of which it is a partial expression. It puts the legal system into cultural perspective.

Of the great variety of living legal traditions, the [civil law and common law] are of particular interest because they are in force in powerful, technologically advanced nations and because they have been exported, with greater or less effect, to other parts of the world.... [T]he civil law tradition is both the oldest and the most widely distributed. The traditional date of its origin is 450 B.C., the supposed date of publication of the XII Tables in Rome. It is today the dominant legal tradition in most of Western Europe, all of Central and South America, many parts of Asia and Africa, and even a few enclaves in the common law world (Louisiana, Quebec, and Puerto Rico). It was the dominant legal tradition in Cuba and in the nations of Eastern Europe — including the [former] Soviet Union — and it continues to exercise an important influence on [the remaining] socialist legal systems. Hence an understanding of the civil law tradition is essential to an understanding of socialist law. The civil law was the legal tradition familiar to the Western European scholar-politicians who were the fathers of international law. The basic charters and the continuing legal development and operation of the European Communities are the work of people trained in the civil law tradition. It is difficult to overstate the influence of the civil law tradition on the law of specific nations, the law of international organizations, and international law.

We in the common law world are not accustomed to thinking in these terms. Hence it bears repeating that the civil law tradition is older, more widely distributed, and more influential than the common law tradition. In these senses, at least, it is more important. It should be added that many people believe the civil law to be culturally superior to the common law, which seems to them to be relatively crude and unorganized. The question of superiority is really beside the point. Sophisticated comparative lawyers within both traditions long ago abandoned discussions of relative superiority or inferiority. But it is to the point that many people think that their legal system is superior to ours. That attitude itself has become part of the civil law tradition.

Hence a lawyer from a relatively undeveloped nation in Central America may be convinced that his legal system is measurably superior to that of the United States or Canada. Unless he is a very sophisticated student of comparative law, he may be inclined to patronize a common lawyer. He will recognize our more advanced economic development, and he may envy our standard of living. But he will find compensatory comfort in thinking of our legal system as undeveloped and of common lawyers as relatively uncultured people. Failure to take this attitude of some civil lawyers toward common lawyers into account can result in misunderstanding and difficulty in communication. One of the purposes of this book is to enable us to understand the origin of this attitude and, incidentally, to show how it is, in some ways, a justified one.

The date commonly used to mark the beginning of the common law tradition is A.D. 1066, when the Normans defeated the defending natives at Hastings and conquered England. If we accept that date, the common law tradition is slightly over 900 years old. It is sobering to recall that when the *Corpus juris civilis* of Justinian (discussed below) was published in Constantinople in A.D. 533, the civil law tradition, of which it is an important part, was already older than the common law is today. As a result of the remarkable expansion and development of the British Empire during the age of colonialism and empire, however, the common law was very widely distributed. It is today the legal tradition in force in Great Britain, Ireland, the United States, Canada, Australia, and New Zealand, and has had substantial influence on the law of many nations in Asia and Africa.

2. ORIGINS OF THE IDEA OF THE CIVIL LAW TRADITION

DAVID S. CLARK, THE IDEA OF THE CIVIL LAW TRADITION, in COMPARATIVE AND PRIVATE INTERNATIONAL LAW: ESSAYS IN HONOR OF JOHN HENRY MERRYMAN ON HIS SEVENTIETH BIRTHDAY 11, 12-16 (David S. Clark ed. 1990)

The first sense in which a "civil law" had wide applicability was *ius civile* developed by the *praetor urbanus*, applicable to actions between citizens, from the time of the Roman Republic. Another moment appeared with the great revival of legal studies in Bologna at the end of the 11th century. Over succeeding centuries, teachers at scores of universities throughout Europe taught a universal "civil" (that is, Roman, non-religious) law based on Justinian's *Corpus juris civilis*. "Civilians" studied and practiced this *juris "civilis."* Together with law universal in the spiritual realm, also taught at universities, the two common laws formed a *jus commune* that in varying degrees influenced the body of legal norms in most parts of continental Europe. *Jus commune* was exported by the Spanish and the Portuguese to America in the 16th century, where it was effectively disseminated through the universities established in the New World.

The wide dispersion of *jus commune* over several centuries and its firm hold on legal norms explains its usefulness today in understanding the national legal systems of a large number of countries....

A ... difficulty in understanding the label "civil law" to classify national legal systems is that European and Latin American comparativists do not themselves generally use it to describe their own legal systems. For instance, the two most widely used comparative law treatises in Europe adopt the terminology "Romano-Germanic family"[13] and "Romanistic" and "Germanic" legal families[14] for European legal systems. The term civil law ordinarily appears in English language commentary.... Europeans and Latin Americans are undoubtedly reticent to adopt the term civil law for their entire legal systems since it already serves to identify the core of their private law norms, distinguishing the core from commercial law and setting it apart from the traditional public law category of criminal law.

[13] David & Brierley 22-24, 35-154.
[14] Zweigert & Kötz 69-186.

The Age of Enlightenment brought the end of *jus commune* in Europe and Latin America. Fervent nationalism, often flavored by Romanticism, suppressed the universal and emphasized the particular in culture and in peoples. In the nineteenth century there was, for instance, a romantic quest for a French history based on the supposition of a unique French spirit. In the German area influential scholars rejected universal natural law and pointed to a positive law that grew with the *Volk* it served. Many disciplines discussed the search for a *Volksseele*. The unity of Spanish America was shattered by the wars of independence, as over 20 nations were created. Everywhere private law, criminal law, and procedural law were codified on a national basis in the vernacular. The universal language of law, Latin, lost its preeminence and was no longer used to instruct at university law faculties. Each of a large number of countries in the nineteenth century started down its own unique road of destiny.

In 1928 Munroe Smith, Bryce Professor of European Legal History at Columbia University, wrote *The Development of European Law*.... Smith returned to the tradition of describing what was general about the European legal systems. Some comparative lawyers provided a taxonomic basis for this effort. Henri Lévy-Ullmann, for instance, in 1922 divided legal systems into the Continental family, the family of English-speaking countries, and the Islamic family, based on differences in sources of law.

F.H. Lawson, the first Professor of Comparative Law at Oxford University, took a similar perspective in his 1953 Cooley Lectures, later published as *A Common Lawyer Looks at the Civil Law*....

The idea of treating the laws of continental Europe as a single unit continued with the 1964 publication of René David's landmark treatise, *Les grands systèmes de droit contemporains*. Translated into English in 1968, David argued for three major legal families in the contemporary world: the Romano-Germanic, the common law, and the socialist law. Within the Romano-Germanic family, David discussed the Latin American variant to an extent unusual for most European law books.

NOTE ON THE CIVIL LAW TRADITION IN EAST ASIA

Either by extension under colonial regimes or as a result of the modernizing — or, more accurately, Westernizing — efforts of nationalist reformers, by the end of the 19th century the civil law tradition had become the dominant influence for the legal orders of East Asia. Although former British colonies, particularly Malaysia and Singapore, retain much of the English common law system, and American legal influence, especially in its former East Asian colony, the Philippines, is strong, nearly all of the non-socialist legal systems in East Asia are today within the civil law tradition. Moreover, as in eastern Europe, the civil law tradition is also the primary source for legal reforms within the three remaining socialist systems — China, North Korea, and Viet Nam.

Historically the introduction of European law in East Asia began during the 16th century in the colonial outposts established to protect Portugal's new-found trading route to China. The Spanish, however, created the first extensive colonial regime in East Asia with the imposition of Spanish rule over the island archipelago that became known as the Philippines subsequent to Magellan's landing in 1521. The Spanish integrated the Philippines into their American colonial empire, subjecting the islands to the jurisdiction of the viceroyalty of Mexico. By the end of the 17th century all the laws in force in the Spanish colonies of Latin America were also in force in the Philippines. This legacy of Spanish and subsequent American rule thus places the Philippines closer to the Latin American than the East Asian experience.

On the eve of the French Revolution both the Dutch and the English controlled major trading ports along the Malay Peninsula and the islands to the southeast, with governing regimes in the principal coastal cities established by chartered trading companies. Territorially the most expansive was the Netherlands East Indies, ruled by the Dutch East Indies Company. Within the company-managed trading posts, Roman-Dutch law applied; beyond these centers a mixture of Islamic and customary (*adat*) law was enforced as "the laws of the land." This pattern of limited application of Western law in both English and Dutch colonies persisted into the 19th century. European law thus remained marginal even within most European colonies until the transformation of European nation-states during and after the Napoleonic Wars, the concomitant European codification efforts, and the advent of state-directed colonial regimes throughout the region. In other words, the expansion of the civil law tradition in East Asia was largely a 19th century phenomenon.

A continuing process of reform and adaptation of civil law institutions and processes by old and new independent states in East Asia also began in the mid-19th century. The emergence of Japan as a world power at the end of the century made its reception of European law the prevailing model either by emulation, as exemplified by the Westernizing monarchs of Siam and the republican reformers of China, or by imposition, as in the case of Japan's two East Asian colonies, Taiwan and Korea. Japan's reemergence from devastating defeat in the Pacific War as an economic power and stable democracy has once again given its laws and legal institutions particular prominence as models to adopt. Today, despite the influence of the United States, particularly in the areas of constitutional and regulatory law, resulting from legal reforms undertaken during the Allied Occupation of Japan (1945-1952), Japan's legal system remains firmly embedded within the civil law tradition.

NOTE ON THE MAJOR RELIGIOUS LEGAL TRADITIONS

The civil, common, and socialist legal systems all derive from a European tradition. They express ideas and embody institutions that have been formed in the European historical and cultural context. Although substantial elements of this tradition have affected all contemporary legal systems worldwide, the extent of their penetration into non-European societies differs widely, depending primarily on the embeddedness of indigenous traditions and the broader institutional and cultural influence of European immigrant communities, particularly evident in the Americas.

The major competing legal influences in the Middle East, Africa, and South and Southeast Asia are the religious legal traditions of Islamic, Jewish, and

Hindu law and the variety of indigenous cultures usually summed up as customary or tribal law. For East Asia, there is the residual influence of the imperial Chinese legal tradition.

Islamic law encompasses the system of duties incumbent upon a Muslim by virtue of his religious belief. It is the expression of Allah's command for the Muslim community. Spread by conquest and trade, it has had a proselytizing appeal, since it recognized no barriers of race or class. It is, as is canon law for Christians or Jewish law for Jews, the law of a religious community. It dominates in the Middle East and much of Africa and Central and South Asia. It is influential in parts of China, India, Indonesia, Malaysia, the Philippines, the Commonwealth of Independent States, and Turkey. Islamic law is a total belief system, since it regulates a person's relationship not only with others and with the state, but also with God. It is a comprehensive code of behavior that embraces both private and public conduct. It thus includes ritualistic practices as well as a system of legal rights and duties. Fundamental to Islamic law is the belief, largely abandoned in Western law, that law is an expression of divine will. With the death of Muhammad in 632, communication of the divine will to man ceased. Unlike secular Western law, which is expected to evolve in response to major changes in society, the dominant Muslim jurisprudence states that it should not be society that frames the law, but rather the divine law that molds and controls society. The "unchanging character of Islamic law" created interesting problems of interpretation for the scholars and operators of Islamic law, and differing views concerning the appropriate solution to such problems account for some of the differences between "schools" of Islamic law (the Ḥanafī, Mālikī, Shāfiʿī, Ḥanbalī, Shīʿī, and others).

Hindu law, like Islamic law, interweaves social, spiritual, and legal teachings, in contrast to our narrowly defined, secular legal categories. The law covers such diverse topics as the structure of the household, religious rituals, and laws of inheritance, always emphasizing the religious dimension in everyday life and the psychological needs of the individual. Until recently, however, the individual hardly counted as a social or legal entity; group identity determined social role and status. Hindu law limited each caste to particular job categories and prohibited most social intercourse between castes, including intermarriage and sharing food. Females enjoyed few rights. Support for these traditions softened until eventually India's 1950 Constitution abolished the harshest features of the caste system, and the Hindu Marriage and Succession Acts of 1955 and 1956 enlarged women's rights. In practical terms, Hindu law has been restricted. It persists as a cultural and spiritual force, but the state has appropriated most of the legal functions. Hindu law applies to the 80 percent of India which is Hindu, and to scattered Hindu populations in Pakistan, Burma, Malaysia, Nepal, and East Africa.

Jewish law stands out as the central, cohesive factor in the history of Jewish culture, dictating the form of religious practice, everyday life, and legal conventions. This national and religious character of Jewish law made possible a remarkable achievement, the survival of the Jewish people as a nation for nearly 3,000 years without independence or homeland. For much of that time the Jews were "a state within a state," politically subjugated but permitted judicial autonomy, and the law could continue to live and grow and structure Jewish life. In the 18th century most Jewish communities were stripped of judicial autonomy, many Jews abandoned strict observance of the Torah, and consequently the law lost much of its dynamism. Jewish law remains, of course, a vital religious force but serves few legal functions. Israel enforces Jewish law only in matters of personal status and in claims brought voluntarily to the rabbinical courts for arbitration. Support exists for greater integration of Jewish law into Israel's legal system, but this is opposed by those who believe that this would produce a separation of religious from legal norms and thus surrender to secular authorities responsibility for the shape and growth of Jewish law.

Law in much of the developing world, but particularly in Africa and Southeast Asia, is a cauldron of custom and of Christian, Muslim, and colonial influences. In many countries independence upset the pot, and one can make only the most tentative generalizations about the shape of the law. Customary law differs radically from community to community, tribe to tribe. It is often unwritten. Like Islamic and Hindu law it orders social, religious, and legal life, and it functions conservatively to preserve traditional forms of family and society. The colonial powers superimposed another layer of law on these cultures, an influence still felt strongly in the court system and elsewhere. Yet custom persists and in some cases has even grown more important as a consequence of post-independence nationalism. Indonesia, for example, has largely preserved the colonial mix of adat custom and Islamic law along with codes and statutes largely derived from Dutch law. Customary law, however, is inadequate as a vehicle for modernization or economic progress, and legislators in the new nations struggle to reconcile their law with their future. Internal diversity of customary laws is an additional complication. Nigeria, for example, must contend with 200 tribes and, not surprisingly, favors internal unification over custom. Increasingly, law is used not to serve existing preferences and institutions but to remake them. Land law has been reformed to meet the exigencies of market economics, and family law has been rewritten to improve the status of women and to eliminate polygamy, dowry, and other practices. The future of customary law in these parts of the globe is uncertain.

NOTES AND QUESTIONS

1. On what grounds could the civil law tradition be considered more important than the common law tradition?

2. Professor Merryman states that many civilians see the common law as "relatively crude and unorganized" and "common lawyers as relatively uncultured people." How well trained are American lawyers in history, the classics, and philosophy? F.H. Lawson, in A Common Lawyer Looks at the Civil Law 3-4 (1955), states:

> It is only when a civilian looks at the Common Law that he fully realizes the affinity between the Civil Law systems, and often enough his first reaction on reading a book on English or American law is to say that it is not a legal system at all, but something queer, outlandish, and barba-

> rous: anything that does not follow the grammar of the Civil Law tends to be for him hardly law at all.

Assess for yourself the indictment that common law rules are unsystematic. How are the statutes in your state organized? By alphabetic categories? By categories based on logic or function? Which rules come first and which follow? Why? How are cases organized? Consider the book review by James R. Maxeiner, 23 Int'l Law. 321, 323 (1989):

> While both these [German language] books evidence substantial interest in American civil procedure in West Germany, it is not an interest born of admiration. Today, when many American lawyers condemn the American system of civil litigation and call for alternative forms of dispute resolution, in Germany an alternative system is in place and seems to work fairly well. German clients are likely to view critically anything less efficient or less just than the system they know. Indeed, Germans view the American system with fear. The first sentence in each book brings this fear home in almost exactly the same words. Lange/Black write: "A lawsuit in the United States is often a traumatic experience for a German business." Schack states: "To be involved in an American lawsuit is a nightmare for most German businesses." In dealing with a German client, the American lawyer ought to be aware that the client may view the U.S. system of litigation as inefficient, expensive, and indeed, fundamentally unjust, if not uncivilized.

3. As late as 1989 it was still common to speak of socialist law as a third major legal tradition, but with the decline of Soviet socialism has come a similar decline in the significance of the Soviet version of socialist law. What will become of the legal systems in former members of the Soviet empire? In most of them, socialist law was little more than a superstructure of socialist concepts imposed on a civil law foundation. With the fall of the empire the superstructure has collapsed, exposing the civil law base. All indications are that these former adherents to the civil law tradition are returning to it. At this writing, some version of socialist law persists in China, North Korea, Vietnam, and Cuba.

4. Is it worth noting that, without significant exception, all former and remaining socialist law nations previously had a civil law system? Why did no common law nation embrace socialist law? Was it mere geography, or was something else at work?

5. The Japanese legal system is classified as a member of the civil law tradition or in a special category on Far Eastern law, despite American-influenced legal reforms under the Allied Occupation (1945-1952). The American influence was confined primarily to constitutional and regulatory law and did not alter the basic features of Japan's European-derived system. Dan Fenno Henderson, *Japanese Law in English: Some Thoughts on Scope and Method,* 16 Vand. J. Transnat'l L. 601, 606 (1983), writes:

> Substituting Japan for France or Germany as the model for the "civil law" legal system may rectify the general academic orientation of comparative law courses and thereby engender more student interest in Japa-

nese law. There are several arguments that support this change: (1) the materials are available in English; (2) Japanese law is arguably more important to the practicing bar than either French or German law because Japan has a much greater economic and business impact on the United States; (3) Japanese law may have more potential for intellectual contrast because of sharper differences in tradition and culture; and (4) it is "civil law," though sui generis.

Should any one country's legal system be used as *the* model of the civil law tradition? Any one region's legal systems (Europe, Latin America, or East Asia)? Are all national legal systems inherently culture bound?

6. Islamic, Hindu, African and Asian customary, and Jewish societies all conceive of law as one element in the moral, spiritual, and social fabric of their culture. They imbue law with religious significance and perceive it, often, as a set of categorical imperatives. In the former Soviet Union, law, until recently, was similarly imbued with ideology; although Marxism-Leninism is not a religion it filled a comparable role in Soviet culture, and the law was required to conform with and to express its spirit and content.

Do the civil law and the common law differ in this fundamental respect from the others? Are they truly "secular" legal traditions? What is the basic content of Western legal culture? Is there any conscious, systematic relationship between our law and a coherent set of moral or spiritual propositions?

NOTE ON FURTHER READING ABOUT THE MAJOR RELIGIOUS AND NON-WESTERN LEGAL TRADITIONS

For an excellent introduction to the major religious and non-Western legal traditions, see René David, chief ed., The Legal Systems of the World: Their Comparison and Unification (2 International Encyclopedia of Comparative Law 1971-1984). Chapter 1 in this volume deals with the different conceptions of law (Western, socialist, Muslim, Hindu, Far Eastern, and African), chapter 2 treats the structure and divisions of the law in these legal traditions, and chapter 3 surveys sources of law. See also John H. Barton, James Lowell Gibbs, Jr., Victor Hao Li, & John Henry Merryman, Law in Radically Different Cultures (1983); René David & John E.C. Brierley, Major Legal Systems in the World Today: An Introduction to the Comparative Study of Law 453-576 (3d ed. 1985).

We discuss the historic importance of canon law later as one of the subtraditions of the civil law in Chapter 3, Section E.

Those interested in a deeper excursion into one of the major religious or non-Western legal traditions might profitably peruse some of the books listed below.

African law. T. Akinola Aguda, ed., The Challenge of the Nigerian Nation: An Examination of Its Legal Development (1985); A.N. Allott, Essays in African Law (1960); *id.*, ed., Judicial and Legal Systems in Africa (2d ed. 1970); *id.*, New Essays in African Law (1970); Hans W. Baade & Robinson O. Everett, eds., African Law: New Law for New Nations (1963); T.W. Bennett & N.S. Peart, A Sourcebook of African Customary Law for Southern Africa (1991);

Martin Chanock, Law, Custom and Social Order: The Colonial Experience in Malawi and Zambia (1985); E. Cotran & N.N. Rubin, eds., 1-2 Readings in African Law (1970); Lloyd A. Fallers, Law Without Precedent: Legal Ideas in Action in the Courts of Colonial Busoga (1969); Max Gluckman, ed., Ideas and Procedures in African Customary Law (1969); *id.*, The Ideas in Barotse Jurisprudence (1965); J.F. Holleman, Issues in African Law (1974); T.W. Hutchison, ed., Africa and Law: Developing Legal Systems in African Commonwealth Nations (1968); Hilda Kuper & Leo Kuper, African Law: Adaptation and Development (1965); Kristin Mann & Richard Roberts, eds., Law in Colonial Africa (1991); A. Kodwo Mensah-Brown, Introduction to Law in Contemporary Africa (1976); H.F. Morris & James S. Read, Indirect Rule and the Search for Justice: Essays in East African Legal History (1972); Charles Mwalimu, The Kenyan Legal System: An Overview (1988); Muna Ndulo, ed., Law in Zambia (1984); Muhammad Haji N.A. Noor, The Legal System of the Somali Democratic Republic (1972); Cyprian Okechukwa Okonkwo, ed., Introduction to Nigerian Law (1980); Arthur Phillips & Henry F. Morris, Marriage Laws in Africa (1971); A.R. Radcliffe-Brown & Daryll Forde, African Systems of Kinship and Marriage (2d ed. 1962); D.A. Reynolds & J.A. Russell, An Introduction to Law (1983) [Zimbabwe]; Simon Roberts, ed., Law and the Family in Africa (1977); Jeswald W. Salacuse, 1-2 An Introduction to Law in French-Speaking Africa (1969, 1975); Julie Stewart & Alice Armstrong, eds., The Legal Situation of Women in Southern Africa (1990); Peter Nanyenya Takirambudde, The Individual Under African Law (1982); University of Ife, ed., Integration of Customary and Modern Legal Systems in Africa (1971).

Hindu law. J. Duncan M. Derrett, A Critique of Modern Hindu Law (1970); *id.*, 1-4 Essays in Classical and Modern Hindu Law (1976-1978); *id.*, Introduction to Modern Hindu Law (1963); *id.*, Religion, Law and the State in India (1968); Sunderlal T. Desai, Mulla, Principles of Hindu Law (15th ed. 1982); Marc Galanter, Law and Society in Modern India (1989); Chakradkhar Jha, History and Sources of Law in Ancient India (1987); Alladi Kuppuswami, Mayne's Treatise on Hindu Law and Usage (12th ed. 1986); Robert Lingat, The Classical Law of India (J. Duncan M. Derrett trans. 1973); B.S. Sinha, Law and Social Change in India (1983); Malladi Subbamma, Hinduism and Women (1993).

Islamic law. In addition to John Makdisi, Islamic Law Bibliography, 78 Law Libr. J. 103 (1986): Norman Anderson, Law Reform in the Muslim World (1976); John Burton, The Sources of Islamic Law: Islamic Theories of Abrogation (1990); Norman Calder, Studies in Early Muslim Jurisprudence (1993); ʿAbdur Raḥmān I. Doi, Shari'ah: The Islamic Law (1984); Daisy Hilse Dwyer, ed., Law and Islam in the Middle East (1990); John L. Esposito, Women in Muslim Family Law (1982); Asaf A.A. Fyzee, Outlines of Muhammadan Law (David Pearl ed., 5th ed. 1986); Nicholas Heer, ed., Islamic Law and Jurisprudence (1990); M.B. Hooker, Islamic Law in South-East Asia (1984); Mohammad Hashim Kamali, Principles of Islamic Jurisprudence (1989); Majid Khadduri, The Islamic Conception of Justice (1984); Daniel S. Lev, Islamic Courts in Indonesia: A Study in the Political Bases of Legal Institutions (1972); Chibli Mallat, The Renewal of Islamic Law (1993); Chibli Mallat & Jane Connors, eds., Islamic Family Law (1990); Syed Ḥabībul Ḥaq Nadvī,

Islamic Legal Philosophy and the Qur'ānic Origins of the Islamic Law (A Legal-Historical Approach) (1989); Jamal J. Nasir, The Status of Women Under Islamic Law and Under Modern Islamic Legislation (1990); David Pearl, A Textbook on Muslim Personal Law (2d ed. 1987); David S. Powers, Studies in Qur'an and Ḥadīth: The Formation of the Islamic Law of Inheritance (1986); S.E. Rayner, The Theory of Contracts in Islamic Law (1991); Joseph Schacht, An Introduction to Islamic Law (1964); R.B. Sergeant, Customary and Shari'ah Law in Arabian Society (1991); Anita M. Weiss, ed., Islamic Reassertion in Pakistan: The Application of Islamic Laws in a Modern State (1986); Bernhard G. Weiss, The Search for God's Law (1992).

Jewish law. Gersion Appel, 1-2 The Concise Code of Jewish Law (1977, 1989); Rachel Biale, Women and Jewish Law: An Exploration of Women's Issues in Halakhic Sources (1984); Arnold Cohen, An Introduction to Jewish Civil Law (1991); Elliot N. Dorff & Arthur Rosett, A Living Tree: The Roots and Growth of Jewish Law (1988); Isaac Herzog, 1-2 The Main Institutions of Jewish Law (2d ed. 1965, 1967); Louis Jacobs, A Tree of Life: Diversity, Flexibility, and Creativity in Jewish Law (1984); Michael Kaufman, The Women in Jewish Law and Tradition (1993); Aaron Kirschenbaum, Equity in Jewish Law: Halakhic Perspectives in Law (1991); Jacob Neusner, Talmudic Thinking: Language, Logic, Law (1992); Emanuel B. Quint & Neil S. Hecht, 1-2 Jewish Jurisprudence: Its Sources and Modern Applications (1980, 1986); Emanuel B. Quint, 1-3 A Restatement of Rabbinic Civil Law (1990-1993); Nahum Rakover, ed., Jewish Law and Current Legal Problems (1984); Phyllis Holman Weisbard & David Schonberg, Jewish Law: Bibliography of Sources and Scholarship in English (1989).

NOTE

As the preceding materials show, an exclusive focus on the civil law would ignore the richness of the world's legal traditions. However, the choice of the civil law as the *initial* tradition for study and comparison makes sense because of the historical power of Europe and the growing importance of Latin America and East Asia in world affairs; because of the relative accessibility to common lawyers of European culture and languages; because of the strong influence of European law in other parts of the world (including Africa and the Middle East); and because of the European origins of contemporary international law, maritime law, commercial law, and the law of international organizations. In addition, the socialist legal systems were built on a civil law base. Accordingly, it makes sense to begin the study of foreign and comparative law with civil law and to go on from there to courses in Islamic law, Chinese law, French law, German law, Japanese law, European Union law, and other special subjects.

B. COMPARISON OF THE COMMON LAW AND THE CIVIL LAW

1. THE COMPARATIVE STUDIES OF SIR WILLIAM BLACKSTONE

DANIEL J. BOORSTIN, THE MYSTERIOUS SCIENCE OF THE LAW 40, 42, 44, 47, 56 (1941)

[T]o the eighteenth-century student of history, and to Blackstone in particular, the study of comparative law was not merely the study of comparisons. According to Blackstone somewhere there existed a general principle of law, which was the perfect form of any rule. This perfect form was merely exemplified and imperfectly reflected in any particular legal system.... In the *Commentaries* [*on the Laws of England*] we are taken "from law to law" and we meet law everywhere.

Certain uniformities, Blackstone says, are inevitable from the nature of society....

Blackstone is concerned to show that even those institutions which the student is accustomed to think characteristic of England have analogues in other legal systems. Consider equity, for example. "This distinction between law and equity, as administered in different courts, is not at present known, nor seems to have ever been known, in any other country at any time: and yet the difference of one from the other, when administered by the same tribunal, was perfectly familiar to the Romans; the *jus prætorium*, or discretion of the prætor, being distinct from the *leges*, or standing laws."...

[Blackstone also observed:] "When the people of Rome were little better than sturdy shepherds or herdsmen, all their laws were contained in ten or twelve tables; but as luxury, politeness, and dominion increased, the civil law increased in the same proportion; and swelled to that amazing bulk which it now occupies, though successively pruned and retrenched by the emperors Theodosius and Justinian.... [I]n like manner we may lastly observe, that, in petty states and narrow territories, much fewer laws will suffice than in large ones, because there are fewer objects upon which the laws can operate."...

From the uniformity of man's nature and the constancy of God's purpose arises the uniformity of the laws of nature which makes relevant all information about the past of English law and the analogous institutions of ancient Rome .... It would be impossible to conceive of a country or an epoch whose experience could not illuminate these eternal, universal laws. Blackstone inevitably appealed to history. But, it is important to notice that the very concept of the uniformity of nature, and of the possibility of a science of human nature, which stimulated him to this interest in history led him to an attitude which seemed to ignore the importance of time and place. Men like Blackstone were interested in the past because its lessons were indistinguishable from those of the present. Past and present were merged into Man as the single object of study.

2. COMPARATIVE STUDY OF LAW IN THE UNITED STATES

ROSCOE POUND, WHAT MAY WE EXPECT FROM COMPARATIVE LAW?, 22 American Bar Association Journal 56, 57-58 (1936)

Under the influence of the rationalist ideas derived from the eighteenth century, Kent and Story made creative use of comparative law in our formative era. On every side they compared the rules of the Roman law, or of the modern Roman law, with those of the common law. They showed, or seemed to show, that the Roman law or the civil law, assumed to be declaratory of reason, laid down rules substantially those which were to be found in the English decisions and English law books....

Although comparative law had done notable service in the shaping of our formative law in the period before the Civil War, it lost its hold upon American law writers and courts and lawyers in the latter part of the nineteenth century. Where the writers of the earlier time had cited and quoted the civilians freely, making good use of the civilian texts in the development of their own views, the writers of a later time made no more than a few perfunctory references, either as deferring to an established fashion, or by way of a display of learning. The causes of this decadence of comparative law were, I suppose, four.

One was the insulation, as one might put it, of American law and Anglo American science of law after the classical era was past. In reaction from the natural-law thinking of our creative era, when we used comparative law, we were busied after the Civil War with organizing and systematizing the results of the period of development. The English texts and English decisions, supplementing our own, sufficed for these purposes. Throughout the world, in the last half of the century, there was this same giving over and even disparagement of the universal conceptions and methods of the eighteenth century. A second reason is to be found in the rise and dominance of the historical jurists. They thought of law as something which grew and must grow up spontaneously in the life of a people. The life of a people impressed its spirit upon experience. Hence a people could not expect to make law. Nor could they borrow law or rules of law with any good results. Why, then, engage in a futile search for what other peoples had done? Nothing for practical purposes was to be achieved by comparison of the laws of one people with those of another. A third and no less effective cause was the vogue of analytical jurisprudence in the English-speaking world at the same time. The analytical jurist thought of law as a body of imperatives of the local sovereign. These imperatives gave us a "pure fact of law," with which alone the jurist had to do. The content of these imperatives was not his concern. Such things were for the legislator. Given the imperatives, the jurist could order and systematize and give logical coherence to them. But he did not need comparative law for this purpose. His analytical method was comparative in that he drew his universal anatomical scheme of law from the materials of the modern Roman law and of the common law. The lawyer and law writer, given the scheme of things legal in this way, could apply it to the pure facts of his local law with no more.

Most of all, however, the decadence of comparative law in nineteenth-century America is due to an exaggerated belief in the self-sufficiency of local law. Nationalism, in the form of faith in a local law existing of itself and for itself, took a strong hold upon the imagination of American lawyers of that time. For a season American jurisdictions took pride in anomalies of local legislation and local judicial decision as things to be cherished for their own sake. There was in many quarters a sort of cult of local law....

Comparative law, and by this I mean more than a mere comparing of rules of law, is the most effective antidote to the idea of the worth of local laws simply as a local possession. It is an effective antidote to the idea that a sufficient number of such anomalies make up a significant local law. Thus comparative law is not the least of the forces in the law of today which are helping bring back the universal ideal to meet the needs of an economically unified world.

3. CONVERGENCE AND DIVERGENCE OF THE CIVIL LAW AND THE COMMON LAW

JOHN HENRY MERRYMAN, ON THE CONVERGENCE (AND DIVERGENCE) OF THE CIVIL LAW AND THE COMMON LAW, 17 Stanford Journal of International Law 357, 359-73, 387-88 (1981)

The root question is whether the Civil Law and the Common Law are getting to be more alike (converging) or less so (diverging). I shall suggest that there are significant tendencies in both directions but that convergence, as I use the term, is the more powerful one.

A. *Philosophies of Convergence*

The answers to questions about the convergence of legal systems depend in the first instance on the view taken of the meaning and purpose of such convergence. A brief description of the principal philosophies of convergence illustrates the variety of attitudes at work.

1. *Return to the Jus Commune*

This attractive thesis is based on an interpretation of history widely accepted among legal scholars, particularly in Europe. Prior to the rise of the nation-state, so the argument goes, the entire civilized world was governed by one legal system: the Roman-Canonic *jus commune*. Lawyers throughout the civilized world attended the same universities, studied the same books in the same language (Latin), and taught in the same way, using the same authorities, to their own students. There was a common law of Europe, a common literature and language of the law, and an international community of lawyers.

The rise of the nation-state disrupted the *jus commune* and eventually destroyed it. In its place has arisen a world composed of separate nation-states, each asserting its own legal sovereignty, each with its own law schools teaching its own law in its own language. From a time when there was a universal law, to which local custom and regulations were treated as inconvenient, if necessary, exceptions, we have passed to a period in which there are national legal systems, with any concession to internationalism regarded as an undesirable, if increasingly necessary, infringement on state sovereignty. Law has become nation-specific; lawyers no longer form an international community.

Many view the rise of the nation-state and the emphasis on state sovereignty as an exaggeration, as one of those periods of history in which the pendulum has swung too far, and the convergence of legal systems as a movement away from the extreme toward a more rational and moderate position. While none argue for a return to the medieval *jus commune*, some would support a movement toward a new *jus commune*, toward a new common law of mankind freed of what they perceive to be the excesses of nation-worship. In any such development, they believe, the differences between the Common Law and the Civil Law would necessarily be reduced; a common law of mankind would emerge as the excesses of legal nationalism declined.

There are obvious difficulties with this thesis. For one, the medieval *jus commune* applied only throughout Christendom, thus excluding large areas of the world which would seem by modern standards to have had a reasonable claim to be considered "civilized." Even within Western Europe it is not clear that the *jus commune* was a normal phenomenon. It was sustained by the existence and the power of a universal Church and by the existence (or the fiction) of a Holy Roman Empire. There is something incongruous about urging a return to the *jus commune* for nations that never were part of it: the large numbers of Common Law and Civil Law nations outside Europe. Even within Europe it is artificial to treat England as a true adherent of the *jus commune*.

A further difficulty is that this thesis neglects to mention the very important unifying effects of the nation-state. Before its emergence every town, commune, dukedom, and principality had its own particular laws. The nation-state abolished this multiplicity of laws, took to itself a monopoly on law-making, and thus accomplished a major convergence of laws within its jurisdiction. To some observers this was the more serious exaggeration, since in abolishing local jurisdictions and the legal authority of intermediate associations, the state made the law monolithic, insensitive to local and group interests. Any movement toward convergence of the Common Law and the Civil Law that would further diminish such sensitivity, that would sacrifice more of the particular to the general, is from this point of view to be avoided rather than welcomed.

2. *Legal Evolution*

This thesis assumes that progressive legal change is a natural process whose pace and direction can be momentarily affected by human actions but will, in the longer run, be controlled by larger forces out of human control. Legal systems are more or less developed or mature, standing at different stages of evolution. When they converge, it is because the less developed system is catching up with the more developed one. Such a view is particularly congenial to civil lawyers, since the Civil Law is far older and, in the opinion of many, far more developed than the Common Law. Thus, the process of convergence is one in which the Common Law becomes more like the Civil Law.

There is some evidence to support this thesis. For example, there is a clear tendency toward codification in major Common Law nations (*e.g.*, the codification activities of the Law Commission in England; the Uniform Commercial Code in the United States). However, there also are countertendencies: Civil Law judges are becoming more consciously active, less inclined to conform to the image of a passive *bouche de la loi* and thus more like Common Law judges. The rights of the defendant in Civil Law criminal proceedings increasingly approach those in the Common Law. Such examples show that legal evolution, if there is such a thing, is not a linear process. Nor is it clear which of the two systems, taken as a whole, could confidently be characterized as the more developed one. Indeed, it is not obvious that the notion of legal evolution, in the sense of movement from a less to a more highly developed legal system, has any validity. There are no universally accepted measures of legal development that are independent of specific social, economic and political objectives. This makes it difficult to discuss legal evolution in the abstract, without reference to the character and movement of the society within which the legal system operates.

3. *Natural Law*

The term "natural law" sums up a variety of philosophies that have in common the premise that human beings, individually and in society, have certain common natural characteristics that lead to similarities in social structures, including laws and legal systems. Significant differences in legal systems are in these terms a denial of what is common in human nature. The convergence of legal systems is a movement toward a situation in which the common nature of human beings is properly observed and expressed by the law.

The principal difficulty with natural law approaches to thinking about the convergence of legal systems is lack of agreement about the common characteristics of human beings and human society that determine, or ought to determine, the character of the legal system. Within both Common Law and Civil Law nations people firmly hold a wide variety of conflicting opinions about politics, society, and economics. This kind of disagreement is, in large part, disagreement about the nature of man and society and hence about law. The argument that we are all one does not take us very far if there is substantial disagreement about the nature of the one.

4. *Law as Superstructure*

The Marxist thesis that law is mere superstructure and that the realities that govern human lives lie quite outside the law, in economics, can be generalized to the notion that law is a social artifact. According to this view of matters, nations that have similar economic, social, and political ideals and systems should be expected to develop similar legal orders. Hence, western bourgeois capitalist nations should have western bourgeois capitalist legal systems with converging tendencies, while truly socialist societies, for example, should have divergent legal systems reflecting the distinct nature of socialist politics, society and economics. The differences between the socialist and the western legal systems are, according to this argument, fundamental and irreconcilable, while the differences between the legal systems of, for example, France and England, are superficial — mere superstructure.

If it is true that legal variations between Common Law and Civil Law nations are often mere matters of superstructure, then convergence is easier to achieve; no sacrifice of principle is involved, no large interest need be compromised. However, the importance of convergence as an objective of policy greatly diminishes; it seems less important that mere superstructures resemble each other. Nothing fundamental is accomplished by convergence of this kind. Conversely, if legal differences between Civil Law and Common Law nations do express social characteristics, and are not mere superstructure, then the true convergence of legal systems can only be accomplished through converging social change. If nations begin to diverge politically, economically, and socially, then their legal systems will also necessarily become less alike.

5. *International Transactions*

Whether or not the differences between legal systems are mere superstructure, they have important practical consequences. They complicate and obstruct international communications, international travel and international trade. The elimination of differences in national legal systems facilitates international transactions, increases the general welfare, promotes the diffusion of culture, and leads to international understanding.

The elimination of superficial differences in order to expedite international transactions is relatively costless. But where the source of differences in legal systems runs deep, convergence becomes a more costly and problematic enterprise. The benefits of smoother international transactions must then be balanced against the loss of cherished aspects of one's own legal system. Further, there is likely to be a conservative inertia, a tendency to cling to the familiar and to treat it as organically rooted in the culture, rather than as mere superstructure. Lawyers generally think of their legal systems as important. They generally resist efforts to deprive their domestic legal order of its unique features. It takes a strongly persuasive case to overcome this kind of legal nationalism.

6. *International Integration*

The growing trend toward formal international economic, social and political integration, expressed most dramatically in the West in the European Communities and in the European Human Rights Convention, argues for convergence of the legal systems of the member states. Common policies require for their realization similar legal rules, institutions and procedures, and the "harmonization" of the laws of the member states. Since the admission of the United Kingdom and the Irish Republic to the European Communities, this process of legal integration is an important force for the convergence of the Civil Law and the Common Law.

This kind of international integration involves harmonizing action within member systems, as well as the adoption of rules binding on and within the member nations. It calls for judicial decisions by a non-national tribunal to provide authoritative interpretations of the constituting treaties and laws of the integrated body. The work of such organs as the European Human Rights Commission and Court and the Court of Justice of the EEC is a unifying legal force, bringing the legal systems of member states, both Common Law and Civil Law, closer to each other....

7. *Simplicity and Certainty*

In some cases the desire for convergence of legal systems merely expresses a yearning for simplicity. It responds to popular discontent with complexity and seeks to induce order where there is untidy diversity. This approach to legal diversity would hardly merit recognition and discussion, since it is little more than an expression of frustration at the fact that the world is complicated, disorderly and uncertain, were it not so firmly rooted in human psychology. It is closely related to an exaggerated demand for certainty in the law. The psychological basis for this attitude has been interestingly explored by Jerome Frank, and the quest for this kind of certainty was one of the principal targets of the legal realist movement in the United States, of which Frank was a leading exponent. Among Civil lawyers, Jhering referred to the idea of a universal law as a quest for the Philosopher's Stone.

The variety of these underlying philosophies complicates the discussion of convergence, since the meaning of the idea so widely varies. To view *rapprochement* as a retreat from the excesses of legal nationalism is one thing; to view it as the mere elimination of superstructure is another. It makes sense to act to remove obstacles to international transactions, but it seems futile to attempt to alter the direction or pace of a legal evolution beyond human control, or to pursue legal *rapprochement* when the underlying social, political, and economic systems are drastically different, as they are in, say, Cuba and New Zealand. Accordingly, it seems best to leave discussion of the philosophy of convergence without attempting to assert the dominance or preferability of any of the competing views. Each has its own area of valid application. Each fails to deal adequately with a number of considerations.

B. *Strategies of Convergence*

The strategies or modes of convergence of the Common Law and Civil Law fall under three main headings: active programs for the unification of law, the transplantation of legal institutions, and the tendency for nations with similar political, economic and social features to develop similar legal systems — a process that might be called "natural convergence."

1. *Unification of Law*

Of these, the first is the easiest to illustrate because it often is accomplished through the use of international institutions specifically intended to promote the unification of law. [See examples in Section C at Note 4 following the Henderson excerpt.]

The unification of law strategy places great faith in the power of legislation and raises all of the questions about the possibility and desirability of reform along foreign lines that were argued in Europe in the early nineteenth century in the context of the Savigny-Thibaut debate. Further, the unification of law movement historically, and perhaps necessarily, focuses on rules of law and is thus at the mercy of the different legal institutions, actors, and procedures existing within nations for uniformity in the interpretation and application of such rules. Such considerations raise important questions about the extent to which unification of law is likely to be accomplished outside a few narrow areas in which there is sufficient international consensus and identity of interest — principally international trade — to ensure a common understanding and a continuing effort to achieve similar results in practice. The experience in the United States with the uniform state law movement illustrates the limits and complexities of unification of law as a strategy even in a highly homogeneous society.

2. *Legal Transplants*

Legal transplantation has a long history. A common mechanism has been imposition of the conqueror's law on the conquered in the wake of military conquest; examples are the extension of Roman law during the military expansion of the Roman Empire, the imposition of French law on Europe during the Napoleonic conquests, and the extension of the great powers' legal systems in the modern age of military and cultural imperialism. All former colonies show obvious marks of legal transplantation in their contemporary legal systems, and in some the result has been to combine elements of the Civil and the Common Law within one jurisdiction; the best known examples are the Philippine Republic, Quebec, Louisiana, and Puerto Rico. In each of these so-called "mixed" jurisdictions a hybrid legal system has emerged from the combination of historical influences, and each represents the playing out of an intensive, concrete process of Common Law-Civil Law convergence.

Transplantation can occur by conscious choice, as when an independent nation chooses to import a legal rule or institution or code. Frequently the motivation is that of a developing nation wishing to modernize its legal system by imitating, through transplantation, some aspect of the law of a more developed nation. The adoption by Ethiopia of European-style codes, including a civil code based on the Code Napoleon, is one example. The adoption by Colombia of the Uniform Negotiable Instruments Law of the United States is another. The adoption of unified judicial systems, an elected chief executive serving a fixed term, rigid constitutions, and judicial review of legislative and administrative action in a number of nations in Latin America, on the model of the United States, is another. Indeed, the French model of codification and the United States model of a constitution are the most widely distributed of such legal transplants in modern history.

Legal transplants across the Civil Law-Common Law boundary obviously lead in the direction of convergence of the two systems. The number and variety of such transplants have never been adequately described, and it would be difficult to compile an exhaustive list. It seems probable that the influence of legal transplants on convergence of the two legal systems has been greater than that exercised by the unification of law movement, although there often is disagreement about whether such legal transplants are successful and, indeed, about how one should go about measuring success in such cases. One can point out that adoption of the British system of criminal procedure in France directly after the French Revolution failed. The French soon found it necessary to alter the system in conformance with their own traditions of criminal procedure, although some vestiges of the attempted English transplant survive. To no one's surprise, the Uniform Negotiable Instruments Law, widely adopted in the United States, failed utterly in Colombia. One gathers that the Ethiopian codes have not penetrated far beyond the cosmopolitan oligarchy in the capital. On the other hand, judicial review growing out of an attempt to transplant the U.S. model seems to work well in some Latin American nations. Some aspects of the trust, that peculiar institution of English law, have been adopted in a number of Civil Law nations and seem to fulfill significant functions in those countries. The law merchant, of Civil Law origin, was successfully received in the eighteenth century by the Common Law. The condominium, a concept developed in the Civil Law, has been widely adopted in the United States without substantial difficulty. The same is true of the community property system, foreign to the Common Law, adopted in a variety of American jurisdictions....

3. *Natural Convergence*

The notion here is that as societies become more like each other their legal systems will tend to become more alike. Thus most Civil Law and Common Law nations are western bourgeois capitalistic democracies, at least in constitutional form. There are forces at work in the world that tend further to homogenize these cultures: increased international communication and travel, increased international trade, the growth in number and reach of international organizations, the growing internationalization of business and technology, increasing awareness of the international consequences of phenomena formerly regarded as national (*e.g.*, pollution, control of energy resources, nuclear proliferation), and growing interchange in the arts and in education and scholarship. These tendencies contribute to the growth of an international culture shared by the western nations.

Much of the movement toward convergence of the Civil Law and the Common Law is traceable not to deliberate efforts to impose unification, nor to transplantation, but merely to the tendency of nations otherwise similar in important respects to have similar problems and to arrive at similar legal ways of perceiving and dealing with them. Examples can be easily supplied: a rather general tendency among western nations, whether Civil Law or Common Law, to provide similar safeguards for the defendant in criminal proceedings; a comparable tendency within both legal traditions toward extension of legal services to needy individuals through legal aid; the widespread adoption of a graduated income tax; a growing uniformity in the definition and protection of individual rights; the recent tendency toward judicial activism, of the sort familiar to the Common Law, in many Civil Law nations; and the rapid spread of judicial review of legislation in this century. Other examples could easily be added. It is sufficient to point out that some of the most fundamental and, assuming political stability, permanent of the tendencies toward legal convergence are of this kind. They build upon cultural convergence and follow it. To one who perceives the law as a social artifact, as something that grows naturally out of the life of the people to whom it applies, this form of convergence is the most convincing of all.

Negative support for the same conclusion can be derived from the converse proposition: Nations that are substantially different in their orientation are likely to have divergent legal systems. This is particularly true if they perceive themselves as different and feel it necessary to emphasize, even perhaps to exaggerate, such differences....

Natural convergence is unquestionably the most effective mode of convergence of laws, superior to legal transplantation and to active unification in the depth and permanence of its consequences. Often legal transplantation and unification of laws are merely ways of formalizing a legal consensus already reached by political-cultural *rapprochement*. Less often legal transplantation or active efforts toward unification of law will incrementally affect the pace and direction of legal change in Common Law and Civil Law nations. In this way there may be a small space for purely legal convergence, independent of the movement of economic, social and political forces. Within this space the convergence of the Civil Law and Common Law is an objective which lawyers, as lawyers, can responsibly and fruitfully seek to achieve. The existence of broad areas of cultural, social and political consensus suggests that the space for active legal convergence among major western nations is comparatively large. The experience with legal transplants and with the unification of laws between major western nations indicates that even under such favorable conditions progress toward the achievement of convergence by active methods is painfully slow.

C. *Convergence and Divergence*

Two opposing forces are at work in international society. One, a universalizing force dramatically expressed in the creation and operation of the United Nations and the European Common Market, moves nations to become more alike. As the world becomes increasingly interdependent, as business and technology are internationalized, as people and information move more widely and freely, a trend can be detected. Extrapolating from these phenomena one would confidently predict (and many have so predicted) the emergence of a genuine international community, a world state, and a common law of mankind.

However, even within nations geographically similar and having comparable economic, social, and political systems and sharing in the same broad cultural tradition there are forces tending to cause legal systems to diverge.... [These] include the nature, variety, and power of the various organized interests working within a nation — business, agriculture, labor, consumer organizations, religious groups, charities, and so on — which while not part of the formal government, exercise an important influence on the way that government operates. The number, distribution, relative wealth, and power of such interests will vary from one country to another, even among nations with similar formal political systems. Such internal political differences will have important effects on the national legal systems concerned and will tend to produce pluralism and diversity, rather than similarity.

A related source of divergence is the importance placed by western nations upon decentralization and differentiation within national governments. These forces are particularly strong today in Western Europe, and a similar phenomenon — the Home Rule Movement — took place in the United States in the second decade of this century, producing a substantial redistribution of power from the state to the local level. The impulse toward decentralization is a powerful one, explicitly based on the proposition that local needs and interests are diverse and call for separate local regulation. The rebirth of intervening institutions of government in the form of regions, provinces, communes, counties, and towns with substantial power to make law complicates the legal system, introduces untidy diversity where there was neat uniformity, and thus limits the area of possible convergence.

Thus a particularizing force is powerfully at work, opposing uniformity, standardization, and the loss of those characteristics by which people define themselves and establish their unique identities. We see it in the emphasis placed on specific attributes of politics, history, language and culture. People's loyalties are commanded by regional, ethnic, organizational, job, religious, class, sex, age, and other social-political-ideological affiliations. The Scots and the Welsh in Britain, the Bretons in France, the Basques and Catalans in Spain, the Québecois in Canada, these and other current manifestations of the demand for ethnic recognition in political terms are only one kind of example.

One interpretation of all this is that an exaggerated emphasis on the state is, after centuries of statism, waning. The state is losing power in both directions. From a time when all political and legal power was focused in the state we are moving toward a more uniform distribution of power along a spectrum extending from the unique individual, the bearer of individual legal rights, through local governments, intermediate organizations and the states, to supranational organizations. If this is indeed what is going on, then to speak of the convergence of state legal systems is to take a partial and distorting view of matters. The redistribution of sovereignty — of political and legal authority — is not unidirectional. To the question: Are legal systems, and in particular the Civil Law and the Common Law, converging, the answer must be yes. But they also are diverging; both processes are going on at the same time. If such a thing can be imagined, and if it would be workable, the product of the present tendency might ultimately be one universal, but highly pluralistic, legal system.

D. *Conclusion*

If the process of redistribution of state legal power occurs in similar ways in Common Law and Civil Law nations, then the resulting complexity and variety can be thought of, curiously, as evidence of convergence. If, for example, there is greater legal protection of human rights, more decentralization of law and government, and substantially increased scope for the formation and activity of political, social, cultural and business associations in, say, Germany and England, then their legal systems may be said to converge. If legal services are available to broader segments of their populations through legal aid or group legal service programs, another point of similarity can be asserted. Such developments illustrate a growing consensus about the law's proper extension within the society. They demonstrate the effort to make the law penetrate more completely, to all socio-economic levels of the population. They indicate an increasingly common legal culture — a broader sharing of basic attitudes about the nature of law and the proper design and operation of the legal system. It is undeniable that a movement of this kind is going on, irregularly and unevenly if one looks only at the short term, massively and with apparent inevitability if one takes the longer view, in the West.

The proposition that increasing scope for diversity, complexity and particularism is evidence of a converging trend in western law is, accordingly, not internally contradictory. It seems so only if one identifies law with primary rules and measures convergence by the extent of their similarity in the two legal families. The similarity of primary rules is of course not in itself undesirable, or even irrelevant. Under many circumstances it is a significant convenience to find similar specific matters treated uniformly in different legal systems. In addition, similar rules often provide outward evidence of a deeper legal similarity. The adoption of uniform rules for a converging or unifying purpose may, under the proper circumstances, add incrementally to *rapprochement*. However, a more convincing measure of convergence is the extent to which legal systems in Civil Law and Common Law nations play out the fundamental values of Western culture. The increasing emphasis on legal protection of human rights and the increasingly sensitive legal recognition of particular regional and social interests within legal systems in both families indicate that the Common Law and the Civil Law are moving along parallel roads, toward the same destination.

4. THE WESTERN LEGAL TRADITION

DAVID S. CLARK, THE IDEA OF THE CIVIL LAW TRADITION, in COMPARATIVE AND PRIVATE INTERNATIONAL LAW: ESSAYS in HONOR of JOHN HENRY MERRYMAN on HIS SEVENTIETH BIRTHDAY 11, 21-22 (Clark ed. 1990)

As one moves away from the particularity of national legal systems and the debate about categorizing countries in Europe and Latin America into legal families, the concept of a Western legal tradition may serve other interesting ends. John Merryman, together with three colleagues, undertook to test this concept using the comparative method in *Law in Radically Different Cultures*.[62] Combining the civil law and common law traditions as part of Western

[62] John H. Barton, James Lowell Gibbs, Jr., Victor Hao Li & John Henry Merryman, Law in Radically Different Cultures (1983).

culture, the book asked: "what do legal systems look like in radically different cultures?" and "[w]hat kinds of social differences are correlated with significant differences in legal systems?" The authors selected four cultures, each with one example: Western (California); Eastern (People's Republic of China); religious (Egypt, Muslim); and traditional (Botswana). Four common social problems were investigated in each legal system:

> (1) someone with property, who holds office and has social status, dies: who gets the property, the office, and the status? (2) a crime is committed: what process does the society use to identify and deal with the criminal? (3) promises are made and relied on but not kept: how does the society deal with "breach of contract"? (4) at a time when there is world-wide concern for population control, in what ways does a society's legal system affect family size?...

One of the major lessons in *Radically Different Cultures* is that our view of a legal system will largely depend on our perspective. If one stands in China, Egypt, or Botswana and observes the law of France and England, his looking glass likely reveals more important similarities than differences. [René] David originally took this approach in 1950 when he combined the civil law and common law into one Western system. Åke Malmström agreed that legal systems that are European in origin have so many common features that the civil law and common law should be classed together in a Euro-American group. Geoffrey Sawer, in the influential *International Encyclopedia of Comparative Law*, took a similar view.

More recently Harold Berman developed this theme historically by tracing in great depth the formation of the Western legal tradition.[72] In particular one must pause to think of the systematization of the church and canon law in the eleventh and twelfth centuries as the first "modern" Western legal system. Mary Ann Glendon, Michael Gordon, and Christopher Osakwe have used the concept of the Western legal tradition to organize teaching materials. Like Berman and others, they also argue for the inclusion of socialist law within the family of Western law.

NOTES AND QUESTIONS

1. Blackstone's *Commentaries*, published in four volumes between 1765 and 1769, was as popular in America as in England and served as the source of organizing authority for English law. Did Blackstone emphasize similarities or differences in his legal comparisons? To what end?

2. How much law does a country or a state require? Blackstone (1723-1780) wrote: "in petty states and narrow territories, much fewer laws will suffice than in large ones, because there are fewer objects upon which the laws can operate." Is this proposition true? What does he mean by "objects"? Does Switzerland need less law than France? Does Colorado need less law than Texas?

[72] Berman, Law and Revolution: The Formation of the Western Legal Tradition (1983); see J.C. Smith & David N. Weisstub, The Western Idea of Law (1983).

3. Roscoe Pound, who was dean of the Harvard Law School when he wrote the article excerpted here, mentions the important comparative law work that James Kent (1763-1847) and Joseph Story (1779-1845) carried out in America. Kent, a lecturer in law and chancellor of New York, published his four-volume *Commentaries on American Law* between 1826 and 1830. Story, a professor at Harvard and United States Supreme Court justice, published nine *Commentaries* on various aspects of American law between 1832 and 1845. For examples of the popularity of comparative studies before the Civil War, see M.H. Hoeflich, *John Austin and Joseph Story, Two Nineteenth Century Perspectives on the Utility of the Civil Law for the Common Lawyer,* 29 Am. J. Leg. Hist. 36 (1985); Peter Stein, *The Attraction of the Civil Law in Post-Revolutionary America,* 52 Va. L. Rev. 403 (1966).

4. Why did the comparative law method of Blackstone, Kent, and Story lose favor in the United States after the Civil War? With which of Merryman's "philosophies of convergence" would they be most comfortable?

5. Is convergence of the civil law and the common law desirable? Why?

6. Which philosophy of convergence seems most persuasive to you? Why?

7. Is the concept of a Western legal tradition useful for comparative law? Should the few remaining socialist law countries be included? *See generally* Craig M. Lawson, *The Family Affinities of Common-Law and Civil-Law Legal Systems,* 6 Hastings Int'l & Comp. L. Rev. 85 (1982); Inga Markovits, *Socialism and the Rule of Law: Some Speculations and Predictions,* in Comparative and Private International Law: Essays in Honor of John Henry Merryman on His Seventieth Birthday 205 (Clark ed. 1990).

8. Consider the opinion of the Barcelona *Audiencia Territorial,* a court of appeal, which affirmed the first instance judge's denial of child custody to the mother:

> This court, on repeated occasions, has recognized that the rule of *bonum filii* has become a universal principle of law: article 187 of the French Code, after the reform of 11 July 1975, confirms "the interest of the child"; the Italian Law of 1 December 1970 in article 6 provides that the moral and material interest of the children will be the "exclusive reference" for the measures adopted for them; section 1671 of the BGB [German Civil Code], amended by the Law of 14 June 1970, confirms the criterion "what is best for the child's welfare"; this "welfare principle" is picked as the inspiration for the "Guardianship of Minors Act 1971" in English law.

Judge D. Rafael Gimeno-Bayón Cobos, *Decision of 12 Sept. 1988,* Chamber 1, No. 763/87, in 88 Revista Jurídica de Catalunya 521, 534 (1989).

Do you suppose that the convergence that led to this "general principle of law" — it is also found in the Spanish Civil Code article 92 — was the result of unification of law, legal transplant, natural convergence, or something else?

9. The rise of the nation-state and the unification of national laws in Europe in the 16th to 19th centuries (and in England at an earlier time) obviously represented a sort of "convergence" of the various legal influences within those nations. Some of the most prominent features of these national unifications are discussed in Chapter 5.

C. ORIGINS, OBJECTIVES, AND METHODS OF COMPARATIVE LAW

1. THE ORIGINS OF COMPARATIVE LAW

RENÉ DAVID & JOHN E.C. BRIERLEY, MAJOR LEGAL SYSTEMS IN THE WORLD TODAY: AN INTRODUCTION TO THE COMPARATIVE STUDY OF LAW 1-3 (3d ed. 1985)

There have always been studies of foreign laws and recourse to comparison in legal scholarship. The comparison of laws, at least in their geographical diversity, is as old as the science of law itself. Aristotle (384-322 B.C.), in considering what form of political community would be best, studied 153 constitutions of Greek and other cities in his treatise, *Politics*; Solon (*c.* 640-558 B.C.), when drafting the Athenian laws, we are told, proceeded on the same basis; the decemvirs appointed in 451-450 B.C. to draw up the law of the XII Tables for Rome are also supposed to have carried out comparative law enquiries in the Greek cities. In the Middle Ages, Canon law and Roman law were compared, and in sixteenth-century England the respective merits of the Canon law and the Common law were debated. The comparison of customary laws in continental Europe was the basis of the formulation of the principles of a "common customary private law" (*droit commun coutumier* in France; *Deutsches Privatrecht* in Germany). Montesquieu (1689-1755) attempted, through comparison, to penetrate the spirit of laws and thereby establish common principles of good government.

Many historical precedents can therefore be invoked. But the development of comparative law, as a science, is rather more recent. Only in the last century was its importance recognised, its method and aims systematically studied, and the term itself *comparative law* (*droit comparé*) received and established in usage.

The reasons for this late development of comparative law as an independent science are not difficult to identify. For many previous centuries, the science of law was devoted to discovering the principles of just law, that is to say law conforming to the will of God, to nature and to reason, and there was little concern for positive law or the law as it applied in fact. Local or customary law was of importance to practitioners and the legislative measures of ruling sovereigns were of interest to governments of other countries, but neither was of any real significance to those who as thinkers in the universities meditated upon and wrote about law. Positive law in either form was neglected in the universities. There the principal study, one thought more noble and more suitable to true legal training, was the search for just rules that would be applicable in all countries. This search, which was to reveal the true science of law, was best carried out in the study not of the various national or local laws but rather in that of Roman law and Canon law, the only laws common to the whole of the civilised (*i.e.* Christian) world.

It was, then, only in the latter part of the nineteenth century that the desirability and later the necessity of comparing national European laws emerged, little by little. This development occurred after the breakdown of the notion of a *ius commune* or law of universal application, which was brought about by the nationalism engendered by the adoption of national codifications and the implantation of these national laws as the proper subject-matter of legal studies in the universities.

2. OBJECTIVES OF COMPARATIVE LAW

GEORGE WINTERTON, COMPARATIVE LAW TEACHING, 23 American Journal of Comparative Law 69, 99-106, 109, 111-12 (1975)

A. *Practical Objectives of Comparative Law*

1. *The International Practice of Law*

The American lawyer is obliged to provide an increasingly wide range of services for his client.... The course offered to the potential practitioner must keep his needs in mind.... Accordingly law schools should offer the future practitioner only a general introductory course in comparative law. The goals of such a course were clearly outlined by Professor Schlesinger whose casebook is often used for such courses:

> If it were possible to state the primary objective of a comparative law course in one sentence, I would say ... that such objective is to convey to the student "that modicum of understanding" and of familiarity with concept and terminology which will make it possible for him "really to grasp an opinion of local counsel" [quoting Professor Jessup], and, I might add, to write an understandable letter asking for such opinion. In litigated cases, moreover, that modicum of understanding should enable the practitioner intelligently to choose as well as to examine and cross-examine the experts testifying as to the foreign law....

2. *Assisting the International Lawyer*

In many areas the international lawyer requires information on the domestic law of a number of countries and here he must call on the assistance of the comparative lawyer. Examples are occasions when regional varieties of international law must be compared, when the law of a number of countries must be studied in the course of preparing a draft treaty and when international lawyers must assess a country's compliance with its international obligations — in which case it is necessary to study the actual practice of a legal system and not merely the "law in the books." An excellent example of partnership between the international lawyer and the comparative lawyer to which further reference is made below is the preparation of conventions for the unification of international trade law, especially the law of international sale of goods, shipping and air transport, and international bills of exchange....

3. *The International Unification or Harmonization of Law*

Comparative lawyers being aware of the many similarities between different legal systems and hoping to assist the search for world cooperation and peace have long sought to use their knowledge to effect a unification of law on a worldwide basis. This movement, which Professor Gutteridge traces to King James I, was reinforced by the enormous expansion of international trade in the late nineteenth century, for international traders and governments as well as jurists could see practical advantages in uniformity of law in areas affecting international trade and intercourse. Considerable success was achieved in the form of the General Postal Convention (1894), the Berne Conventions on Copyright (1886) and Carriage of Goods by Rail (1890), and the 1881 [u]nification of the laws of the Scandinavian countries relating to negotiable instruments. The movement toward unification of laws affecting international trade and commerce has continued and the Hague Conventions on the international carriage of goods by sea, the Paris, Warsaw, and Chicago Conventions on air navigation, the Conventions on the international sale of goods, and the continuing work of UNCITRAL are evidence of the success of the unification movement in this century.

Most comparative lawyers have however come to realize that the wider goal of the international unification of all law — much in vogue at the end of the last century — is not a realistic possibility at present, although notable among the idealists who in recent years still clung to the hope that the unification of all law is feasible in the foreseeable future were such great jurists as Roscoe Pound and Hessel Yntema. The present unfeasibility of worldwide unification of law is an inevitable consequence of the emergence onto the world stage of the countries of Africa, Asia and Latin America, and the Marxist countries. In 1900 comparative lawyers could see their task as merely the unification of the common law of the British Empire and the United States with the civil law systems of the French and German Empires and systems derived from them. Unification of the common law and the civil law probably is feasible and it is likely that the entry of Britain into the EEC will see a greater harmonization of the common law and civil law systems....

A very closely related field of comparative legal research is the elucidation of the "general principles of law" which international and occasionally national courts are directed to apply. For example art. 38(1)(c) of the Statute of the International Court of Justice directs the court to apply *inter alia* "the general principles of law recognized by civilized nations" and art. 215 of the Treaty of Rome establishing the EEC provides that the noncontractual liability of the Community is to be governed by "the general principles common to the laws of the Member States." Although some lawyers have sought to ascertain the "general principles of law" by reasoning solely from their own legal system and not from empirical research the principles thus arrived at are not reliable and only comparative legal research, especially common core research, can ascertain principles of law which can validly be termed "general."...

4. *Developing Policy*

The oldest and one of the most important objectives of comparative law is the framing of policy with a view to legislation and legal reform. The study of foreign laws for this purpose can trace its origins to the Greek city-states, where Lycurgus and Solon drafted laws based on foreign models, but in modern times the study of comparative law for the purpose of framing legislative policy really begins with Montesquieu [1689-1755] and was developed by that great scholar of comparative law, Sir Henry Maine [1822-1888]. In Western nations the formulation of policy is one of the most important objectives of comparative law, and there is no doubt that it is by far the most important function served by comparative law in the economically less-developed countries....

B. *Sociological Objectives of Comparative Law*

Comparative law, wrote Professor Max Rheinstein some years ago, is "the observational and exactitude seeking science of law in general.... It searches for ... laws in the sense in which the word is used in the 'sciences'...." Clearly one who wishes to understand the function of law and its institutions in society must study the role of law in many societies. Hence comparative law is the method by which the legal sociologist explores the world's legal systems with a view to establishing general principles relating to the role of law in society; it is not mere coincidence that two of the great teachers of the sociological school of jurisprudence — Roscoe Pound and Hessel Yntema — were also great comparative lawyers.

We have seen that a sociological examination of law, considering as it does the functions laws and legal institutions perform in society, is an important preliminary to the formulation of public or even private policy, for it is only when these functions are understood that policy-makers know how to use or alter them to achieve their goals. A legislator seeking to frame policy on workers' compensation would do a very poor job if he considered the legislation *in vacuo*, merely as a body of rules; to frame policy it is clearly necessary to understand the purpose of the legislation; and a study of the position in other countries, comparing it with that in his own, will enable him to understand the function to be performed by the legislation....

C. *Political [and Cultural] Objectives*

1. *International Understanding*

One of the causes of dissension among nations and peoples is ignorance of each other; comparative lawyers have long argued that their discipline leads to the breaking down of parochialism and narrow nationalism and hence to greater international understanding and cooperation. This view which was at least partly responsible for the great upsurge in comparative law teaching in the U.S.A. after the Second World War is obviously valid; its validity is demonstrated by the work of comparative lawyers leading to the international harmonization of certain areas of the law relating to international trade....

2. *Understanding a Culture*

Although as observed earlier lawyers are naturally ethnocentric, making law one of the most difficult disciplines with which to study a foreign culture, no study of the culture of a society is complete without a study of the function law plays in that society. The comparative lawyer is the only person professionally qualified to undertake this study; hence comparative lawyers see as one of their tasks the study of foreign legal systems with a view to understanding the culture of those societies.

3. THE PRACTICE OF TRANSNATIONAL LAW

ROGER J. GOEBEL, PROFESSIONAL QUALIFICATION AND EDUCATIONAL REQUIREMENTS FOR LAW PRACTICE IN A FOREIGN COUNTRY: BRIDGING THE CULTURAL GAP, 63 Tulane Law Review 443, 444-51, 453-54 (1989)

A. *Bridging the Cultural Gap*

The most frequent justification for the practice of transnational law is that such a practice offers better service to customary clients from an attorney's home country who prefer to rely on lawyers familiar with their methods of doing business and their specific business requirements....

This justification explains the wave of American transnational lawyers who, in the post-World War II era, followed the export of United States capital and technology initially to Europe and Latin America, then to Asia, Africa, and other parts the world....

It has frequently been said that the pragmatically trained American lawyer provides sophisticated business sense and functional adaptability in handling legal business in widely disparate parts of the world....

Sophisticated commercial legal experience and pragmatic adaptability to different legal systems have ceased to be the monopoly of American transnational lawyers, but, in recent years, have also become the mark of leading law firms in Europe and other parts of the world. European, Canadian, Australian, and Latin American lawyers can now convince their customary clients that they too have transnational legal capacities. Many foreign law firms are moving from their home countries to provide services or to open offices in the United States or other parts of the world. The practice of transnational law is increasingly becoming a two-way street....

Another common justification offered in recent years to encourage the practice of transnational law is that such practice is an increasingly important part of the trade in services on a global basis. As the United States' position in the trade of industrial and commercial products has weakened, the nation has become concerned with the ability of American firms to generate revenue from providing services abroad.... [T]he ability of clients to call upon sophisticated legal assistance provided by experienced transnational lawyers and law firms definitely facilitates overall capital movements, foreign investment, and international trade transactions ....

Without diminishing the importance of these first two justifications, the justification that I prefer for transnational legal practice is the role of the transnational lawyer in bridging the cultural gap. By the cultural gap I mean the tremendously important, yet sometimes hidden, barriers to international business and trade that are created by differing cultural, social, political, and economic systems. I have long been accustomed to telling young lawyers and law students that, although the development of competent legal skills is always important, at least half of the role of the transnational lawyer lies in assisting the client to bridge this cultural gap.

This assistance covers a wide spectrum: helping clients (including in-house counsel and domestic outside counsel unfamiliar with foreign practice) to convert their normal legal and business methods into those that can be successfully employed in a foreign environment; conducting negotiations and general business dealings between a client and his commercial adversary in such fashion as to help both sides understand the reasons for each other's basic concerns and desires so that a successful business deal can be struck; helping a client properly manage a subsidiary or other foreign investment vehicle in the light of the customary ways of operation in a local environment; and drafting a contract in a manner that can facilitate a practical application, by both the client and the other contracting party, which is not basically disruptive of either party's cultural or social traditions....

A legal mindset based totally upon rigid adherence to one country's legal system and practices is a serious but seldom acknowledged obstacle to the successful conduct of international business. A good example is presented by the nature of the contract used for a major international transaction, such as a joint venture agreement, a license, a franchise, or a distribution agreement.

Wall Street law firms all too often pride themselves on the development of long, complex, elaborate, and highly protective contracts designed to cover all contingencies. However, it must be said that foreign businessmen frequently view these Wall Street-style agreements as cumbersome, difficult to understand and apply, excessively limiting the parties' freedom of action, and covering peculiarities produced by case law in the United States rather than the realities of the foreign scene. On the other hand, the traditional civil-law approach common on the continent and in Latin America produces short agreements that constitute bare statements of general principles and rather vague terms and conditions. The American businessman (and many sophisticated foreign businessmen as well) find these short-form civil-law agreements dangerously imprecise and ambiguous, with inadequate coverage of the full scope of the parties' long-term relations.

The solution to this cultural conflict is obvious, and has gained acceptance in contract drafting between sophisticated lawyers on both sides of the transnational law street: an intermediate length contract that is better structured and more precise than the older civil-law form, yet avoids the undue length and complexity of the Wall Street format. Drafting such a contract requires great clarity in presenting the essential business points so they can be understood readily by both parties, using a style that can be easily translated, and weighing boilerplate clauses carefully to determine whether they can be discarded or should be adapted to local usage....

Another risk generated by the cultural gap is the failure to recognize linguistic differences in negotiation and drafting. This can cause fatal misunderstandings, thereby disrupting the making of a business deal or leading to future contract disputes.... Americans all too often chauvinistically assume that it is up to the foreign businessman or lawyer to speak English and to deal with English language instruments. This can be the source of fatal error....

In many cases, the United States-based transnational lawyer must recognize that he is not capable of properly counseling the client about many issues in a foreign legal system. He must therefore devote the time and effort to select a competent foreign law firm, or foreign branch of an American law firm, and deal cooperatively with that firm in providing the appropriate advice to the client.

4. SCIENTIFIC EXPLANATION IN COMPARATIVE LAW

JOHN HENRY MERRYMAN, COMPARATIVE LAW AND SCIENTIFIC EXPLANATION, in LAW IN THE UNITED STATES OF AMERICA IN SOCIAL AND TECHNOLOGICAL REVOLUTION 81, 82-84 (John N. Hazard & Wenceslas J. Wagner eds. 1974)

It is clear that certain kinds of activity sometimes loosely associated with comparative law actually involve no comparison. A description of a foreign legal system is an obvious illustration. The typical symposium is another. Such works may provide a basis for comparison, but they are not in any acceptable sense comparative.

Comparison can be undertaken in order to illustrate a proposition, in order to assist in description, or in order to explain. Thus

(1) Constitutional courts exist in some European nations but not others — in Italy, for example, but not in France.

is comparative in only an illustrative sense. Italy and France are compared in terms of a variable common to both of them (the presence or absence of a constitutional court), but the purpose is merely to provide concrete illustration of a general statement.

In comparative law, description is the most common function of comparison. Thus most descriptions of foreign legal systems employ comparison as a way of adding meaning to a descriptive statement. For example, consider the following paragraph taken from a description of European dogmatic legal science by an American writer:

> Although the common law world has seen occasional brief trends toward the kind of thinking that characterizes legal science, it has never really caught on here. Legal science is a creation of the professors — it smells of the lamp — and our judge-dominated law is fundamentally inhospitable to it. Common law judges are problem solvers rather than theoreticians, and the civil law emphasis on scientism, system-building, formalism, and the like gets in the way of effective problem solving. It also diminishes the role of the judge in the legal process, to the advantage of the legislator and the scholar. Both sociological jurisprudence — which is the opposite of abstraction, formalism, and purism — and legal realism — which rejects scientism and system-building — emphasize the difficulty and the importance of focusing on the judicial process. Both have flourished in the common law world, and particularly in the United States.

The purpose of this sort of statement is to add meaning to a description of one aspect of a foreign legal tradition by contrasting it with a comparable aspect of another legal tradition that is familiar to the reader.

Comparison can be said to have an explanatory purpose if its objective is to produce or to test one or more *general explanatory propositions*. A proposition is *general* if all its terms are general. Thus

(2) California is a community property jurisdiction.

is not a general proposition, but

(3) Developed legal systems contain procedures for controlling administrative legality.

is a general proposition. Not all general propositions are explanatory. Thus

(4) Administrative legality should be controlled.

is general but not explanatory. Proposition (3), however, is both. Its terms are general and it states a relationship between variables, in this case "developed legal systems" and "procedures for controlling legality." It is this quality of expressing or qualifying relationships between two or more variables that constitutes "explanation."

It is important to distinguish between general explanatory propositions and prescriptive statements. Thus

(5) One who wrongly injures another must pay compensation.

is prescriptive, not explanatory. The difference is fundamental; it is the difference between the is and the ought. Proposition (3), which is explanatory, states a conclusion induced from empirical observation. Proposition (5), which is prescriptive, states a desired social outcome if certain facts are found to exist.

Empirical observation for the purpose of generating or testing general explanatory propositions is the essence of the scientific method. Empirical observation for other purposes (e.g. to determine whether a criminal defendant did or did not commit the criminal act) does not fulfill this definition. In general, fact-finding for decision-making purposes, even though done with "scientific" instruments by "scientists," is distinguishable from empirical observation for general explanatory purposes. Conversely, general explanatory propositions that are not based on or tested by empirical observation (for example, certain systems of religious belief) are "unscientific."

Obviously, classification as scientific or unscientific has no invidious connotation; scientific activity and scientific explanation are not necessarily better, worse, or more or less true than other kinds. One kind of objective of comparative law is to establish and test general explanatory propositions on the basis of empirical observation. I shall here use the shorter term "explanation" to refer to this objective. Explanation is distinguished from description of one legal system, even though foreign, which involves no comparison. For the latter type of activity "foreign law" is an appropriate term. Explanation is also distinguished from illustration and description, even though they involve comparison.

Explanation, although not inherently superior to descriptive or illustrative comparative law, is distinguishable in a number of ways from them. One of the most obvious differences is that explanation may provide a basis for prediction. If we know in sufficient detail the nature of certain relationships that have existed between two or more variables in the past, and if we have a reasonable basis for the expectation that such relationships will persist, we can predict the consequences of alternative courses of action with reference to one or the other of such variables. Such ability to predict both satisfies a commonly held desire to penetrate the mystery of the future and has great social utility. Accordingly, those comparative lawyers who would find satisfaction in the pursuit of predictability should eventually be drawn to explanation.

NOTE ON LAW AND DEVELOPMENT

During the 1960s and 1970s there was considerable interest in the U.S. in "law and development," with encouragement and funding from the Agency for International Development (a federal agency), the Ford Foundation, the International Legal Center (a Ford Foundation spin-off), and the Asia Foundation. In its least attractive form, law and development meant American lawyers providing "technical legal assistance" to developing nations in Latin America, Africa, and Asia. The activity, though often well-meant, was characterized by ill-prepared activism, conceptual confusion, and monumental presumption. For example, it was never made clear why American lawyers, even if they were comparative law professors (many were not), were in a position to give useful advice to lawyers in nations with different — often older and, arguably, more "developed" — legal systems. By the latter 1970s the law and development movement began to lose momentum. For informed retrospective evaluations of the movement see James A. Gardner, Legal Imperialism: American Lawyers and Foreign Aid in Latin America (1980); David M. Trubek & Marc Galanter, *Scholars in Self-Estrangement: Some Reflections on the Crisis in Law and Development Studies in the United States*, 1974 Wis. L. Rev. 1062; Merryman, *Comparative Law and Social Change: On the Origins, Style, Decline and Revival of the Law and Development Movement,* 25 Am. J. Comp. L. 457 (1977). Professor Merryman sums it up this way (*id.* at 481):

> These characteristics: unfamiliarity with the target culture and society (including its legal system), innocence of theory, artificially privileged access to power, and relative immunity to consequences, have been typical of many law and development proposals and programs for the third world. Put another way, we were probably incompetent to propose or execute third world law and development action, we were encouraged (by our own self-image, by the foreign assistance psychology and by third-world conditions) to do so, and we did not suffer the consequences of having done so.

Merryman proposed that law and development be revived by changing its program from action (i.e., advising the third world) to inquiry (i.e., studying law and social change in the third world) and changing the field's title from "law and development" to "comparative law and social change," arguing that this provides (*id.* at 483):

> an opportunity to rejuvenate comparative law, to enrich law and society and to strengthen the role of the social sciences and the humanities in legal scholarship. It casts the U.S. scholar in the third world in a more modest and appropriate role, as inquirer rather than adviser, and puts the developing nation in the more dignified position of host rather than target.

For the results of one such study, called SLADE (for Studies in Law and Development), compiling quantitative data on many features of the legal systems of Chile, Colombia, Costa Rica, Italy, Peru, and Spain from 1945 to 1970, see John Henry Merryman, David S. Clark & Lawrence M. Friedman, Law and Social Change in Mediterranean Europe and Latin America: A Handbook of Legal and Social Indicators for Comparative Study (1979); Merryman & Clark, Comparative Law: Western European and Latin American Legal Systems (1978).

5. THE COMPARISON OF JAPANESE LAW

DAN FENNO HENDERSON, THE JAPANESE LAW IN ENGLISH: SOME THOUGHTS ON SCOPE AND METHOD, 16 Vanderbilt Journal of Transnational Law 601, 607-12 (1983)

Issues relating to the concept of law in the culture, the role of law in the society, and the interplay of law and language must be confronted when investigating the law of a country as different as Japan. These issues become more acute in comparative jurisprudence because of the foreign language component. Any comparativist researching English translations of Japanese law must confront these critical issues whether his interest is macrosystemic or microdoctrinal, and whether his focus is directed toward academia or legal practice.

A. *Concept of Law in Japanese Culture*

First, the idea of law itself must be examined. Until the creation of the Great Court of Cassation in 1875, Japan had nothing resembling an independent judiciary, no tradition of justiciable law, and no separation of the judiciary from the administration. Even after 1875, the new courts handled only ordinary civil and criminal cases. Under the Meiji Constitution, which had become effective in 1889, a single administrative court with only token jurisdiction was established to hear administrative law cases. Essentially, the political administration remained above the "law." When the new constitution took effect after World War II, the ordinary courts were empowered to hear all suits against administrative agencies as well as suits involving the constitutionality of legislation. The brief experience of only a century of justiciable law in civil cases and roughly thirty-five years in administrative and constitutional litigation has an important message for comparativists, especially in Japan where traditional social controls have been extraordinarily refined. Indeed, the traditional Japanese society was rule-ridden and behavior was minutely prescribed by society, not justiciable law.

Whatever one's position may be on the usefulness of distinguishing domestic "law" and "administration," or "custom" and "justiciable law" (or "law," "justice," and "politics"), it is misleading and confusing for comparativists to use, without stipulating definitions, the terminology of United States justiciable law (e.g., court, judiciary, bar, bench, appeal, trial) when discussing a system without an independent judiciary. In addition, these terms must be used carefully in a discussion of a system having a brief and superficial experience with justiciable law to avoid exaggerating the role of law. These words are value-laden for the English language reader and inevitably will attribute important characteristics to a system unless the entire legal culture is clearly explained....

B. *The Role of Law in Japanese Society*

For historical reasons, even today the role of law in Japanese society is minimized. As used here, the word "law" has a special meaning: it connotes "justiciable law" or "lawyer's law," which implies a verbalized written rule, typically a statute, enacted by a legislature representing voters. This law is *justiciable* because a plaintiff can obtain a favorable judgment by filing a suit in a court, following proper procedures, and proving his claim by a preponderance of acceptable evidence....

This new alien system of law has been superimposed on a highly unusual society. Isolated from the world for two centuries, Japan became a decentralized system of small feudal domains, each made up of largely self-governing village communities of confucianistic family unity.[23] This kind of society produced a homogeneous, highly immobile, collectivistic people, normally dependent on each other (within the family and the village) for their entire lives. Most community matters were settled communally without a formal "court." If the annual taxes were paid by the village to the overlord, who in turn paid tribute to the Tokugawa Shogun, the villagers were left alone in their dealings with each other.... Behavioral patterns, registries, and written rules and records were precise. On the whole, compliance by the Japanese people was remarkable because it was self-imposed by their own small, closed communities.

The Japanese people may not be described appropriately as "law-abiding" because the controls were more socially ingrained and enforced by immobility and communal adhesion than affected by external law. In the home, workplace, and neighborhood, behavior was so socially prescribed and enforced that state-imposed law was not only absent but quite superfluous in private dealings. It is critical for lawyers to understand that today Japan is still socially disciplined to a remarkable degree.

Despite the country's technological inferiority when opened to the West by Commodore Matthew Perry in 1853, Japan was already quite sociologically

[23] For a capsule presentation of the pre-modern system in the Tokugawa era (1600-1808), see 1 D. Henderson, Conciliation and Japanese Law: Tokugawa and Modern, chs. 2-3 (1965); Hiramatsu, *Tokugawa Law*, 14 Law in Japan: An Annual 1 (D. Henderson trans. 1981).

advanced, indeed quite "modern," if modern means adaptable to the rigors of late twentieth century industrial productivity. The workplace has become what the Japanese wryly call the "second village" because livelihood, welfare, and success in life depend on performance in the same workplace with the same people, ideally for an entire career. This concept of the workplace accounts for the immense corporate dedication of Japanese employees. Today, their ability to focus social energy on the task of improving corporate productivity to compete with rival corporations is incomparable. Japanese competitors also have a strong tendency to group together against foreign businesses.

During the hundred years of experience with imported western justiciable law, the Japanese have developed a sophisticated central bureaucracy, a system of administration, and a structure of private law based on imported codes. The legal literature produced in this period — treatises, commentaries, and case law — is voluminous, systematic, and refined. The mix of social and legal institutions, however, remains subtle and elusive to the comparative lawyer with little exposure to Japanese society.

C. *The Interplay of Law and Language*

The third problem of the comparative method is the relationship of language to law. The language problem is both subtle and complex for the comparativist because of the difficulty of the Japanese language and the inherent parochialism of monolingual lawyers. If the foreign law is in another language and the lawyer is monolingual, he can hardly understand the nuances presented by the problem. The lawyer easily may suppose that "law" and its major concepts are quite platonic; that is, extant "things" in the real world to which his language assigns names. By equating *fuhō kōi, keiyaku,* and *bukken* with English torts, contracts, and property, respectively, a lawyer could assume that he is in command of Japanese law and capable of applying it to his client's problem. This type of lawyer tends to be a chronic, unthinking "word substitutionist," who must obtain the assistance of the comparativist lawyer to avoid making irreparable errors....

The best way to approach the law/language problem in comparative law is by reviewing the problem first in the relatively simple setting of the United States judicial process. The term "interpretation" designates the many meanings that lawyers can find in any rule that is applicable to their particular case. On the other hand, "application" designates the single meaning of the law that is ultimately fixed in the court's holding. Interpretation is the product of the client's interests, multiplied by his lawyer's ingenuity in using and abusing language. Multiple meanings are a normal quality of the abstract language used in statutes. Lawyers do not cause the interpretational malady suffered by a statute, they only exploit its symptoms.

The rule of law and judicial process, which embody the interpretation and application problems accruing from the inherent imperfections in language, are now parts of a political value system embraced by both the United States and Japan. A modicum of understanding of the imperfections of technical language in a single legal system is but a first step for the comparativist working with Japanese law in English. Translation of laws from Japanese to

English (or vice versa) compounds the problems of legal ambiguity.... Translation of Japanese law into English requires sensitivity to structural and conceptual differences in the civil law and common law systems, as well as an awareness of the peculiarities of Japanese legal culture and the uses of law in Japanese society.

NOTES AND QUESTIONS

1. Comparative law as a method is as old as Western law itself. What caused the special emphasis on the differences among laws as a focus of comparative law in the late 19th century? Should comparative law at the end of the 20th century be more concerned with differences or similarities among laws, or with something else altogether?

2. For background on comparative law through the 19th century, see Walther Hug, *The History of Comparative Law,* 45 Harv. L. Rev. 1027 (1932); Gino Gorla & Luigi Moccia, *A Short Historical Account of Comparative Law in Europe and in Italy During Modern Times (16th to 19th Century),* in Italian National Reports to the XIIth International Congress of Comparative Law 67 (1986); Konrad Zweigert & Hein Kötz, 1 Introduction to Comparative Law 47-62 (Tony Weir trans., 2d ed. 1987).

3. Consider the objectives of comparative law described by Winterton. Can the type of comparative law discussed by Goebel, Merryman, or Henderson primarily fit into one of the following categories: professional (practical), scientific, or cultural? Which category do you find the most attractive and interesting? Can you understand why other people might have different preferences?

Reflect on Ferdinand F. Stone, *The End to Be Served by Comparative Law,* 25 Tul. L. Rev. 325 (1951):

> There is a story of the man who went from place to place upon the earth and wherever he went he would pick up bricks and compare them carefully one with another. His conduct excited comment. One man said, "he must be seeking the most perfect of all bricks." Another said, "he must be seeking to describe the qualities inherent in all bricks." Still another of a practical turn of mind said, "he is probably seeking a brick of just the right shape and color to fit into his wall." And still another said, "It is possible that he is not interested in the bricks as such but in their composition. Perhaps, he would set up a kiln of his own for making bricks." Finally, a man of action, impatient with the conjecturing, said, "let us ask him and have done with the questions." And so they approached the stranger and asked, "for what reason do you compare the bricks?" The man answered, "I have no reason other than that it pleases me to compare them."

4. Winterton describes international unification of law activities. U.S. delegates participate in four international organizations involved in private law unification: the Hague Conference on Private International Law; the International Institute for the Unification of Private Law (UNIDROIT, Rome); the United Nations Commission on International Trade Law (UNCITRAL); and the Organization of American States with its Inter-American Specialized Conferences on Private International Law (CIDIP). Draftsmen of proposals carry out elaborate comparative studies so that legal rules can fit into the procedural and substantive law of member states.

The United States has in recent years become more willing to ratify treaties in this field. For instance, the U.N. Convention on Contracts for the International Sale of Goods (CISG) entered into force for the United States in 1988 and in 1990 it had 25 signatories. The Convention applies even if the international sales contract is not in writing. It sets out many aspects of the substantive law to govern the formation of the sales contract and the rights and obligations of the buyer and seller. That law governs if the contract is silent on applicable law, whether that silence is by inadvertence, design, or because the parties could not agree on applicable law. For an interesting look at how comparative law analysis facilitated compromise between lawyers from the common law and civil law traditions, see Alejandro M. Garro, *Reconciliation of Legal Traditions in the U.N. Convention on Contracts for the International Sale of Goods,* 23 Int'l Law. 443 (1989).

For the increasing importance of the Hague conventions on service of process abroad and taking evidence abroad, see Chapter 2, Sections A and C.

For comprehensive reports on U.S. participation in private law unification, see the articles by Peter H. Pfund, assistant legal adviser for private international law, U.S Department of State: 19 Int'l Law. 505 (1985); 20 *ibid.* 623 (1986); 21 *ibid.* 1245 (1987); 22 *ibid.* 1157 (1988). Current work by UNIDROIT is discussed in its journal, Revue de droit uniforme/Uniform Law Review. *See generally* René David, *The International Unification of Private Law,* in 2 Int'l Ency. Comp. L., ch. 5 (The Legal Systems of the World: Their Comparison and Unification, René David ed. 1971).

5. Winterton also mentions comparative law research directed toward establishing "general principles of law recognized by civilized nations." Rudolf B. Schlesinger, *The Common Core of Legal Systems: An Emerging Subject of Comparative Study,* in XXth Century Comparative and Conflicts Law: Legal Essays in Honor of Hessel E. Yntema 65 (Kurt H. Nadelmann et al. eds. 1961) states:

> Somewhat similar terms, such as "common core," "common denominators," and "the common law of mankind," have become current in scholarly discussions. These various forms of words may not be synonymous, but all of them express a basic underlying assumption that the differences between legal systems, described in countless comparative studies and daily observed in practice, relate largely to details; that behind and beyond these details there are shared and connecting elements; that these elements can be identified; and that it should be possible, without resorting to mere generalities, to formulate these elements in normative terms.

For the most ambitious project of this genre, see 1 Formation of Contracts — A Study of the Common Core of Legal Systems (Schlesinger ed. 1968).

Article 3(h) of the European Community's Rome Treaty lists as an objective: "the approximation of the laws of Member States to the extent required for the proper functioning of the common market." The process of approximation or harmonization of legislation among the EC's 12 members accelerated under the 1987 Single European Act, leading to the establishment of a competitive internal market in Europe at the end of 1992. By 1995 the European Union could have 16 members.

6. Professor Goebel sees the transnational or comparative lawyer as a cultural broker. Why might American lawyers be particularly well-suited to this task? Why not? On the other side, by 1992 the District of Columbia and ten states had statutes granting the status of legal consultant to qualified foreign lawyers: Alaska, California, Connecticut, Hawaii, Michigan, New Jersey, New York, Ohio, Oregon, and Texas. *See* Roger J. Goebel, *Lawyers in the European Community: Progress Towards Community-Wide Rights of Practice,* 15 Fordham Int'l L.J. 556 (1991-92).

7. There is a trend in the United States and elsewhere leading to multi-city law firms that are evolving into multi-country law firms. Multi-national corporations desire the convenience in dealing with the same firm on a global basis. The American firms with the most foreign offices include Baker & McKenzie (Chicago), Coudert Brothers (New York), Sidley & Austin (Chicago), White & Case (New York), and Graham & James (San Francisco). Baker & McKenzie in 1992 had 1,600 lawyers in 50 cities worldwide, including all the civil law countries surveyed in this volume.

8. As a matter of professional ethics, American lawyers should be responsible to their clients to recognize questions of foreign law. Once such a question is recognized, the lawyer is obliged either to deal competently with the foreign law point herself or with expert assistance, or to advise her client that another attorney or foreign counsel should be retained. *See* ABA Model Code of Professional Responsibility, Canon 6, EC 6-3 (1980); M.W. Janis, *The Lawyer's Responsibility for Foreign Law and Foreign Lawyers,* 16 Int'l Law. 693 (1982). For an example of a court's public admonishment of an attorney who misrepresented a Mexican judgment due to his lack of knowledge of Spanish, see *In re Disciplinary Action Curl,* 803 F.2d 1004 (9th Cir. 1986).

9. For further material on practical comparative lawyering, see Hans W. Baade, *Comparative Law and the Practitioner,* 31 Am. J. Comp. L. 499 (1983); Dennis Campbell, ed., 1-2 Transnational Legal Practice: A Survey of Selected Countries (1982); Linda S. Spedding, Transnational Legal Practice in the EEC and the United States (1987); Richard H. Wohl, Stuart M. Chemtob & Glen S. Fukushima, Practice by Foreign Lawyers in Japan (1989).

10. Professor Merryman presents five propositions in his article, some of which are useful in scientific comparative law. Why is proposition (3) explanatory and proposition (4) not?

11. Consider Professor Alan Watson's critique of theories of law and development (as well as of law and society):

> Let me sum up my thesis. All legal rules are created by a cause. The cause of their creation is commonly but not always rooted in social, economic or political factors important to the life of the society or its leaders. Likewise reasons can be given for the continuance of existence of legal rules. The reasons for their continued existence are, I believe, often factors which have no direct importance for the life of the society or its

> leaders. Often, indeed, the rules of law are in conflict with the best interests and desires both of the ordinary citizens and the ruling élite. Legal rules, once created, live on. They are frequently remote from the experience and understanding of non-lawyers, and are kept in existence by factors such as the absence of effective machinery for radical change, by indifference, by juristic fascination with technicalities, and by lawyers' self-interest.
>
> One of the most striking features of legal rules is their power of survival. Many, many rules endure for centuries with only minor modifications, both in their own land and abroad. The effect of this for the relationship between law and society is grossly underestimated. Theories of law and society, and of legal development, tend to focus on important innovations. This leads to the impression of a very close inherent relationship between law and the society in which it operates. If one looked more at the continuing life of legal rules a different picture would appear....[21]

Watson, Society and Legal Change 7-8 (1977). How is his criticism different from that of Merryman in the Note on Law and Development, *supra*?

12. What are some of the special difficulties that one might have in researching a Japanese legal question? Do you believe that problems similar to those described by Professor Henderson arise in researching French or Mexican law?

Consider the view of Max Rheinstein, *Comparative Law — Its Functions, Methods and Usages,* 22 Ark. L. Rev. & B. Ass'n J. 415, 418-19 (1968):

> More sophisticated is the comparison of legal terms and concepts. "Mortgage" is a word of the English language. Can it be used as a translation of the French word "hypothèque"? The two terms seem to be equivalent, but on closer investigation it turns out that, while they have a common core, they have different fringes. Is the English term "consideration" equivalent to the French term "cause"? The answer is again: to some extent yes, to others no....
>
> Problems of this kind can be crucial in the translation of a statute, a judicial opinion, an international treaty, or a business contract. The attorney who advises an American firm in negotiations with a firm abroad must know in what meaning a legal term appears in the framework of a foreign system, and he must be loath to assume that it can always be rendered by simply translating it into what may be believed to be its equivalent in American legal parlance.

See Martin Weston, An English Reader's Guide to the French Legal System (1991).

---

[21] The theory of this book is in conflict with the words of L. M. Friedman:

"Some of the old is preserved among the mass of the new. But what is kept of old law is highly selective. Society in change may be slow, but it is ruthless. Neither evolution nor revolution is sentimental. Old rules of law and old legal institutions stay alive when they still have a purpose — or, at least, when they do not interfere with the demands of current life"; *History of American Law* (New York, Simon and Schuster, 1973), p. 14.

13. The following excerpts illustrate the variety of methods available for teaching and scholarship in comparative law. Is the writer principally interested in the practical applications of comparative law, in theory-building about law, in the cultural uses of comparative law, or in something else?

6. FUNCTIONALISM IN COMPARATIVE LAW

KONRAD ZWEIGERT & HEIN KÖTZ, 1 INTRODUCTION TO COMPARATIVE LAW 31 (Tony Weir trans., 2d ed. 1987)

The basic methodological principle of all comparative law is that of *functionality*. From this basic principle stem all the other rules which determine the choice of laws to compare, the scope of the undertaking, the creation of a system of comparative law, and so on. Incomparables cannot usefully be compared, and in law the only things which are comparable are those which fulfill the same function. This proposition may seem self-evident, but many of its applications, though familiar to the experienced comparatist, are not obvious to the beginner. The proposition rests on what every comparatist learns, namely that the legal system of every society faces essentially the same problems, and solves these problems by quite different means though very often with similar results. The question to which any comparative study is devoted must be posed in purely functional terms; the problem must be stated without any reference to the concepts of one's own legal system. Thus instead of asking, "What formal requirements are there for sales contracts in foreign law?" it is better to ask, "How does foreign law protect parties from surprise, or from being held to an agreement not seriously intended?" Instead of asking, "How does foreign law regulate *Vorerbschaft* and *Nacherbschaft*?" one should try to find out how the foreign law sets about satisfying the wish of a testator to control his estate long after his death....

The beginner often jumps to the conclusion that a foreign system has "nothing to report" on a particular problem. The principle of functionality applies here. Even experienced comparatists sometimes look for the rule they want only in the particular place in the foreign system where their experience of their own system leads them to expect it: they are unconsciously looking at the problem with the eyes of their own system. If one's comparative researches seem to be leading to the conclusion that the foreign system has "nothing to report" one must rethink the original question and purge it of all the dogmatic accretions of one's own system.

7. THE LABORATORIES OF COMPARATIVE ANALYSIS

MAURO CAPPELLETTI, MONICA SECCOMBE & JOSEPH H.H. WEILER, INTEGRATION THROUGH LAW: EUROPE AND THE AMERICAN FEDERAL EXPERIENCE, A GENERAL INTRODUCTION, in 1 INTEGRATION THROUGH LAW bk. 1 at 3, 5-6, 9-10 (Cappelletti et al. eds. 1986)

This Project sets out to examine the role of law in the process of European integration as seen against the American federal experience. The Project is divided into two parts: in Part One, in a series of introductory studies written by teams of European and American scholars, the political, legal and economic context in which the integration process has taken, and is taking, place is analyzed. These contextual studies are followed by analyses of the Australian, Canadian, Swiss and German federations, thereby widening the comparative context of the Project. Then the actual process of governance in the European Communities and the United States is examined: a study on political institutions and decision-making precedes an examination of tools and instruments for integration and an analysis of the judicial process. Part One concludes by looking at five core areas of integration which in our view represent the basic elements for the eventual emergence of a European identity. Part Two of the Project, which is open-ended, deals in a comparative manner with areas of substantive law and policy in the Community and the United States. The first five monographs cover environmental protection policy, consumer protection policy, energy policy, corporate law and capital market harmonization and regional policy....

In political, legal and economic analysis one does not have the benefit of the laboratory conditions available to the natural and some of the human sciences. The comparative and historical methods thus become the only available "laboratories" for dealing with the issues, general and specific, which such analysis involves. The purpose of such "laboratories" is two-fold. On the one hand, they provide an empirical basis of concrete data upon which to found realistic, not merely abstract, speculation. On the other hand, especially in legal research, historical and comparative analysis is a fundamental instrument for overcoming the dangers of sheer empiricism and value-free positivism. History and comparison serve to reveal actual societal problems and needs, developments and trends, shared by certain societies — highlighting, say, the problem of pollution or the need for consumer protection in economically advanced societies.

Thus, data can be seen in the light of their contribution to the solution of a given problem and to the satisfaction of a given need, and can therefore be *evaluated* — ultimately, as "progressive" or "backward," "just" or "unjust" — within the context of a given development and trend. Suppose the problem illustrated by historico-comparative analysis consists in the economic inconveniences deriving from certain barriers to movement of persons or goods and the need to overcome such barriers. Comparative legal analysis will then be brought to "evaluate" laws, institutions and techniques in relation to that particular problem and need. This approach represents, in a real way, a "Third School" of legal thinking, different both from mere positivism, for which law is a pure *datum* not subject to evaluation, and from evaluation of such *datum* based on abstract, airy, inevitably subjective criteria such as "natural law" principles. Historico-comparative analysis, on the contrary, provides a yardstick for objective evaluation, even though not an "absolute" one, abstract from the "contingencies" of space and time, but one which is relative to the particular problem and need, to the concrete development and trend which have emerged from that analysis....

Thus comparative analysis contains by its very nature an inevitable dialectical tension. On the one hand the subjects of comparison must have a point of identity or similarity so as to render analysis meaningful. This point may be the function of a political institution or legal mechanism, or the structure or even the material-substantive content of a rule or a policy; or above all, the problem or the politico-economic conditions which suggest the need for a legal "answer" or "solution." But an identity or similarity of one factor will frequently be accompanied by differences in relation to others. Comparative analysis becomes meaningless in conditions of identity. Total identity or total dissimilarity are, thus, equally unprofitable in this kind of enterprise. Instead it is the task of the comparativist to spell out the interplay between similarity and diversity, divergence and convergence.

The specific purposes of this particular method are manifold. There may be a policy objective — to learn about and perhaps eventually transplant or modify existing legal institutions, policies or rules by reference to the experience of others. Another objective may be the attempt to better understand a given legal institution, policy or rule — transcending its specific manifestation in a particular legal-political order. Here one will typically try to identify the causes of any converging (or diverging) trends which spring from the array of problems and needs with which political and legal systems grapple. Last, but not least, the comparison of convergence and divergence gives us a unique perspective in which to analyze, understand and, as we said, to *evaluate* one's own legal institutions and even to foresee the probable future evolution within the trend of which they are a reflection. And, of course, seeing alternative approaches often stimulates us to ask questions about ourselves, questions which otherwise might not have been perceived.

8. LEGAL TRANSPLANTS

ALAN WATSON, SOCIETY AND LEGAL CHANGE 98-99, 102-05, 140-41 (1977)

Comparative Law ... was, I suggested, a study of the relationship of one legal system and its rules with another. This relationship, I thought, was discoverable only by a study of the history of the system or of the rules, and that therefore Comparative Law was Legal History concerned with the relationship between systems. But I suggested Comparative Law was also something more. In studying the similarities and differences between systems which have a relationship, one is better able to understand the particular factors which actually do shape and have shaped legal growth and change, and this, I hinted, may be the easiest approach to an appreciation of how law normally evolves. Hence, Comparative Law is also about the nature of law, especially about the nature of legal development, and is a branch of Jurisprudence.

The main type of relationships between systems arises because one borrowed from the other, or because both borrowed from a third. Since borrowing — often with modifications — is the main way in which the law of any Western system develops, at the centre of study of Comparative Law should be Legal Transplants....

I accepted as true — as I still do — the impossibility of Comparative Law ever being completely systematic ....

A study of legal transplants may tell us a great deal about the nature of law.... [The motivating elements in transplantation are] not necessarily incompatible with the rule adopted being the best available for the borrowing system.

But it seems, in fact, that the factors which determine which system is borrowed from often have nothing to do with the needs of the borrowing society. In the first place, the donor system may be chosen because of the general respect in which it is held. This has been true above all of Roman law, but also of English law and, after the French revolution and the promulgation of the Code civil, of French law. At a rather later date it has also been true of German law, as the influence on Japan and Greece shows....

No doubt the remembrance of past glory would make the reception of Roman law easier in mediaeval Italy, and the theory that the Holy Roman Empire was a continuation of ancient Rome would play a very important role in Germany, but the general high quality of Roman law, the accessibility of the legal materials in the *Corpus Juris Civilis*, and the richness of the materials within a reasonable compass were the final and vital determinants. Obviously Napoleon's conquests helped to spread French law even beyond the conquered territories, but the dominant influence of French law in the nineteenth century was more powerfully due to the Code civil and the absence of plausible rivals. For us, the important fact is that once a system is regarded with enough respect, its rules will be borrowed even when the particular rule is inefficient and inappropriate....

In the second place national pride may determine that borrowings should be made, or should be restricted, from some particular system. The consequence is not that the spiritual nationalists will then invent *de novo* but borrow from some other system.... Scots law is a "mixed system" with roots deep in the Civil Law and the Common Law. At times in her history Scotland has drawn more from one root than the other. The fascinating thing ... is the very real feeling that it is better to borrow consciously from Civil Law systems (including Greece and Ethiopia) than from the Common Law (including England) because the former, but not the latter, is in conformity with Scottish legal principles and tradition....

A third factor which influences the choice of foreign law to be adopted, and which is independent of the quality of the law is language and accessibility. The Reception of Roman law was greatly helped by the fact that the *Corpus Juris Civilis* was in Latin, a language then known to all learned men, and contained the law within reasonable dimensions. Likewise the victory of Common Law over Civil Law in the United States owed much to Blackstone's *Commentaries on the Laws of England* largely because they were written in English and contained so much legal detail in one work....

As a fourth factor one may mention past history. It is enough here to remark that neighbouring countries in Africa may have basically a Common Law or a Civil Law system, depending on who was the colonising power.

9. HORTATORY COMPARATIVE LAW

MARY ANN GLENDON, ABORTION AND DIVORCE IN WESTERN LAW 5-8 (1987)*

The protagonist of [Plato's] *Laws* is a traveler far from his native city, an old man who doesn't even have a name. Plato calls him the Athenian Stranger. In some ways he reminds us of the Socrates of the earlier dialogues, but he is less charming and more pious, less elegant in diction and more urgent in purpose. It may be that this is as close as we get to hearing the voice of Plato himself, but if so, it is the Plato who was approaching the end of his own journey through the world.

The dialogue takes place between the Athenian and two other elderly pilgrims, a Cretan and a Spartan, whom he has encountered on the road from Knossos to the cave and temple of Zeus on the island of Crete. Both Crete and Sparta were renowned in the ancient world for their laws, and the shrine which is the travelers' destination commemorates the divine origin of the laws of Crete. At first it seems that the Athenian may have come to Crete to learn about these laws, for the dialogue opens with his blunt question to the others: "Is it a god or some human being, strangers, who is given the credit for laying down your laws?"[5] When Kleinias the Cretan and Megillos the Spartan reply, somewhat equivocally, that their lawgivers were indeed gods, the Athenian Stranger proposes that it might be pleasant to beguile the time on their journey with conversation about the government and laws of Crete and Sparta. Soon we learn that Kleinias has just been appointed to a commission charged with the duty of establishing a new Cretan colony, complete with a constitution and laws. He has been told that if he and his colleagues should discover some laws from elsewhere that appear to be better than Cretan laws, they are not to worry about their being foreign. It would thus be helpful to him, Kleinias suggests, if the three travelers could spend the day founding a city in speech as they stroll and rest on the way to their common destination.

This request appears to be what the Stranger was waiting for all along. No longer the idly curious student of foreign institutions, he now dominates the ensuing discussion, which ranges over the great perennial questions of the purpose of law; the relations between law and custom, law and power, law and justice, law and what we would today call a particular culture, courts and legislatures; and the extent to which the law should attempt to regulate the private lives of citizens. Along the way no important political or moral principle is left unexamined. Family law, starting with marriage and the upbringing of children, is a central topic.

At the end of the day, the Stranger reminds his companions that their aim has been to devise laws for a real city and not some ideal republic; consequently, the law making process will have to be an ongoing one. Since the city must constantly be reexamining and revising its laws, its Guardians would do well, he advises, to send out mature citizens to study especially good laws elsewhere, and to seek assistance from wise persons wherever they may be

---

[5] Thomas L. Pangle, The Laws of Plato: Translated with Notes and an Interpretive Essay (New York: Basic Books, 1980).

found, even in ill-ordered cities. And, finally, he says that the city should always be willing to receive strangers of either sex who have something important to teach or who have come with a serious desire to learn. How can the comparatist not be enchanted? True, we suspect that for Plato, as for Montesquieu and Tocqueville, discourse about foreign systems is in part just a safe and convenient literary device for raising certain issues about politics and law at home. Even so, we are won over. But won over to what?

From the beginning to the end of the *Laws*, no matter what legal subject is raised, it is education which always comes to the fore. The ultimate concern here, as in *The Republic*, is not so much with the right laws for the state, but with the right education for citizenship.[12] The Athenian Stranger continually brings the discussion around to the classical idea that the aim of law is to lead the citizens toward virtue, to make them noble and wise. The Stranger stresses, further, that the lawgiver has not only force but also persuasion at his disposal as a means to accomplish this aim. He drives the latter point home by comparing the legislator who simply issues commands to a certain kind of doctor whom he calls the slave doctor. The slave doctor, a slave himself, has learned what he knows of medicine by working as the servant of a doctor. His manner of practicing his profession is to make a hurried visit, to order whatever remedy experience suggests, and then to rush off to the next patient. By contrast, the freeman's doctor begins by getting to know the patient and his family. He inquires far back into the nature of the disorder, and when he has got as much information as possible, he then begins instructing the patient with the aim of restoring his health by persuading him into compliance. This doctor gives his prescriptions only after he has won the patient's understanding and cooperation.

As for the law maker, the Athenian Stranger asks, should he merely issue a set of commands and prohibitions, add the threat of a penalty, and then go on to another law, offering never a word of advice or encouragement to those for whom he is legislating? This kind of law may be fit for slaves, he suggests, but surely a legislator for free men should try to devise his laws so as to create good will in the persons addressed and make them ready to receive intelligently the command that follows.

I bring up these old ideas about law for two reasons. First, they are essential to understanding some of the most important differences between the approaches of Anglo-American and continental European law .... In addition, they seem to be closely connected to some of the most interesting contemporary American thinking about law. In England and the United States the view that law is no more or less than a command backed up by organized coercion has been widely accepted. The idea that law might be educational, either in purpose or technique, is not popular among us. But on the European continent, older ideas about law somehow survived the demolition of classical political theory and have persisted, at least as undercurrents, into the modern age. The rhetorical method of law making appears not only in the great conti-

[12]The question in *The Laws* is not about what kind of state is best in the abstract, as in *The Republic*, but about what state is best relative to circumstances.

nental codifications, but also, here and there, in all sorts of contemporary European legislation. It is most especially evident in continental family law.

In England and the United States, where prevailing legal theory tends to deny or downplay any pedagogical aim of law, legislation tends to be in the form of the prescriptions of the slave doctor. But recently a few American scholars have begun to talk about looking at law in a way that would not have sounded entirely strange to Plato. James Boyd White suggests, for example, that "law is most usefully seen not... as a system of rules, but as a branch of rhetoric,... as the central art by which community and culture are established, maintained and transformed."[17] And from another branch of the human sciences has come a related invitation or challenge directed specifically to comparatists. In his Storrs lectures at Yale Law School, the anthropologist Clifford Geertz advised comparative lawyers that they would learn and contribute more if they focused on the fact that law is not just an ingenious collection of devices to avoid or adjust disputes and to advance this or that interest, but also a way that a society makes sense of things. It is "part of a distinctive manner of imagining the real."[18] From this perspective, the interesting comparisons among legal systems should lie, first, in their manner of characterizing factual situations so that rules can be applied to them, and second, in how they conceive of the legal norms themselves. It is to be expected that legal systems compared in this manner will differ in the "stories they tell," the "symbols they deploy," and the "visions they project." The comparatist's task thus becomes a venture into cultural hermeneutics.

10. LAW AS LEGAL SYSTEMS

NOTE ON "LAW" AS LEGAL RULES AND AS LEGAL SYSTEMS

When we use such terms as comparative *law* and foreign *law*, and when we refer to the *law* of France or Italy, what do we mean? Do the authors quoted in this chapter use these terms to mean different things? Does the same person sometimes employ such terms in different senses? The question is basic and important.

Legal rules are what most people think of as law, and a good deal of the work of comparative lawyers is devoted to the description and evaluation of such rules. Much of the concern about differences in legal systems is phrased in terms of rules, and much of the effort toward unification of law is rule-oriented. But there is a very important sense in which a focus on rules is superficial and misleading: superficial because rules literally lie on the surface of legal systems whose true dimensions are found elsewhere; misleading because we are led to assume that if rules are made to resemble each other something significant by way of *rapprochement* has been accomplished.

---

[17] James Boyd White, "Law as Rhetoric, Rhetoric as Law: The Arts of Cultural and Communal Life," 52 University of Chicago Law Review 684 (1985). See also James Boyd White, Heracles' Bow: Essays on the Rhetoric and Poetics of the Law (Madison, Wis.: University of Wisconsin Press, 1985).

[18] Clifford Geertz, Local Knowledge: Further Essays in Interpretive Anthropology (New York: Basic Books, 1983), 175.

Rule-fixation is stronger in the culture of the civil law than in the common law because of the peculiar character and the extraordinary success of the French codification (of rules) and of 19th century German legal science (which was a science of rules). That fixation was easily and naturally transferred to 19th century continental comparative law (commonly called "comparative legislation" at that time, thus indicating both a focus on rules and the attitude that legislation was their principal source). Since comparative law as a field had its origins in Europe it is not surprising to find that the reverence for rules, and the relative absence of attention to other dimensions of the law, are prominent attributes of the work of comparative lawyers everywhere. Comparative law comes late to rule-skepticism.

To speak of the comparison of *legal systems* implies that there are significant differences between them. A focus on rules limits the attention to only one kind of difference and equates "legal system" with "legal rules." A more adequate definition of a legal system, however, would include a number of additional components: legal extension, legal penetration, legal culture, legal structures, legal actors, and legal processes. These are highly interrelated concepts, and each of them is further related to the form and content of the rules of law in the system. Like other social systems, the legal system has boundaries, and its components are interrelated by an internal logic. Legal extension and legal penetration help to define the boundaries of the legal system; the legal culture is its internal logic; legal structures, actors, and processes describe its component parts and the way they function.

In every society, much is left to custom and tradition, to religion, to informal negotiation and settlement, to social convention and peer influence, but the precise location of the boundaries between such nonlegal matters and those of legal concern is unlikely to be always and precisely the same. The range of variation becomes particularly significant if we identify law with the official legal system, manned and operated by the state.

The degree to which that system seeks to penetrate and control social life is often quite different from the extent to which it actually does so. For example, large numbers of Guatemalans, Brazilians, Ethiopians, and Indonesians live much of their lives relatively free of any substantial contact with the official legal system, which actually applies with most force to an urban oligarchy and rapidly loses its power as one moves down the socio-economic scale and away from the major cities. In a substantial number of such nations the paper legal system will look much like that of France or Spain or Italy, or of England or the United States. But if one looks at the actual role of law in the lives of important elements of the population the resemblance is only superficial.

Thus along two dimensions, the aspects of social life that the law proposes to affect and the extent to which it actually does so, the scale of divergence of legal extension and legal penetration between societies can be, and often is, substantial. Both the social reach and the social grasp of the law are important variables.

By "legal culture" is meant those historically conditioned, deeply rooted attitudes about the nature of law and about the proper structure and operation of a legal system that are at large in the society. Law is, among other things, an expression of the culture; ideas about law are part of the intellectual history of a people. Such ideas are very powerful; they limit and direct thinking about law, and in this way they profoundly affect the composition and operation of the legal system. A prominent example is found in the quite different prevailing views of the role of judges in the civil law and common law, but there are many others: the effects of the separate existence of courts of law and of equity during the formative period of the common law; the conflict in pre-Revolutionary France between the king and the provincial *parlements;* the role of the civil jury in the common law; the resistance to Roman law influences in England during the formative period of the common law; the list is endless. Differences in modern legal systems can often be explained only by reference to such historical-cultural influences, which have great contemporary power.

Courts, legislatures, administrative agencies, law schools, and bar associations are all familiar examples of "legal structures." They are the composite units that do the work of the system, and their composition and attributes vary widely among legal systems: one can, for example, contrast the German system of federal supreme courts and the Supreme Court of the United States.

"Legal actors" refers to the professional roles played by participants in the system: advocates, notaries, police, judges, administrative officials, legal scholars, etc. Here again there are substantial areas of divergence: consider the civil law notary and instructing judge, who have no counterparts in the common law.

"Legal processes" refers to legislative and administrative action, judicial proceedings, the private ordering of legal relations, and legal education. Here the range of divergence is illustrated by contrasting criminal proceedings in English and Italian courts, or legal education in, say, Belgium and New Zealand.

Each of these aspects of the legal system is a potential dimension of convergence and divergence. Each is, in a very important way, more fundamental than rules of law to a description and comparison of the civil law and common law. The point can be illustrated by a metaphor: let the complex of legal structures, actors, and processes be thought of as the machinery of law — as the law machine. Certain kinds of rules, the kind Professor Hart[a] calls "primary rules of obligation," are commonly the focus of rule-centered legal study. A typical civil code is made up primarily of such rules, which can be thought of as statements of demand on the law machine. An example of such a rule is Article 1382 of the Code Napoléon, to the effect that one who by his fault injures another is liable for compensation. Thus, if *X* unjustifiably injures *Y* (the "if" part of the rule), it should follow that *Y* will be compensated (the "then" part of the rule).

However, the result does not necessarily follow. Some legal work must be done in order to bring it about. The law machine must be set into operation, in this case by *Y* bringing the appropriate action against *X* in the appropriate French court. Eventually, if the machine functions properly, an official judgment will be issued to the effect that *X* owes *Y* a certain amount of money as

[a] H.L.A. Hart, The Concept of Law 77-96 (1961).

compensation. If *X* does not pay, *Y* can make a further demand on the law machine to have *X*'s property seized and sold in order to satisfy the judgment. Again, if the machine functions properly (and if *X* has property within the court's jurisdiction that can be seized and sold for this purpose), *Y* may be paid.

It is important that the society have appropriate primary rules of obligation, appropriate in the sense that they are directed toward controlling undesirable social behavior and encouraging people to do what is socially beneficial. The determination of what kinds of conduct to encourage and what kinds to discourage is a very complicated and often controversial matter. But, fascinating as such questions are, they are not truly *legal* questions. They are, instead, primarily social, economic, and political questions. For example, the question whether, as a matter of legislative policy, there should be a rule requiring *X* to compensate *Y* if *X* damages *Y*'s property is only incidentally a legal question. The same is true of most other primary rules of law.

What is "legal" about a primary legal rule is that it assumes, or calls into play, the law machine. It is the law machine that does the legal work for the society, that consumes the resources, that determines how and to what extent the precept stated in the primary rule shall be translated into social consequences. The primary legal rule is basically a statement of a desired social outcome. The law machine is the mechanism for bringing it about. When we study primary legal rules we are studying what society asks. The mere request will of course affect social behavior to some extent (although we know very little about the nature and intensity of that effect). But if we are really interested in knowing something about the legal system in any society we quickly have to expand our vision to include the law machine — the complex of legal structures, actors, and processes. We will not get very far in that effort by studying merely the rules of law.

There clearly are important interrelationships in any society between the extension and penetration of the law, the legal culture, the law machine, and the rules of law. Still, it takes little empirical investigation to establish that the legal rules in two societies can look very much alike without insuring that other dimensions of the legal order are equivalent to each other. It may be that similar primary rules exercise (or symbolize) a deeper converging influence, but it is equally possible that the same words have totally dissimilar functional meanings in the two systems.

In brief, an adequate description of the civil law requires attention to all dimensions of the legal system and a de-emphasis on rules of law. This is particularly disagreeable because rules are so easy to find and to read, while it is very difficult to find reliable information in law libraries about legal extension, legal penetration, the legal culture, and the structure, composition, and operation of the law machine.

IT NEUTRALIZES THEM.

NOTES AND QUESTIONS

1. What is functionalism as a methodology? How does it affect the questions posed for investigation? How does the project by Cappelletti, Seccombe, and Weiler illustrate functionalism? What do they mean by the observation that comparison of similarities and differences involves an "inevitable dialectical tension?"

2. In addition to the Florence Integration Project, Professor Cappelletti has directed two other large-scale comparative law research programs. First, the Access to Justice Project, commenced in the early 1970s at the Florence Institute of Comparative Law and concluded in 1981 at the European University Institute, captured the interest of lawyers, sociologists, political scientists, and anthropologists to achieve a better understanding of an important social dimension of law. *See* Mauro Cappelletti, gen. ed., 1-4 Access to Justice (1978-79); *id.*, ed., Access to Justice and the Welfare State (1981); Mauro Cappelletti, James Gordley & Earl Johnson, Jr., Toward Equal Justice: A Comparative Study of Legal Aid in Modern Societies (2d ed. 1981). Second, the Constitutional Guarantees Project dealt with certain human rights and their vindication in courts. *See* Mauro Cappelletti, Judicial Review in the Contemporary World (1981); Mauro Cappelletti & Denis Tallon, eds., Fundamental Guarantees of the Parties in Civil Litigation (1973).

3. Professor Watson argues for the study of legal transplants in comparative law. Is he a functionalist?

4. What does Professor Glendon mean by "cultural hermeneutics" as a method of comparative law? What is hortatory law? Are there important examples of law treated primarily as rhetoric in United States history? The Fifteenth Amendment (right to vote) to the U.S. Constitution between 1870 and 1964? The Eighteenth Amendment (Prohibition) from 1919 to 1933?

5. We have seen a variety of points of view about the objectives and methods of "comparative law," enough to suggest that quite different kinds of teaching and scholarship go on under that name. It will help in using this book to remember that the authors are primarily interested in *description* of legal *systems* — that is, of legal culture and the law machine — with references, where appropriate, to legal extension and legal penetration. Comparison, where it occurs, is there primarily to help describe some aspect of a foreign legal system.

6. The next chapter introduces basic questions arising in comparative law practice: that is, matters involving foreign parties or foreign laws. The following case illustrates how "foreign" law — here Roman, Spanish, and French law — may find its way into a purely domestic controversy.

D. A FIRST LOOK AT THE CIVIL LAW TRADITION

WILLIAMS v. EMPLOYERS LIABILITY ASSURANCE CORP., Ltd.

United States Court of Appeals, Fifth Circuit
296 F.2d 569 (1961)

WISDOM, CIRCUIT JUDGE.

This appeal raises a bizarre question bearing on absolute liability. Article 177 of the Louisiana Civil Code[a] imposes liability on the master of a house for things thrown out of the house. The question for decision is the applicability of

[a] Louisiana is a member of what comparativists call a mixed jurisdiction, combining substantial elements from the civil and common law traditions.

Article 177 to an action against the owner and the manager of an office building by an invitee sexually assaulted within the building.

Liability without fault is a sturdy, ubiquitous, long-lived doctrine that can be traced back to primitive notions of liability based on a person's relation to the instrumentality (thing, ward, servant, or slave) that causes injury, irrespective of fault. Late in the long history of the doctrine, the praetorian quasi delict known to Justinian[b] as *dejectum effusumve aliquid* gave rise to an action against the occupier of a house, whether owner or not, for damage caused by anything being thrown or poured from the house. It was considered a quasi delict[4] because the obligation arose without any kind of fault on the part of the occupier. It survives as a "quasi offense" in Article 177 of the Louisiana Civil Code. This article reads:

> "The master is answerable for the damage caused to individuals or to the community in general by whatever is thrown out of his house into the street or public road, and inasmuch as the master has the superintendence and police of his house, and is responsible for the faults[5] committed therein." La. Civ. Code of 1870, as amended.

A corresponding provision may be found in many codes.

The plaintiff was criminally attacked by an intruder in a ladies' dressing room of an office building. She sued the owner and the operator of the building for damages. The jury found for the defendants. The plaintiff appeals, mainly on the ground that the trial judge erred in refusing to instruct the jury with regard to the effect of Article 177. We agree with the trial judge that Article 177 is inapplicable to the facts of this case.

I

On a Saturday morning in March 1957 the plaintiff, Mrs. Philomene Williams, a widow forty-three years old, reported for her first day of work at a new employer's office in the Pere Marquette Building. This is a large office building in the center of the New Orleans business district. Jesuit High School Corporation owns the Pere Marquette Building and leases it to a building management company, Barcom Corporation. About two o'clock in the afternoon Mrs. Williams went to the ladies' dressing room on the fifth floor, unlocked the door, and entered the room. She saw no one. A few moments later, a tall youth followed her into the room before the door could close. Armed with a knife and using a handkerchief as a mask, he forced her to submit to a sexual assault. Several months later, New Orleans police found

[b] The history of the civil law tradition, and its most important figures, is traced from the time of the Twelve Tables (450 B.C.) in Chapters 3 and 5.

[4] The Louisiana Code follows the French Code in not defining délit (offense) and quasi-délit (quasi offense).... "Injury (*delictum*) is when a person by fraud or malignity causes any damage or wrong to another. ¶ *Quasi delicta,* are facts by which a person causes damages to another, without malignity, but by some inexcusable imprudence." Pothier on Obligations (Evans trans. 1853) p. 164. "[Quasi-Delicts] They were all of praetorian origin and do not appear as a separate class of obligations prior to the time of Justinian .... Quasi delicts were actionable wrongs which were not included in the list of delicts covered by the statutory actions of the jus civile."

[5] Fault is not defined in the Louisiana Civil Code nor is it defined in the French Civil Code, apparently in order to keep the concept fluid.

and arrested the assailant, a juvenile fourteen years old. He admitted the crime. Counsel for the parties stipulated that if the assailant were called to testify he would corroborate Mrs. William's testimony as to the attack.

Mrs. Williams suffered physical injury, shock, and severe nervous disorders requiring psychiatric treatment. She sued for damages in the amount of $150,000 alleging that her injuries, pain, suffering, and humiliation resulted from the defendants' negligence in failing to "take any steps properly calculated to reasonably protect the public from such assaults." This allegation of negligence indicates the plaintiff's uncertainty whether the claim is under the basic torts law of Louisiana Article 2315,[8] or under Article 177, an uncertainty that characterized the trial.

Mrs. Williams alleged that similar incidents known to both the owner and the operator should have put them on notice that the building had been selected by criminals as an habitual place for sexual assaults. Evidence at the trial showed that in July 1956 a man with a knife attempted an attack on a young woman using the stairs between the second floor and third floor. Mr. Songy, the Assistant Building Manager, was aware of this occurrence. Some months after that incident, a man was found in the ladies' dressing room. This was reported to the management. Mr. Songy testified that he knew of two other assaults in the building which had occurred less than six months before the attack on Mrs. Williams; neither was reported to the police. Only about an hour before Mrs. Williams was attacked, a young man, masked with a handkerchief and carrying a knife, threatened a woman in the ladies' dressing room on the third floor. She fought him off, reported the incident to the elevator starter, and asked him to call the police. Instead, he sealed the stairwell and made an unsuccessful search of the premises. The police were not called until shortly after the attack on Mrs. Williams.

The Building Manager, Mr. Lynch, and his assistant, Mr. Songy, testified that they knew of these earlier incidents. Mr. Lynch said that he did not bring any of them to the attention of the police because his tenants had not asked him to do so. None of the tenants testified. Mr. Songy and Mr. Lynch testified that they considered their procedures adequate; some such incidents, they said, cannot be avoided in the operation of a large office building.

On this and other evidence the trial judge properly submitted the issue of negligence to the jury.

Counsel for Mrs. Williams asked the court to give specific instructions that the manager of an office building owes invitees the duties set forth in Article 177 of the Civil Code; that Article 177 requires the defendants to carry the burden of proving that they complied with the duty of superintending and policing the building. The trial judge refused to do so, and instructed the jury that the operators of a building, must use "reasonable and ordinary care to keep such building or premises in such a safe condition that the plaintiff here would not be unnecessarily exposed to danger." After deliberating for two hours, the jury returned for further instructions because, as the foreman said, "There seems to be some misunderstanding about your charge." The trial

[8] Article 2315, in pertinent part, reads: "Every act whatever of man that causes damage to another obliges him by whose fault it happened to repair it." This is almost identical with Article 1382 of the French Civil Code.

judge asked if this misunderstanding related to the question of negligence and the duty of the owner of a building. The foreman answered affirmatively. The court repeated the earlier charge, carefully defining "negligence," "ordinary care," "a reasonably prudent person," and "burden of proof." Then he asked if counsel had anything to add. Counsel for Mrs. Williams again urged the trial judge to give special instructions, particularly with regard to Article 177. The trial judge answered: "No, I don't think that article is applicable.... I think that it would simply tend to be confusing. In some respects if it were given it would be satisfactory but I think that I have covered those portions in my general charge."

II

The plaintiff, concentrating on the last half of Article 177 to the disregard of the first half, reads Article 177 as a law of broad application covering all of the duties of the owner of a building arising out of the "master's" underlying duty of "the superintendence and police of his house." As the plaintiff construes it, the article makes the owner responsible for any faults traceable to lack of proper policing of the premises and the burden of proof is on the owner to prove no-negligence. This construction is erroneous. The article has nothing to do with negligence and the burden of proof. A study of the antecedents of Article 177 shows that the language, *"and[10] inasmuch as the master has the superintendence and police of his house, and is responsible for the faults committed therein,"* is simply an explanation of the vicarious liability absolutely imposed on the master as a matter of public policy in the specific fact situation involving damage caused by objects thrown out of a house. If Article 177 is properly construed, and if it were applicable here, the burden of proof would be unimportant and proof of no-negligence would not save the building owner. There is, of course, a duty on the householder or the owner of a building to furnish a safe place for invitees, but that duty arises under Articles 2315 and 2316 and in an action based on the breach of such duty the plaintiff carries the burden of proof as he would in an ordinary action based on negligence.

Before discussing the derivation of the law, we note that the position of the article in the Code gives some indication of its restricted coverage. It is found in "Chapter 2 — Of Free Servants," In "Book I, Title VI — Of Master and Servant."[11] The pattern of the chapter and the logic of the codal arrangement

[10] Part of the confusion may come from "and." It has no counterpart in the French or English text of the article in the Code of 1808, or in the French text of the Code of 1825. Moreau-Lislet and Brown wrote the Code of 1808 in French. Others translated it into English, and it was printed with the French and English texts on opposite pages; in event of a conflict the French prevailed. The English translation is sometimes imperfect. [Citations omitted.]

Most of the chapter on Master and Servant was carried over into the Code of 1825 without change. "And" crept in, perhaps as a misguided effort to improve the translation or perhaps simply as a printer's error.

[11] The position of an article in a code is more important than the position of a provision in a statute, because a code is conceived of as a complete and systematic compilation of co-ordinated principles of law; a common law statute is not so considered and need not be systematic. Article 177 is one of thirteen articles on "free servants" having its codal origin in Louisiana in the Code of 1808, Book 1, Title VI, "Of the Master and Servant," ["Du Maitre et Du Serviteur"]. Chapter 1 of Title VI Book 1, specifies that there are two classes of servants in the "territory," free servants and slaves; Chapter 2 deals with free servants, Chapter 3 with slaves. The present Article 177

suggest strongly that Article 177 was never intended to regulate broadly the duties of the owner of a building. The law arose out of a special situation characteristic of urban communities in which citizens on the streets were exposed to hazards associated with the absence of plumbing, dispose-alls, and garbage collectors. The master is not liable because of the conjunction of the general duty to superintend and to police his premises and the general duty arising from the doctrine of respondeat superior. He is liable simply because the thing thrown came from his house and presumably was thrown by one of his servants. It is noxal liability arising from the master's relation to the house and the servant (or sometimes a guest) connected with the house, as a result of which a person in the street suffers an injury; the application of the law is limited to these facts. The master cannot escape liability by showing no negligence on his part, that is, that the servants were not chosen carelessly, or that there was nothing he could have done to prevent the injury; nor can he escape by showing his servants were not negligent. (His only relief, in Roman law or under the Louisiana Codes of 1808 and 1825, lay in noxal surrender, for example, forfeiture of the offending slave.) The general law covering the master's delictual liability for the acts of his servant is Article 2320. This article stands, properly enough, in "Chapter 2 — Of Offenses and Quasi Offenses," of "Title V — of Quasi Contracts, and Of Offenses and Quasi Offenses," along with Article 2315 covering wrongful acts, Article 2317 covering "acts of persons for whom we are answerable, or of things which we have in our custody," and other articles of a general nature. Article 2320, which qualifies Article 2317, reads:

> "Masters and employers are answerable for the damage occasioned by their servants and overseers, in the exercise of the functions in which they are employed.
>
> "Teachers and artisans are answerable for the damage caused by their scholars or apprentices, while under their superintendence.
>
> "In the above cases, responsibility only attaches, when the masters or employers, teachers, and artisans, might have prevented the act which caused the damage, and have not done it."

---

was originally Article 14 of Title VI, appearing in Chapter 2 on free servants ["serviteurs libres"]. These articles have remained basically intact, except that Art. 162 of the present Code now provides that "[T]here is only one class of servants in this State, to wit: Free servants," and the Chapter on slaves is entirely excluded. Art. 163 defines free servants. Art. 164 specifies that there are three kinds of free servants. Art. 165 states that the manner and mode by which persons bind themselves to serve are prescribed by special laws [originally by "un acte spécial de la Législature de ce Territoire"]. Art. 166, stating when the engagement of minors shall expire, and Art. 167, regarding the binding of majors, and Art. 168, regarding engagements made in foreign countries, were not among the original thirteen articles in the Code of 1808. Art. 169 covers implied conditions in the contract of apprenticeship. Art. 170 establishes remedies (specific performance and rescission). Art. 171 provides for the case of the master's ill-use of his servant or apprentice. Art. 172 provides for the death of the master, but this article too was not among the original thirteen. Art. 173 sets forth the permissible scope of the master's correction of the apprentice. Art. 174 creates a cause of action in favor of the master for damages caused to his servant by another. Art. 175 sets out the right of the master to defend his servant. Art. 176 sets out the liability of the master for his servant's offenses and quasi offenses. Then, at the end of this series of articles, Art. 177 covers the particular situation of a master's liability for untidy or dangerous objects thrown out of the house into the street, presumably by servants.

The last paragraph of Article 2320, now virtually obsolete, demonstrates that Article 177 was necessary in order to impose liability in cases where otherwise responsibility would attach "only ... when the masters ... might have prevented the act which caused the damage, and have not done it." Article 177 also eliminates the defense set out in the first paragraph of Article 2320, that the act was beyond the scope of employment.

The Louisiana history of Article 177 begins with one of its great jurists, L. Moreau-Lislet. Moreau-Lislet and James Brown compiled the Code of 1808, a digest in codal form of the existing laws in the Territory of Orleans (now the State of Louisiana). Moreau-Lislet, with Edward Livingston and Pierre Derbigny, also prepared the Code of 1825. In between working on these codes, Moreau-Lislet, assisted by Henry Carleton, was commissioned by the legislature to translate the portions of Las Siete Partidas[c] having the force of law in Louisiana.[15]

Article 177 of Louisiana's present Revised Code of 1870 is identical with Article 171 of the Code of 1825 and with Article 14, Title VI of the Code of 1808. There is no corresponding article in the French Civil Code. A preliminary draft of the Code Napoleon, used by the Louisiana codifiers[16] as a source for the Code of 1808, did attempt to codify the law relating to things thrown from houses. The Conseil d'État rejected the proposed provisions. The Code Napoleon, a code to reform the law, perhaps influenced by contemporary philosophical interest in individualism, free will, and moral responsibility,[d] takes the approach that the liability of a master for things thrown out of a house must be based on culpability within the general principle of no liability without fault. Such liability of a master, of course, would be subject to the usual defenses available to defendants in negligence actions and not subject to the burden of proving no-negligence. There are several possible explanations for the drafters of the Code of 1825 rejecting the Code Napoleon approach and deliberately choosing the limited in scope but strict liability approach of Roman law to actions for damages caused by things thrown from houses: the lesser exposure of Louisiana than France to European philosophy, the difference between Paris streets and New Orleans streets, or, perhaps, the influ-

[c] The history and influence of Las Siete Partidas (compiled in 1265 in Spain) is discussed in Chapter 3, Section G.

[15] In the early days of Louisiana the Custom of Paris prevailed. France ceded Louisiana to Spain in 1762 but the laws of Spain were not introduced into Louisiana until 1769, when the Spanish Governor, Don Alejandro O'Reilly abolished French law by proclamation. The short-lived French regime in 1803 made no effort to restore French law. In 1817 the Supreme Court of Louisiana held that Spanish law was still in force, unaffected by the Code of 1808 except where expressly or impliedly changed. *Cottin v. Cottin,* 5 Mart. 93 (1817). This holding led to the Moreau-Lislet and Carleton translation of Las Siete Partidas and, a little later, to the Code of 1825.

[16] The Assembly in 1790, the Convention in 1793 and 1794, and the Directoire in 1796 all promised the French people a code; Cambacérès and his collaborators presented draft codes which failed of adoption. Finally, in 1800, Napoleon, as First Consul, appointed and led the commissions that drew up the Projet du Gouvernement that became the Code Civil des Français, promulgated in 1804. The number of instances in which the Louisiana compilers chose sections of the Projet du Gouvernement rather than the Code as promulgated suggests that either a copy of the Code was not available, which seems highly unlikely, or that they preferred the preliminary draft. It is probable, but it has never been proved that the earlier drafts prepared principally under Cambacérès were available in Louisiana.

[d] For an assessment of the influence of the intellectual revolution on the Code Napoléon, see Chapter 5, Section A.

ence of Louis Moreau-Lislet, who was steeped in Roman law, Spanish law, and the pre-codal French commentaries. The Code of 1825 was a true Code and, like the Code Napoleon, a reform code; the so-called "Code" of 1808, however, was intended as a *digest of existing laws* in the Territory of Orleans, clarifying and systematizing but not remaking the law. There is no doubt that in 1808 Moreau-Lislet regarded absolute liability as the existing law of Louisiana for things thrown out of a house.

The principal sources of the Louisiana Code are well known. Oversimplifying it, the codal roots extend, *on the French side,* through the Code Napoleon, the Code Louis, the Ordinances of D'Aguesseau, the treatises of Pothier and Domat to Justinian; *on the Spanish side,* through the Fuero Juzgo, the Fuero Real, the Récopilaciones de Leyes de los Reynos de las Indias, the Nueva Récopilacion, and Las Siete Partidas to Justinian.

In drafting Article 14, Title VI of the 1808 Code, Moreau-Lislet notched trees so that his trail could be easily followed. In a treasured copy of the Code of 1808, which he annotated on interleaves, there is a notation opposite Article 14, Title VI, reading, "Bk. 1, Tit. 6, L. 25. T. 15. part 7."[21] This is a reference to Title 15, Law 25 of the 7th Partida of the Moreau-Lislet and Carleton translation of "Las Siete Partidas." Title 15, Law 25 of the 7th Partida is as follows:

> "That they who throw bones, or filth into the streets, shall pay for the damage which they cause to persons passing there.
>
> "Men sometimes throw water, bones, or other like things out of the houses in which they live, into the streets, and although they should not do it with the intention of injuring any one, yet if they do damage to the clothes or garments of others, they who dwell in the house, will be bound to pay double the amount of such damage. And if many persons should live in the house from which the substance was thrown, whether it belonged to them or had been hired or borrowed by them, they will be jointly bound to pay for the damage, if it should not be known with certainty who had caused it. But if it should be known who he was, then he alone will be responsible for the damage, and not the others. But if among those who dwell habitually (cotidianamente) in the house, there should be some persons received as guests, these will not be bound to contribute in any manner to the damage caused in this way, unless they were the authors of it." 2 Las Siete Partidas (Moreau and Carleton Translation, 1820), p. 1213.

In his preface to Title 15 of the 7th Partida Moreau-Lislet specifically cites Justinian ("Digest, lib. 9, tit. 3.... De his qui effuderint vel dejecerint") and Domat ("Domat's Civil Law, part 1, b. 2, tit. 8") as sources for this section of his Las Siete Partidas.

---

[21] The Court has examined this copy which is in the possession of the De la Vergne family in New Orleans. The handwriting has never been verified as Moreau-Lislet's handwriting and may be that of an amanuensis, but there is strong internal evidence that he wrote the preface and there is no doubt that he was responsible for the annotations. The De la Vergne family has preserved it from one generation to another as Moreau-Lislet's own copy.

We go then to these two sources. Book 9, Title 3, of the Digest of Justinian concerns "Those Who Pour Anything Out or Throw Anything Down." The Praetor[e] grants a cause of action: "Where anything is thrown down or poured out from anywhere upon a place where persons are in the habit of passing or standing, I will grant an action against the party who lives there for twofold the amount of damage occasioned or done." Ulpian says that this praetorian edict is "of the greatest advantage, as it is for the public welfare that persons should come and go over the roads without fear or danger." D.9.3(1). "This action *in factum* is granted against the party who lodged in the house at the time when something was thrown down or poured out, and not against the owner of the house, because the blame attaches to the former. Mention of negligence or that the defendant denies the fact is not made, in order to authorize an action for double damages, although both of these matters are stated to afford good ground for an action for wrongful damage." D.9.3.1.(4). There is an elaborate discussion on the nature and implications of this edict.

Jean Domat, who exercised an enormous influence on French law and on Louisiana law, refers to this same section of the Digest in the section of his own famous treatise devoted to "That which is thrown out of a house, or which may fall down from it, and do some damage." 1 Domat, The Civil Law in Its Natural Order (Strahan trans., Cushing's ed. 1853) Nos. 1547-57. He, too, discusses at length the ramifications of damages caused by things being thrown out of a house. Domat says: "He who inhabits a house, whether he be proprietor of it, tenant, or other, is liable for the damage which is caused by any thing thrown out or poured out of any place of the said house, whether by day or by night. And he ought to answer for it to him who shall have suffered the damage, whether it was he himself that threw it out, or any of his family or domestics, even although it were in his absence, or without his knowledge." *Id.* No. 1547. "If several persons inhabit the same place from whence any thing hath been thrown or poured out, every one of them will be answerable for the whole damage; unless it can be known which of the masters, or of the persons for whom each master is answerable, has caused it. But if their habitation be distinct, every one is only answerable for what shall be thrown out of the places which he occupies." *Id.* No. 1551.

Article 14, Title VI, of the 1808 Code and its successor, Article 177 of the 1825 Code, follow the Digest and Domat in making the master absolutely liable on pure policy reasons in a particular fact situation in which the state has an interest; they differ from these sources in not dealing with multiple occupancy. There is no suggestion in these sources or in the literature on the subject that liability is based on culpability, on general delictual responsibility, on the doctrine of respondeat superior, or on the close-to-strict liability imposed on a master in early times for the acts of a servant. And there is nothing in the sources extending such liability to injuries taking place *within* a building.

The explanatory language, made much of by appellant, "and inasmuch as the master has the superintendence and police of his house, and is responsible

[e] A praetor was a specialized magistrate, whose office was created in 367 B.C. during the Roman Republic to relieve consuls of the administration of justice. *See* Hans Julius Wolff, Roman Law: An Historical Introduction 33, 72-81 (1951).

for the faults committed therein," does not appear in either of the two principal sources or in the civilian sources we have examined. Blackstone, however, in discussing "how strangers may be affected by his relation of master and servant" does say: "A master is, lastly, chargeable if any of his family layeth or casteth anything out of his house into the street or common highway, to the damage of any individual, or the common nuisance of his majesty's liege people: for the master hath the superintendence and charge of all his household. And this also agrees with the civil law; which holds that the *pater familias*,[f] in this and similar cases, *"ob alterius culbam tenetur, sive servi, sive liberi!"*[g] Blackstone's Commentaries were in Moreau-Lislet's library.

Article 18 of the Code directs courts to construe laws by "considering the meaning and spirit of the law."[27] As is evident from its history, the reason and spirit of Article 177 show that the article is applicable only when an injury results from an object "thrown out" of a house or building.

We turn now from jurists to jurisprudence.

III

In civilian jurisdictions new wine in old bottles is not a deceitful trick. It is inherent in the evolutive construction that is essential to making a code live and work. But Article 177 has seldom been cited; it has never been applied, irrespective of negligence, to an action by one injured within a building; and it has never been used to shift the burden of proof to a defendant. We find only one case decided squarely under Article 177. The cases appellant cites are clearly distinguishable.

In *Simmonds v. Southern Rifle Club,* 1900, 52 La. Ann. 1114, 27 So. 656, 657, a rifle club was held liable for injuries to a little girl struck by a bullet fired from the club's premises by one of its members or a guest. Club members and their guests were firing in the direction of a parapet which, had it been perfectly sound, would have stopped all the bullets. But the parapet had many bullet holes in it, and the wood had rotted. The child was playing in her father's yard, directly in the line of firing, about a hundred feet on the other side of the parapet. At the time of the accident there was no other shooting going on in the neighborhood except at the rifle club. The Supreme Court, in a short opinion, said: "It is not beyond the range of possibility that [the bullet] may have struck the parapet at a point where it had been already partially perforated by one or more bullets, and where the wood had become rotten by reason of the letting of the rain and air into the hole thus made. We, therefore,

---

[f] The Roman concept of *pater familias*, or male head of an extended household, is traced from its legal origins in the Twelve Tables in Chapter 3.

[g] Who is bound for another, whether slave or free man.

[27] "L'office de la loi est de fixer, par de grandes vues, les maximes générales du droit; d'établir des principes féconds en conséquences, et non de descendre dans le détail des questions qui peuvent naître sur chaque matière. *C'est au magistrat et au jurisconsulte, pénétrés de l'esprit général des lois, à en diriger l'application....* Il y a une science pour les législateurs, comme il y en a une pour les magistrats; et l'une ne ressemble pas à l'autre. La science du législateur consiste à trouver dans chaque matière, les principes les plus favorables au droit commun: *la science du magistrat est de mettre ces principes en action, de les ramifier, de les étendre par une application sage et raisonnée aux hypothèses privées.*" Portalis, Discours Préliminaire, reproduced in Fenet, Recueil complet des travaux préparatoires du Code Civil, Vol., 1, 470, 475.

think that the club should be held liable for the injury sustained. Civ. Code, arts. 177, 2315, 2317." The fact situation does not fit exactly into the fact situation covered by Article 177 (the injury did not occur on a street or public road, for example), but the parallel between an object thrown from a house and a bullet propelled from a gun seems close enough to justify application of the article and is in keeping with the civilian concept of the regle juridique.[h] The important fact distinguishing *Simmonds* from other cases the appellant cites is that the injured girl was *outside* of the owner's property. The court referred to Articles 2315 and 2317, but the decision does not suggest negligence; it rests, it seems to us, on absolute liability under Article 177.

The cases appellant relies on in support of the high standard of care imposed on a building owner to superintend and police his property concern restaurant owners and innkeepers. Thus, in *Miller v. De Rusa,* 1955, La. App., 77 So. 2d 748, 749, a guest sued both the owner of a barroom-grocery store and an assailant who struck him over the head with a club while the plaintiff was seated at the bar. The Court did not refer to Article 177, but relied on the general rule, citing authorities, that "the innkeeper must protect his guests." Similarly, in *Matranga v. Travelers Ins. Co.,* 1951, La. App., 55 So. 2d 633, 636, the court affirmed the award of damages to a patron of a restaurant injured in a fracas between the owner and his brother. The court held that "it is the duty of every storekeeper and restaurant operator to use reasonable care in the protection of his patrons and guests."

In *De Hart v. Travelers Ins. Co.,* 1952, La. App., 10 So. 2d 597, 598 the court did cite Article 177. The plaintiff was injured in a Bourbon Street brawl in a cafe-bar when another patron, intoxicated, broke a drinking glass on the counter of the bar at which the plaintiff was seated, and slashed the plaintiff's face with the fragments. The Court of Appeals, reversing and remanding the case, stated that "the proprietor of any public house of entertainment, as a result of an implied contract, though not an insurer of the safety of his guests, owes the duty to exercise reasonable care to protect them." The Court quoted the rule of law governing innkeepers as stated in Ruling Case Law, pointing out that the duty to protect patrons "is not absolute but is limited to the exercise of reasonable care, and the proprietor is liable only when he is negligent." "Such guests or patrons," said the court, "have the corresponding right to believe that the operator, personally, or by his delegated representative, is exercising such degree of reasonable care as shall tend to safety and orderliness. This rule accords with the principles of our Civil Code, which hold the master responsible for the proper policing of his own premises, and the faults committed therein. R.C.C. Art. 177." *Id.* at 599. It is evident that the court did not impose absolute liability under Article 177; the citation of the article was a genuflexion to the civil law.[i]

In *Finney v. Banner Cleaners & Dyers,* 1930, 13 La. App. 101, 126 So. 573, 574, the plaintiff brought suit against the owner of a building to recover

---

[h] The term *"regle juridique"* is here used in a sense similar to the term *"ratio decidendi"* familiar to common lawyers. *See* Arthur L. Goodhart, *Determining the Ratio Decidendi of a Case,* 40 Yale L.J. 161 (1930).

[i] On the felt need to always cite a code provision in the civil law tradition, see Chapter 9, Section A.

damages for injuries he sustained when one of the owner's employees suddenly and violently opened a heavy door which struck the plaintiff and knocked him in front of an approaching truck. The court held the owner liable: "The defendant's employee knew that workmen were engaged in the repair and remodeling of the building and were frequently using the alley.... Defendant's employee was therefore at fault in opening the doors suddenly with force and without warning when he was unable to see if there was any one passing or standing in front of the doors at the time. He failed to use such care and precaution as an ordinary prudent person should have exercised under the circumstances. Civ. Code, art. 2315; Civ. Code art. 177; 45 C.J. 861." As in *De Hart v. Travelers,* although the court cited Article 177, the test required "such care and precaution as an ordinary prudent person should have exercised under the circumstances."

In *Thompson v. Commercial National Bank,* 1924, 156 La. 479, 100 So. 688, Article 177 was correctly construed and narrowly limited to situations where an object is thrown from a house directly causing injury. In *Thompson* the plaintiff was struck on the head by a piece of the metal framework of an awning which fell from a window of one of the rooms occupied by an oil company in a bank's office building. The part fell from the awning to the sidewalk and struck the plaintiff after the canvas and ropes of the awning had been consumed by fire. The plaintiff brought suit against both the oil company and the bank, alleging that they jointly installed the framework and negligently failed to affix it securely to the building and maintain it in a safe condition. The oil company contended that the bank was solely liable under Article 177, since the bank, as master, had the superintendence and police of its building and was responsible for the faults committed therein. The court dismissed this argument, saying: "This is, undoubtedly, a correct principle of law, where the thing thrown out of the master's house is the causa causans of the injury received by a passerby, or third person. Plaintiff's cause of action, however, is predicated squarely upon the legal proposition that, having erected the awning in question conjointly with the owner of the building, the lessee is bound in solido with the owner, and as a joint tort-feasor, for the injury resulting to plaintiff from defects in the original construction and failure to keep said awning in safe repair. In the present case, moreover, we do not find from the evidence that the ignition of the awning and ropes by some unknown third person was the proximate cause of the falling of the framework of the awning." 156 La., at 482, 100 So., at 689.

In view of the restricted scope of Article 177 and in the light of Louisiana jurisprudence, the trial judge correctly refused to charge the jury with regard to the effect of Article 177; he correctly charged that the owner of an office building owes a duty to provide a reasonably safe place for invitees and is liable only when the plaintiff successfully carries the burden of proving the defendant's negligence. [Citations omitted.]

The Court has considered all of the appellant's specifications of error, whether or not discussed in this opinion. There being no harmful error in the proceedings below, the decision is

Affirmed.

NOTES AND QUESTIONS

1. Louisiana and Puerto Rico are the two common law-civil law mixed jurisdictions in the United States. Quebec is a prominent example in Canada. They provide a convenient way to learn something about the civil law tradition, since American law libraries contain much of their legal literature in English. *See* Liana Fiol Matta, *Civil Law and Common Law in the Legal Method of Puerto Rico,* 40 Am. J. Comp. L. 783 (1992).

2. Judge Wisdom, former chief judge of the Fifth Circuit, was trained in the civil law tradition. What are the most significant differences between the way he approaches this tort problem and the approach a common law judge might take? What are the significant differences regarding the source of law, that is, the legal rule used? Regarding the materials used to justify his conclusion?

3. Wisdom commences his opinion with a discussion of the civilian distinction between delict and quasi delict. Consider the origin of the distinction in Roman law, as described by Bruce W. Frier, A Casebook on the Roman Law of Delict 227 (1989):

> Quasi-delict is a murky category that was probably not accepted until the postclassical period, although the law teacher Gaius seems to know it already in mid-second century A.D. The category collects several types of liability, all established in classical law, that for one reason or another are not easily explained as delicts. In all of them, one person has suffered loss, and another person is held liable for that loss even if he or she did not directly inflict it; the defendant may not be at fault, but at least had the opportunity to prevent the loss from occurring. Since the defendant's fault is not necessarily involved, the liability is not delictual; rather, it is said to arise "as if from a delict" (*quasi ex delicto*).
>
> The Praetor's Edict established that if something was poured or thrown from an upstairs dwelling onto a public way, and it caused damage to persons or property beneath, the principal occupant of the dwelling was liable even though he or she was not the culprit. In this sort of situation, a victim may find it difficult to establish the culprit's identity; but whether this is possible or not, the occupant is held liable, perhaps on the theory that he or she had failed to exercise sufficient oversight....
>
> Quasi-delict is mainly interesting for the ways in which it begins to go beyond the classical principles of delictual law, in order to establish liabilities based not on demonstrable fault (*dolus* or *culpa*), but on imputed failure of oversight — a form of strict liability that has become far more prominent in modern law.

Wisdom investigates Justinian's treatment of the quasi delict for those who pour or throw things out of buildings, describing book 9, title 3 of the Digest, one component — along with the Institutes, the Code, and the Novels — of Emperor Justinian's compilation described in Chapter 3.

4. How does the plaintiff argue that article 177 of the Louisiana Civil Code should be interpreted? What do you think of Judge Wisdom's response? Is his a literal interpretation?

5. Wisdom buttresses his conclusions by considering three additional methods of codal interpretation authorized by civilian doctrine: contextual, historical, and evolutive (or teleological or functional).

Compare Donald P. Kommers, Judicial Politics in West Germany: A Study of the Federal Constitutional Court 211-12 (1976):

> [Here are the] general theories of constitutional interpretation developed by the [German Constitutional] Court over the years. We have already made reference to the contextual theory or systematic method, as it is sometimes called, by which the Court derives the meaning of a constitutional norm from its relationship to other parts of the Basic Law. A second approach is the literal method, where the Court tries to assay, frequently at the outset of an inquiry, the plain meaning of the words used in the Constitution. A third approach is the historical method. Here the Court seeks to locate the meaning of constitutional provisions in the intent of the founding fathers.... By the [teleological] method, the Court seeks to specify the "telos," purpose, or function of certain rules laid down in the Basic Law.... More often the "telos" of the Constitution is determined by asking what is the present purpose or meaning of a rule, a rather circuitous way of saying that the Basic Law must be interpreted in light of changing social conditions.

Is the contextual method of interpretation more or less important in common law jurisdictions? In which fields of American law is the contextual method persuasively used? How about evolutive interpretation? We look more closely at methods of interpretation in Chapter 9, Section B.

6. Judge Wisdom lists several possible explanations for the Louisiana rejection of the Code Napoléon negligence approach and the choice of the Roman law strict liability approach to actions for damages caused by things thrown from houses: (1) the lesser exposure of Louisiana than France to European philosophy; (2) the difference between the streets of Paris and those of New Orleans; and (3) the influence of Louis Moreau-Lislet, who was steeped in Roman law, Spanish law, and the precodal French commentaries. Which of these explanations do you find more congenial? Why?

7. Article 177 was repealed in 1990, primarily for the reason that the general liability fault standard of article 2315 was considered adequate and appropriate.

E. RESEARCH IN FOREIGN AND COMPARATIVE LAW

NOTES ON RESEARCH IN FOREIGN AND COMPARATIVE LAW

1. The most comprehensive effort by comparativists since the beginning of this century to present a worldwide picture of law led to the International Encyclopedia of Comparative Law, eventually to appear in 17 volumes. Under the auspices of the International Association of Legal Science, publication began in 1971 as a series of paperback chapters from the various volumes. The editors are Ulrich Drobnig and Konrad Zweigert at the Hamburg Max Planck

Institute for Foreign and International Private Law. Volume 1 provides a concise outline of the basic institutions of each country's legal system, its sources of law, and the main principles of civil, commercial, and procedural law. The comparison and unification of the world's legal systems is the topic of volume 2, while volume 3 deals with private international law. In addition, specific fields of law are treated as follows: family law (volume 4); succession (volume 5); property (volume 6); contracts (volumes 7 to 10); torts (volume 11); business law, including transportation and copyright questions (volumes 12 to 14); labor law (volume 15); and civil procedure (volume 16). Finally, volume 17 discusses the theory and practice of state intervention in the economy.

An earlier effort to provide the English language reader with a thorough survey of European civil law resulted in an 11 volume series (Continental Legal History Series) published from 1912 to 1918 under the direction of the Committee on Translations of Continental Legal History of the Association of American Law Schools. These volumes examine topics of private and public law, historically as well as up to the beginning of the 20th century, concentrating on the experience of France, Germany, and Italy.

Another comprehensive project is Kenneth Robert Redden's multi-volume Modern Legal Systems Cyclopedia, which began publication in 1984 and includes introductions to the legal systems of a large number of countries as well as general studies on subjects such as international arbitration.

2. For the reader limited to English language materials who is interested in research on comparative law or the law of a particular foreign jurisdiction, the indispensable source is Charles Szladits, A Bibliography on Foreign and Comparative Law: Books and Articles in English (1955, 1962, 1968, 1975, 1981, 1989). Thirteen volumes cover the period from 1790 to 1983. This series has been continued by Vratislav Pechota, Szladits' Bibliography on Foreign and Comparative Law, with two volumes for the years 1984-1986 (published 1990) and two volumes for each year beginning with 1987 (published 1992 and after). The Bibliography arranges entries, some annotated, under 12 principal headings with hundreds of systematic subdivisions. A researcher can find the entries for a particular country by using the geographical index.

Also useful is Rex Coleman & John Owen Haley, An Index to Japanese Law: A Bibliography of Western Language Materials, 1867-1973 (1975); Claire M. Germain, Germain's Transnational Law Research: A Guide for Attorneys (1991); Igor I. Kavass, Soviet Law in English: Research Guide and Bibliography, 1970-1987 (1988); Parker School of Foreign and Comparative Law (Columbia University), International Business Transactions: The Parker School 1989 Guide (1989); Matthias K. Scheer, Japanese Law in Western Languages, 1974-1989: A Bibliography (1992); Tim J. Watts, The Japanese Legal System: A Bibliography (1987).

The Current Law Index (also known as Legal Resource Index on microform or as LegalTrac on CD-ROM), the Index to Legal Periodicals (also known as Wilsondisc on CD-ROM), and the Index to Foreign Legal Periodicals provide the means to update one's search for foreign and comparative law materials.

For the most comprehensive guide to research on foreign and comparative law (in English or in other languages), see Juergen Christoph Goedan, International Legal Bibliographies: A Worldwide Guide and Critique (John E. Pickron trans. 1992).

3. Research on foreign and comparative law in languages other than English should begin with Goedan, *supra*. He provides useful information on 17 of the world's important international legal bibliographies.

Valuable bibliographies not discussed in Goedan include: Francisco A. Avalos, The Mexican Legal System (1992); Timothy Kearley & Wolfram Fischer, Charles Szladits' Guide to Foreign Legal Materials: German (2d ed. 1990); Ralph Lansky, Basic Literature on Law: Federal Republic of Germany, A Selective Bibliography (3d ed. 1984); *id.*, 1 Bibliographical Handbook on Law and Public Administration: General Part and Europe (1987) [see Goedan, *supra* at 284-302]; *id.*, Handbook of Bibliographies on Law in the Developing Countries (1981); Rubens Medina & Cecilia Medina-Quiroga, Nomenclatura and Hierarchy: Basic Latin American Legal Sources (1979); S. Pompe, Indonesian Law 1949-1989: A Bibliography of Foreign-Language Materials with Brief Commentaries on the Law (1992); Thomas H. Reynolds & Arturo A. Flores, 1-2 Foreign Law: Current Sources of Codes and Basic Legislation in Jurisdictions of the World (1989, 1991); Renée Sanilevici, 1-2 Bibliography of Israeli Law in European Languages (1985, 1991); Frederick E. Snyder, Latin American Society and Legal Culture: A Bibliography (1985); Charles Szladits & Claire M. Germain, Guide to Foreign Legal Materials: French (2d ed. 1985); Jacques Vanderlinden, 3 African Law Bibliography: 1977-1986, bks. 1-3 (1989).

The primary guide to periodical literature since 1960 (organized by topic, country, and author) is the Index to Foreign Legal Periodicals.

4. Difficulty in the translation of foreign legal terminology is a major source of confusion in comparative law. As with poetry, translation of legal language is not a mechanical matching of words. If a law suit depends upon the precise meaning of a word or phrase in a document, statute, or code, it may be necessary for the skilled advocate to trace the nuances developed by cases, scholarly treatises, or legislative history. Although there are more foreign codes and statutes translated today than previously, their quality is uneven. Moreover, a translation may be accurate enough for one purpose, but inadequate for another.

For a complete listing of foreign language dictionaries of legal terms in English, see Szladits, A Bibliography on Foreign and Comparative Law, *supra*.

5. A number of surveys of the law and legal system of specific countries exist. Of those written in English, especially helpful are: Tuğrul Ansay & Don Wallace, Jr., eds., Introduction to Turkish Law (3d ed. 1987); W.E. Butler, Soviet Law (2d ed. 1988); Mauro Cappelletti, John Henry Merryman & Joseph M. Perillo, The Italian Legal System: An Introduction (1967); G. Leroy Certoma, The Italian Legal System (1985); Albert Hung-yee Chen, An Introduction to the Legal System of the People's Republic of China (1992); J.M.J. Chorus et al., eds., Introduction to Dutch Law for Foreign Lawyers (2d ed. 1993); E.J. Cohn, 1-2 Manual of German Law (2d ed. 1968, 1971); Bernardo M. Cremades & Eduardo G. Cabiedes, Litigating in Spain (1989); René David, French Law: Its Structure, Sources, and Methodology (Michael Kindred trans.

1972); F. Dessemontet & T. Ansay, eds., Introduction to Swiss Law (1983); Ralph H. Folsom, John H. Minan & Lee Ann Otto, Law and Politics in the People's Republic of China in a Nutshell (1992); Nigel G. Foster, German Law & Legal System (1993); Klaus-Albrecht Gerstenmaier, West Germany, in 5 World Litigation Law & Practice (1990); Jean-Marie Nelissen Grade & Johan Verbist, Belgium, in 4 World Litigation Law & Practice (1989); John Owen Haley, Authority Without Power: Law and the Japanese Paradox (1991); Takaaki Hattori & Dan Fenno Henderson, Civil Procedure in Japan (1983); John N. Hazard, William E. Butler & Peter B. Maggs, The Soviet Legal System: The Law in the 1980's (1984); James E. Herget & Jorge Camil, An Introduction to the Mexican Legal System (1978); Norbert Horn, Hein Kötz & Hans G. Leser, German Private and Commercial Law: An Introduction (Tony Weir trans. 1982); Konstantinos D. Kerameus & Phaedon J. Kozyris, eds., Introduction to Greek Law (1988); Zentaro Kitagawa, 1-10 Doing Business in Japan (1980, 1985-1986); Hiroshi Oda, Japanese Law (1992); Mauro Rubino-Sammartano & Girolamo Abbatescianni, Italy, in 2 World Litigation Law & Practice (1986); Sang Hyon Song, Introduction to the Law and Legal System of Korea (1983); Stig Strömholm, ed., An Introduction to Swedish Law (2d ed. 1988); Jaakko Uotila, ed., The Finnish Legal System (2d ed. 1985); Andrew West et al., The French Legal System: An Introduction (1992).

Chapter 2

LITIGATING CASES WITH FOREIGN PARTIES OR FOREIGN LAW ISSUES IN AMERICAN COURTS

NOTE ON INTERNATIONAL LITIGATION

The growing importance of international commerce and travel in the past three decades has had a dramatic impact on civil litigation in United States courts. Today individuals routinely name foreign firms as defendants in lawsuits seeking to enforce U.S. product liability, labor, environmental protection, or consumer protection laws. Equally prevalent are contract and corporate law actions arising out of transnational business activities as well as antitrust or other regulatory actions against foreign businesses.

How does one subject a foreign party to the power of a U.S. court or obtain information relevant to the case from a foreign defendant or foreign nonparty witness? Foreign law may govern when an American state's choice of law rule points to the internal law of a foreign country. Examples include disputes involving contracts made or to be performed abroad, foreign property holdings, torts committed overseas, estates of foreign domiciliaries leaving assets in the U.S. or estates of Americans with real property abroad, and foreign marriages, separations, and child custody or support obligations. How should one plead and prove foreign law in an American court? How does one enforce a foreign country judgment in an American court?

The increase in American lawsuits with a foreign element stimulated substantial changes in federal and state law affecting transnational litigation. On the federal level the Judicial Conference in 1963 approved amendments to the Federal Rules of Civil Procedure: Rule 4(i) — since 1993 Rule 4(f) — provided for alternative methods to serve American judicial documents abroad and Rule 28(b) governed taking depositions abroad and legitimized use of letters rogatory in federal cases. In 1964 Congress added 28 U.S.C. § 1696 and §§ 1781-1782 to improve judicial procedure for serving foreign documents in the U.S. and for obtaining evidence on behalf of foreign and international tribunals. The legislative sponsors hoped that such liberal provision of nonreciprocal national rules might induce other countries to cooperate and follow the U.S. example. Lastly, in 1966 the addition of Rule 44.1 to the Federal Rules of Civil Procedure and Rule 26.1 to the Federal Rules of Criminal Procedure facilitated the proof of foreign law in federal courts.

Meanwhile, in 1963 the United States had joined the Hague Conference on Private International Law and the Rome International Institute for the Unification of Private Law (UNIDROIT), which marked its willingness to enter into treaties related to international civil procedure. Three such international agreements are now in effect for the United States: the Hague Convention on

Service Abroad of Judicial and Extrajudicial Documents in Civil and Commercial Matters (1969); the U.N. Convention on the Recognition and Enforcement of Foreign Arbitral Awards (1970); and the Hague Convention on the Taking of Evidence Abroad in Civil and Commercial Matters (1972).[a]

These developments have led to growth in the federal executive branch of government. First, since the Hague Service Convention requires that each signatory designate a Central Authority through which service might be made, the Department of Justice Civil Division assumed the position of a central office for routine international cooperation in judicial procedure. Second, the Department of Justice further created a Section on International Litigation to represent the U.S. Government in its increasing presence as plaintiff and defendant in foreign courts. Third, the Department of State established the position of Assistant Legal Adviser for Private International Law, responsible, *inter alia,* for the negotiation of new treaties concerning international civil procedure.

In the cases, statutes, and other materials that follow, we consider the various stages in an American lawsuit in which the existence of a foreign issue or party might make a difference. This difference begins with the service of process on a foreign defendant. Domestic rules of civil procedure may tell a lawyer what acts abroad are authorized by local law, but these rules give little guidance as to what is permitted under foreign procedural law. In extreme cases an attorney's acts on behalf of his American client abroad may violate a foreign nation's criminal law; in other cases these acts of service and assertion of judicial jurisdiction simply have no effect under foreign law. A surprise then awaits the victorious plaintiff when he comes into the foreign jurisdiction to enforce his American judgment. The earlier invalid service of process may make his judgment unenforceable.

An analogous problem concerns discovery practice, which often requires access to materials or witnesses located outside the United States. American courts usually have two principal alternatives to obtain evidence located abroad: they can seek judicial assistance from foreign courts, or they can unilaterally apply local discovery rules extraterritorially. The latter choice has produced hostility and retaliation from some foreign nations.

When choice of law rules determine that a claim or a defense is governed by foreign law, the problem of pleading and proving the relevant foreign law occurs. Where statutes do not prescribe the rules governing these procedures, the common law prevails. The basic principle of the common law has been that foreign law is a fact and must be pleaded and proved as a fact. However, in contrast to the firm adherence of the English to this "fact" treatment of foreign law, most American states and the federal courts have now adopted some form of judicial notice provision to facilitate the pleading and determination of foreign law.

---

[a] For the text of these treaties, along with current ratifications and reservations, see the latest edition of the Law Digest volume in the Martindale-Hubbell Law Directory. The history of U.S. abstention and later interest in the unification of international civil procedure is authoritatively traced in Kurt H. Nadelmann, *The United States Joins the Hague Conference on Private International Law: A "History" with Comments,* 30 Law & Contemp. Probs. 291 (1965).

Pleading or otherwise providing sufficient notice of a foreign law issue is, of course, only part of the difficulty. Legal proof must be thought of in terms of statutes, decisions, customs, scholarly commentaries, translations, and expert witnesses to support the necessary contentions. The competent lawyer must interview foreign law experts, study their qualifications, and integrate their knowledge into forms and elements familiar to courts in the United States. We will consider the various approaches that have evolved in the United States in the judicial resolution of foreign law questions, both at trial and on appeal.

Finally, we review what occurs when a litigant asks an American court to recognize or to enforce a foreign country judgment. There is no uniform national standard governing this question, unlike the full faith and credit due sister state or federal judgments. Instead, the recognition and enforcement of foreign country judgments is usually governed by a standard of comity as defined by individual states.

A. SERVICE OF PROCESS ON FOREIGN DEFENDANTS

1. THE INTERPLAY OF SERVICE OF PROCESS AND JURISDICTION

FEDERAL RULES OF CIVIL PROCEDURE

RULE 4
Summons

(f) Service Upon Individuals in a Foreign Country. Unless otherwise provided by federal law, service upon an individual from whom a waiver has not been obtained and filed, other than an infant or an incompetent person, may be effected in a place not within any judicial district of the United States:

(1) by any internationally agreed means reasonably calculated to give notice, such as those means authorized by the Hague Convention on the Service Abroad of Judicial and Extrajudicial Documents; or

(2) if there is no internationally agreed means of service or the applicable international agreement allows other means of service, provided that service is reasonably calculated to give notice:

(A) in the manner prescribed by the law of the foreign country for service in that country in an action in any of its courts of general jurisdiction; or

(B) as directed by the foreign authority in response to a letter rogatory or letter of request; or

(C) unless prohibited by the law of the foreign country, by

(i) delivery to the individual personally of a copy of the summons and the complaint; or

(ii) any form of mail requiring a signed receipt, to be addressed and dispatched by the clerk of the court to the party to be served; or

(3) by other means not prohibited by international agreement as may be directed by the court....

(k) Territorial Limits of Effective Service.

(1) Service of a summons or filing a waiver of service is effective to establish jurisdiction over the person of a defendant

(A) who could be subjected to the jurisdiction of a court of general jurisdiction in the state in which the district court is located, or ....

(D) when authorized by a statute of the United States.

(2) If the exercise of jurisdiction is consistent with the Constitution and laws of the United States, serving a summons or filing a waiver of service is also effective, with respect to claims arising under federal law, to establish personal jurisdiction over the person of any defendant who is not subject to the jurisdiction of the courts of general jurisdiction of any state.

ADVISORY COMMITTEE NOTES

RULE 4

146 F.R.D. 401, 566-72 (1993)

Subdivision (f). This subdivision provides for service on individuals who are in a foreign country, replacing the former subdivision (i) that was added to Rule 4 in 1963....

Paragraph (1) gives effect to the Hague Convention on the Service Abroad of Judicial and Extrajudicial Documents, which entered into force for the United States on February 10, 1969....

Paragraph (2) provides alternative methods for use when internationally agreed methods are not intended to be exclusive, or where there is no international agreement applicable. It contains most of the language formerly set forth in subdivision (i) of the rule. Service by methods that would violate foreign law is not generally authorized. Subparagraphs (A) and (B) prescribe the more appropriate methods for conforming to local practice or using a local authority. Subparagraph (C) prescribes other methods authorized by the former rule.

Paragraph (3) authorizes the court to approve other methods of service not prohibited by international agreements. The Hague Convention, for example, authorizes special forms of service in cases of urgency if convention methods will not permit service within the time required by the circumstances. Other circumstances that might justify the use of additional methods include the failure of the foreign country's Central Authority to effect service within the six-month period provided by the Convention, or the refusal of the Central Authority to serve a complaint seeking punitive damages or to enforce the antitrust laws of the United States. In such cases, the court may direct a special method of service not explicitly authorized by international agreement if not prohibited by the agreement. Inasmuch as our Constitution requires that reasonable notice be given, an earnest effort should be made to devise a method of communication that is consistent with due process and minimizes offense to foreign law....

Subdivision (k)....

Paragraph (1)(D) is new, but merely calls attention to federal legislation that may provide for nationwide or even world-wide service of process in cases arising under particular federal laws....

Paragraph (2) is new. It authorizes the exercise of territorial jurisdiction over the person of any defendant against whom is made a claim arising under any federal law if that person is subject to personal jurisdiction in no state. This addition is a companion to the amendments made in revised subdivisions (e) and (f).

This paragraph corrects a gap in the enforcement of federal law. Under the former rule, a problem was presented when the defendant was a non-resident of the United States having contacts with the United States sufficient to justify the application of United States law and to satisfy federal standards of forum selection, but having insufficient contact with any single state to support jurisdiction under state long-arm legislation or meet the requirements of the Fourteenth Amendment limitation on state court territorial jurisdiction. In such cases, the defendant was shielded from the enforcement of federal law by the fortuity of a favorable limitation on the power of state courts, which was incorporated into the federal practice by the former rule....

There remain constitutional limitations on the exercise of territorial jurisdiction by federal courts over persons outside the United States. These restrictions arise from the Fifth Amendment rather than from the Fourteenth Amendment, which limits state-court reach and which was incorporated into federal practice by the reference to state law in the text of the former subdivision (e) that is deleted by this revision. The Fifth Amendment requires that any defendant have affiliating contacts with the United States sufficient to justify the exercise of personal jurisdiction over that party. [Citation omitted.] There also may be a further Fifth Amendment constraint in that a plaintiff's forum selection might be so inconvenient to a defendant that it would be a denial of "fair play and substantial justice" required by the due process clause, even though the defendant had significant affiliating contacts with the United States....

This narrow extension of the federal reach applies only if a claim is made against the defendant under federal law. It does not establish personal jurisdiction if the only claims are those arising under state law or the law of another country, even though there might be diversity or alienage subject matter jurisdiction as to such claims. If, however, personal jurisdiction is established under this paragraph with respect to a federal claim, then 28 U.S.C. § 1367(a) provides supplemental jurisdiction over related claims against that defendant, subject to the court's discretion to decline exercise of that jurisdiction under 28 U.S.C. § 1367(c).

AVIANCA, INC. v. CORRIEA

United States District Court, District of Columbia
705 F. Supp. 666 (1989)

MEMORANDUM OPINION

LAMBERTH, DISTRICT JUDGE.

Plaintiffs Avianca, S.A., the major airline and flagship international carrier of the Republic of Colombia, and its related Colombian and United States companies and subsidiaries, brought this action against their former attorney, Mark Corriea, a District of Columbia licensed practitioner, and his partner and law firm.... [P]laintiffs allege that after having entered into an on-going attorney-client relationship with one or more of the plaintiff companies in 1980, for which defendants were paid over $1,000,000.00 in legal fees over the next five years, defendants breached their ethical and fiduciary obligations to plaintiffs by, among other things, misappropriating client funds, acquiring and maintaining undisclosed financial interests in transactions involving plaintiffs, and secretly dealing with the then president of plaintiff Avianca, S.A....

I. *Facts*

A. *Parties*

In late 1979, defendant Mark Corriea, while representing his then client-employer, Itel Air Corporation, in a sale-leaseback transaction with plaintiff Avianca, S.A., met plaintiff Avianca S.A.'s then executive vice president, Andres Cornelissen. Apparently impressed with Corriea's work in the transaction, in early 1980, Andres Cornelissen began seeking Corriea's legal services for Avianca, S.A. After briefly representing Avianca and Itel contemporaneously, Corriea left Itel to become a sole practitioner. In 1982, Corriea and defendant Martin J. Tierney formed the defendant law partnership of Corriea & Tierney, which continued to represent plaintiffs in aircraft leasing, corporate financing, and government relations matters until August 1985. Martin Tierney is a licensed attorney, practicing in California. Subsequent to meeting Corriea in 1979, Andres Cornelissen became the president of Avianca, S.A., and then, following a shareholder dispute in 1985, resigned. Cornelissen is a Colombian citizen, who was earlier joined as a party defendant in this case. During the discovery phase of the case, he was ordered to respond to deposition questions regarding his finances and foreign bank accounts by the United States District Court for the Southern District of Florida. Because of his refusal to fully respond, Cornelissen is currently subject to arrest under an outstanding bench warrant issued by that court....

C. *Andres Cornelissen*

Avianca, S.A.'s former president, Andres J. Cornelissen, has been a mysterious, silent party to this litigation for over two years, and has yet to appear before this Court personally or through counsel. The chronology of Cornelissen's role in this case dates back to plaintiffs' July 25, 1986, motion to join Cornelissen as an additional party and amend their complaint....

In their amended complaint, plaintiffs alleged that Cornelissen (1) conspired with Corriea to breach Cornelissen's fiduciary duty as an officer of plaintiff Avianca, S.A., (2) fraudulently misrepresented or failed to disclose material facts in transactions involving plaintiffs and Corriea, and (3) committed civil violations of RICO as a co-conspirator of Corriea.

Following the Court's August 25, 1986 order, plaintiffs were utterly unsuccessful in their attempts to serve Cornelissen, a Colombian citizen and (apparently) frequent world traveller, personally. Nor were they successful in serving Cornelissen through his known District of Columbia contacts. On October 24, 1986, both Corriea and Cornelissen's District of Columbia counsel, Fulbright & Jaworski, objected to plaintiffs' attempts to serve process on Cornelissen through his attorneys. Specifically, Corriea argued that there was no provision for allowing service through another party defendant; ... and that RICO did not authorize service in a foreign country. Fulbright & Jaworski, appearing for the limited purpose of opposing service on Cornelissen through its firm, argued that such alternative service would impermissibly impede their attorney-client relationship with Cornelissen, and that alternative service under the Federal Rules was inappropriate in any event, because neither the D.C. long arm statute nor federal law authorized service under the facts of the case. On October 27, 1986, during a hearing on the matter, the defendants and intervenor conceded that they were not in a position to directly challenge the Court's exercise of personal jurisdiction over Cornelissen, because to do so would have admitted the very agency relationship with Cornelissen they each adamantly repudiated. While the Court agreed that service via a law firm was probably inappropriate, it ordered a further evidentiary hearing to determine the whereabouts of defendant Cornelissen in order to determine a more appropriate means of effecting service of process.

The evidentiary hearing was held on November 5, 1986, and the Court, after hearing testimony from defendant Corriea, found that Cornelissen was aware that he had been joined as a party defendant, and was actively avoiding service of process. In that hearing, Corriea testified that he had last met with Cornelissen in person during the summer of 1986 in the south of France, where Cornelissen was vacationing. Corriea had had frequent telephone conversations with Cornelissen since that meeting, and was keeping Cornelissen apprised of the developments in the case. Further contacts between Corriea and Cornelissen were likely, given their ongoing personal and financial relationships. For example, Corriea, on Cornelissen's request, sold their jointly-owned Rolls Royce, as well as Cornelissen's "small BMW," and sent Cornelissen's share of the proceeds to his estranged wife in California, where she lives with Cornelissen's three children. Furthermore, the law firm of Corriea & Tierney had been paying credit card and other bills for Corriea, and had bought an automobile for and transferred funds to Cornelissen's daughter, a student at Stanford University. Concluding that Cornelissen had ample notice of the proceedings against him, if not valid service of process, and certainly had been given an opportunity to protect his interests, the Court on November 24, 1986, authorized alternative service of process. Specifically, plaintiffs were directed to send the summons and complaint by certified mail to nine addresses within the United States and abroad, with which Corriea was likely to have contact. Having complied with the Court's order, but having received no response whatsoever from Cornelissen, plaintiffs now seek to compel Cornelissen to answer the amended complaint....

II. *Discussion*

C. *Plaintiffs' Motion to Compel Andres Cornelissen to Answer the Amended Complaint*

Resolution of plaintiffs' motion to compel defendant Cornelissen to answer the amended complaint turns on two primary issues: whether there has been effective service of process through the alternative means authorized by the Court, and whether the Court has personal jurisdiction over Cornelissen. Plaintiffs' motion with respect to the former issue is essentially unopposed, and the defendants and intervenor were understandably constrained in fully airing their objections to the latter. However, as will be explained more fully below, the issue of effective service is inextricably connected to that of personal jurisdiction, because the Court must make a determination that it in fact has personal jurisdiction under the District of Columbia long arm statute before it can adequately determine whether there has been effective service.

Rule 4(i)(1)(E) provides that when service upon a foreign party, not an inhabitant of or found within the United States, is authorized by federal or state law, such service is sufficient if made "as directed by order of the court." Fed. R. Civ. P. 4(i)(1)(E). The Advisory Committee Notes indicate that while "the authority for effecting foreign service must be found in a statute of the United States or a statute or rule of court of the State in which the district court is held," the rule nonetheless gives the Court considerable flexibility by "permitting the court by order to tailor the manner of service to fit the necessities of a particular case." Fed. R. Civ. P. 4(i), Advisory Committee Note. Whether specified by statute or rule or fashioned by the Court, however, due process requires that the method of service employed be reasonably calculated to give actual notice and afford an adequate opportunity to be heard. *Mullane v. Central Hanover Bank & Trust Co.,* 339 U.S. 306, 314-15, 70 S. Ct. 652, 657, 94 L. Ed. 865 (1950).

Although RICO authorizes nationwide service of process, 18 U.S.C. § 1965, it does not provide for service of process in a foreign country. [Citation omitted.] Thus, authority for the Court's Order allowing alternative service upon Cornelissen must be found, if at all, in the District of Columbia long arm statute. The D.C. Code permits a court to exercise personal jurisdiction when both a tortious act or omission *and* injury occur in the District, D.C. Code § 13-423(a)(3), or when only the tortious injury occurs in the District, but the tortfeasor "regularly does or solicits business, engages in any other persistent course of conduct, or derives a substantial revenue from goods used or consumed, or services rendered, in D.C.," *Id.,* at § 13-423(a)(4).... The court finds it clear that plaintiffs have sufficiently demonstrated that tortious acts and omissions occurred within the District, resulting in injuries in the District, so that they come within the purview of subsection (3). In meeting the criteria of subsection (3), plaintiffs necessarily rely on Cornelissen's close relationship with Corriea, who had his principal place of business in D.C. For example, Corriea operated AAL, Cornelissen's secret off-shore company, from his law office in D.C. Similarly, Corriea operated Norasco from his D.C. office. Over $3,000.00 of the funds Corriea improperly withdrew from Norasco's account were used to pay for repairs to a Rolls Royce co-owned by Cornelissen. Finally,

Cornelissen directed plaintiffs' business, including in particular the Twin Otter lease transaction, to FSI, which, not surprisingly, Corriea operated from his D.C. law office.

Having confirmed that the Court had authority from the D.C. long arm statute for foreign service, the inquiry now turns to whether the particular means of alternative service authorized met the due process requirement of being "reasonably calculated" to give Cornelissen actual notice of the suit and to afford him an adequate opportunity to be heard. Several courts, when confronted with a foreign party successfully avoiding service of process by conventional methods, have upheld service by registered mail. *E.g., International Controls Corp. v. Vesco,* 593 F.2d 166, 175 (2d Cir. 1979) (allowing service by regular mail where bodyguard at residence made personal service impossible) ....

Moreover, this Court has already expressly found that Cornelissen has actual knowledge that he has been joined as a party defendant, and has been receiving litigation status reports from Corriea. Hence, the Court finds that plaintiffs, in complying with the Court's Order, have made effective service of process, in a manner reasonably likely to provide actual notice and an adequate opportunity to be heard....

ORDER

ORDERED, that Andres J. Cornelissen shall answer or otherwise respond to the amended complaint within twenty days of the date of this Order.

NOTES AND QUESTIONS

1. Federal Rule 4(f) and 4(k) were added with other amendments to Rule 4, which went into effect in December 1993. Rule 4(f) replaced the previous Rule 4(i) cited in *Avianca, Inc. v. Corriea,* but retained the same five alternative Rule 4(i) methods of service now listed in Rule 4(f)(2) and (3). Rule 4(f) introduces an important improvement to the structure of the rule, which now suggests a preference for the use of the Hague Service Convention and other service treaties that the United States has ratified or may later ratify. In addition, Rule 4(f)(2) requires compliance with the Hague Convention in cases in which it applies (article 1 of the Convention states that it "shall apply" in certain cases). By contrast, the Inter-American Convention on Letters Rogatory (see Note 9 following the *Schlunk* case, *infra* this section) is not intended as mandatory, so that an American plaintiff under it has the option of using Rule 4(f)(2)'s alternatives (A), (B), or (C) as long as they are not prohibited by the relevant foreign country's law.

Rule 4(k) replaced the former Rule 4(e), which authorized territorial jurisdiction over nondomiciliaries of the state in which the federal court was located to the extent permitted by federal or state statute or court rule. Rule 4(e) also permitted the assertion of personal jurisdiction over a defendant "found within the state." The new Rule 4(k) continues this authority in 4(k)(1)(A) and (D). Furthermore, Rule 4(k)(2) permits federal courts to consider the aggregate national contacts of foreign defendants in federal question cases to establish personal jurisdiction.

2. How do the facts in *Avianca* show that the personal jurisdiction and the service of process issues can become entwined?

3. The *Avianca* court stated that the authority for its order of service on Cornelissen must be found in the District of Columbia long-arm statute. Is that still the situation under Federal Rule 4(k)?

4. Why do you think the *Avianca* court relied on what is today Rule 4(f)(3) rather than part (2)(c)(ii) of Rule 4(f)? Does the U.S. Constitution's due process clause limit the use of Rule 4? What standard does the Constitution require?

5. Under the new Rule 4(k)(2) for a claim arising under federal law, can a federal court assert personal jurisdiction on the basis of "tag" service, that is, service on a foreigner temporarily in or passing through the United States? Will a foreign corporation be amenable to federal court jurisdiction if the company's president is served process while changing planes at Kennedy International Airport in New York? *See Burnham v. Superior Court,* 495 U.S. 604 (1990).

6. Well over half of the states have adopted the Federal Rules of Civil Procedure in whole or in substantial part for their own courts. The previous Rule 4(i) was thus carried over for state procedure, but it did not mention the preferred use of service of process treaties. Other states have enacted similar rules, such as § 2.01 of the Uniform Interstate and International Procedure Act (in force in four states plus the District of Columbia). *See* 13 U.L.A. 355, 382 (1986).

7. Should at least the summons, if not also the complaint, be translated into the language of the country where the process is served to satisfy the U.S. Constitution's due process clause?

8. Service by mail is relatively inexpensive. However, it is invalid under the laws of some foreign countries and has occasionally provoked diplomatic protests. In addition, if a defendant refuses to cooperate by accepting service, the plaintiff will be left with the difficult task of proving that delivery was actually made. *See* Rule 4(f)(2)(C)(ii).

9. Rule 4(f)(2)(A) permits service "in the manner prescribed by the law of the foreign country for service in that country." This choice minimizes the chance of foreign objection to U.S. service or the later foreign refusal to enforce an American judgment in favor of the plaintiff. It also involves a direct comparative law issue: ascertaining foreign law.

In *United States v. Daneza,* 528 F.2d 390 (2d Cir. 1975), the court of appeals affirmed a district court order holding defendant in civil contempt for failure to comply with a subpoena for a grand jury investigating securities and tax law violations. The district judge issued the subpoena pursuant to 28 U.S.C. § 1783, which the court found referred to the old Rule 4(i) for the manner of service. The American consulate in Milan, Italy delivered the subpoena to the appropriate Italian authorities, who attempted to serve the defendant, an American citizen residing in Milan, in person. Unsuccessful in this attempt, they left the documents at the defendant's residence with the concierge, who took responsibility for their delivery in accordance with Italian law (Civil Procedure Code art. 139, permitting substituted service by delivery to the concierge of the building where the person to be served lives).

10. Traditionally, letters rogatory as a method of service of process, Rule 4(f)(2)(B), provided the greatest certainty of acceptance in a judgment enforcement proceeding in a foreign nation. Some countries, notably Switzerland, forbid extraterritorial service within their borders except by letters rogatory. It is the preferred method in many civil law countries. Nevertheless, the procedure is slow, costly, and unpredictable. It requires the cooperation of a domestic court, a foreign court, usually the U.S. State Department, and the other nation's foreign ministry. See 28 U.S.C. § 1781 (Department of State's role). Often foreign counsel are hired to facilitate the process.

2. THE HAGUE SERVICE CONVENTION

CONVENTION ON THE SERVICE ABROAD OF JUDICIAL AND EXTRAJUDICIAL DOCUMENTS IN CIVIL OR COMMERCIAL MATTERS

Done at The Hague November 15, 1965
Entered into Force for the United States February 10, 1969

20 U.S.T. 361, T.I.A.S. No. 6638, 658 U.N.T.S. 163

The States signatory to the present Convention,

Desiring to create appropriate means to ensure that judicial and extrajudicial documents to be served abroad shall be brought to the notice of the addressee in sufficient time,

Desiring to improve the organisation of mutual judicial assistance for that purpose by simplifying and expediting the procedure,

Have resolved to conclude a Convention to this effect and have agreed upon the following provisions:

Article 1

The present Convention shall apply in all cases, in civil or commercial matters, where there is occasion to transmit a judicial or extrajudicial document for service abroad.

This Convention shall not apply where the address of the person to be served with the document is not known.

CHAPTER I — JUDICIAL DOCUMENTS

Article 2

Each contracting State shall designate a Central Authority which will undertake to receive requests for service coming from other contracting States and to proceed in conformity with the provisions of articles 3 to 6.

Each State shall organise the Central Authority in conformity with its own law.

Article 3

The authority or judicial officer competent under the law of the State in which the documents originate shall forward to the Central Authority of the State addressed a request conforming to the model annexed to the present Convention, without any requirement of legalisation or other equivalent formality.

The document to be served or a copy thereof shall be annexed to the request. The request and the document shall both be furnished in duplicate.

Article 4

If the Central Authority considers that the request does not comply with the provisions of the present Convention it shall promptly inform the applicant and specify its objections to the request.

Article 5

The Central Authority of the State addressed shall itself serve the document or shall arrange to have it served by an appropriate agency, either—

a) by a method prescribed by its internal law for the service of documents in domestic actions upon persons who are within its territory, or

b) by a particular method requested by the applicant, unless such a method is incompatible with the law of the State addressed.

Subject to sub-paragraph *(b)* of the first paragraph of this article, the document may always be served by delivery to an addressee who accepts it voluntarily.

If the document is to be served under the first paragraph above, the Central Authority may require the document to be written in, or translated into, the official language or one of the official languages of the State addressed.

That part of the request, in the form attached to the present Convention, which contains a summary of the document to be served, shall be served with the document.

Article 6

The Central Authority of the State addressed or any authority which it may have designated for that purpose, shall complete a certificate in the form of the model annexed to the present Convention.

The certificate shall state that the document has been served and shall include the method, the place and the date of service and the person to whom the document was delivered. If the document has not been served, the certificate shall set out the reasons which have prevented service.

The applicant may require that a certificate not completed by a Central Authority or by a judicial authority shall be countersigned by one of these authorities.

The certificate shall be forwarded directly to the applicant.

Article 7

The standard terms in the model annexed to the present Convention shall in all cases be written either in French or in English. They may also be written in the official language, or in one of the official languages, of the State in which the documents originate.

The corresponding blanks shall be completed either in the language of the State addressed or in French or in English.

Article 8

Each contracting State shall be free to effect service of judicial documents upon persons abroad, without application of any compulsion, directly through its diplomatic or consular agents.

Any State may declare that it is opposed to such service within its territory, unless the document is to be served upon a national of the State in which the documents originate.

Article 9

Each contracting State shall be free, in addition, to use consular channels to forward documents, for the purpose of service, to those authorities of another contracting State which are designated by the latter for this purpose.

Each contracting State may, if exceptional circumstances so require, use diplomatic channels for the same purpose.

Article 10

Provided the State of destination does not object, the present Convention shall not interfere with—

a) the freedom to send judicial documents, by postal channels, directly to persons abroad,

b) the freedom of judicial officers, officials or other competent persons of the State of origin to effect service of judicial documents directly through the judicial officers, officials or other competent persons of the State of destination,

c) the freedom of any person interested in a judicial proceeding to effect service of judicial documents directly through the judicial officers, officials or other competent persons of the State of destination....

Article 13

Where a request for service complies with the terms of the present Convention, the State addressed may refuse to comply therewith only if it deems that compliance would infringe its sovereignty or security.

It may not refuse to comply solely on the ground that, under its internal law, it claims exclusive jurisdiction over the subject-matter of the action or that its internal law would not permit the action upon which the application is based.

The Central Authority shall, in case of refusal, promptly inform the applicant and state the reasons for the refusal.

Article 14

Difficulties which may arise in connection with the transmission of judicial documents for service shall be settled through diplomatic channels.

Article 15

Where a writ of summons or an equivalent document had to be transmitted abroad for the purpose of service, under the provisions of the present Convention, and the defendant has not appeared, judgment shall not be given until it is established that—

a) the document was served by a method prescribed by the internal law of the State addressed for the service of documents in domestic actions upon persons who are within its territory, or
b) the document was actually delivered to the defendant or to his residence by another method provided for by this Convention,

and that in either of these cases the service or the delivery was effected in sufficient time to enable the defendant to defend.

Each contracting State shall be free to declare that the judge, notwithstanding the provisions of the first paragraph of this article, may give judgment even if no certificate of service or delivery has been received, if all the following conditions are fulfilled—

a) the document was transmitted by one of the methods provided for in this Convention,
b) a period of time of not less than six months, considered adequate by the judge in the particular case, has elapsed since the date of the transmission of the document,
c) no certificate of any kind has been received, even though every reasonable effort has been made to obtain it through the competent authorities of the State addressed.

Notwithstanding the provisions of the preceding paragraphs the judge may order, in case of urgency, any provisional or protective measures.

Article 16

When a writ of summons or an equivalent document had to be transmitted abroad for the purpose of service, under the provisions of the present Convention, and a judgment has been entered against a defendant who has not appeared, the judge shall have the power to relieve the defendant from the effects of the expiration of the time for appeal from the judgment if the following conditions are fulfilled—

a) the defendant, without any fault on his part, did not have knowledge of the document in sufficient time to defend, or knowledge of the judgment in sufficient time to appeal, and *b)* the defendant has disclosed a *prima facie* defence to the action on the merits.

An application for relief may be filed only within a reasonable time after the defendant has knowledge of the judgment.

Each contracting State may declare that the application will not be entertained if it is filed after the expiration of a time to be stated in the declaration, but which shall in no case be less than one year following the date of the judgment.

This article shall not apply to judgments concerning status or capacity of persons....

CHAPTER III — GENERAL CLAUSES

Article 19

To the extent that the internal law of a contracting State permits methods of transmission, other than those provided for in the preceding articles, of documents coming from abroad, for service within its territory, the present Convention shall not affect such provisions.

VOLKSWAGENWERK AKTIENGESELLSCHAFT v. SCHLUNK

United States Supreme Court
486 U.S. 694, 108 S. Ct. 2104 (1988)

JUSTICE O'CONNOR delivered the opinion of the Court.

This case involves an attempt to serve process on a foreign corporation by serving its domestic subsidiary which, under state law, is the foreign corporation's involuntary agent for service of process. We must decide whether such service is compatible with the Convention on Service Abroad of Judicial and Extrajudicial Documents in Civil and Commercial Matters, Nov. 15, 1965 (Hague Service Convention), [1969] 20 U.S.T. 361, T.I.A.S. No. 6638.

I

The parents of respondent Herwig Schlunk were killed in an automobile accident in 1983. Schlunk filed a wrongful death action on their behalf in the Circuit Court of Cook County, Illinois. Schlunk alleged that Volkswagen of America, Inc. (VWoA) had designed and sold the automobile that his parents were driving, and that defects in the automobile caused or contributed to their deaths. Schlunk also alleged that the driver of the other automobile involved in the collision was negligent; Schlunk has since obtained a default judgment against that person, who is no longer a party to this lawsuit. Schlunk successfully served his complaint on VWoA, and VWoA filed an answer denying that it had designed or assembled the automobile in question. Schlunk then amended the complaint to add as a defendant Volkswagen Aktiengesellschaft (VWAG), which is the petitioner here. VWAG, a corporation established under the laws of the Federal Republic of Germany, has its place of business in that country. VWoA is a wholly owned subsidiary of VWAG. Schlunk at-

tempted to serve his amended complaint on VWAG by serving VWoA as VWAG's agent.

VWAG filed a special and limited appearance for the purpose of quashing service. VWAG asserted that it could be served only in accordance with the Hague Service Convention, and that Schlunk had not complied with the Convention's requirements. The Circuit Court denied VWAG's motion. It first observed that VWoA is registered to do business in Illinois and has a registered agent for receipt of process in Illinois. The court then reasoned that VWoA and VWAG are so closely related that VWoA is VWAG's agent for service of process as a matter of law, notwithstanding VWAG's failure or refusal to appoint VWoA formally as an agent. The court relied on the facts that VWoA is a wholly-owned subsidiary of VWAG, that a majority of the members of the board of directors of VWoA are members of the board of VWAG, and that VWoA is by contract the exclusive importer and distributor of VWAG products sold in the United States. The court concluded that, because service was accomplished within the United States, the Hague Service Convention did not apply....

II

The Hague Service Convention is a multilateral treaty that was formulated in 1964 by the Tenth Session of the Hague Conference of Private International Law. The Convention revised parts of the Hague Conventions on Civil Procedure of 1905 and 1954. The revision was intended to provide a simpler way to serve process abroad, to assure that defendants sued in foreign jurisdictions would receive actual and timely notice of suit, and to facilitate proof of service abroad. 3 1964 Conférence de la Haye de Droit International Privé, Actes et Documents de la Dixième Session (Notification) 75-77, 363 (1965) (3 Actes et Documents); 1 B. Ristau, International Judicial Assistance (Civil and Commercial) § 4-1 (1984 and 1 Supp. 1986) (1 Ristau). Representatives of all 23 countries that were members of the Conference approved the Convention without reservation. Thirty-two countries, including the United States and the Federal Republic of Germany, have ratified or acceded to the Convention. [Citation omitted.]

The primary innovation of the Convention is that it requires each state to establish a central authority to receive requests for service of documents from other countries. 20 U.S.T. 362, T.I.A.S. 6638, Art. 2. Once a central authority receives a request in the proper form, it must serve the documents by a method prescribed by the internal law of the receiving state or by a method designated by the requester and compatible with that law. Art. 5. The central authority must then provide a certificate of service that conforms to a specified model. Art. 6. A state also may consent to methods of service within its boundaries other than a request to its central authority. Arts. 8-11, 19. The remaining provisions of the Convention that are relevant here limit the circumstances in which a default judgment may be entered against a defendant who had to be served abroad and did not appear, and provide some means for relief from such a judgment. Arts. 15, 16.

Article 1 defines the scope of the Convention, which is the subject of controversy in this case. It says: "The present Convention shall apply in all cases, in civil or commercial matters, where there is occasion to transmit a judicial or extrajudicial document for service abroad." ... This language is mandatory, as we acknowledged last Term in *Société Nationale Industrielle Aérospatiale v. United States District Court* [see Section C of this chapter]. By virtue of the Supremacy Clause, U.S. Const., Art. VI, the Convention pre-empts inconsistent methods of service prescribed by state law in all cases to which it applies. Schlunk does not purport to have served his complaint on VWAG in accordance with the Convention. Therefore, if service of process in this case falls within Article I of the Convention, the trial court should have granted VWAG's motion to quash.

When interpreting a treaty, we "begin 'with the text of the treaty and the context in which the written words are used.'" [Citation omitted.] Other general rules of construction may be brought to bear on difficult or ambiguous passages. "'Treaties are construed more liberally than private agreements, and to ascertain their meaning we may look beyond the written words to the history of the treaty, the negotiations, and the practical construction adopted by the parties.'" [Citation omitted.]

The Convention does not specify the circumstances in which there is "occasion to transmit" a complaint "for service abroad." But at least the term "service of process" has a well-established technical meaning. Service of process refers to a formal delivery of documents that is legally sufficient to charge the defendant with notice of a pending action. [Citations omitted.] The legal sufficiency of a formal delivery of documents must be measured against some standard. The Convention does not prescribe a standard, so we almost necessarily must refer to the internal law of the forum state. If the internal law of the forum state defines the applicable method of serving process as requiring the transmittal of documents abroad, then the Hague Service Convention applies....

The negotiating history of the Convention also indicates that whether there is service abroad must be determined by reference to the law of the forum state. The preliminary draft said that the Convention would apply "where there are grounds" to transmit a judicial document to a person staying abroad. The committee that prepared the preliminary draft realized that this implied that the forum's internal law would govern whether service implicated the Convention. 3 Actes et Documents, at 80-81. The Reporter expressed regret about this solution because it would decrease the obligatory force of the Convention. *Id.*, at 81. Nevertheless, the delegates did not change the meaning of Article 1 in this respect....

The drafting committee then composed the version of Article 1 that ultimately was adopted, which says that the Convention applies "where there is occasion" to transmit a judicial document for service abroad. *Id.*, at 211. After this revision, the Reporter again explained that one must leave to the requesting state the task of defining when a document must be served abroad; that this solution was a consequence of the unavailability of an objective test; and that while it decreases the obligatory force of the Convention, it does provide clarity....

VWAG protests that it is inconsistent with the purpose of the Convention to interpret it as applying only when the internal law of the forum requires service abroad. One of the two stated objectives of the Convention is "to create appropriate means to ensure that judicial and extrajudicial documents to be served abroad shall be brought to the notice of the addressee in sufficient time." 20 U.S.T., at 362. The Convention cannot assure adequate notice, VWAG argues, if the forum's internal law determines whether it applies. VWAG warns that countries could circumvent the Convention by defining methods of service of process that do not require transmission of documents abroad. Indeed, VWAG contends that one such method of service already exists and that it troubled the Conference: *notification au parquet.*

Notification au parquet permits service of process on a foreign defendant by the deposit of documents with a designated local official. Although the official generally is supposed to transmit the documents abroad to the defendant, the statute of limitations begins to run from the time that the official receives the documents, and there allegedly is no sanction for failure to transmit them. 3 Actes et Documents, at 167-169; S. Exec. Rep. No. 6, 90th Cong., 1st Sess., 12 (1967) (statement of Philip Amram, member of the U.S. delegation); 1 Ristau § 4-33, p. 172. At the time of the 10th Conference, France, the Netherlands, Greece, Belgium and Italy utilized some type of *notification au parquet.* 3 Actes et Documents, at 75.

There is no question but that the Conference wanted to eliminate *notification au parquet. Id.,* at 75-77. It included in the Convention two provisions that address the problem. Article 15 says that a judgment may not be entered unless a foreign defendant received adequate and timely notice of the lawsuit. Article 16 provides means whereby a defendant who did not receive such notice may seek relief from a judgment that has become final. 20 U.S.T., at 364-365. Like Article 1, however, Articles 15 and 16 apply only when documents must be transmitted abroad for the purpose of service. 3 Actes et Documents, at 168-169. VWAG argues that, if this determination is made according to the internal law of the forum state, the Convention will fail to eliminate variants of *notification au parquet* that do not expressly require transmittal of documents to foreign defendants. Yet such methods of service of process are the least likely to provide a defendant with actual notice.

The parties make conflicting representations about whether foreign laws authorizing *notification au parquet* command the transmittal of documents for service abroad within the meaning of the Convention. The final report is itself somewhat equivocal. It says that, although the strict language of Article 1 might raise a question as to whether the Convention regulates *notification au parquet,* the understanding of the drafting Commission, based on the debates, is that the Convention would apply. *Id.,* at 367. Although this statement might affect our decision as to whether the Convention applies to *notification au parquet,* an issue we do not resolve today, there is no comparable evidence in the negotiating history that the Convention was meant to apply to substituted service on a subsidiary like VWoA, which clearly does not require service abroad under the forum's internal law. Hence neither the language of the Convention nor the negotiating history contradicts our interpretation of the

Convention, according to which the internal law of the forum is presumed to determine whether there is occasion for service abroad.

Nor are we persuaded that the general purposes of the Convention require a different conclusion. One important objective of the Convention is to provide means to facilitate service of process abroad. Thus the first stated purpose of the Convention is "to create" appropriate means for service abroad, and the second stated purpose is "to improve the organization of mutual judicial assistance for that purpose by simplifying and expediting the procedure." 20 U.S.T., at 362. By requiring each state to establish a central authority to assist in the service of process, the Convention implements this enabling function. Nothing in our decision today interferes with this requirement.

VWAG correctly maintains that the Convention also aims to ensure that there will be adequate notice in cases in which there is occasion to serve process abroad. Thus compliance with the Convention is mandatory in all cases to which it applies, and Articles 15 and 16 provide an indirect sanction against those who ignore it, see 3 Actes et Documents, at 92, 363. Our interpretation of the Convention does not necessarily advance this particular objective, inasmuch as it makes recourse to the Convention's means of service dependent on the forum's internal law. But we do not think that this country, or any other country, will draft its internal laws deliberately so as to circumvent the Convention in cases in which it would be appropriate to transmit judicial documents for service abroad. For example, there has been no question in this country of excepting foreign nationals from the protection of our Due Process Clause. Under that Clause, foreign nationals are assured of either personal service, which typically will require service abroad and trigger the Convention, or substituted service that provides "notice reasonably calculated, under all the circumstances, to apprise interested parties of the pendency of the action and afford them an opportunity to present their objections." *Mullane v. Central Hanover Bank & Trust Co.*, 339 U.S. 306, 314, 70 S. Ct. 652, 657, 94 L. Ed. 865 (1950).

Furthermore, nothing that we say today prevents compliance with the Convention even when the internal law of the forum does not so require. The Convention provides simple and certain means by which to serve process on a foreign national. Those who eschew its procedures risk discovering that the forum's internal law required transmittal of documents for service abroad, and that the Convention therefore provided the exclusive means of valid service. In addition, parties that comply with the Convention ultimately may find it easier to enforce their judgments abroad. See Westin, *Enforcing Foreign Commercial Judgments and Arbitral Awards in the United States, West Germany, and England*, Law & Policy Int'l Bus. 325, 340-341 (1987). For these reasons, we anticipate that parties may resort to the Convention voluntarily, even in cases that fall outside the scope of its mandatory application.

III

In this case, the Illinois long-arm statute authorized Schlunk to serve VWAG by substituted service on VWoA, without sending documents to Germany. See Ill. Rev. Stat., ch. 110, ¶ 2-209(a)(1) (1985). VWAG has not petitioned for review of the Illinois Appellate Court's holding that service was proper as a matter of Illinois law. VWAG contends, however, that service on VWAG was not complete until VWoA transmitted the complaint to VWAG in Germany. According to VWAG, this transmission constituted service abroad under the Hague Service Convention....

We reject this argument. Where service on a domestic agent is valid and complete under both state law and the Due Process Clause, our inquiry ends and the Convention has no further implications. Whatever internal, private communications take place between the agent and a foreign principal are beyond the concerns of this case. The only transmittal to which the Convention applies is a transmittal abroad that is required as a necessary part of service. And, contrary to VWAG's assertion, the Due Process Clause does not require an official transmittal of documents abroad every time there is service on a foreign national. Applying this analysis, we conclude that this case does not present an occasion to transmit a judicial document for service abroad within the meaning of Article 1. Therefore the Hague Service Convention does not apply, and service was proper. The judgment of the Appellate Court is

Affirmed.

JUSTICE BRENNAN, with whom JUSTICE MARSHALL and JUSTICE BLACKMUN join, concurring in the judgment....

I do not join the Court's opinion because I find it implausible that the Convention's framers intended to leave each contracting nation, and each of the 50 States within our Nation, free to decide for itself under what circumstances, if any, the Convention would control. Rather, in my view, the words "service abroad," read in light of the negotiating history, embody a substantive standard that limits a forum's latitude to deem service complete domestically....

[T]he Convention's language does not prescribe a precise standard to distinguish between "domestic" service and "service abroad." But the Court's solution leaves contracting nations free to ignore its terms entirely, converting its command into exhortation. Under the Court's analysis, for example, a forum nation could prescribe direct mail service to any foreigner and deem service effective upon deposit in the mailbox, or could arbitrarily designate a domestic agent for any foreign defendant and deem service complete upon receipt domestically by the agent even though there is little likelihood that service would ever reach the defendant....

Thus, reading Article 1 "'in the liberal spirit in which it is intended[,]'" to address "'the hardship and injustice, which [the Convention] seeks to relieve,'" [citation omitted], the *Rapport [Explicatif]* interprets the Convention to impose a substantive standard proscribing *notification au parquet* whether the forum nation deems the service "domestic" or "abroad." That substantive standard is captured in the *Rapport*'s admonition that

> "'[a]ll of the transmission channels (prescribed by the convention) *must have as a consequence the fact that the act reach the addressee in due time.* That is a requirement of justice, which assumes its full importance when the act to be transmitted is an act instituting proceedings.'"...

[T]he assumption that the Court imputes to the *Rapport* is inaccurate; as noted above, *notification au parquet* was typically deemed complete upon delivery to the local official. Any requirement of transmission abroad was no more essential to formal service than is the informal arrangement by which a domestic subsidiary might transmit documents served on it as an agent for its foreign parent. See, *e.g.*, 3 Actes et Documents 169. Thus, if the Court entertains the possibility that the Convention bans *notification au parquet* under all circumstances, it can only be because (notwithstanding the Court's stated analysis) the Convention, read in light of its negotiating history, sets some substantive limit on the forum state's latitude to deem such service "domestic."

Significantly, our own negotiating delegation, whose contemporaneous views are "entitled to great weight," *Société Nationale,* took seriously the *Rapport's* conclusion that the Convention is more than just precatory. The delegation's report applauded the Convention as "mak[ing] substantial changes in the practices of many of the civil law countries, moving their practices in the direction of the U.S. approach to international judicial assistance and our concepts of due process in the service of process." S. Exec. Doc. C, at 20. The delegation's chief negotiator emphasized that "the convention sets up the minimum standards of international judicial assistance which each country which ratifies the convention *must* offer to all others who ratify." S. Exec. Rep. No. 6, at 13 (statement by Philip W. Amram) (emphasis in original). Then-Secretary of State Rusk reiterated the same point, as did the State Department's Deputy Legal Advisor, and President Johnson....

My difference with the Court does not affect the outcome of this case, and, given that any process emanating from our courts must comply with due process, it may have little practical consequence in future cases that come before us. But cf. S. Exec. Rep. No. 6, at 15 (statement by Philip W. Amram suggesting that Convention may require "a minor change in the practice of some of our States in long-arm and automobile accident cases" where "service on the appropriate official need be accompanied only by a minimum effort to notify the defendant"). Our Constitution does not, however, bind other nations haling our citizens into their courts. Our citizens rely instead primarily on the forum nation's compliance with the Convention, which the Senate believed would "provide increased protection (due process) for American Citizens who are involved in litigation abroad." *Id.*, at 3. And while other nations are not bound by the Court's pronouncement that the Convention lacks obligatory force, after today's decision their courts will surely sympathize little with any United States national pleading that a judgment violates the Convention because (notwithstanding any local characterization) service was "abroad."

NOTES AND QUESTIONS

1. One of the principal purposes of service of process rules is to guarantee that it is fair to grant a default judgment against an unresponsive defendant. Does the Hague Service Convention satisfy this purpose?

2. What facts in *Schlunk* justify the plaintiff's use of Illinois law rather than the Convention to serve process on a foreign defendant?

3. What is *notification au parquet*? Some civil law nations still utilize it: e.g., the French New Code of Civil Procedure arts. 660-661, 670-672, 684-688. Is substituted service on a corporation's subsidiary analogous to *notification au parquet*? How can it be distinguished?

4. Does the United States Constitution's due process clause, with its reasonable notice requirement, protect foreign defendants against state service of process rules that are unlikely to provide a foreigner with actual notice of a lawsuit?

5. What advantage would a plaintiff, who obtains a default judgment against a foreign defendant without assets in the forum, have by initially using the Convention instead of federal or state service of process rules?

6. Is the Court in *Schlunk* in essence piercing the corporate veil to uphold service on a U.S. subsidiary as effective against the foreign parent VWAG on an alter-ego theory? Or is the Court relying on an assumed agency relationship between the foreign parent and local subsidiary for the purpose of service?

Should either of these approaches justify asserting personal jurisdiction over the foreign parent? The Supreme Court has not dealt with this jurisdiction issue since *Cannon Mfg. Co. v. Cudahy Packing Co.*, 267 U.S. 333 (1925), where it found that the activities of a subsidiary were not necessarily enough to render a parent subject to a court's jurisdiction.

7. A Japanese corporation does some occasional business in New York, but it does not maintain an office or have any agents in New York. However, the company did appoint the New York secretary of state as an agent to accept process so that it could be authorized to do business in New York. Can a plaintiff injured by one of the company's products serve process on the secretary of state rather than use the Hague Convention to serve the defendant in Japan? *See Karaszewski v. Honda Motor Co.,* 537 N.Y.S.2d 975 (Sup. Ct. 1989).

8. Some parties to the Convention, such as Germany, require under article 5 that the process and complaint must be translated into that country's language. The court in *Teknekron Mgt. v. Quante Fernmeldetechnik*, 115 F.R.D. 175, 177 (D. Nev. 1987), illustrated how far this obligation might go in a suit arising out of a stock purchase agreement:

> the plaintiff's initial service on the defendants was clearly improper, in that service was simply mailed to Quante-D in West Germany. The plaintiff, recognizing its error, then attempted to effect service according to the treaty. In so doing, however, it failed to translate a lengthy contract which was attached as an exhibit to the complaint. Under both Federal and Nevada procedure, such an exhibit is considered part of the complaint. *See* Fed. R. Civ. P. 10(c); N.R.C.P. 10(c). Because it was also part of the complaint, the exhibit should also have been translated into German for service to be effective. The defendants' motion to dismiss for insufficient service of process must therefore be granted.

9. Twenty-nine countries are parties to the Hague Service Convention, including Japan and all the European civil law nations discussed in this book (France, Germany, Italy, and Spain). Latin American nations have not ratified the Hague Convention; instead they favor the Inter-American Convention on Letters Rogatory (1975). The U.S. had several objections to this Convention and therefore proposed the Additional Protocol to meet these concerns, which was opened for signature in 1979. The U.S. ratified the Inter-American Convention and Additional Protocol in 1986. Together they provide a service of process mechanism similar to that of the Hague Convention. The U.S. designated the Department of Justice (Office of International Judicial Assistance, Civil Division) in 1988 as the central authority to process and transmit letters rogatory. Among Latin American nations discussed in this book, Argentina and Mexico have ratified both the Convention and Protocol.

3. SERVICE OF PROCESS IN JAPAN

BANKSTON v. TOYOTA MOTOR CORP.

United States Court of Appeals, Eighth Circuit
889 F.2d 172 (1989)

Ross, Senior Circuit Judge.

Appellants Charles Bankston, Sr. and Regina Dixon filed suit in the United States District Court for the Western District of Arkansas against Toyota Motor Corporation, a Japanese corporation, seeking damages resulting from an accident involving a Toyota truck. The appellants first attempted service of process upon Toyota by serving an affiliated United States corporation in Torrance, California, as Toyota's purported agent. Toyota filed a motion to dismiss for improper service of process. The district court denied Toyota's motion but granted the appellants 45 days in which to serve Toyota in accordance with the Hague Convention.

The appellants next attempted to serve process upon Toyota by sending a summons and complaint by registered mail, return receipt requested, to Tokyo, Japan. The documents were in English and did not include a translation into Japanese. The receipt of service was signed and returned to appellants. Toyota renewed its motion to dismiss, arguing that the appellants' proposed method of service still did not comply with the Hague Convention.

The district court concluded that Article 10(a) of the Hague Convention does not permit service of process upon a Japanese corporation by registered mail. In an order dated January 4, 1989, the district court gave the appellants an additional sixty days in which to effect service in compliance with the Hague Convention....

On February 9, 1989, this court entered an order granting appellants leave to take an interlocutory appeal pursuant to 28 U.S.C. § 1292(b).

The crucial article for this discussion is Article 10, under which appellants herein purportedly attempted to serve process upon Toyota by registered mail. [The court sets out Article 10.]

Japan has objected to subparagraphs (b) and (c), but not to subparagraph (a). The issue before this court is whether subparagraph (a) permits service on a Japanese defendant by direct mail.

In recent years, two distinct lines of Article 10(a) interpretation have arisen. Some courts have ruled that Article 10(a) permits service of process by mail directly to the defendant without the necessity of resorting to the central authority, and without the necessity of translating the documents into the official language of the nation where the documents are to be served.

In general, these courts reason that since the purported purpose of the Hague Convention is to facilitate service abroad, the reference to "'the freedom to send judicial documents by postal channels, directly to persons abroad' would be superfluous unless it was related to the sending of such documents for the purpose of service." *Ackermann v. Levine,* 788 F.2d 830, 839 (2d Cir. 1986). *See also Smith v. Dainichi Kinzoku Kogyo Co.,* 680 F. Supp. 847, 850 (W.D. Tex. 1988); *Newport Components, Inc. v. NEC Home Electronics, Inc.,* 671 F. Supp. 1525, 1541 (C.D. Cal. 1987). These courts have further found that the use of the [word] "send" rather than "service" in Article 10(a) "must be attributed to careless drafting." *Ackermann v. Levine, supra,* 788 F.2d at 839.

The second line of interpretation, advocated by Toyota, is that the word "send" in Article 10(a) is not the equivalent of "service of process." The word "service" is specifically used in other sections of the Convention, including subsections (b) and (c) of Article 10. If the drafters of the Convention had meant for subparagraph (a) to provide an additional manner of service of judicial documents, they would have used the word "service." Subscribers to this interpretation maintain that Article 10(a) merely provides a method for sending subsequent documents after service of process has been obtained by means of the central authority. *See, e.g., Hantover, Inc. v. Omet,* 688 F. Supp. 1377, 1385 (W.D. Mo. 1988); *Prost v. Honda Motor Co.,* 122 F.R.D. 215, 216 (E.D. Mo. 1987); *Pochop v. Toyota Motor Co.,* 111 F.R.D. 464, 466 (S.D. Miss. 1986); *Mommsen v. Toro Co.,* 108 F.R.D. 444, 446 (S.D. Iowa 1985); *Suzuki Motor Co. v. Superior Court,* 200 Cal. App. 3d 1476, 249 Cal. Rptr. 376 (1988).

We find this second line of authority to be more persuasive. It is a "familiar canon of statutory construction that the starting point for interpreting a statute is the language of the statute itself. Absent a clearly expressed legislative intention to the contrary, that language must ordinarily be regarded as conclusive." [Citation omitted.] In addition, where a legislative body "includes particular language in one section of a statute but omits it in another section of the same Act, it is generally presumed that [the legislative body] acts intentionally and purposely in the disparate inclusion or exclusion." [Citation omitted.] In *Suzuki Motor Co. v. Superior Court,* 249 Cal. Rptr. at 379, the court found that because service of process by registered mail was not permitted under Japanese law, it was "extremely unlikely" that Japan's failure to object to Article 10(a) was intended to authorize the use of registered mail as an effective mode of service of process, particularly in light of the fact that Japan had specifically objected to the much more formal modes of service by Japanese officials which were available in Article 10(b) and (c).

We conclude that sending a copy of a summons and complaint by registered mail to a defendant in a foreign country is not a method of service of process permitted by the Hague Convention. We affirm the judgment of the district court and remand this case with directions that appellants be given a reasonable time from the date of this Order in which to effectuate service of process over appellee Toyota Motor Corporation in compliance with the terms of the Hague Convention.

JOHN R. GIBSON, CIRCUIT JUDGE, concurring.

I concur in the court's opinion today in every respect. The court correctly interprets the Hague Convention. I write separately only to express nagging concerns I have about the practical effect of our opinion. Automobiles are subject to a plethora of regulations requiring particular equipment and detailed warnings. Should an automobile manufactured in Japan carry a disclosure that, if litigation ensues from its purchase and use, service of process on the Japanese manufacturer can only be obtained under the Hague Convention? Should the purchaser also be informed that this special service of process will cost $800 to $900, as we are told, and must include a translation of the suit papers in Japanese? These decisions we must leave to others. I write only to express my discomfort with the practical effect of Toyota's insistence on strict compliance with the letter of the Hague Convention.

CHIN KIM & ELISEO Z. SISNEROS, COMPARATIVE OVERVIEW OF SERVICE OF PROCESS: UNITED STATES, JAPAN, AND ATTEMPTS AT INTERNATIONAL UNITY, 23 Vanderbilt Journal of Transnational Law 299, 306-09 (1990)

In Japan, "business relating to service shall be administered by the court clerk." [S]ervice of process in Japan, as in most civil law countries, is an official function to be performed by the court. This requirement is consistent with the role the court plays in civil law countries. Their codes of civil procedure grant the judge much power in controlling litigation. Japan and West Germany, for example, give the judge power to clarify the issues of litigation. Both Japan and West Germany authorize the judge to conduct examination of witnesses or parties, and to control the questioning of witnesses by the parties to the litigation. In Japan, the judge may attempt to impose a compromise at any stage of the lawsuit, seek expert testimony to assist in the litigation, examine a party to the lawsuit, or order any necessary investigation pertaining to the litigation.

The methods of service allowed in Japan are personal service, service on the legal representative of one lacking litigation capacity,[60] service on a prison chief for a prisoner, service by mail,[62] and service by publication. Under Japanese law, the places where a person may be served include a person's domicile, place of residence, or place of business, or where the person is encountered. A Japanese court administers service of process by mail by having the clerk stamp "special service" on the envelope, thus designating the postal service as the official effecting agent....

[V]alid service of process in Japan requires that a Japanese court authorize the service. This is the one common thread found in all Japanese service of process rules. Japanese courts are part of the government, and therefore service of process is considered an official act. Under this structure, the Japanese

[60] Service on a legal representative may be made at the place of business or office of the representative.

[62] The Minji Soshōhō [Code of Civil Procedure] allows such service when service by delivery, substitute service, and service by leaving the document all fail. The clerk may then send a copy by registered mail, and service is deemed completed with full effect from the time of dispatch, whether or not the addressee receives it later.

Government and courts are not very tolerant of attempts by foreign governments or persons to circumvent the authority the Japanese courts assert over service of process. Failure to follow the explicit requirements of the Japanese courts may result in a subsequent judgment having no effect. The Japanese Government considers the service of documents directly upon a person residing in Japan by United States courts or litigants to constitute an impermissible exercise of jurisdiction by the United States within the territory of Japan.[76]

NOTES AND QUESTIONS

1. The court in *Bankston* notes that there is a split of authority in the U.S. about how Article 10(a) of the Hague Convention should be interpreted in regard to Japan. Does the court adopt the better interpretation? *Cf. Lemme v. Wine of Japan, Inc.,* 631 F. Supp. 456 (E.D.N.Y. 1986) (mail service permitted).

2. Does the excerpt on service of process in Japan help to convince you that the *Bankston* court was right or wrong in its interpretation? Consider the citation in footnote 76 from the excerpt. In 1987 the Japanese Embassy in Washington informed the U.S. Department of State that the Japanese Government considers direct service of court documents by mail under article 10(a) to be an unlawful exercise of jurisdiction by the United States within the territory of Japan. Should the State Department circular influence the interpretation of article 10(a) by American courts?

In 1983 the Japanese Central Authority accepted U.S. court requests for service of documents in 211 cases for forwarding to the Supreme Court, which sends them to the appropriate district court for administration of service to the addressee. Many requests are denied due to incomplete forms or translation problems. By 1987 the number of accepted requests had risen to 620.

3. Article 200 of the Japanese Code of Civil Procedure provides for the enforcement of foreign civil judgments except in cases where the foreign court is found to lack jurisdiction, there is no proof of reciprocal enforcement of Japanese judgments, or the foreign judgment is against Japanese public policy.

One Japanese court has also refused to enforce a Hawaii judgment because the plaintiff failed to serve a Japanese translation of the proper documents on the defendant. *H. Saeki, Inc. v. Osake* (Tokyo Dist. Ct., 26 Mar. 1990), translated in 34 Japanese Ann. Int'l L. 174 (1991).

4. The Service Convention is only applicable "in civil or commercial matters." Art. 1. Does that include administrative or tax cases? The United States will permit service of process in administrative cases, but France, Germany, and Japan will not. These countries, for example, have refused to serve documents from the Environmental Protection Agency, the International Trade Commission, or the Federal Trade Commission. Egypt excludes family law cases. What about service of a U.S. contract claim requesting punitive damages? Is that essentially a civil or a criminal matter? The German case that follows must answer that question.

---

[76] U.S. Dep't of State, Circular, Service of Process in Japan 3 (June 1987).

4. SERVICE OF PROCESS IN GERMANY

X COMPANY v. BAVARIA

Munich Court of Appeals (9th Civil Chamber)
Decision of 9 May 1989
35 RiW 483, 28 I.L.M. 1570 (1989)

Translated for I.L.M. by Bruno A. Ristau

DECISION

I. The Order [of the Bavarian Ministry of Justice] of December 30, 1988, is vacated.

II. The Bavarian Ministry of Justice is obligated to effect the service requested by the Petitioners, provided Petitioners furnish a complete translation of Plaintiff's Exhibit A to the complaint or provided [in the alternative] that Petitioners declare that they do not wish to have the illegible portions of Exhibit A served.

III. The necessary extrajudicial costs incurred by the Petitioners are to be reimbursed by the State....

REASONS

I

The First Petitioner is an insurance company domiciled in the United States which, among other things, entered into a contract of reinsurance with an insurance company doing business in Munich. In a suit brought in a United States court, the Petitioner asserts claims for restitution and damages, and claims for "malicious and intentional delays in paying the restitution amounts" (punitive damages). The Second Petitioner, counsel for the First Petitioner, acted as the "Requesting Authority" within the meaning of the Hague Convention on the Service Abroad of Judicial and Extrajudicial Documents in Civil or Commercial Matters of 15 November 1965 ("Service Convention"), and requested the Bavarian Ministry of Justice to serve the complaint on the defendant in Munich. Attached to the complaint were documents which are illegible in part and which the translator designated as illegible.

With an [administrative] Order issued on December 30, 1988, the Bavarian Ministry of Justice declined to serve the documents....

[The Petitioners] contend that the Service Convention also applies to a suit seeking punitive damages, since the suit is civil in nature. Service may not be refused since such suit does not concern Art. 13 of the Service Convention — the infringement of the sovereignty or security of the requested state. The clear implication of Art. 13 of the Service Convention is that requests for service may not be denied on mere public policy grounds. Moreover, German public policy would not be offended by the service of a complaint seeking punitive damages. In addition, a complete translation of the Exhibit to the complaint can be furnished at any time.

In opposing the petition, the Respondent contends that the Service Convention does not apply because of the penal nature of the damages sought in the suit, and that the request does not relate to a civil, but rather to a criminal matter. In any event, service of such a complaint would be contrary to German public policy because the assertion of penal powers by private parties and the commercialization of criminal law in favor of damaged parties offends basic principles of due process of law. This, as well as the frequently excessive punitive damage awards rendered by United States courts, mandates that the exception contained in Art. 13 of the Service Convention be interpreted expansively. Finally, the denial of the request here was justified because the Exhibit attached to the complaint was illegible in part and was not translated in part — and thus the request did not comply with Art. 5(1)(a) of the Service Convention and with Sec. 3 of the [German] Implementing Law....

II

2) The petition is ... meritorious.

a) The Service Convention — which applies to civil or commercial matters (Art. 1 of the Convention) — applies also in instances where the complaint to be served asserts punitive damages. The subject matter of such a suit is not criminal in nature.

aa) Under United States law, punitive damages may be awarded in connection with tort or contract claims involving aggravated circumstances, i.e., where the defendant acted in a malicious manner (cf. von Westphalen, RiW [Recht der internationalen Wirtschaft] 1981, 143 ff.). In contrast to other damages which are designed to compensate the damaged party for its losses, punitive damages are designed to punish and to deter (von Westphalen, *supra*; Thümmel, RiW 1988, 613 ff.; Lange/Black, Der Zivilprozess in den Vereinigten Staaten, 1986, no. 128). The assertion of such claims in product liability cases has led to damage awards which, considered from the German vantage point, have been very high. The use of punitive damages has also led to an ever-increasing criticism in the United States (cf. Thümmel, *supra*).

bb) Even though the principal function of punitive damages is to punish and to deter, such claims are nevertheless civil in nature. In the present case it need not be decided whether the characterization of such claims should be made under the law of the requesting state, under the law of the requested state or under the laws of both states, or whether it should be made within the context of the Service Convention.

In each case, the result will necessarily be the same, *viz.*, that punitive damages do not form part of the criminal law. The Court regards the following three criteria as dispositive: punitive damages arise out of individual claims asserted by private parties against other private parties, and the assertion of such claims is discretionary with the private claimants; if the claim succeeds, the damages awarded benefit exclusively the damaged party; above all, an award of punitive damages is not tantamount to a criminal conviction. A defendant against whom punitive damages are awarded is not considered as having been convicted of an offense, nor is the judgment registered in a penal registry. In contradistinction, criminal law has as its purpose the prosecution of an offender by the sovereign. Certain limited exceptions to that principle, such as a private criminal complaint under German law, can be disregarded. In any event, the latter type of proceeding results in a criminal conviction.

b) The Respondent is therefore obligated to effect the requested service under the Service Convention even though the complaint also seeks punitive damages. The Court is not called upon to determine whether the complaint to be served offends German public policy within the context of the Service Convention in the same manner as the Court would be called upon to determine whether a foreign judgment sought to be enforced here would offend German public policy within the context of Sec. 328 of the Code of Civil Procedure.

aa) Under Art. 13 of the Service Convention, a service request can be refused only if the state addressed considers that the execution of the request would endanger its sovereignty or security. Obviously, this is not the case here.

bb) In ratifying the Service Convention, the Federal Republic of Germany made no declarations which go beyond the exception in Art. 13.

cc) Even if one were to assume that Art. 13 of the Service Convention incorporates a public policy exception (cf. Hülsen, RiW 1982, 550, and authorities there cited), such an exception could, consistently with the spirit of the Convention, apply only under very limited circumstances and in exceptionally weighty cases. According to its Preamble, the signatory states desired to improve mutual judicial assistance by simplifying and expediting the procedure so that judicial documents served abroad would be brought timely to the notice of the addressee. This purpose would not be served if at the service stage the state addressed would engage in a detailed public order analysis and condition the execution of the request upon a determination whether the complaint itself violates German law. Aside from the fact that the ultimate outcome of a complaint is, at best, speculative at the [service] stage, everyone who engages in commercial activity abroad runs the risk of being sued in a foreign court. The protection afforded by Sec. 328 of the Code of Civil Procedure, however, is limited to proceedings in domestic courts.

A request for service can, therefore, only be refused in instances where grave injury to the legal order of the state of execution would result (Schlosser, ZZP 1981, 381 ff. with respect to the Hague Service Convention; compare the views of Stiefel on that subject in RiW 1979, 514). If a suit is predicated on facts which are particularly heinous and if a review of the complaint makes it apparent that the service of such a complaint would constitute aiding and abetting violations of basic norms of a free, democratic society, then the service of the complaint should be denied. The Court need not decide whether such a result would flow from an expansive interpretation of Art. 13 of the Service Convention, from an assumed international public policy standard (see Riezler, Internationales Zivilprozeßrecht, 540 ff.), or from the supremacy of constitutional law principles of the state of execution. In the instant case, it is not apparent that service of the complaint seeking punitive damages would offend some higher ranking principles or fundamental constitutional norms.

In particular, we need not be concerned here with a potential misuse of penal powers by private parties. Even though the institution of punitive damages as such is unknown in German law, there are hints and indications [in German law] that certain aspects of the law of damages may serve purposes other than compensation. To begin with, the Civil Code recognizes contractual liquidated damages (§§ 339 ff.). Damages for pain and suffering can be augmented by moral damages. (BGHZ 18, 149; NJW 1976, 1147). Case law acknowledges that a deliberate refusal by an insurer to pay the insurance amount during a prolonged law suit, under circumstances where the obligation to pay the amount is clear, can be compensated by an increase in damages (cf. Palandt-Thomas, BGB, comment 4 to § 847, and authorities cited), thus achieving a result which comes close to punitive damages. Finally, in trademark infringement cases, a punitive addition to ordinary damages may be awarded against the offending party as sanctions and as a preventive measure. It therefore follows that the institution of punitive damages cannot be viewed as being fundamentally at odds with the foregoing principles.

The size of punitive damage awards rendered by United States courts does not call for a different result. It has not been claimed, and it is not apparent, that these high damage awards are rendered arbitrarily or that they are designed to exclude foreign competition. Moreover, at the point in time when a complaint is served, the ultimate damage award is wholly speculative. The Court cannot hold that the principle of proportionality [between damages suffered and compensation sought] is violated when punitive damages are demanded.

dd) The Court is mindful that a defendant domiciled in Germany enjoys greater protection under Sec. 328 of the Code of Civil Procedure with respect to his domestic assets than he does with respect to his foreign assets. It is not, however, the purpose of the Service Convention to protect a person's foreign assets. Here, too, it bears repeating that everyone who engages in international commerce should be aware that his foreign assets may be adversely affected by a foreign legal proceeding.

3) Even though the Respondent is in principle required to honor the service request, the Respondent could decline to serve documents that are illegible or that are not fully translated (Art. 5(1) (a) of the Service Convention, in conjunction with Sec. 3 of the Implementing Law).

But a requesting party's obligation to furnish a translation does not justify a refusal of the service request. In its [administrative] Order of 30 December 1988, the Respondent made it clear that its refusal was based on different grounds. Prior to the 30th of December 1988, Petitioners were given no opportunity to furnish the missing translation. They have now declared that they are prepared to do so. The Court cannot, and does not, determine whether the missing enclosures are an essential part of the complaint. That determination must be made by the Petitioners....

Prof. Dr. Blomeyer Presiding Judge	Mansfeld and Russ Associate Judges

Of the Court of Appeals

NOTES AND QUESTIONS

1. The German Supreme Court has not adjudicated the penal damages issue. Each of the German states, such as Bavaria, has its own central authority under the Convention, and the highest state civil court is the court of appeals. Therefore, although this issue is settled in Bavaria (or at least in Munich, since Bavaria has more than one court of appeals), the state of Northrhine-Westphalia has refused to serve complaints requesting punitive damages or treble damages under a RICO claim. Could this problem be avoided by serving plaintiff's complaint without the punitive damages claim and then, after the German defendant appears in the U.S. suit, by amending the complaint under Fed. R. Civ. P. 15(a)?

The problem of the enforceability of an ultimate penal damages award would of course remain. *See, e.g., North Con I v. Katayama*, Hanrei Jihō (No. 1376) 79 (Tokyo Dist. Ct., 18 Feb. 1991), refusing to enforce a California penal damages judgment on the grounds that penal damages are essentially criminal sanctions and thus not enforceable "civil" judgments and that such awards are also against Japanese public policy.

Consider the following note about an important recent German Supreme Court case in which the plaintiff sought recognition and enforcement of a California judgment in a tort action.

> The petitioner, a U.S. citizen living in California and the plaintiff in the original action, had obtained a California civil judgment against the respondent/defendant, a U.S. and German citizen who had engaged the plaintiff in homosexual activities while the plaintiff was still a minor. The California court awarded $750,260 in damages, consisting of $260 for the costs of medical treatment, $150,000 for the costs of psychiatric treatment, $200,000 for pain and suffering, and $400,000 in punitive damages. After the defendant, who at the time had lived in California, moved to Germany, the plaintiff tried to enforce the judgment in Germany. In its decision of June 1992, the Federal Supreme Court recognized the California judgment only in the amount of $350,260, thus denying recognition of the $400,000 award of punitive damages.[20]
>
> The court stated that to enforce the judgment as far as exemplary and punitive damages were concerned would be incompatible with German public policy because contrary to U.S. law, the policy underlying the German civil law of damages was to compensate the harmed person for injury and loss, but not to punish the perpetrator or deter others. Although it noted that a German court might have awarded damages for pain and suffering only in the area of DM 30,000, the court did recognize the $200,000 award of damages for pain and suffering. In support of this finding, the court considered that when the wrongful actions took place, both parties lived in California and were thus familiar with California's laws of compensation for pain and suffering, as long as the awards were not clearly excessive. In this context, the court left open the question whether different considerations would have applied if the facts had borne a closer relationship to Germany. Commentators have noted that this leaves the door open for a different ruling in a products liability case where stronger German interests may be at stake.

[20] *Judgment of June 4, 1992,* 1992 NJW 3073.

Burkhard Bastuck, *Regional Developments: Germany,* 27 Int'l Law. 218, 224-25 (1993). *See* Hartwin Bungert, *Enforcing U.S. Excessive and Punitive Damages Awards in Germany,* 27 Int'l Law. 1075 (1993); Peter Hay, *The Recognition and Enforcement of American Money-Judgments in Germany — The 1992 Decision of the German Supreme Court,* 40 Am. J. Comp. L. 729 (1992); Joachim Zekoll, *The Enforceability of American Money Judgments Abroad: A Landmark Decision by the German Federal Court of Justice,* 30 Colum. J. Transnat'l L. 641 (1992).

2. Art. 13 of the Convention permits a state to refuse service if it "would infringe its sovereignty or security." Does this language implicitly incorporate a public policy exception to service similar to the public policy exception sometimes used to refuse enforcement of a foreign country judgment?

3. For a thorough discussion of the public policy issue and the relationship between service of U.S. process and enforcement of a U.S. judgment in the context of German law, see Klaus J. Beucher & John Byron Sandage, *United States Punitive Damage Awards in German Courts: The Evolving German Position on Service and Enforcement,* 23 Vand. J. Transnat'l L. 967 (1991); Rolf A. Schutze, *The Recognition and Enforcement of American Civil Judgments Containing Punitive Damages in the Federal Republic of Germany,* 11 U. Pa. J. Int'l Bus. L. 581 (1989); Joachim Zekoll, *Recognition and Enforcement of American Products Liability Awards in the Federal Republic of Germany,* 37 Am. J. Comp. L. 301 (1989).

4. The issues raised in this section often intertwine service of process on foreign defendants with questions about personal jurisdiction. The problem is especially interesting when a corporate relationship exists between a foreign parent and U.S. subsidiary, as illustrated by the *Schlunk* case, *supra.*

Useful reference works on these issues include: Gary B. Born & David Westin, International Civil Litigation in United States Courts: Commentary and Materials, chs. 2-3 (2d ed. 1992); Ved P. Nanda & David K. Pansius, Litigation of International Disputes in U.S. Courts, chs. 1-2 (1990); Bruno A. Ristau, 1 International Judicial Assistance: Civil and Commercial, pts. 1, 3-4, 7 (1990).

Helpful articles include: Gary B. Born & Andrew N. Vollmer, *The Effect of the Revised Federal Rules of Civil Procedure on Personal Jurisdiction, Service, and Discovery in International Cases,* 150 F.R.D. 221 (1994); Committee on Federal Courts of the New York State Bar Association, *Service of Process Abroad: A Nuts and Bolts Guide,* 122 F.R.D. 63 (1988); Ronan E. Degnan & Mary Kay Kane, *The Exercise of Jurisdiction Over and Enforcement of Judgments Against Alien Defendants,* 39 Hastings L.J. 799 (1988); William Temple Jorden, *Beyond Jingoism: Service by Mail to Japan and the Hague Convention on the Service Abroad of Judicial and Extrajudicial Documents in Civil or Commercial Matters,* 16 Law in Japan 69 (1983); Kenneth B. Reisenfeld, *Service of United States Process Abroad: A Practical Guide to Service Under the Hague Service Convention and the Federal Rules of Civil Procedure,* 24 Int'l Law. 55-83 (1990) (with sample forms); Comment, *Jurisdiction Over a Corporation Based on the Contacts of a Related Corporation: Time for a Rule of Attribution,* 92 Dick. L. Rev. 917-46 (1988); Note, *International Service of*

Process by Mail Under the Hague Service Convention, 13 Mich. J. Int'l L. 698 (1992).

B. PLEADING OR JUDICIAL NOTICE OF FOREIGN LAW: APPROACHES TO RECOGNITION OF FOREIGN LAW ISSUES

NOTE ON THE COMMON LAW FACT APPROACH

The common law rule that foreign law is handled as a fact had its beginnings in the 18th century. At that time it was believed that foreign law should be treated like commercial custom, which was similarly outside the purview of the ordinary judge. Unlike domestic law, the judge could not reasonably be presumed to know the applicable foreign rule.

Some logical consequences of treating foreign law as a fact are:

(1) It must be pleaded; a complaint which fails to comply is subject to a demurrer.

(2) Under the traditional view, which is still the law in a few states, questions of foreign law go to the jury.

(3) Ordinary rules of evidence apply, which frequently prevents examination of material that could provide a proper basis for the determination of foreign law.

(4) Courts cannot conduct their own investigation, but must let the parties present the facts.

(5) A judicial decision on a point of foreign law does not constitute a precedent under the doctrine of *stare decisis.*

(6) On appeal, courts normally only consider questions of law. They will not disturb questions of fact decided in the trial court unless they are "clearly erroneous."

1. THE FACT APPROACH IN PRACTICE

ALBERT EHRENZWEIG, FOREIGN RULES AS "SOURCES OF LAW," in LEGAL THOUGHT IN THE UNITED STATES OF AMERICA UNDER CONTEMPORARY PRESSURES 71, 77 (John N. Hazard & Wenceslas J. Wagner eds. 1970)

When I was still willing to engage in this less than dignified game of legal craftsmanship, I was repeatedly employed to "testify" in American courts on foreign laws, German, Austrian, French, — in one case even on Egyptian law, despite my protest that I could not even read Arabic. One of the favorite occasions for such employment is litigation concerning succession to Californian estates of aliens who must prove that their country extends "reciprocity" to American citizens. So long as this was treated as a question of fact, a decision did not create a precedent and it was quite usual to relitigate the same question regarding the same country for other parties and other dates of death. Needless to say courts used for this purpose all time-honored, or should I say time-dishonored, medieval devices of the American law of evidence, including cross-examination of the expert "witness" concerning his "charac-

ter." But even today, when foreign law has been widely recognized as "law," many courts continue to insist on each party producing decisions of foreign courts, however lowly, even of countries in which such decisions are declared to be inconclusive as against statutes, treatises, or learned opinions. This practice, of course, strikes lawyers of those countries as a travesty of their laws which purportedly are sought to be ascertained.

PHILP v. MACRI

United States Court of Appeals, Ninth Circuit
261 F.2d 945 (1958)

HAMLIN, CIRCUIT JUDGE.

This appeal is taken from an order of the District Court, Western District of Washington, dismissing Appellant's complaint for insufficiency.

Jurisdiction of the District Court is based on diversity of citizenship. Jurisdiction of this Court rests on 28 U.S.C. §§ 1291 and 1294.

Appellant (Clyde Philp) alleged three separate causes of action, and all three were dismissed. Appeal is taken only from the dismissal of the first and third causes of action.

In the first cause of action, Appellant seeks an injunction to restrain the Appellees, hereinafter Macri, from proceeding in the Peruvian Courts to enforce a judgment previously obtained against Appellant in a District Court of the United States....

Appellant's third cause of action alleged that Appellant was "slandered" by Macri by his "circulating in financial circles" in Peru the "erroneous story" that Macri "would sue and did sue" Appellant because he did not pay his share of a joint venture.

The pleadings contain conclusions of law, are general in nature, do not allege specific defamatory statements, and appear to refer only to the fact that Appellant was to be sued for not paying money alleged to be owed by him.

Such a suit was actually brought against Appellant.

In this diversity case we must apply Washington rules of conflicts of law. *Klaxon Co. v. Stentor Electric Mfg. Co.,* 1941, 313 U.S. 487, 61 S. Ct. 1020, 85 L. Ed. 1477. [Citation omitted.] Washington follows the general rule that the substantive law applicable to an alleged tort is the law of the place where the tort was committed. Restatement of the Law of Conflict of Laws, §§ 377, 378. [Citations omitted.] Here, there is no question but that the alleged slander occurred in Peru, for the complaint alleges that the defamation was uttered, and Appellant's "credits and reputation" injured, in Lima, Peru.

We are thus faced with a situation where Appellant's cause of action arose in and should be governed by the law of Peru, but no Peruvian law is pleaded or proved.... [T]here is a diversity of views on where this leaves a litigant. Does the cause of action fall for failure to allege an essential of the complaint, or does the forum assume the foreign law is the same as the law of the forum and apply it?

We hold that the instant case is controlled by the principles set forth by Justice Holmes in *Cuba R. Co. v. Crosby,* 1912, 222 U.S. 473, 32 S. Ct. 132, 56 L. Ed. 274. There, the Court was unwilling to assume that the law of Cuba

(*locus delicti*) was the same as the common law. Thus, as the law of Cuba had not been pleaded or proved, the judgment entered for plaintiff in the trial court was reversed. Holmes pointed out that while it might be reasonable to presume that as between two common law countries, the common law of one was the same as that of another; that even as between two such countries there would be no such presumption where a statute was involved; i.e., a statute of one would not be presumed to be a statute of the other; and where both were not common law countries, the limits of the presumption would be narrower still.

Where one country's judicial system is based on the Common Law and the other's on the Civil Law, both systems having been modified by statutory changes, there is little to recommend the employment of a presumption that the law of one is the same as the law of the other.

We do not presume that the law of defamation in Peru is the same as the law of defamation in the State of Washington.

Appellant's complaint, having failed to allege his right to recover, was properly dismissed by the District Court. *Cuba R. Co. v. Crosby, supra; Gordon v. Commissioner of Internal Revenue,* 9 Cir., 1935, 75 F.2d 429; *Walton v. Arabian American Oil Co.*, 2 Cir., 1956, 233 F.2d 541.

The judgment of the District Court is affirmed.

FRANKLIN v. SMALLDRIDGE

Texas Court of Civil Appeals, Corpus Christi
616 S.W.2d 655 (1981)

NYE, CHIEF JUSTICE.

Plaintiff, Hilaria Cabrera Franklin, filed suit for divorce seeking a dissolution of the marriage and a division of the community property. Additionally, plaintiff sought to set aside a deed from her alleged husband, Benjamin T. Franklin, to defendant, M. G. Smalldridge, contending that this was community property which was conveyed without her joinder. Prior to the hearing on the divorce action, plaintiff's alleged husband died, and the divorce proceedings were dismissed. Trial was then to the court on plaintiff's action to set aside the deed and for damages for conversion of plaintiff's nursery business located on the alleged community property. The trial court found for the defendant Smalldridge, whereupon plaintiff appeals.

Plaintiff pled that she and Benjamin T. Franklin had perfected a valid common law marriage; that during this marriage they had acquired the subject property; that they had conducted a nursery business in conjunction with the property; and that Benjamin T. Franklin had conveyed the subject property to defendant Smalldridge without her joinder. The divorce action, the suit to set aside the deed, and the suit for damages resulted.

The plaintiff brings forth 21 points of error in this appeal. However, the main question centers on the validity, vel non, of the common law marriage between her and Benjamin T. Franklin. The facts show that the plaintiff had entered into a ceremonial religious marriage with Luis Chavez in the country of Mexico. Sometime after this relationship, the plaintiff immigrated to the United States in 1955. Plaintiff contends that in 1960, she and Benjamin T.

Franklin entered into a common law marriage which continued until this present action.

In order to constitute a valid common law marriage, it must be established that the parties: 1) entered into an expressed or implied agreement to become husband and wife; 2) that such agreement was followed by cohabitation as man and wife; and 3) that they held each other out professedly and publicly as husband and wife. [Citations omitted.] There is, of course, one additional fundamental rule: that in order to establish any valid marriage, the parties must possess the legal capacity to marry and that there must not be any legal impediment prohibiting the marriage contract. [Citation omitted.]

The trial court, in its findings, found that plaintiff and Benjamin T. Franklin satisfied all of the above requirements to establish a valid common law marriage in the State of Texas, except for the removal of the impediment of the religious ceremonial marriage between the plaintiff and Luis Chavez in Mexico. Plaintiff contends on appeal, however, that this finding of the trial court was erroneous because a party (here, defendant M. G. Smalldridge) who attacks the validity of a present marriage must introduce proof to negate the dissolution of an alleged prior marriage. Therefore, according to appellant, it was incumbent upon defendant Smalldridge to prove the validity of the prior marriage between plaintiff and Luis Chavez to attack the present common law marriage. Alternatively, plaintiff contends that she properly pled and proved the laws of Mexico, thereby proving the invalid Mexican marriage and the lack of any impediment to her common law marriage to Benjamin T. Franklin.

It is true that there is a presumption that the most recent marriage of a party is the valid one, and this presumption continues until one proves the impediment of a prior marriage. [Citations omitted.] However, plaintiff admitted that she entered into a religious marriage with Luis Chavez in Mexico and that this marriage was never dissolved by divorce. It was plaintiff's contention throughout the trial, however, that there was no reason for her to get a divorce from Chavez, because a religious Mexican marriage is not a binding marriage in Mexico. During the trial, plaintiff's attorney made an oral motion for the trial court to take judicial knowledge of the laws of the Republic of Mexico, to fortify plaintiff's position.

Foreign law is regarded as a fact issue in the State of Texas. It must, therefore, be strictly pled and proved by the party relying on such foreign law. [Citations omitted.] Since our Texas courts refuse to take judicial notice of foreign laws, the party relying upon such a foreign law must offer proof and plead the laws themselves. [Citations omitted.] In the absence of pleadings and proof of the laws of a foreign country, it is presumed that the laws of that foreign country are the same as the laws of Texas. *Seguros Tepeyac, S.A., Compania Mexicana v. Bostrom,* 347 F.2d 168, 5th Circuit, 1968. The only evidence offered during the trial of this case as to the marriage laws of Mexico was a deposition by Ramiro Filomeno Rivera Munoz, an attorney from Mexico. Expert testimony such as this, standing alone, is not sufficient to prove such foreign laws.

In the present case, plaintiff admitted the prior marriage and the lack of divorce to dissolve it. It then became her responsibility to prove that she had the legal capacity to marry Benjamin T. Franklin with no legal impediment prohibiting the marriage contract, as well as the subsequent perfection of the common law marriage. Since it must be presumed that the laws of Texas with regard to the validity of a religious marriage are the same in Mexico, her failure to prove a dissolution of that marriage (to Chavez) stood as an impediment to a valid common law marriage in Texas. *Seguros Tepeyac S. A., Compania Mexicana v. Bostrom,* 347 F.2d 168, 5th Circuit, 1968. Plaintiff's points of error one through seventeen are overruled....

Judgment of the trial court is affirmed.

2. FAILURE TO PLEAD FOREIGN LAW

RUDOLF B. SCHLESINGER, A RECURRENT PROBLEM IN TRANSNATIONAL LITIGATION: THE EFFECT OF FAILURE TO INVOKE OR PROVE THE APPLICABLE FOREIGN LAW, 59 Cornell Law Review 1, 2-3 (1973)

A litigant's failure to give notice and to provide information as to the applicable foreign law may be due to many diverse reasons. Perhaps his lawyer is incompetent, and hence does not realize that a case involving foreign elements cannot be handled like an ordinary domestic case. Or maybe the lawyer has recognized that there is a possible foreign law problem, but has wrongly assumed that the court either would apply the forum's own domestic law, or would place the burden of invoking and proving the foreign law on his opponent. In other cases, the lawyer failing to plead and prove the foreign law may be a tricky type. Perhaps he has looked at the foreign law and has found it less favorable to his client than the internal law of the forum. Thus, regardless of the rules on choice of law and burden of proof, he speculates that he might be able to trick his less sophisticated opponent into handling the case as a domestic one until it becomes too late for either party to invoke the foreign law. Sometimes the lawyers on both sides — each analyzing the forum's internal law, the choice of law rule and the burden of proof in a different manner — try to outsmart each other in this way. In still other cases, an attorney, without being either incompetent or tricky, may soundly conclude that to prove the foreign law, or to submit materials relating to it, is simply too expensive for his client. The assumption that a single and simple rule will do justice to all of these motley situations surely is one of the causes of the existing confusion.

NOTES AND QUESTIONS

1. In *Philp v. Macri,* suppose that the alleged slander had occurred in California, but plaintiff did not plead or prove the applicable California law. What would be the result in the case?

2. Why did the federal court in *Philp* state that it must apply the Washington choice of law rules?

3. Suppose the plaintiff in *Philp v. Macri* had alleged in his complaint that "defendant's statements constituted the civil wrong of defamation and entitled plaintiff to damages under Peru Civil Code" (citing article numbers of the applicable provisions of that code). Would the complaint have stated a cause of action? Or would it have been necessary to quote the applicable provisions in the complaint? In Spanish or in English translation? Whose translation?

4. The court in *Philp* considered two options when a party fails to adequately plead a required foreign law for his cause of action or defense. One approach is to dismiss the cause or defense; the other is to adopt a presumption that the foreign law is equivalent to the forum or local law. Which approach did the court of appeals select and why?

Which approach did the Texas court in *Franklin v. Smalldridge* use regarding Mexican law?

After reviewing the above excerpt by Rudolf Schlesinger, which option — dismissal or presumption of equivalence — seems preferable? Does your choice better promote substantive or procedural justice, efficiency, respect for foreign law, or some other policy? Note that the plaintiff lost in both *Philp* and *Franklin.*

5. The excerpt by Albert Ehrenzweig provides insight into some of the problems associated with the common law fact approach to pleading and proving foreign law. Professor Schlesinger, in the article that follows this note, further considers this theme and analyzes the development of judicial notice statutes.

3. THEORIES IN DEALING WITH FOREIGN LAW PROBLEMS AND JUDICIAL NOTICE STATUTES

RUDOLF B. SCHLESINGER, A RECURRENT PROBLEM IN TRANSNATIONAL LITIGATION: THE EFFECT OF FAILURE TO INVOKE OR PROVE THE APPLICABLE FOREIGN LAW, 59 Cornell Law Review 1, 3-5, 16-20 (1973)

A. *Antithetical Theories*

In every legal system it has long been the habit of courts and scholars to pose the problem in the form of the question whether foreign law should be treated as fact or law. This is most unfortunate, because either of these theoretical characterizations, if consistently applied, leads to absurd results. The ultimate absurdity reached under the "fact" theory is that issues of foreign law have to be determined by the jury. It is no less faulty, however, indiscriminately to equate foreign law with domestic "law." Since the ascertainment and interpretation of foreign law require skills which the court simply does not possess, the procedural treatment of a foreign law question cannot be quite the same as that of a question of domestic law. The soundest approach would be to give up all attempts to characterize foreign law as either "fact" or "law" and to start writing a new theory on a clean slate. But in the United States, at least, this seems almost impossible. American common-law doctrines, and in large part the pertinent statutes,[9] are so clearly based on the

[9] One should not overestimate the significance of statutory provisions such as the last sentence of Federal Rule of Civil Procedure 44.1, which provides that the court's determination of the foreign law (if such determination is made) "shall be treated as a ruling on a question of law." This does not mean that a question of foreign law shall for all purposes be treated as a question of law. The effect of this provision is merely to make it clear that an issue of foreign law is to be determined by the court, and not by the jury, and that for purposes of appellate review the trial

fact theory that in dealing with existing law we cannot afford completely to dismiss that unsound theory from our minds.

The difficulties flowing from the use of the fact-law dichotomy are intertwined with, and compounded by, the well-known and tedious battle between two contending conflict of laws theories. The vested rights theory, as preached by Holmes and Beale, had, until recently, a strong impact on the case law in this area. According to the apostles of that theory, it is axiomatic that a foreign cause of action is an *obligatio* created by the command of a particular foreign sovereign. The cause of action does not exist apart from the foreign law which creates and defines it. If one accepts this premise, and combines it with the "fact" theory, it follows with logical necessity that a plaintiff who alleges a cause of action governed by foreign law, but fails to allege and prove the relevant command of the foreign sovereign, has failed to show one of the material "facts" of his case and thus must lose. The same fate befalls a defendant who fails to allege and prove the foreign law on which an affirmative defense is based.

The local-law theory, on the other hand, postulates that the internal law of the forum governs all aspects of a case unless a sufficient justification is shown for displacing it; and according to at least some of the modern anti-Bealeans, such as Professor Ehrenzweig and the late Professor Currie, the law of the forum is never effectively displaced unless the applicable foreign law has been invoked in proper and timely fashion. Thus, if the parties fail to invoke the pertinent foreign law, the court will look to its own domestic law as the rule of decision.

Among the scholars, the antithetical nature of these two theories has engendered a continuing controversy conducted with the earnestness and reckless abandon of a Holy War....

B. *Judicial Notice Statutes*

[About three-fourths] of the states, including all of those in which transnational litigation occurs with some frequency, have enacted statutes or rules either providing for "judicial notice" of foreign-country law or in other ways authorizing the court, in determining foreign law, to consider any relevant material or source, regardless of admissibility under technical rules of evidence, and regardless also of whether or not such material was submitted by a party. These judicial notice statutes, it should be emphasized at the outset, have not displaced the common-law doctrines discussed above. The statutes

court's determination shall be treated as a ruling on a question of law. Plainly, it was not the intention of the draftsmen of Rule 44.1 to equate foreign law and domestic law in all respects. If that had been the intention, the responsibility for ascertaining the foreign law would have been thrown wholly upon the court, and the court would have been instructed to ascertain the foreign law regardless of the assistance or lack of assistance offered by the parties. The most cursory glance at the second sentence of Rule 44.1 shows that such was not the intent of the draftsmen. That sentence leaves it to the discretion of the court whether judicial notice should be taken of the foreign law. It is a well-known fact that in the exercise of that discretion the courts tend not to conduct independent research concerning alien law when they have received no aid from counsel. Thus, it is crystal clear that foreign law is not treated like domestic law, which under all circumstances, and regardless of party presentation, must always be ascertained and determined by the court.

are merely superimposed on the common-law doctrines, which thus retain their vitality in the many situations in which the statutory provisions do not lead to actual notice being taken of the foreign law.

1. *Interaction of Judicial Notice Statutes and Decisional Law*

Even in a jurisdiction which has a judicial notice statute, the statute is not a solvent for every foreign law case. Most of the statutes are permissive only, so that the court's determination, whether or not to take judicial notice of the foreign law, is a discretionary one. In exercising this discretion, courts naturally are disinclined to engage in independent research concerning a strange legal system if they receive no help from counsel. Even when the statute is drafted in mandatory terms, the result is not very different.

Some of the more sophisticated statutes provide that in general it is discretionary with the court whether to take judicial notice of foreign-country law, but that judicial notice becomes mandatory if one of the parties has given timely notice of his intention to rely on the foreign law and has supplied the court with sufficient information concerning such law. The idea of such bifurcation between permissive and mandatory judicial notice, which first emerged in the Uniform Rules of Evidence, has been adopted, *inter alia,* in California and New York. It is clear, however, that such a bifurcated rule is in essence permissive, because it is left to the court to determine whether the information submitted to it is "sufficient." It follows that, no matter how the statute is formulated, cases of a discretionary refusal to take judicial notice of the foreign law will arise with some frequency.

A few of the statutes, moreover, use pleading or notice requirements as a restriction on judicial notice. In California, and arguably in New York, the parties' failure to invoke the foreign law merely has the effect of making judicial notice of foreign law permissible rather than mandatory. But in other jurisdictions, and notably under Federal Rule 44.1, the notice requirement may have stronger teeth. In *Ruff v. St. Paul Mercury Insurance Co.,*[89] the Second Circuit held that unless reasonable written notice of the foreign law issue has been given in the district court, the appellate court cannot look at the foreign law. The result reached in the *Ruff* case was a harsh one, as the court admitted;[90] but the judges of the Second Circuit probably felt that to hold otherwise would render the notice requirement toothless.[91] *Quaere,* how-

[89] 393 F.2d 500, 502 (2d Cir. 1968).

[90] Ruff, a Pennsylvania citizen, was teaching law at the Arthur Grimes School of Law of the University of Liberia when he contracted poliomyelitis, an endemic disease. Ruff sued upon an insurance policy issued to his employer. The district court dismissed the action on the ground that endemic diseases were expressly exempted from the coverage of the policy. On appeal, Ruff for the first time brought up the point that under Liberian law the exemption was ineffective. The court of appeals, however, held the point to be precluded by the first sentence of Rule 44.1. In reluctantly affirming the dismissal of the action, the appellate court stated: "While the result is not one which we like to reach, we cannot rewrite the policy because of our sympathy for Ruff." 393 F.2d at 502.

[91] Alternatively, the court held that even if it were to take judicial notice of the Liberian law, plaintiff would still lose in this action against the insurance company, because Liberian law, although it might enlarge the liability of the employer, could not change the effect of an insurance policy issued by an American insurance company to an American insured (*i.e.,* Ruff's employer). *See* 393 F.2d at 502.

ever, whether the provision really would lose all of its teeth if it were construed differently, *e.g.,* as meaning that nonobservance of the notice requirement should make the court *reluctant* to take judicial notice, but would not completely destroy its *power* to do so.

Whether or not it was correctly decided, the *Ruff* case serves as a reminder that even in jurisdictions where a judicial notice statute is in existence, situations frequently arise in which the court either lacks the power to take judicial notice, or as a matter of discretion will refuse to do so. In every case of this sort, the judicial notice statute in effect becomes inoperative; and just as in the old common-law days, the court is then faced with the question of how it should react to the parties' failure to invoke or prove the foreign law. Most of the statutes are silent on this point. To find an answer, the court must turn to decisional rules — the same rules which would govern in the absence of a judicial notice statute. It follows that these decisional rules continue to play an important role even in those jurisdictions which have adopted a modern statute.

In California and New Jersey, the judicial notice statute itself contains an express direction, telling the court what to do in case the foreign law is neither proved nor judicially noticed. The New Jersey statute, as recently amended, favors application of domestic law in such a case, while the much more sophisticated California provision, by vesting the court with a great deal of discretion, arrives at a result similar to that which has been reached by the most recent judicial decisions. Although essentially declaratory of decisional law, the California statute has two original and valuable features. It warns the court of the constitutional doubts which may be created by imposing domestic law on a legal relationship which lacks any reasonable contact with the forum; and it provides that when an action is dismissed because of the plaintiff's failure to prove the pertinent foreign law, the dismissal should be without prejudice....

2. *Judicial Notice of Uninvoked Foreign Law*

In those cases in which the court actually utilizes its statutory power to take judicial notice of foreign law, the problem of the consequences of the parties' failure to invoke and prove that law becomes moot. True, when the foreign law in question belongs to an alien system, and the parties have given the court no aid in ascertaining it, the court normally will decline to ascertain the foreign law by its own independent efforts; but unless the point is precluded on grounds of lateness, this is completely a matter of discretion. Most of the statutes make it quite clear that the parties' failure to invoke the foreign law does not prevent the court from judicially noticing it, and that the court, even though totally unaided by the parties, has the *power* to undertake its own research.

The combined effect of the court's two alternative holdings seems to be that the plaintiff might have won his case if (1) he had sued his employer rather than the insurance company, and if (2) he had given timely notice of his intention to raise an issue concerning Liberian law.

FEDERAL RULES OF CIVIL PROCEDURE

RULE 44.1
Determination of Foreign Law

A party who intends to raise an issue concerning the law of a foreign country shall give notice by pleadings or other reasonable written notice. The court, in determining foreign law, may consider any relevant material or source, including testimony, whether or not submitted by a party or admissible under the Federal Rules of Evidence. The court's determination shall be treated as a ruling on a question of law.

ADVISORY COMMITTEE'S NOTE

RULE 44.1

39 F.R.D. 69, 117-19 (1966)

Rule 44.1 is added by amendment to furnish Federal courts with a uniform and effective procedure for raising and determining an issue concerning the law of a foreign country.

To avoid unfair surprise, the *first sentence* of the new rule requires that a party who intends to raise an issue of foreign law shall give notice thereof. The uncertainty under Rule 8(a) about whether foreign law must be pleaded [citations omitted] is eliminated by the provision that the notice shall be "written" and "reasonable." It may, but need not be, incorporated in the pleadings. In some situations the pertinence of foreign law is apparent from the outset; accordingly the necessary investigation of that law will have been accomplished by the party at the pleading stage, and the notice can be given conveniently in the pleadings. In other situations the pertinence of foreign law may remain doubtful until the case is further developed. A requirement that notice of foreign law be given only through the medium of the pleadings would tend in the latter instances to force the party to engage in a peculiarly burdensome type of investigation which might turn out to be unnecessary; and correspondingly the adversary would be forced into a possible wasteful investigation. The liberal provisions for amendment of the pleadings afford help if the pleadings are used as the medium of giving notice of the foreign law; but it seems best to permit a written notice to be given outside of and later than the pleadings, provided the notice is reasonable.

The new rule does not attempt to set any definite limit on the party's time for giving the notice of an issue of foreign law; in some cases the issue may not become apparent until the trial and notice then given may still be reasonable. The stage which the case has reached at the time of the notice, the reason proffered by the party for his failure to give earlier notice, and the importance to the case as a whole of the issue of foreign law sought to be raised, are among the factors which the court should consider in deciding a question of the reasonableness of a notice. If notice is given by one party it need not be repeated by any other and serves as a basis for presentation of material on the foreign law by all parties.

The *second sentence* of the new rule describes the materials to which the court may resort in determining an issue of foreign law.... In all events the ordinary rules of evidence are often inapposite to the problem of determining foreign law and have in the past prevented examination of material which could have provided a proper basis for the determination. The new rule permits consideration by the court of any relevant material, including testimony, without regard to its admissibility....

In further recognition of the peculiar nature of the issue of foreign law, the new rule provides that in determining this law the court is not limited by material presented by the parties; it may engage in its own research and consider any relevant material thus found. The court may have at its disposal better foreign law materials than counsel have presented, or may wish to reexamine and amplify material that has been presented by counsel in partisan fashion or in insufficient detail. On the other hand, the court is free to insist on a complete presentation by counsel.

There is no requirement that the court give formal notice to the parties of its intention to engage in its own research on an issue of foreign law which has been raised by them, or of its intention to raise and determine independently an issue not raised by them. Ordinarily the court should inform the parties of material it has found diverging substantially from the material which they have presented; and in general the court should give the parties an opportunity to analyze and counter new points upon which it proposes to rely. [Citations omitted.] To require, however, that the court give formal notice from time to time as it proceeds with its study of the foreign law would add an element of undesirable rigidity to the procedure for determining issues of foreign law.

The new rule refrains from imposing an obligation on the court to take "judicial notice" of foreign law because this would put an extreme burden on the court in many cases; and it avoids use of the concept of "judicial notice" in any form because of the uncertain meaning of that concept as applied to foreign law. [Citation omitted.] Rather the rule provides flexible procedures for presenting and utilizing material on issues of foreign law by which a sound result can be achieved with fairness to the parties.

Under the *third sentence,* the court's determination of an issue of foreign law is to be treated as a ruling on a question of "law," not "fact," so that appellate review will not be narrowly confined by the "clearly erroneous" standard of Rule 52(a). [Citations omitted.]

The new rule parallels Article IV of the Uniform Interstate and International Procedure Act, approved by the Commissioners on Uniform State Laws in 1962, except that section 4.03 of Article IV states that "[t]he court, not the jury" shall determine foreign law. The new rule does not address itself to this problem, since the Rules refrain from allocating functions as between the court and the jury. See Rule 38(a). It has long been thought, however, that the jury is not the appropriate body to determine issues of foreign law. See, e.g., Story, Conflict of Laws, § 638 (1st ed. 1834, 8th ed. 1883); 1 Greenleaf, Evidence, § 486 (1st ed. 1842, 16th ed. 1899); 4 Wigmore, Evidence § 2558 (1st ed. 1905); 9 *id.* § 2558 (3d ed. 1940). The majority of the States have committed such issues to determination by the court. See Article 5 of the Uniform Judicial Notice of Foreign Law Act, adopted by twenty-six states, 9A U.L.A. 318 (1957) (Suppl. 1961, at 134); N.Y. Civ. Prac. Law & Rules, R. 4511 (effective

Sept. 1, 1963); Wigmore, *loc. cit.* And Federal courts that have considered the problem in recent years have reached the same conclusion without reliance on statute.

CALIFORNIA EVIDENCE CODE §§ 310, 311, 452-455, 459, 460

§ 310. Questions of law for court.

(b) Determination of the law of an organization of nations or of the law of a foreign nation or a public entity in a foreign nation is a question of law to be determined in the manner provided in Division 4 (commencing with Section 450).

§ 311. Procedure when foreign or sister-state law cannot be determined. If the law of an organization of nations, a foreign nation or a state other than this state, or a public entity in a foreign nation or a state other than this state, is applicable and such law cannot be determined, the court may, as the ends of justice require, either:

(a) Apply the law of this state if the court can do so consistently with the Constitution of the United States and the Constitution of this state; or

(b) Dismiss the action without prejudice or, in the case of a reviewing court, remand the case to the trial court with directions to dismiss the action without prejudice.

§ 452. Matters which may be judicially noticed. Judicial notice may be taken of the following matters to the extent that they are not embraced within Section 451[a]: ....

(f) The law of an organization of nations and of foreign nations and public entities in foreign nations.

§ 453. Compulsory judicial notice upon request. The trial court shall take judicial notice of any matter specified in Section 452 if a party requests it and:

(a) Gives each adverse party sufficient notice of the request, through the pleadings or otherwise, to enable such adverse party to prepare to meet the request; and

(b) Furnishes the court with sufficient information to enable it to take judicial notice of the matter.

§ 454. Information that may be used in taking judicial notice.

(a) In determining the propriety of taking judicial notice of a matter, or the tenor thereof:

(1) Any source of pertinent information, including the advice of persons learned in the subject matter, may be consulted or used, whether or not furnished by a party.

(2) Exclusionary rules of evidence do not apply except for Section 352 and the rules of privilege.

(b) Where the subject of judicial notice is the law of an organization of nations, a foreign nation, or a public entity in a foreign nation and the court

---

[a] Section 451 refers to matters which *must* be judicially noticed.

resorts to the advice of persons learned in the subject matter, such advice, if not received in open court, shall be in writing.

§ 455. Opportunity to present information to court. With respect to any matter specified in Section 452 or in subdivision (f) of Section 451 that is of substantial consequence to the determination of the action:

(a) If the trial court has been requested to take or has taken or proposes to take judicial notice of such matter, the court shall afford each party reasonable opportunity, before the jury is instructed or before the cause is submitted for decision by the court, to present to the court information relevant to (1) the propriety of taking judicial notice of the matter and (2) the tenor of the matter to be noticed.

(b) If the trial court resorts to any source of information not received in open court, including the advice of persons learned in the subject matter, such information and its source shall be made a part of the record in the action and the court shall afford each party reasonable opportunity to meet such information before judicial notice of the matter may be taken.

§ 459. Judicial notice by reviewing court.

(a) The reviewing court shall take judicial notice of (1) each matter properly noticed by the trial court and (2) each matter that the trial court was required to notice under Section 451 or 453. The reviewing court may take judicial notice of any matter specified in Section 452. The reviewing court may take judicial notice of a matter in a tenor different from that noticed by the trial court.

(b) In determining the propriety of taking judicial notice of a matter, or the tenor thereof, the reviewing court has the same power as the trial court under Section 454.

(c) When taking judicial notice under this section of a matter specified in Section 452 or in subdivision (f) of Section 451 that is of substantial consequence to the determination of the action, the reviewing court shall comply with the provisions of subdivision (a) of Section 455 if the matter was not theretofore judicially noticed in the action.

(d) In determining the propriety of taking judicial notice of a matter specified in Section 452 or in subdivision (f) of Section 451 that is of substantial consequence to the determination of the action, or the tenor thereof, if the reviewing court resorts to any source of information not received in open court or not included in the record of the action, including the advice of persons learned in the subject matter, the reviewing court shall afford each party reasonable opportunity to meet such information before judicial notice of the matter may be taken.

§ 460. Appointment of expert by court. Where the advice of persons learned in the subject matter is required in order to enable the court to take judicial notice of a matter, the court on its own motion or on motion of any party may appoint one or more such persons to provide such advice. If the court determines to appoint such a person, he shall be appointed and compensated in the manner provided in Article 2 (commencing with Section 730) of Chapter 3 of Division 6.

NEW YORK CIVIL PRACTICE LAW AND RULES RULES 3016, 4511

Rule 3016. Particularity in specific actions

(e) **Law of foreign country.** Where a cause of action or defense is based upon the law of a foreign country or its political subdivision, the substance of the foreign law relied upon shall be stated.

Rule 4511. Judicial notice of law

(b) **When judicial notice may be taken without request; when it shall be taken on request.** Every court may take judicial notice without request of private acts and resolutions of the [C]ongress of the United States and of the legislature of the state; ordinances and regulations of officers, agencies or governmental subdivisions of the state or of the United States; and the laws of foreign countries or their political subdivisions. Judicial notice shall be taken of matters specified in this subdivision if a party requests it, furnishes the court sufficient information to enable it to comply with the request, and has given each adverse party notice of his intention to request it. Notice shall be given in the pleadings or prior to the presentation of any evidence at the trial, but a court may require or permit other notice.

(c) **Determination by court; review as matter of law.** Whether a matter is judicially noticed or proof is taken, every matter specified in this section shall be determined by the judge or referee, and included in his findings or charged to the jury. Such findings or charge shall be subject to review on appeal as a finding or charge on a matter of law.

(d) **Evidence to be received on matter to be judicially noticed.** In considering whether a matter of law should be judicially noticed and in determining the matter of law to be judicially noticed, the court may consider any testimony, document, information or argument on the subject, whether offered by a party or discovered through its own research. Whether or not judicial notice is taken, a printed copy of a statute or other written law or a proclamation, edict, decree or ordinance by an executive contained in a book or publication, purporting to have been published by a government or commonly admitted as evidence of the existing law in the judicial tribunals of the jurisdiction where it is in force, is prima facie evidence of such law and the unwritten or common law of a jurisdiction may be proved by witnesses or printed reports of cases of the courts of the jurisdiction.

OKLAHOMA STATUTES §§ 2201, 2203

Title 12 (Civil Procedure) Chapter 40 (Evidence Code)

§ 2201. Judicial Notice of Law

B. Judicial notice may be taken by the court of:....

2. The laws of foreign countries.

C. The determination by judicial notice of the applicability and the tenor of any matter of common law, constitutional law or of any statute, private act, resolution, ordinance or regulation shall be a matter for the judge and not for the jury.

§ 2203. Determining Propriety of Taking Judicial Notice

A. In determining the propriety of taking judicial notice of a matter:

1. The court may consult and use any source of pertinent information, whether or not furnished by a party; and

2. No exclusionary rule except a valid claim of privilege shall apply.

B. A party is entitled upon timely request to an opportunity to be heard as to the propriety of taking judicial notice and the scope of the matter noticed. In the absence of prior notification, the request may be made after judicial notice has been taken.

C. Judicial notice may be taken at any stage of the proceeding.

NOTES AND QUESTIONS

1. The federal courts and most states have now adopted some form of a judicial notice provision to facilitate the determination of foreign law. Rule 44.1 was added to the Federal Rules of Civil Procedure in 1966, while a similar Rule 26.1 was inserted into the Federal Rules of Criminal Procedure at the same time. Today 22 states and the District of Columbia have a provision modeled on Rule 44.1.

California and New York enacted more elaborate statutes, which provide that a party can compel a judge to notice foreign law if she gives adverse parties sufficient notice of her request and furnishes the court with sufficient information to take judicial notice. The issue of sufficiency remains in the discretion of the judge, but these "mandatory" statutes have more bite than the "permissive" Rule 44.1. Nine states — including Florida, Michigan, and New Jersey — have one of these bifurcated permissive-mandatory judicial notice statutes.

Six states have enacted simpler judicial notice statutes, such as the example from Oklahoma, that leave open important questions concerning the treatment of foreign law.

Finally, 12 states — including Illinois — remain in the common law fact camp. Most of these states have provided, however, that a foreign law issue is for the court and not for the jury to determine, and some allow proof of the foreign law issue without use of expert witnesses. Nevertheless, the basic fact approach in these states remains intact. Consider, e.g., *In re Marriage of Osborn,* 564 N.E.2d 1325, 1327 (Ill. App. 1990):

> While we respect the parties' request to consider Canadian law, we are compelled to remind the parties that it has long been the rule that courts will not take judicial notice of the laws of another country, but they must be alleged and proved as facts.... When a party interested in claiming the benefit of a foreign law or statute fails to show by appropriate pleading and proof the status of the law of the place where the contract was made

> or was to be performed, the courts of the state where the suit is brought will apply the law of the latter state to the contract. [Citation omitted.] Under the circumstances, we apply the law of Illinois, without consideration of Canadian law, to determine the issues in this case.

Iowa, another fact-pleading state, illustrates how extreme the presumption of equivalence between foreign law and local law can become. The Iowa Supreme Court, in a child custody case, declared: "Neither party pleaded any statute from another jurisdiction as required.... Neither party attempted to prove Vietnamese law was applicable to any issue raised in this case. Therefore it must be presumed foreign law both statutory and common law is the same as ours." *Doan Thi Hoang Anh v. Nelson,* 245 N.W.2d 511, 516 (Iowa 1976).

A list of the various state rules is found in John G. Sprankling & George R. Lanyi, *Pleading and Proof of Foreign Law in American Courts,* 19 Stan. J. Int'l L. 3, 96-97 (1983).

2. *Philp v. Macri, supra,* was decided in federal court before Rule 44.1 was adopted. Would this rule have made a difference in the outcome of the case? Consider the relevance of *Ruff v. St. Paul Mercury Insurance Co.,* discussed in Professor Schlesinger's excerpt, *supra.*

Should the court in *Philp* have presumed that Peruvian law is the same as that of Washington if the plaintiff could show that Spain made claim to the area now the state of Washington during the height of its empire in America?

3. Texas, in 1984, enacted a judicial notice statute (Rules of Evidence, Rule 203) modeled on Federal Rule 44.1. Would this new rule likely have made a difference in the result of *Franklin v. Smalldridge, supra*?

4. Review the Note on the Common Law Fact Approach, *supra,* which lists six consequences that follow from treating foreign law as a fact. What would be the analogous six consequences from using Federal Rule 44.1? What further differences might there be from using the California, New York, or Oklahoma provisions?

For the interplay between Rules 3016 and 4511(b) in New York, see, e.g., *Dresdner Bank AG v. Edelmann,* 493 N.Y.S.2d 703 (Sup. Ct. 1985).

5. May a federal court under Rule 44.1 apply foreign law even if the required notice by a party is not given? If so, under what circumstances? Most federal courts have found that they are not *required* to apply foreign law if it has not been raised by either party. *E.g., Commercial Ins. Co. of Newark v. Pacific-Peru Constr. Corp.,* 558 F.2d 948, 952 (9th Cir. 1977). In *Commercial Insurance Co.* the court refused to apply Peruvian law and assumed that the parties acquiesced in the application of the local law of the forum, citing the Restatement 2d of Conflicts § 136, comment h (1971). *Id.*

4. THE SUMMARY JUDGMENT HEARING

WALPEX TRADING CO. v. YACIMIENTOS PETROLIFEROS FISCALES BOLIVIANOS

United States District Court, S.D. New York
756 F. Supp. 136 (1991)

LEISURE, DISTRICT JUDGE.

In a previous opinion in this matter, this Court noted that "[t]his extraordinary case has, over the course of several years, consumed more legal, financial and judicial resources in the litigation of essentially threshold issues than scores of cases that have been filed, resolved and forgotten in this Court during the same time period." *Walpex Trading Co. v. Yacimientos Petroliferos Fiscales Bolivianos,* 712 F. Supp. 383, 385 (S.D.N.Y. 1989). The most recent developments constitute an additional chapter in the saga.

This is a breach of contract action brought by Walpex Trading Company ("Walpex"), an American export company, against Yacimientos Petroliferos Fiscales Bolivianos ("YPFB"), an instrumentality of the Bolivian government....

Defendant now moves for summary judgment and dismissal of the case pursuant to Fed. R. Civ. P. 56....

BACKGROUND

Plaintiff is a New York corporation engaged in international commerce. Defendant is a Bolivian government-owned corporation that purchases supplies for the Bolivian government's national oil program. In or around February 1982, defendant publicly invited bids for the supply of piping to be used by the Bolivian oil well industry. The invitation appeared in Spanish in various Bolivian newspapers. As translated into English, it provided as follows:

INVITATION

PUBLIC BID NO. 120-81

SUPPLY OF: PRODUCTION PIPING

Interested firms hereby are invited to present bids of the supply of:

PRODUCTION PIPING

> The List of Specifications may be obtained from the Technical Consulting office of the Materials Department, located at the YPFB building, 4th Floor, 185 Bueno Street.
>
> Bids with the formal requirements set forth in the List of Specifications will be received in the Technical Consulting office until 5:00 p.m., March 2, 1982. [Citation omitted.]

The Specifications referred to in the invitation provided in pertinent part:

> Paragraph 1.0.
>
> The bidding is ruled by the Regulations for Acquisitions and Contracts of

> YPFB, approved by Decree Law 16857 of July 20, 1979 and by related norms in force in the Country....
>
> Paragraph 2.3.3.
>
> The presentation of a bid implies the bidder's submission to the legal system cited in paragraph 1.0 and to all laws in force in the country, as well as to all requirements in this list of Specifications. [Citation omitted.]

Article 120 of the Regulations referred to in ¶ 1.0 of the Specifications provides:

> With respect to contracts with foreign organizations, an express clause shall be included to the effect that all issues emerging from the contract shall be subject to Bolivian law and submitted to the jurisdiction of the courts in Bolivia.

Affidavit of Sergio Palacios De Vizzio, sworn to on December 19, 1989 ("Palacios de Vizzio Aff.") ¶ 18.

The Alleged Formation and Breach of Contract

Walpex received YPFB's invitation for bids and the requisite Specifications through its Bolivian sales agent, Compania de Representaciones Internacionales, S.R.L. ("COREIN"). [Citation omitted.] In March 1982, Walpex submitted its bid for the supply contract through COREIN, and on April 7, 1982, YPFB advised COREIN, in writing, that Walpex had been awarded the contract and that COREIN should come to YPFB's offices in La Paz to sign the formal documents. [Citation omitted.] No formal written contract was ever signed.

During the next fifteen months, YPFB requested numerous extensions on the deadline for payment of the full purchase price of the tubing. [Citation omitted.] Finally, on July 28, 1983, YPFB formally repudiated the contract, stating that it was unable to obtain financing for the project from the World Bank. [Citation omitted.]

Walpex argues that the submission and acceptance of its bid formed a valid contract for the sale of 88,500 feet of three and one half inch seamless steel tubing and accessories. In addition, plaintiff alleges that it took steps in reliance on the contract, including Walpex's entry into a supply contract with Vinson International Supply Company, a Texas pipe manufacturer, and several preparatory actions in Bolivia, such as obtaining a Bolivian corporate charter and designating COREIN as its authorized agent with power of attorney. Walpex also asserts that to satisfy YPFB's requirement of a performance bond, it established an irrevocable letter of credit with Chase Manhattan Bank payable to YPFB. [Citation omitted.] This letter of credit was extended a number of times, and was eventually cancelled after YPFB's repudiation.

Plaintiff alleges that during the fifteen months YPFB was seeking extensions of the performance bond and of its time to pay, YPFB had already decided not to perform under the alleged contract. Plaintiff further alleges that YPFB had made this decision even though it could have obtained the necessary financing from sources other than the World Bank. As a result of its reliance on the contract, induced by YPFB's apparent intent to perform, plaintiff argues that it was "prohibited ... from mitigating its damages by selling the goods in the falling market," and that by the time YPFB formally repudiated the contract, the market for tubing had collapsed completely. [Citation omitted.]

Defendant's Arguments

Defendant denies the existence of an enforceable contract in the absence of a formal written agreement, but argues that even if a contract is deemed to exist, plaintiff's action must still be dismissed. Defendant asserts that the Invitation made ¶¶ 1.0 and 2.3.3 of the Specifications formal elements of any valid bid. [Citation omitted.] Similarly, defendant contends, ¶ 1.0 incorporated Article 120 of the Regulations into plaintiff's bid. Therefore, defendant argues, if a contract exists, it must contain these three clauses, which it contends mandate choice of Bolivian law and make Bolivia the exclusive forum for any disputes arising out of such a contract. In the alternative, defendant argues, even if the Court finds no mandatory choice of forum clause, plaintiff's action must be dismissed under Bolivian law, which, it claims, invalidates any contract between defendant and a foreign party that does not contain such a clause.

DISCUSSION

A. *Standard for Summary Judgment*

Rule 56(c) provides that summary judgment "shall be rendered forthwith if the pleadings, depositions, answers to interrogatories, and admissions on file, together with the affidavits, if any, show that there is no genuine issue as to any material fact and that the moving party is entitled to judgment as a matter of law." "'Summary judgment is appropriate when, after drawing all reasonable inferences in favor of the party against whom summary judgment is sought, no reasonable trier of fact could find in favor of the non-moving party.'" ...

B. *Choice of Law*

Choice of law clauses are routinely enforced by the courts of this Circuit, "if there is a reasonable basis for the choice." *Morgan Guaranty Trust Co. v. Republic of Palau,* 693 F. Supp. 1479, 1494 (S.D.N.Y. 1988) (citing Restatement (Second) of Conflict of Laws § 187 (1971)). New York courts also defer to choice of law clauses if the state whose law is thus selected has sufficient contacts with the transaction.... These cases, however, have involved explicit provisions, clearly incorporated into written contracts signed by the parties. No such document exists in this case. However, the Court need not decide the existence and validity of a choice of law clause, because the Court finds that this action should be governed by Bolivian law even in the absence of such a clause....

When a contract does not contain a valid choice-of-law provision, New York courts choose the controlling law by evaluating the contacts and interests of the competing fora in the transaction in question. In contract cases, New York courts use a "center of gravity" or "grouping of contacts" analysis....

Under this approach, the Court concludes that Bolivian law governs the substantive issues in this action. Bolivia's contacts with the transaction are numerous. The defendant is a Bolivian resident and an instrumentality of the Bolivian government. YPFB's solicitation of bids was published only in Spanish, in Bolivia. Both Walpex's submission of its bid through its agent, COREIN, and YPFB's acceptance of the bid took place in Bolivia. Thus, even under plaintiff's theory, all of the events underlying the formation of the alleged contract took place in Bolivia. [Citation omitted.] In addition, plaintiff alleges performance of several preparatory acts in Bolivia, such as obtaining a Bolivian corporate charter and designating COREIN as its authorized representative with power of attorney.

In contrast, New York state has only two significant contacts with the transaction: (1) plaintiff is a New York resident, and (2) Walpex's international letter of credit was obtained from a New York bank....

Although Walpex's memorandum of law asserts its conclusions as to the proper resolution of this dispute under New York law, it fails to make any argument as to the outcome of the case under Bolivian law....

Walpex also argues that "[d]efendant's belated, unilateral attempt to impose" Bolivian law "is improper, unjust, unreasonable, and unfair under the facts and circumstances at bar." [Citation omitted.] Plaintiff was fully informed before it contracted with YPFB that YPFB intended Bolivian law to govern the contract. The Invitation explicitly stated that bids had to conform to the Specifications, which in turn clearly stated on the first page: "The presentation of a bid implies the bidder's submission to the legal system cited in paragraph 1.0 and to all laws in force in the country, as well as to all requirements in this list of Specifications." Specifications ¶ 2.3.3....

C. *Choice of Forum*

Having decided that Bolivian law governs the substantive issues in this dispute, the Court must turn to the question of whether Bolivia is the exclusive forum for any action arising out of the alleged contract.

In an earlier opinion, this Court denied defendant's motion to dismiss the action on *forum non conveniens* grounds. *See Walpex, supra,* 712 F. Supp. at 392-94. However, the issue of a mandatory forum selection clause raised in the instant motion was not before the Court on the prior motion, and constitutes a separate consideration from the Court's earlier conclusion that "litigation in this forum is permissible." *Id.* at 393.

The Supreme Court has held that forum selection clauses "should be given full effect" when "a freely negotiated private international agreement [is] unaffected by fraud, undue influence, or overweening bargaining power." *The Bremen v. Zapata Off-Shore Co.,* 407 U.S. 1, 12-13, 92 S. Ct. 1907, 1914-15, 32 L. Ed. 2d 513 (1972)....

In this case, however, just as no written instrument signed by the parties contains a choice of law clause, no such instrument containing a choice of forum provision has been produced. While it may be true that, as defendant argues, regulations would have mandated inclusion of such a clause in any formal contract, this Court cannot pass on the validity of a clause that might have been or should have been included in a nonexistent document. Thus, defendant's motion for summary judgment dismissing this action on the basis of an exclusive forum clause is denied.

D. *Unenforceability*

Defendant's argument that the alleged contract is unenforceable if no valid choice of forum clause exists goes to the merits of this action, which must be decided according to Bolivian law.

Plaintiff has not presented any arguments founded on Bolivian law, either in the form of expert testimony or as citations to cases or statutes, despite notice given as long ago as defendant's previous motion to dismiss that defendant contended that Bolivian law controlled. *See Walpex, supra,* 712 F. Supp. at 393. Provided that reasonable notice is given, a party may rely on the law of a foreign country, and this Court "may consider any relevant material or source, including testimony," in determining foreign law. Fed. R. Civ. P. 44.1. The only material offered to the Court concerning Bolivian law is the affidavit of Sergio Palacios de Vizzio, *supra,* submitted in support of defendant's motion.

Mr. Palacios de Vizzio, an attorney admitted to practice in Bolivia and in New York, and licensed by the Appellate Division of the Supreme Court of New York as a Consultant on Bolivian law, does indeed conclude that contracts between YPFB and foreign suppliers must contain mandatory choice-of-Bolivian-law and -forum clauses, and that they are void and unenforceable without such clauses. *See* Palacios de Vizzio Aff. ¶¶ 18-20.

While the Court might be justified in relying on defendant's expert as to this point, defendant has failed to convince the Court that Bolivian courts would necessarily deny plaintiff any relief in a case in which plaintiff's allegations, if proven, may establish that defendant in bad faith induced plaintiff to rely on its promised award of the contract. Defendant has failed to demonstrate that it is entitled to summary judgment on this issue as a matter of law, and its motion accordingly must be denied as to this point.

CONCLUSION

For the reasons set forth above, defendant's motion for summary judgment dismissing the complaint is denied.

NOTES AND QUESTIONS

1. Under Federal Rule 44.1 does a summary judgment hearing in general appear to be the appropriate stage in a civil proceeding at which to resolve a foreign law issue? What are the reasons for or against such an approach? Judge Leisure, in the first paragraph of his 1991 opinion in *Walpex Trading*

Co., quotes a statement from a 1989 decision (denying dismissal based on *forum non conveniens*) expressing the view that this case had already taken too many years without resolution. Judge Leisure revisited *Walpex* in 1992 for another summary judgment hearing, at which he granted defendant's (and denied plaintiff's) motion on the breach of contract theory, but denied defendant's (as well as plaintiff's) motion on the bad faith and equitable estoppel theory. At this hearing the plaintiff had its own expert witness, who submitted an affidavit to the court on Bolivian law. 789 F. Supp. 1268 (1992).

2. In *Walpex Trading Co.* did the plaintiff have sufficient notice under Rule 44.1 for the court to rely on Bolivian law?

3. What is the basis of Judge Leisure's determination that he cannot grant a summary judgment for the defendant on the unenforceability issue under Bolivian law? See the second sentence of Rule 44.1. The defendant submitted an expert affidavit on this issue, while the plaintiff did not. Did the judge conduct his own investigation of Bolivian law?

4. Consider the following comment about the ABA Model Code of Professional Responsibility DR 7-106(B)(1):

> Under the American Bar Association's Model Code of Professional Responsibility, an attorney has the duty to disclose legal authority in the "controlling jurisdiction" known to him which is "directly adverse to the position of his client and which is not disclosed by opposing counsel." One could argue that the forum is the "controlling jurisdiction," unless foreign law is invoked to displace it. This, however, is an overly technical approach to the issue since the purpose of the requirement is to ensure that the court is fully informed of applicable law so that it can make a fair and accurate determination of the merits. The "controlling jurisdiction" is the jurisdiction which should control under the choice of law rules of the forum. In such a situation, then, a party should raise the possible applicability of foreign law whenever it is reasonably certain that his opponent will not do so.

Sprankling & Lanyi, *Pleading and Proof of Foreign Law in American Courts*, 19 Stan. J. Int'l L. 3, 13 (1983). Do you agree? If not, what should an attorney's responsibility be regarding a foreign law issue?

5. For more on these issues see Annotation, *Raising and Determining Issue of Foreign Law Under Rule 44.1 of Federal Rules of Civil Procedure*, 62 A.L.R. Fed. 521 (1983); Stephen L. Sass, *Foreign Law in Federal Courts*, 29 Am. J. Comp. L. 97 (1981). *See also* Adrien K. Wing, *Pleading and Proof of Foreign Law in American Courts, A Selected Annotated Bibliography*, 19 Stan. J. Int'l L. 175 (1983).

C. DISCOVERY WITHIN CIVIL LAW COUNTRIES

1. EXTRATERRITORIAL DISCOVERY AND CIVIL LAW SENSIBILITIES

GARY B. BORN & SCOTT HOING, COMITY AND THE LOWER COURTS: POST-*AÉROSPATIALE* APPLICATIONS OF THE HAGUE EVIDENCE CONVENTION, 24 International Lawyer 393-96 (1990)

It is commonplace to observe that "[n]o aspect of the extension of the American legal system beyond the territorial frontier of the United States has given rise to so much friction as the request for documents associated with investigation and litigation in the United States."[1] Broad pretrial discovery rights in civil disputes are, of course, ingrained traits of the American legal system. Many foreign states, however, have quite different notions of privacy and the acceptable scope of discovery from those prevailing in the United States and have frequently reacted with considerable displeasure to U.S. efforts to obtain discovery of materials located within their territory....

International litigation in U.S. courts frequently requires access to materials or witnesses located outside the United States. When foreign witnesses are willing to provide evidence voluntarily for use in U.S. proceedings, U.S. litigants have generally encountered few insurmountable difficulties in obtaining extraterritorial discovery. Obtaining discovery from recalcitrant foreign litigants or witnesses has often been much more problematic. For U.S. litigants seeking evidence abroad in these circumstances, two basic routes were available historically: obtaining "direct" discovery under U.S. procedural rules and seeking foreign judicial assistance pursuant to letters rogatory.

United States courts have traditionally favored the use of direct discovery orders under applicable federal or state rules of civil procedure to obtain evidence located abroad. United States courts have long held that foreign litigants and witnesses can be required, pursuant to U.S. discovery rules, to provide discovery of documents and other information, even though these are located outside the United States. Direct extraterritorial discovery under U.S. procedural rules will only be ordered, however, from persons subject to the personal jurisdiction of the U.S. court. Persons subject to a court's personal jurisdiction can be required to produce any discoverable information within their possession or "control," regardless whether it is located inside or outside the United States and regardless whether foreign law forbids its disclosure. Failure to comply with extraterritorial U.S. discovery orders is punishable by sanctions, ranging from default judgments to monetary sanctions to less drastic measures.

In many circumstances, foreign persons refusing to provide information voluntarily will not be subject to the personal jurisdiction of U.S. courts. In such cases U.S. courts are unable to order discovery directly and must seek the assistance of foreign courts in obtaining the sought-after evidence. The

[1] Restatement (Third) of the Foreign Relations Law of the United States § 442, reporters' note 1 (1987).

customary method of obtaining foreign judicial assistance in taking evidence abroad, in the absence of a specific treaty obligation, has been by letter rogatory. Letters rogatory have significant disadvantages, most notably the fact that there is generally no legal obligation for foreign courts to execute them; if compliance occurs it is only because of the good will of the foreign tribunal.[10]

Foreign states have often reacted with hostility to unilateral U.S. efforts to obtain discovery of evidence located on their territory. Many nations have seen these U.S. discovery efforts as violating their "judicial sovereignty," as well as their notions of privacy and the appropriate scope of evidence-taking. Some of these countries have responded to extraterritorial U.S. discovery by filing sharp diplomatic protests with the United States government or, more recently, by enacting so-called "blocking statutes" that nominally forbid compliance with U.S. discovery orders.[12]

Because of widely perceived difficulties with existing mechanisms for transnational discovery, the United States acceded to the Hague Convention on the Taking of Evidence Abroad in Civil or Commercial Matters (the Hague Evidence Convention) in 1972. The Convention is a multilateral agreement that prescribes procedures by which litigants involved in civil and commercial disputes may obtain evidence from abroad. There are now some twenty parties to the Convention, including most major Western trading states.[14]

A primary objective of the Convention was to provide a workable and internationally acceptable mechanism for taking evidence abroad. A particular concern was to ensure that the taking of evidence in a foreign state would be consistent with the laws and sovereignty of that country, while nonetheless providing useful results for foreign litigants and courts. Thus, the Convention's framers were careful to avoid offending notions of judicial sovereignty prevailing in many civil law nations, which required that local judicial authorities supervise all evidence-taking.

---

[10] Moreover, because letters rogatory are executed only in accordance with the foreign country's own judicial procedures and customs, a U.S. litigant frequently may not be able to obtain a verbatim transcript and may not have its own counsel conduct the questioning. The letter rogatory process is also typically slow and unpredictable; it often requires six months for completion, and delays of a year or more are not uncommon.

[12] Blocking statutes prohibit, as a matter of law, compliance with U.S. discovery orders for the production of evidence located within the blocking nation's territory. All foreign blocking statutes carry some sort of penal sanction for violating the statutory provisions forbidding disclosure. Recently enacted foreign blocking statutes fall into three broad categories. First, some prohibit the disclosure of documents or other information pursuant to foreign discovery orders, unless the orders are passed through appropriate foreign governmental channels. Second, other blocking statutes provide particular governmental agencies discretionary authority to forbid compliance with specific discovery orders. Finally, the largest number of blocking statutes either grant administrative discretion to prohibit disclosure of information concerning particular industries or automatically prohibit such disclosure.

[14] These include: Argentina, Barbados, Cyprus, Czechoslovakia, Denmark, Finland, France, the Federal Republic of Germany, Israel, Italy, Luxembourg, Monaco, the Netherlands, Norway, Portugal, Singapore, Spain, Sweden, the United Kingdom, and the United States.

FEDERAL RULES OF CIVIL PROCEDURE

RULE 28

Persons Before Whom Depositions May Be Taken

(b) In Foreign Countries. Depositions may be taken in a foreign country (1) pursuant to any applicable treaty or convention, or (2) pursuant to a letter of request (whether or not captioned a letter rogatory), or (3) on notice before a person authorized to administer oaths in the place where the examination is held, either by the law thereof or by the law of the United States, or (4) before a person commissioned by the court, and a person so commissioned shall have the power by virtue of the commission to administer any necessary oath and take testimony. A commission or a letter of request shall be issued on application and notice and on terms that are just and appropriate. It is not requisite to the issuance of a commission or a letter of request that the taking of the deposition in any other manner is impracticable or inconvenient; and both a commission and a letter of request may be issued in proper cases. A notice or commission may designate the person before whom the deposition is to be taken either by name or descriptive title. A letter of request may be addressed "To the Appropriate Authority in [here name the country]." When a letter of request or any other device is used pursuant to any applicable treaty or convention, it shall be captioned in the form prescribed by that treaty or convention. Evidence obtained in response to a letter of request need not be excluded merely because it is not a verbatim transcript, because the testimony was not taken under oath, or because of any similar departure from the requirements for depositions taken within the United States under these rules.

UNITED STATES CODE

TITLE 28, SECTION 1783

Subpoena of Person in Foreign Country

(a) A court of the United States may order the issuance of a subpoena requiring the appearance as a witness before it, or before a person or body designated by it, of a national or resident of the United States who is in a foreign country, or requiring the production of a specified document or other thing by him, if the court finds that particular testimony or the production of the document or other thing by him is necessary in the interest of justice, and, in other than a criminal action or proceeding, if the court finds, in addition, that it is not possible to obtain his testimony in admissible form without his personal appearance or to obtain the production of the document or other thing in any other manner.

ROBERTS v. HEIM

United States District Court, N.D. California
130 F.R.D. 430 (1990)

THELTON E. HENDERSON, DISTRICT JUDGE.

The recommendations of the Special Master are adopted in their entirety and the parties are ordered to comply with their terms....

GERALD A. COHN, SPECIAL MASTER.

I

Introduction

This Recommendation deals with a motion by certain Defendants to compel Plaintiffs to provide further answers to interrogatories and a counter-motion by Plaintiffs to compel one of the moving Defendants, Werner Heim ("Heim"), a Swiss national and resident to appear for deposition in the United States, to produce documents in the United States, and to respond to a request for admissions. These cross motions are being brought in the context of a massive class action wherein Plaintiffs allege a world-wide conspiracy to defraud investors out of hundreds of millions of dollars. In *Roberts v. Heim,* 123 F.R.D. 614 (1989), the alleged scheme was summarized as follows:

> In brief, the crux of the scheme as alleged by plaintiffs is as follows. Plaintiffs claim that certain individuals, led by defendant, Heim, originated the idea of forming these partnerships to sell the investing public on the concept of EOR technology. These individuals recruited the general partners and then arranged for the partnerships to purchase for exorbitant fees from their corporate alter egos the exclusive license to use this "new" technology. Plaintiffs allege this technology was unproven and basically without value....

After a careful review of the extensive briefing and documentation provided by the parties and further research by the Special Master, who has supervised discovery in this case for over four years, it is the recommendation of the Special Master that both motions should be granted....

II

Plaintiffs' Counter Motion

B. *Prior Proceedings Before This Court*

In February, 1989, Friedman & Shaftan, P.C., a Defendant in this case, moved the Court for an order issuing letters rogatory so that it could take Heim's deposition by written interrogatories in Switzerland pursuant to Rule 28(b) as Heim refused to appear in the United States and give his deposition pursuant to Rule 26(a)....

On March 28, 1989, letters rogatory were issued by this Court to the appropriate Swiss authorities....

C. The Special Master's Recommendations Regarding Plaintiffs' Counter Motion

2. *Heim Would Not Be Compelled to Violate Swiss Law Should This Court Order Him to Appear for His Deposition in the United States or to Produce Documents in the United States or to Respond to Plaintiffs' Request for Admissions*

Heim asserts that he would be compelled to violate Swiss law should this Court enter an order which would compel him to give his deposition in the United States or to produce documents in the United States or to respond to any other discovery in the United States. Heim asserts that Plaintiffs must be limited in their discovery to obtaining letters rogatory which can be utilized only through the assistance of Swiss authorities.

As noted above, Swiss authorities did honor this Court's request pursuant to letters rogatory and a Swiss District Judge, on June 2, 1989, before a court reporter, read written interrogatories to Heim who then responded orally.

As the crux of Heim's argument against requiring him to respond to discovery in the United States is that any such order by this Court would compel Heim to violate Swiss law and would subject him to potential criminal prosecution in Switzerland, we must look to pertinent Swiss law to see if this claim is correct. In support of his contention Heim cites Article 273 of the Swiss Penal Code, which provides in pertinent part:

> Whoever makes available a manufacturing or business secret to a foreign governmental agency or a foreign organization or private enterprise or to an agent of any of them, shall be subject to imprisonment and in grave cases to imprisonment in a penitentiary. The imprisonment may be combined with a fine.

Heim also cites further Swiss authority which holds that the term "business secret" as used in Article 273 has been defined to include "all facts of business life to the extent that there are interests worthy of protection in keeping them confidential." *Swiss Federal* [*Attorney General v. A*], 98 BGE IV 209 (September 7, 1972).

First, Heim has made no attempt whatsoever to show that he is in possession of "business secrets" as that term is defined by the Swiss Federal Attorney. In disputes such as this one, the Ninth Circuit has made clear, "The party relying on foreign law has the burden of showing that such law bars production." *United States v. Vetco, Inc.*, 691 F.2d 1281, 1289 (9th Cir. 1981), *In re Grand Jury Proceedings*, 873 F.2d 238, 239 (9th Cir. 1989).

Second, Article 273 of the Swiss Penal Code cited above was carefully analyzed by the Ninth Circuit in *Vetco, supra,* at pages 1286-1289. In that case appellants contended that compliance with summonses issued by the Internal Revenue Service for the production of certain books and records located in Switzerland would result in a violation of Article 273. Appellants, like Heim, also cited the above-quoted statement from the Swiss Federal Attorney. In response, the *Vetco* Court citing further Swiss authority[6] held:

> The Swiss Attorney General has distinguished between cases where there is a public interest in keeping information secret, and cases where only private interests are involved. In the latter type of case, Article 273 prohibits disclosure only if the party whose business secret is being divulged does not consent.... Thus, Switzerland's only interest is in protecting the privacy of its non-consenting domiciliaries. *Vetco*, page 1289.

Heim has made no claim that there is any public interest in keeping information he possesses secret, nor has he attempted to obtain any affidavit or other statement from Swiss authorities which would demonstrate any such public interest in Switzerland with respect to this lawsuit and its possible effect on Heim, the corporations, or other Swiss interests.

As the introductory portion of this Recommendation makes clear, Heim is alleged to be either an owner or control person with respect to the five corporations whose records he holds. Heim has not disputed this contention in response to Plaintiffs' counter-motion. The teaching of the Swiss Attorney General as cited above is that Article 273 does not prohibit a person from divulging his own business affairs but only from divulging the business affairs of others without their consent. Heim has made no showing that he is protecting any interest but his own. No person or entity has filed any affidavit or other statement with this Court claiming that the discovery requested by Plaintiffs would harm or infringe on his or its interest in any manner. Additionally, any interest Heim has in maintaining confidentiality is protected by a protective order previously entered in this case for the benefit of all the litigants.

If any doubt remained as to the correctness of the above interpretation of Article 273 and the ability of Heim to participate in discovery in the United States pursuant to the Federal Rules of Civil Procedure without fear of an Article 273 sanction, it was totally dispelled at the time of Heim's deposition in Switzerland on June 2, 1989, pursuant to letters rogatory. That proceeding was held in the District Court Meilen, Canton Zurich, and was presided over by Judge Egger of that Court.

In making his introductory statement for the record, Judge Egger, who, we may presume, is familiar with Article 273, stated the proceedings were being conducted pursuant to Swiss law, in Switzerland, and therefore would be conducted in German. Then, addressing Heim, Judge Egger stated:

> had you wished to do so, you could have testified in the United States, that would have been one possibility ....

The Special Master has read the entire transcript of the June 2, 1989, proceeding in Switzerland and found nothing which would condition or modify Judge Egger's statement quoted above. At no time did Judge Egger either

---

[6] Gerber, Einige Probleme Des Wirtschaftlichen Nachrichtendienstes, Zeitschrift Für Schweiz 257 (1977). There appears to be a typographical error in this citation which should read: "Zeitschrift für Schweizerisches Recht," which in English means "Journal of Swiss Law."

state or imply that Heim would be subject to Swiss penal sanctions if he were to give his deposition in the United States.[7]

In short, contrary to Heim's assertion, if this Court were to order Heim to come to the United States and give his deposition or to produce in the United States documents he now holds in Switzerland or to respond to a request for admissions, he would not be subject to penal sanctions in Switzerland....

IV

Other Reasons Exist for Granting Plaintiffs' Cross Motion

B. *The Fact That This Case Is a Class Action Imposes Special Obligations on the Court and the Parties*

As previously noted, this case is a very large class action in which Plaintiffs are claiming damages in the hundreds of millions of dollars. In addition to other duties in this case, the Special Master has been ordered by the Court to oversee settlement negotiations among the parties. These negotiations have commenced and the Special Master has had discussions with all the major parties and/or their counsel. In the course of these discussions it became apparent that after four years of very extensive discovery there are still significant gaps in the information presently available.

In particular, one item warrants special mention. The Special Master has been informed that of the cash which was raised from Plaintiffs in the course of this venture, approximately one hundred million dollars ($100,000,000.00) cannot be traced as it "went off shore" to various foreign tax havens which cater to clients who demand bank secrecy.

Even in these days of "soft dollars," one hundred million dollars is not an insignificant sum. Both Plaintiffs and this Court are obligated to ensure to the unnamed Plaintiffs that any settlement of this case is fair, adequate, and reasonable....

VII

Conclusion

In view of the foregoing, it is the recommendation of the Special Master that:

1. Heim be ordered to produce in San Francisco, at a location to be agreed upon by the parties, all the books and records of the five corporations named above so that they may be inspected and copied by all parties to this lawsuit. The cost of such production shall be borne by Heim and/or the corporations.

2. The production described in paragraph 1 above shall take place within thirty (30) days of the date of the Court's order....

4. Heim shall, at his own expense, make himself available in San Francisco for the purpose of having his deposition taken. Heim shall remain in San Francisco until all parties have completed their questioning. The Special Master may attend this deposition in order to expedite it and make immediate

[7] "The Court, in determining foreign law, may consider any relevant material or source, including testimony, whether or not submitted by a party or admissible under the Federal Rules of Evidence." Rule 44.1.

rulings with respect to any questions which may arise in the course of the deposition.

2. DISCOVERY IN JAPAN FOR USE IN THE UNITED STATES

YOSHIO OHARA, JUDICIAL ASSISTANCE TO BE AFFORDED BY JAPAN FOR PROCEEDINGS IN THE UNITED STATES, 23 International Lawyer 10-11, 18-22, 25-27 (1989)

As early as 1905 Japan enacted the Act relating to the Reciprocal Judicial Assistance to Be Given at the Request of Foreign Courts (Reciprocal Judicial Assistance Act). This Act shows that Japanese courts are willing, at the request of foreign courts, to assist in serving documents or taking evidence in connection with cases in civil or criminal matters provided that the request for assistance meets the following criteria:

(i) The request must come through the diplomatic channel.

(ii) If a letter rogatory and documents annexed thereto are not written in the Japanese language, translation thereof into Japanese must be appended to the original.

(iii) The requesting State must guarantee the payment of the expenses incurred in the execution of the letter rogatory.

(iv) The requesting State must assure reciprocal judicial assistance if requested by the Japanese courts.

(v) The letter rogatory must be executed in accordance with the law of Japan.

[Between Japan and the United States] there is no common multilateral Convention as to evidentiary cooperation ratified by both countries. However, both countries have concluded [in 1964] the bilateral Consular Convention, which provides for assistance in gathering evidence. Thus, there are two methods of evidentiary assistance between these countries, namely (1) direct taking of evidence in Japan by the U.S. consular officer stationed there, and (2) a request for taking evidence from the U.S. courts to Japanese courts through diplomatic channels on the basis of bilateral arrangements.

A. *Direct Taking of Evidence in Japan by the U.S. Consul Stationed There*

On the basis of article 17(1)(e)(ii) and (iii) of the bilateral Consular Convention, the U.S. consular officer stationed in Japan may within his consular district take depositions on behalf of the courts or other judicial tribunals or authorities of the United States, voluntarily given, and administer oaths to any person in Japan in accordance with the law of the United States and in a manner not inconsistent with the law of Japan.... The U.S. consul takes depositions within the Consulate General according to the U.S. evidence rules. American attorneys can participate in it. It is said that taking depositions by the U.S. consuls is so frequently employed that applicants are obliged to wait for a few months....

B. *Request for Taking Evidence from the U.S. Courts to Japanese Courts Through Diplomatic Channels*

The U.S. courts may request Japanese courts, through diplomatic channels, to provide assistance for the taking of evidence on the basis of bilateral arrangements for evidentiary assistance.... In addition to the five requirements under the Reciprocal Judicial Assistance Act, the request for taking evidence must be made in writing, stating (a) the names of the parties to the litigation, (b) the manner in which the evidence is to be taken, (c) the name, nationality, and domicile or residence of the person to be examined, and (d) the matters to be investigated ... and statement of the essential facts of the case (the Act, sec. 1-2). The letter of request is forwarded from Japan's Ministry of Foreign Affairs to the Supreme Court and finally to a district court of Japan that has jurisdiction over the evidence to be taken. The district court takes evidence in accordance with the Japanese Code of Civil Procedure (Code).

Under the Japanese Code, modeled after the German Code, taking of evidence is carried out exclusively at the trial stage, unlike American pretrial discovery.[25] Japanese evidentiary rules briefly are as follows: Examination of evidence may be made even in the case of nonappearance of a party on the appointed date. As a rule, the court may examine any person as a witness. In cases where the court is to examine a public servant as a witness regarding official secrets, it must obtain approval from the competent supervising government agency. A writ of summons must state (1) the designation of the parties, (2) the gist of the information to be examined, and (3) the legal sanction to be imposed in the case of nonappearance. A witness who fails to appear without justifiable reason is subject to a nonpenal fine and imprisonment. The court may order that such witness be taken into custody and produced before the court. A witness may refuse to testify in cases where the required testimony relates to matters that may expose himself, his family, or his employer [to criminal prosecution, or may reveal trade or] professional secrets. The presiding judge must have a witness sworn in prior to examination.... Documentary evidence is offered by presentation of the document or by application for a production order addressed to the person who has possession of the said document. The court may, in cases where a party refuses to comply with an order to produce a document, deem the allegation of the other party relating to such document to be true. The court must, in cases where a third person refuses to comply with an order to produce documents, impose upon such person, by ruling, a nonpenal fine. The court may, if it is unable to reach a conclusion upon a question of fact by examination of evidence, examine the parties themselves. The party to be examined is required to take an oath. Should the presiding judge deem it necessary to do so, the parties may be ordered to confront each other, or any witness, in court. In cases where a party does not respond to a summons, refuses to take an oath, or refuses to make a statement without justifiable reason, the court may deem the allegations of the other party to be true. When a party who has taken an oath is found to have made a false statement, the court must issue a ruling that such party is

[25] *See* Harada, *Civil Discovery Under the Japanese Law*, in 16 Law in Japan: An Annual 21 (1983).

subject to a nonpenal fine. In the event that an examination of a party has been conducted, the statement of the party and fact of administration or non-administration of an oath must be entered in the record. Before the Japanese courts, only Japanese attorneys can represent parties (Code, art. 79).

As above stated, a Japanese court has strong power to take evidence *compulsorily,* although a U.S. consular officer can take a deposition only in a *voluntary* manner and obtain copies of documents of a public registry only. Therefore, the consular method is used in cases where the witness voluntarily cooperates in the taking of evidence; otherwise, the compulsory method by courts is employed.

[Between 1980 and 1987 U.S. courts made only ten requests involving 24 people for evidentiary assistance.] It implies that much informal discovery must be carried out in Japan for proceedings in the United States. Such unauthorized discovery is deemed to be illegal, however, and a Japanese court would not recognize or enforce the judgment of the U.S. court based on such discovery because the judgment would be contrary to Japan's procedural public order (Code, art. 200(3)). Of course, it would be contrary to estoppel for a Japanese witness, who cooperated positively in such unauthorized discovery, later to claim the contradiction with procedural public order.

An American lawyer who wishes to conduct discovery formally in Japan must apply to the Japanese Embassy or Consulate General in the United States for a special visa. The Japanese Embassy or Consulate General in the United States will not issue such a special visa to American attorneys who in the past have conducted unauthorized discovery in Japan. The nonissuance of a special visa is the sanction to unauthorized discovery by American lawyers in Japan....

The Reciprocal Judicial Assistance Act of Japan provides assistance to requests from a foreign court only; therefore, the U.S. quasi-judicial tribunals such as the FTC or SEC are not entitled to obtain judicial assistance from Japanese courts directly....

C. *Oral Testimony*

Japanese courts take a rather liberal view as to the degree of admissibility of evidence sought so as to admit hearsay evidence under cross-examination of a witness. Concerning the order of examination, as a rule, a witness is first examined by the party who requested the examination of such witness, and then by the opposing party after such examination has been concluded. The presiding judge may examine the witness after the examination by both parties has been concluded. The presiding judge may, however, if he deems it necessary, examine the witness or permit any of the parties to examine the witness at any time. The presiding judge may exclude testimony in such cases where it relates to matters that have no relevance to the issues (Code, art. 294)....

D. *Privilege*

A witness may refuse to testify in cases in which the required testimony relates to matters that may expose himself, his family, or employer to criminal prosecution or punishment. He may also refuse to testify in cases where (1) he is questioned as to the knowledge of facts that he, being or having been, a doctor, dentist, pharmacist, mid-wife, attorney, patent attorney, notary, or an occupant of a post connected with religion, has obtained in the exercise of professional duties and which facts should remain secret, and (2) he is questioned with respect to matters relating to technical or professional secrets (Code, arts. 280, 281). In the case of *United States v. Matsumura*[40] the U.S. Customs Court requested the Osaka District Court to examine a witness, Mr. Matsumura, Managing Director of Matsushita Electronics Co., about the direct labor cost and sales expenses of electron tubes manufactured by it in connection with the case of *Mitsui & Co., Ltd. v. United States* pending before the court. The Osaka High Court supported the judgment of the District Court, holding that only trade secrets worthy of protection are entitled to the privilege of refusing to testify. The court limited such trade secrets to those disclosures which would incur serious disadvantage to a company. The items to be examined in this case fell under the definition of such trade secrets.

NOTES AND QUESTIONS

1. Under what circumstances might a foreign plaintiff or defendant not want to be deposed within the United States or to produce documents or things for inspection in the United States? Rule 26(c) of the Federal Rules of Civil Procedure permits a party to petition the court for a protective order precluding or limiting discovery when "justice requires [it] to protect a party or person from ... undue burden or expense." On the other hand, if a foreign party fails to appear at his deposition, to serve answers or objections to interrogatories, or to respond to a request for inspection of documents, an opposing party may move to have the court order sanctions under Rule 37, including dismissal or judgment by default. Further recalcitrance by the party may lead to contempt of court.

If the court grants a protective order or if a party needs information or testimony from a nonparty foreign citizen (natural or corporate) who is not a resident of the United States, Rule 28(b) may be useful. In addition, an American citizen or resident is subject to the worldwide subpoena power of the United States and may be required to appear as a witness before a U.S. court or for a deposition and to produce documents or other things. 28 U.S.C. § 1783.

2. In *Roberts v. Heim* a co-defendant requested a letter rogatory under Rule 28(b)(2) for what seemed to be a deposition upon written questions against the defendant Werner Heim in Switzerland. The letter was issued by the federal district court and executed nine weeks later by a Swiss judge.

Whether to request a letter rogatory usually implicates comparative law issues in the area of foreign procedural law and especially foreign discovery practice. For instance, are U.S. officials permitted to administer a deposition in the foreign country? If so, a party may prefer to use a U.S. consular official to administer a deposition under Rule 28(b)(3). *See* 22 U.S.C. §§ 4215, 4221. The State Department's Office of Citizens' Consular Services provides information about each country's relevant laws. Since most countries do not permit

[40] Judgment of Osaka High Court on July 12, 1973. 737 Hanrei Jihō 49.

this notice procedure for their own citizens, or will not permit it for compulsory evidence-taking, an alternative method is a deposition by commission under Rule 28(b)(4). This method is accepted in some nations because the American court appoints the person before whom testimony will be taken and only grants a commission "on terms that are just and appropriate." Some common law countries make compulsory process available to the commission upon petition to the foreign court. Most civil law nations, however, consider evidence-gathering a governmental function and reject commissions as an affront to their sovereignty.

One is then left with the option of a letter rogatory. Because letters rogatory employ the courts of a requested country, their use does not offend that country's judicial sovereignty. These courts often can compel a witness to appear. On the other side, foreign courts normally follow their own procedure. Thus, relevant foreign law questions include: How does a requested court respond to a letter rogatory and how fast can it be executed? Is a blocking statute or a testimonial or document privilege applicable? Is oral examination permitted or is examination limited to written questions? Does a counsel have the right to confront or cross-examine the witness?

3. *Roberts v. Heim* illustrates how a discovery question may involve a foreign law issue. Defendant Heim argued against an order compelling him to respond to discovery in the United States on the ground that he would be forced to violate Swiss criminal law. Did the special master have sufficient materials concerning Article 273 of the Swiss Penal Code to adequately interpret the meaning of "business secret?" Was Heim's attorney too lax in not fully utilizing Federal Rule 44.1? The Swiss case that the court discussed, *Swiss Federal Attorney General v. A*, in fact cites six other cases using the same "definition" of business secret. How persuasive is the secondary authority relied on from footnote 6, or the quotation from Swiss judge Egger concerning Heim's possible testimony regarding business secrets?

4. Japan has not signed the Hague Evidence Convention, mentioned in the article by Born and Hoing. Which of the other three methods from Rule 28(b) for taking a deposition in foreign countries would be permitted in Japan? According to the article by Yoshio Ohara, additional discovery methods beyond those accepted by Japan from Rule 28(b) would be illegal under Japanese law. What does Ohara mean by "illegal" in the absence of any statute or regulation prohibiting such discovery? How would a U.S. court determine whether an order requiring a defendant to provide documents or to permit inspection of manufacturing facilities or records located in Japan violated Japanese law? What sanctions would be available to the U.S. court if the Japanese party did not comply? What would be the consequence for an American lawyer who engaged in discovery in Japan without having obtained the appropriate visa for entry into Japan?

5. What is the major difference between the Japanese professional secrets privilege and the Swiss business secrets rule? To what extent should a U.S. court respect these foreign rules? *See Société Internationale Pour Participations Industrielles et Commerciales v. Rogers*, 357 U.S. 197 (1958).

3. THE HAGUE EVIDENCE CONVENTION

CONVENTION ON THE TAKING OF EVIDENCE ABROAD IN CIVIL OR COMMERCIAL MATTERS

Done at The Hague March 18, 1970
Entered into Force for the United States October 7, 1972

23 U.S.T. 2555, T.I.A.S. No. 7444, 847 U.N.T.S. 231

The States signatory to the present Convention,

Desiring to facilitate the transmission and execution of Letters of Request and to further the accommodation of the different methods which they use for this purpose,

Desiring to improve mutual judicial co-operation in civil or commercial matters,

Have resolved to conclude a Convention to this effect and have agreed upon the following provisions:

CHAPTER I—LETTERS OF REQUEST

Article 1

In civil or commercial matters a judicial authority of a Contracting State may, in accordance with the provisions of the law of that State, request the competent authority of another Contracting State, by means of a Letter of Request, to obtain evidence, or to perform some other judicial act.

A Letter shall not be used to obtain evidence which is not intended for use in judicial proceedings, commenced or contemplated.

The expression "other judicial act" does not cover the service of judicial documents or the issuance of any process by which judgments or orders are executed or enforced, or orders for provisional or protective measures.

Article 2

A Contracting State shall designate a Central Authority which will undertake to receive Letters of Request coming from a judicial authority of another Contracting State and to transmit them to the authority competent to execute them. Each State shall organize the Central Authority in accordance with its own law.

Letters shall be sent to the Central Authority of the State of execution without being transmitted through any other authority of that State.

Article 3

A Letter of Request shall specify—

a) the authority requesting its execution and the authority requested to execute it, if known to the requesting authority;

b) the names and addresses of the parties to the proceedings and their representatives, if any;

c) the nature of the proceedings for which the evidence is required, giving all necessary information in regard thereto;
d) the evidence to be obtained or other judicial act to be performed.

Where appropriate, the Letter shall specify, inter alia—

e) the names and addresses of the persons to be examined;
f) the questions to be put to the persons to be examined or a statement of the subject-matter about which they are to be examined;
g) the documents or other property, real or personal, to be inspected;
h) any requirement that the evidence is to be given on oath or affirmation, and any special form to be used;
i) any special method or procedure to be followed under Article 9.

A Letter may also mention any information necessary for the application of Article 11.

No legalization or other like formality may be required.

Article 4

A Letter of Request shall be in the language of the authority requested to execute it or be accompanied by a translation into that language.

Nevertheless, a Contracting State shall accept a Letter in either English or French, or a translation into one of these languages, unless it has made the reservation authorized by Article 33....

Article 8

A Contracting State may declare that members of the judicial personnel of the requesting authority of another Contracting State may be present at the execution of a Letter of Request. Prior authorization by the competent authority designated by the declaring State may be required.

Article 9

The judicial authority which executes a Letter of Request shall apply its own law as to the methods and procedures to be followed.

However, it will follow a request of the requesting authority that a special method or procedure be followed, unless this is incompatible with the internal law of the State of execution or is impossible of performance by reason of its internal practice and procedure or by reason of practical difficulties.

A Letter of Request shall be executed expeditiously.

Article 10

In executing a Letter of Request the requested authority shall apply the appropriate measures of compulsion in the instances and to the same extent as are provided by its internal law for the execution of orders issued by the authorities of its own country or of requests made by parties in internal proceedings.

Article 11

In the execution of a Letter of Request the person concerned may refuse to give evidence in so far as he has a privilege or duty to refuse to give the evidence—

a) under the law of the State of execution; or
b) under the law of the State of origin, and the privilege or duty has been specified in the Letter, or, at the instance of the requested authority, has been otherwise confirmed to that authority by the requesting authority.

A Contracting State may declare that, in addition, it will respect privileges and duties existing under the law of States other than the State of origin and the State of execution, to the extent specified in that declaration.

Article 12

The execution of a Letter of Request may be refused only to the extent that—

a) in the State of execution the execution of the Letter does not fall within the functions of the judiciary; or
b) the State addressed considers that its sovereignty or security would be prejudiced thereby.

Execution may not be refused solely on the ground that under its internal law the State of execution claims exclusive jurisdiction over the subject-matter of the action or that its internal law would not admit a right of action on it....

CHAPTER II—TAKING OF EVIDENCE BY DIPLOMATIC OFFICERS, CONSULAR AGENTS AND COMMISSIONERS

Article 15

In civil or commercial matters, a diplomatic officer or consular agent of a Contracting State may, in the territory of another Contracting State and within the area where he exercises his functions, take the evidence without compulsion of nationals of a State which he represents in aid of proceedings commenced in the courts of a State which he represents.

A Contracting State may declare that evidence may be taken by a diplomatic officer or consular agent only if permission to that effect is given upon application made by him or on his behalf to the appropriate authority designated by the declaring State.

Article 16

A diplomatic officer or consular agent of a Contracting State may, in the territory of another Contracting State and within the area where he exercises his functions, also take the evidence, without compulsion, of nationals of the

State in which he exercises his functions or of a third State, in aid of proceedings commenced in the courts of a State which he represents, if—

a) a competent authority designated by the State in which he exercises his functions has given its permission either generally or in the particular case, and

b) he complies with the conditions which the competent authority has specified in the permission.

A Contracting State may declare that evidence may be taken under this Article without its prior permission.

Article 17

In civil or commercial matters, a person duly appointed as a commissioner for the purpose may, without compulsion, take evidence in the territory of a Contracting State in aid of proceedings commenced in the courts of another Contracting State, if—

a) a competent authority designated by the State where the evidence is to be taken has given its permission either generally or in the particular case; and

b) he complies with the conditions which the competent authority has specified in the permission.

A Contracting State may declare that evidence may be taken under this Article without its prior permission.

Article 18

A Contracting State may declare that a diplomatic officer, consular agent or commissioner authorized to take evidence under Articles 15, 16 or 17, may apply to the competent authority designated by the declaring State for appropriate assistance to obtain the evidence by compulsion. The declaration may contain such conditions as the declaring State may see fit to impose.

If the authority grants the application it shall apply any measures of compulsion which are appropriate and are prescribed by its law for use in internal proceedings....

CHAPTER III—GENERAL CLAUSES

Article 23

A Contracting State may at the time of signature, ratification or accession, declare that it will not execute Letters of Request issued for the purpose of obtaining pre-trial discovery of documents as known in Common Law countries....

Article 27

The provisions of the present Convention shall not prevent a Contracting State from—

a) declaring that Letters of Request may be transmitted to its judicial authorities through channels other than those provided for in Article 2;
b) permitting, by internal law or practice, any act provided for in this Convention to be performed upon less restrictive conditions;
c) permitting, by internal law or practice, methods of taking evidence other than those provided for in this Convention....

Article 33

A State may, at the time of signature, ratification or accession exclude, in whole or in part, the application of the provisions of paragraph 2 of Article 4 and of Chapter II. No other reservation shall be permitted.

Each Contracting State may at any time withdraw a reservation it has made; the reservation shall cease to have effect on the sixtieth day after notification of the withdrawal.

When a State has made a reservation, any other State affected thereby may apply the same rule against the reserving State....

Article 36

Any difficulties which may arise between Contracting States in connection with the operation of this Convention shall be settled through diplomatic channels.

4. THE HAGUE CONVENTION IN GERMANY

SIEMENS AKTIENGESELLSCHAFT v. BAVARIA

Munich Court of Appeals (9th Civil Chamber)
Decision of 27 November 1980
27 RiW 554, 20 I.L.M. 1025 (1981)

Translated for I.L.M. by Bruno A. Ristau

DECISION

The petition of 7 July 1980 of the corporate Petitioners Siemens AG and Siecor GmbH as well as of the individual Petitioners Bernd Zeitler, Gerhard Blaimer, Werner Schubert, Dr. Wulf-Dieter Seiffert, Dr. Hans Behnke and Heinz Hirthe, who are named as witnesses, concerning the decision of the Bavarian Ministry of Justice of 2 June 1980 is dismissed for lack of merit....

REASONS

A

In a suit pending since 1976 before the U.S. District Court for the Western District of Virginia, the American company Corning Glass Works, plaintiff, prosecutes against the American company International Telephone & Telegraph Corporation (ITT), defendant, claims for damages and injunctive relief because of defendant's alleged infringement of U.S. patents held by plaintiff for optical waveguide fibers; ITT has counterclaimed for damages alleging that Corning has misused its patents by entering into restrictive agreements with dominant telecommunications companies in the United States and throughout the world, including the Federal Republic of Germany.

On motion of ITT, the American court issued a Letter of Request on 17 December 1979 addressed to the Bavarian Ministry of Justice, based on the Hague Convention on the Taking of Evidence Abroad in Civil or Commercial Matters of March 18, 1970 (BGBl, 1977 II S. 1472); [the American court] requested that the individual Petitioners be examined by a court as witnesses and that the corporate Petitioners be ordered to produce numerous documents, identified in Schedule A to the Letter of Request, to the attorneys for the parties to the proceeding for inspection and copying. The complete text of the Letter of Request is contained in a certified translation prepared by a sworn translator for the English language, which translation is attached hereto as Enclosure 1 and forms part of this decision.

With an official reply of 2 June 1980 [citation omitted] the Bavarian Ministry of Justice complied with the request for the examination of witnesses. The request for production of documents was denied on the ground that that part of the request would involve a "discovery of documents" which, in accordance with Article 23 of the Convention the Federal Government declared it would not execute and which could not be executed pursuant to § 14(1) of the Implementing Law of 22 December 1977 (BGBl S. 3105), since to date no implementing regulations have been issued under the authority of § 14(2) of the Implementing Law which would permit execution of such requests under certain conditions.

The petition of ITT of 1 July 1980 challenged the denial to order the production of documents; following this Court's review of the lawfulness of the administrative ruling pursuant to § 23 EGGVG,[a] the petition was dismissed as being unfounded with a Decision issued by this Panel on 31 October 1980. [Citation omitted.]

With a brief dated 7 July 1980, received by the Court the same day, the Petitioners here seek court review of the lawfulness of the approval of the request for an examination of witnesses (which approval was announced on June 6, 1980) and the revocation of this approval on the ground that it constituted an unlawful administrative act which violated the civil rights of the individual Petitioners and the protected business interest of the corporate Petitioners in the enterprises established and carried on by them. The Petitioners contend that the requested examination of witnesses should not have been approved, since such approval would improperly force the individual Petitioners to testify as witnesses before a German judge in aid of a foreign proceeding and the corporate Petitioners could suffer considerable harm in their competitive standing against ITT world-wide. The Letter of Request of the American court was inadmissible because it disregarded numerous formal and substantive requirements mandated by the Convention; moreover, it was

[a] Introductory Law to the Court Organization Act.

contrary to the German public policy ("*ordre public*") because it was inconsistent with fundamental principles of the German law of civil procedure: its purpose was to conduct a fishing expedition which is not sanctioned by German law....

B

I

The petition is admissible for all Petitioners....

II

The petition, however, is not meritorious.

The order requiring the examination of the individual Petitioners issued by the Bavarian Ministry of Justice in its capacity as the competent "Central Authority" pursuant to Articles 2 and 35(1) of the Convention, § 7 of the [German] Implementing Law and Section B 1 of the announcement of 21 June 1979 (BGBl II S. 780) was properly entered, so that the Petitioners' rights were not violated by an unlawful act of judicial administration (§ 28(1) EGGVG)....

2) Contrary to the claim asserted here, there were no formal defects in the American Letter of Request and, therefore, there were no impediments to the approval of the request to the extent that it sought an examination of witnesses. In this connection, the following details are relevant:

a) It is true that the American Letter of Request was — contrary to the stipulation in Article 2, paragraph 2 of the Convention — not transmitted directly to the Bavarian Ministry of Justice as central authority by the requesting American court; according to the uncontroverted statement of the Petitioners, it was submitted by a representative of ITT. But, contrary to Petitioners' contention, this channel of transmission does not constitute a formal defect which would be fatal to an approval of the request by the Ministry of Justice. To begin with, paragraph 2 of Article 2 of the Convention merely excludes the participation of any other authorities of the State of execution; it does not prohibit the transmission of the request [to the Central Authority] through a messenger. Secondly, it is of no moment to the present case — contrary to the argument by the Petitioners — that § 6, para. 2 of the [German] Implementing Law to Article 10 of the Hague Convention on the Service Abroad of Judicial and Extrajudicial Documents in Civil or Commercial Matters of November 15, 1965 (BGBl 1977 II S. 1453), to which the Federal Republic of Germany and the USA are parties, prohibits the "private service" of court documents. For the transmission of the American Letter of Request to the Bavarian Ministry of Justice does not constitute "service" of a court document in the sense of the above-mentioned Service Convention....

b) Petitioners claim that, contrary to paragraph 1(e) of Article 3 of the Convention, the addresses of the witnesses to be examined were missing in the Letter of Request; this constitutes a relatively minor formal defect. Petitioners themselves concede the insignificance [of the omission] and this also follows [from the requirement in the Convention] that an address be given "where appropriate." There was, therefore, no reason to reject the request on that basis. Individual Petitioners ... also contend that they are not domiciled within the district of the "Amtsgericht" (County Court) of Munich although they are employed by the corporate Petitioners 1) and 2) in that district. They argue that if they are required to testify in the Amtsgericht Munich (which is the proper judicial authority within the meaning of paragraph 1, Article 9 of the Convention and § 8 of the [German] Implementing Law) they would be unconstitutionally deprived of the judge of their domicile as their legally competent judge (Article 101, para. 1, sentence 2 of the German Constitution; § 16, sentence 2 GVG [Court Organization Act]). The argument is devoid of merit. To begin with, the term "legally competent judge" refers to the judge who is competent to *decide* a legal controversy (Judgment of the Federal Constitutional Court, NJW 1964, 1020). The present case raises only the question which local judge is competent to execute a request for judicial assistance. Secondly, the venue provisions of § 8 of the Implementing Law are consistent with the venue provisions in paragraph 1 of § 157 GVG [Court Organization Act] for judicial assistance as between German courts, and are also in conformity with the venue provisions for proceedings for the perpetuation of evidence pursuant to § 486, para. 2 ZPO [German Code of Civil Procedure], according to which venue is proper at any place where the witness is to be found ....

3) Petitioners concede, and the Court agrees, that the "nature of the proceedings" — as required by paragraph 1(c), Article 3, of the Convention — is sufficiently specified in Item 2 of the Letter of Request, so that no impediment to the execution of the request is present. On the other hand, Petitioners' other formal objections — which are interrelated — are not without substance. Petitioners claim that the "necessary information in regard to the proceedings" [for which the evidence is required], as required by paragraph 1(c), Article 3 is insufficient, and that the "questions to be put to the persons to be examined or a statement of the subject-matter about which they are to be examined" (paragraph 1(f), Article 3 of the Convention) have not been furnished. These formal requirements — which, Petitioners say, have been insufficiently complied with or disregarded — go to the core of the conflict between German and American procedures, especially as regards fishing expeditions which are not permitted in German procedure.

But these formal objections raised by the Petitioners, which may have a considerable procedural impact, are in the final analysis unfounded. It is true that in the language of the statement of facts in Item 2 of the Letter of Request with respect to the counterclaim of ITT, namely, "that, inter alia, the plaintiff misused its patents by entering into restrictive agreements with dominant telecommunications companies in the United States and throughout the world, including the Federal Republic of Germany" — which forms the basis of the counterclaim — falls far short of the detailed statement of facts which is required by German procedural law. The text of the Letter of Request lacks specific references to occurrences, dates, events and material consequences with respect to which the witnesses are to be examined, which ought to be set forth if the questions to be put to the witnesses are not specified in the request (see the disjunctive "or" in Article 3, paragraph 1(f) of the Convention). However, these defects were not substantial enough to cause the Ministry of Justice, in its capacity as central authority pursuant to Article 5 of the Convention, to question the request ....

The guiding principle mandating this result is the desire of the Federal Republic of Germany to place judicial assistance with the United States, which previously was carried out only on the basis of comity, on a solid treaty basis, as was done in the Convention on the Taking of Evidence here in question, and thereby also to take due account of the procedural device of "pre-trial discovery" which is unknown in German procedural law, but not unfamiliar to Germany's treaty partner, and which was described in the Decision of this Panel of 31 October 1980[b] as a fundamental part of an American civil proceeding. This follows clearly from the fact that the declaration under Article 23 of the Convention excludes "pre-trial discovery of documents," and from paragraph 2, Article 9 of the Convention which basically permits execution of a Letter of Request according to the special method or procedure of the requesting State to the limit of incompatibility with the internal law of the State of execution under paragraph 1, Article 9 of the Convention.

This basic starting point virtually demands the interpretation of the Letter of Request, in the context of Item 3a (examination of witnesses) and b (production of documents), Item 4, and Schedule A, to the end that the witnesses named are to be examined with respect to the documents which are identified by date and subject matter as to their origin, content, business purpose and economic impact. Only to this extent does this Panel authorize the examination of the witness.

The scope of the examination of the witnesses thus authorized is not in conflict with important and governing principles of German law, in particular with German "*ordre public*" in the sense of a violation against the public morals or the policy of a German law (Art. 30 EGBGB [Introductory Law to the German Civil Code]). Nor in the opinion of this Panel does such a holding amount to a disregard of the [German] declaration under Article 23 of the Convention. German law permits the examination of third persons as witnesses concerning the contents of documents, which documents themselves need not be surrendered or produced.

Finally, there can be no question that the sovereignty or the security of the Federal Republic of Germany will be endangered (paragraph 1(b), Article 12 of the Convention). According to paragraph 1 of Article 9 of the Convention, and the relevant provisions of the German Code of Civil Procedure, the examination of witnesses will be conducted by a German judge, in the presence of an American judge familiar with the trial, whose participation has been approved by the Ministry in accordance with Article 8 of the Convention. This manner of proceeding sufficiently ensures that due consideration will be given to the testimonial privileges of the witnesses, in accordance with §§ 383(1)(6), 384 ZPO [German Code of Civil Procedure], the right of the parties and their representatives to examine in accordance with § 397 ZPO, and the limits of discovery of evidence, whose perimeters are doubtful even under German procedural law depending on the type of proceedings and the facts of the case

[b] Translated and set forth in 20 Int'l Legal Materials 1049 (1981).

(Peters, *Ausforschungsbeweis im Zivilprozess*, Beitraege zum Zivilrecht und Zivilprozess, 1966, Heft 16, S. 16, 49, 55, 60-63, 90-91, 120-126). In any event, the prohibition against fishing expeditions in German procedural law is designed for the protection of the adversary who is not required to make available to his opposing party the weapons for the conduct of the lawsuit (BGH, NJW 1958, 1491); but it is not designed for the protection of witnesses who are sufficiently protected by the testimonial privileges provided by law (Peters, S. 58 et seq.).

4) The foregoing considerations also refute Petitioners' other objections, namely that Item 5a of the Letter of Request seeks to have the witnesses examined by the attorneys for the parties, which is contrary to German procedural law and the provisions of the Convention; Item 5c seeks permission for the participation of U.S. judge Glenn Conrad. The Ministry of Justice did not comply with these items of the request. In view of this, the Petitioners have not been aggrieved.

5) Finally, the Petitioners contend that the request should not have been approved because it was issued at the "pre-trial discovery" stage of the proceedings and, therefore, the evidence was "not intended for use in judicial proceedings commenced or contemplated," as required by paragraph 2, Article 1 of the Convention. The Decision of this Panel of 31 October 1980 (9 VA 3/80) establishes, and the legal literature there cited teaches, that the "pretrial discovery" stage not only presupposes a pending judicial proceeding before an American court, but that it is an essential part of the securing of evidence to be introduced at the "trial."

III

For the foregoing reasons, the Petitioners' rights were not violated by an unlawful act of judicial administration. Therefore, their petition must be dismissed as being without merit. (§§ 23, 25, 28 EGGVG).

Dr. Schmadl
Presiding Judge

Prof. Dr. Blomeyer
and Dr. Nägelein
Associate Judges

Of the Court of Appeals

DARRELL PRESCOTT & EDWIN R. ALLEY, EFFECTIVE EVIDENCE-TAKING UNDER THE HAGUE CONVENTION, 22 International Lawyer 939, 975-80 (1988)

Letter of Request

The Federal Republic of Germany [has designated a Central Authority to receive letters of request for each of the federal states.] A letter of request must be sent to the Central Authority of the state in which it is to be executed. The letter of request must be in German or accompanied by a German translation, and should be transmitted from the issuing court to the appropriate Central Authority. Transmission directly to the Central Authority by local counsel in Germany has been criticized by West German courts as contrary to

Convention procedures, although the courts have not refused execution on this basis.

The letter of request will initially be reviewed by the Central Authority, which is [usually] the Ministry of Justice for the particular federal state.... The Ministry's review may include informal contacts between the Ministry and counsel for interested parties and may also involve the submission of written briefs and an informal hearing. After approving the letter of request, the Ministry will send it to the local district court (*Amtsgericht*) for execution in conformance with its ruling. At this point, either the requesting party or the witness may appeal the Ministry's ruling to the Court of Appeal (*Oberlandesgericht*).

A letter of request normally will be executed in West Germany using West German procedures, but in practice some depositions have been taken American style pursuant to a request under article 9 of the Convention for the use of a "special procedure." A German judge will preside over the taking of the evidence. West Germany has declared under article 8 of the Convention that "members of the requesting court" may be present at the taking of the deposition when prior authorization has been granted. This is understood to include counsel for the parties, since they are officers of the court. Counsel for the parties will be permitted to participate in the questioning of the witness. Counsel for the parties may also cross-examine, since this form of questioning is not unknown under West German law. The examination must, however, be conducted in German. The West German court can also administer required oaths and cause a verbatim transcript to be prepared....

When testimony is to be taken in West Germany, the existence of privileges under West German law must also be considered. The most unusual of these to an American practitioner and the most likely to come into play is the privilege for "trade secrets." This privilege extends beyond the concept of "trade secret" as it is understood in the U.S. to include a privilege against disclosing business deliberations, strategies, and plans....

Diplomatic Officers or Commissioners

Because West Germany has not made the permitted declaration under article 15 of the Convention, U.S. diplomatic officers may take the testimony of U.S. nationals in West Germany without prior permission or supervision of the West German Government or court officials. West Germany has declared that such permission is required when testimony is to be taken by diplomatic officers from third state nationals. Such permission must be sought from the Central Authority of the state where the evidence is to be taken. Conditions may be imposed on the granting of such permission, but West Germany has given no indication of what those conditions might be. No compulsion may be used when taking evidence by these methods. Evidence taking by commissioners is disfavored and may be done only with the prior permission of the West German Central Authority. Such permission may be subject to conditions, and the local court is entitled to control the preparation and actual taking of the evidence.

West Germany has declared pursuant to article 33 of the Convention that evidence may not be taken by diplomatic officers where West German nationals are involved. A series of letter agreements between the United States and West Germany, however, allow American litigants to utilize this method for taking the testimony of German nationals when certain conditions are met....

The first condition under these agreements is reciprocity, which was formally granted by the United States in an exchange of notes. No compulsion may be used in the taking of the testimony. The request to give information must not be called a "summons," and the questioning must not be called "interrogatories." No pressure or compulsion of any kind may be imposed upon a person giving evidence to make him sign protocols or other records of the testimony provided. The examination of the witness must take place within the offices of the American Consulate unless the witness agrees otherwise or requests that the evidence be taken at his home or office. The witness must also have the right to be represented by counsel if he wishes.

NOTES AND QUESTIONS

1. In 1993 Federal Rule 28(b) was revised to draw the attention of lawyers to the Hague Evidence Convention. The Committee Notes state: "The party taking the deposition is ordinarily obliged to conform to an applicable treaty or convention if an effective deposition can be taken by such internationally approved means, even though a verbatim transcript is not available or testimony cannot be taken under oath."

What are the purposes and scope of the Hague Evidence Convention? Does it overlap the Hague Service Convention, *supra* Section A?

2. How does the central authority help to accomplish the Convention's purposes? Does *Siemens Aktiengesellschaft v. Bavaria* support your view of a central authority's role?

3. What are the advantages and disadvantages in using chapter II of the Convention (diplomatic officers or commissioners) instead of chapter I (letters of request) in Germany?

4. Does the high court in Munich seem receptive or hostile to the use of the Convention in Germany? Give examples.

5. German procedure does not allow "fishing expeditions." What policy does the court in *Siemens* mention to support such a rule? Can you think of any other supporting policies?

6. Germany has elected under article 23 of the Convention not to permit the pretrial production of documents. The court in *Siemens,* however, states that it is permissible to question a witness about the content of a specific document. How important a loophole is this in practical terms? What role does Germany's trade secrets privilege play in this analysis?

7. In *Siemens* the court mentions the *ordre public* principle as it relates to discovery. Consider what might occur if an American judge decides to order extraterritorial discovery under the Federal Rules rather than use the Hague Convention.

> The concept of *ordre public* is relevant to the extraterritorial discovery conflict in two ways. First, it serves as the basic conceptual reference-point for assessing the validity of U.S. discovery orders relating to conduct in Germany. Accordingly, if an American discovery order violates fundamental principles of the German legal order, it cannot validly be applied to conduct within Germany.
>
> Since, however, an American court applying American discovery rules is not asking a German court to apply foreign law within its borders, the only context in which this "violation" of Germany's *ordre public* can be attacked under German law is in relation to the recognition of an American judgment based on such "invalid" discovery.
>
> According to Section 328(4) of the ZPO, a German court may refuse to enforce a foreign judgment if recognition of the judgment would violate *ordre public* principles. Thus, if a United States court orders discovery that is considered to violate German *ordre public* principles, any U.S. judgment based on, or related to, such a discovery order may thereby be rendered unenforceable under German law....
>
> Scholarly opinion, as well as government statements, ... view U.S. discovery orders relating to conduct on German soil as violations of German *ordre public* principles, at least under certain circumstances. According to one commentator:
>
> > The sometimes crass value differences in substantive law [between the United States and Germany] are so significantly exacerbated by the peculiarities of American procedural law, with its private investigatory rights and decision by the jury, that aid in applying American law must in many cases be classified as a violation of *ordre public* principles.

David J. Gerber, *Extraterritorial Discovery and the Conflict of Procedural Systems: Germany and the United States,* 34 Am. J. Comp. L. 745, 774-75 (1986).

8. For further information about discovery in Germany, see Alex Heck, *Federal Republic of Germany and the EEC,* 18 Int'l Law. 793 (1984); Donald R. Shemanski, *Obtaining Evidence in the Federal Republic of Germany: The Impact of the Hague Evidence Convention on German-American Judicial Co-operation,* 17 Int'l Law. 465 (1983).

5. THE HAGUE CONVENTION IN FRANCE

SOCIÉTÉ NATIONALE INDUSTRIELLE AÉROSPATIALE v. UNITED STATES DISTRICT COURT

United States Supreme Court
482 U.S. 522, 107 S. Ct. 2542 (1987)

JUSTICE STEVENS delivered the opinion of the Court.

The United States, the Republic of France, and 15 other Nations have acceded to the Hague Convention on the Taking of Evidence Abroad in Civil or Commercial Matters.... The question presented in this case concerns the extent to which a federal district court must employ the procedures set forth in the Convention when litigants seek answers to interrogatories, the production of documents, and admissions from a French adversary over whom the court has personal jurisdiction.

I

The two petitioners are corporations owned by the Republic of France. They are engaged in the business of designing, manufacturing, and marketing aircraft. One of their planes, the "Rallye," was allegedly advertised in American aviation publications as "the World's safest and most economical STOL plane."[3] On August 19, 1980, a Rallye crashed in Iowa, injuring the pilot and a passenger. Dennis Jones, John George, and Rosa George brought separate suits based upon this accident in the United States District Court for the Southern District of Iowa, alleging that petitioners had manufactured and sold a defective plane and that they were guilty of negligence and breach of warranty. Petitioners answered the complaints, apparently without questioning the jurisdiction of the District Court. With the parties' consent, the cases were consolidated and referred to a Magistrate. [Citation omitted.]

Initial discovery was conducted by both sides pursuant to the Federal Rules of Civil Procedure without objection. When plaintiffs[5] served a second request for the production of documents pursuant to Rule 34, a set of interrogatories pursuant to Rule 33, and requests for admission pursuant to Rule 36, however, petitioners filed a motion for a protective order. [Citation omitted.] The motion alleged that because petitioners are "French corporations, and the discovery sought can only be found in a foreign state, namely France," the Hague Convention dictated the exclusive procedures that must be followed for pretrial discovery. [Citation omitted.] In addition, the motion stated that under French penal law, the petitioners could not respond to discovery requests that did not comply with the Convention. [Citation omitted.][6]

The Magistrate denied the motion insofar as it related to answering interrogatories, producing documents, and making admissions.... The Magistrate made two responses to petitioners' argument that they could not comply with the discovery requests without violating French penal law. Noting that the law was originally "'inspired to impede enforcement of United States antitrust laws,'" and that it did not appear to have been strictly enforced in France, he first questioned whether it would be construed to apply to the

[3]The term "STOL," an acronym for "short takeoff and landing," "refers to a fixed-wing aircraft that either takes off or lands with only a short horizontal run of the aircraft."

[5]Although the District Court is the nominal respondent in this mandamus proceeding, plaintiffs are the real respondent parties in interest.

[6]Article 1A of the French "blocking statute," French Penal Code Law No. 80-538, provides:

> Subject to treaties or international agreements and applicable laws and regulations, it is prohibited for any party to request, seek or disclose, in writing, orally or otherwise, economic, commercial, industrial, financial or technical documents or information leading to the constitution of evidence with a view to foreign judicial or administrative proceedings or in connection therewith....

Article 2 provides:

> The parties mentioned in [Article 1A] shall forthwith inform the competent minister if they receive any request concerning such disclosures.

pretrial discovery requests at issue. [Citation omitted.] Second, he balanced the interests in the "protection of United States citizens from harmful foreign products and compensation for injuries caused by such products" against France's interest in protecting its citizens "from intrusive foreign discovery procedures." The Magistrate concluded that the former interests were stronger, particularly because compliance with the requested discovery will "not have to take place in France" and will not be greatly intrusive or abusive. [Citation omitted.]

Petitioners sought a writ of mandamus from the Court of Appeals for the Eighth Circuit under Federal Rule of Appellate Procedure 21(a). Although immediate appellate review of an interlocutory discovery order is not ordinarily available, [citation omitted], the Court of Appeals considered that the novelty and the importance of the question presented, and the likelihood of its recurrence, made consideration of the merits of the petition appropriate. 782 F.2d 120 (1986). It then held that "when the district court has jurisdiction over a foreign litigant the Hague Convention does not apply to the production of evidence in that litigant's possession, even though the documents and information sought may physically be located within the territory of a foreign signatory to the Convention." *Id.*, at 124. The Court of Appeals disagreed with petitioners' argument that this construction would render the entire Hague Convention "meaningless," noting that it would still serve the purpose of providing an improved procedure for obtaining evidence from nonparties. *Id.*, at 125. The court also rejected petitioners' contention that considerations of international comity required plaintiffs to resort to Hague Convention procedures as an initial matter ("first use"), and correspondingly to invoke the federal discovery rules only if the treaty procedures turned out to be futile. The Court of Appeals believed that the potential overruling of foreign tribunals' denial of discovery would do more to defeat than to promote international comity. *Id.*, at 125-126. Finally, the Court of Appeals concluded that objections based on the French penal statute should be considered in two stages: first, whether the discovery order was proper even though compliance may require petitioners to violate French law; and second, what sanctions, if any, should be imposed if petitioners are unable to comply. The Court of Appeals held that the Magistrate properly answered the first question and that it was premature to address the second. The court therefore denied the petition for mandamus. We granted certiorari. 476 U.S. 1168 (1986).

II

In the District Court and the Court of Appeals, petitioners contended that the Hague Evidence Convention "provides the exclusive and mandatory procedures for obtaining documents and information located within the territory of a foreign signatory." 782 F.2d, at 124.[11] We are satisfied that the Court of

[11] The Republic of France likewise takes the following position in this case:

"THE HAGUE CONVENTION IS THE EXCLUSIVE MEANS OF DISCOVERY IN TRANSNATIONAL LITIGATION AMONG THE CONVENTION'S SIGNATORIES UNLESS THE SOVEREIGN ON WHOSE TERRITORY DISCOVERY IS TO OCCUR CHOOSES OTHERWISE." Brief for Republic of France as *Amicus Curiae* 4.

Appeals correctly rejected this extreme position. We believe it is foreclosed by the plain language of the Convention. Before discussing the text of the Convention, however, we briefly review its history.

The Hague Conference on Private International Law, an association of sovereign states, has been conducting periodic sessions since 1893. [Citation omitted.] The United States participated in those sessions as an observer in 1956 and 1960, and as a member beginning in 1964 pursuant to congressional authorization. In that year Congress amended the Judicial Code to grant foreign litigants, without any requirement of reciprocity, special assistance in obtaining evidence in the United States.[13] In 1965 the Hague Conference adopted a Convention on the Service Abroad of Judicial and Extrajudicial Documents in Civil or Commercial Matters (Service Convention), 20 U.S.T. 361, T.I.A.S. No. 6638, to which the Senate gave its advice and consent in 1967. The favorable response to the Service Convention, coupled with the longstanding interest of American lawyers in improving procedures for obtaining evidence abroad, motivated the United States to take the initiative in proposing that an evidence convention be adopted. [Citation omitted.] The Conference organized a special commission to prepare the draft convention, and the draft was approved without a dissenting vote on October 26, 1968. [Citation omitted.] It was signed on behalf of the United States in 1970 and ratified by a unanimous vote of the Senate in 1972. The Convention's purpose was to establish a system for obtaining evidence located abroad that would be "tolerable" to the state executing the request and would produce evidence "utilizable" in the requesting state....

III

Initially, we note that at least four different interpretations of the relationship between the federal discovery rules and the Hague Convention are possible. Two of these interpretations assume that the Hague Convention by its terms dictates the extent to which it supplants normal discovery rules. First, the Hague Convention might be read as requiring its use to the exclusion of any other discovery procedures whenever evidence located abroad is sought for use in an American court. Second, the Hague Convention might be interpreted to require first, but not exclusive, use of its procedures. Two other interpretations assume that international comity, rather than the obligations created by the treaty, should guide judicial resort to the Hague Convention. Third, then, the Convention might be viewed as establishing a supplemental set of discovery procedures, strictly optional under treaty law, to which concerns of comity nevertheless require first resort by American courts in all

[13] As the Rapporteur for the session of the Hague Conference which produced the Hague Evidence Convention stated: "In 1964 Rule 28(b) of the Federal Rules of Civil Procedure and 28 U.S.C. §§ 1781 and 1782 were amended to offer to foreign countries and litigants, without a requirement of reciprocity, wide judicial assistance on a unilateral basis for the obtaining of evidence in the United States. The amendments named the Department of State as a conduit for the receipt and transmission of letters of request. They authorized the use in the federal courts of evidence taken abroad in civil law countries, even if its form did not comply with the conventional formalities of our normal rules of evidence. No country in the world has a more open and enlightened policy." Amram, *The Proposed Convention on the Taking of Evidence Abroad,* 55 A.B.A.J. 651 (1969).

cases. Fourth, the treaty may be viewed as an undertaking among sovereigns to facilitate discovery to which an American court should resort when it deems that course of action appropriate, after considering the situations of the parties before it as well as the interests of the concerned foreign state....

We reject the first two of the possible interpretations as inconsistent with the language and negotiating history of the Hague Convention. The preamble of the Convention specifies its purpose "to facilitate the transmission and execution of Letters of Request" and to "improve mutual judicial cooperation in civil or commercial matters." [Citation omitted.] The preamble does not speak in mandatory terms which would purport to describe the procedures for all permissible transnational discovery and exclude all other existing practices.[15] The text of the Evidence Convention itself does not modify the law of any contracting state, require any contracting state to use the Convention procedures, either in requesting evidence or in responding to such requests, or compel any contracting state to change its own evidence-gathering procedures.

The Convention contains three chapters. Chapter I, entitled "Letters of Requests," and chapter II, entitled "Taking of Evidence by Diplomatic Officers, Consular Agents and Commissioners," both use permissive rather than mandatory language. Thus, Article 1 provides that a judicial authority in one contracting state "may" forward a letter of request to the competent authority in another contracting state for the purpose of obtaining evidence. Similarly, Articles 15, 16, and 17 provide that diplomatic officers, consular agents, and commissioners "may ... without compulsion," take evidence under certain conditions. The absence of any command that a contracting state must use Convention procedures when they are not needed is conspicuous.

Two of the Articles in chapter III, entitled "General Clauses," buttress our conclusion that the Convention was intended as a permissive supplement, not a pre-emptive replacement, for other means of obtaining evidence located abroad. Article 23 expressly authorizes a contracting state to declare that it will not execute any letter of request in aid of pretrial discovery of documents in a common-law country. Surely, if the Convention had been intended to replace completely the broad discovery powers that the common-law courts in the United States previously exercised over foreign litigants subject to their jurisdiction, it would have been most anomalous for the common-law contracting parties to agree to Article 23, which enables a contracting party to revoke its consent to the treaty's procedures for pretrial discovery.[22] In the absence of explicit textual support, we are unable to accept the hypothesis that the common-law contacting states abjured recourse to all pre-existing discovery procedures at the same time that they accepted the possibility that a contracting party could unilaterally abrogate even the Convention's procedures. Moreover, Article 27 plainly states that the Convention does not prevent a contracting state from using more liberal methods of rendering evidence than

[15] The Hague Conference on Private International Law's omission of mandatory language in the preamble is particularly significant in light of the same body's use of mandatory language in the preamble to the Hague Service Convention.

[22] Thirteen of the seventeen signatory states have made declarations under Article 23 of the Convention that restrict pretrial discovery of documents.

those authorized by the Convention. Thus, the text of the Evidence Convention, as well as the history of its proposal and ratification by the United States, unambiguously supports the conclusion that it was intended to establish optional procedures that would facilitate the taking of evidence abroad. [Citations omitted.]

An interpretation of the Hague Convention as the exclusive means for obtaining evidence located abroad would effectively subject every American court hearing a case involving a national of a contracting state to the internal laws of that state. Interrogatories and document requests are staples of international commercial litigation, no less than of other suits, yet a rule of exclusivity would subordinate the court's supervision of even the most routine of these pretrial proceedings to the actions or, equally, to the inactions of foreign judicial authorities.... We conclude accordingly that the Hague Convention did not deprive the District Court of the jurisdiction it otherwise possessed to order a foreign national party before it to produce evidence physically located within a signatory nation.[26]...

V

Petitioners contend that even if the Hague Convention's procedures are not mandatory, this Court should adopt a rule requiring that American litigants first resort to those procedures before initiating any discovery pursuant to the normal methods of the Federal Rules of Civil Procedure....

Petitioners argue that a rule of first resort is necessary to accord respect to the sovereignty of states in which evidence is located. It is true that the process of obtaining evidence in a civil-law jurisdiction is normally conducted by a judicial officer rather than by private attorneys. Petitioners contend that if performed on French soil, for example, by an unauthorized person, such evidence-gathering might violate the "judicial sovereignty" of the host nation. Because it is only through the Convention that civil-law nations have given their consent to evidence-gathering activities within their borders, petitioners argue, we have a duty to employ those procedures whenever they are available. [Citation omitted.] We find that argument unpersuasive. If such a duty were to be inferred from the adoption of the Convention itself, we believe it would have been described in the text of that document. Moreover, the concept of international comity requires in this context a more particularized analysis of the respective interests of the foreign nation and the requesting nation than petitioners' proposed general rule would generate.[28] We therefore decline to

[26] The opposite conclusion of exclusivity would create three unacceptable asymmetries....

Second, a rule of exclusivity would enable a company which is a citizen of another contracting state to compete with a domestic company on uneven terms, since the foreign company would be subject to less extensive discovery procedures in the event that both companies were sued in an American court. Petitioners made a voluntary decision to market their products in the United States. They are entitled to compete on equal terms with other companies operating in this market. But since the District Court unquestionably has personal jurisdiction over petitioners, they are subject to the same legal constraints, including the burdens associated with American judicial procedures, as their American competitors. A general rule according foreign nationals a preferred position in pretrial proceedings in our courts would conflict with the principle of equal opportunity that governs the market they elected to enter.

[28] The nature of the concerns that guide a comity analysis is suggested by the Restatement of Foreign Relations Law of the United States (Revised) § 437(1)(c) (Tent. Draft No. 7, 1986) (ap-

hold as a blanket matter that comity requires resort to Hague Evidence Convention procedures without prior scrutiny in each case of the particular facts, sovereign interests, and likelihood that resort to those procedures will prove effective.[29]

Some discovery procedures are much more "intrusive" than others. In this case, for example, an interrogatory asking petitioners to identify the pilots who flew flight tests in the Rallye before it was certified for flight by the Federal Aviation Administration, or a request to admit that petitioners authorized certain advertising in a particular magazine, is certainly less intrusive than a request to produce all of the "design specifications, line drawings and engineering plans and all engineering change orders and plans and all drawings concerning the leading edge slats for the Rallye type aircraft manufactured by the Defendants." [Citation omitted.] Even if a court might be persuaded that a particular document request was too burdensome or too "intrusive" to be granted in full, with or without an appropriate protective order, it might well refuse to insist upon the use of Convention procedures before requiring responses to simple interrogatories or requests for admissions. The exact line between reasonableness and unreasonableness in each case must be drawn by the trial court, based on its knowledge of the case and of the claims and interests of the parties and the governments whose statutes and policies they invoke.

American courts, in supervising pretrial proceedings, should exercise special vigilance to protect foreign litigants from the danger that unnecessary, or unduly burdensome, discovery may place them in a disadvantageous position. Judicial supervision of discovery should always seek to minimize its costs and inconvenience and to prevent improper uses of discovery requests. When it is necessary to seek evidence abroad, however, the district court must supervise

---

proved May 14, 1986) (Restatement). While we recognize that § 437 of the Restatement may not represent a consensus of international views on the scope of the district court's power to order foreign discovery in the face of objections by foreign states, these factors are relevant to any comity analysis:

(1) the importance to the ... litigation of the documents or other information requested;
(2) the degree of specificity of the request;
(3) whether the information originated in the United States;
(4) the availability of alternative means of securing the information; and
(5) the extent to which noncompliance with the request would undermine important interests of the United States, or compliance with the request would undermine interests of the state where the information is located.

[The five factors listed above are now found in § 442(1)(c) of the Restatement (Third) Foreign Relations Law of the United States.]

[29] The French "blocking statute," n. 6, *supra*, does not alter our conclusion. It is well settled that such statutes do not deprive an American court of the power to order a party subject to its jurisdiction to produce evidence even though the act of production may violate that statute. [Citation omitted.] Nor can the enactment of such a statute by a foreign nation require American courts to engraft a rule of first resort onto the Hague Convention, or otherwise to provide the nationals of such a country with a preferred status in our courts.... Extraterritorial assertions of jurisdiction are not one-sided. While the District Court's discovery orders arguably have some impact in France, the French blocking statute asserts similar authority over acts to take place in this country. The lesson of comity is that neither the discovery order nor the blocking statute can have the same omnipresent effect that it would have in a world of only one sovereign. The blocking statute thus is relevant to the court's particularized comity analysis only to the extent that its terms and its enforcement identify the nature of the sovereign interests in nondisclosure of specific kinds of material.

pretrial proceedings particularly closely to prevent discovery abuses. For example, the additional cost of transportation of documents or witnesses to or from foreign locations may increase the danger that discovery may be sought for the improper purpose of motivating settlement, rather than finding relevant and probative evidence. Objections to "abusive" discovery that foreign litigants advance should therefore receive the most careful consideration. In addition, we have long recognized the demands of comity in suits involving foreign states, either as parties or as sovereigns with a coordinate interest in the litigation. See *Hilton v. Guyot*, 159 U.S. 113 (1895). American courts should therefore take care to demonstrate due respect for any special problem confronted by the foreign litigant on account of its nationality or the location of its operations, and for any sovereign interest expressed by a foreign state. We do not articulate specific rules to guide this delicate task of adjudication.[30]

VI

In the case before us, the Magistrate and the Court of Appeals correctly refused to grant the broad protective order that petitioners requested. The Court of Appeals erred, however, in stating that the Evidence Convention does not apply to the pending discovery demands. This holding may be read as indicating that the Convention procedures are not even an option that is open to the District Court. It must be recalled, however, that the Convention's specification of duties in executing states creates corresponding rights in requesting states; holding that the Convention does not apply in this situation would deprive domestic litigants of access to evidence through treaty procedures to which the contracting states have assented. Moreover, such a rule would deny the foreign litigant a full and fair opportunity to demonstrate appropriate reasons for employing Convention procedures in the first instance, for some aspects of the discovery process.

Accordingly, the judgment of the Court of Appeals is vacated, and the case is remanded for further proceedings consistent with this opinion.

It is so ordered.

JUSTICE BLACKMUN, with whom JUSTICE BRENNAN, JUSTICE MARSHALL, and JUSTICE O'CONNOR join, concurring in part and dissenting in part.

Some might well regard the Court's decision in this case as an affront to the nations that have joined the United States in ratifying the Hague Convention. [Citation omitted.] The Court ignores the importance of the Convention by relegating it to an "optional" status, without acknowledging the significant

[30] Under the Hague Convention, a letter of request must specify "the evidence to be obtained or other judicial act to be performed," Art. 3, and must be in the language of the executing authority or be accompanied by a translation into that language. [Citation omitted.] Although the discovery request must be specific, the party seeking discovery may find it difficult or impossible to determine in advance what evidence is within the control of the party urging resort to the Convention and which parts of that evidence may qualify for international judicial assistance under the Convention. This information, however, is presumably within the control of the producing party from which discovery is sought. The district court may therefore require, in appropriate situations, that this party bear the burden of providing translations and detailed descriptions of relevant documents that are needed to assure prompt and complete production pursuant to the terms of the Convention.

achievement in accommodating divergent interests that the Convention represents. Experience to date indicates that there is a large risk that the case-by-case comity analysis now to be permitted by the Court will be performed inadequately and that the somewhat unfamiliar procedures of the Convention will be invoked infrequently. I fear the Court's decision means that courts will resort unnecessarily to issuing discovery orders under the Federal Rules of Civil Procedure in a raw exercise of their jurisdictional power to the detriment of the United States' national and international interests. The Court's view of this country's international obligations is particularly unfortunate in a world in which regular commercial and legal channels loom ever more crucial.

I do agree with the Court's repudiation of the positions at both extremes of the spectrum with regard to the use of the Convention.... I dissent, however, because I cannot endorse the Court's case-by-case inquiry for determining whether to use Convention procedures and its failure to provide lower courts with any meaningful guidance for carrying out that inquiry. In my view, the Convention provides effective discovery procedures that largely eliminate the conflicts between United States and foreign law on evidence gathering. I therefore would apply a general presumption that, in most cases, courts should resort first to the Convention procedures. An individualized analysis of the circumstances of a particular case is appropriate only when it appears that it would be futile to employ the Convention or when its procedures prove to be unhelpful....

II

By viewing the Convention as merely optional and leaving the decision whether to apply it to the court in each individual case, the majority ignores the policies established by the political branches when they negotiated and ratified the treaty. The result will be a duplicative analysis for which courts are not well designed. The discovery process usually concerns discrete interests that a court is well equipped to accommodate — the interests of the parties before the court coupled with the interest of the judicial system in resolving the conflict on the basis of the best available information. When a lawsuit requires discovery of materials located in a foreign nation, however, foreign legal systems and foreign interests are implicated as well. The presence of these interests creates a tension between the broad discretion our courts normally exercise in managing pretrial discovery and the discretion usually allotted to the Executive in foreign matters.

It is the Executive that normally decides when a course of action is important enough to risk affronting a foreign nation or placing a strain on foreign commerce. It is the Executive, as well, that is best equipped to determine how to accommodate foreign interests along with our own. Unlike the courts, "diplomatic and executive channels are, by definition, designed to exchange, negotiate, and reconcile the problems which accompany the realization of national interests within the sphere of international association." [Citation omitted.] The Convention embodies the result of the best efforts of the Executive Branch, in negotiating the treaty, and the Legislative Branch, in ratifying it, to balance competing national interests. As such, the Convention represents a political determination — one that, consistent with the principle of separation of powers, courts should not attempt to second-guess.

Not only is the question of foreign discovery more appropriately considered by the Executive and Congress, but in addition, courts are generally ill equipped to assume the role of balancing the interests of foreign nations with that of our own. Although transnational litigation is increasing, relatively few judges are experienced in the area and the procedures of foreign legal systems are often poorly understood.... A pro-forum bias is likely to creep into the supposedly neutral balancing process and courts not surprisingly often will turn to the more familiar procedures established by their local rules....

IV

I can only hope that courts faced with discovery requests for materials in foreign countries will avoid the parochial views that too often have characterized the decisions to date. Many of the considerations that lead me to the conclusion that there should be a general presumption favoring use of the Convention should also carry force when courts analyze particular cases. The majority fails to offer guidance in this endeavor, and thus it has missed its opportunity to provide predictable and effective procedures for international litigants in United States courts. It now falls to the lower courts to recognize the needs of the international commercial system and the accommodation of those needs already endorsed by the political branches and embodied in the Convention. To the extent indicated, I respectfully dissent.

DARRELL PRESCOTT & EDWIN R. ALLEY, EFFECTIVE EVIDENCE-TAKING UNDER THE HAGUE CONVENTION, 22 International Lawyer 939, 964-70 (1988)

Letters of Request

France views litigation as a process supervised by public officials and thus views international judicial assistance as assistance rendered by one court for the benefit of another court. It is preferable, therefore, to transmit a letter of request directly from the U.S. court to the French Central Authority, rather than submit it by U.S. or local counsel. The letter of request must be in French or accompanied by a translation into French. The French Central Authority will send the letter of request to the *ministère public* (district attorney) of the jurisdiction in which it is to be executed. The *ministère public* then directs the letter to the competent court, which in turn assigns it to a magistrate for execution.

The French [New Code of Civil Procedure] (*Nouveau Code de Procédure Civile*) was specifically amended in 1975 to accommodate letters of request received pursuant to the Convention. The letter of request will be executed in accordance with French law unless the foreign court has requested a special procedure. A verbatim transcript (not just a summary) is taken if the issuing court has so requested. Upon authorization by the French judge, foreign counsel and their clients may be present and ask questions, which (along with the answers) must be translated into French. The U.S. judge may also attend.

Echoing article 12 of the Convention, the ... Code provides that enforcement of letters of request cannot be denied solely on the ground that France claims exclusive jurisdiction of the subject matter or does not recognize the substantive cause of action that is the subject of the litigation. The French court does not assess costs or taxes for execution of letters of request, although fees will likely be due to witnesses, experts, interpreters, and a reporter who takes a verbatim transcript. In permitting questioning by counsel and the taking of a verbatim transcript, and in making powers of compulsion available in pursuance of causes of action that may not even be recognized in France, articles 739-748 represent a major concession by France to the common law style of taking evidence.

A French court, either "*sua sponte* or upon demand of any interested person" may refuse to execute a letter of request if it considers that its execution is beyond its jurisdiction or is likely to threaten the sovereignty or security of France. The judge has discretionary power in making this determination. Any adverse decision may be appealed by any of the parties or by the *ministère public* to the Court of Appeals, which ultimately decides whether to perform the requested acts.

The French court may employ various methods of compulsion in executing the letter of request. A party or nonparty may be ordered to disclose any and all written documents in his possession and a daily fine for noncompliance may be imposed. Witnesses must give evidence under oath unless they have a legitimate excuse for not doing so or are a relative of a party. A fine of from 100 to 10,000 francs may be imposed against a witness who refuses to appear or to give evidence or to take an oath. Parties may be ordered to appear; if they fail to do so, adverse inferences may be drawn against them with respect to issues about which they would be expected to provide evidence. Witnesses who give false evidence may be fined from 500 to 7,500 francs and may be imprisoned for two to five years.

Although France initially declared under article 23 that it would not execute letters of request issued for the purpose of obtaining pretrial discovery of documents, an August 19, 1986 letter from the French Minister of Justice to the Minister of Foreign Affairs states that France will not object to the execution of letters of request seeking the production of documents, provided that the requested documents are enumerated in the letter of request and have a direct and clear nexus with the subject matter of the litigation. In its amicus brief, filed August 22, 1986, in the *Aérospatiale* case before the U.S. Supreme Court, the Republic of France stated that it "will use its compulsory powers to require production [of documents] if the demand is formulated pursuant to the Convention, and meets minimum standards of relevance and specificity."

Diplomatic Officers and Commissioners

Evidence may be taken by diplomatic officers or commissioners in France only pursuant to a commission issued under rule 28(b)(4) by the court in which the action is pending. Attendance before a consul or commissioner will not be compelled in France.

American diplomatic officers in France may take evidence from American nationals without the prior approval of French authorities, since France did not exercise its right under article 15 of the Convention to require such permission. Prior French Central Authority authorization is required, however, when evidence is to be taken by diplomatic officers from French or third-state nationals....

France's prior permission is required whenever evidence is to be taken by commissioners. Permission is granted on the same terms as for the taking of evidence by diplomatic officers from French or third-state nationals....

The French "Blocking Statute"

France's concern for the integrity of its territorial and judicial sovereignty is manifested in French penal statutes that prohibit persons from requesting or producing evidence for use in foreign judicial proceedings other than through the procedures provided by the Convention, other applicable international treaties, or specific provision of French law. The French statute, enacted in 1980, imposes significant fines and, in the case of individuals, up to six months' imprisonment, or both....

First, it is not, as it has often been characterized, a "blocking" statute, insofar as it merely relegates U.S. litigants to Convention procedures. The 1980 law was passed after France ratified the Convention and made the above outlined changes in the internal French [New Code of Civil Procedure] to accommodate Convention requests. The 1980 law was passed specifically in response to many U.S. litigants' disregard of Convention procedures. Thus, the law does not seek to impede access to evidence but rather to channel requests for evidence through procedures that have been established by means of a negotiated international agreement — an agreement that, significantly, has been implemented in France through changes in French law that represent unprecedented concessions to the United States' desire to facilitate U.S.-style discovery abroad. Second, contrary to the views expressed by some American courts and litigants, the 1980 law does not allow the French Government to waive the penal prohibitions against discovery outside of the Convention. No such waiver has ever been granted. Third, its prohibitions apply to those who request as well as those who produce evidence and nothing would prevent the French Government from using it to halt broad and unfocused "legal tourism" that offends its concepts of sovereignty.

NOTES AND QUESTIONS

1. The *Aérospatiale* litigation engendered substantial academic, practitioner, and government interest. For instance, the governments of France, Germany, Switzerland, and the United Kingdom, along with the Italy-America Chamber of Commerce, each filed an amicus curiae brief with the Supreme Court. For some flavor of practitioner views (together with a bibliography), see Symposium, *Compelling Discovery in Transnational Litigation,* 16 N.Y.U. J. Int'l L. & Pol. 957 (1984).

2. Justice Stevens, writing for the majority in *Aérospatiale,* identifies four interpretations of the relationship between the Federal Rules on discovery and the Hague Convention. Why would France support the exclusive use interpretation? (See footnote 11 of the opinion.) How persuasive is the Court's rejection of that option?

What about the first use interpretation? Could a trial court in appropriate circumstances prevent undue delay by fixing a time limit on the use of Convention procedures or by precluding a foreign party from obtaining discovery until he has provided evidence requested under the Convention?

3. At the end of part V of Justice Stevens's opinion he states: "American courts should therefore take care to demonstrate due respect for any special problem confronted by the foreign litigant on account of its nationality or the location of its operations, and for any sovereign interest expressed by a foreign state." Should the attorney representing a foreign client be prepared to introduce foreign law under Federal Rule 44.1 at a discovery hearing for a protective order? The Supreme Court is not particularly helpful: "We do not articulate specific rules to guide this delicate task of adjudication." Is footnote 28 on comity analysis helpful? *See* Joseph P. Griffin & Mark N. Bravin, *Beyond* Aérospatiale: *A Commentary on Foreign Discovery Provisions of the Restatement (Third) and the Proposed Amendments to the Federal Rules of Civil Procedure,* 25 Int'l Law. 331 (1991).

4. The Evidence Convention was the product of intense negotiations between common law and civil law nations that wished to bridge the gap between their respective procedural systems to facilitate international litigation. The countries intended to replace vague concepts of comity and broad judicial discretion with concise treaty obligations to create more order and certainty in the field of international evidence gathering. *See Siemens, supra.* Does *Aérospatiale* in essence redelegate broad discretion to federal and state trial courts, which will likely return litigants to an unpredictable system of comity that the Convention was specifically designed to replace?

5. How persuasive is Justice Blackmun's separation of powers argument in part II of his concurring and dissenting opinion? Do the inherent comparative and international legal issues in transnational litigation make their resolution more appropriate for the political branches of government?

6. Have the French by enacting articles 739 to 748 in the New Code of Civil Procedure shown more accommodation to American procedural interests than *Aérospatiale* showed to French procedural interests? Did the Supreme Court fully understand France's so-called blocking statute? *See* Note, *Discovery in France and the Hague Convention: The Search for a French Connection,* 64 N.Y.U. L. Rev. 1073 (1989).

7. Twenty-one countries have signed the Hague Evidence Convention, as listed by Born and Hoing (see footnote 14 in Born & Hoing excerpt, *supra*), plus Mexico. This includes all of the European civil law countries discussed in this book, and Argentina and Mexico in Latin America, but none of the East Asian countries discussed. Most Latin American countries have ratified the Inter-American Convention on Letters Rogatory, but the United States has taken a reservation against art. 2(b), which provides (art. 2(b)) for "taking of evidence and the obtaining of information abroad." See Section A at Note 9 following *Schlunk.*

8. In addition to articles excerpted or cited in this section, useful commentary includes George A. Bermann, *The Hague Evidence Convention in the Supreme Court: A Critique of the* Aérospatiale *Decision,* 63 Tul. L. Rev. 525 (1989); David J. Gerber, *Obscured Visions: Policy, Power, and Discretion in Transnational Discovery,* 23 Vand. J. Transnat'l L. 993 (1991); *id., International Discovery After Aérospatiale: The Quest for an Analytical Framework,* 82 Am. J. Int'l L. 521 (1988).

Major reference works on these issues include Gary B. Born & David Westin, International Civil Litigation in United States Courts: Commentary and Materials, ch. 5 (2d ed. 1992); Ved P. Nanda & David K. Pansius, Litigation of International Disputes in U.S. Courts, ch. 6 (1990); Bruno A. Ristau, 1 International Judicial Assistance: Civil and Commercial, pts. 3, 5, 7 (1990).

D. PROVING FOREIGN LAW: EXPERT WITNESSES AND OTHER SOURCES

NOTE

Federal Rule 44.1, *supra* Section B, states: "The court, in determining foreign law, may consider any relevant material or source, including testimony, whether or not submitted by a party or admissible under the Federal Rules of Evidence."

Review the advisory committee's note to Rule 44.1 and the state statutory materials, *supra* Section B, regarding information that may be used in proving foreign law.

In this section we focus on some practical questions associated with the use of expert witnesses, English language translations of foreign words, laws, case reports, and treatises. We then consider under what circumstances it might be appropriate for the court to select its own expert witness or special master to resolve a foreign law problem.

1. THE USE OF EXPERTS AND DOCUMENTS

JOHN G. SPRANKLING & GEORGE R. LANYI, PLEADING AND PROOF OF FOREIGN LAW IN AMERICAN COURTS, 19 Stanford Journal of International Law 3, 43-45, 48-50, 58-60 (1983)

A. *Experts*

1. *The Role of the Expert*

Both as a consultant and as a witness, an expert serves two primary functions. First, he must find and synthesize the sources of foreign law. Second, he must "translate" the foreign law into terms comprehensible to nonexperts. Since foreign law must undergo a double interpretation — once within its own legal framework and again when it is brought into the American legal system — before it can be applied, the expert must be trained and fluent in both languages and legal cultures.

As part of his synthesizing function, the expert can ascertain and attest to: (1) the authenticity and authoritativeness of a source of foreign law; (2) the most current state of that law; (3) the law which controlled at the pertinent time and place; and (4) other laws which might apply to the situation. The expert also can provide information on the decisional and unwritten law of a foreign country. Additionally, the expert must evaluate and select among conflicting legal doctrines, decisions, statutes, and criticism to determine the law which the appropriate foreign court would most likely apply. He then must determine the appropriate interpretation and application of that law.

Once the expert has ascertained the law to his satisfaction, he must perform a comparative function and explain the foreign-law concepts in terms comprehensible to domestic lawyers and laymen. The expert will need to consider and explain, for example, differences in translations of the law, including the accuracy, potential to mislead, and analogical meaning of the various translations. He must also explain the reasoning that a foreign court would be likely to follow in a given situation and assert how that court would apply such reasoning to the facts.

A testifying expert normally will repeat the translating function for the benefit of the court, which generally is ignorant of the nature and structure of the foreign legal system and often is implicitly biased against it, if only out of excessive zeal for the system in which the court operates. The process of establishing foreign law thus requires the expert to provide basic, fundamental instruction about the foreign legal system. Two types of testimony are helpful in this regard. First, the expert should describe the rules of construction employed in the foreign jurisdiction and the nature and weight of sources used to interpret the law. Second, the expert should integrate his conclusions with the concepts of domestic law familiar to the court. Thus, the ideal expert would have a working knowledge of both the foreign and domestic legal systems, together with the skill to bridge the gap between the two.

The major advantage of expert testimony is that the expert can measure and respond to the sophistication, comprehension, background knowledge, and questions of the court and counsel. A well-framed affidavit or other substitute for testimony is less flexible, although more persuasive than documentary sources of law....

2. *Methods of Providing Expert Opinion*

The most common means to present expert testimony on foreign law is through an affidavit or similar written statement. Such a statement sets forth the applicable foreign law and analyzes it in the light of the facts of the case. Translated copies of the key legal authorities upon which the expert relied generally are attached. The statement is then filed with the court, usually without cross-examination of its author....

When a foreign-law issue is complex or actively contested, however, the effectiveness of the affidavit is limited. Even in isolation from the form of proof offered by the adverse party, an affidavit may be less persuasive to the court than oral testimony. The role of the expert is to show the judge how the foreign law meshes with the facts of the case. An affidavit, however, cannot respond to unique questions or concerns of the court which may arise during the proceedings. In addition, judicial predispositions toward the adversary approach may make the court suspicious of any "evidence" which has not been subjected to cross-examination....

The problem can be more pronounced when the affidavit is compared to the form of proof used by the adverse party. If both parties rely on affidavits, the court will have few means to determine which interpretation is more accurate, aside from a crude scrutiny of the authorities cited and of the qualifications of the respective experts. If, on the other hand, one side employs an affidavit while the other provides oral testimony, the party providing the expert witness in court may reap substantial advantages in persuasiveness....

B. *Documentary Sources of Law*

[D]ocumentary sources of law often may suffice to dispose of a case. Especially when the parties do not dispute the foreign law, presentation of documents alone may be sufficient. When there is some dispute over the substance or application of a foreign law, however, counsel should be prepared to rely on more than naked documents....

Statutes in particular require interpretation in order to be applied to the facts at bar, because the public policy embodied in them is rarely clear on their face. Consequently, courts sometimes have been willing to look beyond the commonly accepted notion that precedent carries no weight in civil-law systems and have relied on decisions from the foreign jurisdictions. Where admissible as evidence, treatises and other scholarly commentaries on the law can help fill the gaps between statutes and reality. In many legal cultures — especially among nations of the civil law tradition — tribunals give great weight to commentaries....

The greatest disadvantage to documentary sources of foreign law is their lack of power to persuade and explain. A statute usually cannot answer questions about its meaning. Expert testimony can guide the court through the vagaries and contortions of the process by which a foreign court would derive and apply its law. If one party employed an expert, the other side would be imprudent to rely on documents alone.

DIAZ v. SOUTHEASTERN DRILLING CO. OF ARGENTINA, S.A.

United States District Court, N.D. Texas, Dallas Division
324 F. Supp. 1 (1969), *affirmed,* 449 F.2d 258 (5th Cir. 1971)

BREWSTER, DISTRICT JUDGE.

This is a suit against Southeastern Drilling Company, et al., for an accounting of the net profits realized from a contract between Southeastern and Yacimientos Petroliferos Fiscales (YPF) for the drilling of 1500 oil wells in a government owned, proven field in Argentina. YPF was the agency of the Argentine government which had jurisdiction over that country's petroleum fields and activities.

By written agreements, Southeastern gave 20% of its net profits from such operation to Diaz, O'Neall and Dillin for their services in securing the contract. It was originally contemplated that the commission would be divided among those three persons as follows: Diaz, 10%; O'Neall, 5%; Dillin, 5%.

However, Diaz had to assign some of his interest to other persons in Argentina, and wound up with only 4%.

The first drilling contract was so satisfactory that the parties decided to go after a second one. Diaz claims that O'Neall and Dillin each assigned him 1% of the net profits out of their respective interests to help take care of the expenses hereinafter explained. Diaz says that while such assignments gave him 6% of the profits insofar as Southeastern was concerned, they in fact resulted in a net equal interest of 4% each among O'Neall, Dillin and him, with his having an additional 2% to defray expenses.

O'Neall and Dillin have repudiated their respective assignments. O'Neall claims that he transferred all of his 5% interest to Trefina, A. G., a Swiss corporation. Dillin alleges that he sold his entire 5% to Great American Investment Corporation, a company organized under the laws of the Bahama Islands.

Diaz' claims to the two interests of 1% interest each from O'Neall and Dillin are based upon two written instruments, one signed by O'Neall and the other by Dillin. They were not executed at the same time and the wording of them is materially different.

Trefina challenges the claim of Diaz to the 1% interest he says he got from O'Neall, and insists that it owns all of the full 5% O'Neall had. Great American takes a similar position in regard to the 1% Diaz alleges he got from Dillin.

There is an argument over whether the law of Argentina applies to the instruments above mentioned, and, if so, what the pertinent Argentina law is.

The document signed by O'Neall which Diaz claims assigned a 1% interest to him is dated March 30, 1959, and reads as follows:

> TO WHOM IT MAY CONCERN
> KNOW ALL MEN BY THESE PRESENTS:
>
> That I, Charles F. O'Neall, hereby authorize and direct Southeastern Drilling Company of Argentina, S. A. (now in formation) to pay, from such sums as are payable to me, one (1%) percent of the net profits realized by said company on the contract it now expects to obtain from Y.P.F. pursuant to Bid Invitation No. 10,338, to the order of Antonio Angel Diaz. Dated this 30th day of March, 1959, in Buenos Aires, Argentina.
>
> /s/ Charles F. O'Neall
>
> WITNESSETH: I, Antonio Diaz, do, this ______ day of ________, hereby exercise the power specified above by directing that such payments be made to the order of ______.
>
> /s/ Antonio Angel Diaz

Trefina contends that this letter constituted only an authorization for a limited and conditional purpose which never materialized, that no consideration was ever paid therefor, that by said authorization O'Neall did not intend to convey any interest to plaintiff, and that it was timely cancelled and revoked.

Diaz testified that at the time this letter was executed, O'Neall signed an identical instrument on behalf of Dillin but that Diaz preferred to have such an instrument signed personally by Dillin and wrote him to that effect. Dillin did not comply with the request of Diaz, but, instead, drafted a letter containing different wording, which he mailed to Diaz in Buenos Aires. That letter, dated July 8, 1959, reads as follows:

> Dear Antonio:
>
> Reference is made to the Commission Agreement dated February 1959, between Southeastern Drilling Company, represented by Mr. Clements as president, the Houston Brothers, O'Neall, yourself, and me. As you will recall, that agreement provides that I am to receive five (5%) per cent of the net profits, if any, from the contracts contemplated thereby.
>
> I also refer to previous conversations and agreements reached between you, O'Neall, and myself with respect to the special use to be made of twenty (20%) per cent of my commission, namely one (1%) per cent out of the five (5%) per cent.
>
> This letter constitutes written confirmation of my agreement and constitutes your authorization to collect on my behalf one-fifth of the five (5%) per cent commission payable to me under the Southeastern agreement for the purposes we have agreed to.
>
> In order to be sure you will receive this confirmation promptly I am sending a carbon copy to your hotel in New York, with the original being mailed to your office in Buenos Aires.
>
> Sincerely yours,
> /s/ W. N. Dillin

Great American argues that this letter constituted merely an authorization in the nature of an agency, not coupled with any transfer of interest in the property thereof. It asserts that it was timely revoked, that no personal benefit for Diaz was intended by it, that no consideration was paid, and that there was a conditional purpose which was never completed.

The evidence shows that on September 17, 1959, Southeastern paid an advance "signing bonus" to each of the parties entitled to a percentage of the net profit under the February agreement. On the same date, O'Neall and Dillin each wrote checks to Diaz for amounts equalling 1% of the total advance payment.

Diaz argues that the two per cent was assigned to him by these letters in exchange for personal expenses he had incurred in connection with the drilling contract and for expenses which he contemplated in the future to secure a second contract for Southeastern for an additional number of wells. He argues that the payments of September 17, 1959 should be interpreted as a ratification or confirmation of these instruments as assignments.

The substantive rights of the parties are to be governed by the laws of Texas, including its choice of law rules. [Citations omitted.] Under Texas conflict of laws rules, the validity, interpretation and effect of an assignment, and of contracts generally, are determined by the law of the place where the contract is made. [Citations omitted.] Under Texas law, a contract is generally held to be made at the place where the offer is accepted. [Citations omitted.] Even under the trend toward application of the law of the place having the most significant relationship to a case, it is clear that the law of Argentina would be applicable.

The evidence shows that the debtor, Southeastern Drilling Company, is a Panama corporation which was formed for the sole purpose of performing this drilling contract in Argentina. The commission contract of February 13, 1959, for services rendered in Argentina, was entered into by all parties in Buenos Aires. The alleged assignee, Diaz, is domiciled in Argentina. The letter from O'Neall was drafted and signed by him in Buenos Aires and was received and accepted there by Diaz. The Dillin letter was drafted and signed by him in Washington, D.C., but it was received and accepted by Diaz in Buenos Aires. The only connections which the State of Texas has had with these transactions were insignificant. For example, the payments of September 17, 1959 were made to Diaz by O'Neall and Dillin in Corpus Christi; the balance of the money associated with the claimed assignments is on deposit in a Dallas bank; and an office of Southeastern Drilling Company is located at Dallas. The State of Texas has had no contact with the assignments and there is no evidence that Diaz, O'Neall or Dillin negotiated with reference to Texas law. Argentine law controls the issues presented here.

A major portion of the trial was devoted to the introduction of evidence to prove the applicable laws of Argentina, including the testimony of three witnesses offered as experts on Argentine law and designated articles from the Argentine Civil Code (Joannini Translation) published by the Comparative Law Bureau of the American Bar Association (Boston Book Company, 1917). The determination of Argentine law is a question of law on which the Court may consider any relevant material or source. Rule 44.1, Federal Rules of Civil Procedure.

Professor Julio Lezana, Professor of Law at the University of Buenos Aires, the largest university in Argentina, testified for plaintiff with respect to the effect of the March 30, 1959 letter. He stated that he received his equivalent of an L.L.B. degree in 1924 and his doctorate degree in Jurisprudence in 1932; that he began the practice of law in 1924; and that he has been a professor at the University since 1956. He testified that he had written many articles for legal publications and that he is a member of the Law Institute of Buenos Aires, a doctorate program specializing in Civil Law.

The Professor stated that a power, referred to in the Argentine Civil Code as a "*mandate*" exists "when one person is authorized to act on behalf of and under directions of another person, in accordance with the instructions given."[1] He stated that an assignment, called a succession of credits in Argentina, exists "when the credit is assigned to another person and that person can dispose of it freely."[2] As explained by the Professor, a mandate may be gratuitous or onerous, and it will be presumed gratuitous in the absence of a stipulation that the *mandatary,* the recipient of the power, is to receive compensation for his work.[3] He further stated that a *mandate* is revocable by the principal, provided that it has been given only in the interest of one party.[4]...

[1] Art. 1869.
[2] Arts. 1434, 1444, 1448, 1454, 1460.
[3] Art. 1871.
[4] Arts. 1963(1), 1970, 1977.

Professor Lezana concluded that the O'Neall letter was not a power or *mandate* because "it does not state that Mr. Diaz has to do anything with reference to Mr. O'Neall," whereas a *mandatary* is one who acts "on behalf of the principal generally following his instructions."

The Professor was of the opinion that the portion of the instrument above the signature of O'Neall itself constituted a valid assignment in favor of Diaz, perfected at the moment at which it was accepted by Diaz, and that it was ratified by the second part of the document which showed, by the words "to the order of," that Diaz could do anything with that part of the profit which was assigned to him. Professor Lezana explained that blank spaces were common in the business world in Argentina in commercial transactions and that Diaz could put any name there, even his own.[5]

As to the requirement of consideration for a contract under Argentine law, the Professor pointed out that if it were not expressed, Article 1016 of the Civil Code would "suppose" that it existed.[6] The contract, as an assignment, would not be revocable by one party, but would require consent of both parties for its modification or cancellation.[7]

If the parties were unable to agree upon the terms of a contract in Argentina or if the terms were ambiguous, the Professor testified that the issue would be for the judge to determine by attempting to locate the intent of the parties from the contract or from their conduct, such as payment, under its provisions.

Great American offered the testimony of Harry Wright, a Professor of Law at the University of Texas School of Law, on the issue of the application of Argentine law to the letter of July 8, 1959. Professor Wright holds a Bachelor of Science degree in Foreign Service from the School of Foreign Service at Georgetown University and received his L.L.B. in 1952 from the University of Texas where he was Editor-in-Chief of the Texas Law Review. Following his graduation from law school, he served in the Army for a year and a half, some of which time was spent in Puerto Rico. He engaged in private practice for 10 years, including 5 years with a law firm in Mexico City and 5 years with a Houston, Texas firm. He has been a Professor of Law for about six years at the University of Texas Law School, where he teaches Civil Law and Latin American Law with emphasis on Argentine and Mexican law. From time to time, he also teaches such courses as Latin American Commercial Law and International Business Transactions.

Professor Wright testified that the letter of July 8, 1959 fit squarely into the definition of a *mandate* and clearly indicated on its face that it was to be this type of contract. He pointed out that the language of the letter, "Your authorization to collect on my behalf," contained all the essential elements of a *mandate* — (1) a power, (2) to represent the principal in the execution of some act, and (3) in the name and for the account of the principal. Professor Wright pointed out that under the Argentine Code, *mandates* may be general or special[8] and that a special *mandate* must be limited to the act or acts for

[5] Art. 1016.
[6] Arts. 500, 501.
[7] Arts. 1200, 1197.
[8] Art. 1879.

which it is given.[9] He concluded that since the letter conferred authority for only one transaction, it was a special *mandate* and that the authority of Diaz was limited to that act. The witness testified that the authority given was further limited by the express statement that the debt was to be collected "for the purposes we have agreed to," and that this limitation could not be exceeded under Article 1905 of the Civil Code, and that if any amounts were collected by Diaz for purposes other than that for which the authority had been granted, Diaz would be obligated to account for it to Dillin.[11]

Professor Wright found no words in the letter of July 8 indicating an assignment and thought that the letter seemed expressly to negate any intention to make an unconditional transfer of ownership in the claim.[12] He felt that the payment of September 17, 1959 could not be interpreted as a "confirmation" that the letter was an assignment under Article 1059. He explained that "confirmation" was an act which removed or waived a defect in a transaction, that there was no evidence of any such defect in the letter, and, further, that confirmation could not be made until the defect, such as minority of a party, had ceased to exist.[14] On the other hand, he was of the opinion that the payment would be entirely consistent with and would, in fact, strengthen the construction of the letter as a *mandate,* since the principal must advance amounts to the *mandatary* which are necessary for the performance of this *mandate* and if the *mandatary* has advanced them the principal must repay him.[15] Thus, the payment could be viewed as an advance or repayment of amounts advanced in performance of the *mandate.*

Finally, the Professor noted that under the interpretation of the letter as a *mandate* the authorization could be revoked at any time by Dillin and at his will.[16]

The Court is of the opinion that the credentials and reliability of these witnesses as experts were established beyond dispute and that the testimony given by each of them should be accepted. From their testimony and the excerpts from the Argentine Civil Code introduced into evidence, together with other evidence offered on these issues, the Court concludes: (1) that the letter of March 30, 1959, from Charles F. O'Neall to Antonio A. Diaz constitutes a valid assignment under Argentine law; and (2) that the letter of July 8, 1959, from Wm. N. Dillin to Diaz is not an assignment but is a revocable power or "*mandate.*"

The evidence shows O'Neall was a successful attorney. If he intended the instrument prepared by him to have the effect of a power, he failed to indicate that intention in any manner. On the other hand, the refusal of Dillin, also a lawyer, to sign an identical letter, and his insistence upon drawing up an entirely different instrument established to the satisfaction of the Court that he was seeking to avoid a construction such as has been placed upon O'Neall's letter; and it is the opinion of the Court that he succeeded.

---

[9] Art. 1884.
[11] Art. 1909; ... Art. 1911.
[12] Art. 1434.
[14] Art. 1060.
[15] Art. 1948; ... Art. 1949.
[16] Art. 1963; ... Art. 1970; ... Art. 1972; ... Art. 1966.

NOTES AND QUESTIONS

1. A foreign law expert may act as a consultant to an attorney, a witness before a court, or both. How are these roles likely to differ and what ethical norms should apply to each role?

2. Under what circumstances should an attorney submit an expert's affidavit to the court instead of offering the expert's oral testimony (by deposition, at a hearing, or at the trial)?

When might an unsworn statement from a party's attorney be sufficient? Consider *Swiss Credit Bank v. Balink,* 614 F.2d 1269, 1271-72 (10th Cir. 1980):

> The parties stipulated in the pretrial order that Swiss law controlled the relationship between the Bank and Wyoming. Balink contends that the Swiss law was never adequately proved. But the Bank submitted a letter from its legal counsel in Switzerland that set forth the applicable law and the legal conclusion that the Bank could not charge the account. Balink presented no evidence to the contrary, relying entirely upon the argument that the evidence is of little probative value. Fed. R. Civ. P. 44.1 gives the court wide latitude in determining foreign law, and it can consider any relevant material. The unrefuted evidence presented here is sufficient to establish the determination of Swiss law.

3. What are the advantages and disadvantages of submitting only documentary evidence of foreign law — translations of statutes, judicial decisions, or treatise excerpts — to a court?

4. Would it have been adequate in *Diaz v. Southeastern Drilling Co.* for a party to have provided only a translation of the relevant Argentine Civil Code articles? Plus judicial decisions? Plus treatise excerpts?

What was effective about the plaintiff Diaz's expert? What was effective about the defendant Great American's (Dillin's) expert?

5. For an explanation of why O'Neall assigned his interests to Trefina, A.G. (Switzerland) and Dillin assigned his interests to Great American (Bahamas), see Judge Brewster's memorandum in *Diaz* (at 324 F. Supp. 1, 7-19) on the IRS's intervention in the case regarding its $1.1 million assessments against these two Texas lawyers.

6. An American law professor discusses some of the difficulties involved in serving as a foreign law expert in Boris Kozolchyk & Martin L. Ziontz, *A Negligence Action in Mexico: An Introduction to the Application of Mexican Law in the United States,* 7 Ariz. J. Int'l & Comp. L. 1 (1989). He asks:

> If Mexican substantive law is applied, what does it encompass? Will Mexican federal law suffice if the accident took place on federal property such as federal highways or "maritime zones," or are Mexican state or local versions of substantive law equally relevant, and if so, which state law should apply?; With respect to a "codified" system of laws such as Mexico's, is the restatement of Mexican codal, statutory and administrative law provisions enough, or should court and doctrinal interpretation also be alleged and proven?; What is the precise ranking of the various sources of law, such as constitutions, codes, statutes, administrative regu-

> lations, court decisions, doctrinal comments and so forth?; Once all applicable sources have been identified and ranked, how does the litigant establish the appropriate Mexican counterpart to United States litigational concepts such as "cause of action," "proximate cause," "contributory or comparative negligence," "assumption of the risk," "act of God," "punitive damages," and so on?; How can one effect the application of a Mexican standard of diligence in the United States if such a standard differs from that which prevails in the jurisdiction in question?

Id. at 4.

2. LÉSION CORPORELLE IN FRENCH LAW

EASTERN AIRLINES, INC. v. FLOYD

United States Supreme Court
111 S. Ct. 1489 (1991)

JUSTICE MARSHALL delivered the opinion of the Court.

Article 17 of the Warsaw Convention sets forth conditions under which an international air carrier can be held liable for injuries to passengers. This case presents the question whether Article 17 allows recovery for mental or psychic injuries unaccompanied by physical injury or physical manifestation of injury.

I

On May 5, 1983, an Eastern Airlines flight departed from Miami, bound for the Bahamas. Shortly after takeoff, one of the plane's three jet engines lost oil pressure. The flight crew shut down the failing engine and turned the plane around to return to Miami. Soon thereafter, the second and third engines failed due to loss of oil pressure. The plane began losing altitude rapidly, and the passengers were informed that the plane would be ditched in the Atlantic Ocean. Fortunately, after a period of descending flight without power, the crew managed to restart an engine and land the plane safely at Miami International Airport. 872 F.2d 1462, 1466 (CA11 1989).

Respondents, a group of passengers on the flight, brought separate complaints against petitioner, Eastern Airlines, Inc. (Eastern), each claiming damages solely for mental distress arising out of the incident. The District Court entertained each complaint in a consolidated proceeding. Eastern conceded that the engine failure and subsequent preparations for ditching the plane amounted to an "accident" under Article 17 of the Convention but argued that Article 17 also makes physical injury a condition of liability. [Citation omitted.] Relying on another federal court's analysis of the French authentic text and negotiating history of the Convention, *see Burnett v. Trans World Airlines, Inc.*, 368 F. Supp. 1152 (NM 1973), the District Court concluded that mental anguish alone is not compensable under Article 17. See 629 F. Supp., at 314.

The Court of Appeals for the Eleventh Circuit reversed, holding that the phrase "lésion corporelle" in the authentic French text of Article 17 encompasses purely emotional distress. See 872 F.2d, at 1480. To support its conclusion, the court examined the French legal meaning of the term "lésion corporelle," the concurrent and subsequent history of the Convention, and cases interpreting Article 17....

II

"When interpreting a treaty, we 'begin "with the text of the treaty and the context in which the written words are used."'"... Moreover, "'treaties are construed more liberally than private agreements, and to ascertain their meaning we may look beyond the written words to the history of the treaty, the negotiations, and the practical construction adopted by the parties.'"...

A

Because the only authentic text of the Warsaw Convention is in French, the French text must guide our analysis. [Citation omitted.] The text reads as follows:

> Le transporteur est responsable du dommage survenu *en cas de mort, de blessure ou de toute autre lésion corporelle* subie par un voyageur lorsque l'accident qui a causé le dommage s'est produit à bord de l'aéronef ou au cours de toutes opérations d'embarquement et de débarquement. 49 Stat. 3005 (emphasis added).

The American translation of this text, employed by the Senate when it ratified the Convention in 1934, reads:

> The carrier shall be liable for damage sustained *in the event of the death or wounding of a passenger or any other bodily injury* suffered by a passenger, if the accident which caused the damage so sustained took place on board the aircraft or in the course of any of the operations of embarking or disembarking. 49 Stat. 3018 (emphasis added).

Thus, under Article 17, an air carrier is liable for passenger injury only when three conditions are satisfied: (1) there has been an accident, in which (2) the passenger suffered "mort," "blessure," "ou ... toute autre lésion corporelle," and (3) the accident took place on board the aircraft or in the course of operations of embarking or disembarking. As petitioner concedes, the incident here took place on board the aircraft and was an "accident" for purposes of Article 17. See 872 F.2d, at 1471. Moreover, respondents concede that they suffered neither "mort" nor "blessure" from the mishap. Therefore, the narrow issue presented here is whether, under the proper interpretation of "*lésion corporelle*," condition (2) is satisfied when a passenger has suffered only a mental or psychic injury.

We must consider the "French legal meaning" of "lésion corporelle" for guidance as to the shared expectations of the parties to the Convention because the Convention was drafted in French by continental jurists. [Citation omitted.] Perhaps the simplest method of determining the meaning of a phrase appearing in a foreign legal text would be to consult a bilingual dictionary. Such dictionaries suggest that a proper translation of "lésion corporelle" is "bodily injury." See, *e.g.*, J. Jéraute, Vocabulaire Français-Anglais et

Anglais-Français de Termes et Locutions Juridiques 205 (1953) (translating "bodily harm" or "bodily injury" as "lésion ou blessure corporelle"); see also *id.*, at 95 (translating the term "lésion" as "injury, damage, prejudice or wrong"); *id.*, at 41 (giving as one sense of "corporel" the English word "bodily"); 3 Grand Larousse de la Langue Française 1833 (1987) (defining "lésion" as a "[m]odification de la structure d'un tissu vivant sous l'influence d'une cause morbide"). These translations, if correct, clearly suggest that Article 17 does *not* permit recovery for purely psychic injuries. Although we have previously relied on such French dictionaries as a primary method for defining terms in the Warsaw Convention, [citation omitted], we recognize that dictionary definitions may be too general for purposes of treaty interpretation. Our concerns are partly allayed when, as here, the dictionary translation accords with the wording used in the "two main translations of the 1929 Convention in English." [R. Mankiewicz, The Liability Regime of the International Air Carrier 197 (1981) (hereinafter Mankiewicz)]. As we noted earlier, the translation used by the United States Senate when ratifying the Warsaw Convention equated) "lésion corporelle" with "bodily injury."... We turn, then, to French legal materials, [citation omitted], to determine whether French jurists' contemporary understanding of the term "lésion corporelle" differed from its translated meaning.

In 1929, as in the present day, lawyers trained in French civil law would rely on the following principal sources of French law: (1) legislation, (2) judicial decisions, and (3) scholarly writing. See generally 1 M. Planiol & G. Ripert, Traité élémentaire de droit civil, pt. 1, Nos. 10, 122, 127 (12th ed. 1939) (Louisiana State Law Inst. trans. 1959); F. Gény, Méthode d'Interprétation et Sources en Droit Privé Positif Nos. 45-50 (2d ed. 1954) (Louisiana State Law Inst. trans. 1963); R. David, French Law: Its Structure, Sources, and Methodology 154 (M. Kindred trans. 1972). Our review of these materials indicates neither that "lésion corporelle" was a widely used legal term in French law nor that the term specifically encompassed psychic injuries.

Turning first to legislation, we find no French legislative provisions in force in 1929 that contained the phrase "lésion corporelle." The principal provision of the French Civil Code relating to the scope of compensable injuries appears to be Article 1382, which provides in very general terms: "Tout fait quelconque de l'homme, qui cause à autrui un dommage, oblige celui par la faute duquel il est ... arrivé, à le réparer." See 2 Planiol & Ripert, *supra*, at pt. 1, No. 863 (translating Article 1382 as, "Every act whatever of man which causes damage to another obliges him by whose fault it happened to repair it").

Turning next to cases, we likewise discover no French court decisions in or before 1929 that explain the phrase "lésion corporelle," nor do the parties direct us to any. Indeed, we find no French case construing Article 17 of the Warsaw Convention to cover psychic injury. The only reports of French cases we did find that used the term "lésion corporelle" are relatively recent and involve physical injuries caused by automobile accidents and other incidents. These cases tend to support the conclusion that, in French legal usage, the term "lésion corporelle" refers only to physical injuries. However, because they were decided well after the drafting of the Warsaw Convention, these cases do not necessarily reflect the contracting parties' understanding of the term "lésion corporelle."

Turning finally to French treatises and scholarly writing covering the period leading up to the Warsaw Convention, we find no materials (and the parties have brought none to our attention) indicating that "lésion corporelle" embraced psychic injury. Subsequent to the adoption of the Warsaw Convention, some scholars have argued that "lésion corporelle" as used in Article 17 should be interpreted to encompass such injury. See, *e.g.*, Mankiewicz 146 (arguing that "in French law the expression *lésion corporelle* covers any 'personal' injury whatsoever"); G. Miller, Liability in International Air Transport 128 (1977) (hereinafter Miller) (arguing that "a liberal interpretation of [Article 17] would be more in line with the spirit of the Convention"). These scholars draw on the fact that, by 1929, France — unlike many other countries, see *infra* [Part II.B] and n. 10 — permitted tort recovery for mental distress. See, *e.g.*, 2 Planiol & Ripert, *supra*, at pt. 1, No. 868A (citing cases awarding damages for injury to honor and for loss of affection). However, this *general* proposition of French tort law does not demonstrate that the *specific* phrase chosen by the contracting parties — "lésion corporelle" — covers purely psychic injury.

We find it noteworthy, moreover, that scholars who read "lésion corporelle" as encompassing psychic injury do not base their argument on explanations of this term in French cases or French treatises or even in the French Civil Code; rather, they chiefly rely on the principle of French tort law that any damage can "giv[e] rise to reparation when it is real and has been verified." 2 Planiol & Ripert, *supra,* at pt. 1, No. 868. We do not dispute this principle of French law. However, we have been directed to no French case prior to 1929 that allowed recovery based on that principle for the type of mental injury claimed here — injury caused by fright or shock — absent an incident in which *someone* sustained physical injury.[7] Since our task is to "give the specific words of the treaty a meaning consistent with the shared expectations of the contracting parties," [citation omitted], we find it unlikely that those parties' apparent understanding of the term "lésion corporelle" as "bodily injury" would have been displaced by a meaning abstracted from the French law of damages. Particularly is this so when the cause of action for psychic injury that evidently was possible under French law in 1929 would not have been recognized

[7] Of the two cases cited by Mankiewicz to demonstrate that French law did compensate mental injuries, one involved recovery by a stepdaughter for emotional distress resulting from the death of her stepmother and the other involved recovery for injury to honor arising from adultery. See Mankiewicz 145 (citing decisions of the highest French court in 1923 and 1857). See also XI International Encyclopedia of Comparative Law: Torts ch. 9, § 9-39, pp. 16-17, and nn. 114-115 (A. Tunc ed. 1972) (citing, as the first personal injury cases permitting recovery for nonpecuniary damages, an 1833 French decision in which "counsel for the plaintiff took as an illustration of *dommage moral* for which recovery should be permitted the grief of a family upon the death of one of their members" and an 1881 Belgian decision in a wrongful death case). Whether the "shared expectation" of the Warsaw Convention parties was that the distress experienced by relatives of injured or dead airline passengers qualified under Article 17 as "*dommage survenu* en cas de mort, [ou] de blessure ... subie par un voyageur" ("*damage sustained* in the event of the death or wounding of a passenger") is a different question from whether psychic injury actually suffered by a passenger is encompassed by the term "lésion corporelle."

in many other countries represented at the Warsaw Convention. See *infra* [Part II.B] and n. 10.

Nor is this conclusion altered by our examination of Article 17's structure. In the decision below, the Court of Appeals found that the Article's wording "suggests that the drafters did not intend to exclude any particular category of damages," because if they had intended "to refer only to injury caused by physical impact," they "would not have singled out and specifically referred to a particular case of physical impact such as *blessure* ('wounding')." 872 F.2d, at 1472-1473 (citing Mankiewicz 146). This argument, which has much the same force as the surplusage canon of domestic statutory construction, is plausible.... However, because none of the other sources of French legal meaning noted above supports the Court of Appeals' construction, we are reluctant to give this argument dispositive weight.

The same structural argument offered by the Court of Appeals was advanced by one of the German delegates to the Warsaw Convention. [Citation omitted.] Accordingly, the official German translation of "lésion corporelle" adopted by Austria, Germany, and Switzerland uses German terms whose closest English translation is apparently "infringement on the health."[a] See Mankiewicz 146. We are reluctant, however, to place much weight on an English translation of a German translation of a French text, particularly when we have been unable to find (and the parties have not cited) any German, Austrian, or Swiss cases adhering to the broad interpretation of Article 17 that the German delegate evidently espoused.

In sum, neither the Warsaw Convention itself nor any of the applicable French legal sources demonstrates that "lésion corporelle" should be translated other than as "bodily injury" — a narrow meaning excluding purely mental injuries. However, because a broader interpretation of "lésion corporelle" reaching purely mental injuries is plausible, and the term is both ambiguous and difficult, see *supra* [Part II], we turn to additional aids to construction.[8]

B

Translating "lésion corporelle" as "bodily injury" is consistent, we think, with the negotiating history of the Convention. "The treaty that became the Warsaw Convention was first drafted at an international conference in Paris in 1925." [Citations omitted.] The final protocol of the Paris Conference contained an article specifying that: "'The carrier is liable for accidents, losses, breakdowns, and delays. It is not liable if it can prove that it has taken reasonable measures designed to pre-empt damage....'" [Citation omitted.] It appears that "this expansive provision, broadly holding carriers liable in the event of an accident, would almost certainly have permitted recovery for all types of injuries, including emotional distress." [Citation omitted.]

---

[a] The German version of Article 17 is: "Der Luftfrachtführer hat den Schaden zu ersetzen, der dadurch entsteht, daß ein Reisender getötet, körperlich verletzt oder sonst gesundheitlich geschädigt wird...." BGBl. 1958 II 317.

[8] We will refer to these alternative interpretations of "lésion corporelle" as the "narrow" and "broad" readings of the term.

The Paris Conference appointed a committee of experts, the Comité International Technique d'Experts Juridiques Aériens (CITEJA), to revise its final protocol for presentation to the Warsaw Conference. [Citations omitted.] The CITEJA draft split the liability article of the Paris Conference's protocol into three provisions with one addressing damages for injury to passengers, the second addressing injury to goods, and the third addressing losses caused by delay. The CITEJA subsection on injury to passengers introduced the phrase "en cas de mort, de blessure ou de toute autre lésion corporelle." [Deuxième] Conférence Internationale de Droit Privé Aérien, 4-12 Octobre 171-172 (1929) (Article 21, subsection (a) of the CITEJA draft). This language was retained in Article 17 ultimately adopted by the Warsaw Conference. See 49 Stat. 3005. Although there is no definitive evidence explaining why the CITEJA drafters chose this narrower language, we believe it is reasonable to infer that the Conference adopted the narrower language to limit the types of recoverable injuries. [Citation omitted.][9]

Our review of the documentary record for the Warsaw Conference confirms — and courts and commentators appear universally to agree — that there is no evidence that the drafters or signatories of the Warsaw Convention specifically considered liability for psychic injury or the meaning of "lésion corporelle." See generally Minutes. Two explanations commonly are offered for why the subject of mental injuries never arose during the Convention proceedings: (1) many jurisdictions did not recognize recovery for mental injury at that time, or (2) the drafters simply could not contemplate a psychic injury unaccompanied by a physical injury. [Citations omitted.] Indeed, the unavailability of compensation for purely psychic injury in many common and civil law countries at the time of the Warsaw Conference[10] persuades us that

[9]Courts and commentators, including the Court of Appeals, have cited the doctoral thesis of a French scholar, Yvonne Blanc-Dannery, as extrinsic evidence of the Warsaw parties' intent. [Citations omitted.] According to Mankiewicz, the Blanc-Dannery thesis was written under the supervision of Georges Ripert. Mankiewicz 146, citing Blanc-Dannery, La Convention de Varsovie et les Régles du Transport Aérien International (1933) (hereinafter Blanc-Dannery). Georges Ripert was a leading French delegate at the Warsaw Convention and an expert of the French Government at the CITEJA proceedings. Minutes, Second International Conference on Private Aeronautical Law, October 4-12, 1929, Warsaw 6 (R. Horner & D. Legrez trans. 1975) (hereinafter Minutes). Mankiewicz translates a passage from the Blanc-Dannery thesis as follows: "'The use of the expression *lésion* after the words 'death' and 'wounding' encompasses and contemplates cases of traumatism and nervous troubles, the consequences of which do not immediately become manifest in the organism but which can be related to the accident.'" Mankiewicz 146. Eastern offers persuasive evidence that Mankiewicz's translation may be overbroad. See Reply Brief for Petitioner 2 (noting that the French word "perturbations" should be translated to connote a disturbance or aberration in a bodily organ or function rather than mere traumatisms or nervous troubles). Even if Mankiewicz's translation is accurate, however, Blanc-Dannery's asserted definition is not supported by evidence from the CITEJA or Warsaw proceedings. See Blanc-Dannery 62. In the absence of such support we find the Blanc-Dannery thesis to have little or no value as evidence of the drafters' intent.

[10]Although French law recognized recovery for certain types of mental distress long before the Convention was drafted, see Mankiewicz 145, in common-law jurisdictions mental distress generally was excluded from recovery in 1929. See Miller 113. Such recovery was not definitively recognized in the United Kingdom until the early 1940's. See Mankiewicz 145; J. Fleming, Law of Torts 49 (1985) (hereinafter Fleming). American courts insisted on a physical impact rule long after English courts abandoned the practice.... Several of the civil law and socialist signatories to the Warsaw Convention were slow to recognize recovery for nonpecuniary losses such as pain and suffering, grief caused by the death of a relative, or mental distress. See XI International Encyclopedia of Comparative Law: Torts, Ch. 9, §§ 9-39, 9-40. The Netherlands, for example, did not

the signatories had no specific intent to include such a remedy in the Convention. Because such a remedy was unknown in many, if not most, jurisdictions in 1929, the drafters most likely would have felt compelled to make an unequivocal reference to purely mental injury if they had specifically intended to allow such recovery....

The narrower reading of "lésion corporelle" also is consistent with the primary purpose of the contracting parties to the Convention: limiting the liability of air carriers in order to foster the growth of the fledgling commercial aviation industry. [Citations omitted.] Indeed, it was for this reason that the Warsaw delegates imposed a maximum recovery of $8,300 for an accident — a low amount even by 1929 standards. [Citation omitted.] Whatever may be the current view among Convention signatories, in 1929 the parties were more concerned with protecting air carriers and fostering a new industry than providing full recovery to injured passengers, and we read "lésion corporelle" in a way that respects that legislative choice.

C

We also conclude that, on balance, the evidence of the post-1929 "conduct" and "interpretations of the signatories," [citation omitted], supports the narrow translation of "lésion corporelle."

In the years following adoption of the Convention, some scholars questioned whether Article 17 extended to mental or emotional injury. See, *e.g.*, Beaumont, *Need for Revision and Amplification of the Warsaw Convention,* 16 J. Air L. & Com. 395, 402 (1949); R. Coquoz, Le Droit Privé International Aérien 122 (1938); Sullivan, *The Codification of Air Carrier Liability by International Convention,* 7 J. Air. L. 1, 19 (1936). In 1951, a committee composed of 20 Warsaw Convention signatories met in Madrid and adopted a proposal to substitute "affection corporelle" for "lésion corporelle" in Article 17. See International Civil Aviation Organization Legal Committee, Minutes and Documents of the Eighth Session, Madrid, ICAO Doc. 7229-LC/133, pp. xiii, 137 (1951). The French delegate to the committee proposed this substitution because, in his view, the word "lésion" was too narrow, in that it "presupposed a rupture in the tissue, or a dissolution in continuity" which might not cover an injury such as mental illness or lung congestion caused by a breakdown in the heating apparatus of the aircraft. See *id.,* at 136. The United States delegate opposed this change if it "implied the inclusion of mental injury or emotional disturbances or upsets which were not connected with or the result of bodily injury," see *id.,* at 137, but the committee adopted it nonetheless, see *ibid.* Although the committee's proposed amendment was never subsequently implemented, its discussion and vote in Madrid suggest that, in the view of the 20 signatories on the committee, "lésion corporelle" in Article 17 had a distinctly physical scope.

permit nonpecuniary damages until 1943, and the German and Swiss Civil Codes generally barred nonpecuniary damages, though with certain exceptions — including an exception for cases of personal injury. See *id.,* at § 9-41. In addition, the Soviet Union, another original signatory, has never recognized compensation for nonpecuniary loss. *Id.,* at § 9-37.

In finding that the signatories' post-1929 conduct supports the broader interpretation of "lésion corporelle," the Court of Appeals relied on three international agreements: The Hague Protocol of 1955, The Montreal Agreement of 1966, and the Guatemala City Protocol of 1971. See 872 F.2d, at 1474-1475. For each of these agreements, the Court of Appeals emphasized that English translations rendered "lésion corporelle" as "personal injury," instead of "bodily injury." In our view, none of these agreements supports the broad interpretation of "lésion corporelle" reached by the Court of Appeals....

We must also consult the opinions of our sister signatories in searching for the meaning of a "lésion corporelle." [Citation omitted.] The only apparent judicial decision from a sister signatory addressing recovery for purely mental injuries under Article 17 is that of the Supreme Court of Israel. That court held that Article 17 does allow recovery for purely psychic injuries. See *Cie Air France v. Teichner,* 39 Revue Française de Droit Aérien, at 243, 23 Eur. Tr. L., at 102.

Teichner arose from the hijacking in 1976 of an Air France flight to Entebbe, Uganda. Passengers sought compensation for psychic injuries caused by the ordeal of the hijacking and detention at the Entebbe Airport. While acknowledging that the negotiating history of the Warsaw Convention was silent as to the availability of such compensation, *id.*, at 242, 23 Eur. Tr. L., at 101, the court determined that "desirable jurisprudential policy" ("la politique jurisprudentielle souhaitable") favored an expansive reading of Article 17 to reach purely psychic injuries. *Id.*, at 243, 23 Eur. Tr. L., at 102. In reaching this conclusion, the court emphasized the post-1929 development of the aviation industry and the evolution of Anglo-American and Israeli law to allow recovery for psychic injury in certain circumstances....

Although we recognize the deference owed to the Israeli court's interpretation of Article 17, [citation omitted], we are not persuaded by that court's reasoning. Even if we were to agree that allowing recovery for purely psychic injury is desirable as a policy goal, we cannot give effect to such policy without convincing evidence that the signatories' intent with respect to Article 17 would allow such recovery. As discussed, neither the language, negotiating history, nor post-enactment interpretations of Article 17 clearly evidences such intent....

Moreover, we believe our construction of Article 17 better accords with the Warsaw Convention's stated purpose of achieving uniformity of rules governing claims arising from international air transportation. [Citation omitted.] As noted, the Montreal Agreement subjects international carriers to strict liability for Article 17 injuries sustained on flights connected with the United States. [Citation omitted.] Recovery for mental distress traditionally has been subject to a high degree of proof, both in this country and others. See Prosser and Keeton on Torts, at 60-65, 359-361 (American courts require extreme and outrageous conduct by the tort-feasor); Fleming 49-50 (British courts limit such recovery through the theory of foreseeability); Miller 114, 126 (French courts require proof of fault and proof that damage is direct and certain). We have no doubt that subjecting international air carriers to *strict* liability for purely mental distress would be controversial for most signatory countries. Our construction avoids this potential source of divergence.

III

We conclude that an air carrier cannot be held liable under Article 17 when an accident has not caused a passenger to suffer death, physical injury, or physical manifestation of injury....

The judgment of the Court of Appeals is reversed.

3. *SHUBUN* IN JAPANESE LAW

DAN FENNO HENDERSON, THE JAPANESE LAW IN ENGLISH: SOME THOUGHTS ON SCOPE AND METHOD, 16 Vanderbilt Journal of Transnational Law 601, 616-20 (1983)

International litigation often focuses sharply on law/language issues .... In important cases, both parties use their own experts who give differing interpretations of the law. The differing expert opinions pose problems for the judge, who lacks the language competence necessary to find the correct interpretation on his own. In this context an extraordinary stress is placed on the translated law; a single mistranslated word may result in victory or defeat.

Clarity is elusive in an English language discussion of Japanese Code concepts that are seldom identical to comparable United States legal concepts. Bilingual litigation is the ultimate form of the law/language problem in United States-Japanese comparative law methodology. Anyone concerned with the practical aspects of this type of litigation will soon be disenchanted after a few court experiences.

Several years ago, some rather technical rules concerning res judicata were nearly misapplied in a California court case because of an EHS[a] [*Eibun Hōrei-sha*] mistranslation of a critical word, *shubun,* as "text" instead of "order" or "holding." The summary below briefly discusses the typical lawyer-related problems in the case presented by the differences between the civil law and common law doctrines of res judicata (claim preclusion) and collateral estoppel (issue preclusion).

The California suit was *Farmland & Development Co. v. Toho Co. Ltd.*[56] Hachitsuka (Farmland) and Yonemoto (Toho) had planned to export a United States film for showing in Japan. Hachitsuka, believing that Yonemoto had promised to obtain the necessary license for importing the film into Japan, bought through Farmland the rights to show the film in Japan for $14,000. Yonemoto, however, was unable to acquire the import license in Japan and the whole venture failed. Hachitsuka, having allegedly lost $93,000, sued Toho Corporation and Yonemoto in California on two separate legal theories: (1) breach of contract; and (2) tort (deceit). Yonemoto filed suit in Tokyo[57] to obtain a declaratory judgment absolving him of tort liability and damages. Although he pleaded to negate the tort claim, Yonemoto failed to seek negation of the contract liability. Two independent suits, based on the same grounds and seeking opposite results, were pending on each side of the Pacific.

---

[a] EHS is a useful compendium of translations of the major codes, statutes, and regulations.

[56] No. 69-2762 (Los Angeles, Cal. Super. Ct. 1968) (no opinion was filed, thus the summary provided in the text is from the author's files).

[57] *Toho Inc. v. Hachitsuka Chieko,* 16 Kakyū minshū 923 (1965), *reprinted in* 11 Japan Ann. Int'l L. 197 (1967) (English trans.).

The Tokyo court found no tort liability and duly rendered a judgment that Toho was not liable to Hachitsuka in tort. The California action, however, sought damages on two theories, contract and tort, a key difference that determined whether the Japanese judgment for Toho precluded Hachitsuka's later California recovery. Because the Tokyo judgment was handed down before the trial in California, Toho lawyers asserted the Tokyo judgment as a res judicata defense to the California suit. The question was whether judicially determined facts underlying the Japanese tort judgment estopped Farmland from making contrary assertions in the contract claim in California.

Pursuant to California law, a foreign (Japanese) judgment bars the tort claim by res judicata and a previously litigated "fact" (here, no promise by Toho) necessary to such a judgment bars the contract claim by collateral estoppel. The California court, applying its choice of law rule, found that it must apply Japanese law and give the Japanese judgment the effect it would have had as a Japanese judgment under Japanese law. The critical question for the contract claim became: is there a doctrine of collateral estoppel (*sotenko*) in Japanese law?

To determine the scope of a declaratory judgment and the existence of collateral estoppel in Japanese law, the California court heard conflicting expert testimony on provisions of the Japanese Code of Civil Procedure. The English translation (EHS) of the pertinent provision of the Code, although clear, is a bit awkward: "As far as the matters contained in the text of a judgment which has become final and conclusive are concerned, they have *res judicata.*" Because the findings of fact are included in the published text of the court's opinion, res judicata (*kihanryoku*) seemingly would result under the pertinent Code section. This, however, is not the law in Japan. The word "text" in the English translation is the EHS "English equivalent" for the Japanese word *shubun*. The *shubun,* which makes no findings of fact, is only a short order as opposed to the full text of the court's opinion. In this case the *shubun* read: "[I]t shall be confirmed that the plaintiffs [Toho and Yonemoto] are under no obligation to compensate for damages amounting to $93,000 due to the torts set forth in the annexed list.... The expense of the suit shall be borne by the defendant."

Under California law, Japanese law may be proven by expert witnesses. To ascertain the meaning of the applicable Code of Civil Procedure section, Toho, the California defendant, offered the English translation of the section quoted above through his expert witness. The expert stated that the Code provision should be interpreted to give effect to the facts underlying a Japanese judgment. Although this is a view held by some professors in Japan, it is not Japanese law. The Supreme Court of Japan consistently has refused to yield to the criticisms of several excellent young scholars and, following the opinion of Kaneko Hajime and other older scholars, has declined to make "collateral estoppel" a part of Japanese law.

This author was the plaintiff's expert on Japanese law at the California trial and had great difficulty opposing the defendant's expert. The California judge naturally tended to favor the expert interpretation which was similar to California's own collateral estoppel practice. By finding that the EHS translation of *shubun* was misleading and reviewing the supporting court cases and the writings of Professor Kaneko, the judge properly limited the effect of the Japanese judgment and held that the judgment barred only the tort claim by res judicata. The plaintiff was then given the opportunity to submit evidence of the contract.

NOTES AND QUESTIONS

1. *Eastern Airlines v. Floyd* illustrates — as does much of this chapter — that the line between international law and comparative law can be quite porous. The Warsaw Convention (for the Unification of Certain Rules Relating to International Transportation by Air, 49 U.S.C. App. § 1502) is a multilateral treaty that derives much of its meaning from French internal law.

2. How many distinct methods of treaty interpretation can you identify in Justice Marshall's opinion for a unanimous Court in *Eastern Airlines*? Are these methods analogous to those we saw for codal interpretation in *Williams v. Employers Liability, supra* Chapter 1, Section D? Is the similarity of methods likely a matter of convergence between the civil law and common law traditions or simply the influence of civil law methodology on U.S. treaty interpretation?

3. Justice Marshall mobilized a large amount of material to support the Court's interpretation that the phrase "lésion corporelle" in article 17 of the Warsaw Convention does not allow recovery for purely mental injuries. Which among the following provides persuasive support for the Court's conclusion:

(a) bilingual French-English dictionaries;
(b) the U.S. Senate and United Kingdom Parliament translations of "lésion corporelle" as "bodily injury";
(c) review of French statutes and Civil Code article 1382 in force in 1929;
(d) review of pre- and post-1929 French judicial decisions using the term "lésion corporelle";
(e) review of French doctrine (treatises and scholarly writing) pre- and post-1929;
(f) the German translation of "toute autre lésion corporelle" as "sonst gesundheitlich geschädigt wird" (other injury to health);
(g) the 1929 Convention's drafting history of article 17 beginning with the Paris Conference in 1925;
(h) comparative law research showing the unavailability of compensation for purely psychic injury in many common law and civil law countries in 1929;
(i) post-1929 conduct of the International Civil Aviation Organization;
(j) the article 17 interpretation made by the Supreme Court of Israel; and
(k) the general purposes of the Convention?

4. Are you surprised that the Court did not refer to any foreign law experts? Could they have helped the plaintiff Rose Marie Floyd? How? What is the primary difference between the nature of the foreign law issue in *Eastern Airlines* and in *Diaz*?

5. Was the California court's experience with "*shubun*," described in Professor Henderson's excerpt, similar to that of the U.S. Supreme Court with "lésion corporelle?" What special problems are likely to exist when dealing with an East Asian legal issue?

4. THE COURT APPOINTED EXPERT OR SPECIAL MASTER

FEDERAL RULES OF EVIDENCE

RULE 706
Court Appointed Experts

(a) Appointment. The court may on its own motion or on the motion of any party enter an order to show cause why expert witnesses should not be appointed, and may request the parties to submit nominations. The court may appoint any expert witnesses agreed upon by the parties, and may appoint expert witnesses of its own selection. An expert witness shall not be appointed by the court unless the witness consents to act. A witness so appointed shall be informed of the witness' duties by the court in writing, a copy of which shall be filed with the clerk, or at a conference in which the parties shall have opportunity to participate. A witness so appointed shall advise the parties of the witness' findings, if any; the witness' deposition may be taken by any party; and the witness may be called to testify by the court or any party. The witness shall be subject to cross-examination by each party, including a party calling the witness.

(b) Compensation. Expert witnesses so appointed are entitled to reasonable compensation in whatever sum the court may allow. The compensation thus fixed is payable from funds which may be provided by law in criminal cases and civil actions and proceedings involving just compensation under the fifth amendment. In other civil actions and proceedings the compensation shall be paid by the parties in such proportion and at such time as the court directs, and thereafter charged in like manner as other costs....

(d) Parties' experts of own selection. Nothing in this rule limits the parties in calling expert witnesses of their own selection.

FEDERAL RULES OF CIVIL PROCEDURE

RULE 53
Masters

(a) Appointment and compensation. The court in which any action is pending may appoint a special master therein.... The compensation to be allowed to a master shall be fixed by the court, and shall be charged upon such of the parties or paid out of any fund or subject matter of the action, which is in the custody and control of the court as the court may direct....

(b) Reference. A reference to a master shall be the exception and not the rule .... [I]n actions to be tried without a jury, save in matters of account and of difficult computation of damages, a reference shall be made only upon a showing that some exceptional condition requires it ....

(c) Powers. The order of reference to the master may specify or limit the master's powers .... Subject to the specifications and limitations stated in the order, the master has and shall exercise the power to regulate all proceedings in every hearing before the master and to do all acts and take all measures necessary or proper for the efficient performance of the master's duties under the order. The master may require the production before the master of evidence upon all matters embraced in the reference, including the production of all books, papers, vouchers, documents, and writings applicable thereto. The master ... has the authority to put witnesses on oath and may examine them and may call the parties to the action and examine them upon oath....

(e) Report.

(1) Contents and filing. The master shall prepare a report upon the matters submitted to the master by the order of reference and, if required to make findings of fact and conclusions of law, the master shall set them forth in the report. The master shall file the report with the clerk of the court and serve on all parties notice of the filing. In an action to be tried without a jury, unless otherwise directed by the order of reference, the master shall file with the report a transcript of the proceedings and of the evidence and the original exhibits. Unless otherwise directed by the order of reference, the master shall serve a copy of the report on each party.

(2) In non-jury actions. In an action to be tried without a jury the court shall accept the master's findings of fact unless clearly erroneous. Within 10 days after being served with notice of the filing of the report any party may serve written objections thereto upon the other parties. Application to the court for action upon the report and upon objections thereto shall be by motion and upon notice as prescribed in Rule 6(d). The court after hearing may adopt the report or may modify it or may reject it in whole or in part or may receive further evidence or may recommit it with instructions....

(5) Draft report. Before filing the master's report a master may submit a draft thereof to counsel for all parties for the purpose of receiving their suggestions.

JOHN HENRY MERRYMAN, FOREIGN LAW AS A PROBLEM, 19 Stanford Journal of International Law 151, 154-55, 172-73 (1983)

Suppose the lawyer consults an expert and learns that the foreign law could be used to the client's advantage. That opinion can be useful in advising the client, negotiating for a settlement, and planning legal and trial strategy. But, looking down the road a bit, counsel has to consider a number of relative unknowns: Will opposing counsel retain an expert? Will the matter go to trial? Will there be a "battle of the experts?" Will "their" expert be measurably more authoritative, prepare a more persuasive affidavit, be a more imposing witness, or hold up better on cross-examination than "our" witness? Once one starts down that road, it is difficult to stop: How much can the client afford? How much will litigation about the foreign-law question and the antecedent choice-of-law question lengthen and complicate the case? How competent is counsel to deal with the foreign-law question in the litigation context? Somehow the lawyer will resolve these questions and pursue or seek to evade the foreign-law issue. If the decision is in favor of pursuit or if subsequent developments compel it because opposing counsel or — in the rare instance —

the court raises the foreign-law issue, then resort to an expert becomes a practical necessity.

If the foreign-law issue does emerge as the case proceeds to trial, each party typically will engage its own expert. Experts in such situations perform two related but fundamentally distinguishable functions: expert witness and expert consultant. They may submit affidavits to the court, appear to testify, or both. They will also be consulted from time to time by counsel in developing the strategy and tactics of the case. The experts may — indeed very probably will — disagree, and if they testify at trial they will be subjected to hostile cross-examination. The case may turn on a point of foreign law and the point of foreign law may turn on the effectiveness of one's expert witness.

This brief narrative is sufficient to demonstrate three factors that ought to concern us in evaluating the way in which the law concerning pleading and proof of foreign law usually works in the United States: (1) the difficulty of access to the applicable foreign law, including the difficulty of identifying a qualified expert; (2) the added expense that the reference to foreign law entails; and (3) the tendency for experts to become partisans and for the resolution of foreign-law questions to degenerate into a "battle of the experts."...

The foreign-law problem will not go away. It will be brought under control only by judges who exercise the power that they already have by regularly appointing expert witnesses or special masters in cases raising foreign-law questions. That solution has ample legislative and theoretical support. Since it promises to improve the quality of foreign-law determinations and to make the process simpler and cheaper for parties and the court, use of the impartial expert appears to be a highly desirable practice. Until it has had a fair try, there is no apparent reason, other than habit or inertia, to ignore it. The only remaining difficulty is that appointment of an impartial expert requires judicial initiative. The court itself will have to appoint the impartial expert witness or the special master. The best answer to the foreign-law problem is before us, merely waiting for judges to act.

CORPORACION SALVADORENA DE CALZADO (CORSAL), S.A. v. INJECTION FOOTWEAR CORP.

United States District Court, S.D. Florida, Miami Division
533 F. Supp. 290 (1982)

ARONOVITZ, DISTRICT JUDGE.

The Nature of the Action

This cause came on to be heard before the Court on February 5, 1982, upon Plaintiff's Objections and Amended Objections to Report of the Special Master and Motion for Rejection of same....

In September, 1980, this Court entered an Order of Reference pursuant to Fed. R. Civ. P. 53, appointing Professor Daniel Murray of the University of Miami School of Law as Special Master in this cause and directing Professor Murray to file a Report to the Court addressing eight (8) enumerated issues presented (Order of Reference, docket # 125). At that time, Cross-motions for Summary Judgment were pending before the Court in this action brought by

Plaintiff to domesticate a judgment against Defendant obtained in the Fifth Civil Court for the District of San Salvador of the sovereign state of El Salvador.

The dispute in El Salvador arose out of a contract between the parties whereby Defendant was to supply Plaintiff with raw materials for the manufacture of footwear. The contract provided that in the event of a dispute, the parties would proceed through an arbitration procedure in El Salvador. Plaintiff commenced arbitration proceedings in El Salvador and, despite Defendant's absence, obtained an arbitrator's award in favor of Plaintiff which was ultimately reduced to judgment in the Fifth Civil Court. It is this judgment which Plaintiff seeks to domesticate in this United States District Court for the Southern District of Florida.

Defendant contends that the proceedings which resulted in the judgment against it not only violated El Salvador law in every respect, from the commencement of the arbitration proceedings in its absence to the confirmation of the award without prior notice to Defendant by the Fifth Civil Court, but also that for this Court to domesticate the El Salvador judgment would violate Defendant's right to due process of law under both the United States and State of Florida constitutions.

The issues thus presented for resolution are extremely complex, involving issues of the law of El Salvador, the United States and the State of Florida, in addition to conflicts of law.... The matter at hand is further complicated by the language barrier, in that many of the relevant documents are in Spanish, as well as the fact that in various pertinent respects, the law of El Salvador comes within the Bustamante Code, to which El Salvador is a signatory but the United States is not. An additional problem is that El Salvador does not, of course, follow the common law system of jurisprudence.

In support of their respective Motions for Summary Judgment, the parties submitted several affidavits from "experts" familiar with El Salvador law, who stated their opinions as to whether El Salvador law was complied with in the instant case. Most of these affidavits are in the original Spanish with English translations. However, as set forth in the Order of Reference, the experts for the respective sides contradict each other in every material respect. This difficulty is compounded by the need to translate not only the affidavits of the parties, but the statutes upon which those affidavits are based. At the filing of the Cross-motions for Summary Judgment, as now, there were no material facts in dispute so as to preclude an award of summary judgment. The material facts were known to the parties and evident in the record essentially as set forth in the Special Master's Report and Recommendations (docket # 157), and reached independently by the Court. Thus, what was referred to the Special Master for determination were questions of law, not fact, which are susceptible of resolution on summary judgment. Under Fed. R. Civ. P. 44.1, the determination of foreign law is a question of law which can properly be resolved on summary judgment.

Based upon the foregoing, this Court concluded that the most satisfactory means of reaching an ultimate decision in this case was through the appointment of a special master pursuant to Fed. R. Civ. P. 53, who has expertise in Latin American law and is fluent in the Spanish language, as set forth in this

Court's Order of Reference. [Citation omitted.] Although the Court recognizes that the appointment of a special master is the exception and not the rule, the Court determined that the exceptional circumstances here presented justify the reference. This Court has by prior Order denied Plaintiff's Motion to Vacate the reference of this matter to the Special Master ....

The Special Master held two hearings in this cause to obtain testimony by experts in the law of El Salvador offered on behalf of both parties....

Findings of Fact

This Court hereby adopts the Special Master's Statement of Facts as set forth in his Report and Recommendations ....

On August 21, 1976, Plaintiff instituted proceedings for the compelling of arbitration and the appointment of "friendly arbitrators" with the filing of its petition in the Fifth Civil Court, San Salvador. The Fifth Civil Court accepted the petition of Plaintiff and ordered that a writ be issued directing Defendant to designate its "friendly arbitrator" within thirty (30) days after it was notified of the court's order. A Letter Rogatory was issued by the court and it was delivered to the Foreign Minister of El Salvador, who delivered it to the American Embassy in San Salvador.

Mr. James P. Bell, Jr., who was the Commercial Attache in the American Embassy, mailed the Letter Rogatory directly to the Defendant by using certified United States mail, addressed to 8730 N.W. 36th Street, Miami, Florida. The letter was received by someone in Defendant's plant on December 6, 1976, and the return receipt was filed by Mr. Bell on January 7, 1977, with the Fifth Civil Court.

The Defendant did not respond to this letter-notice and the Fifth Civil Court appointed a "friendly arbitrator" for Defendant on January 29, 1977. The Fifth Civil Court submitted the matter to the arbitrators on February 3, 1977. The arbitrators, all of whom were and are practicing attorneys, conducted *ex parte* hearings without communicating with the Defendant and the arbitrators awarded Plaintiff the sum of 1,706,723.59 *colones* (approximately $817,307.28 in U.S. currency).... This award was confirmed by a judgment entered by the Fifth Civil Court on April 28, 1977.

The Defendant was not given personal notice of the application to the Fifth Civil Court for a confirming judgment of the award. The only attempt to notify the Defendant was by means of a subsequent notice of the judgment rendered, which was posted on a judicial bulletin board in San Salvador. Subsequent to the entry of this judgment, a certified copy of the judgment was allegedly mailed to the Defendant and allegedly received on June 3, 1977. Plaintiff is seeking to domesticate this foreign judgment under the law of the State of Florida and jurisdiction of this Court is predicated solely on diversity....

Conclusions of Law

The Special Master undertook an extensive review of the applicable statutory provisions under the law of El Salvador, as well as a thorough analysis of due process standards under both state and federal law, as set forth in detail in the Report and Recommendations, in addressing the issues mandated by this Court. In summary, the Special Master rendered the following conclusions and recommendations regarding the enumerated issues:

1. The Special Master concluded that the sequence of events set forth in the factual statement failed to comply with the procedural requirements of El Salvador law, both in commencing the arbitration proceeding and in reducing the arbitration award to judgment....

2. The Special Master concluded that the American Embassy's delivery of certain papers to the Defendant in the United States, which was accomplished by certified mail, does not constitute sufficient service of process to support the commencement of arbitration proceedings under El Salvador law. Specifically, as a signatory to the Bustamante Code, El Salvador requires that Letters Rogatory or Letters Requisitorial be sent by the issuing El Salvadorean judge through the executive department of his country to the named judge or court in a foreign country. This was the procedure initiated in this case, but it was aborted when the Commercial Attache of the United States Embassy, Mr. James P. Bell, Jr., mailed the letters to the Defendant, using certified mail (docket # 157 at page 19), rather than transmitting said letters to a United States District Court pursuant to 28 U.S.C. § 1696 as requested by Plaintiff....

3. As to whether an arbitration award entered by default may be reduced to judgment by an El Salvador court without any notice to the defaulting party, the Special Master concluded that the answer is in the negative. Under the Code of Civil Procedure of El Salvador, when a defendant fails to answer a complaint, judicial proceedings must be held to declare that the defendant is in default. (Docket # 157 at pages 26-27.) The record fails to demonstrate that this procedural step was complied with in the instant case....

In conclusion, the Special Master sets forth the following specific recommendations:

1. The judgment of the court of El Salvador should be denied comity recognition because said judgment was not obtained by complying with the procedural requirements of the law of El Salvador both in the commencing of arbitration proceedings and in reducing the award to judgment.

2. The judgment should also be denied comity recognition because the method of service of process did not comply with the law of El Salvador nor with the law of the State of Florida.

3. The judgment should also be denied comity recognition because the procedures utilized were not consistent with the Due Process Clause of the Fifth Amendment of the United States Constitution and with Article 1, Section 9 of the Florida Constitution....

As set forth in Fed. R. Civ. P. 53, the standard for this Court's review of the Special Master's Findings of Fact is the "clearly erroneous" standard. The Master's factual finding may be disturbed only where the Court, after reviewing the entire evidence, is left with the definite and firm conviction that a mistake has been made, even though there may be some evidence to support the erroneous finding....

The Special Master's Conclusions of Law carry no weight with the Court. [Citations omitted.] Since Plaintiff has challenged the Special Master's Conclusions of Law, this Court is obligated to undertake a sufficient review of the record herein to determine whether the findings are correct. [Citation omitted.] Accordingly, this Court has carefully and thoroughly reviewed the Report and Recommendations as well as pertinent portions of the record herein. Neither in its Memoranda nor at oral argument was Plaintiff able to controvert any specific conclusion of law arrived at by the Special Master. Rather, Plaintiff relied upon general allegations that the Master's conclusions were contrary to the law of El Salvador, the law of the United States and the law of Florida in unspecified respects....

ORDERED AND ADJUDGED as follows: ...

3. The Special Master's Report and Recommendations are hereby ACCEPTED, ADOPTED AND RATIFIED by this Court.

NOTES AND QUESTIONS

1. Professor Merryman favors greater use of court-appointed experts or special masters. What reasons would support this proposal? What reasons argue against it? Which cases in this chapter illustrate your points? The American Academy of Foreign Law was established to improve the use and understanding of foreign law in American legal proceedings, including the use of nonparty sources of foreign law expertise. *See* 22 Int'l Law. 318 (1988). For a more favorable view of party-retained foreign law experts, see Hans W. Baade, *Proving Foreign and International Law in Domestic Tribunals,* 18 Va. J. Int'l L. 619, 640-48 (1978).

2. What are the advantages of a special master over a court-appointed expert witness? Should all cases involving the law of a civil law country be deemed to have an "exceptional condition," as required under Rule 53(b)?

In *Corsal* the special master held two hearings at which party-retained experts testified on the law of El Salvador. Is this permitted under Rule 53? Would it generally be a good idea? *See Roberts v. Heim, supra* Section C, and especially conclusion 4 at the end of the case.

E. RESOLUTION OF FOREIGN LAW ISSUES ON APPEAL

NOTE

Federal Rule 44.1, *supra* Section B, states: "The court's determination shall be treated as a ruling on a question of law." The advisory committee's note declared that since foreign law is to be treated as a legal issue, appellate review should not be confined to the "clearly erroneous" standard of Rule 52(a).

Review the advisory committee's note to Rule 44.1 and the state statutory materials, *supra* Section B, concerning the treatment of foreign law issues on appeal. Ask yourself whether any of the rules permit a foreign law issue to be raised for the first time on appeal.

1. FOREIGN LAW ON APPEAL

RUDOLF B. SCHLESINGER, A RECURRENT PROBLEM IN TRANSNATIONAL LITIGATION: THE EFFECT OF FAILURE TO INVOKE OR PROVE THE APPLICABLE FOREIGN LAW, 59 Cornell Law Review 1, 21-23 (1973)

[F]requently it happens that the parties and the court neglect a decisive foreign law point until after the trial. Perhaps the point is raised by the parties, or discovered by the court, for the first time in connection with a post-trial motion, such as a motion for judgment n.o.v. or for a new trial. Or — and this is not infrequent — the foreign law point turns up for the first time on appeal. Is the point now waived or precluded by lateness?

The answer to this question depends, in the first place, on whether the statute contains a notice requirement, and whether the courts have added teeth (or perhaps dentures) to that requirement. In this respect, the judicial notice statutes differ among each other. On the one hand, there is Federal Rule 44.1, with its express notice requirement, which, at least in the Second Circuit, has been taken so seriously that the foreign law point is dead unless introduced in good time.[109] On the other hand, most of the state statutes (except those patterned after Federal Rule 44.1) either have no notice requirement at all, or provide that the parties' failure to give timely notice does not preclude the court from looking into the foreign law.

This, however, is not a complete answer to the question of preclusion. Even when, as in California and New York and a number of other states, the judicial notice statute itself contains no preclusionary rule, belated resort to the foreign law may be precluded by general principles of procedure. Suppose, for instance, that in a jury case the judge has instructed the jury in accordance with domestic law, and the parties have failed to raise the foreign law issue by timely requests or exceptions. In such a case, it might well be too late to argue on appeal that the judge committed error by charging the jury in accordance with the law of the forum.

Even in a nonjury case, a foreign law issue may be similarly precluded if raised too late. Suppose, for instance, that in an action brought in a state court the complaint alleges invasion of privacy. Although the allegedly tortious acts occurred in Ruritania, where the plaintiff lived at the time, the case is tried on the assumption that it is governed by the law of the forum. After a trial without a jury, the court holds for the plaintiff. On appeal, the defendant for the first time claims that the law of Ruritania controls, and he submits ample materials demonstrating that under the law of that country an invasion of privacy such as shown in this case is not actionable. Even though the forum state's judicial notice statute contains no notice requirement, the point may be precluded. It is true, of course, that pursuant to the classical rule the defendant may at any time, and even for the first time on appeal, point to the legal insufficiency of the complaint. But the classical rule has been changed in a number of states. Under the influence of Federal Rule 12(h), several states

---

[109] *Ruff v. St. Paul Mercury Ins. Co.*, 393 F.2d 500, 502 (2d Cir. 1968).

now provide that after the end of the trial a defendant may no longer attack the sufficiency of the complaint unless he has previously raised the objection.

These preclusionary rules are technical and refined. Suppose that in the hypothetical invasion of privacy case the trial court, although applying domestic law, for some reason had dismissed the complaint, and the plaintiff had appealed. In that event, it might be possible for the defendant, *as appellee,* to urge affirmance on the basis of Ruritanian law. Some cases, at least, seem to suggest this distinction in favor of the appellee.

In many jurisdictions, moreover, there is a more general rule that prohibits the parties, or at least the appellant, from raising new points of any kind for the first time on appeal. True, this rule is applied with considerable flexibility, and it is generally thought that an appellate court, in its discretion, can disregard the rule whenever its strict application would lead to injustice. In spite of its flexibility, however, the rule lurks in the appellate practice of most jurisdictions. A lawyer devising litigation strategy in a foreign law case thus should keep in mind that even under the most liberal judicial notice statute, it may be dangerous to hold a foreign law point in reserve for an eventual appeal.

In any event, in order properly to appraise the consequences of a failure to invoke or prove the applicable foreign law, one must realize that the pertinent common-law rules interact not only with judicial notice statutes but also with other, more general rules of trial and appellate procedure, and that under rules of the latter kind a foreign law point may be precluded unless seasonably raised.

2. STANDARDS OF REVIEW

JOHN G. SPRANKLING & GEORGE R. LANYI, PLEADING AND PROOF OF FOREIGN LAW IN AMERICAN COURTS, 19 Stanford Journal of International Law 3, 89 (1983)

Appeals on questions of foreign law fall into four general categories. First, a party may contend that the court did not apply the law of the correct jurisdiction. This issue can arise as a matter of conflict of laws or on the related matter of presumptions, and includes the question of whether the parties or court properly invoked the foreign law. Second, a party may seek review of the judge's decision to dismiss the action — either with or without prejudice — or to apply local law as a result of inadequate proof of the foreign law. However, determinations about the sufficiency of the materials presented, the taking of judicial notice, and the qualification and credibility of experts are matters within the discretion of the court and in most jurisdictions the judge will be reversed only for an abuse of that discretion. Third, a party may appeal the court's determination of the substance of the foreign law. Finally, a party may seek review of the application of the foreign law to the facts of the case.

When an appeal concerns the interpretation of foreign law, the reviewing court has four options. It can: (1) affirm the construction placed on the foreign law by the lower court; (2) remand the case to the lower court for a new evaluation of the foreign law; (3) redetermine the law based on the materials sent up on appeal; or (4) where judicial notice applies, seek and consider new sources of information to make a *de novo* determination of the foreign law.

QUESTIONS

1. After reading Professor Schlesinger's excerpt, would you hold a foreign law issue in reserve for an eventual appeal?

2. Of the four options facing an appellate court on an interpretation of foreign law (as set out by Sprankling and Lanyi), which would you expect an appellate court to generally choose? Does your choice depend on whether you assume that appellate courts by their nature have superior resources and expertise to determine *legal* issues, while trial courts are organized to primarily deal with factual questions? If an appellate court felt it could not affirm, which of the remaining three options is best designed to promote justice and efficiency?

F. DOMESTIC ENFORCEMENT OF FOREIGN COUNTRY JUDGMENTS

NOTE

We have already seen in Section A of this chapter that an attorney who wishes to serve process on a foreign defendant must at the earliest stage of a lawsuit consider the law of that defendant's country if the plaintiff later must enforce his U.S. judgment there. A similar comparative law inquiry into the judgment enforcement law of another country was also recommended (*supra* Section C) if a plaintiff intends to use U.S. discovery rules to obtain extraterritorial testimony or documents.

In this section we discuss the reciprocal problem: recognition and enforcement of a foreign country judgment in a United States federal or state court. Foreign law issues may again appear concerning, for instance, the finality of the judgment, the impartiality of the tribunal, or the adequacy of the rendering court's subject matter or personal jurisdiction.

Recognition and enforcement often go together, but they are distinct procedural concepts. If a U.S. court precludes litigation of a particular foreign claim because it was previously litigated abroad, and instead relies on the foreign judicial decision, the court recognizes the decree or judgment. *See Panama Processes, S.A. v. Cities Service Co., infra* this section. If the plaintiff further requests that a court use its coercive power to compel the defendant to satisfy the recognized judgment, usually in money damages, the court may enforce the foreign judgment. *See* Uniform Recognition Act § 3, below, and *Ackermann v. Levine, infra* this section.

1. THE UNIFORM RECOGNITION ACT

UNIFORM FOREIGN MONEY-JUDGMENTS RECOGNITION ACT

13 U.L.A. 261, 264-65, 268, 272, 274 (1986)

§ 2. [Applicability]

This Act applies to any foreign judgment[a] that is final and conclusive and enforceable where rendered even though an appeal therefrom is pending or it is subject to appeal.

§ 3. [Recognition and Enforcement]

Except as provided in section 4, a foreign judgment meeting the requirements of section 2 is conclusive between the parties to the extent that it grants or denies recovery of a sum of money. The foreign judgment is enforceable in the same manner as the judgment of a sister state which is entitled to full faith and credit.

§ 4. [Grounds for Non-recognition]

(a) A foreign judgment is not conclusive if

(1) the judgment was rendered under a system which does not provide impartial tribunals or procedures compatible with the requirements of due process of law;

(2) the foreign court did not have personal jurisdiction over the defendant; or

(3) the foreign court did not have jurisdiction over the subject matter.

(b) A foreign judgment need not be recognized if

(1) the defendant in the proceedings in the foreign court did not receive notice of the proceedings in sufficient time to enable him to defend;

(2) the judgment was obtained by fraud;

(3) the [cause of action] [claim for relief] on which the judgment is based is repugnant to the public policy of this state;

(4) the judgment conflicts with another final and conclusive judgment;

(5) the proceeding in the foreign court was contrary to an agreement between the parties under which the dispute in question was to be settled otherwise than by proceedings in that court; or

(6) in the case of jurisdiction based only on personal service, the foreign court was a seriously inconvenient forum for the trial of the action.

---

[a] Section 1(2) reads: "'foreign judgment' means any judgment of a foreign state granting or denying recovery of a sum of money, other than a judgment for taxes, a fine or other penalty, or a judgment for support in matrimonial or family matters."

§ 5. [Personal Jurisdiction]

(a) The foreign judgment shall not be refused recognition for lack of personal jurisdiction if

(1) the defendant was served personally in the foreign state;
(2) the defendant voluntarily appeared in the proceedings, other than for the purpose of protecting property seized or threatened with seizure in the proceedings or of contesting the jurisdiction of the court over him;
(3) the defendant prior to the commencement of the proceedings had agreed to submit to the jurisdiction of the foreign court with respect to the subject matter involved;
(4) the defendant was domiciled in the foreign state when the proceedings were instituted, or, being a body corporate had its principal place of business, was incorporated, or had otherwise acquired corporate status, in the foreign state;
(5) the defendant had a business office in the foreign state and the proceedings in the foreign court involved a [cause of action] [claim for relief] arising out of business done by the defendant through that office in the foreign state; or
(6) the defendant operated a motor vehicle or airplane in the foreign state and the proceedings involved a [cause of action] [claim for relief] arising out of such operation.

(b) The courts of this state may recognize other bases of jurisdiction.

§ 6. [Stay in Case of Appeal]

If the defendant satisfies the court either that an appeal is pending or that he is entitled and intends to appeal from the foreign judgment, the court may stay the proceedings until the appeal has been determined or until the expiration of a period of time sufficient to enable the defendant to prosecute the appeal.

§ 7. [Savings Clause]

This Act does not prevent the recognition of a foreign judgment in situations not covered by this Act.

NIPPON EMO-TRANS CO., LTD. v. EMO-TRANS, INC.

United States District Court, E.D. New York
744 F. Supp. 1215 (1990)

DEARIE, DISTRICT JUDGE.

In this action, plaintiff, Nippon Emo-Trans Co., Ltd. ("NET"), seeks recognition of a judgment it obtained against defendant, EMO-Trans Inc. ("ETI"), in the Tokyo District Court of Japan. Currently before the Court are (i) NET's motion to confirm an attachment pursuant to Sections 6211 and 6212 of the New York Civil Practice Law and Rules [citation omitted], and (ii) ETI's cross-motion to vacate or modify the attachment and to stay this action pursuant to Section 5306 ....

BACKGROUND

NET is a Japanese corporation with its principal operations in Japan; ETI is a New York corporation with its principal place of business in New York City. Since the Court's jurisdiction is based on diversity of citizenship, this action is governed by New York law, including New York principles of conflict of laws. *Klaxon Co. v. Stentor Electric Manufacturing Co.*, 313 U.S. 487, 61 S. Ct. 1020, 85 L. Ed. 1477 (1941).

NET and ETI are freight forwarders; their business involves assembling goods from various sources for shipment, arranging shipment, and arranging to have the shipments broken down and delivered to the ultimate recipient. Between August 1982 and February 1986, NET and ETI had a contractual relationship pursuant to which each would act as the receiving end for shipments assembled by the other. At some point in 1985, a dispute arose as to the allocation of profits between the two companies in connection with freight charges collected from consignees. NET claimed that ETI had failed to remit approximately $354,000 due to NET. ETI claimed that NET's calculation was based on a misinterpretation of the contract.

In June 1986, NET filed an action (the "Japanese Action") in the District Court of Tokyo (the "Tokyo Court"), seeking to recover the money it claimed was owing from ETI. In April 1988, ETI filed a parallel action in this court entitled *Emo-Trans, Inc. v. Nippon Emo-Trans Co., Ltd.*, CV-88-1332 (RJD); that action was stayed pending the outcome of the Japanese Action. In the Japanese Action, ETI initially contested the Tokyo Court's jurisdiction over it; that Court ruled on December 8, 1988, that it had personal jurisdiction over ETI. Thereafter, ETI appeared and defended in Japan. A trial was conducted, and on November 14, 1989, the Tokyo Court issued a decision awarding NET 51,331,204 [yen] (approximately $354,000) plus interest and costs (the "Japanese Judgment"). On November 28, 1989, ETI filed an appeal with the Tokyo High Court; that appeal is pending.

On February 1, 1990, NET commenced the present action by filing an application for an *ex parte* order of attachment which would permit it to attach any property of ETI found in New York, up to a limit of $400,000. The application was granted and the order of attachment was signed on February 2, 1990. In accordance with New York law, NET was required to make a motion to confirm the attachment within five days after levy was first made. Notices of levy were served on various banks and on the Queens County Clerk on February 5, 1990; NET timely moved to confirm the attachment on February 9, 1990.

In order to prevail on the motion to confirm, NET must show (i) that there is a cause of action, (ii) that it is probable that NET will succeed on the merits, (iii) that one or more grounds for attachment exist, (iv) that the amount demanded from ETI exceeds all counterclaims known to NET, and (v) the need for continuing the levy.

In this case, the question whether to confirm the attachment turns on two issues. The first is whether the Tokyo Court had *in personam* jurisdiction over ETI. If so, then a cause of action arises under New York's version of the Uniform Foreign Money-Judgments Recognition Act, N.Y. Civ. Prac. Law & R. §§ 5301-5309 ("Article 53"), NET will probably succeed on the merits (barring a reversal on appeal in Japan), and the Japanese Judgment would provide a basis for the attachment. The second issue is whether there is a need to continue the attachment....

JURISDICTION OF THE TOKYO COURT

ETI asserts that the Tokyo Court did not have *in personam* jurisdiction over it, and that as a result, Section 5304(a)(2) precludes recognition of the Japanese Judgment. ETI argues that (i) because it has preserved its jurisdictional objection in Japan, it did not "voluntarily appear" in Japan within the meaning of Section 5305(a)(2); (ii) none of the other bases of jurisdiction described in Article 53 is applicable in this case; and (iii) the Tokyo Court found that it had jurisdiction on the basis of principles which do not warrant recognition under Article 53. NET responds that ETI has misinterpreted Japanese law; it argues further that by defending on the merits, ETI has, under Article 53, foregone any right to claim that the Tokyo Court did not have jurisdiction. In addition, it asserts that New York courts will recognize the jurisdiction of foreign courts on any basis under which they themselves would be permitted to take jurisdiction. Finally, NET claims that even under more conservative standards, the Tokyo Court could properly have taken jurisdiction.

A. *Background of Article 53*

New York had a long-standing liberal tradition regarding recognition of foreign country judgments prior to the passage of Article 53. In the late 1960's, the Judicial Conference of the State of New York commissioned Professor Barbara Kulzer to conduct a study on the desirability of enacting the Uniform Foreign Money-Judgments Recognition Act (the "Uniform Act"); Professor Kulzer generally supported passage of the Uniform Act, while recommending minor changes to bring the statute closer to New York caselaw.

In 1970, when the Uniform Act was enacted as Article 53, a brief commentary on the bill was included in the *New York State Legislative Annual — 1970*. The commentary indicated that its primary purpose was "to procure for New York judgments in foreign countries much better reciprocal treatment at the hands of foreign courts than they now receive." *Id.* at 10. It indicated further that the legislation was intended to "incorporate [the Uniform Act] in New York law."...

B. *"Voluntary Appearance"*

Although ETI lost its jurisdictional challenge in the Tokyo Court and was ordered to proceed on the merits, it has preserved its jurisdictional objection on appeal in Japan. ETI contends that under Japanese law it is not deemed to have voluntarily appeared, and thus cannot be precluded from raising the jurisdictional issue here under Section 5305(a)(2). NET argues that it is error under Japanese law to equate the notion of preserving an objection on appeal with that of involuntary appearance. The parties support their arguments with affidavits from Japanese attorneys and impressive citations to Japanese legal authorities.

The Court is of the view that it need not decide which of these arguments is correct as a matter of Japanese law, for there is no indication in Section 5305 that the question whether a party has "voluntarily" appeared was intended to turn on the law of another jurisdiction. If anything, Article 53 was meant to simplify the task of a court in determining what effect to give to the judgments of foreign courts, often based on legal principles vastly different from the common-law and constitutional traditions familiar to New York judges and attorneys. To introduce, even potentially, a difficult legal issue requiring the pleading and proof of the law of another jurisdiction would magnify the cost and effort required beyond reasonable bounds. While Japanese law is relevant to the jurisdictional inquiry in other ways, without some firm indication in the statute pointing the Court to the law of the foreign country, it appears eminently more reasonable to view this as a question of New York law.

Of course, New York law also provides that a party who, after losing on a jurisdictional objection, proceeds to defend the merits, will not be deemed to have submitted to the court's jurisdiction by virtue of appearance, unless the jurisdictional objection "is not ultimately sustained."...

(E) *Common-Law Approaches*

(3) *The Tokyo Court's Jurisdictional Ruling*

The Tokyo Court based its assertion of jurisdiction on two factors: first, it found that ETI's duty to remit payments to NET constituted an obligation which was to be performed in Japan; second, it found that ETI had an affiliate in Japan, from which it received assistance in pursuing the lawsuit. The questions of the "place of performance" of ETI's obligation to make payments and the relationship between ETI and its Japanese affiliate are, at best, mixed questions of fact and law. Under these circumstances, the approach outlined above, [described in Restatement (Third) of the Foreign Relations Law of the United States § 482 comment c (1986),] would require a court to look behind the judgment to see if the facts supported the exercise of jurisdiction.

It is clear that neither of the bases of jurisdiction articulated by the Tokyo Court would support jurisdiction under New York law....

Simply because the articulated bases of jurisdiction would have been deemed insufficient under New York law does not lead to the conclusion that the Tokyo Court improperly asserted jurisdiction, however; if ETI's contacts with Japan were sufficiently well-developed to support jurisdiction, there would be little reason to deny recognition to the Japanese Judgment just because the Tokyo Court's stated rationale differed from that which a New York court would follow. In this case, uncontested facts readily lead to the conclusion that, judged by the standards of New York and federal constitutional law, jurisdiction could properly have been asserted in Japan....

(4) *Jurisdiction Under New York Law*

Between 1982 and 1986 ... the president of ETI had been a director of NET, and he had travelled to Japan to help solicit business for both NET and ETI....

There can be no question but that the value of shipments sent by ETI to Japan is "substantial."... In this context, the "substantiality" requirement is satisfied by the gross value of business transacted by ETI in Japan, in excess of half a million dollars annually....

In view of the volume and continuity of activity initiated by ETI and directed toward Japan, the Court concludes that, were it necessary to reexamine the facts to determine whether ETI is amenable to suit in Japan, it would find that, judged by the standards of Section 301, a New York court would conclude that ETI was doing business in Japan on a substantial, continuous and permanent basis, and that as a result the Tokyo Court could properly have asserted jurisdiction over it. In consequence, whether under Section 5305(a)(2) or under common law, NET has demonstrated a probability of success on the question of the Tokyo Court's jurisdiction, and thus on the merits of this action.

THE NEED TO CONTINUE THE ATTACHMENT

It remains to be seen whether NET has demonstrated a need to continue the levy, as required by Sections 6212(a) and 6223(b) of the New York Civil Practice Law & Rules....

The Court concludes that NET has not met its burden of proof regarding the need to continue the attachment; as a result, the motion to confirm is DENIED, and the order of this Court dated February 2, 1990, granting such attachment, is vacated subject to the conditions described in the following section....

STAY PENDING APPEAL IN JAPAN

FIRST, the stay shall take effect only upon ETI's posting a bond for the full amount of the Japanese Judgment, plus a reasonable reserve to cover interest for an eighteen-month period; ETI may, in its discretion, post such bond in this Court or in the appropriate court in Japan; and

SECOND, in order to avoid creating any incentive for "strategic behavior" on ETI's part, the effective time of the vacatur of this Court's order of attachment shall be postponed until such time as ETI posts the bond described above....

Subject to the conditions described herein, (i) the motion for an order confirming the attachment is DENIED, and (ii) the proceedings in this action are hereby STAYED pending the outcome of ETI's appeal of the Japanese Judgment.

NOTES AND QUESTIONS

1. The Uniform Recognition Act of 1962 largely codified existing American common law rules on the recognition and enforcement of foreign country judgments. The usual starting point in most states under the common law approach was the classic dictum from the 1895 United States Supreme Court decision in *Hilton v. Guyot,* 159 U.S. 113 (1895):

> [W]here there has been opportunity for a full and fair trial abroad before a court of competent jurisdiction, conducting the trial upon regular proceedings, after due citation or voluntary appearance of the defendant, and under a system of jurisprudence likely to secure an impartial administration of justice between the citizens of its own country and those of other countries, and there is nothing to show either prejudice in the court, or in the system of laws under which it was sitting, or fraud in procuring the judgment, or any other special reason why the comity of this nation should not allow it full effect, the merits of the case should not, in an action brought in this country upon the judgment, be tried afresh.

Id. at 202-03. The Court also required reciprocity (the foreign court must enforce a U.S. judgment in similar circumstances), but only in the particular situation in which a citizen of the foreign country won a lawsuit against a noncitizen (e.g., American) defendant and brought the judgment to the United States for enforcement. For an illustration of this common law approach, see *De la Mata v. American Life Ins. Co.,* 771 F. Supp. 1375, 1380-90 (D. Del. 1991).

In what ways does the Recognition Act clarify the common law and make an enacting state's law more certain and predictable? What does it omit from *Hilton*? Which elements are clearly new? The Act has been substantially adopted in 22 states, but five of these states (including Georgia, Massachusetts, Ohio, and Texas) added lack of reciprocity as a discretionary (Georgia as a mandatory) ground for nonrecognition.

2. Section 4 of the Recognition Act divides grounds for nonrecognition into mandatory and permissive grounds. Does the distinction seem reasonable as implemented?

3. Does the federal district court in *Nippon Emo-Trans Co.* use federal or New York state rules for recognition of foreign country judgments? Why? Should distinctively federal rules exist for service of process and discovery abroad and for pleading, proof, and appeal of foreign law issues, but not for recognition and enforcement of foreign country judgments? What is the distinguishing factor?

4. In *Nippon Emo-Trans Co.* the central issue concerned the Tokyo court's personal jurisdiction over the defendant, ETI. Must the plaintiff NET show that in sections 4(a)(2) and 5 (sections 5304(a)(2) and 5305 in New York) of the Recognition Act the Tokyo court had personal jurisdiction under both Japanese law and New York law?

Does the Recognition Act permit a stay of the enforcement proceedings under the circumstances in this case?

5. Review *Corsal v. Injection Footwear Corp., supra* Section D, where the plaintiff attempted to enforce its judgment from El Salvador in the Miami federal district court. Florida has not enacted the Uniform Recognition Act. How would you analyze *Corsal* under the *Hilton* dictum and under section 4 of the Recognition Act? Would the federal court have been correct in denying plaintiff's enforcement claim?

2. THE PUBLIC POLICY DEFENSE AND OTHER DEFENSES

ACKERMANN v. LEVINE

United States Court of Appeals, Second Circuit
788 F.2d 830 (1986)

PIERCE, CIRCUIT JUDGE:

This is an appeal from a judgment and final order of the United States District Court for the Southern District of New York, Irving Ben Cooper, *Judge,* entered May 20, 1985, 610 F. Supp. 633, following an enforcement proceeding, holding unenforceable the default judgment issued by the Regional Court of Berlin in West Germany on December 12, 1980 in favor of plaintiffs and against defendant for 190,708.49 deutschemarks (DM), or approximately $100,000, plus interest, for legal fees allegedly owed by appellee....

BACKGROUND

Peter R. Ackermann is a German citizen practicing law in West Berlin in the appellant law firm. Ira Levine is an American citizen engaged in the real estate business in New York, where he lives, and New Jersey, where he was the general partner of a limited partnership entitled Hudson View Associates in 1979, and at all pertinent times herein. In the spring of 1979, Levine was considering financing, developing and selling a proposed real estate project in Edgewater, New Jersey (the Edgewater Project). The total cost of the completed project was estimated at approximately $21 million, of which Levine's interest was approximately $6 million. In May of 1979, Levine was introduced to Gottlieb Bauer Schlictegroll ("Bauer"), a West German business promoter en route from Costa Rica to West Germany via New York, and Walter Pfaeffle, a friend of Bauer and a West German journalist living in New York whom Bauer introduced to Levine as a "financial consultant." Bauer informed Levine that he knew potential German investors, including Peter Kuth. At a meeting at the Regency Hotel in New York, Levine gave to Bauer financial documents and written specifications of Edgewater Towers. It was agreed that Levine would pay Bauer a $600,000 commission if he raised the needed capital. The district court found that Bauer was "a devious opportunist ...."

Later in May, 1979, Levine received two telephone calls involving the potential interest of a German investment group called the Titan Group. Levine then visited Frederic Coudert, Esq., of the international law firm of Coudert Brothers, in New York, and asked if Mr. Coudert could represent him in West Germany. When Coudert replied that he did not have an office in West Berlin, Levine said, "I do not wish to go to Germany and sit down and hopefully sign a contract without any type of representation." Coudert then recommended three West Berlin law firms, including that of Ackermann.

In late May or early June, 1979, Levine went to West Berlin, with Coudert's list of firms, to talk with Kuth. Bauer met Levine at the airport and explained that Kuth was unavailable. Bauer suggested that Levine talk to Bauer's attorney and friend, Peter Ackermann. Noting the coincidence that Ackermann was affiliated with one of Coudert's recommendees, Levine met with Bauer and Ackermann....

It is undisputed that the parties never discussed attorneys fees or the nature of their relationship. Ackermann testified, however, that Levine told him that he had been referred to Ackermann by the Coudert firm. The district court found "that the parties discussed, in general terms only, tax shelter schemes — a plan that benefitted both Mr. Ackermann, who wanted to develop this approach, and Mr. Levine, who stood to gain financially from a German purchaser." The court also found that while there was no agreement for Ackermann to begin talks with any bank, it was resolved that Levine, Bauer and an accountant would commence talks with the Grundkreditbank in West Berlin. This conversation at the bank immediately followed the meeting with Ackermann, and was conducted entirely in German, which Levine apparently does not speak....

On June 8, 1979, Levine wrote to Ackermann, stating:

Ackerman & Shuetze-Zeu
Kampftrasse 13
1 Berlin 12
Attn: Peter Ackerman

Dear Peter:

I am very pleased to address this letter to you regarding our real estate project in Edgewater, New Jersey.

I wish to authorize your firm to negotiate this matter in the behalf of Hudson View Associates and I am looking forward to a successful completion of these negotiations.

Sincerely,
Ira Levine,
General Partner
Hudson View Associates

The district court found Ackermann to be a "moral, upright 'officer of the Court,'" [citation omitted], who reasonably believed that Levine wanted him to structure the deal as part of his duties in negotiating with the bank, rather than to act as a real estate broker, which Judge Cooper found lawyers may not lawfully do in Germany. *Id.*

On June 14, 1979, Ackermann sent Levine the following telex:

6/14/79 2:30 p.m.
att: mr. ira levine
re: edgewater towers

dear ira,

during a 2 hour session i have presented this project to the president of grundkreditbank and his two directors.

> they have qualified your offer as 'very interesting' but too large to handle on their own.
>
> they will attempt to convince another bank in frankfurt to run this as a joint venture. appropriate contacts will be made tomorrow.
>
> in the event that the frankfurt bank — which has not yet been disclosed — shows serious interest, do you want me to negotiate the project with them?
>
> best regards,
> peter r. ackermann

Levine testified that he then called Ackermann, disappointed that the original proposal to the Grundkreditbank was rejected, and that in response to the question in Ackermann's letter, he said, "That's up to you."

On June 21, 1979, Ackermann went to Frankfurt to present the deal to the second bank. That effort failed....

Ackermann testified before Judge Cooper that by the end of July he had spent fifteen to twenty full working days on the project. However, Ackermann stated in a deposition that neither he nor his firm had prepared any written studies or formal memoranda, and that he did not believe that his files would contain any handwritten notes regarding the project....

On October 22, 1979, Ackermann sent his bill for legal services to Levine. The fees were computed in accordance with the German legal fee statute called Bundesrechtsanwaltsgebuehrenordnung, or BRAGO. Under the statute, each legal step taken in an action constitutes a fee unit which in turn is converted into a price that reflects both the value of the legal questions or financial transaction and the percentage (from 50 to 100%) of the total fee unit that the attorney decides to charge.[3] As most German lawyers do in non-litigation work, Ackermann charged Levine 75% of the allowable fee units. Ackermann's letter itemized the bill in two main parts: 89,347.50 DM for studies and client counseling, and the same for discussions with banks.

On January 11, 1980, suit was initiated herein to recover legal fees when the German court sent a summons and complaint to the German Consulate in New York, which mailed them by registered mail to Levine's former New Jersey address. Although a receipt postmarked March 13, 1980, was received, Levine claims that he never received such process. A second summons and complaint was sent by the same method to Levine's Manhattan apartment, and was received by a building employee, Ortiz; the receipt was postmarked October 14, 1980. Levine acknowledges receipt of the summons and complaint and actual knowledge of the suit. Indeed, Levine testified that on at least one occasion before judgment was entered, he consulted with Frederic Coudert, Esq. about the suit, and he decided to ignore it. A default judgment was entered on December 12, 1980....

Plaintiffs commenced an action seeking enforcement of the foreign judgment in the United States District Court for the Southern District of New

[3] The attorney may also charge more than the value of a fee unit if he has the client's written consent.

York on February 8, 1982. Levine appeared and the matter was tried to the court....

DISCUSSION

We are confronted here with issues relating to the recognition and enforcement of a foreign judgment in a case involving attorney-client relations in an international business context. The district court appropriately framed the issues in accordance with the well-settled rule that a final judgment obtained through sound procedures in a foreign country is generally conclusive as to its merits *unless* (1) the foreign court lacked jurisdiction over the subject matter or the person of the defendant; (2) the judgment was fraudulently obtained; or (3) enforcement of the judgment would offend the public policy of the state in which enforcement is sought....

I

To be subject to *in personam* jurisdiction,[5] a defendant must have had certain "minimum contacts" with the forum state.... We agree with the district court that under the "minimum contacts" test of *International Shoe* and its progeny, Levine had sufficient contacts with West Germany such that he was "avail[ing] himself" of the privileges arising therein....

Service of process must satisfy both the statute under which service is effectuated and constitutional due process.[7] The statutory prong is governed principally by the Hague Convention on the Service Abroad of Judicial and Extrajudicial Documents in Civil or Commercial Matters (Hague Convention)....

The service of process by registered mail did not violate the Hague Convention. Plaintiffs declined to follow the service route allowed under Article 5 of the Convention, which permits service via a "Central Authority" of the country in which service is to be made. Instead, plaintiffs chose to follow the equally acceptable route allowed under Articles 8 and 10. [Citation omitted.] Article 8 permits each contracting state "to effect service of judicial documents upon persons abroad ... directly through its diplomatic or consular agents." The Regional Court of Berlin availed itself of this method by first sending the summons and complaint to the German Consulate in New York. As to the forwarding of those documents by registered mail from the Consulate to Levine's residence, the method of service was appropriate under Article 10(a), which states in pertinent part:

> Article 10 — Provided the State of destination does not object, the present Convention shall not interfere with —

---

[5] As to the issue of subject matter jurisdiction, which appellee does not contest, this case arose under the district court's diversity jurisdiction. The Regional Court of Berlin apparently had jurisdiction in Germany to hear actions arising under the BRAGO statute.

[7] Defendant-appellee also argues that service violated service of process laws of West Germany. [S]ince foreign law is to be determined by the court, in light of both evidence admitted and the court's own research and interpretation, see Fed. R. Civ. P. 44.1, [an earlier case] did not preclude Judge Cooper or this court, upon review, from finding that, under the evidence presented herein, service did not violate current German law.

(a) the freedom to send judicial documents, by postal channels, directly to persons abroad....

Since the United States has made no objection to the use of "postal channels" under Article 10(a), service of process by registered mail remains an appropriate method of service in this country under the Convention....

Nor was service ineffective because it did not satisfy the Federal Rules of Civil Procedure. The old Federal Rule 4 was superseded by the Hague Convention and thus presumptively should not limit application of the Convention.... Thus, the Convention "supplements" — and is manifestly *not* limited by — Rule 4....

Finally, service by registered mail does not violate constitutional due process. *See Mullane v. Central Hanover Bank & Trust Co.,* 339 U.S. 306, 314, 70 S. Ct. 652, 657, 94 L. Ed. 865 (1950) (due process permits service of process by mail so long as such service provides "notice reasonably calculated ... to provide interested parties notice of the pendency of the action")....

III

The district court held that, based on the undisputed fact that Ackermann never discussed fees with Levine, the German judgment was rendered unenforceable as violative of New York's public policy that "the attorney, not the client, must ensure the fairness, reasonableness and full comprehension by the client of their compensation agreement."...

A judgment is unenforceable as against public policy to the extent that it is "repugnant to fundamental notions of what is decent and just in the State where enforcement is sought."... In the classic formulation, a judgment that "tends clearly" to undermine the public interest, the public confidence in the administration of the law, or security for individual rights of personal liberty or of private property is against public policy. *See Somportex v. Philadelphia Chewing Gum,* 453 F.2d 435, 443 (3d Cir. 1971), *cert. denied,* 405 U.S. 1017, 92 S. Ct. 1294, 31 L. Ed. 2d 479 (1972) (quoting *Goodyear v. Brown,* 55 Pa. 514, 26 A. 665, 666 (1893)); *see also, Loucks v. Standard Oil Co.,* 224 N.Y. 99, 110, 120 N.E. 198 (1918) (Cardozo, J.) (vested rights may be withheld when "the cause of action in its nature offends our sense of justice or menaces the public welfare").

The narrowness of the public policy exception to enforcement would seem to reflect an axiom fundamental to the goals of comity and res judicata that underlie the doctrine of recognition and enforcement of foreign judgments. As Judge Cardozo so lucidly observed: "We are not so provincial as to say that every solution of a problem is wrong because we deal with it otherwise at home." *Loucks,* 224 N.Y. at 110-11. Further, the narrowness of the public policy exception indicates a jurisprudential compromise between two guiding but sometimes conflicting principles in the law of recognition and enforcement of foreign judgments: (1) res judicata [citations omitted], and (2) fairness to litigants [citation omitted], or fairness regarding the underlying transaction [citation omitted].

The question presented here involves the extent to which local public policy will permit recognition and enforcement of a foreign default judgment. Since a foreign default judgment is not more or less conclusive but "*as* conclusive an adjudication" as a contested judgment, *Somportex,* 453 F.2d at 442-43 & n. 13 (citing authority) (emphasis added), the district court quite properly afforded Levine the same opportunity to contest the enforceability of the German judgment in light of the public policy issue.[12]...

However, we believe that the district court erred in holding that the failure of German law regarding attorneys fees to meet our more rigorous principles of fiduciary duties sufficiently offended local public policy as to justify nonenforcement of the entire judgment, and thus total vitiation of the values of comity and res judicata that enforcement would promote. We so hold in light of the consistency with which *stare decisis* has followed Judge Cardozo's maxim, *Loucks,* 224 N.Y. at 110-11, 120 N.E. 198, that mere variance with local public policy is not sufficient to decline enforcement.

The narrow public policy exception to enforcement is not met merely because Ackermann did not inform Levine of the BRAGO billing statute. [Citation omitted.] Nor is the exception met in the event that Ackermann's bill should exceed the amount which American lawyers might reasonably have charged. *See Somportex,* 453 F.2d at 443 (exception not met where a British default judgment of $94,000 against an American defendant to a contract action included in substantial part damages for loss of good will and for attorneys fees and other costs, none of which would be awarded by Pennsylvania, the state in which enforcement was granted). Certainly it is not enough merely that Germany provides a billing scheme by statute rather than by contractual arrangements subject to an attorney's fiduciary duties. We note that even New York policy permits statute-based billing systems in certain instances....

We hold that the public policy that charges an American lawyer with ensuring fair and reasonable compensation, fully disclosed to and understood by the client, does not warrant nonenforcement of the German judgment, given that there was no finding of "fraud, overreaching or bad faith" on the part of Ackermann, the foreign lawyer, *cf. Spann,* 131 F.2d at 611, and that Levine, the American client, was a sophisticated business person with access to competent American international legal counsel....

We hold that the applicable theory of public policy requires that recovery of attorneys fees be predicated on evidence of, at a minimum, (1) the existence of some authorization by the client for the attorney to perform the work allegedly performed [citations omitted], and (2) the very existence of that work [citation omitted]. These evidentiary predicates, we hold, constitute the *sine qua non* of a client's liability for legal fees. Without these predicates, there is a grave risk that American courts could become the means of enforcing uncon-

[12] Under the Uniform Foreign Judgments Recognition Act, 13 U.L.A. 417 (1980), which New York has adopted, *see* N.Y.C.P.L.R. §§ 5301-5309 (McKinney's 1986), a plaintiff seeking enforcement of a foreign country judgment granting or denying recovery of a sum of money must establish *prima facie:* (1) a final judgment, conclusive and enforceable where rendered; (2) subject matter jurisdiction; (3) jurisdiction over the parties or the *res;* and (4) regular proceedings conducted under a system that provides impartial tribunals and procedures compatible with due process. These requirements approximate those required at common law. *See, e.g., Hilton v. Guyot,* 159 U.S. 113, 16 S. Ct. 139, 40 L. Ed. 95 (1895). [Citation omitted.] A defendant may then raise, e.g., fraud and public policy.

scionable attorney fee awards, thereby endangering "public confidence" in the administration of the law and a "sense of security for individual rights ... of private property." *Somportex,* 453 F.2d at 443. Further, to forsake this fundamental public policy would impose upon American citizens doing business abroad an undue risk in dealing with foreign counsel — a result that, ironically, could undermine the very processes of transnational legal relations that the doctrines of comity and res judicata seek to promote....

In applying this evidentiary-based public policy, we note that courts are not limited to recognizing a judgment entirely or not at all. Where a foreign judgment contains discrete components, the enforcing court should endeavor to discern the appropriate "extent of recognition," *cf.* 18 C. Wright & A. Miller, Federal Practice and Procedure § 4473, at 745 (1981), with reference to applicable public policy concerns.

Ackermann has laid the predicate in support of his bill for "detailed discussions with prospective buyers" and for the related travel and office expenses, but he has not done so for the "basic fee for the study of the project files, [and] discussion with client and his counsel."...

As to the fifteen to twenty days of work that comprise the bulk of the "basic fee for study of the project files," the record reflects no evidence of an authorization to do such work or of the existence of any work product....

IV. CONCLUSION

This case involved an unfortunate disagreement between parties of different countries and legal cultures. As the district court found, both parties behaved honorably, and their dispute was born of mutual mistake. Although the defendant chose to default in a German action commenced by valid service of process, he did not thereby waive his right to contest the enforceability of the foreign judgment on grounds of public policy. The increasing internationalization of commerce requires "that American courts recognize and respect the judgments entered by foreign courts to the greatest extent consistent with our own ideals of justice and fair play." [Citation omitted.] In light of that important imperative, we hold the German judgment to be enforceable in all respects except for the first item of DM 89,347.50 for the "[b]asic fee for the study of project files, discussion with client and his counsel," for which there was no evidence of authorization or of work product. The judgment of the district court is accordingly affirmed in part and reversed in part, and the cause is remanded to the district court for entry of an order not inconsistent with this opinion.

QUESTIONS

1. Is Judge Pierce in *Ackermann v. Levine* using federal or New York state rules for recognition and enforcement of the German judgment? Would it be constitutional for federal courts to develop a uniform, national federal common law standard for the recognition and enforcement of foreign country judgments? Would it be desirable?

2. How does the service of process issue in *Ackermann* relate to the personal jurisdiction issue? What is this relationship under the Uniform Recognition Act? Must the plaintiff show that service was valid under both German law and United States law? For the latter are we concerned with federal or New York state law? See *supra* Section A.

3. How broad is the public policy exception to the enforcement of foreign country judgments? Did the court in *Ackermann* use an "evidentiary-based public policy" rule to readjudicate the merits of plaintiff's underlying claim? Is this desirable? In default judgment suits? In attorney fee recovery suits?

PANAMA PROCESSES, S.A. v. CITIES SERVICE CO.

Supreme Court of Oklahoma
796 P.2d 276 (1990)

OPALA, VICE CHIEF JUSTICE.

The appeal presents four issues for decision: [1] Did the district court err in recognizing a prior Brazilian declaratory judgment? [2] Does Brazilian law apply to the issue whether a majority stockholder owes a fiduciary duty to a minority stockholder? and if so [3] Does Brazil's Civil Law system recognize that majority stockholders owe a fiduciary duty to minority stockholders? and [4] Does Brazilian law permit an individual stockholder's suit against a majority stockholder for breach of a statutory duty? We answer the first, third and fourth questions in the negative and the second in the affirmative.

THE ANATOMY OF LITIGATION

This is an appeal from summary judgment rendered for the defendant, Cities Service Company [Cities], and against the plaintiff, Panama Processes, S.A. [Panama]. The dispute involves a Brazilian corporation, Companhia Petroquimica Brasileira-Copebras [Copebras]. Before 1965 Copebras had three shareholders: Panama, Columbian Carbon Company [Columbian] and Celanese Corporation [Celanese]. Columbian is Cities' predecessor in interest and a wholly owned subsidiary of Cities. Celanese advised Panama and Columbian in 1965 that it wanted to sell its Copebras stock. To accomplish this purpose Panama and Cities agreed that Copebras would redeem the Celanese-owned stock and retire its interest. This redemption effectively reduced the number of shareholders from three to two, with Cities owning 70% and Panama 30% of Copebras stock. As a precondition to the transaction, Panama wanted Cities to provide certain assurances concerning Copebras' future dividend, expansion and board representation policies. Negotiations then occurred in New York between Panama's representative and Cities' counsel, which resulted in a September 7, 1965 letter of agreement outlining these assurances.[2] The day after the letter was signed, Panama executed an agreement for the purchase and retirement of the Celanese-owned shares in Copebras.

---

[2]The September 7, 1965 letter from Columbian Carbon Company to Panama Processes, S.A., states as follows:

Gentlemen:

In the event Columbian Carbon Company, (Columbian) [Cities' predecessor in interest] attains a majority position in the stock interest of Companhia Petroquimica Brasileira (Copebras), you as a minority shareholder have expressed your concern as to the dividend policy Columbian would adopt.

It must be recognized that future policy of this kind may be affected by the industrial, fiscal, and political situation in Brazil, and that the corporate objectives and competitive position of Copebras may change from time to time.

Prior New York Federal Litigation

In 1973, after Copebras announced its intention to enter into transactions that would restrict dividend payments and after Cities advised Panama that it no longer considered the 1965 letter binding, Panama sued Cities in federal court,[3] seeking a declaratory judgment that the letter was a binding contract. The claim was dismissed because the relief Panama sought was inconclusive.

Six years later Panama again sued Cities in federal court, alleging breach of the letter agreement and of a fiduciary duty owed by a majority to a minority shareholder.[5] The court dismissed the suit on grounds of *forum non conveniens* upon Cities' consent to accept service of process in Brazil and to contest Panama's claims on the merits.

The Present State and Concurrent Brazilian Litigation

Panama commenced this action against Cities in 1981 on two theories of liability — breach of contract and breach of fiduciary duty — in the District Court, Tulsa County. The trial court in 1982 denied Cities' motion to dismiss on grounds of *forum non conveniens*. Cities then unsuccessfully sought on the same grounds a writ of prohibition in the Oklahoma Supreme Court. In 1983, while the Oklahoma action was still pending, Cities, along with Copebras and three wholly-owned Cities subsidiary companies, filed a declaratory judgment action in Brazil against Panama and its Brazilian subsidiary. The Brazilian trial court held itself competent over Panama's objections that (a) the place of performance of the 1965 letter was to be Oklahoma and (b) an action was pending in an Oklahoma court concerning the same letter. The Brazilian court rendered judgment for the plaintiffs in 1984, holding that the letter was unenforceable.[13] The appellate court affirmed this decision.[14]

It is definitely the intention of Columbian after due consideration of the above factors to cause Copebras to declare dividends, insofar as it may legally do so, to the extent of at least 50% of each year's net income after taxes.

Any declaration or omission of dividend will be voted only after full consultation and, if possible, agreement with all minority shareholders....

Very truly yours,
WITNESS: COLUMBIAN CARBON COMPANY
__________ By ____________________
Executive Vice President

ACCEPTED and AGREED TO:
This 8th day of September, 1965.
WITNESS: PANAMA PROCESSES, S.A.
__________ By ____________________

[3] *Panama Processes, S.A. v. Cities Service Co.*, 362 F. Supp. 735 [S.D.N.Y. 1973], affirmed 496 F.2d 533 [2d Cir. 1974].

[5] *Panama Processes, S.A. v. Cities Service Co.*, 500 F. Supp. 787 [S.D.N.Y. 1980], affirmed 650 F.2d 408 [2d Cir. 1981].

[13] The Brazilian trial court based its decision on the following grounds: (1) the purposes of the 1965 letter agreement were illegal under Brazilian law in that it required dividend payment of a certain percentage of profits and of cumulative dividends to a holder of common stock, and in that it contravenes Copebras' interests; (2) changes in Brazil's fiscal and political situation occurring after the signing of the letter caused the letter to lapse under its own terms and (3) even assuming the 1965 letter agreement was valid and had not lapsed, since it was for an indeterminate term it could be, and was, effectively terminated by Cities' 1973 letter.

[14] Panama's request for an "extraordinary appeal" to the Brazilian Federal Supreme Court was denied.

Cities then moved for partial summary adjudication in the Tulsa trial court on the breach of contract theory, asserting that the Brazilian judgment should be recognized and enforced and that the *res judicata* doctrine bars relitigation of Panama's breach of contract theory, which had been fully and fairly litigated in the Brazilian court. On January 18, 1988 the district court sustained Cities' motion on the basis of comity. The following July it gave summary judgment to Cities on both of Panama's theories of liability. The decision on the status-based prong of the dispute ... rested on several grounds: (1) Brazilian law applies to this issue; (2) neither Brazilian Corporation Law [Code] nor any other Brazilian law creates a fiduciary obligation of majority to minority shareholders; (3) any recovery for abuse of majority shareholder power must be sought under Article 246 and in accordance with Articles 116 and 117 of the Brazilian Corporation Law; and (4) an action pursuant to these provisions is derivative, thus a shareholder has no individual cause of action under Brazil's Corporation Law for damages suffered by it as a shareholder.

I

The Brazilian Judgment Is Entitled to Recognition

The full faith and credit clause of the United States Constitution does not extend to foreign nation judgments, but state courts have the power to recognize them. The present trend in the United States clearly favors recognition of foreign nation judgments. Strong policies support recognition, such as the protection of party expectations, prevention of harassment of one party by the other, conservation of judicial resources and promotion of consistency and uniformity of law.

This trend parallels the Restatement (Second) of Conflict of Laws § 98, which states that

> [a] valid judgment[21] rendered in a foreign nation after a fair trial in a contested proceeding will be recognized in the United States so far as the immediate parties and the underlying cause of action are concerned.

A

The Public Policy Defense

Panama argues that the Oklahoma court's assertion of jurisdiction over this case precluded the Brazilian court from simultaneously hearing the declaratory judgment action. It further asserts that the May 19, 1983 denial of Cities' general and special demurrers to its two theories of recovery is a final adjudication of the enforceability and validity of the 1965 agreement and operates to bar relitigation of that issue by the trial court. Recognizing the Brazilian

[21] The Oklahoma legislature has adopted the Uniform Foreign Judgments Recognition Act, 12 O.S. 1981 §§ 710 *et seq.* Although the act does not apply here because the Brazilian judgment was not one "granting or denying recovery of a sum of money" (§ 710(2)), § 716 provides that "this act does not prevent the recognition of a foreign judgment in situations not covered by this act."

judgment under these circumstances, Panama argues, would violate the public policy of Oklahoma.

A foreign-country judgment may be denied recognition when it is contrary to the crucial public policies of the forum in which enforcement is requested. This rule concedes that a state is not required to give effect to foreign judicial proceedings grounded on policies which do violence to its own fundamental interests. In the Restatement (Second) of Conflict of Laws, Comment c, the drafters explain that the original claim must not be "repugnant to the fundamental notions of what is decent and just in the State where enforcement is sought." The standard for refusing to enforce judgments on public policy grounds is narrow in scope; the present trend has been to recognize this defense only in exceptional cases. We find no basis here for invoking a public policy defense to preclude recognition of the Brazilian judgment.

Under the doctrine of res judicata, only terminal judicial rulings — whether they be judgments or postjudgment dispositions — are given preclusive effect. A prejudgment order that overrules or sustains a demurrer to a pleading under the pre-1984 Oklahoma pleading regime does not bear the attributes of a complete and final disposition entitled to res judicata effect.

The principle of concurrent jurisdiction applies here. Where a similar controversy between the same parties is pending in separate jurisdictions, each forum is generally free to proceed to a judgment. The first final judgment would be res judicata as to issues that were or could have been raised in that action. The important principles of comity compel deference and mutual respect for concurrent foreign proceedings. Because the Brazilian court's final judgment was the first to be rendered, it is conclusive as to the underlying cause of action and will be accorded res judicata effect....

Even if the Brazilian court had misperceived the choice-of-law doctrine, that would not create an infirmity in the court's power. The Brazilian judgment cannot be made vulnerable for legal error in the application of law; it is assailable, if at all, only for a defect in jurisdiction....

C
The Due Process Argument

Panama also attacks the Brazilian legal system on due process grounds. Our attention is directed to certain "due process deficiencies" in the "judicial process and procedures" of the Brazilian courts which operate as a defense against recognition of a foreign nation judgment. Panama asserts that in Brazil: (1) no witnesses of any party may be subpoenaed, (2) testimony of corporate employees is inadmissible, (3) there is no available process for requiring testimony of indispensable U.S. witnesses; (4) there is no right of cross-examination, and (5) the parties may neither conduct pre-trial discovery nor subpoena documents. Panama does not contend that it failed to receive full and fair notice or that it was not given the opportunity to be heard in the Brazilian court.

This argument, rather than having its basis in a denial of due process, actually rests on the procedural differences between United States and Brazilian courts.[35] Although Brazilian norms of procedure differ from ours, that is not a basis for their condemnation as falling short of the minimum due process standards in the Anglo-American sense....

III

Breach of Duty "Claim" Under Brazilian Law

Lastly, we must determine whether the trial court erred in rendering judgment for Cities on the statutory breach of duty prong.

A

The Statutory Duty Theory Did Not Survive the Res Judicata Effect of the Brazilian Judgment

Panama asserts that Cities *qua* controlling shareholder of a Brazilian corporation breached the duties and obligations owed by it under both the 1965 contract and Articles 116 and 117 of Brazil's Corporation Law. Because these theories of recovery are predicated on the same alleged conduct of Cities, it follows that the contractual obligations are identical to those imposed by Brazilian law on a controlling shareholder.

Assuming the duties are the same, this fact could have been tendered by Panama as another defensive theory in the Brazilian litigation because a declaration of the contract's invalidity would not relieve Cities of its statutory duties. In other words, Panama could have defended against the quest for rescission by showing that it would not result in any effective relief.

The Brazilian judgment is a complete claim-preclusion bar to this theory because res judicata in the Anglo-American sense bars not only the defensive theories actually interposed therein, but any defenses that could have been raised in that action. Panama failed to urge, in the Brazilian lawsuit, the defense of Cities' statutory duties and is hence barred from pressing this theory as the basis of a second action involving the same subject matter and the same parties.

Assuming as a matter of comity that preference would be given to Brazilian law in determining the preclusive effect of the judgment,[70] we must still apply here the domestic law of res judicata. This is so because we are without the benefit of proof as to the scope of Brazil's res judicata jurisprudence and must conclude that its outer limit is the same as our own.

B

Brazilian Law Does Not Recognize a Duty Owed by a Majority to a Minority Stockholder

Even if this theory had survived the preclusive effect of the Brazilian judgment, we would still conclude there was no error in the trial judge's determi-

---

[35] Panama made a general appearance in the Brazilian court, thus waiving any defense it may have asserted for lack of notice.

[70] Once a foreign-nation judgment has been recognized, some American courts, *on the basis of comity,* have given a foreign judgment the same effect to which it is entitled in the jurisdiction where rendered. [Citations omitted.] By way of limitation, most courts have refused to give foreign-country judgments any greater force or effect than that afforded to sister-state judgments.

nation that Brazilian law does not permit an individual stockholder's claim against a controlling shareholder for breach of statutory duty.

[The supreme court then reviewed the trial court's judicial notice of Brazilian civil and corporation law under 12 Okla. Stats. §§ 2201 and 2203, reprinted *supra* Section B, and concluded that the trial court had correctly resolved the foreign law issues.]

[CONCLUSION]

In sum, we recognize the Brazilian judgment for reasons of practicality, fairness and policy and because no defense has been shown for not according it res judicata effect as to the breach of contract theory of recovery. Brazilian law is applicable to the breach of duty theory because (1) the fiduciary duty arises out of the agreement, (2) the agreement was to be performed in Brazil and (3) application of Oklahoma or New York law would be in sharp conflict with Brazil's legal tradition. Panama cannot recover under the breach of duty prong because a fiduciary duty is not recognized under Brazil's civil law system and its statutory law does not permit an individual stockholder's action for damages.

The trial court's judgment is affirmed.

[Four justices concurred in Justice Opala's opinion, one concurred in part and dissented in part, one concurred in the judgment, and two dissented.]

NOTES AND QUESTIONS

1. From the cases in this section can you derive the policies supporting the doctrine of comity? What additional policies support the enforcement of foreign country judgments? Note that the Panama Processes and Cities Service litigation began in 1973 and employed attorneys in New York federal courts, Oklahoma state courts, and Brazilian courts for almost 20 years.

2. Oklahoma has adopted the Uniform Recognition Act. Why does it not directly apply to *Panama Processes*? Does the Act's inapplicability seem to affect Justice Opala's analysis of the recognition claim?

3. The defendant in *Panama Processes* argued the public policy defense as did the defendant in *Ackermann*. Did the Oklahoma Supreme Court take a narrower or broader view of the exception than the federal court in *Ackermann*?

4. In granting recognition of the Brazilian judgment, did the court in *Panama Processes* give it effect under the res judicata law of Brazil or Oklahoma? If this should be a foreign law issue, is it appropriate to presume that foreign law is the same as local law? See *supra* Section B.

5. Practical commentary on the enforcement of foreign country judgments in the United States includes: Annotation, *Judgment of Court of Foreign Country as Entitled to Enforcement or Extraterritorial Effect in State Court,* 13 A.L.R.4th 1109 (1982); Gary B. Born & David Westin, International Civil Litigation in United States Courts: Commentary and Materials, ch. 9 (1989); Ronald A. Brand, *Enforcement of Foreign Money-Judgments in the United States: In Search of Uniformity and International Acceptance,* 67 Notre Dame

L. Rev. 253 (1991); Werner F. Ebke & Mary E. Parker, *Foreign Country Money Judgments and Arbitral Awards and the Restatement (Third) of the Foreign Relations Law of the United States: A Conventional Approach,* 24 Int'l Law. 21 (1990); Robert E. Lutz, *Enforcement of Foreign Judgments, Part I: A Selected Bibliography on United States Enforcement of Judgments Rendered Abroad,* 27 Int'l Law. 471 (1993); Ved P. Nanda & David K. Pansius, Litigation of International Disputes in U.S. Courts, ch. 11 (1990); Eugene F. Scoles & Peter Hay, Conflict of Laws 996-1018 (2d ed. 1992).

For a comparative view of the enforcement issue, see Ulla Jacobsson & Jack Jacob, eds., Trends in the Enforcement of Non-money Judgments and Orders: The First International Colloquium on the Law of Civil Procedure (1988); Friedrich K. Juenger, *The Recognition of Money Judgments in Civil and Commercial Matters,* 36 Am. J. Comp. L. 1 (1988); Robert E. Lutz, *Enforcement of Foreign Judgments, Part II: A Selected Bibliography on Enforcement of U.S. Judgments in Foreign Countries,* 27 Int'l Law. 1029 (1993); Charles Platto & William Horton, eds., Enforcement of Foreign Judgments Worldwide (2d ed. 1993); Philip R. Weems, ed., Enforcement of Money Judgments Abroad (1992).

Chapter 3

THE CIVIL LAW TRADITION IN EUROPE BEFORE THE REVOLUTION

We now begin an examination of those historical components of the civil law tradition that are essential to an understanding of the contemporary civil law systems of Europe, Latin America, and East Asia.

In this chapter we consider Roman law, canon law, and commercial law. Since the earliest and most complex influence came from Roman law, we treat it in three separate sections — the Roman civil law legacy from the time of the Republic and the Empire; revival of Roman law after the Dark Ages in the 12th century at the universities in Italy and elsewhere; and reception of the Roman part of the *jus commune* throughout continental Europe. We illustrate continuity in the civil law tradition with the development of the institution of forced inheritance and the concept of *patria potestas* from the time of the Twelve Tables (450 B.C.) to Justinian's *Corpus juris civilis* (533 A.D.) to the *Siete Partidas* of the 13th century.

Although the civil law tradition grew out of European legal life, it has been accepted in widely varying circumstances. To understand the variety that exists among civil law jurisdictions today, we shall briefly look at the indigenous substratum with which the civil law elements blended. Thus we consider in this chapter local and feudal law in medieval Europe. In the next chapter we take up precolonial Latin America law and the development of Europeanized law and legal institutions in Latin America from the 16th through the 18th century, followed by consideration of the primary legal traditions in East Asia.

The incorporation of Roman law, canon law, and commercial law into the legal systems of Europe and Latin America (but not of East Asia) brings the civil law tradition up to the eve of the Revolution, which is discussed in Chapter 5.

A. THE ROMAN CIVIL LAW, CANON LAW, AND COMMERCIAL LAW SUBTRADITIONS

JOHN HENRY MERRYMAN, THE CIVIL LAW TRADITION: AN INTRODUCTION TO THE LEGAL SYSTEMS OF WESTERN EUROPE AND LATIN AMERICA 6-13 (2d ed. 1985)

The civil law tradition is a composite of several distinct subtraditions, with separate origins and developments in different periods of history.... [T]hese subtraditions will be described under the following headings: Roman civil law, canon law, commercial law, the revolution, and legal science. A brief discussion of each of them provides a convenient way of summarizing the historical development of the civil law tradition and indicating something of the complexity of that tradition.

The oldest subtradition is directly traceable to the Roman law as compiled and codified under Justinian in the sixth century A.D. It includes the law of persons, the family, inheritance, property, torts, unjust enrichment, and contracts and the remedies by which interests falling within these categories are judicially protected. Although the rules actually in force have changed, often drastically, since 533, the first three books of the Institutes of Justinian (Of Persons, Of Things, Of Obligations) and the major nineteenth-century civil codes all deal with substantially the same sets of problems and relationships, and the substantive area they cover is what a civil lawyer calls "civil law." The belief that this group of subjects is a related body of law that constitutes the fundamental content of the legal system is deeply rooted in Europe and the other parts of the world that have received the civil law tradition, and it is one of the principal distinguishing marks of what common lawyers call the civil law system. The expansion of governmental activity and the increasing importance of public law have not seriously altered this outlook. "Civil law" is still fundamental law to most civil lawyers. Hence a problem of terminology. Common lawyers use the term "civil law" to refer to the entire legal system in nations falling within the civil law tradition. But the legal terminology of lawyers within such a jurisdiction uses "civil law" to refer to that portion of the legal system just described....

Justinian, a Roman emperor residing in Constantinople, had two principal motivations when he ordered the preparation, under the guidance of the jurist Tribonian, of what is now called the *Corpus Juris Civilis*. First, he was a reactionary: he considered the contemporary Roman law decadent; he sought to rescue the Roman legal system from several centuries of deterioration and restore it to its former purity and grandeur. Second, he was a codifier: the mass of authoritative and quasi-authoritative material had become so great, and included so many refinements and different points of view, that it seemed desirable to Justinian to eliminate that which was wrong, obscure, or repetitive, to resolve conflicts and doubts, and to organize what was worth retaining into some systematic form. In particular, Justinian was concerned about the great number, length, and variety of commentaries and treatises written by legal scholars (called jurisconsults). He sought both to abolish the authority of all but the greatest of the jurisconsults of the classical period and to make it unnecessary for any more commentaries or treatises to be written.

On publication of the *Corpus Juris Civilis,* Justinian forbade any further reference to the works of jurisconsults. Those of their works that he approved were included in the *Corpus Juris Civilis,* and henceforward reference was to be made to it, rather than to the original authorities. He also forbade the preparation of any commentaries on his compilation itself. In other words, he sought to abolish all prior law except that included in the *Corpus Juris Civilis,* and he took the view that what was in his compilation would be adequate for the solution of legal problems without the aid of further interpretations or commentary by legal scholars. He was able to make his prohibition against citation of the original authorities more effective by having some of the manuscripts of their work that had been collected by Tribonian burned.

The prohibition against citation of works not included in the *Corpus Juris Civilis* effectively destroyed an even greater amount of material, because it naturally diminished interest in preserving and copying the works of the jurisconsults who had produced them. (These two influences have, understandably, complicated the work of persons interested in studying the pre-Justinian Roman law.) His command that there be no commentaries on the compilation was less effective, however, and was disregarded during his lifetime.

The *Corpus Juris Civilis* of Justinian was not restricted to Roman civil law. It included much that had to do with the power of the emperor, the organization of the empire, and a variety of other matters that lawyers today would classify as public law. But the part of Justinian's compilation that deals with Roman civil law is the part that has been the object of the most intensive study and has become the basis of the legal systems of the civil law world. Other parts of Justinian's compilation have been less carefully studied and used because they have seemed to be less applicable to the problems of other peoples and governments in other times and places. In any event, the part of the *Corpus Juris Civilis* that is devoted to Roman civil law is much the larger part.

With the fall of the Roman Empire, the *Corpus Juris Civilis* fell into disuse. Cruder, less sophisticated versions of the Roman civil law were applied by the invaders to the peoples of the Italian peninsula. The invaders also brought with them their own Germanic legal customs, which, under their rule that the law of a person's nationality followed him wherever he went, were applied to themselves but not to those they had conquered. Even so, a fusion of some Germanic tribal laws with indigenous Roman legal institutions did begin to take place in parts of Italy, southern France, and the Iberian peninsula. Over the centuries this produced what Europeans still refer to as a "vulgarized" or "barbarized" Roman law, which is today of interest primarily to legal historians.

As light returned to Europe, as Europeans regained control of the Mediterranean Sea, and as that extraordinary period of feverish intellectual and artistic rebirth called the Renaissance began, an intellectual and scholarly interest in law reappeared. What civil lawyers commonly refer to as "the revival of Roman law" is generally conceded to have had its beginning in Bologna, Italy, late in the eleventh century. There was, however, an earlier revival of interest in the *Corpus Juris Civilis* in the ninth century, in the Eastern Roman Empire, resulting in the publication (in Greek) of a compilation called the *Basilica.* Although the *Basilica* had much less general influence than the subsequent Italian revival, it remained an important source of civil law in Greece until the adoption of the first Greek civil code after World War II.

It was at Bologna that the first modern European university appeared, and law was a major object of study. But the law that was studied was not the barbarized Roman law that had been in force under the Germanic invaders. Nor was it the body of rules enacted or customarily followed by local towns, merchants' guilds, or petty sovereigns. The law studied was the *Corpus Juris Civilis* of Justinian.

There were several reasons for this attention to the *Corpus Juris Civilis* and neglect of other available bodies of law. First, the conception of a Holy Roman Empire was very strong and real in twelfth-century Italy. Justinian was thought of as a Holy Roman Emperor, and his *Corpus Juris Civilis* was treated as imperial legislation. As such it had the authority of both the pope and the temporal emperor behind it. This made it far superior in force and range of applicability to the legislation of a local prince, the regulations of a guild, or local custom. Second, the jurists recognized the high intellectual quality of the *Corpus Juris Civilis*. They saw that this work, which they called "written reason," was superior to the barbarized compilations that had come into use under the Germanic invader. The *Corpus Juris Civilis* carried not only the authority of the pope and the emperor, but also the authority of an obviously superior civilization and intelligence.

Within a short time, Bologna and the other universities of northern Italy became the legal center of the Western world. Men came from all over Europe to study the law as taught in the Italian universities. The law studied was the *Corpus Juris Civilis,* and the common language of study was Latin. There was a succession of schools of thought about the proper way to study and explain the *Corpus Juris Civilis*. Of special prominence, for both their views of the law and their styles of scholarship, were the groups of scholars known as the Glossators and the Commentators. They produced an immense literature, which itself became the object of study and discussion and came to carry great authority. Those who had studied in Bologna returned to their nations and established universities where they also taught and studied the law of the *Corpus Juris Civilis* according to the style of the Glossators and Commentators. In this way, the Roman civil law and the works of the Glossators and Commentators became the basis of a common law of Europe, which is actually called the *jus commune* by legal historians. There was a common body of law and of writing about law, a common legal language, and a common method of teaching and scholarship.

With the rise of the nation-state and the growth of the concept of national sovereignty, particularly from the fifteenth century on, and with the demise of the Holy Roman Empire as anything but a fiction, the age of the *jus commune* — of a common law of Europe — waned, and the period of national law began. In some parts of Europe (e.g. Germany), the Roman civil law and the writings of the Bolognese scholars were formally "received" as binding law. (Civil lawyers use the term "reception" to sum up the process by which the nation-states of the civil law world came to include the *jus commune* in their national legal systems.) In other parts of Europe the reception was less formal; the *Corpus Juris Civilis* and the works of the Glossators and Commentators were received because of their value as customary law or because of their appeal as an intellectually superior system. But, by one means or another, the Roman civil law was received throughout a large part of Western Europe, in the nations that are now the home of the civil law tradition.

Eventually, in the nineteenth century, the principal states of Western Europe adopted civil codes (as well as other codes), of which the French Code Napoléon of 1804 is the archetype. The subject matter of these civil codes was almost identical with the subject matter of the first three books of the *Insti-*

tutes of Justinian and the Roman civil law component of the *jus commune* of medieval Europe. The principal concepts were Roman and medieval common law in nature, and the organization and conceptual structure were similar. A European or Latin American civil code of today clearly demonstrates the influence of Roman law and its medieval revival. Roman civil law epitomizes the oldest, most continuously and thoroughly studied, and (in the opinion of civil lawyers) most basic part of the civil law tradition.

Roman law is often said to be the greatest contribution that Rome has made to Western civilization, and Roman ways of thinking have certainly percolated into every Western legal system. All Western lawyers are in this sense Roman lawyers. In civil law nations, however, the influence of Roman civil law is much more pervasive, direct, and concrete than it is in the common law world. We have had no reception of Roman law.

The second oldest component of the civil law tradition is the canon law of the Roman Catholic Church. This body of law and procedure was developed by the Church for its own governance and to regulate the rights and obligations of its communicants. Just as the Roman civil law was the universal law of the temporal empire, directly associated with the authority of the emperor, so the canon law was the universal law of the spiritual domain, directly associated with the authority of the pope. Each had its own sphere of application, and a separate set of courts existed for each: the civil courts for Roman civil law and the ecclesiastical courts for canon law. There was, however, a tendency toward overlapping jurisdiction, and before the Reformation it was common to find ecclesiastical courts exercising civil jurisdiction, particularly in family law and succession matters, as well as jurisdiction over certain types of crimes. The canon law had its beginnings early in the Christian era and has a fascinating history, including forged documents treated for centuries as though they were genuine. Various collections and arrangements of canon law materials were assembled, and by the time of the Bolognese revival there was a substantial body of written canon law available for study.

The study of canon law came to be joined with the study of the Roman civil law in the Italian universities, and the degree conferred on a student who had completed the full course of study was *Juris Utriusque Doctor,* or Doctor of Both Laws, referring to the civil law and the canon law. (The J.U.D. degree is still granted in some universities in the civil law world.) Because the two were studied together in the Italian universities, there was a tendency for them to influence each other; and the canon law, as well as the Roman civil law, helped in the formation of the *jus commune* that was subsequently received by the European states. Canon law influenced the *jus commune* mainly in the areas of family law and succession (both parts of the Roman civil law), criminal law, and the law of procedure. By the time the ecclesiastical courts of Europe were deprived of their civil jurisdiction, many substantive and procedural principles and institutions they had developed had been adopted by the civil courts themselves.

This Roman civil law-canon law *jus commune* was the generally applicable law of Europe. There was also, of course, a great amount of local law, some of it customary and some in the form of legislation by princes, lords, towns, or communes. In general, such law was regarded as exceptional in nature and of only local interest. The attention of the legal scholar was focused on the *jus commune,* rather than on local variations. Still, local law had some effect on the development of the *jus commune.* Many of the most important law teachers and scholars were also practicing lawyers in constant contact with the law in action. What they saw of customary and local law, particularly in fields such as criminal law, where Roman law was undeveloped or considered inapplicable, helped form their ideas about the *jus commune.* At the same time their scholarly bent and their conviction of the superiority of Roman civil law strongly affected the development of local law. The two tended to converge along lines favored by the scholars.

The reception of the *jus commune* in European nations eventually aroused a nationalistic concern for the identification and preservation — and in some cases the glorification — of indigenous legal institutions. The *coutumes* of the various French regions generally classified as the *pays de droit coutumier* (regions of customary law) — in contrast to those regions generally classified as *pays de droit écrit* (regions of written law), where Roman law was the dominant influence — became a source of national pride and scholarly interest as France became self-consciously a nation-state. After the Revolution, an effort was made during codification to include institutions from the *coutumes* in the new centralized legal order. In Germany a dispute arose during the preparatory work of codification between the so-called "Germanists" and "Romanists," and the draft of a civil code originally proposed for unified Germany was rejected because of the opposition of the Germanists. Their complaint was that the draft was purely Roman in form and substance, to the neglect of native legal institutions, and they were able to force a revision for the purpose of giving the code a more German, less purely Roman, flavor.

In these and other ways, the development of a national legal system in each of the major European nations took on certain characteristics directly traceable to the desire to identify, perpetuate, and glorify indigenous legal institutions. This tendency is indeed one of the main reasons for the substantial differences that exist between contemporary civil law systems. But what binds such nations together is that these indigenous legal institutions have been combined with the form and substance of Roman civil law, under the influence of the *jus commune.* The Roman influence is very great; the native legal contribution, while substantial, is generally of subsidiary importance. It does not go to such matters as basic legal attitudes and notions, or to the organization and style of the legal order. These are drawn from the older, more fully developed and sophisticated Roman civil law tradition.

The third subtradition, after Roman civil law and canon law, is commercial law. Although it is obvious that some form of commercial law is as old as commerce, the commercial law of Western Europe (and also, as it happens, of the common law world) had its principal development in Italy at the time of the Crusades, when European commerce regained dominance in the Mediterranean area. Italian merchants formed guilds and established rules for the conduct of commercial affairs. Medieval Italian towns became commercial centers, and the rules developed within these towns — particularly Amalfi, Genoa, Pisa, and Venice — were influential in the development of commercial law. Unlike Roman civil law and canon law, which were bookish and dominated by scholars, commercial law was the pragmatic creation of practical men engaged in commerce. Interpretation and application of the commercial law went on in commercial courts, in which the judges were merchants. The needs of commerce and the interests of merchants, not the compilation of Justinian or those of the canonists, were the main sources of the law.

The commercial law that developed out of the activities of the guilds and of the maritime cities soon became international in character. It became a common commercial law that penetrated throughout the commercial world, even into areas, such as England, where the Roman civil law had met with resistance. This common commercial law of Europe was later received by the nation-states and eventually was incorporated into the commercial codes adopted throughout the civil law world in the eighteenth and nineteenth centuries.

These three subtraditions within the civil law tradition — Roman civil law, canon law, and commercial law — are the principal historical sources of the concepts, institutions, and procedures of most of the private law and procedural law, and much of the criminal law of modern civil law systems. In modern form, as affected by revolutionary law and legal science, ... they are embodied in the five basic codes typically found in a civil law jurisdiction: the civil code, the commercial code, the code of civil procedure, the penal code, and the code of criminal procedure.

NOTES AND QUESTIONS

1. Professor Merryman here introduces the notion that there are five major civil law subtraditions. The first three: Roman civil law, canon law and commercial law, are the focus of this chapter. The remaining two: the Revolution and German legal science, are the topic of Chapter 5. But how about the notion itself that there are five (and only five) subtraditions? Is it possible to summarize a history extending from 450 B.C. to, say, 1896 so simply? Obviously, each of these five categories is itself a vague sort of catch-all, and anyone with a serious interest in pursuing any of the subtraditions will quickly find whole libraries of relevant material. In addition, much that does not fall into any of these five categories is simply excluded by this analysis of the civil law tradition. One major example is what Professor K.W. Ryan, An Introduction to the Civil Law 1 (1962), refers to as "the folk laws of Germanic origin." There is no doubt that, heavily Romanized, such an influence was exerted on the private law, and eventually the codifications, in France and Germany. However, one significant distinguishing feature of civil law systems is that competing legal traditions were engulfed, transformed, and absorbed — co-opted, if you will — by the scholars who have been the main custodians of the civil law tradition. The lack of any such process of thorough Romanization of domestic law is, indeed, what leads many scholars to exclude Scandinavian legal systems from the civil law and to treat them as a separate family.

2. *Jus commune,* common law, is a Latin term used by comparatists to identify the two bodies of law, medieval Roman law and canon law, prior to national codifications that aspired to universality and were important enough to be studied in Latin at universities throughout Europe (including England) and Latin America. The Latin term is necessary to distinguish the English law common to the realm that we inherited in the United States. Adding to the potential for confusion, some writers use *jus commune* to refer only to Roman law (as developed by scholars at the universities). We examine the reception of the Roman *jus commune* in Europe in Section G of this chapter.

B. THE ROMAN CIVIL LAW LEGACY

NOTE ON DATES IN ROMAN LEGAL HISTORY

Republic

B.C. 451-450	Twelve Tables
367	*Leges Liciniae Sextiae*
	Admission of plebeians to consulate
	Institution of urban praetorship and curule aediles
c.286	*Lex Aquilia*
c.242	Institution of peregrine praetorship
241	First province established (Sicily)
c.125	*Lex Aebutia*
44	Julius Caesar assassinated
43	Death of Cicero

Principate

B.C. 27	Augustus' power constitutionalized
A.D. 14	Death of Augustus
117-138	Reign of Hadrian
c.130	Consolidation of the praetorian Edict
c.161	Gaius' Institutes
161-180	Reign of Marcus Aurelius (to 172 with Lucius Verus)
c.212	*Constitutio Antoniniana*
c.150-230	Classical juristic literature of Julian, Papinian, Paul, and Ulpian

Dominate

A.D. 284-305	Reign of Diocletian
306-337	Reign of Constantine the Great
313	Toleration of Christianity
330	Transfer of capital to Constantinople
395	Death of Theodosius the Great
	Final division of the empire into eastern and western parts
426	Law of Citations
438	*Codex Theodosianus* (Theodosius II)
476	End of western empire
506	*Lex Romana Visigothorum* (Alaric II)
527-565	Reign of Justinian

528-529	First Code
530	Fifty Decisions
530-533	Digest
533	Institutes
534	Second Code
533-555	Novels

1. CONSTITUTIONAL HISTORY

BARRY NICHOLAS, AN INTRODUCTION TO ROMAN LAW 3-14 (1969)

The Struggle Between the Orders, and the Republican Constitution

[T]he Roman Republic emerges as a small city-state, based mainly on agriculture but already acquiring some commercial importance and showing signs of those military abilities which were to extend her frontiers far beyond the Mediterranean world. However, the first century and a half of the Republic (510-367 B.C.) was devoted largely to the internal struggle between the two Orders or classes into which the citizen body was divided — the Patrician nobility and the Plebeians who formed the bulk of the population. The struggle was for equality, partly economic but mainly political. It was important for the early development of the Roman constitution, but since it was finally over by at the latest 287 B.C., and the significant development of the private law did not begin for at least another century after that, we may be content merely to glance at the relevant features of the Republican constitution. This constitution consisted from the beginning of three elements — the magistrates, the Senate, and the assemblies.

The magistrates were the inheritors of the royal power. For the principal political consequence of the revolution which inaugurated the Republic was simply the replacement of the King by two magistrates, eventually known as Consuls. They were endowed with full executive power (*imperium*), subject only to three limitations: in the first place, though each had full power, each was subject to the veto of the other; in the second place, they held office only for a year; and lastly, their power might be limited by legislation. As Rome developed, other major magistracies were created to relieve the Consuls of their duties in specific spheres, but the principle of the *imperium* remained — each such magistrate had full power within his own sphere, subject to the same limitations and subject also to the veto of magistrates superior to him. How sweeping this power was can be seen from the fact that it was only by legislation that a citizen had the right of appeal to the Assembly from a magisterial order for his execution.

The magistracy which most vitally concerned the private law was the Praetorship, created in 367 B.C. to take over that part of the Consuls' duties which concerned civil (as opposed to criminal) jurisdiction. The Praetor was thenceforth responsible for the administration of the civil law, though the period of his great formative influence upon it was not to come for another two centuries. In about 242 B.C. a division of his functions became necessary and thereafter two Praetors were appointed. One had jurisdiction in cases in which both parties were citizens and was called the Urban Praetor (*praetor urbanus*), and the other had jurisdiction in cases in which at least one party was a foreigner (*peregrinus*), and was called the Peregrine Praetor (*praetor peregrinus*, or, in full, *praetor qui inter peregrinos ius dicit*). In the later Republic the number of Praetors was greatly increased, but only these two were concerned with the private law.

The two Curule Aediles, also appointed for the first time in 367 B.C., were the magistrates responsible for what might be called public works in the city, and also for the corn supply, but their importance for the private law lies in their control of the market place, in connexion with which they exercised a limited civil jurisdiction. This jurisdiction enabled them to make an important contribution to the law of sale.....

The Senate was a council of elders, recruited in historical times almost entirely from the ranks of ex-magistrates and numbering until the last century of the Republic three hundred. In form its function was merely advisory, but it came in substance to be the most powerful element in the constitution. For the Assembly, as we shall see, had no power of initiative, and a magistrate, holding office only for a year, would rarely act against the assembled wisdom of the Senate, the more so as he could only do this to any purpose if he could carry with him his colleague.

The Assembly was a very different body from a modern legislature. Like all ancient assemblies it was composed not of representatives but of the entire citizen body.... There were three assemblies of the whole people, differing in the unit on which the voting group was based....

[T]he struggle between the Orders had been substantially settled ... by the *leges Liciniae Sextiae* of 367 B.C. This legislation conceded the main economic demands of the Plebeians and also their most important political demand, that one of the Consuls must in each year be a Plebeian; and it was not long before Plebeians were admitted to all magistracies. It was, however, only the wealthier Plebeians who benefited from this political emancipation, and what in fact emerged from the struggle was not a classless society, but a new nobility based on office. The distinction was now not between Patrician and Plebeian but between those families whose members had held one of the higher magistracies and those which could point to no such distinction....

The Later Republic

The most important phase of internal political strife may therefore be said to have ended in 367 B.C., and in the next century and a half Rome turned her energies to territorial expansion. By 272 B.C. her control over Italy was virtually complete — partly by direct rule, partly by nominal but unequal alliances — and Rome faced Carthage, her only rival for the control of the Western Mediterranean. In two wars (264-241, 218-201 B.C.) Carthage was eventually defeated, but at heavy cost to Rome in life and in the dislocation of Italian agriculture. As a result of these two wars, however, Rome acquired her first provinces — territories outside Italy which were placed under the government of a magistrate with *imperium*. The first province was Sicily, created in 241 B.C.; Sardinia was added ten years later, and two provinces in Spain at the end of the second war with Carthage. It is no coincidence that it was in this period also that the number of peregrines in Rome increased to such an extent as to make necessary, as we have seen, the appointment of the *Praetor peregrinus* to exercise jurisdiction in cases in which they were parties....

This period of territorial expansion in the second century B.C., and Rome's meeting with the older civilization and commercial wealth of the Near East, had far-reaching consequences in Roman history. Rome became a great commercial power, and capital flowed in from the East and from the other new provinces. And not the least important form that this capital took was slaves in vast numbers. This influx of wealth, coupled with the depletion of the citizen body at home — partly by constant wars and partly by emigration to the newly conquered territories — changed the face of Italy. It was no longer a country of yeomen farmers; the land came more and more into the hands of the rich, who cultivated it in large estates with slave labour. This replacement of the small holding by the large estate was accompanied by a radical change in the use to which the land was put. Egypt and North Africa could now supply corn in larger quantities and more cheaply than could Italy, and Italian landowners therefore concentrated on those products (principally the grape and the olive) which would find the best market overseas and which at the same time were best suited to exploitation by the farmer with capital.

All this in turn produced a great change in Roman society. The old compact citizen body had disappeared. There was now a gulf between the wealthy man of capital and the poor. Now for the first time there emerged a proletariat....

In the later years of the second century the Republican structure began to break down. It was plain that a state dependent for her strength, as Rome was, on her citizen army could not afford to see her citizen body degenerate into a landless proletariat dependent on the rich man's dole. But the rich filled the Senate, and no reform was possible. Indeed a public corn-dole was instituted for citizens, and this secured the perpetuation of a proletariat interested only in "bread and circuses." The next step followed before the century was out. Citizens were no longer sufficiently numerous or sufficiently willing to fill the army, and Rome had to resort to the use of a professional army drawn from the lowest class of the citizen body. Henceforward any ambitious general, with an army prepared to serve him as long as he could pay them and with the means to secure by largess the votes of the populace in Rome, could make himself virtually master of the Empire. A succession of such generals provides the pattern of the last century of the Republic. Further sources of danger were a mutinous slave population on the great estates, with little to lose by revolt, and Rome's Italian allies, resentful at her refusal to grant them the citizenship. This grievance came to a head in the frightful Social War of 91-88 B.C., which resulted militarily in victory for Rome but politically in the concession of what she had fought to refuse — citizenship for all Italy.

And yet in this period territorial expansion continued without pause. The frontiers were pushed forward to the Channel, the Rhine, the Danube, and the Euphrates, and each fresh conquest brought in new wealth....

From the succession of contending generals, and from the civil wars to which their contentions gave rise, there eventually emerged alone Octavian, better known by his title of honour, Augustus. The constitution had long been in effect in suspense, but in 27 B.C., with peace restored, he claimed to have restored constitutional government. The restored constitution was only in form, however, Republican, and it is from this moment that we date the beginning of the Empire.

The Empire is usually divided into two periods, that of the Principate (27 B.C.-A.D. 284) and that of the Dominate or absolute monarchy which followed.

The Principate

Julius Caesar had been assassinated because he made too naked an assertion of personal power. Augustus learned the lesson of Caesar's fall, and dressed his power in Republican forms. There was no ostensible alteration in the constitution. The magistracies remained; what was new was the concentration in the hands of Augustus of powers which had never before been held by one man, and the fact that he held them in practice for life. He was in form merely *princeps* — first citizen — but in substance his authority extended into every department of government. The popular assemblies were not abolished, but were allowed gradually to die. Their acts were never more than ratifications of the wishes of the Emperor, and they became progressively rarer as the Principate wore on, disappearing altogether by the end of the first century A.D. By contrast, the power of the Senate was, formally at least, enhanced. Political authority was shared between Emperor and Senate, so that the constitution of the Principate has been described as a dyarchy, but there was never any doubt as to which was the predominant member of the partnership. The legislative power which had formerly belonged to the assemblies passed now to the Senate, so that by the early second century A.D. it was beyond question that its resolutions (*senatusconsulta*) had the force of law. But here too the effective voice was that of the Emperor: the Senate was virtually his mouthpiece....

The centre of balance of the Empire was being shifted from Italy and from the old Roman families.... The imperial civil service, on whom increasingly devolved the effective powers of government, was drawn largely from freedmen or the descendants of freedmen — men, therefore, not of Roman stock. More important still was the change in the composition of the army. The recruits came increasingly not merely from outside Italy but from the frontier peoples of the north, peoples without Roman traditions and with more affinity with the potential enemies of Rome than with Rome herself.

The seeds which were thus sown bore fruit in the last hundred years of the Principate. Marcus Aurelius, the last of the great Emperors of the second century, died in 180. For nearly twenty years there had been trouble on the frontiers — invasions across the Rhine and the Danube, wars with Persia.... This period of economic crisis, accompanied by frontier wars, culminated in 235 in a collapse of imperial authority. The following fifty years saw a bewildering succession of Emperors or claimants to the title, very few of whom died a natural death. The Empire was torn by civil wars and subjected to invasions along its frontiers. The result was economic and political chaos. If Rome's enemies had been sufficiently politically developed to seize their opportunities, the history of Rome might well have ended in the third century. Towards the end of this period, however, a few strong Emperors began to restore order, and their work was completed by Diocletian (284-305), whose reign is customarily taken to mark the opening of the Dominate.

The Dominate

The Dominate is so called because the last vestiges of the Republican constitution and of the Emperor as merely the first citizen were cast aside, and the Emperor was openly accepted as *dominus,* as lord and master of the Roman world. In this, however, the division of history into periods is even more than usually misleading. The fact of the absolute power of the Emperor — that the constitution was, as it has been put, "an autocracy tempered by the legal right of revolution" — had been manifest for a century and more. Diocletian's work was not, any more than that of Augustus had been, one of sweeping innovation. Both merely brought together what had grown up in the confusion of the age and made it into a system. The achievement of Diocletian, as of Augustus, was to take facts as he found them and order them into a constitutional form.

The Empire in the third century had suffered from three defects, political, administrative, and economic. Politically, the Emperor was at the mercy of the army; he had continually to be on his guard against the setting up of a usurper who would offer the soldiers more attractive terms. Administratively, a single central authority was not capable of ruling so widespread an Empire, still less of repelling invasions along perhaps ten thousand miles of frontier. Economically, the heavy increase in taxation, in a period when invasion and civil war had drastically weakened the ability of the tax-payer to meet the imperial demands, had led to a continual devaluation of the currency, with its attendant evils. The character of the later Empire is in part summed up in the remedies which Diocletian found for these three defects.

For the political defect the remedy was the completion of the Emperor's transformation from *princeps* to *dominus*. He was now a monarch in the oriental style, appearing rarely, hedged about with an elaborate ceremonial maintained by a numerous court, a figure whose every aspect was sacred and on entering whose presence even the highest in the land must prostrate himself. The forms of Republican government were finally discarded. All power was in the Emperor and was administered by him through a civil service responsible only to him. The Senate lost even the appearance of legislative power and dwindled to scarcely more than the municipal council of Rome. The Consuls survived, but their office was purely honorific. They could indeed claim a certain immortality because it was by their names that the years were still dated; and they had also the costly duty of providing the games for the city. So burdensome indeed did this duty become that in 541 Justinian abolished the office.

The administrative defect of overcentralization was met by a division and subdivision of the Empire. For future history the most important feature of this was Diocletian's sharing of his power with a co-Emperor, Maximian, Diocletian administering the Eastern part of the Empire and Maximian the West. This feature did not, however, become permanent until 395, and even then it was not a division of the Empire: it was a division of the rule of an undivided Empire. All legislation, even though the work of one Emperor, was issued under the names of both. Division was carried even further. For each Emperor appointed an assistant, a Caesar, who administered a part of his territory and was marked out as his successor. And under the Emperors and their Caesars there was an administrative hierarchy of four prefectures, each divided into dioceses, which were in turn divided into provinces.

To remedy the economic ills the Emperors resorted to compulsion and to state control. State factories were common, and the state regulated the internal and external commerce of the Empire. A rigid hereditary class system grew up. For example, the son of an artisan was bound to his father's trade, and peasants were commonly tied to the land in the manner of the medieval villein.

With Diocletian's successor, Constantine, the Roman Empire becomes the Byzantine Empire. He created in Byzantium a New Rome, thenceforth known as Constantinople, to which in 330 he transferred his capital. The shift in the centre of gravity of the Empire from West to East was thus finally recognized. And seventeen years earlier he had taken the far more momentous step of ending the persecution of the Christians and granting imperial favour to the new religion. There then began the close association of Emperor and Church which was to be so marked a feature of the Byzantine Empire.

By the end of the fourth century the Western Empire was threatened. In 410 Rome was sacked by the Goths, and thereafter successive invasions reduced the imperial power to a shadow. We place the end of the Western Empire in 476, when the Emperor Romulus Augustulus was deposed.

So it was that when, in 527, Justinian succeeded to the throne, he ruled over a Roman Empire of which Rome was no longer a part. But Justinian was a man with a vision, the vision of restoring the glory of the Roman Empire. He set out to recover its lost territories and to revive and perpetuate its greatest intellectual achievement, the Roman law. His territorial ambitions were only momentarily realized: he restored the imperial rule to Italy, North Africa, and southern Spain, but he had over-estimated the strength of the Empire, and his conquests did not last. The law, however, he did perpetuate, but in a way which he could not foresee.

NOTES AND QUESTIONS

1. The readings on Roman law may seem dense, distant, and difficult. However, the history of Roman law is a fundamental element in the development of Western civilization and an essential subtradition of the civil law tradition. In particular, the student should be able to identify or to explain the following:

(1) the conflict between the patricians and plebeians during the Republic and how it was resolved;
(2) the three elements of the Republican constitution;
(3) limits on executive power during the Republic;
(4) the office of praetor *peregrinus*;

(5) the consequences of Rome's territorial expansion from 241 B.C. to the end of the Republic;
(6) how the Republic's three constitutional elements changed during the Principate;
(7) how the emperor's role changed from *princeps* to *dominus*; and
(8) why the western Roman empire fell.

2. How does the Republican constitution's tripartite division compare to the checks and balances in the United States Constitution? In what other ways was American governmental power limited? Were the motivations behind the Roman and American designs similar or different?

2. SOURCES OF LAW: STATUTES, EDICTS, AND JURISTIC INTERPRETATION

THE INSTITUTES OF GAIUS 19, 21, 23 (W.M. Gordon & O.F. Robinson trans. 1988)

BOOK ONE

2. The laws of the Roman people are based upon acts, plebeian statutes, resolutions of the Senate, imperial enactments, edicts of those having the right to issue them, and answers given by jurists.

3. An act is law which the people decide and enact. A plebeian statute is law which the plebeians decide and enact. Plebeians and people differ in that the people is the whole citizen body, including the patricians; but the plebeians are the citizens without the patricians. This is why formerly the patricians used to say that they were not bound by plebeian statutes, which were made without their authorisation. Subsequently, however, the Hortensian Act was passed providing that plebeian statutes should bind the whole people; and so they were placed on the same level as acts.

4. A resolution of the Senate is law decided and enacted by the Senate; this also has the status of an act, although this point has been questioned.

5. An imperial enactment is law which the Emperor enacts in a decree, edict or letter. It has never been doubted that it has the status of an act, since it is by means of an act that the Emperor himself assumes his imperial authority.

6. The magistrates of the Roman people have the right to issue edicts. The right is found most fully in the edicts of the two Praetors, Urban and Peregrine (whose jurisdiction in the provinces is exercised by provincial governors) and again in the edicts of the curule aediles ....

7. Juristic answers are the opinions and advice of those entrusted with the task of building up the law. If the opinions of all of them agree on a point, what they thus hold has the status of an act; if, however, they disagree, a judge may follow which opinion he wishes. This is made known in a written reply of the Emperor Hadrian.

1 THE DIGEST OF JUSTINIAN 2 (Theodor Mommsen, Paul Krueger & Alan Watson eds., Watson trans. 1985)

BOOK ONE

1. JUSTICE AND LAW

7. PAPINIAN, *Definitions, book 2.*

Now the *jus civile* is that which comes in the form of statutes, plebiscites, *senatus consulta,* imperial decrees, or authoritative juristic statements.
1. Praetorian law (*jus praetorium*) is that which in the public interest the praetors have introduced in aid or supplementation or correction of the *jus civile.* This is also called honorary law (*jus honorarium*), being so named for the high office (*honos*) of the praetors.

BARRY NICHOLAS, AN INTRODUCTION TO ROMAN LAW 14-25, 27-34, 36-38 (1969)

The sources of Roman law may be broadly classified under three heads: statutes, edicts of magistrates, and the *interpretatio* of the jurists.

1. *Statutes*

Lex and plebiscitum. By "statute" we mean an express enactment of a general rule by a legislator or a legislative body....

The Twelve Tables were an early product of the struggle between the Orders. The law was at that time administered by Patrician magistrates, and evidently even the knowledge of its contents was denied to the populace at large. One of the demands of the Plebeians was therefore for the publication of the law. The traditional story — compounded in what proportions of legend and of fact we do not know — is that in 451 B.C., after a delegation had been sent to Greece to study the legislation of Solon, ten men compiled a code which was set up in the marketplace on ten bronze tablets. A further two were added by another commission of ten in the following year (450). In a sense, therefore, the Twelve Tables were both a statute and a code, but one must beware of pressing either word too far. They were not a code in the modern sense of a complete and coherent statement of the law; and though they were in form a statute, it is unlikely that in substance they departed much from the traditional customary law....

Although *lex* was thus in a sense the foundation of the law, it played, as we have said, only a small part in its development. In the four centuries between the Twelve Tables and the end of the Republic we know of only some thirty statutes affecting the private law. The *lex Aquilia* was of fundamental importance in the law of delict, and others, especially the *lex Aebutia,* effected important reforms in the law of actions and procedure, but the remainder are for the most part significant only for the detail of the law.

Senatusconsulta. We have seen that in the Republican constitution the Senate had in form no legislative power. Its resolutions (*senatusconsulta*) were merely advice to magistrates, and though this advice was unlikely to be ignored, it had no legal effect until it had been embodied either in a resolution of the assembly or in a magisterial edict. The advent of the Principate brought no immediate change. *Senatusconsulta* continued for some time to take effect only through the medium of a magistrate's edict, but they increased in importance as the assembly withered away. It became plain that they had for practical purposes replaced the old forms of legislation, and constitutional theory accommodated itself to the new facts. Thus Gaius records that in his time (the middle of the second century A.D.) *senatusconsulta* were acknowledged to have the force of *lex*....

But the life of the Senate as a substantial source of law was short. By the end of the second century even the semblance of initiative has gone. The Senate merely confirms what the Emperor puts before it, and the jurists when they wish to refer to the measure thus passed speak of it simply as a speech (*oratio*) of the Emperor. The *senatusconsultum* has merged into direct legislation by the Emperor....

Constitutiones principis. *Constitutiones* took several forms, and not all were statutes in the sense in which we have used the term. Many were more akin to what an English lawyer would call precedents. The closest to statutes were *Edicta*. The Emperor held magisterial powers and therefore, like all higher magistrates, could issue edicts setting out his orders or the policy he intended to follow in his sphere; and since the sphere of the Emperor was unlimited, his edicts covered a large variety of subjects. The most famous is the *constitutio Antoniniana* (*c.* A.D. 212), which gave Roman citizenship to the bulk of the free inhabitants of the Empire. *Mandata* also had a certain general character. They were in form administrative instructions to officials, especially provincial governors, but by accumulation they formed what amounted to standing orders. These were, however, of only minor and sporadic importance for the private law. On this the Emperor's influence was most vigorously and regularly exercised through his decisions in individual cases, and these provide the great majority of surviving *constitutiones*. They took two main forms — *decreta* and *rescripta*. *Decreta* were judicial decisions of the Emperor, who exercised jurisdiction either as a trial judge or on appeal. In general there was in Rome no idea of the binding or even persuasive force of precedents, but the unique authority of the Emperor gave to his decisions the character of authentic statements of the law. *Rescripta,* on the other hand, were not judgments but written answers to questions or petitions. Such questions or petitions might be submitted either by officials or public bodies or by private individuals. Many of them would have no bearing on the private law, but it was permissible for either a judge or a litigant to seek a decision on a point of law involved in a case. There was no judgment, since there was no investigation of the facts, but the imperial ruling would determine what the decision must be if the facts were as stated in the petition. This practice of submitting a preliminary issue of law to the Emperor became increasingly common from the reign of Hadrian onwards, and a great many rescripts from the time before Constantine are preserved, mainly in the *Codex* of Justinian....

2. *Edicts of Magistrates*

The power of higher magistrates to issue edicts has already been mentioned. From the edicts of those magistrates whose sphere included jurisdiction, and above all from that of the Urban Praetor, there derived the *ius honorarium* or magisterial law. This stood side by side with, and either supplemented or qualified, the *ius civile* — i.e. the traditional common law as embodied in or modified by statute and the *interpretatio* of the jurists. It was the Urban Praetor's edict which, more than any other single factor, transformed the Roman law from the rigid narrow set of rules which we see in the fragments of the Twelve Tables into the flexible and comprehensive system which was to serve the needs of Europe through many changing centuries. And it achieved this work of transformation while leaving the *ius civile* ostensibly unaltered. It reconciled conservatism with the need for change. For the Praetor had no more than any other magistrate the power to make law: his power was only over the remedies, i.e. the means by which the law was enforced. But this power enabled him indirectly to alter the law. For an understanding of this central contradiction of the Roman law some further explanation of the functions of the Praetor is necessary.

We have seen that the sphere of the Praetor is the administration of the private law between citizens. Within this sphere he can be said to have a particular and a general function. The particular function is the day-to-day control of litigation; the general function is the issuing of the Edict in which he sets out the circumstances and ways in which he will discharge his particular function during his year of office. It is the general function which gives him his importance as a source of law.

The general function of the Praetor. "Ubi ius, ibi remedium" is the modern principle. The right, not the remedy, is the primary concept. The law is made up of rights (and correlative duties), and remedies are merely the procedural clothing of these rights. But this was not the approach of the Roman lawyer. He thought in terms of remedies rather than of rights, of forms of action rather than of causes of action. A claim could only be pursued in a court of law if it could be expressed in a recognized form. In the same way it has been said that it was with writs and not with rights that the older English law was concerned. The difference is of course mainly one of emphasis, but it has the important practical consequence that the man who controls the granting of remedies controls also the development of the law. In Rome that man was the Praetor. By creating a new form of action or extending an old form to new facts he could in effect create new rights. In form there was merely a new remedy, in substance there was new law.

For the first two centuries of his existence, however, this power of the Praetor lay dormant. A claim could be initiated only in one or other of five ritual modes recognized by statute (*legis actiones*). The Praetor could, it seems, neither create new forms of action nor extend the existing *legis actiones* to claims not recognized by the law. He only began to make his influence felt when a new and more flexible system of actions — the formulary system — was introduced. This system, which was the framework of the Roman law throughout its classical period, is remarkable for its simplicity, economy, and adaptability. By the use of a very small number of typical "parts" or elements, the essentials of any dispute could be concisely and clearly expressed.

The characteristics of this system were that for each cause of action there was an appropriate form of action, and that each action was expressed in a set of words or *formula,* which constituted the pleadings. Thus, if there had been a contract of sale (*emptio venditio*) and the seller refused to deliver what he had sold, the buyer had an action on the purchase (*actio empti*), and conversely if the buyer refused to pay the price, the seller had an action on the sale (*actio venditi*); and each action had an appropriate *formula* in which the issue was defined. It was this principle that each cause of action should have its appropriate form of action which gave the Praetor his opportunity. For obviously if he could create new forms of action he could thereby in substance create new causes of action; and the structure of the *formula* was such that it could comfortably accommodate any new action which he might thus create.

Precisely how and when the formulary system was introduced is uncertain. The decisive step was evidently taken by statute — a *lex Aebutia.* What evidence there is suggests that this *lex* must have been passed in the first three-quarters of the second century B.C., and most probably towards the end of this period, but all that is certain is that in the last quarter of the second century the new system was in force, and with it the Praetor's free power to create new actions. Nor is it surprising that this crucial innovation should have occurred in the period when so much else in Roman life, and particularly in Roman economic and commercial life, was on the move. The rigid system of the *legis actiones* and the narrow *ius civile* which it enforced could never have met the needs of the emerging Roman Empire.

The principal instrument by which the work of adaptation was carried out was the Praetor's Edict. At the beginning of his year of office the Praetor issued an Edict which consisted of a series of statements of policy (themselves referred to as edicts). These individual edicts varied greatly in length and complexity and to some extent in grammatical structure, but the purpose of all was to define the circumstances in which the Praetor would exercise his power to grant new remedies. In theory each Praetor's Edict was independent of his predecessor's and was valid only for his year of office, but obviously a system in which a substantial part of the law changed every year would be unworkable, and though in the earlier years there was no doubt a certain amount of experimentation, the main body of the Edict was carried over from year to year, successive Praetors making only such additions and deletions as seemed necessary. In this way the Edict acquired the character, though not the form, of a legislative document, to be commented on and expounded by the jurists. It must also have been the jurists who were substantially responsible for its contents, since the Praetor would not usually be learned in the law and would therefore rely upon the advice of those who were. This natural inclination must, moreover, have been reinforced by the Roman habit of consulting an informal council of advisers before making any important decision in public or private life.

In addition to the statements of policy, the Edict contained pattern *formulae* for each of the remedies promised and also for those which already existed to enforce the traditional *ius civile*. Of these last there was no other mention in the Edict, since it was superfluous for the Praetor to declare that he would carry out his primary function, the enforcement of the *ius civile*.

The publication of the Edict did not exhaust the Praetor's power to innovate. He could at any time, if he thought fit, either on the facts of a particular case or on more general grounds, grant a new remedy. Such remedies would often presumably be made permanent in the next year's Edict.

The building of the Edict seems largely to have been completed by the end of the Republic. In the first century of the Empire the initiative in the development of the law was increasingly left to the interpretative activity of the jurists and to the various forms of imperial intervention. It was indeed inconsistent with the emerging constitution of the Empire that a magistrate should have what amounted to legislative power, and it was, once again, in the reign of Hadrian that the new facts were openly acknowledged and given permanent form. The great jurist Julian was commissioned to make a final revision of the Edict, which thenceforth was not to be altered. The career of the Praetor as a source of law was thus terminated. The only way in which the *ius honorarium* could develop was by juristic interpretation of the words of this final Edict, or by the granting of new "Praetorian" remedies by the Emperor.

The Urban Praetor's Edict was not the only source of *ius honorarium*. The Peregrine Praetor also issued an Edict, and many of the features which we find in the Urban Praetor's Edict may well have originated in that of his colleague. For the Peregrine Praetor, since he did not work within the framework of the traditional law, must have built faster and more freely than the Urban Praetor.... [T]he Curule Aediles' Edict ... was confined to the contract of sale and to a special provision concerning liability for animals....

The particular function of the Praetor. The Praetor's day-to-day function was the granting of remedies in individual cases. In any system of litigation there must be something to correspond to what the English lawyer calls pleadings, some method of ensuring that the issues between the parties are clearly defined before the actual trial begins. In the formulary system the place of pleadings was taken by the *formula*. The proceedings in an action were divided (as they had also been under the system of *legis actiones*) into two stages. The first took place before the Praetor (*in iure*) and was devoted to the drawing up of the *formula*, and the second took place before a *iudex* or lay arbitrator (*apud iudicem*) and was devoted to the trial of the issues set out in the *formula*. The Praetor's function was therefore not to try the action but to satisfy himself that it could be expressed in a *formula* included in his Edict, or, exceptionally, to grant a new *formula* to meet the facts of the case. The *formula* consisted essentially of a direction to the *iudex* to condemn the defendant if he found the plaintiff's case proved and to absolve him if he did not....

[T]he *iudex* is chosen by agreement between the parties from an official list of well-to-do laymen who undertake this function as a public duty. The whole *formula* is then put into writing and finally approved by the Praetor. This is the moment of joinder of issue (*litis contestatio*), i.e. the moment by reference to which the issues between the parties must be decided and after which there can be no alteration of the pleadings and no fresh action on the same issue.

At some time after *litis contestatio* the hearing of the case by the *iudex* took place. The parties were represented by advocates and adduced evidence, either documentary or oral, but there were no such strict rules of evidence or procedure as govern the trial of an English action. Within the limits of the *formula* the *iudex* had a wide discretion. He was judge of both fact and law, and took what advice he chose in arriving at a decision. Since he was not a jurist, he would be guided in matters of law by the opinions of those who were. His decision was binding as between the parties, but since the Roman law knew no system of precedent, it had no wider significance....

Actions and procedure of the late law. When, with the consolidation of the Edict by Julian, the general function of the Praetor lost its importance, the particular function none the less continued. But already there was growing up beside the formulary system another system of procedure more akin to those found in the modern world and more congenial to the increasingly bureaucratic character of the Empire. The characteristic features of the formulary procedure were that the trial was divided into two stages and that it was in form a voluntary submission to arbitration in which the only part played by the state was the approval of the *formula* and of the appointment of the *iudex*. There was no direct state enforcement of the appearance of the parties or of the execution of the judgment, and there were no professional judges. In the new, "extraordinary," procedure (*cognitio extraordinaria*) all this was changed. The magistrate, either in person or through an official delegate (*iudex pedaneus*), heard the whole case and took steps for the enforcement of his decision. The *formula* gave place to an informal system of pleadings. This new procedure was introduced at first only for particular purposes.... By the beginning of the Dominate, however, the formulary system had disappeared and the "extraordinary" procedure alone survived. But the law had taken shape in the mould of the *formula* and of the contrast between the *ius honorarium* and the *ius civile*, and to recast it would have required a greater zeal and capacity for reform than were to be found in the late Empire. Justinian did indeed cut away much that was obsolete, but, as we shall see, the very method and purpose of his compilation was incompatible with any radical reform. Hence it is that just as the English lawyer still very largely thinks in terms of the forms of action which were abolished a century ago, so also the greater part of Justinian's law is intelligible only in terms that had lost their practical importance two hundred and fifty years before.

3. *Juristic Interpretation*

All law requires interpretation. The need is most obvious where, as in a statute or Edict or a modern Code, the law is embodied in specific words, but it is none the less present where it is not. Moreover the function of interpretation will necessarily fall to those who are in some sense professional lawyers. In England it is discharged principally by the courts. In Rome, where, in the formative period of the law, there were, as we have seen, no professional judges and no regular courts, it was discharged until perhaps the end of the fourth century B.C. by the priestly "college" of *pontifices,* but thereafter by lay jurists.

Interpretatio prudentium. The Roman jurists have no exact parallel in the modern world. In the formative years of the later Republic they were men from the leading families who undertook the interpretation of the law as part of their contribution to public life. They were not professional men in our sense: they received no remuneration and the law was only one facet of their public career; they were statesmen who were learned in the law. In the closing years of the Republic and thereafter there was some widening of the class from which they came and a few, even of the most eminent, seem to have taken no other part in public life than as jurists, but their essential character and cast of mind remained the same. They were men of affairs, interested in practical rather than theoretical questions, and yet not immersed like the modern professional lawyer in the details of daily practice. To English eyes they have some of the characteristics of both the academic and the practising lawyer. For on the one hand they built up a great legal literature and also undertook what legal teaching there was, and on the other hand they influenced the practice of the law at every point. They advised the Praetor in the formulation of his Edict and in the granting of remedies in individual cases; they advised the *iudex* in the hearing and decision of a case; and they advised private individuals in the drawing up of documents and the making of other legal acts, and also in the conduct of cases before the Praetor or the *iudex*. But they were advisers, not practitioners, and in particular they did not appear in court to argue cases. That was the province of the advocate; and though a distinguished advocate, such as Cicero, might have a very fair knowledge of the law, his main interest was in the art of persuasion rather than in the science of law.

The jurist as we have described him was a product of Republican political and social life, and he could not remain wholly unaffected as the forms of Republican government were cast aside and the new bureaucratic structure of the Empire emerged. He retained his eminence in public life, but was now more and more commonly to be found among the highest officials in the Emperor's service. [Julian is an example of] this new type of imperial jurist.... Born in what is now Tunisia, he held a great variety of official positions: he served on the official staff of Hadrian (and was, it is recorded, given double the usual salary because of his learning), was in charge of the state treasury and of the military treasury, was Praetor and Consul (148), and subsequently governor of Lower Germany, Nearer Spain, and Africa. He was a member of the Imperial Council in the reigns of Hadrian, Antoninus Pius, and Marcus Aurelius and Lucius Verus.

The great jurists of the early third century A.D., to whom we owe most of the surviving legal literature, were even closer to the centre of imperial authority. Papinian, often considered the greatest of the Roman jurists, is first heard of as head of the department of the imperial chancery which dealt with petitions by individuals, and from A.D. 203 until A.D. 212, when he was put to death by Caracalla, he held the most powerful appointment in the Empire, that of Prefect of the Praetorian Guard. The careers of Paul and Ulpian were similar. Both held the Prefectship of the Praetorian Guard under Alexander Severus (222-35), Ulpian being murdered by his own troops in 223.

Not long after this the long line of jurists ends. For half a century the very existence of the Empire is at stake, and when from this period the Dominate emerges, there is no room for individual *interpretatio,* even by jurists as identified with the Emperor's service as were Papinian, Ulpian, and Paul. The sole source of law is now the Emperor, and the place of the jurist is taken by the anonymous civil servant in the imperial chancery. The life has gone out of the Roman law....

Ius respondendi. We have seen that one of the functions of the jurists was to give opinions on questions of law submitted to them. How far were such opinions (*responsa*) authoritative? How far were they binding on a *iudex*? This is one of the unsolved problems of Roman law. Certainly in the Republic the matter was unregulated: a *iudex* was free to make his own assessment of the weight to be given to a *reponsum,* though in doing so he would no doubt take account of the reputation of the jurist who gave it. In a passage preserved in the Digest, however, Pomponius, a jurist of the reign of Hadrian, tells us that Augustus, in order to give greater authority to the law, conferred on some jurists the privilege of giving *responsa* with the Emperor's authority, and that this practice was continued by his successors. It is the nature of this *ius respondendi* which is in doubt. Pomponius does not tell us what the effect of Augustus' innovation was. It is inconceivable that Augustus, reluctant in so many other respects to make an open break with the past, should have made these *responsa* formally binding. It is more likely that he wished to mark out certain jurists as peculiarly eminent, knowing that a *iudex* would not lightly disregard this sign of imperial favour. It is even possible that only such authoritative *responsa* could be cited in court, in somewhat the same way as in an English court, at least according to the traditional rule, only the writings of dead authors may be cited. From an obscure passage of Gaius it seems that by the second century this *de facto* authority was no longer confined to *responsa* given for the particular case, but had extended to all writings of patented jurists, living or dead. This would present the scrupulous *iudex* with a difficult problem when, as would be increasingly likely, there was a conflict of juristic opinion. Hadrian, apparently, had little sympathy with such scruples: Gaius refers to a rescript of his which declared that if juristic opinion was unanimous it had the force of *lex,* but that otherwise the *iudex* was free to choose. This must have been cold comfort to the inquirer, since the most difficult questions in law are precisely those over which learned opinion is likely to differ....

Forms of legal literature. In the perspective of history the most important function of the jurists was to write, and their literature was vast and varied. We owe almost all that survives to the Digest, and that, large as it is, contains only a fraction even of what still survived in Justinian's day. This literature took many forms and had many names, but it can be very broadly classified under four headings: the expository textbook, introductory or more advanced, the commentary, the problematic work, and the monograph. Only of the textbook do we possess a virtually complete example, the Institutes of Gaius. The rest are preserved only in fragments, though often very substantial fragments, in the Digest and in a few small intervening compilations. The largest category in point of surviving bulk is that of the commentary. In addition to commentaries on the Edict, which contribute more than a third of the Digest, there were commentaries on individual *leges* and *senatusconsulta* and, more especially, commentaries on the works of earlier jurists. Pomponius, Paul, and Ulpian, for example, all wrote works *ad Sabinum* — commentaries on Sabinus' textbook on the *ius civile* — and works of other jurists were treated similarly. Even in such commentaries dogmatic exposition is freely interspersed with illustrations and problems, but the casuistic approach of the Roman jurist is best seen in the problematic literature, which makes up some third of the Digest. In works of this category we find loosely strung together an immense number of problems, sometimes with a citation and discussion of the opinions of other jurists, sometimes simply with the writer's own conclusion. It is this problematic literature which gives Roman law its extraordinary richness of detail. It provides the case law of the Roman system. But whereas the development of the Common law has largely depended on the appearance of problems in the actual practice of the courts, the Roman lawyer elaborated his system with the aid often of hypothetical problems. For though some of the problems discussed arose in actual practice and were submitted to the jurist for his *responsum,* others arose in discussion with pupils, and others again were simply the product of the writer's own speculations....

The post-classical period. We have seen that the day of the independent jurist ended in the upheavals of the middle of the third century. Something of the old quality could still be found in the rescripts issued from Diocletian's chancery, but the decline had already set in. It was hastened by the growth of what is called the "vulgar law."

By the *constitutio Antoniniana* (*c.* A.D. 212) the peregrine population of the Empire was accorded Roman citizenship and was therefore required to conduct its affairs according to a system of law of which it knew little or nothing. In the result, the law which was in fact applied in the provinces was a mixture of debased Roman law and local practice, varying from area to area but far removed from the refinement and elaboration of the classical law. Something of this vulgar law can be seen in the codes promulgated for their Roman subjects by the Germanic rulers in the West after the downfall of the Western Empire. Of these the most important is the *lex Romana Visigothorum*, promulgated in 506 by Alaric II, King of the Visigoths (and sometimes therefore called the Breviary of Alaric). It consists of some imperial constitutions, an abridgement of Gaius' Institutes, a selection from a post-classical and much edited anthology of the writings of Paul (the *Sententiae*), and one *responsum* of Papinian, all, except the abridgement of Gaius, accompanied by a commentary or paraphrase. The result is but a thin, distorted echo of the Roman law.

The metropolitan lawyers of the East, trained in the law schools of Beirut and Constantinople, maintained a greater continuity with the classical law, but even they were unable to manipulate the vast mass of juristic literature. Doubts arose as to the authenticity and authority of different works, and these doubts eventually called forth the famous Law of Citations of A.D. 426. This singled out as authoritative the writings of Papinian, Paul, Ulpian, Modestinus, and Gaius. Where there was a conflict, the majority opinion was to be followed; if numbers were equal, Papinian's view was to prevail; only if numbers were equal and Papinian silent was the judge to decide for himself....

[One] difficulty was that of obtaining access to so diffuse a mass of material. Surprising as it may seem, there had been in classical times no system of permanently accessible publication, it being presumably the function of the jurists to keep professional opinion informed. But now that such jurists had disappeared other means were necessary. The first attempt to meet the need was the publication, probably under Diocletian, of two private collections, the *Codex Gregorianus* and the *Codex Hermogenianus*. Neither survives, but constitutions are quoted from them in later collections, and the compilers of Justinian's *Codex* drew on them. It was not however until 438 that, under the auspices of Theodosius II, an official compilation was made, the *Codex Theodosianus*. This was indeed more than a compilation, since the commission entrusted with the work was directed to make alterations and amendments in the interests of clarity and consistency. It was superseded in the East by Justinian's *Codex* but it continued to be used in the West and a substantial part has been recovered from various manuscripts and from other sources, especially the *lex Romana Visigothorum*.

NOTES AND QUESTIONS

1. Gaius lists the Roman sources of law as: *leges* (legislation, i.e., acts or statutes from the two assemblies known as *comitia centuriata* and *comitia tributa*), *plebiscita* (acts of the plebeian assembly, the *concilium*), *senatusconsulta* (senate resolutions), *constitutiones principis* (imperial enactments), *edicta* (edicts from consuls, praetors, aediles, and provincial governors), and *responsa prudentium* (opinions from jurists known as *juris consulti*). Compare Justinian's view of the official sources of law as expressed in the Digest.

In the long history of Roman law the relative importance of distinct categories of these sources varied. The period of primary importance for each category is listed in parenthesis as follows. First, *jus civile* (450-27 B.C.): the Twelve Tables, *leges, plebiscita,* and *senatusconsulta*. Second, *jus honorarium* (367 B.C.-117 A.D.): *edicta,* primarily from the praetors. Third, *jus respondendi* (27 B.C.-230 A.D.): juristic *responsa*. Fourth, imperial *constitutiones* and *leges* (117-555 A.D.): their bulk is evidenced by the compilations from the *Codex Gregorianus* (292 A.D.) to Justinian's *Codex* and Novels.

2. Which among the sources of law enabled the rigid fifth century B.C. Roman law to become a flexible and comprehensive system required to serve an empire? How did it develop?

3. Differences between imperial *constitutiones* known as *decreta* and *rescripta* seem clear enough. Can one as easily distinguish between imperial "judicial" decisions and imperial "administrative" decisions?

4. How did the two-stage formulary procedure for civil cases operate? Why was knowledge of it still relevant for understanding the judicial process once the "extraordinary" procedure prevailed during the Dominate?

5. Describe the position and work of jurists (*juris consulti*) during the Republic and Principate. Why did their influence on legal development end during the Dominate?

6. The *constitutio Antoniniana* (212 A.D.) signaled a shift from the personality principle in choice of law to the territoriality principle. Did this encourage the growth of vulgar law?

3. FAMILY LAW: *PATRIA POTESTAS*

SAMUEL P. SCOTT, 1 THE CIVIL LAW iii-iv, 64-65 (1932)

THE LAWS OF THE TWELVE TABLES (450 B.C.)

Table I:	Concerning the Summons to Court
Table II:	Concerning Judgments and Thefts
Table III:	Concerning Property Which Is Lent
Table IV:	Concerning the Rights of a Father, and of Marriage
Table V:	Concerning Estates and Guardianships
Table VI:	Concerning Ownership and Possession
Table VII:	Concerning Crimes
Table VIII:	Concerning the Laws of Real Property
Table IX:	Concerning Public Law
Table X:	Concerning Religious Law
Table XI:	Supplement to the Five Preceding Ones
Table XII:	Supplement to the Five Preceding Ones

TABLE IV

Concerning the Rights of a Father, and of Marriage

Law I

A father shall have the right of life and death over his son born in lawful marriage, and shall also have the power to render him independent, after he has been sold three times.

Law II

If a father sells his son three times, the latter shall be free from paternal authority.

Law III

A father shall immediately put to death a son recently born, who is a monster, or has a form different from that of members of the human race.

Law IV

When a woman brings forth a son within the next ten months after the death of her husband, he shall be born in lawful marriage, and shall be the legal heir of his estate.

H.F. JOLOWICZ & BARRY NICHOLAS, HISTORICAL INTRODUCTION TO THE STUDY OF ROMAN LAW 118-120 (3d ed. 1972)

The complete power of the Roman father over his children has become proverbial, and the Romans knew that it was an institution peculiar to themselves. It extended not only over all sons and daughters (so long as they had not passed into the *manus* of a husband), but also over the children of the sons and more remote descendants through males, without any limit other than that imposed by the span of human life.

The oldest male ancestor (*paterfamilias*) has complete control over the persons of his descendants, even to the extent of inflicting the death penalty on them. This *vitae necisque potestas* was not, however, an arbitrary power, but was subject to the requirement, certainly by custom and perhaps by law, that a *consilium* be convened to hear the case; and it seems that the *paterfamilias* was bound by the verdict which this *consilium* passed. Again, only the *paterfamilias* has any rights in private law: no subordinate member of the family can own any property, and any acquisitions that they make go straight to the *pater,* just as the acquisitions of a slave become the property of his master. No person, male or female, *in potestate* can marry without the consent of the *pater,* and if the sons marry with *manus* it is the *pater* who obtains authority over their wives. One limitation there was, presumably from the earliest times: *patria potestas* has no concern with public law, and a son under power could vote and hold a magistracy just as freely as a *paterfamilias.* In private law the only limitation, if it can be called one, which we know to have existed at the time of the XII Tables, was the rule that if a father sold his son three times the son was to be free from the father. This rule, as we have seen, was used to make emancipation possible.

If the tie between father and child can be artificially broken by emancipation it can also be artificially created by adoption. Desire for continuity of the family was always strong at Rome, and it was of especial importance that there should be a son to carry on the *sacra* or religious cult of the family. In republican law as we know it there were two entirely different forms of adoption, according as the person to be adopted was one under *potestas* (i.e. *alieni iuris*), who was merely to be transferred to another *potestas,* or a *paterfamilias* (i.e. a male *sui iuris*), who was to give up his independence and come under the *patria potestas* of someone else. In the former case the process was *adoptio* (in the strict sense) and the rule about the three sales was again pressed into service to break the *potestas* of the real father. The child (or rather "person to be adopted" — for he might be of any age) is twice sold to a third party and after each sale manumitted; then he is sold a third time, so that the *patria potestas* has gone irretrievably. The next step is that the adopting father should bring an action against the third party who now holds the child in *mancipio,* claiming that he is his son. The action is of course collusive, so that the third party makes no defense and the magistrate adjudges the child to the adopter, into whose *patria potestas* he thus passes. This is one of a number of cases where the Roman jurists used a collusive action to bring about results for which no direct method was provided by law.

Adrogatio was a more important affair; first there was an investigation by the pontiffs into the desirability of the transaction and then, if they had no objection, the *comitia curiata,* meeting probably under the presidency of a pontiff, had to give their approval, the institution taking its name from the *rogatio* or bill which was submitted to them. The reason why there was need here of approval by the religious authorities and by the assembly, whereas none was needed for *adoptio,* is not difficult to see. *Adrogatio,* being the adoption of a person *sui iuris,* meant that a family was extinguished and merged into another. The family might consist only of the person adrogated himself, or of him together with those whom he held in his *potestas* (who would follow him into the *potestas* of the *adrogator*), but in either case it was extinguished, and provision might have to be made for the continuation of its domestic cult. This no doubt was the special interest of the pontiffs.

NOTES AND QUESTIONS

1. Note the almost absolute *patria potestas* at the time of the Twelve Tables. We will follow its history in Roman and civil law later in this chapter. At this point, however, it is a useful medium by which to emphasize the formalism of early Roman law. Suppose a father wished to emancipate his son. Do you see how this could be done? Do you see how the same rule could be used to accomplish adoption? Does this sort of thing remind you of the formalism of the early common law?

2. Comparisons between Roman law and the common law are tempting. Consider the following two paragraphs from Franz Wieacker, *The Importance of Roman Law for Western Civilization and Western Legal Thought,* 4 B.C. Int'l & Comp. L. Rev. 257, 267-68 (1981):

> I. The last characteristic feature of ancient Roman law is that new law was created by giving legal advice (*consilia, responsa*) in contrast to the European way of creating law by legislation and the Anglo-American way of doing it by judicial decision. In this extremely closed society, the public actions both of private persons and of magistrates required the constant social backing of political, religious or legal authority. One might, for example, consult an oracle. In legal matters, one consulted the oracles of the law (*oracula iuris*), the jurists, who offered counsel (*consilium*). The *consilium* was used to determine the appropriate form of action (*agere*) or the appropriate document for a transaction (*cavere*) or — in its noblest form — to frame a legal opinion (*respondere*) addressed to the praetor, a private judge (*iudex privatus*) or a client. By means of these advisory activities, the Roman jurist maintained constant contact with actual cases. The fact that legal development came out of actual cases makes ancient Roman law much more like Anglo-American law than the practice of deducing law from statutes (continental legalism) or from scientific legal concepts (as in the *Begriffsjurisprudenz* of German Pandectism).
>
> II. A unique quality of Roman jurisprudence is that it did not stop at a purely pragmatic and precise casuistry. On the contrary, the greatest achievement of the Roman jurists was their ability to "purify" the case of its accidental elements, of the *species facti,* thus, to specify the essential

legal problem as a *quaestio iuris*. The first occasion to do this was presented by the *disputatio fori*, i.e., the discussion held by the older jurist, who had been asked for a *consilium*, with his apprentices. This later developed into legal instruction and was finally set down in a legal literature. Under these conditions, legal science and literature were molded out of their original raw material; they were derived from the simple nature of the *formulae* and *responsa* which had been honed by practical experience, sorted and recorded. In this way, the decisions of a new science were reduced to common denominators, and the literary presentation of its professional knowledge became rationalized. A process of intellectual reasoning and the evolution of general propositions had begun.

Do you understand how the first paragraph expresses something that characterizes the common law and distinguishes it from the civil law, while the second paragraph describes something that characterizes the civil law and distinguishes it from the common law?

3. Is the following comparison of Roman law and English common law persuasive?

For the last fifty years it has been a commonplace among writers on the character of classical Roman law that it shared what Fritz Pringsheim called "an inner relationship" with English common law. This relationship was in the first place based on the fact that both Roman law and English law were built up through the discussion and decision of cases. Their rules were not in the form of broad propositions laid down by a legislature but rather were narrow statements declared in the context of particular sets of facts. Despite the number of statutes and other examples of *ius scriptum*, the essence of both laws was seen to be *ius* rather than *lex*, that is, law "discovered" in debates among experts — the Roman jurists and the English judges — and elaborated by them.

A second, and related, feature of both laws is that legal development centred around the scope of particular forms of action — the *iudicia* promised by the Roman praetor in his edict and the writs set out in the English Register of Writs. So in both laws substantive rules grew out of the elaboration of remedies.

Thirdly, both Roman law and English law contain two more or less distinct bodies of rules: on the one hand, the traditional rules, which in the course of time became rigid and unsuited to new conditions, and, on the other hand, a more flexible set of rules based on ideas of fairness and justice, which mitigated the harsher aspects of the old law. The latter were based on magisterial innovation: the *ius honorarium* in Rome and the equity administered by the Chancellor in England. However, despite the obvious similarities, the fact that in Rome the praetor applied both the traditional *ius civile* and the new *ius honorarium* in one jurisdiction, whereas in England equity and law were administered in separate courts prevents us from pressing this parallel too far.

These [are the common] three features of both laws, their casuistic character, their development in relation to remedies, and the parallel between *ius honorarium* and equity.

Peter G. Stein, *"Equitable" Remedies for the Protection of Property*, in New Perspectives in the Roman Law of Property: Essays for Barry Nicholas 185, 185-86 (Peter Birks ed. 1989). *See* Giovanni Pugliese, *Ius Honorarium and English Equity*, in Comparative and Private International Law: Essays in Honor of John Henry Merryman on His Seventieth Birthday 275 (David S. Clark ed. 1990).

4. The principal general works on Roman law in English are: W.W. Buckland, A Text-book of Roman Law from Augustus to Justinian (Peter Stein 3d ed., rev. 1963); H.F. Jolowicz & Barry Nicholas, Historical Introduction to the Study of Roman Law (3d ed. 1972); Max Kaser, Roman Private Law (Rolf Dannenbring trans., 4th ed. 1984); Wolfgang Kunkel, An Introduction to Roman Legal and Constitutional History (J.M. Kelly trans., 2d ed. 1973); Barry Nicholas, An Introduction to Roman Law (1969); Hans Julius Wolff, Roman Law: An Historical Introduction (1951).

For a practical approach to pronouncing Latin, see H.A. Kelly, *Lawyers' Latin: Loquenda ut Vulgus?*, 38 J. Legal Educ. 195 (1988).

For a series of volumes on the substantive law of the last 200 years of the Roman Republic, see Alan Watson's The Law of Obligations in the Later Roman Republic (1965), The Law of Persons in the Later Roman Republic (1967), The Law of Property in the Later Roman Republic (1968), and The Law of Succession in the Later Roman Republic (1971), as well as his Roman Private Law around 200 B.C. (1971).

4. A ROMAN LAW CASE

CAECINA v. AEBUTIUS

Praetor Urbanus (69 B.C.)

[This case is described in an article by Professor Bruce W. Frier in the Cardozo Law Review, which is excerpted below.]

BRUCE W. FRIER, AUTONOMY OF LAW AND THE ORIGINS OF THE LEGAL PROFESSION, 11 Cardozo Law Review 259, 262-66 (1989)

In 69 B.C. Aulus Caecina, a wealthy Roman from the Etruscan city of Volterra, brought suit against Sex. Aebutius. Caecina, as the principal heir of his late wife, sought to enter a farm that was, he alleged, in her estate. However, he found his way barred by Aebutius, who claimed that the farm was his property and not part of the estate, and who gathered and armed his neighbors and their slaves to prevent Caecina from entering. Caecina then returned to Rome, where he applied for and received an interdict "concerning armed force" (*de vi armata*) from the Urban Praetor. This interdict was a procedural form ordering Aebutius to surrender the farm if he had used armed violence to thrust out Caecina.

Aebutius resisted the interdict, and as a consequence the Urban Praetor appointed a panel of (probably three) "recoverers" (*recuperatores*) to decide the merits of Caecina's case. During the trial that followed, Caecina was represented by the eminent late Republican orator Cicero, while Aebutius was represented by C. Calpurnius Piso. Because the *recuperatores* were uncertain about the correct interpretation of the interdict, they required three hearings to reach a verdict.[16] Cicero's *pro Caecina* is a lightly edited version of the speech he delivered at the third and final hearing.

As the trial developed, its outcome came to hinge almost entirely on the correct legal interpretation of the interdict *de vi armata*. The legal details of this dispute are of considerable interest. Briefly, depending on the exact interpretation given to the interdict's wording, Caecina either did or did not have standing as a plaintiff. Cicero of course argued that his client did have standing, while Piso, speaking for the defendant, denied this. Both Cicero and Piso presented lengthy rhetorical arguments in favor of their respective positions; these arguments rested on the tacit presupposition that the *recuperatores* were to decide the question of law for themselves.

However, both advocates also used another method to buttress their positions: they introduced *responsa*, statements of law, that they had obtained from jurists. This method was probably a bit unusual; all four of Cicero's published private orations (delivered between 81 and 69 B.C.) concern important questions of law, but the *pro Caecina* is the only speech that mentions juristic *responsa* in the context of a trial....

In Caecina's lawsuit the question therefore arose: What weight should the judges accord these *responsa* in interpreting the interdict *de vi armata*? Although Piso, speaking for the defendant, introduced such a *responsum*, he argued that the *responsa* should not be accorded great weight, and that the judges were free to depart from the *responsa* if they wished. Cicero rejected this view, but admitted that he often heard other talented advocates maintain that *iudices* did not always have to defer to jurists, nor the rules of the *ius civile* to prevail in trials; instead, *iudices* could rely on their own unaided judgment as to legal rules. Piso, however, went still further by publicly identifying and attacking the jurist used by Cicero, C. Aquilius Gallus, perhaps the foremost jurist of the day.

Piso's attack opened the way for Cicero to deliver a long and passionate eulogy of the *ius civile*, the jurists in general, and Aquilius in particular.... The eulogy is obviously conditioned by Cicero's immediate forensic purpose, to win the case for Caecina. Nonetheless, despite the passage's overtly rhetorical tone, it constitutes a major document in explaining the evolution of the Roman judicial system from its Ciceronian form (in which jurists still played only a marginal role in settling questions of law) to its early imperial form (in which legal questions arising in trials were regularly settled through juristic opinions).

In this passage Cicero distinguished three "levels" of law, with progressively greater degrees of fallibility and contingency. The first and highest level is the *ius civile* itself: an apparently independent body of rules and institutions that together constitute the bonds of "social welfare and life" (*Caec.* 70: *vincula ... utilitatis vitaeque communis*). These rules, knit together by their intelligible intellectual structure (78: *iuris civilis ratio*), offer the sole reliable basis for determining rights to ownership and general legal interrela-

[16] The verdict is unknown, but circumstantial evidence indicates that Cicero's client prevailed.

tionships (70), and for then protecting these rights "against a third party's influence" (74: *contra alicuius gratiam*). Here Cicero thought mainly of the secure tenure and devolution of property: boundaries, possessory relationships, servitudes, usucapion, and testamentary succession (74). Law is the incorruptible guarantor of such rights; and as such, *ex hypothesi*, influence cannot bend it, nor personal power break it, nor wealth corrupt it (73). In this sense, at least, the *ius civile* is removed and set apart from ordinary political and social life; it is autonomous. Further, as between citizens it is neutral, "uniform among all and identical for everyone" (70: *aequabile inter omnes atque unum omnibus*). This autonomous *ius civile* is a great inheritance (74), which Romans should defend as tenaciously as they defend private property itself (75).

The jurists constitute the second level of law, intermediate between the incorruptible *ius civile* and the judicial system. They are the "interpreters of law" (70: *interpretes iuris*), whose prerogative it is to "determine" law (68, 69: *statuere*). At several points Cicero suggested that their authority is bound up with that of the *ius civile*; an attack on them must inevitably be an attack on law as well (67, 70), and their attacker thus "weakens statute and law" (70: *leges ac iura labefactat*). Aquilius Gallus, the jurist Cicero relied on, is in this respect a paragon, whose talent, hard work, and fidelity were constantly available to the Roman people (77-78); he was so skilled that both his knowledge of civil law and his goodness seemed innate, and he never separated legal science from fairness (78). Yet there are also "stupid men" who should not be considered jurists when they make rulings "which ought not to be applied as law" (68: *stultis hominibus ... quod non oporteat iudicari*). Likewise, even skilled jurists may disagree with one another on questions of law; but if so, either opinion is good law, and the *iudex* must choose between them (69). Thus, Cicero plainly believed it possible for jurists to make rulings that are not law, just as it is possible for *iudices* to reach verdicts that are law despite the opposition of jurists (69).

The third and most fallible level of law comprises the courts themselves. Cicero asserted that *iudices* must decide in accord with juristic *responsa* that correctly declare the law (68); to this extent, the *ius civile* binds courts (70). Naturally, this does not mean unchallenged domination by jurists; judges may also determine that a jurist's opinion incorrectly states the law, or they may choose between conflicting juristic opinions (69). But Cicero carefully distinguished this position from the view, which he described as common among advocates, that "the jurists need not be followed, nor the *ius civile* always prevail in trials" (67: *nec iuris consultis concedi nec ius civile in causis semper valere oportere*). On the contrary, although Cicero readily admitted the fallibility of judicial fact finding (false witnesses and evidence are common, and judges may be bribed: 71), he maintained that even a corrupt judge will not dare to decide against recognized rules of law (72-73). The sanction against such misbehavior is entirely moral: general public censure resulting from the fear that legal rules will weaken (69) and legal insecurity will then increase (73, 76). Nonetheless, this weight of public opinion generally ensures that corrupting influences are unable to break the rule of law within the courts (72).

5. THE HAVES COME OUT AHEAD

PAUL VEYNE, THE ROMAN EMPIRE, in 1 A HISTORY OF PRIVATE LIFE: FROM PAGAN ROME TO BYZANTIUM 5, 166-68 (Veyne ed., Arthur Goldhammer trans. 1987)

Although technically complex, Roman civil law was more verbal than conceptual, and scarcely deductive. It afforded professional students plenty of opportunity to demonstrate their virtuosity. Did it enable ordinary people to obtain justice, however? Did it enforce respect for the rules when people violated them and oppressed their neighbors? In a society as unequal and inegalitarian as the Roman, it is obvious that formal rights, however clear, had no reality, and that a weak man had little to gain by going to court against powerful enemies.... One example will suffice, I think, to show that the public authorities did not so much supplant private vendettas as organize them.

Suppose I lend money to someone who decides not to pay me back. Or, better still, suppose that all I own in the world is a small farm, to which I am attached because my ancestors lived there and the country is pleasant. A powerful neighbor covets my property. Leading an army of slaves, he invades my land, kills those of my slaves who try to defend me, beats me with clubs, drives me from my land, and seizes my farm. What can I do? A modern citizen might say, go to court (*litis denuntiatio*) to obtain justice and persuade the authorities to restore my property (*manu militari*). And this was indeed what would have happened toward the end of antiquity, when provincial governors finally succeeded in imposing their ideal of public coercion. But in Italy in the first two centuries A.D. events would have taken a different turn.

For one thing, the aggression against me by my powerful neighbor would have been considered a strictly civil offense; it would not have been covered by a penal code. It would have been up to me, as plaintiff, to see to it that the defendant appeared in court. In other words, I would have had to snatch the defendant from the midst of his private army, arrest him, and hold him in chains in my private prison until the day of judgment. Had this been beyond my power, the case could never have been heard (*litis contestatio*). But suppose that I did manage to bring the defendant into court and, thanks to the intervention of a powerful man who had taken me on as client, succeeded in obtaining justice, meaning that the court declared the law to be on my side. It then would have been up to me to enforce that judgment, if I could. Was I obliged to recapture my ancestral farm by myself? No. By an inexplicable twist in the law, a judge could not sentence a defendant simply to restore what he had taken. Leaving my farm to its fate, the judge would authorize me to seize my adversary's chattels real and personal and sell them at auction, keeping a sum equal to the value placed on my farm by the court (*aestimatio*) and returning the surplus to my enemy.

Who would have considered recourse to a system of justice so little interested in punishing social transgressions? Most likely two types of people. When powerful, stubborn men quarreled over a piece of land, both parties wished to be judged to have the better case by the many Romans who followed trials in the courts because they found chicanery or legal eloquence to their taste. Such men would have settled their dispute in the courts, as they might have settled it at other times in history in a duel before witnesses. Or a creditor might bring suit against a debtor in default, who was scarcely in a position to put up a fight. The creditor would already have seized the debtor, who might at first have attempted to hide. Ulpian tells of one debtor who stayed away from the public market in order to avoid running into his creditor. When he saw him, he quickly hid behind the columns of the courtyard or one of the many kiosks in the marketplace. Recourse to the law was therefore just one of many possible moves in the social game, and some people begged that it never be used against them: *Juris consultis abesto,* "No lawyers in this business!"

Apart from its strategic uses, the law formed part of the substance of the old Roman culture. To have recourse to law, to make learned use of the ins and outs of civil law, was sophisticated behavior.

NOTES AND QUESTIONS

1. Is it likely in the case *Caecina v. Aebutius* that the judges were free to give their own legal interpretation to the interdict *de vi armata*, or were they bound by the *ius civile*? How were judges held accountable to the law?

For a fuller discussion of the *jus civile*, judges, and jurists, see Bruce W. Frier, The Rise of the Roman Jurists: Studies in Cicero's *pro Caecina* (1985).

2. For whom was the Roman judicial system useful? Does your answer surprise you? Cf. Marc Galanter, *Why the Haves Come Out Ahead: Speculations on the Limits of Legal Change,* 9 Law & Soc'y Rev. 95 (1974). *See* J.A. Crook, Law and Life of Rome (1967).

6. JUSTINIAN AND THE *CORPUS JURIS CIVILIS*

BARRY NICHOLAS, AN INTRODUCTION TO ROMAN LAW 39-42 (1969)

Justinian's first project was the relatively modest one of doing again for his own time the work which, ninety years before, Theodosius II had done for his. In February 528 he appointed a commission of ten, including Tribonian, then head of the imperial chancery, to make a new collection of constitutions. They were to omit all that was obsolete and were to make such consolidations, deletions, and alterations as were necessary to remove contradictions. The work was quickly completed and the Code was promulgated in April 529. It remained in force, as we shall see, only until 534 and has not survived.

Justinian then turned his attention to the juristic law. Theodosius himself had intended to make a collection of juristic writings but had abandoned the project. Justinian seems at first to have envisaged only the settling of outstanding controversies and the formal abolition of obsolete institutions. The constitutions by which these reforms were enacted are referred to as the Fifty Decisions, but as such they have not come down to us, though many must be contained in the second Code.

It was apparently at this point that Justinian conceived the far more ambitious project of a compilation, the Digest or Pandects, which would both preserve the best of the classical literature and provide a statement of the law in force in his own time. This task was entrusted, on 15 December 530, to Tribonian, who by this time was, in modern terms, Minister of Justice, and who was to choose a commission to help him. He chose sixteen men — one great officer of state, eleven practitioners, and four professors, two from Constantinople and two from Beirut. They were to read and make excerpts from the old literature, and these excerpts were to be collected into fifty books, divided into titles (chapters) according to subject-matter. Moreover they were to abridge and alter as much as was necessary to ensure that the work contained no repetitions, no contradictions, and nothing that was obsolete.[1] At the same time, they were to record the provenance of each excerpt, giving the name of the author, the title of the work, and the number of the book. (This is called the "inscription," e.g. "Ulpian, first book *ad Sabinum*.")

Even to envisage such an undertaking was remarkable, and supports the view, for which there is some other evidence, that there had been a revival of classical learning in the law schools of Constantinople and Beirut. Tribonian was to be the central figure and his may well have been the inspiration. Certainly Justinian records, in the constitution promulgating the Digest, that a large part of the books used came from Tribonian's library and that many of them were unknown even to the most learned. The scale of the undertaking was heroic. Justinian declares that nearly 2,000 "books" were read, containing 3,000,000 lines, and that they were reduced to 150,000 lines. And even these 150,000 lines give us a work one and a half times the size of the Bible. The excerpts are taken from thirty-nine authors, ranging from Q. Mucius Scaevola, who died in 82 B.C., to two otherwise unknown jurists who probably wrote early in the fourth century A.D., but the great bulk (95 per cent.) of the work is taken from authors of the period between A.D. 100 and 250. Even in this period a few predominate. Ulpian contributes well over a third, and Paul more than a sixth, of the whole. Nevertheless the frequent citations by these later classical authors of their predecessors in the early Principate give us a much wider picture than these figures would suggest.

The time allotted for the work was ten years, but it was completed within three. It was promulgated by Justinian on 16 December 533, and came into force fourteen days later. To many it has seemed astonishing that so vast a work should have been completed in so short a time, particularly since Justinian says the alterations made were "many and very great".... As we shall see, the compilers appear to have split up into three committees for the preparatory work, and there may well have been a still further division of labour within each committee. And the work was very imperfectly done.

Meanwhile Tribonian and two of the professors (Theophilus from Constantinople and Dorotheus from Beirut) had been entrusted also with the task of producing an official elementary textbook for students, the Institutes. This too was promulgated in December 533, and was even given legislative force. No more than the Digest, however, is it an original work. It is a patchwork of passages of classical institutional works, filled out, where a change of

[1] These alterations are now referred to as "interpolations." The term is misleading, since it includes not merely the insertion of new matter but any alteration even if only by abridgement or omission.

law or some other reason makes this necessary, with pieces of the compilers' own composition. In this respect it differs from the Digest only in that the provenance of the individual passages is not indicated. This is often, however, discoverable. For a large part of the Institutes is borrowed from the Institutes of Gaius, and a fair number of other passages are reproduced in the Digest. This patchwork character accounts for the rather disjointed and occasionally contradictory appearance of the text.

The Institutes are indebted to those of Gaius not only for a large part of their substance but also, to an even greater extent, for their arrangement, and especially for the division of the law into three main parts, concerning Persons, Things, and Actions....

By this time the enactment not only of the Fifty Decisions but also of a great many other reforming constitutions had made the Code of 529 obsolete, and Tribonian was accordingly commissioned, with Dorotheus and three of the practitioners from the Digest commission, to prepare a new edition. Once again the commissioners were given wide powers of alteration, rearrangement, and deletion. The work was published on 16 November 534, and came into force on 29 December of the same year. It is this second Code (*Codex repetitae praelectionis*) which survives, though its manuscript tradition leaves a great deal to be desired. It is about half the size of the Digest and contains some 5,000 constitutions dating from the reign of Hadrian onwards.

The work of codification was now complete, but the flow of constitutions continued. Justinian had envisaged an official collection of these new constitutions (*novellae constitutiones* — hence their modern name, "Novels") but the project was never carried out, and the collection which appears as the final part of the *Corpus Iuris* in modern editions is derived from three unofficial or semi-official collections. The Novels are for the most part concerned with public law or ecclesiastical affairs, but they include also a number of important reforms of the private law, particularly in matters of family law and succession.

CHARLES DONAHUE, JR., BOOK REVIEW, ON TRANSLATING THE DIGEST, 39 Stanford Law Review 1057, 1058-59 (1987) (reviewing *The Digest of Justinian*, Mommsen, Krueger & Watson eds. 1985)

The 9,127 extracts that make up the *Digest*[3] range in length from a few words to several pages. Most approximate the length of a modern paragraph. Each is headed by the name of the jurist to whom it is ascribed, the title of the work from which it comes, and the number of the book in the original work — e.g., "Ulpian in the eighteenth book on the Edict"; "Modestinus in the first book of Rules." The extracts are gathered into titles, the rubrics of which indicate the subject that the extract was meant to illustrate — e.g., "On the *lex Aquilia* [the basic Roman statute on wrongful damage to property]"; "On the rite of nuptials." The 430 titles are arranged in fifty books of roughly

[3] The *Digest* actually contains 9,950 extracts from juristic works, but some of the extracts are combined under a single heading.

equal length.[8] The titles themselves, however, vary greatly in length, ranging from *De legatis et fideicommissis* ("Concerning legacies and 'trusts'"), which occupies all of books 30-33, to the thirty-three brief titles on interdicts that make up book 43.

The order of the titles and books is puzzling. It is related to the course of legal education in Justinian's time, but is determined more by the order of the praetor's edict, a collection of formulae and official promises to allow actions that had formed the basis of the private law in the period of the jurists. The edict had grown over time. Some of the topics covered in the edict are related to others close by, but the edict as a whole is not systematic.

The order of the extracts within the titles of the *Digest* is also puzzling. We occasionally find groups of texts that go together and some that make no sense unless they are read together. By and large, however, the order of the extracts is not dictated by the sense of the texts but by the largely arbitrary order in which the compilers did their extracting.

NOTE

Some passages taken from the *Corpus juris civilis* are set out below to familiarize you with the real thing. These passages deal with three major institutions of Roman law: the *lex Aquilia,* the *legitim,* and *patria potestas.*

7. TORTS: *LEX AQUILIA*

1 THE DIGEST OF JUSTINIAN 277, 292-93 (Theodor Mommsen, Paul Krueger & Alan Watson eds., Watson trans. 1985)

BOOK NINE

2. *THE LEX AQUILIA*

1. ULPIAN, *Edict, book 18*

The *lex Aquilia* took away the force of all earlier laws which dealt with unlawful damage, the *Twelve Tables* and others alike, and it is no longer necessary to refer to them. The *lex Aquilia* is a plebiscite, the enactment of which by the plebs was procured by the tribune Aquilius....

52. ALFENUS, *Digest, book 2.*

If a slave were to die as the result of an assault and without any contributory factor like neglect on the part of his owner or lack of professional skill in a doctor, an action may properly be brought for killing him wrongfully.

1. One night a shopkeeper had placed a lantern above his display counter which adjoined the footpath, but some passerby took it down and carried it off. The shopkeeper pursued him, calling for his lantern, and caught hold of him; but in order to escape from his grasp, the thief began to hit the shopkeeper with the whip that he was carrying on which there was a spike. From this

[8] A "book" in the ancient world was roughly the length of a papyrus roll. Although the *Digest* books vary in length, they average about 10,000 words, or roughly 40 modern double-spaced typewritten pages.

encounter, a real brawl developed in which the shopkeeper put out the eye of the lantern-stealer, and he asked my opinion as to whether he had inflicted wrongful damage, bearing in mind that he had been hit with the whip first. My opinion was that unless he had poked out the eye intentionally, he would not appear to have incurred liability, as the damage was really the lantern-stealer's own fault for hitting him first with the whip; on the other hand, if he had not been provoked by the beating, but had started the brawl when trying to snatch back his lantern, the shopkeeper would appear to be accountable for the loss of the eye.

2. Some mules were pulling two loaded carts up the Capitoline. The front cart had tipped up, so the drivers were trying to lift the back to make it easier for the mules to pull it up the hill, but suddenly it started to roll backward. The muleteers, seeing that they would be caught between the two carts, leaped out of its path, and it rolled back and struck the rear cart, which careened down the hill and ran over someone's slave-boy. The owner of the boy asked me whom he should sue. I replied that it all depended on the facts of the case. If the drivers who were holding up the front cart had got out of its way of their own accord and that had been the reason why the mules could not take the weight of the cart and had been pulled back by it, in my opinion no action could be brought against the owner of the mules. The boy's owner should rather sue the men who had been holding up the cart; for damage is no less wrongful when someone voluntarily lets go of something in such circumstances and it hits someone else. For example, if a man failed to restrain an ass that he was driving, he would be liable for any damage that he caused, just as if he threw a missile or anything else from his hand. But if the accident that we are considering had occurred because the mules had shied at something and the drivers had left the cart for fear of being crushed, no action would lie against them; but in such a case, action should be brought against the owner of the mules. On the other hand, if neither the mules nor the drivers were at fault, as, for example, if the mules just could not take the weight or if in trying to do so they had slipped and fallen and the cart had then rolled down the hill because the men could not hold it when it tipped up, there would be no liability on the owner or on the drivers. It is quite clear, furthermore, that however the accident happened, no action could be brought against the owner of the mules pulling the cart behind; for they fell back down the hill not through any fault of theirs, but because they were struck by the cart in front.

BRUCE W. FRIER, A CASEBOOK ON THE ROMAN LAW OF DELICT 3 (1989)

The Lex Aquilia, proposed by an otherwise unknown plebeian tribune named Aquilius, was intended to replace most earlier statutory law on damage to another's property (Ulpian, D. 9.2.1). Its date is uncertain, but probably early third century B.C.

The new statute established liability under two heads: in the First Section, for the unlawful "slaying" (*occidere*) of slaves or four-footed herd animals; and in the Third Section, for the unlawful "burning, breaking, or rending" (*urere, frangere, rumpere*) of property in general, except for acts included under the First Section. (The statute's Second Section, on an apparently unrelated topic, soon became obsolete.) The Lex Aquilia thus attempted to create a general basis whereby a person could bring suit if his or her property was wrongfully damaged by a third party. The Urban Praetor implemented the statute by providing a private action in his Edict.

The Lex Aquilia was not skillfully drafted, and it soon required interpretation; this early and rather awkward interpretation exercised a strong influence on later juristic writing about the statute. In particular, the words "slay" and "rending" were given rather unexpected meanings. "Slaying" was narrowly interpreted, and acts not strictly encompassed by the narrow meaning of the verb were excluded from coverage; by contrast, "rending" was very broadly interpreted. But both Sections required a high degree of physical directness; if this was not present, no action was available under the Lex Aquilia.

In order to prevent injustice, the Urban Praetor intervened by granting what are variously called, without distinction, either "analogous actions" (*actiones utiles*) or "actions on the facts" (*actiones in factum*) that were modelled after the statutory action. The Praetor gave such actions in situations where, for instance, a defendant had not directly "slain" a slave, but had indirectly caused his death to occur. The classical jurists struggled, without great success, to explain the legal basis of the distinction between statutory and analogous actions; the difficulties they encountered are somewhat similar to those involved in the older common law distinction between Trespass and Trespass on the Case, which was also based on the difference between direct and indirect causation of harm.

The later history of the Lex Aquilia is also heavily influenced by its ambiguous purpose: was it chiefly intended only to compensate the owner for property losses, or did it also aim to punish the offender for a wrongful act? The jurists concede that the Lex Aquilia has at least a partially punitive purpose, and this purpose is illustrated by one of its provisions, whereby a defendant who initially denies liability, and so forces the issue to trial, is condemned to pay to the plaintiff double the loss.

8. INHERITANCE LAW: *LEGITIM*

JUSTINIAN'S INSTITUTES 79 (Paul Krueger ed., Peter Birks & Grant McLeod trans. 1987)

2.18 IRRESPONSIBLE WILLS

Heads of families often disinherit or omit their children without good reason. Those aggrieved at being unfairly cut out or passed over are allowed the complaint of an irresponsible will. The form of this is that the balance of the testator's mind was disturbed when he made his will. But the suggestion is not that he really was insane, rather that in making an otherwise valid will he failed to keep his mind on his family responsibilities. The will of someone really insane is of course a nullity.

1. The right to complain of an irresponsible will is not only given to children against parents but also vice versa. A brother or sister is allowed to challenge disreputable appointees. That is laid down in imperial pronouncements. They cannot go against every type of heir. Relatives remoter than brother or sister cannot sue, or if they do cannot win.

2. Real children and adopted children covered by our pronouncement can make this complaint provided they have no other claim to some of the deceased's property. Those who have some other right to all or part of the estate can never bring the complaint of an irresponsible will. Posthumous children too may use this claim if they have no other.

3. That must be construed as meaning they can do so if the testator made no provision for them in the will. Our pronouncement on this subject maintains respect for natural ties. If some part — however small — of the estate or its contents is left to someone in the will, he cannot bring the complaint of irresponsibility. Instead he can claim supplementation to a quarter of his entitlement on intestacy. This supplementation, worked out by the standards of the reasonable man, is an automatic right, not dependent on the intention of the testator....

6. The bar to a complaint for irresponsibility is receipt of your quarter entitlement. It can come to you as heir, legatee, beneficiary under a trust, donee in contemplation of death, or — though here only in the cases specified in our pronouncement — as donee inter vivos, or in any other way specified in imperial pronouncements.

7. Our references to the quarter share are to be taken in this way: whether there is one person in the category allowed to make the complaint of irresponsibility or more than one, it is enough to give a single quarter for proportionate division between them. That works out at one quarter of the intestate entitlement for each claimant.

1 THE DIGEST OF JUSTINIAN 174-75, 179-80 (Theodor Mommsen, Paul Krueger & Alan Watson eds., Watson trans. 1985)

BOOK FIVE

2. THE UNDUTIFUL WILL

1. ULPIAN, *Edict, book 14.*

It should be noted that complaints against the undutiful will are common; for it is possible for everyone to argue want of duty, parents as well as children. For one's cognates beyond the degree of brother would do better not to trouble themselves with useless expense since they are not in a position to succeed.

2. MARCIAN, *Institutes, book 4.*

The supposition on which an action for undutiful will is brought is that the testators were of unsound mind for making a will. And by this is meant not that the testator was really a lunatic or out of his mind but that the will was correctly made but without a due regard for natural claims; for if he were really a lunatic or out of his mind, the will is void....

4. GAIUS, *Lex Glitia, sole book.*

For parents should not be allowed to treat their children unjustly in their wills. They generally do this, passing an adverse judgment on their own flesh and blood, when they have been led astray by the blandishments or incitements of stepmothers....

19. PAUL, *Questions, book 2.*

A mother on her deathbed appointed an outsider as heir to three quarters of her estate, one daughter as heir to one quarter and passed over the other. The latter successfully brought a complaint of undutiful will. The question is: How should help be given to the daughter in the will? My answer was that the daughter passed over should claim what she was going to have on her mother's intestacy. Now it can be said that if the one left out were successfully to claim the whole inheritance, she might even have the succession entirely to herself, as she would if the other daughter had foregone her statutable inheritance. But we cannot allow her complaint of undutiful will to be accepted to the detriment of her sister. Moreover, it should be stated that she who accepted in accordance with the will is not in a similar position to one foregoing an inheritance. For this reason, half the inheritance should be claimed from the outsider and the justice of taking a whole half should be maintained on the ground that a whole half is the daughter's due. According to this, the will is not broken completely, but the deceased is made intestate only in part, although her last judgment is condemned as that of a lunatic. Furthermore, if anyone thinks that with the daughter's success the whole will is broken, it should be stated that the daughter appointed can still enter into her inheritance on intestacy. For a daughter who has entered in accordance with a will she thinks valid is not considered to be repudiating her statutable inheritance, which indeed she does not know is on offer to her, since even those who do know do not lose their rights when they opt for what they think suitable for them. This happens in the case of a patron who under a false impression has accepted the judgment of the deceased; for it is not considered that he has rejected the idea of being given possession of the estate contrary to the will. From this it is clear that the daughter passed over was wrong to claim the whole inheritance, since, although the will has been broken, the right of the one appointed to enter into her inheritance is still intact....

25. ULPIAN, *Disputations, book 2.*

If a gift has been made not *mortis causa* but *inter vivos* with however the expectation that it would be considered part of the quarter, it can be said that a complaint of undutiful will is inoperative if the recipient has his quarter in the gift or, if he has less, if the deficiency is made up in accordance with the estimate of a good man; certainly the gift should be counted in.

DAVID JOHNSON, THE ROMAN LAW OF TRUSTS 2-4 (1988)

Roman law, from its earliest days and its earliest rules incorporated in the XII Tables, had been bound to the principle of universal succession. A testator's only necessary act in making a will was to appoint an heir; and this is what Gaius means when he speaks of the institution of an heir as the *caput et fundamentum* of a will.[2] The heir did not simply acquire the property of the deceased: he succeeded him as a person, and so was entitled to benefit from and was bound by (almost) all obligations in favour of or against the deceased. He was heir, moreover, for good: *semel heres semper heres.*

Freedom and formality are a paradoxical pair, but they are the two words which best characterize the Roman civil law of succession. Roman law from the XII Tables onwards was notable for the freedom it allowed the testator: *uti legassit suae rei, ita ius esto* are the words Gaius quotes from them,[3] and this was the way the law for long remained. A testator was free to dispose of his property as he wished; the concept of legitim or *Pflichtteilsrecht* lay in the future.

This is not to say the law of succession was unregulated. On the contrary. Civil law provided that formal requirements must be met. No will was valid if it was not duly made and witnessed, if it did not begin with the institution of an heir in prescribed form; no legacy was valid if it did not follow the institution and itself satisfy the time-honoured wordings. Depending on the words used, the legacy was classified as one of four different types, and the actions available to claim it were determined accordingly.

Nor was this all. The civil law protected the expectations of children, particularly male children, with various provisions. Male children, if not instituted heirs, had to be disinherited by name. Female children need not be mentioned by name, but had to be covered at least by a general clause of disherison. These requirements do not in any way inhibit freedom of testation. They demand only that proper forms be followed. Their rationale is plain: it is desirable that a testator should make his intentions quite clear, and in the case of heirs in his family this rightly takes on a sense of urgency.

Only with the evolution of the *querela inofficiosi testamenti* did Roman law arrive towards the end of the Republic at the principle that the descendants (or ascendants) of a testator actually had a legitimate expectation of acquiring a share of his estate, by virtue of the law itself rather than the testator's own fancy. The *querela* lay to any descendant or ascendant who could show that he had received less than a quarter of the share of the estate he would have received had the testator died intestate; and that the testator had no good reason for cutting him out. Yet even here it is clear how cautiously Roman law advanced towards a concept of legitim, for a quarter of the prospective intestate share is not really very much. Take the case of a testator with three children. Each has a prospective intestate share of one-third of the estate; to bar the *querela* each must be left at least a quarter of that, that is one-twelfth. The consequence is that the testator's hands are tied only in respect of a

---

[2] G. 2.229.

[3] G. 2.224; the words probably related to the original pre-mancipatory will and might be translated something like "as he declared with respect to his own property, so let the law be."

quarter of his entire estate, and he is free to give away the remaining three-quarters as he pleases.

9. PATRIA POTESTAS REVISITED I

JUSTINIAN'S INSTITUTES 43, 45, 47, 67, 71 (Paul Krueger ed., Peter Birks & Grant McLeod trans. 1987)

1.9 FAMILY AUTHORITY

The people within our authority are our children, the offspring of a Roman law marriage.

1. Marriage, or matrimony, is the union of a man and a woman, committing them to a single path through life.

2. Our authority over our children is a right which only Roman citizens have. Nobody else has such extreme control over children.

3. Any child born to you and your wife is in your authority. The same is true of one born to your son and his wife. That is to say, your grandson and granddaughter are equally within your authority, and your great grandson and great granddaughter, and so on. Your daughter's child is not in your authority but in its father's....

1.12 EMERGENCE FROM FAMILY AUTHORITY

Now to ways in which dependent persons emerge from authority. For slaves, these can be gathered from what we have already said about manumission. By contrast free people within family authority become their own masters on the head of the family's death. But distinctions must be made. The death of a father who is head of the family makes his sons and daughters completely independent at once. The death of a grandfather does not always do so, but only if the grandchildren do not fall into their father's authority on their grandfather's death. If at the time of their grandfather's death their father is alive and within his authority, they do then pass into the authority of their father. If at the grandfather's death their father is already dead or has emerged from family authority, the grandchildren cannot pass into their father's authority. They become independent.

1. Next, since someone who is transported to an island for some crime loses his citizenship, his removal from the Roman citizen-body releases his children from his authority just as though he had died. The same logic means that a dependent person who is transported to an island passes out of the authority of the head of his family. If an imperial pardon lets such people back they completely recover their original status.

2. By contrast fathers merely detained on an island keep their children within their authority; and, vice versa, sons so detained stay within family authority.

3. Someone condemned to penal slavery ceases to hold family authority over his sons. Penal slaves are those sentenced to the mines or thrown in with wild beasts.

4. A son who has done military service or become a senator or a consul remains in his father's authority. Neither such service nor the honour of a

consulate makes a man his own master. But by our own pronouncement attainment of the patriciate, the highest of honours, releases a son from family authority as soon as he is given the imperial patent. It would be intolerable for a father to be able to release a son from the bonds of his authority by emancipation while the high majesty of the emperor had no power to remove from another's authority a man he chose to rank among his fathers.

5. If the head of the family is captured by enemies the status of the children is in suspense because of his right of rehabilitation. This is true even though his captors make him a slave, because prisoners of war who come back recover all their former rights. He will have his children in his authority again when he gets back, because his right of rehabilitation allows him to be treated as if he had never stopped being a citizen. If he dies as a prisoner, the son's independence is back-dated to the moment of his father's capture....

6. Next, children also emerge from family authority by emancipation. That used to be done by an old legal procedure involving pretended sales and intervening manumissions or else by imperial writ. Here too our meticulous pronouncement has introduced an improved regime. We have put an end to the play-acting. The head of a family can now go straight to competent judges or magistrates and there discharge sons, daughters, grandchildren, and so on, from his control. As for the property of the discharged son, daughter, or grandchild, the praetor's edict gives the head of the family the same rights as are given to a patron over the property of his freedman. If the son or daughter, and so on, is still a young child the head of the family himself becomes its guardian by virtue of the emancipation.

7. We should note that where the head of a family has a son and by that son a grandchild it is a matter entirely for him whether to discharge the son from his authority but keep the grandchild or, vice versa, to discharge the grandchild and keep the son. It is the same for great grandchildren. Equally, he is free to make them all independent.

8. The bond of the real father's authority is also broken when he allows a son within his authority to be adopted by his real grandfather or great grandfather under our legislation, i.e. where he makes a properly documented declaration of his assent before a competent judge in the presence of the adoptee and without objection voiced by the adoptor. But here the authority passes to the adoptive head of the family. As we have already said, with that category of adoptor the adoption takes full effect.

9. Note too that if your daughter-in-law conceives by your son and during her pregnancy you emancipate the son or give him in adoption the baby is still born into your authority. A baby conceived after emancipation or adoption is subject to the authority of its emancipated father or its adoptive grandfather.

10. Notice finally that children, whether real or adopted, have virtually no means of compelling the head of their family to discharge them from his authority....

2.9 ACQUISITION THROUGH OTHER PEOPLE

Property passes to us not only through our own acts but through those of the people within our authority. This is true of slaves in whom we have a usufruct, also of free people and slaves belonging to others whom we possess in good faith. We must consider each of these more closely.

1. First, male and female descendants within your authority. The old rule was that everything which came to them, with the exception of the military fund, was acquired for the head of the family. No distinctions were drawn. The property vested in the head so absolutely that he was free to take what one member of his family had acquired and give it away to another or to an outsider or sell or use it in any way he pleased. To us that seemed harsh. We have made a general pronouncement both easing the lot of children and preserving the rights of fathers. We have laid down that anything which comes to a child from using the father's property shall become the father's absolutely in the old way — for what could be wrong with the father getting the return on his own capital? — but anything which a son acquires in any other way shall vest in himself as owner, subject to a usufruct in the father. The aim is to ensure that what he obtains by his own work or good fortune does not bring profit to another and bitterness to himself.

2. We have also dealt with this problem in another situation. A father in emancipating a child was entitled under earlier imperial pronouncements to keep back, if he wanted to, as a kind of price for the emancipation, one third of the child's assets which had escaped his automatic right of acquisition. Here the harshness consisted in the possibility of the son's being stripped of some of his assets, losing in wealth the value of the enhanced, independent status conferred by his emancipation. We have enacted that instead of ownership in the third the head should be allowed a usufruct over half. This will keep the son's property intact, while the father will enjoy a larger sum by gaining control of a half rather than a third....

2.12 PERSONS INCAPABLE OF MAKING A WILL

Not everyone has the capacity to make a will. First, someone within another's authority has no power to do so, not even with the consent of the head of the family. There are exceptions which we have already spelled out, notably soldiers in family authority, to whom imperial pronouncements have given the power to make a will of their military acquisitions.

SAMUEL P. SCOTT, 14 THE CIVIL LAW 318-19 (1932)

THE CODE OF JUSTINIAN

Book VIII

TITLE XLVII
Concerning Paternal Control

1. *The Emperors Antoninus and Verus to Titius.*

If you allege that your son is under your control, the Governor of the province will determine whether he ought to hear you, as you have for a long time permitted his affairs to be transacted as those of the head of a family, by the persons appointed his guardians under his mother's will.

2. *The Emperor Antoninus to Maronia.*

Whatever property you have obtained while under the control of your father belongs to him, excepting such as he cannot legally acquire.

Published on the sixteenth of the *Kalends* of March, during the Consulate of Laetus and Cerealis, 216.

3. *The Emperor Alexander to Artemidorus.*

While your son is under your control, he cannot alienate any property which he has acquired for you. If he should not show you the respect due to a father, you will not be prevented from punishing him by the right of paternal authority, and you can use even a harsher remedy if he should persevere in his obstinacy, for having brought him before the Governor of the province, the latter will impose the sentence which you desire.

Published on the sixth of the *Ides* of December, during the Consulate of Albinus and Maximus, 228.

4. *The Emperors Valerian and Gallienus to Cala.*

It seems to be more proper for the disputes which have arisen between you and your children to be settled at home. If, however, the matter is of such a nature that you deem it necessary to have recourse to the law in order to punish them for the wrong which they have inflicted upon you, the Governor of the province, if applied to, will order what is usually prescribed by law with reference to pecuniary disputes, and will compel your children to show you the respect which is due to their mother, and if he should ascertain that their disgraceful conduct has proceeded to the extent of serious injury, he will severely punish their want of filial affection.

Published on the fifteenth of the *Kalends* of June, during the Consulate of Æmilianus and Bassus.

5. *The Emperors Diocletian and Maximian to Donatus.*

If your daughter does not show you proper respect, but also refuses to furnish you with the necessaries of life, she can be compelled to do so by the Governor of the province.

Published on the *Kalends* of March, during the Consulate of Diocletian, Consul for the third time, and Maximian, 287....

7. *The Same Emperors and Caesars to Dupliana.*

If your husband, although a soldier, was still under the control of his father, and himself had a son in lawful marriage, there is no doubt that he will remain subject to the authority of his grandfather.

Ordered on the second of the *Nones* of April, during the Consulate of the Caesars....

9. *The Same Emperors and Caesars to Niconagoras.*

The Decrees of the Senate enacted with reference to the acknowledgment of offspring clearly set forth that no one can deny his child, as is shown by the penalty prescribed, as well as the prejudicial action authorized by the Perpetual Edict, and the fact that support can be demanded before the Governor by a child over three years of age, if applied for in its own name.

Ordered at Sirmium, on the fifth of the *Kalends* of May, during the Consulate of the Caesars.

1 THE DIGEST OF JUSTINIAN 19-24 (Theodor Mommsen, Paul Krueger & Alan Watson eds., Watson trans. 1985); 4 ibid. 819

BOOK ONE

7. ADOPTIONS AND EMANCIPATIONS AND THE OTHER FORMS OF RELEASE FROM POWER

1. MODESTINUS, *Rules, book 2.*

Sons-in-power can be made such not only by nature but also by forms of adoption. The term "adoption" denotes a genus, which is divided into two species, of which one is called by the same word "adoption," the other *adrogatio.* Sons-in-power are subject to adoption; people who are *sui juris,* to *adrogatio*....

12. ULPIAN, *Sabinus, book 14.*

Someone who has been set free from his father's power cannot afterward honorably return into his power except by adoption....

15. ULPIAN, *Sabinus, book 26.*

If a head of household (*pater familias*) should be adopted, everything which belonged to him and which can be claimed by him is by tacit operation of law transferred to his adopter. Stating this more fully: his children who are in his power go with him. But also those of his children who by right of *postliminium* return [to full citizenship from being enslaved by an enemy] or who were *in utero* at the time of *adrogatio* are likewise brought into the power of the adrogator.

1. If a man who has two sons and has a grandson by each of them wishes to adopt one of the grandsons on the fiction that he is the son of the other son, he can do this by emancipating the grandson and then adopting him on the fiction that he is the son of the other son. For he does this as anyone at all, not as grandfather, and since the *rationale* is that he can adopt the child as though he were born of anyone at all, so also he can adopt the child as if born of the other son.

2. In cases of *adrogatio,* the scrutiny of the court is directed to the question whether perhaps the adrogator is less than sixty years old, because then he should rather be attending to begetting his own children — unless it should so happen that sickness or health is an issue in the case or there is some other

just ground for *adrogatio,* such as his being related to the person he wishes to adopt.

3. Likewise, one ought not to adrogate several people unless on some just ground. And *adrogatio* of someone else's freedman or of an older person by a younger is out of the question....

21. GAIUS, *Rules, sole book.*

For females also can be adrogated under imperial rescript....

25. ULPIAN, *Opinions, book 5.*

After the death of a daughter who had been living as a *mater familias* as if lawfully emancipated and who had appointed testamentary heirs before her death, her father is estopped from initiating proceedings which would give the lie to his own act by raising the allegation that he did not carry out a lawful emancipation or did not do so in the presence of witnesses....

28. GAIUS, *Institutes, book 1.*

A man who has in his *potestas* a son and through him a grandson has a free choice as to releasing the son from his power while retaining the grandson or *vice versa* as to keeping the son in power while manumitting the grandson or as to making them both *sui juris.* The same propositions we may take as read in relation to the great-grandson....

30. PAUL, *Rules, book 1.*

Even bachelors can adopt sons.

31. MARCIAN, *Rules book 5.*

A son who is in his father's power is unable by any means to compel his father to emancipate him, whether he be a natural or an adoptive son....

34. PAUL, *Questions, book 11.*

It has been asked if there is any actionable right in a case where I gave a son to you in adoption subject to the condition that you should give him back to me in adoption after, say, three years. Labeo holds that there is nothing actionable here, since it is not at all agreeable to our customs that someone have a temporary son....

40. MODESTINUS, *Distinctions, book 1.*

On the adrogation of a head of household (*pater familias*), those children who were in his power become grandchildren to the adrogator and come into his power at the same moment as does their father. But the same proposition does not apply in a case of adoption; for then the grandchildren are retained in the natural grandfather's power. 1. Not only when someone is adopting but also when he is adrogating, he must be older than the person he is making his son by *adrogatio* or by adoption. What is more, he must be of complete puberty, that is, he must be eighteen years older than the person in question. A eunuch can by *adrogatio* obtain for himself a *suus heres*; his bodily defect is no hindrance to him....

45. PAUL, *Lex Julia et Papia, book 3.*

There are transferred to an adoptive father any legal burdens incumbent on the person given in adoption....

BOOK FORTY-EIGHT

8. *LEX CORNELIA* ON MURDERERS AND POISONERS

2. ULPIAN, *Adulterers, book 1.*

A father cannot kill his son without giving him a hearing but must accuse him before the prefect or the provincial governor.

10. *PATRIA POTESTAS, EMANCIPATIO,* AND *PECULIUM*

ALAN WATSON, SOCIETY AND LEGAL CHANGE 23-29 (1977)

Patria potestas, the power of a Roman head of family over his children and remoter descendants, was the core of the Roman law of persons. In the second century A.D. the jurist Gaius could write:

> Also in our *potestas* are the children whom we beget in civil marriage. This right is peculiar to Roman citizens; for scarcely any other men have over their sons a power such as we have.[1]...

The unusual features of Roman *patria potestas* were both that it was so extensive and also that it ended only with the death of the *paterfamilias*....

[A] person in *potestas* could not own any property. It is immediately apparent to us that a system in which the majority of adults, even of the upper classes, males as well as females, could own no property but were dependent on their father or father's father, and were always subject to parental discipline, can scarcely have been economically satisfactory for the society as a whole. The main questions for us, therefore, are whether it corresponded to something deep in the Roman psyche, to the "spirit of the people," and it worked to the advantage of the political élite.

The first thing to notice is that two devices developed early, *emancipatio* and the *peculium*, which profoundly modified the working of *patria potestas* though they had little effect on legal rules.

Emancipatio did not exist as early as the XII Tables, but was a new institution created apparently by the early guardians of the law, the pontiffs, by a deliberate misinterpretation of the provision of the XII Tables that if a father sold his son three times the son was free from his father. According to Gaius writing in the second century A.D., the father mancipates the son to a third party who in turn manumits the son *vindicta*. The son reverts to the father's

[1] G.1.55.

potestas, and he mancipates the son again, and again the recipient manumits him. The process is repeated once again, and the son is then free from paternal power and independent. The XII Tables had spoken only of a son, and a very forced interpretation decided that only one mancipation would end *potestas* for all other descendants, male and female. The procedure was clumsy — in the case of a son which would be the most common situation — but effective.

Thus *patria potestas* could be brought artificially to an end when the father wished. The need for such a possibility was obviously felt at a very early date and among the upper classes (who alone would have the necessary incentive, and the necessary influence with the pontiffs) — but no statistical evidence is available to show how common the practice was. Some statistical evidence for the early post-classical period — when *patria potestas* was still in full swing — is, however, provided by Justinian's *Code*. For the period A.D. 235-284 for instance, there are 53 rescripts which deal in any way with parent and child and 14 of these show there was an *emancipatio*. For the succeeding reign of Diocletian the corresponding figures are 112 and 36. Since there may in some of the cases have been an *emancipatio* which is not mentioned because irrelevant, and since some of the rescripts concern infants, adoption and other topics, it emerges that at that time *emancipatio* was very common indeed. The precise significance of this is not easy to judge. It may be that as a consequence of the *constitutio Antoniniana* which extended Roman citizenship to most of the free inhabitants of the Empire, a large proportion of the population — unused to Roman tradition — preferred to opt out of the system of *patria potestas*, and that *emancipatio* became much commoner. At the very least, however, one can say that during the third century A.D. very many Romans preferred not to live with the much vaunted *patria potestas*.

The other device modifying *patria potestas* is very much more important. Only persons, male or female, not subject to another's power could own property. But from very early times, fathers allowed their sons a fund (called a *peculium*) which they dealt with virtually as if it were their own. *Peculia* for free descendants are not evidenced in the XII Tables, but *peculia* to slaves are; hence a *fortiori, peculia* to descendants existed. All the evidence suggests that in historical times, virtually every (male?) person in *patria potestas* — apart from the large class of have-nots — had a *peculium*. Though the *peculium* existed and had legal recognition, there was little legal content to the *peculium*. Its legal recognition is apparent, above all, in the *actio de peculio et de in rem verso* and in *praelegata* of *peculium*. The *actio de peculio* which was probably invented in the first century B.C. was a modified action brought against a *paterfamilias* in respect of a contract made by someone in his *potestas* or ownership. The *pater* could be condemned to pay damages up to the amount in the *peculium* and to the extent to which he had benefited. Until the introduction of this action and the other *actiones adiecticiae qualitatis* (as such modified actions are called) no contractual remedy lay against a *paterfamilias* for contracts entered into by his dependants. This must have restricted the commercial usefulness of sons and slaves very severely. A *praelegatum* was a legacy left to an heir when there were more heirs than one. Commonly each heir who was in the *potestas* of the testator was left a *praelegatum* of his *peculium*.

The inability of a person in *potestas* to own property of his own should be the aspect of *patria potestas* of greatest social importance. Yet so far were the wealthier Roman citizens from accepting the values inherent in their much vaunted life-long power of the father that they evaded the effects by granting *peculia*. The resulting situation, however, can scarcely be regarded as satisfactory. If a son, of whatever age, made a contract with a third party and failed to perform adequately, that third party could not enforce against him a judgement for financial compensation since the son owned no property. Again even when a son was granted the right of full administration of his *peculium* this did not entitle him to make gifts. And when he died, no property rights passed since he owned no property. In keeping with this, a son, a *filiusfamilias*, could not make a will.... So far as property is concerned, it is no exaggeration to claim that in practice the Roman citizens largely abandoned the pure conception of *patria potestas* without putting in its place a system which was really satisfactory, economically or socially.

In evaluating *patria potestas* as a reflection of the spirit of the Roman people, some aspects should be stressed more than others. It is, of course, true — at least for periods in Roman history — that new-born infants might legally be exposed and left to die, that infants and young children might be sold into slavery by indigent parents, that parental consent might be required for marriage and might control divorce, and that fathers might have the legal right to punish recalcitrant children, and that all these are very important aspects of *patria potestas*. But all these are commonly to be found in other systems and would not justify Gaius' opinion of *patria potestas* as unique, or our singling out *patria potestas* as something peculiarly Roman. What does require our attention, apart from questions of property, are those elements which are very uncommon in other systems (or not found at all) and which give the *pater* extreme powers especially over adult descendants. Three elements appear particularly striking: the power of life and death, the power of sale into real slavery, and the right to surrender a wrongdoing descendant to the victim instead of paying compensation or a penalty....

[I]n fact there is textual evidence that the XII Tables themselves contained a clause that the *paterfamilias* could put a son to death only with good reason, which presumably would mean that the son had to have committed a serious crime.

The father's power to sell "across the Tiber" certainly existed but we seem to have no record of the power ever having been used. Cicero talks as if the power existed in his day, but this may have been so only in theory. It is hard to resist the conclusion that in practice the right became obsolete long before the Empire.

The right to surrender a son, daughter, or remoter descendant instead of paying compensation or the penalty for a delict committed by the descendant also existed but the right to surrender a female had disappeared by the time of Gaius,[24] and the surrender of males was abolished by Justinian.[25] We cannot tell how often the right was used. Though it does seem to have existed in

---

[24] G.4.75ff.

[25] J.4.8.6.

practice in classical law, Justinian tells us that it was obsolete before he abolished it....

All in all, it seems to me that *patria potestas* was harmful to the Roman economy and not at all beneficial to the ruling élite. The system was fundamentally inconvenient and remained so despite everything which could be done to mitigate its effects. Yet *patria potestas* does not seem to have corresponded to any deep-felt need in the Roman psyche. It could be, and frequently was, artificially terminated by *emancipatio*, and its most far-reaching social consequence, that *filii* could have no property, was very largely negatived by the virtually universal grant of a *peculium*. The extreme powers of the *pater* are scarcely in evidence. The adherence of the Romans in the later Republic and the Empire to the concept of *patria potestas* can scarcely be described as reasonable....

It is a supreme example of the power of inertia.

NOTES AND QUESTIONS

1. For a study of the methods by which Justinian's four part *Corpus juris civilis* was accomplished, see Tony Honoré, Tribonian (1978).

2. The *Corpus juris* is cited by subdivision. For the Digest, the citation is by book, title, and extract or fragment. E.g., the fragment on sources of law set out *supra* Section B, Part 2 — book 1, title 1 (Justice and Law), fragment 7 — is ascribed to Papinian from book 2 of his *Definitions,* and would be cited D. 1.1.7.

Most fragments are further divided into a *principium* (introduction) and paragraphs. The example above came in two divisions, D. 1.1.7. pr. and D. 1.1.7.1.

3. The *lex Aquilia* is cited D. 9.2. The two fragments reproduced *supra* Section B, Part 7, are cited D. 9.2.1. and D. 9.2.52. pr., 1, 2 (*principium* and paragraphs 1 and 2). Ulpian states that the *lex Aquilia* was a plebiscite. Consider Alfenus's extract. Do you think his opinions resulted from actual cases or hypotheticals discussed with students?

4. Formulate the law of succession based on the extracts from Justinian's Institutes and Digest. The procedural device to enforce these rules was the *querela inofficiosi testamenti* (complaint of undutiful or irresponsible will). Do the rules make sense? What social policies are promoted by the rules?

5. Formulate the law of *patria potestas* based on Justinian's *Corpus juris.* Who is speaking, and to whom, in the excerpts from the Institutes, the Code, and the Digest?

6. Notice the distinctive styles among the different parts of the *Corpus juris.* Which excerpts appear most similar to a modern statutory enactment? To the *ratio decidendi* in a judicial opinion? To language in a treatise?

7. One of the rules associated with *patria potestas* was that a person *in potestate* could not own property. Was this rule a part of the Roman *Volksgeist* (spirit of the people), a Marxian example of the elite exploiting an underclass of citizens, or something else? What other idea could explain the continuity of such a rule for a thousand years?

8. Augustus invented a special privilege to encourage voluntary recruitment of citizens into his professional army. It was a new *peculium*, the *peculium castrense* (military fund). This fund consisted of what a son *in potestate* acquired by military service. A son could alienate this property or devise it by will without interference by his *paterfamilias*.

9. For research on the role of women in Roman society, see Eva Cantarella, Pandora's Box: The Role and Status of Women in Greek and Roman Antiquity (1987); Jane F. Gardner, Women in Roman Law and Society (1986); Judith P. Hallett, Fathers and Daughters in Roman Society: Women and the Elite Family (1984); Mary R. Lefkowitz & Maureen B. Fant, Women's Life in Greece and Rome: A Source Book in Translation (1982).

For the foundations of parental authority in historical and comparative perspective, see S.J. Stoljar, *Children, Parents and Guardians,* in 4 International Encyclopedia of Comparative Law ch. 7 (Max Rheinstein ed. vol. 4, Persons and Family, 1973).

C. LAW AND GOVERNMENT IN MEDIEVAL EUROPE

1. THE DECAY OF ROMAN LAW

PAUL VINOGRADOFF, ROMAN LAW IN MEDIEVAL EUROPE 13, 15-18, 24-29 (2d ed. 1929)

My tale begins at the epoch of decay during which the Western Empire was engaged in its last struggles with overwhelming hordes of barbarians. It was the time when the new languages and nations of Western Europe were born; when the races gathered within the boundaries fixed by Augustus, Trajan, and Septimius Severus were permeated by Latin culture; when the elements of Romance and Teutonic Europe were gradually beginning to assume some shape. The period may be studied from two opposite points of view: it was characterized by the Romanization of the provinces and by the barbarization of Rome....

Roman Law, even so far as it was recognized and practised by the barbarians in the provinces, began to take the shape of a body of debased rules. Though many of the characteristic institutions of Roman legal antiquity were still in vigour, they had ceased to represent a high level of juridical culture. Three principal statements of barbarized Roman Law arose at the close of the fifth and at the beginning of the sixth century: the Edicts of the Ostrogothic kings, the *Lex Romana Burgundionum*, and the Roman Law of the Visigoths (*Breviarium Alaricianum*) compiled in 506 by order of King Alaric II. Of these three, the last exerted the greatest influence. While the Edicts of the Ostrogothic kings lost their significance after the destruction of their kingdom by the Byzantines, while the law of the Romans in Burgundy remained local, the Visigothic compilation became the standard source of Roman Law throughout Western Europe during the first half of the Middle Ages. The *Breviarium Alaricianum* purposed to be, and indeed was, a more or less complete Code for the usage of the Roman populations of France and Spain. And it deserves attention as evidence of the state to which Roman Law had been reduced by the beginning of the sixth century....

The *Corpus Juris* of Justinian, which contains the main body of Roman Law for later ages, including our own, was accepted and even known only in the East and in those parts of Italy which had been reconquered by Justinian's generals. The rest of the Western provinces still clung to the tradition of the preceding period culminating in the official Code of Theodosius II (A.D. 438). In the fifth century, lawyers had to take account of the legislative acts of Constantine and his successors up to 438, of fragments of earlier legislation gathered together in the private compilations of Gregorius and Hermogenes, of the *Novellae* of fifth-century emperors, and of a vast unwieldy body of jurisprudence as laid down in legal opinions and treatises of the first three centuries A.D. Even after the achievement of the commissioners of Theodosius, the despairing remarks of Theodosius II on the state of the law in his time remained to a great extent true. One of the principal reasons of the "pallid hue of night studies of Roman Law," as he expresses it, was undoubtedly connected with the "immense quantity of learned treatises, the variety of actionable remedies, the difficulties of case law, and the huge bulk of imperial enactments which raised up a dense wall of fog against all attempts of the human mind to master it." It was a rather fine performance of the "barbarian" Visigothic king to attempt, in 506, with the help of his nobles, his clergy, and the representatives of provinces, to do for the Roman population under his sway what Justinian did some thirty years later with infinitely greater resources at his disposal for the Eastern Empire....

We must next inquire in what way, and how far, the degenerated legal customs of Rome were applied in the early Middle Ages. It must be noticed firstly, that no State of this period was strong enough to enforce a compact legal order of its own, excluding all other laws, or treating them as enactments confined to aliens. Even the most powerful of the barbarian governments raised on the ruins of the Empire, such as the Lombard or Frankish, dealt with a state of affairs based on a mixture of legal arrangements. The Carolingian rulers, and especially Charlemagne, introduced some unity in matters of vital importance to the government or to public safety, but, even in their time, racial differences were allowed to crop up everywhere. Law became necessarily personal and local in its application. Both facts must be considered in connexion with the survival of Roman legal rules.

The forcible entry of the Goths, Lombards, and Franks into the provinces did not in any sense involve the disappearance or denationalization of the Roman inhabitants. The legal status of the latter was allowed to continue. The personality of a Roman was valued in a peculiar way, differing from the barbarians that surrounded him. If it cost 200 *solidi* to atone for the homicide of a Frank, it cost 100 *solidi* to kill a Roman in Frankish Gaul. All intercourse between Romans was ruled by the law of their race. When a Roman of Toulouse married a girl of the same race, she brought him a *dos* in accordance with Paul's *Sententiae*, II, 22, 1; he exercised a father's authority over his children, on the strength of the ancient custom of *patria potestas*, as modified by the laws of Constantine. If a landowner wanted to sell his property, he would do it of his own free will, according to the rules of *emptio venditio*. If he wished to dispose of his property after his decease, he would be able to draw up a will making provision for bequests to be paid out by his heir....

In all these and in many other respects the legal rights of the Roman would be at variance with those of his German neighbours. These, again, would act differently, each according to his peculiar nationality, as Salian Franks or Ripuarians, Bavarians or Burgundians, &c. The position became very intricate when members of different nationalities, living under different laws, were brought together to transact business with each other....

We find, in fact, in these cross-relationships very striking examples of so-called conflicts of law. Before proceeding to examine the material questions at issue, it was necessary for the judges to discover to what particular body or bodies of law the case belonged. The report of a trial between the monasteries of Fleury on the Loire and St. Denis provides a good illustration of the points raised on such occasions. The case was brought before the tribunal of the Frankish Court. It was found necessary to adjourn it, because both plaintiff and defendant were ecclesiastical corporations, and as such entitled to a judgement according to Roman Law, of which none of the judges was cognisant. Experts in Roman Law are summoned as assessors, and the trial proceeds at the second meeting of the tribunal. The parties would like to prove their right by single combat between their witnesses, but one of the assessors of the court protests against the waging of battle, on the ground that such a mode of proof would be contrary to Roman Law. The point at issue is therefore examined and decided according to Roman rules of procedure, that is, by production of witnesses and documents. St. Benet, however, the patron of the Abbey of Fleury, was seemingly prejudiced in favour of the Frankish mode of proof-by-battle, as he revenged himself on the too forward assessor by striking him dumb.

The rules as to allowing or disallowing recourse to one or the other personal law were necessarily rather complicated. For instance, the payment of fines for crimes was apportioned according to the law of the criminal, and not of the offended person. As regards contracts, each party was held bound by the rule of its own law; but if the contract was accompanied by a wager, it was interpreted according to the law of the party making the wager. In the case of a contract corroborated by a deed (*carta*), the legal form and interpretation depended on the status of the person executing the deed....

The confusion resulting from such cross-relations of personal legal status was not lessened by the fact that in almost every jurisdictional district, local customs arose to regulate the ordinary dealings of its population. In districts with a clearly preponderating racial majority these customs assumed a specific national colouring — Lombard, Frankish, Roman, as the case might be. Local customs become in course of time a very marked characteristic of the Middle Ages. They tend to restrict the application of the purely personal principle, although the latter was not entirely abolished for a long time. The way in which the light of Roman legal lore was transformed while breaking through the many-coloured panes of local custom was most varied. It is sufficient for our present purpose to note the geographical boundaries of the regions where legal customs were built up on the basis of Roman Law. The area was a wide one. It covered, firstly, Southern Italy, where the Byzantine Empire upheld its authority, until the advent of the Saracens and of the Normans. Here the courts administered not only Roman Law as laid down in the

Corpus Juris, but also the legislation of Justinian's successors. In the centre, the district forming the so-called Romagna was characterized by the application of Justinian's Code. Thirdly, in Southern France and Northern Spain, the *Breviarium Alaricianum* reigned supreme.

Now, by laying stress on these geographical limits, I do not mean that Roman legal customs did not assert themselves outside the mentioned regions. On the contrary, throughout the proper domain of barbaric laws, in Northern France, in Germany, and even in England, the influence of certain Roman institutions was manifest in many ways. Even where there was no numerous Roman population to represent the Roman racial element, the clergy, at least, followed Roman Law, and many rules of the latter were adopted for their practical utility.

2. CUSTOMARY LOCAL LAW

HAROLD J. BERMAN, LAW AND REVOLUTION: THE FORMATION OF THE WESTERN LEGAL TRADITION 52-59, 76, 81, 297-98 (1983)*

The earliest known legal orders prevailing among the peoples of northern and western Europe were mainly tribal in character. Every tribe or "stem" (*Stamm*) had its own law: the Franks, Alemanns, Frisians, Visigoths, Ostrogoths, Burgundians, Lombards, East Saxons, Vandals, Suevi, and other peoples that were eventually combined in the Frankish Empire, embracing much of what later became Germany, France, and northern Italy; the Angles, West Saxons, Jutes, Celts, Britons, and other peoples of what later became England; the Danes, Norwegians, and other Norsemen of Scandinavia and later of Normandy, Sicily, and elsewhere; and many others, from Picts and Scots to Magyars and Slavs. In the period from the sixth to the tenth centuries, the legal orders of all these peoples, though largely independent of one another, were nevertheless remarkably similar. On the one hand, the basic legal unit within the tribe was the household, a community of comradeship and trust based partly on kinship and partly on oaths of mutual protection and service. Violation of the peace of the household by an outsider would lead to retaliation in the form of blood feud, or else to interhousehold or interclan negotiations designed to forestall or compose blood feud. On the other hand, there were territorial legal units consisting typically of households grouped in villages, villages grouped in larger units often called hundreds and counties, and hundreds and counties grouped in very loosely organized duchies or kingdoms. In the local territorial communities, the chief instrument of government and law was the public assembly ("moot," "thing") of household elders. Besides kinship and local territorial communities, there were also various kinds of lordship (feudal) bonds, often formed by households "commending" themselves to great men for protection.

At the head of the tribes and of the local and feudal communities stood royal and ecclesiastical authorities. In the course of time the larger territorial and religious units represented by these higher authorities became more and more

*For permission to photocopy this selection, please contact Harvard University Press.

Figure 3.1
Western Europe circa 1050

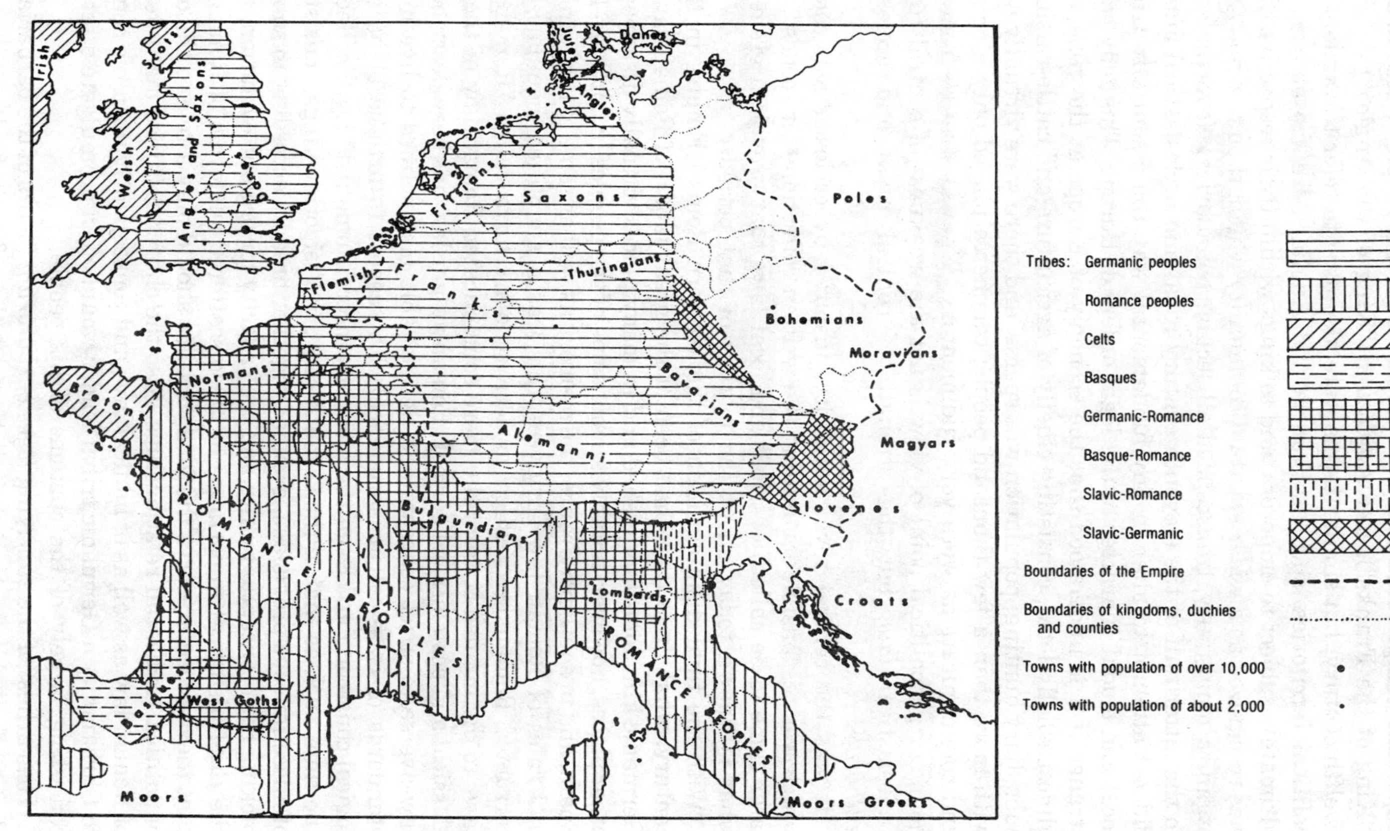

important. Kings continued to be called kings of a people — *Rex Francorum* ("King of the Franks"), *Rex Anglorum* ("King of the Angles") — until the twelfth century, but similar terms were also used to refer to vaguely defined political territories, such as Francia and Anglia. Also the church, though ultimately subject to emperors, and to kings within their respective domains, was recognized as a wider spiritual community which, though wholly without organizational unity, transcended all secular boundaries. Nevertheless, prior to the latter half of the eleventh century royal and ecclesiastical authorities did not attempt to alter in any fundamental way the essentially tribal and local and feudal character of the legal orders of Europe. This may seem less strange if it is understood that the economy of Europe at the time was also almost wholly local, consisting chiefly of agriculture and cattle-raising, with subsidiary hunting; population was sparse, and there were virtually no towns with more than a few thousand people; commerce played only a small role, and communications were very rudimentary. What is strange from an economic or geopolitical point of view is not the weakness of central royal and ecclesiastical *law*, but the strength of central royal and ecclesiastical *authority*.

It was the central royal authority, inspired by ecclesiastical counselors which was responsible for issuing the written collections (or "codes," as they later came to be called) of tribal and local laws that provide a great deal of what is known today about the folklaw of that period.

With the final disintegration of the Western Roman Empire in the fifth century, what little there had been of the great fabric of Roman law in the Germanic kingdoms diminished and in many places virtually disappeared. In other places, however, notably among some of the peoples in northern Italy, in Spain, and in southern France, the memory as well as some of the terminology and rules of Roman law survived. This was a simplified, popularized, and corrupted Roman law, which modern scholars have called "Roman vulgar law" to distinguish it from the more sophisticated Roman law of the earlier classical and postclassical periods. Roman vulgar law has been described as "a law averse to strict concepts and neither able nor inclined to live up to the standards of classical jurisprudence with respect to artistic elaboration or logical construction." Even the most advanced "Romanist" legal collections of the time, such as that of the seventh-century Visigothic kings, consisted only of miscellaneous provisions, grouped together broadly according to subject but lacking both conceptual unity and the capacity for organic evolution. Perhaps the chief historical importance of these scattered survivals of Roman law is that they helped preserve the idea that law should play a role in the ordering of political and social relationships. Also the church retained many remnants of Roman law as well as of biblical law; and consequently upon his conversion to Christianity a Germanic tribal leader would often promulgate a set of laws consisting largely of the customs of his people.

The earliest of the surviving *leges barbarorum* ("laws of the barbarians"), as they are called by historians to distinguish them from *leges Romanae*, was the law of the Salic Franks, the Lex Salica, issued by the Merovingian king Clovis shortly after his conversion to Christianity in 496. It starts by listing monetary sanctions to be paid by a defendant to a plaintiff for failure to respond to the plaintiff's summons to appear in the local court. It also lists monetary sanctions to be paid by wrongdoers to injured parties for various kinds of offenses, including homicides, assaults, thefts. These are typical provisions of primitive law; one of their principal purposes was to induce the parties to a dispute to submit to a decision of the local assembly (the hundred court) instead of resolving their dispute by vendetta, or else to provide a basis of negotiations between the household of the victim and that of the offender....

Somewhat more sophisticated ... was the so-called Edict of the Lombard chieftain, or king, Rothari, written down in 643, seventy-five years after the Lombards had moved from what is now Hungary and Yugoslavia to what is now northern Italy. Of the 363 articles in the edict almost 140 deal with penal measures. For the murder of a free man or free woman by a free person, compensation of 1200 shillings (*solidi*) was required, whereas the price for the death of a household servant was only 50 *solidi*, and for a slave 20. (Murder of a free person by an unfree person was "compensated" by death.) Various prices were stated for hitting someone on the head, cutting off someone's hair, breaking various named parts of the skull, gouging out the eyes....

The institution of fixed monetary sanctions payable by the kin of the wrongdoer to the kin of the victim was a prominent feature of the law of all the peoples of Europe prior to the twelfth century ....

In addition to the settlement of disputes by blood feud and by interhousehold or interclan negotiations, the Germanic peoples from earliest times held public assemblies (moots) to hear and decide disputes. However, jurisdiction in most types of cases depended on the consent of the parties. Even if they consented to appear, they might not remain throughout, and even if they remained, the moot generally could not compel them to submit to its decision. Thus the procedure of the moot had to assume, and to help create, a sufficient degree of trust between the parties to permit the system to operate, just as the procedure for interhousehold or interclan negotiations, with its reliance upon sureties, pledges, and hostages, had to assume, and to help create, such a degree of trust. Yet it is clear that both the trial before the assembly and the negotiations between the households or clans were apt to be intensely hostile in character....

In Germanic society, the "trust-mistrust" syndrome was closely related to the overriding belief in an arbitrary fate, and this belief, in turn, was reflected above all in the use of the ordeal as a principal method of legal proof. The two main types of ordeal were those of fire and water, the former for persons of higher rank, the latter for the common people. Originally, these were invocations of the gods of fire and water, respectively. Those tried by fire were passed blindfolded or barefooted over hot glowing plowshares, or they carried burning irons in their hands, and if their burns healed properly they were exonerated. The ordeal of water was performed either in cold water or in hot water. In cold water, the suspect was adjudged guilty if his body was borne up by the water contrary to the course of nature, showing that the water did not accept him. In hot water he was adjudged innocent if after putting his bare arms and legs into scalding water he came out unhurt ....

The system of trial by ordeal was combined with, and sometimes replaced by, trial by ritual oaths ("compurgation"). First came the fore-oaths....

These oaths opened the lawsuit. The moot would then decide which party should be allowed to give the oath of proof. On the appointed day both parties would appear, and the party allowed to give the oath would swear to a set formula. To complete his oath, however, he would have to have a number of compurgators, or oath helpers, swear to supporting formulas. The number of required oath helpers depended on their *wer*[a] and on the offense being tried. They might swear, for example: "By the Lord, the oath is clean and unperjured [the complainant or the defendant] has sworn."

All the fore-oaths, denials, final oaths, and supporting oaths had to be repeated flawlessly, "without slip or trip," if they were to succeed. All were cast in poetic form, with abundant use of alliteration....

The formality of proof and its dramatic character were connected with the fact that the law was almost entirely oral. "So long as law is unwritten," Maitland states, "it must be dramatized and acted. Justice must assume a picturesque garb or she will not be seen." Maitland's remark echoes that of the nineteenth-century German historian and linguist Jakob Grimm, who speaks of the "sensuous element" in Germanic law, as contrasted with the more abstract or conceptual element which is prominent in more "mature" legal systems....

Some examples of the symbolic and ceremonial character of Germanic law are the transfer of land by the handing over of twig and turf or hat and glove or by the touching of the altar cloth or the bell rope; the leaving of the house key upon the bier of her dead husband by a widow who wished to free herself from liability for his debts; the use of the staff in legal transactions (for instance, its delivery in a contract of pledge); the handclasp as the usual confirmation of pledges of faith and of contracts; and the use of various ceremonials in seating oneself when taking possession of land or of an office....

[S]een from the perspective of the twelfth century, the institutions of legislation and adjudication of the peoples of northern and western Europe in the year 1000 were very rudimentary. Although kings issued laws, they did so only rarely, and largely in order to reaffirm or revise preexisting customs. The lawmaking authority of popes, metropolitans, and bishops was also largely restricted to occasional reaffirmance or revision of preexisting rules laid down in Scripture or by the church fathers or by church councils. There was no idea that royal or ecclesiastical authorities had the task of systematically developing a body of statutory law. The so-called codes, whether of worldly law or of God's law, were incomplete collections of specific customs, or specific rules, elliptical in character, without definitions of principles or concepts. Similarly with regard to adjudication, there were no professional courts, that is, courts staffed with professional judges, and no idea that cases should be decided according to a developed system of general principles. There were, of course, established rules and procedures for punishing offenses, for compensating for harm, for enforcing agreements, for distributing property on death, and for dealing with many other problems related to justice. Each of the peoples of

[a] *Wer* refers to a person's social status, which varied depending on whether he was, e.g., a Roman or Lombard, clergy or lay, man or woman, and young or old. Cf. the modern German *wer*, which means "who." In a suit for compensation for death, *wergeld* (one's value) was the value fixed for a person's life.

Europe had its own rather complex legal *order*. But none had a legal *system*, in the sense of a consciously articulated and systematized structure of legal institutions clearly differentiated from other social institutions and cultivated by a corps of persons specially trained for that task....

Before the great upheavals of the late eleventh and early twelfth centuries, the peoples of Europe were organized politically in a loose, complex, and overlapping structure of (1) local units, (2) lordship units, (3) tribal (clan) units, (4) large territorial units such as duchies or principalities, which might include a number of tribes (clans), and (5) kingdoms, of which the Frankish kingdom, from the year 800, was also called an empire. The kingdoms were conceived not as territorial units but primarily as the community of the Christian people under a king (emperor), who was considered to be Christ's deputy and supreme head of the church as well as of the nobility, the clans, and the army. The church itself was not conceived as a political unit but primarily as a spiritual community led ultimately by the king or emperor and intermediately by bishops, of whom the Bishop of Rome was by tradition the most important.

Within this general classification, there were very wide differences from locality to locality, lordship unit to lordship unit, tribal unit to tribal unit, and so on. The economy of Europe before the eleventh century was largely local and agrarian. There was very little intercommunication; apart from monks and some others of the clergy and a small number of merchants, and except for military campaigns, only the higher nobility and kings traveled.

3. THE GERMANIC ROMAN EMPIRE AND THE ROMAN CHURCH

DAVID S. CLARK, THE MEDIEVAL ORIGINS OF MODERN LEGAL EDUCATION: BETWEEN CHURCH AND STATE: 35 American Journal of Comparative Law 653, 661-67 (1987)

Charlemagne and the Creation of the Germanic Roman Empire

After the dramatic coronation of Charlemagne (the German-speaking king of the Franks, Karl der Grosse) as Roman emperor in 800, his successor Otto I the Great (936-973) used Christianity as a unifying force to fuse Germanic tribes into an incipient state (*regnum Teutonicum*). He appointed bishops and archbishops as he named other governmental officials, to spread royal authority, thus making the German church a national proprietary institution only weakly tied to Rome. Otto defeated ducal resistance in Germany, compelled tribute from the king of Denmark, forced the dukes of Poland and Bohemia to accept him as their feudal lord, secured the eastern border against the Hungarians, and invaded Italy finally to be crowned Roman emperor by Pope John XII in 962.

In the tenth and eleventh centuries, German kings were more powerful than other monarchs in western Europe. A long struggle between popes and emperors — that is, German kings crowned emperors — prevented the development of a central power in Italy and allowed many urban authorities to exist by competing one against another. Bologna, where the revival of legal studies began, was one of these communes. Papal territory at the time of John XII included only the duchy of Rome and a few other areas in central Italy. Lombardy, in northern Italy, and Burgundy were absorbed into a Roman empire which became a dependency of the German crown.

The Roman Empire as Ideology

From these political and military events German kings concluded that Italy should be part of their patrimony. They saw themselves as successors of the ancient Caesars; their empire was the Roman empire of antiquity. Germans in the late Middle Ages assumed that since the time of Charlemagne this empire had been in their hands, that it and its functions were sacred, and that the emperor was the supreme monarch of the world (*caput mundi*), above all other secular rulers.

An emperor's spiritual mission was to spread Christianity and to bring peace and justice to the Christian world. The medieval *Weltanschauung* before the Investiture Controversy (1075) equated the *imperium Romanum* and *imperium Christianum*; the two spheres should work hand in hand: Emperors argued that by asserting their power they could forestall the prophet Daniel's prediction of the world's end, which would accompany the antichrist's arrival when the Roman empire ceased to exist.[28]

Dominant eleventh century political theory embraced Pope Gelasius I's fifth century doctrine of the two swords, seasoned by additional metaphors: the sun and the moon, gold and lead, soul and body. There was, under this theory, only one holy society in the relevant world: a single Christian society as Saint Augustine had written in his *City of God* (*De civitate Dei*). Under God this society had two rulers, the emperor and the pope, who with their separate hierarchies of governing officials shared respectively the direction of bodies and souls. No man could possess both *imperium* and *sacerdotium*, for each realm was subject to divine law. There should be in principle no conflict between the two, although sinful pride or greed might lead the office holders of either power to exceed the boundaries allotted by divine plan. The emperor was *ex officio* protector of the Church, as Charlemagne had been *rector ecclesiae*, while the pope owed aid and support to the emperor for his mission of maintaining peace and justice.

The coronation of Charlemagne set the stage for subsequent rivalry between church and empire .... When the church was building its power in the eleventh and twelfth centuries, the coronation provided precedent for the proposition that civil authority derived from ecclesiastical conferment; no one could become Roman emperor except by papal coronation (*translatio imperii*). The theory of two swords was reinterpreted to support hierocracy (*kurialistische Theorie*), requiring secular power to follow the church's spiritual guidance, just as the moon receives its light from the sun.

---

[28] To squelch the opposing ascending thesis of government underlying customary law (that a group's consent to a particular practice is needed to create a binding rule), Constantine I expressly decreed that customary law could not derogate from positive written law. (*Jus positivum* evolved as a copying mistake in the twelfth century from the correct Roman term *jus positum*: posited law.)

Alternatively, under a dualistic view (*imperiale Theorie*) the coronation had strengthened Charlemagne and his successors, especially against baronial disaffection, by making the emperor a direct vicar of God (*divus imperator*) for secular matters, advancing the theory of a divine right of kings (*Dei gratia*). Moreover, the fact that Charlemagne continued to make Aachen, not Rome, his capital signaled a shift of political power northward, from Latin peoples to Teutons, creating what later would be called the first German Reich. Charlemagne and his advisors thought of his added authority as a revival of old imperial power. An ideal of Roman culture (*kulturelle Romidee*), with its remembered glory and unity, was ideologically useful. However, it was only with Otto I that the distinctively new political character of the regime became obvious. The Roman empire only became explicitly "holy" when Frederick I Barbarossa (1152-1190) introduced the word *sacrum* into his title in 1157.

The Roman Church as Ideology

Constantine, by granting the church status as a corporation, raised it from its subterranean existence and converted it into a lawful Roman public body. This meant that the church as an entity was now subject to Roman public law, of which emperors had always been held to be the source. Law regulating sacred matters (*jus in sacris*), which provided a constitutional basis for the emperor as *pontifex maximus*, was an essential portion of Roman public law.

On the question of governing the "church universal," the imperial government at Constantinople and the papacy in Rome diverged in the fifth century. Nourished by neoplatonic cosmology — with its theme of totality and indivisibility precluding distinctions between religion, politics, law, or ethics — Christianity claimed to seize the whole of man. According to this wholeness viewpoint, the church universal was a new divinely created society, composed of members who through baptism entered a new life (*novitas vitae*). Its members were bound by God-given laws, found in the Bible, which would be made known by church officers with special Platonic qualifications for government.

The emperor's asserted role as sole governor of the church, according to the church's argument, must be denied for two reasons. First, the forged Donation of Constantine purported to grant the papacy secular authority over Rome and other territories. Second, an emperor would be insufficiently qualified. It was the pope, successor of Saint Peter, who was entitled to issue laws for and to govern Christian society. This doctrinal and jurisdictional primacy, directly founded on the Petrine commission, had three major consequences. First, it constituted the church as a body of all faithful, cleric (*clericus*) and layperson (*laicus*) alike. Second, Christianity seized the whole man, not just his religious and moral spheres. All of his actions — including the political, cultural, and economic — were accessible to judgment by Christian norms. Third, Jesus' commission to Peter established a government over Christian society. The *societas christiana* was an entity to be governed as a hierocracy. It was, in summary, a *corpus* of Christians over which the Roman church exercised plenary monarchic *principatus* through the medium of a pope as the vicar of Saint Peter.

Political Realities in Twelfth and Thirteenth Century Germany

With the expansion of Europe's economy in the twelfth and thirteenth centuries, early nation states, particularly England and France, became more centralized. It is curious that Germany, as the Holy Roman Empire (*das Heilige Römische Reich Deutscher Nation* as it was called in the fifteenth century) and Europe's greatest state in the eleventh century, started to disintegrate during this same period. Economic prosperity in agriculture and commerce added to the strength and pretensions of local German dukes, counts, bishops, and margraves, who were naturally uncomfortable under imperial domination.

The Hohenstaufen emperors (1138-1254) were intoxicated with the idea of reconquering Italy, which kept Rome on an anti-imperial balance of power policy. As this struggle evolved German emperors felt compelled to bargain with their vassals, to employ servant-knights (*ministeriales*), and to grant concessions in return for support. These privileges gave princes and knights the right to maintain their own law courts, to build castles and raise armies, to collect taxes and mint money, and to control roads, markets, and towns lying within their territories. Increased trade at the same time spawned a hundred towns, many of them with charters of self-government. Fortified (*Burg*), administering their own law, these towns became islands of liberty for their middle class (*Bürgertum*).

Frederick I Barbarossa (1152-1190) put the government of Germany on a new footing by accepting these developments. Imperial peace statutes contained much new Romanized law that was enforced at the imperial level. In addition, some of this new law penetrated the territorial law of the developing German cities, duchies, and principalities. Feudalism over the next century triumphed in Germany at the very time that it was succumbing to royal power in France and England. A Germany of princes (*Reichsfürsten*) had arrived.

By the thirteenth century, consequently, Germany had fragmented into a bewildering number of political units, governed locally with only the vaguest obligation to weakened imperial authority. Bishops, furthermore, whom earlier emperors had appointed and favored to offset the power of princes, became a second nobility, fully as rich and independent as secular lords. Rome supported in 1267 an electoral monarchy, later confirmed in the Golden Bull of Emperor Charles IV in 1356. Seven nobles (the archbishops of Mainz, Trier, and Cologne, the duke of Saxony, the king of Bohemia, the count palatine of the Rhine, and the margrave of Brandenburg) were eventually named to elect the Holy Roman emperor.

These electors (*Kurfürsten*) might have attempted to give Germany unity. Instead, between elections they and other princes went their separate ways, usurping royal prerogatives and seizing crown lands. They were first Saxons, Swabians, Bavarians, Thuringians or Franks. The Golden Bull was a *magna charta* of German particularism. A loose bureaucracy of *ministeriales* appointed by the emperor to administer the royal demesne provided some continuity in imperial government, but the *Reichstag* (an imperial diet founded in the twelfth century) languished feebly until 200 years later. No one capital focused the people's loyalty; no one system of laws governed.

The physical Holy Roman Empire was merely a shadow of the ideological Roman empire. Emperors, therefore, were tempted to utilize Roman law to buttress the empire's decaying structure, to lend support to a weakened polity with such lofty ambition.

4. FEUDALISM

MUNROE SMITH, THE DEVELOPMENT OF EUROPEAN LAW 166-73 (1928)

After the dissolution of the Frank Empire, feudalism attained its full development. So long as land remained the most important source of wealth, the economic basis of the whole system was found in the land. It is on the yield of the land tilled by serfs bound to the soil that the whole structure of feudalism primarily rests. Not only is the fighting man, the knight, dependent upon this labor for his maintenance, but his feudal superior and that superior's superior and finally the king himself (where there is a king) has his own manors. The king and his court are maintained primarily by the yield of the royal domains.

Each feudal superior has against his inferior certain rights of economic value. Even when fiefs have become heritable, the feudal superior is entitled to a payment when the fief passes to the heir — the payment known as a relief and amounting usually to one year's income. If the heir is a minor, the feudal superior has the rights of a guardian, which again may involve payment for his services. If, as happened in many parts of Europe, the fief may pass to a daughter, if the deceased vassal had no son, the feudal superior has a voice in determining the marriage of the heiress; it is his right to see that she marries a man capable of discharging the duties that run with the fief; and the lord's consent to marriage may involve a payment and become an additional source of revenue. In certain emergencies the lord may call upon his vassals for aids or contributions — for example, to ransom him from captivity or to provide his daughter with a dowry when she marries. When such aids are demanded from vassals, they in their turn are entitled in this emergency to aids from their inferiors. Thus these taxes, as we may call them, are shifted down the line until they are paid in last instance in whole or in part by the serfs on the manors. There was a possible reversion of the fief to the feudal superior; it came back to him by escheat when there was no heir and by forfeiture in case of a breach of fidelity.

In the manor or demesne itself the servile tillers of the soil not only pay rent in money or in kind but owe to the lord of the manor certain services limited as to amount but not as to character. The serf or villein is bound to work for the lord only so many days in the week, but he must do whatever he is ordered to do. The villein may not give his daughter in marriage (at least, not to a villein on another manor), nor may have his son ordained a priest, nor may he sell a horse or an ox without the lord's permission. For leave to marry, the villein has to pay. His holding passes to his heir, but the heir pays heriot in cattle or other chattels or in money just as the vassal paid relief. The villein might also be called upon for an extraordinary contribution in a special emergency just as the vassal might be called upon for aids; and as already noted, the payment of an aid by the seigneur was an emergency to be met by contributions from his villeins. In the Norman terminology these contributions are described as *tallages*.

In so far as a fief included jurisdiction — and we have seen that the office of count, with the right and duty of holding the county courts, had come to be regarded as a benefice or fief — costs and fines collected in the administration of justice were a source of revenue.

Under the feudal system medieval society fell into marked classes. Above the serfs or villeins stood the knights and other nobles and in the nobility itself there were sharp gradations of rank. We find these most elaborately worked out in the thirteenth century in Germany. At the top of the social hierarchy stand the princes, secular and ecclesiastical. Then we have the free lords whose fiefs are held, not directly from the crown, but from ecclesiastical or secular princes. Then come the freemen who have seat and voice in the county court. These are for the most part knights, but where there were still peasant freeholders, these freeholders or, as the English called them, yeomen, are in the same class as the knights. In the next lower class stand the *ministeriales*, the knights of servile origin who were still in legal theory unfree but whose social position is higher than that of the landless freeman or of the burgess or townsman.

In other parts of Europe the social classification was less elaborate but everywhere those feudal magnates who hold authority over considerable territories as the immediate vassals of the crown constitute the highest nobility, and everywhere the ecclesiastical magnates — bishops and abbots — belong to this class. Under them is the lower nobility, and then comes what the French call the Third Estate — the free burgesses or townsmen....

Regarded as a system of government, feudalism was capable of very different developments. Regarded as a system of tenures, the fact that all lands and offices were held in last instance from a supreme lord — from the king or, where there was no king, from the territorial prince — tended to consolidation of political power. Regarded, on the other hand, from the point of view of the personal bond between lord and vassal — that is, between the immediate feudal superior and his feudal inferior — it could be argued that the king or territorial prince could demand political services only from his immediate vassals and that these in turn could receive orders only from their immediate lord. This latter theory became dominant in western continental Europe. It was expressed in the saying, "The man's man is not the lord's man." This meant disintegration of political authority: it placed in the hands of the great territorial princes, dukes, marquises or counts, a degree of power which tended to make them largely independent of the crown. Until the middle of the thirteenth century, as already noted, the authority of the German kings, who had become also Roman emperors, was greater than the authority exercised by the kings of France. The disintegrating tendencies of feudalism had revealed themselves first in France. From the middle of the thirteenth century, however, German monarchy steadily grew weaker and the chief territorial princes, both in Germany and in northern Italy, became practically independent of the crown. In France, on the other hand, largely through the absorption in the crown of one or another of the great duchies, partly through escheat, partly through marriage, the power of the crown steadily increased. Of no little importance, of course, was the fact that the French crown had become hereditary while the German kingship continued to be elective....

In Spain the practically continuous war between the Christian kingdoms of the north and the Moors, who in the eighth century had obtained control of the greater part of the peninsula, tended, as war always does, to strengthen the central power; and the Spanish royal authority in the separate kingdoms, all of which except Portugal were finally brought by intermarriage into the hands of a single family, became practically absolute ....

In England as a result of the Norman conquest the disintegrating tendencies of feudalism were successfully resisted. At the outset, William's victory over Harold placed in the hands of the conqueror all the English royal domains and the domains of Harold's supporters. A series of rebellions that were crushed and were followed by the seizure of the domains of the rebels brought practically all the land of England into the possession of the Norman crown....

When we consider the development of law on the continent we see that the disintegration of central authority made the development of national law an impossibility. The court of the king was a court for the immediate vassals of the crown and for them only. The courts of these crown vassals had jurisdiction only over their immediate vassals and only in matters of feudal law. The administration of justice, except in feudal matters, remained in the hands of local courts administering local customs. The tradition that the king had a supreme right and duty of drawing into his court all cases of delay or denial of justice never wholly disappeared; but the kings and even the great territorial princes had not the power to enforce this tradition.

When we consider the extent to which feudal law has influenced modern law, we note that little of the feudal system is left except in the law of real property. In so far as feudalism constituted a system of public law, its principles were superseded on the continent by the development of absolute monarchy in Spain and in France and by the development in Germany and in Italy of an equally absolute authority exercised by territorial princes, or by the development of independent or autonomous republics.

In considering feudalism as a system of land tenures, it is to be noted that, just as political authority was dissolved into fragments, so rights in land were separated in medieval jurisprudence into two great groups — *dominium eminens* and *dominium utile*. Eminent domain included at once the political authority of the feudal superior — not merely of the king but of each feudal superior in his relation with his immediate inferior — but it included also all the economic advantages, guardianship, marriage, reliefs, aids, etc., which accrued to the superior. *Dominium utile*, which we may perhaps translate as practical ownership, was held by the seigneur in that property which was under his immediate and direct control. It belonged equally to the king in the royal domains, to every mesne lord in his immediate domains and to the knight in his fee held on tenure of military service. Where, as was usually the case, the serf had a permanent and heritable right in land, we sometimes find that practical ownership was held to be his while the seigneur's right was that of eminent domain.

Practical ownership consists of a life interest, inalienable in most cases, and of a reversion or remainder which again, when vested, is simply another life interest....

On the continent of Europe the modern law of real property shows few traces of feudal principles. Nowhere on the continent were landholdings even in the open country so thoroughly feudalized as in England. What was more important, in the European cities, when these became autonomous and developed each its own law in its own city court, all land was converted into freehold, and rights in land became alienable and capable of devise by will. With the reception of the law books of Justinian as subsidiary law, the Roman conception of ownership became applicable in all cases not governed by the existing local law or by feudal law. Feudal law, as such, had never been administered by any but feudal courts, and when feudal tenures were swept away by the great revolutions of the eighteenth and nineteenth centuries, real property previously governed by feudal law came to be governed by Roman rules.

NOTES AND QUESTIONS

1. In the Dark Ages choice of law rules were primarily based on a person's nationality. This nationality (or personality) principle was gradually replaced for many purposes by the territoriality principle. Is one principle superior in some way for a system of justice to the other principle?

2. *Barbarus* was a person not Roman or Greek. Many barbarians were used by Roman emperors in the fourth and fifth centuries to staff the armies that fought other barbarians. Whole nations, such as Burgundians, Visigoths, Ostrogoths, and Franks, were admitted as allies and settled within the borders of the Roman empire. Can an argument be made that the barbarians "saved" Roman law for Western civilization when, around 500, they published compilations of Roman law (the Ostrogoth Theodoric the Great's *Edictum Theodorici*, King Gundobad's *Lex Romana Burgundionum*, and King Alaric II's *Lex Romana Visigothorum* or *Breviarium Alaricianum*) intended to regulate the affairs of Roman subjects and the clergy within the German kings' domains?

3. Under the personality principle, Germanic invaders continued to live under their own customary law. The kings, however, found it necessary to improve the law for their barbarian subjects and accordingly issued compilations in Latin influenced by Roman and Christian law. The Romanization of the *leges barbarorum* varied from significant in the *Lex Visigothorum* of King Euric (466-484) to little in the *Lex Salica* (c. 496). Other important barbarian laws include the *Edictus Rothari* (Lombards, 643), and the eighth century *Lex Ribuaria* (Ripuarian Franks), *Lex Alemanorum* (Alemans), and *Lex Baiuvariorum* (Bavarians). Around 800 Charlemagne's envoys also wrote down the laws of the Frisians, the Thuringians, and the Saxons. For an English translation of Rothair's Edict and other Lombard laws, along with commentary, see The Lombard Laws (trans. by Katherine Fischer Drew 1973).

In some parts of Europe the division of peoples by nationality began to break down and form territorial groups to whom a common law could be applied. This fusion occurred, for instance, in Visigothic northern Iberia with King Reckesvinth's *Fuero Juzgo* (654) — also called *Liber Iudiciorum* or *Lex Visigothorum* — which suppressed the *Breviarium Alaricianum* and was applicable to all subjects.

4. Medieval law can be characterized by the dramatic character of its proof-taking procedures. Frederic Maitland, the English legal historian, found that "Justice must assume a picturesque garb," while Jacob Grimm, who with his brother Wilhelm compiled the Grimm fairy tales, spoke of the "sensuous element" in early German law (see the Berman excerpt, *supra*). Does U.S. civil and criminal trial procedure, with its champion lawyer, lay factfinders, and forceful cross-examination exhibit these medieval sensuous elements? *See* Wendy Davies & Paul Fouracre, eds., The Settlement of Disputes in Early Medieval Europe (1986).

5. Law, to be effective, requires persuasive ideological support. Can you see how the combined ideologies of the Roman Church and the Holy Roman Empire, despite their differences, favored Roman law?

6. The term "feudalism" has many different meanings. It was a social and economic system establishing rights and obligations associated with lord-vassal relationships and dependent land tenures. But it also was a military system linked to the armed cavalryman — the knight. Feudalism varied significantly from the eighth to the 15th centuries and from place to place. The Enlightenment throughout Europe was in many ways a reaction against feudalism. See Chapter 5, Section A. One way to distinguish the common law and civil law traditions is by the extent to which they have been "defeudalized." The best topic for such a comparison is the law of property. As the Smith excerpt, *supra,* shows, the civil law of property has been more thoroughly defeudalized than the common law. For details see the materials in Chapter 11, Section C.

D. REVIVAL OF ROMAN LAW

1. THE UNIVERSITY AS THE CENTER FOR THE REVIVAL OF ROMAN LAW

DAVID S. CLARK, THE MEDIEVAL ORIGINS OF MODERN LEGAL EDUCATION: BETWEEN CHURCH AND STATE, 35 American Journal of Comparative Law 653, 671-75, 681-93, 696-700 (1987)

A. *The Spontaneous Rise of Universities*

The university added a new institution to family, church, and school as the primary agents for transmission of culture. Characterized by student or teacher corporations enjoying privilege and autonomy, universities were divided into recognized faculties, with specified courses of study, examinations, and degrees. It was within the university framework that the first academic discipline in Europe's history developed, the scholarly and holistic examination of Roman law.

The earliest universities, later called *studia generalia*, date from the twelfth century. Stimulated by a general renaissance of commerce and interest in ancient learning, and perhaps by a specific interest in the continuing Investiture Controversy, they grew spontaneously (*ex consuetudine*) out of needs among teachers and students for protection and out of a desire by professors to formalize examinations and to control issuance of the teaching license (*licentia docendi*). The twelfth century, especially in central and northern Italy, saw the rapid growth of urban life with the formation of municipal institutions, increased exchange of goods, birth of financial capitalism, and the appearance of a lay-spirited middle class. The commune of Bologna, known for its secular, democratic, and egalitarian attitudes, partook of all these developments. It was here that the first modern university evolved.

In the thirteenth century many *studia generalia* were founded by papal or imperial bulls (*ex privilegio*), as the pope and Holy Roman emperor took greater interest in higher education. Even the oldest universities, at Bologna and Paris, by century's end felt it useful to obtain a bull from Pope Nicholas IV. Few new *studia* after this time could acquire the power of conferring a valid teaching license usable throughout Europe (*jus ubique docendi*) without a papal or imperial charter.[63]

B. *The Holy Roman Empire and Roman Law*

The great revival of legal studies occurred in Bologna around 1076, when Pepo began lecturing on Justinian's *Codex* and *Institutiones*. It is probable that a primitive school of notarial arts existed at that time. Other teachers joined Pepo, and between 1085 and 1090 the rebirth was definitely established through the lectures of Irnerius. Irnerius, a layman, interpreted Justinian's *Corpus juris*, and especially its rediscovered *Digesta*, in a direction similar to the tradition at the school in Ravenna to favor the supremacy of imperial over ecclesiastical power.[66] The descending theme of government and law found in Justinian's *Codex* and *Novellae* proved too attractive for emperors to resist. They supported the new lecturing and writing, which helped to establish Bologna as the center for Roman law studies and to attract thousands of students from throughout Europe, including Germany and England.

Clerici who studied Roman law enjoyed certain privileges and immunities, such as the right to invoke ecclesiastical jurisdiction and freedom from taxes. Anxious to stimulate lay travel to Bologna to guarantee a continuous supply of educated legal personnel for administering his empire, Holy Roman Emperor Frederick I Barbarossa in an 1155 decree (repeated in his 1158

[63] The principle of mutual recognition of doctorate degrees for teaching was scarcely recognized by the better *studia generalia*. Many universities required examinations for graduates from elsewhere before allowing them to teach their own students. For most graduates, therefore, the *jus ubique docendi* was no more than a titular honor.

[66] The only surviving manuscript of the Digest was written around 600 in the Byzantine part of Italy. Located in Pisa until 1406 — hence called the *Pisana* — the Florentines removed it when they captured Pisa and renamed it the *Florentina*. It was a copy of the *Pisana*, made in the eleventh century and placed in Bologna, which formed the basis of teaching and scholarship until the humanists became concerned with restoring an uncorrupted text. It is probable that Pope Gregory VII's supporters, searching the libraries of Italy for legal ammunition to use against Emperor Henry IV in their controversy over investiture, found this manuscript.

Authentica habita) granted lay students the same privileges which clerical students possessed. These included immunity from taxes and tolls during the trip to Bologna, freedom from reprisals (liability for debts or damages incurred by a fellow student countryman), and the right to trial before one's own master or bishop. The *Authentica habita* was viewed as the University of Bologna's charter, which gave the student *universitas ultramontanorum* a certain autonomy vis à vis the commune. Law professors soon interpreted Frederick's imperial privilege as one protecting all lay students traveling to and attending any university.

Bolognese professors reciprocated for Frederick at the Diet of Roncaglia (1158), finding that an emperor under Roman law held sovereign rights (*regalia*), especially jurisdiction, over all parts of the empire. Martinus, one of the famous *quattuor doctores*, contended that Frederick was *dominus mundi* with respect to property within his empire and might modify private rights whenever he felt it necessary (*justa causa*) for the state. The adjective holy or sacred in front of the Roman empire, furthermore, implicitly asserting jurisdiction over the church, was justified on the basis of the Roman public law principle controlling sacred matters (*jus in sacris*). The four doctors, who in addition to teaching at Bologna served as counselors to the imperial government as well as to other public officials, also declared along with the commission of judges at Roncaglia that Frederick had the power to tax Lombard cities. Pope Alexander III, who saw the ideological implications of these developments, repudiated them and excommunicated Frederick in 1160 after he intervened in the papal schism to support the antipope.

Hohenstaufen emperors, following the example of Bolognese jurists who inserted extracts from the *Novellae* (*novae leges*) into appropriate places in Justinian's *Codex*, decreed the insertion of their own new laws into the Code as laws of Roman emperors. As a result, a medieval user of the Code might find a law enacted by Frederick I sandwiched between a decree issued by Constantine and one issued by Valentinian....

C. *Students and Their University*

1. *The Number of Students and Their Social Origins*

Men flocked to study law at the University of Bologna after about 1130 from every part of western Europe, including England and Germany. One must admire the motivation (whether for love of learning or for career advancement) of students who traveled across Europe in conditions as dangerous as any encountered by explorers of the American West. The number of law students at Bologna during the thirteenth century probably averaged between 500 and 1500, with substantial fluctuation in attendance due to the contingencies of medieval life. They were mostly older, many in their thirties.

The medieval university student (*studens*) — usually referred to as a scholar (*scholaris*) — was expected to know Latin and to be able to pay a small sum to each master (*magister*) or teacher whose course he took. He might be helped financially — if he were poor — by his town, by a private benefactor, or by his church or bishop. Half the students in the German nation at Bologna, for instance, were financed by ecclesiastical benefices. Many students were aristocrats, who could easily pay the lecture and examination fees, the boarding and travel expenses, as well as the very high prices for books. The remainder were either laymen, clergymen, or secular nonmonastic "clerics" looking to improve their opportunities for advancement. Many were successful, especially graduates of Bologna, in reaching positions as notaries, scribes, counselors, or judges in either imperial, royal, or papal service. Others became judges, notaries, diplomats, mayors, or advisors for cities.

2. *The Commune of Bologna*

Bologna was an independent city-state, with a population between 35,000 and 40,000, precariously playing off the rival power of emperor and pope against each other while simultaneously trying to maintain its own independence. The city council and mayor (*podestà*) recognized that the *studium* was worth cultivating, but they were suspicious of students who wanted to elect their own rectors and confer jurisdiction and allegiance to their own corporate entities.

The *universitas* represented an attempt to create artificial citizenship in place of the natural citizenship which non-Bolognese students had temporarily renounced to pursue knowledge. The great commercial value which a *studium* contributed to Bologna, along with medieval familiarity with the personality principle for choice of law, convinced city fathers to recognize what became an *imperium in imperio* — an extensive civil and penal jurisdiction controlled by the elected officers of student guilds. The threat of student migration, once carried out, severely harmed the town's trade as well as masters' income. After papal intervention and support for students, first against the city in 1217 and later against Emperor Frederick II, who attempted to close the *studium* at Bologna by edict in 1225, the city recognized substantial exemptions and privileges for scholars attending the university. Students won exemption from municipal taxes and military service, while securing jurisdiction through the university over certain town citizens — landlords of student halls and tradesmen engaged in renting or producing books — in matters affecting scholars. By 1245, foreign scholars were accorded the same civil rights as Bolognese citizens, excepting political rights to vote or to hold office....

3. *Student Organizations*

During the thirteenth century, law students at Bologna formed two *universitates* — guild-like corporations, each with its own rector, to confirm by combination those rights that they could not claim as town citizens, as well as to provide mutual protection, social assistance, and a form of self-government. This concluded a stage in the gradual process of amalgamation of smaller student societies, beginning in the twelfth century. The *universitas citramontanorum* represented students from Italy, while the *universitas ultramontanorum* included students from beyond the Alps. These *universitates scholarium* were further subdivided into nations (*natio*, place of birth) that in 1265 numbered 13 for the ultramontane university.

Leaders (*consiliarii*) from the two law *universitates* formed by the fourteenth century a deliberative assembly that consulted on matters of common concern with student *rectores*, Bologna's chief academic officers. The rectorship was something more than the presidency of a private society. According to medieval Roman law every trade had a right to form a *collegium*, elect magistrates, and carve out judicial jurisdiction for disputes concerning members of its trade. Scholars, in setting up a *universitas*, relied on this analogy in electing a rector with judicial authority which, although resisted by professors, was ultimately accepted by them and by the townsmen.

Each of the two law school rectors was elected on an annual basis by its university *consiliarii*. A rector was usually over 25 years old, a cleric, unmarried, and from a prominent family, since wealth was required to support his rank. As chief magistrates, rectors claimed civil and criminal jurisdiction over both scholars and masters. An appeal might be taken from a rector to the university assembly, and from there to the papal legate. In addition, rectors carried out a full range of administrative duties.

D. *Teachers*

Teachers formed their own guilds, *collegia doctorum*, mainly for the task of regulating examinations and granting teaching licenses. Professors were excluded from student *universitates*, not so much because they were teachers, but because the earliest Bolognese professors were town citizens with the rights and privileges that status guaranteed.

The locus of university power resided originally with students, who had the right to organize boycotts (*cessationes*) of unsatisfactory masters and ultimately could threaten to migrate to another town. Teachers swore obedience to the university rector, who appointed student committees (*denunciatores doctorum*) to observe their conduct. The expected coverage of lectures (*lecturae*) was strictly regulated, with fines for omissions. Professors were not supposed to miss class without first obtaining the permission of their students and rector; they could not leave town without providing monetary security guaranteeing their return.[116]

Teachers were in effect free lance lecturers whom students engaged to instruct them. Their income was primarily derived from student lecture fees (*collectae*), but the most famous also earned money by responding to princes, cities, and private inquirers about matters of public or private law.

When other Italian cities desired to attract Bolognese masters to their new universities in the late thirteenth century, by paying an annual stipend, the city of Bologna responded by offering a few teachers *salaria*. More teachers in the fourteenth century were paid municipal salaries and finally the city gained the power to select teachers. In 1381, 23 salaried law professors received annual *salaria* varying from roughly $13,000 to $81,000 (100 to 620 *librae*), while the budget for all faculties at the University of Bologna was $8.3 million.

---

[116]In the fifteenth century, most Italian cities (or princes) established boards (*reformatores studii*) to govern their relations with *studia*. By the sixteenth and seventeenth centuries, these boards succeeded in largely eliminating student autonomy.

E. *Roman Law Studies*

1. *Glossators*

Irnerius, in his *Summa codicis*, collected glosses on the *Corpus juris* according to a scholarly (scholastic) dialectical method derived from the teaching of grammar and logic in the *trivium* and also used in canon law and theology. The syllogism and the orderly marshaling of arguments for and against particular theses characterized the intellectual climate of the age, based in large part on Aristotle's rediscovered logic. Abélard's book *Sic et non* was also tremendously influential. He first stated in the form of a thesis the question on which doubt existed. *Sic et non* contained 158 such questions, such as "a lie is never permissible, *et non*." Abélard brought together for each question the conflicting opinions of various authorities. His view was that by doubting we are led to inquiry, and by inquiring we attain truth.

Irnerius's disciples, among whom the lay four doctors were the most famous — Bulgarus, Hugo, Jacobus, and Martinus — became known as glossators by their use of the gloss as a typical literary form. Their method involved the task of restoring the text of the *Corpus juris civilis* — the title later used for Justinian's compilation consisting of the *Digesta, Codex,* and *Institutiones*, supplemented with the *Novellae* — by eliminating the many summaries and extracts that had been used in the early Middle Ages. Glosses were explanations, corrections, and variant interpretations written between the lines and in the margins of the rediscovered text. *Glossae* helped future scholars improve their study of the legal text and served as notes for teachers orally presenting *lecturae.*[123]

Glossators derived from glosses other literary forms, stimulated by their lectures. *Summae* were comprehensive statements concerning a title or groups of titles from part of the *Corpus juris.* They grew out of the introductory portion (*introductio titulorum*) of lectures. Some, like Azo Portius's (1150-1235) *Summa Codicis*, were extremely popular with practitioners. *Casus* were hypothetical or actual cases that illustrated one or more legal texts. Writings that generalized from issues posed by groups of cases were called *commenta*, precursors to a form of literature popular with postglossators. *Quaestiones legitimae* dealt with important unresolved issues that arose from conflicting texts, frequently with the author's *solutio.* Some manuscripts were organized in the form of queries (*quaere*); others followed Abélard's *sic et non* approach; still others were written as dialogue between teacher and student of the type one might hear at a disputation. It is here that one finds a harbinger for the modern Socratic dialogue in law....

Glossators considered the *Corpus juris* to be truly organic, theoretically containing no contradictions, and surviving as living law. Although not the law actually in force anywhere — even in Italy, degenerated Roman law and Lombard customs were used — Bologna graduates used the new learning

[123] Glossators symbiotically developed their lectures and writings, since transcripts of lectures (*lecturae reportatae*) circulated widely. Some glossators also brought glosses together to form a collection (*apparatus*), which was useful in preparing lectures....

The first edition actually called *Corpus juris civilis*, combining the *Digesta, Codex*, and *Institutiones*, was edited by Dionysius Gothofredus in 1583.

when they took up positions in chanceries and courts all over Europe, exerting great influence on the law's development. The last great glossator, Accursius, created a collection (*apparatus*) of glosses between 1220 and 1260 in his *Glossa ordinaria*. This became the standard authority used by jurists working for kings and towns to help break the grip of local feudal lords and to fight assemblies of commoners as well as the papacy.[128]

The two principal legitimating sources of ultimate knowledge in the late Middle Ages were authority (*auctoritas*) and reason (*ratio*). Glossators helped to establish the *Corpus juris* as *auctoritas* in the same way that the Bible or Aristotle's writings were *auctoritas*. But they also brought reason — in essence, logic — to create systematic order for Roman law. They used their learning to understand and to explain the text, as well as to make sometimes obvious contradictions fit within a larger framework. An incipient legal science was used not to question the *Corpus juris*'s authority, but rather to be dogmatic in the sense of *ratio*. Glossators learned, from the classical Roman jurisconsults, the art of solving human problems by discussing an isolated legal issue in light of general rules. Reason as a source for order and justice was now an alternative to inflexible custom or violence.

2. *Commentators*

The cultural climate of the late thirteenth century — influenced by the increasing economic, political, and social complexity of growing towns and rising nation states — stimulated the practical application of learned law, especially through *consilia*, and the use of more complicated literary forms such as the comment (*commentarium*). In harmony with the sophisticated scholastic philosophy of St. Thomas Aquinas (1225-1274), the comment as a characteristic literary genre built upon established glosses but was more likely to also consider the statutory law of Italian or other European cities, guild law, or feudal customs and statutes in striving toward a more systematic and practical treatment of legal themes.

Today, in selecting the date of Accursius's death (1263) as the watershed to separate two schools of legal scholarship, we can say that glossators laid the foundation for a systematic study and explication of Roman law. A subsequent group of scholars, whom Friedrich von Savigny called postglossators, are now usually referred to as commentators, although Franz Wieacker and others also refer to them as *Konsiliatoren* to emphasize their role in applying Roman law in specific *consilia* to the legal issues of feudal Europe.

The huge number of independent political jurisdictions faced with economic change and periodic turmoil increased interest in conflict of laws principles and in the relationship between a learned Roman law and relatively primitive local statutes and customs. Commentators developed new doctrines to meet this situation; in fact they developed whole fields of law. In conjunction with canonists, commentators worked out principles in the context of actual cases

[128] Accursius's *Glossa ordinaria* became the basic text used for law study. Printed editions between 1468 and 1627 exist in five large size volumes....

Glossators, although primarily law teachers, also gave expert opinions (*consilia*) to clients, acted as advocates in lawsuits, and resolved disputes as judges.

for criminal law, procedure, choice of law, and for the law of matrimonial property, land utilization, commerce, and corporations. From the middle of the thirteenth century, throughout Europe — from Italy north to Scotland and Scandinavia, from Portugal east to Hungary and Poland — learned jurists worked at interpreting what would become a European common law (*jus commune*). The initial path for the reception of Roman law in western Europe was paved and smoothed by the efforts of commentators and their brethren in canon law. Masters at newly established French and Italian universities in particular played a major role complementing the work at Bologna. French jurists, such as Guido de Cumis, Jacques de Révigny, and Pierre de Belleperche in the second half of the thirteenth century, were influenced by developments in philosophy, especially the rediscovered parts of Aristotle's logic. Dialectic, always a staple at the University of Paris in theology and philosophy, more starkly colored jurists' literary forms enunciating legal issues. After a burst of important commentaries, ending with the influential work of Pierre de Belleperche at the University of Orléans about 1300, the locus of major writing returned to Italy.

Norbert Horn divides commentator scholarship into four types with various subtypes. First, exegetic literature included commentaries (*commentaria*) as its most important form....

Second, commentators accumulated substantial literature based on their discussion of complex problems and expert opinions, which reflected their interest in how society was developing. Problems (*quaestiones*) grew out of glossators' *quaestiones legitimae* and disputations, following the pattern: facts (*casus*), legal issue (*quaestio*), *argumenta pro et contra,* and decision (*solutio, decisio*). Expert opinions (*consilia*) resembled *quaestiones,* but might devote less attention to opposing views: the *contra. Consilia* offered advice on whole lawsuits based on the record. A commentator usually gave his *consilium* to the court itself, although he might send it instead to one of the parties involved in a dispute who paid for the opinion. Some Italian cities encouraged by statute the practice of judges seeking *consilia. Consilia* tended to emphasize the jurist's view in *argumenta,* buttressed by other scholars who supported the same position. Some *consilia* achieved the authority of custom.

Third, monographs, especially treatises (*tractatus*), appeared more regularly....

Finally, the spread of learned law throughout western Europe created a demand for books to guide the growing corps of university law graduates. Commentators wrote compilations of short *quaestiones*, encyclopedias (*repertorien*) of key words organized alphabetically, dictionaries, and introductions to law. Specifically for practitioners, and especially notaries who handled documents, jurists also developed form books.

Cinus de Pistoia (1270-1336), an early commentator, influenced by the writings of French masters, helped to develop what would for centuries be known as the Italian method (*mos italicus*) of legal scholarship....

Cinus took a position in 1310 with Emperor Henry VII as assessor in Rome, which brought him into daily contact with governmental affairs. In juxtaposing Roman law with contemporary French and municipal statutes, he emphasized a practical comparative study of law. He demonstrated the relevance of current judicial decisions, while referring to classical Roman jurists, in interpreting what would become a European *jus commune*.

Cinus's greatest pupil, Bartolus de Saxoferrato (1313-1357), received his doctorate at Bologna and taught law at Pisa and Perugia. His massive commentaries on virtually the whole *Corpus juris* were used by jurists for centuries (*nemo jurista nisi Bartolista* — no jurist unless Bartolus). In addition, he wrote 40 treatises on various topics of public and private law as well as on political questions. His conception of sovereignty, for instance, illustrated the application of Roman law to contemporary conditions. It supported the ascending theme of government, looking toward popular acquiescence and representation in lawmaking, which became more significant in political theory.... His reputation spread throughout Europe so that copies of his works proliferated in Germany, England, and France, while his opinions had legal force in Spain and Portugal, where they were translated into the vernacular.

Academic commentators issued thousands of *consilia*. Clients included popes and antipopes, emperors, kings, and dukes as well as monasteries, municipalities, baronial families, and prosperous merchants. Masters spoke out on private law matters dealing with issues such as property boundaries, inheritance, or fishing rights and public law questions concerning citizenship, taxation, military duties, reprisals, or maritime rights....

F. *Methods of Instruction*

1. *The Lectura, Disputatio, and Repetitio*

Universities were centers for the characteristic *lectura, disputatio,* and *repetitio*....

The purpose of a lecture was to read and explain the text of a book for the course. Since many students did not have access to a manuscript, most of a lecturer's time was spent reading aloud the standard text together with glosses and comments.

A typical glossator's lecture proceeded with the following steps. First, he introduced the title (*titulus*) under consideration, showing how it fit within the larger section. Second, he systematically summarized each individual law (*lex*) or constitution (*constitutio*) in the title along with its purpose. Third, he read the text aloud, dealing with any grammatical problems. Fourth, some Bolognese masters, such as Odofredus (1200-1265), repeated the text. Fifth, a glossator mentioned similar (*similia*) and contrary (*contraria*) legal provisions, solving apparent contradictions (*solutiones contrariorum*) by revealing how a distinction (*distinctio*) might lead one text to apply in a certain situation and another text in a different situation. Sixth, he continued to clarify the text with *argumenta* and pairs of opposing arguments (*brocardica*). Seventh, he might formulate further distinctions (*distinctiones*), finally concluding with his own interpretation (*solutio*). This was then followed by questions and discussion from the students.

Commentators' lecturing continued to follow the order of introducing rules established at Bologna. Although the emphasis was still on authoritative texts and glosses (*lectio textus et apparatus*), commentators gradually added more of the material characterizing their school of scholarship....

Masters as well as scholars also presented disputations (*disputationes*), with which they maintained in a dialectical style of argument, *quaesita et opposita*, a thesis against all comers. These evolved out of the *quaestio* part of lectures. They stimulated student interest in points of law and helped to develop student ability to argue *pro et contra*.

Professors also presented — usually during the evening — *repetitiones*, which consisted of elaborate discussions of some particularly difficult or important question reserved from a recent lecture.

2. *Books*

Lectures as a mechanism to communicate knowledge made sense at a time when books were scarce and costly. To secure the necessary supply of correct and reasonably priced volumes, the university early in its history took on regulation of the book trade (*librarii* or *stationarii*) as one of its privileges. The accuracy of each copy — of course, made by hand — was supervised, while restrictions curbed the flow of books out of town. Before the invention of printing, books were extremely expensive. It is estimated that Bolognese books varied in price from 4 lire (or *librae*) to 300 lire, with 35 lire ($4,550) the average price. Naturally, only a few students could afford to buy even one book. Books were commonly rented rather than owned, at a fixed price per quire (*pecia*) (four sheets with writing on both sides in a portfolio).

The overwhelming majority of books existing in Bologna in the thirteenth and fourteenth centuries were law books. In a sample of notarial registries made in Bologna between 1265 and 1330 Antonio Martin identified 3,295 registered books, predominantly made with goat skin pages, 98 percent of which dealt with law in the 1260s, a figure falling to 90 percent by the period's close. Of the 121 law books, which *stationarii* were required to stock by university statute, Martin found 112 in the registries. In addition, 55 other law titles were located. The most popular book (with 571 handmade copies) was the *Digestum vetus*, of which almost half contained Accursius's *Glossa ordinaria*. Closely following in popularity was the *Codex* (books 1 to 9), over half of which had Accursius's gloss. The most common canon law book (480 copies) was Gregory IX's *Liber extra*, most with glosses and organization by Bernardo da Pavia.

G. *Examinations and Degrees*

No examination was required at Bologna for the baccalaureate, which was not really a distinct degree as it later became at other universities. After four years of residency in canon law or five years in Roman law, a student, upon application to the rector, might be licensed to lecture on a single title of canon or civil law. Completing a series of lectures entitled these students — who were actually apprenticing teachers — to be called *baccalarii*. Bachelors admitted "to read" a whole canon law decretal or a Roman law book could give extraordinary lectures or *repetitiones*.

Scholars who continued their studies for at least two more years to earn a doctorate in canon law or a doctorate in Roman law were entitled to teach in that field. Formal testing began in the early thirteenth century. Time spent in the study of one discipline was counted to reduce the time necessary for graduation in the other, so that it was possible to become a doctor of both civil and canon law (*doctor utriusque juris*) in ten years.

A doctoral candidate initially applied through the *consiliarius* of his nation to the rector for permission to initiate the promotion or graduation process. He swore to the rector that he had complied with all statutory requirements, paid the rector his fee, and then petitioned (along with another fee) a master in the *collegium doctorum*, who arranged for a private exam followed by a public session (*conventus*) before the archdeacon and college of teachers.

At a public examination the presenting doctor (*promotor*) introduced to the archdeacon and *collegium* his candidate, who gave a lecture on two assigned passages (*puncta*). Two doctors appointed by the college examined him, followed by questions and comments from the assemblage. The doctors voted, requiring a majority for promotion. The *licentia docendi* was then formally conferred by the archdeacon after the new master gave his first doctoral disputation at the cathedral....

Pope Nicholas IV in a 1291 bull conferred on all doctors licensed by the archdeacon of Bologna a permanent rank, which included the right to teach not only at Bologna but worldwide. According to Hastings Rashdall,

> the doctorate became an order of intellectual nobility with as distinct and definite a place in the hierarchical system of medieval Christendom as the priesthood or the knighthood.

2. LEGAL HUMANISM

MAURO CAPPELLETTI, JOHN HENRY MERRYMAN & JOSEPH M. PERILLO, THE ITALIAN LEGAL SYSTEM: AN INTRODUCTION 36-38 (1967)

By the end of the fifteenth century, Italian legal science showed signs of excessive rigidity and pedantry. Nevertheless, during the sixteenth and seventeenth centuries, students from all over Europe continued to enroll in the Italian universities, and the style of the Commentators — the Bartolistic method — was widely used in many European universities.

The movement known as legal humanism arose in the fifteenth and sixteenth centuries in reaction to the Bartolistic method. Liberty of interpretation was its slogan. It rejected doctrinal precedent and the supine acquiescence of many scholars to the *communis opinio doctorum*. It had its genesis in the world of letters, where jurists were criticized for their wretched Latin, their lack of sensitivity in facing the problems of a critical reconstruction of the Roman texts, their neglect of literary style, and, indeed, their lack of intelligence. The more able jurists accepted much of this criticism and acknowledged the need to deepen their knowledge of philology and history. From this era came the first critical editions of Justinian's texts and of works of postclassical Roman law. The first proposal to put together a critical edition of the *Digest* was made in the fifteenth century by Politian, a master of erudition as well as a great poet.

During this period Italian legal science lost its preeminence. The humanist school centered elsewhere in Europe, for the most part in the French universities. There came to be a clear contrast between the *mos italicus jura docendi*, the Italian manner of legal teaching, and the *mos docendi gallicus*, the French manner. The former, in the tradition of the Glossators and Commentators, looked to Roman law for practical ends. The latter sought to obtain an historical, scientific knowledge of Roman law without practical preoccupations. The French school was interested in Roman law as an historical phenomenon rather than as an existing body of law. They sought to reconstruct the original text, freeing them from interpolations made by Justinian's codifiers and from the Glossators.

The leader of the French school, Andrea Alciato (1492-1550), was an Italian. He was both an expert philologist and a master jurist. Born in Lombardy, he taught in Italy and in France (Bourges). To comprehend his importance it is enough to know that he founded the so-called "School of the Cultured Men" or "Cultured Jurisprudence" (*Scuola dei Culti*), which reached its apex with Jacques Cujas (Cujacius). In Germany the principal exponent of the French approach was Ulrich Zasius. It is commonly stated that the teaching of Alciato, followed to such a great extent in France, had extremely limited influence in Italy. This statement is essentially true, although there were a number of scholars who continued his work in Italy.

Implicit in the formation of the *"Scuola dei Culti"* was the birth of legal nationalism. When, in France and Germany, scholars claimed to study the *Corpus Juris Civilis* as if it were just another ancient text, they obscured its status as living law. In this era of refined classicism it was natural that scholars would search for the original textual formulation and meaning of the components of the *Corpus Juris*. The difficulty was that for centuries the practice and doctrine had been based on the interpolated text and the glosses. The contradiction could be resolved by a new codification designed to govern organically and completely given subject matters, such as civil, criminal, or procedural law. This idea appears, for example, in the *Antitribonien* (1567), the celebrated work of the Frenchman Francis Hotman. The *Antitribonien* is an indictment of Justinian and his chief scholar, Tribonian, and a plea for the codification of French law. The idea triumphed two centuries later.

NOTES AND QUESTIONS

1. The glossators, the commentators, and the humanists were all scholars — learned men who wrote and taught about the law. Many of them were also active as practicing lawyers, advisors to princes, and so on, but it was their scholarship that has had historical importance. The commission that prepared the *Corpus juris civilis*, headed by Tribonian, was dominated by scholars. Much of the material with which they worked was the product of earlier generations of scholars. Thus, over a very large part of its history prior to the Revolution, Roman law has been peculiarly a law of the scholars (and legislators), rather than a law of the judges. The same is true of canon law. This strong scholarly tradition in the civil law continues up to the present, as the materials in later chapters show. The contrast with the common law tradition is obvious and significant.

13 **De Iustitia, & Iure.** 14

a [I]N nomine Domini.] Hoc in cōpilatione Digestorū fuit dictū non[a] quando leges factę fuerūt: quia pagani erāt: vt C. de vet. iu. en. l. j. sic & aliàs facit Inst. in proœ. in pr.
b ¶ Perpetui. id est generalis [b].
c ¶ Augusti. Quia semper huius propositi debet esse vt augeat imperiū, licèt non semper augeat. sic & matrimoniū indiuidua coniunctio dicitur: tamen diuiditur quādoque: vt C. de repud. l. cōsensu. Sed propositū[d] cōsideratur: vt Instit. de pat. pot. in pr.
d ¶ Enucleati. per similitudinē vocat ius enucleatum, quod nobis est traditum in libris Pandectarum. Sicut enim antequam[e] perueniatur ad nucleum interiorem nucis, vnū amarissimū, & aliud durum, & aliud amarum, & quartò ad nucleū dulcem peruenitur: ita & in multitudine antiquorū librorū amaritudines inueniūtur. i. discordiæ infinitę. item duritiæ. i. iniquæ sententiæ, & aliæ nō sic iniquæ, in quibusdā tamen locis quædā latebāt dulcedines. i. æquissimæ sententię, velut lilia inter spinas: & illas dulces sententias Iustinianus ex aliis excerpsit, & nobis tradidit legendas: vnde ipse dicitur tradere ius enucleatū, secūdùm IOAN.
e ¶ Collecti. ex his. i. ex eo quod dixit in princ. poterit colligi quis fuerit author[f], siue compilator: quia Iustinianus filius Iustini[*]: vt Instit. de donat. §. est & aliud.
2. ¶ Item quę materia. i. omnia vetera iura antiquorum prudentum.
3. ¶ Quæ intentio, id est, vt colligas ius enucleatum in vnum volumen.
4. ¶ Vtilitas per se patet: quia minori pecunia poterit nunc emi liber iste: & quia citiùs adipisci potest quàm olim.
5. ¶ Cui parti philosophiæ supponatur: & quidem Ethicæ, quia de moribus tractat hoc volumen, sicut alia duo volumina.

a Hoc est non à iurisc[o]nsultis quorum ex libris cōposita.
b Male est enim legendū, perpetuo.
c Similis gloss. in constitutione, amorem, §.
† Inclusa desunt Florētiæ.
d Propositum consideramus in nominū appellationibus.
† Inclusa desunt Florētiæ.
* Hic titulus est lib. 2. Basilicōn. tit. 1.
e Hinc Plaut. Curcul. act. 1. qui è nuce nucleum esse vult, frangit nucem.
† τὰ πάντα, quatuor libris contenta.
f De Pādectarum authore, materia, vtilitate, obiectio.
* Intellige per adoptionē, quia reuera nepos eius ex sorore fuit.

f ¶ Iuri. scilicet addiscendo, vel pertractando [a].
g ¶ Prius. quàm [b] noscat substantiam iuris per diuisiones, quæ dicuntur ∫. eo. §. huius study. Nec ob. quod dicitur ∫. in proœm. §. & primò quidē. ¶ Et quod dicit, oportet [c], impropriè[d] dicit. i. decet. sic C. de bon. qua lib. l. cùm oportet. in pr. & de rap. vir. l. j. §. oportet enim. & c. sic econtra decet pro oportet: vt C. de capt. & postli. reuer. l. fin.
h ¶ Iustitia. Est autem ius à iustitia, sicut à matre [e] sua: ergo priùs fuit iustitia quàm ius. Sed contra ∫. eod. l. iustitia, ibi, ius suum, & c. ex quo colligitur quòd statim fuit ius, postquā fuit iustitia. Sed dic ibi, ius suū, id est, hominis meritum. 2. Vel dic, prout in actione & obligatione: bene dico ius à iustitia appellari: si enim ius est ars boni & æqui. vt subiicit: & iustitia nihil aliud est quā ipsa æquitas & bonitas: ergo iustitiam habet matrem: & hoc subiicit, nam, & c. [f] sic & obligatio [g] dicitur mater actionis: vt ∫. de procur. l. licèt. §. ea obligatio.
i ¶ Ius est ars. hoc potest intelligi tribus [h] modis. 1. Primò, vt dicas definitū ius in genere. & sic est ars, id est scientia finita, quæ arctat infinita. nam ars est de infinitis finita doctrina, secundùm Porphyrium. 2. Secundò dic describi quamlibet speciem iuris, vt prætorium, vel ciuile, vel naturale, vel gentium: & tūc ponetur pro præcepto [i] coarctante. sed hoc non placet, cùm istæ partes iuris nō sint artes, sed artis partes. 3. Vel tertiò, ars, id est artificium. nam auctor iuris est homo, iustitiæ Deus Et quod subiicit, boni & æqui, id est eius quod est æquū & vtile.

a Vel etiam docendo.
b Absurdū est ignoratis principiis ad alia, & alia coniequētia trāsire. facit l. j. ∫. si. s.
c Oportet pro decet: & decet pro oportet.
d Vt totā hanc dubitationem dissoluamus: duplex principiū statuēdum est. vnde priore ignorato, sequētia principij scire possumus: v. g. nosse possumus Titium, ignorato eius patre ac matre. Altero verò ignorato, non possumus consequentia nosse. atq; ita verbū oportet, hic sumi potest propriè.
e Iustitia an iuris mater & prior iure?
f Vel dic, Ius in habitu cōsideratum, iustitię, vt ita dicatur, coætaneū. Vt autem ars dicitur collecta ex multis præceptis, ius a iustitia esse dici potest.
† Vt Deam.
† Vt artem.
g Obligatio materactionis.
h Ius ars dicitur, & quō.
i Ars quid sit. Hāc interpretationē reprehēdit Corras. 3. Miscel. 18.
k artis vocabulo hic sciētiā intelligēs.
k Hic locus reprehēditur à Ferrando, in …
l Salomonius putat nihil bonum esse quod nō sit æquum: quo nomine reprehenius à Corras. ibid. n. 6. Bonum & æquum genus, … species: quæ duo cōfundit Bud.
m nihil interest, … an merito legas. nā & merito iuris seu iustitiæ sacerdotes & qui in iuris arte aut iustitia versantur, meritò sacerdotes. idque probatur ex cultu, professione, & aliis quæ sequūtur. Reprehenditur hic Accurs. à Bud. ab Antonio Vac.
n l. … §. … de off. praef. … & … l. … Leges … de … l. … ex caus. maior.
o Idem in … mentis. l. … de …
p Metu pœnæ.

[IN NOMINE † DOMINI [a] AMEN.]

D. NOSTRI SACRATISS.

PRINCIPIS

IVSTINIANI

[† PP. [b] * AVGVSTI [c]]

Iuris enucleati [d] ex omni vetere (iure) collecti [e]

DIGESTORVM,

seu

PANDECTARVM

PARS PRIMA †.

LIBER PRIMVS.

DE IVSTITIA, ET IVRE.

TITVLVS I.

Meritò incipit à virtute, quam iuris auctores colūt: & à iure, quod profitētur. ¶ *Et est* IVSTITIA *constantia perpetua voluntatis ius suum cuiq; tribuendi, vt liberalitas constantia perpetua benignitatis.* ¶ *Ius est scientia æqui, & iniqui, vel ars. Ars enim est eorū, quæ sciuntur.* ¶ *Et huius artis, iurisve partes hoc titulo proponuntur summā. Sed & alia significationes iuris.* CVIACIVS.

1. VLPIANVS *libro primo Institutionum.*

[I]VRI [f] operam daturum priùs [g] nosse oportet vnde nomen iuris descendat. Est autem à Iustitia [h] appellatū. nam, vt eleganter Celsus definit, Ius est ars [i] boni & æqui. 1. ¶ Cuius [k] meritò quis nos sacerdotes [l] appellet. Iustitiam namq; † colimus [m], & boni & æqui notitiam † profitemur [n], æquum ab iniquo [o] separantes, licitum ab illicito [p] discernētes: bonos nō solùm metu pœnarū [q], verùmetiam præmiorum quoque exhortatione efficere cupiētes: veram (nisi fallor [r]) philosophiam, non simulatam affectantes.

Hic iurisconsultus incipit tractare per modum diuisionis, & procedit vsque ad l. Iustitia. infrà eo. exem-

DE IVSTITIA, ET IVRE.

[I]Vri.] hoc prin. vsque ad §. huius study, diuiditur in quinque partes. 1. In prima ponit, quid oportet facere volentem studere in iure. 2. In secunda docet vnde ius dictum sit. 3. In tertia definit ius authoritate Celsi. 4. In quarta ponit quid habeat quis cōsequi ex hoc studio. 5. In quinta ponit vnde sequatur hic honor. Secunda ibi, est autem. Tertia ibi, nam vt eleganter. Quarta ibi, cuius meritò. Quinta & vltima ibi, iustitiam namque. B. ¶ CASVS vsque ad fi. l. sic figuratur. Aliqui leges, siue iura audire volebant: inde quæstionem Vlpiano fecerūt quis esset modus quo oportet addiscere. ad quod dicit Vlpian. quod prius est necesse quòd aliquis sciat vnde nomen iuris descendat. 2. Secundò dicit, vnde appelletur ius. 3. Tertiò dicit, quid sit ius. Nam nos ministri iuris separamus æquum ab iniquo, licitum ab illicito. 4. Item dicit quod ius pluribus modis facit [g] aliquos bonos: vt apertè in litera dicit. 5. ¶ Diuiditur quidē ius in duas species: quia aliud priuatum, aliud publicum. & hæc omnia plene & apertè exemplificat. 6. Item diuiditur ius priuatū in tres species. nam colligitur ex iure naturali, & ex iure gentiū, & ex iure ciuili: & de his omnibus exempla ponit. Nam ius gentium commune tātùm hominibus est. nam debet erga Deum habere religionem, & obedire patri & patriæ: quę bruta nō faciunt. Item licet de iure naturali vim vi repellere: cū omnes ab Adam ortū habuerimus: & ideo vnus alteri insidiari non debet. Ponit etiam quòd manumissio ab hoc iure processit. nam iure naturali omnes nascebātur liberi: sed iure gentium sunt hodie tria genera hominum. Item ex iure gentium introducta sunt bella, & alia multa. VIVIAN. ff. Vetus.

g Finis hic est iuris.

¶ Et not. quòd aliud [k] est bonum, & aliud est æquum: vt hic: est enim quoddam bonum, & æquum: vt ∫. si cert. pet. l. si & me. in fin. est bonum & non [l] æquum: vt vsucapio: vt ∫. de vsucap. l. j. & ∫. de reg. iur. l. iure natura. in fin. sit. est tertium æquum, & non bonum: vt C. de pact. con. l. hac lege. est etiam æquo æquius: vt ∫. de furt. l. si seruus communi. §. quod verò.
k ¶ Cuius. istud, cuius, si referatur ad ius: hæc dictio, merito [m], in vim nominis ponetur. (meruit enim ius appellari sacrum, & ideo iura reddentes sacerdotes vocantur) si ad artem, in vim aduerbij, secundum Azo. ADDITIO. malo referre ad iustitiā. CONT.
l ¶ Sacerdotes. quia vt sacerdotes sacra ministrant & conficiunt, ita & nos, cùm leges sint sacratissimæ: vt C. de leg. & const. l. leges. & vt ius suum cuique tribuit sacerdos [n] in danda pœnitentia, sic & nos in iudicando: vt ∫. eod. l. iustitia.
m ¶ Colimus. id est eius voluntatem seruamus, quæ est vt ius suum cuique tribuatur: vt ∫. eod. l. iustitia. §. j.
n ¶ Profitemur. id est docemus.
o ¶ Ab iniquo. vt in contractibus [o], secundùm Ioannem.
p ¶ Illicito. vt in matrimoniis: vt ∫. de ritu nupt. l. semper.
q ¶ Metu pœnarum. metu [p] sit quis bonus: vt in transactione iurata: vt C. de transact. l. si quis maior. Item vbique pœna vnius est metus multorum: vt C. ad leg. Iul. rep. l. j. præmio fit bonus: vt C. quib. ex caus. ser. pro præmio liber. acci. per totum. & de stat. & imagin. l. & virtutum. & de fam. lib. l. j. ∫. ad Silla. l. antequā. §. fin. & in authent. de non alien. §. fin. collat. 4. vnde versus:

Oderunt peccare boni virtutis amore.
Oderunt peccare mali formidine pœnæ.

r ¶ Nisi fallor. nullo q modo fallimur. nam ciuilis sapientia vera philosophia dicitur, id est amor sapientiæ: à philos, quod est amor: & sophia, id est, sapientia: vt ∫. de var. & extraord. cogn. l. j. §. proinde.

A 4

& præmij spe boni euadimus. q Nisi, pro nullo modo.

Note 5

First page of Justinian's digest as presented to us in the ordinary gloss

2. For the past 900 years the scholarly tradition of the civil law has been associated with instruction in law at the university. Why did the first great university specializing in law arise in Italy? What would explain the emphasis in instruction on reading the text? Why was the relationship between law students and professors at the University of Bologna in the 13th century different from the relationship existing in modern legal education? Explain the division of control between matters of general administration and issues concerning examinations and degrees.

3. The terms "glossators," "commentators," and "humanists" all refer to different periods of intellectual history — to different schools of thought about the proper way to study and to employ the *Corpus juris civilis*. The form their work took, whether as a gloss written in the margins or as a separate comment, is secondary to a larger issue. The important point is that they had different sets of working assumptions and objectives. Can you characterize these three scholarly styles?

4. Return to *Williams v. Employers Liability Assurance Corp., supra* Chapter 1, Section D. Note 5 following *Williams* identified certain civilian methods of codal interpretation, including the literal, contextual, and historical methods. How do these three methods parallel the schools of legal thought discussed in this section? We will further examine this topic in Chapter 9, Section B.

5. The Florentine copy of the Digest was first printed in 1553. The most important publication of the whole *Corpus juris civilis*, however, was an edition by Dionysius Gothofredus (1549-1622). It was considered the standard working text until the 19th century. Subsequent versions of the *Corpus juris* appeared with only the text or with Accursius's standard gloss or with Gothofredus's notes. The first page of a 1627 edition of the *Corpus juris* is reproduced below: 1 Corpus Iuris Civilis Iustinianei: Studio et opera Ioannis Fehi 13-14 (1627, reprinted by Otto Zeller, Osnabrück 1965). This edition includes both Accursius's gloss and Gothofredus's notes. Notice that Justinian's text in D.1.1.1. is surrounded by two perimeters of notes, clarifications, and elaborations. It was this accretion of scholarly material that lawyers and judges relied upon for their standard reference source.

E. CANON LAW

1. THE CHURCH, UNIVERSITIES, AND CANON LAW

DAVID S. CLARK, THE MEDIEVAL ORIGINS OF MODERN LEGAL EDUCATION: BETWEEN CHURCH AND STATE, 35 American Journal of Comparative Law 653, 675-78, 693-96 (1987)

The Church and Canon Law

The secular character of Roman law studies and their connection to German emperors' claims (*renovatio imperii Romani*) aroused papal ire. The Bolognese monk Gratian, who may have been a pupil of Irnerius and later a teacher at Bologna, helped to meet this secular challenge. He systematically applied the theologian Abélard's method of solving contradictions to canon law, publishing his textbook and compilation *Concordia discordantium canonum* in 1140.

The *Concordia* stimulated papal pretensions and rendered previous collections of canon law obsolete ....

Gratian's *Concordia* — later referred to as *Decretum Gratiani* — provided canon law with an authoritative and learned sourcebook, analogous to Justinian's *Corpus juris*. This made it an appropriate subject to study at the university. The *Decretum* went a long way toward clarifying the writings of church fathers, apostolic and conciliar canons, and papal decretals and decrees, as well as demarcating the boundary between ecclesiastical and civil courts, and between church and state in general. It systematized approximately 3,800 canonical texts on the nature and sources of law, ecclesiastical offices and behavior, church dogma, ritual, religious orders, and other issues of administration and organization. It contributed to rational procedure in episcopal and papal courts, and effectively preempted the fields of family and inheritance law.

Gratian explored various sources of law and placed them in a hierarchical order. He fitted natural law between divine law and human law. Divine law, as the will of God reflected in the Bible's revelation, was supreme. Natural law also reflected God's will, but it could be found in human reason and conscience as well as in revelation. Gratian concluded that neither human law (*leges*) of secular rulers or the church could contravene natural law (*jus naturale*).

Furthermore, adopting a principle stated by Ivo, Gratian declared that princes were bound by their own laws. Although a lawmaker could change existing norms in a lawful manner, he could not lawfully disregard them. This new theory varied from the older Roman and Germanic principle that a good emperor ought to observe his own laws as a moral question, but was not legally bound to do so.

Gratian explicitly favored the church in a text (mistakenly attributed to Pope Nicholas II) declaring that Christ had conferred "on the blessed key-bearer of eternal life rights over a heavenly and an earthly empire." He found that princely *leges* and enactments (*constitutiones*) were subordinate to ecclesiastical *leges* and *constitutiones*. In addition, at a time when most legal norms were legitimate because they comprised practices accepted as binding by the communities in which they prevailed, Gratian asserted that customs (*consuetudines*) should yield to enacted laws of secular and ecclesiastical authority. Most enacted norms were still justified as restatements of preexisting custom, but canonist theory now provided a basis for pruning those customs that did not conform to reason, conscience, or positive law.

The medieval church after Gratian assumed more and more the character of a legal corporation. Canon law became clearly differentiated from theology. The cry "freedom of the church" (*libertas ecclesiae*) involved a battle to emancipate the clergy from its former subservience to temporal government, which was now considered a betrayal of the church's divine mission. Educated canonists were the generals in this war....

Canon Law Studies

Canon law in the twelfth century was largely contemporary law, a living law that had grown out of societal exigencies. Canon law differed in this respect from its model, Roman law, which even at the time of its sixth century compilation in the *Corpus juris* was in some ways outdated. By the twelfth century, Roman law was constantly in need of adaptation. Canon law continued to develop through primary sources. On controversial points of doctrine, liturgy, or discipline, it commonly issued from the papacy as needed in the form of decretal letters (*epistolae decretales*) addressed to one or more bishops or princes.

For instance, Alexander III's chancery issued over 700 decretal letters. The decretal, modeled on a Roman emperor's rescript to a subordinate official, was the vehicle by which the papacy as a monarchic institution governed western Europe. The scope of public jurisdiction expanded as decretals dealt with matters such as royal elections, sanctions against individuals and corporations, tithes, currency counterfeiting, class privileges, and the creation of crimes....

Since Gratian's *Decretum* drew from a range of frequently conflicting sources, the first generation of Bolognese masters lectured in a manner and wrote with literary forms similar to those used by civil law teachers. Paucapalea, a student of Gratian, and Rolandus Bandinelli, for instance, wrote *summae* before 1148. These early writers considered the *Decretum* the authoritative statement of canon law, in much the same way that civilians looked at the *Corpus juris*. Called decretists, their approach quickly spread to France, the Rhineland, and England. But Bologna remained the center for decretists. Rufinus completed his lengthy *summa* (1157-1159) there, which was later overshadowed by master Huguccio's *summa* (1188), cited by jurists for centuries. In addition, Johannes Teutonicus wrote the standard gloss (*Glossa ordinaria*, 1216) for the *Decretum* in Bologna. Johannes added his own notes to those of earlier glossators in the margins of the text. This manuscript, supplemented by others, was popular in university instruction.

Canon law depended on Roman law — minus its ideology — for the proper technical legal tools to systematically organize its own body of rules. Juristic theologians, therefore, frequently studied Roman law to adequately develop their legal skills. An intimate connection between the earliest generation of canonists, especially the scholars at Bologna, and the papacy's judicial branch involved universities in ecclesiastical law creation. Papal decretals frequently were the concrete implementation of abstract Bolognese canonistic scholarship. Canon law professors, in a process of reciprocity, then interpreted these decretals utilizing the underlying principles that they themselves had promoted in their lectures and writings. They also issued *consilia* like their civilian colleagues in response to questions on sovereignty, elections, schisms, tithes, and taxation. Juristic interpretation stimulated further decretal legislation, which in turn was subjected to additional academic explication.

By the end of the twelfth century, it was clear that the vast production of ecclesiastical law needed further systematization. Popes continued to churn out a substantial number of decretals while general councils issued decrees, which collectively were considered to be wandering outside Gratian's *Decretum (extra decreta vagantium)*. The Bolognese professor Bernardo da Pavia, following the model of Justinian's *Codex,* collected these canons along with some older material that he found in repositories throughout Europe. He organized them into five books, subdivided as titles and chapters. Bernardo's enterprise, the *Breviarium extravagantium*, finished between 1188 and 1192, along with the scholarly doctrine of other canonists now known as decretalists, was published in 1234 as *Liber extra*, the papacy's first official law book.

Decretists and decretalists, like their colleagues in civil law, developed literary genres — such as *casus, summae, notabilia, brocardica,* and *distinctiones* — out of different types of glosses.... In the thirteenth century, some canonists favored literary forms similar to those used by Roman law commentators, in particular *commentaria, summae, consilia, quaestiones,* monographs, and *repertorien.*

The fame of Bolognese canon law professors in the thirteenth and fourteenth centuries was almost as great as their civilian brethren. Tancred, an early specialist in decretals, wrote between 1210 and 1220 the ordinary gloss on three of the five *compilationes* of canons commonly used at Bologna, in addition to a monograph on marriage law. Guilelmus Durantis (died 1296), following the *Liber extra*'s order in his encyclopedic *Speculum juris*, treated questions regarding the law of persons, civil and criminal procedure, as well as other contemporary governmental issues by drawing on both theory and practice. Guido de Baisio (died 1313) wrote an influential commentary on the *Decretum* and an *apparatus* on the *Liber sextus*. Johannes Andreae (died 1348), a layman, was a prolific writer who authored important commentaries on the *Liber extra* and *Liber sextus*. Both Guido and Andreae promoted a hierocratic ideology to accentuate papal monarchic powers. The doctrine of the pope's personal sovereignty in his function as governor placed secular rulers as "sons" or subjects of the pope. The pope's governing role was to be protected by law, including elaboration of the crime of high treason.

Harold Berman contends that scholastic jurists, both Romanists and canonists, created a legal "science" in the modern sense of that word. The phenomena they studied were decisions, rules, and customs. Canonists concentrated on the law promulgated by church councils, bishops, and popes along with the Holy Scriptures. Romanists also considered the Bible, but focused on the law used by city magistrates, dukes, kings, and emperors along with Justinian's *Corpus juris*. These legal materials were treated as data to be observed, classified, and systematically explained in terms of general principles. The explanations, in turn, were subject to verification by both logic and experience.

2. JURISDICTION OVER PERSONS AND OVER SUBJECT MATTER

HAROLD J. BERMAN, LAW AND REVOLUTION: THE FORMATION OF THE WESTERN LEGAL TRADITION 222-23, 226-34, 237-41, 245-48, 250-53 (1983)*

[J]urisdiction was said to be divided into two types: jurisdiction over certain kinds of persons (*ratione personarum,* "by reason of persons") and jurisdiction over certain kinds of conduct or relationships (*ratione materiae,* "by reason of subject matter"). The church claimed "personal jurisdiction" over: (1) clergy and members of their households; (2) students; (3) crusaders; (4) *personae miserabiles* ("wretched persons"), including poor people, widows, and orphans; (5) Jews, in cases against Christians; and (6) travelers, including merchants and sailors, when necessary for their peace and safety. This was the famous — or notorious — *privilegium fori* ("privilege of court" or "benefit of clergy"), against which secular rulers struggled hard, and often with some success.

Clergy were forbidden by canon law to waive the privilege of ecclesiastical jurisdiction; however, in practice they were subjected to secular justice in certain types of crimes and certain types of civil actions. There were also some recognized exceptions to ecclesiastical jurisdiction over crusaders and over students; and they could waive such jurisdiction if they wished. Personae miserabiles, who prior to the Papal Revolution had been treated primarily as wards of emperors and kings, were thereafter subject also to ecclesiastical jurisdiction, principally in cases where the secular authorities did not offer adequate protection to them. The same was true with regard to Jews and travelers (including merchants and sailors): the church did not attempt to eliminate but only to supplement imperial or royal jurisdiction over them.

The personal jurisdiction of the church extended, in principle, to all types of cases in which these six classes of persons were involved, although the principle sometimes yielded to the competing interests of the secular authorities. The "subject-matter jurisdiction" of the church, by contrast, extended in principle to all classes of persons, laymen as well as clerics, in certain types of cases, although — again — there were qualifications and exceptions. The principal types of cases over which the church claimed jurisdiction were so-called spiritual cases and cases connected to spiritual cases. Spiritual cases were chiefly those arising out of: (1) administration of the sacraments; (2) testaments; (3) benefices, including administration of church property, patronage of church offices, and ecclesiastical taxation in the form of tithes; (4) oaths, including pledges of faith; and (5) sins meriting ecclesiastical censures. It was on this jurisdictional foundation that legal science in the twelfth century began to develop various branches of substantive law, including family law (on the foundation of jurisdiction over the sacrament of marriage), the law of inheritance (on the foundation of jurisdiction over testaments), property law (on the foundation of jurisdiction over benefices), contract law (on the foundation of jurisdiction over pledges of faith), and criminal and tort law (on the foundation of jurisdiction over sins). Presupposed was the jurisdiction of

*For permission to photocopy this selection, please contact Harvard University Press.

the church over its own jurisdiction; on this basis it constructed the body of corporation law.

The church also extended its jurisdiction to other kinds of causes by offering it to all who wished to choose it. This was done through a procedure called prorogation, whereby parties to any civil dispute could, by agreement, submit the dispute to an ecclesiastical court or to ecclesiastical arbitration. Such an agreement might take the form of a clause in a contract renouncing in advance the jurisdiction of a secular court and providing for recourse to an ecclesiastical court or to ecclesiastical arbitration in the event of a future dispute arising out of the contract. Because of the primitive character of most secular procedure in the twelfth and thirteenth centuries, parties to civil contracts often wrote in such renunciation clauses.

In addition, according to canon law any person could bring suit in an ecclesiastical court, or could remove a case from a secular court to an ecclesiastical court, even against the will of the other party, on the ground of "default of secular justice." Thus the church ultimately offered its jurisdiction and its law to anyone and for any type of case, but only under exceptional circumstances, that is, when justice itself, in the most elementary sense, was at stake....

The Canon Law of Marriage

From earliest times, the church had a great deal to say about marriage and the family. In pagan cultures in which polygamy, arranged marriages, and oppression of women predominated, the church promoted the idea of monogamous marriage by free consent of both spouses. In the West this idea had to do battle with deeply rooted tribal, village, and feudal customs. By the tenth century ecclesiastical synods were promulgating decrees concerning the matrimonial bond, adultery, legitimacy of children, and related matters; nevertheless, children continued to be married in the cradle and family relations continued to be dominated by the traditional folkways and mores of the Germanic, Celtic, and other peoples of western Europe. In the folklaw of the European peoples, as in the classical Roman law, marriage between persons of different classes (for example, free and slave, citizens and foreigners) was prohibited. Also divorce was at the will of either spouse — which usually meant, in practice, at the will of the husband. There were not even any formal requirements for divorce. Paternal consent was required for a marriage to be valid. Few obligations between the spouses were conceived in legal terms.

It was the great upheaval of the late eleventh and twelfth centuries, symbolized by the Papal Revolution, that made it possible to effectuate to a substantial degree ecclesiastical policy concerning marriage and the family....

The church had long held that no formality was required to effectuate a marriage; the two parties were themselves "ministers of the sacrament of marriage." (The presence of a priest was first made obligatory in the sixteenth century; the common law marriage of English and American law is, in fact, a survival of canon law marriage as it existed before the Council of Trent.)...

The rules concerning consent to a marriage were developed into a whole body of contract law. The consent must have been given with a free will. A mistake concerning the identity of the other party, or a mistake concerning some essential and distinctive quality of the other party, prevented the consent and hence nullified the marriage. Duress also nullified the marriage by interfering with the freedom of consent. It was also ruled that a marriage could not be validly contracted under the influence of fear or fraud....

Canon law also laid down conditions necessary for the validity of a marriage, apart from consent. In the twelfth and thirteenth centuries the regulations as to age imposed by Roman law were maintained in general, but exceptions were permitted in the light of local custom, provided that the parties were able to beget children and to understand the nature of the act they were performing. Impotence at the time of marriage was a cause of nullity, however. Also a marriage between a Christian and a heathen was void, since baptism was a necessary condition for participation in any sacrament....

Finally, canon law offered considerable protection — as contrasted with the folklaw of the society in which it first developed — to the female partner in the marriage. "Before God the two parties to marriage were equal and this doctrine of equality was first taught by Christianity. In practice it meant, above all, that the obligations, especially that of fidelity, were mutual. Nevertheless, the husband was head of the household, and in virtue of his position as such, he might choose the place of abode, reasonably correct his wife, and demand from her such domestic duties as were consonant with her social position." Although the church, for the most part, accepted the severe restrictions placed by secular law upon women's property rights (and their civil rights generally), nevertheless, to protect the widow it insisted that no marriage could be contracted without a dowry, that is, the establishment of a fund which could not be reduced in value during the marriage....

The Canon Law of Inheritance

The folklaw of the Germanic peoples of Europe did not provide for testamentary succession. Devolution upon heirs of the rights and duties of a decedent was regulated initially by tribal custom, latter also by village custom, and still later also by feudal custom; the main concern was that the family or household or fief should survive the death of its individual members, and especially of its head....

With the introduction of Christianity, the dead man's portion was no longer buried or burned with the corpse; instead, it was distributed for pious works, for the benefit of the dead man's soul. Customs varied throughout Europe, but typically the property subject to distribution was divided into thirds: one-third for the clan chieftain or king, one-third for the heir, and one-third as "God's portion."

The clergy, of course, had a great interest in God's portion. Particularly when a person was known to be about to die, a priest was apt to be present to remind him of his duty to atone for his sins and to leave his belongings for religious or charitable uses, such as the building of a chapel or relief of the poor. Throughout Europe the rule was introduced that a dying man's "last words" were to be given legal effect, whether or not they were reduced to writing. A Latin phrase was attached to the practice: *donatio causa mortis* ("gift in anticipation of death"). It was not exactly a will, although in most cases it had the same effect. In the rare event that the dying man recovered, the gift lost its effect....

It was partly on the basis of the Germanic Christian gift *causa mortis* ... that the twelfth-century canonists created a new law of wills — and partly on the basis of the classical Roman law of testaments, which was known to the church and used by the church from early times. The Romans had a law of intestate succession that was similar to that of the Germanic folklaw, in that its primary purpose was to provide a successor to the head of the household (*pater familias*). Roman law, however, spelled out the legal aspects of succession much more fully. The inheritance itself was called a *universitas juris*, a single complex legal unit; this comprised the *familia* itself, with its ancestral privileges and obligations, its property, its slaves, and all the legal rights and duties of the decedent. All this devolved upon the heir instantaneously at the death of the decedent. However, from the time of the Twelve Tables, Roman law also provided that the "universal succession" of the heir to the legal personality of the decedent could be governed, alternatively, by a testament....

The canonists treated the very making of a will as a religious act, and the will itself as a religious instrument. Typically it was made in the name of the Father, Son, and Holy Spirit....

In the twelfth century the canonists established a body of rules for determining the validity of wills and for interpreting and enforcing them. In contrast to Roman law, testamentary formalities were minimized. Not only were "last words" spoken to one's confessor on one's deathbed treated as full-fledged testaments, but oral wills generally were considered valid. The Roman requirement of signatures and seals of seven qualified witnesses yielded to the rule stated in a decretal letter of Pope Alexander III to the Bishop of Ostia: "We decree as permanently valid the testaments which your parishioners may make in the presence of their priest and of three or two other suitable persons." In addition, individual bequests to pious causes were valid, according to another regulation of Alexander III, if witnessed by two or three persons. Thus canon law added charitable bequests to the two kinds of testaments which also under Roman law were exempt from the usual legal requirements, namely, testaments of soldiers and sailors in active service and testaments of parents conferring a benefit on those descendants who would have received property in the absence of a testament.

The canonists also strengthened the protection of the surviving spouse and children against disinheritance by the testator. Roman law had provided that an heir could not be deprived of his "legitimate share"; this was originally fixed at one-fourth of what he would have received if the testator had died without a will, and later was raised to one-third (or one-half, if the testator was survived by five or more children). However, the heirs entitled to this share were the children and grandchildren or, if there were none, the parents, but not the wife. Canon law increased the share and included the wife within the protection, but not the grandchildren or the parents of the decedent. If a wife and children survived, neither could be deprived by will of more than one-third of the property subject to disposition by will; if only a wife or only children survived, she or they were entitled to one-half....

The fact that the making of a will was a religious act explains the church's assumption of jurisdiction over intestacy as well. The church, in fact, considered intestacy to be in the nature of a sin. If a man died intestate, it was likely that he had died unconfessed. Moreover, the goods of the intestate ought to be distributed for the welfare of his soul. Thus the goods of the intestate were at the disposal of the ecclesiastical judge, that is, the bishop or his deputy, the "official." The bishop might trust the next of kin of the intestate to do what they thought best for his soul, but they had no claim to inherit anything more than their "legitimate part." Under the new canon law, the part that could not be taken from the wife and children by will was also the part that they inherited without a will; and all other kin had no right of inheritance at all unless the decedent had named them in a will. Thus the church claimed jurisdiction over intestate succession not only in order to protect the decedent's widow and orphaned children but also, for the good of his soul, to distribute the residue of his estate for charitable purposes....

The canon law of inheritance constituted a direct intervention by the church in feudal economic and political relations. The secular authorities offered strenuous resistance, especially with respect to ecclesiastical claims of jurisdiction over devises of land.

The Canon Law of Property

The ecclesiastical courts could hardly claim so extensive a jurisdiction over property relations as they exercised over family relations and inheritance. Yet their jurisdiction in property matters was by no means meager, and out of it came a substantial body of law. The church had enormous wealth, acquired through gifts and taxes as well as through its own agricultural, manufacturing, and commercial enterprises. Indeed, it is said to have owned between one-fourth and one-third of the land of western Europe. It is hardly surprising that not only the church's legal scholars but also church courts and church legislators had a great deal to say about rights and duties pertaining to the possession, use, and disposition of such wealth. In addition, canon law had something to say about rights and duties pertaining to secular property as well....

The canonists of the time not only systematized the law of property for the first time; they also introduced some wholly new concepts and rules of property law — concepts and rules that had a profound and lasting effect on the Western legal tradition....

The canonists also developed a legal device called a "foundation" or "corporation of goods" (*universitas bonorum*), as contrasted with "corporation of persons" (*universitas personarum*). This had been wholly missing from the older Roman or Germanic law. Although it has no exact parallel in later English secular law, it was received into the secular legal systems of other European countries. (In German it is called a *Stiftung*, in French a *fondation*.) It consisted of a personification of the purposes to which property, money, land, and incorporeal rights had been dedicated. Thus an ecclesiastical benefice itself — the property rights and duties connected with a clerical office, the income from economic activities adhering to the office, and all other perquisites of it — was treated as a legal person, with power through its officers to conduct its own economic and legal affairs as a single entity. A hospital or poorhouse or educational institution, or a bishopric or abbey, could be viewed not only as a corporation of persons but also as a corporation of goods.

In addition to developing the modern concepts of corporate ownership, trust, and foundations, the canonists also developed modern concepts of possessory remedies. In particular, they developed in the twelfth century a legal action for the recovery of possession of land, goods, and incorporeal rights, whereby a prior possessor who had been violently or fraudulently dispossessed could recover against a present possessor merely by proof of the wrongful dispossession and without the necessity of proving a better title.

Possessory remedies were needed because of the widespread practice of violent taking and retaking of land by rival claimants.... The forcible ejection of the possessor was called *spoliatio* ("spoliation" or "despoiling")....

In Causae II and III of his *Decretum* (called originally *The Concordance of Discordant Canons*), Gratian dealt with the question of spoliation in the context of two fairly complex cases, each involving a bishop who had been forcibly dispossessed because of alleged crimes....

Gratian then drew from these two papal epistles, which had been written with reference to specific cases, a rule of very great breadth. Anyone is entitled to a judicial decree of restitution of everything that has been taken from him, including incorporeal rights and powers, whether it has been taken by force or by fraud; and further, the remedy lies not only against the initial wrongdoer but also against third persons.... Gratian's rule was called the *canon redintegranda* ("rule of restitution")....

The Canon Law of Contracts

A developed body of contract law was needed by the church in the twelfth century, if only to regulate the myriads of economic transactions between ecclesiastical corporations. In addition, the ecclesiastical courts sought and obtained a large measure of jurisdiction over economic contracts between laymen, where the parties included in their agreement a "pledge of faith" — and for that, too, it was important that the canon law of contracts should command respect. Moreover, the canon law of marriage contained important elements of contract law.

In contract law, more even than in property law, the canonists were able to incorporate a great many of the concepts and rules that were being developed contemporaneously by the glossators out of the rediscovered texts of Justinian. The reasons for that were twofold: first, the older Roman law (especially the ius gentium) had achieved a very high level of sophistication in the field of contracts, and much of its vocabulary in that field, as well as many of its solutions to individual questions, could be applied in the twelfth century to the newly burgeoning commercial life of western Europe; second, the twelfth-century glossators of the Roman law were particularly sophisticated in their reconstruction and transformation of the older Roman law of contracts, in part just because of the demands placed upon them in that respect by the rapid economic changes of their time....

The theory of contract which was developed by the postglossators in the fourteenth century was built, however, not only on the foundations of the Romanist legal science of the twelfth- and thirteenth-century glossators — as viewed through Aristotelian concepts, categories, and definitions — but also on the foundations of the legal science, and, above all, the legal *system*, of the twelfth- and thirteenth-century canonists. What the canonist added to Romanist legal science was, first, the principle that promises are in themselves binding, as a matter of conscience, regardless of whether or not they are "clothed"; and second, that the causa which forms the basis of a contract, and which — if it is a proper causa — gives it validity, is to be defined in terms of the preceding moral obligation of the parties which justifies their having entered into the particular contract.

The canonists started from the principle of penitential discipline that every promise is binding, regardless of its form: *pacta sunt servanda* ("agreements must be kept"). Therefore it is not a defense to an action on a contract that the contract was not in writing or not made under oath. An oath and a promise without an oath are equal in the sight of God, they said; not to fulfill the obligations of a pact is equivalent to a lie.

Yet it did not follow that all promises are binding. Only agreements supported by a proper causa — in the sense of justification — were considered legally binding. "There was *causa* if the promisor had in view a definite result, either some definite legal act or something more comprehensive such as peace. And in order that morality might be safeguarded, it was not only necessary that the promisor should have an object but that this object should be reasonable and equitable."

In contract law, "reason" and "equity," for the twelfth-century canonists and Romanists alike, required a balancing of gains and losses on both sides. In every contract the things or services exchanged should have an equal value. This was called the principle of "just price." The phrase itself, *pretium iustum*, was taken from a passage in the Digest which provided that where the seller of an estate (*fundus*) had received less than half the "just price" he might sue the buyer, who would, however, retain the choice of the manner of discharging the obligation (presumably either by paying the balance or by rescinding the contract)....

The canonists were also concerned, however, with another aspect of a sale at other than the just price, namely, the excess profit derived by one of the parties. Profit making in itself — contrary to what has been said by many modern writers — was not condemned by the canon law of the twelfth century. To buy cheap and sell dear was considered to be proper in many types of situations.... What was condemned by the canon law was "shameful" profit (*turpe lucrum*, "filthy lucre"), and this was identified with avaricious business practices. These, in turn, were defined partly by whether they deviated from normal business practices. Thus for the canonists the doctrine of the just price became, in essence, both a rule of unconscionability, directed against oppressive transactions, and a rule of unfair competition, directed against breach of market norms....

Procedure

The canonists borrowed much both from the old Roman texts and from the contemporary Germanic custom. Yet they gave a new twist to both (if only by combining them), and the resulting ensemble was much different from either.

This appears nowhere more strikingly than in the procedure of the ecclesiastical courts. (1) In contrast to both the older Roman and the Germanic systems of procedure, canonical procedure was written. A civil or criminal action could only be commenced by a written complaint or accusation containing a short statement of the facts. The defendant was supposed to reply in writing to the points set forth by the plaintiff or accuser. By the early thirteenth century a written record of the proceedings was required. The judgment had to be in writing, although the judge did not have to give his reasons in writing. Parties examined witnesses and each other on written interrogatories. (2) Testimony, whether written or oral, was required to be under oath, with heavy penalties for perjury. The oath itself was a Germanic institution, but the canonists were the first to use it systematically as a testimonial device in the modern sense. In contrast to the Germanic system of compurgation (oath-helping), in which a party by oath "purged" himself of charges and others supported him by swearing the same oath, the canonists required a party or witness to swear an oath in advance to answer truthfully any proper questions that might be put to him. (3) Canonical procedure permitted the parties to be represented by counsel, who argued the law before the judge on the basis of the facts disclosed by the evidence. Earlier, both in the classical Roman law and in Germanic law, one who acted for another had assumed the rights and duties of the other; he was a substitute rather than a representative. The concept of legal representation was first introduced by the canonists, and was closely linked with both theological concepts and ecclesiastical concerns. (4) The canonists also invented the concept of a dual system of procedure, one solemn and formal, the other simple and equitable. The simple procedure was available for certain types of civil cases, including those involving poor or oppressed persons and those for which an ordinary legal remedy was not available. It dispensed with legal counsel as well as with written pleadings and written interrogatories. (5) Finally, in criminal proceedings the canon law, in contrast to both the Roman and the Germanic systems, developed a science of judicial investigation of the facts of the case, whereby the judge was required to interrogate the parties and the witnesses according to principles of reason and conscience. One of these principles was that the judge must be convinced, in his own mind, of the judgment he rendered. The system of procedure was said to be designed "to inform the conscience of the judge" — a phrase later used in the equitable procedure of the English chancery....

The emphasis on judicial investigation was associated not only with a more rational procedure for eliciting proof but also with the development of concepts of probable truth and of principles of relevancy and materiality. Rules were elaborated to prevent the introduction of superfluous evidence (matters already ascertained), impertinent evidence (matters having no effect on the case), obscure and uncertain evidence (matters from which no clear inferences can be drawn), excessively general evidence (matters from which obscurity arises), and evidence contrary to nature (matters which it is impossible to believe).

The more modern, more rational, more systematized procedure of the canon law of the twelfth century offered a striking contrast to the more primitive, formalistic, and plastic legal institutions that had prevailed in Germanic judicial proceedings in the earlier centuries. Indeed, the principles of reason and conscience were proclaimed by the ecclesiastical jurists as weapons against the formalism and magic of Germanic law. The most dramatic example of this was the decree of the Fourth Lateran Council in 1215 prohibiting priests to participate in ordeals. This law effectively ended the use of ordeals throughout Western Christendom, thereby forcing the secular authorities to adopt new trial procedures in criminal cases. In most countries the secular courts adopted procedures similar to those in use in the ecclesiastical courts....

Yet despite its sophistication, and despite its emphasis on reason and conscience, the canon law also contained its own elements of magic. These were evident throughout, but most strikingly in the solemn ("ordinary") as contrasted with the summary ("plain") procedure. Above all, the emphasis on writing was so exaggerated as to strongly suggest a magical element. As Mauro Cappelletti has said, "Procedural acts not reduced to writing were null and void .... The judge was required to base his decision exclusively upon the written record." Eventually, in the most formal types of ordinary procedure, the judge did not himself examine the parties and the witnesses but only studied the written record of their examination drawn up by subordinate court officials. This, of course, defeated the original purpose of judicial investigation, which was to enable the judge to form an "inner conviction" of the truth of matters in dispute.

Coupled with the sanctity or magic of the writing was the elaboration of a set of formal rules for evaluating evidence, which existed alongside the rational rules of relevancy and materiality. Two oracular or auricular witnesses were required to establish a fact (although judicial notice could be taken of notorious facts). The testimony of a woman counted only one-half and had to be supplemented by the testimony of at least one man. The testimony of a nobleman counted more than that of a commoner, that of a priest more than that of a layman, that of a Christian more than that of a Jew. The artificial weighing of evidence — full proof, half proof, one-fourth proof, even one-eighth proof — assumed increased importance as the judge became removed from the examination of witnesses and had nothing else to go on but the written record.

The rigors of proof, both formal and rational, were such as to make it often very difficult to establish grounds for conviction in criminal cases. It was this fact, more than any other, that eventually led to the widespread use of torture to extract evidence, and especially to extract that "queen of proofs," a confession. In cases where the state of mind of the accused was at issue — heresy cases were a prime example — there was no one more qualified to testify concerning his state of mind than the accused himself, and no more effective way to secure his admission of a criminal state of mind than the use of physical force.

In civil cases not only the rigors of proof but also, and more especially, the complexities of taking evidence by written interrogatories, without participation of the judge, led inevitably to the widespread use of dilatory tactics by the lawyers. This, in turn, was counteracted by the establishment of a series of compulsory stages, with separate rulings by the judge at each stage. However, the system could not resist the pressure to allow appeals to be taken from the separate rulings, and then to require such appeals to be taken at the risk of waiver of the right to object to the rulings at a later stage. It is not surprising that some cases went on for years and even decades.

These vices in the Romanist-canonical procedure were more characteristic of its use in the secular courts than in the ecclesiastical courts, where the judge's participation was more extensive and judicial discretion was given more scope. They were also more characteristic of its later development than of its use in the twelfth and early thirteenth centuries. It is likely that the increased reliance on written proofs, on formal rules of measuring evidence, and on confessions in criminal cases all reflected a decline in respect for oaths, which itself, paradoxically, may have reflected the increased emphasis upon rationality in the law.

NOTES AND QUESTIONS

1. Why would the church be interested in controlling universities? Who controls universities today?

2. Some of Gratian's ideas are distinctly modern. For instance, consider how his view of natural law relates to modern constitutionalism and how the notion that princes are bound by their own laws suggests the concept of the rule of law.

3. How was the scholarly work of the decretists and decretalists similar to or distinct from that of the glossators and commentators?

4. The church had general ecclesiastical jurisdiction over six classes of persons. Why were these groups included but not others?

5. A person might under canon law remove a suit from a secular court to an ecclesiastical court for "default of secular justice." Is the rationale for such a procedure similar to that allowing a defendant in an American state court to remove to a United States district court in "diversity of citizenship" or "federal question" cases? Is the rationale analogous for prorogation?

Consider the concept of "denial of justice" in modern international law. It triggers the conversion of a national civil or criminal case involving an alien — when there is denial of access to courts, inadequate procedures, or unjust decisions — into an international claim by the alien's state against the violator state.

Finally, a person could directly bring a suit to an ecclesiastical court alleging default of secular justice. How does this compare to the justification for the expansion of equity jurisdiction in 16th century England at the expense of the king's courts?

6. Review the canon law of marriage, inheritance, property, contracts, and procedure. Pick one of these areas of law and defend the proposition that the church either improved the law or worsened it.

7. As we will see in Chapter 10, civil and criminal procedural systems in the civil law world are direct descendants of the medieval procedural reforms in the ecclesiastical courts. Given the relation between procedure and substance ("In the law, all questions of procedure are, at bottom, questions of substance, and vice versa"), it is not surprising that much substantive canon law also grew out of ecclesiastical jurisdiction and procedure. Consider for instance, Gratian's *canon redintegranda*, which evolved into the *actio spolii*:

> The *actio spolii* first appeared around 1180; by this action the victim of any unjustified loss of possession, indeed of any obstacle to the exercise of a right, could claim restitution. The action went beyond the protection of possession given by the interdicts of Roman law, and far beyond the assize of novel disseisin and other feudal remedies, in that it covered any subject of alleged benefit, including movable property or an office or benefice. All the claimant had to do was to show that he had held this benefit peacefully before the present possessor; the question of right, of title, could be settled afterwards.

O.F. Robinson, T.D. Fergus & W.M. Gordon, An Introduction to European Legal History 151 (1985).

See R.C. van Caenegem, *History of European Civil Procedure,* in 16 Int'l Ency. Comp. L. (Civil Procedure) ch. 2, § 18 (1973).

3. PAPAL GOVERNMENT

HAROLD J. BERMAN, LAW AND REVOLUTION: THE FORMATION OF THE WESTERN LEGAL TRADITION 208-09, 212 (1983)*

Not only the electoral principle and the necessity to accommodate the cardinals, bishops, and clergy generally but also the very complexity of the ecclesiastical system of government served as a substantial limitation upon papal absolutism. Although legislation was their sole prerogative, popes in the twelfth and thirteenth centuries nevertheless felt the need to summon general councils periodically to assist them in the lawmaking process. These were Europe's first legislatures. Similarly with respect to administration, the papacy developed a highly efficient bureaucracy of specialists in various fields .... The papal chancery was in charge of drafting and issuing documents, including writs initiating judicial cases, and of keeping records of decrees, regulations, and decisions of the papal government; the chancellor was the keeper of the papal seal. The papal exchequer, called the Apostolic Chamber, operated both as a treasury for papal revenues and as a ministry of finance; in addition, the chamber had its own court for civil and criminal cases connected with taxation and other financial affairs. The papal court of general jurisdiction, both original and appellate, was called, in the twelfth century, the consistory; the pope himself presided over it. As papal jurisdiction expanded, the popes began to appoint judicial auditors (cardinals, bishops, or simple chaplains), whose decisions were binding, subject to papal ratification. In the thirteenth century the auditors became a permanent court, called the Audience of the Holy Palace, which deliberated as a body (often divided into sections), and at the end of that century a separate court of appeals was established for civil and criminal cases. (In the fourteenth century a supreme court was established, eventually named the Rota.) In addition, the papal household had a "penitentiary," which heard cases in the "internal" forum, that is, cases of sins to be dealt with not as criminal or civil offenses but by way of confession and penance. The Grand Penitentiary heard appeals from penances administered by bishops, and he administered censures and absolutions reserved to the pope.

The papal government also operated, at the regional and local level, through papal legates as well as through other appointees and subordinates.... There were three kinds: the proctorial legate, who was sent out to a locality or region with "full right" to act in place of the pope, under either a general or a special mandate; the judge-delegate, who exercised the judicial power of the papacy in particular cases; and the nuncio, who until the sixteenth century had only a limited capacity to represent the pope, for example, to transmit messages, gather information, or negotiate and conclude agreements on particular matters. Of these, the proctorial legate was the most powerful; he was sometimes authorized to preside over bishops in council and to bring sentences of deposition against them. However, decisions of all these types of papal legates were subject to appeal to the pope himself....

Moreover, archbishops and bishops, as well as heads of the major religious orders and of those individual monasteries that came directly under papal authority, were also in one sense the pope's officers. From the end of the eleventh century on, they were required at installation to swear an oath of loyalty to the pope. His approval was necessary for their appointment, and all their decisions were subject to his review.

Yet bishops were more than the pope's officers, both in theory and in practice. Each was also supreme on his own level of authority. Even after the Papal Revolution, every bishop remained the supreme judge, legislator, and administrator in his own diocese — unless the pope intervened. Therefore, it is only half the truth to say that the pope ruled the whole church through a corps of bishops; the other half of the truth is that the bishops ruled their respective dioceses subject to the pope....

At the same time, the bishop was surrounded in his diocese by various functionaries, who in practice wielded considerable countervailing power. The canons of the cathedral chapter elected the bishop just as the cardinals elected the pope. The canons also elected a provost or dean, who presided over the assemblies of the clergy of the cathedral. The chapter had power to try its own members, before its own courts, for disciplinary infractions. The chapter's consent was required for various acts by the bishop — for example, for the alienation of church property. Privileges of cathedral chapters varied from diocese to diocese; in many places, tensions between the chapter and the bishop led to appeals to Rome by one side or the other.

Officers of the bishop's household began to multiply at the end of the eleventh century, just as officers of the papal curia multiplied. The archdeacon assumed more power as chief executive officer; generally selected by the bishop, he ran the day-to-day affairs of the diocese. The chancellor emerged as the keeper of the episcopal seal and the officer in charge of correspondence and of the external affairs of the diocese. The "official" (*officialis*), trained in law, sat as judge in place of the bishop. Judicial seal-bearers, notaries, clerks of court, advocates, procurators, agents for executing court orders, assessors, and other types of judicial or quasi-judicial officers emerged in the bishop's court, just as archpriests, coadjutors, and other types of clergy emerged to assist the bishop in his liturgical functions.

NOTE

The levels in the governmental pyramid described by Professor Berman, beneath the pope in descending order, were the archdiocese (also called metropolitan archbishop), diocese (bishop), deaconry (deacon), and parish (priest). The regular court of first instance was that of the bishop. He or his delegate (*officialis*) was known as the "ordinary judge" or simply "ordinary." From him an appeal normally would go to the metropolitan (archbishop).

The Latin Church has lasted longer than any comparable Western institution. Its legal system has had a special impact on the civil law tradition. Direct influence continues today primarily in countries with a largely Roman Catholic population.

The two excerpts that follow illustrate this continuity. First, the 1983 Code of Canon Law is a revision of the 1918 Code, which served to bring order to canon law developments since the earlier *Corpus Juris Canonici*. The 1983 Code, intended for the whole Latin Church, has only one official version — in Latin. The canons are organized into 7 books: (1) general norms; (2) the people of God; (3) the teaching office of the Church; (4) the office of sanctifying in the Church; (5) the temporal goods of the Church; (6) sanctions in the Church; and (7) processes. The specific canons reproduced here come from book IV, part I (the sacraments), title VII (marriage). The introduction to title VII includes canons 1055-1062, and chapter IV (matrimonial consent) includes canons 1095-1107.

Second, the case *M v. E*, decided in Spain in 1988, concerns the nullification of a marriage under canon law, utilizing the norms mentioned above. Spain divides family law jurisdiction between ecclesiastical courts and ordinary civil courts. Mr. M brought this suit against his wife, Mrs. E, to the first instance ecclesiastical tribunal of Palma de Mallorca on February 15, 1988. The court issued its decision on June 20, 1988 (which is reported below), and it was confirmed by a decree of the metropolitan tribunal of Valencia on July 26 of the same year.

4. *CODEX IURIS CANONICI*

CODE OF CANON LAW: LATIN-ENGLISH EDITION xvii-xix, xxviii, 387, 399, 401 (Canon Law Society of America trans. 1983)

In the middle of the twelfth century, this mass of collections and norms, not infrequently contradicting one another, was put in order again through the private initiative of the monk Gratian. This concordance of laws and collections, later called the *Decretum Gratiani*, constituted the first part of that significant collection of laws of the Church which, in imitation of the *Corpus Iuris Civilis* of the Emperor Justinian, was called the *Corpus Iuris Canonici* and contained the laws which had been passed during two centuries by the supreme authority of the Roman pontiffs with the assistance of experts in canon law called glossators. Besides the Decree of Gratian, in which the earlier norms were contained, the *Corpus* consists of the *Liber Extra* of Gregory IX, the *Liber Sextus* of Boniface VIII, the *Clementinae*, i.e. the collection of Clement V promulgated by John XXII, to which are added the *Extravagantes* of this pope and the *Extravagantes communes*, decretals of various Roman pontiffs never gathered in an authentic collection. The ecclesiastical law which this *Corpus* embraces constitutes the classical law of the Catholic Church and is commonly called by this name....

Subsequent laws, especially those enacted by the Council of Trent during the time of the Catholic Reformation and those issued later by various dicasteries of the Roman Curia, were never digested into one collection. This was the reason why during the course of time legislation outside the *Corpus Iuris Canonici* constituted "an immense pile of laws piled on top of other laws." The lack of a systematic arrangement of the laws and the lack of legal certainty along with the obsolescence of and *lacunae* in many laws led to a situation where church discipline was increasingly imperiled and jeopardized.

Therefore during the preparatory period prior to the First Vatican Council, many bishops asked that a new and sole collection of laws be prepared to expedite the pastoral care of the people of God in a more certain and secure fashion. Although this task could not be implemented through conciliar action, the Apostolic See subsequently addressed certain more urgent disciplinary issues through a new organization of laws. Finally, Pope Pius X, at the very beginning of his pontificate, undertook this task when he proposed to collect and reform all ecclesiastical laws and determined that the enterprise be carried out under the leadership of Cardinal Pietro Gasparri.

The first issue to be resolved in such a significant and difficult undertaking was the internal and external form of the new collection. It was decided to forego the method of compilations of laws whereby individual laws would have been expressed in the extensiveness of the original text; rather the modern method of codification was chosen. Hence texts containing and proposing a precept were expressed in a new and briefer form. However, all of the material was organized in five books which substantially imitated the system of Roman law institutes on persons, things and actions. The work took twelve years with the collaboration of experts, consultors and bishops throughout the Church. The character of the new Code was clearly enunciated in the beginning of canon 6: "The Code generally retains the existing discipline although it introduces appropriate changes." Therefore it was not a case of enacting a new law but rather a matter of arranging in a new fashion the operative legislation at that time. After the death of Pius X, this universal, exclusive, and authentic collection was promulgated on May 27, 1917 by his successor Benedict XV; it took effect on May 19, 1918.

Everyone hailed the universal law of this Pio-Benedictine Code, which made a significant contribution to the effective promotion of pastoral ministry throughout the Church, which in the meantime was experiencing new growth. Nevertheless, both the external situation of the Church in a world which had experienced sweeping changes and significant shifts in customs within a few decades as well as progressive internal factors within the ecclesiastical community necessarily brought it about that a new reform of canon law was increasingly more imperative and was requested. The Supreme Pontiff John XXIII clearly recognized the signs of the times, for when he first announced the Roman Synod and the Second Vatican Council, he also announced that these events would be a necessary preparation for undertaking the desired renewal of the Code.

Shortly after the Ecumenical Council had begun, the Commission for the Revision of the Code of Canon Law was established on March 28, 1963....

Now, however, the law can no longer be unknown. Pastors have at their disposal secure norms by which they may correctly direct the exercise of the sacred ministry. To each person is given a source of knowing his or her own proper rights and duties. Arbitrariness in acting can be precluded. Abuses which perhaps have crept into ecclesiastical discipline because of a lack of legislation can be more easily rooted out and prevented. Finally, all the works, institutes and initiatives of the apostolate may progress expeditiously and may be promoted since a healthy juridic organization is quite necessary for the ecclesiastical community to live, grow and flourish....

TITLE VII
MARRIAGE

Can. 1055 — § 1. The matrimonial covenant, by which a man and a woman establish between themselves a partnership of the whole of life, is by its nature ordered toward the good of the spouses and the procreation and education of offspring; this covenant between baptized persons has been raised by Christ the Lord to the dignity of a sacrament.

§ 2. For this reason a matrimonial contract cannot validly exist between baptized persons unless it is also a sacrament by that fact.

Can. 1056 — The essential properties of marriage are unity and indissolubility, which in Christian marriage obtain a special firmness in virtue of the sacrament....

Can. 1061 — § 1. A valid marriage between baptized persons is called ratified only if it has not been consummated; it is called ratified and consummated if the parties have performed between themselves in a human manner the conjugal act which is per se suitable for the generation of children, to which marriage is ordered by its very nature and by which the spouses become one flesh....

Chapter IV
Matrimonial Consent

Can. 1095 — They are incapable of contracting marriage:

1° who lack the sufficient use of reason;

2° who suffer from grave lack of discretion of judgment concerning essential matrimonial rights and duties which are to be mutually given and accepted;

3° who are not capable of assuming the essential obligations of matrimony due to causes of a psychic nature.

Can. 1096 — § 1. For matrimonial consent to be valid it is necessary that the contracting parties at least not be ignorant that marriage is a permanent consortium between a man and a woman which is ordered toward the procreation of offspring by means of some sexual cooperation.

§ 2. Such ignorance is not presumed after puberty....

Can. 1099 — Error concerning the unity, indissolubility or sacramental dignity of matrimony does not vitiate matrimonial consent so long as it does not determine the will....

Can. 1101 — § 1. The internal consent of the mind is presumed to be in agreement with the words or signs employed in celebrating matrimony.

§ 2. But if either or both parties through a positive act of the will should exclude marriage itself, some essential element or an essential property of marriage, it is invalidly contracted.

5. A CANON LAW CASE

M v. E

Ecclesiastical Court of Palma de Mallorca (Spain)
Decision of 20 June 1988
88 Revista Jurídica de Catalunya: Jurisprudència 521 (1989)

Don Antonio Pérez Ramos, president and reporter.

I. *Species facti*

1. The parties met each other casually in Barcelona at a party in December 1984. Shortly thereafter the relationship became intimate and toward the middle of 1985 they began to live together in Mallorca. Advised from Chile that M's brother had died in an accident, the pair traveled there. The boy's family was not pleased with the irregular arrangement that M had with E, so they forced them to quickly have a civil wedding, which took place on 10 July 1985. After a few weeks the couple returned to Palma, where E's family insisted that they have a religious marriage, which was the traditional model that Mr. and Mrs. E desired. The couple, again solely to please the family members participating in the canonical wedding, agreed against their own wishes and, on 17 August 1985, celebrated their nuptials in the parish church of P. They have not had any children.

2. The beginning of conjugal life went well; but when the pair moved to Chile on account of the husband's work, the first problems arose, in large part because the wife did not adapt to Chilean customs. There developed a growing remoteness in interpersonal communication, with a grave deterioration in mutual affection.

3. With practically nothing in common other than the physical fact of dwelling beneath the same roof and with the failure of romantic relations, poorly established *ab initio*, the spouses separated in September 1987 by consent.

4. On 15 February 1988 Mr. M brought the present claim for a declaration of the marriage's nullity. On the 24th we accepted the complaint and a summons for the defendant. On March 9 the defendant stipulated to the facts in plaintiff's libel [complaint] and signaled her wish not to take an active part in the lawsuit. On the 11th the following issue was established: "Was there a nullity in the marriage in this case due to the exclusion of the benefits of sacrament and due to the lack of interest by both parties in having children (*prole*)?"

II. *In iure*

5. Because of the lack of normative autonomy in both [the old and new canon law] codes concerning false pretenses (*simulación*) as it relates to the benefit of children [*bien de la prole*] as a ground for matrimonial nullity, doctrine today looks for the legal seat of the element in question in canon 1055(1), canon 1061(1), and canon 1096(1). These canons prohibit the deliberate avoidance of natural procreation, an intention that definitely rejects the rights and obligations given and received in the conjugal pact — canon 1095(2), (3) — and acts to exclude an essential element of marriage as expressly stated in canon 1101(2). Cf. Aznar, El Nuevo Derecho Matrimonial Canónico 367 (1985); Bernárdez, Compendio de Derecho Matrimonial Canónico 176 (1986); López Alarcón-Navarro Valls, Curso de Derecho Matrimonial Canónico y Concordato 172-73 (1984). Case law recently deduced the notion of the rejection of the benefit of children from its comparison of canon 1055(1) with canons 1061(1) and 1084(3). Palestro, Decision of 29 Jan. 1986: Monitor Eccles. 414 (no. 4, 1986).

6. In this context the norm about children seems to be considered an essential property of marriage (De Luca, Un singolare caso di esclusione del bonum prolis; Ephemerides J.C. (1962)), equal to the rule about the good of the spouses (Serrano, Decision of 3 Apr. 1973: Il Diritto Eccles. 552 (no. 4, 1982)). The classic properties in canon 1056 fail to be a *numerus clausus*; the aforementioned canons 1101(2) and 1056 — in the prior code canons 1086(2) and 1013(2) — are no more than declarative of natural law. Cf. De la Hera, Intentio contra bonum prolis: 7 Jus Canonicum 224, 227 (pt. 1, Jan.-June 1967); Viladrich, Código de Derécho Canónico 629 (1987).

7. Likewise, since false pretenses as a legal concept lacks delimitation, it is appropriate to exegetically interpret canon 1101(2) to integrate the rejection of the benefit of children, which Castaño better understands as a right to conjugal acts (La "exclusio boni prolis," causa de nulidad de matrimonio?: R.E.D.C. 173 (no. 70, 1979), with both the exclusion of marriage itself, and its right constituting in essence the communion of life together, and the exclusion of the unity and indissolubility of marriage, which refers to a will completely contrary to the attributes of the matrimonial bond. Martinell, Matrimonio Canónico y Simulación: Jus Canonicum 189-90 (no. 41, 1981).

Graziani already in 1956 had taught that the exclusion of marriage itself could suitably include rejection of *bonum prolis* [benefit of children]. Volontá attuale e volontá precettiva nel negozio matrimoniale canonico 192 (1956)....

9. It is well known that current jurisprudence and doctrine — of course not unanimously — go beyond considering only the bride or groom's thoughts or state of mind as influences on one's will, and see them as something external to the will, to motivate one to marry. Now they affirm that we should assess a person's personality, the formation of his being and his habitual behavior and attitudes, not only as relevant data to procedurally explain the reason for exclusion, but as the factor so integrated into the bride or groom that it substitutes for or ranks equally with the act of exclusion itself. Cf. Serrano, Incapacidad y exclusión, in: Curso de Derecho Matrimonial 183-95 (1982); Decision of 23 Oct. 1981: Ephemerides Juris Canonici 147 (pts. 1-2, 1983); De Lanversin, Decision of 23 Mar. 1981, and Felici, Decision of 17 Mar. 1959: 51 S.R.R.D. 167; Viladrich, Código de Derecho Canónico (commentary to canon 1099) 662-63 (1987)....

11. In any case, as Fiore observes, the question of the validity or not of a marriage is not resolved by cold and abstract principles or axioms, since it is principally a question of fact. Each fact has its own history, dialectic, and individual circumstances. Decision of 23 July 1981: Ephemerides Juris Canonici 246 (pts. 3-4, 1983).

III. *In facto*

12. The fact of the exclusion [of the benefit of sacrament], more than the exclusion of the marriage itself or its indissolubility, as well as the reason for the exclusion and the reason that the parties went to the ceremony, appear clearly from the statements of the plaintiff and defendant, under oath. "I only believed," confessed M, "in the union of the couple, without the necessity therefor of any bond or process whatsoever. E and I agreed about this. I had learned in the school where I studied, which was Catholic, the concept of Christian marriage, but I did not accept that concept, especially that it should be for a lifetime." ... They went to the ceremony, nevertheless, since "E's family, which is traditional, at least regarding marriage, told us that since we were now living together and had been married by the civil authorities, we should also be married by the Church." ...

13. The witnesses, close friends to the protagonists and to the disarray that hardened on their hasty marriage, supported this view.... [Excerpts from the statements of P.P.G., J.Ch.F., M.P., and C.S.]

14. The rejection of the benefit of children is also evidenced in our opinion by each sworn statement. The simulated fact and its motivating causes emerge from them. The *causa simulandi* is the same here as for the exclusion of the benefit of sacrament, that is the contracting parties' firmly rooted error against marriage in general and against two of its properties: indissolubility and the rule of procreation.... In respect to *bonum prolis*, the contrary will of the bride and groom, coming from the irregular logic of a union lacking a true foundation, would bring its effects primarily on innocent third persons. In addition, there is the egoism that refused to make a profound and lifetime

commitment and preferred to dedicate itself to the realization of personal or professional goals.... [Excerpts from the statements of the parties and from the witnesses M.P.G., J.Ch.F., M.P., and C.S.]

17. On these merits we decide and sentence *affirmatively*; that is, the nullity of marriage in this case is evident due to the exclusion of the benefits of sacrament and the rejection of children by both parties.

NOTES AND QUESTIONS

1. Canon law procedure influenced the procedure used in secular courts, including the style of judicial opinions. Notice the opinion's division: (1) *species facti* (view of the facts); (2) *in iure* (the legal situation); and (3) *in facto* (the factual situation, i.e., consideration of the facts and application of the law to the facts). This style is today used in a number of civil law nations.

2. Consider the sources of authority used by the court: (1) the code of canon law; (2) doctrine, i.e., the articles, treatises, and commentaries of jurists; and (3) case law (jurisprudence), usually edited by or with comments by a jurist. The sources of law in secular courts are reviewed in Chapter 9, Section A.

3. Do you understand the court's reasoning and its application of the canons to the facts in *M v. E*? Does the result seem correct?

4. Spain adopted in articles 117.1 and 117.3 of its 1978 Constitution the Enlightenment principle that the state should have complete and exclusive control over judicial jurisdiction. The exception for ecclesiastical courts is narrow — a mere shadow of the church's past power — and is shrinking. Under the concordat of 23 August 1953 with the Vatican, ecclesiastical court judgments in matters of the nullity of a marriage or judicial separation of husband and wife were granted full effect in Spain, so that Spanish courts could not reconsider the underlying facts, including those for child custody decisions. Since the 1978 Constitution seemed to violate this international concordat, the Spanish government signed a new treaty with the Vatican in 1979 that led to certain changes in the 1888 Civil Code under Law 10 of 7 July 1981. Now only ecclesiastical cases concerning nullity or non-consummation of a marriage will be recognized by Spanish courts, and then only according to the general rules for recognition of foreign judgments. *See* Ignacio de Otto, Estudios Sobre el Poder Judicial 84-88 (1989).

F. COMMERCIAL LAW

1. THE LAW MERCHANT

HAROLD J. BERMAN, LAW AND REVOLUTION: THE FORMATION OF THE WESTERN LEGAL TRADITION 333-35, 339-41, 346-50 (1983)*

The Spread of Urbanization

[It] was [in] the late eleventh and twelfth centuries ... that the basic concepts and institutions of modern Western mercantile law — *lex mercatoria* ("the law merchant") — were formed, and, even more important, it was then that mercantile law in the West first came to be viewed as an integrated, developing system, a *body* of law.

The changes in mercantile law were even more striking than the changes in feudal and manorial law: informal, customary feudal and manorial relations had been widespread in the ninth and tenth centuries, although they had not then been given systematic legal expression, whereas, since the decline of the western Roman Empire, commercial relations had existed only on a very limited scale. To be sure, trade had never entirely died out. Some agricultural products continued to be sold by traveling merchants, who also bought and sold small luxuries and local handicrafts. Fairs and markets also existed, though they were not widespread, and some towns, especially seaports, survived from Roman times. Nevertheless, the Frankish Empire, in contrast to the Roman Empire, was not a Mediterranean civilization with abundant maritime trade, but a land-centered economy, hemmed in — in Henri Pirenne's phrase, "bottled up" — on all sides by Norsemen, Arabs, Magyars, and Slavs. Also, unlike the Roman Empire, the Western economy between the sixth and the tenth centuries was based not on thousands of cities but on perhaps a hundred thousand agrarian villages and manors. In the year 1000 only about two dozen towns of western Europe had more than a few thousand inhabitants, and probably only Venice and London had more than ten thousand. (Constantinople, in contrast, had a population of hundreds of thousands, possibly even a million.)

Then in the eleventh and twelfth centuries there occurred a rapid expansion of agricultural production and a dramatic increase in the size and number of cities. [From a mid-11th century European population of about 20 million, with perhaps 200,000 living in villages, the number of inhabitants doubled by 1200 with about 4 million living in thousands of towns and cities. Many of these urban centers had a population over 20,000 and a few even exceeded 100,000.] At the same time there emerged a new class of professional merchants, who carried on large-scale commercial transactions both in the countryside and in the cities. [From 1050 to 1200 the number of merchants increased from a few thousand to several hundred thousand.] It was primarily to meet the needs of the new merchant class that a new body of mercantile law was developed....

The New System of Commercial Law

To say that the basic concepts and institutions of modern Western commercial law were formed in the period of the late eleventh and twelfth centuries does not ignore the debt which the creators of those concepts and institutions owed to the Roman law as it was reflected in the newly discovered texts of Justinian. The Roman texts contained a highly sophisticated set of rules for forming contracts of various types, including loan of money, loan of goods, pledge, sale, lease, partnership, and mandate (a form of agency). These rules, however, were not consciously conceptualized; they were classified but not explicitly interrelated with one another and not analyzed in terms of general principles. Moreover, no conscious distinction was made between commercial contracts and noncommercial contracts; all were treated as civil contracts.

The old Roman jurists had also recognized that many contracts were governed not by the civil law but by customary law, including the *jus gentium*. Indeed, it was the *jus gentium*, the (customary) "law of nations," applicable to those who were not Roman citizens, that governed most types of commercial transactions within the Roman Empire, especially those involving carriage of goods over long distances. Included in the customary law of commerce of the Roman Empire was the Sea Law of Rhodes, usually thought to date from about 300 B.C., as well as the customs of maritime trade that had been developed subsequently by eastern Mediterranean traders. Some of the rules of the Roman customary law of commerce, as well as some of the rules of Roman civil law, had survived in the West from the fifth to the eleventh centuries, independently of the texts of Justinian; they are to be found, for example, in Lombard law as well as in customs of the merchants of Venice, which remained as a flourishing trading center throughout the period.

Nevertheless, neither the newly rediscovered Roman civil law nor the barely surviving Roman customary law, including the *jus gentium*, was adequate to meet the kinds of domestic and international commercial problems that arose in western Europe in the late eleventh and twelfth centuries.

It is conceivable that the learned Romanists in the European universities of the late eleventh, twelfth, and thirteenth centuries could have created a new body of mercantile law out of the Roman texts, just as they created a new body of civil law out of those texts. It is also conceivable that the canon lawyers at the same universities, together with their colleagues in the papal and episcopal chanceries, could have done the same, especially in view of the fact that ecclesiastical corporations engaged heavily in commercial activities. It is characteristic of the time, however, that the initial development of mercantile law was left largely, though not entirely, to the merchants themselves, who organized international fairs and markets, formed mercantile courts, and established mercantile offices in the new urban communities that were springing up throughout western Europe.

Occasionally, rules of mercantile law developed by merchants were collected and circulated. One of the earliest examples was a collection of maritime laws adopted about the time of the First Crusade (1095) by the Republic of Amalfi on the Italian coast of the Tyrrhenian Sea; known as the Amalfitan Table, its authority came to be acknowledged by all the city republics of Italy. About 1150 a compilation of maritime judgments by the court of Oléron, an island off the French Atlantic coast, was adopted by the seaport towns of the Atlantic Ocean and the North Sea, including those of England. The Laws of Wisby, a port on the island of Gotland in the Baltic Sea, were adopted about 1350; they were similar to and possibly derived from the Laws (or Rolls) of Oléron, and they gained wide authority in surrounding Baltic countries. About the same time the Consolato del Mare, a collection of customs of the sea observed in the Consular Court of Barcelona, based partly on the earlier collections and partly on statutes and compilations of the Italian cities, came to be accepted as governing law in the commercial centers of the Mediterranean. All these collections dealt exclusively with maritime law, including contracts of carriage of goods by sea.

At the same time a large body of law was created that governed overland trade. Markets and fairs had existed since the seventh or eighth century, but on a relatively small scale and without a highly developed legal character. From the eleventh and twelfth centuries on, however, great international fairs were held regularly in scores of cities and towns throughout Europe. International markets were also common, especially in seaport towns. These fairs and markets were complex organizations, and with the growth of legal systems, both ecclesiastical and secular, there developed the concept of a special law merchant, which included not only the customary law of fairs and markets but also maritime customs relating to trade and, finally, the commercial laws of the cities and towns themselves. The Italian cities took the lead in collecting systematically and enacting the customary rules by which commercial activity was governed.

The law merchant, then, governed a special class of people (merchants) in special places (fairs, markets, and seaports); and it also governed mercantile relations in cities and towns....

Participatory Adjudication: Commercial Courts

Commercial courts included courts of markets and fairs, courts of merchant guilds, and urban courts. Although guild and urban courts were not concerned exclusively with commercial matters, their commercial jurisdiction was sufficiently extensive to warrant their being treated as commercial courts.

Market and fair courts, like seignorial and manorial courts, were nonprofessional community tribunals; the judges were elected by the merchants of a market or fair from among their numbers. Guild courts were also nonprofessional tribunals, usually consisting simply of the head of the guild or his representative, but often he chose two or three merchant members of the guild to sit as assessors in mercantile cases. Occasionally, a professional jurist would sit with the merchant assessors. Professional notaries often acted as clerks to take care of legal formalities. Urban mercantile courts, too, often consisted of merchants elected by their fellows. A law of Milan of 1154 authorized the election of "consuls of merchants" to sit on commercial cases, and this system of merchant consular courts spread to many Italian cities. It permitted foreign merchants to choose judges from among their own fellow citizens. The courts of the merchant consuls in the city republics of northern Italy gradually extended their jurisdiction over all mercantile cases within the city. Other European cities adopted the Italian institution of the merchant consul or else developed similar institutions for adjudication of commercial cases by merchant judges. In some countries, royal authority was asserted over merchant guilds and over town markets and fairs, but even then the law merchant continued, in general, to be administered by merchant judges....

Another type of commercial court was the local maritime court in seaport towns, with jurisdiction over both commercial and maritime causes involving carriage of goods by sea. These courts — called admiralty courts — would sit on the seashore "from tide to tide."

In all types of commercial courts the procedure was marked by speed and informality. Time limits were narrow: in the fair courts justice was to be done while the merchants' feet were still dusty, in the maritime courts it was to be done "from tide to tide," in guild and town courts "from day to day." Often appeals were forbidden. Not only were professional lawyers generally excluded but also technical legal argumentation was frowned upon. The court was to be "ruled by equity ... whereby every man will be received to tell his facts ... and to say the best he can" in his defense. A typical statute of a merchant guild provided that commercial cases "are to be decided *ex aequo et bono*; it is not meet to dispute on the subtleties of the law." These procedural characteristics sharply distinguished commercial law from the formalistic procedure of urban and royal courts and also from the written procedure of the canon law in ordinary cases.

The procedure of the commercial courts was, however, related to the summary (as contrasted with the ordinary) procedure in ecclesiastical courts. Summary procedure in special types of cases, including commercial cases, was authorized by a papal bull of 1306, the Decretal "Saepe Contingit" (from the opening words, "It often happens"). The bull referred to the pope's practice of sometimes referring cases to (ecclesiastical) judges with the instruction that the procedure "be simple and plain and without the formal arguments and solemn rules of the ordinary procedure." To explain these words, the bull stated that the judge in such a case need not require a written complaint, that he should not require the usual type of pleading, that he might proceed even in time of vacations, that he should cut off dilatory exceptions, and that he should reject unnecessary appeals that caused delay as well as the "shouting" of advocates, prosecutors, parties, and superfluous witnesses. In such cases, the bull stated, the judge "shall interrogate the parties, either at their instance or on his own initiative wherever equity so requires." This decretal found its way into later Italian statutes establishing mercantile courts; it also influenced German, French, and English commercial and maritime courts, including the English chancellor's court in its equity jurisdiction....

The Integration of Mercantile Law

Western mercantile law acquired in the late eleventh, twelfth, and early thirteenth centuries the character of an integrated system of principles, concepts, rules, and procedures. The various rights and obligations associated with commercial relations came to be consciously interpreted as constituent parts of a whole body of law, the lex mercatoria. Many diverse commercial legal institutions created at that time, such as negotiable instruments, secured credit, and joint ventures, together with many older legal institutions that were then refashioned, were all seen as forming a distinct and coherent system.

The following distinctive characteristics of Western mercantile law were introduced during these centuries:

the sharp separation of the law of movables (chattels) from the law of immovables (land and fixtures attached to land);

recognition of rights in the good-faith purchaser of movables superior to those of the true owner;

replacement of the older requirement of delivery of goods in order to transfer ownership by the device of symbolic delivery, that is, transfer of ownership (and of risk of loss or damage) by transfer of transportation documents or other documents;

the creation of a right of possession of movables independent of ownership;

recognition of the validity of informal oral agreements for the purchase and sale of movables;

limitation of claims for breach of warranty, on the one hand, and development of the doctrine of implied warranties of fitness and of merchantability (*merchandise loyale et marchande*), on the other hand;

the introduction of an objective measure of damages for nondelivery of goods, based on the difference between the contract price and the market price, together with the introduction of fixed monetary penalties for breach of some types of contracts;

the development of commercial documents such as bills of exchange and promissory notes and their transformation into so-called abstract contracts, in which the document was not merely evidence of an underlying contract but itself embodied, or was, the contract and could be sued on independently;

the invention of the concept of negotiability of bills of exchange and promissory notes, whereby the good faith transferee was entitled to be paid by the drawer or maker even if the latter had certain defenses (such as the defense of fraud) against the original payee;

the invention of the mortgage of movables (chattel mortgage), the unpaid seller's lien, and other security interests in goods;

the development of a bankruptcy law which took into account the existence of a sophisticated system of commercial credit;

the development of the bill of lading and other transportation documents;

the expansion of the ancient Graeco-Roman sea loan and the invention of the bottomry loan, secured by a lien on the freight or by shares in the ship itself, as means of financing and insuring a merchant's overseas sales;

the replacement of the more individualistic Graeco-Roman concept of partnership (*societas*) by a more collectivistic concept in which there was joint ownership, the property was at the disposition of the partnership as a unit, and the rights and obligations of one partner survived the death of the other;

the development of the joint venture (*commenda*) as a kind of joint stock company, with the liability of each investor limited to the amount of his investment;

the invention of trademarks and patents;

the floating of public loans secured by bonds and other securities;

the development of deposit banking.

Thus a great many if not most of the structural elements of the modern system of commercial law were formed in this period. Implicit in them were certain basic legal principles which were shared by all the legal systems of the time and which were adapted to the special needs of the mercantile community. These included the principle of good faith, which was manifested particularly in the creation of new credit devices, and the principle of corporate personality, which was manifested particularly in the creation of new forms of business associations.

NOTE

> That Italy exercised a dominant influence in the development of the general law merchant was apparently due to the fact that the Italian cities first contested the supremacy of Constantinople in the oriental trade and first revived Mediterranean trade on a large scale; but it was due also to the fact that the Italian cities were not making wholly new law, such as was being made at the fairs and at the seaports of France and Germany; the Italian cities were in touch with the East, where the Mediterranean custom of merchants as embodied in the Roman law had never lost its force.

Munroe Smith, The Development of European Law 223 (1928).

Italian businessmen devised instruments that permitted them to remain more at home and to conduct widespread commerce through agents. This "modern" development depended on insurance, letters of credit, bills of exchange, and other devices. The decline of fairs in the 13th century indicated that a new, sedentary merchant had replaced his itinerant predecessor.

2. PARTNERSHIPS AND CONTRACTS

O.F. ROBINSON, T.D. FERGUS & W.M. GORDON, AN INTRODUCTION TO EUROPEAN LEGAL HISTORY 172-73, 176-77 (1985)

The firms which dealt in money and in goods — such as spices and dyestuffs, skins, silk and wool — were no longer either associations for one voyage or lifelong partnerships based on community of family property. These kinds of partnership did indeed survive, fitting well into the Roman models of the *societas unius rei* (partnership for a single deal) and *societas omnium bonorum* (partnership in all property), but it became more common to arrange an association for a term of years, after which profits were distributed in proportion to the shares which members had contributed. This sort of partnership, with joint and unlimited liability for the partners, was known as the *compagnia*. Although it was not unlike the Roman *societas quaestus* (partnership for all business matters), it was more concerned with questions arising from relationships with third parties, in effect with agency; Roman law had been primarily concerned with the internal relationship between the partners. *Compagnia* was not incompatible with the contract of commission, whereby one merchant took care of another's business for a percentage or a fixed fee. In firms like the Bardi or the Peruzzi the family connection remained strong, and hence membership stayed fairly constant at each renewal of the partnership. Partners shared profits proportionately, but investments by outsiders usually drew only a fixed rate of interest; the number of investors increased greatly in the early fourteenth century. Accounting methods improved; double-entry bookkeeping was introduced around the middle of the century. Although the Italian economy collapsed in the later fourteenth century when huge numbers of firms went bankrupt under the pressures of the Black Death, warfare, bad debts and other troubles, the skills acquired were not lost but were taken over by such firms as the Medici of Florence in the fifteenth century and the Fuggers of Augsburg and also the great banking houses of Bruges and Antwerp in the sixteenth....

As well as dealing with money, negotiable instruments, forms of partnership and insurance, mercantile custom also had its own view of the contract of sale and its related agreements. Perhaps the most dramatic new usage introduced by the growth of trade was the rule that the buyer in good faith at a public market — market overt — immediately acquired title to the goods bought. This was at variance with both Roman and Germanic law. In the former the original owner never lost his title if the property had been stolen, and by Germanic law, while the owner could raise an action against someone who stole from him, if he had lent the property to a friend, that friend acquired the right of action for the stolen goods. It might well be hard for a merchant, constantly travelling, to produce the seller from whom he had bought goods, and he was not in a good position to know if the seller actually had the right to sell. It took time for this usage of merchants to be accepted by the ordinary courts, but provided such protection was firmly linked to the market or fair it was likely to be agreeable to the feudal lord as another inducement for men to frequent the market from which he profited. The Church's stress on the value of good faith and the importance of supporting agreements, however informal, also worked to protect the merchant.... In a few areas, in the Netherlands and in certain German sea-ports, all possession in good faith was protected, but for the most part the rule was restricted to the open market, and in this form passed into later law.

Another tendency arising from mercantile custom was to give effect to formless contracts. Roman law had recognized only a limited number of contracts as being created by consent alone, and it had not given effect to nude pacts; Germanic law recognized only formal and real contracts. The Church's insistence on the honouring of any agreement slowly helped the custom enter the law, and it was accepted in fifteenth century France, as it generally had been throughout northern Italy, on the grounds of equity. Nor was it mercantile custom to require grounds to be stated in any document recording an obligation; this applied particularly to negotiable instruments. Writing was nevertheless a normal feature of commercial usage. This was another area in which the influence of notaries was considerable in bringing about standard clauses to meet the standard situations encountered by merchants.

NOTES AND QUESTIONS

1. Why did the new system of mercantile law develop apart from the rediscovered Roman law and from canon law? Did Roman law or canon law, nevertheless, have an impact on commercial law or on the procedure of commercial courts?

2. It was fundamental to Roman law that a nude or bare pact (an agreement that did not come within the limits of any recognized type of contract) was unenforceable. This rule was obviously inadequate for the needs of commerce in the late Middle Ages. Canon law (and the rule *pacta sunt servanda*) along with the standard clauses of notaries offered a solution to this legal problem.

3. The law merchant provided the content for the 19th century commercial codes in Europe, Latin America, and East Asia. Compare the development of commercial law in England:

> At first, the law merchant developed in England in much the same way as in other European countries. In the sixteenth and early seventeenth centuries, however, it was applied chiefly in special courts of Admiralty and of Chancery. In the later seventeenth century, the common-law courts of King's Bench and Common Pleas succeeded in usurping jurisdiction over commercial cases. Questions of mercantile custom were then submitted to juries of merchants for decision.
>
> As a body of customary law pleaded by merchants and implicit in jury verdicts, the law merchant was hardly suited for a leading commercial power, which England became in the eighteenth century. From the point of view of the individual merchants, there was a need for the law to be more clearly defined; from the point of view of national policy, there was a need for the law to be developed officially and not merely informally by commercial experience. These needs were finally met by Lord Mansfield (1705-1793), who became Chief Justice of the King's Bench in 1756. In the case of *Pillans v. van Mierop,*[14] Lord Mansfield held that the rules of the law merchant were questions of law to be decided by the courts rather than matters of custom to be proved by the parties and, further, that such rules applied not only to merchants but to all persons. Thus the law merchant was made an integral part of the substantive English common law....
>
> [T]his benefit to English common law was to some extent, at least, offset by the detriment to the continuing development of commercial law on a transnational basis. British jurists did not think of the common law — now including the law merchant — as a highly flexible set of principles to be continually reinterpreted in the light of new customs. Once the court declared a custom, it was not generally to be disturbed by inconsistent practices and understandings of merchants.

Harold J. Berman & Colin Kaufman, The Law Of International Commercial Transactions (*Lex Mercatoria*), 19 Harv. Int'l L.J. 221, 226-27 (1978).

---

[14] 3 Burr. 1663, 97 Eng. Rep. 1035 (K.B. 1765).

G. RECEPTION OF THE *JUS COMMUNE* IN EUROPE

NOTE ON ITALY AND THE *JUS COMMUNE*

Italy is the starting point for the revival of Roman law, its mixture with canon law, the rise of commercial law, and development of modern civil law systems. Although the term *jus commune* sometimes refers only to post-revival Roman law, it more often is associated with the single normative system resulting from the fusion of Roman law, as developed by the glossators and commentators, with canon law. The two parts symbiotically influenced each other and were considered to be the law of Christendom ruled by two supreme authorities: the emperor as its temporal head and the pope as its spiritual head. Intrinsic to both systems was a thrust toward universality, which helps to explain the reception in Europe.

In Italy the jus commune was the personal law of its citizens; there was no need for importation. From the centers of higher learning in Italy, the diffusion of a revitalized jus commune proceeded to the rest of Europe, to the point where it could be said (and often was said) that there was a common law of the civilized (by which was then meant "Christian") world.

Lawyers throughout Europe studied and used the same materials in the same way in the same language (Latin). The idealization of this period of dominance of the jus commune is at the bottom of a special attitude that might be called "the nostalgia of the civil lawyer." It refers to a desire to reestablish a jus commune — a common law of mankind — in the West.

The story of the reception of the jus commune is a complicated one that forms an important part of the legal history of contemporary European nations. By 1500 canon law, the *Corpus juris canonici*, had been accepted by all Christian peoples because of their allegiance to the Roman church. Canon law was binding everywhere in ecclesiastical courts, which had an extensive jurisdiction. For Roman law, however, the situation was different. In southern Europe, including Spain and southern France in addition to Italy, Roman law had never wholly expired. Revived Roman law was seen as perfecting what had been preserved in the *Lex Romana Visigothorum, Lex Romana Burgundionum,* and other compilations. In northern Europe customary law (*jus proprium*) alone survived. Hostility to the new learned law came partly from local lay courts, protecting their customary law, and often from rulers. In northern France the imperial origin of the *Corpus juris civilis* was an obstacle to its acceptance, until it was seen that the king could present himself as emperor within his own territory and thereby apply to himself texts supporting absolute imperial power.

The relationship between canon and Roman law and their reception was further supported by the use of canon law in some secular courts, which normally followed Roman rules. The general rule was that both laws should be interpreted in such a way as to avoid contradictions; the aim was to achieve harmony between canon and Roman law. Each law supplemented the other. If a matter was only clearly covered by canon law, the rule of canon law should be used. Furthermore, if obedience to Roman law would lead people into sin — by allowing interest on loans that was by canon law usury, for instance —

Roman law should not be followed. Finally, canon law was absorbed by significantly influencing the procedure used in many secular courts.

The agents for transmission of the jus commune throughout Italy and beyond were the university-trained lawyers, described in the next excerpt.

1. THE DEMAND FOR ACADEMIC LAWYERS

DAVID S. CLARK, THE MEDIEVAL ORIGINS OF MODERN LEGAL EDUCATION: BETWEEN CHURCH AND STATE, 35 American Journal of Comparative Law 653, 678-81, 717 (1987)

Bologna became in the twelfth century the principal European center for Roman law and canon law. The university, as seat for both laws, served to varying degrees and in different ways the interests of state and church. This was true even though both Roman law and canon law could be interpreted to embrace a strict monarchic system of government supported by unitary descending themes of law creation and administration.

On the secular side, a proliferating class of lawyers — trained at Bologna and other law faculties — promoting rationalism and secularization, labored to reduce the role of the church in government and to expand the authority of other political entities. For example, a staff of educated notaries, attorneys, judges, and accountants from the thirteenth century on worked at the imperial chancery to process the flow of petitions directed to Hohenstaufen emperors. Other graduates worked as legal advisers, notaries, or judges to cities, kings, princes, and lords of manors.

On the religious side, many of the major medieval popes after the time of Gratian were canonists rather than theologians. Pope Alexander III (1159-1181) brought thc papal chancery into close contact with Bolognese canon law. Legal training facilitated the tasks of legislating for Christian society and administering a complex hierarchical organization.[92] Alexander III, for instance, ended from a legal standpoint the Investiture Controversy by issuing decretals inspired by Gratian's juristic theory.

The papal curia, and especially its evolving chancery (*Rota romana*) which handled an increasing flow of disputes sent to Rome, required a large cadre of legally trained assistants, whom Bologna and other newly formed universities educated. These learned jurists brought with them Roman law and their law professors' scholastic techniques, which influenced both procedural and substantive canon law. Episcopal chanceries, furthermore, sought canonistic students for archdeacon offices and for numerous judicial positions (especially the position of *officialis generalis*) that proliferated after 1150. Ecclesiastical court jurisdiction was extensive by the late Middle Ages, encompassing — in addition to strictly religious matters or cases involving clerics — family and inheritance law issues as well as many questions concerning contracts and corporations. The church, in fact, was the first important entity to absorb large num-

---

[92] Popes after Alexander III, including Innocent III and IV, Gregory IX, and Boniface VIII, until the fourteenth century were usually highly qualified jurists. They frequently intervened personally in the vast litigation which flowed into the curia. Most secular rulers, in contrast, were barely able to write a Latin sentence.

bers of learned jurists, and so became the first home for the new legal profession.

In the twelfth century, both imperial and papal authorities became well equipped with lawyers to help with their controversies. Emperors now had Roman jurists to provide ideological support for their German armies; popes had a newly ordered canon law with a growing international bureaucracy to apply it....

Success generated imitation. Universities — 46 by 1400 — modeled on either the example at Bologna or Paris, began when masters and students migrated to a new town — as at Padua or Orléans — or when founded by secular rulers or by ecclesiastical authority.

Many princes and city leaders founded universities because they felt that it would be advantageous to have a center where lawyers could be trained to assist in the political development and administration of their regimes. At first lawyers worked as general counselors, diplomats, judges, or notaries. At distinct tempos in various European polities, centralizing administrative systems — orchestrated by civil servants at the center and implemented by officials at the local level — gradually replaced feudalism. These evolving administrative and judicial bodies stimulated great demand for academically educated jurists, who took places formerly occupied by noblemen. The medieval theory of pluralistic sources of law, moreover, facilitated acceptance by judges or administrators of a Roman legal norm over a territory's or city's statutes and customs. Roman law, as *ratio scripta*, further accentuated demand for university trained lawyers.[244]

2. A *JUS COMMUNE* CASE

FABRONIS v. MARRADI BALL PLAYERS

Rota Fiorentina (1780)

[This case is described in an article by Gino Gorla in the Tulane Law Review, which is excerpted below.]

GINO GORLA, A DECISION OF THE ROTA FIORENTINA OF 1780 ON LIABILITY FOR DAMAGES CAUSED BY THE "BALL GAME," 49 Tulane Law Review 346-55 (1975)

The *Rota Fiorentina* was one of the highest courts in the Grandduchy of Tuscany under the rule of the Medicis (until 1737) and the Lorenas. It was the most authoritative Court in the Grandduchy and enjoyed great prestige and authority in the world of the *ius commune*. The *Rota* acted at times on the

244 The prevalent theory of sources of law, as developed by university law professors, considered Roman law to be *ratio scripta*. Thus, although a judge should apply a local statute or custom when it was clearly appropriate to the case at hand, if a custom could not be proved or a statute was not directly on point, he could refer to Roman law to fill the gap in local law. In addition, a judge was entitled to construe local law within the framework of Roman legal science....

An incident from Germany in 1259 illustrates how Roman law infiltrated local law. A representative of Lübeck asked the Hamburg council what rules it applied to some questions of maritime law. An advisor could not find for one of the issues an appropriate rule in the Hamburg statutes or customs. However, since he was an educated jurist, he translated certain passages from the Digest into German and responded to Lübeck that these represented the Hamburg rule.

commission of another Supreme Court, *Il Magistrato Supremo*, where the lieutenant of the Grandduke sat. The decision discussed probably echoes the policy of the Medicis and the Lorenas to protect the middle and lower classes against overwhelming pretensions of the nobility. The decision is given in appeal on a commission by the *Magistrato Supremo* to a judge of the *Rota Fiorentina*.

The judge was Giuseppe Vernaccini, a prominent personage in the *Rota* and the council of the Grandduke....

Judicial decisions at that time were given a title. The decision discussed in this article is entitled *Marradiensis Praetensae Refectionis Damnorum*. There are difficulties in the presentation of this decision due to the judicial style of the *Rotae*, to the language,[7] and to the fact that we have lost the art of reading a case of those times.

I have tried to overcome these difficulties by paraphrasing the text of the decision, occasionally abridging it. However, on the whole I have tried to follow the text of the decision. Similarly, I have tried to reproduce Vernaccini's narration of the "facts of the case," since it is important to comprehend how the judge visualizes facts and where he puts emphasis or color; this seems to be particularly interesting in this case. The courts of the Grandduchy of Tuscany, as many other Italian courts (not all of them), had the duty to give "motives" or "grounds" for a judgment. The judgment had to be grounded ("motivated") on the basis of *auctoritates et rationes, i.e.,* authorities and reasons. The latter were displayed especially when the former were lacking or when they were not binding.

The authorities were, in order of importance:

(1) Roman texts (which had the force of law), statutes, and *legal* customs. These authorities were binding (*auctoritates necessariae*) only when the provision was precisely on point and clear. If the provision considered a case similar to the case at stake, then it was a matter of an *argumentum a similibus*;

(2) judicial precedents of the Supreme Courts of the State, whose decisions, if on point, were binding as law, where there were a series of them constituting a *consuetudo iudicandi, i.e.,* a judicial custom;[10]

(3) judicial precedents of the Supreme Courts of other States (Italian or European), and especially the *Rota Romana*, which, besides being one of the Supreme Courts of the Pope's temporal State, was the Supreme Court of the Catholic Church legal order;

(4) the *Doctores*, in their legal writings, *i.e., Glossae* (of the famous *Glossa*), commentaries and treatises, *Consilia* (legal advice), and *Allegationes* or advocates' briefs when published in volumes.

Authorities mentioned in (3) and (4) were not binding, *i.e.,* they were only persuasive, even when they were on point.

[7] The decision is written in Italian. However, this is the Italian of the 18th century, or rather the Tuscan language of those times. It is interesting that most decisions of Tuscan Supreme Courts were written in Latin.

[10] In some Italian States, like Piedmont and Naples, a single decision of the Supreme Court was binding as law. However, in Tuscany and other States, two decisions (*binae judicaturae*) were sufficient to create a *consuetudo iudicandi.*

All authorities, binding and not binding, had to be on point, in order that they could be alleged as (pure) authorities. If they considered a case similar to the case at stake, then they were a matter of an *argumentum a similibus*, which could be a matter of discussion according to the degree of similarity. The *argumentum a similibus* was middle way between *auctoritates* and *rationes*, because maintaining similarity and drawing an argument from it involved a certain reasoning. In the absence of authorities on point, the *argumentum a similibus* was a way of developing or creating law. It was used largely by the Glossators and Commentators of the 12th to the 15th centuries, to adapt Roman texts to the times. Thus, *argumenta a similibus* were often artificially stretched. During the 16th to 18th centuries, Supreme Courts were at work in the various Italian States, and they used the same method of *argumenta a similibus* to develop or create the law according to the changing times. The Supreme Courts applied that method not only to Roman texts but also to judicial decisions and [the writing of] *Doctores*....

The Decision

The Facts of the Case

In the Tuscan town of Marradi since time immemorial, it was customary during the summer for a team of amateurs (*dilettanti*) to play a ball game in the public square. According to a similar usage existing in other towns of Italy, the game was played mostly as an amusement or public feast for the citizens, rather than as an athletic exercise for the local youth. The owners of houses surrounding the square never opposed the use of the area for the game. It was also customary that the team would notify the owners of the day during the summer on which the games would be commenced, in order that they might adopt measures to avoid damages to their houses, especially to the windows.

At the beginning of the season of 1778, the team, as usual, gave formal notice to the homeowners that the games would commence on July 24. The Fabronis, a noble family of Marradi, having restored the facade of their house located in the public square, asked the Community Magistrate for an injunction prohibiting the game or for a *cautio de damno infecto*.[19] The team, resenting the fact that one family would oppose the public games, claimed that the game had to be absolutely free and "immune" from any liability for damages as it had been in the past.

[19] In the *ius commune*, the *cautio de damno infecto* dealt with in the Digest 32.9 had become a kind of suretyship or warranty to be given for a person building or making a work on his land from which damages could result to neighboring property, or where it is probable that damages would result from an existing building, work, or situation of the property of that person. *See* the present articles 1171 and 1172 of the Italian Civil Code. In the Digest, the *cautio* was not a suretyship; it was a solemn promise (*stipulatio*) to be made by that person, that he shall pay those damages. Further, from Vernaccini's decision it seems that the *cautio de damno infecto* could be extended to damages probably resulting from acts other than building or making a work *on land*, *i.e.*, in the instant case from playing a ball game.

On July 20, 1778, the Community Magistrate, composed of seven members, unanimously rendered a decree that:

> The amateurs' team can continue giving such *licit* amusement in the public square; however, the question of damages is to be left open and discussed in the ordinary course of justice.

On the same date, the Community Magistrate issued a decree stating that in the territory of Marradi there was no place, other than the public square, where the ball game could be conveniently played. This decree was given at the request of the *Auditore Fiscale*, who asked, at the solicitation of the Fabronis, whether it was possible to find another place "adaptable" to the game without inconvenience to neighbors and the "ornament" of their houses.

No appeal or recourse was taken by the Fabronis from the two decrees. They did, however, file an action before the ordinary local court of the "*Vicario*," for a *cautio de damno infecto* and for the payment of any damages caused by the games. The *cautio* was also sought for future damages that would result from games during subsequent summer seasons. On July 26, 1778, the team gave the *cautio* by way of a personal suretyship of one citizen of Marradi, in order to avoid delay of the public amusement. However, the *cautio* was given "without any prejudice of the question of liability for damages, to be examined in the subsequent course of procedure." During the games of that season, damages of eight lire were caused to the windows and shutters of the Fabronis' house. Further, the facade was soiled by the ball being dirtied in sand and lime on the ground that was used to restore the Fabronis' house, and damages were estimated at forty lire.

On January 20, 1779, the *Vicario* gave a judgment for payment of the former damages, but acquitted the team for the latter damages, since the ball was dirty due to the sand and lime heaped on the ground by order of the Fabronis. Both parties appealed to the Magistrato Supremo in Florence: the Fabronis asked for the payment of damages for soiling the facade, the team to be acquitted for damages caused to the windows and shutters of the Fabronis' house.

The Motives

(1) According to the common opinion of *Doctores* interpreting the *Lex Aquilia*, the basic Roman law on torts, the act causing damage must be committed with *dolus*, or, at least, with *culpa* in order to constitute an *iniuria* or wrong, and thereby give rise to liability for damages. There is no *iniuria* without at least *culpa*.

(2) Further, there is no *culpa* and, therefore, no *iniuria* and no liability when the act causing damage is *"licit and permitted by law."*

(3) According to the *communis opinio* of the *Doctores*, the ball game is considered a licit and permitted act which cannot be prohibited: *est de iure permissus, nec potest de iure prohiberi.* Further, in the particular case the game is to be considered licit and permitted precisely in the public square of Marradi, since there was an immemorial custom of playing it in the public square and, more importantly, because it was authorized by the Community

Magistrate's decree of July 20, 1778, that there was no other place where the game could be conveniently played; this decree, for lack of appeal, has become a *res iudicata.*

(4) Therefore, since the game is an act *licit* and *permitted*, which in the particular case was *licit and permitted precisely* in the square of Marradi, the team was not liable for damages caused by the game to the houses surrounding the square.[27]

(5) Moreover, as was customary, the team notified the owners of the houses surrounding the square of the day on which the games would begin in order to allow them to adopt measures to protect items likely to suffer harm from blows by the ball. This notification represents an act of "diligence," to avoid damages ensuing from a licit and permitted act. Indeed, some of the *Doctores* require that even in the case of a *licit and permitted* act, *diligentia* (care) must be used to avoid damages.

(6) The Fabronis ignored the notice and left exposed to possible damage items that could have been protected from harm. Similarly, they had embellished the facade of their house located where they knew the game was customarily played. Thus, the Fabronis willingly exposed themselves to the damages which could derive from the game. Therefore, the text of the Digest 11 *ad legem Aquiliam* is to be applied.[30]

(7) The Fabronis raised two objections to these arguments. First, they argued that the rules of immunity from liability in case of an act licit and permitted are applicable only when, as a consequence of that act, nothing is introduced onto the neighbor's property: *nihil in alienum immittitur.*[31] This objection must be rejected. While this is true where a work to be done is new

[27] Here the decision, besides citing again the authorities cited in paragraph (2), cites other authorities. First of all, it cites the Digest 9.2 (on *Lex Aquilia*), 7, § 4 (*si quis*). This text says that there is no *iniuria* in the case of boxing or other fighting in a public game when one of the parties is killed, because the harm is caused for the sake of glory and virtue, and not to commit an *iniuria.* Then, the decision cites *Doctores* interpreting that text; among them it again cites Bonfini. This author says that such custom (*consuetudo*) of boxing or fights excuses the fighting party (*ludentem*) from punishment for assault and battery or homicide, if the game is done without fraud (*sine dolo*) in a place established for that purpose (*in loco ordinato et consueto*); however, he adds, if harm or death is caused in *loco non ordinato*, and in an illicit game, then according to the *Lex Aquilia*, there is punishment. This citation of the Roman text, the *Doctores*, and Bonfini is an instance of Vernaccini using the *argumentum a similibus.*

[30] The text of Digest 9.2 (*Ad Legem Aquiliam*), 11, is a case involving the following facts: In the course of a ball game, the ball was pitched with great force striking the hand of a barber shaving a customer whose throat was cut. The *jureconsult* Proculus held that the barber, not the player, was at fault (*culpa*), because the barber conducted his business near an area where it was customary (*ex consuetudine*) to play the ball game, or where people passed frequently. Thus the barber is liable for damages towards his client, although it would not be wrong to say that the client could not complain if he permitted the barber, who keeps his shaving chair (*sellam*, not a shop) in a dangerous place, to shave his face. Here the *argumentum a similibus* seems to be nearer to the case in Vernaccini's decision. The barber had *willingly* put his trade chair in a place where it was *customary* to play the ball game, and in a similar manner the Fabronis did not protect the windows and embellished the facade of their house in a place where it was customary to play the ball games. Despite that fact, there are some differences between the two situations.

[31] The text invoked by the Fabronis was Digest 8.5 (*si Servitus Vindicetur*), 8, § 5. According to the Fabronis' objection, in the ball game what is introduced in the neighbor's property is the ball launched by the players. The Roman text deals with quite different cases of "immission," *i.e.*, "immission" of smoke or water *from a factory or a land* onto the neighbor's property, whereas here the ball is "immitted" by a group *of persons.* Here we find an *argumentum a similibus* adopted by the Fabronis' lawyer and discussed as such by Vernaccini.

and unusual, it does not apply, however, to a work already *pre-existing and usual*. Thus, the rule is not applicable in the instant case, since the ball game was not introduced for the *first time* in the public square of Marradi, nor played in a *new and unusual manner*, but rather was played in the public square since time immemorial, and it was intended that the game would continue there in the *ancient and usual* manner.

(8-11) Secondly, the Fabronis objected that future damages and the *cautio de damno infecto* for such damages were the main object of their action. Therefore, they argued that the pertinent law was not the *Lex Aquilia*, concerning damages already caused and requiring *culpa*; rather, the applicable law was *cautio de damno infecto*, under which the *cautio* has to be given also for future damages deriving from a licit and permitted act even if no *culpa* occurs. This objection too must be rejected. While this might be true in the case of future damages that one fears would derive from a *new and unusual* work, it is not true in the case of damages which one fears would derive from a *pre-existing and usual* work. In the latter case, the obligation of giving the *cautio de damno infecto* presupposes *culpa*, if not a *culpa in committing* something, at least a *culpa in omitting* something, that is *negligentia*.[34]

(12) Moreover, the law of the *cautio de damno infecto* has no bearing on the present case, since the object of the *cautio* is that of safeguarding against future damages deriving from *extrinsic and accidental* defects of the work, and not against future damages deriving from *natural and intrinsic* defects such as wind.[35]

(13) Because the ball cannot always be directed by the players precisely where they want and, therefore, may strike surrounding houses, this constitutes a *natural and intrinsic* defect of the ball game. Thus, damages deriving from such a game cannot be the subject matter of the *cautio de damno infecto*. On the contrary, this is a damage that the owners of houses located in a public square, where a game is played, have to suffer in good peace (*in buona pace*) as a natural and inevitable consequence of the location of their houses, similar to that suffered by the owner of inferior land from the natural and inevitable flow of water from the superior land of a neighbor.

NOTES AND QUESTIONS

1. The *Ball Players* case can be read on several levels. First, merely as a story, it is timeless. Here are rough, boisterous ball players (they could be stickball players in the Bronx or street basketball players in any town) and the householder, who is worried about property damage and probably objects to the noise and congestion as well. At this level, what do you think of the decision? Suppose you think of the ball players as the proletariat and the householder as a wealthy capitalist — there you have it: the class struggle epitomized.

[34] Here the decision cites Donellus (a French author of the 16th century) in a work where, *inter alia*, he deals with cases of a house or similar work which was badly built, built with bad materials, or which the owner neglected or omitted to repair (*i.e.*, three cases of *culpa* or *negligentia*).

[35] Here Vernaccini cites *Doctores* and decisions of the *Rota Romana* concerning buildings or other similar works.

2. From another point of view the case illustrates the vitality of the *jus commune* in Tuscany in the late 18th century and the use of the Digest of Justinian as primary authority for the decision of cases 12 centuries after its promulgation. U.S. courts occasionally cite old materials, but never as primary authority, never as the principal legal basis for the decision in the case (and never anything 12 centuries old). Citations to old sources in American court reports are usually there for other purposes: as historical background to help understand modern law; as an aid to interpreting today's law; or merely to enrich the opinion with history, to make it more interesting to read, or to display judicial erudition.

3. The case is also interesting as an exercise in interpreting and applying law. (This characteristic activity of judges in all periods of Western law will be discussed in Chapter 9.) How would you describe Judge Vernaccini's process of interpreting the authorities? Do you agree with the decision or disagree? Why?

3. THE RECEPTION IN FRANCE AND GERMANY

K.W. RYAN, AN INTRODUCTION TO THE CIVIL LAW 15-22 (1962)

The Development of French Law

[I]n the ninth century three bodies of law applied in France. Under the system of personality of laws, the Germanic and Roman laws were the personal laws of the Germanic and Roman sections of the community respectively. In addition, the Imperial capitularies bound everyone in France independently of racial origin. With the progress of time, the intermixture of the races made it almost impossible to adhere to the system of personality, and this was replaced by the system of territoriality. The territorial unit was not however the country of France. The change from the system of personality to that of territoriality coincided in time with the development of feudal institutions in France, so that the area controlled by a particular seigneur was decisive as to what law was to be applied. In general it may be said the law of a territory was that of the dominant race. Since the Roman element of the population was most pronounced in the south of France, and the Germanic element in the north, the whole country was effectively divided into two regions, the country of written law (*pays de droit écrit*) where the law was basically Roman and the country of customary law (*pays de droit coutumier*) in which the law was Germanic in origin. Moreover, the break-down of the system of personality meant that the laws which were recognised in a territorial unit could no longer be the *leges* of a particular race. The laws therefore no longer took effect as the enactments of the legislative organs recognised by the various national groups, but as the customary law of the territory.

In the *pays de droit écrit,* the law in force was a customary Roman law, modified somewhat by those parts of the capitularies which were still accepted as being in force and by the canon law. Roman law was the common law of the south; and since the authoritative expression of Roman law was to be found in Justinian's codification, the Roman law revival in Italy, which as we have seen was based on the critical analysis of Justinian's texts, found a ready response in southern France. As Esmein says, it was like a country which, having lost its codes, had lived for some centuries only on its recollection of them and then rediscovered them one fine day. As early as the end of the eleventh century studies based on Justinian's texts appeared in France, and in the following century the summary of Justinian's code named *Lo Codi* shows that the work of the Glossators was well known in southern France.

In the regions of the centre and north, on the contrary, the common law was the customary Germanic law, and Roman law could only make its way by a process of infiltration into the body of the customary law. The reception of Roman law took place therefore not by virtue of any theory of its continued validity as part of the positive law, but in consequence of its own inherent worth, that is, as *ratio scripta*, not as *ius scriptum*. This reception occurred on two planes. First, Roman law was early regarded as a supplementary system available to fill up the gaps in the customary law; and secondly, in certain areas of the law, particularly in the field of obligations, the Roman system was seen to be so superior to the customary law that the prescriptions of the latter were ultimately rejected throughout the regions of customary law in favour of the alien Roman rules.

From the beginning of the thirteenth century there appeared a number of works by French jurists on customary law. These books, though modelled on the Roman law compilations, were written in the vernacular, mainly by judicial officers....

Subsequently, official compilations of customary law made their appearance. At first these *chartes des coutumes* were issued under the authority of the local seigneurs, and so naturally they were concerned mainly with local variations in the customary law, rather than with the general body of law which formed the customary common law. The first official measure designed to reduce the general customary law to writing was an Ordinance of Montils-les-Tours issued by Charles VII in 1453, which directed that the customs of all the regions of France be written down. This direction was largely ignored, but it was repeated by subsequent sovereigns, and by the middle of the sixteenth century the customs of all the more important regions had been published.

This official publication of the customs was a matter of the highest significance in the history of French law. The authentic statement of the customary law left no room for the reception *en bloc* of the Roman law which occurred about the same time in Germany; Roman law could henceforth infiltrate into the fixed customary law only by way of interpretation. The risk that Roman law would replace the customary law was no longer a real one. Furthermore, the character of the customary law was changed. It was no longer, strictly speaking, customary law at all; the customs had become statutes, deriving their effect not from the consent of the people but from the royal authority.

The publication of the customs undoubtedly did much to eliminate many local differences, but at the same time it confirmed such differences between the major regions of France as did in fact exist. Voltaire's quip that in France a traveller changed law as often as he changed horses was not far from the truth. It was not till the promulgation of the Code Napoléon in 1804 that France became a legal unit. Moreover, the customs did not constitute a code.

The status of persons, donations, succession law, feudal tenures, and matrimonial relations were in general regulated in them; but other areas of the private law were not touched at all or only at some points, and the Roman law therefore still had application over many provinces of the private law. It is in the marriage of the customary law with Roman law on a basis of rough equality that French law in the regions of customary law attained its distinctive character towards the close of the *ancien régime.*

The publication of the customs resulted in the existence of a set of texts of customary law which corresponded to the *Corpus Iuris Civilis* of the Romanists and the *Corpus Iuris Canonici* of the canonists, and naturally enough commentaries upon them were soon written as they were upon the older texts. The great Commentators upon the customary law were Du Moulin in the sixteenth century, Domat in the seventeenth, and Pothier in the eighteenth. Since the majority of Commentators wrote their observations upon the *coutume de Paris*, that particular custom became in course of time the most developed, refined and influential, and the *coutume de Paris* as explained particularly by Pothier is the main source to which Napoleon's commission turned in its task of codifying the civil law of France.

We have seen that Roman law took effect as the customary law of the *pays de droit écrit*, and that in the north it was in part a supplementary system and in part it superseded the customary law. The interpretation placed upon Roman law in the French courts and universities was that of the Italian Commentators, particularly Bartolus....

Judicial decisions were a minor but not unimportant source of law in pre-Revolutionary France. Prior to the publication of the customs, the existence and scope of customary rules were declared by the courts, and after their publication the courts had the function of interpreting them. In addition, the *Parlements* (regional courts) occasionally rendered decisions (the so-called *arrêts de règlement*) which were legislative in character in that they bound all persons within the *Parlement's* jurisdiction, and not merely the litigants before the court.

From the middle of the sixteenth century a certain number of royal Ordinances were enacted which were concerned mainly with procedural and commercial law, but which also left permanent marks on the civil law of France....

The Development of German Law

The history of German law from the ninth to the fifteenth century closely parallels the development in northern France. The law applied throughout the Reich was customary law, which, in consequence of the change from the personality principle to the territorial principle, became local territorial law only. Such Imperial law as existed was concerned almost exclusively with constitutional questions. In addition, feudal and manorial courts existed to settle litigation arising out of the feudal relation, and municipalities obtained a large degree of legal autonomy. The whole tendency from the period of the interregnum (1250-72) was towards the disintegration of the Empire into a loose confederation of states, and of the states into regional leagues of towns and princes. In these circumstances, the emergence of a native common law for the whole of Germany based upon the Germanic customs was clearly impossible.

In the thirteenth and fourteenth centuries there appeared a number of compilations of local customary law, like the works which appeared about the same time in France. The outstanding work in this field is the *Sachsenspiegel* (the Mirror of the Saxons) composed about 1215 by Eike von Repgow, which records the territorial customary law of lower Saxony. A south-German adaptation of this work was published about 1260 under the name of the *Deutschenspiegel* (the Mirror of the Germans). Later in the century this was superseded by the *Schwabenspiegel* (the Mirror of the Swabians). The latter two works aimed to reproduce not merely local law but the common customary law of Germany. They probably had some effect in countering the particularist tendencies of the period, but the forces leading towards disintegration were far too strong to be stemmed by them.

The purely local character of the law in Germany became intolerable when the growth of trade towards the end of the fifteenth century led to constant commercial intercourse between different territorial groups. The need for a common law was obvious, but at the same time the lack of an effective central government made its attainment by legislative action a most unlikely event. But if a common law could not be developed out of the Germanic sources, there was another system which could supply it, and there was a good theoretical argument to support the practical considerations which induced lawyers and traders to have recourse to it. The basic concept of the Holy Roman Empire was that of continuity with the Empire of the Caesars. It followed that the Roman law continued in full effect within the Empire as its common law. In addition, the German universities which were founded in the fourteenth century completely ignored the German customary law, and taught only Roman and canon law in the spirit of Bologna. Roman law was accordingly regarded by German scholars as in force in Germany both as *ius scriptum* by virtue of the Imperial tradition and as *ratio scripta* through its own inherent worth.

These ideas formed the theoretical grounds for the reception of Roman law in Germany, and German scholars refer to their development as constituting the theoretical reception. But more was required before one could speak of a practical reception in the sense of the application of Roman law as the common law of Germany by the courts. Two factors above all led to such a practical reception. First, there occurred a gradual replacement of the lay judges, the *Schöffen*, by lawyers who had been trained in Roman law or canon law at the universities. The *Schöffen* were permanent judges, who under the Carolingian system corresponded with the Anglo-Saxon Witan, and were obliged to attend all court sessions in their district and declare what the law was on the particular issue before the court. The law they applied was the customary law of the region, but their lack of any systematic legal training and the archaic nature of the customary law itself had provoked general dissatisfaction with their administration. The new judges naturally applied the Roman system in which they had been trained. Secondly, in 1495 the Imperial Court of Justice, the Reichskammergericht, was reconstituted and directed to decide cases "according to the Imperial and Common law and also according to just, equitable and reasonable ordinances and customs." Since the personnel of the court was composed at first as to half, and later wholly, of doctors of the civil law, the term "common law" was naturally interpreted to mean the Roman law. The example of the Reichskammergericht was followed by the territorial courts of appeal. This fact, combined with the introduction of civil lawyers as judges into the courts of first instance, meant that in the course of the sixteenth century the alien system triumphed over the native and became firmly established as the common law of Germany.

It must be stressed that in Germany the reception of Roman law was not merely partial, as it was in northern France. Instead, the German jurisprudence became essentially Roman jurisprudence. Germany had not succeeded in the course of the Middle Ages in developing its own native system of law with the help of the Roman law. At the end of that period, therefore, its system was too primitive to sustain the load placed upon it by the changed political and economic conditions, and it was rejected almost totally in favour of the more developed system. One might perhaps say that because the German customary law had not been gradually immunised by suitable injections of Roman law, it succumbed almost completely to it in the end. The only thing which could have saved it was the vigorous growth and development of the native institutions themselves such as occurred in England, but the absence of a strong central government made this practically impossible.

At the same time, the indigenous law was not wholly ousted, and Roman law was regarded, as in France, as essentially a supplementary system, so that it would not prevail against local customary or statute law. This principle was expressed in the maxims "Municipal law breaks regional law" (*Stadtrecht bricht Landrecht*) and "Regional law breaks imperial law" (*Landrecht bricht Reichsrecht*). At the time of the Reception these maxims were explained as an application of the rule that the municipal or regional laws being later in point of time than the Roman law, which was regarded as having always applied in Germany since it became part of the Empire, would prevail over it; but subsequently the view was taken that Roman law was merely supplementary and left the local laws intact. However, the Imperial courts applied a rule which did in fact do much to destroy the customary law. This was the rule that every local law had to be proved by the party who relied on it, whilst the Roman common law would not have to be proved, as it was a matter of which the courts would take judicial notice. In most cases it would be extremely difficult or even impossible to prove the custom, and consequently in the vast majority of cases the issue was tried by the principles of the Roman law alone. Nevertheless, in certain areas, particularly in Saxony, the Germanic law held out for a considerable time, and certain institutions, such as agreements relating to the institution of an heir, testamentary executorship and real charges, which are of Germanic origin, still appear in the present German civil code.

The Roman law which was thus "received" as the common law of Germany was so much of the *Corpus Iuris Civilis* as was glossed by Accursius, so that it was said in Germany: "*Quidquid non agnoscit glossa, nec agnoscit forum.*" Moreover, the adaptations which had been made by the Commentators to the Roman law to fit it to the conditions of mediaeval Italy were retained in Germany and further modifications were made in Germany itself. The process of moulding into one system the Roman, canon and German law was carried out mainly by practitioners from the sixteenth to the eighteenth century, who thus created what has been termed the *usus modernus pandectarum*.

JOHN P. DAWSON, GIFTS AND PROMISES: CONTINENTAL AND AMERICAN LAWS COMPARED 41-42 (1980)

The *légitime*, essentially as defined in late Roman law, was well established in most districts of southern France by the year 1100. As knowledge of Roman law was diffused more widely in the north, the *légitime* received much praise from late medieval authors and became well known. It was not until the middle of the sixteenth century that a real break-through came, when the Parlement of Paris, the leading royal appellate court with a jurisdiction that extended widely over northern France, declared that the *légitime* had been accepted as a part of local usage and incorporated in the Custom of Paris. This conclusion was formally ratified some thirty years later when an assembly of the three estates of the Paris area included the *légitime* in the revised text of the Custom of Paris, which was promulgated in 1580. It was somewhat more than a century later, in 1688, that in the Custom of Paris the protection of the heir's "legitimate part" was definitively extended beyond wills to inter vivos gifts.

Throughout most of the customary districts of northern France the *légitime* was adopted by similar means, a combination of court decisions and revision by local assemblies of the texts of the published customs. There were variations between the districts as to the classes of heirs protected (for example, only descendants in the Custom of Paris) and as to the shares guaranteed (in the Custom of Paris one-half of the intestate share, in other customs one-fourth). In many districts these restrictions were carried back to include not only gifts by last will but those made by owners in their lifetimes, as had been true from the beginning with the restrictions on gifts of inherited land. The two types of restriction persisted side by side, overlapping and reinforcing each other. Certainly by the seventeenth century the *légitime*, as a limitation on the power to disinherit close relatives, was conceived by most persons to have a secure place in that ideal construct, the "common law of the customs" of France. When, after the Revolution, the minds of many turned toward the drafting of a national code, this form of limitation was accepted without question as part of the national heritage.

NOTES AND QUESTIONS

1. Whether in the *pays de droit écrit* or the *pays de droit coutumier*, by the 17th century Roman law was accepted as generally applicable law throughout France. In an individual case the only question was whether or not the Roman law-canon law *jus commune* was displaced by specifically applicable royal legislation (*ordonnance*) or, in the *pays de droit coutumier*, by a specifically applicable custom. Thus Domat:

> [Consider] Jean Domat's *Les Lois Civiles dans Leur Ordre Naturel* (which first appeared between 1689 and 1697). Domat's grand plan was to

> set out a scheme of Christian law for France in an easily comprehensible arrangement. Four kinds of law, he said, ruled in France. First, the royal ordinances had universal authority over all of France. Second, customs had particular authority in the place where they were observed. Third, Roman law had two uses, first as custom in some places in several matters, second over all of France and on all matters, "consisting in this that one observes everywhere these rules of justice and equity that are called 'written reason,' because they are written in Roman law. Thus, for this second use, Roman law has the same authority as have justice and equity on our reason." Fourth, canon law also contained many rules accepted in France.

Alan Watson, Failures of the Legal Imagination 11-12 (1988).

2. It is also important to remember that, to French judges trained in the Roman law, it seemed natural to interpret ordinances and customs consistently with Roman law. The practice was analogous to that of common law judges during the same period, summed up in the principle: "Statutes in derogation of the common law are strictly construed." Thus there was a tendency for non-Roman sources of law to be Romanized in practice.

3. As a concrete example of the Romanization of non-Roman sources of law, observe that the Roman *legitim*, widely adopted in southern France because it was a Roman law institution, eventually prevailed in northern France by "a combination of court decisions and revision by local assemblies of the texts of published customs."

4. Why was there both a "theoretical" reception of the Roman part of the *jus commune* and a "practical" reception of the Roman-canonic *jus commune* in Germany? Why would the French king or Germanic dukes be nervous about accepting the authority of the *Corpus juris civilis*? How and to what extent did the practical reception in Germany occur? To what does the German *usus modernus pandectarum* refer?

5. Italy was the home of the Roman-canonic *jus commune*, and thus no Italian reception was necessary. Roman law, canon law, and commercial law all were indigenous law, and to this extent Italy is the archetypical civil law nation. It was the revolution and legal science, both discussed in Chapter 5, that moved the center of interest from Italy to France and Germany. The comparatively recent nature of these phenomena (both have occurred in the last two centuries) gives them particular significance. It is interesting, however, to observe that if we think of the civil law tradition as beginning in 450 B.C., it is now over 24 centuries old. In all but the last two of those centuries the civil law tradition was primarily an Italic phenomenon.

6. The Roman civil law was indigenous law in Italy. It was formally received in Germany. A different kind of reception took place in France. These three examples show that the influence of Roman civil law, canon law, and commercial law may typically have varied in degree, form, and style from one civil law nation to another. The following excerpt, on the reception elsewhere in Europe, confirms this notion.

4. THE RECEPTION IN SPAIN, PORTUGAL, AND ELSEWHERE IN EUROPE

MAURO CAPPELLETTI, JOHN HENRY MERRYMAN & JOSEPH M. PERILLO, THE ITALIAN LEGAL SYSTEM: AN INTRODUCTION 31-33, 35-36 (1967)

Spain, too, had a substratum of Roman law. For a time, Roman personal law, expressed in the *Lex Romana Wisigothorum*, coexisted with the laws of the Visigoths. With the fusion of the two peoples, a territorial law, permeated in form and substance by Roman law, was promulgated by King Recceswinth (perhaps in 654). This *Liber iudiciorum*, commonly called the *Lex Wisigothorum*, was the fundamental basis of Spanish law until the fifteenth century.[a] At about the same time, local customary laws with a primarily Germanic content, called *usus terrae* or *fueros*, began to appear. In later centuries these *fueros* became obstacles to national legal unification.

In the twelfth, thirteenth, and fourteenth centuries Spanish legal culture underwent a more thorough process of Romanization. Students from Spain were so numerous at Bologna that in 1364 the Spanish Cardinal Gil of Albornoz founded a boarding institution there for them. (The Collegio di Spagna is still in existence). Spanish universities sprang up: Valencia (1208-9), Salamanca (c. 1227-28), Seville (1254-60), and Lérida (1300). These institutions were to spread the knowledge of Roman and canon law, and the methods of the Glossators and the Commentators, throughout the Iberian peninsula.

The major product of this vigorous growth of the study of Roman law was the principal legislative monument of medieval Spain: the *Libro* (or *Fuero*) *de las leyes*, commonly called the *Ley de las Siete Partidas*, compiled in 1265 by order of Alphonse the Wise, King of Castille and León. This work, divided into seven books, was intended to unify law throughout his realm. The text, drafted largely by doctors of the University of Salamanca, brought together various parts of the compilation of Justinian, the *Decretum* of Gratian, and the *Decretales* of Gregory IX, as well as the textual interpretations made by the most famous of the Glossators, especially Azo and Accursius, on civil law, and Goffredo of Trani and Raymond of Peñafort on canon law. With this text, Roman and canon law would have become, by will of the King, the common law of Spain. However, Spanish traditionalists, loyal to their local customs, were so strongly opposed to the *Siete Partidas* that it was not promulgated until 1348 and then only as an appendix to the *Ordenamiento de Alcalá*. It was relegated to the role of a subsidiary statute, effective only where the *Ordenamiento* and the local customs were silent. Despite the lack of its promulgation as the common law of the realm, the fate of Roman law in Spain was decided: the *Siete Partidas* was recognized and applied as the official law of Spain. The accompanying reception of Italian legal doctrine was so massive

[a] The *Liber iudiciorum*, a comprehensive compilation that was revised several times up to 694, is today primarily referred to as the *Fuero Juzgo*. Although heavily influenced by Roman law, the *Fuero Juzgo* also drew from Visigothic custom and edicts. Displaying an amazing life span, it continued in force as a supplementary source of Spanish law up to codification in the nineteenth century.

that the monarchs decreed that the courts, in case of gaps or doubts in the law, should rely on the authority of the major Glossators and Commentators, and should not follow the opinions of jurists later than Bartolus on the civil law and Giovanni d'Andrea on canon law.

Thus Roman law, although opposed by some kings and local interests and objected to because of the pretensions of the Empire, became the nucleus of Spanish legal life and the basis for the scientific study of law in the universities. Indeed, until the eighteenth century the only subject studied in the universities was Roman and canon law.

In nearby Portugal the legislation at first was the same as in Visigothic Spain: the *Liber iudiciorum*, with additions in 1054 by Alphonse V of León, as well as the various local customary laws. Portugal, too, received the *jus commune* with the foundation of legal studies at its universities (Coimbra and Lisbon). The consequences are clear in Portuguese legislation. The first systematic collection, the *Ordenações Alfonsinas*, promulgated by Alphonso V in 1446, in large part consisted of Roman and canon law. This collection was followed by the *Ordenações Manuelinas* of King Manuel in 1521, and finally in 1603, after Philip II became king of Portugal, by the *Ordenações Filipinas*, which remained in effect until modern times not only in Portugal, but also in its colonies, including Brazil. These enactments embody the principle that Roman law, the glosses, and the comments are the common law of the kingdom and applicable whenever the local legislation or customs are silent or ambiguous....

Elsewhere in Europe the foundation of universities, whether at Prague or Dublin, further spread Roman law and the methods of the Italian school. A true *koiné*, a union of legal thought and practice, existed throughout Europe in the late middle ages. Naturally the penetration of Roman law often caused reactions, opposition, and confusion, especially in areas without a substratum of Latin culture and institutions.

Even where Roman law was not received in a normative sense, there was nonetheless a doctrinal reception. Roman rules might be rejected, but the conceptual structure created by the Italian scholars gave a Roman form to indigenous rules. For example, in Norway and Hungary, although there was no adoption of the *jus commune*, local legislation was marked by a certain Romanist influence. The Code of 1274 of King Magnus VI of Norway, the *Lagaböter* (lawgiver), while intended to be a written draft of ancient Viking custom, shows the influence of Roman and canon law in its organization and in many of its institutions. In areas as far off as Byelorussia and the Ukraine, where there was no reception, but where Roman law from Byzantium was applied, for example, to matrimonial matters, Roman law was looked to as a remote paradigm to be used as a guide. Aside from the "reception," Roman law impregnated all of the indigenous systems of law in Europe, accomplishing a civilizing mission.

5. LEARNED LAWYERS IN CASTILE

RICHARD L. KAGAN, LAWYERS AND LITIGATION IN CASTILE, 1500-1750, in LAWYERS IN EARLY MODERN EUROPE AND AMERICA 181, 184-87 (Wilfrid Prest ed. 1981)

Castile's legal profession in the sixteenth century was subdivided into three principal branches — *abogados* or advocates, *procuradores* or attorneys, and *solicitadores* or solicitors. Advocates — the profession's learned elite — were the only practitioners required to possess university degrees in law and were known consequently as *letrados*, whereas most attorneys and solicitors had learned their law merely through clerkship or apprenticeship. In theory, the advocate was the legal expert, to be consulted on the fine points of law necessary to substantiate a particular case, while the attorney was primarily responsible for planning strategy, rounding up witnesses, and seeing to it that the proofs, testimonials and other documents which made up a case were prepared properly and then filed with the appropriate court official. In practice their duties often overlapped. [Solicitors aided attorneys in the preparation of law suits.]...

Practitioners known as *voceros* — the forerunners of advocates — were mentioned in the *Liber Judiocorum* (c. A.D. 550) and in the *Fuero Viejo* (late thirteenth century) they appear as men skilled in the *fueros* or local usages which then governed most of Castile. Reference to clerics expert in the canon law who pleaded in ecclesiastical courts appear in the eleventh century, although the first evidence of civil lawyers (*abogados*) comes only at the end of the twelfth century, when Roman law first seeped into the kingdom from Italy. Advocates are noted as such in Book III of the *Siete Partidas* (*c.* 1248) which also contained laws regulating their work. Thereafter, the legal profession developed slowly until the Cortes in 1348 agreed to accept the *Siete Partidas* as the law by which appeals to royal justice would be judged. The *Ordenamiento de Alcalá de Henares*, as this agreement became known, gave rise to the wider use of written procedures and arguments drawn from the Roman law, paving the way for the development of a large class of practitioners expert in such matters.

Both advocates and attorneys crop up with increasing regularity in the documents and literature of the fifteenth century, when *letrados* first received regular appointments to the councils and tribunals of the king. Ferdinand and Isabella (1474-1503) continued this policy, and in 1480 granted *letrados* exclusive rights to places on their *chancillería* as well as the *consejo real*. It should be noted, however, that Charles V and the later Habsburgs preferred university law professors to practising lawyers and thus effectively denied most lawyers access to positions high on the royal bench. Even so, it was largely in response to new openings for lawyers that the law faculties of the universities of Salamanca and Valladolid, dormant for well over a century, suddenly acquired new life. By 1495 the *letrados*, qualified and unqualified, were proliferating so rapidly that the crown required every new advocate to have studied both civil and canon law at a recognised university for a fixed term of years (later set at five) and then to be examined by the judges of the tribunal in which they intended to plead. Attorneys, whose number was also increasing, also came under some form of governmental control. Most cities enacted legislation limiting their number, and in royal tribunals attorneys not only had to be licensed but were also required to purchase their offices, the number of which was strictly controlled. *Procuradores de número* in the *chancillería* of Valladolid, for example, were limited to 30 until Philip II, responding to demands to expedite the administration of justice in this important tribunal, created five additional places despite opposition from established attorneys who feared that the value of their own offices would decline as a result. By 1596, however, one of these offices fetched 2,300 ducats, as compared with only 500 ducats a half-century before, an increase best explained by the heightened profitability of these exclusive practices in an era of abundant litigation....

In 1589 a record number of 56 registered. By this time the *chancillería* of Granada, the Andalusian counterpart of Valladolid's tribunal, had some 35 advocates, possibly more, and Madrid, seat of the royal council and other courts, had as many as 100 in 1595. Nor were advocates found only in major cities and attached to important courts. At least six to eight advocates practised in each of the 67 courts headed by the king's *corregidores*, many of which were located in small provincial towns. In sum, the evidence suggests that the number of practitioners was increasing rapidly during the sixteenth century, possibly at a rate comparable to that of the law faculties which had more than doubled their number of graduates in less than fifty years.

6. PATRIA POTESTAS REVISITED II

NOTE ON THE *SIETE PARTIDAS*

King Alfonso the Wise, ruler of Castile and Léon, began the task of unifying the diverse laws in his kingdom in 1255. Heavily influenced by the Spaniards who had studied Roman and canon law in Bologna, his achievement, the *Siete Partidas*, was completed ten years later. Even though the nobility and towns resisted Alfonso's attempt to expand royal power by refusing to recognize the king as chief lawmaker, the *Siete Partidas* went into effect in 1348, exerting tremendous influence on Spain and its colonies up to the era of codification.

The excerpt that follows includes the Spanish interpretation of the doctrine of *patria potestas*. Ask yourself to what extent it deviates from or elaborates on the Roman formulation as traced in Section B of this chapter.

SAMUEL P. SCOTT, LAS SIETE PARTIDAS 960-63 (1931)

The Fourth Partida

Title XVII

Concerning the Authority, of Every Description Whatever, Which Fathers Have Over Their Children

Fathers have power and authority over their children, both according to natural reason and according to law. First, because they are born of them; second, because they are to inherit their property. Wherefore, since in the preceding title we treated of legitimate children, and of all others of every description whatsoever, we intend to speak here of the authority which fathers have over them. We shall show what authority is; and in how many ways this word can be understood; how it should be established; and what force it has.

LAW I

What the Authority Is Which a Father Has Over His Children

Patria potestas, in Latin, means, in Castilian, the authority which a father has over his children. This authority is a right which those especially enjoy who live under, and are judged by, the ancient laws and regulations made by philosophers, by the command and with the permission of the emperors; and they possess this authority over their children and grandchildren, and all others descended from them in the direct line who are born in lawful wedlock.

LAW II

Over What Children a Father Does Not Possess This Authority

Children which men have by concubines, are called natural, as stated in the title which treats of them, and such children are not under the control of their fathers, as legitimate children are; nor are children who are called in Latin *incestuosi*, which means those that men have by their female relatives within the fourth degree; or by women connected with them by affinity; or by those belonging to religious orders. Persons of this kind are not worthy to be called children, because they are begotten in great sin. And although a father may have legitimate sons or grandsons, or great-grandsons who are descended from his sons, under his control, it is not understood by this that the mother can have authority over them, or any other relative on the mother's side. Moreover, we decree that children who are born of daughters should be under control of their fathers, and not under that of their grandfathers on the mother's side....

LAW V

What Force the Authority Which a Father Possesses Over His Children Has With Respect to the Property Which Said Children Obtain

The earnings obtained by children, while under the control of their fathers, are divided into three different kinds. First, such as children earn by means of the property of their fathers, and gain of this kind is called in Latin *profectitium peculium*; for, although it is obtained in this way or on account of their fathers, it all belongs to their fathers who have control of it. Second, where anyone's child earns something by the labor of its hands, by means of some trade or through any other knowledge which it may possess, or in any other manner; or it acquires a gift left to it by will, or through inheritance from its mother, or from some of its relatives, or by any other means; or where it finds a treasure or other property accidentally.

Any profits made by a child, in any of these ways, and which are not derived from the property of its father or grandfather, should belong to the child who obtained them, and the usufruct of the same to the father during his lifetime, by reason of the authority which he has over said child. This kind of gain is called in Latin, *adventitia*, because it is derived from an exterior source, and not through the property of the father; we decree, however, that the father must protect and preserve this adventitious property belonging to his son, during his whole life, in court as well as out of it. The third kind of property and profit, is that called, in Latin, *castrense vel quasi castrense peculium*, which will be explained hereafter.

LAW VI

Sons Can Do What They Please With Property Which Is Obtained in a Castle, or in the Army, or at Court, Even Though They May Be Under the Control of Their Father

Castra is a Latin word which is understood in three senses. The first and most common is every castle and stronghold surrounded by walls or other fortifications. The second is an army or fortified camp where many persons are assembled, and which is protected by defenses, and, for this reason is called, in Latin, *castra*. The third is the Court of the King, or of some other prince, where many persons are assembled, as around a lord who is a fortress and the bulwark of justice. Wherefore, the profits which men obtain in any of said places derive their name from this Latin word *castra*, and, for this reason, they are called *castrense vel quasi castrense peculium*. And also, since men obtain profits of this kind through great hardship and danger, and because this is done in such noble places, they become absolutely the property of those who claim them, and enjoy greater exemptions than profits of other kinds; for owners of property of this description can dispose of it as they wish, and neither a father, nor a brother, nor any other relative that they may have has any right to it, or can interfere with it in any way....

LAW VIII

For What Reasons a Father Can Sell or Pledge His Child

Where a father complains of great hunger, and is so poor that he cannot have recourse to anything else, he can then sell, or pledge his children in order to have something to buy food with. The reason why he can do this is the following, namely; since neither the father nor his child has any other means to escape death, it is proper that he should sell the latter, and make use of the price, so that neither of them may die. There is another reason for which the father can do this, for, according to the loyal *fuero* of Spain, where a father is besieged in a castle, which he holds of his lord, and is so afflicted with hunger that he has nothing else to eat, he can eat his son without incurring reproach, rather than surrender the castle without the order of his lord. Wherefore, if he can do such a thing for his lord, it is but proper that he should be able to do it for himself. This is another right growing out of the authority which a father possesses over his sons who are under his control, which a mother does not have. This, however, can only be done in such a case where it is publicly understood that the father has no other means to avoid death, if he does not sell or pledge his son.

LAW IX

How a Son Who Is Sold by His Father Can Be Redeemed and Restored to Liberty

When a father sells his son through stress of hunger, as stated in the preceding law, and he himself pays for him the price for which he was sold, or someone else does this for him, the son should be restored to freedom. But if the party, after he purchased him, should teach him some trade or science, on account of which he would be worth more than at the time when he bought him, he will not be required to surrender him for merely the price which he paid for him, but he should be given, in addition to said price, as much as reliable and intelligent men truly estimate that his value has been increased on account of what the party had afterwards taught him, or had expended out of his own property in order to have him taught.

LAW X

A Father Can Ask a Judge to Again Place His Son Under His Control, When He Does Not Have Such Control Over Him, or His Son Is Unwilling to Obey Him

A father has still another kind of authority over his son. For although some party may keep him in subjection by force, or with the son's consent, the father can claim him in court, and have him placed again under his control. The same rule applies where a son voluntarily wanders over the country and refuses to obey his father; for the father can ask the judge of the district where he is found to place him again under his control, and the judge in the discharge of his official duty is obliged to do so.

NOTES AND QUESTIONS

1. Notice that the *jus commune* was received in Spain and Portugal by the end of the 15th century. This was the time of the age of discovery, when the *jus commune* was carried to the Spanish and Portuguese colonies established in the Americas. See Chapter 4, Section B.

Roman law is still used in judicial argument in the Spanish region of Cataluña, which had fully received the *jus commune*. It has not been carried over intact, however, but is used to interpret the Compilation of Catalan Civil Law. The Spanish Supreme Court, for instance, recently said: "Justinian's Institutes do not have per se application in Cataluña, but can only serve as interpretive guides to the Catalan Compilation, according to the provisions of article 1." Supreme Tribunal (Civil Chamber 1), decision of 24 Jan. 1989, 56 Aranzadi Repertorio de Jurisprudencia, case 117 at 123, 125 (1989). For a discussion of article 1, see Pablo Salvador Coderch, La Compilación y su Historia 313-90 (1985).

2. How did the Castilian legal profession, particularly the *abogados*, facilitate reception of the *jus commune*?

3. In what ways does the treatment of *patria potestas* in the *Siete Partidas* differ from the treatment in the *Corpus juris civilis*?

How would you compare the style of the *Siete Partidas* with the various parts of the *Corpus juris civilis*? With a modern statute?

4. Consider *patria potestas* as received in France:

> By the later Empire, considerable limitations on this power had developed, both in relation to control over the child's person and to control over his property, and in this ameliorated form paternal power was a settled institution in the *pays de droit écrit* until the Revolution. It gave the father the right to custody of the child, to chastise him, and to enjoy the profits of his property; and it lasted during the life of the father, unless the child was expressly or impliedly emancipated. In the *pays coutumiers*, the father's *Mund* (or "Mainbournie") was based on a similar conception and entailed much the same consequences, though it differed considerably in point of detail. In particular, it ceased upon attainment of majority; it could be exercised by the mother; and it did not entitle the father to a usufruct over the child's property.

K.W. Ryan, An Introduction to the Civil Law 279 (1962).

7. RESISTANCE TO ROMAN LAW IN ENGLAND

R.C. VAN CAENEGEM, JUDGES, LEGISLATORS AND PROFESSORS: CHAPTERS IN EUROPEAN LEGAL HISTORY 114-15, 118-22 (1987)

Right through the early Middle Ages and up to the mid-twelfth century English and continental law belonged recognisably to one legal family, Germanic and feudal in substance and in procedure. Except for possible linguistic complications, a traveller from the Continent in the days of King Stephen would have had no problem in recognising the rules, arguments and modes of proof in an English manorial, borough or feudal court. A century later the landscape had changed: Roman law and Roman-canonical procedure were transforming life in many parts of the Continent (and others were to follow), whereas in England a native law, common to the whole kingdom, that was — and remained — free from the substance and the procedure of the new continental fashion, had arisen. The moment when this dichotomy arose can be pinpointed exactly. It was in the reign of King Henry II, when certain reforms in judicial organisation and procedure were carried out which modernised English law before Roman law entered the scene with such wide and immediate success that no need was felt in later centuries, when the neo-Roman model was available, to give up the native system. The main changes of King Henry II's reign were the foundation of one group of royal judges with competence in first instance for the whole kingdom to settle litigation of certain types of land (which meant feudal litigation), and the introduction of the jury in civil and in criminal cases as the standard mode of proof (instead of ordeals and judicial combat). Litigants flocked to these new courts and their new procedures — and paid for the privilege of being heard there — and the judges built up a common feudal law. Their role was expanded by the creation of new writs, bringing ever more types of cases before them. The old local courts were sadly left behind, not because of any law or crafty scheme on behalf of the king, but because of the quality of justice that was dispensed by his judges. It should never be forgotten that this important innovation was not a solely or typically English event, it was, in more than one sense, Anglo-Norman. Henry II introduced the new scheme of writs and juries in his Norman duchy as well as in his English kingdom; the feudal law administered in the ducal and royal courts — at Rouen and at Westminster — was the same and the judges belonged to one and the same class of French-speaking knights, who often possessed at the same time their old family lands in Normandy and their newly-acquired lands in England (all feudally held directly or indirectly from the same king-duke, Henry II Plantagenet). It was the conquest of Normandy by the French monarchy and the gradual introduction of Roman-inspired French law into the duchy that turned Anglo-Norman into purely English law....

During the crucial thirteenth and fourteenth centuries, the English common law was safely and firmly embedded in national life. It had its own courts, occupied by the best lawyers in the country. It had its Glanvill and its Bracton, comprehensive expositions which presented the common law as a self-sufficient and reasonable whole, its registers of writs, some of which were official texts, its bar and the serjeants at law, a well established and self-assured corporation from whose ranks the senior justices were appointed, and its Year Books, with up-to-date reports of what happened in the courts. Its practitioners were conscious of its distinctness and, insofar as they ever looked across the Channel, were convinced of its superiority.... Lastly, and this was probably the most important consideration, the common law was the safeguard of lawful landholding and therefore the cornerstone of every fortune of every notable family and every church in the country. Power and prestige were based on land, and the safety of the land was based on the common law....

If the possibility of continental borrowing from English law was slight, the occasions for the penetration of civilian influence in England were serious and numerous. Roman law and Roman-canonical procedure made their influence felt if not in the common-law courts then in other courts, such as those of the Church....

In the Court of Chancery the chancellor exercised his equitable jurisdiction, as a correction of, or complement to, the harshness or deficiencies of the common-law courts. Indeed, Chancery offered remedies which were a matter of course in the professional procedure, but not available in the common-law courts, such as injunction, specific performance and rectification of documents. Since the chancellor was almost always a bishop whose court had arisen long after the new Roman-canonical process was established, it is not surprising that its procedure was much closer to that of the Church than of the common law — the jury was a notable absentee and the interrogation of witnesses on "articles" one of the most striking loans from the *ordines judiciarii*. The Court of Admiralty, which left regular records from 1524 onwards, followed a procedure of the civilian type and administered a commercial and maritime law that was cosmopolitan rather than English and familiar with various forms of business unknown to the common law. The Star Chamber also proceeded more forcefully and intervened more directly in the course of litigation than did the common law: it was extremely active and popular, *inter alia*, because it did not suffer from the rigged and intimidated juries which were the bane of the time. Not only could these un-common-law-like moves be observed by everyone interested in the law, but the theory of civil and canon law was being taught in the two English universities as in so many others on the Continent and in Scotland. And, of course, those Englishmen who found that their own universities did not quench their thirst for knowledge could and did go to study abroad.

The high tide in the fortunes of Roman law, with a "reception" in Germany and Scotland and a much-debated possibility of a "reception" in France, was in the sixteenth century. It is not surprising therefore that in England also various circles showed an earnest desire for the cobwebs of the medieval law to be swept away and Roman law — "common to all civilised Europe" — to be introduced in their stead. Such, naturally enough, was the opinion of some scholars who had studied on the Continent, but it was also the opinion of certain people in authority. The foundation of regius chairs of civil law by King Henry VIII is witness to it. This monarch had great respect for everything imperial, notably the law of imperial Rome, and also the great Christian emperors of Rome, in whose line of monarchs he saw himself — England being his "Empire." The "danger" to the common law in those heady Renaissance days has been exaggerated and its power of internal renewal underrated, so that scholarly opinion does not now hold that the common law was ever in real peril.

NOTES AND QUESTIONS

1. Roman civil law and canon law have had their influence on English law, but no one would think of classifying England as a civil law nation. What is different about the influence of the *jus commune* in England? Why was there no English reception of Roman law?

2. We have seen the important part that learned lawyers from the universities played in facilitating the acceptance of the *jus commune* throughout continental Europe. Roman law was also taught at Oxford and Cambridge, but it was taught as an academic, rather than as a professional, subject. English barristers and solicitors were trained at the Inns of Court in London. They emphasized a pragmatic knowledge of procedural law in whose interstices English substantive law was firmly embedded. Could it have been the power of the English legal profession (including judges, who came from the senior ranks of barristers) that saved the common law for England?

3. For more on the development of private law in Europe after the fall of the Roman empire, including the English example, see R.C. van Caenegem, An Historical Introduction to Private Law (D.E.L. Johnston trans. 1992); Reinhard Zimmermann, The Law of Obligations: Roman Foundations of the Civilian Tradition (1990).

NOTE ON COMPLEXITY WITHIN THE CIVIL LAW TRADITION

Life in medieval Europe was governed by a bewildering variety of laws and jurisdictions. The residents of Florence and Toulouse, like those of other towns and communes, were subject to a variety of local laws. Outside the towns, in the countryside, feudal laws and feudal jurisdiction still exercised substantial influence. The working lives of artisans, merchants, professionals, and others of the growing middle class were regulated by the statutes of the guilds or corporations that dominated their *metiers*. Commercial law (the law of merchants) was a particularly important institution which attained an international stature that distinguished it from, say, the statutes of a local drapers' guild or a corporation of vintners. But at bottom the phenomenon was the same: these so-called "intermediate associations" produced and applied law that governed much of the secular lives of their members. Add to these canon law and ecclesiastical jurisdiction, the temporal legal authority of kings and princes, and finally, the *jus commune* studied and taught by the scholars in the universities and propagated by them throughout Europe, and it may be seen that the medieval legal universe was very complicated. As we shall see in Chapter 5, one of the purposes of the French Revolution was to abolish this multiplicity of laws and to lodge all lawmaking power, and all jurisdiction, in the state.

Chapter 4

THE LEGAL TRADITIONS OF LATIN AMERICA AND EAST ASIA

The Americas and East Asia had their own indigenous legal traditions before the arrival of Europeans or the influence of European ideas. It is this fact that even today largely accounts for the distinctive legal cultures existing in Latin America and East Asia. This chapter first presents some examples of law in precolonial Latin America and examines the transplantation of the *jus commune* and other European legal institutions in the Americas from the 16th through the 18th century. Then we turn to East Asia to survey law and legal institutions as they existed on the eve of the introduction of Western legal forms.

A. LAW IN PRECOLONIAL LATIN AMERICA

NOTE ON THE ORIGINAL AMERICAN INHABITANTS

People entered America from Asia via the Bering Strait between 25,000 to 40,000 years ago. Over the course of time they spread to both American continents, reaching Tierra del Fuego by 9,000 B.C. From their beginnings as groups of nomadic hunters and food gatherers, some "Indians" shifted to plant and animal domestication around 7,000 B.C. in central and northeastern Mexico. In Peru Indians cultivated crops and domesticated llamas as early as 5,000 B.C. Techniques were later invented to provide irrigation, terraces, and artificial islands in shallow lakes, which greatly increased agricultural production that would support larger populations.

Social stratification and political organization began as bands and tribes evolved into chiefdoms with populations normally ranging between 5,000 and 20,000, but sometimes up to 60,000. In Mesoamerica and the Andes chiefdoms were transformed into states characterized by a network of towns and cities. At the time of the Spanish conquest, Tenochtitlán, capital of the Aztec empire, was a major manufacturing, trading, and military center with a population between 150,000 and 300,000. Cuzco, center of the Inca empire, was organized with nobles, bureaucrats, and priests residing in a core area with a supporting peripheral population between 100,000 and 200,000.[a] Although there is considerable controversy over the size of the aboriginal population in Latin America around the year 1500, a recent estimate places it at 53 million, consisting of 21 million in Mexico, 6 million each in Central America and in the Caribbean, 12 million in the Andes, and 8 million in lowland South America.

---

[a] At this time only four European cities had a population greater than 100,000: Paris, Venice, Milan, and Naples. Seville, from which the Spanish *conquistadores* set sail, had about 40,000 inhabitants.

See The Peoples: Pre-Columbian Settlement, in The Cambridge Encyclopedia of Latin America and the Caribbean 128 (Simon Collier, Harold Blakemore & Thomas E. Skidmore eds. 1985); Maria Luiza Marcílio, *The Population of Colonial Brazil,* in 2 The Cambridge History of Latin America: Colonial Latin America 37 (Leslie Bethell ed. 1984); Nicolás Sánchez-Albornoz, *The Population of Colonial Spanish America,* in 2 *ibid.* 3. *See also* The Native Population of the Americas in 1492 (William M. Denevan ed. 1976).

1. THE INCAS AND THEIR LEGAL SYSTEM

NOTE ON THE INCA LEGAL SYSTEM

When the Spanish conquistador Francisco Pizarro first reached Peru, the Incas governed an empire that stretched along the Pacific coast and through the Andes from what is now the northern border of Ecuador to central Chile. They ruled about 12 million people who spoke at least 20 unrelated languages. A century earlier, by contrast, the Incas had controlled little territory beyond their own village in the Cuzco Valley.

The Inca political system was a hierarchical one. The aristocracy distinguished between those individuals who claimed descent from one of the 12 Inca rulers and those who belonged to one of the Quechua-speaking ethnic groups from the Cuzco area. At the top of the pyramid was the emperor, called the Inca, who not only ruled by divine right, but also claimed lineal descent from the sun. Immediately below the Inca in the administrative hierarchy were the *apocunas* (prefects) of the four territorial divisions of the empire. Both the Inca and the *apocunas* belonged to the highest level of Inca nobility. Below them were the *t'oqrikoq* (provincial governors) who resided in the various regions and were the lowest government officials that had to be Incas.

The *t'oqrikoq* had wide judicial and administrative responsibilities and directed the activities of the *curacas,* who formed the lower levels of the Inca bureaucracy. The *curacas* governed units of 10,000, 1,000, 100, or ten families. (A *curaca* who had authority over 10,000 families was called a *hunu* and one who governed ten families was known as a *chunca.*) These positions were probably held largely by the traditional leaders of the ethnic groups conquered by the Incas. Succession to these offices was usually hereditary, subject to the approval of the Inca.

What the Inca government primarily insisted upon as law was the universal acceptance of its authority, its taxes, the sun cult, and the Quechua language. One of the Inca's overwhelming concerns was with collecting taxes. These were owed by a *curaca* for his ethnic group as a whole rather than by the individuals who belonged to it. Taxes were paid in the form of labor. They were calculated as a certain number of man-days in the army, working on public works projects, or farming for the Inca or his priests.

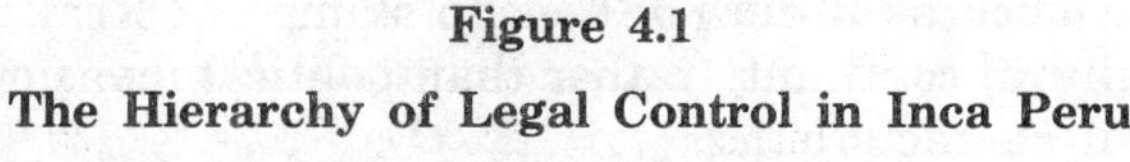

Figure 4.1
The Hierarchy of Legal Control in Inca Peru

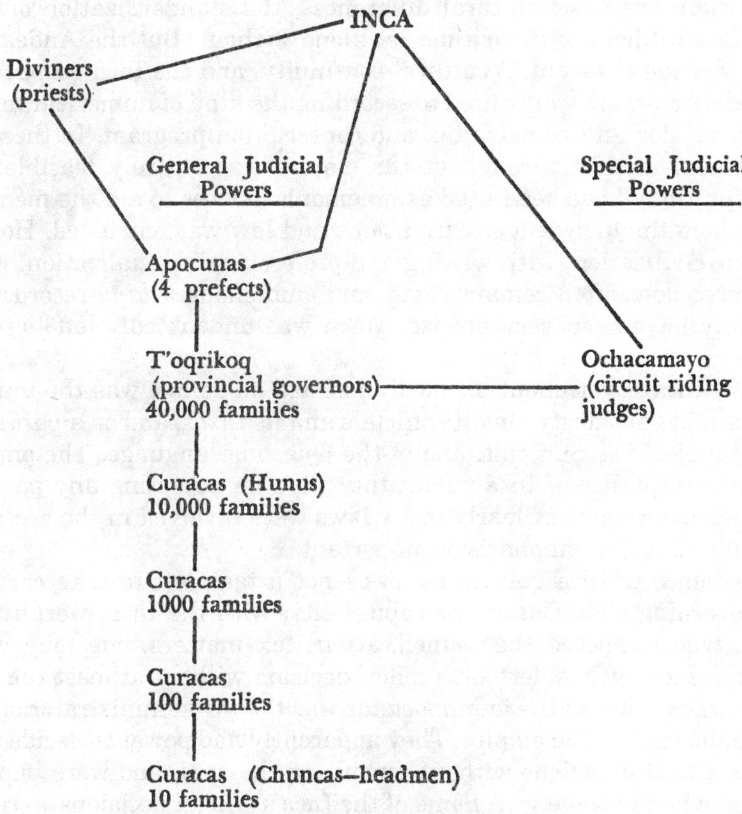

SALLY F. MOORE, POWER AND PROPERTY IN INCA PERU 74-81, 83-84, 100, 102, 111-13, 115-20 (1958)

The Inca Legal System

The Inca were invaders and conquerors. In each new territory they superimposed Inca government on an already existing one. The degree of governmental development of the conquered peoples varied, but in many instances it appears to have been considerable, as for example in the Chimu kingdom. The Inca altered the apportionment of some of the land, but they did not do away with the local government and replace it. They did not disturb local hereditary interests. They simply added themselves at the top and made full use of the already existing administrative machinery, incorporating the local hereditary aristocracy into the decimal system....

In spite of the fact that the sources say the Inca imposed their law wherever they ruled, this must not be naïvely understood to mean that laws affecting all matters were changed on conquest, even though it is stated clearly that laws were universal in the empire. Many local differences of custom seem to have been tolerated. The Inca government does not seem to have tried to stamp them out, much as it did not seek to stamp out local religious cults. Wide Andean cultural continuity rather than political invasion may account for many general characteristics.

Where there are basic cultural differences, the standardization of law is difficult. It is difficult with writing, let alone without. But the Andean area probably was one of essential cultural continuity, and the Inca *quipus* [knotted colored cords] were well suited to recording the kind of numerical information necessary for an extensive tax and conscription program. In these matters, universal method throughout the empire was entirely feasible.

The *quipus* may have been used as mnemonic devices to aid the memory of those to whom the knowledge of traditions and law was entrusted. However, even in our civilization, with writing and professional specialization, legislation and precedent often remain vague and ambiguous. *Quipu*-recorded laws could hardly have been very precise. Much was undoubtedly left to judicial discretion.

What the Inca government primarily insisted on as law was the universal acceptance of its authority, and its officials and its taxes, and as a part of this, the acceptance of the Sun cult, and of the Quechua language. The emphasis was on the acceptance of Inca rule rather than on accepting any particular body of Inca law as such. Clearly many laws were involved in the acceptance of Inca rule, but the emphasis is important.

The obedience to Inca government was not a task left to take care of itself.... Governing from Cuzco, the capital city, with the Inca, were the four *apocunas*, who composed the council. As in tax matters, one may wonder whether the Inca ever undertook a major decision without at least the advice of the *apocunas*. Each of the four *apocunas* was the top administrator of one of the "four quarters" of the empire. They apparently had power to decide all but the most difficult questions without consulting the Inca, and were important in deciding when to wage war. Some of the Inca's official decisions were made on the basis of divination which suggests a crucial role for the diviners....

With respect to the punishment of crimes affecting the government, there appears to have been a close connection between the reports made by annual inspectors and the sending out of judges by the central government with power to punish. These judges were sent out when the inspectors disclosed that there had been violations of law. The judges punished crimes and fixed penalties as they saw fit, and were not bound by any rules as to the applicability of particular penalties. The *ochacamayo*, as these judges apparently were called, used divination and torture when more rational methods of obtaining information were unsatisfactory. They apparently received presents from the local *curaca* when they came on their much-feared business....

[T]his brings out a fundamental characteristic of Inca administrative structure: Higher officials had power to invade the offices of lower officials. This was, of course, most true of the Inca himself. Whenever the Inca was present, he alone was the judge before whom all wrongs were pleaded. When he was not present, justice was administered by his governors and *caciques*.[a] One has the strong impression that the Inca could take any matter out of the gover-

[a] *Cacique* refers to any official who was not required to be an Inca, that is *curacas* and below.

nor's hands if he chose. In fact, in any difficult or complex matter, the governor was obliged by law to consult the Inca.

In the same manner the provincial governor could intervene in the official life of his province. Officials beneath the rank of *t'oqrikoq* had to get permission from the governor to impose the death penalty, and they kept their superiors informed of events in their jurisdiction. It was an uneasy delegation of power, all the way down the line....

Annually at the feast of Raymi, the *t'oqrikoq* went to the court, reported the state of affairs in his district and presented to the Inca the tribute which had been required from his area. He supervised all the rulers of smaller units of population, and had charge of the raising of armies, the census taking, the tax collection, and the Inca and Sun lands in his province. The provincial governor also had powers to administer justice and to punish crimes. He had judicial powers in all criminal cases relating to the Inca, witchcraft, or speaking against the Inca, Indians fleeing the place where they were supposed to live, and any neglect of the *tambos*[b] or neglect of duty by the *chasquis*.[c] He could sentence by himself if he did not consider it an important enough case to refer to the Inca....

When criminal trials were conducted by the governor all persons concerned or having any knowledge of the delict were assembled. They sat in a circle with the accused in the center. Each one stated his accusation. The defendant then had an opportunity to deny and explain. If the result was uncertain the governor sent to the man's *curaca* to discover whether he had a good reputation. If the answer was negative, he was tortured until he confessed and then was punished appropriately....

The *hunus* and lower officials had cognizance of lesser offenses. They had charge of the allocation of land, and where the land was irrigated, of water. They supervised the mining of gold and silver and the marriage of their subjects in the official annual ceremony.

It is significant that, at least toward the bottom of the hierarchy — if not above — the *cacique* was personally responsible for the performance of tax duties by those in his charge. If there were any omission in the service of the *tambos*, the local *cacique* in charge of the *tambo* was punished for it; and he passed the punishment along to those under him....

The unspecialized nature of Inca offices is notable. All functions of government were in some measure invested in each decimal official. There was no separate judiciary except possibly for the special judges sent out by the central government. In the decimal hierarchy, judge, tax collector, and governor were one, and so up and down the line.

One senses that the duties of the governing officers — of whatever rank — were much more emphasized and more clearly defined than their powers. The job of government was to maintain itself, to produce taxes, armies, and to keep the peace, with some national-religious proselytizing thrown in. The powers associated with office were to conduct these affairs in the customary way (about which custom we know miserably little) and with great care not to

[b] Royal lodgings or storehouses located along the royal highways.

[c] Messengers who ran the Inca's orders to governors and *caciques*. These runners were stationed at intervals of about a kilometer, which permitted them to use a relay system.

usurp the power of any higher official. The hierarchy seems to have been very sensitive to disrespect. There was great fear of usurpation of power from below — not surprising for an invader government which has been superimposed on a pre-existing government accustomed to independence. There was great fear of rebellion, and the many shades of incipient rebellion from disrespect to treason.

The modern Anglo-American constitutional concern for the limitation of the power of government and the protection of the rights of the individual are seen here in reverse. The concern in the Inca state was for the protection of government. The great fear was of challenges of its authority. The fear was not that the government would exceed its power, but that it would be weakened by the usurpation of its power by subordinates and subjects.

The Judicial Function

In the decimal system, the higher the official, the more important to the state were the matters he could decide. Minor local questions and presumably all contentions between individuals were resolved finally at the lowest levels of the hierarchy. There were no appeals. But officials were obliged to report their judicial activities to superior officials as a part of keeping the government informed about what was taking place in the communities.

The provincial governor had judicial powers in all criminal cases relating to the Inca. One may infer that crimes and private contentions in which the Inca government had no such direct interest were tried by the various levels of *curacas*. One would also guess in this case that local customary laws applied....

In trying to reconstruct the sort of justice which was dispensed at the *curaca* level, particularly in the communities, one should bear in mind that at the lowest ranks, the local *curacas* probably were the senior kinsmen of the kin group, and that there was a face to face relationship within the community. The *curaca* had charge of allocating the annually divided shares of communal land and dealt with whatever conflicts arose in connection with the individual shares. In conflicts about other property the sources justify the assumption that there was often recourse to the local *curaca* in his judicial capacity. For example, theft was variously punished, depending on the circumstances, by penalties including reprimand, public beating, and death. In all of these instances punishment was an official act; it was not the job of the wronged party to avenge himself. On the other hand, where flocks damaged a field, the owner of the field had the right to take from the herd the equivalent in value of the damage done. Whether disagreement in this case ultimately would result in bringing the matter to the *curaca* is not stated. There is no mention of blood feud. Homicide appears to be entirely a matter for official intervention.

Outside the decimal system were special judges sent out by the Cuzco government to deal with crimes involving a refusal to accept fully the obligations to and authority of the Inca state and the state religion. These ranged from refusal to pay tribute, to witchcraft against the Inca. There were the *ochacamayoc*, judges who were dispatched to punish crimes discovered by the regular investigating officials when the crimes touched on Inca power. The crimes called *capaocha* included having relations with one of the chosen women or women of the Inca or Sun, having performed witchcraft against the Inca, or having failed to pay tribute....

There did exist a customary trial procedure, certainly from the administrative level of provincial governor up the ladder. Yet there were no lawyers and it appears that there were no fees or taxes paid to the Inca in law cases. This suggests a limited development of formal courts.

In a criminal trial if the matter was not clearly settled by testimony, the judge could apply to the *curaca* of the accused for information as to his character. When matters remained in doubt, divination, torture and ordeals were used....

Rules of Substantive Law

Striking, though certainly not unique to the Inca,[d] was the privilege granted to the ruler and in part to the ruling class to commit certain crimes, or rather acts which were crimes if committed by a commoner. Leaving out sumptuary laws entirely, and turning to certain of the major offenses which could carry the capital penalty — incest, homicide and theft — a most interesting phenomenon is seen. The Inca emperor was permitted all three in certain forms. The Inca could commit incest with his sister, who was also his principal wife. The Inca and his governors could apply the death penalty as they saw fit, that is, they could commit a legal homicide. One may wonder what limitations of process there were on this privilege, if any. The Inca could confiscate the property of those who were considered to have committed a crime against him, and could in some, if not in all cases, apply the property to his own use. The Inca could, in short, with certain limitations, commit a legal theft.

The nobility, though it did not enjoy all of these special privileges of the Inca emperor, had considerably more than the commoners. Any illegal act committed by a noble invariably carried a lesser penalty than the same act committed by a commoner. Incest, which carried the death penalty for commoners, involved merely a public reprimand for the nobility....

The use of state power to shield the rulers of the state from certain criminal penalties, or to soften these penalties is an extremely significant one. It gives the lie to the conception of the noble noble, of the purer morality of the nobility. It suggests that the nobility, as enforcer of the law, was moved by a singularly convenient double standard. Rather than regard the exemption of the noble from common penalties as the emblem of the ethically high-minded, one could say that it was simply the privilege of the powerful. Just as it was easier for a Greek aristocrat equipped with a chariot and horses to be more heroic at war than a foot soldier accompanying him, so was it possible for the Inca nobility to be more moral than the commoners who could not cloak their anti-social acts with legal privilege. With what delicacy of feeling did the Inca

[d] "The authority [*potestas* and power of *imperium*] of the [Roman] magistrates was so great that they might even disregard the law." Hans Julius Wolff, Roman Law: An Historical Introduction 28 (1951).

(or Cobo[e] for them) rationalize this differentiation by saying that to an Inca of royal blood, public reprimand meant as much as the death penalty to a commoner....

That Inca punitive methods ordinarily did not include fines, nor most forms of slavery, nor our type of imprisonment, but consisted largely of physical punishments is closely related to Inca economic development. The Aztecs regularly used fines and slavery and it suited their economic system. In the Andean culture area, fines and slavery were less practical. To pay a fine a man must either own something he can pay with or have a means of acquiring it. For the Inca taxpayer, the opportunity to accumulate property was very limited. As for slavery, the Inca agriculturalist would not have had the means either of supporting or exploiting a slave, while government officials had an ample supply of labor through the tax system for personal service, as well as for government projects....

[T]here appear to have been certain tort-like situations as well as some crimes in which compensation for economic damage seems to have had a part in determining the penalty. There is some slight evidence that restitution and repayment may have had some role in compensating the victim of a theft. However, punishment involving no economic aspect is more commonly mentioned. Some exceptions follow: Cobo tells us that if any flocks damaged neighboring fields, the owner of the fields had the right to take animals to the extent of the damage done. One who injured another in such a way that he could no longer work at ordinary tasks, was obliged to support the injured man in addition to sustaining punishment for having caused injury. If he had no estate out of which to support his victim, the Inca fed him out of his estate, and the wrongdoer's punishment was augmented. One who burned down a house was put to death, but he also had to pay for the damage out of his property. If he burned down his own house out of negligence and the house of another burned down in consequence, he was obligated to make good the damage. In spite of the fact that these are instances of economic penalties, they tend to confirm the impression that such penalties were the exception rather than the rule. In the instance of livestock doing damage, the existence of a source of compensation is identical with the cause of the damage. In the case of personal injury the possibility that there were no resources from which to support the victim is recognized by the rule itself. In the burning of a house, rebuilding principally involved the contribution of labor. Labor might also be the principal means of supporting an injured man. The payment of goods is involved with certainty only in the livestock damage....

[T]he central government jealously reserved for itself the exclusive right to punish homicide. Neither the *ayllu*[f] nor family of the murdered man, had any right to take the law into its own hands. The immediate governing official had to obtain permission from above. The central government alone had the authority to act independently.

This is an extremely important indicator of the development of Inca government. One has only to compare it with more primitive arrangements where

[e] Father Bernabe Cobo (1580-1657) was one of the New World's outstanding historians. *See* Cobo, History of the Inca Empire (Roland Hamilton ed. & trans. 1979).

[f] Kin unit, usually in the landowning class.

self-help, clan feuds, and retaliatory killings are the order of the day to realize what the state had become by Inca times....

Homicide by witchcraft resulted in death, not only of the killer, but of his whole family. This may be a remnant of some former family responsibility for the actions of its members. But we are told that the rule was in order that no one should survive who knew witchcraft. It is evident from the accounts that not only the Inca believed in witchcraft, but that their Spanish chroniclers also did....

Inca criminal law has striking characteristics which reflect in a single application much that was true of the social and political system as a whole. The emphasis on the sacredness of government, its symbols, its property, its officials, the punitive distinctions made among criminals on the basis of rank and sex; the reservation to the central government of the power to condemn to death; the emphasized use of physical rather than economic punishment; the comparative lack of state concern for the individual as against the overwhelming concern that government remain unchallenged; the same seen in the existence of administrative review rather than appeal; the pervasive belief in supernatural punishment and in supernatural tests of crime; the frequent lack of administrative specialization; the placing of sexual acts on a level of culpability comparable to that of the most serious crimes meriting the death penalty — all these are characteristic of Inca criminal law, yet they have innumerable implications for Inca ideals, standards and behavioral norms. They serve to inform more precisely of the type and level of Inca development.

In comparing Chibcha, Inca, and Aztec lawbreaking, Trimborn sees the possibility of differentiating phases of development of the high culture state, and ascertaining the legal mentality that goes with it. He notes a developing shift from self-help to state enforcement. He also concludes that deterrence gradually replaced revenge as a motive for punishment, and asserts that an older "objective" test gave way to a "subjective" phase in which the state of mind of the lawbreaker was taken into account. He charts a reconstructed evolutionary history of punishment. In Trimborn's view, the death penalty was the original and sole penalty in some primal culture. Step by step in his scheme are added (in order): restriction of freedom, corporal punishment, penalties to honor, and fines and compensation for damage. The Inca rate high on such a scale, the Aztec still higher.

Yet to much of this one must take exception. Underlying it there is an implied concept of the civilized mind as the opposite of the primitive. Has any people ever had a wholly subjective or wholly objective set of criminal law standards? Is there no question of deterrence being involved in retaliatory blood feud as well as revenge? Can one assume that revenge is not a significant element in the state enforcement of criminal penalties? Has it not, for example, been made clear from the studies supporting the abolition of the death penalty, that its deterrent effect is questionable?

It is not the evolutionary element in Trimborn's approach, per se, which raises question, but the way it is used. There is no denying that law has evolved from simpler forms to more complex ones, and that there is a general historical trend which can be discerned from the comparison of peoples of various cultural levels. Hoebel has put it this way in his excellent discussion:

> As for law, simple societies need little of it. If the more primitive societies are more lawless than the more civilized, it is not in the sense that they are *ipso facto* more disorderly; quite the contrary. It is because they are more homogeneous; relations are more direct and intimate; interests are shared by all in a solid commonality; and there are fewer things to quarrel about. Because relations are more direct and intimate, the primary, informal mechanisms of social control are more generally effective. Precisely as a society acquires a more complex culture and moves into civilization, opposite conditions come into play. Homogeneity gives way to heterogeneity. Common interests shrink in relation to special interests. Face-to-face relations exist not between all the members of the society but only among a progressively smaller proportion of them.

2. THE AZTECS AND THEIR LEGAL SYSTEM

NOTE ON THE AZTEC LEGAL SYSTEM

The Aztecs, like their Inca counterpart in Peru, were relative latecomers to empire, having built their civilization on the efforts of earlier Indian occupations. Like the Incas, the Aztecs were at the height of empire in the 16th century. The Aztec emperor Moctezuma II had recently expanded his conquest to the Indian towns along the gulf coast of Mexico when the Spanish arrived.

The Aztecs, a Nahuatl-speaking nation, sometimes called the México or Tenochcas, were thus the dominant people in Mesoamerica in 1519. They ruled over an empire of 5 to 6 million people. From Tenochca the name of their capital was derived, Tenochtitlán, which was founded circa 1325 on the islands of Lake Texcoco. This city was sometimes known as México, which later was applied to the surrounding valley. In the early 15th century the Aztecs, with their allies, won a series of battles that led to the emergence of Tenochtitlán as the center of an extensive empire ruled by Moctezuma II from 1502 to 1520.

Aztec and other Mesoamerican social and political organization was characterized by corporate groups known as *calpulli,* which consisted of perhaps 50 to 500 extended families. *Calpulli* lands were owned communally, but were distributed among households that enjoyed a right of use. This right of use could be transferred within a family through inheritance. The right could be lost for failure to exploit the land for two consecutive years. *Calpulli* lands were also used to support religious cults, military service, the administration of justice, and later for tribute to the Aztecs. A *calpulli* was ruled by a council of households, headed by a chief selected by the council. Only the chief could sell or rent communal lands. Within the state a *calpulli* served both as a military unit and as a unit for taxation and labor.

Prior to the Aztec expansion in the 15th century, a large number of states existed, each organized around a central town. The head of state was called a *tlatoani,* a position fixed within a particular lineage. There was a tradition among these states that respectable nations had to have a *tlatoani* with noble

Toltec blood descended from the god Quetzalcóatl. The Aztecs met this condition as early as 1383. Their king, a descendant of Quetzalcóatl, married several *calpulli* chiefs' daughters and thereby formed the foundation for a hereditary nobility.

Aztec kings were assisted in the rule of their empire by a council of 12 to 20 nobles called *tlalocan*, perhaps consisting of *calpulli* chiefs. In addition, a Council of Four, relatives of the Aztec king (*tlatoani*) selected by him, elected the new *tlatoani* from among themselves and advised the king on various matters. The chief legal officer, and the second most powerful post in the empire, was the *cihuacoatl*. He appointed lifetime judges and performed various military, religious, and administrative functions.

As the empire expanded near the end of the 15th century, a corps of hierarchically organized tribute collectors was recruited to supervise the flow of goods from the imperial provinces to Tenochtitlán, Texcoco, and other cities. Although tribute deliveries were technically under the jurisdiction of local rulers, after 1450 stewards (*calpixque*) were assigned to conquered provinces. These were consolidated into 38 tributary provinces, each controlled by an Aztec governor or high steward. The system as a whole was coordinated by a single official in Tenochtitlán.

In addition to the military success of the Aztecs, an important feature of its civilization was a highly developed commercial activity. Professional merchants (*pochteca*) undertook journeys lasting up to a year. Merchant wards in many towns were organized under a central trading guild in Tenochtitlán. These wards administered town markets held in great plazas. Merchants enjoyed high prestige and had their own special tribunals to adjudicate commercial disputes and to regulate trade.

Near the end of the Aztec empire, certain laws were codified, primarily for the use of judges. Nevertheless, outside the areas of major Aztec interest — military control, tribute, and commerce — there was little uniform imperial law. The Aztecs were content to allow conquered peoples to retain their own form of government and laws. In the field of Aztec criminal law, capital punishment was common, but other sentences included mutilation, exile, slavery, imprisonment, confiscation of property, destruction of home, loss of job, or fines. There is some evidence that a defendant's nobility was an aggravating circumstance, suggesting a type of *noblesse oblige*.

Courts of various types existed in the Aztec empire. Minor matters were heard in courts of limited jurisdiction staffed by annually elected judges. More important cases went to three-judge general jurisdiction courts, where judicial appointment was by the king's *cihuacoatl*. Appeals could be taken to the king's court, which met about once a month.

Special commercial courts, consisting of ten to 12 judges, heard cases arising from designated markets (*tianguis*). A hereditary class of merchants controlled these markets and the prices charged. The king benefited through heavy taxes on market transactions. Since there was no money, merchants accepted cacao, copper bars, and valued fabric or feathers in exchange for their goods. Because commerce was very important to the empire, theft from *tianguis* was dealt with more harshly by commercial courts than ordinary theft was punished by general jurisdiction courts. There were also special jurisdiction courts for family matters, taxes, and military crimes.

Aztec judicial procedure was primarily oral. The judge could allow both parties and witnesses to testify, apparently under oath, but he also used presumptions and accepted documents in evidence (e.g., property maps have been found in court records). Advocates (*tepantlatoanis*) assisted the parties. Major decisions were recorded in hieroglyphics and filed in official archives.

After the Spanish conquest of Mexico, the crown did not want to eliminate all indigenous law, and expressly authorized its use when compatible with the crown's or church's interests. Recopilación de Leyes de las Indias (1680) 2.1.4; 5.2.22. Even now, in the shadow of Mexico City, old customary legal practices continue *contra legem*. For instance, a 15th century Aztec would have no difficulty understanding today's collective labor on certain land, and the use of a portion of the yield to support the cult of a sacred virgin or saint. Only the name of the revered image has changed.

For a sketch of Olmec, Maya, Chichimex, and Aztec law, see Guillermo Floris Margadant, Introducción a la historia del Derecho mexicano 7-26 (7th ed. 1986), roughly translated from the third edition in An Introduction to the History of Mexican Law (Eugenio Ursúa-Cocke trans. 1983). *See also* Edward E. Calnek, *Patterns of Empire Formation in the Valley of Mexico, Late Postclassic Period, 1200-1521,* in The Inca and Aztec States, 1400-1800, at 43 (George A. Collier, Renato I. Rosaldo & John D. Wirth eds. 1982); J. Rounds, *Dynastic Succession and the Centralization of Power in Tenochtitlán,* in *ibid.* 63.

NOTES AND QUESTIONS

1. It was a basic policy of the Roman legal system to permit its non-Roman subjects to live according to their own laws, i.e., to exist under a principle of personality or nationality. Thus in large parts of the empire Roman law served primarily administrative functions, and the bulk of ordinary legal activity proceeded according to personal or local law. There was no attempt to Romanize the legal system. The apex of the indigenous social pyramid was replaced by Roman administrators, and certain matters (e.g., taxation and public order as it affected the empire) were changed to suit Roman preferences, but for the rest, what was traditional and familiar was allowed to go on. This also seems to have been the policy in the Inca and Aztec empires. When the Spanish conquerors came they merely replaced the Inca and Aztec rulers at the top of the social pyramid. The great indigenous masses of people below them of course felt the weight of the new regimes, but for large areas of traditional life things went on much as before. For most purposes, traditional law remained in force, interpreted and applied in traditional ways by traditional institutions.

Such an approach to colonial administration has the obvious attraction of economy, since it makes only minimal demands on the colonizing power. It is, indeed, the standard administrative approach to colonization, particularly in its initial stages, and has been widely employed by colonial powers in modern times. The occasional effort to transform the entire legal system of a colonized area has been relatively unsuccessful. For an excellent discussion of a spectacular failure, see Gregory J. Massell, *Law as an Instrument of Revolutionary Change in a Traditional Milieu: The Case of Soviet Central Asia,* 2 Law & Soc'y Rev. 179 (1968). Thus, most present and former colonies are legally pluralistic: there is a certain area for the operation of the colonial power's law, but the rest is left to indigenous law. For an authoritative survey, see M.B. Hooker, Legal Pluralism (1975).

With independence in Spanish America, cosmopolitan elites replaced the Spanish crown at the top of the pyramid. Even today in Latin America, after almost five centuries under European law, legal pluralism is still an important fact. Large Indian elements of the populations of Mexico, Guatemala, El Salvador, Bolivia, Ecuador, and Peru, for example, are relatively untouched by the official legal system and live by customary law. For an interesting study see Jane Fishburne Collier, Law and Social Change in Zinacantan (1973). In other Spanish-American nations, like Argentina, Chile, and Uruguay, the indigenous inhabitants were so thoroughly eliminated that little trace of traditional societies remains, and the official legal system penetrates further down the social pyramid.

2. By the beginning of the 16th century, the Inca empire controlled approximately 12 million people. This was larger than any European political unit at the time (e.g., England at 3 million, Spain at 8 million), and may be compared to the Roman empire of the second century A.D. (110 million) or the Chinese empire of the first to 10th century A.D. (50 million).

List the similarities and differences you can find between the Roman and Inca legal systems with regard to the following:

(1) method of developing law and communicating it to others;
(2) choice of law rule for conquered subjects;
(3) degree of state involvement in punishing ordinary crimes;
(4) access to formal adjudicatory processes for enforcing legal rules;
(5) rationality of proof-taking methods;
(6) existence of a legal profession;
(7) legal treatment of the nobility compared to commoners; and
(8) legal regulation of familial, commercial, and other private relationships.

3. What is the relationship between the type of legal punishments used and the type of economy in the Inca, Aztec, and Roman empires?

4. The seventh part (*partida*) of the *Siete Partidas* listed 14 kinds of treason. Was this concern of 13th century Spanish government more like the Inca view of the relationship between the state and the individual or more like the 18th century view in the U.S. Constitution?

5. Notice the quotation from A.E. Hoebel at the end of Professor Moore's excerpt: "As for law, simple societies need little of it." He goes on to suggest that more "law" is needed as societies become more heterogeneous. What does he mean? How does one measure the degree of simplicity or complexity, homogeneity or heterogeneity, of a society? How does one measure the amount of "law" a society has or "needs"?

B. THE DEVELOPMENT OF LAW IN COLONIAL LATIN AMERICA

1. THE SPANISH CONQUEST OF MEXICO

FRED R. HARRIS, MEXICO: HISTORICAL FOUNDATIONS, in LATIN AMERICA, ITS PROBLEMS AND ITS PROMISE: A MULTIDISCIPLINARY INTRODUCTION 261, 262-63 (Jan Knippers Black ed. 1984)

When Hernán Cortés and the conquistadores came over the snowy pass to the east and first saw Tenochtitlán and the other cities in and around the lake, they could hardly believe their eyes. Bernal Díaz del Castillo, who was in the party, later wrote that "we were amazed and said that it was like the enchantment they tell of in the legend of Amadis, on account of the great towers and cues and buildings rising from the water, and all built of masonry." Within three years thereafter, Cortés was the ruler of all he had at first surveyed — except that, by then, the great city was in ruins.

Why did Moctezuma II, the Aztec ruler, let the Spaniards come freely into Tenochtitlán? Cortés's monstrous use of terrorism as a tactic must have been puzzlingly and terrifyingly different from any kind of war that Moctezuma II had known. Why destroy a huge tribute city like Cholula and the income one could derive from it, as Cortés did? Why kill such great numbers of people for no useful purpose? Moctezuma II must also have let the Spaniards come because he was certain that at any later moment when he wanted to, he could easily defeat and capture Cortés and his army. Moctezuma must have been influenced, too, by Cortés's continued and effusive expressions of friendly intention. And, philosopher and thinker that he was, intellectually curious, Moctezuma must have been intrigued by these strange white men and anxious to know more about their identity and their place of origin.

In any event, Cortés did indeed come on. Once inside Tenochtitlán, he seized Moctezuma and held him prisoner. But Cortés soon had to leave for the Gulf Coast to defeat a rival Spanish army sent by the governor of Cuba. While he was away, the Aztecs at last rose up and attacked the Spaniards. Moctezuma was killed in the bloody fighting. Cortés, with his Tlaxcalan allies, marched back to Tenochtitlán to relieve the embattled Spanish garrison there. But the Aztecs had had enough, and they drove Cortés and the Spaniards from the city.

Then came into play one of the most terrible factors in the success of the conquest — European disease, in this case, smallpox. The European plagues — smallpox, influenza, typhus, typhoid, diphtheria, measles, whooping cough, and others — were unknown in the New World. The native peoples of the Western Hemisphere had built up no immunities to them. Time after time, then, with first contact, one or another of the European diseases decimated whole populations in the Americas. Such was now the fate of Tenochtitlán. Smallpox swept through the city with devastating effect, throwing social and political organization into disarray and shaking religious beliefs.... Cortés had time to regroup. When he attacked, he fought a weakened enemy. Still, Cuauhtémoc and the Aztecs resisted fiercely until, at last, they were defeated

— and Cuauhtémoc captured — in the suburb of Tlatelolco on August 21, 1521. By that time, Tenochtitlán had been destroyed.

2. THE SPANISH CONQUEST OF PERU

EDWARD P. LANNING, PERU BEFORE THE INCAS 171-72 (1967)

A small corps of Spaniards under Francisco Pizarro invaded Peru in 1532. In six short years, they conquered the whole of the Inca Empire, looted it of all the gold and silver in sight, and drove the last remnants of the Inca government into exile in the *montaña*. Their feat was one of the most spectacular military accomplishments in the history of man.

How could a handful of adventurous Europeans take over the mightiest empire of ancient America? Though they used both horses and firearms, they were scarcely better armed, armored, or organized than their Inca opponents and they were vastly outnumbered in the bargain. The answer lies, not in European military superiority, but in a concatenation of circumstances which, though they affected the outcome of the conquest, arose independently of it. Four principal factors combined to give the Spanish the victory.

First and most important, Pizarro and his men arrived just at the end of a disastrous civil war. Huayna Capac had died in 1527 without leaving clear the succession to the throne. Two of his sons, Huascar and Atahuallpa, rived the empire through five bloody years. The Spanish arrived just as Atahuallpa's army had won the final decisive battle, but enmities were still strong and either side was willing to make an alliance with the newcomers against the other.

Secondly, the Spaniards found allies among some of the disaffected provincial people. The Cañari of Ecuador, for example, had suffered Atahuallpa's wrath during the civil war and they eagerly joined the Spanish in their march on Cuzco. In the first years of the conquest, before Spanish reinforcements began to arrive en masse, the invading army could well have been described as an Indian army under Spanish command.

In addition the Incas were weakened by a series of epidemics that swept through the empire. They were caused by European diseases, such as smallpox and measles, to which the Indians had no immunity. Starting in Central America, these diseases swept down across South America in great waves, debilitating and demoralizing the Inca defenders. The Inca civil war itself was, in a sense, a result of the epidemics, since Huayna Capac's sudden death was due to the first epidemic, which arrived in Peru before the Spaniards who had originally carried it.

Finally, there was an important difference in diplomatic tactics which worked to the Spaniards' advantage. The Incas had always fought by a traditional code which had served them well, announcing their coming and attempting to frighten their enemies into submission. There was never any doubt about their intentions. The Spanish, militarily weak, looking for gold and not territory as such, chose to hide their intentions in the guise of a diplomatic mission. Any European power would have been suspicious of them, but these tactics were new to the Incas. By the time the conquerors' role became clear, Atahuallpa had been kidnapped and his armies were paralyzed in fear for his safety....

The Spanish conquest was consolidated by 1538 and the Incas, in spite of resistance in exile and a series of bloody uprisings in the seventeenth and eighteenth centuries, never succeeded in breaking the grip of their conquerors. After 1538, the history of Peru became part of the history of Europe and of modern America.

NOTE ON THE PORTUGUESE SETTLEMENT AND LEGAL SYSTEM IN BRAZIL

The Treaty of Tordesillas (1494) granted Portugal possession of lands in America eastward of a vertical line drawn 370 leagues west of the Cape Verde Islands. The Portuguese crown first attempted to establish an organized government in this region in 1533, when the colony of Brazil was divided into 15 hereditary captaincies, parallel strips ten to 100 leagues wide that extended from the coast to the inland line of Tordesillas. These lands were donated to loyal wealthy individuals who were willing to assume the costs of settlement in exchange for broad governing privileges. When this feudal system failed, the crown in 1549 switched to a unified administration centered in the city of Salvador, captaincy of Bahia. The original donatories had to surrender their political privileges to a governor-general.

The growth of sugar cane plantations thereafter stimulated a slave trade that attracted many new Portuguese settlers. In the north, settlement was pushed by missionaries, who established missions along the Amazon. In the northeast, cattlemen from the sugar growing areas of Bahia and Pernambuco drifted inland in search of new pastures. But the greatest movement went west, led by Paulistas — the settlers of São Paulo — who organized expeditions (*bandeiras*) to capture Indian slaves and to find gold and precious stones.

Spain and Portugal were united during the reign of Philip II of Spain for a period known as the Spanish captivity (1580-1640). Philip II (Philip I of Portugal, 1580-1598) began the reorganization of Portugal's law and legal institutions. He reformed the judicial system and ordered a recompilation of Portuguese law, which was a mix of Roman and canon law, customs, municipal statutes, and Portuguese legislation. It was published in 1603 as the Ordenações Filipinas. This compilation continued in force as Brazil's general law until a civil code was adopted in 1917. In 1604 the king created a Portuguese Council of the Indies, which played a role similar to its Spanish counterpart. This became, in 1642, the Conselho Ultramarino.

NOTE ON THE SPANISH LEGAL SYSTEM IN AMERICA

The political and legal organization of the Spanish empire in America reflected the recently centralized regime by which Spain itself was governed. The Council of the Indies, chartered in 1524, stood at the head of the Spanish imperial administration. Its membership consisted predominantly of lawyers. Under the king, it was the supreme legislative, judicial, and executive organ of colonial government. One of its most important functions was the nomination of all high colonial officials. It also framed a vast body of legislation.

The principal royal agents in the colonies also shared executive, legislative, and judicial powers. They were the viceroys, captains general, and the judges of the *audiencias*. The viceroys and captains general had essentially the same administrative and military functions, differing only in the greater territory assigned to the former. In the first centuries after the conquest there were two viceroyalties: one in New Spain, with its capital at Mexico City, and the other in Peru, centered at Lima. The two viceroys, and the larger number of captains general, were assisted in the performance of their duties by an *audiencia*. Their joint decisions had the force of law.

The provincial administration was entrusted to royal officials who governed districts of varying sizes. The *corregidor* possessed supreme political authority in his district and represented the royal interest in the town council.

Figure 4.2 illustrates that certain civil and criminal cases could be appealed from the municipal magistrates (*alcaldes* or *jueces*) to the *corregidor* and from him to the *audiencia* (a multi-judge tribunal on which the viceroy or captain general generally sat). This judicial structure was imposed on top of a separate Indian judicial structure that existed much as before the Spaniards arrived.

Figure 4.2

Legal Organization of the Spanish Empire in America

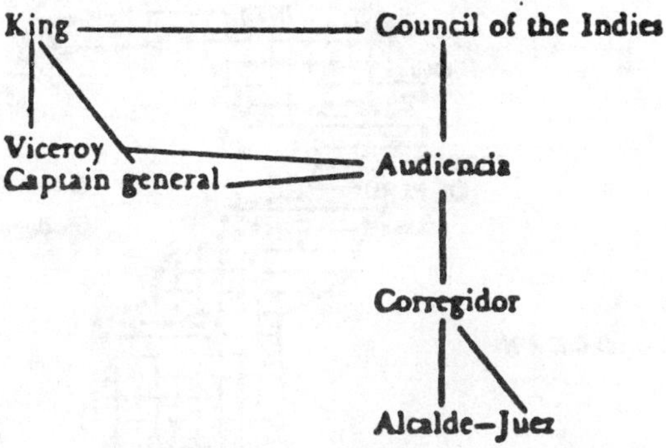

Although royal authority was dominant in the capitals, large landowners had great power in the more distant countryside. On the large, self-sufficient estates they dispensed justice in the manner of feudal lords, holding courts and imprisoning peons in their own jails.

By the last quarter of the 18th century, as shown in Figure 4.3, the Spanish New World was divided among four viceroys (and a larger number of captains general), extending well into what is now part of the United States.

Figure 4.3
Extension of the Spanish Viceroyalty System in America in 1800

3. THE *ENCOMIENDA* IN AMERICA

P.E.B. COY, JUSTICE FOR THE INDIAN IN EIGHTEENTH CENTURY MEXICO, 12 American Journal of Legal History 41-42 (1968)

Christopher Columbus's discovery of the Americas occurred in the same year which saw the end of the seven-century-long reconquest of Spain from the Arabs. The conquest of the American mainland was therefore in many ways a continuation of the reconquest of the Iberian Peninsula and many of the same legal and administrative devices which had been used successfully in the Peninsula were used initially in the New World. A case in point was the *encomienda* system, by which conquered Moslems on Iberian soil were entrusted to Spanish overlords; the latter were charged with the conversion and taxing of the Spanish Crown's new subjects in return for a part of the tribute and considerable prestige.

The transfer of this system across the Atlantic Ocean introduced the new factor of distance between crown and trustee; this simple variant was sufficient in itself to assure the inappropriateness of the device in the new context: the Spanish king was to experience great difficulty in regulating the conduct of his *conquistadores* when they did not choose to co-operate.

The *encomienda* was interpreted by the men who had borne the peril and hardship of the military conquest as an opportunity to enrich themselves, and their consequent exploitation of the indigenous inhabitants of the Caribbean islands was not only to develop into a type of accidental genocide, but was to arouse the indignation of the spiritual conquerors who had followed. An active campaign against the *encomienda* was undertaken by the mendicant orders both from the pulpit and at the court of the new King of Spain, Charles, Holy Roman Emperor. Charles sent out observers to the islands to experiment with free communities of Indians unsupervised other than by priests. In the meantime, however, Hernán Cortés had manned his expedition to the mainland by promising *encomiendas* to whomever would accompany him. The conquest of Mexico in 1521 overtook the experiments and added new factors to the problem: the vastness of the new territory and the large numbers of new souls available for conversion. The price for holding the way open for evangelization was now no longer the entrusting of Indians, with their lands, to a *conquistador* for life, but in perpetuity.

Persuaded by Cortés that evacuation was the only alternative to the *encomienda,* Charles permitted the system to continue, but caused his Council for the Indies to enforce, where they could, "Ordinances for the good treatment of the natives." In 1542, however, Fr. Bartolomé de las Casas, a Dominican friar who had been granted, and had given up, an *encomienda* in Cuba in 1515, who had taken part in the experiments with free Indian communities and who had become a violent opponent of the *encomienda* system, presented to the Spanish court his reasons for regarding continuation of the system as a "Mortal sin." Charles was so impressed that he caused to be promulgated the New Laws of the Indies in the same year. These were based on las Casas's "Remedies" and effectively placed the disposal of the *encomienda* Indians in the hands of the crown. Chapter 30, revoking the concession whereby an *encomi-*

enda could be inherited, especially enraged the Spanish settlers in the Americas: in Peru they assassinated the Viceroy Vaca de Castro; in Mexico the Viceroy Mendoza prudently ignored the New Laws. In 1545 Chapter 30 was rescinded, which no doubt has led to the later "black legend" that the New Laws of the Indies were no more than a dead letter. Nevertheless, the Laws of 1542 were the beginning of the end for the *encomiendas*, which now fell into the hands of the crown as they became vacant and were thenceforth ruled by government officials or were sold by the government as land. Thus there grew up side by side the huge private estates, often more than 2,500 acres in area, and the crown lands.

4. THE SPREAD OF IBERIAN LAW TO LATIN AMERICA

DAVID S. CLARK, JUDICIAL PROTECTION OF THE CONSTITUTION IN LATIN AMERICA, 2 Hastings Constitutional Law Quarterly 405, 407-13 (1975)

The pattern of Iberian administration in the American colonies reflected the steady growth of centralized rule in Spain and Portugal. The colonies, treated as direct and exclusive possessions of the king, were separate kingdoms united with those of the Iberian peninsula, but under a common sovereign. The Spanish king's power over his subjects was, although ample, not unlimited. America was a vast and distant land. Communication was slow. Totalitarian control, even if desired, was physically impossible. Furthermore Portugal, with her limited resources already committed to exploitation of Africa and the Far East, had administrative difficulties in controlling Brazil.

Administration and law enforcement in a complex society require the existence of courts or their functional equivalent to interpret and apply laws and regulations. To meet this need, the Spanish and Portuguese administrators adapted the royal court system to a new environment. One of the most striking characteristics of colonial government was its heavy reliance on judicial devices, procedures, and on legally trained officials — what Professor Parry refers to as the "rapidly increasing body of officials, lawyers, notaries and miscellaneous quill-drivers." The interpretation of the various legal codes lay in the hands of a numerous and powerful judiciary, at whose head stood the king. Spain and Portugal carried over from the age of feudalism to the age of sovereignty the notion of jurisdiction as the essential function of authority. At least during the sixteenth century the king, though he legislated continually, was still regarded as the chief of judges. The principal task of government, accordingly, was adjudicating between competing interests rather than deliberately planning and constructing a new society.

After several temporary groups of advisers, Charles V of Spain decided in 1524 to create the Council of the Indies, modeled after the Council of Castile, to act in matters related to the colonies. The council's authority extended beyond judicial review, as the highest court of appeal, to practically all fields of government action: legislative, financial, military and ecclesiastical. The principal royal agents in the colonies were the viceroys, the captains general, and the *audiencias*. Viceroys and captains general had the same duties. The former, however, were more important due to the larger expanse of territory assigned to their jurisdiction. Both viceroys and captains general were the supreme civil and military officers within their regions. The major restraint upon the arbitrary exercise of power by these officials, however, lay in the royal *audiencias*, nine of which were created in the sixteenth century. The *audiencia* was essentially a court of appeals with jurisdiction over roughly the same territory governed by the viceroy or captain general. It served, in addition, as a consultative council to the executive officials and had a limited degree of legislative power.

The *audiencia* system reflected two important characteristics of Spanish imperial government in America: the division of authority and responsibility, and the king's distrust of initiative on the part of his colonial officials. Although these characteristics often prevented effective administration in the colonies, they aided the king and his council in maintaining political control in Spain. Spanish imperial government was one of checks and balances, although not secured by the separation of powers into executive, legislative, and judicial branches seen in modern constitutional regimes, but rather secured by a division of authority among different individuals or tribunals exercising the same powers.

It is in the *audiencia*, as a result, that one can find the germination of what will be judicial review of legislative and executive acts in Latin American nations in the nineteenth and twentieth centuries.

> It was the center, the core, of the administrative system, and the principal curb upon oppression and illegality by the viceroys and other governors. Viceroys came and went; the *audiencia* was a more permanent and continuous body, which acquired a long line of corporate tradition.... [*Audiencias*] embodied a "tendency toward jurisdictional autonomy in spite of royal pragmatics and the ill-concealed jealousies of viceroys and governors."...

As a court of law the *audiencia* maintained an unquestioned supremacy; the technical right of appeal from its decisions to the king and Council of the Indies, furthermore, was made so difficult as to be nearly impossible by the eighteenth century.

The jurisdiction of the *audiencia* was extensive. All colonial *audiencias* exercised a general supervision over the conduct of inferior magistrates within their territory. They possessed, in addition to their appellate powers over civil, criminal, administrative and some ecclesiastical matters, original jurisdiction in cases concerning royal patronage and revenue, and might take the initiative in investigating any usurpation of royal authority, even to the point of sitting in judgment on the acts of a viceroy. The protection of interests of Indians, moreover, was one of the *audiencia's* more important functions.[22]

In the interests of impartiality, the seventeenth century code, *Recopilación de las Leyes de las Indias*, prescribed a semi-monastic life for the *audiencia*

[22] "The Indian very rapidly assimilated ... juridical sense, and then defended himself against the acts of the colonizer not with bows and arrows but with lawsuits."... Up to forty percent of an *audiencia's* time was occupied with suits between Indians, or between Indians and Spaniards. The Indians, furthermore, were relieved in some regions of legal costs and had attorneys designated to defend them in court.

judges, the number of which varied from four to eighteen, depending on the importance of the territory. Many of the code articles laid down strict rules of daily life for these judges, showing them to be a highly specialized and respected professional group upon which the crown placed particularly heavy reliance. For their many duties and responsibilities, *audiencia* judges received salaries much higher than those of any other colonial officials except viceroys, and considerably higher than those paid to corresponding judges in Spain.

The Portuguese judicial system in Brazil differed somewhat from that in colonial Spain, although there were important similarities. During the sixty year period of Spanish-Portuguese union after Philip II of Spain inherited the crown of Portugal in 1580, for instance, the *Conselho da India*, resembling the Spanish Council of the Indies, was created to administer the king's policies in Brazil. The Conselho da India, however, and its successor, the Overseas Council (*Conselho Ultramarino*), did not have the judicial function of the Spanish Council of the Indies. Final appellate jurisdiction resided in the *Casa de Suplicação* in Lisbon for a few captaincies general and in the *relações* in Bahia or, after 1751, also in Rio de Janeiro for most of the Brazilian captaincies general. As with the *audiencia* in Spanish America, the *relação* acted as the principal check on the arbitrary exercise of power by a Brazilian captain general. *Relações* were both judicial and administrative bodies, but they were not subordinate to the captain general. The harbinger of today's Supreme Court in Brazil finds its roots in the *relação*.

Even though the *audiencia* and *relação* were important institutions in colonial America in curbing the arbitrary exercise of official power, two points should be emphasized. First, these two partially judicial organs were not upholding a higher law, natural or secular, against the legislative or administrative acts of the king. On the contrary, *audiencias* and *relações* were the most consistently loyal and effective institutions of the colonial bureaucracy. Legality was defined by the king and his councils. Aggrieved individuals could complain, and many thousands did, against official action that was contrary to the king's law. The second important fact to remember is that the New World was enormous in size, especially compared to the Iberian peninsula. The scattered pattern of settlement,[28] the lack of resources, the tremen-

[28] Table 4.1 presents a rough impression of the distribution of the 22 million people living in Latin America at the beginning of their period of political independence from Europe.

Table 4.1

Population of Latin America in 1830, by Country

Country	Population
Argentina	754,000
Bolivia	1,714,000
Brazil	4,692,000
Chile	905,000
Colombia	1,765,000
Costa Rica	59,000
Cuba	704,000
Dominican Republic	139,000
Ecuador	564,000
El Salvador	222,000
Guatemala	440,000
Haiti	463,000

dous distances involved, the often complex nature of judicial procedure in the sixteenth to eighteenth centuries, corruption, especially at lower levels in the hierarchy — all naturally made the task of extending royal authority in an effective manner to all parts of the colonies a difficult one. The actual administration of justice probably only approximated the model in and near the larger towns where *audiencas* and *relações* were located.[29] Outside these areas, large landowners frequently ruled arbitrarily; from their rule there was no appeal.

To sum up, the principal task of government during the colonial period was to adjudicate between competing interests. The *audiencia* and *relação* were the institutions that fulfilled this function. The high salaries received by the magistrates, in addition, reflect the prestige and importance of their position in the Iberian imperial governments. The colonial government was one of checks and balances, of divided authority and responsibility. The *audiencia* and *relação*, forerunners of today's high courts, exercised the principal restraint on the arbitrary use of power by viceroys or captains general. These agencies protected what rights the colonials and Indians had under the king's law. When the age of revolution arrived in Latin America at the beginning of the nineteenth century, new institutions were fashioned. They were not completely hewn from the abstract political ideology of the time, however. Many were based on the practical experience of the previous centuries.

Country	Population
Honduras	194,000
Mexico	6,365,000
Nicaragua	226,000
Panama	—
Paraguay	421,000
Peru	1,585,000
Uruguay	95,000
Venezuela	453,000
TOTAL	21,760,000

Surprisingly, there were probably fewer people living in Latin America in 1830 than when the Europeans first landed. It is estimated, for instance, that there were [21 million] Indians living in Mexico in 1500. In every area of the New World, the European invasion was followed by a steep decline in the numbers of the native population, caused chiefly by foreign pestilence: smallpox, malaria and yellow fever. The estimated number of Indians in Mexico by 1580 was 1,900,000. Even though there were huge numbers of Negro slaves imported into Brazil, especially during the eighteenth century, their death rate was also extremely high.

Although Indians had substantial access to the high courts, most judicial review probably dealt with those of European ancestry living in Latin America, whose number had risen from 225,000 in 1600 to 3,400,000 by 1800.

[29] Brazilians were served by high courts in Bahia and Rio de Janeiro. In addition, there were thirteen *audiencias* in Spanish America during the latter part of the eighteenth century. There were two *audiencias* for Mexico (one each in Guadalajara and Mexico City), one for the Caribbean islands located in Santo Domingo, one for all of Central America in Guatemala, one each for Panama, Venezuela, Colombia and Ecuador, two for Peru (one each in Lima and Cuzco), one for both Bolivia and Paraguay, one for Chile and one for both Argentina and Uruguay.

5. THE JUDICIARY IN MEXICO

COLIN M. MacLACHLAN, CRIMINAL JUSTICE IN EIGHTEENTH CENTURY MEXICO: A STUDY OF THE TRIBUNAL OF THE *ACORDADA* 21-28, 31 (1974)

Evolution of the Viceregal Judicial Structure

In New Spain the needs of justice were served by political institutions that exercised various judicial functions as an adjunct to their political authority. The subordination of justice within political institutions was a natural result of the philosophical development of the monarchy. Jurisdiction constituted the essence of the medieval concept of sovereignty accepted by the Castilian crown. Such a concept drew no real distinction between judicial and political objectives.... Thus, the viceroy of the kingdom of New Spain became the chief magistrate of the realm, although his political functions were more important than his judicial responsibilities. In addition, the physical distance separating the king of Spain from his empire tended to emphasize the political duties of the viceroy as well as other royal officials charged with both political and judicial functions. All crown officials, including the viceroy, combined judicial functions with political and administrative responsibilities that in reality were of paramount importance.

The audiencia, the highest court in the viceroyalty, provides a clear example of the fusion of justice and political administration. Divided into two salas, civil and criminal (*sala del crimen*), the audiencia possessed appellate authority over all cases decided upon by crown or municipal magistrates. In addition to accepting appeals, the court approved, before execution, all major sentences of judicial officials, thus technically reviewing the actions of inferior magistrates throughout the viceroyalty. In the immediate area of its residence and for a radius of five leagues around the capital, the audiencia, through the sala del crimen, legally exercised justice in the first instance. In actuality the sala del crimen of the audiencia of Mexico also appointed agents outside the five league area.... As a primary tribunal within the prescribed area, the audiencia directly engaged in law enforcement. Agents of the criminal chamber patrolled the streets apprehending delinquents and bringing them before the *alcaldes del crimen* of the court. Certain crimes, occurring within the viceroyalty, which fell into the category of *casos de corte*, such as murder, rape, arson, treason, criminal acts of inferior justices, and crimes against widows and orphans, could also be processed by the audiencia in the first instance. Such judicial responsibilities were extremely important by themselves. When compared to the political functions of the court, however, it becomes obvious the audiencia was an important political institution. In the viceregal capital it served as the viceroy's council of state. All major decisions or departures from established procedures required the agreement of the oidores of the audiencia. The *acuerdo* (agreement) of the judges served as an interim ruling on the constitutionality of the viceroy's actions. Only a politically naive viceroy failed to value the audiencia's support. In the case of a viceroy's death, and in the absence of any instructions to the contrary, the court assumed supreme executive authority. As has been noted, the audiencia served the crown's political objectives in a very effective manner.... Unfortunately, the political success of the court contrasted sharply with its judicial failure [in the field of criminal justice]....

The [frequent] suspension of the audiencia's authority over sentences imposed by inferior magistrates resulted in a further subordination of its judicial duties to its active political responsibilities. Even under normal circumstances the judges of the criminal sala, in keeping with the importance placed on political functions, did not enjoy the higher status accorded the civil judges, the oidores....

While the audiencia engrossed in its political duties offered little assistance in maintaining order, other royal officials were equally as ineffective and for the same reason; the subordination of judicial responsibilities to political duties. The corregidor, who functioned as a district political officer, automatically became a member of the municipal council in the city or town of his residence, representing the king. His political duties overshadowed all other responsibilities, although as a judicial officer he shared the responsibility of maintaining civil order — apprehending and sentencing malefactors. Another crown official, the alcalde mayor, possessed much the same responsibilities of the corregidor exercising both political and judicial duties. The only judicial officials relieved of pressing political responsibilities were the municipal magistrates. The ordinary magistrates of the city council (*jueces ordinarios*) were not crown officers and, although not entirely free of political duties, their main functions were judicial.

Unfortunately, municipal magistrates, while free of the political preoccupations of crown officials, could not be relied on to bear the burden of law enforcement. Territorially restricted to their districts, they proved no match against bandits who crossed into other jurisdictions to avoid capture. Local judges, selected from respected residents by the council for a one-year term, lacked professional interest in law enforcement, accepting the post more for the status that it conferred than from a sense of civic responsibility. These judges, in small urban centers in particular, inclined toward a paternalistic approach to law enforcement, an attitude that preserved a reasonable degree of local harmony at the expense of the exact observance of the laws....

Complementing this essentially Spanish system of justice was a separate Indian judicial structure. The placing of limited judicial power in the hands of the native inhabitants was inspired by Spain's willingness to recognize the authority of Indian nobles, the caciques, when it did not conflict with the crown's sovereignty. Spain preferred not to see itself as a usurper. Rather, control of Indian communities could best be accomplished through Indian officials under the watchful eyes of a Spanish corregidor or alcalde mayor. Initially the caciques exercised the authority of a *gobernador* (governor) with virtually the same political and judicial responsibilities of a corregidor. The idea of political power vested in a hereditary nobility, even an Indian one, was, however, basically repugnant to the crown and in violation of its already well-established policy of making political power dependent on royal appointments rather than inherited feudal rights. As a consequence, a royal cédula in 1538 ordered the election of Indian gobernadores who would also be invested with the functions of a cacique thus moving toward a nonhereditary Indian officialdom. In 1549 the crown required Indian communities to choose their own municipal officials, governing themselves along the same lines as a Spanish municipality, electing councilmen (*regidores*) and municipal magistrates as well as the standard assortment of town functionaries. It became the responsibility of these Indian officials to administer justice in a manner consistent with Spanish practices. The audiencia exercised the usual appellate functions, hearing cases in the second instance, as well as approving major penalties imposed by Indian officials....

A system of justice formulated more to further the political objectives of the crown than to facilitate the ordering of society was only viable in a static situation. The relatively simple society of the first half century of conquest required a minimum of European judicial intervention. The Indian social structure did not collapse after 1521 but continued to function. Indian officials, acting in accordance with native tradition and norms, maintained order with little difficulty. An orderly Indian society permitted the crown to devote its energy to the more pressing problem of establishing royal authority in New Spain. Events indeed justified the crown's political preoccupations. The judicial system, designed to protect royal prerogatives, failed to adjust to the needs of a more varied situation as the society of conquest evolved. The rapidly growing number of mestizos and other racial mixtures, without a secure position in society, because of their mixed parentage, added a complex element to the previously simple division between the conquerors and the conquered. Such groups were not governed by an automatic allegiance to either Indian or European values but would develop their own norms to reflect social reality. The growth of a disorderly group of Spanish vagabonds further complicated the administration of order. Not being skilled artisans or suitable for positions in the expanding viceregal government, such people failed to find the opportunities they had expected. Even the need for unskilled labor could be adequately filled by the Indian population. Unable to fit into the Spanish economy at any level, they were content to live a parasitic existence among the Indians, using their undefined status as Spaniards to require goods and services from the confused villagers. Small groups of vagabonds moved across the kingdom of New Spain, corrupting Indian customs and imposing their will on a society still awed by the conquest. Moreover, the concentration of economic power in principal urban centers made it difficult to build a network of viable towns. Rural inhabitants drifted from their marginal communities into the cities only to find the attractions of city life more myth than reality. Crime and frustration became part of their urban existence....

The ability of the viceregal judicial structure to maintain order weakened when Indian society began to deteriorate as a consequence of the introduction of European epidemic disease. The great epidemics of 1576 and 1579, smallpox and measles in particular, virtually decimated the hapless Indian population. New Spain entered the seventeenth century still staggering from these demographic disasters. The Indian gradually acquired a degree of immunity and began a slow recovery. A population decline of such magnitude, however, necessitated social and economic adjustments by every class and caste.

The demand for Indian labor to meet the expanding economy of New Spain far exceeded the number of laborers readily available, causing both economic problems and social tension. The shortage of Indian labor resulted in active competition among employers to secure an adequate labor force. By 1627 the labor demands of the viceregal government could be met only with difficulty. It became necessary to draft Indians from towns and villages outside the valley of Mexico to meet governmental labor requirements. Textile factories (*obrajes*), which had always experienced difficulty in holding their labor force because of bad treatment and hard work, turned to convict labor. Local officials imposed obraje sentences for a variety of crimes, often in cooperation with factory owners. Even Indian officials, formerly exempt from forced labor, were pressed into the labor market. The critical shortage broke down Indian class distinctions, reducing all Indians to the same level. Increasing pressure forced many Indians to seek the protection of willing landholders, who incorporated them into their labor pool. Such rural labor, in spite of many drawbacks, was more acceptable and in line with Indian traditions than labor in factories, mines, or public works. Nor were mestizos immune from the voracious demand for labor, although they could aspire to a more exalted status as foremen or supervisors of Indian labor. Such significant social changes could not be accomplished without bitterness and violence. Temporary vagrancy and vice were natural consequences of the time....

The inefficient judicial structure, with the sala del crimen at its highest level, appeared unable to cope with the disorders brought about by far-reaching changes in colonial society. The ineffectiveness of the judicial system at such a critical moment magnified the degree of disorder in the viceroyalty. The crown, rather than face the problem, attributed the disorders to the many mixtures and races in the population of New Spain. The inhabitants of the viceroyalty were accused of having a natural propensity for violence and disorder. Undoubtedly, maintaining order in the colony was more difficult than it was in Spain; many of the king's New World subjects were not philosophically attuned to the Spanish judicial system. A large number, on the very fringes of Spanish culture or even beyond its influence, had no active contact with the law. Mexico had all the problems encountered in a frontier region.

6. THE JUDICIARY IN PERU

STEVE STERN, THE SOCIAL SIGNIFICANCE OF JUDICIAL INSTITUTIONS IN AN EXPLOITATIVE SOCIETY: HUAMANGA, PERU, 1570-1640, in THE INCA AND AZTEC STATES, 1400-1800: ANTHROPOLOGY AND HISTORY 289, 293-94, 307-08, 310-11 (George A. Collier, Renato I. Rosaldo & John D. Wirth eds. 1982)

Spanish legal philosophy associated sovereignty with the idea of jurisdiction, which was conceived as responsibility for reconciling life on earth with the principles of a higher, divinely ordained law. The state was fundamentally a dispenser of justice, and its officials were invariably known as "judges" or the like. The great burst of legislation and political reform in the 1570s gave new life to this tradition. The reforms included detailed statements of the natives' legal rights and procedures for claiming them. In addition, the state's administrative network included bureaucrats like the "protectors of Indians," whose stature, money-making possibilities, and power depended upon their potential as formidable legal defenders of the natives. In short, the juridical institutions that sponsored the extractions of a colonial ruling-class also gave the natives an opening by which to constrict exploitation. As long as some bureaucrats or colonial powers found it in their interest, in some cases, to back an assertion of the natives' legal rights, the Indians could find ways to impede, obstruct, or subvert extraction....

From early on, the natives earned a reputation as litigious peoples. By the 1550s, they had flooded the viceregal court, or *audiencia*, in Lima with petitions and suits — the majority of them between native communities, *ayllus* [kin units], and ethnic groups. In the 1570s, Viceroy Toledo hoped that local reorganization might streamline the litigation and avoid overtaxing the Lima jurists. In practice, however, the consolidation of a harsh exploitative system administered through a set of justices and legal guidelines did little to discourage litigation. Instead, the natives learned how to press aggressively for the "rights" allowed them. By the 1600s, they had developed legal forms of struggle into a major strategy for protecting individual, *ayllu*, and community interests....

The Indians' juridical strategy inflicted considerable hardships upon many colonials, but nevertheless brought unfortunate consequences to native Andean society. Given the bitter conflicts over lands, *kurakazgos* (chieftainships), and tribute-*mita* burdens that shaped *ayllu* and ethnic life, one could not expect that the natives would limit judicial politics to peasant actions against colonial exploitation. Andean litigants used their juridical rights and skills against one another — a practice that left native society divided and dependent upon colonial authorities to settle internal disputes. In addition, access to Spanish power and legal institutions encouraged a certain individualization, or privatization, of interest and perspective on the part of natives who acquired private land titles, secured legal exemptions from *mita* or tribute, mediated *ayllu* relationships with *corregidores* or other colonial powers, and the like. By reinforcing *ayllu* and ethnic strife and fostering class dynamics that tied privileged Indians to the colonial power structure, a working system of colonial justice weakened the capacity of native societies to unite around a more ambitious, radical assault upon the exploitative structure as a whole. A more fragmented strategy pursued more limited victories — that is, the particular causes of particular native groups or individuals. And the Indians grew increasingly dependent upon the legal institutions and favor of their exploiters to advance such causes, even when the disputes involved only Indians....

Even within an ethnic group, access to colonial juridical institutions fostered conflicts that undermined internal authority and cohesion. Succession to major chieftainships had always constituted a difficult, thorny process in Andean societies. The potential heirs of a *kurakazgo*, or chieftainship, almost always included several rivals — sons, and even nephews or brothers of the incumbent chief....

By offering defeated aspirants a tool with which to overturn the status quo, access to colonial judges kept disputes and local polarization alive, and left ethnic chiefs dependent upon Spanish power to back up their standing even with local kinfolk....

The Indians' struggle for Spanish justice subjected a good many colonials to constraints and hardships and even forced some of them to search for alternative ways to extract labor and profits. What it could not do, however, was challenge colonialism itself. Spanish justice, in some instances and on some issues, favored the natives against their exploiters. But for that very reason, it set into motion relationships that sustained colonial power, weakened the peasantry's capacity for independent resistance, and contributed to the oppression of Andean peoples.

7. THE JUDICIARY IN BRAZIL

STUART B. SCHWARTZ, SOVEREIGNTY AND SOCIETY IN COLONIAL BRAZIL: THE HIGH COURT OF BAHIA AND ITS JUDGES, 1609-1751, at xiv-xv, 173-74, 185-86, 293-94, 304-05 (1973)

In Portugal, the House of Aviz depended on mercantile and lower-class support in its struggle to establish a centralized monarchy, but like Castile it also turned to bureaucratic administration to formalize its achievement.... Both kingdoms reserved places of distinction and service for the titled nobility so long as they tied their fortunes to the rising star of the crown.... But in both Spain and Portugal the professional bureaucrats, that quasi-estate of royal servants and officers, were commonly non-noble lawyers or judges whose training in, emphasis on, and respect for legal procedure and the Roman Law tradition eventually pervaded society as a whole....

The crown used two methods to insure the loyalty, impartiality and administrative effectiveness of the judges. First, because, the *desembargadores*[a] were representatives of royal authority, every effort was made to raise them above society and to give them by means of prestige, wealth, and social standing a position of unassailable respect. Colonial society placed great emphasis on ascriptive status. A wealthy landowner with pretentions of nobility would not readily accede to law enforcement by men whom he viewed as his social inferiors....

While trying to insure their status, the crown also sought to cut off the magistrates from the society in which they lived. *Desembargadores* were expected to live in close residential proximity to each other and to limit their social intercourse with others in society. Marriage to women in Brazil was expressly forbidden by an *alvará* of 22 November 1610, although upon request the crown could and sometimes did grant exceptions to the law. Royal ordinances also prohibited a magistrate from conducting business or owning land within the area of his jurisdiction. Behind such measures lay a basic belief that the magistracy could operate in a social vacuum, devoid of the pressures of family, friends, or interest. Such an idea was utopian....

One way to evaluate the independence of the High Court is to examine its relationship to the sugar aristocracy. In the seventeenth century this sector more than any other exerted considerable political pressure both in the colony and in the metropolis.... The development of the colony depended directly on the agricultural inputs of the sugar sector. Despite the continuing but declin-

[a]*Desembargadores,* i.e, those who disembarked, were the relação (high court) judges.

ing dyewood trade and the constant search for minerals, sugar and Brazil had become synonymous and the sugar industry was always a creation of the private sector, a fact that the crown recognized. The planter elite controlled the municipal councils of northeastern Brazil and formed a significant lobby at the councils of the king, but it never fully controlled the magistrates of the Relação.

Clearly, the High Court's enforcement of the Indian protection law of 1609 had quickly dashed any hopes that the planters may have nurtured about finding the tribunal a pliant ally. From that point on it became clear that the services which the High Court could provide to the sugar planters would be more than balanced by the potential threat it presented to the dominance of the planters.

The presence of the Relação in Bahia did facilitate some matters for the planters. Disputes between equals could now be settled at less cost and in less time.... Land survey and demarcation was another service which the tribunal provided. Statute required that such surveys be performed by a *letrado*, and throughout the history of the Relação the desembargadores often performed this task. This service was a mixed blessing for the planters, however. On one hand, water and property rights were firmly established, but in the Recõncavo, where much of the land had been acquired without formal title, such surveys threatened the status quo in which the planters had a vested interest. The elimination of fraud, the enforcement of regulatory legislation, and the ordering of an unruly society in which personal power had formerly settled most disputes all made the Relação a potential threat to the sugar planter elite....

Whatever the failings of legal training as preparation for the tasks of government, the Coimbra experience produced a number of effects which gave the Portuguese bureaucracy its distinctive character. First, since all the magistrates had to secure a law degree at Coimbra, no matter what their social origin or place of birth, the university served as a centralizing agent. Attempts to establish other universities in the empire, such as that made in 1675 to turn the Jesuit College of Bahia into a university, were unsuccessful. The result was a system of bureaucratic preparation centered on the metropolis and thus more subject to royal control. Second, the common university experience created conditions among the personnel of the magistracy and among the lawyers which were counterproductive in terms of bureaucratic aims but which facilitated the rise of a *letrado* class. Friendships and clientage resulted from the shared experience of Coimbra, so that there was often little social distance between the bar and the bench. This fact may also help to explain the relative ineffectiveness of *residencias* which investigated judicial behavior, since these were generally carried out by other magistrates....

Although the magistracy had developed as a corps of professional bureaucrats with specific functions within the political structure, the magistrates had also, over the course of time, sought to turn their position into the basis of social status. Having emerged under royal tutelage as a counter-weight to traditional groups like the titled nobility, the crown judges began to demand the privileges, symbols, and recognition of the very groups whose power they had most inhibited. Portugal shared this historical process with other nations in western Europe, and as in Prussia and France the magisterial bureaucrats did not become the implacable enemies of the aristocracy, but instead sought to penetrate its ranks. Two tendencies in this process can be identified. First, the magistrates justified their social ascendancy by developing a theoretical basis of their own nobility.... By the eighteenth century, jurists argued that the study of law by itself literally ennobled an individual, and that by extension all judges should be considered the equals of the landed and military nobility....

But in the Portuguese empire the magistracy did not become a *noblesse de la robe*, an identifiable nobility based on office and function. Individual magistrates might be, and often were, integrated into the traditional nobility by marriage, or they might achieve this position through the action of the crown; but a magisterial class, either in competition with or as an adjunct of the landed and military aristocracy never developed as an autonomous entity with independent class goals beyond those prescribed by the crown.

NOTES AND QUESTIONS

1. Hernán Cortés studied law at the University of Salamanca in Spain for two years, after which he sailed for the island of Hispaniola. There he worked as a farmer until he was appointed to head an expedition to help establish a colony on the American mainland.

2. Is it surprising to you that the Spanish conquistadores with their small numbers could defeat the Aztecs and Incas? How would you explain it?

3. The principal task of the judiciaries in colonial America was to promote the crown's law and policy. What factors made this objective difficult to achieve? Can these factors be grouped under the following categories:

(1) legal rules;
(2) legal structures;
(3) legal processes;
(4) legal culture; and
(5) legal penetration.

4. Try to imagine the interests of the following groups in colonial America: the crown; the church; conquistadores; and Indians. How were these groups served by the legal framework that developed?

5. Notice that Colin MacLachlan does not concern himself with the civil jurisdiction of the courts or with the private ordering function of the legal system (e.g., wills, contracts, business and commerce, the recordation of property interests). What are some of the differences that he describes between Spanish law in colonial Mexico and Spanish law in Spain? Are any of these differences analogous to the variations between law in the eastern United States and law in the western United States in the first half of the 19th century? The law in France and the law in Algeria before World War II?

6. Why were Indians so litigious in colonial Peru? Did their use of the *audiencia* system, according to Steve Stern, ultimately better or worsen their situation? Do you agree with Stern?

7. Lawyers and judges were important agents of the Portuguese crown in Brazil. How was their loyalty and effectiveness promoted? Was the crown successful in its efforts?

8. THE ACCOMMODATION OF SPANISH AND INDIAN LAW

WOODROW BORAH, JUSTICE BY INSURANCE: THE GENERAL INDIAN COURT OF COLONIAL MEXICO AND THE LEGAL AIDES OF THE HALF-*REAL* 27-32, 34-35, 38-40 (1983)

During the sixteenth century, a long series of discussions and experiments attempted to settle the relations of the dominant and the subjugated communities. From perhaps 1511 on, some members of the royal bureaucracy, sincerely disturbed by the destruction of the Indian population in the Antilles and on the mainland, initiated discussions aimed at finding less murderous systems of exploitation....

The discussions were characterized by almost innumerable variations of opinion and proposal, but in general three schools of thought emerged. One, led eloquently by Francisco de Vitoria, held that the Indians, having developed their own society, were entitled to their own institutions and law. Should they come under the rule of a foreign sovereign (like the Spanish king), he was bound to uphold and defend native institutions and laws and the rights of existing nobles and chiefs, since he served as the native prince. The most that might be conceded as imposed change was the minimum necessary for extirpating idolatry and introducing Christianity. Such views, which required undoing a profitable occupation imposed by conquest, met a frigid reception from crown and settlers.

Diametrically opposed to the Vitoria school, other men advanced the idea of one society. That meant sweeping assimilation of the Indians to Castilian institutions, laws, and procedures. Castilian law was to be applied to the Indians in full rigor. Their customs and institutions were to be assimilated to Christian and European ones without restriction or special accommodation. Although the adherents of this view never developed the eloquence in exposition or defense of their position that flowed from the pens and teaching of the upholders of the other schools of thought, their position had very real strength, for it accorded best with the interests of the crown and the settlers. Most crown jurists held this view. Men trained in law (*letrados*), they were developing a unitary legal system which would replace feudal diversity with a uniform royal administration. In deciding questions affecting the Indians, they tended to apply Castilian procedure and law....

The third school of thought might be called one of two republics. Recognizing that the Spanish were in America to stay, it urged that the Indians and Spaniards be organized into two separate commonwealths, each with its own laws, customs, and system of government. This was the position of Alonso de Zorita, judge of the Audiencia of Mexico, although he was exceptional among his colleagues in holding these views. Jerónimo de Mendieta, one of the foremost proponents of this position, held that the Spaniards were so corrupt and given to vice that the Indians should be kept as isolated as possible. Their institutions and law should be modified to conform to Christianity and to ensure proper governance, but the Indians should retain as much as possible of the old or be moved to a new [system] that would be different from the world of the Spaniards. He went so far as to urge that the Indian commonwealth be so completely separate that it would be linked with the Spanish only by being subject to the same viceroy. In general, the missionaries held to some form of these views and attempted to keep the two communities apart, even to the extent of further propagating the use of Nahuatl as a lingua franca among the various Indian linguistic groups, rather than favoring Spanish.

Interestingly enough, the proponents of the two-republics position proceeded from contradictory views of the nature of the Indians. Most of the missionaries, including Mendieta, held that the natives were childlike in their understanding and, although industrious, were weak-willed, easily led astray whenever error was presented to them. They lacked the will power and physical force to resist anyone, especially Spaniards who wished to abuse them, seize their goods and women, or force them into harmful or sinful behavior. Only through rigid separation from the Europeans could the Indians be saved from corruption in their ways and physical extinction. Others, such as Vasco de Quiroga and Las Casas, took the opposite view that the Indians were able, civilized people, who had governed themselves well except in matters of religion and were fully able to understand the way of civilized polity. The Indians should be kept separate from the Spaniards because under proper guidance there lay in them the possibility of a better society than the European....

Official royal policy steered an ambiguous course among all schools. It wavered between the theory of the two republics and that of one society, but occasionally showed some slight adherence to that led by Vitoria. To a considerable extent, the difficulty of detecting clear lines in royal policy arises because there were few explicit formulations of it. The crown proceeded by decisions on specific cases and problems as they arose, the decisions setting a precedent for the future and for other regions of America....

In the course of the sixteenth century, although a thorough-going decision was never reached, the crown issued a number of rules which tended to keep the two racial communities separate. Encomenderos were forbidden to settle in their Indian towns. Indeed, any Spaniards, Negroes, and mixed-bloods were forbidden to settle in such towns. The ordinances were so stringent that Spanish bachelors and merchants, both of whom were regarded as especially prone to teach the natives bad habits or to abuse them, were permitted to tarry only three days in an Indian town, even if they were there on proper business. Furthermore, the royal government tried to keep Indians and Spaniards in separate settlements even when the needs of the Spanish required that Indians live near them in order to be available for service....

In practice, of course, the policy of separation proved unworkable, since the needs of the Spanish for tribute and labor meant very substantial, continuing contact between them and the Indians — so that, even if the two groups remained in separate settlements, there could be no real isolation. Actually there was very considerable intermingling, since numbers of Spaniards took up residence in Indian towns in order to establish businesses and care for properties, at the same time that large numbers of Indians were drawn into Spanish households as permanent or semi-permanent workers....

In consequence, the royal program for organizing Indian society in northern Mesoamerica, as it developed during the course of the sixteenth century, contained contradictory elements. On the one hand, the crown officially accepted the idea of preserving Indian organization and custom. The first comprehensive regulations for the guidance of provincial governors in New Spain, issued in 1530, expressly [so] stated.... The injunction was confirmed in the New Laws of 1542....

On the other hand, whatever the theory or rhetorical justification, and despite all palliative measures, the imposition of Spanish rule meant sweeping change for the natives, for the Castilian crown and its European subjects responded to a series of imperatives inherent in the imposition of alien sovereignty and an alien religion as well as the insertion of an alien upper class. In some instances, Spanish officials mistakenly considered that they were continuing the custom of the time of Montezuma; in other instances, they held that the Indians were being brought to proper rational and Christian practice. At all times the crown had to keep what its subjects had conquered. If it was unthinkable that the Spanish permit continued practice of idolatry and human sacrifice or continued existence of the heathen religious hierarchies, it was equally unthinkable that the Castilian crown and its officials not replace the old native political superstructures and their administrative hierarchies. In any case, religious and political functions were so deeply intertwined that extirpating the one meant a wrenching effect upon the other. So there disappeared the imperial political structures of Tenochtitlán and its allies in the Triple Alliance, of the Zapotec kingdoms, and of the Tarascan state, even though the crown and its officials accepted the policy of preserving the status of pre-conquest chieftains. The chieftains were forbidden to use the title lord or natural lord, which would have implied a challenge to the legitimacy of Spanish rule. Instead, they were given the title caciques and the status of nobles. Lesser members of the Indian upper classes became *principales*, with the status of lesser nobles....

Further, the Spanish — probably without malice, but also without genuine understanding — imposed a number of their own conceptions in important aspects of Indian life. They were strongly influenced by sixteenth-century European beliefs in natural law and in a universal substratum of civilized custom to which all peoples might properly be held. Among these conceptions were ... the nature of ownership and use of land, the nature of slavery, and proper administration and relief within it.... Differences in conceptions of ownership and use of land ... brought substantial change. For the Indians, land was essentially a means of production, held by the community or clan and allocated to support certain offices or functions. Tenure was fundamentally conditional and subject always to the requirement of use. Indian conceptions of the nature of land-holding most closely approximated those of the feudal linkage of land tenure to service or office. It is unlikely that aboriginal Indian society had any conception of the owning of land in the sense of Roman law, that a man could be the master of land which was his to allow to remain idle, destroy, or till as he chose, subject only to the right of the sovereign to tax or take for public use on due compensation.

The Spanish, on the other hand, not only were moving to the conception of land-ownership embodied in the Roman or Civil Law, but further declared that all land not actually occupied by Indians or used by them was vacant and thus royal domain available for grant or purchase. For the Spanish, land was not merely a means of production; ownership of far larger stretches of it than the owner could make use of directly or through tenants was a visible sign of prestige in the community and one of the few safe forms of investment. The results were a vast series of conflicts between Spanish and natives, and far-reaching readjustments within the Indian towns as their more powerful and more alert members strove to assert and extend ownership in Spanish fashion, usually at the expense of the peasantry and other members of the pre-Conquest upper class.

Slavery is another illustration of the way in which almost unwitting imposition of a Spanish conception brought sweeping change, so that a fairly benign native institution became a harsh and destructive form of exploitation. Slavery was widely known among the pre-Conquest Indians of northern Mesoamerica. It seems, in general, to have been a mild affair which entitled the owner of the slave to service for life, but left the slave very substantial rights. The latter, for example, could hold property and himself own slaves. Families might agree to provide a slave, but shift the role among members. The only truly harsh aspect of aboriginal slavery was the selection of some slaves, upon repeated resale, for fattening and eventual sacrifice and eating; but this affected only a very small percentage of the total. Under Spanish law, on the other hand, slaves had far fewer rights. They were civilly dead, chattels who might be worked like domestic animals and transported and sold like any other form of merchandise.

The initial Spanish equation of slavery under Indian custom with slavery under Castilian and Civil Law meant that Indian slaves could be subjected to merciless exploitation. Enterprising Spaniards acquired Indian slaves by purchase, levy on tributary villages, or straight kidnapping, and worked them to death in mines or shipped them for sale to new and very different lands and climates, where they soon died.... There was for a time serious danger that the experience of the Antilles would be repeated on the mainland, through the slave trade, until the danger was averted by royal legislation. Finally put into effect in the 1550s, it abolished Indian slavery save for captives taken on the northern frontier.

A third Spanish conception, which had especially far-reaching consequences, was that of appeal against the acts or decisions of judicial and administrative officials; indeed, that any person, however high his status, including the monarch himself through his agents, could be brought into court. It is unlikely that pre-Conquest Indian society had this concept except in highly restricted and attenuated form. For the Spanish, on the other hand, the idea of appeal and accountability was part of the very fabric of the state. Castilian law and procedure made elaborate provision for appeals in judicial cases, for delaying the actions of executive officials until they could be reviewed either by a superior or by a court, and for formal accounting for an official's acts after his term of office. Today some may object that the result often was long delay and even near-paralysis, with a consequence of substantial injustice, but there can be no doubt that behind the conception lay a concern for orderly and just administration. It was unthinkable to the crown bureaucracy that a civilized and Christian state should deny the right of appeal to any subject. Furthermore, keeping open the channels for appeals greatly increased the chance that the royal government could examine the acts of its officials and implant a centralized, uniform administration.

So the Indians of New Spain, after enduring the shocking losses and disruption of the first years of conquest, found that once a relatively orderly royal administration began under the Second Audiencia in 1531, they could haul any official into court and challenge his decisions; that any grant of land could be disputed; that boundaries and political arrangements could be challenged; and that any private person or corporate entity could be held to redress for damage done or be forestalled through petition for an order of *amparo*. They found very quickly, furthermore, that any decision once rendered could be appealed up the long line of reviews provided by Castilian law. The conquerors thus placed a potent weapon at the disposal of the conquered, one that might be used against them as well as the subjected. Fear of direct, extralegal reprisal, and the reluctance of Spanish judges and officials to rule against fellow Spaniards, undoubtedly limited its use against Europeans, especially those of superior status, but the Indians made very great use of their right.

Within the Indian community, litigation before Spanish courts and petitions for administrative review and protection became the principal means of carrying on the long series of disputes unleashed by the Conquest over land, status, and virtually all other relationships. The conquerors were amazed that subjects so meek showed such ferocity and tenacity in litigation.

9. INDIAN CASES IN THE ROYAL COURTS OF MEXICO

WOODROW BORAH, JUSTICE BY INSURANCE: THE GENERAL INDIAN COURT OF COLONIAL MEXICO AND THE LEGAL AIDES OF THE HALF-*REAL* 44-51, 53-54 (1983)

Indian cases which poured into the Spanish courts and the audience chambers of administrators fell into two primary categories: Church and royal. Church cases might involve civil litigation or criminal offenses under ecclesiastical law, or dispensations and permissions under that law. Included were such matters as tithes, marriage, and orthodoxy of belief and religious practice. All fell within the jurisdiction of Church tribunals and administrators, who functioned under Church rules of procedure and canon and diocesan law in a gradation of levels of jurisdiction beginning with the parish and extending through the diocese, with a theoretical but rarely used right of appeal to the Rota in Rome. Judges, lawyers, notaries, and secretaries qualified under canon law and held Church appointment. Recourse to the royal jurisdiction was possible when the Church authorities appealed for the support of the *brazo secular* to enforce or execute its decisions, or when a party objected to Church jurisdiction through *recurso de fuerza*, a plea before the audiencia that rights guaranteed by royal law were being abridged....

Royal cases fell within three basic groups: civil, criminal, and administrative, each with different laws and procedures. Involved in civil cases were the relations of people with each other and questions of personal status, essentially disputes in which the state acted as arbiter between or among subjects.... They were the differences of towns with each other over lands, water, and woods (in other words, boundary disputes) and the fight of dependent towns to free themselves from their *cabeceras*, or head towns. Boundary disputes became matters of community prestige and were carried on at heavy cost, which in many, perhaps most, instances far exceeded the total value of the land or water at issue. The relations of *sujeto* and cabecera also involved matters of prestige and further substantial financial and social advantages, for the cabecera collected tributes, administered justice, and forced the natives of its dependencies to contribute in money, goods, and labor for community enterprises, which were centered in the head town and benefited its inhabitants far more than those of the dependencies.

These two kinds of disputes were rife long before the coming of the Spaniards, but the reshuffling of relationships after the Conquest afforded a chance to demand a more favorable settlement. When the Second Audiencia attempted to insure that all of the conquered had their day in court, it opened the floodgates. The audiencia probably had little choice, since the disputes, if left unsettled or not given more peaceful outlet in litigation, frequently threatened to lead to riot and civil war....

Another major subcategory of civil suit among Indians involved inheritance, especially inheritance of the property and rights of caciques. While the number of such cases was far less than those involving towns, all such suits, like those of towns, had to be brought before the Spanish courts, both because of the assimilation of the caciques to Spanish noble status and the value of the lands and privileges in dispute. Aboriginal custom in succession varied from region to region and even within regions, but was seldom strictly patrilineal. In the Valley of Mexico, inheritance more frequently moved through brothers before entering the next generation, with an element of election among a group of potential heirs....

Although these customs did differ from Spanish law, there is nothing in them contrary to natural law or Christian doctrine. Nevertheless, as disputes over succession were brought to Spanish judges for decision, the judges began to apply Spanish ideas of rights in inheritance, holding that the cacicazgo must go to the oldest son or, in default of a son, to the nearest heir by Castilian rules. Indian custom was refused validity as contrary to reason....

Many of the civil suits were between Indians and Spaniards — for suits were one of the few means by which Indian towns and caciques and commoners could defend their possessions from the European population settling among them. Under the prevailing rule, suits of Indians against Spaniards had to be brought in Spanish courts; the legal quality of towns and caciques equally brought cases by Spaniards against them into Spanish courts. A substantial proportion of the suits arose over land, which the Spanish acquired in one or more of three ways. (1) They might receive title to vacant land by royal grant. Such grants were always subject to revocation or modification if they prejudiced the interests of a third party. Initially the proceedings took place under administrative law; but the grant, if made despite protest, could be challenged before the Spanish courts. (2) In many instances, the Spanish simply took lands they wanted. When they dared, the Indians sued for restitution or payment. Thus, upon the death of Hernán Cortés, many of the Indian towns within his marquisate instituted suit for such seizures and recovered judgment. (3) A third method by which Spaniards might acquire Indian lands was purchase or rental, usually an amicable arrangement without suit. But this method too meant a great deal of business before the Spanish justices, since the crown very early insisted that any such purchases or rentals must be made under judicial supervision....

In addition to disputes over ownership of land, Spanish agriculture led to a long series of disputes over the extent to which Spanish-owned livestock might graze upon Indian land. Under Castilian custom, once the crop was harvested the stubble became common pasture which might be grazed by any livestock, however much towns and individual proprietors objected. Most of the livestock wandered loose with insufficient guard the year around, being rounded up in an annual drive for branding and slaughter. Inevitably, many Spaniards let their livestock invade the Indian villages before crops were harvested....

Yet another major category of civil dispute between Indians and Spaniards arose from the demand of the Spanish community for labor: Indian labor. In the first decades of the sixteenth century, many of the suits concerned demands by Indians held as slaves that they be recognized as free. After the virtual abolition of Indian slavery, the mass of business before the courts involved the attempts of the European community to bind its Indian laborers through the use of debt. The Indians were advanced money, to be repaid by service, the practicc being that the Indians were always kept in debt and hence remained bound for service. Petitions by Spaniards demanding that Indians be turned over to them for working off debt, and the counterbalancing petitions of Indians that they be freed, on the grounds that they either did not owe money or long ago had worked off the debt, became a standard part of the business before Spanish colonial justices....

A second major group of Indian cases within the royal jurisdiction dealt with criminal offenses. From the first the crown planned to take jurisdiction, for its long-term policy in Spain as in America was to bring to royal judges all decisions of death or mutilation. Judgment or review in such cases was expressly reserved to the audiencia. Royal judges thus found themselves forced to deal with a large number of Indian offenses against native custom. They had to decide whether to honor the custom or disallow it as contrary to reason or Christian precept. More importantly, infractions of custom and statute by Indians in and around Spanish settlements, which were regarded as the special preserve of Spanish judges, whether local or royal, gave rise to a vast number of criminal charges. Many offenses occurred as infractions of laws and ordinances which were new to the natives, or covered actions that under their custom were not improper. Many others occurred in the general weakening of Indian custom after the Conquest, with the appearance of the usual patterns of behavior of subject races. However virtuous and well-behaved the Indians may have been in their relations with each other and the state power before the Conquest, they astonished their conquerors by their proneness to theft, assault, homicide, rape, riot, drunkenness, and a host of other transgressions, most of which called for infliction of the more gory penalties of Castilian law.... With royal consent, the audiencia during the 1530s adopted a policy of branding and selling as slaves Indians convicted of crimes that otherwise would have been punished by torture, mutilation, service in the galleys, or death.

This solution became impossible in the 1540s when the New Laws abolished Indian slavery. The audiencia again laid the problem before the crown, pointing out that the full rigor of the laws could not be enforced against the Indians, who were weak people and committed many crimes.... In 1555 the crown gave way, although it did pay respect to the New Laws by stipulating that no Indian might be condemned to service for life.

Thereafter sale of service became standard throughout the colony as punishment for serious offenses by Indians. The practice rapidly became a profitable source of labor for the Spanish community, so that justices soon began to sell Indians for offenses which should not have been punished so severely, or even delivered them over without formality of trial as a substitute for imprisonment pending hearing. Once turned over to a Spaniard for whatever reason, an Indian rarely regained his freedom....

A third major group of Indian cases within royal jurisdiction was those calling for administrative decision and remedy. Very often they involved a series of proceedings that at viceregal level were not easily distinguishable from judicial process, except that the final order issued as an administrative decree rather than as a judicial writ. The number of Indian cases advanced for administrative determination may well have exceeded all other kinds of Indian suits and petitions, for most of the new relationships arising from the Conquest called for executive determination, which the crown and its agents could not forego without surrendering control of the new territories.

Because of the bewildering variety, only the more important kinds can be indicated. I have mentioned already that grants of land by the crown automatically meant validating proceedings to insure that the interests of third parties were not adversely affected. Institution of the encomienda and royal tribute meant a long series of administrative hearings and petitions for virtually each town; for, whether held in encomienda or by the crown, its tribute was assessed at fairly frequent intervals, very often with a good deal of dispute and appeal. Furthermore, all exactions by encomenderos or corregidores in excess of the schedule set and all other kinds of abuse, if the Indians dared object, meant petitions for redress to the executive. Similarly, the reduction of Indian government and the caciques to a fairly uniform pattern characterized by annual elections and written schedules of payments meant executive inspection to arrive at the proper assessment, continuing supervision to prevent abuse and extortion, demands for reassessment either by the peasants or by the officials and caciques, and annual confirmation of elections....

Two forms of administrative intervention became especially important in Indian affairs and proved of considerable effect. One, the colonial version of the present-day writ of amparo, was an order to the appropriate officials that the petitioner be protected in the possession of land or the exercise of some function which he feared might be unjustly disputed or forbidden. The writ was especially effective in quieting title to lands held by Indians. The second form of intervention was a writ to an official to carry out his duty. For example, an Indian who could not get his complaint or suit heard by the local official would petition the viceroy for an order compelling a hearing....

Finally, a great many Indian petitions concerned release from Spanish restrictive legislation. To insure control of the native population, the viceroys and audiencia imposed a number of prohibitions. For example, Indians might not own firearms, swords, or daggers; they might not ride horses, nor might they wear European dress. Within a few years, caciques, governors of towns, and many principales were permitted exemption from these restrictions if they petitioned for special license. Within a few decades, as European customs, agriculture, and industry spread among the Indians, there was sound reason for granting many more licenses to Indian nobles, merchants, and commoners, since explicit or unwritten restrictions which impeded their living and working in the new ways threatened to curtail a production of goods and services which the Spanish community itself needed. The raising of livestock by natives, for example, usually was authorized by special license, as was engaging in European crafts. In these instances, the licenses avoided possible difficulties with local officials rather than exempted [them] from specific prohibitions. Petitions for special licenses thus became another substantial category of Indian business before the viceroy.

The total amount of business represented by Indian cases under civil and criminal law and petitions for administrative relief or remedy was clearly enormous and left untouched few of the more important aspects of Indian life. As already indicated, it was one of the principal instruments of the upheaval that took place within native society after the Conquest. Further, the mass of Indian litigation and petitions served to nullify the recognition of native custom by the crown in the regulations for provincial governors of 1530 and in the New Laws. Despite continuing royal injunctions validating Indian usage, Castilian procedure and law became the basis for handling Indian suits and complaints in royal courts and administration. Inevitably the European ways moved downward into native society, displacing the older aboriginal ones.

TEXCOCAN VILLAGES v. HACIENDA LA BLANCA

Audiencia of Mexico City
(1744 to 1757)

[This case is described in an article by P.E.B. Coy appearing in the Journal of Legal History, which is excerpted below.]

P.E.B. COY, JUSTICE FOR THE INDIAN IN EIGHTEENTH CENTURY MEXICO, 12 American Journal of Legal History 41, 43-46, 49 (1968)

The particular cases ... were selected because they related to a group of irrigating villages in the municipality of Texcoco.... The municipality lay, and still lies, on the eastern slopes of the highland Valley of Mexico and was separated from the metropolis of Mexico City by the lake of Texcoco. The roads joining the two urban centres ran north and south about the lake and were seven leagues and eight leagues long respectively. In the eighteenth century the township of Texcoco was separated from the irrigating villages under its supervision by a ring of estates. These *haciendas* were owned either by corporations, like the Jesuits' Hacienda de Chapingo (now the national agricultural college), or by individuals, like the Molino de Flores (now a public park for week-end picnics). Three quite different groups were therefore competing for the natural resources of a strip of gently sloping land about five miles wide: the townsfolk of Texcoco, the cattle-estate owners and the crop-growing villagers.

The Indian villagers were not altogether at the mercy of the Spanish estate-owners, for the old Indian kingdom, of which Texcoco town had been the capital, was now land held by the crown of Spain, not land entrusted to private individuals, and was ruled by an *Alcalde Mayor*. The villagers learned, during the course of three collective representations to the Royal Audience in Mexico City, that they might expect a sympathetic hearing. Thus in 1667 the villagers alone were able to obtain enforcement of the old royal decree which prohibited Negroes, Mulattoes and Mestizos from living in Indian villages.

The same villages, well supported by both Spanish and Mestizo witnesses from the town, fought a protracted case before the Audience, from 1744 to 1757, against a local hacienda-owner and his tenants over wood-cutting rights. This second case began on the 7th August 1744, when the legal representative of the Indian villages between Texcoco and the mountains lodged a complaint with the Audience in Mexico City. He alleged that the owner of the hacienda called La Blanca was allowing his cattle to stray into the corn patches of the villages and, furthermore, was preventing the villagers from collecting firewood from a hill which had belonged to them from time immemorial. Evidence was also given that the sale of charcoal from the wood gathered had been the only means whereby the villagers had been able to pay their tribute to the Crown. If their ability to cut wood were curtailed, the tribute would not be forthcoming. The case dragged on across a decade and through 284 folios of manuscript; both sides brought forward a stream of witnesses to justify their opposing claims.

The 1744 case, because of its length, discloses a number of situations and legal institutions. The situations illustrate the special problems of the social environment within which the colonial government attempted to operate. The legal institutions indicate the manner in which the colonial government tried to ensure if not an equal measure of justice for all, then at least sufficient of it to prevent grievance sharpening into revolt.

A few of the situations disclosed merely confirm some of the characteristic features of Mexican colonial society which are already well-known: the fact that it was possible for a rural estate to be owned by a priest residing in Mexico City; the fact that the powerful Audience in Mexico City might extend its protection to groups of Indians without being able to compel the good behaviour of the adjacent hacienda-owners. Some of the situations which may be inferred from the testimony in the manuscripts may only have had local historical interest: the fact that one witness, only fifty-four years old, was personally acquainted with the previous five owners of the hacienda in question — implying a very rapid turnover in ownership, something quite contrary to the classical concept of the laboriously amassed estate, entailed so as to remain in the possession of the same lineage for centuries; the fact that witnesses were prepared to give evidence across ethnic barriers — some Spanish citizens of Texcoco supported the Indians' case, whilst at least one Indian, the governor of the neighboring village of Tepetlaoztoc, gave evidence for the hacienda-owner.

The most constructive interest, however, is afforded by the description of the ritual which gave substance to the legal decision to "protect the Indians." The ceremony of *Amparo de los Naturales* is interesting twice over: it is redolent of the sort of legalism to be found in the sixteenth century *Requerimiento*, the necessary ritual prelude to the waging of a just war; it is, moreover, a vestige of mediaeval symbolism which could still perform a useful function in the eighteenth century. In the case of the Texcocan villages versus the hacienda La Blanca in 1744, the Royal Audience was persuaded that a *prima facie* case had been made out against the hacienda-owner and gave protection to the Indians, and declared that his cattle were not to be allowed to stray into their corn patches, indeed, that cattle were not allowed within one and a half leagues of Indian reductions. Cattle should, moreover, have a herder to prevent them from straying and, pronounced the Audience, the Indians might kill any cattle found in their corn patches without penalty.

Once the supreme court had thus declared its especial protection of a specific group of Indians, a physical manifestation of the import of the legal decision followed as a matter of course. Representatives of both the contending parties assembled on the wooded slopes under dispute, together with all the executive authorities of the area. The latter included the Lieutenant of the Alcalde Mayor of Texcoco, the Indian Governor, the two Judges of the two groups of villages concerned and the "Sergeant Major" of Texcoco. In the presence of these the official interpreter requested the senior police officer present (the Lieutenant of the *Alguacil Mayor*) to protect the natives in the lawful execution of their right to cut wood in the area. (The fact that the ritual request was in a language readily intelligible to the Indians, unlike what must usually have occurred in the case of the Requerimiento, would seem to disclose a more compromising attitude on the part of the eighteenth-century authorities.) The Indians were then invited to exercise their right, under the eyes of the assembled company, and the hacienda manager was required to acknowledge, on the spot, that he had been served with the Audience's fiat. A similar statement was extracted from the hacienda owner himself, a few days later: he had (conveniently?) been away from his estate at the time of the ceremony.

The 1744 case between the Texcocan villages and the hacienda La Blanca had been initially about the right to cut wood but eventually about the right to water. This was consistent with both Spanish and Indian land tenure systems: the common lands of villages might provide pasturage, water, firewood, beekeeping and slaughtering facilities to the members of their communities; if the ownership of land conferred wood-gathering rights it also conferred rights to the water which flowed through the land. If the ownership of the hill was in dispute between two adjacent users of its facilities, it was easier to test ownership in the courts by challenging the collection of firewood than by challenging the use of its water: the waters arising from a hill could be used by leaving a sluice-gate open many miles from the hill with the beneficiary asleep in his bed; for the collection of firewood the beneficiary, or his agents, needed to be on the spot and usually in daylight....

The series of cases involving a small corner of eighteenth century Mexico discloses a regular pattern of relationships between three major strata of colonial society: the Spanish administration; Spanish and *criollo* property-owners; and the Indian population in town and village. Negative relationships involving antipathy and friction between adjacent strata in Texcocan colonial society were balanced by the impression that alternate strata seemed to have had a common aim: the maintenance of existing arrangements regarding the tenure and usufruct of land, based on traditional usages and the directives of the Crown. Between these two corporative strata comprising bureaucrats and Indians were wedged uncomfortably the individualistic, restless exploiters of land. Faced with the choice of giving justice to the Indians or acceding to the landowners' increasing demands, the vice-regal administration seems to have favoured justice for the Indians, in one small corner of Mexico at least. Whilst, according to modern standards, this may have been an admirable choice, it can hardly be calculated to have endeared the administration to the *criollo* landowners. The path of honour does not always lead to success and, in this case, may be considered to have led straight to 1821 and political rebellion.

10. THE GENERAL INDIAN COURT

WOODROW BORAH, JUSTICE BY INSURANCE: THE GENERAL INDIAN COURT OF COLONIAL MEXICO AND THE LEGAL AIDES OF THE HALF-*REAL* 79, 120-21, 125-30, 144-47, 187, 189-90 (1983)

A. *Establishment of the Court*

By the 1580s, the efforts of the crown and its administrators in New Spain to ease introduction of the Indians into Spanish law and legal procedures clearly had failed. The Indians still lacked access to relatively simple, inexpensive, quick and effective legal remedies. Awareness of this failure by the clergy and many of the higher officials in the royal bureaucracy in both the colony and the Peninsula led in the last years of the sixteenth century to renewed efforts at an effective solution. During these years the investigations and concern of the imperial government bore fruit in a number of reforms for easing the burden on the Indians in New Spain and the rest of Spanish America, notably in the great labor measures embodied in the *reales cédulas* of 1601 and 1609. In the Audiencia of Mexico, they also resulted in establishment of the General Indian Court and the special Indian agents of the half-real....

The General Indian Court, an integral unit of the Spanish colonial government in central Mexico from 1592 until its abolition in 1820, functioned for more than two centuries.... Under the royal cédulas that established the court and defined its competence, it had alternate but not exclusive jurisdiction in first instance in suits of Indians with each other and in those of Spaniards against Indians. Suits of Indians against Spaniards, the major avenue of complaint seeking relief, were specifically removed from the competence of the court; but under colonial Mexican practice since the time of Viceroy Mendoza, they could be heard by the viceroy as petitions for administrative remedy. The court further had alternate but not exclusive jurisdiction in criminal cases against Indians....

Let us turn now to the nature or mix of business that came before the viceroy sitting in audience as the General Indian Court: in short, what kinds of cases and in what proportions?...

All observers alive in the years the court existed were agreed that the largest proportion of cases and complaints concerned land, in the form of disputes over ownership, questions of grants, petitions for amparo (writs granting formal government protection in possession), sale and rental, or division among heirs....

Table 4.2

Kinds of Cases Before the General Indian Court, Declarations of August-September 1784

Land and easements on land	32%
Other property	6
Inheritance	3
Licenses affecting land	2
Subtotal	43%
Complaints against local Spanish officials	26%
Complaints against priests	1
Labor: Indians vs. Spaniards	12
Complaints arising from town government	5
Private Indian suits (not over land)	5
Money (not peonage)	1
Extension of time on debts	2
Family quarrels and offenses	1
Miscellaneous	3
Not stated	2
Total (due to rounding)	101%

The next-largest category might be complaints against local Spanish officials, to which might be added those against priests. Other categories of relative importance were relations with Spaniards other than in disputes over land (questions of debt, service, and treatment as workers), and conflicts arising over relations within Indian towns, i.e., disputes over elections, government, mistreatment and extortion by officials, or refusal of respect or obedience by commoners.

B. *A Selection of Case Abstracts*

1. *Land and Property Rights*

Complaints and disputes over land and property rights were at all times the largest category. Indian villages would fight each other or hacendados for decades and even centuries over boundaries, frequently spending in the suits far more than the value of the land in dispute. Contrary to a widely held current opinion, Indian villages fought more with each other in these suits than with Spaniards.

a. *Disputes in General*

....

2. March 6, 1634, Mexico City. Ixtlán, province of Antequera, vs. Calpulalpan and two of its sujetos, a long suit over land and status. Ixtlán claims that the two villages are tenants on its land and exhibits the latest version of the agreement of rental, dated September 11, 1629. The two villages, declaring themselves sujetos of Calpulalpan, province of Ixtepeji, claim that the agreement is fraudulent, entered into in order to obtain water. Each side sues in different courts, Ixtlán in the General Indian Court. The viceroy orders the alcalde mayor of Antequera to investigate with personal inspection of the lands and of Indian pictographic records. On May 15, 1631, the alcalde mayor hears the case, with inspection of the agreement transcribed and translated from Zapotec in a sworn version. He reports that the lands are Ixtlán's. On August 2, 1632, the viceroy decides in favor of Ixtlán, the other side being allowed thirty days to comply or appeal. This decision is to be enforced even if contrary judgment has been rendered elsewhere.

Calpulalpan and its two sujetos manage to get the case reopened; the alcalde mayor of the Antequera is instructed to hold new hearings and to suspend criminal proceedings for failure to comply with the previous decision. In the new hearing, Ixtlán presents two viceregal decrees of August 1632 in its favor. Again the alcalde mayor recommends judgment for Ixtlán, but with the proviso that Indians of the cabecera of Calpulalpan may enter the lands without wand of justice for collection of tribute. He negotiates a new agreement of rental, one clause of which sets a fine of 500/ [silver pesos] for reviving the suit, half for the other party and half for the crown, plus payment of all costs. In his report to the viceroy, May 20, 1633, he includes all papers, and comments that suits are being brought in a number of courts besides the General Indian Court and both sides are incurring heavy expense. (The rent asked by Ixtlán was 6/ a year.)

Calpulalpan again asks that the case be reopened, on the ground that the agreement has been signed by people not authorized to act for the town and the two sujetos and that the alcalde mayor is prejudiced. The viceroy appoints the corregidor of Tecocuilco as special judge to investigate. All parties then give testimony before him, Calpulalpan and its two sujetos repeating their plea that the agreement of May 1633 is void and the alcalde mayor prejudiced. On January 5, 1634, the corregidor renders his opinion that the lands are clearly Ixtlán's. On February 16 the assessor of the General Indian Court recommends a decision in favor of Ixtlán on the basis of the corregidor's report, and on March 6, 1634, the viceroy signs the formal judgment as recommended. All judges and justices elsewhere are enjoined to observe the final sentence. The two sujetos are to pay 6/ a year rent, to help maintain the church of Ixtlán, and to show up with flowers and festive arches for the feast of St. Thomas, patron saint of Ixtlán.

This case is an excellent example of the tenacity of Indian litigation, especially in land disputes in Oaxaca. The suits were carried on simultaneously in various jurisdictions, repeatedly renewed, and piled up costs far in excess of the value of whatever was in dispute. In this case, legal costs and the expense of sending delegations to Mexico City, Antequera, and other towns must have run to hundreds, perhaps thousands of pesos, as against a rental of 6/ a year and minimal acts of dependence....

b. *Amparo*

Since the Constitution of 1857, Mexicans have pointed with pride, as a great advance in the assurance of human rights, to the writ of amparo: the granting of protection in some right that is likely to be threatened, or the guarantee of existing dimensions of that right. Actually, as one Mexican legal scholar has proved, the issuance of writs and orders of amparo was common colonial practice. Orders of amparo, valid within the Audiencia of Mexico, fell within the administrative prerogative of the viceroy, and their issuance began with the first viceroy. Petitions for many of them were heard in the General Indian Court, once that was established. Most orders concerned land and water, but any other right under threat of infringement might be protected....

34. June 7, 1616, Mexico City. The town of Chiautla presents evidence that Lic. Diego Landeras y Velasco as visitador-general of New Spain ordered that it be protected in its use of water from the arroyo of Salepango, and set penalties for Cristóbal Osorio and other persons who tried to seize the water; but the owners of the haciendas involved transferred their claim for water to others, who refuse to allow the Indians any use, even to irrigate the kitchen garden of the convent. The town asks for protection in its use of the water and that an inspector be sent to set boundaries to their lands in accordance with the Indians' titles and grants. On the advice of the assessor, the viceroy orders the justice of Texcoco to force all people to observe the decision on water rights issued by Lic. Landeras y Velasco. The town is to be protected in peaceful use, and if there is any complaint, it is to come before the viceroy in the General Indian Court. If no judge has yet been named to set boundaries to the Indians' lands, Alonso Sánchez Redondo is hereby commissioned to do so under the ordinances and with due regard to titles. All neighbors, residents, and interested parties are to be cited to the proceedings. If a judge already has been named or a suit is being heard on the matter, it is to be brought to conclusion promptly, with due opportunity for the Indians to present their claims....

40. March 20, 1630, Mexico City. Melchor López de Haro, Indian solicitor, on behalf of Melchor de los Reyes, *indio chino*, born in Manila, petitions for an order of amparo to protect his client from molestation by any justice in New Spain in his occupation of making and selling the maguey liquor called *agua*

ardiente de maguey. On the advice of his assessor, the viceroy issues the order of amparo.

This document is notable because a Filipino, as a "Chinese Indian," is held to be entitled to the services of the court, and because the reference to the "burning water from the maguey" is one of the earliest references to distilled liquor from the fermented juice of the maguey. We cannot be sure just which species of agave was used, but the order of amparo certainly refers either to an early version of tequila or mezcal or to something similar....

2. *Indian vs. Indian*

One of the major purposes of the establishment of the General Indian Court was to handle disputes of Indian with Indian. The court was to settle such matters with as little litigation and as expeditiously as possible, reducing costs and fees or even eliminating them entirely.... Many of the complaints against Spanish officials and clergy included Indians, either as agents or partners and even as allies, for towns might split into factions over their priest, their Spanish justice, or a resident non-Indian....

a. *Caciques and Indian Town Officials*

A long series of sixteenth-century royal cédulas and viceregal ordinances attest to both the existence of, and attempts to curb, abuses by caciques and by the Indian officials in the new governmental system the Spaniards instituted. Later royal cédulas, ordinances, and reports testify to the prevalent and continued abuse of power throughout the seventeenth century and to the end of the colonial regime. There were, to be sure, changes, in that the power of the caciques as a group steadily declined, even more than might be easily apparent, for less and less did they occupy the foremost posts of town government. These increasingly came to other men who had or acquired wealth and prestige. But the newcomers proved equally adept at using their posts for personal profit and for burdening and mistreating their fellow Indians within the town. One avenue of seeking remedy lay in the Spanish custom that permitted complaint or suit before the Spanish authorities. So the famous capítulos came to be applied also to caciques and Indian town officials....

116. January 27, 1616, Mexico City. Dr. Galdós de Balencia, fiscal protector, for Bartolomé García, Indian of Cuistla, province of Miahuatlán, complains that Don Martín de Almaraz was the lover of García's wife before the two were married, and seeks to have her continue as his mistress. Although the ecclesiastical judge of the bishopric of Oaxaca has ordered him to desist, on pain of 100/ fine and exile, Almaraz, who is an Indian alcalde and a friend of the lieutenant of the alcalde mayor of Miahuatlán, and hence a man of power, has seized five mules García uses to earn his livelihood, to cover the expenses of the suit in the Church court. Almaraz was town alcalde last year and is again so this year, and thus justice is impossible except from outside.

On the advice of his assessor, the viceroy orders the alcalde mayor of Miahuatlán, if the story is true, to go in person to Cuistla and force return of the five mules; if Almaraz has any claim against García, the alcalde mayor is to hear the case by summary procedure; if Almaraz has been alcalde the past year, he is not to hold office in the current year; and he is to be ordered not to molest García or his wife, under suitable penalties to be assigned by the alcalde mayor. Furthermore, Almaraz is to be forced to comply with the sentence pronounced against him by the ecclesiastical judge.

NOTE ON JUSTICE FOR THE INDIANS

Although Indians had some legal protection, they have suffered a great deal under the mantle of Western civilization. Indians disappeared from some Latin American countries as the result of policies of extermination and isolation, and those remaining often find little justice. In Paraguay, for example, the remaining 80,000 Indians suffered mass arrests and torture and faced annihilation at the hands of the government, according to a 1976 report from the International League for the Rights of Man. One tribe, the Ache Indians, has been hunted down, killed and enslaved until its population has been reduced from 10,000 to several hundred. In the prairies of Colombia, the Llanos, Indian-hunting has been such common sport that they even have a special verb for it, *guahibiar*. In 1972 a Colombian jury attracted world attention by acquitting eight cowboys who lured a score of Indians to a feast and massacred them with guns, machetes, and clubs. The defendants were shocked that *guahibiar* was considered a crime at all. Indian-hunting was common practice in that region and they believed the Indians were no different than animals, "except that other animals don't steal our pigs." The jury found the defendants innocent on grounds of "invincible ignorance." The verdict generated outcries from Church and government officials and newspapers and at a new trial, ordered by the judge, the men were convicted. New York Times, July 9, 1972, at 9:4; April 6, 1976, at 5:1.

In 1993 Brazilian gold miners, bringing "shotguns, malaria, and mercury poisoning," ran thousands of Yanomama Indians off their preserve in Brazil and stripped the land in the neighboring Yanomama rain forest in Venezuela. Newsweek, Mar. 1, 1993, at 6.

NOTES AND QUESTIONS

1. Analyze the different schools of thought in 16th century Spain about the nature of Indians and the type of legal regime to which they should be made subject. Did the Spanish crown tend to preserve Indian law, organization, and custom or did it bring sweeping change for the natives?

2. Between Spanish and Indian conceptions, which were more appropriate for 16th century America regarding:

(1) the nature of land ownership and the use of land;
(2) the nature of slavery; and
(3) the legal accountability of governmental and judicial officials?

3. Consider the caseload involving Indians that was filed in audiencias and other Spanish courts in Mexico. Why did so many cases concern land? Was Spanish or Indian law used to resolve land disputes? Was the *Hacienda la Blanca* case that Coy describes typical of the administration of justice in colonial America?

4. The General Indian Court in New Spain (Mexico) was a special jurisdiction vested in the viceroy and a staff of legal aides. Expenses for this court were paid from a small contribution (a half *real*) by each Indian family. Thus, we have an early example of a type of legal insurance. How did this court's caseload compare with those involving Indians in the other Spanish courts?

5. For further information on Latin American legal institutions, see Kenneth L. Karst & Keith S. Rosenn, Law and Development in Latin America, ch. 1 (1975); Colin M. MacLachlan, Spain's Empire in the New World: The Role of Ideas in Institutional and Social Change (1988); and Guillermo F. Margadant, *Spanish Colonial Policy Towards Indians: The Tlaxcalan Actas (1545-1627),* 22 Tex. Int'l L.J. 419 (1987).

C. THE LEGAL TRADITIONS OF EAST ASIA

East Asia has no unifying legal tradition or experience. Indeed, geographically and culturally East Asia is almost too diverse to attempt to describe it as a single region. Stretching north to south from the Russian Far East to Indonesia and west to east from Thailand to Japan, East Asia encompasses the arid plateau of landlocked Mongolia as well as the 7,100 islands of the tropical Philippine archipelago. Its many parts have as little otherwise in common. At different times and to widely varying degrees, its indigenous peoples have been subjected by conquest or conversion to nearly all of the world's major political regimes and religious beliefs. Indian princes, Islamic traders, Portuguese missionaries, Dutch merchants, British bankers, American sailors, and Russian soldiers have each left their mark. East Asia was the site of the last battle of the 1917 Russian Revolution as well as the American military debacle in Vietnam. It contains the last of the hardline Communist regimes separated by a mere border from the world's most dynamic market economies. It includes the world's fastest growing Christian and Muslim communities as well as persistent animist believers. From bullet-trains to ox-carts, East Asia combines in extremes whatever we think of as most modern with the still-enduring elements of its multifaceted traditions.

Within this mosaic the influence of the two dominant Asian civilizations — India and China — stand out. At least before the expansion of Islam into Central, South, and Southeast Asia between the 11th and 15th centuries and the arrival of the Portuguese in the late 15th century, most of East Asia could be divided into two spheres of competing political and cultural influence. As reflected today in language, religion, and the arts, the Indian Hindu-Buddhist influence prevailed in the south and west while that of Confucianist imperial China dominated the north and east.

1. THE HINDU-BUDDHIST TRADITION AND LAW IN THE KINGDOM OF SIAM

NOTE ON THE HINDU-BUDDHIST TRADITION

By the end of the second century the influence of Hindu-Buddhist civilization had been extended beyond the Malay Peninsula. For a millennium thereafter various, frequently warring, Indianized states flourished in the region from Burma to Java. Only one, however — the kingdom of Siam — managed to survive, as an independent polity (today Thailand), the successive incursions of first Islamic and then European merchants, missionaries, and finally, colonial conquerors.

In the earliest of these Brahmanical states, such as the Champa in Cambodia, the sacred Hindu law books — the *dharmašatra* or laws of Manu — quite naturally served as a primary source of principles and rules for ideal governance, as well as the rites and tenets of Hindu religious belief. Even with the spread of Buddhism in the region, the Hindu *dharmašatra* retained importance as the basis for law and legal institutions, especially in Siam, as a result of the efforts of the Mon (Raman or Taleng) people of southern Burma. The Mon, after their conversion to Buddhism, rewrote the *dharmašatra*, expurgating references to Hindu religious practice while retaining portions compatible with Buddhism and those that dealt with ideal governance. The Pali (vernacular Sanskrit) version they produced was thus more akin to a manual — albeit still sacred — for just administration of government than a religious text.

Until the 19th century, for the rulers of successive Siamese kingdoms — Sukothai (1278-1318), Ayudhaya (1350-1767), and the reigning Bangkok (Chakkri) monarchy (1793-present) — the Pali *dharmašatra* along with other sources of Indian tradition and the collected supplementary edicts (the *ratchašatra*) of their predecessors comprised the wellsprings of law and justice.

The most important era in the formation of the Hindu-Buddhist tradition in Siam was under the Ayudhayan kings. They restructured the Siamese state to enhance the authority and power of a central monarch and more clearly defined the notion of paternal kingship.

Much of what we know today about traditional law in Siam is based on its first comprehensive compilation of law in 1805 under Rama I, the founder of the reigning Chakkri dynasty. Generally referred to as the "Three Seal Code," this 1805 compilation was an attempt to reconstruct the edicts of the Ayudhayan kingdom, which were lost in a Burmese invasion.

Litigation and lawsuits in the Kingdom of Siam should not be equated with a system of private rights and duties similar to those in Roman law. Law in the Hindu-Buddhist tradition of Siam, like that in China, was essentially penal. In Siam no less than in imperial China law was an instrument of governmental power designed to maintain and perpetuate the existing political and social order.

SARASIN VIRAPHOL, LAW IN TRADITIONAL SIAM AND CHINA: A COMPARATIVE STUDY, 65 Journal of the Siam Society 109-15, 124 (1977)

[The Siamese King]

[W]ith the introduction of Indian political principles and institutions, the role of the Siamese king led to significant political consolidation. The traditional father-figure of the monarch was elevated to that of the *Chakravatin* (Hindu for "Lord of the Universe"). He attained a status similar to the Chinese emperor who acted as intermediary between heaven and earth. According to the Hindu interpretation, the Ayudhayan monarch was regarded as the apex of the pyramidal model of human government and his status was, in actual fact, set in the border realm between the human and cosmic spheres.

Although they never went so far as to accept the Hindu cosmological order completely, Ayudhayan kings nevertheless capitalized upon the latter's concept of the divinely sanctioned kingship to fortify their traditional paternal status. To make it even more complete and absolute, Buddhist doctrines from India were introduced to strengthen further the ideal of the kingly righteousness in government and administration. (And with this, the picture of an absolute and virtuous *Chakravatin* was made complete.) Possessed with the three cardinal principles of *dhammakamata* ("desire for righteousness"), *attakamata* ("desire for others' welfare"), and *rattapipalanopaya* ("policy of governance"), the Ayudhayan monarch, like his Chinese counterpart, was armed with an important moral-ethical weapon to govern (*i.e.* to protect, lead, and set an example for his people to follow)....

[The Three Seal Code]

Because the monarch's principal duty as a *Chakravatin-Bohisattva* was to govern, it goes without saying that the administration of justice was one of his main concerns. The effort by King Rama I in the 1805 Code in a sense represents only the culmination of a long series of attempts by previous Ayudhayan kings to produce a practical code of laws.

Siamese rulers borrowed substantially from Indian laws. In the 1805 Code, prominence was given to a corpus of legal treatises known collectively as the *Dharmasatra* (in proper Siamese pronunciation, it should be romanized as *Thammasart*)....

The 1805 Code is arranged in an order of 29 titles, each representing one fundamental division of function though not always clear-cut. These titles as a whole represent a relatively co-ordinated body of legislation reflecting a composite of the *Dharmasatra* (with moral admonishments), the *Ratchasatra*, (with modified and expanded civil legal concepts drawn from the original Manu Code and entitled *laksana*), as well as other special royal decrees, regulations and decisions. This *corpus* had served the Siamese monarchical state for centuries ....

[A]t least in form, [the Three Seal Code evidenced] the continuing heavy influence of the Indian moral-ethical code; but what is more important is how the Siamese regarded and utilized it. While under each title in the code there were written short introductory comments in Pali upholding the spirit of the Manu Code, these were intended primarily to lend sacredness to the main body of the legislation which dealt with secular matters.

As mentioned above, the *Dharmasatra* served as the "basis" (*mulkadi*) for the Siamese legal development. In the Three Seal Code, it is represented essentially by the first two titles, the *Dharmasatra* and *Intarapard*, supposedly timeless and unchanging. These two titles purported to represent the universal truth, serving as an inviolable constitution which even the monarch himself must observe. The true value of the two titles (notwithstanding the rather fascinating account of the creation of earth in the first title) was an admonition to rulers of men to maintain justice constantly, and specifically to uphold justice in law. The first title spoke generally of the king's obligation to ensure peace by being just and righteous; the second title spoke out more specifically on legal justice, and amounted to a set of instructions to men of law on the proper mental attitude to maintain, and the proper process of litigation to observe, in dispensing justice.

The remainder of the Code may be classified as *Ratchasatra* in the broad sense of the term, and can be broken down into the categories of criminal, civil, and administrative laws. In the area of civil law, the section on this subject in the original code of Manu was adopted but was modified by successive Ayudhayan reigns. This reflected the necessity for having proper regulatory devices to govern the relationships between individuals in material transactions. Titles 14 (slaves), 15 (husband-wife), 17 (miscellaneous infractions), 18 (inheritance), and 19 (loans) may be classified as belonging to the civil category in the 1805 Code. As for the criminal section, one may cite titles 21 (robbery), 22 (officials' public violations), 23 (offenses in general), 24 (treason), 16 (abduction), and 20 (violent quarrels). These titles represent activities deemed as disrupting public peace and order, which throughout Ayudhaya were heavily sanctioned against. Traditional Siamese administrative law was, in fact, quite elaborate though not to the same extent as the Chinese. In the Three Seal Code, the titles pertaining to this category were: 5 (scheme of compensation), 6 (civilian ranking), 7 (military ranking), 4 (*Pra Tammanoon* [authority of judges and courts]), 9 (litigation basis), 10 (witnesses), 11 (ordeal), 12 (judges, corollary of the *Intarapard*), 13 (appeal), 8 (dispute basis). The remainder of the Code, titles 25, 9 and 3, may be treated as a special subgroup of administrative law concerned more with the king's private sphere....

[The Judicial System]

Due to the very diverse and complicated nature of the mechanism of administration of justice and the elaborate procedures adopted in the state's dispensation of justice, almost all aspects of state administration were somehow tied in, directly or indirectly, with the question of litigation....

[I]n the days when the state was still small and uncomplicated, the monarch was personally in charge of all administration, including the administration of justice. Soon, as administration grew more complex, the monarch had to delegate his judicial authority. Hence there developed an elaborate system of justice administration which lasted for over three centuries.

According to the *Laksana Sakdina Fai Polaruan* (Art. 6), instituted in the reign of Trilokanart, there were 22 law courts, each with specific jurisdiction within the capital of Ayudhaya alone. Such a system of court decentralization was based on an ingenious judicial scheme for the separation of the advisory and executive authorities; the rationale being that the monarch, though having to delegate his judicial power, still wished to ensure the proper administration of justice carried out on his behalf. The system was supposedly effective in checking on the officials who carried out his delegated authority, and, at the same time, ensuring justice to his subjects. Nevertheless, naturally at the apex of judicial power was still the monarch himself.

At the capital as well as in the provinces, courts were classified into the court of first instance and the court of appeal, or second instance, and these governed most classes of society except the monks and the nobility. At the head of the first-instance court system in the capital ... was the department of the *Krom Wang* ("Department of the Palace") with its *Krom Rub-fong* ("Litigation Station") appointed by the king to receive written suits. The station was staffed by a body of Brahman priests, called *luk khun*, which reviewed the suits on the basis of the *Dharmasatra* and recommended if they had sufficient substance in law to be brought to trial. The recommendations were then passed on to another committee, the *Pra Racha Pichai* which decided under the jurisdiction of which of the twenty-odd departmental courts the case should fall. The departmental court's sole function was to hold proceedings necessary to gather all material evidence and to make a summary of the case before it. The findings were then returned again to the Brahman *luk khun* ("jury") who decided the appropriate verdict. If the sentence should be a serious one, the king's approval was necessary before it was executed by yet another committee (attached to the *Krom Vieng*, "Department of the City") called the *Pra Krai Si*. In the outlying districts, a committee of senior officials took the place of the *luk khun* in the capital, with the various district departments (more or less identical with their city counterparts) taking on the task of the trial proceedings.

The courts of second instance in the capital and the provinces were called *Sarn Luang* and *Sarn Na Rohng* respectively. Appeals (*dika*) could be made against misjudgments by judges or other improper proceedings in court — primarily on the principles of the *Dharmasatra*, against the misconduct of the judge or the improper admission of evidence. *Dikas*, in the case they were filed in the capital, must be submitted to the monarch, while in the outlying areas, the ones who heard the *dikas* were the provincial rulers with authority delegated by the king.

Among special courts established outside of the regular court system for specific purposes and mentioned in the *Pra Tammanoon*, several merit one's attention. A special court, the *Sarn Raj*, dealt exclusively with infractions of judges who had been accused by the people in the capital — with its counterpart in the provinces as well. The duty of *Sarn Khun Prachaseb* was to deal with officials' dishonesty and violation. In addition, a *Sarn Ayachak* was established to deal with "litigation tricksters" like the Chinese *sung-kun* ("professional litigants") who incited litigation, made false representation in court, and represented litigious parties for a fee.

As far as trial procedures were concerned, Siamese judicial administrative laws were also rather detailed. Prominent among the *Ratchasatra* legislation on this matter were chapters dealing with the questions of litigation basis, witnesses, and methods of arriving at the truth.

The *Laksana Rub-fong*, promulgated quite early in the Ayudhayan reign (in A.D. 1356) set the basis for litigation which was to be instituted in the courts of the monarch. It is of interest to note that, despite the monarch's determination to give justice to all his subjects, qualifications were made at the very start of the *Laksana* which excluded certain types of people from filing suits and initiating litigation. Nevertheless, it should be noted that such restrictions were placed mostly on those with some type of physical limitation, the seven categories to be excluded being the insane, the deaf, the crippled, the blind, the beggar, the senile, and the mentally incompetent or "babbling infant." Furthermore, the *Laksana* was quick to point out that suits filed by persons neither on their own behalf nor on behalf of their close relatives such as grandparents, parents, spouse, brother or sister, uncle or aunt, would be rejected, and if found to be guilty of any intention to disrupt the peace, such litigants would also be fined.

Finally, the law also required that all writs initiating litigation must bear the full name of the person(s) filing them, or the party submitting them would be punished. This is in line with the Chinese laws against anonymous accusations....

The legal provisions on witnesses or the *Laksana Payarn*, promulgated in A.D. 1351, served as a guideline for the courts in dealing with witnesses. They were based upon the *Dharmasatra*'s emphasis on the role of witnesses in bringing out the truth or helping clear up doubts. In this respect, Siamese law seemed to see more importance in witnesses than did the Chinese where little regard was actually paid to direct statements; what apparently seemed more vital was wringing out the truth from litigants than taking witnesses seriously.

The law excluded 33 types of people from appearing as witnesses in litigation because of physical impediments or intellectual incapacity. The list ranged from slaves, children under seven, elders over 70, dancers, beggars, the deaf and blind, wizards and witches, quacks, executioners, fishermen, vagabonds, madmen, prostitutes, gamblers and thieves, and so forth. The *Laksana*, in addition, followed the *Dharmasatra* in classifying people who were eligible as witnesses into three kinds whose testimony would bear varying weight.... However, the Siamese law on witnesses did not merely take this triple classification as determining the value of a witness's testimony; circumstantial considerations were also important. Hence, a witness who was at the scene would be worth more than one who had second-hand information, and so on.

The practice of swearing in witnesses was also adopted by the Siamese. The *Laksana* described the oath administered to witnesses as a long and elaborate curse on perjurers including the prayer that should the particular witness suffer one way or another within three to seven days after taking the oath, the litigant party who cited him stood to lose his case automatically.

Furthermore, law required that judges follow witnesses' testimony very closely. Ayudhayan courts are known to have practiced the issuing of subpoenas, and as for those who had the privilege of not being compelled to appear as witnesses in court, such as monks and nobles, the judge must go to them for their testimony....

The most fascinating section of Siamese laws concerning methods and procedures for arriving at truth in litigation ... is the *Laksana Lui Nam Lui Fai* ("trial by ordeal"). The law, following the tradition of the *Dharmasatra*, prescribed that when witnesses' testimony was unclear, or the judge could not ascertain the truth in the trial, the litigant parties could be made to, or could themselves request to, use trial by ordeal to determine which side held the truth. The rationale behind this was that each party should prove ... himself through a process of purification or purgation by fire or water. For it was held that truth would be most likely to be on the side of the party which survived the ordeal better. The parties involved in the test were further required to take extremely lengthy oaths which could easily fill three printed pages, invoking all the gods to help the party who spoke the truth by supporting him successfully through the ordeal and causing the one who spoke falsehood to fail.

Nevertheless, trial by ordeal was normally reserved as the very last resort of the court when every other means had failed. Siamese law was explicit about circumstances where this type of a test would not be allowed, such as when statements by litigants and witnesses were in contradiction, or when one litigant did not have any witnesses while the other did....

As the practical expression of natural law, positive law could not be taken lightly: any violation or transgression, no matter how mild or severe, must be regarded as disruption. This served as the basis for the Siamese judicial attention to the *munlamert* ("theories on transgression or violation"), punishable always by corporal means.

QUESTIONS

1. How did the notion of "law" in the Hindu-Buddhist tradition differ from that in the Roman system and pre-Columbian traditions in the Americas? Were there important differences, for example, in the concepts of legal "rights" and adjudication? Was the role of the Siamese monarch more like that of an Inca or Aztec ruler or like that of a European monarch after the rise of nation states?

2. Viraphol notes a practice in Siamese law similar to "trial by ordeal" in Europe. How did they differ? What did they have in common?

3. Compare litigation and judicial procedure in Siam with that in the Inca empire. What striking similarities or differences can you find?

2. THE IMPERIAL CHINESE TRADITION: ORDER WITHOUT LAW

NOTE ON THE IMPERIAL CHINESE TRADITION

China's legal tradition, the longest of any enduring political system in the world, rivals that of Roman law in its historical importance and lasting influence. The Chinese legal legacy continues to shape the legal cultures of Northeast Asia as well as the large Chinese communities of Southeast Asia.

The idea of law that developed in imperial China has much in common with the prevailing features of any contemporary administrative state. This is not surprising. Law in the imperial Chinese system was an instrument of state regulatory control. With remarkable consistency, from the fragmentary evidence of the first known codes and statutes of the Ch'in (3rd century B.C.) and Han (206 B.C.-220 A.D.) dynasties through the great T'ang (618-906), Ming

(1368-1644), and Ch'ing (1644-1911) codes, imperial Chinese law represented a detailed set of administrative regulations with penal proscriptions and elaborate punishments. Included was a highly rational procedural system with heavy emphasis on confession, coerced if necessary. Although legislated rules did reflect the norms of various ethical or social philosophies, especially those influenced by China's familial orientations and Confucianist beliefs, the idea of law remained purely secular without any claim to deistic origin.

Law in the Chinese tradition differed fundamentally from law in the West in its lack of any notion of private ordering by law. While not devoid of rules related to property, contracts, commercial transactions, and familial relations, the imperial Chinese codes and statutes covered these matters only to the extent necessary to protect or promote state interests. Such rules were, however, implemented by administrative processes or enforced by penal proscription and punishment. Totally alien was the idea of a comprehensive corpus of legal principles, rules, and categories designed to govern private relationships and to be enforced within a remedial system of rights and duties through formal adjudicatory processes subject to the initiative and control of litigants. Unless a matter was of state concern and therefore subject to official regulation, no law existed. What might be considered "rights" of property or contract were thus more the creation of custom and practice as recognized in the interstices of administrative and penal regulation. Their enforcement, however, was left largely to extralegal remedies and sanctions applied by community, guild, or family. An ideological emphasis on social harmony, ordered relationships, and observance of ritual, based primarily on Confucian thought, was antithetical to the development of private legal ordering. Proper behavior and social order were to be maintained more by education and example than by legal rules. All individuals were to act benevolently to inferiors and deferentially to superiors so as not to disturb the natural order. It was therefore considered better to suffer social wrongs than to seek redress for them, even if they could be punished by law. Conflict was to be avoided. Dispute resolution was not a question of which parties had the "law" on their side; what was important was to suppress conflict by making the adversaries understand how to behave according to the higher order of Confucian morality.

Without any claim to deistic source or divine intervention, the Chinese legal process reflected high regard for rationality and developed into a sophisticated system of fact-finding, documentary proof, and appeals. At least by the time of the Ch'ing dynasty, review and approval of individual cases by the emperor was necessary for infliction of capital punishment. The system also stressed confession and set out complex rules for the degrees of torture permitted for its extraction, if necessary, from both witnesses and the accused.

Although obstacles of cost, delay, and personal risk confronted litigants in imperial China, they did not deter all parties to private quarrels from resorting to the formal legal process. Furthermore, the threat of a complaint to a magistrate was often used effectively as leverage in negotiating a private settlement. Even such motives as personal revenge might lead to charging acquaintances with commission of a crime. Law remained, nevertheless, a secondary instrument of social control. At least for the strict Confucianist, ritual observance and rule by moral example were the ideologically preferred methods of inducing correct behavior. Chinese political ideology recognized a natural moral, rather than a legal, order, which governed sovereign as well as subject. The idea of justiciable claims against the state could not germinate from belief in the mandate of heaven and in obligations to ancestors. However, to the extent that Confucianist values were actually internalized by those with political authority, they offered alternative constraints against arbitrary exercises of political power.

China's contributions to the intellectual and political life of the neighboring states of East Asia are difficult to exaggerate. The influence of Chinese civilization endures today in the arts, language, religion, and technology of East Asian countries. The effect of the Chinese legacy on patterns of social ordering, political authority, and statecraft has been equally important. Most fully emulated under *Lê* rule in Vietnam (1428-1788) and in *Yi* dynasty Korea (1392-1910), the institutions and ideological foundations of imperial Chinese governance provided models that have been formally replaced only within the past century.

THOMAS B. STEPHENS, ORDER AND DISCIPLINE IN CHINA: THE SHANGHAI MIXED COURT, 1911-27, at 3-5, 7-9, 11-12 (1992)

When traditional Chinese concepts and ideals of social order, inter-personal relations and obligations, and dispute resolution are viewed against the familiar models of Western jurisprudence, it is found that the two by no means coincide. This nonconformity has long embarrassed Western jurists attempting to interpret the Chinese system in terms of Western juristic thought and to analyze it in terms of comparative law. The disparities are notorious and profound....

The fundamental difficulty is that the Chinese system simply does not yield to treatment in terms of Western jurisprudence or legal theory. The realities of dispute resolution and the maintenance of social order in traditional China do not fit, and cannot be made to fit, into the categories, constructs, and relationships of Western jurisprudence. An entirely different framework of theory, unrelated to jurisprudence, is called for if the realities of the Chinese system are to be made intelligible in Western thought patterns....

In Western thought, the antithesis of chaos is order, and order is conceived of, both cosmologically and philosophically, as an artificial objective deliberately brought about, managed, and controlled in predetermined forms according to the conscious will of a transcendent power exterior to the flux, by the enforcement of codes of rigid, universal, specific, imperatives constraining conduct.

In Chinese thought and cultural tradition, the antithesis of chaos is harmony, which is thought of simply as a natural characteristic of a state of affairs that arises and persists automatically in a hierarchical universe so long as all the individual parts of that universe, even the smallest, and all persons in it, perform their duties and offices faithfully "according to the internal necessities of their own natures" in whatever station or function in life they find themselves born to or assigned to by superior authority.

The difference between these two contrasting states of order and of harmony is reflected in the means adopted to sustain them. In Western society, where concepts of order prevail, disputes are resolved and breaches of order are corrected by measuring them against rigid, universal codes of imperatives external to the parties, in an adjudication. This adjudication is conducted by an authority equally subject to the codes, independent of each of the parties, and not committed to the interests of either one more than the other, and regardless of the consequences to the existing social and political order and the policies of its rulers. The outcome turns on the balancing of the rights and duties of each party in relation to the other according to the predetermined codes. This may be designated an "adjudicative" system. Rules of obligation are the heart and center of this system....

In the society of traditional China, where concepts of harmony prevailed, disputes were resolved and disturbances of harmony corrected (ideally within the immediate group where they arose) by relating them to the personalities, the exigencies, and the surrounding circumstances of the particular case, with a view to the instruction of the parties in the conduct expected of them, and the punishment of those disturbing harmony. This process was carried out by, and according to the values of, an authority superior in rank to both parties (generally from among the leaders of the immediate group), and primarily in the interests of maintaining the existing hierarchical order, the superior position of the authority figures in it, and the cohesion of the group. The outcome in such a system turns upon the enforcement of duties without rights. This may be designated a "disciplinary" system. Obedience to superiors in a hierarchy of authority is the heart and center of this system. It does not use the idea of transcendent, rigid, predetermined, universal, and imperative rules....

It is characteristic of the adjudicative system that political rulers applying it act as the "fountain of justice," that is to say they concern themselves in their subjects' quarrels and actively enforce their subjects' rights according to the transcendent codes of imperatives and the independent adjudicator's judgments.

It is characteristic of the disciplinary system that the political rulers or supreme hierarchical authorities applying it concern themselves as little as possible with the quarrels of subordinates. It is the very definite duty of the lower ranks and the common people not to quarrel at all, and if they do they must at all costs settle it among themselves, and certainly not on any account trouble their ruler or any government officials with it. If they do, they must expect to be treated harshly — especially the complainant who brought the trouble to the notice of the officials....

Table 4.3

Characteristics of the Adjudicative and Disciplinary Systems

The Adjudicative (or "Legal")	*The Disciplinary (or "Parental")*
Contemplates: a confrontation between parties on an equal footing, an external fixed code of conduct not pre-	*Contemplates:* a confrontation between unequals — a status superior and an inferior — where an alleged insubor-

The Adjudicative (or "Legal")	*The Disciplinary (or "Parental")*
scribed by either, and enforced by an authority equally subject to it, independent of each of the parties, and not committed to the interests of either one more than the other, regardless of the consequences to the existing political order. The proceedings turn on rights.	dination is investigated and punished by one of the parties, i.e., the superior (or a delegate) and primarily in the interests of that party, and of maintaining the existing hierarchical order and the superior's own authority in it. The proceedings turn on duties.
Rules prescribing conduct are: central, indispensable, and of the essence.	*Rules prescribing conduct are:* peripheral, dispensable, and, if used at all, for convenience only.
Observable in: the West, the United States, Europe, and in sports.	*Observable in:* Asia, China, Japan, and in the armed forces.
Appropriate to a society classed as: individualistic and egalitarian, "contract oriented," "*Gesellschaft*," or "organized."	*Appropriate to a society classed as:* group hierarchical, "status oriented," "*Gemeinschaft*," or "fragmented."
Links that bind society together are: reciprocal ties of mutual rights and obligations enforced horizontally between equals.	*Links that bind society together are:* unilateral ties of duty only, enforced vertically downward upon inferiors.
Behavioral guides: please yourself so long as you do not break the rigid rules. Lawyers, courts, and judges tell you what you must do according to universal fixed codes, e.g., acts of Parliament.	*Behavioral guides:* please your group leaders at whatever cost. Your group leaders will tell you what to do (in traditional China, even what man or woman you must marry), according to what is best for the group in the particular circumstances of each case.
Theory of this category: jurisprudence.	*Theory of this category:* nowhere systematically formulated.

In 1934, Marcel Granet observed, "La notion Chinoise de l'Ordre exclut, sur tous ses aspects, l'idée de Loi" (The Chinese notion of Order excludes, in all its aspects, the idea of Law). Joseph Needham, after the most extensive and searching investigations, approved Granet's observation, finding that the Chinese see order in the universe, and therefore in society, as a case of "Order which excludes Law." What is present is the harmony of pattern arising spontaneously from within. The idea of predetermined, rigid, universal imperatives governing conduct and imposing order from without is not there. Nor is there any word in the Chinese language which projects that idea, as does the English word "law." The character *fa,* 法, is often translated "law" but the two words are not by any means equivalent. The expression *fa* conveys primarily a signification of "model" or "method." Its connotations are primarily persuasive and exemplary rather than imperative. Even when it is used to convey specifically an imperative signification, that signification does not project the idea of universal, compulsive, rigid rules of general behavior external to the parties, but only the idea of the immediate command of a present superior in a hierarchical social context. Watt sharply distinguishes *fa* from law, rejecting the translation "law" and rendering it as "methods."

In the teaching of the *Fa Jia*, the so-called School of Legalists, the art of government was not seen as resting only, nor even chiefly, in *fa*. The role of *fa* was similar to that of the standing orders of a military or command headquarters, issued from time to time for obedience by all under command as a manifesto expressing the commander's will for the time being and as a means of maintaining instant response to that will at all times. The use of the word *legalism* in this connection is unfortunate and misleading. As Fung Yu-lan has pointed out, "It is wrong to associate the thought of the Legalist School with jurisprudence." The teaching of the legalists was directed to administration, organization, and leadership, not legalism. Waley calls the followers of this way of thought "realists," not "legalists."

Szaszy, investigating the concept of the legal rule in different cultures, found that in China legality as a principle was abhorred, and that, according to Chinese theory,

> the notion of subjective law, of the legal relation, rigidly opposes the idea of natural order. Subjective law, or the legal relation, is a form of social disease. The making of legal rules is the original evil; honesty and morals, and not the law, have to be the guides of human conduct....

Living for more than two thousand years in a relationship with their rulers that they themselves characterized as a parent-child relationship, the Chinese were very experienced in the practical application of a parental or disciplinary system of order. There developed moreover in China a considerable literature on dispute resolution and the maintenance of order in society. Interest, however, was concentrated on the substantive specifications of preferred behavior in particular circumstances, on the proper punishments for misbehavior, and on the realities of particular cases. It was not directed to the theory of the systems as such.

There never developed in China any sustained interest in the investigation and study of the system or process of the maintenance of order considered in the abstract, apart from the substantive content of the norms it upheld. Escarra puts it thus:

> There lacked in China that tradition of jurisconsults succeeding one another through the centuries, whose opinions, independent of the positive law and whatever its practical application might be, built up, on account of their methodical, doctrinal, and scientific character, the "theory" or speculative part of law.

Chinese genius was never inspired to erect the analysis of the Chinese system into a formal science of the theory of the maintenance of order that might stand in the same relation to the Chinese system as jurisprudence stands to the legal systems of the West.

SHUZO SHIGA, SOME REMARKS ON THE JUDICIAL SYSTEM IN CHINA: HISTORICAL DEVELOPMENT AND CHARACTERISTICS, in TRADITIONAL AND MODERN LEGAL INSTITUTIONS IN ASIA AND AFRICA (David C. Buxbaum ed.) 46-51 (1967)

Studies reveal that the courts and trials in imperial China, while changing in technical points in the course of more than two thousand years, were fundamentally of an immutable character, which may be defined as "the executive character of the judicature" or "trials as an aspect of administrative activities."

Despite the rise and fall of many dynasties, the same political system, in which public power was ultimately and integrally in the hands of the emperor and delegated through the branches of a bureaucracy staffed with officials whom the emperor appointed and dismissed as he wished, was maintained down to the nineteenth century. There was, as a rule, no one person or group of persons who had even subordinate and partial power which was inherent in his position, and was thus independent of the emperor. History has recorded several epochs of disunification in the empire, but these were nothing less than interludes in the process of reunification which would be completed when the last of the rival chiefs became the single possessor of public power, i.e., the emperor. Consequently, judicial procedure was no longer in a position to function as a means of adjusting the political order itself as in ancient times. Competitions for jurisdiction among various types of authority, which were notable occurrences in European history, were unknown in China. There was no concept of a constitutional organization, an independent court, or a parliament of elective members, which derived authority from the law or from the will of the electorate (i.e., from a source other than the imperial will) — and was thus able to restrict the power of the emperor. The state power was undivided.

Law (*fa*) was essentially nothing more than the regulations issued by the emperor to officials, prescribing the way to discharge their administrative office routines. Settling litigations among the populace and punishing criminals — that is, adjudication — was one of the most important of administrative routines which had to be discharged according to the law in the aforesaid sense. Officials who acted contrary to the law, whether in trial procedure or in the content of judgments, incurred disciplinary or even criminal punishments in serious cases. While the officials' whim was restrained, the people reflectively enjoyed the effects of law. But it was not the direct intention of law to determine rights and duties for each person. The people were generally not in a position to demand judgments in accordance with law and to resist judgments, especially those of punishment, which had no foundation in the letter of the law. Law was a restriction upon the officials, but not upon the emperor; on the contrary, his word was the law. He not only theoretically held the power to mete out punishment for crimes not previously provided for by law, but he actually exercised this power as occasion demanded when rendering an exceptional decision. Such a decision by the emperor gave precedent for future similar cases and quite often came to be formulated into an article of law. The principle of *nulla poena sine lege* was unmistakably accepted as a restriction imposed on officials by the emperor, but never as a restriction imposed on the imperial government as a whole by a social contract with the people.

No institutional distinction was made between civil and criminal procedures, although of course particular cases varied in coloration, some being more civil, others more criminal. In the documents of the Ch'ing, criminal and civil cases were called "important cases" and "trifling matters" respectively. That is to say, the grade of importance of a case was measured by the grade of punishment which might result.

Criminal cases were brought to court either by the accusation of a private party — ordinarily, the victim of the crime, or on initiative of the official who detected and arrested the criminal. In the former situation, the petitioner was under threat of the same punishment as the accused, should the accusation prove false. In the latter situation the same official, the magistrate who acted as the judge, functioned also as the prosecutor — and the procedure was inquisitional. At any rate, it was an accepted principle that in cases of a serious criminal nature a person should be found guilty only on the basis of his own confession. The magistrate enjoyed wide latitude of action; strict law of evidence was little known. The proceedings as a whole were in reality a process aimed at the confession of the suspect. Torture, which was approved and regulated by the law, was an indispensable means to obtain a confession from a stubborn suspect if suspicion was strong enough. The final confession was written by a clerk in a document, to which the confessor was forced to affix his signature. This signature meant the end of the trial in court. The application of law to the fact proved by the confession was an internal matter of the officialdom, not the subject of debate in court.

Civil cases were concluded when both parties, in writing, agreed to and promised to follow the decision of the magistrate. If one of the parties stubbornly withheld his consent, final settlement could not be reached. The magistrate could inflict a punishment of bamboo strokes on a party if his assertions were obviously absurd, for the law not only provided for punishments for innumerable civil iniquities but also authorized the magistrate, while conducting trials, to inflict slight punishments generally on whomever he saw fit. But on the other hand, either the fact or the pretext that the magistrate had resorted to irresistibly coercive measures in order to obtain the party's consent afforded a satisfactory basis for an appeal to higher authorities. In conclusion, it may be said that the main task before the magistrate was to induce both parties, sometimes under threat of punishment, to accept some settlement gracefully.

In summation, trials in imperial China were essentially procuration in criminal cases and mediation in civil cases. In either case there was no judgment in the genuine sense of the word, that is; there was no concept of a conclusion which, being reached through fixed rules or procedure, was to be regarded as the best substitute for the absolute truth and justice of God. As a natural consequence, the theory of *res judicata* or *ne bis in idem* was little known in China. The notable lack of magical factors, such as ordeal, in the courts of imperial China, and lack of strict formalistic rules of procedure as well, can also be explained by the fact that the judge was not a servant of a

SCORES (Q) THE FOURS: TERROR. 4 USA O

mechanism aimed at objective truth beyond personal wisdom but was a representative of an almighty and merciful government which held the mandate of heaven to realize harmony in this world.

It is easily understandable under such circumstances that the prerequisites for recognition of the practice of law as an honorable profession were lacking. The parties, as a general rule, personally appeared in court, where they remained kneeling on the floor while the magistrate gave a hearing. People were not in want of a sort of legal advisor called "master of law suits (*sung-shih*)," equipped with a superficial knowledge of law and formalities, who offered their services secretly; but these were generally men of bad reputation, who provoked unsophisticated people to raise wasteful law suits, and suffered suppression by the government. It was inconceivable, too, that a sort of governmental agency could stand at the bar, like the public procurator in modern states. There is, therefore, little to be said on the subject of judicial organization other than to describe the hierarchical bureaucracy itself.

The governmental organization of the empire consisted, generally speaking, of several bureaux in the central government and three levels of local government; which may be called, for the sake of convenience, the province, the prefecture and the magistracy. At the central level, and (since the Sung era [960-1279]) also at the provincial level, there were special bureaux of justice. But at the level of the magistrate, who was something like a minor emperor over the district under his jurisdiction, and in the personal jurisdiction of the emperor, judicial functions together with all the other administrative functions were charged upon one and the same person.

The magistrate acted as the judge of the first instance in almost every case which occurred in his district. But in criminal cases of some consequence he was required after the hearing was concluded to prepare a draft sentence and submit it to the prefect, for re-examination together with the person and the record of the case. The prefect, if he agreed with the original draft but was not authorized for final decision, was required to forward it in the same way to the provincial government, which in turn might send the case to the bureau of justice in the central government, although at this last stage, only the documents, not the person, were to be sent. Thus a case, without any action of either party, might undergo a certain number of retrials to reach final judgment by the authorized superior, whose level was specified according to the grade of the punishment. A case involving capital punishment generally had to be submitted to the emperor for his personal sanction. Furthermore the superior supervised his inferiors' judicial activities by inspection or through several types of obligatory reports on cases pending or concluded and, if necessary, overruled their decisions. People were little restricted in taking an appeal to the superior if discontented with their treatment in lower courts, which was in its nature nothing but a petition asking for the superior's supervision of his inferior. On the other hand, lower officials were allowed, sometimes even encouraged, to apply to their superiors, especially to the bureau of justice in the central government, for an interpretation of some provision of the law concerned with a case under trial in his court. The idea that the trial in each level of court should be a self-contained process was lacking, although its conclusion, after being given decisively, might once again be overruled by an upper court through a self-contained process.

As a consequence of the Confucian theory which required the officialdom to be composed of gentlemen educated in classical literature, the chiefs or the main staff of each office whether central or local who were charged with general responsibility, were not usually expected to be specialists in technical points of law; therefore, they relied upon the preparatory and advisory services of subordinate officials, clerks or private secretaries (*mu-yu* or *shih-yeh*), especially the latter in the local government under the Ch'ing. Various sorts of assistance, either clerical or physical, indispensable for the actual functioning of an office were offered by almost non-salaried clerks (*hsü-li*) or government runners (*ya-i*), who lived on innumerable customary fees paid by the people who had dealing with the office. Law suits were golden opportunities for them to make an income at the expense of the persons involved, often abusively.

In the bureau of justice in the central government, each case to be decided was first allotted to a subordinate official to be dealt with substantially. His draft was then submitted to the main staff for sanction, to be given by the consent of all the members of the staff, not by majority. Therefore the tribunal could not be truly identified in this highest judicial organ. All in all, it was the well-known mechanism of bureaucracy that brought forth judgments in judicial cases. It functioned in precisely the same way as it did concerning administrative matters.

These general descriptions do not mean at all that China remained static throughout imperial times. It is a task of vital importance to trace various aspects of dynamism notable within the unchanged framework of the imperial regime.... It may be noted that the central control over the local officials became more and more elaborate in the course of years. The aforementioned systems of the necessary retrials and obligatory reports were most fully developed under the Ch'ing, the last dynasty, and fettered the lower officials with piles of documents. At the beginning under the Han, these systems were still unformulated. Local officials were given a free hand to govern their territories and were only responsible for the results of their management. They even seem to have been invested with the power of passing and executing a capital sentence without asking for the emperor's sanction in advance. And as the means of control, superiors' rounds of inspection were more significant under the Han than in later eras.

It should not be overlooked that the maintenance of social order and the settlement of troubles in social life did not wholly or even in the main depend upon the governmental administration of justice thus far dealt with. A sort of justice (that is, mediation, social sanctions or even lynchings) administered in an informal manner by autonomous organizations of the people — clans, villages, guilds, etc., and even more informally by mere neighbourhoods or by curious crowds on the streets — was far more effective in minor cases than the time-wasting and expensive formal law suits. The government favoured such self-controlling and peace-making activities unless they ran to extremes such as death, for "few litigations in official courts" was an ideal of Confucian theory. The people, on the other hand, recognized the governmental court as the force they could rely on for solution of problems beyond their capacity. Thus two sorts of peace-making mechanisms, governmental and popular, were complementary to each other in their social functions, but with regard to the institutional framework, they were clearly separated. People neither enjoyed, nor even sought, formal authorization by the government for their spontaneous activities, because the system of government was thoroughly bureaucratic. In this connection, the institution of *li-lao-jen* (village elder) in early Ming times attracts our attention. *Li-lao-jen*, nominated from among the people by the government, were officially invested with jurisdiction over minor cases. To bring minor cases directly to the magistrate skipping over the *li-lao-jen* was prohibited. But this institution eventually fell into desuetude because, presumably, men of truly good character were unwilling to accept such nominations. Therefore, no attempt was successful to combine governmental and popular factors into an institutional organization of judicature. That may be regarded as a notable peculiarity of imperial China and derived from the people's general attitude of non-commitment toward the government.

NOTES AND QUESTIONS

1. In making comparisons one must constantly guard against the temptation to exaggerate in order to make a point. Consider, for example, Stephens's description of Western law. Is it properly characterized as "the enforcement of codes of rigid, universal, specific, imperatives constraining conduct"? Is that what law is like in America? Do our private law rules of contract, property, and inheritance fit that description? Or do many such rules seek to effectuate the actual or presumed intentions of people engaged in private ordering? Are tort rules created in order to constrain conduct or to protect the reasonable expectations and desires of people against the negligence or malice of others? Is the expectation that I will be liable for damages if I fail to exercise reasonable care in my conduct toward others a rigid constraint? Are the concepts of social order and social harmony all that different?

2. Are you persuaded by Stephens that Western legal categories and concepts do not apply to imperial China? To what extent does Shiga rely on Western terminology and classifications to describe the imperial Chinese "legal" system? Would Stephens object to Shiga's terminology? Give specific examples.

3. Explain what Stephens means by "disciplinary" and "adjudicatory" systems of governmental control. How would Stephens label the Roman legal system? Canon law? The Inca and Aztec traditions? Law in the Kingdom of Siam?

4. How did the role of praetor in Roman law differ from that of magistrate in the Chinese system? What other differences or similarities can you find in the judicial procedure of imperial Rome, China, and Inca Peru?

5. For more on imperial Chinese law, see Derk Bodde & Clarence Morris, Law in Imperial China (1967); Paul Heng-chao Ch'en, Chinese Legal Tradition under the Mongols: The Code of 1291 as Reconstructed (1979); Phillip M. Chen, Law and Justice: The Legal System in China, 2400 B.C. to 1960 A.D. (1974); Jerome Alan Cohen, R. Randle Edwards & Fu-mei Chang Chen, eds.,

Essays on China's Legal Tradition (1980); Wallace Johnson, trans., The T'ang Code (1979); John R. Oldham, ed., China's Legal Development (1986); Sybille van der Sprenkel, Legal Institutions in Manchu China: A Sociological Analysis (1977); Ann Waltner, Getting an Heir: Adoption and the Construction of Kinship in Late Imperial China (1990); Arthur P. Wolf & Chieh-shan Huang, Marriage and Adoption in China, 1845-1945 (1980).

3. THE CONFUCIANIST TRADITION IN YI KOREA

WILLIAM SHAW, SOCIAL AND INTELLECTUAL ASPECTS OF TRADITIONAL KOREAN LAW, in TRADITIONAL KOREAN ATTITUDES 15, 25-32 (Bong Duck Chun, William Shaw & Dai-kwon Choi eds. 1980)

The Role of Chinese Law

No understanding of the Yi-dynasty legal tradition is possible without coming to grips with the role of Chinese law and legal concepts in Korea during the Yi period. The penal code of the Ming dynasty, the *Ta-Ming lū*, though modified in some particulars by the effect of subsequent Korean legislation, was the basis for criminal law in Korea from the time of its reception in the fifteenth century. Some provisions, notably those pertaining to flogging as a penalty for Korean subjects, were retained in the code revisions of 1907-1908, which took place under Japanese auspices after the Japanese assumption of protectorate control over Korea.

Chinese law, particularly that of the T'ang and Sung periods, was known in Korea before the Yi dynasty. During the final decades of the preceding Koryō dynasty (918-1392), there had even been a short-lived attempt to make use of Yūan legislation. Partly due to the pro-Ming diplomacy of the new regime of Yi Sōng-gye, however, and partly due to the greater clarity and level of organization of the Ming Code, it was the latter that was finally adopted in Korea. "Intelligibility of the law must be a primary concern of the ruler," argued a 1388 proponent of the Ming Code.

This law appealed to the Yi-dynasty founder and his advisors because of its clarity and for legal, institutional, and conceptual reasons. These included a desire to establish clear jurisdictional lines between confused and competing judicial agencies, concern for careful review of death-penalty cases, and a determination that officials trying cases must adhere to code provisions and not introduce extraneous considerations into their judgments. Discussions in the late Koryō and early Yi periods of these and related questions reveal not only the shortcomings of the Koryō legal system but also the general familiarity of Korean thinkers and administrators with these fundamental values of the Chinese legal tradition.

In sum, an important characteristic of Ming law for the bureaucrats and statesmen of the early Yi period was its rationality. The Ming Code was seen as valuable in the task of imposing order on the administration of justice and in the establishment of systematic disciplinary reform. As a system of criminal law, the Ming Code was a coherent and self-consistent body of statutes that attempted to cover all possible circumstances, thereby reducing the risk of unwarranted judicial discretion. Officials were expected to use code provisions and not their subjective moral or other insights in settling cases, and penalties were provided for failure to accurately and fully cite the statute being applied.

The Ming Code not only provided a basic foundation for criminal law during the Yi period, but also served as the basic foundation for a comprehensive social reform along neo-Confucian lines. This was accomplished by the increased criminalization of offenses among family members, for example, as well as in other ways. The Ming Code was in this respect the most thoroughly "Confucian" avatar of Chinese legal development.

Korean Legislation

Of course, Ming law was not the only law in effect in Korea, even during the early decades of the Yi period. A native administrative and penal code, the *Kyōngje yukchōn* (Six-Division Code for Administration), was promulgated as early as 1397. Each of the six divisions of this code corresponded to one of the principal administrative boards of the central government, which generally was organized along Chinese lines as in the preceding Koryō period. Three revisions of this code were produced between 1413 and 1433. These became in turn the basis for the central legislative accomplishment of the early Yi dynasty, the *Kyōngguk taejōn* (Great Code for Administering the Country). This code stated explicitly that the Ming Code would be the basic criminal law of the dynasty, even while adding to Ming criminal law in important ways. Major supplements to the *Kyōngguk taejōn* appeared in 1746, 1785, and 1865. There is every indication that such legislative activity received a high priority in terms of personnel and other resources. Many scholars active in helping to draft the *Kyōngguk taejōn* were among the foremost literary and academic minds in the government, equally adept and accomplished in such diverse fields as Chinese phonology, history, and classics. As important as Chinese law was in the Yi dynasty, then, it would be misleading to slight the significance of domestic codification and other forms of lawmaking.

What was the content of this Korean legislation? Essentially, Korean law developed to regulate positive programs of administration, including tax and population policies, ritual matters, and military organization, for which contemporary Chinese law offered little that could be applied to specifically Korean conditions. Thus, although the fifteenth-century *Kyōngguk taejōn* code stated that the Ming criminal code was to be used, the penal statutes of the Korean compilation went on through more than twenty sections of law that amplified or differed from Ming law. Later, as Chinese and Korean case law continued to develop, supplementary codifications appeared in both countries, accentuating procedural and substantive divergences between the two. Reflections of such divergences are not difficult to trace even in the first century of Yi rule. Korean slave-ownership customs and inheritance rules did not correspond to Chinese practice. Korea's conceptions of social-status distinctions were more ramified than those of China and found expression in sumptuary regulations and in criminal procedure. In some instances, actions not mentioned in the Ming Code were criminalized or penalties for specific offenses under Ming law were raised or lowered.

Despite the existence and growth of such distinctions, however, Korean criminal law never departed significantly from the fundamental theoretical categories of Chinese criminal law. A hypothetical visiting Chinese jurist might have been puzzled by the details of Korean penal statutes, but he would have found little theoretical novelty in Korean legislation or judicial reasoning. Many Korean code provisions remained keyed to the Ming Code, either explicitly or by analogy. As in China, the categories of Ming law remained fundamental for generations of subsequent jurists (and officials).

QUESTIONS

Was the Korean reception of Chinese law similar to the German or French reception of Roman law? Were the reasons for reception similar?

4. JAPAN'S AMBIVALENT LEGAL TRADITION

NOTE ON JAPANESE INSTITUTIONAL HISTORY

Chinese conceptions of imperial governance and patterns of bureaucratic rule also transformed Japan. Adapting the T'ang Code, the sinicizing rulers of the emergent Japanese state had established by the end of the eighth century a new legal order, the foundations of which lasted until Japan's Western law reforms of the late 19th century. Centrifugal political forces, however, disabled Japan from ever fully replicating the Chinese state. Powerful clans with familial ties to the Japanese imperial throne prevented the establishment of a merit-based bureaucracy, and claims to deistic ancestry by the occupants of Japan's imperial throne precluded the introduction of any notion of a heavenly mandate for imperial rule that could be withdrawn as well as bequeathed. Finally, grants of largely autonomous, tax-exempt estates (*shōen*) to the nobility, powerful Buddhist temples, and others in positions of control and influence gradually dissipated the powers of the center and led to the gradual collapse of effective governance from the imperial capital.

By the 13th century the throne had been forced to yield most of its administrative powers to a warrior caste organized through consensual arrangements in which loyalty and service were exchanged for protection and reward. Although the offices, titles of appointment, and forms of a sinicized administrative state remained along with a jurisdictionally truncated imperial government, new patterns of legal ordering were developed. These relied on customary rules, recognized through an essentially judicial process and adherence to precedent, that were only partially supplemented by administrative edict. Japan thus began to evolve legal institutions and processes that more closely resembled those of feudal Europe than of any of its East Asian neighbors.

Only vestiges of the centralized institutions of imperial governance remained in Japan by the mid-16th century. Successive wars left the nation divided into hundreds of competing domains whose warrior-lords, unlike their predecessors, had not the faintest claim to legitimacy by office or title from a now impoverished and powerless throne.

Without any ties to imperial rule, the new 16th century *daimyō* began for the first time in Japanese history to legislate as territorial sovereigns, issuing edicts applicable to all inhabitants within their domains. Until then the T'ang-based imperial code — *ritsuryō* — along with an accretion of supplemental statutes and regulations (*ryaku-shiki*), stood as the only national territorial law. The private *shōen* manors, like the temples and other organizations, had their internal rules, and past daimyō had generally claimed only the prerogative to legislate (and adjudicate) matters affecting the warrior caste.

The pivotal event of the mid-to-late 16th century was the sudden development of castle towns (*jōkamachi*) and the relocation of the samurai from the villages. Within the span of only a few decades various daimyō throughout Japan built new fortifications and began the movement, ultimately completed under Hideyoshi, to require their samurai retainers to establish residence in these new centers where they could be more closely supervised. In addition whatever proprietary rights in land they may have had were converted into fixed stipends for service measured by estimated yields of rice from their prior holdings. Recognition of cultivator proprietary rights, nationwide cadastral surveys, and the reorganization of local communities into administrative units were among the other important reforms during this period.

Sixteenth century Japan also witnessed the consolidation of power by the three warrior "unifiers" of late medieval Japan: Oda Nobunaga, Toyotomi Hideyoshi, and finally, Tokugawa Ieyasu. Nobunaga and his successor, Hideyoshi, managed to establish control by force of arms and the adoption nationwide of many of the innovations for effective governance introduced by local daimyō.

Tokugawa Ieyasu completed the reforms begun by his two predecessors and in the process created a system of national governance that continued until the mid-19th century. His more immediate political reforms included a seclusion policy that limited all contact between Japan and the outside world to the small port of Nagasaki in southern Japan, with the Dutch granted the monopoly for trade with Europe. Stringent anti-Christian measures enforced through compulsory temple registration and a surveillance system with internal border checks were also instituted. Other new measures for political control included holding hostage the wives and children of all daimyō in the vicinity of the Tokugawa stronghold at Edo (now Tokyo), along with mandatory personal attendance of all daimyō and renewal of fealty every two years.

Tokugawa Ieyasu and his successors introduced few if any legal innovations. Rather they perfected preexisting forms of political and legal control. As a result of their efforts, however, Japan's legal order reverted partially to the older sinicized forms of law and legal institutions. They too legislated as territorial rulers and freely borrowed the forms and style of the *ritsuryō* and Chinese law, including the Ming Code. Often hortatory in tone despite their regulatory intent, the sumptuary edicts issued by the Tokugawa rulers increased over the years to constitute a vast volume of administrative and penal regulation. The 1742 *Osadamegaki* of Tokugawa Yoshimune, the eighth shogun, was the Tokugawa equivalent in nearly all respects to an imperial *ritsuryō*. Finally the transformation of the warrior caste completed the recreation of a sinicized administrative state. This caste, now divorced from land and village, changed into an hereditary elite as Japan's version of the Chinese literati-bureaucracy, with new emphasis on neo-Confucianist thought as the ideological basis for stable Tokugawa rule.

Nevertheless, much that was native to older forms of warrior governance also continued to develop. The adjudicatory processes of legal ordering remained strong despite a repeated emphasis on negotiated settlement of disputes and mediation. Although the parties might be instructed as to their mutual shortcomings and responsibilities, giving Tokugawa conciliation its "didactic" quality, they still could and did resort to administrative officials for adjudicatory redress of grievances. In the precedents that developed, along with the customary law that was made, Japan developed a nascent system of private "rights" at least for property and commercial transactions.

The lives of the vast majority of Japanese, however, were regulated less by law than by the consensual and customary rules governing village communities. The relocation of warriors from villages and the pattern of indirect rule through village headmen perfected under the Tokugawa shogunate meant that village Japan was, for the most part, self-governing. So long as taxes were paid and peace maintained, outside intervention by the ruling military overlords was rare. The consequence was the development of a dense fabric of extralegal community controls that regulated the affairs of most Japanese in the village and town.

JOHN OWEN HALEY, AUTHORITY WITHOUT POWER: LAW AND THE JAPANESE PARADOX 38-40 (1991)

With the establishment of the Kamakura *bakufu* [in 1181, literally, "tent government"], a remarkably sophisticated system of adjudication became an integral feature of Japanese governance. As noted, the court in Kyoto remained institutionally intact and maintained a parallel system of law enforcement. The Kamakura rulers, however, were compelled to adapt to new political conditions and demands. Pressed to reestablish order, the warrior-administrators found in adjudication an ideally suited means of legal control. First, adjudicatory emphasis on processes for resolving rival claims and land disputes allowed them to restore and preserve order with minimum cost. A bureaucratic public law regime would have required an extensive force of policing officials and the sort of extensive internal controls of the Chinese administrative state that for Japan had earlier been unattainable. More to the point, an official bureaucracy would have demanded a restructuring of *bakufu* organization — essentially its defeudalization — by either replacing vassals with appointed officials or transforming vassalage into official service, which occurred much later in the sixteenth and seventeenth centuries. Law enforcement by adjudication, on the other hand, amounted to a form of indirect rule with only isolated tests of power. It required less manpower and fewer resources.

Adjudication also complemented *bakufu* authority. Those who dispensed justice did so as neutral arbiters deciding claims based on local practice, custom, and official documents, not legislated codes. Both those who sought relief or defended against a claim could submit to the authority of the Kamakura *bakufu* as equals or near equals obliged to obey out of bonds of allegiance. "Kamakura," as Jeffrey Mass concludes, "thus remained outside and above the suits it sought to resolve, and in the process insulated itself from undue partisanship or criticism."[a] ...

Kamakura jurisdiction extended to three categories of suits. Those involving land tenure and title were classified as *shomusata* and were tried in both Kamakura and *bakufu* offices in Kyoto. What would today be classified as criminal cases — actions involving rebellion, theft, brigandry, homicide, rape, violent assaults, and similar conduct — were tried by special *bakufu* offices in either Kamakura or Kyoto under *shomusata* procedures. The third category of miscellaneous cases, referred to as *zatsumusata,* encompassed various claims to property, other than land, arising from interest-bearing loans, bills of exchange, mortgages, and sales. At least by the fourteenth century these suits were being tried in Kamakura before the *monchūjo* under direct control of the *bakufu.*

Law enforcement by the Kamakura authorities could only be activated by outside complaint or accusation generally, and the process remained subject to the initiative and direction of the litigants. "In this way," Mass correctly observes, "the Bakufu was fundamentally judicial in character and not merely a policing agency." Also evident is the procedural sophistication and inherent rationality of the Kamakura adjudicatory process. Upon receipt of a petition with attached documents, the authorities reviewed it to assure that the controversy was properly within their jurisdiction. If so, the next step was to assign the case to the proper *bakufu* agency, taking into account the parties, the issues, and the location of the property at issue or wrongdoing. Unless the matter could be decided or resolved after the initial pleading, the authorities would subpoena the accused to submit a response and, if necessary, submit to a hearing. The outcome of the process depended primarily upon the persuasiveness of the parties' documentary evidence, especially the availability of official instruments or records issued by the court officials or the *bakufu.* If testimony were needed, the authorities could take statements from witnesses — ordinarily it appears at the request of one of the parties. A witness could be summoned either to appear at Kamakura (or Kyoto) or a convenient site such as the headquarters of the local *bakufu*-appointed military governor [*shugo*]. A form of affidavit or deposition by a witness or the parties (*kishōmon*) could also be arranged by the litigants and submitted in lieu of live testimony. Cases could be reopened for reconsideration, and as the system later evolved, a system of appeals [*osso*] was instituted. As in Chinese practice, no substantive conceptual distinction was made between civil and criminal matters. Coupled with the requirements of party initiative to bring an action, there could be "no penalties for crimes not included in original indictments." Yet, the system represented the mirror image of the Chinese system in its reliance on party initiative and control.

---

[a] Jeffrey P. Mass, The Development of Kamakura Rule (1979).

YOSHIRŌ HIRAMATSU, TOKUGAWA LAW, 14 Law in Japan 1, 27-28, 31-38 (Dan Fenno Henderson trans. 1981)[a]

Enforcement of Law

Shogunal hearing procedures [by the late 18th century under Tokugawa rule] were divided into "inquisitorial proceedings" and "adversary proceedings."... The inquisitorial proceedings were procedures for exercising the penal power, and can be called criminal hearings, but in the adversary proceedings, besides hearing disputes over private powers, they also imposed light penalties. So it became a mixed civil and criminal hearing. For the petitioning private person, the inquisitorial or adversary proceedings were optional. Did he seek to punish his opponent, or to resolve the quarrel? The official could start inquisitorial proceedings at any time. It was also possible to convert an examination begun as an adversary proceeding into an inquisitorial one. Conversely, there were legal limits on changing an inquisitorial proceeding into an adversary one.

Thus the two procedures had a common element, but the distinction between them was based on whether the procedural progress was carried forward by the authorities, or whether it could be maneuvered according to the wishes of a private person. The subjects of inquisitorial proceedings were criminal cases which were involved with the lord's authority itself and with social discipline. Thus, they were carried forward by the lord's authority and the procedure progressed throughout as the lord's affair (*goyō*).

The subject of an adversary proceeding was a private quarrel which had few connections with the lord's interests, but it was a matter, originally between the parties, in which the authorities were specially asked to intervene in order to dispose of and settle the case. Because this was a matter of gracious "mercy," the parties were required to compromise and conciliate as quickly as possible and leave the "court." In a technical legal sense, all cases in which "conciliation" and "requests for withdrawal of inquisitions" were not permitted were definitely inquisitorial matters; others could become adversary matters....

Inquisitorial Proceedings

Inquisitorial proceedings had two stages: determination of the facts of the crime and the decision on the penalty. In the first stage, legal controls were extremely weak; in the second, prudence was carried to an extreme. In the determination of the criminal facts, the ever abiding pursuit of a confession was the special feature. To hand down a decision of guilt at all, a confession of the principal was essential, and moreover a confession was sufficient to establish guilt. Even if there was other evidence, the examination could not be concluded without a confession; so they tried to induce a confession even by applying torture. With a confession, if there was a confirming statement from persons concerned, background physical evidence was not necessarily required....

[a] Certain Japanese terms are omitted.

The confession was finally prepared as a protocol, and then the commissioner would assemble in the court all persons concerned, read it to them and have the principal seal it. This was called the "record of the conclusion of inquiry," and with it, the penalty was decided at an examination-by-document.

The scope of penalties within which the Commissioners and the Deputies could decide "summarily" was fixed, and in cases outside that scope (or cases difficult to decide), an executive inquiry was submitted to a higher agency in accordance with the channels of control. Since these inquiries eventually were gathered at the Senior Council, all of the important cases from Shogunal hearing offices all over the country were recorded by the Senior Council, and it could thus issue instructions with uniformity. This was the so-called central concentration of authority by limiting the inferior administrators' powers. The Commissioners and Deputies, in practice, drafted the inquiries in accordance with the *Osadamegaki* and precedents. Under the Senior Council, the Inner-secretary-in-charge-of-executions specially studied their propriety under the *Osadamegaki* and precedents, and if there was no problem, the Senior Council issued its instructions. The Senior Council, when necessary, handed cases down to the Chamber-in-Bank and had it deliberate. The Chamber would search the *Osadamegaki* and precedents in depth. The consultation was but a reference opinion, but in fact the Senior Council accepted the recommendation in most cases. The Chamber-in-Bank had the function of unifying to a degree the decisions of the hearing offices all over the country.

The Senior Council could also put questions regarding interpretation of the *Osadamegaki* to the Three Commissioners in Charge of the *Osadamegaki*. If a case became a moral problem, they could seek an opinion from a confucianist or Hayashi Daigaku-no-kami,[b] but as the theory of precedent crystallized Hayashi Daigaku-no-kami said: "If I adhere entirely to the phrasing of the Chinese penal statutes, it must run counter to the national polity," and did not especially offer counterarguments. When a sentence was delivered, the case was concluded. Since there was no system of appeal, the penalty was immediately executed.

The purpose of the penalties was to deter the people in general, to eliminate criminals ("one killed; many live"), and to satisfy the victims' feeling of vengeance. Thus the policy of maintaining discipline predominated, and the retributive concept which punishes because crime is evil was comparatively weak.

Private Authority

Deeds

In the Tokugawa law, it was not quite proper, actually, to use the word, "rights" (*kenri*) concerning private persons. This is because both the concept that private individuals possess and enjoy equally rights from birth as in the modern law, and the state agency to guarantee them by trial, were lacking.

---

[b] The head of the Hayashi family or school of advisors to the Shogunate, founded after the appointment in 1608 of Hayashi Razan by Tokugawa Ieyasu, as his official Confucian advisor.

But of course the individual's so-called sphere of autonomous activity did exist, and its nature was close to that of "rights." The individual could exercise his authority himself, and also it was possible, according to circumstances, for the lord or others to assert it for him. Private authority (*shiken*) in this sense (and we use it with this meaning here) followed from moral standards or social status. In other words, it was granted as a natural or customary thing flowing from one's position in his community, and at times it was facilitated by the lord's *ad hoc* order, proclamation of a statute or license, or resulted from his non-intervention .... Also it could be asserted by a "contract" or will based on the volition of the individual. Originally private authority was a matter which the individual or group had to defend itself, but there were also situations where either the lord defended it with punishments, or where it was given protection through the hearing agencies. The degree and method of that participation was governed by the interest and policy of the lord, and accordingly the efficacy of private authority was not of constant strength. The individual, in order to insure the enforcement of his own wishes made "deeds." Deeds were also called "notes" or "bonds," and a great variety and volume of these exist today. They, along with a variety of forms, and collections of drafts, represent the general popular law of the Tokugawa period. We can consider two reasons why these deeds were specifically made so frequently. First, for purposes of evidence at a later date, they added social pressure to force the performance of the other party, and documents were required in presenting a petition to the hearing officer .... Second, they were necessary to decide the substance and condition of right between the parties, since actual private law rules were practically non-existent. The requirements for submitting a petition to the hearing offices regulated the form and content of the deeds and standardized them, and the right to petition began to cause a kind of private law to develop. In the Tokugawa period there was no civil code, but in the deeds and in the courtyard there was civil law, whatever the extent of it.

Tokugawa period deeds, to give them compelling force, sought reliability by requiring the participation of the village or block officials and also witnesses, but that was not the only method to strengthen their contractual effectiveness. There is something which legal historians call an outrage clause. It is said to be a contract phrase whereby the obligee and public make the person not performing submit to an insult, and we know in the Tokugawa period of the called "ridicule deeds" as examples of this. Stories were written in the miscellanies of that time to the effect that there were deeds in the past saying, if by chance borrowed money was not repaid, "even if I [borrower] should be laughed at among the people, on such occasion, there will be not a word of protest." These deeds were dated in the Manji period (1658-1661) and Genroku period (1688-1704). Originals of such deeds have not been found, but in the latter half of the Edo period, these stories of an ancient period perhaps have some credibility. Actually using one's honor as security was something that could be quite real, and it may be regarded as consistent with transactions between businessmen. As to the customs of Osaka businessmen, the *Nihon shōji kanrei ruishū* says, "Most of them concluded their sales with an oral promise and hand clasp, also the exchange of written promises agreed upon went no further than using simple sales slips." Thus it is reported that oral contracts were made with a hand clasp, and only simple memoranda were issued. Concerning their effect, the same source says, "In past transactions, naturally they were in good faith, and even if it was an oral promise, there was a custom that it could not be intentionally broken, and if one caused disputes or such by seizing an unprovable oral promise as an opportunity to gain for oneself, or in order to avoid one's own loss, one's credit in transactions would immediately crash to the ground, and one would not be able to stand upright among businessmen." Here we can see that honor in vocation and status had more power than law.

Main Suits and Money Suits

Filings by individuals at the offices were uniformly called complaints (*uttae*) or petitions (*soshō*). Submissions of complaints for hearings, as well as requests, memorials, applications, reports and the like were all embraced in these terms.

The commoners were not necessarily fearful or reluctant to file at the offices. Assertions of their "rights" based on status such as house-rank or seating order were extremely fierce, from the daimyō down to the commoners. The "Sitting Places" or "Sit-down Tea Houses," serving as waiting places for persons connected with petitions and attached to the Chamber and Commission offices, were generally busy and crowded. Most "suit inns" were established as businesses. The premise for hearing adversary proceedings was the classification of them into "main suits," "money suits" and "mutual affairs." Their formalities had been minutely defined, at the latest in the Meiwa period (1764-1772). But in the beginning they were derived from the clerical necessity of limiting the filings of complaints. Claims for borrowed gold or silver might be regarded as the representative money suit; and for main suits, it was hardship disputes, land disputes and disputes over illegality. But main suits also included: house management, pledged lands, pledged houses, bills of exchange, tenancy, wages of servants, shop construction, and breaches of village practices.

Money suits were obligations bearing interest but without security. It can be said the main suits were all suits outside those transactions. Money suits were simply complaints seeking repayment or borrowed gold and silver; so there was little need for participation of the authorities, but main suits, along with confirming status and land boundaries, disposing of security and priority payments, eliminating or preventing damage and restoring to the original state and the like, had a high degree of need for disposition and determination by the authorities. Obligations designated as money suits generally received cold treatment as compared to main suits. Frequently, by several Mutual Settlement Ordinances in 1661, 1719, 1789 and 1843, the offices ordered the parties to settle among themselves, and refused to receive money petitions, designating them as matters "not to be taken up." Furthermore under Cancellation Ordinances pronounced in 1789, 1842 and 1843, the obligations were declared worthless.

The discrimination seen against money suits was more pronounced in mutual affairs, and this was confirmed by the *Osadamegaki*. Quarrels centering on profit-and-loss accounting in joint enterprises of several persons, mutual funds, and capital shares in the theatre were (all three) listed in the *Osadamegaki*, Second Book, article 33, and in 1843 pleasure girl fees were added. It was provided that, as mutual affairs, they were "not to be taken up" even if a petition was filed. With main suits as the standard, protection of money petitions was weak, and in mutual affairs, there was no authority to petition. Even in matters "not to be taken up," if payment was made between the parties, it was an effective payment, and not unjust enrichment; the obligation was discharged. In present day law, this came to be called a natural obligation, and it is an exceptional thing, but in Tokugawa law, this kind of thing (what we might call a weak "right" not protected by hearings) was quite widespread. The grounds for the discrimination against money suits and mutual affairs was found in "mutual contract" based on the "actual intent" of both parties. In Tokugawa law, underlaid by the principle of party self-reliance, naturally the parties should have been prepared to settle between themselves. There were two theories: (1) what might be called the "mutuality" theory, which held it improper to demand intervention by the authorities and (2) the "immoral" theory which held that from the standpoint of feudal morality, this type of claim was considered vulgar. Their emphases differ. Money suits were simply payment problems. Originally the reason for discriminating may be thought to be in the degree of need for participation by Tokugawa hearing offices, which, being essentially administrative anyway, had little enthusiasm for such settlements. We can say that when the relief it afforded warriors became quite plain, then the immoral quality of this type of claim came to be asserted with special strength.

Adversary Proceedings and Conciliation

The lord controlling the parties' place of registry had the hearing authority for adversary proceedings. "Disputes involving (two) different jurisdictions," as they were called, or petitions concerning another fief were accorded collegial hearings by the Shogunal Chamber-in-Bank. The headman's seal at the end was necessary on the complaint, that is, the petition. To file a petition with the Shogunate and make a person from another jurisdiction your opponent, an "accompanying messenger" from the domain (or in the case of fiefs of bannermen and the like an "accompanying letter") was required. In both cases some lord's officer went along and appeared at the hearing office to prove the registry and jurisdiction. Petitions were not an individual's problem; they were prosecuted on the basis of consent and support from the block, village or domain.

Adversary proceedings began with a procedure called "examination of the complaint." This was an investigation of the petitioner (plaintiff) and his petition by professional officers, and the main subjects were the jurisdiction to hear it and the "suit title." The suit titles were headings (e.g., dispute-over-a-shop; dispute-over-changes-in-agreements, or the like), and they had legally standardized the types of plaintiffs' claims. The relationship between the suit title and the actual legal problem shown in the deed was studied, and it was decided whether the petition was to be classed as a main suit or money suit, or as acceptable or unacceptable. In the adversary proceeding, the professional law was most developed concerning forms of suit titles and the methods of disposing of them, and the complaint examination had an aspect rather judicial in nature.

These questions in the complaint — what might be called the drafting of its legal structure — were too much for amateurs; they usually went as clients to a suit inn. The commission which received the complaint wrote an "endorsement-on-the-back." This became the writ of summons to the "opponent" (or defendant). The commissioner sealed the endorsement-on-the-back, and this "august stamp" certified participation by the authorities. The plaintiff put this in a box (made of paulownia wood), hung it around his neck and took it himself to the place of the defendant, and at a meeting with the block or village officials delivered it to the defendant. The defendant submitted an answer to the hearing office, and this was the refutation from the defendant's side. On the designated day both parties appeared at "court," and had a confrontation, and there traded answers to the official's questioning. Both sides submitted evidence, but the office could also investigate *ex officio*. The officers were not necessarily bound by statements of the parties; they assessed the circumstances and put forward a solution from an independent standpoint. If the Commissioner pronounced it as a decision, a Deed-of-Receipt-of-Decision, jointly sealed by the parties was submitted. The plaintiff was then given the complaint and answer joined together by the office; he obtained the commissioner's seal to cancel the endorsement-on-the-back; he filed these documents in the commission office, and thus ended the petition.

It is accurate to say that the decision was like an administrative disposition. It was not a question of whether or not the plaintiff's allegations as illuminated by legal rules were reasonable. It was rather an authoritative determination and disposition of various problems centering around the particular dispute. When necessary, light penalties could also be imposed on persons concerned. In reality, there was no big difference, on this point, between these suits and the conciliatory settlements explained later. Each party bore his own expense of suit, the loser did not pay all.

In conciliation, a third person mediated and caused both parties to compromise, and the third person's acts were called "to conciliate." The person was called a "conciliator." Conciliation could be conducted either before or after the issuance of the endorsement-on-the-back. Also in inquisitional proceedings concerned with quarrels, wounding, immorality and the like (or crimes with a strong personal quality), there were instances where the offender and offended both might conciliate and discontinue the dispute, then request a stay of the inquisition. The office would end the examination by the formality of allowing it with some flexibility; this was "withdrawal of the inquisition request." At the block or village level, the conciliators were block or village officials, or persons of repute in the district. When it came to petitions concerning diverse jurisdictions, the appropriateness of such persons as conciliators was weakened, and pressures of the hearing office and coordinating activity of the suit inns became necessary. On reaching a settlement, both parties made a deed ("settlement deed"), and it had the same effect as a "judgment," on being announced by the commissioner.

In money suits, especially, conciliation was encouraged and the plaintiff alone could approve a settlement ("settlement by one side"). In water disputes, conciliation on the spot was made a precondition to filing a petition ("matter of negotiating on the spot"). Because conciliation sought only to cause a concrete accord between the parties in order to settle the dispute, an authoritative investigation of proof was not usually conducted and the pattern of facts not necessarily publicly clarified. Also differing from the decision, compulsory execution or "[to take all] to the extent of belongings" was not practiced. The commissions and officials led and persuaded the parties concerned toward a proposed solution fair in all the circumstances, and at times threatened to impose punishment and also made attempts to brow beat.

The reasons that conciliation was made, in principle, the method to settle private disputes are many: (1) legal sentiment favored a particular concrete solution over a legalistic determination; (2) priority of community custom and discipline; (3) confucianistic ideas of respecting harmony in social discipline; (4) lack of development in the private law; (5) lack of facilities and efficiency in the hearing agencies; (6) the Shogunate's policy of non-interference with its territorial interests. Also pressure for compromise was promoted by concepts favoring autonomy and disposition by the parties, or that in quarrels and breaches of discipline the merits were 50-50. So in the *Kentei hikki*[c] there is the following criticism: "In suits and disputes it is not good to order conciliation, if justice becomes a compromise, the one in the wrong gets some benefit." Conciliation in principle prevented the nurturing of rights consciousness in either the commoners or the officials. Adversary proceedings also promoted the tendency to pursue only the political and concrete propriety of the result.

Suit inns were hostels where persons could stay who had come to Edo to petition. Their masters and underlings and the like came to participate in petitions, and by natural growth they came to be something vocationally resembling a lawyer.... [W]e know that in 1774 there were in Edo 198 such inns, and that finally they formed a company with three groups: (1) the travellers' inns; (2) the group of 82 inns; and (3) the group of 30 inns.

In the inquisitorial proceedings which were "Shogunal affairs," there was no room for advocacy, and in the *Koruishū* (Old classified complication) we have the following: "When suitors stay in the Edo inns, it is improper above all else to gossip about the Commission office. Therefore he who estimates the range of the penalty and tells it to others is wrong-headed and a rude person." Thus if one predicted the penalty and told it to his client, he would be punished. Since in adversary proceedings, both decisions and settlements emphasized disposition by the principals or parties, the suit inns as a rule could not be suit representatives. They could only assist their clients in or out of court. The inns helped private persons in hearings, which had become complex or technical. They stuck close by while clients were in the commission offices and were good at mediating between the offices and parties. As mediators who

[c] Official compilation of rulings.

caused settlements eventually along lines suggested by the offices, they were indispensable, even as seen from the eyes of the offices.

QUESTIONS

1. What features distinguished "inquisitorial" from adversary proceedings in Tokugawa law? To what extent did these categories correspond to criminal and civil proceedings in most contemporary legal systems?

2. How important were confessions in Tokugawa inquisitorial proceedings? Why?

3. Hiramatsu mentions an underlying principle of "party self-reliance" in Tokugawa law as well as an evident willingness to assert "rights" of status and other interests in formal proceedings. Were these tendencies encouraged in official Tokugawa policy?

4. Contrast the adjudicatory procedures in 17th and 18th century Japan with those in Siam. Which were the more rational? Is this explained by the lack of a deistic source for law in the Chinese tradition?

5. The institutions of Japanese "feudal" law are frequently compared to those in Europe, especially England. What similarities and differences do you consider significant?

JOHN OWEN HALEY, AUTHORITY WITHOUT POWER: LAW AND THE JAPANESE PARADOX 58-62 (1991)

The pivotal element of the Tokugawa legal order was not, however, this amalgam of regulatory and adjudicatory legal controls. Instead it was the paradox of a highly judicialized administrative state characterized by the autonomous village [*mura*]. The bureaucratic apparatus of the Tokugawa system was not pervasive. Urban centers may have been "overgoverned" as Hall puts it, but the Japanese *mura* remained largely autonomous. Unlike Europe, no warrior-ruler remained to become the manorial lord and ultimately the local gentry and landed aristocracy of a postfeudal generation, nor was Tokugawa Japan like Korea where a *yangban* aristocracy remained close at hand. Legal controls did not penetrate to the village level through a resident official *yamen* "runner" as in imperial China or the *sōri* clerk as in Yi dynasty Korea. The Japanese *mura* was linked to the Tokugawa or *han* [local domain] authorities solely through the formal accountability of the headman. However, any sense of responsibility or loyalty felt by headmen toward the ruling authorities was diluted by their identity of personal interests and priorities as well-placed villagers with those of the village community in general. As a result the vast majority of Japanese were freed from effective oversight and control by either a European-styled aristocracy or a Chinese-styled officialdom.

The Japanese *mura* as a self-contained, semi-autonomous economic and political unit was also a product of the late sixteenth century. The dissolution of the *shōen* estates and the consolidation by Hideyoshi of various local units — the *shō, gō, hō* and *ri* — into a single unit called the *mura* had enabled it to become the smallest territorial unit of a three-tiered political structure — provinces (*kuni*), districts (*kōri*) and villages (*mura*) — of the Tokugawa domains. Hideyoshi had also successfully defined peasant status through a series of edicts: the prohibition against peasant possession of swords and other implements of warfare, restrictions defining exclusive occupational roles for warriors and peasants and removal of the warrior from the village all served to reinforce village identity as separate community and caste.

Once the *mura* was recognized as a administrative unit, village offices were also established. The most important was that of headman. Completing a triad of village officers were the offices of *kumigashira,* comprising the three or four heads of leading households who assisted the headman, and *hyakushōdai,* representatives from a board of overseers that included all landholding families. Thus within the village a hierarchy of rank and status, presumably determined at least initially by wealth, prevailed. With the vicissitudes of economic change, however, family pedigree was as often divorced from wealth in the village as the town.

The office of headman was, at least in Tokugawa domains, ostensibly appointive or at least subject to formal *daikan*[a] approval. In practice, however, in some villages the position became an hereditary office, while in others the headmen were selected by agreement among those eligible and not uncommonly rotated at regular intervals. In some instances, the headman held the office for life. Several of the village documents collected by Henderson hint at the intrigue involved in the process of selection. In one, six village elders meet and agree to rotate the office among themselves and their descendants for five-year terms. Anticipating, however, the possibility of a retirement or the appointment of an outsider, they agree that one of the six would keep custody of a copy of village survey records and maintain a common front. In another, unable to find a successor, a village contracts with a neighboring headman to assume its office as well. In return all agree to cooperate, put an end to past disagreement and pay their respective share of village taxes as instructed by village officials. In a third, the village apparently preferred the appointment of a more wealthy farmer who lacked the requisite family status. The solution was an arrangement separating authority from power at the village level by supporting the appointment of a person who was eligible but, by agreement, recognizing the other as the one with actual responsibility.

Viewed from above, the *mura,* like its urban counterpart the *machi,* appeared to be an intensively regulated community. At least there was no dearth of regulatory proscriptions, and no facet of personal or community life was beyond the potential purview of administrative fiat. In addition to registration, tax and *corvée* labor obligations, villagers were increasingly subject to a wide variety of regulatory controls designed primarily to maximize revenue yields from rice production and closely related efforts to restrict social and geographic mobility. Villagers could not possess weapons, alienate land or legally leave the village. Even dress was prescribed to inhibit social mobility. In Akita *han,* Kōta Kodama reports, an 1807 edict prohibited peasants from wearing any rain gear other than straw hats and straw coats. Liability for any individual infraction was vicarious, with households, the five-household

[a] The daikan was the lowest legal official in the Tokugawa administrative hierarchy, with functions similar to those of an imperial Chinese magistrate.

groups and the village as a whole collectively liable for any individual misconduct and the headman individually accountable as well.

Focus on the volume and scope of regulatory edicts alone is misleading, however. Viewed over time, Tokugawa legislation manifests a consistent pattern. The greater the decline of shogunal and *han* resources and power in favor of an increasingly prosperous and autonomous rural elite whose growing manufacturing and commerce activities were outpacing their agricultural income, the more stringent became the legal controls imposed in the Tokugawa village....

From the mid-eighteenth century most Tokugawa and *han* legislation directed toward the village reflected an attempt to increase the resources under their control and at least to contain the threatening processes of economic and social change taking place in rural Japan.... In response to these social ills — all symptomatic of the diversification and growth in nonagricultural sectors of the economy — the authorities renewed old proscriptions and imposed new controls on the alienation and reclamation of land, commodity markets, rural mobility and the administration of lawsuits. These and other attempts to stem the tide of social change by edict failed. The regulatory apparatus of the Tokugawa administrative state was incapable of preventing the erosion of the foundations of Tokugawa rule.

By the end of the eighteenth century Japan had a total population of about 26.5 million persons. Eighty percent of the population comprised peasant farmers residing in one of 60,000 plus villages. Roughly four to five million lived in Tokugawa domains. With only forty *daikan* in ten districts to oversee their activities, the impracticability of adequate enforcement of Tokugawa controls is evident. Without the cooperation of village officials Tokugawa edicts could not be effectively enforced. Moreover, since most if not all Tokugawa regulation took the form of instructions issued to *daikan* and other shogunate officials and were usually not made public, even the remote possibility of voluntary village compliance was also quite limited. Where restrictions were widely publicized, villagers — especially the leading landowning families and most active commercial entrepreneurs who dominated official village posts — can hardly be expected to have submissively complied with legal restrictions designed to transfer wealth to outside authorities or deny them new sources of income. To the contrary, official reliance on village self-government and indirect rule through the mediation of village headmen enabled the village to disregard unwanted restrictions. One of the most telling of Henderson's[b] village documents is indicative of the most likely village response. In 1832 officials from six neighboring villages colluded to resist *daikan* approval of a petition to open a new field in a nearby river bed. In addition to details on the apportionment of expenses, the memorial of their agreement even anticipated and attempted to preclude the prisoner's dilemma:

> If a single village or individual [among us] should be interrogated alone, in accordance with [this agreement] petitions for opening of new fields

[b]Dan Fenno Henderson, Village "Contracts" in Tokugawa Japan 179-82 (1975).

> will not be accepted no matter where [the proposed reclamation might be located].

Japanese villagers were, it appears, quite adept at collective action to protect their own interests.

Autonomy had a price. For the community and the individual, conflict avoidance and deference to authority were the prerequisites of self-governance and independence. So long as peace prevailed and taxes were paid, there was little to draw official attention and scrutiny. However, any open conflict or breach of peace threatened that autonomy and invited investigation and more stringent controls. By suppressing intracommunity quarrels and satisfying formal fiscal obligations, a village community could restrain or avoid unwanted official regulation. The consequence was an institutional structure that in allowing evasion of official legal controls also promoted external deference and internal cohesion. In effect the village had the security of the administrative state along with the freedom of the outlaw.

To achieve or maintain such autonomy with ostensible conformity the community itself had to develop mechanisms of control. The most prominent included the psychological sanction of collective community displeasure as well as more severe forms of community coercion, such as ostracism and expulsion. Because rice cultivation necessitated a high degree of cooperation, community action had substantial coercive impact. Moreover, as the protection afforded by the community rather than outside or higher official authority was more important to the individual and the household, the threat of community sanction became an even more effective means of control. Outside one's village the individual no longer shared the material or psychological benefits of membership. The alternative was flight to urban centers without introduction and guarantees, often in defiance of legal restrictions on travel and change of residence, possibly offering the unattractive alternative of more direct supervision and stringent legal regulation within *machi,* which were also semi-autonomous and subject to similar community controls. Consequently, community sanctions of both formal and informal stripe, not the samurai's sword, were the real deterrents to wrongdoing in Tokugawa Japan. Moreover, inasmuch as such sanctions were as readily imposed on the family for the misconduct of its members as other village documents in the Henderson collection suggest, the family tended to parallel the village in both its need for a means to control its members and the forms of coercion it used.

In this environment individual interests were generally subsumed by community and family concerns. At each level of social organization from the larger village to the nuclear family and the individual, a greater measure of effective autonomy was achieved by outward display of dependence and deference to authority. All stood to gain therefore by overt submission to those with power at each level in the hierarchy of authority and to control by whatever means the conduct of others for whom one might be vicariously liable. In other words, the Tokugawa scheme of indirect governance set into motion a process that fostered social cohesion as a means of maximizing autonomy, coinciding neatly with the neo-Confucian norms of loyalty and respect for authority. In other words Japan evolved a self-enforcing process of autonomy with dependence.

NOTES AND QUESTIONS

1. Viraphol in his comparison of Siamese and Chinese law also notes the prevalence of corruption in both systems:

> Operating, as they did, in a setting of monarchical absolutism, both the Siamese and Chinese legal systems were inevitably susceptible to abuses, despite their presupposed foundation upon a divine set of ethics and morality. The main problem was, of course, human frailty. No matter how perfect a structure for the administration of justice could be drawn up, under the operating system of *pouvoir arbitraire,* the human element was ever ready to undermine it. Consequently, the main drawbacks to the traditional systems stemmed from such factors as unscrupulous judges and other officials concerned with the administration of justice, including the king himself.

Similar observations have been made by others in accounts of the problems in the administration of justice in Korea as well as other traditional systems in East Asia. Studies of traditional Japanese law are notably silent on the issue. There thus appears to have been remarkably little corruption, at least in its more venal forms, in Tokugawa Japan. Can this be explained in terms of either institutional or cultural characteristics of the Japanese legal process?

2. Do the developed legal traditions in East Asia have any features in common? If so, what are they? To what extent do these characteristics resemble or differ from the Roman and pre-Columbian legal traditions? How do they compare in regard to the following features:

(1) method of developing law and communicating it to others;
(2) choice of law rule for conquered subjects;
(3) correcting private wrongs;
(4) formality of procedure and courts;
(5) rationality of proof-taking methods;
(6) existence of a legal profession;
(7) legal treatment of the nobility compared to commoners;
(8) legal regulation of familial, commercial, and other private relationships; and
(9) access to formal adjudicatory processes for enforcing legal rules.

3. Contrast the legal institutions of 12th century Europe (as discussed by Berman in Chapter 3, Section C) with those described below in 12th and 13th century Japan. How would you explain the similarities and differences?

4. For more on Japanese legal history, see the bibliography in John Owen Haley, Authority Without Power: Law and the Japanese Paradox 233-45 (1991).

Chapter 5

THE INTELLECTUAL REVOLUTION AND LEGAL SCIENCE

In Chapters 3 and 4 we surveyed the history of the civil law tradition from its Roman origins to its spread throughout Europe and Latin America. In this chapter we complete the historical survey and bring the civil law tradition up to modern times. We are here concerned with the two remaining components of the civil law tradition: the intellectual revolution (with particular reference to the 1789 Revolution in France and its consequences) and legal science, primarily a German phenomenon. It is the combination of these modern intellectual and political developments with the materials and traditions of the Roman-canonic *jus commune* and European commercial law that produced contemporary civil law systems.

We also encounter here some of the diversity that characterizes the civil law world. From 450 B.C. until the intellectual revolution (more than 2,000 years), the civil law was an Italic, Roman-law based international tradition revived and nourished by the Renaissance. With the Revolution the life of the civil law continued, but in the context of the nation-state. And, inevitably, different national experiences led to different legal developments. The first and most significant divergence is between France and Germany.

> Of both France and Germany it is often said that they follow "the civil law" tradition, as though there were only one. But the account already given should indicate that before 1800 they had used Roman law in very different ways. The divergences between their legal systems was not as great as the gulf between them and English law, for Frenchmen and Germans had in Roman law at least a common vocabulary. On the issues that are of interest here — the role of courts and of the law that courts manufacture — it seemed that France and Germany around 1800 were poised in a kind of tacit agreement; they both placed case law far down on the scale among available sources of law. But the forces that had brought them to this momentary agreement were entirely different. Faced thereafter with great social changes and unexpected demands, the legal systems of the two countries have responded in very different ways.[a]

We first look at France, the enactment of its five codes, and the impact of the Revolution in Europe and Latin America. Next we turn to Germany and consider its development of legal science. Finally, we take up the reception of European law in East Asia at the end of the 19th century and in the 20th century.

[a] John P. Dawson, The Oracles of the Law 374 (1968).

A. THE INTELLECTUAL REVOLUTION

1. THE FRENCH *PARLEMENTS*

BAILEY STONE, THE FRENCH *PARLEMENTS* AND THE CRISIS OF THE OLD REGIME 18-20 (1986)

[F]ourteen provincial *parlements* shared with the primal *parlement* at Paris (and with a few more specialized law courts) a multiplicity of judicial roles. Each tribunal was officially styled a "sovereign court" — that is, sovereign in the sense that it adjudged appeals from all presidial courts, *bailliages* or *sénéchaussées,* and lesser royal courts in its jurisdiction, and could only be overruled in such cases by the king's Council or by such high tribunal as the king himself should designate on appeal. In addition, each tribunal functioned as a court of first instance for certain privileged litigants and in certain fields of litigation....

[T]his judicial role carried with it an administrative function in a society whose justice and administration had always been closely intertwined. It is true that each provincial tribunal had to share this latter function with the intendant, the military governor and/or lieutenant-general, the Estates if still active, the archbishop or bishop, and various municipal officers. And even the mighty Paris Parlement increasingly had to reckon in the eighteenth century with the *lieutenant-général de police* in the capital and with the intendants and their subordinates in the surrounding regions. Nonetheless, the judges all over France continued to have their fingers in a thousand and one administrative pies. In times of emergency, these justices could arrest or detain "seditious" individuals, ban public gatherings in city, village, or countryside, and impose curfews. Of greater moment on a day-to-day basis were the *parlementaires'* use of *arrêts de règlement.* By means of such regulatory decrees they helped to ensure the provisioning of foodstuffs and firewood to their communities, maintain the upkeep of urban thoroughfares and the sound condition of public and private buildings, and regulate hospitals, religious foundations, and prisons. Through their supervision of merchants, butchers, bakers, and a myriad of guilds and other associations the magistrates had much to say about wages, commodities, and working conditions in their cities and towns. They helped supervise universities, *collèges,* and academies, and charged the officers of lower courts with the same function. Further, the judges, in conjunction with the police, acted as censors of public morals and literature, investigating the conduct of public officials and sociable sons of nobility and sanctioning or burning books and pamphlets. Finally, the *parlementaires* could launch full-scale inquests into controversies within their jurisdictions. Let overseers of work upon the king's bridges and highways be accused of abusing their laborers, for instance, and the *parlement* within whose jurisdiction such malfeasance was reported would require from subordinate courts all particulars upon the matter....

Unfortunately for the cause of harmony between monarch and magistrates, the latter had in the eighteenth century a more potent excuse for challenging the government on the legislative front. In the continuing absence of the Estates General, the *parlements* had been conceded the right to legalize many of the king's public policies. They did so by transcribing legislation implementing such policies upon their official registers in formal plenary sessions. This ceremony of *enregistrement* was essential for the legitimization of the monarch's edicts, for it — and it alone — made them enforceable as law throughout the kingdom. *Enregistrement* simultaneously reaffirmed the legality of French kingship itself. On the other hand, the *parlementaires* could protest against legislation they deemed "illegal" and/or harmful to the king and his subjects. It was in playing this quasi-legislative role that the judges loomed so large in the political calculations of Louis XVI's ministers in the late 1780s.

LENARD R. BERLANSTEIN, THE BARRISTERS OF TOULOUSE IN THE EIGHTEENTH CENTURY (1740-1793) 1-4, 104-05 (1975)

Legal institutions determined the pace and tone of life in eighteenth-century Toulouse, so the city assumed a new sense of animation each year after November 12, Saint Martin's Day. This date marked the annual convocation of the Parlement, after which the city was busy handling the legal affairs of the huge province of Languedoc whose capital it was. Litigants came to Toulouse in very large numbers, on foot, by coach, or by sedan. Everyone, from the sharecropper to "Monsieur," the king's brother, brought cases to the bar of Toulouse. The courts in this proud capital were numerous, and anyone who contested a will, attempted to collect a debt, or defended himself against criminal accusations might well have found himself called before a Toulousan magistrate.

This renewed flow of litigants was supplemented by the arrival of nearly 400 law students. Toulouse was the home of the most important law faculty in the Midi. Some revered legal scholars, Cujas in particular, had lectured there and endowed it with much prestige. That academic standards had become scandalously low by the late eighteenth century did not diminish the éclat of a degree from the Law Faculty of Toulouse. On the contrary, low standards probably encouraged more students to matriculate.

With its tribunals and law school, Toulouse was the legal city par excellence. In one corner of the city stood the Palace of the august Parlement. This was the second Sovereign Court of the kingdom in age and extent of jurisdiction, the court of last resort for an immense area encompassing fourteen present-day departments. The Parlement received cases on appeal from fifteen seneschal-*présidial* courts, ten seneschal courts, and thirty-one royal jurisdictions. Near another end of Toulouse stood the University, whose heart was the Law Faculty. Between the Parlement and the University were the numerous tribunals which, though far humbler than the Parlement, were nonetheless active. These included the Seneschal-*Présidial* Court of Toulouse, the Mastery of Waters and Forests, the Salt-Tax Court (*Grenier à sel*), the Court of Coinage (*Cour des Monnaies*), the Municipal Tribunal, the Merchants' Court (*Bourse des Marchands*), the Bureau of Finances, and numerous others. The judicial institutions of Languedoc were heavily concentrated in Toulouse; they gave the city its profound sense of being a capital....

At the very pinnacle of Toulousan society were the magistrates of the Parlement. Indisputably the richest men in the city — more than ten times wealthier than the average commoner — they served also as the cultural and political elite. These *parlementaires* were the "fathers of the people," from whom the populace expected paternalistic guidance. When the Garonne River inundated the city, when a bad harvest raised bread prices, Toulousans looked to the *parlementaires* to deal with public disaster. The stern justice issuing from the Parlement was thought to be the bulwark of religion, morality, and order. The magistrates of Toulouse, more than judges of other sovereign courts, enjoyed the reputation of being austere, learned, and upright. It was a commonplace encouraged by the provincial resentment of the capital to compare the stern virtue of the Toulousan magistrates to the foppishness and immorality of Parisian aristocrats.

Since the Law Faculty and the courts had such a profound influence upon the economic and social structure of Toulouse, it is not surprising that the cultural life of the city had a strong legal foundation. Before the educated Toulousan read Voltaire he studied the *Digest*. The aristocratic salons buzzed with discussion of the most interesting cases; the man who could not talk of their legal implications with insight was considered uncultivated....

The éclat of the magistrature, the reverence for legal knowledge, and the pomp of the court ceremony dazzled the minds of Toulousans and heightened the prestige of legal careers. Young men were avid for the respectability of a career in one of the courts, especially the Parlement, and their fathers shared their enthusiasm. Toulousans themselves claimed that the centuries of cultural domination by the Parlement and the university had turned the "genius" of the residents from commerce to law. There was a general awareness that the legal institutions virtually determined the way of life in the city. It was probably of a provincial capital like Toulouse that the municipal officers of Lyon were thinking when they denounced all plans to establish a superior court or university in their city; they feared that this would undermine its commercial mentality. In Toulouse these Lyonnais had an example of complete social domination by legal professions....

In comparison to the urgent and deeply-felt criminal reform movement among the Toulousan barristers, demands to alter civil legislation were hardly voiced. Perhaps civil laws themselves are more protected from currents of changing opinion because they are often social norms stated in juridical language. But the barristers had other reasons for not favoring civil reform. As students and masters of Roman law, they identified with it, and they saw the jurisprudence of the Parlement as partly their own work. When changes in civil law were attempted, they were often seen as royal interference with provincial customs and prerogatives, so opposition to reform engaged the barristers' sense of localism and attachment to the Parlement. This suspicion of civil law reform can best be seen in the barristers' response to codification, which had had the support of celebrated jurists since the sixteenth century, at least, and was being effected by royal officers in the early eighteenth century.

The resistance of the Parlement to royal initiatives at private law reform, especially codification, was hardly new by the mid-eighteenth century. Louis

XIV's Ordinance of 1667, which attempted to unify civil procedure only, had met with open hostility from the Sovereign Court of Toulouse.

JOHN P. DAWSON, THE ORACLES OF THE LAW 369-71 (1968)

The Parlement refused to register edicts that created new offices, it opposed and threatened to interfere with royal administration of monetary and fiscal controls, it became embroiled for decades in controversies over religious doctrine and church administration, it refused to register royal edicts that imposed new and more equal taxation on the nobility and on wealthy investors. For a time, in 1720, the Parlement of Paris was exiled in a provincial town. When the king threatened exile again, in 1732, the whole Parlement went on strike and collectively resigned. Peace was restored and for a time thereafter there was an interlude of relative calm. But for the future it was more ominous that the provincial Parlements, which had been engaged in their own separate forms of turbulence, began to echo increasingly the views and the claims of the Parlement of Paris. It was not long before they all would claim that they were a single indivisible body and would organize a united front in opposition to the crown, at all times under the leadership of the Parlement of Paris.

This is not the place to retell the story of the helpless drift toward revolution. By 1750 the Parlements had emerged as an articulate and determined opposition, resisting every effort at moderate reform that successive ministers sought to propose. The Parlements rested their claims on the highest grounds. They invoked the fundamental laws of the kingdom and claimed to be guarding its liberties. At times they rallied much popular support, though their consistent line of policy was defense of the privileges of the nobility and resistance to all change in administration. At one stage, in 1771, the Parlement of Paris again went on strike, but this time their collective resignation was accepted. A vigorous chancellor, Maupeou, announced an intention to buy back their offices and actually set up a new system of appellate courts to displace the Parlements. Ingeniously contrived, the reforms of Maupeou had a reasonable chance of succeeding, but on the death of the king three years later his successor cancelled them all and restored the Parlement with honor. This episode if anything served to incite it more. Finally in 1788, when royal finances had reached a desperate state, the government proposed some new taxation, also some important administrative reforms and a transfer to a new "plenary court" of the power to register royal edicts. Even the king's command in *a lit de justice*[a] could not persuade the Parlement of Paris to accept these measures. It was then that it made its great mistake. Supported by all the Parlements, which threatened collective resignation, the Parlement of Paris demanded the convocation of the Three Estates.[b] With the whole country in a state of intense excitement, the king acquiesced. The Three Estates assembled on May 4, 1789.

---

[a] This was a royal hearing of the king and his chancellor to witness the transcription of the king's acts upon the judges' register.

[b] The Three Estates consisted of the clergy, nobility, and the bourgeoisie.

The Parlements soon had their reward. On November 3, 1789, the Three Estates, by that time transformed into a Constituent Assembly, voted to place the Parlements on indefinite vacation. Within a year thereafter they were wholly dissolved. When one considers the savagery of popular feelings against them, it is surprising that so few of their members were actually guillotined, though this is largely because so many escaped into exile.

It should be plain that the French and American revolutions were sure to project quite different roles for the judges in these two societies. In both countries the judiciary had revived and reasserted some ancient ideals to justify resistance to political power. Partly as a result of this experience, there entered deeply into our own inheritance the conception of judges as guarantors of our liberties. Much more than in our own colonies, the courts in France under the old regime were the center of opposition to authoritarian government. In a very direct and immediate sense they brought on the French Revolution. But for this they earned no gratitude. They earned instead a lasting distrust, which in France is not yet overcome. The French codifications were achieved under a new dictatorship, but they came soon enough so that the effects of the Revolution were not yet spent. The French codifications and the thinking that inspired them had enormous influence throughout western Europe and in very large parts of the civilized world. This influence gave a new and more telling effect to the conception of the judge's subordinate role that had been expressed in the ancient maxim — *non exemplis sed legibus iudicandum*.[c] Announced by another dictator, Justinian, more than 1200 years before, and repudiated altogether in French experience under the old regime, the idea expressed in this truncated maxim could now become a symbol of representative government, a rallying cry of liberty against the *imperium* of the judge.

NOTES AND QUESTIONS

1. The magistrates of the French *parlements* resisted royal authority. Judges in the American colonies also resisted royal authority. Contrast the reasons for and the consequences of these contemporaneous, but quite different, legal phenomena.

2. What similarities can you identify between the French *parlements* and the 16th century Spanish *audiencias*? What characteristics made them pre-revolutionary?

3. For additional discussion of the *parlements* and their role as whipping boys of the French Revolution, see Philip Dawson, Provincial Magistrates and Revolutionary Politics in France (1972).

---

[c]Judgment is given according to the laws, not according to examples (precedents).

2. ELEMENTS OF THE INTELLECTUAL REVOLUTION

JOHN HENRY MERRYMAN, THE CIVIL LAW TRADITION: AN INTRODUCTION TO THE LEGAL SYSTEMS OF WESTERN EUROPE AND LATIN AMERICA 14-18 (2d ed. 1985)

Three of the five principal subtraditions of the civil law tradition — Roman civil law, canon law, and commercial law — are, as we have seen, the historical sources of much of the law embodied in the five basic codes in force in most civil law jurisdictions. The reader will observe that much of public law, particularly constitutional law and administrative law, is conspicuously absent from this listing. The reason is that the public law in contemporary civil law nations is in large part a product of a revolution that took place in the West in the century beginning with 1776. This movement, which affected most Western nations, included such dramatic events as the American and French revolutions, the Italian Risorgimento, the series of wars of independence that liberated the nations of South and Central America, the unification of Germany under Bismarck, and the liberation of Greece after centuries of Turkish domination.

But these events were themselves products of a more fundamental intellectual revolution. Certain long-established patterns of thought about government and the individual were finally overcome, and newer ways of thinking about man, society, the economy, and the state took their place. Even in parts of the West that escaped violent revolutions (e.g. England), these newer ideas came to prevail. It is in this intellectual revolution that we find the main sources of public law in the civil law tradition. Although a careful historical investigation could undoubtedly trace the origin of a number of contemporary governmental institutions to legal materials that preceded this revolution, the fact is that the guiding spirit of European public law and many of the concepts and institutions in which it is expressed are of modern origin, and do not have deep roots in the Roman or medieval periods of European history.

The effect of the revolution was not, however, limited to public law. It also had a profound influence on the form, the method of application, and, to a lesser extent, the content of the basic codes derived from Roman and *jus commune* sources. The intellectual revolution produced a new way of thinking about law that had important consequences for the organization and administration of the legal system and for rules of substantive and procedural law.

One of the principal driving intellectual forces of the revolution was what has since come to be called secular natural law ("secular" because it was not derived from religious doctrine, belief, or authority: revolutionary thought was severely antireligious and anticlerical). It was based on certain ideas about man's nature that find expression in the American Declaration of Independence and in the French Declaration of the Rights of Man and of the Citizen. All men, so the reasoning goes, are created equal. They have certain natural rights to property, to liberty, to life. The proper function of government is to recognize and secure these rights and to ensure equality among men. Government should be carried on by elected representatives. And so on.

The surviving institutions of feudalism, which conferred social status and public office on the basis of land ownership, were clearly inconsistent with

these ideas. So were aristocracies of other kinds, based on considerations other than the ownership of land, such as the aristocracy of the robe. Before the French Revolution, judicial offices were regarded as property that one could buy, sell, and leave to one's heir on one's death. Montesquieu himself inherited such an office, held it for a decade, and sold it. The judges were an aristocratic group who supported the landed aristocracy against the peasants and the urban working and middle classes, and against the centralization of governmental power in Paris. When the Revolution came, the aristocracy fell, and with it fell the aristocracy of the robe.

A second tenet of the intellectual revolution was the separation of governmental powers. A number of writers, notably Montesquieu in his *Spirit of the Laws* and Rousseau in *The Social Contract*, had persuasively argued the fundamental importance to rational democratic government of establishing and maintaining a separation of governmental powers, and in particular of clearly distinguishing and separating the legislative and the executive, on the one hand, and the judiciary, on the other. The purpose was to prevent intrusion of the judiciary into areas — lawmaking and the execution of the laws — reserved to the other two powers. This attitude toward the judicial power did not exist in the United States either before or after the American Revolution. The system of checks and balances that has emerged in the United States places no special emphasis on isolating the judiciary, and it proceeds from a philosophy different from that which produced the sharp separation of powers customarily encountered in the civil law world. It is important to emphasize this point and to understand why this was the case.

In France the judicial aristocracy were targets of the Revolution not only because of their tendency to identify with the landed aristocracy, but also because of their failure to distinguish very clearly between applying law and making law. As a result of these failings, efforts by the Crown to unify the kingdom and to enforce relatively enlightened and progressive legislative reforms had frequently been frustrated. The courts refused to apply the new laws, interpreted them contrary to their intent, or hindered the attempts of officials to administer them. Montesquieu and others developed the theory that the only sure way of preventing abuses of this kind was first to separate the legislative and executive from the judicial power, and then to regulate the judiciary carefully to ensure that it restricted itself to applying the law made by the legislature and did not interfere with public officials performing their administrative functions.

In the United States and England, on the contrary, there was a different kind of judicial tradition, one in which judges had often been a progressive force on the side of the individual against the abuse of power by the ruler, and had played an important part in the centralization of governmental power and the destruction of feudalism. The fear of judicial lawmaking and of judicial interference in administration did not exist. On the contrary, the power of the judges to shape the development of the common law was a familiar and welcome institution. It was accepted that the courts had the powers of *mandamus* (to compel an official to perform his legal duty) and *quo warranto* (to question the legality of an act performed by a public official). The judiciary was not a target of the American Revolution in the way that it was in France.

The age was also the Age of Reason. Rationalism was a dominant intellectual force. It was assumed that reason controlled men's activities and that all obstacles would fall before the proper exercise of careful thought by intelligent men. The subconscious had not yet been discovered, and the power of irrational forces in history was not yet recognized. It was optimistically assumed that existing laws and institutions could be repealed and new ones, rationally derived from unimpeachable first principles, put in their place.

The emphasis on the rights of man in the revolutionary period produced statements about individual liberty of the sort found in our Declaration of Independence and in the French Declaration of the Rights of Man and of the Citizen. There was, however, a very important difference. Feudalism (in the general, nontechnical sense of the term as it was used by many European and Latin American revolutionaries) had survived in Europe and Latin America in a form that kept alive many of the social injustices inherent in its origins, whereas in the American colonies, legal institutions of undeniably feudal origin had already been deprived of much of their ability to produce the kind of social and economic evils that characterized feudal societies. As a consequence the intellectual revolution in the civil law world was more intensely antifeudal in orientation than it was in the United States. The emphasis on the right of a man to own property and on the obligation of the law to protect his ownership was in part a reaction against dependent tenure under feudalism. The emphasis on a man's right to conduct his own affairs and to move laterally and vertically in society was a reaction against the tendency under feudalism to fix a man in a place and status. The revolution became, to use Sir Henry Maine's famous phrase, an instrument for the transition "from status to contract." The result was an exaggerated emphasis on private property and liberty of contract, similar in effect to the exaggerated individualism of nineteenth-century England and America. But the reaction in the civil law world carried a special antifeudal flavor.

The revolution was also a great step along the path toward glorification of the secular state. Henceforward the temporal allegiance of the individual would be owed primarily to the state. Feudal obligations and relationships were abolished. Religious obligations lost most of their remaining legal importance. The ecclesiastical courts lost what little remained of their temporal jurisdiction. Family relationships were now defined and regulated by law (i.e. by the state). Local governmental autonomies were abolished; guilds and corporations were deprived of regulatory power. Separate legal traditions were merged into a single body of national law. The legal universe, formerly very complicated, was suddenly simplified: henceforward it would in theory be inhabited only by the individual and the monolithic state.

Nationalism was another aspect of the glorification of the state. The objective was a national legal system that would express national ideals and the unity of the nation's culture. Such a national law should be expressed in a national language and should incorporate national legal institutions and concepts. The authority (but not the content) of the *jus commune* was rejected; a common law of the civil law world was now history. In the future all law would be national law, and variation from the *jus commune* was not merely accepted, but valued as evidence of national genius and identity.

Thus the revolution was composed of such intellectual forces as natural rights, the separation of powers, rationalism, antifeudalism, bourgeois liberalism, statism, and nationalism. These are all respectable enough as ideas or points of view, so long as they are kept in proportion. But during and following the revolution a general atmosphere of exaggeration prevailed (as is typical of revolutionary movements). The hated past was painted in excessively dark colors. The objectives of the revolution were idealized and the possibility of their accomplishment assumed. The problems in the way of reform were ignored or oversimplified. Ideological passion displaced reason; revolutionary ideas became dogmas; the revolution became utopian.

In France in particular, just as in the Soviet Union after the October Revolution, the utopian flavor was very strong. Tocqueville said that the Revolution "developed into a species of religion." This development profoundly affected the revolutionary reforms in France, and since the revolutionary law of France has been extremely influential outside of France, the legal systems in many parts of the civil law world show the effects both of the fervent utopianism that characterized the French Revolution and of reactions against it. The emphasis on separation of powers led to a separate system of administrative courts, inhibited the adoption of judicial review of legislation, and limited the judge to a relatively minor role in the legal process. The theory of natural rights led to an exaggerated emphasis on individual rights of property and contract and to an oversharp distinction between public and private law. Glorification of the state, nationalism, and rationalism combined to produce a peculiar civil law theory of what law is and to determine the form and style of the basic codes.

NOTE

Of the intellectual revolution's principal tenets that Professor Merryman identifies, natural law has the longest association with Western legal thought, as the following excerpts illustrate.

3. NATURAL LAW

O. F. ROBINSON, T. D. FERGUS & W. M. GORDON, AN INTRODUCTION TO EUROPEAN LEGAL HISTORY 354-55, 357-58, 360-61 (1985)

The roots of Natural Law theory (that certain legal rules are in some sense "natural" and not purely arbitrary creations) lie in Plato and Aristotle, the great philosophers of ancient Greece. For Plato, the idea of justice was the pattern to which law ought to conform; in his thinking, however, justice was a virtue accessible only to the philosopher-kings who were to rule his ideal society and to legislate as far as possible in conformity with justice. This view, that law should conform to an ideal of justice but that knowledge of what justice demands is not granted to everyone, was transmitted to the early mediaeval world by St. Augustine. Aristotle had taken a more practical approach to natural law. He made a clear distinction between morality and law, and he introduced the concepts of distributive and commutative justice. The former requires that we should give to each his due; the latter requires that we should make up inequalities brought about by our actions and give due return for what we have received. To determine what is due Aristotle relied on observation of nature, since he held that the natural world was created with a discoverable purpose; for example, observation shows that reason distinguishes men from other animals and consequently men should act rationally. Aristotle's ideas were taken up by St. Thomas Aquinas in the thirteenth century and amplified in his *Summa Theologica.* The Stoic philosophers, whose ideas were reflected by Cicero, had applied the idea of natural law to a wider world than Plato's city state of Athens; the world was of its nature orderly, but natural law was a moral rather than a legal order and justice a private virtue. Both Aristotle and the Stoics believed in versions of the "social contract" as an explanation of the existence of a legal order within any particular state; the state itself was seen as formed by agreement among the members of the society constituting the state. The "social contract" was a concept much used in political and legal theories of the seventeenth and eighteenth centuries.

Aquinas was philosophically an idealist, believing that values such as justice have a real existence; he also believed that human reason, being the creation of a rational God who is the source of natural law, could discern justice. Positive law created by human authority could and should try to conform to divine justice....

Hugo de Groot (1583-1645), better known as Grotius, studied at the University of Leiden, acquired a law degree from Orléans, engaged in practice at the bar and at the age of twenty-four was appointed Advocate-General of Holland, Zeeland and West Friesland. His religious and political views eventually brought him into conflict with the government of Holland, and he was charged with treason and with disturbing the established religion of the United Provinces; after serving nearly two years (1619-20) of a life sentence of imprisonment he escaped and left the Netherlands for France.... It was in France that he wrote his treatise, seminal for the development of Natural Law, *De Jure Belli ac Pacis* (*On the Law of War and Peace*)....

The practical problem Grotius was trying to meet in this treatise was that of providing a law which would be binding on all nations without necessarily having its basis in any particular legal tradition. The difficulty was that there was no longer — even in theory — any universally accepted authority, such as pope or emperor, as a result of the Reformation and the growth of national sovereign states. Grotius tried to provide an international law by the application of Natural Law, which he based on human experience as testified by tradition....

Grotius was deliberately trying to deal in abstractions and to avoid being tied to particular times or places; although inspired to write by the misery of contemporary warfare, he claimed that his theories were not related to current events. The system he proposed could apply in any time or circumstance....

[A]lthough he is most commonly known as the father of modern public international law (and he was the institutional founder of Dutch law), Grotius was also a starting point for the codifying lawyers of the Enlightenment and a support for an increasingly mercantile society, in which good order and a clearly defined system of rules of property and obligations were seen as highly desirable. He provided an overall scheme, not merely a set of rules for particular application. It is somewhat ironic that, in basing the law on the subjective rights of the members of a community, that is such rights as the right to property or to reparation for injury, his approach to the presentation of law could be taken up by the legal positivists — a strange fate for the originator of a system of Natural Law.

HUGO GROTIUS, DE JURE BELLI ET PACIS I, Prolegomena §§ 6, 8 (William Whewell trans. & ed. 1853)

For man is an animal indeed, but an animal of an excellent kind, differing much more from all other tribes of animals than they differ from one another; which appears by the evidence of many actions peculiar to the human species. And among these properties which are peculiar to man, is a desire for society; that is, a desire for a life spent in common with fellow-men ....

And this tendency to the conservation of society, which we have now expressed in a rude manner, and which tendency is in agreement with the nature of the human intellect, is the source of *Jus* or Natural Law, properly so called. To this *Jus* belong the rule of abstaining from that which belongs to other persons; and if we have in our possession anything of another's, the restitution of it, or of any gain which we have made from it; the fulfilling of promises, and the reparation of damage done by fault; and the recognition of certain things as meriting punishment among men.

CONSTITUTION OF FRANCE OF 1791

The national Assembly irrevocably abolishes the institutions that wounded liberty and equal rights:

there is no longer nobility, not peerage, nor hereditary distinctions, nor feudal regimes, not *justices patrimoniales*, nor any of the titles, denominations, and prerogatives deriving from any order of chivalry, nor any of the corporations or dedications requiring proof of nobility or which suppose distinction of birth, nor any other superiority than that of public functionaires in the performance of their functions;

there is no more sale or inheritance of public office;

there is no longer for any part of the nation or for any individual a privilege or exception to the law common to all French;

there are no guilds nor professional, trade, or arts corporations;

the law no longer recognizes religious vows nor any other obligation contrary to natural rights or to the Constitution.

QUESTIONS

1. Do the major elements of the intellectual revolution mutually support each other?

2. How would you explain the difference, in concept and in consequence, between natural law and legal positivism?

4. INTERMEDIATE LAW AND DRAFTING THE FRENCH CIVIL CODE

KONRAD ZWEIGERT & HEIN KÖTZ, INTRODUCTION TO COMPARATIVE LAW: THE FRAMEWORK I, 82-85 (Tony Weir trans., 2d ed. 1987)

The "droit intermédiaire," the law of the revolutionary period between the first session of the Assemblée Constituante of 1789 and the coming to power of Napoleon Bonaparte in 1799, altered the traditional social order with almost unparalleled speed and thoroughness. All the institutions of the *ancien régime* were rooted out in very short order — the absolute monarchy, the interlocking powers of King, nobility, clergy, and judiciary (*noblesse de robe*), the old territorial division of the country into provinces, the feudal regime of land, the courts system, and the tax system. In its place was put the vision of the Enlightened Society, as sketched by Diderot, Voltaire, and Rousseau: according to this, man is a rational and responsible creature who acquires at birth an inalienable right to freedom of conscience, belief, and economic activity. No longer does man have to deal with the intermediary status groups of the *ancien régime*, but only with the state itself, which is bound through its legislation to free its citizens from the traditional authority of feudal, church, family, guild, and status groups, and to equip all its citizens with equal rights.

In pursuit of these aims the hectic legislation of the early years of the Revolution was sometimes too radically individualistic in the area of private law, and many of the extreme positions it adopted had to be abandoned by the more composed draftsmen of the Code civil. In 1791, decrees of the Assemblée Constituante abolished without compensation all feudal servitudes and cancelled all the privileges of primogeniture along with all the other differences based on age and sex which existed in the laws of succession. Estates both moveable and immoveable were to be divided completely and equally between the descendants or other heirs in intestacy: "All heirs of equal degree succeed in equal parts to the property which vests in them by law." This still left the possibility that the decedent might by *will* seek to prefer some persons over others, or to attempt to bind the inheritance for a long period of time. This possibility the Revolution also did away with; fideicommissary substitutions ... were forbidden, and they even went so far, in the interests of dividing up landed property, as to abolish freedom of testation and donation. The National Convention in 1793 decreed that "the power of disposing of one's goods whether on death, or inter vivos, or by contractual donation in direct line, is abolished: in consequence all descendants will have an equal part of the property of ascendants." The testator with children could dispose by will of only one-tenth of his estate....

The changes in family law were equally far-reaching. *Patria potestas*, which in the *pays du droit écrit* had allowed the father to exercise some paternal power even over adults, was abolished as being inconsistent with the rights of man. Restraints on marriage laid down by canon law were severely curtailed, and the requirements of marriage, particularly the requirement of parental consent, reduced to a minimum. Marriage itself was regarded as a civil contract (*contrat civil*), with the consequence, amazing for its time, that either spouse could announce a wish to terminate the contract and then obtain a divorce; it was sufficient to assert that there was "incompatibility of temperament or character" between the spouses. The justification for this principle was made clear: "individual freedom entails the freedom to divorce, since it would be lost if the engagement of marriage were irrevocable." Only civil marriages were lawful, and the central register of civil status was introduced. Illegitimate children recognized by their parents were equated with legitimate children....

One of the most important aims of the Revolution from the very beginning was to unify the private law. The Assemblée Constituante itself had decreed: "A code of civil law common to the whole kingdom will be drawn up." In 1793 Cambacérès tendered a first draft which was immediately rejected on the ground of being too comprehensive and complicated, although it had only 697 articles: what was wanted were "simpler and more philosophical conceptions."... The next year Cambacérès offered a second draft with only 297 articles, but this time the National Convention found it too sparse and terse. The indefatigable Cambacérès produced a third draft in 1796 and laid it before the Council of Five Hundred, the Directorate's legislative organ, but its protracted consideration of the draft was rudely interrupted by Napoleon's taking power at the end of 1799.

Things now began to move more briskly. Under the constitution introduced by Napoleon the executive power and the power of initiating legislation was vested in three Consuls; Napoleon was the First Consul, and the two others had only advisory roles. Draft legislation was to be prepared by the Conseil d'État on the proposal of the Consuls, and was then to be referred by the Consuls to the Tribunat, who could adopt or reject the draft, but not alter it. Then the draft had to be laid before the Corps Législatif, which was just a caricature of a Parliament, since it also had no power to discuss the draft, but only to hear the views of the representatives of the government and the Tribunat and then to adopt it as a law or to reject it. After this constitution was adopted, Napoleon devoted himself with energy and circumspection to the creation of a Code civil. He appointed a Commission of only four persons to draft it; these were no revolutionary hotspurs, but experienced practitioners. The representatives of the *droit coutumier* were Tronchet, President of the Court of Cassation, and Bigot de Préameneu; both had previously been advocates at the Parliament of Paris; the representatives of the *droit écrit* were Portalis, a high administrative official and a brilliant speaker and writer, and Maleville, judge of the Court of Cassation. In the astonishingly short period of four months this Commission produced a draft. It was shown to the Court of Cassation and the Courts of Appeal and then, along with their views on it, laid before the Conseil d'État for discussion under the chairmanship of a Consul, normally Napoleon himself. There the decision was taken to divide the Code into large sections and to submit these sections separately to the legislative process. But the very first section met with opposition in the

Tribunat. Some of its members were very suspicious of the abolition of the Directorate and the rise to power of the young General Napoleon....

Suspicion and envy rather than reasons of substance led the Tribunat to reject the first portions of the Code, and the Corps Législatif to follow suit. Napoleon's reaction must have surprised them. He withdrew the whole legislative project, saying that the calmness and unanimity required for so important a project had not yet been achieved. He then purged the Tribunat of all the members hostile to him.... After the lapse of only a year, Napoleon set the legislative process in motion again, and in 1803 and 1804 thirty-six separate statutes were passed without opposition; they were finally consolidated by the law of 31 March 1804 and brought into force under the title of "Code civil des Français."

What part did Napoleon himself take in the creation of the Code civil? As we have seen, his energy and determination were needed to force the Code through the legislative process, but we are now interested in his influence on its form and substance. Napoleon, as chairman, took a very lively part in no less than 57 of the 102 meetings at which the Conseil d'État considered the text of the drafting committee. Of course, Napoleon had no legal training; he was a soldier, and indeed was heavily preoccupied at the time in question by military adventures against the English. He was absent when some important matters, such as, for example, the law of obligations and the law of matrimonial property, were being discussed by the Conseil d'État, and he took very little part in purely legal debates. Yet his contribution to the formation of the Code civil was quite substantial. Then a man of 34 and head of state, Napoleon had, according to all contemporary evidence, a most powerful and fascinating personality. At the meetings of the Conseil d'État he constantly focused attention on the realities of life rather than the technicalities of law; he immediately saw the practical relevance of abstract rules; he put an abrupt end to any hair-splitting discussions, and by clear and simple questions kept bringing the discussion back to the practical and concrete; above all, he insisted on a style of drafting which was transparently clear and comprehensible to a non-lawyer like himself. It has been said that the Code civil owes the clarity and comprehensibility of its language to the fact that its draftsman had constantly to ask himself whether the words he had chosen would withstand the criticisms of a highly intelligent layman like Napoleon, unfamiliar with the jargon of the law.

5. IDEOLOGY OF THE FRENCH CIVIL CODE

JOHN HENRY MERRYMAN, THE CIVIL LAW TRADITION: AN INTRODUCTION TO THE LEGAL SYSTEMS OF WESTERN EUROPE AND LATIN AMERICA 27-30 (2d ed. 1985)

The ideology of the French codification, though more temperate than that of the immediate postrevolutionary period, accurately reflects the ideology of the French Revolution. For example, one reason for the attempt to repeal all prior law, and thus limit the effect of law to new legislation, was statism — the glorification of the nation-state. A law that had its origins in an earlier time, before the creation of the state, violated this statist ideal. So did a law that had its origin outside the state — in a European common law, for instance. The nationalism of the time was also an important factor. Much of the prerevolutionary law in France was European rather than French in origin (the *jus commune*), and was consequently offensive to the rising spirit of French nationalism. At the same time, much that was French (the *coutumes* of the northern regions in particular) now appeared as the logical object of preservation and glorification. The drive toward a centralized state made it important to bring some unity out of the diversity of legal systems and materials in the French regions. The secular natural law ideal of one law applicable to all Frenchmen pointed the same way.

The rampant rationalism of the time also had an important effect on French codification. Only an exaggerated rationalism can explain the belief that history could be abolished by a repealing statute. Such an attitude is implicit also in the hypothesis that an entirely new legal system, incorporating only certain desirable aspects of the generally undesirable prior legal system, could be created and substituted for the old system. The assumption was that by reasoning from basic premises established by the thinkers of the secular natural law school, one could derive a legal system that would meet the needs of the new society and the new government. The legal scholars of the time were, of course, trained in an earlier period, and they found their working legal conceptions, institutions, and processes in the old law. Those who participated in drafting the French codes consequently incorporated a good deal of the prior law and legal learning into them. In this way some continuity with the prior legal culture was retained. This tempered the legal consequences of the French Revolution, but it did not entirely avoid them. For several decades after the enactment of the Code Napoléon (the French Civil Code of 1804), the fiction was stoutly maintained by a large group of French jurists that history was irrelevant to interpretation and application of the code. This point is illustrated by the frequently quoted statement of a French lawyer of the period: "I know nothing of the civil law; I know only the Code Napoléon."

As in many utopias, one of the objectives of the Revolution was to make lawyers unnecessary. There was a desire for a legal system that was simple, nontechnical, and straightforward — one in which the professionalism and the tendency toward technicality and complication commonly blamed on lawyers could be avoided. One way to do this was to state the law clearly and in a straightforward fashion, so that the ordinary citizen could read the law and understand what his rights and obligations were, without having to consult lawyers and go to court. Thus the French Civil Code of 1804 was envisioned as a kind of popular book that could be put on the shelf next to the family Bible. It would be a handbook for the citizen, clearly organized and stated in straightforward language, that would allow citizens to determine their legal rights and obligations by themselves.

Fear of a "gouvernement des juges" hovered over French post-revolutionary reforms and colored the codification process. The emphasis on complete separation of powers, with all lawmaking power lodged in a representative legislature, was a way of insuring that the judiciary would be denied lawmaking power. Experience with the prerevolutionary courts had made the French wary of judicial lawmaking disguised as interpretation of laws. Therefore some writers argued that judges should be denied even the power to interpret legislation.... At the same time, however, the judge had to decide every case that came before him. The premises of secular natural law required that justice be available to all Frenchmen; there could be no area for judicial selection or discretion in the exercise of jurisdiction.

But if the legislature alone could make laws and the judiciary could only apply them (or, at a later time, interpret and apply them), such legislation had to be complete, coherent, and clear. If a judge were required to decide a case for which there was no legislative provision, he would in effect make law and thus violate the principle of separation of powers. Hence it was necessary that the legislature draft a code without gaps. Similarly, if there were conflicting provisions in the code, the judge would make law by choosing one rather than another as more applicable to the situation. Hence there could be no conflicting provisions. Finally, if a judge were allowed to decide what meaning to give to an ambiguous provision or an obscure statement, he would again be making law. Hence the code had to be clear.

If insistence on a total separation of legislative from judicial power dictated that the codes be complete, coherent, and clear, the prevailing spirit of optimistic rationalism persuaded those in its spell that it was possible to draft systematic legislation that would have those characteristics to such a degree that the function of the judge would be limited to selecting the applicable provision of the code and giving it its obvious significance in the context of the case. Actually, the Code Napoléon is not the most extreme example of this type of codification. That dubious honor falls to the Prussian Landrecht of 1794, enacted under Frederick the Great and containing some seventeen thousand detailed provisions setting out precise rules to govern specific "fact situations." The French civil code was drafted by experienced and intelligent jurists who were familiar with the rather spectacular failure of the Prussian attempt to spell it all out. Indeed, if we read the comments of Jean-Etienne-Marie Portalis, one of the most influential of the compilers of the code, we find a constant realistic concern to avoid the extremes of rationalist ideology. Portalis shows us that the code builds on much prerevolutionary law and legal scholarship; and he remarks that the provisions of the code are best thought of as principles or maxims, "féconds en conséquences," to be developed and applied by judges and other jurists.

This kind of professional realism was, however, easily and quickly submerged by the rhetoric of the Revolution and by the excesses of the prevailing rationalism. The code became a victim of the revolutionary ideology and was uniformly treated as though it were a conscious expression of that ideology, both in France and in the many nations in other parts of the world that were heavily influenced by the French Revolution.

CIVIL CODE OF FRANCE

Articles 4, 5, 7, 544, 545, 1123, 1134

Article 4

The judge who refuses to decide on the pretext of the silence, obscurity, or insufficiency of the law may be prosecuted for denial of justice.

Article 5

Judges are forbidden to pronounce decisions by way of general regulatory provisions on cases that are submitted to them.

Article 7

Roman law, *ordonnances*, general or local customs, statutes, and regulations cease to have legal effect in matters governed by the present Code from the date its provisions take effect.

Article 544

Ownership is the right to enjoy and dispose of things in the most absolute manner, provided use is not made of them that is prohibited by statutes or regulations.

Article 545

No one can be required to give up his property, unless for a public purpose, and with prior just compensation.

Article 1123

Any person who is not declared incompetent by statute may enter into contracts.

Article 1134

Legally formed agreements have the force of law for the parties.

NOTES AND QUESTIONS

1. Compare the results of the French Revolution and the American Revolution. What does it mean to say for the French: "rights were created and secured *through* law; rights were not something that could be enforced *against* the law?"

2. Consider the Civil Code articles set out above. Do any of them illustrate the effects of the French revolutionary ideology?

3. For fuller discussion of the forces leading up to the French Revolution, see Alexis de Tocqueville, The Old Regime and the French Revolution (Stuart Gilbert trans. 1955); Georges Lefebvre, The Coming of the French Revolution, 1789 (R.R. Palmer trans. 1947).

On the evolution of the French Civil Code, see Christian Atias, The French Civil Law: An Insider's View (Alain A. Levasseur trans. & ed. 1987); Rudolfo Batiza, *Origins of Modern Codification of the Civil Law: The French Experience and Its Implications for Louisiana Law,* 56 Tul. L. Rev. 477 (1982).

NOTE ON THE INFLUENCE OF THE FRENCH CODES

The spirit of the intellectual revolution led the French to promulgate five codes: *les cinq codes.* These include — after the *Code civil* (1804) — the *Code de procédure civile* (1806), *the Code de commerce* (1807), the *Code pénal* (1810), and the *Code d'instruction criminelle* (1810). The idea of codification, the notion of *les cinq codes* as a core system of rules, and the content of these codes spread throughout much of the world in the 19th century.

The French experience was particularly influential in Europe, for several reasons. For one, obviously, France was a part of Europe; French ideas and events seemed both more immediate and more comprehensible than what was happening across the sea in the New World. Second, France was a part of the civil law world, a participant in the *jus commune*, while the American colonists were common lawyers. French legal developments were for this reason more readily comprehensible to European lawyers. Third, it appeared to many Europeans that the desirable features of American (and English) law and government had already been considered and, where applicable to European conditions, had been adopted in post-Revolutionary France. For example, trial by jury in criminal cases on the British model, had been adopted in 1790 in France; at the same time, trial by jury in civil actions was considered and rejected. The French Declaration of the Rights of Man and of the Citizen contained much that had previously been stated in the American Declaration of Independence, and the mutual debts of French and American publicists were well-known. Accordingly, nations influenced by the French reforms could assume that they were actually receiving the benefits of the most desirable features of both traditions. Finally, French laws and institutions were imposed on much of Europe during the Napoleonic conquests and, despite the restorations following Napoleon's fall, left their mark. One result was a tendency to confuse specifically French events and ideas, growing out of peculiarly French circumstances, with the more general movement of ideas and events then transforming Western society, government, and law. The Revolution (in the broad sense) was easily assumed to be the same as the French Revolution.

Frenchmen, in particular, found this tendency congenial, and for them it was an easy step to the belief that the French Revolution and post-Revolutionary reforms in French law and government expressed, not only in a general way but in detail, the best aspects of enlightened Western culture. This belief had two major consequences for the modern world. One, mentioned above, was the imposition of French laws and institutions on the nations conquered in the Napoleonic campaigns; French imperialism carried French law with it because Frenchmen believed that they were bringing enlightenment and progress to the peoples they conquered (to many Frenchmen the proper word was "liberated"). The other, and much more far-reaching, consequence is of the sort that would today be called "cultural imperialism." French men of law and of letters became active propagandists for the superiority and universal applicability of the French codes, legal culture, and legal institutions. The extraordinary success of this thesis, which is still actively advanced by the French today, is shown by the extent to which new nations and new governments throughout the world, in the present century as well as the preceding one, have adopted French law and French ideas about law.

Much that has been exported by France in this way was enlightened and beneficially adaptable to foreign conditions. The difficulties have arisen from the tendency to generalize those aspects of the French experience that grew out of conditions peculiar to France. Louis XVI's (and his predecessors') difficulties with the provincial *parlements* during the 18th century, for example, have had no convincing equivalents in many other parts of the world, but the French doctrine of separation of powers and the French theory of sources of law, which are products of that struggle, continue to cripple the judicial systems of developing nations in every part of the globe.

The tendency for influential nations to exercise their influence by exporting their own culture and institutions is by no means limited to France. What is remarkable about the French is their success in convincing the world of the superiority and the transplantability of French law. In the United States this tendency in the late 1960s and 1970s took the form of what was called the "law and development movement." The notion was that the less developed nations could be helped along the road to development by improving their legal systems and that lawyers and legal scholars from the United States could assist them. For a critical discussion, see John Henry Merryman, *Comparative Law and Social Change: On the Origins, Rise, Decline and Revival of the Law and Development Movement,* 25 Am. J. Comp. L. 457 (1977). See also the Note in Chapter 1, Section C.4.

6. THE REVOLUTION IN ITALY

MAURO CAPPELLETTI, JOHN HENRY MERRYMAN & JOSEPH M. PERILLO, THE ITALIAN LEGAL SYSTEM 40-46, 52 (1967)

Legislative Policy in Italy Before the French Revolution

On the Continent the period from the sixteenth to the latter part of the eighteenth century was one of increasing princely absolutism and a corresponding decline in the autonomy enjoyed by the communes. In contrast with France, where the *ordonnances* of the kings were enacted as instruments in the unification of the kingdom, there was little in the way of important legislative compilation in Italy. The medieval legal system remained the basis of law in Italy. Numerous laws were promulgated to supplement or modify the inherited mass of legislation, but these changes tended to be fragmentary, unsystematic, and designed to meet the contingencies of the moment. In the seventeenth century, to facilitate research in the mass of legislative, judicial, and doctrinal material of diverse origin and authority, there was an outpouring of private compilations of law organized in chronological or systematic order....

Italy was influenced by various contemporary European cultural movements. As a result, Italian culture became considerably less provincial and pedantic. The effects on legislation were considerable. Ancient feudal privileges, guild-controlled economic structures, and rules and customs that hindered the free circulation of goods and persons were in part removed. Punishment became more humane. Torture was abolished in Tuscany and in other Italian states. The abolition was in large part due to the enormous impact of Beccaria's book *Of Crimes and Punishments* (1764), an acute and lucid indictment of torture, the death penalty, and other evils of criminal law.

This climate of renewal was evident in much of the legislation that preceded the Napoleonic codes, but an overview of the legislative work of the eighteenth century demonstrates that, important as it was in the simplification and development of the law, it was at best a prelude to codification. It did not completely abrogate the ancient Roman common law and substitute new, complete, coherent laws to govern matters heretofore regulated by Roman law. Nevertheless, the codifications of the nineteenth century owe much to the legislative compilations of the eighteenth.

Revolutionary and Napoleonic Legislation in Italy

With the arrival of the French revolutionary armies in Italy in 1796, and the foundation of several Italian republics and, later, vassal kingdoms, came the new revolutionary legislation. This legislation was generally well received in Italy, both because it satisfied social and economic needs and because France and Italy shared a common legal tradition based on the Roman law and the standard glosses and comments. This tradition, in great part, was absorbed into the Napoleonic codes.

The republics that were formed on the French model usually copied the legislation of revolutionary France; they abolished feudal rights, the procedural privileges of the clergy and nobility, and most future interests in property; they confiscated a part of the ecclesiastical mortmain, introduced civil marriage, and lowered the age limits of majority....

The French Civil Code of 1804 was made effective in the Kingdom of Italy in 1806. The Civil Code was followed by the Code of Civil Procedure, the Commercial Code, and the Penal Code, all mere translations of the corresponding French codes. The same process occurred in the Kingdom of Naples. An exception in the Kingdom of Italy was the Code of Criminal Procedure, in effect on September 8, 1807; although inspired by the principles of the French code, it varied from the model in several notable respects, for example, elimination of the jury.

The new codes were an expression of the power of the middle class at the expense of the aristocracy. In addition, they represented both a substantive and a formal departure from the preceding consolidations. Prior organic collections of law were normally compilations of preexisting legislation; the codes born from the revolution were new law that would entirely replace the old. Even the many rules and institutions with ancient roots incorporated into the codes were effective (in theory) only because of their reenactment as part of the new, complete legislative system. There was a formal rupture with the *jus commune*; no longer was it to be considered as a kind of general residual law. Despite the formal rupture with the past, however, the codes were, of necessity, built up of culturally familiar concepts, institutions, and ways of thinking about law derived from the preceding system.

Among the elements that spurred the rising Italian ruling class to seek political unity in the era of the Risorgimento was the realization that unitary legislation, such as the Napoleonic codes, was a necessary condition for the material and moral development of the country. Its fractioned legal systems, the direct consequence of political disunity, constituted a serious impediment to the improvement of its standard of living.

The Legislation of the Restoration

After the restoration of the old regime in 1815, most Italian princes ordered the immediate reenactment of the prerevolutionary legislation. Soon thereafter they authorized the drafting of new codes, almost always turning to the French codes as models. The Napoleonic codification contained too many legal and technical virtues to be ignored in the changed ideological and political context of the time.

In Piedmont the restored King Victor Emmanuel I of Savoy reenacted pre-Napoleonic compilations. His successor, Charles Albert, was responsible for the drafting of a constitution that later became the constitution of a united Italy, and an almost complete codification, including a Civil Code, Penal Code, Military Penal Code, Commercial Code, and Code of Criminal Procedure. The work was completed by his successor, Victor Emmanuel II, the last king of Piedmont (officially known as King of Sardinia) and the first king of Italy, with the promulgation in 1854 of the Code of Civil Procedure, and in 1859 of a new Penal Code that was later extended throughout Italy (with the exception of Tuscany) and remained in effect until 1890.

Despite the conservative, if not reactionary, intentions of almost all of the restored monarchs, the Napoleonic experience left its mark on the Italian law of the restoration. It was not possible to reestablish the ancient feudal jurisdictions, municipal and noble privileges, and restrictions on the alienability of property. Indeed, the restored princes found many of the Napoleonic reforms congenial to their aims because they involved the suppression of privileges of the aristocracy, who, in the ancien régime, had set boundaries upon the central power of the monarch. Despite the repeal of some reform legislation, Italy's legal condition did not regress to its pre-Napoleonic state.

Legislative Unification

The proclamation of the new Kingdom of Italy in 1861 brought about a rapid and sometimes artificial process of unification of law and centralization of administration. At first the process involved the simple introduction of the codes and principal public laws of Piedmont (the Kingdom of Sardinia headed by the House of Savoy) into the annexed territories. In some cases the introduction of these codes involved a regression to local laws. The second stage was the promulgation, in 1865 and following years, of new codes for the Kingdom of Italy: the Civil Code, Code of Commerce, Code of Civil Procedure, Navigation Code, and Code of Criminal Procedure....

The French and German codifications, in particular, reflect contrasting attitudes toward the nature and functions of codification, and are cast in quite different forms. In a sense they constitute the polar extremes of the European codification movement. Each has strongly influenced the legal development of unified Italy. The first Italian codes were French in form, and Franco-Belgian exegetic scholarship for a time dominated the Italian doctrine. Later the rise of the Pandectist school in Germany and the enactment of the German codes profoundly affected the style of Italian legal thought and, through it, of the new Italian codifications of the 1930's and 1940's.

The result of these forces is a legal order that combines (1) the legal tradition and many of the historically derived concepts and institutions of the *jus commune* and (2) the quite different French and German contributions of the nineteenth century.

NOTE ON THE REVOLUTION IN SPAIN

The 18th century, under the enlightened despotism of the Bourbon dynasty, was an age of reform in the social and political life of Spain. The many royal laws required a new compilation to replace the Nueva Recopilación (1567); it and its many supplements were thus rearranged into 12 books and published as the Novísima Recopilación de las Leyes de España (1805). But the Novísima was inadequate by Enlightenment standards: it was too long and it lacked clarity and theoretical unity. Jurists continued to consult the doctrinal works of scholars, judicial case law, and the Roman-canonic *jus commune*.

Napoleon's pretensions to rule Europe forced the king of Spain, Charles IV, to abdicate in 1808. Napoleon placed his brother, Joseph Bonaparte, on the Spanish throne, which led to the War of Independence (1808-1813). Spanish patriots, in alliance with Great Britain, finally succeeded in expelling the French. But during the chaos of war, Spanish liberals, influenced by the ideas of revolutionary France, acted in various regions to resuscitate the medieval Cortes as a legislative body and initiated Spain's first constitutional government with the Cadiz Constitution (1812). The Cadiz Constitution declared the joint sovereignty of the people and the king, separation of governmental powers, abolition of feudal relationships and jurisdictions, reform in ecclesiastical jurisdictions and abolition of judicial torture, equality of rights between *peninsulares* and Americans, emancipation of black slaves, elimination of imprisonment for Indians who refused baptism, and natural law rights of liberty, property, and equality before the law.

This liberal experiment ended in 1814, when Ferdinand VII regained absolute monarchical power aided by the conservative Spanish nobility and clergy and by French military intervention. The remainder of the 19th century was characterized by a bitter struggle between the supporters of absolute monarchy and the advocates of constitutional government, with each side temporarily gaining control.

National codification was supported in articles 258 and 259 of the Cadiz Constitution, which called for a national civil code, commercial code, and penal code. But Spain in general was late to codify due to the continuing political disorder of the 19th century. The first enactment was the Penal Code (1822), which was repealed with the reestablishment of the old regime in 1823. A new Penal Code appeared in 1848, modeled on the French (1810) and Brazilian (1830) codes; it was substantially reformed in the Penal Code of 1870. Next came the Commercial Code (1829), based on the French model, and modified slightly in the Commercial Code of 1885. The Civil Code was not enacted until 1889, and is still in effect. It was the result of a decade-long process and built on an earlier *proyecto* (1851) inspired primarily by the French Civil Code. Nevertheless, older Castilian law provided many of the rules for family and inheritance matters, and canon law controlled marriage for Roman Catholics. Civil procedure was first codified in the Ley de Enjuiciamiento Civil (1855), rooted in medieval Spanish procedure and reformed in the Ley de Enjuiciamiento Civil of 1881. The Code of Criminal Procedure (Ley de Enjuiciamiento Criminal) was enacted in 1872, but its inadequacies led to a new code in 1882 based on Enlightenment principles and foreign examples, such as the Austrian Code (1873).

See José Antonio Escudero, Curso de Historia del Derecho: Fuentes e Instituciones Político-administrativas 829-45, 871-932 (3d ed. 1987); Antonio Torres del Moral, Constitucionalismo Historico Español 13-165 (1986); Rafael Altamira, *Spain*, in A General Survey of Events, Sources, Persons and Movements in Continental Legal History 579, 675-96 (1912).

NOTES AND QUESTIONS

1. There were differences in the reception of the intellectual revolution in France, Italy, and Spain. Did these differences affect the process of codification in these nations?

2. For an interesting study of criminal law and procedure in Italy, see John A. Davis, Conflict and Control: Law and Order in Nineteenth-Century Italy (1988).

7. THE REVOLUTION IN LATIN AMERICA

R. A. HUMPHREYS & JOHN LYNCH, INTRODUCTION, in THE ORIGINS OF THE LATIN AMERICAN REVOLUTIONS: 1808-1826, at 3-5, 10-14, 24, 26-27 (R.A. Humphreys & John Lynch eds. 1965)

The Spanish and Portuguese empires in America were the first great European land empires overseas. They were already old when Captain John Smith and his associates founded Jamestown in 1607. They were still growing when the English colonies in North America declared their independence in 1776. And although by the beginning of the nineteenth century Spain had abandoned her exclusive claims to the northwest coast of North America and had parted with the ill-defined area of Louisiana, her empire still stretched, through nearly a hundred degrees of latitude, from California to Cape Horn. As for the small state of Portugal, she commanded in Brazil a territory which, gradually extended both westward and southward, had come to comprise the half of South America.

Twenty-five years later, of all these vast dominions there remained to Spain only the two islands of Cuba and Puerto Rico, and to Portugal nothing. In the last quarter of the eighteenth century the thirteen mainland colonies of England became one United States. In the first quarter of the nineteenth century thirteen states — twelve new republics and one new monarchy — replaced the empires of Spain and Portugal. When at Ayacucho, the Yorktown of South America, in December 1824, the last Spanish viceroy laid down his office and his arms, European dominion in the New World south of the Great Lakes had been reduced to a chain of islands in the West Indies, to the British settlement of Belize in Central America, and to the three colonies of British, French and Dutch Guiana in South America.

The Napoleonic invasions of Portugal and Spain in 1807-1808 precipitated this great movement of political emancipation. Fleeing before the march of Napoleon's armies the royal family of Portugal sought safety in Brazil. There it remained for thirteen years. And in this vast and empty land the transition from colony to kingdom and from kingdom to independent empire was a gradual process. There was no abrupt break with the colonial past, no prolonged and devastating civil war. When the royal family returned to Portugal in 1821, the heir to the crown of Portugal himself became the emperor of Brazil, endowed the country with its constitution, and secured its entry into the family of nations, and, with the support of a powerful plantation aristocracy, the throne thus peacefully established survived for sixty-five years.

The fate of the Spanish colonies was very different. Spain's American dominions were the property of the crown. Strictly speaking, they were not colonies at all, but kingdoms, united to the kingdoms of Spain merely by a dynastic tie. That, at least, had been the Habsburg view. It was still the Spanish American view. But whereas the Portuguese crown escaped the clutches of Napoleon, the crown of Castille was captured. A usurper, Joseph Bonaparte, was placed upon the throne, and the bond which united Spanish America to Spain was severed. The Spaniards rose against an alien hand; and the nationalist, monarchist movement of resistance in Spain was paralleled by a semi-nationalist, semi-monarchist movement of resistance in Spanish America. But here Spaniards born in America stepped into the shoes of Spaniards born in Spain. The latent hostility between Creoles and *peninsulares* flared into open war; and a movement which began as an assertion of freedom from French control ended as a war of independence from Spain.

The Napoleonic invasion of Portugal, therefore, led finally to the peaceful dissolution of the Portuguese empire in America, the Napoleonic invasions of Spain to the violent dissolution of the Spanish empire in America. Had these invasions not occurred, Spanish America might well have remained Spanish for some years to come, and the empire of Brazil might never have come into existence at all; Brazilian independence, when it was ultimately achieved, would almost certainly have taken a different form. In this sense "the French Revolution in its Napoleonic expression" may properly be regarded as the "greatest of all the forces which made a revolution in Latin America inevitable."

What were these forces? Though much was said of "popular sovereignty" and of the reversion of power to the people, it is clear that the revolutions on which the modern states of Spanish America were founded were not "popular" movements, except in a very restricted sense. They were the work of the few, not of the many. The wars which they precipitated were civil wars. Spanish Americans fought Spaniards, but Spanish Americans also fought each other; and while the loyalists, or royalists, were proportionately more numerous than they had been in the English colonies during the war of North American independence, a large part — perhaps the greater part — of the population was indifferent and indifferently changed sides....

But to what extent did the Enlightenment penetrate to Spanish America and what was its effect? The ideas of the *philosophes* — their criticisms of contemporary social, political, and religious institutions — were, of course, known to an educated minority both in Spain and in Spanish America. But they were not accepted uncritically. The majority of Spaniards remained Catholic in conviction and devoted to absolute monarchy. They sought not new philosophical ideas but practical answers to practical problems. In effect, Spain drained the Enlightenment of its ideology and reduced it to a program of empirical reform within the existing political and social order. The empire was included in this program; and imperial reform meant binding America closer to Spain and making it a more fruitful source of wealth and power. Thus, reforming ministers, viceroys, and ecclesiastics, many of whom were acquainted with the thought of the Enlightenment, worked not to dissolve the empire but to improve it. They advocated new administrative and economic, but not new political, ideas.

The political and social views of the Creoles, too, were usually conservative. Those who responded to the thought of the Enlightenment acquired, for the most part, not so much new information or ideas as a new approach to knowledge, characterized by a preference for reason and experiment rather than for authority and tradition; and while this might lead them to demand reforms in the colonial regime, it did not lead them to question the regime itself. The work of the economic societies which, from the 1780's, spread from Spain to Spanish America is an admirable illustration. The object of these societies was simply to encourage agriculture, commerce, and industry by study and experiment. Their members were a small elite of clerics, officials, merchants, and scholars: the dozen or so societies in Spanish America had a total membership of no more than 700. Their anxiety to improve the economic and social position of the Creoles — most of their members were Creoles — and their plea for agricultural and industrial expansion, which, by implication, was obstructed by Spain, did have the effect of underlining the difference between the interests of America and those of Spain. But the societies themselves were concerned with the empirical rather than the theoretical side of the Enlightenment, and their most recent historian has concluded that "the Creole members were generally moderate men of property and position, sometimes intellectually 'advanced,' but socially and politically moderate; many in the coming years of independence were to be conservatives."...

Insofar as the Enlightenment reached Spanish America through Spain, therefore, it was a conservative, not a revolutionary, force. But Spanish America also received the Enlightenment directly from its original sources in England, France, and Germany. Despite the censorship of the Inquisition, its literature entered and circulated with comparative freedom. Newton, Locke, Adam Smith, Descartes, Montesquieu, Voltaire, Diderot, Raynal, Rousseau, Condillac, and d'Alembert all were read in New Spain, for example; and the readers included higher civil servants, professional men and ecclesiastics, merchants, and even officials of the Inquisition itself. The flow seems to have reached its height in the 1790's, and it was then that the Inquisition, hitherto halfhearted and inefficient, began to bestir itself, alarmed principally by the political and seditious content of some of the new writing, which was regarded as "contrary to the security of states," imbued with "general principles of equality and liberty for all men," and even spreading news of "the frightful revolution in France which has caused such damage."...

But what was its significance? Altogether it involved a very small group of men, a minority within an upperclass minority, lost among the intellectually inert mass of Creoles. The fact of possessing or reading a book did not mean that the reader accepted or was influenced by its ideas. He might read it to condemn it, or merely out of intellectual curiosity, anxious to know what was happening in the outside world and resentful of any attempt to keep him in ignorance. But such an attitude was not necessarily subversive....

The mass of the Creoles had many objections to the colonial regime, but these were not ideological objections. Some, no doubt, were already dissenters. These, when they read the forbidden literature of the Enlightenment, found further inspiration in it for their own ideas, and when they came to power their policy naturally reflected this inspiration. But though the ideas of the Enlightenment were important in Spanish America, it may be questioned whether they were important as a "cause" of independence. It is more significant that there was a transmission of ideas from the Enlightenment, across the movement for independence and into the new republics, whose governments continued the traditions of eighteenth-century enlightened despotism in the search for administrative, economic and educational improvement....

The independence movement cannot be explained solely in terms of antagonism between Creoles and Spaniards. For the Creoles, politically radical, were socially conservative and considered themselves the dominant group in the country. Therefore, while they aspired to oust their political superiors, they were also concerned to keep in their place the mass of the people below themselves....

At the root of the desire for independence was Creole nationalism. This was the result of a long process of alienation from Spain in which the peoples of Spanish America had come to regard themselves as different from Spaniards with interests and identities of their own.

From what sources was this national consciousness fed? The first thing which separated Creoles from Spaniards was their place of birth. For Creoles their *patria* was America, and in the eighteenth century they were becoming increasingly conscious of this, and the more anxious to know their own countries so that they could better exploit their resources. Americans, as the Creoles now began to call themselves, were rediscovering their own land in a uniquely American literature. Creole writers in Mexico, Peru, and Chile expressed this feeling and helped to nurture it, for, as the *Mercurio Peruano* put it, "it interests us more to know what is happening in our own nation." The best examples of this cultural expression of "Americanism" were the Jesuit exile writers, and they, perhaps, were the literary precursors of American nationalism. The idea of America as a great homeland was very easily converted into a national attitude. As Viscardo wrote, "The New World is our homeland, and its history is ours, and it is in this history that we ought to seek the causes of our present situation, to make us determined thereby to take the necessary action to save our proper rights and those of our successors." Furthermore, distance from Spain, demands for economic autonomy and for monopoly of public office reflected a deeper antagonism between Spanish interests and American interests, and a sharper appreciation that these two interests were basically different. For the foreign policy of Spain in the second half of the eighteenth century, and the many wars in which she was engaged, especially after 1796, needlessly but complacently involved America too. America's problems were neglected while her resources were plundered, simply to satisfy the international interests of Spain. As well as promoting criticism, this also stirred Americanism and a desire for independence, which would enable American interests to be decided in their own right. In his defense of the revolt begun in Mexico by Hidalgo, Fray Servando Teresa de Mier wrote, under a pseudonym, his *Historia de la Revolución de Nueva España,* in which he criticized the Spanish government and its policy, and its neglect of the colonies, referring to Europe as "this small part of the world" where Spain was continually involved in war which Mexicans unwillingly and unfortunately had to enter simply because of their dependence on Spain; "and as Spain is unable to protect her commerce and unwilling to allow others to export our products and us to import theirs, and has deprived us of factories and industries, the war is more cruel for us than for her, and is ultimately waged with our money. We simply need to stay neutral to be happy."

NOTE ON THE LATIN AMERICAN VARIATION

It was shown in Chapter 3 that the reception of the Roman-canonic *jus commune* took place in different ways and to varying extents from one European nation to another. As the materials in the present chapter show, there also was substantial variation in the influence of the Revolution, which took different forms and had different consequences in France, Italy, Spain, Brazil, and in Spanish America.

One important distinguishing feature of the Revolution in Latin America was the greater influence of the American and the lesser influence of the French examples. Relative proximity to the United States and remoteness from Europe may have had some effect. The fact that they, like us, had been colonies of European powers may have made our case seem more like theirs. Unlike the European nations, Latin America had not been conquered and occupied (liberated?) by the French. Whatever the reasons may have been, there was an important result: Latin American legal systems acquired special, typical features unlike those in Europe or elsewhere in the civil law world. While still recognizably civil law systems, participants in and products of the civil law tradition, they constitute a special variation with its own recognizable features.

These characteristic features of Latin American legal systems will be described in greater detail in later chapters but can be briefly summarized here. In the structure of the various branches of government, in the idea of the nature and function of a constitution, in the approach to review of the legality of legislative, administrative, and judicial action, Latin America was strongly affected by the United States model. This feature of Latin American legal systems can be simply, with only partial accuracy, summarized by saying that Latin American public law is more North American than European in character. In the structure and content of the civil, commercial, and procedural codes, in the roles assigned to legislator, scholar, and judge in the legal process, in the pattern of legal education and the legal professions, in the style of legal scholarship, Latin American legal systems are more orthodox — sometimes more European than the Europeans themselves. This can briefly, but with great risk of misrepresentation, be summarized by saying that Latin American private law is more European than North American.

Further, as Humphreys and Lynch show, Latin American independence movements had complex ideological motivations significantly different from those in the United States and France. Most Latin American nations seem to have achieved independence from Spain and Portugal without fully accepting the ideologies of the American and French revolutions. Since the Code Napoléon (and, by association with the code concept, any other modern civil code) was widely perceived as embodying revolutionary ideas, codification on the French (or any other) model had to await the penetration of such ideas into the ideologies of governing oligarchies in the new nations of Central and South America. With this in mind, consider the following materials on independence and codification in Mexico, Brazil, Chile, and Colombia.

8. THE REVOLUTION IN MEXICO

FRED R. HARRIS, MEXICO: HISTORICAL FOUNDATIONS, in LATIN AMERICA, ITS PROBLEMS AND ITS PROMISE: A MULTIDISCIPLINARY INTRODUCTION 261, 264-67 (Jan Knippers Black ed. 1984)

"To say Benito Juárez is to say Mexico. To say Mexico is to say sovereign nation." Those were the beginning words of a patriotic speaker at the annual Mexico City ceremony on Benito Juárez Day, March 21, 1982 — the 176th anniversary of the birth of the Zapotecan Indian who rose to be president of Mexico. Virtually every Mexican town and city has a monument to Juárez or a principal street named for him — this stern "man of law" who stripped the Catholic Church of its property and privileges; reformed Mexican politics; instituted public education; ended the rule of the Mexican dictator Santa Anna; and later, drove the French from Mexico.

Reform. Respect for law. Nationalism and resistance to foreign aggression. Civilian control of the government. The importance of "great leaders." Public morality. Separation of church and state. Pride in Indian history. These are some of the concepts that the memory of Benito Juárez evokes for Mexicans — and is used to evoke. To Mexicans, Juárez was an Indian who became a

Mexican, as Mexico was an Indian nation that became a Mexican nation. But it was Indian first....

Spanish Colonialism

After 1700, the Mexican and Spanish economies, both of which had been depressed, began to revive. The population in Mexico began to grow — mostly among the mestizos. The numbers of the *criollos* (Spaniards born in the New World) also grew, and they began to develop a pride in Mexicanness, which paralleled their increasing resentment of the privileged position of the *peninsulares*, who had been born in Spain.

Spain's wars in Europe meant more taxes in Mexico, more "forced loans" to the crown, and confiscation of Church charitable funds. Then, Napoleon Bonaparte imposed his brother on Spain as its ruler. At this, some *criollos* in Mexico attempted a revolt against the *peninsulares*, but this revolt was put down. Political dissatisfaction was soon joined by economic troubles.

Independence and Empire

Throughout Mexico, groups of dissidents began to meet in 1809, some to plot. One such group met regularly in Querétaro. Among its members were a young cavalry captain, Ignacio Allende, thirty-five, and a fifty-seven-year-old priest, Miguel Hidalgo y Costilla, whose parish was in the small nearby village of Dolores. Hidalgo, a *criollo*, had been investigated twice by the Inquisition for his political views. When word leaked out about the conspiracy in Querétaro, its members were warned by the wife of the local *corregidor*, or governor (she is celebrated in Mexican history as *la corregidora*). In Dolores, with Allende by his side, Father Hidalgo rang his church bell to summon his parishioners and issued what came to be called the *grito de Dolores*, a call to rebellion, on September 16, 1810. Many *criollos* were alarmed by the excesses of the mestizos and Indians who fought for Hidalgo and independence. Government forces rallied. Hidalgo and Allende were defeated, captured, and killed.

A mestizo priest, José Maria Morelos y Pavón, took up the sword of leadership, and in the Congress that he called in 1813, he made clear by his stirring speech to the delegates that the sword he carried was meant to cut the *criollo*, as well as the *peninsular*, bonds that had for so long held down the mestizos and Indians of Mexico. The constitution adopted by this Congress was a liberal document. Principles could not stand up to guns, however. *Criollos* and *peninsulares* joined together in opposition to this rebellion, and by 1815, Morelos, too, had been captured and killed. Still, the war — or wars — for independence sputtered on for another five years.

In Spain, Ferdinand VII had been restored to the throne in 1814, but the *criollos* of Mexico felt increasingly separate from Spain. In 1823, led by a conservative military man, Agustín de Iturbide, the *criollos*, backed by the Church, declared Mexican independence — a conservative independence, much different from that for which Morelos and Hidalgo had fought and died. Spain, after years of war, had no alternative but to agree to Mexican independence. The Mexican economy was in shambles. And after all the fighting, the lives of the great mass of the Mexican people had not changed. The identity of their oppressors had changed, but the nature of the oppression remained the same. Iturbide had himself declared emperor of Mexico — the first of its *caudillo*, or strongman, rulers. But the imperial grandeur in which Iturbide lived and ruled lasted only ten months.

Now, there rode onto the Mexican scene one of the most flamboyant and most enduring *caudillos* of Mexican history, the Veracruz military commander, a twenty-nine-year-old *criollo*, Antonio López de Santa Anna. Santa Anna had switched from the Spanish army to support Iturbide. After Iturbide dissolved the Mexican Congress, Santa Anna switched and led forces that unseated Iturbide. He could be a monarchist or an antimonarchist. He could be a liberal or a conservative. He could be a defender of his country, or he could sell it out. For him, expediency and self-interest were the first principles. In February of 1823, Iturbide was driven into European exile, and his rule was replaced by that of a provisional government, run by a three-man military junta.

Needless to say, there are no statues in Mexico honoring Iturbide. By contrast, both Hidalgo and Morelos had states named after them, and there are many monuments to them. On each anniversary of the *grito de Dolores*, the president of the Mexican republic rings the old bell, now at the National Palace, in commemoration of that important event.

The Mexican Republic

A new Mexican constitution was promulgated in 1824. It established the Estados Unidos Mexicanos, which consisted of nineteen states and four territories. Patterned after the constitution of the United States and influenced by the writings of the French philosopher, Montesquieu, the Mexican Constitution established a national government of three branches — executive, legislative, and judicial — a bicameral legislature, and a president to be elected by nationwide popular vote. Roman Catholicism was continued as the established religion. Military men and priests were guaranteed their special privilege of the *fuero* — that is, the right to be tried for any offense not by the civil courts but by the military or Church courts.

After Manuel Félix Fernández Guadalupe Victoria was elected as the first president, poor Iturbide mistakenly thought he heard a call of the Mexican people — all the way over in Italy. He unwisely returned home, where he was arrested and executed. In 1827, Santa Anna put down another attempted revolt. In 1830, he was called on to defend the country and the government once more. When the second republican president had pushed through legislation expelling all Spaniards from Mexico, Spain had invaded Mexico at Tampico. Santa Anna laid siege to the Spanish forces and eventually forced their surrender. By then, he was easily the most popular figure in Mexico. The president of Mexico was then thrown out of office and executed by his vice-president. Santa Anna rose up and threw this usurper out of office. He was then elected president of Mexico in 1833.

It turned out that Santa Anna was not very much interested in governing. His vice-president, though, began to push through liberal reforms. So the army, the Church, and the other conservatives banded together to overthrow the constitutional government and rescind the reforms. And who should lead this revolt but the president of the republic himself, Antonio López de Santa Anna. Now the foremost conservative, Santa Anna abolished the Constitution of 1824 and made the states into military districts. He required that he be addressed as Your Serene Highness. He was to occupy the presidency again and again, off and on, until 1855. During those years, the army became larger and larger, the bureaucracy became ever more bloated, taxes became higher and higher, the economy stagnated, bribery and corruption of officials became outrageous, and there were conflicts with foreign governments — first with the Republic of Texas, then with France, and finally, and disastrously with the United States.

For years, Mexico had encouraged emigration from the United States to the sparsely settled, vast lands of Texas — provided only that the new emigrants were Catholics, would be loyal to the Mexican government, and would use Spanish as their official language. As the years passed, little was done to enforce these requirements. The flood of emigration swelled. Eventually, people from the United States greatly outnumbered Mexicans in Texas, and they became increasingly critical of the central government, until, at last, they rebelled and declared the establishment of the Lone Star republic in 1836. Santa Anna took personal command of the Mexican army and marched to San Antonio, where, at the Alamo on March 6, 1836, he defeated the Texas defenders there and killed them all. Another part of the Mexican army captured the small town of Goliad, taking 365 prisoners, all of whom Santa Anna had executed. Then, on April 21 of that same year, Santa Anna was himself defeated at the San Jacinto River and was taken captive.

To save himself, Santa Anna promised the Texans that Mexico would not again fight against Texas and that the Mexican cabinet would receive a formal mission from the Lone Star republic. When the cabinet heard of these agreements, they immediately repudiated them and sent Santa Anna back to his estate near Veracruz. Soon, however, the trumpets sounded again for Santa Anna. Provoked by Mexico's refusal — actually an inability — to pay its French debts, France ordered a shelling and invasion of Veracruz. Santa Anna led the Mexican forces that eventually drove the French away.

War With the United States

Then came the war between the United States and Mexico (1846-1848). U.S. attitudes toward Mexico and Mexicans were highly derogatory, even racist — especially after the war with Texas. Furthermore, the people and government of the United States felt that it was their Manifest Destiny to stretch their country's boundaries westward, all the way to the Pacific. The United States annexed Texas as a state of the Union in 1845. Mexican officials seethed, but were largely powerless to do anything else. Then, without any discoverable basis in law or fact, Texas claimed that its border went, not just to the Nueces River, but much past it to the Rio Grande (which the Mexicans call the Rio Bravo). Not only had Mexico suffered the loss of Texas, but it was now expected to accept the doubling of Texas territory — to include additionally, for example, San Antonio, Nacogdoches, and Galveston in Texas as well as Albuquerque, Santa Fe, and Taos in present New Mexico.

NOTE ON CODIFICATION IN MEXICO

Political disorder in Mexico precluded codification until decades after independence, and some 19th century federal codes lasted only a few years. The first code, promulgated by President Santa Anna, was the Commercial Code (1854) based on the French (1807) and Spanish (1829) codes. After Santa Anna's overthrow, an 1855 law abolished the commercial courts and procedure and effectively repealed the Code, which was replaced with the medieval Spanish Ordinances of Bilbao that remained in effect until the new Commercial Codes of 1884 and 1889 were adopted.

The most important early period of codification occurred a few years after the end of French intervention and the reign of Emperor Maximilian (1864-1867). The "republican, representative, democratic, and federal" Constitution of 1857 was restored, while work continued on what would become the federal Civil Code of 1871. The Code commission commented that it had relied on the "principles of Roman law, our own complicated legislation, the codes of France, Sardinia, Austria, Portugal ... in addition to past drafts completed in Mexico and Spain." Since a national code is only applicable in the Federal District (Mexico City) and in federal territories, the individual states commonly adopt a code that is the same as or similar to the federal code. The 1871 Civil Code was replaced by the 1884 and 1928 codes.

President Benito Juárez in 1867 ordered a commission to draft a penal code that, based on an earlier version and on the Spanish Penal Code of 1870, was completed in 1871. The 1871 Penal Code was followed by the codes of 1929 and 1931. One year following the original Civil Code and Penal Code, the Code of Civil Procedure was enacted in 1872. It was followed by the federal codes of 1880, 1884, and 1932. The last of the *cinq codes* to be adopted was the Code of Penal Procedure (1880), which included the right to trial by jury. It was later replaced by the codes of 1894, 1929, and 1931.

See Helen L. Clagett & David M. Valderrama, A Revised Guide to the Law and Legal Literature of Mexico (1973).

9. THE REVOLUTION IN BRAZIL

MICHAEL L. CONNIFF, BRAZIL: FROM INDEPENDENCE TO 1964, in LATIN AMERICA, ITS PROBLEMS AND ITS PROMISE: A MULTIDISCIPLINARY INTRODUCTION 475-79 (Jan Knippers Black ed. 1984)

The First and Second Empires

Brazilian independence came at the hands of Prince Pedro of Alcantara who governed the prosperous colony on behalf of his father, King João VI of Portugal. João and the entire Portuguese court had resided in Brazil's capital city, Rio de Janeiro, from 1808 until 1821 in order to elude Napoleon's hostile armies and then to manage the burgeoning economy of their giant tropical possessions. By long tradition, the British had played a role in protecting the

Portuguese Empire, in exchange for which England was granted free access to Brazilian resources and trade. João had more to fear than foreign threats to his colony, however: Independence wars were raging across the continent, and similar movements had erupted in Brazil as well. Thus, when João returned to Portugal, he instructed his son Pedro, who remained as prince regent, to assume the leadership should independence become inevitable. Thereby a dynastic, if not a colonial, relationship would continue between Portugal and Brazil.

Pedro — brash, impetuous, ambitious, and advised by persons sympathetic to independence — was all too ready to take command of the colony. On September 7, 1822, in response to insults from the Portuguese Parliament (temporarily in the ascendancy), Pedro declared Brazil independent and soon received the crown of the newly created empire. With the help of the British, he quelled several pro-Portuguese rebellions and received recognition from the United States, England, Portugal, and finally, the Vatican. True to the spirit of the Enlightenment, which inspired many of his supporters, Pedro gave the country a quasi-parliamentary government in the Constitution of 1824. He retained and exercised an overriding authority, however, the so-called moderating power.

Pedro's reign, known as the First Empire (1822-1831), proved turbulent and ill starred. The great prosperity of the preceding decades broke in the mid-1820s as a hemisphere-wide depression set in. Even coffee, rapidly becoming Brazil's leading export, experienced a slump. Pedro's authoritarian style, deemed necessary during the independence period, now irritated Brazilians, as did a scandalous extramarital affair. The decline in his popularity was also due to prolonged meddling in the Portuguese succession struggles (João VI died in 1826) and to a costly and unsuccessful war against Argentina over the Banda Oriental (to become Uruguay in 1828). In 1831, confronted with financial insolvency, street demonstrations, and a hostile Brazilian elite, Pedro abdicated.

The end of the First Empire contributed to a prolonged period of internal conflict, because the emperor's son (also named Pedro) was only five years old and could not ascend to the throne until he was eighteen. Brazilian political leaders quickly formed a regency triumvirate to rule in the prince's name. They lacked the legitimacy a true monarch would have enjoyed, however, and the country drifted toward dissolution. Nearly every region experienced an uprising of some sort, and two — the Cabanagem in Amazonas (1835-1840) and the Farroupilha in Rio Grande do Sul (1835-1845) — were outright civil wars. Ineffectual central rule permitted considerable authority to shift into the hands of officers, typically *coronéis* ("colonels"), of the newly created National Guard. Most *coronéis* were in fact prominent planters or cattlemen who used their commissions to legitimate armed control over their rural dominions.

Pedro II, it is generally agreed, symbolically and personally brought peace to the country in the 1840s and made it a true nation in the 1850s. In 1840, he was approached by leading politicians who proposed that Parliament declare him of age immediately in order to stem the provincial warfare and aimlessness of government. Young Pedro agreed, and the following year he was duly crowned Pedro II, ushering in the Second Empire (1841-1889).

In the 1840s, two principal parties became consolidated, the Liberals and the Conservatives, and Pedro II relied on each in alternation to staff high executive posts in the government. Within several years, a workable, albeit authoritarian, version of the British parliamentary system was in operation, allowing Pedro to exercise the moderating power while more experienced men ran the affairs of state on a daily basis. From 1853 to 1868, in fact, Pedro managed a bipartisan government of some sophistication during the conciliation era. Powers that had been ceded to the provinces during the 1830s were reconcentrated in the imperial court, and in several major cases (notably the Queiros Law of 1850, which ended the African slave trade), Pedro displayed considerable statesmanship.

The Brazilian economy recovered its dynamism during the 1840s, aided by the growth of coffee exports from the Paraiba Valley northwest of Rio de Janeiro. Since the time of independence, landowners in the region had secured their hold on huge tracts, which were planted in coffee. By mid-century, Brazil had become the world's leading supplier of coffee, and the new planter elite dominated imperial government....

The Old Republic

The beginnings of civilian-military rivalry in Brazilian government are rooted in the five-year transition period during which [the ranking general, Marshal Deodoro de Fonseca] (1889-1891) and army Marshal Floriano Peixoto (1891-1894) ruled the country more or less dictatorially. To be sure, Deodoro declared Brazil a federal republic, but once in power, he and his successor found it difficult to step down, for political as well as circumstantial reasons. For one thing, the country had very few persons experienced in representative government and quite a few who desired restoration of the monarchy. Civil uprisings of various sorts punctuated the 1890s and made strong rule necessary. For another, the country was plunged into a depression following a crisis in the London capital market, the economic effects of which were extremely harmful for Brazil.

The United States quickly recognized Deodoro's government and initiated trade overtures designed to end the long-standing advantages enjoyed by the British....

Ruy Barbosa, a firebrand republican appointed minister of government in 1890, held a constitutional convention and orchestrated the adoption of a charter like that of the United States. The Constitution of 1891 provided for a federal republic, a broad bill of rights, a president elected for a nonrenewable four-year term, a bicameral legislature, a separate judiciary, and important powers vested in the states. Among the last were supervision of all elections, collection of export taxes (important for the coffee states), maintenance of militias, financial autonomy, and state-enacted constitutions. Although for several years the constitution was unenforced, due to army control, depression, and civil wars, it did last until 1930 and gave shape to the country's modern administration.

NOTE

The order of codification in Brazil was the Penal Code (1830), the Code of Criminal Procedure (1832), the Commercial Code (1850), and finally after a number of attempts in the 19th century, the Civil Code (1916). The structure of the Civil Code is similar to the German Code (1896), with a general part followed by four books on the family, property, obligations, and successions. A constitutional mandate to unify procedure led to the Code of Civil Procedure (1939).

10. CODIFICATION IN CHILE

JUAN G. MATUS VALENCIA, THE CENTENARY OF THE CHILEAN CIVIL CODE, 7 American Journal of Comparative Law 71-77 (1958)

Background

The need for a codification of private law, comporting with the status of Chile as a free and independent state, was felt from the very first days of the Republic.... The existing legal system was most unsatisfactory; the Spanish law was a great mass of enactments and decisions, whose application was not clear because there were many conflicting compilations with obsolete provisions written in old Spanish and repugnant to the republican constitution.

Fortunately, a brilliant Venezuelan, Andrés Bello, arrived in Chile in 1829. Few men of his time had his encyclopedic knowledge and classical culture, not only in the field of law in which, though he never received a law degree, he was an authority on Roman and Spanish law, but equally so in philosophy, languages, and literature. The influence of Bello was soon felt. In 1831, the vice-president of the Republic proposed a law of codification. Meanwhile, Bello had started on his own, without any official aid, the monumental work of drafting a new civil code for Chile....

The Law of Codification was finally approved on September 10, 1840; it provided for the creation of a commission, composed of two senators and three deputies, charged with "codifying the civil laws, reducing them to an orderly and complete body, leaving aside the superfluous or that which was against the republican institutions of the State and deciding the points controverted among the interpreters of the Law." The commission was to take into consideration suggestions made by the government, the courts, or any individual. Bello was at the time a senator in the Chilean Senate and undoubtedly had a decisive voice in drafting the Law of September 10, 1840.

The members of the legislative commission were immediately appointed, including Andrés Bello and Mariano Egaña, representing the Senate, and Manuel Montt as one of the representatives of the Chamber of Deputies. In this commission, Andrés Bello was the key man. The discussion soon centered about his work; he missed only one meeting; and after 1844 he continued practically alone.... In 1852, the Project of the Code was completed. In its publication the following year, Bello added various notes which are now of great value in the study of the historical development of the provisions of the Code. This is known as the 1853 Project.

The 1853 Project was revised twice before being submitted to the Congress, on November 22, 1855, with a magistral message of the President of the Republic that Bello prepared. As recommended in the message, the discussion of the Code was brief, and it was promulgated on December 14, 1857....

Contents and Merits of the Chilean Code

The Presidential message, notable in style and in substance, is regarded as a primary auxiliary for the interpretation of the Code. In this it is observed, after a reference at the outset to the need of codification, that in Chile advantage should be taken of foreign codes, not merely copying their provisions, but without losing sight of the peculiar circumstances of the country. Thereafter, the provisions of the Code are reviewed: the elimination of custom as a source of law; time in the law; personality and presumption of death in the case of missing persons; promise of marriage, which pertains to "the honor and conscience of the individual," but does not produce a civil obligation; marriage, the matrimonial regime, the relation of father and child, majority, guardianship; real property, dismemberment of ownership, easements; law of inheritance; contracts and quasi-contracts; proof of obligations; annuity, partnership, antichresis; priority of creditors; prescription — all these are described and explained in eloquent and concise terms. Recommending the adoption of the Code, the message concludes with the famous words: "I do not presume to offer under these respects a perfect work, none as such has come until now from the hands of man."...

These modest words were belied by the outstanding merits of the Chilean Civil Code, regarded as of its time.... While conservative in respect to the status of married women, the progress that the Code represented led to its adoption in various countries: Colombia and Ecuador adopted it almost in its entirety, while Argentina and Paraguay, Uruguay, Venezuela, El Salvador, and Nicaragua modelled upon it many of the provisions of their own civil codes....

Basic Principles of the Code

The most important principles upon which the structure of the Chilean Civil Code rests are:

(1) *Omnipotence of the Law.* The 1833 Chilean Constitution was based upon the Portalian theory of a government of law; the Civil Code expressly states that everyone must obey the law, when duly promulgated. Law replaced the king: above all stands the supreme law of the land, the Constitution, and thereafter the statutes enacted according to the provisions of the Constitution. Article 1 of the Chilean Civil Code declares that "The law is a manifestation of the sovereign will, which, expressed in the manner prescribed by the Constitution, orders, forbids, or permits." The law, once promulgated, obliges all. Even the judges, the Civil Code provides, are subject to law: they cannot create law; their decisions form law only for the cases for which they are rendered and have no effect as precedent; custom is not law, save in exceptional cases when the law expressly provides that custom has the force of law. A law is valid until repealed by another law; nonuse does not invalidate law.

(2) *Equality Before the Law.* The Chilean Civil Code in article 56 defines persons as including all individuals of the human species "whatever may be their age, sex, birth, or condition." In this, the Code followed the French Civil Code, which as a result of the French Revolution had emphasized equality, and also accorded with the provisions of the 1833 Constitution and the measures taken by the first Supreme Director O'Higgins, abolishing titles of nobility and primogeniture.

This equality was taken to include also foreigners. No distinction between nationals and foreigners in the acquisition and enjoyment of civil rights regulated in this Code is recognized, declares the Code, with generosity indeed rare for its epoch....

(3) *Private Property.* The French Revolution abolished all feudal institutions that encumbered title to land, thus forcefully reviving the individualistic Roman notion of ownership. This principle was adopted by Bello as one of the fundamental pillars of the Civil Code and forms the basis of the law of real and personal property and of succession. Also as in France, the danger of allowing landed property to accumulate in the hands of private corporations was apprehended; consequently, corporations and foundations were restricted. These required license by the legislature to own land after a certain period; partnerships and corporations organized for profit, however, were completely free consistently with the ideas of economic liberalism that underlie the Code....

Article 582 of the Chilean Civil Code closely resembles Article 544 of the *Code Napoléon*,[a] declaring the principle of *ius utendi, fruendi et abutendi* of the classical Roman law.

(4) *Freedom of Contract.* The principle of freedom of contract, or autonomy of the will, is another cornerstone of the Code. Article 1545 states "that every contract legally concluded, is a law for the contracting parties and cannot be voided but by their mutual consent or for legal causes." Thus, as in the French model, private contracts are elevated to the category of law. The requirements for a valid contract are few and simple: legal capacity, consent free of vice, licit object, and licit cause ("causa"). The Code regulates the typecontracts, but individuals are free to enter into any other kind of agreement that they may conceive. Few rules on contracts hamper the will of the parties. In the courts, this principle has been applied as if there were a constitutional clause of absolute freedom of contract.

Principal Sources of the Chilean Civil Code

In Article 19, second paragraph, the Code provides that in the interpretation of law the intention or spirit of the law as manifested in the law itself or in the true history of its enactment may be considered. The true history of the enactment of law includes the reasons taken into account by the legislature in enacting law. In the case of the Civil Code, those reasons can be found only in the works of Andrés Bello.

The sources which most frequently are cited as contributing to the formation of the Code are:

---

[a] See French Civil Code art. 544, *supra* Section A.5.

(1) Roman law, the principal source of all the Codes of the so-called "civil or continental system of law";

(2) Spanish law in force in Chile before the Civil Code. Among these, may be mentioned the *"Novísima Recopilación," Las Siete Partidas* with the glosses of Gregorio López, and the *Fuero Real;*

(3) The *Code Napoléon* of France, with the commentaries of Rogron;

(4) Other civil codes in force at the time of the preparation of the Chilean Civil Code, viz., of Louisiana, Sardinia, Austria, Prussia, and the two Sicilies;

(5) Works of French, German, and Spanish authors: e.g., Delvincourt, Pothier, Merlin, Escriche, Tapia, Gomez, Molina, Matienzo y Goyena, and Savigny.

Exemplifying the importance of the sources, Barros Errazuris states that the provisions respecting easements are based on the French Civil Code, aqueduct on the Sardinian Code, father and children on Spanish law, and contracts on the works of Pothier.

11. CODIFICATION IN COLOMBIA

ROBERT C. MEANS, CODIFICATION IN LATIN AMERICA: THE COLOMBIAN COMMERCIAL CODE OF 1853, 52 Texas Law Review 18, 20-24 (1973)

The enactment of a commercial code in 1853 was merely one episode in an effort to codify the major branches of Colombian law, an effort that provided a major and recurring theme of legal reform for half a century after the country secured its independence. The reasons given for codification varied with the area of law concerned, but common to all was the expressed conviction that the administration of justice suffered from faults so grave that they endangered the bases of an orderly society. Throughout the eighteenth century judicial delay had ranked with such problems as smuggling and inadequate roads as staple items of each viceroy's *Relacion de Mando.* Independence perhaps brought a new sensitivity to the problem; certainly, it brought a new view of its causes and thus of the appropriate remedy.

The Spanish viceroys had regarded the problem as basically one of inadequate judicial resources, stemming from the *audiencia's* increasing case load and nonjudicial duties and from the age and ill health of some members. This theme did not altogether disappear after independence, but the emphasis shifted to other and apparently more fundamental causes. The new diagnosis differed little from that offered by postindependence reformers in the United States: voluminous and ill-ordered legal sources, slow and complicated procedures, and a legal profession that found profit in intricacies that only it could unravel. None of these phenomena was new to Colombia, but, as in the United States, reaction against the former colonial power and a new instrumental conception of law apparently combined to move them to center stage.

Until superseded by national codes, the prerevolutionary Spanish legislation, with its legendary bulk and disorder, continued to serve as Colombia's basic private law following independence. A sixteenth-century Spanish effort to impose order on this mass of legislation in the *Nueva Recopilacion* had been largely a failure, and the problem had grown worse with the accumulation of decrees and orders since the *Recopilacion's* last edition. Describing the governing law as a "vast chaos," an 1823 report sounded the theme that was to be repeated again and again:

> With later laws repealing in large part earlier ones, they give rise to continuous doubts, interpretations and delays; there is hardly a transaction for which two contradictory laws are not found. For this reason, and because of the great defects existing in Spanish procedure, suits both criminal and civil last for years without conclusion. For this reason, families are ruined; there is no greater misfortune for an honorable citizen than to find himself involved in litigation, which must for a long time cost him his tranquility and perhaps his fortune, even when the right is on his side.

The problem of Spanish law was compounded by that of the growing republican legislation, "increased each year by one or more volumes enacted by the legislature, always following the same system of repealing or reestablishing in part articles or even isolated clauses, leaving it to the person applying the law to discern which are the provisions contrary to that most recently repealed."

The 1845 *Recopilacion Granadina* provided a partial solution to the chaos of the republican legislation, and to mitigate the problems of the inherited Spanish law, one writer proposed substituting the 1805 *Novisima Recopilacion* for the older *Nueva Recopilacion*. But the ultimate solution must have been obvious in a new republic whose legal traditions place it within the civilian family of legal systems. The new European codes offered, packaged in a readily exportable form, order to replace chaos and new procedural systems to supplant the old. What is surprising is not that Colombia ultimately codified its law, but that codification was so long delayed.

Codification efforts began early enough. The constitutions of 1811 and 1812, adopted after the first declarations of independence, referred to codification, and efforts began soon after the permanent organization of a republican government in 1821. Vice President Santander appointed a commission to draft civil and penal codes in 1822, and discussion about codifying the substantive and procedural sides of the civil and penal law continued during the 1820's and 1830's. But the first code, covering the substantive penal law, was not adopted until 1837, and no further code was enacted prior to the Commercial Code of 1853. A civil code did not appear until 1859, nearly four decades after Colombia's effective independence.

The delay evidently was not due to any opposition to the idea of codification. Occasionally, an official warned against adopting foreign models without regard to the Colombian milieu, but these cautions had more the ring of elementary prudence than of the historicism that underpinned opposition to codification in Germany and the United States. Although the Spanish tradition had its defenders in nineteenth-century Colombia, there is no indication that they drew codification into this conflict. In the civil and penal areas the root cause for the delay was underdevelopment. The resources necessary for codification were in short supply, and the capacity for mobilizing them was limited.

Lawyers were in adequate supply, at least in Bogota, but legal scholars were another matter. Until well after the adoption of the first Colombian codes, apparently no one devoted himself to the serious study of private law. In contrast to public law and its borderlands with the social sciences, until late in the century private law was the subject of no Colombian work above the level of pamphleteering. The law schools taught civil law, of course, but as late as the middle of the century the courses apparently were based on Juan Sala's *Illustracion del derecho real de Espana,* a work most charitably described as pedestrian in quality. This dearth of legal scholarship probably had several causes. The decade-long war for independence took its toll of men and resources, and after independence public law and related areas of philosophy and social science attracted the most attention. Part-time faculty, inadequate library facilities, and a complete absence of legal journals made a bad situation worse. Whatever the reasons, the result was that few if any Colombian lawyers had the background, inclination, or institutional base for a major codification effort.

Moreover, the government was unable fully to mobilize even the existing resources. The European codes could serve as models, and with sufficient time a competent lawyer should have been able to make the changes necessary for their adoption in Colombia. The Colombian government, however, could not readily employ persons for an extended project. Revenues that invariably fell short of expenses made it difficult to fund any dispensable project, however well regarded, and even with funding political instability made extended projects difficult to sustain. The contrast with the nineteenth-century codification efforts of two non-Latin American countries is notable. Three draftsmen and their secretaries worked full time for five years to produce the Quebec Civil Code of 1866; preparation of the Louisiana Civil Code of 1808 occupied a pair of men for nearly two. The former effort would have been inconceivable in Colombia, and even the Louisiana Code required a sustained effort that was seldom if ever applied to nineteenth-century Colombian legislation.

Even with the limited resources at hand, codification might have come sooner if the government had assigned it a sufficiently high priority. But codification was not the first order of business. Institution-building took precedence, and the Colombian legislature devoted most of the remaining time to narrow and pressing problems, such as awarding pensions and making land grants to road builders.

NOTES AND QUESTIONS

1. How did the reception of the intellectual revolution in Latin America compare to its reception in Europe?

2. Benito Juárez, the Zapotec Indian from Oaxaca who courageously supported liberalism and the Constitution of 1857, was one of Mexico's greatest presidents. Does the fact that an Indian was selected president imply that Mexicans might be more willing to preserve indigenous laws and legal institutions against the importation of European laws and legal institutions than people from other Latin American societies in which Indian culture was eliminated or weak?

3. Can the influence of natural law be seen in the Chilean Civil Code?

4. Why did Colombia import and adapt European codes after independence? Was the continuation of Spanish colonial law or the drafting of an eclectic national code (like that of Bello) feasible?

5. For a fuller treatment of 19th century codification in Colombia, see Robert Charles Means, Underdevelopment and the Development of Law: Corporations and Corporation Law in Nineteenth-Century Colombia (1980).

B. GERMAN LEGAL SCIENCE

Of all the civil law nations in Europe the one that seems to have been most resistant to the influence of the French Revolution is Germany. The reasons for and the significance of the German variation are so intimately bound up with the flowering of what we here call German legal science that they cannot conveniently be separated for discussion. Instead we now turn to a description of that great scholarly movement and, incidentally, we observe some of the special ways in which the Revolution took form in Germany and affected German law.

1. THE THIBAUT-SAVIGNY DEBATE

MATHIAS REIMANN, THE HISTORICAL SCHOOL AGAINST CODIFICATION: SAVIGNY, CARTER, AND THE DEFEAT OF THE NEW YORK CIVIL CODE, 37 American Journal of Comparative Law 95, 97-98 (1989)

In the wake of the defeat of Napoleon and of the deliverance from French rule, a wave of patriotism and enthusiasm for national unity swept through the fragmented German lands in 1814. This led the Heidelberg professor of Roman law, Anton Friedrich Justus Thibaut, to write a small pamphlet entitled *Über die Notwendigkeit eines allgemeinen bürgerlichen Rechts für Deutschland* [*On the Necessity of a Common Civil Law for Germany*]. He passionately advocated the codification of the major areas of the law for all of Germany. Thibaut lamented that German law was not only geographically disunited but also ridden with the complexities of Roman law, which led to delays and uncertainty. He believed that a uniform code could remedy these problems, and that such a code could be completed within two to four years.

Thibaut's pamphlet immediately triggered the famous essay in response by Savigny, *Vom Beruf unsrer Zeit für Gesetzgebung und Rechtswissenschaft.*[10] Savigny's principal argument against codification was that his own age lacked the ability necessary to do it properly. In his view, a proper code had to be an organic system based on the true fundamental principles of the law as they had developed over time. A thorough understanding of these principles was an indispensable prerequisite to codification. Savigny found such mastery of principles lacking among his contemporaries and feared that a codification in his time would therefore do more harm than good by perpetuating misun-

[10] The only English translation is Abraham Hayward, *On the Vocation of Our Age for Legislation and Jurisprudence* (1831).

derstandings. Thus, he urged his contemporaries to study the historical evolution of the basic principles first and to turn to codification — if at all — later.

Savigny used the occasion, however, to present his general view of law, going way beyond Thibaut's proposal and the issue of codification as such, and turning his pamphlet into the basic charter of the historical school. Two features are most salient in Savigny's rather romantic theory. First, law is, like language, an expression of the "common consciousness of the people"; it is therefore essentially custom. Second, along with this common consciousness, it grows organically over time, driven by "internal, silently operating powers"; it is thus an evolutionary phenomenon, subject to constant change, and can be properly understood only in its historical dimension.

Thibaut's and Savigny's booklets spawned an extensive debate among contemporary German academics. In the end Savigny's side prevailed and codification was postponed for many decades. The reasons for this outcome are not clear. It is unlikely that Savigny's essay was the main cause of this postponement.[16] But his pamphlet was soon regarded as the standard polemic against codification — a reputation which spread beyond Germany, and even across the Atlantic.

NOTE ON GERMAN ROMANTICISM

The revolutionary, rationalist, and natural law aspects of the French Revolution and the French codification were products of the interaction of specific French conditions with the intellectual currents prevailing in Europe in the latter half of the 18th century. By 1814, when Thibaut's article appeared, faith in rationalism had begun to languish, and in Germany, in particular, its intellectual foundations were seriously weakened by the critical success of Immanuel Kant's *Critique of Pure Reason.* German Romanticism (and German nationalism) expressed in the literary product of Herder, Goethe, and others filled the gap, capturing the minds of scholars as well as politicians, and the concepts of the *Volk* and the *Volksgeist* were taken seriously. History — more specifically, German history — was emphasized at the expense of rational invention. Romantic nationalism became a strong intellectual force throughout the West, but Germany is where it had its strongest impact on legal scholarship and codification.

2. IDEOLOGY OF THE GERMAN CIVIL CODE

JOHN HENRY MERRYMAN, THE CIVIL LAW TRADITION: AN INTRODUCTION TO THE LEGAL SYSTEMS OF WESTERN EUROPE AND LATIN AMERICA 30-32 (2d ed. 1985)

In contrast to the essentially revolutionary, rationalistic, and nontechnical character of the Code Napoléon, the German Civil Code of 1896 (effective in 1900) was historically oriented, scientific, and professional. A large share of the credit (or blame) for the differences between the German and the French

[16] [E]ven without Savigny's opposition it is, in light of the political fragmentation of Germany at the time, highly unlikely that a national code would have been drafted and enacted.

civil codes is owed to Friedrich Karl von Savigny, one of the most famous names in the history of the civil law tradition.

The idea of codification aroused widespread interest in Germany and other parts of Europe and in Latin America during the first parts of the nineteenth century. The French code was widely admired and copied, and in the course of time it was proposed that Germany follow France's lead. However, Savigny and his followers — influenced by Kant, Hegel, and German Romanticism — opposed this effort, persuasively arguing a thesis that became very influential in Germany. Proponents of what came to be known as the "historical school," these scholars maintained that it would be wrong for Germany to attempt to devise a civil code by reasoning from principles of secular natural law. In their view, the law of a people was a historically determined organic product of that people's development, an expression of the Volksgeist. Consequently, a thorough study of the existing German law and of its historical development was a necessary prelude to proper codification. Since the Roman civil law as interpreted by the medieval Italian scholars had been formally received in Germany some centuries before, a thorough historical study of German law had to include Roman law and old Germanic law as well as more recent elements of the contemporary German legal system. Under the influence of Savigny and the historical school, many German scholars turned their energies to the intensive study of legal history.

Savigny's idea was that by thoroughly studying the German legal system in its historical context legal scholars would be able to draw from it a set of historically verified and essential principles. These features of the law could then be individually studied, studied in relation to other such principles, and eventually systematically restated. The result would be a reconstruction of the German legal system according to its inherent principles and features. This, in turn, would provide the necessary basis for the codification of German law.

The components of the German legal system, in their historical context, came to be thought of by certain successors of Savigny as something like natural data. Just as natural data in biology, chemistry, or physics could be studied in order to determine the more general principles of which they were specific manifestations, so the data of German law could be studied in order to identify and extract from them those inherent principles of the German legal order of which they were specific expressions. Hence the proposed reconstruction of the German legal system was to be a *scientific* reconstruction.... Finally, the Germans were convinced that it was neither desirable nor possible to rid the world of lawyers. The idea that the law should be clearly and simply stated so that it could be correctly understood and applied by the popular reader was expressly rejected. The German view was that lawyers would be needed, that they would engage in interpreting and applying the law, and that the code they prepared should be responsive to the needs of those trained in the law.

Consequently, the German Civil Code of 1896 is the opposite of revolutionary. It was not intended to abolish prior law and substitute a new legal system; on the contrary, the idea was to codify those principles of German law that would emerge from careful historical study of the German legal system. Instead of trying to discover true principles of law from assumptions about man's nature, as the French did under the influence of secular natural law, the Germans sought to find fundamental principles of German law by scientific study of the data of German law: the existing German legal system in historical context. Rather than a textbook for the layman, the German civil code was thought of as a tool to be used primarily by professionals of the law.

Tool for Code is for prof'ls of the law

NOTE ON GERMAN CODIFICATION

The Civil Code (Bürgerliches Gesetzbuch, or BGB) was the last of the principal German national codes to be enacted. The first was the General German Commercial Code (Allgemeines deutsches Handelsgesetzbuch), issued in 1861. It was introduced by local legislation into the member states of the North German Confederation. After Otto von Bismarck's efforts toward unification led to the creation of the German Empire (*Reich*) in 1871, the Commercial Code was reissued that year as imperial law. Also in 1871 the imperial Penal Code (Strafgesetzbuch) was enacted, which was largely based on the North German Confederation Penal Code, itself borrowed from the Prussian Penal Code (1851). Two imperial procedure codes were adopted in 1877: the Code of Civil Procedure (Zivilprozeßordnung) and the Code of Penal Procedure (Strafprozeßordnung).

NOTES AND QUESTIONS

1. Thibaut, as a representative of the natural law school, desired a series of codes to encompass private law, criminal law, and procedure. His proposed civil code looked to contemporary models: the Prussian Landrecht (1794), the Austrian General Civil Code (1811), in which natural law concepts predominated, and the Napoleonic Code (1804).

Do you understand how Savigny undercut the premises of natural law thinking?

2. Consider the principal tenets of the historical school of law. Does a nation have only one *Volksgeist* or do ethnically diverse nations have a *Volksgeist* for each cultural group? What are the implications of your answer for a civil code?

3. For a symposium on Savigny and his influence, see *Savigny in Modern Comparative Perspective,* 37 Am. J. Comp. L. 1-184 (1989). *See also* Note, *A Very German Legal Science: Savigny and the Historical School,* 18 Stan. J. Int'l L. 123 (1982). For a discussion of 19th century German codification and the enactment of the BGB, see Michael John, Politics and the Law in Late Nineteenth-Century Germany: The Origins of the Civil Code (1989).

3. LEGAL SCHOLARS AND THE ELEMENTS OF LEGAL SCIENCE

JOHN HENRY MERRYMAN, THE CIVIL LAW TRADITION: AN INTRODUCTION TO THE LEGAL SYSTEMS OF WESTERN EUROPE AND LATIN AMERICA 57, 59-67 (2d ed. 1985)

The preeminence of the scholar in the civil law tradition is very old. The Roman jurisconsult — who advised the praetor and the judge, was recognized as an expert on the law, but had no legislative or judicial responsibility — is considered to be the founder of this scholarly tradition. His opinions had great weight, and during the second century A.D. the opinions of certain jurisconsults were binding on judges. Their opinions were written down, collected, and treated as authoritative. Much of the most important part of Justinian's *Corpus Juris Civilis* — parts of the *Digest* and all of the *Institutes* — is made up of the work of jurisconsults.

After the revival of Roman law in Italy, those responsible for the revival and development of the medieval *jus commune* were scholars. The work of the Glossators and the Commentators, added to Justinian's *Corpus Juris Civilis*, made up the body of Roman law received throughout Western Europe. During this period the responses of scholars to questions of law were in some places given binding authority in courts, a practice analogous to the use made of jurisconsults during the classical period of Roman law. For a time in Germany, for example, cases were frequently sent by courts to law faculties for decision. Many of the codes drafted in Europe and in Latin America during the nineteenth century were the work of scholars, and all were based on the writings of earlier generations of scholars. The great debate about codification in Germany was begun and conducted by scholars.

We begin to understand the true importance of the civil law scholar when we look at a typical book on Continental legal history. Much of what is called legal history in the civil law tradition is baffling to the common lawyer who first approaches it. He is used to thinking of legal history as an account of legal rules and institutions in their historical, economic, and social contexts. The legal history he reads is full of great cases, occasional statutes, and historical events. But when he picks up a book on legal history in the civil law tradition, he is likely to find the bulk of it devoted to a discussion of schools of legal thought and of disputes between legal scholars and their followers. He will read about the Glossators, the Commentators, the Humanists, about the differences among the French scholars of the eighteenth century, and about the debate between Savigny and Anton Thibaut on codification in Germany. All in all, it is a peculiar form of intellectual history, almost entirely divorced from socio-economic history on the one hand, and from discussion of the origin and development of specific legal institutions on the other. The protagonist of this form of legal history is the legal scholar, and its subject matter is currents of thought about the structure and operation of the legal order.

This is what we mean when we say that the legal scholar is the great man of the civil law. Legislators, executives, administrators, judges, and lawyers all come under his influence. He molds the civil law tradition and the formal materials of the law into a model of the legal system. He teaches this model to law students and writes about it in books and articles. Legislators and judges accept his idea of what law is, and, when they make or apply law, they use concepts he has developed. Thus although legal scholarship is not a formal source of law, the doctrine carries immense authority.

In the United States, where the legislature is also theoretically supreme, there is a well-known saying (originated by a judge) that the law is what the judges say it is. This is, properly understood, a realistic statement of fact. The judge has to decide how to characterize a legal problem presented to him, which principles of law to apply to the problem, and how to apply them in order to arrive at a result. Whether the principles he chooses are embodied in legislation or in prior decisions, they achieve substantive meaning only in the context of a specific problem, and the meaning attributed to them in that context is necessarily the meaning supplied by the judge. In a similar sense it is reasonably accurate to say that the law in a civil law jurisdiction is what the scholars say it is....

At any given moment in the history of the civil law tradition a number of different points of view will be in competition with each other, but one or another will always tend to dominate. The contemporary civil law world is still under the sway of one of the most powerful and coherent schools of thought in the history of the civil law tradition. We will call it legal science. It is the fifth component of the civil law tradition (after Roman civil law, canon law, commercial law, and the legacy of the revolutionary period) and the final one to be discussed in this book....

Legal science is primarily the creation of German legal scholars of the middle and late nineteenth century, and it evolved naturally out of the ideas of Savigny.... Savigny argued that German codification should not follow the rationalist and secular natural law thinking that characterized the French codification. He maintained that a satisfactory legal system had to be based on the principles of law that had historically been in force in Germany. Therefore a necessary preliminary step to codification was a thorough study of the legal order to identify and properly state these principles and to arrange them in a coherent system.

Because private law, and particularly that part of it we have called Roman civil law, was thought to be the heart of the legal system, the German scholars put their principal efforts into study and restatement of the principles of Roman civil law as received in Germany and as modified by the addition of Germanic elements. They concentrated their study on the *Digest* (in German, *Pandekten*, from the Latin *Pandectae*) of Justinian, and thus came to be called the Pandectists. They produced highly systematic treatises based on principles they drew from their study of Roman law. The *Digest* had been studied systematically for centuries, but the mid-nineteenth-century Germans brought this study to its highest and most systematic level. Their work culminated in the publication of influential treatises and, impelled by the unification of Germany under Bismarck in 1871, in the promulgation of the German Civil Code of 1896 (the BGB). The treatises and the BGB were influential throughout the civil law world (and also, to some extent, in the common law world, where there was a flurry of enthusiasm for legal science). The methods and the concepts developed by the German scholars were applied to other fields of law, both private and public, and hence came to dominate legal scholarship. Despite a variety of criticisms and reactions against it from the time of Savigny to the present, legal science continues to affect the thinking of civil law scholars, and hence of other men of law, in the civil law tradition.

The concept of legal science rests on the assumption that the materials of the law (statutes, regulations, customary rules, etc.) can be seen as naturally occurring phenomena, or data, from whose study the legal scientist can discover inherent principles and relationships, just as the physical scientist discovers natural laws from the study of physical data. As a leading German scholar of the time, Rudolph Sohm, put it: "The scientific process, by means of which principles are discovered that are not immediately contained in the sources of law, may be compared to the analytical methods of chemistry." Under the influence of this kind of thinking, legal scholars deliberately and conscientiously sought to emulate natural scientists. They intended to employ the scientific method, and they sought admission to the community of scientists. (It should be added that similar assumptions, but with less emphasis on science and the scientific method, underlay some of the work of legal scholars in the United States in the late nineteenth century and still constitute one source of justification for the famous case method of teaching in American law schools.)

Like the natural sciences, legal science is highly systematic. Principles derived from a scientific study of legal data are made to fit together in a very intricate way. As new principles are discovered they must be fully integrated into the system. If new data do not fit, either the system must be modified to accommodate them, or they must be modified to fit the system. In this way the preservation of systematic values becomes an important consideration in criticizing and reforming the law.

This emphasis on systematic values tends to produce a great deal of interest in definitions and classifications. Much scholarly effort has gone into the development and refinement of definitions of concepts and classes, which are then taught in a fairly mechanical, uncritical way. The assumption of legal science that it scientifically derives concepts and classes from the study of natural legal data on the one hand, and the generally authoritarian and uncritical nature of the process of legal education on the other, tend to produce the attitude that definitions of concepts and classes express scientific truth. A definition is not seen as something conventional, valid only so long as it is useful; it becomes a truth, the embodiment of reality. Serious arguments are conducted by grown men about the "autonomy" of certain fields of law, such as commercial law or agrarian law, or about the "true" nature of specific legal institutions. Law is divided up into clearly delimited fields. Public law and private law... are treated as inherently different and clearly distinguishable. There is a precisely defined legal vocabulary and an accepted classification of law that are reflected in the curricula of the law schools, in the professorial chairs in the faculties of law, in the arrangement of books in law libraries, in the subject matter of works written by legal scholars, and in the approach of legislators to lawmaking.

The order thus imposed on the legal system by legal science represents a great systematic achievement. Civil lawyers are justly proud of their legal structure and methodology and of the very real contribution it makes to the certain, orderly, and efficient statement, elaboration, and administration of the law. Every phase of the legal process is a beneficiary of this systematic jurisprudence, and the absence of anything equivalent to it in the common law is one of the reasons why civil lawyers think of the common law as crude and undeveloped.

Because the components of this systematic restatement of the law, although theoretically inherent in the existing positive legal order, did not exist there in identified, articulated form, and because the legal order was a universe of data within which inherent principles were to be identified, new concepts had to be invented to express these components and principles. The novelty of these concepts and their prominence in the work of scholars committed to legal science eventually led critics to call this kind of doctrine "conceptual jurisprudence." Since communication without concepts is difficult, it hardly seems fair to criticize legal science for using them. What was peculiar to legal science was that its concepts were new (or were given a new emphasis), that the accent was on their "validity" rather than their functional utility, that their proper arrangement and manipulation were thought to be the province of scholars, and that they tended to be highly abstract.

This high level of abstraction — this tendency to make the facts recede — is one of the most striking characteristics of legal science to a lawyer from the United States or England. The principles developed by legal scientists have been taken out of their factual and historical context, and are consequently lacking in concreteness. The legal scientist is more interested in developing and elaborating a theoretical scientific structure than he is in solving concrete problems. He is in quest of the ever more pervasive legal truth, and in the process of making statements more abstract, "accidental" details are dropped. The ultimate objective is a general theory of law from which all but the essential elements have been removed.

The work of legal science is carried on according to the methods of traditional formal logic. The scholar takes the raw materials of the law and, by an inductive process sometimes called "logical expansion," reasons to higher levels and broader principles. These principles themselves reveal on further study the even broader principles of which they are only specific representations, and so on up the scale. The principles derived by logical expansion are, at one level, the "provisions that regulate similar cases or analogous matters" and, at a higher level, the "general principles of the legal order of the state" that judges should employ in dealing with the problem of lacunae in the interpretation of statutes .... Intuition and the subconscious, despite their powerful influence on human affairs, are excluded from this process. The result is something that Max Weber called "logically formal rationalism."

Finally, legal science attempts to be pure. Legal scientists deliberately focus their attention on pure legal phenomena and values, such as the "legal" value of certainty in the law, and exclude all others. Hence the data, insights, and theories of the social sciences, for example, are excluded as nonlegal. Even history is excluded as nonlegal — and this seems peculiarly inconsistent in view of the fact that Savigny and his disciples are called the historical school. It is of interest to historians (including legal historians) but not to legal science. Nor is the legal scientist interested in the ends of law, in such ultimate values as justice. These may properly be the concern of philosophers, including legal philosophers, but the legal scientist is concerned only with the law and with purely legal values. The result is a highly artificial body of doctrine that is deliberately insulated from what is going on outside, in the rest of the culture.

However, although legal scientists sought to be value-free and pure, they were ideological captives of their era. The creative work of the legal scientists took place in nineteenth-century Europe, in the intellectual climate that has since come to be called nineteenth-century European liberalism. Among the more relevant aspects of this ideology was a strong emphasis on the individual and his autonomy. Private property and liberty of contract were treated as fundamental institutions that should be limited as little as possible. It was an era of what we would now consider exaggerated individualism. The heart of the law was the Roman civil law, and the Roman civil law was basically a law of property and contract. Legal scientists concentrated their work in this area of civil law, and the body of doctrine they eventually produced embodied the assumptions and values central to the thought of their time. Under the banner of legal science they built ideologically loaded concepts into a systematic conceptual legal structure that is still taught in the faculties of law of the universities, that limits and directs the thinking of the legal scholars who perpetuate it, that provides the parameters of judicial interpretation and application of laws, precedents, and legal transactions, and that, in a word, dominates the legal process. The role of these assumptions and values is concealed behind a façade of ideological neutrality, of the scientific study of purely legal phenomena. In this way European systematic jurisprudence embodies and perpetuates nineteenth-century liberalism, locking in a selected set of assumptions and values and locking out all others.

The special attitudes and assumptions about law that characterized the work of the Pandectists and that make up what is here called legal science can thus be summarized in the following terms: scientism, system-building, conceptualism, abstraction, formalism, and purism. These characteristics of legal science are apparent to many civil lawyers, and there have been many reactions against it in the civil law world. These reactions have taken a variety of forms, and they seem to have been gathering force in the period since World War II; but legal science is far from dead. In all except the most advanced civil law jurisdictions it reigns practically undisturbed. It dominates the faculties of law, permeates the law books, and thus is self-perpetuating. The average law student is indoctrinated early in his career and never thinks to question it: its characteristics, and the model of the legal system that it perpetuates, are all he knows. Legal science has been subjected to direct attack and to subversion from many sides. Its critics have tried to introduce consideration of concrete problems, to see that the existence of a subconscious and of intuition are taken into account, to bring nonlegal materials to bear on the legal consideration of social problems, and to involve legal scholars in the conscious pursuit of socioeconomic objectives. Nevertheless, the average civil lawyer still forms his own ideas of the law according to the teachings of legal science....

Although the common law world has seen occasional brief trends toward the kind of thinking that characterizes legal science, it has never really caught on here. Legal science is a creation of the professors — it smells of the lamp — and our judge-dominated law is fundamentally inhospitable to it. Common law judges are problem solvers rather than theoreticians, and the civil law emphasis on scientism, system-building, formalism, and the like gets in the way of effective problem solving. It also diminishes the role of the judge in the legal process, to the advantage of the legislator and the scholar. Both sociological jurisprudence — which is the opposite of abstraction, formalism, and purism — and legal realism — which rejects scientism and system-building — emphasize the difficulty and the importance of focusing on the judicial process. Both have flourished in the common law world, and particularly in the United States.

It is true that the famous case method of instruction, which is a creation of law professors in the United States, originated under the influence of German legal science; the idea was that decisions of courts, being sources of law, should be studied as data with the aim of deriving principles of law from them and finally arranging them into a coherent system. The end product of this line of thought in the United States was *The Restatement of the Law* (prepared mainly by professors), and its publication provided the occasion for a thorough, devastating attack by the legal realists. Since that attack, legal science has been essentially discredited in the United States, and the emphasis in legal education has subtly shifted. Cases are still studied, but they are no longer studied as the data of legal science. Instead, they are seen as convenient records of concrete social problems and as convenient examples of how the legal process operates.

The basic difference is epitomized in another quotation from the German legal scientist Rudolph Sohm: "A rule of law may be worked out either by developing the consequences that it involves, or by developing the wider principles that it presupposes.... The more important of these two methods of procedure is the second, i.e. the method by which, from given rules of law, we ascertain the major premises they presuppose.... The law is thus enriched, and enriched by a purely scientific method." An American legal realist would resist the implication that rules of law should be the principal objects of his study or the suggestion that there are only these two ways of studying them. But if pushed to Sohm's choice, most law professors, judges, and lawyers in the United States would easily and quickly choose the first of his two methods. Most civil lawyers would still choose the second.

4. THE SCHOLARLY ORIGINS OF GERMAN LEGAL SCIENCE

JOHN P. DAWSON, THE ORACLES OF THE LAW 196, 198-201, 203, 206-07, 227-28, 231, 240-41, 450-52, 454-60 (1968)

The Triumph of the Learned Men

Expert opinions (*consilia*) had been, as we have seen, the principal means by which the learning of the great doctors had been put to use in the law practice of late medieval Italy. Germans who had been trained in the Italian mode would naturally expect to render similar service when called on in Germany. In expert counselling as in other respects the canonists led the way. Even as early as the 1200's and increasingly thereafter difficult legal questions were referred by church courts to expert canonists. Training in Roman law, organized in German universities in the late 1400's, rapidly multiplied the number of men who could give *consilia* on problems of secular law. Zasius and his followers were much engaged in rendering expert opinions. A volume of *consilia* by Zasius was published in 1538. Thereafter a considerable market developed for literature in this form. By 1600 there had been published forty-one volumes of *consilia* written by Germans trained in Roman law....

Most expert opinions by lawyers trained in the Italian tradition were still given, as in Italy, by individual jurists. Yet for more than 100 years there had been isolated instances of opinions given by university faculties acting collectively. After 1550 they became somewhat more common, enough so that a few universities drew up their own internal regulations for the preparation of collective opinions. Yet until 1600 the great and growing bulk of published *consilia* consisted overwhelmingly of works by individual jurists who spoke for themselves alone.

On other hand, Germany had known since the Middle Ages collective responses on legal questions — the judgments of *Schöffen* in local courts, the declarations of custom in the *Weisthümer*, and especially the responses of those law-speakers wise in German law who functioned in the *Oberhöfe*. It was not a great change but merely a fusion of German and Romanist traditions for the law professors to coalesce into collegiate groups whose responsibility became collective....

Some collective responses by the faculties were written in German, but it was more natural for them to write in Latin, the normal medium for their own disputations. Whether written in German or Latin, the responses would usually be cast in technical language. If reasons were given or authorities cited, they would be, in any event, barely intelligible to their questioners. Under these circumstances the convenience of the inquiring court was actually served if the response was drawn up as a draft decree.... It became more common for the inquiring court to escape the task of formulating the legal questions that troubled them and merely to forward the documents. So it became the practice for the inquiring court simply to ship a full written record of the case to its expert advisers, who would thus have before them all the materials needed for a final decree. Thus the way was fully prepared for that astonishing practice which one wise scholar long ago termed "the decisive turning point" in the reception — the practice of "dispatching the record" (*Aktenversendung*) to university faculties for their collective and binding decision....

Under developed *Aktenversendung* procedure, when the record of a case was dispatched to a law faculty, the decree returned had no coercive effect until it had been issued by the inquiring court and thus made enforceable by its own process.... The inquiring court had no independent power of review over content; even if the decree appeared on its face to be erroneous as a matter of law, the court's only recourse was to ship the record to another law faculty in the hope of receiving a different decision....

The law professors were not, even in a formal sense, members of the inquiring court; indeed they had not been appointed to any judicial office whatever. No political agency had conferred on them executive power, for this was retained by the inquiring court. They could issue no process, even to compel attendance by the parties; in fact their practice was to conduct no hearings either of the parties or their counsel. They often resided and did their work in the land of another ruler....

When one searches for reasons why the practice was originally developed and so long maintained, one finds a theme that constantly recurred, the need for the "impartiality" that the law professors provided. The resulting delays and higher costs, the professors' ignorance of local conditions (including deviant rules of local statutes or custom), their remoteness from the human issues that came to them in piles of papers — all these seemed not too high a price to pay for small groups of decision-makers who were free from political influence and could be trusted to adhere to rules. The fact that their responsibility was collective seemed to offer a further guarantee. In the early nineteenth century when the whole system came under review, the "palladium of German liberty" was found by some to be, not the jury of laymen that we ourselves have enshrined, but collective judgments of law professors rendered after "dispatch of the record."...

The leadership assumed by the law professors, both through court decrees after *Aktenversendung* and through advisory opinions to individual questioners, was sure to influence decisively the content of the new mixed system that was being produced. Working in libraries on the piles of paper submitted to them, the professors could not know the whole environment in which the problems arose or the diversified customs of which the traditional law of Germany still largely consisted. For the law professors, as for the *Reichskammergericht* and the appellate courts of the territories, custom was another fact to be proved; if not proved, it could be ignored. Where custom was sufficiently proved or local legislation was encountered, men who were thoroughly Bartolized tended to employ the techniques of restrictive interpretation that had been developed long before by the Italian doctors (*statuta stricte sunt interpretanda*). The washing out of local diversities was further promoted by the resort to distant faculties, often to faculties located in other German states. The choice of the faculty that would be addressed was made by the court, not by the parties, in *Aktenversendung* procedure; indeed, to discourage attempts to bribe or persuade elaborate precautions were taken to keep secret the identity of the faculties that the courts had chosen. In making their choices, the dispatching courts must often have felt that distance from the local scene was a positive advantage, a further assurance of the neutrality that was so much desired. The records of the faculties show that cases flowed in to them from most of Germany. Especially those with high prestige cast their influence out in all directions. Exchange of ideas among the faculties themselves was powerfully aided by the printing press. Great folio volumes of judgments and *consilia* served as law reports, used both by the professors themselves and by their expanding public. As the years went by the activities of the faculties thus built a great body of common doctrine, penetrated with Italianate learning and transcending the boundaries of the German states....

The judicial powers that the faculties were acquiring through *Aktenversendung* made their decisions a kind of hybrid case law.... This highly sophisticated literature was all very well for the law professors, but for persons interested in the work of other courts some methods of condensation were needed....

It would be difficult to characterize all the "reports" that thereafter poured out over Germany during the late seventeenth and eighteenth centuries. Their volume was great, there were many diversities in form and content.... The audience evidently wanted most of all to know the relevance of particular solutions to a superstructure of legal ideas. The "reports" that acquired influence were doctrinal essays by experts; many centered on problems that had been raised in litigation but hypothetical questions would do as well. The courts whose decisions seemed worth reporting were mainly those whose members met the standards of academic excellence, whether they were the surviving *Schöffen* courts, the law faculties themselves, or appellate courts that were staffed by equally learned men. Even the solutions that these "courts" reached acquired significance only after they had been filtered through the minds of learned authors and assigned a proper place in a setting of organized legal doctrine. Among the industrious problem-solvers at work all over Germany, courts (at least, the "learned" courts) had been elevated to the rank of a junior partnership. Serious efforts and numerous volumes were devoted to recording the work that courts were doing. Germany had acquired a kind of case-law, secreted in the interstices of learned writings....

Germany's own commitment to its special version of "legal science" must be explained, I suggest, not by the activities or ambitions of governments but by the primacy already acquired by learned academicians who were almost wholly exempt from political control. Academicians had been brought into prominence through the importation of Roman law, which they were best able to explain, but France was to show that large-scale Romanization does not necessarily transfer effective leadership to academicians. I have argued earlier that the rate and extent of the German reception were greatly increased at critical times by the pressure of the new appellate courts; the *Reichskammergericht* had a part in this but still more the courts in the territories. This pressure from courts that had been created by rulers through political motives had, however, an anomalous result. It promoted the transfer of effective powers of judicial decision to law faculties and to their allies, the surviving *Schöffen*-courts. After 1600, when *Aktenversendung* had become fully organized, their judicial powers gave these detached groups of learned experts effective leadership in the shaping of doctrine, not only over the whole range of private law but still more in the criminal law....

The Pandectist System

In following the progress after 1800 of efforts to organize German law one has the strange sensation of observing a great wheel loaded with human passengers, revolving slowly but inexorably so as to bring them back to their starting point. The wheel was to spin off in new directions after 1900, when the new Civil Code took effect. During the intervening century (1800-1900) the ascendancy of academic jurists was re-established more firmly than ever before, the heavy deposit left by three centuries of German experience was largely sloughed off, and a great conceptual system was constructed — a system that seemed all the more pure and all the more valid because it was based on a rediscovered Roman law. This was the Pandectist system, so-called because it rested mainly on the principal available source of classical Roman law, the Pandects (i.e., the Digest) of Justinian....

The influence of Savigny was so enormous and has been described so often that only a sketch will be attempted here. It was due not only to the power of his intellect, his aristocratic birth and bearing, the key positions that he held (professor in the University of Berlin, later Prussian minister of legislation), but above all to the timeliness of the ideas he advanced. He is most often remembered in the outside world for his theory that law is the product of the *Volksgeist,* embodying the whole history of each nation's culture, responding to organic processes of growth in society itself, and reflecting inner convictions that are rooted in common experience. These contributions to sociology have been sufficiently criticized. One of his immediate objectives has already been mentioned, to postpone attempts to codify; in this respect his influence was decisive. His reasons for postponement included not only the effect of a code in arresting processes of organic growth but the deficiencies of German lawyers and even of the German language. His program, essentially, was a call to arms for a two-front campaign — to recreate the nation's past and to perfect the method of German legal science. Success in each would promote the other.

To most scholars of his time, and to others as well, this program had a powerful appeal. It included a rejection of natural law styles of logical demonstration which had degenerated, many thought, into sterile exercises. It was to be a national movement, though its nationalism was not narrowly conceived, and it was proposed at a time when liberation from foreign rule was releasing the forces of German patriotism. The campaign on both fronts was to be conducted with the weapons of scholarship; expert jurists were to be the spokesmen of the *Volk* in transmuting its convictions into law. But others besides lawyers were to be enlisted. Savigny had many ties with the larger world of scholarship, with historians, linguists, and intellectual leaders like Goethe. He was familiar with and encouraged the promising work already begun in German legal and institutional history. His theories of the *Volksgeist* no doubt added some strains of mysticism and romanticism that suited the mood of the times. But quite without them, the substance of his proposals offered twin objectives that many of his generation were ready and eager to pursue....

For Savigny himself history and "legal science" were opposite sides of the same phenomena; they could "no more be separated than light and shadow." He was drawn to classical Roman law not only by his admiration for antique culture and his belief in the continuity of historical experience, but because he believed he could find in the classical jurists an ordered system of ideas. To him the clarity and internal consistency of these ideas offered the greatest hope for rapid improvement in German legal method. But on this voyage of discovery the explorer was forced to supply much of his own equipment. In describing their own conceptual apparatus the Roman classical jurists had been extraordinarily taciturn, since their attention had been concentrated on specific problem-solving. The objective now was to find and unveil an ideal system that Roman jurists 1600 years before had themselves not tried to articulate and that would also serve the needs of nineteenth century Germany. The experience and recurring problems of nineteenth century Germans were imported into the system as its outlines became more precise and refined in the work of Savigny's followers. The system purported to be drawn from Justinian's Pandects, but the aim, as its authors themselves declared, was a *modern* legal science. They wanted a system perfectly suited to resolving all problems that a mature society could present.

As time went on this universe of concepts began to seem to its admirers not only complete but self-sufficient. Contemporary conduct, depicting the "inner convictions" of the *Volk,* had early dropped from view. Ethics and explicit value judgments had gone out with natural law. Even the Roman law texts from which the concepts had been drawn were treated more selectively. They receded to an outer fringe, where they served more as flying buttresses to maintain the firmness of the main structure. More and more attention was devoted to the upper reaches of the superstructure. Emphasis shifted from monographs on specific topics to comprehensive treatises, fitting and extending conceptual girders at high levels of generality. "Concepts were labored over, to be got into the broadest terms men's minds might reach, for system's sake. The edges of definitions were stated and taped with the explicit precision of a tennis court." There were to be no gaps. Increasingly it seemed that legal problems could be resolved by simple subsumption under categories, with a rigorous exclusion of moral judgments and with no concern for consequences to those affected by the rules. Decades were required for the system to be perfected and for these attitudes to harden. The end result has been well described as "scientific positivism." Instead of legislation, sanctioned by the power of the political state, the academic profession transferred its allegiance to the categorical imperatives that its own efforts had created....

Several causes combined to radiate Pandectist methods of analysis far outside the cloisters in which they had originated. One of these was the existing vacancy that they helped to fill. They were intended to be and were in fact an agent for unification in a society that was still divided politically but was bound together by a common language and culture and a growing sense of a common destiny. Lacking a national code and (until 1879) the unifying influence of a central court with a generalized and nationwide jurisdiction, Germans could look to the "heavenly city of juristic conceptions" as Frenchmen could gaze with pride and admiration on Napoleon's Code. The heavenly city had been made in Germany, by German jurists to serve the needs of their own nation, though it was also invested with the authority of the Roman law from which it had been at least nominally derived.

The eventual triumph of the Pandectists was due even more to their own self-imposed limitations. They were concerned almost exclusively with private law, as Justinian's Pandects had been; they could pursue their work in relative peace, untroubled by the surrounding turbulence over the limits and purposes of governmental action. From their own analysis the Pandectists excluded all explicit value judgments and abstained from conscious weighing of competing social interests. But this had the positive advantage of casting them in the role of political neutrals. The German nineteenth century was sufficiently troubled by political and social conflict so that these very disclaimers of responsibility, for which they were later reproached, gave their product at the time an added attraction. As in medieval Italy, where there was even greater need for trustworthy neutrals, the neutrality of the jurist could be assured by an intricate, technical and impersonal system that purported to exclude subjective judgments. For courts whose relations with political superiors were as yet uncertain, recourse to the Pandectist system defined and narrowed judicial power and thus justified and reinforced claims to judicial independence. In committing themselves to its relentless logic courts did not hamper but rather promoted the progressive forces of the time. The Pandectists disclaimed philosophy, as they disclaimed so much else, but at the core of their thinking were theories of individualism — free contract, protection of private ownership, maximum scope for individual self-assertion. These theories could have a special appeal for members of the middle class from which the judiciary was increasingly recruited. To many it must have seemed that the Pandectists' ideal system of private law, designed to work automatically, promised a release of private energies as did the economists' ideal market. The social debris and conflict caused by advancing industrialism could be disregarded by a pure science of law if it left the way clear for the powerful forces that were promoting economic growth....

Their product could not have been accepted to the degree that it was if it had not coincided in so many ways with the needs and dominant trends of the time. But it should be said that its triumph was at least equally due to the care, precision and thoroughness with which the work was done. When looked at now, a hundred years later, it has the perfection of a still-life in which dream figures appear from another world, with all motion suddenly frozen. Despite this remoteness and unreality, despite everything else that has been said against it, one can still look at it with admiration as one of the great achievements of the human intellect.

The culmination came with [Bernhard] Windscheid, whose three-volume handbook of *Pandektenrecht* appeared in stages between 1862 and 1870. The influence of this book can only be compared with that of the Accursian gloss in medieval Italy. Indeed its function was similar. It was a great work of summation, extracting from a great accumulated mass of legal literature the useful and important ideas, discarding the irrelevant or out-of-date, and condensing into highly usable form the intellectual product of earlier decades. As with Accursius, the chief merit of Windscheid was not his originality. "He was no leader or prophet ... merely first among equals"; but in the range of his influence he was indisputably first. His Pandects were adopted as the statute law of Greece. They were and still are the primary source both in and out of Germany for those seeking access to Pandectist learning. Windscheid's concern for the needs of practice and his numerous references to court decisions made his book useful to practitioners as well. In the seven revised editions that he published before his death in 1892 he constantly added new material and gave respectful attention to the views of others. He had an objective, precise, and discriminating mind which ranged over all important areas of private law and assembled it all in an intricate, complete and ordered system. It was indeed a monument.

An even more lasting monument was the national Civil Code which took effect on January 1, 1900. The Code was prepared with utmost deliberation. A preliminary draft of a general law of obligations had been drawn up in 1865 by a commission that had worked for four years. In 1874, three years after the new *Reich* was organized, planning began for a code drafting commission, which began its meetings in 1881 and then worked intensively for six years. Of its eleven members only four were professors, but one of these was Windscheid. In this First Drafting Commission his influence was commanding. The judges and lawyers who formed a majority had all been trained in the Pandectist system and were intimately familiar with Windscheid's writings. When the first draft, accompanied by the Commission's *Motives*, was published in 1887, a storm of criticism broke out, much of it directed at the abstractness and formalism that Windscheid had contributed. For three years the text was debated and defended; then in 1890 a Second Drafting Commission set to work. It made many changes during five years of study. Windscheid was not a member of this Commission, and he did not live to see the final text, which was approved by the legislature in 1896 with its effective date postponed to 1900. This prolonged study brought to bear in a collective effort the trained legal intelligence of Germany. It somewhat diluted but could not efface the personal influence of Windscheid. More than this, through a deliberative process as extensive as it could well be, the nation adopted and embodied in a code the methods and the instruments of cerebration that Windscheid had best exemplified.

The structure and style of the Civil Code clearly mark it as the ultimate triumph of the Pandectists. It opens with a General Part that arches over the whole, cast at the highest level of abstraction. It then proceeds through descending levels of generality — all obligations, then contractual obligations, then particular contracts and noncontractual obligations, and so on. These provisions all interlock and all must be constantly kept in mind. The language is in effect copied from Pandectist textbooks, though extremely condensed; it is a special language, artificial and refined, and is used throughout with rigorous consistency. Intelligibility to laymen could have been no object. It was addressed to lawyers, for whom each key word should strike a chord resonating back on their own well-tempered scale. Regulation in detail was rarely attempted. The bias of the draftsmen and their faith in the results already achieved led them repeatedly to prefer general over more specific language. Furthermore, they were well aware that some scope was needed in interpretation and that problems would arise in forms not precisely foreseen. But for all such problems the Code should provide answers when read against the great accumulated reservoir of doctrine which the Code expressed in shorthand.

NOTES AND QUESTIONS

1. Consider the role of legal scholars in the history of the civil law tradition. Which legal actors have performed equivalent functions in the common law tradition?

2. Do the principal characteristics of the Pandectist school of legal science referred to by Professor Merryman reinforce each other?

3. Why did legal scientists want their discipline to be value free and pure? Does purism enhance the attractiveness of legal science for import into countries where there is substantial distrust between the political branches of government and the judiciary?

4. Rudolph Sohm, quoted in the Merryman excerpt in subsection 3 above, said: "A rule of law may be worked out either by developing the consequences that it involves, or by developing the wider principles that it presupposes." Compare Chief Justice Rehnquist, dissenting in *Anderson v. Liberty Lobby, Inc.*, 477 U.S. 242, 269 (1986):

> The Court, I believe, makes an even greater mistake in failing to apply its newly announced rule to the facts of this case. Instead of thus illustrating how the rule works, it contents itself with abstractions and paraphrases of abstractions, so that its opinion sounds much like a treatise about cooking by someone who has never cooked before and has no intention of starting now.

5. What do you think of the practice of *Aktenversendung*? Why did it develop? How was it related to the proliferation of books of *consilia*?

6. What part did Bernhard Windscheid, 1-3 *Pandektenrecht* (1862-1870), play in the process of codifying the BGB?

NOTE ON THE INFLUENCE OF GERMAN LEGAL SCIENCE

The Civil Code has been the most successful of the five German codifications. Its acceptance beyond the borders of Germany is one way legal science has traveled. The BGB substantially influenced: the Japanese Civil Code (1898), with the exception of family and succession law; the Swiss Civil Code (1907) and Code of Obligations (1911); the 1914-1916 revisions of the Austrian General Civil Code; the Brazilian Civil Code (1916); civil codes in some republics of the former Soviet Union and private law statutes in Hungary and the former Czechoslovakia and Yugoslavia from the 1920s; the Turkish Civil Code and Code of Obligations (1926), modeled on the Swiss codes; the Chinese Civil Code (1930); and the Greek Civil Code (1940).

Civil codes aside, it is difficult to overstate the influence of German legal science on the way civil lawyers think, write, and teach. In particular, the power of an orderly, systematic general theory of law has been difficult to resist. In its most pervasive, highly simplified form it supplies the content of the manuals on "introduction to law" or "introduction to the study of law," on which courses of the same title in civil law universities are based. These courses, given in the first year of law study in universities throughout Europe, Latin America, and East Asia, have a permanent effect on the way civil lawyers think. Such courses supply them with a coherent theory and a set of mutually consistent hard-edged concepts and propositions that they carry with them throughout their lives. In other words, these courses supply to law students in civil law universities exactly the sort of thing that teachers refuse (or fail) to supply to first year law students in U.S. law schools.

The general theory of law emerging from the tradition of German legal science, particularly as presented in the manuals, would today be rejected by sophisticated philosophers and theorists of law, both within Germany and outside it. It is a product of the 19th century, and much has happened since then; the jurisprudence of interests, sociological jurisprudence, and legal realism are only three examples of major competing schools of legal thought. Further, the manuals so simplify matters that much of the subtlety, complexity, and elegance of the great general theories of law are lost in them. Still, their use in introductory courses in law, particularly in Latin America, and their hold on the ways of thinking among civil lawyers everywhere seem unshakeable.

The best way to capture some of the flavor of such manuals is to examine one of them. For this purpose the following excerpt samples and comments on one of the very best of such manuals. In reading it, keep in mind that something of this sort constitutes the bulk of the first course in law taken by all law students in universities in most of Europe, Latin America, and East Asia.

5. LEGAL SCIENCE IN INTRODUCTION TO LAW COURSES

JOHN HENRY MERRYMAN, THE CIVIL LAW TRADITION: AN INTRODUCTION TO THE LEGAL SYSTEMS OF WESTERN EUROPE AND LATIN AMERICA 69-79 (2d ed. 1985)

The book begins with some "preliminary notions," the first of which is "the legal order." We are told that "no society ... is able to live in an orderly way without an aggregate of rules governing the relations among the persons who compose the group (*ubi societas ibi ius*) and individuals who are charged with enforcing their observance." Applying this observation to the state, "we ... establish the necessity both for an aggregate of norms that regulate the relations among citizens and for ... organs and institutions that ... enforce observance of the norms established by the state." [It will be observed that this definition of the legal order, limited to rules, or norms, and institutions for their enforcement, omits processes. This is a typical traditional approach. The legal order is seen as something static. Law is viewed not as a process for the perception and resolution of problems, but as a set of established rules and institutions. Instead of studying how such institutions perceive and resolve problems, or how they make, interpret, and apply the law, the doctrine focuses on the substantive content of the existing rules as its major object of study.]

The author begins his examination of the first component of the legal order in this way: "The legal norm ... is ... a command addressed to the individual by which a determined conduct ... is imposed on him." [Actually, not all norms command; the text statement is inaccurate. There are many norms, particularly in the field of private law, that merely state the legal consequence of a state of fact: e.g. if a person dies intestate, half of his property passes to his children.] Many norms, including all those of private law, not only require or prohibit, but "correlatively attribute to another person a power." The debtor is told to pay the debt, and the creditor is given the power to obtain payment. Hence the distinction between objective law and subjective right. "Objective law is the rule to which the individual must make his conduct conform; subjective right is the power of the individual that is derived from the norm." Objective law can be distinguished into natural law and positive law. "Our study is directed exclusively toward positive law." [Here are two very significant and ideologically loaded fundamental notions. The first is that of the "subjective right." In private law, this is the foundation of a legal system in which private, individual rights, i.e., property, contract, personal, and family rights, exist. The second is the rejection of "natural law," and hence of any normative system external to the state by which the validity of the positive law can be judged.]

The legal norm is more than mere advice; to the precept is joined a threat of "an evil administered by ... the state" if it is not observed. The nature of this sanction distinguishes the legal norm from rules of custom, rules of etiquette, religious norms, and moral norms, whose nonobservance leads to other kinds of consequences (social disapproval, pangs of conscience). [This emphasis on sanctions is very misleading. Many legal norms bear no express or implied "threat of an evil administered by the state." It distorts legal reality to speak in such a way about rules of intestate succession to property, rules defining the different types of contract (sale, loan, lease, etc.), and rules stating which courts have jurisdiction to hear and decide what kinds of cases (civil or criminal, large or small claims, etc.), to select only three examples.] The legal norm is also general; its command is not addressed to specific individuals but to a model "fact situation": the debtor who does not pay is liable for damages. If a concrete fact corresponds to this model, e.g. Smith does not pay his debt to Jones, then the effects established by the norm follow, i.e. Smith is liable to Jones for damages. [The reader will recognize that the traditional view of the judicial function described earlier is implicit in this statement. Once the facts of the case are found, the judge compares them with the model fact situations in the legal norms, selects the norm whose model corresponds to the facts of the case, and applies the consequence stated in that norm.] One difficulty with the model fact situation is that occasionally the application of the abstract norm to the concrete case "gives place to consequences that offend the sense of justice." Equity is the power to vary application of the norm; it is "the justice of the individual case." But "the legal order frequently sacrifices the justice of the individual case to the demands of certainty in the law, inasmuch as it is believed that subjecting the legal order to the subjective valuation of the judge is dangerous; it is better that individuals know in advance the precepts they must observe and the consequences of nonobservance (the principle of certainty of law)."...

These "preliminary notions" having been described, the author now moves to "the general part" of the civil law. He first distinguishes public law from private law: "The first governs the organization of the state and the other public entities ... and the relations between them and the citizen, relations in which the state and the public entities are in a position of supremacy with respect to the citizen, who is ... in a state of subjection and subordination....

The private law regulates the relations among citizens.... A characteristic of private law, in contrast to public law, is thus equality of position among subjects."... At this point the discussion turns exclusively to private law. The author points out that private law norms are either dispositive or imperative. "The first can be modified by private arrangements or agreements; the second, insofar as they refer to the protection of fundamental social interests, are not subject to modification by individuals."

Next comes a discussion of the sources of law, i.e. of legal norms, which are said to be statutes, regulations, and custom, in that order.... This is followed by a discussion of the temporal effect of legal norms: rules for determining when statutes shall take effect, methods of abrogation, the rule against retroactivity, and the effect of a change in a statute on partly completed or continuing states of fact. Then the author discusses interpretation of the legal norm, ... ending with a brief discussion of "the conflict of laws in space," which shows how to determine what legal norms apply when those of two or more nations are possibly applicable.

The author then turns from the legal norm to the legal relation. "Human relations can be of various kinds: they can be inspired by affection, by sentiment, by friendship, by interest, by conviviality, by cultural interests, etc. Everyone instinctively grasps the difference between those relations and that which exists between me and my debtor. This relation is regulated by the law, which attributes to me the power (subjective right) to obtain payment of the debt, and puts on my debtor the obligation to pay. Thus the legal relation is the relation between two subjects regulated by law. When one wishes to allude to the persons who have put a legal relation into effect (for example, a contract), one uses the expression parties. Opposed to the concept of parties is that of third persons. The third person is, in general, one not a party and not subject to a legal relation. It is a general rule that the legal relation does not produce effects either in favor of or against third persons (*res inter alios acta tertio neque prodest, neque nocet*)." [This rule is subject to so many exceptions that its usefulness is questionable; actually there are many situations in which the private legal relation does affect the legal interests of third persons. The tendency in the general part to overstate general propositions and to submerge exceptions is here clearly illustrated. Leaving aside the inaccuracy of the generalization, note that there is no reference to the very interesting question of whether, and if so under what circumstances, third persons *should* be affected by private legal relations. The tenets of traditional scholarship — particularly the belief that only legal considerations, narrowly defined, are of interest to the legal scholar — exclude these matters from discussion. The rule is stated as the product of scientific investigation. No normative judgment on it is expressly made, but the methods and objectives of legal science and the authority of the doctrine give it a normative impact. In terms of the "is" and the "ought," the statement in question misstates the "is," avoids discussing the "ought," and implies a normative judgment that the misstated "is" is the desirable rule.]

In general, the term "subjective right" is used to indicate the legal interest of the person who has the benefit of a legal relation in private law. "The ultimate end that the norm seeks is always the protection of general interests.

In many cases, however (and it is the rule in private law), it is the view that the best way to pursue this end consists in promoting individual interests, in stimulating individual initiative. The legal order recognizes the interests of the individual and seeks to effect the realization of his intention. Therefore the subjective right is defined as the primacy of intention, as the power to act for the satisfaction of one's own interests, protected by the legal order." [Here again we encounter the fundamental importance of the subjective right in private law. In addition, the reference to "the primacy of intention" conceals a long, voluminous scholarly debate. Some argued that private rights could be created, and private obligations imposed, only with the conscious assent of the individuals concerned. They were seeking the ultimate source of private legal relations, and they found it in the individual intention, or will. The *Willenstheorie* and the rule, criticized above, concerning the effects of legal relations on third persons, are logically related to each other. If the will or volition of the individual is taken as the true source of the legal obligation, then it seems right to conclude that one who has not expressed the will or volition to enter into the relation — i.e. one who is not a party to it — cannot be subjected to the obligation and cannot claim the benefits of it. (The parties to the contract are bound by it only because they voluntarily entered into the contract.) But if the *Willenstheorie* is abandoned, and if the view is generally taken that the true source of the rights and obligations arising out of the legal relation is the positive legal order itself, then the third persons rule does not necessarily, or even logically, follow. Instead, one is freer to adopt a more eclectic approach to the problem of whether and under what circumstances third persons should be legally affected by the agreement of the parties to the legal relation. The author does not discuss the point.]

The holder of a subjective right is not required to compensate others for any prejudice that the exercise of the right may cause to them, except where he abuses the right. [The criticisms made above of the rule that third persons are unaffected by a private legal relation apply to one interpretation of this statement. If it means anything, it is far from accurate, and it embodies a set of value judgments that the author never discusses. Is it true that the holder of the right is free to exercise it to the injury of others, so long as he does not "abuse" the privilege? Why? In addition, we could argue that the statement is nothing more than a tautology. If we say that the holder of a subjective right is liable to others for the exercise of that right only if he abuses it, then we have said that he is not liable for exercise of the right except when he is liable for the exercise of the right.] In some jurisdictions, such as France, courts use a general doctrine of scholarly origin to define "abuse of right." In others it is thought dangerous "to entrust the determination of the limits of the subjective right to the discretionary and variable criteria employed by judges." In the interests of certainty, then, the judge has this power only in selected, legislatively defined cases. [Observe the repeated emphasis on certainty in connection with the concern about giving discretionary power to judges.] ...

"The first and fundamental division of subjective rights" is into "*absolute rights*, which guarantee to the owner a power that he can exercise only against all others (*erga omnes*), and *relative rights*, which give him a power that he can exercise only against one or more determined persons. Typical absolute rights are the *real rights*, that is to say, rights in a thing. These attribute sovereignty, either full (ownership) or limited (real right in another's thing), over a thing to the owner. The immediate relation between the man and the thing stands out clearly, and is effective without need for the cooperation of others. Other subjects must merely abstain from interfering in the peaceful exercise of this sovereignty. In an obligatory relation, however [where only relative rights are involved], the conduct of another subject who is held to a determined conduct is of primary importance. The category of relative rights coincides with that of *rights of credit* (which are also called *personal rights* in contrast to real rights); that of the absolute rights include not only the real rights but also so-called *rights of personality* (right to a name, to one's image, and so on). The reverse, whether of the right of credit or the real right, is the *duty*: negative duty of abstention in the real right, and duty (more precisely, *obligation*) of one or more determined persons in the right of credit.

"The legal relation is constituted when the subject acquires the subjective right. Acquisition indicates the association of a right with a person, who then becomes its owner: in substance, a subjective right becomes a part of the person's patrimony. The acquisition can be of two kinds: by *original title*, when the subjective right arises in favor of a person without being transmitted from another; and by the *derivative title*, when the right is transmitted from one person to another. In acquisition by derivative title, one observes this phenomenon: the right that appertains to one person passes to another. This phenomenon is called *succession*. It indicates a change in the subject of a legal relation. In acquisition by derivative title, the new subject has the same right that the preceding titleholder had, or a right derived from it. This justifies the following rules: (1) The new titleholder cannot exercise a right greater than the one the preceding titleholder had (*nemo plus iuris quam ipse habet transferre potest*); (2) The validity and efficacy of the new title depend as a rule on the validity and efficacy of the preceding title." [Here again, these "rules" are subject to so many qualifications and exceptions that their usefulness as rules is dubious. In any legal system, there are cases in which the transferee of a right may get more or less than the transferor had, and the validity and efficacy of the new title can depend on factors other than the validity and efficacy of the preceding title. And as is often the case, these "rules" embody normative judgments about a variety of undisclosed issues.]

The author next turns to "the subject of the legal relation," discussing the legal characteristics of physical persons and legal persons (e.g. companies, foundations). Then, under the heading "the object of the legal relation," he discusses the legal concept of a thing (corporeal and incorporeal, movable and immovable, fungible and nonfungible, divisible and indivisible, consumable and nonconsumable, and so on).

Having discussed the basic characteristics of the legal relation in private law, typified by the subjective right and the subjective duty, the author turns to the proudest achievement of the civil law doctrine: the "juridical act." [This is the archetypal product of the methods and objectives of legal science .... Whole libraries of books and articles have been written on it. In some nations the notion has been employed in legislation (for example, in the German civil code, where it is called the *Rechtsgeschäft*). In others it is found only in the doctrine. But in any civil law nation it functions in two major ways: as a central concept in the systematic reconstruction of the legal order produced and perpetuated by scholars; and, together with the concept of the subjective right, as the vehicle for assertion and perpetuation of the role of individual autonomy in the law.]

The concept of the juridical act is based on another concept, the "legal fact." It will be recalled that the legal norm contains a statement of a model fact situation and a legal result. If the concrete facts that fit the model fact situation occur, then the legal result becomes operative. A legal fact is an event (e.g. birth or death of a person, a contract) that fits a model fact situation and that therefore has certain legal consequences. It is a legally relevant fact, as distinguished from those that have no legal relevance. Legal facts include "natural facts that come into being without the participation of our intention (the death of a person from sickness, an earthquake), as well as acts deliberately and voluntarily performed by men." Thus the distinction of legal facts into two categories: legal fact in the strict sense (i.e. mere legal fact) and deliberate, voluntary legal acts.

"Legal acts are distinguished into two large categories: acts that conform to the requirements of the legal order (*licit acts*) and acts that are performed in violation of legal duties and that produce injury to the subjective rights of others (*illicit acts*). The licit acts are subdivided into *operations*, which consist of modifications of the external world (for example, the taking of possession, the construction of a ship), and *declarations*, which are acts directed toward communicating one's thought, one's state of mind, or one's intention to others. The acts intended to communicate one's thought or one's state of mind are called *declarations of knowledge* (for example, notification); the acts intended to communicate one's intention constitute *juridical acts*. These last have been the object of significant doctrinal elaboration; as to the others, which are also called *legal acts in the strict sense*, the single point of certainty seems to be the nonapplicability of principles relative to the juridical act. In general, one can say that legal acts in the strict sense are acts that presuppose intention and deliberation in the actor, but not the intention to produce a legal effect: this is attached automatically by the legal order to the performance of the act. For example, if a person declares in writing in an unequivocal manner that he is the father of a child conceived out of wedlock, the child has a right to support according to the civil code, even if the declarer did not have any intention to attribute such a right to him by the act of declaration.

"Among legal acts, the juridical act is of fundamental importance. In fact, it constitutes the most complete and interesting expression of legal activity. To understand the notion of the juridical act well, it is desirable to move to an empirical demonstration. He who executes a will or the parties who enter into a contract intend to produce legal effects: to distribute one's goods among the persons that the testator will leave at the moment of his death or to transfer by sale the ownership of a thing in exchange for the price, and so forth. It is easy, therefore, to understand the definition given by the prevailing doctrine: the juridical act is a declaration of intention directed toward legal effects that the legal order recognizes and guarantees. And it is this direction of the intention toward legal effects that constitutes the characteristic element of the concept of the juridical act, and distinguishes it from legal acts in the strict sense, which — as we have seen — are also voluntary and deliberate acts, but produce their effects without requiring that the intention of the person who performs them be directed toward the production of these specified effects. These legal effects at which the parties aim are recognized and guaranteed by the legal order: this distinguishes the juridical act from illicit acts which — as we have seen — violate duties established by the legal order. The juridical act is a general figure elaborated by the writers drawing upon the study of particular legal figures (contracts, will, and so on). These figures present common characteristics. The fundamental characteristic consists in the fact that these are expressions of private autonomy, of the power that the legal order recognizes in individuals to regulate their own interests. This power is not, however, unlimited: the liberty of the subject to put transactions into being is subordinated to observance of rules dictated by the order, which establishes a series of burdens and limits. (For example, if one wishes to transfer real property, it is necessary to use the written form.) Above all, it is required that the purpose to which the act is directed be recognized as worthy of protection by the legal order. The study of the general theory of the juridical act is very important. Since the legal order recognizes the power of the will of individuals in regulating their own interests in the field of private law, the greater part of legal activity consists of juridical acts."

[The preceding paragraph illustrates several characteristics of legal science: the emphasis placed in the traditional doctrine on "private" juridical acts and the "private" legal relations arising out of them; the empirical stance of the doctrine ("the juridical act is a general figure elaborated by the writers drawing upon the study of particular legal figures"); and the remoteness of the doctrine from concrete problems. How, for example, does one go about determining whether a specific act is or should be considered "worthy of protection by the legal order"? Who decides, and by what criteria? How does the legal process function to place this kind of limit on private autonomy?]

Next follows a description of the various types of juridical acts (unilateral or multilateral, *inter vivos* or at death, gratuitous or onerous, and so on). Then the author begins an extensive discussion of the elements of the juridical act. "The elements of the juridical act are divided into *essential elements*, without which the act is void, and *accidental elements*, which the parties are free to include or not. The essential elements are called *general* if they apply to every type of act (such as intention, cause); *particular* if they refer to the particular type being considered. Thus in a sale, besides intention and cause, the thing and the price are essential." Then follow discussions of the general essential elements (intention and cause) and of the general accidental elements (condition, time limit, mode). And finally come discussions of interpretation and effects, and of the consequences of voidness and voidability of the juridical act.

The general part of this manual then closes with brief general discussions of the judicial protection of subjective rights and the proof of legal facts in civil actions. The general part is contained in 236 pages — more than a fourth of the entire volume. More than a hundred of those pages deal with the juridical act. Nowhere in the general part is there a discussion of specific subjective rights or specific legal institutions. The progress is from the more general and abstract to the less general but still abstract. The discussion of specific subjective rights and specific legal institutions later in the volume goes on within the conceptual structure established in the general part. More important, the later discussion has the same tone and style; the emphasis is on inclusive definitions, clean conceptual distinctions, and broad general rules. There is no testing of definitions, distinctions, and rules against reality. Indeed, the tone set trains the lawyer to make the concrete facts fit into the conceptual structure. The tendency is to preserve the rule from the exception, to smooth out the rough spots.

The law of the general part is thus doctrinal law; it is a law purely of the scholars, and if we encounter it in the enacted, living law of a civil law nation, as in Germany, it is because the lawmaker has chosen to put the doctrine into statutory form. The civil codes that preceded the German BGB naturally contain no similar general part, but even those that followed it have, on the whole, preferred to maintain a formal separation between the scientific work of the scholar and the lawmaking work of the legislator. The result, in most modern civil codes, is that the legislation reflects but does not expressly embody the general doctrinal scheme here described. However, it is enacted, interpreted, and applied by people whose minds have been trained in the doctrinal pattern and to whom the scheme here described seems basic, obvious, and true. The conceptual structure and its inherent, unstated assumptions about law and the legal process constitute a kind of classroom law that hovers over the legal order, deeply affecting the way lawyers, legislators, administrators, and judges think and work.

Attempts to introduce a similar systematic reconstruction of the basic elements of positive law in the common law world have, on the whole, been failures. There was a time, toward the end of the nineteenth century, when legal scholars in England and the United States sought to emulate German legal science. The introduction of the case method of instruction in the Harvard Law School during the 1870's was based partly on the assumptions of legal science. Early in this century English and American analytical jurists produced a good deal of scholarship that resembles the work of legal science in a number of ways, and from time to time there are revivals of interest in analytical jurisprudence in the common law world. The ambitious undertaking called *The Restatement of the Law*, begun in the 1920's and carried on by a group of outstanding professors at major American law schools, has had much in common with the civil law doctrine typified by the discussion of the general part described in this chapter. But there have also been a number of counter-influences: the impact of sociological jurisprudence and of legal realism, the lesser role of legal scholars and their work, the dominance of the problem-solving judge, and the different style and objectives of American legal education are among them. Most thoughtful legal scholars in the United States and England recognize the value of order and system, and they long, at least occasionally, for the introduction of a similar degree of order into our law. At the same time, most of them believe that the price is likely to be too high. They fear that this kind of order costs more in terms of sensitivity to the needs of a highly complex, constantly changing society than people should be willing to pay. Even those who are willing to pay that price lack the power within the legal process that is needed to establish a doctrinal system. They are teacher-scholars, and the protagonist of our legal process is still the judge.

CIVIL CODE OF GERMANY

Title 2: Declaration of Intention (Willenserklärung)

Sections 116-122

Section 116 [Mental reservation]

A declaration of intention is not void when the declarant secretly reserves the fact that he does not will what he has declared. The declaration is void if made to a person who is aware of such a reservation.

Section 117 [Sham act]

(1) If a declaration of intention is made only in pretense, with the agreement of the person to whom it is made, it is void.

(2) If another juridical act (Rechtsgeschäft) is concealed behind a sham act, the provisions applicable to the concealed juridical act apply.

Section 118 [Lack of seriousness]

A declaration of intention not seriously intended, which is made in the expectation that it will be understood not to be seriously intended, is void.

Section 119 [Avoidance on account of mistake]

(1) A person who when making a declaration of intention was under a mistake as to its meaning, or did not intend to make a declaration of that meaning at all, may avoid the declaration if it appears that he would not have made it with knowledge of the situation and with reasonable appreciation of the case.

(2) A mistake concerning such characteristics of a person or thing that are regarded in business as essential is also deemed to be a mistake as to the meaning of the declaration.

Section 120 [Avoidance on account of incorrect transmission]

A declaration of intention, which has been incorrectly transmitted by the person or institution employed for its transmission, may be avoided under the same conditions as a declaration of intention voidable for mistake under § 119.

Section 121 [Period for avoidance]

(1) Avoidance in the cases provided for in §§ 119 and 120 must be sought without culpable delay (promptly), after the person entitled to avoid has obtained knowledge of the grounds for avoidance. An avoidance as against a person who is not present is deemed to have been effected in due time if the avoidance has been forwarded promptly.

(2) Avoidance is barred if thirty years have elapsed since the making of the declaration of intention.

Section 122 [Avoiding a person's duty to compensate]

(1) If a declaration of intention given to another person is void under § 118 or voidable under §§ 119 and 120, the declarant shall compensate him or any third party for damage that the other or third party has sustained by relying upon the validity of the declaration; however, the damages shall not exceed the value of the interest that the other or third party has in the validity of the declaration.

(2) The duty to compensate does not arise if the injured party knew the ground of the nullity or avoidance or he did not know it due to negligence (he should have known it).

NOTE ON THE INFLUENCE OF GERMAN LAW IN THE UNITED STATES

John Merryman mentions above that German legal science has influenced two major developments in American law: (1) the case method of instruction at Harvard Law School under Dean Christopher Langdell in the 1870s, and (2) the American Law Institute's program of Restatements for many areas of the law. For more on how Americans borrowed from German models the case method and the structure of the modern Harvard Law School, see David S. Clark, *Tracing the Roots of American Legal Education — A Nineteenth-Century German Connection*, 51 Rabels Zeitschrift 313 (1987).

Another important area of German influence is the most successful codification in the United States: the Uniform Commercial Code. *See* James Whitman, *Commercial Law and the American* Volk: *A Note on Llewellyn's German Sources for the Uniform Commercial Code*, 97 Yale L.J. 156 (1987).

German legal thought also stimulated other currents in American law. Consider the discussion about Rudolf von Jhering:

> That Jhering successfully conquered the United States with his ideas — which are related to the pragmatism, American style, of such "fresh-air" philosophers as William James and John Dewey — has been frequently and openly acknowledged. The famous statement by Justice Holmes, who had read the *Geist des römischen Rechts* in a French translation in 1879, that "the life of law has not been logic: it has been experience," has a precise parallel in Jhering's passage:
>
> > "That particular cult of the logical, which tries to twist jurisprudence into a mathematics of law, is an aberration and rests on ignorance about the nature of law. Life is not here to be a servant of concepts, but concepts are here to serve life. What will come to pass in the future is not postulated by logic but by life, by trade and commerce, and by the human instinct for justice, be it deducible through logic or unlikely to happen at all."

> Holmes' trail-blazing address, *The Path of the Law*, in which he advocated the reading of eminent German jurists, breathes the clear air of Jhering's spirit. However, the decisive breakthrough came with Roscoe Pound and the publication of his five-volume comparative treatise on *Jurisprudence* and his book, *The Spirit of the Common Law*. [In his "sociological jurisprudence," Pound relied on Jhering,] whom he considers to be the German Bentham — because, contrary to the earlier Utilitarians like Comte or Mill, Jhering's ideas represented a social and not an individually oriented utilitarianism. In 1907 Pound became the first to point to the necessity of creating such a "school of sociological jurisprudence."

Konrad Zweigert & Kurt Siehr, *Jhering's Influence on the Development of Comparative Legal Method*, 19 Am. J. Comp. L. 215, 225-26 (1971). *See* James E. Herget, American Jurisprudence, 1870-1970 (1990): On Jhering and Pound (at 158-70), and *The Contributions of the Migrant Scholars, 1940-1970* (at 262-83). *See generally* Marcus Lutter, Ernst C. Stiefel & Michael H. Hoeflich, eds., Der Einfluß deutscher Emigranten auf die Rechtsentwicklung in den USA und in Deutschland (1993) (many articles in English); Mathias Reimann, ed., The Reception of Continental Ideas in the Common Law World, 1820-1920 (1993).

NOTES AND QUESTIONS

1. Why do most American law schools fail to provide the first-year student with an "Introduction to Law" course for the purpose of orientation? Would it be a good idea?

2. Does German legal science approach law basically as process or as substance? What is the usual American approach?

3. What is a subjective right? Can you distinguish between absolute rights and relative rights? To which does a legal relation attach?

4. What is a legal norm? Give an example illustrating its two parts.

5. Diagram the derivation of the private juridical act from the category of legal facts. Try to understand the terms and categories involved.

6. Sections 116 to 122 from the German Civil Code are found in book 1 (general part), section 3 (juridical acts), title 2 (declaration of intention). Is it possible from the sections excerpted above to foresee how a German lawyer, as a preliminary matter, would analyze a situation where a real property transfer, the creation of a testament, or the acceptance of a contract were intended as a joke? Would compensation be due?

7. John Merryman ends his excerpt above with a comment about legal scholars in the United States and the interest of some in establishing a doctrinal system. Is this desirable? Is it possible?

For an interesting discussion of the roles of judge and scholar in the United States, see David R. Barnhizer, *Prophets, Priests, and Power Blockers: Three Fundamental Roles of Judges and Legal Scholars in America,* 50 U. Pitt. L. Rev. 127 (1988):

> Judicial thought in America generates the categories, language, purposes, and values of the academic legal scholar. While judges and legal

scholars are two aspects of a single system, this in no way means that the relationship is exclusive, that it is one of master-servant or that the categories of judicial thought are the only ones possessed by academic legal scholars. It is instead an assertion that the judge-scholar relationship is central to what American legal scholars do and that the judicial thought pattern dominates the system.

Id. at 127.

8. The American Restatements borrow much from 19th century German legal science and the historical school of law. Reflect on the following comment:

> [T]he restatements of the law [are] perhaps the high-water mark of conceptual jurisprudence. Work began in the late 1920s, under the sponsorship of the American Law Institute (founded in 1923). The proponents were hostile to the very thought of codification. They wanted to head it off, and save the common law, by reducing its principles to a simpler but more systematic form. The result would be a restatement, not a statute. Judges and professors would do the work, hacking away at the major common-law fields: contracts, trusts, property, torts, agency, business corporations, conflict of laws. They took fields of living law, scalded their flesh, drained off their blood, and reduced them to bones. The bones were arrangements of principles and rules (the black-letter law), followed by a somewhat barren commentary. The first restatement, on contracts, was finished in 1932. The restatements were, basically, virginally clean of any notion that rules had social or economic consequences. The arrangements of subject matter were, on the whole, strictly logical; the aim was to show order and unmask disorder. (Courts that were out of line could cite the restatement and return to the mainstream of common-law growth.) The chief draftsmen, men like Samuel Williston and Austin W. Scott of Harvard (contracts, trusts), were authors of massive treatises in the strict, conceptual, Langdell mold. They expended their enormous talents on an enterprise which, today, seems singularly fruitless, at least to those legal scholars who adhere to later streams of legal thought. Incredibly, the work of restating (and rerestating) is still going on.

Lawrence M. Friedman, A History of American Law 676 (2d ed. 1985).

How would a German legal scientist respond? For a thoughtful discussion of clarity in legal rules, see James Gordley, *European Codes and American Restatements: Some Difficulties*, 81 Colum. L. Rev. 140 (1981).

6. *PATRIA POTESTAS* REDEFINED

MARY ANN GLENDON, THE TRANSFORMATION OF FAMILY LAW: STATE, LAW, AND FAMILY IN THE UNITED STATES AND WESTERN EUROPE 97-99 (1989)

The [French] Civil Code originally gave a father unchecked power over a child's person and property until the child reached the age of 21. This *puissance paternelle* included the right to control the child's mode of life and education and to give or withhold consent to the child's marriage or emancipation. Until 1935, a father who had grave cause for dissatisfaction with the conduct of his child could even obtain a court order for the child's arrest and detention in an "appropriate place." In 1942, the role of the mother began to be recognized. The Code was amended in that year to provide that authority over a child "belonged" to both parents, even though it was to be "exercised" by the father in his capacity as head of the family. It was not until 1970, however, that a thoroughgoing revision of the law in this area took place.

The 1970 law was ... a landmark in the development of legal equality of the sexes in France. It was, in addition, the culmination of a steady trend to modify the degree and kind of control to which children were subjected. It not only provided that mothers and fathers should exercise their authority jointly from then on, it replaced the *puissance paternelle* with what is now called *l'autorité parentale*. The change from *power* to *authority* was as significant as that from *paternal* to *parental*. *Puissance*, like the Roman law concept of *potestas*, signified dominion over the children; *authority* in the new law was the name given to a scheme which encompassed parental duties as well as powers. The Code still recites, as it did in 1804, that: "A child of any age owes honor and respect to its father and mother." But now parents have obligations too: to protect the child's "safety, health, and morals," and to furnish him or her with care, supervision, and education. Far-reaching as the 1970 changes were, they nevertheless stopped short of establishing full equality between father and mother. The father's right to administer and receive the income from his children's property remained predominant until 1985, and his right to transmit his surname to his legitimate children remains to this day.

In Germany, the Civil Code of 1896 had already substituted *parental*, for *paternal*, power (*elterliche Gewalt*) and had assigned parents duties as well as rights. But except for a few specific rights given to mothers, parental power over the child's person and property was to be "exercised" by the father, who also was given the last word in the event of disagreements between the parents. An early inroad on this patriarchal model, however, was made in a 1921 statute on the religious upbringing of children. Under this law, which is still in effect, the religious education of a child up to the age of fourteen is supposed in principle to be determined by both parents acting together. In the event of disagreement, the child is to be raised in the religious denomination of the parents at the time of their marriage. If the parents did not have a common religion at that time, the guardianship court can accord the right of decision to one parent. The law goes on to specify that the religious denomination of a child over twelve cannot be changed against his or her will and that a child over fourteen can decide the matter alone.

In other areas, despite the equality command of the 1949 Constitution, the 1957 Equality Law specified that the father's decision would prevail in the event of disagreements between parents regarding the child. It also provided that only the father could act as the child's legal representative. Equality between parents thus had to await a court decision which declared these provisions unconstitutional. The legislature then remained silent on these matters until 1979, when it completely redesigned the legal image of the relationships between parents and children. The 1979 law replaced the term *parental power* with *parental care* (*elterliche Sorge*) and established mutual duties of parents and children to assist and respect each other. The new law also provided for participation by a child in decisions regarding his or her education and upbringing. It admonished parents to take into consideration the child's aptitudes and needs for independent responsibility at various stages of development and instructed them that their child-raising methods were not to include "humiliating treatment."

QUESTION

Which subtradition, the intellectual revolution or legal science, most altered the legal nature of parent-child relationships inherited from the *jus commune*?

C. RECEPTION OF EUROPEAN LAW IN EAST ASIA

NOTE ON THE CIVIL LAW TRADITION AND THE TYPICALITY OF CIVIL LAW SYSTEMS

We have completed our survey of the five subtraditions within the civil law tradition and have seen that they occur in different ways, with different intensities, in contemporary civil law systems. In the presence of such diversity does it make sense to perpetuate the notion of a "civil law" family, to be contrasted with a "common law" family of legal systems? The answer would seem to be that it does make sense, not so much because of the theoretical utility of such concepts, but for their practical value. The notion of a civil law tradition and its five subtraditions, properly qualified, is a useful way of conveying information about some of the basic characteristics of legal systems in more than half the world. It is a way of explaining why and how their legal systems are different from our own. Still, the amount of variation one encounters within the civil law world is very great, and we are right to be careful to avoid over-generalization.

Which of the contemporary civil law systems is the most typical? The question is an interesting one. It would be useful, for example, for someone who wished to study a concrete civil law system and had no predispositions in favor of one or another to know which to choose, and typicality is certainly a consideration. (No one can be an effective comparative lawyer without a fairly comprehensive grasp of one foreign legal system in all its various aspects, and hence one must choose.) One of us, who became a comparative lawyer rather late, was actually in such a position and, after a good deal of study and consultation, chose Italian law. Typicality was not the only consideration, but it was an important one (see John Henry Merryman, *The Italian Style I: Doctrine*, 18 Stan. L. Rev. 39, 40-42 (1965)).

The practice in comparative law teaching and scholarship in England and the United States has been to focus on French and German law. There are sound reasons for this practice. Germany and France are relatively wealthy, powerful nations that play important parts in our commercial, cultural, and strategic relations. The French and German contributions to the civil law tradition, as this chapter has shown, are basic. Comparative law has become an important academic and practical study only recently in the United States, and that interest was in large part fostered, and commanding academic posts filled, by refugee scholars, particularly from Germany. Such men as Rudolf Schlesinger at Cornell and Hastings and the late Max Rheinstein at Chicago, to name only two of the most prominent of them, found it natural and congenial to teach and write about what they knew best — their own legal system and its most prominent civil law rival. France has particular importance in the United States because of the French influence in Louisiana, and a similar consideration applies to Quebec in Canada. These regions of lively interest in French law add color and texture to the national legal systems of nations otherwise dominated by the common law. French and German legal scholarship still play leading roles in the literature of the civil law. A substantial literature in English has grown up about French and German law, making their study more accessible to faculty and students in common law nations.

Thus considerations other than typicality have in the past determined the focus of comparative law teaching and scholarship and will probably continue to do so in the future. It has seemed important, for excellent reasons, to focus on France and Germany. Typicality, however, is not one of the reasons. On the contrary, France and Germany are, in important ways, among the least typical of the civil law nations. If we define the civil law world to include Europe (exclusive of Scandinavia) and Latin America, plus the civil law nations of Africa, the Middle East, and Asia and civil law enclaves like Quebec, Louisiana, and Puerto Rico, we find few nations that are, in terms of size, wealth, social and natural conditions, and culture, truly comparable to France or Germany. But even on the strictly legal plane, France and Germany are extraordinary. Their legal systems, like the others, are built on a base composed of the *jus commune* (Roman civil law and canon law) and commercial law as they grew in practice and were organized and systematized by scholars in pre-revolutionary Europe. But much of the ideology of the French Revolution and its aftermath, which has enormously influenced codification and the structure of government throughout the rest of the civil law world, was, through the efforts of Savigny and others, deliberately rejected in Germany. Conversely, of all civil law nations, France seems to have been the most resistant to German legal science. Elsewhere in the civil law world, particularly in Europe, Latin America, and East Asia, German legal science has been extremely influential. What one finds in those legal systems is an acceptance and utilization of both the French and German contributions to the civil law tradition. They are in this sense the more "typical" civil law systems (but in view of the Latin American and East Asian variations noted in Chapter 6, Sections D and E, can any Latin American or East Asian legal system be considered typical of the civil law?).

As we have done so far, we will continue in the rest of this book to deal with the legal systems of France and Germany, but also with those of other civil law nations in Europe, Latin American, and East Asia. France and Germany may not be typical, but they are important; other nations may be less important, but they present a fuller and more accurate view of the contemporary civil law world.

NOTE ON JAPAN AS A MODEL IN EAST ASIA

By the mid-19th century China, Japan, Korea, and Thailand were the only remaining independent states in East Asia. Most of Indochina was under French rule; the British controlled South Asia, the Malay peninsula, and Hong Kong; and the Dutch had extended control over Sumatra, Java, and the other islands of the Indonesian archipelago. Like most of Latin America, the Philippines had been subjected to Spanish colonial rule since the 16th century. But by 1900 the Philippines had begun to experience its half-century of American military rule. In this context the opening of Japan in the 1850s, initiated by the United States but sustained and expanded by the European powers, was the catalyst for dramatic changes that eventually engulfed not only Japan but also East Asia as a whole.

Successfully emulating the West in comprehensive political, economic, educational, and legal reforms, Japan emerged within half a century as a military and industrial rival, if not quite a peer, of Great Britain, France, Germany, and — also newly acknowledged as a world power — the United States. This achievement was for Japan a source of deep national pride and of a widely shared belief in a mission to free the region from European domination by means of Japanese imperial tutelage. By 1910 Japan had thus established colonial control over both Taiwan and Korea. Japan's experience, however, also inspired in other East Asian nations a sense of regional pride and nationalism and made Japan a model to emulate. In both China and Thailand, Japan's experience was closely followed and functioned as a source for their own reforms. Thus, like other aspects of East Asia's modern transformation, the reception of European law too begins with Japan.

1. CODIFICATION AND LEGAL SCIENCE IN MEIJI JAPAN

NOTE ON CODIFICATION

The process of legal reform in Japan began in the early 1870s. The abdication of the last Tokugawa shōgun and assumption of direct rule by the newly enthroned 16-year-old emperor Mitsuhito[a] in January 1868 brought into power a small group of new leaders, drawn mostly from the Western domains least supportive of the Tokugawa shōgunate. After a short-lived attempt to revert to a Chinese-styled *ritsuryō* system, they realized that their goal of national autonomy through strength could only be achieved by breaking with the past completely and restructuring the Japanese polity on the basis of Western models. Legal reform was thus only a part of a much more comprehensive package of reforms that reached into every area of Japanese life.

External pressures contributed to the decision. In the 1858 Treaty of Amity and Commerce with the United States, Japan conceded jurisdiction over American nationals in Japan in both civil and criminal cases. Japan's subsequent diplomatic and commercial treaties with the European powers contained similar provisions. The West justified special extraterritorial rights on

[a] Mitsuhito's reign was designated Meiji from the Chinese character compound ("bright rule") he selected at its inception. He was known thereafter as the Meiji emperor. The Meiji era lasted from 1868 to 1912.

the basis of the perceived superiority of Western law, an apparent affront to Japanese sovereignty and national pride that was readily understood. By conditioning the elimination of consular jurisdiction as well as the more economically significant restoration of control over customs and trade policies on legal reforms acceptable to the "civilized" states of the West, the European powers added an important impetus for legal reform. However, it would be a mistake to view Japan's efforts as merely a response to Western demands. Legal reform was an essential element of the Meiji leadership's broader reconstruction of Japan into a modern military and industrial power.

The chronicle commences in 1870 with the organization of a code compilation project headed by Shinpei Etō under the Institutions Bureau of the Great Council of State (*Dajōkan seido kyoku*) and the 1871 publication of Rinsho Mitsukuri's translations of the French Penal Code and Civil Code. In 1871 a Western-styled Department of Justice (*Shihō-shō*) was organized, and by 1872 a rudimentary system of local trial courts had been established along with Japan's first law faculty, the *Meihō-ryō* Law School in the Justice Department. By the mid 1870s the basic institutional structure for Japan's modern judiciary was completed with the creation of the Great Court of Cassation (*Daishin'in*) and a system of intermediate appellate courts and local prefectural courts. Also in 1875 the role of private advocates (*daigennin*) was officially recognized.

The prevailing influence of French law and institutions was apparent from the outset. French jurists Georges Hilaire Bousquet and Émile Gustave Boissonade de Fontarabie were prominent among the foreign law advisors invited to Japan. Indeed the initial efforts at reform involved hardly more than an attempt to translate the French civil, commercial, penal, and procedure codes into Japanese. These early efforts were rejected, however, in favor of a deliberate effort to ensure compatibility of Japanese customs with the new law. As the process proceeded, the result was a radical institutional transformation.

The first full draft of a Civil Code was completed in 1878. Reflecting Etō's preferences for French law and for speed, it was quickly rejected as a flawed translation incompatible with Japanese tradition. A second drafting effort began almost immediately with Boissonade as the primary foreign advisor. Every effort was made this time to ensure that the code would accommodate Japanese traditional practices and customs. Over a decade later the final product was eventually enacted, after considerable debate, in 1890, along with a Commercial Code dealing primarily with company law, initially drafted by the government's principal German legal advisor, Hermann Roesler. Almost immediately, however, both codes became embroiled in a vehement dispute between Japanese legal factions — the French versus English schools — that also pitted traditionalists against more internationalist reformers. Although the family law provisions were the primary target of criticism, the controversy resulted in postponement of enforcement of both codes and eventually their abandonment. (However, the company law provisions of the 1890 Commercial Code did go into effect on a temporary basis.) New drafting committees were then organized and, finally, in 1896, based on the German model, the first three books of the current Civil Code were enacted, covering General

Provisions (book I), Real Rights (book II), and Obligations (book III). Two years later the remaining two books on family relations and succession were adopted. By 1899 a new Commercial Code was also completed. The codification process finally ended in 1907 with enactment of the Penal Code, also based on German law.

The controversy over the 1890 codes was a pivotal event in the Japanese codification process. Yet despite rhetoric protesting the adoption of Western legal principles and forecasting the ruin of Japan's "virtuous ways and beautiful customs" (*junpu bizoku*), the outcome was not a rejection of European law but rather a shift from French to German models.

Japan's reception of European law did not end, however, with the enactment of the codes. Their completion merely marked the conclusion of one phase. A gradual but profoundly influential process followed through which the theory and concepts underlying the codified rules of German law were introduced and incorporated into Japanese law, despite the mixed origin of the Japanese codes, by scholarly interpretation and judicial decision.

RICHARD W. RABINOWITZ, LAW AND THE SOCIAL PROCESS IN JAPAN, 10 Transactions of the Asiatic Society of Japan 36-37 (Third Series 1968)

In 1892 a truly impassioned conflict raged between defenders of what was conceptualized as British and French points of view, and yet four years later a Civil Code, essentially German sourced, was adopted. Consider in this connection that it was not until 1890 that Japanese students graduated with majors in German law from Japanese institutions of higher education. And there have been explicit assertions that when the Dispute raged the German law faction, if it existed at all, was of no significance whatever. How could this happen if a German tradition did not exist, and if intellectually committed men were involved in the 1892 incident?

First, I believe the new Civil Code was adopted in 1896 and 1898 because it was politically necessary. This is a very simple-minded explanation, but it cannot be overlooked merely because it is at a low level of abstraction. Those in charge of the Meiji government, those dealing on a day-to-day basis with foreigners, those handling diplomatic relations were well aware that there would be serious problems with foreign states if codes were not adopted, and most fundamental in this regard was the Civil Code. Those running the government in the 1890s, just as in the day of Etō, still felt it perfectly reasonable that a French-type code be adopted. After all, these were men trained in the French language, French law and French culture, and they had formulated their ideas at a time when the evidence available to them indicated that the French Civil Code was more highly regarded than any other in Europe. But they had no particular commitment as a matter of philosophical principle to French-based codes. They merely wanted to get the job done.

Secondly, we should keep in mind that much of the emotional heat generated by the Dispute was a manifestation of the fact that the Meiji elite began to perceive that the non-material culture of Europe was not the simplistic thing they at first had thought it was, and which they certainly would have preferred it to be. Indeed, they found themselves faced with alternative models, and decision-making in the domain of non-material culture had a range of complexity which did not inhere when decisions were being made as to the use of the narrow or broad gauge railroad tracks. Those out of political power were best suited to explore these complexities, they could deal with national character, traditional folkways; they did not have direct responsibility for getting rid of extraterritorial jurisdictions. However, once the Dispute had been won by the proponents of postponement, those men who had articulated a more sophisticated intellectual position, those in what had been identified as the English law faction, had to take on some of the responsibility for code drafting, and they rapidly lost interest in demanding the working out of subtle interrelationships between law and custom. They, too, had to turn out codes.

Both groups, those who had advocated postponement of enforcement of the old Civil Code and those who had advocated its adoption, could accept the German Code as a model precisely because neither group had a really deep intellectual commitment to what it had been espousing during the Dispute, and both groups were sufficiently empirical to want to get on with the job — the losers did not want to retire to monasteries after their defeat. There could be no winners.

The German Code was particularly acceptable as a model because it was perceived as being even more modern, scientific and correct than the French, and Japan was intent upon acquiring that which was most modern, scientific and correct. Furthermore, and we should not overlook this very important fact, by accepting the German Code, both groups, those who had trained in English and those who had trained in French, would be similarly disadvantaged in obtaining positions in the bureaucracy, the universities and in the profession. Both factions had to acquire a new orientation. The adoption of the new Civil Code on the German model constitutes a prime exemplification both of the Japanese skill at compromise and of the lack of intellectual commitment within the social system.

For those of us interested in legal phenomena in general rather than in their specific Japanese manifestation, that which is of perhaps greatest interest about the period of introduction of Western law in Japan is not so much the literalism with which the task was undertaken, nor the purely fortuitous character of the Dispute, nor the fact that after the violent verbal battle of 1892 the Civil Code was adopted very quietly in 1896. What is of more significance, I believe, is the fact that when Western law finally was adopted none of the dire consequences predicated to flow thereupon came about. The social fabric was not rent and vast reorganization of the society was accomplished.

NOTES AND QUESTIONS

1. What was similar or different between the rejection of the French Civil Code in Germany and in Japan during their respective codification debates?

2. What aspects of Western law might have been perceived as a threat to Japan's legal culture?

3. What does Rabinowitz mean by "a lack of intellectual commitment" in explaining the outcome of the dispute over adoption of the codes?

4. For more on the making of the Japanese Civil Code, see Robert Epp, *The Challenge from Tradition: Attempts to Compile a Civil Code in Japan 1866-78*, 22 Monumenta Nipponica 15 (1967); Michiatsu Kaino, *Some Introductory Comments on the Historical Background of Japanese Civil Law*, 16 Int'l J. Soc. L. 383 (1988); and Ken Mukai & Nobuyoshi Toshitani, *The Progress and Problems of Compiling the Civil Code in the Early Meiji Era*, 1 Law in Japan 25 (1967).

ZENTARO KITAGAWA, THEORY RECEPTION: ONE ASPECT OF THE DEVELOPMENT OF JAPANESE CIVIL LAW, IN 1 LAW AND THE LEGAL PROCESS IN JAPAN 270-72 (John Owen Haley & Dan Fenno Henderson eds. 1988)

Soon after the codification of the Japanese Civil Code, Japanese scholars looked almost exclusively to German legal theory in order to assimilate the received foreign legal elements. We can call this German influence on the development of Japanese law the period of "Theory-Reception." The basic system of the Japanese law was shaped therefore by legal conceptions and doctrines introduced into Japan during this time for the most part from German legal theories. The Theory-Reception sometimes went so far that the compatibility of the theory with the corresponding article of the Codes was either neglected or lightly considered....

[T]he reception of foreign legal institutions and their assimilation are two different things. Certainly, it is not always easy to clearly distinguish between the reception itself and the assimilation of the received legal elements. In the case of Japan, however, these two processes can be distinctly separated. The Theory-Reception involving German doctrine may be identified with the process of assimilating the accepted foreign elements, which were entirely strange to the Japanese tradition. The Theory-Reception made these strange legal institutions practicable....

As to the second aspect, namely the role of the Theory-Reception in the overall reception process, we should note the reception of Roman law in Germany as described by Franz Wieacker. He stresses the "scientification" (*Verwissenschaftlichung*) of legal life as the most important aspect of reception in general. This is very important for Japanese civil law since the assimilation of received foreign legal elements took place in Japan in the form of this "scientification" of legal materials. And, of course, German legal theory naturally lent itself to this role. Without this step of "scientification," of Theory-Reception, the foreign legal concepts embraced by the general reception would have remained inaccessible to Japanese lawyers for some time after their formal adoption.

What advantages or disadvantages for development of Japanese civil law were incurred as a result of this Theory-Reception from German law?

Unquestionably the Theory-Reception enabled Japanese legal systemization in a much shorter time than otherwise would have been possible. Before the codification of the Japanese Civil Code, French influence on the Japanese civil law was predominant. Many French legal doctrines were more popular than German doctrine at that time. Had the French influence continued to dominate Japanese law after codification, it would have taken much longer to form a viable legal system from the received foreign concepts. Here we must recall the quality of the German Civil Code. It is recognized as a masterpiece of civil law codification throughout the world. It is, moreover, a body of highly systematic legal thinking. All legal problems, according to this way of thinking, can and should be resolved by deductive reasoning from basic axioms (*Begriffsjurisprudenz*). Although the validity of such a method can indeed be questioned, such a system of legal reasoning undoubtedly made it easier for Japanese jurists to comprehend otherwise strange legal importations....

We see [an] example of the extreme reception of German legal doctrine in the law of damages. In short, the main article on damages of the Japanese Civil Code follows the Anglo-American principle of *Hadley v. Baxendale*, but it has been construed exclusively according to the German theory of "adequate causation." Article 416 of the Japanese Code [in summary states:] Where a party has not performed his duty, the other party may recover (1) such damages as usually arise from such nonperformance and (2) such damages arising out of special circumstances, that the parties have foreseen or could have foreseen. In spite of this dependence on an Anglo-American principle, Japanese legal doctrine has incorporated the German theory of "adequate causation," under which the whole injury caused by nonperformance should be compensated. Certainly, there is an important difference between this causation theory and the Anglo-American theory in regard to the scope of recoverable damages. Thus German legal doctrine has in effect repealed some provisions of the Code. Similarly, the legal construction of various basic concepts has taken a different shape from that which would have been expected from the structure of the Civil Code (e.g., the law of warranty, the right to rescission, the theory of contractual liability).

It is difficult today to ascertain why Japanese legal doctrine followed German legal theory so closely, accepted at times without adequate consideration of its compatibility to the Code structures. Nevertheless, as a result of this somewhat questionable Theory-Reception from German law, received foreign legal principles became available and practicable to Japanese lawyers as the elements were fit into an understandable, overall system of civil law. Here we must note that German legal doctrine was the heir of the so-called *Pandektensystem* of the 19th century in Germany. The logical clarity and consequence of this German system was very appropriate for the assimilation of the imported legal elements. Thus, by the end of World War I, a miniature model of the German legal system had been constructed in Japan.

In conclusion, the legal structure of Japanese civil law has a double nature; namely, one that has arisen from the reception of many foreign legal institutions, and another from the Theory-Reception of German legal doctrine.

NOTES AND QUESTIONS

1. Kitagawa and other Japanese scholars generally attribute article 416 of the Japanese Civil Code (1896) to the influence of the English case *Hadley v. Baxendale*, 9 Exch. 341, 156 Eng. Rep. 145 (1854). Article 416 provides:

> A demand for damages shall be for the reparation by the obligor of such damage as would ordinarily arise from the non-performance of an obligation.
>
> The obligee may recover the damages that have arisen through special circumstances too, if the parties had foreseen or could have foreseen such circumstances.

Ironically, the decision in *Hadley v. Baxendale* is a prime example of early to mid-19th century influence of civil law principles on the common law, in this case by the French Civil Code, article 1150 of which provides:

> The obligor is liable only for the damages foreseen or which could have been foreseen at the time of the contract, so long as it is not due to his fraud that the obligation has not been performed.

2. What does Kitagawa mean by "theory reception"? How did it occur? Was it necessary or inevitable?

2. THE MEIJI CONSTITUTION

NOTE

The codification process paralleled the more central reform of Japan's governmental structure. Once all thoughts of reverting to traditional *ritsuryō* models had been dismissed, the reorganization of national governmental institutions based on European patterns proceeded quite rapidly. The organization of the judiciary came early, but only as part of the comprehensive package of institutional reforms the Meiji leaders designed to create an effective national government. Demands within both the ruling elites and the public at large for a constitution and representative democratic institutions led in 1881 to an imperial decree promising a parliament by 1890. At that point governmental reforms, headed by Hirobumi Itō, began in earnest.

As they had with the code compilation project, the Japanese sought foreign models and advice in reforming government structure. Itō himself spent several months in Europe, especially in Germany and Austria, consulting with leading constitutional jurists such as Rudolph Gneist, Albert Mosse, and Lorenz von Stein. He also met Clemenceau in France and attended a lecture on representative government by Herbert Spencer in England. Itō's first reform upon his return was to establish a new peerage based on the German system. This was followed by the creation of a national cabinet (*naikaku*), comprised of a presiding Minister President of State and Ministers for Foreign Affairs, Home Affairs, Finance, War, Navy, Justice, Education, Agriculture and Commerce, and Communications, with their respective administrative establishments. All were responsible to the emperor.

In 1886 Itō turned to the problem of drafting a constitution. Hermann Roesler, the German jurist who had drafted the Japanese Commercial Code, was teaching at the newly established Imperial University in Tokyo was appointed as advisor. Roesler's draft, translated into Japanese, was complete by April 1887. After intensive discussion and several redrafts, a constitution and an Imperial House Law were ready to be ratified. Deliberations in the Privy Council continued throughout the year, and in January 1889, the Council finally approved the constitution, the Imperial House Law, the Law on the House of the Diet, the Election Law, and an Imperial Ordinance on the House of Peers. Finally, on February 11, 1889, the anniversary of the accession of the Emperor Jimmu, the Emperor read a prepared statement granting the constitution to his subjects.

JOHN OWEN HALEY, AUTHORITY WITHOUT POWER: LAW AND THE JAPANESE PARADOX 78-80 (1991)

In outline, the constitution provided for ministers of state as the basis for a cabinet government who were to "advise" the emperor on matters of state and take responsibility for advice given. A Privy Council to deliberate on matters of state "when consulted by the Emperor" completed the executive organs of government. A judiciary with powers to adjudicate "in the name of the Emperor" civil and criminal cases but not hear direct appeals from administrative measures was also recognized. In addition, the constitution provided for a two-house legislature, the Imperial Diet. The upper chamber was a House of Peers comprising "members of the Imperial Family, of the orders of nobility, and of those who have been nominated thereto by the Emperor." The only governmental organ with any direct accountability to the electorate was the House of Representatives [*Shūgi-in*]. On the one hand, all statutes required the consent of both houses of the Diet and countersignatures of each minister of state. On the other, however, administrative ordinances [*meirei*] required no legislative action, only ministerial advice. Thus, except for the elected House of Representatives and the autonomous judiciary, all other branches of government were either constituted by or accountable only to the throne. In the words of the constitution:

> Article IV. The Emperor is the head of the Empire, combining in himself the rights of sovereignty, and exercises them, according to the provisions of the present Constitution.
>
> Article V. The Emperor exercises the legislative power with consent of the Imperial Diet.
>
> Article VI. The Emperor gives sanction to laws and orders then to be promulgated and executed....
>
> Article IX. The Emperor issues or causes to be issued, the Ordinances necessary for carrying out of the laws, or for the maintenance of public peace and order, and for the promotion of the welfare of the subjects.

The Meiji Constitution did not even in theory, however, grant the imperial institution absolute powers. Chapter II set out an extensive list of constitutionally protected fundamental rights of all subjects. These included the "freedom of abode" or freedom of all Japanese subjects to determine their permanent and temporary residence; freedom from arrest, detention, trial, and punishment except in accordance with law; the right to judicial trial; freedom from unlawful entry and searches; freedom from censorship of correspondence; guarantee of property rights with a right to compensation for lawful takings in the public interest; the freedom of "speech, writing, publication, public meetings and association"; and the right to petition. These were not empty guarantees. The phrase "as provided by law" or equivalent did hedge each provision, but the English translation is misleading. The Japanese "*hōritsu ni yoru*" referred to statutory law.

The Meiji Constitution was therefore less absolutist and authoritarian than it first appears. The Constitution by its own terms bound all institutions including the emperor, and these rights could not be modified except by statute requiring the consent of an elected lower house. The absolutism of the Meiji Constitution thus depended on how broadly the electorate was defined, as provided by separate statute, not the constitution itself. Nevertheless, no change from the initial institutions established under the control of those in power in 1889 and 1890 would be possible without the affirmative action of the upper chamber and the ministers of state. The Meiji Constitution had created a system that would be remarkably resistant to change.

More detrimental than the controls against unwanted progressive change, however, was the role of the emperor. For Hermann Roesler and other Western jurists, the imperial institution was pivotal for a workable constitutional order. The accountability of the political and administrative organs of government to the emperor meant that the throne in exercising its prerogatives and powers could ensure desired change and adjustment of conflict....

The Meiji Constitution was consistent with Japanese tradition. The emperor was to be the locus of national sovereignty and the authority of the state, but the occupant of the imperial throne was not to exercise power or be responsible for the consequences of decisions made pursuant to the imperial will. In turn, responsibility and access to the throne meant autonomy and accountability.

The lawmakers of Meiji Japan confronted a dilemma they did not fully appreciate or articulate. Only by describing the authority of the imperial institution in absolutist terms as exercisable power could they maintain the sanctity of the institution as the locus of sovereignty and source of all authority and power. To have attempted to separate the emperor's authority from exercisable powers and to have described accurately his institutional role in a written constitution would have been impossible. To do so would have impaired the full sovereignty of the institution. This is perhaps tacitly understood in the United Kingdom and explains why the role of the crown is not defined in a written instrument of law.

The consequences were profound. Japan's new constitutional order had a fatal flaw that, by misconstruing the role the emperor could play, Western advisors like Roesler failed to appreciate and thus to correct. Without an active emperor, no institutional mechanism existed to regulate or to mediate the inevitable tensions and conflicts between Diet and cabinet, or between the military and civil bureaucracies. Each branch or institution of governance was accountable only to the emperor with seemingly limited powers to "advise" or consult. No organ or branch of government was supreme. None had the power to direct or check the others. Only the judiciary could claim full autonomy from all direct outside interference — hence judicial independence — as it alone had both the authority and power to act "in the name of the Emperor." The military would at a later time similarly base its claims to independence from control from the civilian political branches of government on the emperor's prerogative as commander-in-chief and the "right of supreme command." In other words, by centralizing all legal powers in the person of the emperor who by convention could not or would not exercise them, the Meiji Constitution ensured that there could be no effective centralized control. The consequence was, to paraphrase Masao Maruyama, a failure of political integration and a fatal fragmentation of governance. Western legal forms were unable to express or articulate the basic premises of the Japanese political tradition, the separation of power from authority.

3. ADAPTABILITY OF WESTERN LAW IN JAPAN

JOHN OWEN HALEY, AUTHORITY WITHOUT POWER: LAW AND THE JAPANESE PARADOX 70-72 (1991)

Several aspects of the Meiji transformation of Japanese law illustrate the adaptability of Western law as well as the residual problems Japan encountered. The first is a point too often neglected: For the most part, Western legal institutions, processes, and even derivative legal rules proved to be easily integrated into the Japanese cultural and institutional matrix. This transferability can be explained on the one hand by the existence of analogous institutions, processes, and even norms in Tokugawa law. As one observer — presumably John Henry Wigmore — wrote in a long series of essays for the *Japan Weekly Mail*, nearly all of the presumably new, Western-derived institutions of the 1890 Codes with respect to property rights and commercial practices were analogous to preexisting institutions and practices. Although stressed by Wigmore for purposes of influencing enactment of the 1890 Code, fundamental similarities in practice did exist. The series concluded:

> We have seen that the leading ideas of Code and custom (where comparison is possible) have the same content; that where latitude could be given, the new Code has allowed to local varieties of usage the freest play; and that where novelties or inflexible rules have been determined on, the conditions were such as to admit the exercise of legislative discretion. Looking once more over the detailed comparisons of the foregoing chapters, we cannot see how there can be more than one answer to the question we started with — the answer that in any fair sense the Codes are not in conflict with existing custom.

Japan had also long been familiar with registry systems, complex procedures for adjudication, and sophisticated commercial instruments. Official land registers were maintained in village offices throughout Japan. They recorded the names of proprietors, the location and size of the parcel, as well as the assessed yield for tax purposes. The Tokugawa shogunate had also — as noted previously — expanded personal registration with Buddhist temples as a means of enforcing its ban against Christianity as well as with village officials for census and other control purposes. Births, marriages, adoptions, and deaths were all recorded and reported to *daikan* officers and ultimately to Edō....

With respect to commercial instruments, by the end of the eighteenth century Japanese merchants and traders were using a wide variety of commercial instruments analogous to contemporary, Western forms. These included shares [*kabu*] in commercial enterprises, guaranty certification [*hikiawase*], various types of bills of exchange [*kawase*], and promissory notes [*tegata*]. Special summary trial procedures [*naka-nuki-saiban*] for actions on commercial paper had also been introduced.

The drafters of Japan's new codes also took particular care not to incorporate derivative rules or norms that directly contradicted desired preexisting ones. As Boissonade would later point out in defense of the 1890 Civil Code and Code of Civil Procedure, the code drafting commission had before it extensive sources on traditional law and procedure. These included a set of 7556 volumes of manuscripts and other materials containing country wide records evidencing extant customary practices encompassing the last two centuries of the *bakufu*, a Ministry of Justice compilation of local judicial practices in ten volumes, and a summary of the Ministry of Justice compilation prepared for the draftsmen of the civil and commercial codes. The drafting process was methodical. Every effort was made to ensure continuity.

Individual Japanese were quick to take advantage of new institutions introduced from the West. As shogunate and *han* restrictions on internal trade and entry into new occupations were abolished, enterprising Japanese from all classes took advantage of their new opportunities. For example, Japan's first modern banking regulations were promulgated in 1872. These were quite restrictive, requiring newly formed national banks to transfer over half of their cash holdings to the government in return for government securities. Only four banks were established under the regulations, with an aggregate capital of about two and a half million yen. The restrictions were eased by amendments decreed in 1876, and by 1880 Japan had 151 banks with an aggregate capital of over 43 million yen. Not then nor thereafter did anyone seriously question the applicability of new commercial institutions and norms.

It would be a mistake, however, to view the growth of new commercial ventures, whether joint-stock companies, banks, or other Western-inspired forms of commercial enterprise, as the product of law reform, new statutes, and codes. As Ryōsuke Ishii notes, a number of new banks were initially organized as joint-stock companies and were actively engaged in the banking business before 1876, only they could not be called banks. For the most part the new codes and statutes were responses as a means of regulation and control rather than catalysts to entrepreneurial activity. New legislation was prompted less by the desire to initiate or stimulate economic growth than a felt need to channel and control economic activity. The lawmakers of Meiji Japan thus construed Western law in traditional East Asian terms: law as an instrument of the pervasive administrative state. Only gradually, if at all, did they adjust to the underlying premises of private law in a liberal political order.

NOTES AND QUESTIONS

1. As related to the Meiji Constitution, what does the phrase "authority without power" mean?

2. What were the "underlying premises of private law" in the 19th century liberal Western state? Could they have been accommodated within either the East Asian Hindu-Buddhist or Chinese traditions discussed in Chapter 4, Section C?

3. Japan was the only non-Western, independent nation during the 19th century to undertake and complete a comprehensive reform of its legal system based on European models. Other countries, such as Thailand and China, had made substantial progress before World War II. Most countries in East Asia, however, only began to establish legal systems as independent, autonomous states in the post-independence era after World War II. What contrasts would you expect to discover as a result of these differences in the timing of legal reforms? How had concepts of law and legal ordering changed in Europe and the West between the mid-19th and mid-20th centuries? To what extent, for example, did civil, commercial, and other private law codes still occupy a position of primacy?

4. TAIWAN AND KOREA UNDER JAPANESE COLONIAL RULE

EDWARD I-TO CHEN, THE ATTEMPT TO INTEGRATE THE EMPIRE: LEGAL PERSPECTIVES, in THE JAPANESE COLONIAL EMPIRE, 1895-1945, at 268-74 (Ramon H. Myers & Mark R. Peattie eds. 1984)

Except for a brief initial period of vacillation after the annexation of Taiwan, its first colony, the Japanese government during its fifty years as a colonial power was committed to achieving the legal integration of its empire. The goal of Japanese colonial policy was to create a tightly welded, centrally controlled empire within the legal framework of the Meiji Constitution. All colonies eventually were to be governed by laws and regulations originating from Tokyo. At no time were self-governing colonies, similar to the British Dominions, the goal of the Japanese government.

On the other hand, the Japanese government recognized the need to allow each colony to develop its own legal system, tailored to meet the need of local conditions. Thus, each colonial government was given power and responsibility far more extensive than any of the prefectural governments of Japan. In certain colonies the governors were even permitted to enact laws independent of the Imperial Diet. In all but one colony the judicial system was independent, and the Supreme Court of Japan had no jurisdiction over colonial courts. While these arrangements appear to undercut the ultimate goal of the legal and administrative integration of the empire, the Japanese government always regarded local colonial laws as an interim structure, to be replaced gradually by the laws and regulations of Japan. The ultimate design of the Japanese government was to replace all colonial laws by Japanese laws and to end the distinction between Japanese and colonial legal systems....

Yet it is clear that Japan did not achieve this goal. For example, those provisions of the constitution related to the political rights of the people were never extended to the colonial populations. Nor did the Japanese government enforce in any colony the Election Law of the House of Representatives of the Japanese Diet, the most visible symbol of total legal integration. Even in those colonies where Japanese settlers outnumbered the indigenous population, certain special features inconsistent with the ultimate goal of integration were retained in their legal and administrative systems....

With no large Japanese population to hasten the process of integration[a] or any legal restriction which would prevent the application of Japanese laws, Taiwan and Korea are better examples [than Karafuto, the Benin Islands, and other colonial territories] by which to measure the degree of success in legal integration of the empire. The most visible signs of success were the application of the constitution (except for those provisions related to the political rights of the people) and the extension of a significant number of Japanese laws. Another important evidence of integration was that the two colonies after 1942 were brought under the jurisdiction of the Ministry of Home Affairs, and the two governors-general were placed under the supervision of several cabinet ministers in the central government. On the minus side was the system of "delegated legislation" which authorized the two governors-general to enact their own laws. While the original intention of such a system was to give the colonial government the flexibility to cope with local unrest, in 1945 their power to legislate colonial laws was the greatest barrier separating the colonial legal systems from the Japanese legal system.

In Korea, Japan faced an additional disadvantage. The political prominence of the governor-general, as recognized in the imperial rescript of 1910, ... enabled him to spurn successfully, until 1942, the efforts of the Japanese government to bring him under full control. In contrast, the Japanese government was able to expand steadily its supervisory power over the colonial government of Taiwan. After the installation of a civilian governor-general, it even succeeded in limiting his legislative power so that he could exercise it only when no comparable Japanese laws were available. The upshot was that a far greater number of Japanese laws were enforced in Taiwan than Korea, making Taiwan the more legally integrated colony....

What the Japanese government had accomplished in its fifty years of colonial experience was the integration of *systems* and *institutions*. Behind the appearance of an integrated empire, the indigenous populations, especially those of Taiwan and Korea, remained adamant in refusing to accept the Japanese culture as their own. Without their support and loyalty, the extension of all portions of the constitution and the Election Law of the House of Representatives would have been a disaster for Japan. To extend to Taiwanese and Koreans, for example, the right to the freedom of speech and assembly would

[a] In 1942 the population of Taiwan was 6,427,932 and that of Korea 26,361,401. Of these, Japanese residents in Taiwan numbered 384,847 and in Korea 752,823, representing 6 and 2.9 percent, respectively, of their total populations.

have been tantamount to giving sanctions to their criticism of Japanese rule and encouraging the growth of their nationalistic aspirations. To allow the Koreans and Taiwanese (numbering nearly 33 million in 1942) to elect members to the Japanese House of Representatives would have placed in the Diet a large number of persons whose loyalty to Japan was an unknown factor. Their combined votes could adversely influence the legislative process of the entire empire.

When the Meiji leaders followed the counsel of the French adviser and adopted integration as Japan's ultimate goal in Taiwan, they assumed that the Taiwanese could easily be assimilated because they "belong to the same race and use the same script." They believed that, unlike Western colonialism, which they characterized as the rule of the white race over non-whites, the "ethnic similarity" in Taiwan should help to promote integration. When Korea was annexed, a similar goal was proclaimed, based on the even stronger assumption that there had been frequent mixing of blood between Japanese and Koreans in their distant past. What the Japanese failed to realize was that the ethnic similarity had little, if any, effect on the assimilation of Taiwanese or Koreans. In both colonies the Japanese were always regarded as aliens, and assimilation was a means of destroying and replacing indigenous cultures and traditions. Confronted by intense resistance, the Japanese government could only make slow ... progress in acculturation. On the other hand, the legal and administrative integration of the empire was speeded up following Japan's military intervention in China in the 1930's....

Naive confidence in their ability to transform the Taiwanese and Koreans into "loyal subjects of the emperor" caused the Meiji leaders to reject the British system of colonial administration. As Japan grew in size in the first two decades of the twentieth century, creation of one empire under one emperor, run from the center, Tokyo, became a national passion. Following the Japanese invasions of China in the 1930's, integration was no longer just a passion but a strategic and economic necessity upon which the fate of the entire empire rested. Japan's scheme for integration came to an abrupt end only with her defeat in World War II.

5. WESTERNIZATION AND JUDICIAL REFORM IN SIAM (THAILAND)

FRANK C. DARLING, AMERICAN INFLUENCE ON THE EVOLUTION OF CONSTITUTIONAL GOVERNMENT IN THAILAND 29-35 (Ph.D. dissertation, American University, 1961)

As Mongkut (Rama IV) ascended the throne [1851] only he and a few Siamese officials were aware of the vast changes taking place in the Far East. Observing the European advances in the surrounding countries Mongkut realized that all of Asia was being confronted with a vastly superior military and technological order, and he decided that the only realistic course for Siam was to cooperate with the Western nations and adopt their modern techniques in an effort to preserve the independence of the country. He consequently reversed the traditional isolationist policy and opened the country to extensive intercourse with the West. Within a few years he negotiated new treaties with almost every European country and the United States, and he welcomed the arrival of Western traders, diplomats, and advisers into the country....

Mongkut made modest attempts to promote the Westernization of Siam, and he became deeply interested in Western techniques and learning. He studied several Western languages himself and gained some knowledge of Western history, geography, and astronomy. He encouraged his subjects to learn European languages, especially English, and he adopted a few Western innovations to make Siam appear as though it were becoming a modern country. During his reign he began the construction of roads and canals, and he supported a shipbuilding program to provide Siam with its own merchant fleet. He also established a printing office and modern mint, and published a government newspaper.

To assist in the Westernization of Siam Mongkut employed eighty-four European advisers who quickly assumed an important role in the administration of the country.... These advisers included military officers, a harbor master, a custom house director, and a superintendent of a police force. Mongkut also employed an English governess to tutor the Crown Prince, Chulalongkorn. These persons exerted a profound influence in modernizing the country and in disseminating some understanding of Western methods and values.

Like other Oriental rulers Mongkut was only interested in adopting the modern innovations of Western technology, and he made no attempt to import the values of Western political theory or the practices of Western political institutions. He continued to uphold the traditional monarchical rule and strongly opposed any attempt to impose limitations on his absolute power.... Instead of apologizing for his absolute power Mongkut used his position to force the adoption of modern Western techniques on his more conservative and less ambitious people....

Mongkut likewise began to mitigate some of the more stringent features of the Siamese legal system which was still based on the Hindu law of Manu. These changes showed considerable influence of the Western values of equality, individual rights, and respect for law. He altered the law to facilitate the payment of redemption money by debt slaves, and he raised the status of women by an order allowing them more freedom in deciding whom to marry. He also made it more difficult for parents to sell their children into slavery. He recognized the baneful effects of gambling, opium-smoking and drinking, and in spite of the restrictions in the treaties with the Western nations he endeavored to curtail the importation of spiritous liquors....

When Mongkut died in 1868 few tangible changes had been made in modernizing the country and by Western standards Siam was still very backward....

When Chulalongkorn was designated to succeed to the throne in 1868 he was only sixteen years old, and a Regent was appointed until 1873 to manage royal affairs. Chulalongkorn had been considerably influenced by Western ideas from his English governess, Anna Leonowens, who tutored him for five years. To expand his contacts with Western innovations he traveled in 1871 to India, Java, and Singapore to observe the advances made by European influence in other parts of Asia. This trip made a deep impression on Chulalongkorn and on his return to Siam he was determined to hasten the process initiated by his father of transforming his backward country into a modern nation. He was convinced that Siam could preserve its independence and achieve an equal status among the nations of the world only by rapidly adopting Western technological and administrative methods.

DAVID M. ENGEL, LAW AND KINGSHIP IN THAILAND DURING THE REIGN OF KING CHULALONGKORN, 9 Michigan Papers on South and Southeast Asia 16-17, 63-65, 69-70, 74-76 (1975)

The process of change was ... to prove a difficult task, characterized by eager bursts of reforming zeal followed by extended periods of political difficulty and inactivity. These peaks and valleys have been charted by one historian as follows: an initial period of enthusiastic reform lasted from 1873 until the "Front Palace Incident" of December 1874. This crisis, involving an attempted coup by the *upparat* or "second king," very nearly resulted in British intervention against the throne, and was followed by more than ten years of political caution and quiescence on the part of King Chulalongkorn. A new period of activity began in the second half of the 1880s, leading to the establishment of a Cabinet system of government in 1892. Again, however, a period of political crisis ensued and, in 1893, a conflict with France nearly brought the two countries to war. For three years, until 1895, the king rested and recovered both politically and emotionally, but then began once again his task of reform. It was during this period, from 1895 until the king's death in 1910, that he permanently consolidated his power, reorganized the government bureaucracy, reformed the legal system, and twice travelled to Europe.

Despite the varying pace of reform and governmental change, however, a certain consistency and logical continuity may be observed throughout the entire thirty-eight years of King Chulalongkorn's reign. While change was encouraged and promoted in many ways, it was resisted when it threatened the structure of the monarchy itself. While European laws and methods of government were studied and adopted to some extent, the fundamental theory of constitutional government was held at arm's length. While parliamentary forms and methods were used in appointed legislative bodies, the notion of a truly representative system never became more than a suggestion or a prophecy.

The Early Period

King Chulalongkorn's first attempts to cure the confusion and ineffectiveness of the judiciary were, like his early experiments with new legislative bodies, short-lived. In 1874 he resorted to an instrument of royal control over the judicial function known as the *rap sang* court, a temporary court created by and accountable to the king for the resolution of a particular case or group of cases. The *rap sang* court was established by royal edict on July 14, 1874 to decide cases pending in the four major ministries — *mahatthai*, *kalahom*, *tha* (*khlang*), and *nakhọnban*. This court, which had been suggested by the Council of State, was intended to alleviate the problem of increased crime throughout the country, and to assist the *nakhǫnban* ministry whose chief was ill and whose work was not being completed. It is also likely, however, that the *rap sang* court was intended as a radical challenge to the traditional court system, with the ultimate purpose of ending the delay, expense and corruption which had become endemic in the courts of the major ministries.

The edict establishing the *rap sang* court dealt primarily with major crimes of violence, both in Bangkok and the provinces. It required that all cases of any type then pending trial at *nakhǫnban* be transferred to the *rap sang* court. The court would then retain those suits involving major offenses and redirect the petty offenses to an official in *nakhǫnban* for speedy decision. The heads of *mahatthai*, *kalahom*, and *tha* were ordered to do the same for all cases then pending in their departments which had arisen in the provinces and been sent on to Bangkok. In this way the *rap sang* judges, who were directly accountable to the king, would acquire jurisdiction over most of the important cases then pending in the Bangkok courts and, at least in the case of *nakhǫnban* suits, would apparently retain such jurisdiction on a semi-permanent basis.

The fact that the king's motive went beyond mere criminal punishment is evidenced by several provisions which were aimed at the elimination of improper influence and corruption in the judicial process. In Paragraph 5, for example, it was made a punishable offense to coach the defendant during the trial, to announce during the trial that the defendant had friends in high positions, or to obstruct the process of justice in any other way. Paragraph 7 required that the king be informed of any instance in which a defendant or a witness could not be brought before the trial court because he resided in the royal palace, in the house of a *senabǫdi*, or in the residence of a prince or high government official. In all of these situations there was a likelihood that the influence of status and power might prevent the trial from taking place. Paragraph 10 prohibited private communications between litigants and judges in the *rap sang* court which might serve as channels for bribery and corruption.

The *rap sang* court, not surprisingly, created resentment among those who had long depended on the traditional system for their livelihood. It was threatening not only because it removed many cases from courts where jurisdiction had previously been exercised, but also because it announced new standards of behavior to be observed by judges and by litigants. The edict was modified and weakened after the Front Palace Incident of 1874-1875, during the same period when King Chulalongkorn's early legislative reforms were to enter a period of quiescence....

The Ministry of Justice and the Bangkok Courts

On March 25, 1892 King Chulalongkorn proclaimed the establishment of a new Ministry of Justice and a streamlined organization for the Bangkok courts. He was, he announced, determined to end the delay and corruption which resulted from the divided judicial responsibilities of the old system. His solution was to regroup all the Bangkok courts under one minister who would oversee the judicial process, resolve important problems which arose, and make certain that the procedure was both convenient and just. The division of responsibility between the *tralakan* and *lukkhun* was also changed. In charge of each of the new courts was an *athibǫdi*, or chief judge, whose role it was to decide the cases and to supervise the trial process. Under him was a staff of examiners who would actually conduct the trials (Paragraph 4). The practice of sending the case out of the court to a separate *lukkhun* department for a verdict was thereby eliminated. Each case was to be supervised from beginning to end by the *athibǫdi* of the court in which it was brought.

Seven courts were established under the proclamation to replace the numerous courts which formerly existed in the various ministries. The new courts were: (1) Royal Appeals Court (performing the appellate function of the *dika* court), (2) People's Appeals Court (replacing the *mahatthai* appeals court), (3) Court for Punishable Offenses, (4) *phaeng kasem* court (a civil court), (5) *phaeng klang* court (a civil court), (6) *sanphakǫn* court (a tax and inheritance court), (7) International (extraterritorial) Courts. A department was also established within the Ministry of Justice to receive all plaints brought by the people. Its function was to channel the suits into the appropriate courts and to prevent the parties from exercising improper influence upon the *athibǫdi* of the court by bringing their pleadings directly to him. As time went on, however, this department caused more problems than it resolved. Many would-be litigants misunderstood its function and believed that their suits had been disallowed because of corruption within the judiciary, although in fact the department had rejected the pleadings on technical grounds. When a later effort of the king to clarify the work of the department had failed, he finally abolished it entirely and established new standards for receiving plaints in each court....

The Ministry of Justice and the Provincial Courts

Until 1896 the Ministry of Justice exercised control only over the Bangkok courts. No sweeping reform of the provincial courts had been made when the Bangkok courts were restructured from 1892 to 1896. Indeed, very few changes of any kind had been made in the provincial court system to that time. With the transformation of the traditional bureaucracy, however, the control which the three great ministries had exercised over their respective geographical regions was eventually removed. As a consequence, the court system which they had administered together with the provincial governor and provincial council had also to be changed. *Mahatthai* and *nakhǫnban* were left with temporary authority over the judiciary outside of the capital, but meaningful centralized control would not be asserted until the provincial courts underwent a restructuring similar to that of the Bangkok courts from 1892 to 1896....

New Laws and Procedures for the Thai Judiciary

Concurrent with King Chulalongkorn's restructuring of the Thai court system was an equally thorough revision and restatement of the procedures which the courts were to follow....

Adjustments in the rules of evidence dated back to the earliest days of King Chulalongkorn's reign. Later, on April 1, 1895, a royal edict set forth new and elaborate evidentiary rules together with charts and tables showing which of the traditional laws were eliminated or retained. These rules were applied first in the Bangkok courts and then, to an increasing extent, in the provincial courts which became incorporated into the central system.

Civil procedure came to be controlled by a royal edict of November 15, 1896, which proclaimed a set of provisional rules to be followed until the committee in charge of revising the laws had prepared a complete new code. This edict was followed by a proclamation on November 29, 1898 specifying the old laws which were replaced or amended by its provisions. In 1908 the new code of civil procedure was promulgated by royal edict, defining in elaborate detail such matters as jurisdiction of the court over the defendant, procedures to be followed in ordinary and in petty cases, requirements and procedures for appeals, the role of counsel, the appointment of special masters, offenses against the status and power of the court, and the assessment of costs. With this new code, Thai civil procedure took on an unprecedented degree of detail and precision, set forth in a form readily understandable to most western observers.

The law of punishable offenses underwent an analogous revision and restatement. On April 27, 1896, a royal edict established a provisional procedural law for all cases involving punishments imposed by the government. This procedure was to be followed until final codification was completed. On June 1, 1908 the new code of substantive "criminal" law was promulgated, containing significant provisions dealing with such matters as crimes against the king and the country, internal and external threats to the nation's security, crimes against diplomats and foreign relations, offenses against government officials, misuse of official position, obstruction of justice, and crimes against religion....

In a preface to the new criminal code in 1908, the king provided a fitting summary of his accomplishments in the area of judicial reform. Since ancient times, the king observed, the Thai monarch had defended and interpreted the *thammasat* as the basis for the administration of all laws in the nation. Whenever legal matters arose which could not be resolved easily by reference to the *thammasat* or to Thai customs, then the king would enact laws to deal with such issues. But with the passage of time and the change of conditions, such laws had proliferated and become confused and difficult to apply in the courts of the land. When such situations arose it was customary for the king, together with his advisers and the *lukkun* legal experts, to revise and reform the laws.

The king had undertaken the present revision of the law of punishable offenses for these very reasons. The last revision of the laws had occurred more than a century before, and in the interim they had become outmoded and self-contradictory. In addition, the king pointed out, the unequal treaties with the western countries had provided another incentive to reform Thai law. Extraterritoriality required the application of many different bodies of law within Thailand itself, and as a result there was much uncertainty and confusion in dealings with aliens. All countries like Thailand, which had agreed to the establishment of extraterritorial courts, had subsequently desired to put an end to them and to make their own laws applicable to all people within their boundaries.

For this reason, concluded the king, he had chosen to follow the example of Japan, which was the first country to solve this difficult problem. By commissioning foreign legal experts to work together with local officials, Japan had revised its legal system so that the laws would resemble those of the western countries and would be administered in modern courts of justice throughout the land. Foreign nations had been willing to abolish their extraterritorial courts when they saw that order had been brought to Japan's judiciary. Similarly, foreign legal experts had been brought by the king into Thailand and a committee established to revise the Thai laws. It was clearly the expectation of King Chulalongkorn that this process of revision, together with the reorganization of the Thai courts, would lead directly to the end of extraterritoriality in Thailand and a recovery of her full rights of sovereignty.

NOTES AND QUESTIONS

1. The modernizing rulers of 19th century Japan and Thailand viewed legal reforms as part of a broader program to achieve economic and military strength. To what extent were they correct? For example, did European-derived legal rules, processes, and institutions contribute in either theory or practice to economic growth? Is the East Asian experience relevant for other non-Western states or perhaps even eastern Europe today?

2. How did the role of the monarch differ in Japan and Thailand in terms of the initiation and effective implementation of legal reforms?

3. The process of European law reception in Thailand continued until the eve of World War II under King Chulalongkorn's sons: King Vajiravudh, Rama VI (1910-1925) and King Prajadhipok, Rama VII (1925-1935, d. 1941). The initial codification effort ended in 1935 with the promulgation of the final books of the Civil and Commercial Codes and new Codes of Civil and Criminal Procedure. In 1932 a bloodless revolution had led to the establishment of a constitutional monarchy. In 1939 the kingdom of Siam was renamed Thailand.

6. INDONESIA UNDER DUTCH COLONIAL RULE

DANIEL S. LEV, JUDICIAL INSTITUTIONS AND LEGAL CULTURE IN INDONESIA, in CULTURE AND POLITICS IN INDONESIA 248-57 (Claire Holt ed. 1972)

A national legal system did not exist in Indonesia until Dutch colonialism produced an archipelago-wide state. Before then many different legal orders existed independently within a wide variety of social and political systems. These ranged from the Hinduized, hierarchical, territorially organized states of Java, founded on highly regulated irrigation systems, to the clan-based societies of Sumatra and elsewhere, with other types in between. In some cases, as among the patrilineal Batak and matrilineal Minangkabau of Sumatra, legal and judicial forms developed out of prevailing family systems. A basic "law-job" in these societies was to maintain the integrity of kinship groups and to uphold the consequences of their organization and supporting beliefs. In Java and other aristocratic societies the purpose of law was not different but more complex, and the organization of royal government independent of kin associations in a bilateral society gave rise to more specific functions of law enforcement and adjudication. Written law was more characteristic historically of the latter kind of society than the former, and possibly more necessary, in that family organization provided less thorough social control. But even when, as in old Java, there were written laws and enforcement officials, relatively few matters were brought within the purview of formal government. Administrative resources were inadequate to anything like full control of the population. Most issues of conflict were therefore left to the village or family, and the usual mode of settlement was probably compromise.

Nowhere in traditional Indonesia was written law important to social cohesion. This depended, rather, primarily on either kin organization or on highly developed status concepts supporting aristocratic elites. In both cases authority was ascriptive, suffused with family and religious significance, and concepts of law were bound to eternal orders of family, locality, religion, and status, changeable in fact but not in theory. It was not a distinct idea of law, but rather these notions — family, locality, religion, status — that gave meaning to society. Even in the kingly polities there was less a concept of the law than of discrete laws (in Java, the *angger*) which emanated sporadically from the palace as edicts of the reigning prince, each standing independently with a name of its own and more or less specific subject matter. In societies where only the elites were literate, as in early medieval Europe as well, such laws were far less compelling than the power of the palace and the authority of the aristocracy.

Islam introduced a new legal tradition into the archipelago.... Yet Islam did not produce a national legal culture in Indonesia any more than it did or could produce a unified state....

Along with the specific legal categories that it brought to Indonesia, Islam also contributed a novel conception of law itself. Sunni Islam is divided among four different doctrines of law (*madhab*) — the school of Sjafi'i was eventually adopted in Indonesia — but the idea of law in Islam is divorced from the particular interests of local communities and generalized to the entire *ummat* (community of Islamic believers), conceived originally in universal terms including all Moslems. Through the medium of Islam a supralocal level of social and political conception became possible even before the Dutch began to link the country together administratively....

In Indonesian the most basic notions of law itself (*húkum*), justice (*keadilan*), custom (*adat*), right (*hak*), judge (*hakim*), are borrowed from Arabic. In some places the word *hukum* used alone still means Islamic law, and elsewhere it often also means national law as opposed to local custom. In both cases it is clearly supralocal....

Dutch colonial authority [established] new nationally relevant administrative and legal functions as Islam had earlier provided new nationally applicable law concepts.

The colony, eventually encompassing all of modern Indonesia, created the framework of the state. Local change aside, Indonesians head little more control over the process than they had over the devastating economic effects of the "culture system" in nineteenth-century Java. New institutions, new skilled roles, and new social and political symbols were imposed from another tradition, which in part became that of Indonesians who gradually entered the world of colonial law. With independence these institutions, roles, and symbols would be challenged, bent to new shapes, and rearranged, but they could not be rejected altogether without threatening the very idea of a national state. There was little else to fall back on that was not inherently divisive....

What was the character, then, of the colonial legal order which Indonesia inherited? Only the briefest introduction is possible, but it is necessary.

In the first place the colonial legal order, like the social order, was a plural one, based implicitly on an assumption of racial inequality. This was true in varying degree of all colonies in the age of imperialism. The striking characteristic of the Netherlands-Indies legal system was its remarkable adherence to the internal logic of colonial society and purposes, not complete but more so than in most colonies. What other colonial governments were usually satisfied to achieve through stratificatory pressures, the Dutch tended to ensure with a statute. Each major social group had its own law, applied differentially by two distinct judicial hierarchies — three, actually, including the Islamic family law courts, which the colonial government did not establish but did regulate. European law was not restricted to Europeans, however. Indirect rule and the political alliance between the Dutch and Javanese nobility required privileges for the latter. The uppermost reaches of the aristocracy (*prijaji*) were thus accorded a special forum for their legal disputes and the right to register births and deaths in the civil registry (*burgerlijke stand*). This last privilege was also extended, for the same reasons, to high-level civil servants and commissioned military officers. The only other Indonesians served by the burgerlijke stand were those who in some way had opted for European status, either by formally submitting to European law or by converting to Christianity. But among non-Europeans the highest prijaji alone enjoyed the guarantees of European criminal procedure. All others were subject to the procedural code for Indonesians (the Inlandsch Reglement, Native Regulation, later revised as the Herziene Inlandsch (Indonesisch) Reglement, HIR) which was simpler, less demanding of authorities, and therefore less protective of individual rights.

The racial criterion of colonial law was similarly qualified by other special functions of particular groups. Economic position was a compelling determinant of legal parity. As commercial efficiency has everywhere demanded common norms of transactions, it was probably inevitable that Dutch commercial power would insist on applying its law to a group as economically significant as the Chinese. In addition, Indonesians who engaged in certain kinds of urban business or specific transactions were presumed by a useful fiction to have acquiesced in the relevant rules of Dutch commercial law — e.g., contracts, notes, checks, and the like. This was a matter of convenience. Otherwise Indonesians were assumed — and the assumption helped to ensure the reality — to live an autonomous legal life little concerned with "modern" commerce. They were governed in theory by their own customary (*adat*) law, applied either by traditional courts or by the government courts (landraden) for Indonesians. Relations between the several law groups in the colony, when not dominated by European law, were governed by a highly developed body of conflicts rules.

Whatever the inconveniences caused by legal pluralism, they were outweighed by the disadvantages of weakening the myths of Indonesian economic and political incapacity. By the twentieth century, when the great debate took place over unification of the law for all groups — a debate which the unifiers lost during the colonial period but won after independence — the fear that Indonesians might compete economically with the Dutch and Chinese was probably minor. But too many fundamental assumptions of colonial authority depended upon a functional separation of population groups to permit even symbolic unification. Van Vollenhoven and ter Haar, the learned adat law scholars who successfully opposed unification, were in no way disingenuous in their arguments; both men were sympathetic toward Indonesian cultures and no doubt feared the consequences of, and probably saw injustice in, an abrupt imposition of unified codes derived largely from European models. But although the scholars' motives were different from those of the colonial authorities, these views were consistent with colonial conservatism. During the nineteenth century, the seedtime of colonial administrative and legal development, the priority given commercial agriculture required the maintenance of an exploitable mass agrarian base, which the notion of "different people, different needs" helped to achieve. Later, however insignificant an explicit policy of differentiation was for economic purposes, it was imbedded in the supporting myth of the colonial state.

During most of the nineteenth century the Dutch believed that Indonesian customary law was based largely on Islamic law, and the jurisdiction of Islamic courts was accordingly recognized over a wide range of family law matters. This may have been a boon for Islam in areas like Central and East Java where antagonism toward the religion was powerful enough to stem its expansion. The Dutch were drawn into this historical religious conflict between the forces of Islam and pre-Islam in Java, Sumatra, and elsewhere. Along with European prejudice against Islam, a growing sophistication about Indonesian society gradually enabled the Dutch to revise their earlier views of Islamic influence. When the adat law scholars of Leiden emerged in the twentieth century, the additional factor of tendencies peculiar to ethnologists (and also to the continental school of historical jurisprudence) placed them on the side of "tradition" against the claims of Islam. Thereafter Islam was no longer regarded *a priori* as a fundamental source of Indonesian law, but had to prove the fragmentary reception of its legal norms into adat law. This was a significant turning point in colonial policy, one in which the adat law scholars won out over the more complex vision of the famous Islamicist, C. Snouck Hurgronje, who had favored accommodation with Islam and a general political and social (and legal) modernization. Islamic leaders today still regard Van Vollenhoven, ter Haar, and the new adat law policy with as much resentment as their opponents regard them with favor. In the 1930's, as one consequence of the new outlook, the colonial government transferred jurisdiction over inheritance disputes from Islamic courts to the landraden; Islamic groups have tried to get it back ever since. The conflict between adat and Islam, which basically involves the limits of Islamic expansion, remains an essential theme of political and therefore legal culture in Indonesia.

Although no extended discussion of adat law itself can be undertaken here, two general points about colonial adat law policy deserve attention. One is that, here more than in any other European colony the Dutch built an appreciation for customary law into the legal order through legal structure, education, and ideology. This appreciation, however, was probably more Dutch than Indonesian. The views of Indonesian leaders toward adat law were (and are) ambivalent. For although adat was distinctly Indonesian and symbolically attractive, the European codes smacked of social prestige, political superiority, and modernity; adat law acquired overtones of backwardness.

Second, despite Dutch emphasis on the place of adat law, its future was inevitably jeopardized by the emergence of a national level of politics and administration. In the Netherlands Indies, as in other colonies, the several ethnic groups could not represent much more to the government than units of population whose sensitivities should be respected if only to keep the peace. The relationship between colonial elite and subject people obviously did not constitute an integrated political community, and therefore was most easily treated as an administrative one. As a result, the law of colonial Indonesia looked vaguely like that of medieval France, except that customary differences between provinces in Indonesia grew from incomparably greater variations of social structure, religion, and culture. But after independence, though the process had already begun with the expansion of Dutch authority, as in old France, in Indonesia too a more intense effort was made to extend the *Pays du Driot Écrit* at the expense of the *Pays du Droit Coûtumier.* When an Indonesian elite assumed national power, a prolonged and painful attempt was begun to transform the colonial administrative state into a national political community, and local adat law felt the impact early.

The development of a national Indonesian "law community" — meaning here all related legal roles within the legal system — was more closely connected with *droit écrit* than *droit coûtumier.* Under indirect rule traditional Indonesian legal officials were not all eliminated, but a higher Dutch authority was imposed upon them, circumscribing their functions even as their positions were maintained. The plural legal system gave rise to informal linkages between the traditional and colonial legal orders, mainly in the form of special Indonesian roles concerned with understanding and manipulating unfamiliar Dutch legal machinery. One such link between the two legal universes was the *pokrol bambu*, an untrained but often knowledgeable "bush lawyer" about whom more will be said in our discussion of procedure. But it was in the major cities, in the colonial administrative service, in the government courts, and in the law schools of Holland and Batavia that a new group of professional lawyers began to emerge from within the colonial legal order. As legal studies became an evident route to success in the colony, a full term law faculty was finally opened in Batavia in 1924, though Indonesian students had gone to the Netherlands for advanced training before then. Most early Indonesian law students were high born Javanese who, from their knowledge of the Dutch language, were already familiar with the national level of colonial authority. Upon graduation most joined the Indonesian part of the judicial service. None was appointed to higher European jurisdictions before the Japanese occupation, and only one or two were given posts at higher levels of the European procuracy. A handful became private advocates. A few became highly respected legal scholars, primarily under the adat law research program of the Department of Justice; one of these, R. Supomo, became a law professor.

The legal traditions and symbols to which these men and many other professionals became committed could not easily be defended in the independent state, not basically because trained lawyers were so few but because the political and social order changed so radically. Colonial government was in fact based on the rule of law — a term used here in the Weberian sense of an essentially "rational-legal" organization of the state. That violent force implicitly underlay the colonial system as it applied to most Indonesians is irrelevant, for the primary clientele of the Netherlands-Indies government was not Indonesian but European. The immediate and central audience of the courts, procuracy, advocacy, notariat, and higher bureaucracy, was one that lived by a larger measure of contract than status, to use Maine's terms. These institutions of the law were nearly as powerful as in the Netherlands itself, and the law community was substantial, an integral part of a specialized government apparatus serving well-defined private interests. Law officials were themselves symbols of the law, and the law represented the consensus of the Dutch colonial community and its interests. In the independent state, this would disappear. The governmental structures inherited by the new state were explicitly based on contract conceptions, ideas related to the rule of law, but politics was much more a matter of status.

NOTES AND QUESTIONS

1. What were the salient contrasts in colonial policy with respect to legal reform between Japanese rule in Taiwan and Korea and Dutch rule in Indonesia? Do these contrasts help to explain differences in the extent of legal penetration in these societies?

2. One explanation for the greater resistance to Japanese rule shown by Koreans in contrast to the Taiwanese is Korea's historical experience as an independent nation. Taiwan, after all, was in 1895 a remote and relatively recently annexed part of China populated largely by successive generations of emigrants from the mainland. To what extent did the Indonesian experience differ from that of both Taiwan and Korea?

3. Family law is the one area of law in which the drafters of modern law codes have conscientiously tried to incorporate traditional customs and practices. Hence the family law provisions in most East Asian civil codes tend to reflect indigenous rather than European concepts and rules. To what extent, however, is it possible to incorporate traditional familial regimes in Western law codes? For example, how effectively can notions of filial piety and paternalism be expressed in terms of private law rights and duties?

4. Significant legal reforms continued to be made in both Japan and Thailand after World War II. In the case of Thailand, these tended to be self-directed efforts. For Japan, however, the most far-reaching changes were those imposed under the Allied Occupation (1945-1952). They included a new constitution and an extensive array of regulatory statutes, including foreign exchange and trade controls, antitrust legislation, securities regulation, labor and tax law reforms, and land reforms. Remarkably few changes were actually made, however, in the basic private law codes or to the institutional structure of the legal system established in the Meiji period. Even in areas of substantial institutional change, such as administrative law, and in civil and criminal procedure, the new rules tended to be enveloped in a theoretical gloss originally developed in Germany in the late 19th and early 20th centuries. The result has been a hybrid between the goals of the American reformers and the predominantly German prewar system. Today this is still seen even in fields of law based on American models, such as antitrust and constitutional law, where contemporary developments in German law exert considerable influence.

5. For fuller treatment of the codification of law in Japan, see Ryosuke Ishii, Japanese Legislation in the Meiji Era (William J. Chambliss trans. 1958). One of the few detailed studies on legal reform in Taiwan under Japanese rule is Tay-sheng Wang, Legal Reform in Taiwan Under Japanese Colonial Rule (1895-1945): The Reception of Western Law (Ph.D. Dissertation, University of Washington School of Law, 1992). For a study of early colonial legal reform in Indonesia, see John Ball, Indonesian Legal History, 1602-1848 (1982). For Thailand, see also Apirat Petchsiri, Eastern Importation of Western Criminal Law: Thailand as a Case Study (1987).

Chapter 6

THE STRUCTURE OF LEGAL SYSTEMS

NOTE ON POPULATION AND ECONOMIC DATA

The purpose of this chapter is to provide an overview of the constitutional and institutional structure of contemporary civil law systems. Europe, Latin America, and East Asia are separately treated in this chapter because there are important structural differences between them. In addition there are significant differences in legal penetration and legal culture, to which we also give special attention in Section D (Latin America) and Section E (East Asia).

We set out below some basic social data for the regions and specific countries to be considered. One should remember that each particular legal system is structured and operates within its own social and cultural milieu.

Population statistics in Table 6.1 provide a comparative overview for the three regions and the United States, with information about selected countries appearing in Table 6.2.

Table 6.1

Total Population (000,000), by Region and Year

Region	1980	1990	2000 (proj.)	Growth Rate[1]	1990 Density[2]
USA	228	250	268	0.9%	69
Europe	484	500	514	0.3%	266
Latin America	364	449	537	2.1%	57
East Asia	1,181	1,335	1,508	1.2%	293

[1] Annual rate of population growth (1980-1990).
[2] 1990 population per square mile.

Table 6.2

Total Population (000,000), by Country and Year

Country	1980	1990	2000 (proj.)
Europe			
France	54	56	59
Germany	78	79	82
Italy	56	58	59
Spain	37	39	40
Latin America			
Argentina	28	32	36
Brazil	123	153	181
Colombia	27	33	40
Mexico	70	88	109

Country	1980	1990	2000 (proj.)
East Asia			
Indonesia	155	190	224
Japan	117	124	128
South Korea	38	43	46
Taiwan	18	20	22
Thailand	47	56	64

Seven of the world's ten largest metropolitan areas are located in the countries chosen for study. See Table 6.3.

Table 6.3

World's Largest Metropolitan Areas in 1990, by Rank and Population (000,000)

Name	Rank	Population
Tokyo-Yokohama, Japan	1	27
Mexico City, Mexico	2	20
São Paulo, Brazil	3	18
Seoul, South Korea	4	16
New York, USA	5	15
Osaka-Kobe-Kyoto, Japan	6	14
Buenos Aires, Argentina	9	12
Rio de Janeiro, Brazil	10	11

There is also great diversity in per capita economic production among the various nations that we will examine, both within a region and between regions. See Table 6.4. In general we can see that the European nations are, along with Japan (and the United States), the world's leading economic powers. But there is variability within western Europe: Spain had only half the gross national product (GNP) per capita of Germany in 1989. The eastern European countries, of course, are only now transforming their economies to the capitalist model in the 1990s and are still far behind in GNP statistics.

Table 6.4

Gross National Product Per Capita (in Constant 1989 US $), by Country and Year

Country	1980	1989
USA	17,670	20,910
Europe		
France	14,660	17,000
Germany (West)	16,410	19,520
Italy	12,500	14,940
Spain	7,711	9,471
Latin America		
Argentina	2,289	1,694
Brazil	3,124	3,090
Colombia	1,077	1,139
Mexico	2,415	2,170
East Asia		
Indonesia	334	479
Japan	16,750	22,900

Country	1980	1989
South Korea	2,409	4,920
Taiwan	4,104	7,390
Thailand	766	1,246

All four Latin American examples in Table 6.4 are illustrative of developing economies, with only a fraction of the per capita productive output of a European nation. The rapid population growth rates for Latin America (see Table 6.1) make the task of improving the economic lot of the average citizen very difficult. The 1980s were particularly bad, as the real GNP per capita declined in Argentina, Brazil, and Mexico. A weak economic base translates into minimal penetration of the national legal system outside major cities and gives Latin America its distinctive civil law variation.

The East Asian selections show greater range in per capita GNP than the countries in either of the other two regions, which makes generalization for East Asia more risky. This difference is obvious when one considers Japan, which has an economy functioning at the world's highest levels, compared to Indonesia, which produces less than half the per capita GNP of Colombia, the poorest of the Latin American nations considered. On the other hand, all of the East Asian countries grew significantly in per capita economic terms during the 1980s, some at an astounding rate.

For general information on the constitutions and legal structures of countries examined in this book, see Viktor Knapp, ed., *National Reports*, 1 International Encyclopedia of Comparative Law (1972-1991); Kenneth Robert Redden, ed., 1-10 Modern Legal Systems Cyclopedia (1991); Albert P. Blaustein & Gisbeth H. Flanz, 1-19 Constitutions of the Countries of the World (1991). Statistical data on legislatures is provided in Inter-Parliamentary Union, 1-2 Parliaments of the World: A Comparative Reference Compendium (2d ed. 1986).

A. EUROPE

1. FRANCE

RENÉ DAVID, FRENCH LAW: ITS STRUCTURE, SOURCES, AND METHODOLOGY 19-33, 35-36, 38-39, 41-45 (Michael Kindred trans. 1972)

A. *The Constitution*

The Constitution of the French Republic, adopted October 4, 1958, is relatively new, and it is still difficult to predict the future development of a structure that was dominated until 1969 by the personality of General de Gaulle. We will limit ourselves here to a brief description of the political institutions set up by the Constitution of 1958. We shall mention in passing certain French traditions, attitudes, and feelings that are at least as important to a true understanding as the text of the Constitution itself.

Like every French constitution since 1791, the Constitution of the Fifth Republic is based on the principle of separation of powers.[1] French constitutional law scholars since the eighteenth-century philosophers have erected this principle into a dogma. Frenchmen grow up with the assumption that France's difficulties during the monarchy were the result of failure to respect the principle of separation of powers. A Frenchman can imagine only tyranny, arbitrariness, and corruption if this principle is ignored. Rationally and intuitively he is upset by real or imagined violations of it, in either the structure of his institutions or their activities....

1. *Executive Branch*

A Frenchman raised and educated under the Third or Fourth Republic would be disturbed to begin his study of French political institutions by looking at the executive branch. He takes for granted the supremacy of the legislative branch, represented by Parliament. The Constitution of 1946 was particularly clear in this regard. Article 3 stated: "The people exercises [its national sovereignty] in constitutional matters by the vote of its delegates .... In all other respects, it exercises it through its representatives in the National Assembly." No reference was made to the executive branch, which was composed of a figurehead president of the republic and a council of ministers drawn almost entirely from members of Parliament and overturned by Parliament with notorious frequency. In French political tradition, parliamentary supremacy has been intimately associated with the very concept of democracy, since French experience had indicated that a strong executive was a threat to democracy and freedom.

The Constitution of 1958 repudiated this tradition. It put the executive branch on an equal footing with the legislative and even, at least temporarily, above it.... The dominant theme of the Constitution is the establishment of a new equilibrium between the executive and legislative branches by the imposition of strict limits on a Parliament that recently was omnipotent. In fact, the point of equilibrium has been passed; the Constitution institutes clear executive supremacy. Under the new Constitution, therefore, the executive branch deserves, both theoretically and practically, to be discussed before the legislative.

Executive power, according to the Constitution of 1958, is in the hands of the President of the Republic and his Government.[2]...

[T]he President's main function continues to be as the chief executive officer. This position is indicated by the various prerogatives and powers granted

[1] The First Republic existed from 1792 to 1804; the Second from 1848 to 1852; the Third, established after the war of 1870, lasted until 1940; the Fourth from the liberation of France in 1944 until 1958; the Fifth was set up following the events of May-June, 1958.

[2] Translator's Note: The French term *gouvernement* has two distinct meanings, which can be confusing for an English-speaking reader. The first meaning is the same as our meaning of "the government," the totality of political organs that govern society, including the executive, legislative, and judicial branches. The second meaning has no precise equivalent in English and refers to a group of officials in the executive branch comprising the Council of Ministers and a significant number of other high appointed executive branch officials. It is contrasted with the lower-rank, civil service bureaucracy, or *administration*. For clarity the term *gouvernement* is translated "government" with a small "g" when used in its broadest, usual English sense, and "Government" with a capital "G" when it is used in its special French sense.

him by the Constitution: appointment of the Prime Minister and, on the nomination of the latter, of the other ministers (article 8), presidency of the Council of Ministers (article 9), promulgation of statutes (article 10), signatory of ordinances and decrees adopted by the Council of Ministers (article 13), appointment of civil and military employees of the state (article 13), commander-in-chief of the armed forces (article 15), and others. Since 1958 the position of the President of the Republic has been further strengthened through constitutional amendment. The Constitution originally provided for his election by an electoral college, but was amended in 1962 to provide for direct election by universal suffrage.

The Government is headed by the Prime Minister, who is appointed by the President. The other ministers are also appointed and dismissed by the President, but his decision in their case must be based on a proposal from the Prime Minister (article 8). The Prime Minister can submit the Government's resignation to the President (article 8) and he must do so where the National Assembly has adopted a motion of censure or has failed to approve the platform or a general policy statement of the Government under conditions stated in article 49. The constitutional act of June 3, 1958, posed as its third principle that "the Government must be responsible to Parliament." The Constitution did incorporate this principle; so from this point of view France is still a parliamentary democracy, despite the increased power given to the executive. Finally, the 1958 Constitution creates an incompatibility between the function of member of the Government and the status of member of Parliament (article 23).

The Government determines and implements the nation's policies (article 20). On a more narrowly legal plane, it is important to know how this power is to be exercised. There is a crucial division between subjects within the legislature's jurisdiction and those of a "regulatory" nature. With respect to the former, the Government can only act if and to the extent that Parliament delegates power to it; then it acts through ordinances (article 38). In the "regulatory" sphere, however, the Government acts at its own discretion; the only limitation is that it must act through decrees proclaimed with the advice of the Council of State where its action will amend legislatively passed statutes. The regulatory power granted to the Government constitutes a substantial part of what is theoretically the function of the legislative branch. This redistribution of power toward the executive is particularly great because under the Constitution the regulatory area seems to be the rule and the statutory area the exception....

Reoriented as it is with respect to the legislative branch by the reestablishment of a balance that had previously been destroyed in the legislature's favor, the executive has retained its traditional independence from what used to be called the judicial branch and is now called the judicial authority. Here, French institutions can be explained historically. The supreme courts of prerevolutionary France, the *parlements*, made themselves very unpopular by opposing all reforms to the traditional legal system. Assiduous in their defense of an antiquated system based on the inequality of social classes and on self-serving premises, they failed in their ambition of becoming the nation's representatives. Nor did they succeed in really controlling government action or in imposing procedural rules upon it. Of their many ill-advised interferences in politics and government, people remember their opposition to those organizational reforms that the monarchy did attempt from time to time. Abolition of the *parlements* was one of the first acts of the French Revolution, on November 3, 1789. The following year a law on judicial organization, which is still in force, proclaimed that "the judicial functions are distinct and will always remain separated from the executive functions" (law of August 16-24, 1790, title II, article 13). Judges are forbidden to concern themselves with executive action. Article 5 of the Civil Code clearly states that they cannot enact regulations. Nor can they give any order to a government agent: the common law's writ of mandamus disturbs Frenchmen greatly. The courts cannot even judge cases in which executive activities are at issue; such litigation might lead them to criticize or condemn such conduct, and indirectly to try to subordinate the executive to judicial control. A practical procedure, that of the "conflict," has been set up by statute; the executive can require the regular courts to renounce jurisdiction when the case in question is one over which, by virtue of the principle of separation of powers as thus understood, they lack jurisdiction. A special tribunal called the Court of Conflicts (*Tribunal des Conflits*), composed partly of judges and partly of administrators, has been created to handle jurisdictional disputes between the regular courts and the executive. [See Figure 6.1, *infra* this subsection.]

The lack of jurisdiction in the regular courts to hear cases involving the executive is a principle that dominates French law and has led some foreign jurists to question whether individual citizens are adequately protected against abuse of governmental power and whether France really subscribes to the rule of law. An affirmative answer to such questions is beyond doubt today. The Frenchman is at least as well protected as anyone against state power; often he is better protected. The only difference is that, in France, litigation involving the executive branch goes before tribunals that are independent of the regular courts. Although these tribunals, of which by far the most important is the Council of State, are "administrative courts" within the executive branch, the necessary precautions have been taken to insure their full independence from the "active administration." The independence and impartiality of these courts are unquestioned. In short, the French division between regular and administrative courts, like the separation in common law countries between courts of common law and those of equity, is explained by history. There, too, the existence of the equity courts was once contested; they seemed dangerous, subject to abuse, likely to encourage arbitrariness and destroy the "rule of law." Today these fears have faded and English equity is unquestionably "legal." It has come to be regarded as a progressive, rather than a regressive, force in the development of the law. Frenchmen view their administrative law in the same way. In the beginning, the exclusion of regular court jurisdiction over litigation involving the government was risky and on principle hard to defend. In practice, however, it has turned out well and has contributed to the development of French law. The administrative courts, totally independent of the executive in fact, have been able, because of their position at the very center of the executive branch, to establish a control over governmental action that would have been thought intolerable if attempted by regular judges.

2. *Legislative Branch*

Before 1958, the legislature had in fact gained almost unlimited power. It closely supervised executive action. Because the courts could not declare a statute passed by Parliament unconstitutional, constitutional limits on legislative power were purely formal.

The Constitution of 1958 reflects a strong reaction against this system. It severely restricted legislative prerogatives. The powers of the legislature today can be summarized into two principal points: (1) Parliament helps prepare and passes legislation; (2) it can force the Government to resign.

Although these are virtually the same powers that permitted past Parliaments to establish their omnipotence, various new rules in fact change everything. The National Assembly can still turn out the Government, but in doing so it now risks dissolution by the President of the Republic. The Government is no longer recruited from the National Assembly, or at least a member of Parliament who is appointed minister must give up his parliamentary seat until the next election. While these two rules do not restrict the rights of Parliament in theory, in reality a demand for the Government's resignation has ceased to be an attractive, risk-free operation for members of the National Assembly....

Parliament helps to prepare statutes. Here again nothing is changed in theory. Parliament retains the legislative initiative and the right of amendment, and only Parliament can pass statutes. In reality, however, two new rules change everything. In the first place, bills and amendments formulated by a member of Parliament are inadmissible where their adoption would either reduce public resources or create or increase a public charge (article 40). A second and no less important limitation is that the legislative domain is restricted to specific subjects listed by the Constitution (article 34), beyond which one is in the regulatory area, reserved for executive action....

The legislative branch provided for by the Constitution of 1958 is composed of a Parliament of two assemblies, the National Assembly and the Senate. The National Assembly is elected for five years by direct, universal suffrage. Senators are elected for nine years by indirect suffrage. One-third of the Senate changes every three years. In most respects, the two chambers have the same functions, but only the National Assembly can require the resignation of the Government, and it can also override the Senate's opposition to a bill....

3. *Judiciary*

Traditional doctrine recognizes the existence of a third branch, or power (*pouvoir*), of government, in addition to the legislative and executive. This third power is the judiciary. Frenchmen have always had some difficulty, however, thinking of the courts as exercising a "power" comparable to those exercised by Parliament and the executive. The judiciary does not have the prestige in France that it has in England. Nor does it have or aspire to the functions and responsibility of judges in the United States. Few political questions of concern to the nation's executive come before the judiciary, since French courts are not allowed to review the constitutionality of legislation or to control the activity [of] the executive. Jurisdiction in this latter area is entrusted to a body within the executive branch, the Council of State. Even in the private and criminal law areas, the courts' powers are restricted by the codification, which at least theoretically seems to solve all problems. In these circumstances, a Frenchman must exert himself if he is to think of the courts as constituting a true branch, or power, given what this somewhat poorly chosen term, *pouvoir*, connotes for him. The Constitution of 1958 reconciled theory with facts by speaking of the judiciary simply as the "judicial authority" (articles 64-66), instead of the judicial power, or branch....

French courts, while independent in their judicial activities, readily accept legislative and executive jurisdiction over the organization of the administration of justice. They do not regard the Ministry of Justice as threatening their prerogatives in any way. Nor do the courts claim any exclusive power to establish their own procedure or to organize and regulate the judiciary, lawyers, and other auxiliaries of the judicial system. Civil and criminal procedure are regulated in France by legislatively enacted codes. Similarly, statutes and decrees fix the organization and regulation not only of judges, but of others who hold legal jobs as well.

4. *Authority and Strength of Constitutional Rules*

French constitutions have traditionally been rigid documents. Constitutional rules are adopted and are subject to amendment only by special procedures. The Constitution of 1958 has followed tradition in this regard. The Constitution itself was approved by a referendum, and amendments to it require approval either in a referendum or by a special majority of Parliament. In 1962 the electorate approved, by a substantial majority, an amendment providing for the direct election of the President by universal suffrage. In 1969, on the other hand, it rejected a proposal to establish "regions" in France with considerable autonomy and, in connection therewith, to change the Senate fundamentally. The rejection of this proposal led to the resignation of the President of the Republic, who had placed his prestige behind it. Nevertheless French tradition has never accepted a real supervision over the constitutionality of legislation. There has been a refusal to conceive of the people as a separate, fourth factor.

During the period when Parliament established its supremacy, the distinction between the legislative branch and the people was regarded simply as a device to limit the sovereignty of Parliament, and in reality to give supremacy to one of the other branches of government, the executive or the judicial. To distinguish between the legislative branch and the people appeared to Frenchmen in principle illegitimate and in practice a threat to individual liberties, which could be guaranteed effectively only by the elected Parliament. Frenchmen had become used to fearing an executive dictatorship, but not a legislative one. Nor were they prepared to accept what one of them called, with a kind of Jacobin emotion and sense of protest, a "government by judges."

The Constitution of 1958 has taken a step forward in this area. It clearly has not given the right to examine the constitutionality of legislation to the judiciary as a whole, or even to a constitutional court especially created for that purpose. Nevertheless the principles proclaimed by the Constitution are better protected than in the past against possible legislative infringement, while earlier institutions have been retained and continue to provide protection against possible infringements of these principles by the executive.

What happens if there are violations of the Constitution by the legislative branch? The Constitution of 1958 has created an organ to prevent such violations: the Constitutional Council (title VII, articles 56-63). In addition to various other functions, the Constitutional Council determines the constitutionality of statutes *prior to their taking effect* whenever the law is an "organic statute" by virtue of its object,[5] and whenever the council is requested to do so by the President of the Republic, the Prime Minister, the President of the Senate, or the President of the National Assembly.

[In 1974 the National Assembly and Senate approved by more than the required three-fifths majority an amendment to article 61. It broadened standing to request the Constitutional Council to rule on the constitutionality of proposed legislation to include any group of 60 deputies or senators. This reform was intended to strengthen the power of the political minority. The Council's] decisions are final, unappealable, and binding on all branches of government and all administrative and judicial officials (article 62). The Constitutional Council has had to determine on several occasions whether a particular bill transgresses the regulatory power which the Constitution grants to the executive branch....

What happens if the executive violates the Constitution? Here the pre-1958 rules remain in force. The Constitution is treated just as any other statute. The Constitutional Council has no jurisdiction other than that just described. Only the Council of State has jurisdiction to determine whether acts of the executive are illegal or unconstitutional. In this area, the new Constitution seems inadequate, and one wonders whether it gives sufficient attention to the matter of regulations. Their use is no longer restricted to the creation of subsidiary legislation and implementation in areas already covered by statute. Regulations now have their own sphere of operation, parallel to that of legislative action. In such a situation it is shocking to have an administrative court, at least theoretically part of the executive branch, as the only body able to review the constitutionality of regulations. Although the independence of the Council of State within the executive branch is universally recognized, the Constitution can be criticized on this point for having ignored the principle of separation of powers and sanctioned a degree of executive supremacy that may be dangerous.

Respect for the Constitution, and especially for the principle of independence of the executive from judicial control, is imposed on the judiciary by binding jurisdictional rules, which are enforced by the Court of Conflicts and by various Civil and Penal Code rules such as that forbidding judges to give

[5]This term denotes statutes of particular constitutional importance for which the Constitution has provided or which are necessary to implement the Constitution's provisions. The Constitution of 1958 called for eighteen organic statutes; these were promulgated between November 7 and December 29, 1958.

general or regulatory decisions on issues submitted to them (Civil Code, article 5).

B. *Administrative Organization*

The administration plays a considerable role in all modern countries by reason of the importance of the services people expect from it and the development in modern states of the notion of public services and the "public sector" of the economy.

In consequence, there has been a steady evolution since the Revolution, with a progressive increase in the tasks assumed by the administration. This evolution has been accelerated recently during two periods of extensive nationalization, first in 1936 when the "Popular Front" took control of the government and then in 1945 with the liberation and the establishment of the Fourth Republic. In the first period, the railroads and the Bank of France were nationalized and a national social security administration was created. Immediately after the liberation, there were important nationalizations in banking, insurance, energy (coal, gas, and electricity), radio, maritime and air transport, and other specific industries (the Renault industrial complex, defense industries, and the like).

These ever-increasing administrative functions have been carried out until recently through a variety of public law entities, the most important of which was the state itself. As the tendency toward governmental direction and guidance of activities in the private sector has become more prominent, the situation has grown much more complex. Along with the traditional public law entities, the state has created other bodies to assist in the performance of its new functions. Often these bodies seem superficially to be ordinary private organizations. For a variety of reasons the government has found it advantageous to "disguise itself" in directing a "public service," and has thus organized a corporation of which it is the sole shareholder. In numerous other cases it has joined with private individuals to form a "mixed corporation," in which it may or may not have a controlling voice. [In the mid-1980s the French Government began a process of privatization that included selling many of the companies it owned or in which it controlled shares. Nevertheless, by 1994 the Government still controlled about 2,000 firms.]

The administrative agencies and public services run by the state are grouped into ministerial departments under the authority of various ministers, although the precise number of departments and the allocation of services between them changes from time to time.... The central administration is situated in Paris and deals with matters arising throughout the country. The external services, on the other hand, are composed of ministerial agents stationed in specific localities with authority to settle minor problems themselves. Their existence corresponds to the need for some deconcentration of administrative power and personnel.

The most important central administrative officials outside the capital are the prefects, who are stationed in each of France's ninety-five departments. The office of prefect was created by Napoleon on the pattern of the intendant of prerevolutionary France and has many special functions. But the prefect is above all, in addition to his special functions, the Government's chief official in his department, and as such, supervises all of the various ministries' external offices in his department. In addition, he has a power of administrative tutelage, and thus some control, over the manner in which departments and communes manage the affairs designated by law as within their sphere of primary responsibility. Deconcentration through external offices of the ministries is contrasted in French legal terminology with decentralization, which delegates certain powers in the jurisdiction of particular administrative agencies either to territorial subdivisions or to autonomous institutions with specific functions.

Administratively, metropolitan France is divided into ninety-five departments. These are subdivided into arrondissements, the arrondissements into cantons, and the cantons into communes....

The French civil service, always conscious of its responsibilities and particularly so since it achieved complete independence from the judiciary in 1790, has understood that it must fight the dangers that threaten the powerful, such as arbitrariness and corruption. As its recruitment and esprit have become democratic, the civil service has placed limits on its own power and has developed an institution designed to regularize its operation and minimize abuses. This institution is the Council of State, the true control mechanism of the French civil service.

Divided into sections, the Council of State is often asked — and sometimes it must be asked — for its advice on government legislative and regulatory proposals. But it has another function, equally essential, that makes it unique. The Council of State is best known to jurists as the supreme court of administrative law, with jurisdiction to control administrative action in almost all areas. On the petition of private individuals, the Council of State can either invalidate administrative actions or award damages or other remedies to individuals wrongly injured by such action. Every French executive official, from the President of the Republic to village mayor, with ministers and prefects between the two, is subject in his official actions to the Council of State's criticism and censure. And the Council also has control over the activity of independent administrative agencies and their officials, and over the activity of certain elected bodies, such as the departmental general councils and the municipal councils. It has created the French "administrative law" over the last one hundred years. The result is that a legal structure has, perhaps more completely in France than in any other country, replaced an earlier structure that allowed much arbitrary action and many situations in which the government could not be held liable for improper action on its part. French public law can be understood only through a knowledge of the Council of State and particularly its unique esprit. This esprit has grown out of its participation, aside from its judicial functions, in the work of the active civil service, its members' devotion to public service, their comprehension of administrative necessities, and also its determination to curb abuses and misuses of power, to guarantee the equality of citizens, and to insure a healthy civil service....

[The Council of State is divided into five sections. The first four are administrative sections: interior, finance, public works, and social affairs. The fifth section is the judicial section (*Section du contentieux*), which consists of over

100 members divided into ten subsections. Since 1980 each subsection is competent to proceed independently with a case and render judgment in the name of the Conseil d'Etat, although normally two subsections combine in reaching a decision.]

The independence of the Council of State is illustrated by numerous decisions where it has readily affirmed the rule it thought most just under the law, even at the risk of provoking a serious governmental crisis and embarrassment, whether political or financial.

The Council of State was at one time the court of first instance in all administrative law disputes, but in 1953 it was relieved of this function and new lower administrative courts were created to lessen congestion in the Council of State. There are [26] lower administrative courts in metropolitan France, each with three members to give judgment and often a fourth to act as commissioner of the Government....

[There are seven additional administrative tribunals in the French overseas departments. In 1986 there were 375 judges in the *tribunaux administratifs*. After years of trying to reduce the delay in hearing cases (averaging about 8,000 annually) in the Council of State's judicial section by increasing the number of its judges, Parliament created five intermediate *cours administratives d'appel* that began in 1989 to hear appeals from first instance tribunals. These new courts hear appeals in which the primary dispute is factual, involving, for instance, taxes, procurement contracts, public official liability for injury, and civil service matters. For questions of law, decisions of the courts of appeal (as well as those of special administrative courts) may be attacked by cassation before the Conseil d'Etat with a motion to quash. The Council retains its original first instance jurisdiction where the constitutional or legal status of an administrative act is challenged. In addition, it was given a new task in 1989. Any lower administrative court, faced with a novel question of law contested in several cases, may send the issue to the Council for an *avis* that, although not binding on the referring court, will likely be followed.]

C. *Judicial Organization*

Separation of powers, as that concept is ordinarily understood in France, dictates that administrative courts be regarded as an administrative service and be studied with administrative law, rather than as part of the judicial structure. To the French jurist, therefore, the words *judicial organization* refer only to those courts which decide cases in the private and criminal law areas. [See Figure 6.1, *infra* this subsection.]...

[French private law courts were substantially reorganized in 1958, and subsequently modified in particulars during the 1970s and 1980s. The general jurisdiction ordinary civil court for first instance is the *tribunal de grande instance*. The court's geographic jurisdiction usually covers a department, and in the late 1980's there were 181 *tribunaux*. It decides all cases, subject to appeal, not expressly within the jurisdiction of another court. For most cases this means that the amount in controversy exceeds 30,000 F. In some matters, such as personal status actions (marriage, divorce, filiation, nationality), execution of judgments or executory titles, patents, trademarks, or certain real estate cases, it has exclusive jurisdiction. If the amount in controversy in these cases is less than 13,000 F, there is no right of appeal, but recourse to cassation is available. The principle of judicial collegiality requires that three judges hear cases dealing with personal status, those in which a party so requests, or those in which a single judge refers a case back to the court. Since 1970, however, a single judge in other situations may hear a case if the presiding judge (president) so decides. In addition, the president has some judicial powers of his own: he passes judgment in urgent cases *en référé* and he deals with ex parte applications for certain measures.

The *tribunal d'instance* is a limited jurisdiction civil court, whose geographic power normally includes an arrondissement. There were 470 tribunals of this type in the late 1980s. Disputes are heard by a single judge and include actions for possession of land or determination of boundaries, leases, alimony, attachment of movables, and other cases where the amount in controversy is less than 30,000 F. There is no right of appeal if the amount at issue is under 13,000 F.]

Courts are divided into chambers where their workload justifies it. Thus, the Paris court of appeals has twenty-five chambers and the Paris court of major jurisdiction has twenty-seven, themselves subdivided into sections.

For criminal cases, different courts have jurisdiction depending on whether the offense alleged, judged by the penalty involved, is classified as a major offense (*crime*), an intermediate offense punishable by brief imprisonment or fine (*délit*), or a minor offense (*contravention*). Major offenses are judged, in first and last instance, by the court of assize (*Cour d'assises*), a court composed of three magistrates and nine jurors, who are selected by lot for each session of the court of assize from a previously established list. Intermediate offenses are judged, in first instance, by the correctional court (*tribunal correctionnel*), the criminal law equivalent of the court of major jurisdiction. Appeals, if any, go to the correctional appeals chamber (*Chambre des appels correctionnels*) of the court of appeals. Minor offenses are handled by the police court (*tribunal de police*), which corresponds to the court of minor jurisdiction. Appeals, if any, go to the court of appeals....

Finally, children up to eighteen years of age who commit intermediate or minor offenses are tried by special children's courts, made up of one professional judge and two nonprofessional assistants. A major offense committed by a sixteen- or seventeen-year-old minor is judged by the court of assize for children (*Cour d'assises des* [*mineurs*]), made up of one court of appeals judge, two special children's judges, and nine jurors.

Above all these civil and criminal courts sits the French supreme court, called the Court of Cassation (*Cour de cassation*). It is composed at the present time of one criminal and one civil chamber; with the latter itself subdivided into three civil sections, a commercial section, and a social section. Cases taken to the Court of Cassation are generally heard by a single section. Particularly delicate cases and those likely to create conflicts with earlier decisions can be referred to "mixed chambers" (formerly the civil assembly [*Assemblée plénière civile*]), a special grouping of the president and one representative of each civil section of the civil chamber, and in some cases, the president and a councilor from the criminal chamber. Finally, there are circumstances, which we will discuss presently, where a case can be heard by the full court (*Assemblée plénière*, formerly called the *Chambres réunies*) of the Court of Cassation.

Within the judicial hierarchy, the Court of Cassation is unique. As a rule, it considers only questions of law and leaves all factual questions for determination by other courts. It is impossible to reach the Court of Cassation by complaining that the lower courts have made a mistake of fact, such as having incorrectly evaluated the amount of damage suffered by the plaintiff or having found X guilty of theft when he was innocent. The Court of Cassation hears only questions of law, or so at least goes the general rule.... The Court of Cassation's role is not, as scholars sometimes seem to think, to guard the purity of this distinction. Rather, it is to insure the consistency of French judicial decisions, so as to avoid there being a better chance of winning a lawsuit in a Marseille court, say, than in a Le Havre court. The Court of Cassation intervenes wherever intervention seems required to fulfill the court's function, without too much concern as to whether the question to be considered ought, strictly speaking, to be called a question of law. Only two primary factors limit the overextension of its jurisdiction. The court may fear a loss of effectiveness through overexposure. And its own procedures prevent the court, for example, from taking evidence freely.

Since it generally considers only questions of law, the Court of Cassation seldom considers the whole of a lawsuit. Thus, exceptional cases aside, it cannot dispose of disputes definitively. Either of two things happens. If the court decides that the law has been correctly interpreted in the case, it will reject the petition. If it decides that the lower court judges have made an error of law, it will quash their decision and send the dispute back to a new court of the same level as the one whose decision is quashed. This new court — the court of rehearing — has jurisdiction over the whole dispute. On the point of law that was submitted to the Court of Cassation, it may adopt the court's point of view, in which case the litigation is terminated and the new court's decision is final. If the court of rehearing, however, refuses to follow the Court of Cassation, as it has the right to do, a new petition to that court can be taken. In such a case, the dispute comes before the full court of the Court of Cassation. Where the full court quashes the decision against which the second petition is brought, it again sends the case back to a court of the same level. On the point of law which the Court of Cassation has decided, this new court must yield to the opinion of the full court.

Any decision of any court whatsoever can be brought before the Court of Cassation, without regard to the amount in controversy, provided only that the decision involved is not appealable to another court.... This is possible even where the amount in controversy in the case is too small to allow an appeal to the court of appeals. A case that seems to be a trifling matter can raise basic issues of law, on which the Court of Cassation can usefully speak so that the people throughout France will be subject to the same law and judged in the same way.

Among the French courts of general jurisdiction, only the court of minor jurisdiction and the police court in the criminal area are composed of a single judge. And among the courts of exceptional jurisdiction, the landlord-tenant courts, the referees' courts (*juridiction des référés*), and the court of the president of the court of major jurisdiction (*juridiction du président du tribunal de grande instance*) are single-judge tribunals. In [most] other cases, the principle of judicial collegiality prevails. In most courts, three judges collaborate in a decision, and in the Court of Cassation the minimum number is seven. The courts of assize are composed of three professional magistrates and nine jurors.[29] Similarly in other courts (labor boards, joint rural lease commissions), laymen are associated with judges in the settlement of disputes. Various attempts have been made in France to establish more single-judge courts, most notably in 1945. But these attempts have failed; the statutes in question have been repealed, in large part because of the resistance of the judiciary itself to the idea of giving judgment singly in criminal cases.

Although criminal and civil courts have different names, the same judges in fact sit in the courts of major jurisdiction and the correctional courts, on the one hand, and in the courts of minor jurisdiction and the police courts, on the other. Except in courts where the volume of litigation justifies several specialized chambers, the same judges hear civil cases one day and criminal cases the next. Similarly, the courts of appeals hear on appeal both civil and criminal cases.

NOTE ON THE STRUCTURE OF THE FRENCH COURT SYSTEM

The preceding excerpt by the late professor René David mentions or describes each of the four principal high "courts" within the French legal system. We will further consider the functioning of these courts in Chapter 7 (Judicial Review).

Two of these high courts, the *Cour de cassation* and the *Conseil d'Etat*, have their own hierarchical structures. The Court of Cassation system essentially consists of three tiers as set out in Figure 6.1. The first instance specialized tribunals involve many laypersons in the administration of justice and process a substantial percentage of all the cases before the "civil jurisdiction." These specialized tribunals include, among others, commercial tribunals (*tribunaux de commerce*, 227 in number), labor conflict councils (*conseils de prud'hommes*, 282), social security affairs tribunals (*tribunaux des affaires de sécurité sociale*, 110), and rural lease tribunals (*tribunaux paritaires des baux ruraux*, 409). Commercial tribunals consist of at least three lay judges, who are business persons elected by their peers for short terms and who serve without pay. Labor councils are established for different trades, industries, and professions. Each council has an equal number of employee and employer representatives elected to six-year terms without pay to resolve disputes over individual employment contracts. In case of an even split on a panel, a judge from the local *tribunal d'instance* casts the deciding vote. Social security tribunals and rural lease tribunals have one professional judge assigned to a panel together with elected laypersons. Social security tribunals each have

[29] Since 1941 the judges and jurors have joined together to decide both on the question of guilt and on the penalty.

Figure 6.1
Structure of the French Court System

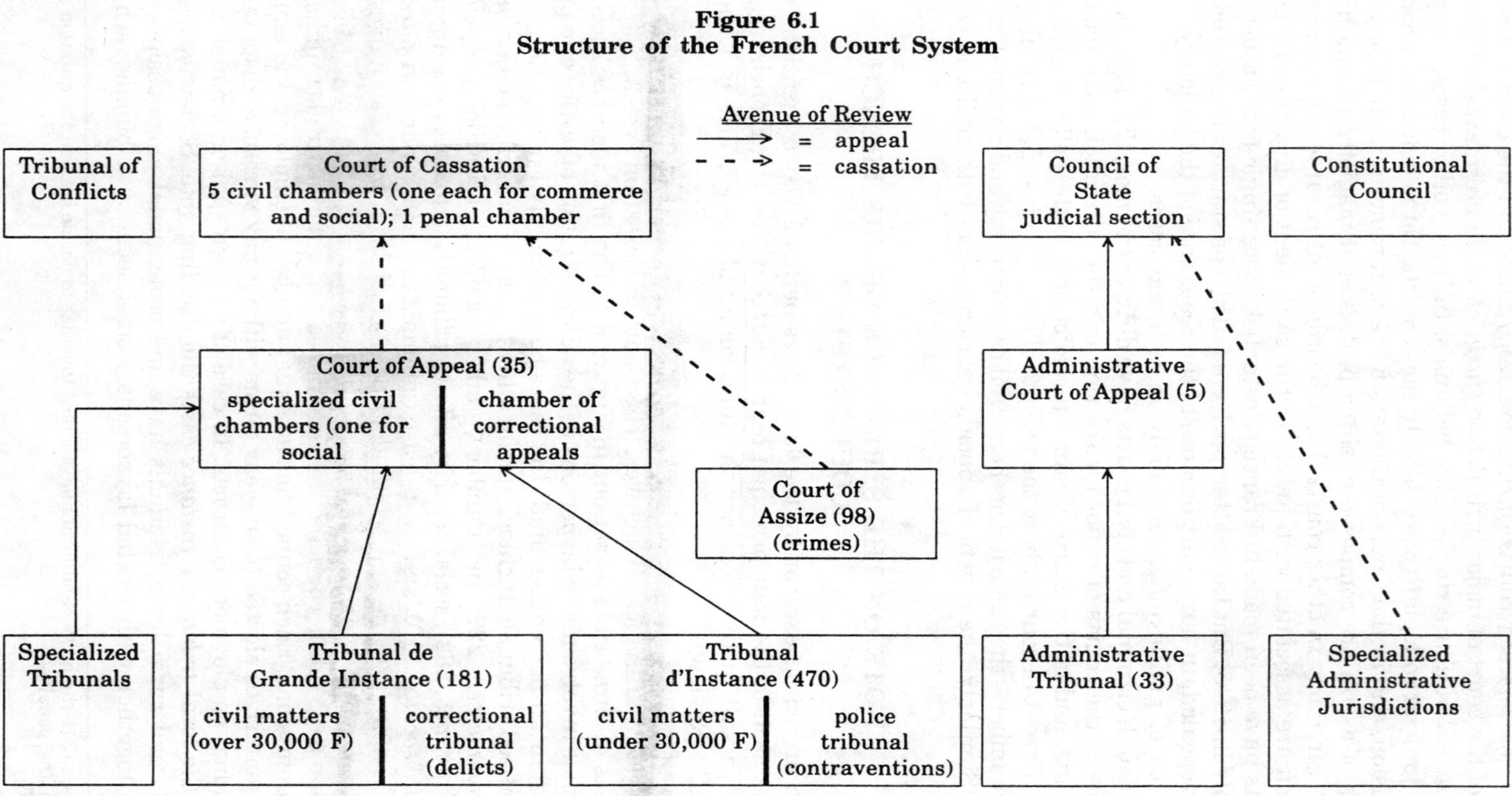
Avenue of Review
→ = appeal
- - -> = cassation
Tribunal of Conflicts
Court of Cassation
5 civil chambers (one each for commerce and social); 1 penal chamber
Council of State
judicial section
Constitutional Council
Court of Appeal (35)
specialized civil chambers (one for social
chamber of correctional appeals
Administrative Court of Appeal (5)
Court of Assize (98)
(crimes)
Specialized Tribunals
Tribunal de Grande Instance (181)
civil matters (over 30,000 F)
correctional tribunal (delicts)
Tribunal d'Instance (470)
civil matters (under 30,000 F)
police tribunal (contraventions)
Administrative Tribunal (33)
Specialized Administrative Jurisdictions

one lay judge representing employers and one lay judge representing employees. The laypersons are designated by organizations to serve five-year terms. Rural lease tribunals each have two elected representatives of farm lessors and two elected representatives of farm lessees, who serve for five years.

The Council of State since 1989 has had a three-tier system. See Figure 6.1. The specialized administrative jurisdictions include the Court of Accounts, the Court for Review of Public Expenditures, the Jurisdiction of Pensions, the National Council of the Physicians' Order, the Commission of Discipline for Firemen, and about 40 others.

The method for reviewing first instance decisions is indicated in Figure 6.1. For certain cases, usually less important matters in a *tribunal de grande instance, tribunal d'instance*, or a specialized tribunal, no appeal is permitted. An unsatisfied party is then left with only a petition for cassation on legal issues before the Court of Cassation.

Some idea of the caseload volume in French ordinary courts is provided by the following statistics. In 1987 the number of civil cases filed, by court, was: *tribunaux de grande instance* (423,490), *tribunaux d'instance* (472,045), *tribunaux de commerce* (281,076), *conseils de prud'hommes* (139,804), *tribunaux des affaires de sécurité sociale* (84,160), and *tribunaux paritaires des baux ruraux* (9,948). The number of penal cases terminated in 1987, by court, was: *tribunaux de grande instance* (correctional) (413,884), *tribunaux d'instance* (police) (9,609,296), and *cours d'assises* (2,410). At the *cours d'appel* level 145,463 civil cases were filed and 33,389 penal cases were terminated in the chambers of correctional appeals. Finally, 26,178 cases — civil and penal — were filed at the *Cour de cassation.*

For an American view of the capability of a French commercial court, see *Allendale Mut. Ins. Co. v. Bull Data Sys., Inc.*, 62 U.S.L.W. 2326 (7th Cir., 9 Nov. 1993, No. 93-2389) (C.J. Posner), in which an injunction was issued against the parties litigating in the foreign forum.

CONSTITUTION OF FRANCE

Title V: On Relations Between the Parliament and the Government Articles 34, 37, 38

Article 34

Laws (*loi*) are enacted by Parliament.

Laws govern:

- civil rights and the fundamental guarantees of citizens in the enjoyment of their public liberties; national defense obligations imposed on the persons and property of citizens;
- nationality, the status and capacity of persons, matrimonial regimes, successions, and gifts;
- definition of crimes and misdemeanors (*délits*) and the applicable punishments; criminal procedure; amnesty; the creation of new kinds of courts and the status of magistrates;

- the budget, taxes, and the methods of collecting imposts of all types; the issuance of money.

Laws also govern:

- elections to Parliament and local assemblies;
- the creation of categories of public agencies;
- fundamental guarantees granted to civil and military personnel employed by the State;
- nationalization of enterprises and transfer of enterprise from the public to the private sector.

Laws establish fundamental principles:

- of the general organization of national defense;
- of the free administration of local organizations; their competence and their resources;
- of education;
- of the property regime, real rights, and civil and commercial obligations;
- of labor law, union law, and social security.

Article 37

Matters other than those governed by laws (*loi*) are of a regulatory character.

Legislative texts concerning these matters may be modified by decrees (*décrets*) issued after consultation with the Council of State. Those legislative texts produced after this Constitution comes into force cannot be modified by decree unless the Constitutional Council declared that they have a regulatory character according to the first paragraph of this Article.

Article 38

The Government may, to carry out its program, ask Parliament to authorize it through ordinances (*ordonnances*) for a limited period to take measures that are normally governed by laws.

Ordinances shall be enacted in meetings of the Council of Ministers after consultation with the Council of State. They shall enter into force upon their publication, but shall become void if the bill for their ratification is not submitted to Parliament before the date set by the enabling act.

At the expiration of the time limit mentioned in the first paragraph of the present Article, ordinances may be modified only by laws for those matters that are within the legislative domain.

NOTES AND QUESTIONS

1. What is unusual from an American perspective about the French principle (dogma?) of separation of powers? Which branch of government is supposed to be supreme? How does the Constitution of 1946 differ from the Constitution of 1958 in this regard?

2. What type of executive system do the French have: parliamentary or presidential? We will see later that the Germans, Italians, and Japanese have a classic parliamentary system. The United States has the paradigmatic presidential system. What special prestige and powers does the French president have that puts the French executive system into a hybrid category?

3. What is the "Government" and its responsibilities? In particular, what lawmaking powers does the Government have? Identify the distinction between an ordinance and a decree. See the French Constitution, Articles 37-38.

4. How is the executive branch separate (independent) from the judicial branch (authority)? What role does the Tribunal of Conflicts play in this separation? See Figure 6.1.

5. How does the power of the French parliament compare with the power of an American state legislature? See the French Constitution, Article 34.

6. Define the boundaries of the judicial power? Does it include the Council of State court system? See Figure 6.1.

7. Which legal entities protect constitutional rules and individual liberties? What does the phrase "government by judges" mean to the French? How has that phrase been applied to the legal situation in the United States?

8. How does the Constitutional Council differ from the U.S. Supreme Court in its jurisdiction to protect the nation's constitution?

9. The Council of State is the control mechanism for the executive branch and the civil service. How is it organized and how does it function?

About one-half of the total capacity of the Council of State is absorbed by tasks other than the adjudication of disputes. *See* Bernard Ducamin, *The Role of the Conseil d'Etat in Drafting Legislation*, 30 Int'l & Comp. L.Q. 882 (1981).

10. Compare the judicial organization and jurisdiction of the French courts under the Court of Cassation to the organization and authority of a state judiciary in the United States. See Figure 6.1. What are the significant similarities and differences? What important differences are there in procedures?

11. For more on the French legal system, see John S. Bell, French Constitutional Law (1993); L. Neville Brown & John S. Bell, French Administrative Law (4th Ed. 1993); Andrew West et al., The French Legal System: An Introduction (1992).

2. GERMANY

OLIVER PASSAVANT & GERHARD NÖSSER, THE GERMAN REUNIFICATION — LEGAL IMPLICATIONS FOR INVESTMENT IN EAST GERMANY, 25 International Lawyer 875-76, 878-79 (1991)

The reunification of Germany on October 3, 1990, was a historic event in world affairs. Before the Berlin Wall opened on November 9, 1989, hardly anybody believed that the fierce division of postwar Germany could be overcome in the foreseeable future. On March 18, 1990, the first free elections after World War II were held in the German Democratic Republic (GDR or East Germany). The German-German Treaty of May 18, 1990, established a monetary, economic, and social union as of July 1, 1990. Pursuant to another treaty, signed on August 31, 1990, the GDR acceded to the Federal Republic of Germany (West Germany) as of October 3, 1990. The first free elections of the unified Germany were held on December 2, 1990....

Two treaties accomplished the harmonization of the two fundamentally different German legal systems: The Treaty Between the Federal Republic of

Germany and the German Democratic Republic Establishing a Monetary, Economic and Social Union (Economic Treaty) and the Treaty Between the Federal Republic of Germany and the German Democratic Republic on the Establishment of German Unity — Unification Treaty (Unification Treaty). In two steps these treaties combined two sovereign countries and their legal systems. The Economic Treaty declares important West German business laws applicable in the territory of the GDR....

The political unification of the two German states was accomplished by the Unification Treaty of August 31, 1990. As of October 3, 1990, the GDR ceased to exist; East Germany became a part of the Federal Republic of Germany and subject to its laws.

The German Basic Law, as enacted in 1949, envisioned two different technical ways for a future reunification. Article 146, for a long time viewed as the only path to unification, provided that the Basic Law would be replaced by a new constitution adopted by a free decision of all German people. During the negotiations in 1990, however, article 23 of the German Basic Law proved to be a more viable approach to bring about the unification. Article 23 provided that the Basic Law would become applicable in other territories upon their accession to West Germany. To comply with article 23 and to prepare for the federal structure of the Federal Republic of Germany, the GDR recreated five *Länder* or states: Brandenburg, [Mecklenburg-West Pomerania, Saxony, Saxony-Anhalt, and Thuringia. The smallest of these new states is Mecklenburg-West Pomerania (2.1 million) and the largest is Saxony (5 million).] On October 3, 1990, these states became part of the Federal Republic of Germany. Berlin, including the former East Berlin, was designated as [a new state and as] the capital of the new Germany. Since then, the legislators have decided that the seat of the parliament and the government will be Berlin.

As a general rule, the laws of the Federal Republic of Germany are now also applicable in the territory of the former GDR; any exceptions are set forth in the Unification Treaty.

DONALD P. KOMMERS, GERMAN CONSTITUTIONALISM: A PROLEGOMENON, 40 Emory Law Journal 837-38, 845-47 (1991)

Germany's written constitution is known as the Basic Law (*Grundgesetz*), so labeled because it was conceived in 1949 as a transitional document pending national unification. The more dignified term "constitution" (*Verfassung*) would be reserved for a governing document applicable to the nation as a whole and designed to last in perpetuity. Yet, over the years, having survived the test of time, the Basic Law has taken on the character of a genuine constitution. In fact, following the bloodless coup of March 18, 1990 — the day on which East Germans voted to end Germany's division — a new and freely elected East German government chose to accede to the Federal Republic of Germany within the framework of the Basic Law. This decision and the Unification Treaty signed later by East and West Germany transposed the Basic Law from a temporary instrument of governance for one part of Germany into a document of force and permanence for the entire German nation.

An imposing document of 146 articles, the Basic Law draws much of its inspiration from previous German constitutions in the democratic tradition.[5]...

The Basic Law marks a radical break with Germany's past. Previous constitutions in the democratic tradition were easily amended and not regarded as binding in all respects. By contrast, the Basic Law is a binding document. As several of its provisions make clear, it controls the entire German legal order, in which respect Articles 1, 19, 20, and 79 are particularly relevant. Article 1, paragraph 3, declares that the fundamental rights listed in the Basic Law, including the inviolable principle of human dignity, "shall bind the legislature, the executive, and the judiciary as directly enforceable law." In reinforcing this provision, Article 20 subjects "legislation" to the "constitutional order" and *binds* "the executive and the judiciary to law and justice."

In binding executive and judicial authority to "law" (*Gesetz*) and "justice" (*Recht*), the Basic Law's founders were recreating the formal *Rechtsstaat* — a state based on the rule of positive law (*i.e., Gesetz* or *Rechtspositivismus*) — but now, unlike the situation under previous constitutions, positive law is subject to the supra-positive notion of justice or *Recht*, a notion that appears to include unwritten norms of governance. In one of its landmark decisions the Federal Constitutional Court declared that laws "must also conform to unwritten fundamental constitutional principles as well as to the fundamental decisions of the Basic Law, in particular the principles of the rule of law and the social welfare state." In short, the *Rechtsstaat*, far from being an end in itself, now serves the constitutional state (*Verfassungsstaat*).

Articles 19 and 79 carry the principle of the Basic Law's supremacy even further. Article 19, paragraph 2, bans any law or governmental action that invades "the essential content of [any] basic right." But this is not all. Article 79, paragraph 3 — the so-called "eternity clause" — bars any amendment to the Basic Law that would tamper with the principle of federalism or impinge upon "the basic principles laid down in Articles 1 and 20." Article 1, as already noted, sets forth the principle of human dignity and imposes upon the state an affirmative duty "to respect and protect it," whereas Article 20 proclaims the basic principles governing the polity as a whole — *i.e.,* federalism,

---

[5] The Basic Law currently includes 14 sections. They are: Section I (Basic Rights [articles 1-19]), Section II (Federation and the States [articles 20-37]); Section III (Federal Parliament or Bundestag [articles 38-49]); Section IV (Council of States or Bundesrat [articles 50-53]); Section IVa (Joint [Federal-State] Tasks [article 53a]); Section V (Federal President [articles 54-61]); Section VI (Federal Government [articles 62-69]); Section VII (Legislative Powers of the Federation [articles 70-82]); Section VIII (Execution of Federal Laws and the Federal Administration [articles 83-91]); Section VIIIa (Joint [Federal-State] Tasks [articles 91a-91b]); Section IX (Administration of Justice [articles 92-104]); Section X (Finance [articles 104a-115]); Section Xa (State of Defense [articles 115a-115*l*]); Section XI (Transitional and Concluding Provisions [articles 116-146]); and Appendix (articles 136-139 and 141 of the Weimar Constitution). Under the Unification Treaty ... several articles of the Basic Law, including the preamble, are to be revised or repealed in the light of reunification. The Treaty, for example, repeals Article 23, which provides for the accession of "other parts of Germany" into the Federal Republic. The repeal of this article effectively freezes Germany's present borders, barring any further legal claim on the part of Germany to territory lost to Poland and the Soviet Union as a consequence of World War II. By the same token, Article 146 no longer incorporates the "achievement of unity" as a major aspiration of the Basic Law; the preamble underwent a similar change. Article 51 (2), as amended by the Treaty, changes the allocation of votes in the Bundesrat.

democracy, republicanism, separation of powers, the rule of law, popular sovereignty, and the social welfare state.[30] The Basic Law's framers believed, quite clearly, that the best way to realize human dignity, now and in the future, is to freeze certain principles of governance into the constitutional structure itself.

Finally, the authority conferred upon the Federal Constitutional Court, as well as upon the judiciary as a whole, assures every person that the Basic Law will prevail over all legal rules or state actions that would subvert or offend it. Accordingly, Article 19, paragraph 4, grants a judicial hearing to any person whose rights the state violates. Indeed, "recourse shall be to the ordinary courts" in the event that some other judicial remedy is not specified by law. In addition, Article 80 (1) helps to insure the protection of the rule of law against the decisions of executive officials. It requires that any law delegating the power to make legally enforceable regulations specify the "content, purpose, and scope of the authorization." The right of administrative judges — and indeed all judges — to refer constitutional questions to the Federal Constitutional Court in cases where they seriously doubt the constitutionality of a statute under which an action is brought backs up this guarantee. Failing these protections, the individuals affected have the option, once their legal remedies have been exhausted, of filing a complaint with the Constitutional Court.[32]

NORBERT HORN, HEIN KÖTZ & HANS G. LESER, GERMAN PRIVATE AND COMMERCIAL LAW: AN INTRODUCTION 16-23 (Tony Weir trans. 1982)

The System of Government

The provisions of the Basic Law fall into two groups. One group contains the "basic rights," which regulate the relationship between the citizen and the state, while the other provisions relate to the governmental institutions of the Bundesrepublik and the functions they perform. We shall take the latter group first.

The most important governmental institution in the Bundesrepublik is the *Bundestag*. It represents the people, and its members are elected by the people for four years at a time. The Basic Law states that elections must be "general, direct, free, equal and secret," but leaves all the details of electoral procedure to be determined by federal enactment (art. 38). Thus the decision whether to adopt the majority system or some form of proportional representation was left by the constitution to the federal legislature. So far it has opted for a slightly modified form of proportional representation, which ensures that Par-

[30] Article 20 defines West Germany as a "democratic and social federal state," provides for representative institutions through "elections and voting," and channels the exercise of state authority into "specific legislative, executive and judicial organs." (Article 28 requires the adoption of these principles at the state level. It reads, "The constitutional order of the *Länder* [states] must conform to the principles of republican, democratic, and social government based on the rule of law within the meaning of the Basic Law.").

[32] By 1990 German citizens had filed more than 78,000 such complaints, the overwhelming majority against judicial decisions allegedly in conflict with fundamental rights secured by the Basic Law.

liament accurately reflects the political forces in the country. The danger of such a system is that it can give rise to many small splinter groups, but this is countered by a provision of the federal electoral law which ensures that no party obtains any seat in Parliament at all unless it has attracted at least 5 per cent of the votes cast.

Of the powers which the Basic Law explicitly allocates to the Bundestag, the most important are its power to legislate and its power to nominate the Chancellor; but almost as important, though unmentioned as such in the Basic Law, is its role in the formation of public opinion. The Bundestag is the forum in which the central controversies of politics are debated, the viewpoints of the different parties formulated, and the Opposition's powers of control exercised.

About the function and powers of the *federal government* the Basic Law does not say very much. According to art. 62, the federal government consists of the Federal Chancellor and the federal ministers. The Chancellor's position is a strong one. He determines the "principles of policy," and the policies he prescribes must be followed by the ministers in the conduct of their departments, although they are otherwise independent (art. 65). The federal ministers are chosen by the Chancellor, and the president is bound to execute his proposals for their appointment or dismissal. Thus only the Chancellor himself is selected by the Bundestag. The Bundestag may call upon the Chancellor to dismiss a particular minister with whose performance it is dissatisfied, but whether the Chancellor follows such a resolution or not depends entirely on his view of what is politically expedient. It is only the Chancellor himself whom the Bundestag can require to withdraw, but a simple vote of no confidence is not sufficient for the purpose: the Bundestag must *at the same time* nominate his successor (art. 67). The purpose of this provision is to prevent the instability of an interregnum such as occurred several times under the Weimar Constitution, when there was a majority in Parliament for dismissing the head of government, but not for choosing his replacement. The position of the Federal Chancellor is thus particularly powerful and influential ....

In the Bundesrepublik the head of state, the *Federal President*, has but little scope for exercising political influence. His main function is to accord formal validation to decisions taken by others: he promulgates the laws that have been voted in Parliament, appoints the Federal Chancellor chosen by the Bundestag and the ministers proposed by the Chancellor, and represents the Bundesrepublik in the sphere of international law, for example in the accreditation of diplomats. The Federal President symbolizes the unity of the state and can thus exercise considerable influence on public opinion; but this depends more on his personal authority than on his constitutional powers.

The most important attribute of the Bundestag is its power to *legislate*. This power is subject to two constraints. First, the Bundestag can enact laws only on matters which the Basic Law allocates to the legislative competence of the Federation rather than to that of the Länder; and second, such legislation needs the co-operation of the *Bundesrat*.

The constitution starts out from the proposition that legislation is a matter for the Länder: federal laws can only be enacted where express power has been granted to the Federation in the Basic Law (art. 70). The areas in which *exclusive* power to legislate is granted to the Federation include foreign affairs, national defence, nationality, the currency, and the law relating to patents, trade-marks, and copyrights. In areas where the Federation has *concurrent* legislative power, the Länder may legislate, but only if the Federation has failed to exercise its power; in fact, the Federation has exercised its power so fully by now in these areas that there is hardly any room left for the Länder to legislate. Such areas include the whole of private and criminal law and procedure, labour law, the law of social security, and the vast field of law concerning the economy and agriculture. Finally, there are areas in which the Federation only has the power to enact *skeleton laws*. For example, the Federation may legislate on the status of civil servants within the Länder, the protection of the countryside, and the structure of universities, which are run exclusively by the Länder. Any such law, however, may contain only skeleton provisions, and must leave other matters to be filled in by legislators in the Länder. The matters for which the Länder retain exclusive competence today are in reality only collateral and residual, such as the law relating to local administration and cultural institutions, notably education.

The Länder do, however, take part in federal legislation through the Bundesrat. It is composed of members of the governments of the Länder, and they vote as instructed by the Land that sends them. A Land has a minimum of three votes, four if it has more than two million inhabitants, and five if it has more than six million.

[Since each of the five new eastern states has between 2 and 6 million inhabitants, each receives four votes in the Bundesrat. To appease the most populous of the western states — Northrhine-Westphalia — the Basic Law was amended (art. 51, para. 2) to give it six votes (as a state with more than 7 million inhabitants).]

If the Bundesrat disapproves of a bill which has been voted by the Bundestag, it can enter an objection (*Einspruch*). The Bundestag must then consider the bill anew, and only if the majority in the Bundestag in favour of the bill is as great as the majority in the Bundesrat against it may the law come into force. Often, however, the Bundesrat has a more effective veto, for the Basic Law expressly provides that the concurrence of the Bundesrat is required for any law that significantly affects the interests of the Länder, as many laws in fact do. In all these cases agreement between the Bundestag and the Bundesrat may be facilitated by the Vermittlungsausschuss or Committee of Mediation for which the Basic Law provides: it consists of equal numbers of members of the two bodies, and works out compromise proposals to lay before them (art. 77).

The Bundesrat's involvement in federal legislation is of great importance in two practical respects. First, it permits the input of the Länder's administrative experience and technical expertise. In principle, it is for the authorities in the Länder to implement federal laws (art. 83), and it might be very difficult or impossible for them to do this if bills promoted by the zealous reformers in the Bundestag could not be modified on technical administrative grounds on their way through the Bundesrat. Second, the role played by the Bundesrat in federal lawmaking can be of critical political importance, especially when the parties that have a majority in the Bundestag, and have therefore chosen the

Federal Chancellor and formed the government, are in a minority in the Bundesrat. In such a situation, which is by no means rare, the Bundesrat can obviously obstruct the legislative policies of the federal government. It is questionable whether it is right for a Land to use its voting power in the Bundesrat for general political purposes, to frustrate the legislative policies of the federal government and the majority in the Bundestag, rather than to protect any special interest of its own. However this may be, the part played by the Bundesrat in the process of federal lawmaking is certainly great — somewhat greater indeed than the draftsmen of the Basic Law had in mind.

If the place of the Länder in the Bundesrat has enabled them to increase their influence on federal policy-making, the past twenty years have seen a marked decrease in their ability to take independent measures on their own territory. It is not that the Basic Law has been amended to this effect; it is just that technological, economic, and social changes have made it much more sensible to do the planning and set the goals at the federal level rather than in the individual Länder. In the event, the Länder have developed various forms of mutual co-operation, often involving the Federation as well; these permit the assimilation of conditions in the different Länder and the harmonization of administrative practice, but they also tend to reduce the Länder's individual freedom of action. Furthermore, the Federation has powers whose exercise tends to weaken the powers of the Länder. For example, when the Basic Law was amended in 1959, the Federation was granted the power to give the Länder and local communities financial assistance with very costly projects (art. 91a). It may also now help the Länder with improving their regional economies and with constructing and extending their universities, matters that fall within the competence of the Länder. In these cases the Federation bears half of the costs involved (art. 91a). It will be evident that the offer of half the cost of a project which the Federation fancies is bound to curtail the practical options of the Land in question....

The Federal Constitutional Court

The resolution of disputes between the organs of state under the constitution of many countries is a matter for compromise and agreement. Other constitutions, including the Basic Law, provide for an independent court. In Germany this is the Bundesverfassungsgericht, or Federal Constitutional Court, and the Basic Law gives it a particularly important position (arts. 92-94). It decides disputes between the Federation and the Länder, or between different Länder, and also resolves any difficulties regarding their respective rights and duties under the Basic Law that may arise between the Bundestag, the Bundesrat, the federal government, the Federal President, and certain other institutions with constitutional roles....

Basic Rights

The first chapter of the Basic Law is entitled "Basic Rights" ("Grundrechte"). These are in line with the general human and civil rights now recognized in all constitutional states in the West, and covered by the European Convention for the Protection of Human Rights. Here one finds the basic principles that everyone has the right to life, corporeal integrity, and the unhampered development of his personality (art. 2); that everyone is equal before the law (art. 3); that freedom of belief, conscience, religion, and ideology is inviolable (art. 4); and that everyone has the right to express himself freely in speech, writing, or pictures (art. 5). Here, too, are the basic right of assembly (art. 8), the inviolability of the home (art. 13), and the right of petition (art. 17). In addition, all Germans are granted the right to form associations and societies, especially in the field of industrial relations (art. 9), to make a free choice of their career, place of work, and place of training (art. 12), and to refuse on grounds of conscience to serve in the armed forces (art. 4). The state affords special protection to marriage and the family (art. 6), and it guarantees the right of property and inheritance by providing that there shall be no expropriation except for the common good and against a fair compensation (art. 14). Some other basic rights are conferred elsewhere in the Basic Law, such as the right to a hearing in the courts, the freedom from punishment under retroactive laws, and the freedom from double punishment for a single act (art. 103). There are also provisions on the citizen's rights in relation to arrest and detention (art. 104).

According to art. 1 par. 3 of the Basic Law, these basic rights constitute directly applicable law binding on the legislature, the executive, and the judiciary. However great the majority in Parliament, therefore, the legislature may not enact any law that conflicts with these basic rights; nor may the courts affect them by the form of their proceedings or the substance of their decisions; and the executive is bound to respect these basic rights both in imposing burdens on individuals and in distributing benefits.

It follows that, whenever the outcome of any civil, criminal, or administrative proceeding depends on its validity, the court may inquire whether a law or other act of the public power is unconstitutional and void as infringing a basic right. Usually it will be an interested party that draws the court's attention to the question, but the court must inquire into it *ex officio* if need be. As to the constitutionality of a *law*, a distinction must be drawn: if the court can dispose of any objections to the constitutionality of the law, it must apply the law and make its decision accordingly; but if it is convinced that the objections are sound, it cannot decide that the law is unconstitutional, but must stay the proceedings and submit the question to the Bundesverfassungsgericht (art. 100).[3] The name given to this submission procedure is "Vorlageverfahren"; but there is another, more important, method by which the Bundesverfassungsgericht can be seised of the question whether an official act is constitutional or not: it is open to a citizen to complain directly to the Bundesverfassungsgericht that one of his basic rights has been infringed by an act of the public power. The name given to this remedy is "Verfassungsbeschwerde" (compare art. 93 par. 1 no. 4a).

Several conditions must be satisfied before a Verfassungsbeschwerde is admissible. In particular, the complainant must have exhausted all the other remedies, including litigation, that are open to him in respect of the harmful

[3]This only applies to laws which came into force after the Basic Law: see *BVerfGE* 11, 126. It is open to any court to hold unconstitutional and void any law adopted before the Basic Law and any regulation made by the executive pursuant to delegated legislative power.

official act. Furthermore, a Verfassungsbeschwerde is only admissible if the complainant has *locus standi*: he must be personally affected by the act in question, rather than just a member of the public. If the act in question is a decision of an *administrative authority*, only the person to whom the decision was addressed may complain of it. If the act in question is a *law*, the citizen must in principle wait until a court or administrative authority has applied the law to his disadvantage; only when this has been done, and he has exhausted his legal remedies against the administrative or judicial decision, may the citizen raise a Verfassungsbeschwerde. This, however, does not apply where the mere enactment of the law has "directly and immediately" affected the complainant in his basic rights. It was so held in a case in which the complainant claimed that the Law of 1957 on the Equal Rights of Man and Woman was unconstitutional in so far as it provided that, in cases of a difference of opinion between spouses, the husband was entitled to the final decision. The Bundesverfassungsgericht held that the Verfassungsbeschwerde was admissible because the complainant was "directly and immediately" affected by the law; furthermore, it held that the complaint was justified, because the Basic Law declares that men and women are equal in law (art. 3 par. 2) and there was no adequate justification for giving the husband a superior right in this way.

A Verfassungsbeschwerde may likewise be raised against a *court decision*, for decisions of the courts are acts of the public power as well. Of course, the complainant must allege that the judgment in question misconstrued the Basic Law, but this requirement does not entirely remove the danger that a litigant who is dissatisfied by the judgment of the ultimate civil, criminal, or administrative court may try to use the Verfassungsbeschwerde in order to give himself yet another level of appeal. The Bundesverfassungsgericht has therefore enunciated a number of restrictive tests, notably by insisting that the judgment under attack must contain a "material" or "particularly grave" infringement of the complainant's basic rights.

DONALD P. KOMMERS, THE CONSTITUTIONAL JURISPRUDENCE OF THE FEDERAL REPUBLIC OF GERMANY 67-68, 85-86 (1989)

Federalism and separation of powers are controlling principles of the German Constitution. Both are deeply anchored in Germany's constitutional tradition. What is new about their reincarnation in the Basic Law is their linkage, in Article 20, to the ideas of democracy and justice as well as to the more traditional principle of the rule of law. The adoption of federalism as a master feature of the new polity reflected postwar Germany's determination to avoid the extremes of particularism and authoritarianism. Too little power at the center would inhibit, as it did throughout most of German history, the full flowering of parliamentary democracy, whereas too much power at the center would retard the growth of constitutionalism. Separation of powers, in turn, was expected to moderate the exercise of power at all levels of government and thus prevent the reemergence of political absolutism. Together, fused with democracy and bound by justice, the two principles were calculated to lock liberty and the rule of law in a firm, mutual embrace....

The German states are autonomous governments with their own legislative, executive, and judicial institutions. Like the American states, they share power with the federal government within the same territory and over the same people. But the comparison between the two federal systems ends here. In West Germany the bulk of legislative power is vested in the federal government, while the administration of federal law is the main responsibility of the states. This system of "legislative-executive," or "administrative," federalism, as it is sometimes called, encourages flexibility in adjusting general policy to local conditions. But the system is also very complex. At least forty-three articles of the Constitution deal with relations between state and national governments. Many of these articles, such as those on fiscal administration (Articles 104a and 109) and the execution of federal law (Articles 82-86), contain exceedingly detailed provisions. The specificity of these provisions has invited numerous constitutional amendments over the years, in many instances shifting power from the state to the federal level, usually to meet needs not contemplated by the framers and occasionally in response to Federal Constitutional Court decisions.

The national government's legislative power extends to subjects falling within parliament's "exclusive" or "concurrent" authority. A short list of powers covering such areas as foreign affairs, customs policy, postal and telecommunications services, and federal railroads encompasses the federation's exclusive authority (Article 73). The states may legislate in these fields only to the extent expressly authorized by federal law. Article 74 embraces a list of twenty-seven topics concerning which the federation has concurrent power. These topics include ordinary civil and criminal law, public welfare, most economic matters, and, following a series of amendments over the years, subjects such as environmental protection, production of nuclear energy, and promotion of scientific research. Article 72 permits the states to legislate on these topics "as long as, and to the extent that, the federation does not exercise its right to legislate." Article 72 also limits the federation. Its concurrent authority may be exercised only when there is a *need* for federal regulation because state legislation (1) cannot effectively regulate the matter, (2) might prejudice the interests of other states, or (3) would threaten "the maintenance of legal or economic unity, especially the maintenance of uniformity of living conditions beyond the territory of any one state" (Article 72 [2]).

THE ATOMIC WEAPONS REFERENDA CASE

Federal Constitutional Court of Germany
Judgment No. 14 of 30 July 1958
8 BVerfGE 104 (1958)

English translation published in Kommers, The Constitutional Jurisprudence of the Federal Republic of Germany 86-88 (1989)

[In the mid-1950s equipping the German army with tactical nuclear weapons was at the top of the Adenauer government's military agenda. Germans debated this issue at great length while Social Democrats bitterly opposed the plan for nuclear armaments. In an effort to show that public opinion was against the placement of nuclear weapons on German soil, several Social Democratic-controlled cities and states planned to hold referenda on the issue. The Adenauer government challenged the constitutionality of these referenda as an invasion of the federation's exclusive power over military affairs. This case, brought in the form of an abstract review proceeding, challenged the validity of referenda in Hamburg and Bremen.]

Judgment of the Second Senate

B. III. In a federal state, the constitution of the national state limits the authority of states — and therefore the jurisdiction within which the state organ of the state's body politic can generally become active. The referendum laws of Hamburg and Bremen transgress constitutional limits drawn by the Basic Law.

1. Matters of defense fall within the exclusive jurisdiction of the federation; Article 73, no. 1, of the Basic Law sets out the domain of the legislature, and Articles 65a, 87a, and 87b confirm the domain of the executive (including the government).... Thus the federation has sole and unlimited authority over the task of "defense" as far as it concerns the federal army and its equipment....

Neither the two laws nor the participation of the people of Hamburg and Bremen in the referenda interfere with the federation's exclusive authority so as to determine or technically regulate a matter of defense — for example, equipping the federal army. However, that is not the decisive point. What is decisive is the clearly recognizable purpose of the laws and referenda of Hamburg and Bremen. In the area of defense, especially with respect to equipping the army, the federal government has chosen a particular policy with the *Bundestag*'s approval. The opposition in the *Bundestag* considers this policy wrong and has fought it passionately. The opposition has not been able to win in the *Bundestag* but believes that a majority of the people shares its view. It hopes that political pressure resulting from successful referenda will force the federal government to reverse its policy. Speeches of Social Democrats in the *Bundestag* have clearly expressed this belief....

The clear goal of these two referenda — to force the competent constitutional organs of the federation to change a decision about a matter of defense that these organs consider right — represents an attempted infringement upon the exclusive jurisdiction of the federation. States infringe on the exclusive, autonomous authority of federal organs not only when they try to regulate a matter themselves, but also when they schedule a referendum in an effort to pressure federal organs into changing their decisions. The infringement occurs when a state attempts to form a "will of the state" to oppose the constitutionally formed "will of the federation."

2. [One] reaches the same result if one examines legislative authority to order referenda.... [I]n a merely consultative referendum the people take part in the exercise of state authority just as they do in elections and plebiscites. The general catalog of authority in the Basic Law (Articles 73-75) does not contain any provision relating to the authority of the federation or states to enact electoral laws. Nevertheless, until now it has never been seriously

doubted that the federation cannot pass electoral laws for a state parliamentary election or that a state cannot pass electoral laws for the *Bundestag* election. A state cannot permit either a referendum or a plebiscite on a question belonging exclusively to the competence of the federation or a state referendum on a matter of exclusive federal jurisdiction.

DAVID S. CLARK, THE SELECTION AND ACCOUNTABILITY OF JUDGES IN WEST GERMANY: IMPLEMENTATION OF A *RECHTSSTAAT*, 61 Southern California Law Review 1795, 1808-14 (1988)

The structure of German courts is defined by four characteristics: (1) political division into federal and state courts; (2) appeal through unitary hierarchies; (3) geographical decentralization so that even small towns have civil and criminal courts; and (4) specialization by subject matter.

Figure 6.2 illustrates these characteristics. The first three features also describe the system of courts in the United States, although the federal-state division is almost totally different. In Germany the unitary judicial hierarchies are more thoroughly integrated so that most kinds of litigation may find its way into a federal court of last resort. These federal courts, except for the Federal Constitutional Court (*Bundesverfassungsgericht*), have almost no original jurisdiction; they primarily hear cases appealed from lower state courts. There is nothing comparable to the United States district courts, which have important concurrent subject matter jurisdiction that would allow the same cases to be heard in state trial courts.

The dominance of federal courts in the German system is accentuated because about 95 percent of the law involved in litigation is federal. The five principal codes — civil, commercial, criminal, civil procedure, and criminal procedure — promulgated by the end of the nineteenth century were nationwide in scope. Federal law established the network of state and national courts and today prescribes the status, duties, and compensation for all judges. The responsibility of state governments is to appoint and promote state judges and to provide for their financial support.

The primary distinguishing feature of the German court structure, however, is its specialization by subject matter. The most important jurisdiction in terms of caseload, shown quantitatively in Table 6.5, is the hierarchy of ordinary courts (*ordentliche Gerichte*) for civil and criminal matters. At the bottom local courts (*Amtsgerichte*) operate in towns and cities where single judges handle minor civil cases (up to a value of 5,000 DM), certain agricultural disputes (with two lay judges), and petty criminal and juvenile offenses. Furthermore, they deal with landlord-tenant disputes, the supervision of guardians, testamentary administrators, bankruptcy trustees, and the maintenance of commercial registers and a land register. Since 1977 family cases — involving divorce, marital property, child custody, or alimony — have been heard by a special division in *Amtsgerichte*. From this division, an appeal proceeds directly to a court of appeals rather than to a district court. District courts (*Landgerichte*), in addition to their appellate function for civil and criminal cases from *Amtsgerichte*, are also general jurisdiction first instance

Figure 6.2
Structure of the German Court System

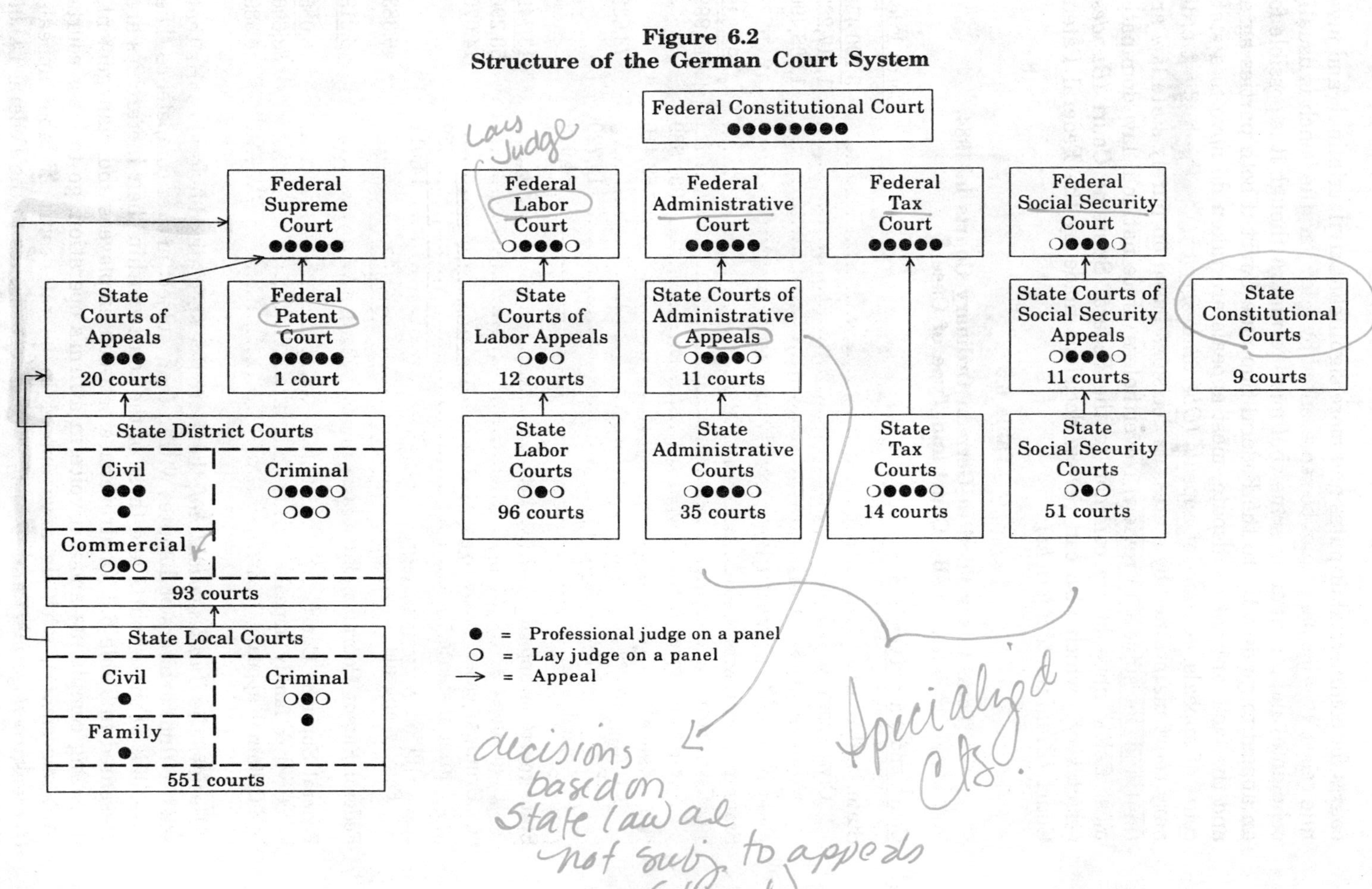

courts for commercial disputes and more significant civil, criminal, and juvenile cases. Parties here must be represented by a lawyer, the bench is usually collegiate, and procedure is somewhat more formal. Although it is possible for an appeal to go directly to the Federal Supreme Court if both parties agree and the facts are not in dispute, most appeals are taken de novo to a state court of appeals. A court of appeals (*Oberlandesgericht*) is the highest ordinary court maintained by states; its decisions based on purely state law are final and not subject to review. Nevertheless, since national law dominates most fields, appeals are common to the Federal Supreme Court (*Bundesgerichtshof*), which also can review decisions made by the Federal Patent Court (*Bundespatentgericht*).

Table 6.5

Total Cases Filed in German Ordinary Courts in 1984, By Court and Type of Case

Court and Case Type		Cases Filed
State local courts		3,100,456
Civil cases		1,217,282
Criminal cases		1,508,490
Family cases		374,684
State district courts		492,632
Civil cases		413,999
First instance	331,589	
Appeal	82,410	
Criminal cases		78,633
First instance	13,720	
Appeal	64,913	
State courts of appeal		113,749
Civil appeals		53,296
Criminal cases		14,070
First instance	59	
Appeal	14,011	
Family appeals		46,383
Federal Patent Court		6,219
Federal Supreme Court		8,085
Civil & family appeals		3,696
Criminal appeals		4,389

Besides the *Bundesgerichtshof*, there are five specialized federal courts that are the final arbiters of disputes within their subject matter competence. The caseloads of these courts and those of the courts within their hierarchies are presented in Table 6.6. Controversies between employees and management, including complaints about a voice in a firm's operation, go to labor courts (*Arbeitsgerichte*), with de novo appeal to a state court of labor appeals (*Landesarbeitsgericht*) and final appeal on legal issues to the Federal Labor Court (*Bundesarbeitsgericht*). Lay judges, selected from labor and management groups, vote on a court's decision.

Table 6.6

Total Cases Filed in German Specialized Courts in 1984, By Subject Matter and Court

Subject Matter and Court	Cases Filed
Labor cases	
State labor courts	361,435
State courts of labor appeals	17,483
Federal Labor Court	674
Administrative cases	
State administrative courts	129,107
State courts of administrative appeals	54,771
Federal Administrative Court	3,442
Tax cases	
State tax courts	61,843
Federal Tax Court	3,100
Social security cases	
State social security courts	184,499
State courts of social security appeals	18,483
Federal Social Security Court	824
Constitutional cases	
State constitutional courts	226
Federal Constitutional Court	3,484

A series of administrative courts adjudicate public law controversies. When one has a complaint about executive action or inaction that has not been satisfactorily resolved with an agency, a lawsuit may be filed in an administrative court (*Verwaltungsgericht*), appealed de novo to a state court of administrative appeals (*Oberverwaltungsgericht*), and finally appealed on the legal issues to the Federal Administrative Court (*Bundesverwaltungsgericht*). A parallel system of courts exists for social insurance and other welfare matters culminating in the Federal Social Security Court (*Bundessozialgericht*) that, like the high labor court, uses two lay judges on its five judge panels. For tax litigation, there is a two tier system with a right of appeal to the Federal Tax Court (*Bundesfinanzgericht*).

Complicating this system of courts, a number of specialized jurisdictions is interwoven into the network variously denominated as courts, chambers, senates, or jurisdictions. These judicial bodies adjudicate questions concerning discipline and personnel in the military, judiciary, and civil service as well as discipline and ethics among certain professionals, such as lawyers, notaries, medical doctors, dentists, pharmacists, architects, and tax consultants. These bodies normally use lay judges together with career judges, and appeal usually runs either to a special senate in the Federal Supreme Court (for judges, lawyers, notaries, and tax consultants) or to a special senate in the Federal Administrative Court (for civil servants and soldiers).

At the apex of this system of courts and jurisdictions in terms of prestige and ultimate authority is the Federal Constitutional Court (*Bundesver-*

fassungsgericht). This Court only adjudicates issues of national constitutional law; it is the guardian of institutional boundaries and the protector of fundamental human rights. Individuals (or juridical persons) may lodge constitutional complaints (*Verfassungsbeschwerden*) before the Court alleging that governmental acts — legislative, executive, or judicial — violate their basic rights. This procedure constitutes about 97 percent of the Court's filings. The remaining caseload consists of issues referred to the Court either by other courts, which have concluded that they cannot decide cases until certain constitutional questions have been resolved, or by certain federal institutions such as the *Bundestag* or by state governments that desire rulings on constitutional matters. Each of the states, except for Berlin and Schleswig-Holstein, also has a constitutional court that hears cases raising purely state constitutional issues.

NOTES AND QUESTIONS

1. Was the German reunification in 1990 an accession or a merger? What role did article 23 of the Basic Law serve? For a thorough study of the issues, see Peter E. Quint, *The Constitutional Law of German Unification*, 50 Md. L. Rev. 475-631 (1991). For a discussion of legal institutions and the legal professions during the transitional phase, see Daniel J. Meador, *Transition in the German Legal Order: East Back to West, 1990-91*, 15 B.C. Int'l & Comp. L. Rev. 283 (1992).

2. The German Basic Law is unusual in that parts of it may not be amended. Why did the framers in 1949 place this restriction on politicians and in fact on the German people?

3. Germany is a federal republic with 16 states. By contrast France has a unitary political structure in which the central government substantially defines the powers of local government. Where federalism has been adopted, the idea is to seek an equilibrium between unity and diversity, to achieve centralized authority for the nation as a whole without sacrificing regional cultures or institutions. Did the federal model serve Germany well for the reunification process in 1990?

The United States is considered a strong federal system since local political units have substantial power vis-à-vis the national government. Switzerland is a good European example of this situation. Alternatively, some commentators classify Germany as a quasi-federal nation, since the autonomy of the states is reduced, although significant cooperation is necessary between the federal and state governments to implement "administrative federalism."

What limits are there on the German federal government in the realms of legislation, administration, and adjudication? For an excellent treatment, see Philip M. Blair, Federalism and Judicial Review in West Germany (1981).

4. Germany has a parliamentary type of executive. The chief executive officer is thus not the president but the chancellor, chosen by the federal parliament (Bundestag). The federal government consists of the chancellor and 16 ministers, who run the various departments. Both the Bundestag, with 662 deputies elected in 1990, and the federal council (Bundesrat), with representatives from the state governments, participate in federal lawmaking. Describe the relationship between the Bundestag and the Bundesrat. How does it support federalism?

See David P. Currie, *Separation of Powers in the Federal Republic of Germany*, 41 Am. J. Comp. L. 201 (1993); Nevil Johnson, State and Government in the Federal Republic of Germany: The Executive at Work (2d ed. 1983); Uwe Thaysen, Roger H. Davidson & Robert Gerald Livingston, eds., The U.S. Congress and the German *Bundestag*: Comparisons of Democratic Processes (1990).

5. In the *Atomic Weapons Referenda Case*, the Hamburg and Bremen referenda were clearly intended to be nonbinding. In the Constitutional Court's discussion of the federalism issue, what constitutional value from an American's perspective seems to be missing? Should the states as a policy matter have greater say regarding the placement within their boundaries of army units with tactical nuclear weapons?

6. Do you find any significant differences between the German list of basic rights and the constitutional liberties and rights recognized in the United States?

7. The Constitutional Court, which hears disputes involving basic rights, has a large caseload. See Table 6.6, *supra*. Its justiciability rules, finality doctrine, and other norms limiting access are liberal compared to the U.S. Supreme Court. What is the difference between the procedures of *Vorlageverfahren* and *Verfassungsbeschwerde*?

8. Compare the judicial organization and jurisdictions of the German courts with those of the French courts. What are the major similarities and differences? See Figures 6.1 and 6.2, *supra*.

9. Should the German judicial system of specialization by subject matter be imported to the United States? What would be the advantages and disadvantages? *See* John Langbein, *The German Advantage in Civil Procedure*, 52 U. Chi. L. Rev. 823, 851-52 (1985).

10. For more on the German legal system, see Nigel G. Foster, German Law & Legal System (1993).

3. ITALY

MAURO CAPPELLETTI, JOHN HENRY MERRYMAN & JOSEPH M. PERILLO, THE ITALIAN LEGAL SYSTEM: AN INTRODUCTION 53-54, 56-58, 60-70, 72-83 (1967)

Introduction. Italy is a relative newcomer to the family of nations. Before 1861, Italy was a conglomeration of petty states, dismissed by the European powers as nothing more than a geographical expression. Since the downfall of Rome — with a few parentheses — Italian territory had been fragmented into numerous states, often existing in some form of dependence on non-Italian rulers....

The formation of the Italian state in 1861 (with Venice, Rome, Trent, and Trieste not yet included) did not unify Italian society. Disunity continued in a different framework. Elections were sometimes rigged, and violent demonstrations, although always kept in hand, showed a deep social malaise. World War I exhausted Italy economically, killed 600,000 of her men, and brought little reward at the peace table. The postwar struggles between Marxist, reform, clerical, liberal (conservative), and nationalist groups disrupted state action and provided the opportunity for a fascist coup.

The downfall of fascism, brought about by the Allied armies in conjunction with widespread popular uprisings in northern and central Italy, was the occasion for a coalition of parties, dominated by the Church-inspired Christian Democrats, ranging from the Communists to the conservative Liberals. Fascists and Monarchists were excluded. In retrospect, the degree of sound compromise that went into the 1948 Constitution, adopted by a national convention representing such a spectrum of parties, is striking. It can only be explained by one of the central facts of Italian history — the resistance. Over 100,000 Italians died in the fight against fascism, more persons than the allies lost in the long Italian campaign. The ideal of anti-fascism and the memories of a common struggle against the fascist regime temporarily overcame ideological difficulties, but the lack of a national consensus on fundamental political principles has prevented the implementation of many constitutional provisions. However, despite the lack of a national consensus, viable constitutional government survives and is slowly making progress....

Fundamental Provisions of the Constitution. The Constitution of January 1, 1948, adopted certain fundamental principles that have traditionally been recognized by liberal states. Separation of powers, checks and balances, procedural due process, equal protection of the laws, universal suffrage, freedom of expression, association and assembly, freedom from unreasonable search and seizure, freedom to travel, and other fundamental liberties find expression in the Constitution. Judicial review of legislation, not traditionally recognized as a fundamental principle of government outside the Western Hemisphere, was also adopted....

Social goals have also been incorporated into the Italian Constitution. Paragraph 2 of article 3 provides: "It shall be the task of the Republic to remove obstacles of an economic or social nature that, by restricting in practice the freedom and equality of citizens, impede the full development of the human personality and the effective participation of all workers in the political, economic, and social organization of the country." The right to employment, free medical aid to the indigent, eight years of compulsory free education, paid vacations for all workers, the right to strike and to form trade unions, and other social goals are proclaimed.

Some of the provisions of the Italian Constitution are said to be enforceable (*precettive*) and others to be programmatic (*programmatiche*). Many of the social goals of the Constitution impose a duty upon Parliament to act, but create no legally enforceable right in the individual. Consequently, for example, the right to employment, guaranteed by the Constitution, has been held not to create the right of unemployed individuals to undertake public works not authorized by competent public organs. Thus, in a sense, the "right" to employment is merely a platform plank elevated to constitutional status. Despite often unwieldy political coalitions, however, the programmatic provisions are slowly being acted upon....

Disputes on church-state relations still plague Italian politics. The Constitution incorporates by reference the Lateran agreements entered into by Italy and the Vatican in 1929, which place the Roman Catholic Church in a privileged position.

[A concordat ratified in 1985 between Italy and the Vatican modified some of these privileges. Signed by the socialist prime minister of Italy, Bettino Craxi, and the Vatican secretary of state, it instituted the following changes. First, Roman Catholicism would no longer be deemed the state religion of Italy. Second, Vatican annulment of marriages would be subject to review by an Italian court if one of the spouses so requested. Third, church marriages would not be automatically recognized. And fourth, religious instruction in state schools would be optional and Catholic schools would be administered with "full freedom."]

The state exercises certain controls over the Church. It has a limited power to veto the appointment of bishops and parochial pastors. Acquisition of real property by, and donations and testamentary gifts to, churches and religious organizations are contingent upon state approval.

Freedom is guaranteed to all other religions, and organized non-Catholic religions do find toleration. Article 8 of the Constitution provides that relations between the state and non-Catholic religions are to be regulated by laws based on agreements entered into by the state and representatives of those religions. Evangelical preachers who are not ministers of religions that have reached agreements with the state have sometimes been hampered in the performance of missionary work....

Local Government. Government in Italy is largely based on the centralized system instituted in France by Napoleon. Centralized government was favored and implemented by the leaders of Italian unification, who feared divisive regionalism, and was further extended by fascist leaders who feared any opposition to dictatorial control. The provinces and communes of Italy are not to any large degree autonomous.

The Constitution grants a greater degree of autonomy to the twenty regional governments of Italy. [By 1975 the national government had enacted laws and decrees to implement this constitutional scheme throughout Italy. The Constitution] also invests the regions with legislative competence, so long as their legislation does not conflict with the national interest or the interests of another region, in such matters as urban planning and the promotion and regulation of tourism and the hotel industry. In addition, local public works, hunting and fishing, artisans, and local police are to be placed under regional control.

Regional government is vested in a single-chamber legislative council, which elects an executive committee whose president is also the regional president. The acts of the region are closely controlled. The central government assigns a commissioner to the region to protect national interests. Under certain circumstances the commissioner may veto administrative acts of the regional government. Parliament may quash regional laws that conflict with the interests of the state or of another region, while the Constitutional Court may quash regional laws that violate the Constitution.

The basic working units of local government today are the approximately 8,000 communes. Some communes consist of a large city, such as Rome, others may be a collection of rural hamlets and their countrysides, but all have the same governmental structure. A communal council is chosen by popular election. The council then elects an executive committee and a mayor....

Most of the functions of communes are delineated by state laws. Communes are entrusted with zoning power, police powers in matters of food marketing, and traffic control. Some communes have assumed ownership of utilities. The prefect has wide powers to prevent communes from undertaking activities or entering into contracts that are either illegal or undesirable. In many cases he has the power to substitute his judgment for that of the commune. He is also in charge of the major police units. His activities, in turn, are subject to scrutiny in Rome....

The provinces are larger geographical units than the communes, but have narrower functions. Local elections provide a provincial council, which in turn selects a provincial executive committee, one of whose members is designated provincial president. The provinces maintain provincial roads, undertake certain public works, and engage in some welfare functions. The prefect has wide supervisory powers over provincial government, similar to those he exercises over communal government.

Governmental Participation in the Economy. The government of Italy, from its unification until the fascist coup, was dominated by the Liberal Party. This party espoused economic policies that, roughly speaking, find their American counterparts in the policies of Hamilton, rather than in those of Jefferson. Industry was protected and supported by the state.

In the immediate pre-fascist period, the government began to purchase shares of stock in private corporations. During the fascist era, a governmental corporation, the Institute for Industrial Recovery (IRI — Istituto per la Ricostruzione Industriale), purchased a controlling interest in many large corporations, particularly those that had fared badly during the depression and whose survival was considered essential to the national economy. In many instances, the old management was retained, and shares of these corporations continued to be traded on stock exchanges.

Before the creation of the Republic, Italy, almost by accident and with little ideological stimulus, developed a mixed economy. The Constitution of 1948, drafted, it will be recalled, by a coalition representing conservative, center, and leftist parties, institutionalized a compromise between liberty for private economic initiative and state ownership of the means of production. Freedom for private enterprise is proclaimed, but state regulation is permitted. Economic planning to direct private enterprise toward social ends is made the duty of the state, and the unlimited right of the state to own property seems to be proclaimed. However, the state may expropriate only those enterprises that are monopolistic or relate to essential public services or sources of energy.

The post-fascist government has continued the existence of IRI, which is actively engaged, directly or through holding companies, in the production of iron and steel, autos (Alfa-Romeo), machinery, and ships. It also controls shipping lines, telephone communications, toll roads, most steel production, major banks, the airline Alitalia, and the Italian television network....

A ministry, the Ministero delle Partecipazioni Statali, has been created to supervise industries in which the state has an interest, and to coordinate their activities with overall governmental policy....

Despite these insufficient controls, it is widely believed that the Italian bureaucracy stifles industry and commerce. That the government itself realizes this is shown by the institution of a ministry of bureaucratic reform. Many permits, licenses, and authorizations are required, and often the bureaus that issue them do not effectively control or regulate anything. Most permits must come from Rome, and are often received only after delays, frustrations, and perhaps invitations for bribery. Big business can go to the top of the administrative hierarchy for quick results, but much of the Italian economy is in the craft and entrepreneurial tradition of individual enterprise.

Italian industry is concentrated in the North, whereas southern Italy and the islands of Sardinia and Sicily still have a primitive economic structure. One of the keystones of governmental policy has been to induce industry to locate in the South and the islands....

Parliament. At the center of the Italian governmental structure is Parliament, the only national organ selected by popular suffrage. It selects the Chief of State and approves the selection of the head of the government. Consequently, neither of these personages may claim to represent the national will in opposition to Parliament.

Parliament is bicameral. Both the [630 seat] Chamber of Deputies and the [315 seat] Senate are elected by proportional representation [for one-fourth of their seats, with the remainder chosen directly by the voters. Each chamber has equal powers.]... [M]embers of both houses serve for five years, unless new elections are called sooner....

Although the enactment of legislation is the principal function of Parliament, it also, in joint session, elects the President of the Republic, five judges to the Constitutional Court, and seven members to the Superior Council of Magistrature. When electing the President of the Republic, delegates from the regions join Parliament as electors. Although the ministers are appointed by the President of the Republic, Parliament controls their installation and continuation in office by votes of confidence and no confidence. Investigatory and watchdog committees check the government's activities, and ministers are subjected to regular question periods. Parliament may indict the President of the Republic for high treason or for attempting to overthrow the Constitution. It may indict a minister for crimes committed in the scope of his functions. No member of Parliament may be prosecuted for any crime without the authorization of the house to which he belongs.

Legislation may be introduced into Parliament by any senator or deputy, by the Council of Ministers, by certain independent state agencies, or by the petition of 50,000 voters. Among the major liberal democracies of Europe, only Italy has no limitation on private-member bills. A substantial number of laws originate in this way. Many of these bills are presented on behalf of small vested interests, which explains the excessive fragmentation of Italian laws.

Both houses of Parliament are organized into standing committees. These are selected on the basis of proportional representation of the political groups represented in Parliament. Usually, the presiding officer of the house, upon introduction of a bill, assigns it to the competent standing committee, instructing the committee either to report the bill out to the house with its recommendations, or to take final legislative action for the house. The power of a committee to take final action on a bill is unique to Italy. Before and during the fascist regime, governments often issued decree-laws to compensate for Parliament's inability to act swiftly in matters of urgency, and it was partly through the abuse of its power to issue decrees that the fascist government achieved its dictatorship. The framers of the republican Constitution invested legislative powers in the committees to speed legislative action, thereby lessening the necessity for governmental decrees....

Article 75 of the Constitution provides that laws or decrees having the force of law may be repealed by popular referendum. Upon the petition of 500,000 voters or five regional councils, a referendum may be called to repeal legislation on any subject except tax and budgetary laws, laws concerning amnesties and pardons, and laws authorizing the ratification of treaties.

[Implemented by statute in 1970, the first referendum was an attempt by the Christian Democratic party to repeal the recent legislation permitting divorce. The referendum, held in 1974, was defeated when it obtained only 39 percent of the vote.]...

The Council of Ministers. The Council of Ministers, which is also known as the Government or the Cabinet, is responsible to Parliament. After a national election or a governmental resignation, the President of the Republic consults with political leaders and selects the Prime Minister, or, as he is usually called, the President of the Council of Ministers. The person so selected in turn selects the ministers whom he wishes to serve on the Council. These designees, who are usually members of Parliament, are then invested by the president of the Republic....

The realities, however, are somewhat different from the constitutional procedure just outlined. Governments rise and fall by decisions made within the central committees and congresses of political parties and by complex negotiations between parties. The President of the Republic usually does little more than catalyze the negotiations. Parliament, in a sense, acts as a rubber stamp. Many parliamentarians, however, have leading roles in the party committees and congresses.

Although the President of the Council of Ministers is charged with the duty of coordinating policy among Council members, he is often unable to control his ministers. Coalition governments have been the rule, and the Christian Democratic Party, which has supplied [most] prime ministers since December 1945, is itself a coalition of various currents of opinion....

Control of a ministry by its minister, rather than by the Prime Minister, produces a significant degree of autonomy within each ministry. Since ministers are frequently changed, the permanent bureaucracy, "overstaffed, underpaid, inefficient and insubordinate," functions with considerable autonomy.

The Council of Ministers has the power to initiate legislation in Parliament. In addition, Parliament may delegate to the Council the power to issue legislative decrees (*decreti legislativi*) that have the same effect as laws enacted by Parliament. In delegating this power, Parliament must set the general principles and criteria to be followed in drafting the decree, delimit its subject matter, and limit the delegation to a specific period of time. The Council of Ministers, in extraordinary cases of necessity and urgency, may issue decree-laws (*decreti legge*), which must be presented to Parliament for ratification on the day of issuance. A decree-law loses its effect, retroactively to the date of its issuance, if not approved by Parliament within sixty days. Legislative decrees are issued quite frequently, [and in recent years the number of decree-laws has increased. In the interest of "governability," decree-laws are sometimes even reissued when their conversion into law by Parliament proves impossible within sixty days. Both delegated legislative decrees and decree-laws must be issued with the signature of the President of the Republic to be effective. Upon promulgation they are published with an annual sequential number as *decreti del Presidente della Repubblica* (D.P.R.).]

The President of the Republic. The President of the Republic is elected for a seven-year term by a joint session of Parliament and by electors appointed by regional councils....

The role of the President of the Republic is not rigidly defined. He is nominally invested with broad powers. For example, he must give his authorization before the ministers may present a bill to Parliament. He promulgates the laws, ratifies treaties, sets the elections, commands the armed forces, grants pardons and commutations, may call Parliament into special session, and dissolve the national and regional parliaments....

The present concept of the President is that of an elder statesman, standing above the clamor of political controversy, a symbol of national unity and balance. If today a President wanted to wrest from the government the actual rather than symbolic exercise of all his powers, he would be in danger of violating the Constitution and could be indicted before the Constitutional Court; but in future decades the seeds of presidential power may find fertile soil for development....

The Constitutional Court. Judicial review of the constitutionality of laws is new to Italy. Before 1948, the Constitution of Italy was the Statuto, granted in 1848 by Carlo Alberto, King of Sardinia and Piedmont. Because it could be overridden by simple act of Parliament or by Royal Decree, the Statuto was the type of constitution that is called "flexible." No court could refuse to enforce, or strike down, a law as unconstitutional. Such an attempt would have been regarded as a presumptuous violation of the principle of separation of powers....

The present Constitution, which can be overridden only by a special amending procedure, is said to be "rigid." The constituent assembly that approved the Constitution considered and rejected the American system under which an ordinary court can, under the rule of *Marbury v. Madison,* refuse to apply a law that it deems unconstitutional. Since in Italy stare decisis is not a recognized principle, the highest ordinary court (Corte di cassazione) might find a law to be unconstitutional, and lower courts or the highest court itself in subsequent decisions might refuse to follow the decision. Consequently, a Constitutional Court with power to abrogate a law *erga omnes* was felt to be necessary. It was also considered desirable to concentrate in one court all constitutional matters, including the power to adjudicate controversies on the division of powers among the supreme organs of the state as well as among the regions and between the state and the regions, to decide the admissibility of referenda, to try the President of the Republic for high treason or an attempt to overthrow the Constitution, and to try a minister for crimes committed within the scope of his functions.

In creating a separate Constitutional Court, the framers of the Constitution also took into account that the ordinary judiciary had neither the prestige nor the importance of the American judiciary, and moreover that the incumbent Italian judges had been selected, trained, and promoted under the fascist system and were unlikely to interpret the Constitution in the progressive spirit intended by the framers. Traditional notions of separation of powers also may have played a role. There was some feeling that the Constitutional Court was to be not a judicial, but a legislative, control body; however, this theory has lost general acceptance.

The Constitutional Court consists of fifteen judges who serve for [one nine-year term]. Five are chosen by the President of the Republic, five by Parliament in joint session, and five by the judges of the highest ordinary and administrative courts. Judges of these high courts, law professors, and lawyers who have practiced for twenty years are eligible....

The Constitutional Court may not rule on the constitutionality of a law except in a concrete case. In any civil, criminal, or administrative proceeding, a party or the court in which the case is pending has the right to refer a constitutional issue to the Constitutional Court if the court in which the proceeding unfolds finds the issue relevant and not patently groundless....

Actions also may be initiated in the Constitutional Court by the state against a region, or by a region against the state or against another region, on the charge of invasion of the plaintiff's competence. The Court may adjudicate conflicts of competence between the fundamental organs of the state, such as the President of the Republic, Parliament, the Council of Ministers, the Corte di cassazione, and the Constitutional Court itself....

The Civil and Criminal Courts. Italy has a unified national court system. No regional, provincial, or municipal courts exist. The ordinary courts, which exercise civil and criminal jurisdiction, are the *conciliatori, pretori,* tribunals, courts of appeal, and Corte di cassazione.

At the bottom of the pyramidal organization of the ordinary courts are the *conciliatori,* competent only in some civil cases that involve claims under [1,000,000 lire. There is no appeal, but a petition of cassation goes directly to the Court of Cassation.] Parties may agree to have a *conciliatore* mediate any case, regardless of its value. The *conciliatori,* who serve for prestige and in fulfillment of a civic duty, are not paid and are not necessarily law school graduates.

The *pretori* ... serve as courts of first instance, with some exceptions, in cases involving claims under [5,000,000 lire] and in certain other cases specifically provided by law [such as possessory actions, and for some provisional remedies]. They are competent in criminal matters for which the penalty is three years or less of imprisonment. They, like the *conciliatori,* adjudicate alone. Though higher courts use jurymen in certain criminal cases, in the courts of the *pretori* no jurymen sit. There are about [900] pretorial districts. Except for a limited number of honorary appointees, the *pretori,* like the judges of the higher courts, are career members of the judiciary.

The [159] tribunals hear civil and criminal appeals on questions of fact and law from the *pretori*. They are competent in all civil cases that are not within the competence of the *pretori* or *conciliatori,* and are exclusively competent in tax cases, in matters that concern the status and capacity of persons or honorific rights, in proceedings to test the authenticity of a document, in cases having an undeterminable monetary value, and in proceedings to levy execution on immovable property. Three judges sit on the panel that adjudicates a case.

Tribunals are often divided into sections that in practice specialize in particular subject matters. In addition, the law provides for certain specialized sections for cases dealing with minors, certain sharecropping matters, and other agrarian problems; laymen serve on these cases, not as jurymen, but as "popular" or "expert" judges, deciding along with ordinary judges issues of law and fact.

Criminal cases that are not within the competence of the *pretori* are allocated to the tribunals and the courts of assizes. The courts of assizes are now organized as specialized sections of the tribunals; nevertheless, there is a division of competence between the tribunals as tribunals and the courts of assizes. Many of the most serious criminal cases are heard by the courts of assizes. Here, two ordinary judges and six laymen, acting as "popular" judges, sit on the bench for a case. All eight vote on the facts and law. A majority vote convicts; a tie vote acquits.

The [24] courts of appeal, sitting in panels of five, hear appeals on questions of fact and law from the tribunals. They have limited competence as courts of first instance: they alone may give a foreign judgment domestic effect or approve a consensual adoption. Courts of appeal of assizes, in panels of two ordinary judges and six "popular" judges, hear appeals on questions of law and fact from the courts of assizes and are organized as special sections of the courts of appeal....

The highest of the ordinary courts is the Corte di cassazione, often called the Supreme Court, which may either uphold or quash decisions of the lower courts. Since there is a constitutional right to obtain the review of all provisional orders relating to personal liberties and of all judgments of the ordinary courts, the Corte di cassazione has a heavy work load. It is divided into a number of criminal and civil sections. A panel of [five] judges sits on each case. In an attempt to maintain uniformity of interpretation of the laws, united civil and criminal sections, composed of [a total of nine judges from] the regular sections, hear and determine cases that involve particularly controversial issues.

Administrative Courts.... Special courts have been instituted to review administrative acts, and the ordinary courts may also entertain certain actions against the state or a public body. The jurisdictions of the administrative courts and the ordinary courts are related to the dichotomy between the Italian concepts of "rights" and "legitimate interests." A right is defined as an interest directly guaranteed by law to an individual, whereas a legitimate interest is defined as "an individual interest closely connected with a public interest and protected by law only through the legal protection of the latter." For example, if an individual enters into a contract with a public body, the contract gives him contractual *rights*. Redress for breach of the contract may be obtained in the ordinary courts since they are vested with jurisdiction when an individual's rights are violated. If, however, the state requests competitive bids from the public for the formation of a contract, an individual who is unlawfully excluded from competing for the contract cannot show that a right has been violated. Italian law deems that the public competition was opened in the public interest and not for the benefit of individual bidders. A qualified individual, however, has a legitimate *interest* in competing and can seek relief in the administrative courts.

In an action against the state in the ordinary courts, only declaratory judgments and judgments for a sum of money may be obtained. The administrative court may vacate the administrative act attacked and sometimes may substitute its own....

In order to reduce uncertainty, a large number of the cases that involve mixed questions of rights and legitimate interests [e.g., public employment issues] have been invested exclusively in the administrative courts. The Corte di cassazione, the highest civil court, determines, in the last resort, issues of jurisdiction.

[Regional administrative tribunals undertake within their jurisdiction the first instance judicial review of administrative acts. Created in 1971, each *tribunale amministrativo regionale* (TAR) has a president and at least five judges. It sits in panels of three judges. In addition to a tribunal's exclusive jurisdiction (e.g., public employment contracts) and its general jurisdiction over legitimate interests, it also has the power to enforce an ordinary court money judgment against the public administration when the government will not voluntarily pay.

The Council of State (Consiglio di Stato), along the lines of the French model, has both judicial and consultative functions. The judicial functions are carried out by three sections, allocated according to the ministries from which an administrative act under attack originated. Each section adjudicates with a collegiate panel of seven members. A plenary session exists to resolve conflicts among the three sections. Its membership includes the president of the Council and four councilors from each of the sections. Today the primary judicial role of the Council of State is to hear appeals from the TARs. In addition, it has exclusive first instance jurisdiction over a few specified matters.]

Independent of the Council of State is the Court of Accounts (Corte dei conti), which is primarily concerned with the handling of public money. It hears cases against public officials involving their management of public funds. Six of its eight judicial sections in Rome are concerned with pension claims.

FREDERIC SPOTTS & THEODOR WIESER, ITALY: A DIFFICULT DEMOCRACY 158-61 (1986)

Despite its difficulties, the Italian *magistratura* remains a select profession, a career service with entry through a stiff annual public examination. Magistrates are the elite of the civil service and again stand at the top of the government wage scale. In contrast to the United States, Britain, and many other countries, the Italian judiciary comprises not only judges but also investigating magistrates and prosecuting attorneys. In other words the functions of a grand jury, district attorney, and trial judge are all exercised within the same organization. Entrants, usually fresh from a university law school, serve an initial period of internship with either a judge or a prosecutor. From then on they normally remain in one or the other branch of the judiciary. Appointed for life, magistrates are responsible only to the Superior Judicial Council [Consiglio Superiore della Magistratura] and therefore have a great latitude of personal discretion. They are promoted by seniority throughout their career; transfer, by the Superior Judicial Council, requires their agreement. The purpose of establishing a separate and autonomous judiciary with its members subject only to other magistrates was to create a system that would be both independent of government and immune from politics. The postwar history of the Italian judiciary is essentially a struggle over this ideal.

Today the principal defect of the Italian judiciary is precisely its immersion in politics and ideology. The problem began in the Fascist era when the Piedmontese model of a politically neutral judiciary was increasingly compromised. By 1945 Italy was in the hands of a judiciary that was deeply conservative in its approach to the law and the role of the courts. The senior judges, being at the top of a tightly organized judicial system, tacitly imposed their own points of view on the new judges as they rose through the ranks. But when they lost control of promotions, they lost their hold on the subordinate judges. A sense of intellectual liberation swept through the judiciary. Younger judges in particular began to challenge both their superiors' authority and their theory of law.

This disagreement coincided with the wave of student and worker unrest in 1968-69, which radicalized a large number of judges, especially the younger ones in the North, driving many of them to the extreme left. By the end of the 1960s the judiciary was split from top to bottom over issues as basic as the nature of law and the role of judges. The consequence was a political polarization that fractured the unity of the judiciary and has impeded the administration of justice. Probably a majority of judges adhere to the conventional view that the operation of the courts is essentially mechanical rather than discretionary. Even so, the judiciary as a whole is deeply divided over how laws are to be interpreted, how old statutes and the new constitution are to be reconciled, and the extent to which legislation should be molded to meet the changing needs of society.

Conservative and right-wing judges have explicitly endorsed the most restrictive view of the judicial role. But in practice they impose their own conservative ideology on the law and its application. In the past some of them have regularly banned books, plays, films, and magazines and have taken action against those whose mode of social behavior — the wearing of bikinis at the beach, for instance — they found distasteful....

For the leftist judges, organized in a group called the "democratic magistrates," the use of ideology goes even further and is explicit. These judges openly, indeed proudly, acknowledge their ideological commitment, occasionally even expressing it on cases that are *sub judice*. For them, the courts are an instrument in the class struggle. In their view, as summed up by a noted jurist, Federico Mancini, "All laws should be interpreted with this yardstick: partisanship is a virtue and neutrality a misconception or a fraud; so is independence; a judiciary cloaking itself with these sham values is a servant of power and ought to be told as much; judges must defend the oppressed and the downtrodden, cooperate with the labor movement, act as a countervailing force *vis-à-vis* the political and industrial government."

It was in this spirit that many younger judges, conducting political crusades from the bench, earned the title *pretori d'assalto,* "fighting judges." In their hands the social provisions of the constitution, up to then considered platitudes about economic equality and social justice, were treated as an enforceable legal code. In labor disputes these judges almost invariably decided in favor of workers and unions. "For an employer," Mancini remarked, "to emerge from their hands as a winner was harder than for a camel to go through the eye of a needle." At the same time they were also responsible for much judicial legislation by establishing new standards of environmental protection against industrial pollution and real estate speculation, outlawing food adulteration, and the like. In seeking to be the country's social conscience, these judges hoped to revolutionize the role of the Italian judiciary. In the course of the 1970s some "democratic magistrates" became increasingly radical, occasionally denouncing other judges as "trucklers to the bourgeoisie" and appearing at public meetings at the side of extremist leaders. Ultimately a few even became involved with the Red Brigades.

Given the pronounced politicization of every other area of Italian public life and the ideological cleavages in the country, the political infection of the judiciary was probably unavoidable and once it occurred was destined to be more virulent than anywhere else in Western Europe. Since the mid-1970s, it has gradually subsided. The old right-wing judges have now retired. The "democratic magistrates," splintered by repeated secessions, have been stepping back from political causes. And the Communist party, seeking to enter the government after 1976, told the Communists on the bench to leave social reform to the party in parliament.

But political differences remain and have damaged the various judicial organizations. The National Association of Magistrates, the judges' professional organization to which all judges traditionally belonged, was already in the hands of the younger judges by 1969. The senior judges walked out a short time later and formed their own strongly conservative body, the Union of Italian Magistrates, which they dissolved in 1979. The political factions in the association itself hardened over time into groups as distinct and hostile as those among the political parties. Of those identifiable in the early 1980s, roughly 37 percent belonged to the conservative "independent magistrates," 45 percent to the center-left "unity for the constitution," and the remainder to the "democratic magistrates."

Inevitably these divisions have been carried into the Superior Judicial Council, subverting its political autonomy and neutrality. Even at the best of times the council's independence was far from immaculate. The ten members appointed by parliament have in fact always been selected by the parties, with four falling to the Christian Democrats, three to the Communists, two to the Socialists, and one to the lay parties. After the judges themselves became politically factionalized, the remaining twenty appointments — chosen by the judiciary — were also subject to ideological selection, each faction voting for its own adherents. In practice this works out to the Christian Democrats and Communists having a decisive voice in selecting members of the council. And that is only the beginning. Judges argue long and hard to ensure that the panels of the courts are formed in accord with factional divisions. Assignments to the courts themselves — unlike promotions, which are automatic, based on seniority — are also subject to political considerations. The result is a political spoils process that infects the judiciary as it does other public institutions. Even the council's disciplinary function has been compromised; by appealing to their faction for support, offenders are almost always absolved.

The judicial system is also prey to a different type of problem: external pressures, political and other, that are occasionally brought to bear both on individual magistrates and on the *pubblico ministero,* "district attorney's office." Whether these influences come from the government, a political party, or some group or individual, the intent is to cajole or intimidate magistrates into redirecting their activities or dropping a case. The atmosphere in which some magistrates work can at times be tense and dangerous, and many an individual prosecutor has shown tremendous moral and physical courage in the face of threats and blandishments. Others have given in. Three cases in Western Sicily illustrate the situation. Giangiacomo Montalto, deputy district attorney in Trapani, was murdered in 1983 because he would not be deterred from his probe of mafia activities. His successor on the other hand cooperated with the mafia, was exposed, and landed in prison. *His* successor in turn again went after the mafia and was promptly the object of an assassination attempt.

The situation is somewhat similar for one or another *pubblico ministero.* Some are hard hitting and courageous. The Rome office, however, has had a reputation for being "sensitive" to the interests of political parties and the concerns of persons with good political connections. Cases that properly lay in the jurisdiction of the magistrates in Milan or other cities have at times been transferred to Rome for that reason. The result has on occasion been skewed investigations and even downright judicial iniquity.

NOTE ON LITIGATION IN ITALIAN COURTS

Examine Tables 6.7 and 6.8. Is it apparent what type of case is most important to the Italian judicial system? Does this finding seem to fit the Italian legal culture? Compare the Italian judicial statistics to similar data for Germany in Tables 6.5 and 6.6. What are your conclusions?

Table 6.7

Total Cases Filed in Italian Ordinary Courts in 1987, by Court and Type of Case

Court and Case Type	Cases Filed
Conciliazioni (civil cases)	91,820

Court and Case Type		Cases Filed
Preture		4,132,979
Civil cases		512,693
Criminal cases (instruction or instruction & trial)		3,620,286
Tribunals		1,390,157
Civil cases		363,525
First instance	320,238	
Appeal	43,287	
Criminal cases		1,026,632
Adjunct instruction	864,488	
Trial	147,499	
Courts of Assizes (trial)	917	
Appeal	13,728	
Courts of Appeal		127,058
Civil cases		32,163
First instance	4,271	
Appeal	27,892	
Criminal cases		94,895
Appeal	93,878	
Courts of Assizes (appeal)	1,017	
Court of Cassation		43,581
Civil cases		10,687
Criminal cases		32,894

Table 6.8

Total Cases Filed in Italian Administrative Courts in 1987, by Court

Type of Court	Cases Filed
Regional Administrative Tribunals	62,234
Council of State	5,198
First instance	310
Appeal	4,888
Court of Accounts	11,381

FREDERIC SPOTTS & THEODOR WIESER, ITALY: A DIFFICULT DEMOCRACY 283, 290-92 (1986)

A journey through the labyrinth of Italian politics ends as it began — with a deep sense of the uniqueness, subtlety, tension, paradoxes, confusion, vitality, and resilience of the Italian mode of self-government....

Government Instability

The most obvious symptom of political dysfunction is the acute instability of government. Statistics sum up the situation dramatically. Between 1945 and 1985 there were forty-five governments and seventeen different prime ministers. Governments lasted on an average less than ten months. Parliament itself had on four successive occasions to be dissolved ahead of its full term because incompatible party interests made impossible the formation of any type of governing coalition. In the second half of the life of the republic, twice as much time was required to form a regime as during the first half....

Prosperity and Peace

The long succession of Italy's postwar governments may not have accomplished much in a positive sense, but they committed few errors and by their conspicuous inaction gave free reign to the country's social forces to develop at will. The economy was the key element. Apart from its intervention in the South, no other government in postwar Europe was so singularly lacking in programs to promote economic growth, industrial modernization, or foreign trade. In part by design but in larger part by abdication, the government followed a course of laissez-faire that has probably not been seen anywhere else in the West after 1945. The "underground economy" — based on an inability or unwillingness to enforce tax regulations and other laws — is the epitome of its approach.

For a nation of such pronounced individualism, industry, and ingenuity, this unbridled freedom unleashed the native energies of the people and produced economic growth as miraculous in its way as that in Germany. Overall there has been a rise in the standard of living of all social groups, even if unequally shared, that has reinforced popular support for the constitutional order under which it occurred. The economic success is the success not of the government but of the hard work and entrepreneurial spirit of workers and managers alike. The contrasting decline of the public sector enterprises after their annexation by the Christian Democrats is clear evidence of how — and why — Italy works best when government is not involved....

In addition there are several important psychological elements that help to explain why and how the country's problems have been managed and some defects overcome.... The Italian's political fatalism and mistrust of the state are a great liability but have another side: the popular capacity to absorb crises, shocks, and scandals because nothing much better is expected from the governing authority. Being skeptical, Italians have no false hopes; being on their own in an "asocial social welfare state," they know how to protect themselves by either making the system minimally effective or getting around it entirely....

Beneath all these various explanations of why Italy moves despite the manifold flaws of the system lies yet a deeper consideration: Italian national character. Italians have, in a word, a genius that they have learned over centuries for patience, resilience, and improvisation in the face of looming disaster. They possess a much higher tolerance for uncertainty, confusion, and complexity than any other Western people and enjoy an uncanny ability to bring at least a minimum of order out of a maximum of chaos. Although such abstract traits are easy to overlook beneath the more tangible defects and weaknesses of the political systems, they ultimately provide the country with an underlying emotional strength that helps it ride out every storm.

Ultimately Italians have in their political system the sort of government that most of them want. Although they crave the security the state can offer, they are natural Jeffersonians — knowing from experience that that government governs best that governs least — and consider little and weak government safer than strong and effective government. The institutions may not work smoothly and may arouse derision, but they are the institutions Italians feel safest with.

NOTES AND QUESTIONS

1. The French, German, Italian, and Japanese constitutions are all products of the post-World War II period. All four establish representative democracies built on the basic premises of Enlightenment liberalism, but with an overlay of mid-20th century social welfare thought. What role in this respect do the programmatic provisions of the Italian Constitution play?

2. Does the 1985 concordat between Italy and the Vatican represent a secularization of the Italian legal system?

3. The Italian political structure is somewhere between the unitary French system and the quasi-federalism of Germany. Five of the 20 Italian regions have special autonomy under Article 116 of the Constitution. Four of the special regions — Sardinia, Sicily, Trentino-Alto Adige, and Valle d'Aosta — were constituted in 1948 and Friuli-Venezia Giulia was given its specific constitution by Parliament in 1963 after Yugoslavia settled the political question of Trieste. All five enjoy broader autonomy than the other regions because of an historic legislative and administrative self-sufficiency, their relative geographic isolation, or the existence of linguistic minorities.

What differences between the legal structures of Germany and Italy justify the German use of the title "federal?"

4. Contrast the lawmaking power in Italy between the *Parlamento* and the Council of Ministers. Which entity has the greater power? How does this compare to the French structure of lawmaking?

5. Is the Italian Constitutional Court more like the German Constitutional Court or the French Constitutional Council? Is the usual constitutional issue in Italy heard in a process more like the German *Vorlageverfahren* (indirect) or *Verfassungsbeschwerde* (direct)?

6. Is the Italian judicial organization more like that of France or Germany? In what ways is it different from both? The work of the French Tribunal of Conflicts is handled in Italy primarily by the Court of Cassation. In 1987, apart from its ordinary cases, the Court heard 1,250 special petitions related to conflicts of jurisdiction and the regulation of court competence. In addition, the Italian Constitutional Court has the responsibility to decide conflicts of competence between the organs *(poteri)* of the state (Const. art. 134).

7. How has the Italian judiciary become politicized? Does a comparable phenomenon exist in the United States? *See* Giuseppe di Federico, *The Crisis of the Judicial System and the Referendum on the Judiciary,* 3 Italian Politics: A Review 25 (1989).

8. Beginning in 1992 a corps of Italian prosecutors in Milan began a probe called Clean Hands into the pervasive political corruption existing in Italy. During a two-year period more than 3,000 politicians and businessmen were arrested, most linked to the Christian Democrats or Socialists, including former Socialist prime minister Bettino Craxi. Prosecutors during the campaign used their controversial power to place suspects under preventive detention without charges.

9. Every legal system has its own characteristic legal culture: the attitudes and values held by a distinct population related to law and legal institutions. To a large degree this is what makes the Italian legal system "Italian," or the German legal system "German," and so on. *See* Joseph LaPalombara, Democracy: Italian Style (1987); *A Symposium on the Political and Social Aspects of Italian Law,* 4 Ind. Int'l & Comp. L. Rev. 219 (1994). At some point in comparing the structure of national legal systems, the surface similarities are so overshadowed by cultural differences that one must make a special effort to examine the legal culture. We shall do so later in this chapter for Latin America (Section D) and for East Asia (Section E).

10. For a summary description of Italian substantive law, see G. Leroy Certoma, The Italian Legal System (1985).

4. SPAIN

PETER J. DONAGHY & MICHAEL T. NEWTON, SPAIN: A GUIDE TO POLITICAL AND ECONOMIC INSTITUTIONS 10-13, 19-21, 98, 100, 103-04, 112-13, 117-18 (1987)

The Constitution of 1978

The 1978 Constitution is divided into eleven major sections (*títulos)* including the Introductory Section (*Título Preliminar),* which lays down the guiding principles which regulate the functioning of the new Spanish state and Spanish society. Section I enumerates a whole range of civil, political and socio-economic rights. The remaining nine Sections deal with the division of the powers of the state, the nature and functions of the different institutions of the state and the territorial organisation of the country. Section II examines the role of the monarchy, laying particular stress on its role *vis-à-vis* the Constitution and the question of the succession. Section III outlines the composition, functions and powers of both Houses of Parliament. Section IV deals with the organisation of the government and public administration, while Sections V and VI respectively refer to the relationship between the government, the legislature and the judicial authorities. Section VII breaks new ground in Spanish constitutional history by laying down the basic principles by which the economy shall be run. Section VIII concerns the territorial organisation of the state and thus the whole question of the relationship between central government and the regions and peoples of Spain. Section IX outlines the composition and competences of the constitutional court and Section X the processes by which the Constitution may be reformed. It is worthy of note that, compared to its predecessor, the 1978 Constitution devotes much more attention to such key aspects as rights (forty-six Articles), the legislature, which embodies popular sovereignty (thirty-one Articles) and the rights of the regions of Spain *vis-à-vis* the state (twenty-three Articles).

The more idealistic clauses of the Constitution are contained in the Introductory Section. Article 1, for instance, proclaims that Spain is a "social and democratic state based on the rule of law" and that "national sovereignty resides in the people from whom all powers derive." Article 2, while referring to the "indissoluble unity of the Spanish nation" recognises and guarantees the "right of the nationalities and regions of Spain to autonomy." Article 3 recognises regional languages as co-official in the regions concerned alongside Castilian, the official language of the Spanish state. It is interesting to note that on two occasions the Constitution refers to the concept of "political pluralism" (Articles 1 and 2) and in this context both political parties and trade unions, the internal structures and functioning of which are to adhere to democratic practices, are expressly recognised. Article 9.1 affirms that both citizens and the authorities are subject to the Constitution and to the law in general. Clause 2 of this Article puts an obligation on the public authorities to create the conditions in which the freedom and equality of the individual and groups can be genuine and effective, and to remove obstacles to the full participation of all citizens in the political, economic, social and cultural life of the country. Though not inserted in this outline of general principles, there is no doubt that the concept of decentralisation enshrined in Article 103, referring to the government and civil service, was also a major guiding principle.

Two major provisions refer to Spain's major socio-political institutions, the armed forces and the Catholic Church, often referred to by contemporary politicians and commentators as the *de facto* powers (*poderes fácticos*). These institutions, as is well known, have played such a dominant role in the political and constitutional history of Spain that their interests have always, to some extent at least, had to be accommodated and their role clearly defined. Even the Constitution of 1978 has had to take them into account and indeed has tried to ensure that, unlike the case in 1931, they are not alienated to the point where they become forces of dissension and opposition....

Unlike the armed forces, the Church would seem to play only a minor role within the new Constitution, especially when we consider the importance [the former dictator, General Francisco] Franco, attached to it in his fundamental laws. However, unlike the 1931 Constitution, which effectively paved the way for the establishment of a completely secular state and thus provoked the conservative elements of Spanish society, the 1978 document merely states in Article 16 that there will be complete religious freedom and that there will be no state religion. However, Clause 3 goes on to say that "the public authorities shall take into account the religious beliefs of Spanish society and shall maintain consequent links of co-operation with the Catholic Church and other faiths." While in theory this prepared the way for a gradual move towards the separation of Church and state — involving, for example, the eventual financial independence of the former — the Church, which has basically accepted the new order, has in practice retained much of its influence, not least within the education system. Moreover, both under UCD and PSOE governments, the Church has not been averse to lending both moral and material support to groups protesting against government policies on education, divorce and abortion.

[The UCD or Unión de Centro Democrático, a center-right coalition of Christian democrats, social democrats, and liberals, controlled the Cortes or Parliament from the first fully democratic elections in 1977 until 1981 under

Prime Minister Adolfo Suárez. The PSOE or Partido Socialista Obrero Español, a center-left coalition of socialists and social democrats, succeeded to power in 1982 under Prime Minister Felipe González, who remained in office through the mid-1990s.] Statistics show, however, that society is becoming increasingly secularised and it is highly unlikely that the Church will again be the predominant factor that it has been in the past.

By far the longest section of the Constitution deals with fundamental rights and the obligation of the state to uphold and guarantee these rights, except in the most exceptional circumstances. It is worthy of note that Article 10 declares that such rights shall conform to those listed in the Universal Declaration of Human Rights. Following a now classical categorisation, three types of rights can be identified: basic human or civil rights; political rights; and socio-economic rights. The latter involve some positive action on the part of the state to benefit the public....

Needless to say even in the most advanced and developed democratic system difficulties are often expressed in translating constitutional ideals into everyday realities. In the case of Spain, which has only recently emerged from a dictatorial regime where civil and political liberties were constantly denied, this task will be all the harder, especially in view of the fact that not all sections of society accept the desirability of constitutional rule. As far as the socio-economic rights are concerned, whatever obligations theoretically bind the authorities, in the final analysis their protection and consolidation will depend on the success of the economic policies pursued by successive governments. In the short term at least such goals may be considered utopian. A court ruling may be sufficient to ensure that a woman has the right to equal treatment to a man either in marriage or in terms of job opportunities, but only an increase in the overall economic prosperity of the country, coupled with the will of central and regional governments to distribute fairly their resources, will ensure improvement in such vital areas of education, health and housing that have, even in years of relative prosperity, been severely neglected.

The Constitutional Court

The constitutional court, envisaged in Section IX of the Constitution, is the supreme interpreter of the Constitution and a theoretically impartial body which has the final say in the settling of appeals arising from legislation that emanates from the Constitution. There is no appeal against the decisions of this court.

The constitutional court consists of twelve members formally appointed by the king: of these, four are elected by the Congress by a majority of three-fifths of its members, four by the Senate by a similar majority, two by the government and two by the general council of the judiciary (*Consejo General del Poder Judicial*). The members of the court must be lawyers of recognised competence with more than fifteen years' experience in the legal profession. They are appointed for a period of nine years; a third of their number will be replaced every three years. No member of the court can simultaneously be a public representative, i.e., as national or regional deputy, a member of the government or any branch of public administration, an office holder in a political party or trade union; neither can he practise privately in the legal profession. All members are expected to be independent and permanent in the exercise of their duties (Article 159). The court elects a president, appointed for three years, from among its members by secret ballot prior to formal appointment by the king.

According to Article 161 the court has jurisdiction throughout the national territory. Its judgments (*sentencias)* may be sought in the following cases:

1. *Appeals against unconstitutional laws and regulations* (*recursos de anticonstitucionalidad*). These can be made in the case of statutes of autonomy, organic laws, ordinary laws of the national or regional parliaments and international treaties.

2. *Appeals for protection* (*recursos de amparo*). These can be lodged when a citizen's fundamental rights or freedoms have been allegedly violated by the state, the autonomous communities or other official bodies or authorities.

3. *Official appeals concerning the autonomous communities*. Such appeals can be submitted in cases of dispute between the state and the autonomous communities over areas of competence. The government, for example, can appeal to the court if it feels that certain legislation adopted by the autonomous communities is unconstitutional; in such cases the legislation is suspended for a maximum of five months while the court decides whether to ratify or lift the suspension.

In recent times one of the most publicised appeals to the constitutional court was initiated by the autonomous communities of the Basque Country and Catalonia who claimed that certain Articles of the controversial Law on the Harmonisation of the Autonomy Process contravened the Constitution. In fact the court, to the great embarrassment of the government, found in favour of the autonomous communities, thus leaving a dangerous constitutional void in August 1983. Other appeals, presented under both the *recurso de anticonstitucionalidad* and under the *recurso de amparo* were filed by the right-wing AP [Alianza Popular] party during the first period of Socialist government between 1982 and 1986, when the latter was trying to push through legislation relating to education and abortion. In all cases the appeals were rejected. None the less, in the absence of an effective Upper House of Parliament, the court is likely to retain its semi-political, as well as its judicial, role for the foreseeable future and its rulings are likely to provide a substantial corpus of case-law related to constitutional issues.

Ombudsman (Defensor del Pueblo)

The ombudsman (or defender of the people) is a post envisaged in Article 54 of the Constitution. This figure is designated by both Houses of Parliament and his role is to defend the rights enshrined in Section I of the Constitution, monitoring the activities of all branches of public administration and reporting to both Houses of Parliament.

The role of the ombudsman was explicated in an organic law of April 1981. This law permits him to watch over the activities of ministers, administrative authorities, civil servants and persons working for any branch of public administration. All public authorities are obliged to assist him in his investigations, giving him preference over other claimants on their time. In practice this post was left unfilled throughout the period when the Centre-Right (UCD) was in power; after the 1982 elections, when the Socialists (PSOE) came to power, Parliament voted to appoint to this prestigious office a jurist of international repute, the former Christian Democrat leader, Joaquín Ruiz-Giménez....

Regional Government

Regional Autonomy in the Post-Franco Era

The political map of Spain is now radically different from what it was only a few years ago. Instead of a unitary state divided into some fifty provinces, the role of which was merely to administer the services of the central government, the country now has a semi-federal structure in which the powers of the state are shared with seventeen newly created autonomous communities, each endowed with its own president, parliament, executive and high court of justice. In the modern history of Spain there is no precedent for such a major change in the structure of the state nor for such a fundamental shift of power from the centre to the periphery....

[P]artly as a reaction to centuries of stifling centralism, culminating in the dictatorship of General Franco and partly in response to deep-seated cultural differences — particularly manifest in the case of the Basques and the Catalans — the post-Franco era has witnessed considerable popular and official support for some form of decentralisation. This has been conceived as an essential ingredient of the return to democracy. In the summer of 1977, following the UCD victory in the June elections of that year, Adolfo Suárez appointed a Minister for the Regions whose specific brief was to take some steam out of the clamours for regional autonomy and to negotiate provisional autonomy agreements with representatives of the regions.

Subsequently, between September 1977 when Catalonia's historic regional government, the *Generalitat,* was restored and the end of 1978, most of Spain's regions were endowed with institutions which, while enjoying only limited powers, represented an important symbolic first step on the road to self-government. The conversion of these provisional bodies into fully fledged autonomous organs of government had to await the promulgation of the Constitution in December 1978.

Autonomy in the 1978 Constitution

During the sixteen-month constitutional debate, the autonomy issue was by far the most controversial. In some way a balance had to be struck between the fears of the parties of the Right that any reference to the "nationalities" of Spain represented a threat to national unity and the obvious preference of the Left for a federal-type solution. Certain parliamentarians were equally concerned that autonomy might be a disguise for mere administrative decentralisation, without any effective decision-making power being devolved to the regions. Many regionalists were unhappy about the distinction, drawn in Article 2, between the "nationalities" and the "regions" of Spain, especially when Transitional Provision 2 of the Constitution suggested, although it did not actually state, that the former corresponded to the Basque Country, Catalonia and Galicia, which would be able to accede to autonomy through an accelerated procedure.

Not surprisingly, the formula eventually agreed on was very much a compromise between the various political groups represented in Parliament, a compromise that applied to both the procedure for attaining autonomy and the powers to be exercised by the new regional institutions. However, with the possible exception of the Basque Nationalists, who urged their electorate to abstain in the constitutional referendum, arguing that the pre-existence of Basque rights or *fueros* had not been expressly recognised, all major parties could accept the basic proposition of Article 2. This is stated as follows:

> The Constitution is based on the indissoluble unity of the Spanish Nation, the common and indivisible motherland of all Spaniards, and recognises and guarantees the right to autonomy of the nationalities and regions of which it is composed and the common links that bind them together.

This basic principle is developed in considerable, if not always clear, detail in Section VIII of the Constitution entitled, "The Territorial Organisation of the State." Article 143.1 spells out the territorial basis for the establishment of self-governing regions:

> Exercising the right to autonomy recognised in Article 2 of the Constitution, adjoining provinces with common historical, cultural and economic characteristics, the islands and the provinces with a historical regional identity will be able to accede to self-government and form autonomous communities in accordance with the provisions of this section of the Constitution and of their respective statutes....

Establishment of the Autonomous Communities

The first regions to attain autonomy under the 1978 Constitution were the Basque Country and Catalonia, where successful referendums were held in October 1979 and where statutes of autonomy ... were ratified in the *Cortes* by an organic law of December of that year. In March of the following year elections were held to the Basque and Catalan Parliaments, as a result of which the first regional governments of the post-Franco era were sworn in. On the same day a referendum was held in Galicia to approve that region's statute of autonomy. Elections, however, were not held until October 1981 when, simultaneously, the referendum to approve the Andalusian statute was held. The delay in holding these polls was partly due to the attempted *coup* of February 1981, which came close to destroying Spain's hard-won democracy....

Nature and Implications of Autonomy

Autonomy is not the easiest term to define and has a variety of different senses. In the Spanish case, however, whatever the limitations of the new decentralised structure and whatever state control over regional institutions still exists, autonomy is undoubtedly of a political nature. A serious attempt has been made to create alternative region-based centres of political power which, while in the last resort subservient to the central power, enjoy a generous degree of freedom to run their own affairs. It is generally accepted that political autonomy consists of a capacity to take decisions and to implement them on the basis of adequate resources. For it to be effective, political autonomy must include statutory, legislative and, above all, at least some financial autonomy....

All seventeen autonomous communities are now subject not only to the Constitution but to their own statutes of autonomy which govern all aspects of political life at a regional level. In effect they constitute regional constitutions. Having been approved in the *Cortes* as organic laws, they can only be amended by an overall majority in both Houses of Parliament and only after a complicated procedure can they be overruled by Madrid. At the simplest level, a statute enables a region to organise its own institutions of self-government and establish the parameters of its own particular relationship with the central authorities.

It is interesting to note that, although the statutes have many features in common, because each is the result of a long process of political negotiation, they all have individual features which reflect their own special relationship with Madrid. The Basque Statute enshrines the restoration of the economic agreements *(conciertos económicos),* involving certain tax-raising privileges, while the Catalan Statute grants the region considerable freedom in matters related to education, culture and language....

Powers of the Autonomous Communities

It is in the key area of powers (*competencias)* devolved to the autonomous communities that we see most clearly where contemporary Spain, at least for the moment, seems to differ from the classical federal state. In the latter, the regions tend from the outset to assume control over a clearly defined area and inherit clearly structured institutions. In Spain, however, not only has each region been free to decide whether or not to request autonomous status, but it has been, and will be, able to decide on the level of autonomy required and, where applicable, the time-scale of progression to full autonomy.

According to the Constitution, the powers granted to the communities will depend on the route by which autonomy has been achieved. Basically the slow-route autonomous communities can assume responsibility for areas of responsibility listed in Article 148 of the Constitution. In reality these include little more than one might expect of a local authority in a fairly centralised state like the UK ....

Article 148 of the Constitution lists a series of powers to which slow-route regions can accede. These include: the organisation of their own institutions of self-government; town-planning; housing; public works; forestry; environmental protection; museums; libraries; cultural affairs; the regional language (where applicable); tourism; sport and leisure; social welfare; health and hygiene; and non-commercial ports and airports....

Conclusion

It is clear that the process of devolving political power to the regions is far from complete and daunting problems remain to be surmounted. At the root of many basic problems are theoretical and constitutional considerations. It may well be that in the end Adolfo Suárez and the constitution makers will not be thanked for adopting an open-ended, *laissez-faire* approach in which fundamental matters, such as the final form of the Spanish state, were avoided and serious political problems were glossed over by imprecision in Section VIII of the Constitution. It is far from clear ... whether Spain is moving slowly toward a federal state or is likely to remain basically a regional state comparable to Italy. Neither is it clear what the limits are for regions that may wish to transfer to full autonomy, especially when the experiences to date of the rapid-route regions do not bode well in this respect. Even more daunting are the economic and administrative implications of devolution. Not only is the whole process of transferring powers, department by department, sector by sector, inevitably going to be very protracted, but the sheer cost of creating an extra tier of authority, involving seventeen extra governments and administrations, is bound to impose severe strains on an already fragile economy. In theory, as a result of devolution, areas of the central bureaucracy that have been transferred to the new regional authorities should have been either closed down or substantially reduced; as yet, however, there is little evidence of this happening and, if anything, the ministries in Madrid are continuing to expand, albeit under the pretext of rationalisation and the assumption of a coordinating role.

The acid test of the autonomy process, however, is likely to be political and cultural and relates to that much used, if not abused, word "solidarity." Sadly, during recent years "insolidarity" between the regions and peoples of Spain seems to have been the order of the day. This has been exemplified in the constant squabbles between Madrid and the Basque governments and by the apparent resentment shown by Basques and Catalans when the distribution of the Inter-regional Compensation Fund seems to have favoured the poorer regions, Andalusia for example. One of the basic questions lying at the heart of the autonomy issue, a question which could make or break the whole operation, is the extent to which substantial powers can be granted to the "region-based" communities (e.g., Castilla y León, Murcia) without giving offence to the "nation-based" communities (e.g., Basque Country, Catalonia) which, for a whole series of historical, cultural and economic reasons, feel that they merit preferential status. If the former were to be given powers in any way comparable to those enjoyed by the Basque Country and Catalonia and if substantial resources were transferred to them at their expense, what then would be the reaction of these historical nationalities? This and many other questions relating to autonomy remain, for the moment, unanswered.

BERNARDO M. CREMADES & EDUARDO G. CABIEDES, LITIGATING IN SPAIN 39, 41-46, 71 (1989)

The Organic Law for the Judiciary [(1985), implemented by Law 38 of 28 December 1988,] has introduced profound changes into the organization and structure of the Spanish judicial system. Nevertheless, the basic structure has been maintained. In general, courts are divided into those with a single judge (courts of the first instance, called *juzgados)* and those with three or more sitting judges (appellate courts, called *audiencias* or *tribunales),* which can also serve as courts of original jurisdiction in certain types of cases....

The court system is divided into the types of matters heard. Thus, there are courts of civil jurisdiction, courts of administrative jurisdiction, labor courts, criminal courts and the Constitutional Court....

Types of Courts

There are four types of ordinary jurisdiction in the Spanish judicial system: civil, judicial-administrative, labor and criminal. All multi-judge courts, including the Supreme Court, are divided into chambers for each of these areas over which they have jurisdiction. The various levels of courts within each type of jurisdiction are empowered to hear specific types of cases, depending on subject matter or amount of the claim.

The Supreme Court *(Tribunal Supremo),* which sits in Madrid, has nationwide jurisdiction and, pursuant to Article 123 of the Constitution, "is the supreme judicial body in all areas, except as provided in the area of constitutional guarantees. The presiding Magistrate of the Supreme Court shall be appointed by the King, on proposal of the General Council of the Judiciary." It is divided into four chambers. Each autonomous region (except La Rioja) has a superior justice court *(tribunal superior de justicia),* with supreme jurisdiction within the region over cases arising from regional law, which is divided into four chambers. The National Court of Justice *(Audiencia Nacional)* has nationwide jurisdiction, and is divided into three chambers (it lacks jurisdiction over civil matters). Provincial courts of justice *(audiencias provinciales)* are divided into two chambers, hearing criminal cases and some civil appeals. There is one such court in each province, sitting in the provincial capital, although sections of the court may be created elsewhere in the province.

Courts of the first instance *(juzgados de primera instancia)* have full jurisdiction over most civil cases in the first instance. They sit in the major town of a judicial district *(partido judicial)* which contains several municipalities, with major cities having more than one such court.[9] In towns without courts of the first instance, justice of the peace courts *(juzgados de paz)* perform certain minor functions in civil and criminal matters. There are also lower judicial-administrative and labor courts *(juzgados de lo contencioso-administrativo* and *juzgados de lo social,* respectively), located in provincial capitals, and several types of lower-level courts with criminal jurisdiction.[11] This basic structure is shown in Figure 6.3.

[9] In most municipalities, a single court — the court of the first instance and lower criminal court *(juzgado de primera instancia e instrucción)* — has jurisdiction over both civil and criminal matters in the first instance. When necessary, however, criminal jurisdiction may be separated from civil jurisdiction in the first instance, with criminal cases being heard by lower criminal courts *(juzgados de instrucción)* and civil cases heard by courts of the first instance *(juzgados de primera instancia)*.

[11] In criminal matters, the Criminal (Second) Chamber of the Supreme Court hears appeals, and criminal proceedings brought against various high public officials. The Criminal Chamber of the

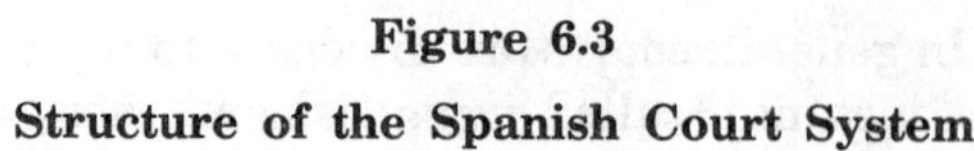

Figure 6.3

Structure of the Spanish Court System

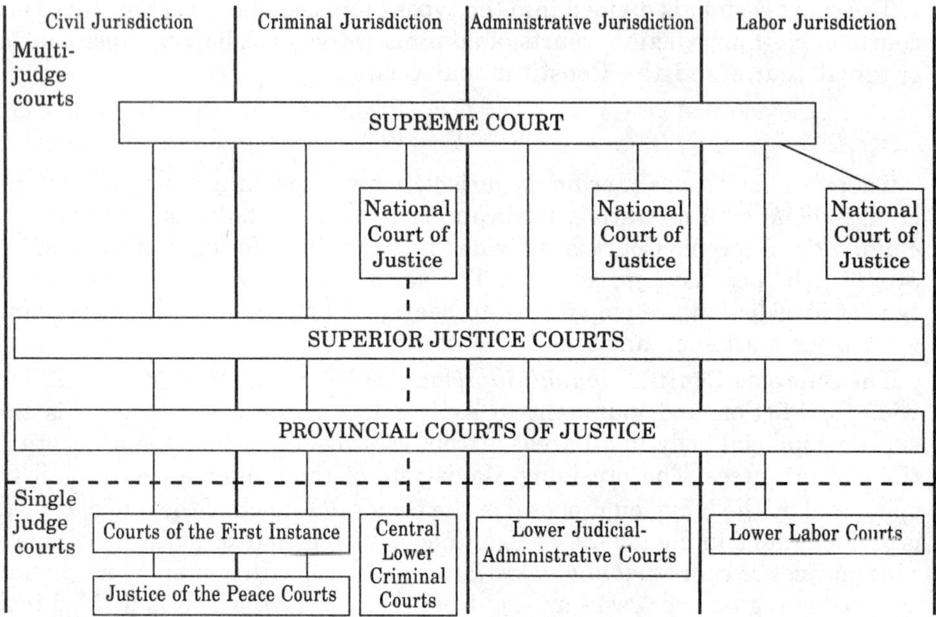

[The superior justice courts are the high courts for each of the regions that has created an autonomous system of courts. Not shown in Figure 6.3 are the lower courts for the regional government.]

National Court of Justice hears: crimes against the Crown, high government bodies, and the form of government; counterfeiting and other monetary crimes; price-fixing and food and drug offenses affecting more than one province; extraterritorial crimes, criminal proceedings initiated abroad and execution of foreign sentences to be heard or handled by Spanish judges by virtue of law or treaty; and extradition proceedings. Superior justice courts hear criminal proceedings as provided in the regional autonomy statutes, those against judges and prosecutors for crimes committed in the performance of their functions and conflicts of jurisdiction between lower criminal courts located within the region. Provincial courts of justice hear felony cases and appeals from lower criminal courts. Central lower criminal courts (*juzgados centrales de instrucción)*, located in Madrid, hear the initial stages of cases to be decided on by the National Court of Justice. Lower criminal courts hear: felony and misdemeanor proceedings as provided by law, the initial stages of cases to be decided on by the provincial courts of justice, appeals from decisions rendered by justices of the peace in misdemeanors, *habeas corpus* proceedings and conflicts of jurisdiction between justice of the peace courts in their jurisdiction. Justice of the peace courts hear misdemeanor proceedings as provided by law. Minor courts (*juzgados de menores),* located in each province, perform functions as provided by law for minors who commit felonies or misdemeanors. Penal supervision courts (*juzgados de vigilancia penitenciaria),* located in each province, execute sentences, control the disciplinary powers of prison authorities and protect the rights of prisoners).

1. *Courts of Ordinary Civil Jurisdiction*

In civil matters, the Civil (First) Chamber of the Supreme Court has jurisdiction over cassation appeals, appeals for review and other extraordinary appeals. It also hears in original jurisdiction petitions for enforcement of foreign judgments and claims for civil liability brought against high executive, legislative and judicial officials for acts committed in the performance of their duties, including the President of the Government.

The superior justice courts have jurisdiction over: cassation appeals and appeals from the decisions of lower civil courts within their respective regions, provided they are based on regional law, and that the region's autonomy statute has granted such jurisdiction; claims for civil liability against officials of the autonomous region; and certain conflicts of jurisdiction among lower courts located in the region.

Provincial courts of justice hear appeals from the decisions of courts of the first instance within the province, certain conflicts of jurisdiction between lower courts in the province and petitions for recusal of their magistrates in certain cases.

Courts of the first instance hear all civil cases and *ex parte* proceedings in the first instance not attributed to other courts, appeals from decisions of justices of the peace and conflicts of jurisdiction among justice of the peace courts. Also, judges of the first instance are responsible for the civil registry in their jurisdiction.

Justice of the peace courts hear in the first instance such cases as the law provides. They are also responsible for the civil registry in their municipalities.

[2. *Courts of Criminal Jurisdiction*

The Spanish Constitutional Court, in its Decision of 12 July 1988, held that the impartiality of a judge to try a penal case and to sentence the defendant is compromised when he also acts as the investigating judge. In response the Parliament in 1988 enacted an organic law to establish the new "criminal courts." These single judge courts, organized by provinces, hear cases involving crimes with penalties of up to six years' incarceration. The investigating courts (central lower criminal courts) retain the task of preliminary investigation. See *supra* footnote 11.]

3. *Courts of Administrative Jurisdiction*

In administrative matters, the Administrative (Third) Chamber of the Supreme Court hears: judicial-administrative proceedings[14] brought against administrative acts and provisions of the Council of Ministers, the General

[14] Any citizen whose rights or legitimate interests have been injured by illegal administrative action or a general administrative provision of a rank lower than a statute has standing to bring judicial-administrative proceedings (*recurso contencioso-administrativo)*.... In acts of general application, the municipality or public agency affected by the act has exclusive standing, although any acts and enforcement of general administrative provisions may be appealed by affected citizens. If an individual legal status is sought to be recognized and restored, only the holder of the right considered violated by the contested act or provision will have standing.

Council for the Judiciary and other high public bodies in original jurisdiction; cassation appeals from judicial-administrative decisions rendered by superior justice courts (relating to administrative provisions issued by the State or by the autonomous regions which violate State law) and the National Court of Justice; and appeals for review as provided by law.

The National Court of Justice has original jurisdiction over judicial-administrative proceedings brought against administrative acts and provisions issued by ministers and secretaries of state. In original jurisdiction, superior justice courts hear judicial-administrative appeals from administrative acts and provisions issued by the executive body of the autonomous regions, and those issued by the State not attributed by law to other courts; judicial administrative proceedings brought against certain acts and provisions of the regional legislative assembly; appeals from election results; and conflicts of jurisdiction between lower judicial-administrative courts sitting in their region. On appeal, these courts also hear appeals brought from decisions of lower judicial-administrative courts in their region. Lower judicial-administrative courts hear judicial-administrative proceedings not attributed to other courts.

4. *Courts of Labor Jurisdiction*

In labor matters, the Labor (Fourth) Chamber of the Supreme Court hears cassation appeals, appeals for review and any other extraordinary appeals provided by law. The National Court of Justice hears, in original jurisdiction, special proceedings challenging collective bargaining agreements applicable in more than one autonomous region and proceedings concerning such agreements when the judgment will affect more than one autonomous region. Superior justice courts hear labor proceedings affecting more than one judicial district within their autonomous region, appeals from decisions of the lower labor courts and conflicts of jurisdiction between lower labor courts within the region. Lower labor courts hear labor proceedings not attributed to other courts....

Territorial Jurisdiction

Judicial bodies are assigned a territory over which they exercise jurisdiction. Some judicial bodies (the Supreme Court and the National Court of Justice) exercise nationwide jurisdiction. Other courts extend their jurisdiction over certain defined territories: municipalities, judicial districts, provinces or autonomous regions.

Superior justice courts are limited in jurisdiction to the autonomous region in which they sit, as defined in their respective autonomy statutes. Some autonomy statutes, such as that of La Rioja, make no provision for superior justice courts. There are 51 provincial courts of justice, with jurisdiction over the province in which they are located.

CONSTITUTION OF SPAIN

Articles 3, 14, 23

Article 3

1. Castilian is the official Spanish language of the State. All Spaniards have the duty to know it and the right to use it.

✓ **2.** The other languages of Spain are also official in their respective autonomous communities in accordance with their Statutes.

3. The richness of Spain's linguistic diversity is a cultural patrimony entitled to special respect and protection.

Article 14

Spaniards are equal before the law, without being subject to any discrimination for reasons of birth, race, religion, opinion, or any other personal or social condition or circumstance.

Article 23

2. [Citizens] have the right on conditions of equality to perform public functions or to hold public employment, according to the requirements established by law.

VIZCAYA v. DIPUTACIÓN FORAL DE VIZCAYA

Supreme Court of Spain
(Contentious-Administrative Chamber No. 4)
Decision 10,274 of 31 December 1988
55 R.J. 10,081 (1988)

The attorney general, in the name of the governor of Biscay [the Spanish province Vizcaya], brought a petition of revocation against the Biscayan Legal Commission concerning a competitive examination summoned on 6 and 7 November 1985. Open were 46 jobs for computer operators. The examination consisted of 4 exercises: the first 3 were obligatory; the fourth was voluntary and tested one's knowledge of Basque. [The latter exercise consisted of 5 of the exam's total score of 41 points.] The Commission refused to respond.

The attorney general then brought a contentious administrative petition to the provincial court (audiencia) in Bilbao, which in a decision of 7 February 1988 denied the petition.

The petitioner now appeals to the Supreme Court, which denies the petition and confirms the lower court decision.

MR. JUSTICE JOSÉ MARÍA REYES MONTERREAL delivered the opinion of the Court....

Legal Bases

First. It is clear that the development of the autonomy process in its functional aspects — which in a concrete way is at issue in this appeal — makes certain demands in those autonomous communities where two official languages coexist. When the public sector is hiring for jobs, it may favor the selection of those candidates who have, among other characteristics, bilingual ability. This seems required by article 3 of the Constitution, so long as both languages are conferred identical official character. It takes into account the linguistic diversity integral to a cultural patrimony.

Second. Nevertheless, since a specific principle of equality can be deduced from article 3, and above all, since the same more general and ample principle, without any exception whatever, is confirmed in article 14 of the Constitution, the autonomous communities at the time of recruiting their personnel cannot establish any condition or characteristic, directly or indirectly, that would result in discrimination of some type against a candidate....

Third. Naturally, given what is stated in article 3 of the Constitution, it cannot be understood that the equality principle, just referred to and constitutionally confirmed, would be weakened when the same Constitution, at least for the present situation, permits the exception of article 3. In addition, article 6 of the Statute of the Basque Country... reiterates the right of all citizens to use whichever of the two official languages they elect.... The Constitutional Court found this provision in its decision of 26 June 1986 to be in conformity with the Constitution....

Fourth.... The court considers that the provincial Commission was permitted to assign as a characteristic relevant for positions of employment the acquisition of a knowledge of Basque, measured by a voluntary exercise — not to be a necessary condition — scaled from 0 to 5 points. It is well understood that, to conform with the cited decision of the Constitutional Court and with this chamber's decision [of 25 January 1988,] "this measure must give the necessary respect to what is stated in articles 14 and 23 of the Constitution, without producing in its application discrimination."

NOTES AND QUESTIONS

1. Spain is a parliamentary monarchy, while Germany and Italy are parliamentary republics. Which officer in the latter two countries do you believe would serve the same governmental functions as the king of Spain?

2. The ombudsman may be a worthwhile legal institution for a country only recently emerging from the long dictatorship of General Francisco Franco (1936-1975). Which governmental officers serve the function of the ombudsman in the United States?

3. Is the Spanish political structure more like the quasi-federalism of Germany or the regionalism of Italy? What are the institutional differences and similarities? Is it accurate to say that the form of the Spanish state is still rapidly evolving?

4. How is the Spanish judicial organization different from the examples we have seen for France, Germany, and Italy? What are the similarities and how might they be explained?

5. Does the Spanish Supreme Court in *Vizcaya v. Diputación Foral de Vizcaya* adequately accommodate the values present in articles 3 and 14 of the Spanish Constitution? How important is it for an autonomous community to be able to promote the use and understanding of its own language?

5. COMPARATIVE LITIGATION RATES

NOTE ON THE COMPARISON OF CIVIL LITIGATION RATES AMONG NATIONS

In Section A we have seen litigation statistics for the courts of France (*supra* Section A.1), Germany (*supra* Section A.2), and Italy (*supra* Section A.3). Cross-national comparisons confront serious methodological difficulties; at the very least population size must be removed as a variable. Table 6.9 does this for our European examples.

Table 6.9

Total Civil Cases Filed in First Instance Courts in Europe, by Country and per 100,000 Population[a]

Country (and Year)	Cases Filed	Per 100,000 Population
France (1987)	1,326,363	2,412
Germany (1984)	2,291,209	3,756
Italy (1987)	929,022	1,630

In the United States approximately 14.8 million civil cases were filed in state and federal courts during 1989. About one-quarter of these dealt with family law and another quarter were small claims cases.[b] In relative terms this caseload translates to 5,968 cases per 100,000 population.

How would you explain the different civil litigation rates in France, Germany, and Italy? Why is the U.S. rate 59 percent greater than that in Germany? What methodological problems do you see in attempting to make a meaningful comparison?

For an early effort to collect accurate figures on litigation (and other elements of a legal system) in a cross-national context, see John Henry Merryman, David S. Clark & Lawrence M. Friedman, Law and Social Change in Mediterranean Europe and Latin America: A Handbook of Legal and Social Indicators for Comparative Study (1979).

What does the following excerpt tell us about litigation trends and cross-national comparisons? Why might some Latin American nations have a higher rate of civil litigation than certain European nations?

DAVID S. CLARK, CIVIL LITIGATION TRENDS IN EUROPE AND LATIN AMERICA SINCE 1945: THE ADVANTAGE OF INTRACOUNTRY COMPARISONS, 24 Law & Society Review 549, 563-65 (1990)

Figure 6.4 sets out the total number of civil cases filed since 1945, per 100,000 population, for Italy, Spain, Chile, Costa Rica, and Colombia. What relationships do we find between these caseloads and socioeconomic development at a national level?

---

[a] Excludes administrative, tax, and social security cases, but includes commerce and labor cases.

[b] David S. Clark, *Civil Procedure*, in Introduction to the Law of the United States 367, 377-79 (David S. Clark & Tuğrul Ansay eds. 1992).

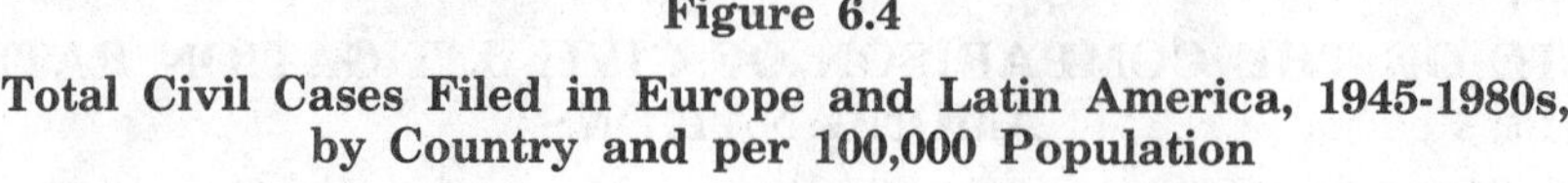

Figure 6.4
Total Civil Cases Filed in Europe and Latin America, 1945-1980s, by Country and per 100,000 Population

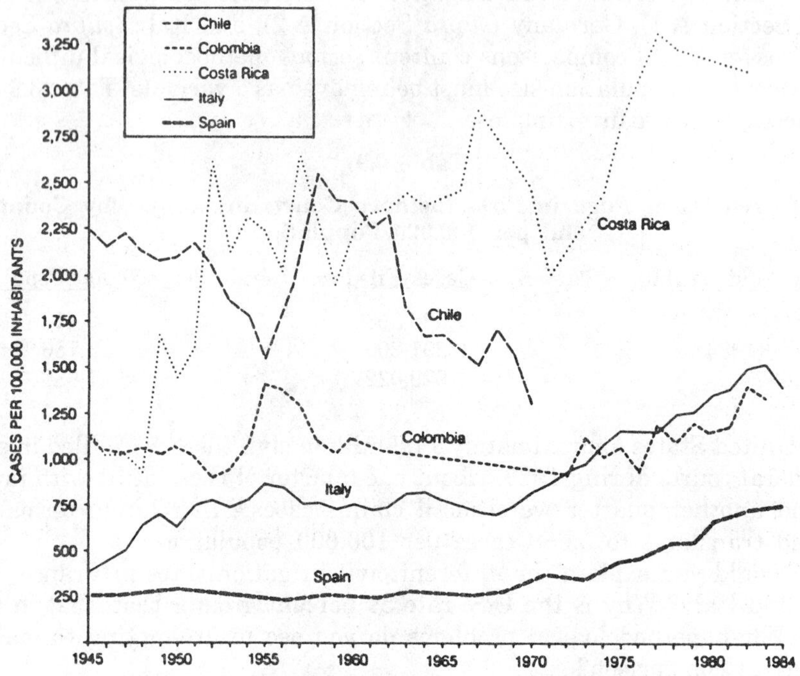

Litigation rates in Chile and Colombia decline overall between 1945 and 1970, and although thereafter in Colombia the filing rate generally climbs until 1982, it is at that point still lower than the rate in 1955. In contrast, the rate in Costa Rica climbs dramatically from 1948 to 1952, but it is higher in that latter year than in 1970. It is then during the period of reduced economic growth after 1970 that litigation rapidly rises until 1977. In Italy and Spain, furthermore, civil filings per capita remain stagnant for most of the 1950s and 1960s in spite of enormous economic development and social dislocation.

What single explanation might fit the disparate patterns represented in Figure 6.4? In the four nations for which information is available after 1970, the civil filings rate rises significantly during the 1970s even though that was a period of sharply reduced real per capita economic growth. Perhaps the litigation rate increases *because* that was a time of slowing economic expansion, with fewer benefits to distribute among the population than before. Since the economic pie was not growing as fast as previously, citizens and businesses may have felt that litigation about the pie's distribution was more compelling.

We might expect, based on the level of economic development, that civil court litigation rates in the five countries would rank from highest to lowest: Italy, Spain, Chile, Costa Rica, and Colombia. In fact, in Figure 6.4 from 1945 to 1970 Italy and Spain were at the bottom, with fewer than a thousand filings per 100,000 inhabitants, Colombia was in the middle with around a thousand filings, and Chile and Costa Rica had more then fifteen hundred filings for most of the period. The failure of a socioeconomic variable to predict the level of civil litigation rates [is surprising].

NOTE ON THE COMPARISON OF CRIMINAL LITIGATION RATES AMONG NATIONS

Criminal litigation statistics may be even harder to compare across nations, since each country can define for itself what is deviant and may choose to rely primarily on forms of social control other than courts. Furthermore, differences in classification make comparison difficult: for instance, France (*supra* Section A.1) includes traffic cases in its police jurisdiction and Italy (*supra* Section A.3) double-counts cases at the instruction and trial stages in its criminal procedure.

We will attempt, nevertheless, to compare first instance criminal litigation rates between Germany and the United States. During 1984 in Germany 1,522,269 cases were filed (*supra* Section A.2, Table 6.5) for a rate of 2,496 criminal cases per 100,000 population. In contrast, 12.6 million criminal cases were filed in the United States in 1989, which does not count 1.5 million juvenile cases or 67 million traffic and other ordinance violation cases.[a] This provides a rate of 5,081 criminal cases per 100,000 inhabitants in the U.S., about double the German rate.

The underlying crime rate in the two countries supports this comparison, as illustrated in Table 6.10.

Table 6.10

Crime Rates (per 100,000 Population) in a German and an American State in 1981, by Type of Crime[b]

Crime	Baden-Württemberg	Texas
Homicide	1.8	16.5
Rape	12	46
Robbery	34	193
Aggravated assault	94	276
Burglary & theft	2,923	4,947
Motor vehicle theft	268	564
Total violent & property crime	3,334	6,042

What does this comparison tell us about the functioning of the criminal justice system in Germany and the United States? About the two societies? Does the following excerpt help to answer these questions?

---

[a] David S. Clark, Civil Procedure, in Introduction to the Law of the United States 367, 376, 378 (Clark & Tuğrul Ansay eds. 1992).

[b] Baden-Württemberg's population was 9.3 million, while Texas' population was 14.8 million. Harald Arnold & Raymond H.C. Teske, Jr., *Factors Related to Fear of Crime: A Comparison of the Federal Republic of Germany and the United States*, in Crime and Criminal Justice 357, 377 (Günther Kaiser & Isolde Geissler eds. 1988).

DAVID S. CLARK, THE AMERICAN LEGAL SYSTEM AND LEGAL CULTURE, in INTRODUCTION TO THE LAW OF THE UNITED STATES 1, 10-11 (Clark & Tuğrul Ansay eds. 1992)

A too-large underclass is related to crime and violence, the ultimate indicator of a breakdown in community and the failure of a legal system to maintain order and justice. A 1991 Senate Judiciary Committee report found that the United States is "the most violent nation on earth," surpassing in killing, raping, and robbing every other country that maintains crime statistics. For instance in 1990 Americans killed 23,300 people, which when adjusted for population is a rate twice that of Northern Ireland, four times the rate in Italy, nine times the rate in England, and 11 times the murder rate in Japan. The comparative figures for rape and robbery were even worse. For rape the U.S. rate was 15 times higher than in England, 23 times higher than in Italy, and 26 times higher than in Japan. For robbery the U.S. rate exceeded that of England by a factor of six, Italy by a factor of seven, and Japan by a factor of 150. The U.S. Department of Justice reports that 34 million Americans were victims of crime in 1990. Of that number 19 million were victims of crime against their person, while 15 million were victims of crime against their property. These people lived in 27 million separate households, which means that 24 per cent of American households experienced crime in 1990.

Historians show us that high crime rates in the United States go back almost as far as the collection of statistics. Lawlessness is part of American legal culture, a part of the wild West mystique, a part of individualism somewhat too rugged. But recent trends seem too high compared to other industrialized nations. There is the perception of a crisis, a social breakdown. It is not that the United States ignores its legal system. There are 792,000 lawyers and judges. In 1988 all governmental units spent $61 billion on the justice system: 12 per cent by the federal government, 33 per cent by states, and 55 per cent by localities. This illustrates the extreme decentralization of the American legal system. Of the $61 billion, police forces cost $28 billion, courts and legal services cost $14 billion, and corrections (for example, prisons, parole) cost $19 billion. About 1.1 million Americans in 1990 were in federal or state prisons or local jails. This gives the United States the world's highest incarceration rate at 455 per 100,000 people, followed by South Africa's 311 per 100,000 population. Canada imprisons, by comparison, at a rate of 111; the United Kingdom at 97. The U.S. imprisonment rate for black males is 3,370 per 100,000, a level five times higher than that in South Africa.

B. LATIN AMERICA

1. INDEPENDENCE AND THE FIRST LATIN AMERICAN CONSTITUTIONS

DAVID S. CLARK, JUDICIAL PROTECTION OF THE CONSTITUTION IN LATIN AMERICA, 2 Hastings Constitutional Law Quarterly 405, 413-16 (1975)

During the first quarter of the nineteenth century, the Spanish and Portuguese empires in America, which had existed for more than three centuries, were broken up. The struggles for independence represented the first efforts of the patriots to liquidate the colonial system in government and society. For example, there were frequent attempts to remove legislative and executive duties from the high courts and to restrict the judiciary to the administration of justice.

In the nations which emerged from the Spanish empire, the removal of the mother country as a common enemy severed a bond of cohesion; divisive political forces erupted throughout the Americas. In fact, the next few decades in many regions of Latin America could be best characterized as in a condition of anarchy. Independence had brought pressing economic problems. The principal cause of protests and revolutions, however, was the delay in reaching a consensus as to the form of government to be adopted. In spite of unsatisfactory experiments with monarchy in Haiti and Mexico, debate persisted in many countries between advocates of monarchy and those in favor of a republic. Where republics were established there were lengthy conflicts between federalists and those in favor of centralized government, between the city commercial class and rural landowners, between those favoring separation of church and state and those supporting clericalism, and between ideological conservatives and liberals.

The first constitutions of the Latin American nations are important because they indicate political traditions as well as the controversial issues which emerged. The political thought of Hobbes, Locke, Rousseau and Montesquieu had become well-known to the educated elite in the Americas, as censorship became less strict and travel abroad by colonials increased. These writings contained theoretical discussions of the practical issues that later confronted the authors of the Constitutions of the United States and France. The influence of social contract theories, especially as they related to issues of natural rights, and ideas on the proper functions for a limited government, particularly the separation of powers, pervaded the constitutional formulations of the revolutionary era. Many leaders of the cause for independence in Latin America, familiar with constitutional developments in the United States and France, drew on translations of the French Declaration of the Rights of Man and of the Citizen and certain major political documents of the United States, including the Declaration of Independence, the constitutions of Maryland, Massachusetts and Virginia, the Articles of Confederation and the Constitution of 1789.

The history of Latin American constitutional theory and practice portrays the elaboration of a set of values — including liberty, equality, justice, and the sanctity of private property — widely shared with other Western nations. One hundred and fifty years of experience, however, amply demonstrates that these values are not self-executing. Their implications are by no means unambiguous. On the contrary, these values are frequently contradictory. Freedom of contract and the private ownership of property, for example, have clashed with modern notions of social justice. Similarly, concepts of equality may conflict with notions of liberty, and so on. Furthermore, the values incorporated into Latin American constitutions have never been universally accepted.

All Latin American governments are obliged by their constitutions to respect the basic rights of man enumerated in the provisions that define liberty, equality, justice and property. In construing these matters, Latin American regimes are often misunderstood. Since political unrest impedes the proper functioning of political and legal institutions, all too often generalizations are based on such situations of unrest. The generalities in turn lead to assertions that the constitutional guarantees are deceptive and that Latin Americans' desire for liberty and justice expresses itself in words and not action. This conclusion applies to some nations generally, but for the large nations with major populations it is true only for relatively short periods of time.

There have been two major epochs in the establishment of constitutional guarantees in Latin America. The first stage includes the decades subsequent to the wars for independence, influenced by the liberal thought of the eighteenth century. The second stage dates from the Mexican Revolution. Beginning in 1910, the first successful socialist revolt spelled out its goals of social justice and expressed them in the Constitution of 1917. This document, emphasizing nationalism, the concept that private property must serve a social function and containing a social program for land reform and the protection of labor, has had an important impact on constitution-making since that time.

The central issue that faced the framers of Latin American constitutions, and has confronted Western political theorists in general was the problem of ensuring that governmental power, which is necessary for the realization of constitutional values, be constrained so that it would not impinge upon these same values. The resolution of the problem lies in a system of effective restraints upon government action. Such controls involve some division of power, since those who are expected to do the restraining must act with some authority. The principal division of governmental power has generally taken one, and frequently two forms. First, there is a functional division into legislative, executive and judicial spheres. Second, there may be a territorial division of sovereignty between a central government and smaller political units.

2. LATIN AMERICA: EXECUTIVE DOMINANCE

HOWARD J. WIARDA & HARVEY F. KLINE, THE LATIN AMERICAN TRADITION AND PROCESS OF DEVELOPMENT, in LATIN AMERICAN POLITICS AND DEVELOPMENT 1, 81-94 (H. Wiarda & H. Kline eds., 3d ed. 1990)

In Latin America, the state has historically held an importance that it lacks in the classic models. The state is viewed as a powerful and independent agency in its own right, above and frequently autonomous from the class and interest-group struggles. Whether in socialist regimes such as Cuba's or capitalist ones like Brazil's, it is the state and its central leadership that largely determine the shape of the system and its developmental directions.

The state not only reflects the class structure but, through its control of economic and political resources, shapes the class system. The state is viewed as the prime regulator, coordinator, and pacesetter of the entire national system, the apex of the Latin American pyramid from which patronage, wealth, power, and programs flow. The critical importance of the state in the

Latin American nations helps explain why the competition for control of it is so intense and sometimes violent. Determining who controls the pinnacles of the system is a fundamental, all-important, and virtually everyday preoccupation.

Related to this is the contrasting way citizens of North America and Latin America tend to view government. In North America government has usually been considered a necessary evil that requires elaborate checks and balances. Political theory in Iberia and Latin America, in contrast, views government as good, natural, and necessary for the welfare of society. If government is good, there is little reason to limit it or put checks and balances on it. Hence, before we fall into the trap of condemning Latin America for its powerful autocratic executives, subservient parliaments, and weak local government, we must remember the different assumptions on which the Latin American systems are based....

The Theory of the State: Constitutions and Legal Systems

After achieving independence early in the nineteenth century, the Latin American nations faced a severe legitimacy crisis. Socialism had not yet produced its major prophets and therefore was not an alternative. Monarchy was a possibility (and some nations did consider or experiment briefly with monarchical rule), but Latin America had just struggled through years of independence wars to rid itself of the Spanish imperial yoke, and monarchy had been discredited. Liberalism and republicanism were attractive and seemed the wave of the future, but Latin America had had no prior experience with liberal or republican rule.

The solution was ingenious, though often woefully misunderstood. The new nations of Latin America moved to adopt liberal and democratic forms of government while at the same time preserving many of the organicist, elitist, and authoritarian principles of their own tradition. The liberal and democratic forms provided goals and aspirations toward which society could strive; they also helped present a progressive picture to the outside world. But the liberal and republican principles were circumscribed by a series of measures authoritarian in content that were truer to the realities and history of the area and to its existing oligarchic power relationships. The ongoing challenge of Latin American politics has been to blend and reconcile these conflicting currents.

Virtually all Latin American constitutions have provided for the historical, three-part division of power among executive, legislature, and judiciary. But in fact, the three branches are not coequal and were not intended to be. The executive is constitutionally given extensive powers to bypass the legislature, and judicial review is largely outside the Latin American legal tradition. Knee-jerk condemnation of a Latin American government that rules without giving equal status to the legislature or courts often reveals more about our own biases, ethnocentrism, and lack of understanding than it does about the realities of Latin America.

Similar apparent contradictions exist in other areas. Although one part of a constitution may be devoted to civilian institutions and the traditional three branches of government, another may give the armed forces a higher-order role to protect the nation, preserve internal order, and prevent internal disruption. In this sense, the military may be considered a fourth branch of the state. Military intervention, therefore, should not necessarily be condemned as an extraconstitutional and illegitimate act since it is often provided for in the constitution and is an implied prerogative of the armed forces. The military thus generally sees itself as the defender of the constitution, not its usurper — although it is the military leaders who decide when the constitution needs defending.

The same situation exists for human rights. Even though all the Latin American constitutions contain long lists of human and political rights, the same constitutions also give the executive the power to declare a state of siege or emergency, suspend human rights, and rule by decree. The same applies to privilege. While one section of a constitution may proclaim democratic and egalitarian principles, other parts give special privileges to the church, the army, or the landed elites. Although representative and republican precepts are enshrined in one quarter, authoritarian and elitist ones are legitimated in another....

The most important issues of Latin American politics, therefore, revolve, not around haughty condemnations from the point of view of some "superior" political system, but around the dynamics of change and process from the Latin American perspective. North Americans and others cannot understand the area if they look only at the liberal and republican side of the Latin American tradition and ignore the rest; nor should one simply condemn some action from the point of view of the North American constitutional tradition without seeing it in the Latin American context. If the civil and military spheres are not strictly segregated, as in the U.S. tradition, then what are their dynamic relations in Latin America and what are the causes of military intervention? If strict separation of powers is not provided for in Latin America and if the branches of government are not equal, what are their respective powers and interrelations? If hierarchy, authority, and special privilege are legitimate principles along with democratic and egalitarian ones, then how are these different principles reconciled, glossed over, or challenged, and why?

The fact that Latin American countries have generally each had a number of constitutions is also frequently misunderstood. People in the United States frequently smile condescendingly on Latin America because of its many constitutions (thirty-odd in Venezuela, Ecuador, and the Dominican Republic), but in doing so they ignore the fact that in Latin America a new constitution is generally promulgated whenever a new amendment is added or when a major new interpretation requires official legitimation. The situation is comparable to the United States' proclaiming a new constitution every time an amendment is passed or a major judicial reinterpretation decided upon. The facts are first, the Latin American constitutional tradition has been far more stable than the number of constitutions implies, and second, in most countries of the area only two main constitutional traditions, one authoritarian and the other liberal and democratic, reflect the main currents of Latin American politics....

[A]n understanding of the code-law system and its philosophical underpinnings can carry one a considerable distance toward understanding Latin American behavior. The truths embodied in the codes and constitutions and the deductive method have their origins in and reflect the Roman and Catholic-scholastic traditions. The authoritarian, absolutist nature of the codes is also reflected by (and helps reinforce) an absolutist, frequently authoritarian political culture. The effort to cover all contingencies with one code and the almost constant constitutional engineering to obtain a "perfect" document tend to rule out the logrolling, compromise, informal understandings, and unwritten rules that lie at the heart of the U.S. and British political systems. And because courts and judges, in their roles as appliers and enforcers of the law rather than creative interpreters of it, are bureaucrats and bureaucratic agencies, they do not enjoy the respect their counterparts do in the United States, thus making judicial review and even an independent judiciary difficult at best.

Executive-Legislative-Judicial Relations

The tradition of executive dominance in Latin America is part of the folklore. Power in the Latin American systems has historically been concentrated in the executive branch, specifically the presidency, and terms like *continuismo* (prolonging one's term of office beyond its constitutional limits), *personalismo* (emphasis on the person of the presidency rather than on the office), to say nothing of *machismo* (strong, manly authority) are all now so familiar that they form part of the political lexicon. The noted Latin America scholar Frank Tannenbaum has argued that the power of the Mexican president is comparable to that of the Aztec emperors; it can also be said that the present-day Latin American executive is heir to an imperial and autocratic tradition stemming from the absolute, virtually unlimited authority of the Spanish and Portuguese crowns. Of course, modern authoritarianism has multiple explanations for its origin (a reaction against earlier mass mobilization by populist and leftist leaders, the result of stresses generated by modernization, and the strategies of civilian and military elites for accelerating development) as well as various forms (caudillistic and more-institutionalized arrangements). In any case, the Latin American presidency is an imperial presidency in ways never dreamed of in the United States.

The formal authority of Latin American executives is extensive. It derives from a president's powers as chief executive, commander in chief, and head of state and from his broad emergency powers to declare a state of siege or emergency, suspend constitutional guarantees, and rule by decree. The presidency in Latin America is such a powerful position that the occupant of the office can rule almost as a constitutional dictator.

The powers of a Latin American president are far wider then is implied in the provisions of the constitutions. The presidency has been a chief beneficiary of many twentieth-century changes: among them, radio and television, concentrated war-making powers, broad responsibility for the economy. In addition, many Latin American chief executives serve simultaneously as head of state and president of their party machine; if the leader's route to power was the army, the president also has the enormous weight of armed might for use against foreign enemies and domestic foes. Considerable wealth, often generated because the lines between the private and the public spheres are not so sharply drawn as in North American political society, may also be an effective instrument of rule.

Perhaps the main difference lies in the fact that the Latin American systems, traditionally and historically, are more centralized and executive oriented than in the United States. The president is the focal point of the system. It is around the person occupying the presidency that national life swirls. The president is responsible not only for governance but also for the well-being of society as a whole. A Latin American president is the symbol of the national society in ways that a U.S. president is not. Not only is politics concentrated in the office and person of the president, but it is by presidential favors and patronage that contracts are determined, different clientele are served, and wealth, privilege, and social position are parceled out. The president is the national *patrón,* replacing the local landowners and men on horseback of the past. With both broad appointive powers and wide latitude in favoring friends and people who show loyalty, the Latin American president is truly the hub of the national system. Hence, when a good, able executive is in power, the system works exceedingly well; when this is not the case, the whole system breaks down.

Various stratagems have been used to try to limit executive authority, but none has worked well. They range from the disastrous results of the experiment with a plural (nine-person government-by-committee) executive in Uruguay to the various unsuccessful efforts at parliamentary or semiparliamentary rule in Chile, Brazil, Cuba, and Costa Rica. Constitutional gimmickry does not work in limiting the power of the executive because such power is an area-wide tradition and cultural pattern, not just some legal article.

The role of the congress in such a system is not generally to initiate or veto laws, much less to serve as a separate and coequal branch of government. Congress's functions can be understood if one begins, not with the assumption of an independent branch, but with the concept of an agency that is subservient to the president and, along with the executive, a part of the same organic, integrated state system. The congress's roles are thus to give advice and consent to presidential acts (but not much dissent), to serve as a sounding board for new programs, to represent the varied interests of the nation, and to modify laws in some particulars (but not usually to nullify them). The legislature is also a place to bring some new faces into government as well as to pension off old ones, to reward political friends and cronies, and to ensure the opposition a voice while guaranteeing that it remains a minority.

Except in a handful of countries, only a very brave or foolhardy legislature would go much beyond these limited functions. Legislatures that do are often closed, and their members are sent home. Most legislative sessions in Latin America are of relatively short duration, since to fulfill the limited functions listed above requires little time. Because of the legislative restrictions and short sessions, few legislators see their jobs as being full-time ones. Nor do their limited functions and part-time role demand elaborate staffs and offices.

If the president in Latin America is the heir of royal absolutism, then the congress is in a sense a descendant of the old royal curia or cortes. The curia, which generally represented the major estates or elites, was a body of royal advisers to the Spanish and Portuguese crowns, and it evolved into the cortes. But the cortes never had the independent budgetary and law-making capacities of the British Parliament, nor did the supremacist doctrines put forth by the British Parliament ever become a part of Spanish or Portuguese public law. The king remained the focus, not the cortes. In all these ways, the modern-day Latin American congress is a direct descendant of the cortes. Moreover, in some countries it was determined early on not only that the congress would be just an advisory body but that it would chiefly represent society's major corporate groups — army, church, hacendados, industrialists, and perhaps some middle sectors and labor groups (though generally only those recognized and legitimated by the state). Popular representation — the idea of one person, one vote — has only recently been institutionalized in Latin America, and only partially and not altogether enthusiastically. Many countries have combined systems of geographic, political, and functional representation.

Still, one cannot say that the legislatures of Latin America are worthless. Their functions are sometimes important ones; and in some countries (Chile in the past, Colombia, Costa Rica, Venezuela), the congress has come to enjoy considerable independence and strength. A few congresses have gone so far as to defy the executive — and gotten away with it — and some have strong staffs and do important committee work. The congress may serve additionally as a forum that allows the opposition to embarrass or undermine the government, as a means of gauging who is rising and who is falling in official favor, or as a way of weighing the relative strengths of the various factions within the regime.

Many of the same comments apply to the courts and the court system. First, the court system is not a separate and coequal branch — nor is it intended or generally expected to be. A Latin American supreme court would declare a law unconstitutional or defy a determined executive only at the risk of embarrassment and endangering itself, something the courts have assiduously avoided. Second, within the prescribed limits, the Latin American court systems do manage to function; particularly in the everyday administration of justice they are probably no worse then the U.S. system. Third, the courts, through such devices as the writ of *amparo* (Mexico and Argentina), popular action (Colombia), and *segurança* (Brazil), have played an increasingly important role in controlling and overseeing government actions, protecting civil liberties, and restricting executive authority even in dictatorial regimes....

Local Government and Federalism

There have been four full-fledged federal systems in Latin America: in Argentina, Brazil, Mexico, and Venezuela. Federalism in Latin America emerged from exactly the reverse of the situation in the United States. In the

United States in 1789, a national government was reluctantly accepted by thirteen self-governing colonies that had never had a central administration. In Latin America, by contrast, a federal structure was adopted in some countries that had always been centrally administered.

It is difficult to judge where federalism works best or least. In the United States, the federal principle survives, however inefficiently and precariously at times, in the face of a long-term trend toward the gradual centralization of power in the national government. In Latin America, the principle of unitary government has survived, also precariously at times, despite such weak central power sometimes that regionalism and an almost de facto form of federalism exist whether specified in the constitution or not.

The independent power of the states in those few Latin American countries organized on a federal basis was greatest in the nineteenth century when the central government was weak. For a long time Mexico, Argentina, and Venezuela were dominated by caudillos operating from a regional base that often corresponded to federal boundaries. In Argentina, the disparity of wealth and power between Buenos Aires and the interior was so great that the adoption of federalism seemed eminently sound. Brazil was so large that the federal principle also made sense there.

Although these nations were federal in principle, the central government reserved the right to "intervene" in the states. As the authority of these central governments grew during the 1920s and 1930s, their inclination to intervene also increased, thereby often negating the federal principle. These major countries have since been progressively centralized so that virtually all power is now concentrated in their national capitals. Nevertheless, the dynamics of the relations and tensions between these central governments and their component states make for a most interesting political arena.

Local governments in Latin America may be described by employing many of the same caveats. The Latin American countries are structured after the French system of local government. Virtually all power is concentrated in the central government. Authority flows from the top down, not from the grass roots up. Local government is ordinarily administered through the ministry of interior, which is also responsible for administering the national police. Almost all local officials are appointed by the central government and serve as its agents at the local level.

Local governments have almost no power to tax or to run local social programs. These activities are administered by the central government according to a national plan....

And yet, even though the theory calls for a centralized state, the reality in Latin America has always been somewhat different. Spanish and Portuguese colonial power was concentrated mostly in coastal enclaves, and the vast hinterland was subdued but only thinly settled. The Spanish and Portuguese crowns had difficulty enforcing their authority in the interior, which was far away and virtually autonomous.

With the withdrawal of the colonial powers early in the nineteenth century, centrifugal tendencies were accelerated. Formerly large viceroyalties and captaincies general fragmented into smaller nation-states, and within the new nations, decentralization proceeded even further until the local region, parish, municipality, or hacienda became the focal point of the system. Power drained off into the hands of local landowners or regional men on horseback, and these people competed for control of the national palace. With a weak central state and powerful centrifugal tendencies, a strong de facto system of local rule emerged in Latin America, despite what the laws or constitutions proclaimed.

Thereafter, nation building in Latin America consisted of two major tendencies: populating and thus "civilizing" the vast empty interior and extending the central government's authority over the national territory. Toward the end of the nineteenth century national armies and bureaucracies were created to replace the unprofessional armed bands led by the local caudillos; national police agencies enforced the central governments' authority at the local level; and the collection of customs duties was centralized, thereby depriving the local strongmen of the funds for their *pronunciamientos*. Authority became concentrated in the central state, the regional isolation of the *patrias chicas* broke down as roads and communications grids were developed, and the economies were similarly centralized under the direction of the state. In most of Latin America the process of centralization, begun in the 1870s and 1880s, is still going forward. Indeed, that is how development is often defined throughout the area.

A developed political system is one in which the central agencies of the state exercise control over the disparate and centrifugal forces that make up the system. In many countries this process is still incomplete, and in the vast interior, in the highlands, in diverse Indian communities, and among some groups (such as landowners, large industrialists, the military, and big multinationals), the authority of the central state is still tenuous. Even today there is little government presence in isolated areas (especially those in the rugged mountains or tropical jungles), and local strongmen — sometimes guerrillas or drug traffickers — may be more powerful than the national government's representatives. This situation also constitutes one of the main arenas of Latin American politics: the efforts of the central government — any government — to extend its sway over the entire nation and the efforts of the local and component units (be they regions, towns, parishes, or Indian communities) to maintain some degree of autonomy.

A Fourth Branch of Government: The Autonomous State Agencies

One of the primary tools in the struggle to centralize power has been the government corporation or the autonomous agency. The growth of these agencies, which in many ways has paralleled that of the regulatory "alphabet agencies" in the United States, has given the central governments a means to extend their control into new areas. These agencies have become so large and so pervasive that they could be termed a separate branch of government, and some Latin American constitutions even recognize them as such.

The proliferation of these agencies means that in some countries they number in the hundreds. Many are regulatory agencies, often with far broader powers than their North American counterparts, with the authority to set or regulate prices, wages, and production quotas. Others administer vast government corporations: among them, steel, mining, electricity, sugar, coffee, tobacco, railroads, utilities, and petrochemicals. Still others are involved with social programs: education, social security, housing, relief activities, and the like. Many more participate in the administration of new services that the state has been called upon to perform: for example, national planning, agrarian reform, water supplies, family planning.

The reasons why these agencies have been set up are diverse. Some, such as the agrarian-reform or family-planning agencies, have been established as much to please the North Americans and to qualify a country for U.S. and World Bank loans as to carry out actual agrarian reform or family planning. Others have been created to bring a recalcitrant or rebellious economic sector (such as labor or the business community) under government control and direction. Some have been intended to stimulate economic growth and development; to increase government efficiency, and hence its legitimacy; or to create a capitalist structure and an officially sanctioned entrepreneurial class where none had existed before. They also enable more job seekers to be put on the public payroll.

But a common feature of all these agencies is that they tend to serve as agents of centralization in the historic quest to "civilize" and bring order to what was, in the past even more than now, a vast, often unruly, nearly empty territory with strong centrifugal propensities. The host of official agencies, bureaus, boards, commissions, corporations, offices, directorships, and institutes that are now part of the state structures are all instruments in this process.

The growth of these agencies, specifically the government corporations, has meant that the degree of central government control and even ownership of the means of production has increased significantly as well. It is a fundamental mistake to think that the Latin American economies are private enterprise-dominated systems. It is not just socialist Cuba that has a large public sector; in fact, all the Latin American economies are heavily influenced by the state.

If one asks who "owns" Brazil, for example, the answer will not be Coca-Cola, General Motors, or International Telephone and Telegraph (ITT) but the Brazilian government. The Brazilian national government, either by itself through the ownership of major public corporations or through joint ventures with private entrepreneurs, generates 35-40 percent of the total gross national product (GNP). The second-largest generator of GNP in Brazil is not Ford or Volkswagen but the Brazilian state governments, and the third-largest, municipal governments. Between these three levels of government, roughly 55-60 percent of the GNP is generated by the public sector. It is only after these three levels of public ownership that one can begin talking about General Motors, Chrysler, and other multinationals. The situation is similar, although the percentage of public ownership varies somewhat, throughout Latin America. Contrary to the popular notion, these countries do not have free-enterprise, capitalist economies but state-capitalist ones (state-socialist in Cuba) with a very high percentage of the GNP generated by the public sector.

This fact has important implications. It means the stakes involved in the issue of who controls the central government, with the vast resources involved, are very high....

Army and Church: Fifth and Sixth Branches of Government?

Although most Latin American constitutions proclaim that the government should be civil and republican and that the armed forces are to play an apolitical role, they also give certain special functions to the army that make it constitutionally the ultimate arbiter of national affairs. The army not only plays a moderating role but is frequently given the power to defend national integrity and preserve order. If these functions are not mentioned in the constitution, they are often given full expression in the organic law of the armed forces, literally a separate constitution that both establishes the internal structure of the military and defines its relations with the state.

All this is foreign to the U.S. experience. The usual distinction implied by the term *civil-military relations* is inapplicable in Latin America. There the distinction between the military and the civilian spheres is blurred, and in fact most regimes are coalitions, albeit in varying degrees, of civil and military elements. Not only do the armed forces have the right and obligation to intervene in politics under certain circumstances, but they are urged and expected to do so by the rest of the population. In this sense, the army is an integral part of the central state apparatus, and it functions almost as a separate, perhaps even coequal, branch of government. Although often internally divided, the army may still act as a monolith to protect itself when its own institutional interests are threatened.

Some of the same comments apply to the church, although in most Latin American constitutions church and state are now officially separated. Still the church, like the military, has its organic law, usually in the form of a concordat, signed by the government and the Vatican, that defines the rights and obligations of both. The concordat may give the church certain privileges in the areas of education, social services, charity, health care, and the like; it may obligate the state to aid the church with public funds; and it may grant the church autonomy in the appointment of ecclesiastic authorities.

In addition, the church can participate in a variety of quasi-official ceremonies (openings, blessings, and dedications of bridges, highways, and public buildings) and take quasi-official stands on a variety of matters that are undefined in any official document — for example, stands on abortion, divorce, family planning, or unofficial advice proffered the president or the voting population. In this more secular age, the church is not as strong or as influential as it once was, and it is certainly not as powerful as the army or the business elites. But its position remains more than that of a mere pressure group. In this way, the church could also be said to function as a distinct branch of government, no longer of first-rank importance but probably at least as influential as the legislature or the judiciary.

3. ARGENTINA

PETER G. SNOW & GARY W. WYNIA, ARGENTINA: POLITICS IN A CONFLICT SOCIETY, in LATIN AMERICAN POLITICS AND DEVELOPMENT 129, 159-61 (H. Wiarda & H. Kline eds., 3d ed. 1990)

The organizational structure and the formal powers of most government institutions in Argentina closely resemble their counterparts in the United States. Political authority is divided between a national government and twenty-two semiautonomous provinces, each of which has a constitution that allocates power among the various branches of the provincial government. At the national level, there is a president chosen for a fixed term of office by an electoral college, a bicameral Congress composed of a Senate and a Chamber of Deputies, and a judiciary headed by a Supreme Court. Nevertheless, in practice there is a great deal of difference between the two countries.

To begin with, Argentina has long been a highly centralized state. Ever since the federal district was created in 1880 there has been near-total hegemony on the part of the national government, which now dominates the allegedly autonomous provinces both politically and financially.

All the constitutional provisions to ensure provincial autonomy are easily negated by the power of the national government to intervene in any province to guarantee a republican form of government. The fact that it is the national government itself that is empowered to define republicanism means the national government may assume total control of a province at any time; however, more often than not, the mere threat of intervention is sufficient to obtain provincial compliance....

The centralization of authority does not stop there, for within the national government the president holds most power. Except for a brief period between 1912 and 1930, the Congress was a preserve of the Conservatives, who appear to have seen their function as that of rubber-stamping the proposals of the chief executive. Decisions tended to be made by the president and a small group of friends and advisers; some of the members of this group may have been congressional representatives, but it was their socioeconomic status that made them members of the political elite, not the offices they held. Between 1912 and 1930 the Congress did gain a degree of political influence, because after the election of Radical and Socialist representatives to the Congress, it became an open arena for conflict and, to a lesser extent, for conflict resolution. This short-lived situation ended with the 1930 revolution, and by the late 1930s "representative institutions like the Congress were discredited and useless." Once again it was the president who was almost completely dominant.

The Argentine judiciary has never played a prominent political role. Although possessing the power of judicial review, the Supreme Court has used considerable restraint in its exercise. Like its U.S. counterpart, it has always refused to hear political questions, and it has defined as *political* any issue that might lead to a major conflict with the executive branch — a conflict that all justices realize they would certainly lose. Damaging to both the power and the prestige of the court is the fact that in spite of constitutional guarantees of life tenure for its members, there were major purges in 1946, 1955, 1966, and 1976. Also detrimental to its public image is its tradition of formally recognizing the de facto status of revolutionary governments. (In fact, during periods of military rule, the court seems to limit itself to attempting to protect individual liberties.) Although it would be an overstatement to claim that the Argentine judiciary has no political power, it is certainly true that all the courts are exceptionally weak in comparison to the president and even in comparison to their counterparts in the United States.

4. BRAZIL

IÊDA SIQUEIRA WIARDA, BRAZIL: THE POLITICS OF ORDER AND PROGRESS, in LATIN AMERICAN POLITICS AND DEVELOPMENT 167, 190-93 (H. Wiarda & H. Kline eds., 3d ed. 1990)

Given the size and diversity of Brazil, federalism made sense to the people who drafted the first republican constitution in 1891. The Rio de Janeiro government was weak and unwilling to challenge powerful regional centers, and while the central government remained vulnerable, for the next three or four decades, the states had a great deal of freedom. São Paulo, Minas Gerais, and Rio Grande do Sul showed so much independence that they maintained diplomatic relations with foreign governments, displayed their state flags above the national one, and even called their state governors "presidents."

The Vargas era lessened these centrifugal pulls. The 1934 constitution clearly gave preeminence to the national executive, state flags and anthems were abolished, and most economic functions were now handled by the national government. Vargas's Estado Novo strengthened and reinforced centralization to the extent that even after his departure in 1945 the national government's powers far outpaced states' rights. Only during the turbulent and short Goulart years did some states again act on their own, perhaps secure in the knowledge that the federal government had enough other problems and would not worry about states' initiatives. Governor Leonel Brizola of Rio Grande do Sul, without a clear mandate to do so, expropriated U.S.-owned utilities in that state ....

From 1964 to 1985 the military regimes revised the constitution with institutional acts and decrees, and sometimes these gave the national executive carte blanche in the restructuring of the government and in the proclamation and implementation of all types of policies. The taxing powers of the federal government ensured that all governors and mayors, even those of powerful states and metropolises, would comply with the wishes of the president if they hoped to get any funding for essential services. The 1988 constitution is still untested. It promises greater freedom and power to [the 22 states and to] local administrations, but few Brazilians believe it will reverse the decades-old trend toward centralization.

The new constitution does give Congress greater power than ever before and strengthens civil liberties, labor rights, and social benefits. Its proclamation, in October 1988, abolished the authoritarian charter of 1967. Under the new constitution, Brazilians elected a president by direct popular vote in

November 1989, for the first time since 1960. The constitution also provides for the right to strike, sets the voting age at sixteen, abolishes censorship, and gives more power and income to state and municipal governments....

The Constitutional Assembly did not discard the presidential system, but the president, who will now hold office for five years, has been made accountable and in some instances subordinate to Congress. The legislature, composed of a Chamber of Deputies and a Senate, can sanction the president, alter the national budget, and determine international treaties. The text of the constitution is sufficiently ambiguous concerning the power of Congress that it is possible the legislative branch will assert itself against a president, or vice versa.

A similar ambiguity surrounds the role of the military as the guarantor of the constitutional order, the old *poder moderador* concept, but the armed forces retain their claim of being the ultimate arbiter of political life in Brazil. Land reform, on the other hand, one of the most controversial issues in Brazil and practically as old as the *poder moderador* question itself, is not resolved in the new constitution. Not surprisingly, the left complains that the constitution protects large private landowners and further weakens the sputtering efforts to distribute plots to landless peasants, at a time when 4 percent of the country's population owns half the arable land.

The new constitution is one of the world's longest with a total of 245 articles. Its length and detail ensure that it does not fully please or irritate all Brazilians. Some provisions are impractical, and they are the likeliest to be the first to be modified or ignored. Among them is an article that sets a ceiling of 12 percent on interest rates. It is widely assumed that a *jeito* (practical twist) will be found to cover the difference in a market where interest rates in real terms are now close to 22 percent. Perhaps the people who drew up the constitution realized the inevitability of having to modify the overly ambitious charter, because the document itself provides that amendments for the next five years will require only a simple majority.

Regardless of the tinkering to which the new constitution is already being subjected, some structural mainstays are not likely to change. Thus, traditionally, Brazilian ministries have been very large bureaucracies with a plethora of subcabinets, councils, and other agencies, many of them powerful in their own right, plus institutes, autonomous agencies, and the like attached directly or indirectly to the ministries themselves. In this bureaucratic maze, personal and political linkages are of great importance and often override considerations of merit, efficiency, or organizational rationalism. With so many people involved, many of them moving toward contradictory goals and policies, it is not surprising that Brazilian bureaucracy is notorious for its red tape (*papelada*) and unpredictability. Antibureaucratic czars have been appointed, to no avail. It is not corruption that is pervasive; what is, at all levels, is the sheer dead weight of myriad legal rules and enacted codes that long ago outlived their usefulness. About the only saving grace is the proverbial ability of the Brazilian bureaucrat to bend the rules just a little, apply a little humor or a *jeito,* so that some business can be transacted daily and the whole machinery of government does not come to a grinding halt....

Both federal and state courts exist in Brazil, and the federal Supreme Court has usually enjoyed a reputation for judicial learning and impartiality. The federal system is made up of the Supreme Court [with its inferior general jurisdiction courts] and the specialized military, electoral, and labor courts. The size of the Supreme Court has varied, as military presidents have added members in an effort to obtain more favorable judgments.

5. COLOMBIA

HARVEY F. KLINE, COLOMBIA: THE STRUGGLE BETWEEN TRADITIONAL "STABILITY" AND NEW VISIONS, in LATIN AMERICAN POLITICS AND DEVELOPMENT 231, 251-52 (H. Wiarda & H. Kline eds., 3d ed. 1990)

Colombia's national government is very similar, in appearance at least, to that of the United States: three branches of government with separation of powers and checks and balances. There are some important differences, however. The executive is clearly the most powerful branch of government, with that power centered in the president, who is elected for a four-year term with no immediate reelection allowed. Congress is bicameral, with both chambers elected on the basis of population, and is clearly secondary in power. Legislation is rarely written by the Congress, but it is not merely a rubber stamp — projects initiated by the executive are often dramatically changed, or indeed blocked altogether, by Congress. In comparative terms, probably only the congresses of Venezuela and Costa Rica have more power than the Colombian one. The Supreme Court has the right of judicial review, and its members are appointed by the president, with approval of Congress, for fixed terms.

[Colombia adopted a new Constitution effective 5 July 1991, designed partly to strengthen the judiciary]. The Colombian system is an extremely centralized one. *Departamentos* have only slight independent taxation abilities, and their governors are appointed by the president. *Municipios* (townships) have even lower taxation abilities, and until 1988 the mayors (with the exception of the mayor of Bogotá) were appointed by the governors. In 1988, for the first time in the country's history, Colombians elected the mayors, despite the fear of some that this constitutional change would increase the power of the drug dealers. Although *departamentos* might have some independent bureaucracy, most bureaucrats are national employees and report back to officials in Bogotá....

Colombians take pride in having a "mixed" economy — one that is not purely capitalist or socialist. Therefore, certain industries are government owned and run, such as communications, electricity, and natural resources. Others, especially in the area of consumer goods, are financed purely by private capital, either Colombian or foreign. In still others the government is one of several stockholders. The end result is a society in which the government plays a much larger part in the economy than it does in the United States, and government spending represents a larger percentage of the GNP.

6. MEXICO

MARTIN C. NEEDLER, MEXICAN POLITICS: THE CONTAINMENT OF CONFLICT 87-90, 94-96 (2d ed. 1990)

The citizen of the United States would find little that is unfamiliar about the government of Mexico if he looked solely at the nation's constitution, or at a formal organizational chart. To be sure, the president is elected for six years and may never be reelected, and there is no elected vice president. But there are two houses of the legislature and a separately structured judiciary. The president appoints cabinet members and ambassadors, with the consent of the Senate. There is a federal system, with governors and state legislators. Constitutional amendments must be voted by two-thirds of the Congress meeting in joint session and must be approved by a majority of the [31] state legislatures. (A permanent commission, composed of 29 members, may act in certain essential matters in place of the Congress, between legislative sessions.) Each state has two senators; however, so does the Federal District, unlike the situation in the United States.

The Legislature

But that is the form. The content is of course different. The dominance of the PRI in the legislature, and the president's position as head of the PRI, mean that the Congress passes all government legislation. Representatives of the opposition parties, whose numbers were substantially increased by the reforms of the López Portillo [1976-1982] and de la Madrid [1982-1988] administrations, participate in the debates and criticize the government position where it seems appropriate; the PAN is particularly proud of instances where it has found anomalies and inconsistencies in government bills, causing them to be modified. Although the Congress is thus acquiring greater significance in the Mexican system, its influence remains limited. Today, as in the 50 years prior to the electoral reform, one role of the national legislature remains that of providing another source of sinecures, a place for young politicians to pause on the way up, or for old ones to rest on the way down; of providing another salary for a deserving political worker, or cold storage for one for whom an appropriate job cannot at the moment be found. The Congress also serves as a place where recognition — in lieu of real power — can be given to second-level leaders of the PRI's less potent sectors, the labor and agrarian. And it socializes into national-level politics the politician who has heretofore made his career at the state level and is ready to try the big time.

However, another function of the Congress now is to give a stage to opposition leaders, to channel their activity into peaceful channels, to ease the pressure that would build up if they were totally closed out of significant roles. Accordingly, the electoral law has been changed several times to increase opposition representation. As a result, by the 1988 elections, the Chamber of Deputies was enlarged to 500 members. Three hundred deputies were to be elected, as before, in districts each of which returned a single member; but in addition, 200 deputies were to be chosen by proportional representation in order to reflect the percentage of votes cast for parties whose total vote was not fairly represented by the number of seats they had won in the single-member district elections — that is, for parties other than the PRI. The original provision for limited proportional representation, or party-list deputies, had been introduced during the presidency of López Mateos; under that system parties were allowed one deputy for every one-half of 1 percent they polled nationally, up to a total of 20 deputies, provided they polled at least 2.5 percent of the vote. This provision had never resulted in a total opposition representation of more than 40 seats in the Chamber of Deputies. In 1977 the number of "party list" deputies was increased to 100 and ten years later it was raised to the present 200....

The members of the Senate were, for a long time, all from the PRI, except that the leader of the Popular Socialist Party, Jorge Cruikshank, was, in effect, given a seat from the state of Oaxaca in 1976; the PRI candidate withdrew from contention, and in return the PPS agreed not to make a fuss over the gubernatorial election in another state, Hidalgo, where the PPS candidate had been unfairly treated. In 1988, four opposition senators were elected, however, all from left-wing parties.

In the Chamber elections, the PRI won only 233 of the 300 single-member districts, with 38 going to the PAN and 29 to left-wing parties. Proportional list seats were then allocated, bringing the parties to the figures shown in Table 6.11....

Table 6.11

The Mexican Chamber of Deputies (1988-1991), by Party Representation

Party	Seats
Partido Revolucionario Institucional (PRI)	260
Partido de Acción Nacional (PAN)	101
PFCRN*	34
Partido Popular Socialista (PPS)	32
Partido Auténtico de la Revolución Mexicana (PARM)	31
Frente Democrático Nacional (FDN)	22
Partido Socialista Mexicano (PSM)	19

*Partido de la Frente Cárdenista de Reconstrucción Nacional.

Note: The FDN is not a party but was an *ad hoc* coalition of pro-Cárdenas parties united to contest single-member districts.

Thus it may be that the legislature will assume a more important role than it has played in the past. But for all practical purposes, the Mexican government still means the executive branch, and especially the presidency. Even a great deal of Mexican legislation has taken the form of presidential decrees, whose legal basis may lie either in specific grants of power to legislate by decree — for example, during war or insurrection — or in the president's power of *reglamento*, of issuing decrees that specify the manner in which legislation passed by Congress is to be enforced. In addition, there are standing grants of power to the president; for example, the law governing the budget gives the president a great deal of freedom in transferring funds among budgetary categories and in exceeding expenditures envisioned in the original budget. In fact, the powers of the executive are very broad indeed.

The Judiciary

The judiciary, however, does have a limited measure of independence from the executive, and has rendered decisions against the executive. Especially significant here is a Mexican contribution to jurisprudence, the writ of *amparo*. This is issued by a court in response to the suit of an individual claiming that a legally guaranteed right had been violated by an official act. The writ may either command or prohibit specific government acts; in this respect, it has no equivalent in Anglo-Saxon jurisprudence, combining features of the injunction with those of specific writs such as habeas corpus or mandamus. However, the judiciary normally limits itself to a nonpolitical role and has not mounted frontal challenges to Mexican presidents, as the U.S. Supreme Court has sometimes done with respect to presidents of the United States.

The Power of the President

Thus the principal factor in governing Mexico is the president, which means in fact the executive branch — both the low-level bureaucrats and the top-level political administrators who come into office with a new president and are directly responsive to his policy preferences. When the presidency changes, the top echelon of office holders changes, too, as the new president puts in his own choices as heads of cabinet departments and of independent agencies. Each of these appointees brings along with him members of his network, his *camarilla*, some of whom are themselves developing cliques of friends, supporters, and clients, who will collaborate with each other, exchange favors, and promote each other's careers as they move up the hierarchy....

The public service in Mexico contains people of a wide range of capabilities. Many of the people at the top levels of the system are intelligent, well-educated, and dynamic political entrepreneurs with well-developed conceptions of the public interest; but, frequently, in his dealings with government, the citizen encounters mostly corrupt, self-serving, time-wasting incompetents. Between those extremes are many dedicated public servants, especially among the technically trained; but there are also others, particularly among middle- and lower-level administrative personnel, such as office managers, who are primarily interested in their bank accounts, who take kickbacks from lower-level employees, divert supplies, and pocket fees on purchases and contracts....

Sometimes one almost feels surprise that anything at all gets done, and that any public funds do find their way to the designated purpose. But there are forces making for effectiveness in the system. At the top levels, the political administrators want to promote their careers, and that means acquiring a reputation for competence and ability to deliver; this implies not only working hard and achieving assigned objectives, but also trying to build up a staff or cadre which performs effectively. So there is a continual sifting process, as a result of which merit is recognized and rewarded. People who can take charge, perform effectively, and meet the targets set are in demand; they are spotted and picked up by aspiring political entrepreneurs, whose coattails they ride up the bureaucratic career ladder.

State and Local Government

As in the United States, each state has authorities chosen by the voters of that state; of course, the role of the official party is critical. Because of the dominance of the same party at the national and state levels, it is unusual for a state government to defy federal directives, and, in extreme cases, the constitution provides that the federal Senate may, in fact, remove an elected governor, and, upon the nomination of the president, designate his successor. This provision is used today less frequently than in the earlier, more turbulent, days of Mexican history. However, since gubernatorial and presidential terms do not necessarily coincide, a governor may represent a faction of the party different from the president's even if the president personally approved all gubernatorial nominations made during his term.

The distance of the state capital from Mexico City gives a governor a certain amount of autonomy, although the military-zone commander (if he is not in cahoots with the governor) may be used by the federal government to check up on governors whose actions are reputed to be too notoriously repressive, venal, or bizarre. Otherwise, the governor dominates his state as the president dominates the country. The fact that the country is structured on federal lines would not necessarily in itself mean that the state governments were genuinely autonomous, given the dominant position of the executive, and especially the president, within the national government, and the fact that all state governors were, from the party's founding till 1989, nominees of the PRI, as were the majorities in all state legislatures. In fact, however, the state governments do enjoy a great measure of autonomy in their day-to-day activities, with the federal government intervening quite infrequently, principally at times of notorious gubernatorial misconduct....

Fiscal relations among the three levels of government are quite complex. State governments levy a range of taxes, which may include property, general-sales, excise, and even income taxes. They also receive federal subsidies earmarked for specific purposes. Local government is heavily dependent on subsidies from the state, but also raises funds by charging fees for municipal services and for licenses and permits of various kinds....

The structure of state government parallels that of the federal level except that all state legislatures are unicameral and are generally quite small in size. Neither state deputies nor state governors (there are no lieutenant governors) are eligible for immediate reelection, although the structure of each state government is established by the state constitutions, which differ from each other.

A basic unit of local government is the *municipio*, comparable, in Anglo-Saxon terms, to a township, county borough, or consolidated city-county government; that is, it consists of the town plus the surrounding rural area. Like other elected officials in Mexico, mayors and councilmen are not eligible for immediate reelection.

It is at the *municipio* level that opposition parties have been most successful; the PAN especially has captured *municipio* governments in the more developed northern states along the U.S. border and in Yucatán.

NOTE ON THE STRUCTURE OF THE MEXICAN COURT SYSTEM

Courts in Mexico can be divided between those within the judicial branch and those outside the judicial branch. First come the national federal courts within the judicial branch (*poder judicial de la federación*). At the top is the Supreme Court (*Suprema Corte de Justicia de la Nación*), with 26 justices (*ministros*) working in four ordinary chambers and one auxiliary chamber. Each chamber sits with five justices, while the president of the Court sits only in plenary session. Cases reach the Supreme Court via the writ of *amparo* and are divided up by subject matter:

First chamber — penal cases,
Second chamber — administrative cases,
Third chamber — civil cases,
Fourth chamber — labor cases, and
Auxiliary chamber — "left-over" cases.

The plenary Court (21 ordinary justices excluding the five supernumerary justices from the auxiliary chamber) hears constitutional cases (e.g., conflicts between federal branches) and certain other suits and judicial administration matters.

The circuit courts of appeal appear next in the federal judicial hierarchy. They consist of 30 collegiate circuit courts, each with three judges (*magistrados*), divided among 16 circuits. They hear all *amparo* cases outside the jurisdiction of the Supreme Court. In addition, there are 19 unitary (single-judge) circuit courts, which hear appeals from the decisions of district court judges in civil and penal matters.

District courts — 104 located in 44 judicial districts — are at the bottom of the hierarchy. These single-judge (*juez*) courts hear first instance civil and penal cases, indirect *amparo,* and constitutional *amparo* cases.

Almost one-quarter of the Mexican people live in the Federal District, which has its own system of courts (*poder judicial del Distrito Federal*). The highest court is the Superior Court of Appeal, with 34 judges working in 11 three-judge chambers. The chambers hear appeals in civil cases (chambers 1 to 5), penal cases (6 to 9), and family cases (10 and 11). The plenary court (including the president) assembles for important judicial administration matters. There are 99 first instance courts, divided by subject matter: civil (43), penal (33), and family (23). Below these courts are the limited jurisdiction peace courts (*juzgados mixtos de paz*), which handle minor civil and penal cases.

Each of the 31 states in Mexico has its own constitution, which establishes the structure of its state judicial power, along with an implementing *ley orgánica.* For appeals there is a supreme court or a superior court of appeal. Disputes are initially heard, depending on the importance of the question, in:

(1) first instance courts (civil, penal, and family cases); (2) limited jurisdiction courts (civil and penal cases); or (3) peace courts or other municipal courts (small claims or petty criminal cases).

There are also tribunals outside the federal and state judicial powers, which are regulated and budgeted within the executive branch. These courts fall with two categories: labor tribunals and administrative tribunals.

Federal labor tribunals operate under *La Junta Federal de Conciliación y Arbitraje*. There are 61 tribunals (*juntas especiales*), with 18 in Mexico City and 43 located among the 31 states. Each tribunal sits with three judges: one selected by labor, one by management, and the court president by the federal secretary of labor. Federal jurisdiction concerns 21 industrial activities (e.g., textiles) and three types of businesses (e.g., those that undertake projects in federal zones or territorial waters). Disputes are between laborers and management, a union and management, or between unions themselves. The Federal District and each state has its own system of labor tribunals (*juntas locales*), with residual jurisdiction existing outside the enumerated categories for the federal tribunals. Since 1976 federal caseloads have expanded at the expense of state *juntas locales*. Workers favor federal *juntas especiales* in each state, because they have more independence *vis-à-vis* local businesses.

For federal government employees there is the Federal Civil Service Tribunal. It has three judges: one chosen by the federal government, one by the employees, and the court president by agreement between these two sectors. The tribunal hears cases between executive or legislative branch employees and their governmental entity. Some states have also established this type of tribunal based on the federal model. Disputes between judicial employees and the federal courts are resolved by the plenary Supreme Court.

Administrative tribunals are the other major type of courts within the executive branch. At the apex is the Federal Superior Administrative Tribunal (*Tribunal Fiscal de la Federación*), with nine judges who hear appeals from the 13 three-judge federal regional administrative tribunals. These lower courts have jurisdiction to annul federal fiscal acts and to resolve certain cases involving administrative law (e.g., social security of public employees, governmental civil responsibility, public works contracts). The Federal District has an analogous tribunal (*Tribunal de lo Contencioso Administrativo*), with ten judges working in three chambers. Some states follow this federal model to review state governmental fiscal or administrative acts; other states permit these cases to go to the ordinary courts within the judicial branch.

The pattern of interaction among all these courts is very complicated. In general the control of legality and constitutionality is handled through the writ of *amparo*, with the ordinary federal courts carrying out this function. In 1982, 108,298 *amparo* cases (*juicios de amparo*) were filed in federal district courts, categorized as follows: 9,964 civil; 71,910 penal; 23,433 administrative; and 2,991 labor. We will review the Mexican *amparo* in Chapter 7.

NOTES AND QUESTIONS

1. What is similar about the political history of the United States and the Latin American republics? As compared to the history of Germany and Italy?

Does this help to explain the important influence of the U.S. Constitution on the legal structures found in Latin American constitutions? Is geography important?

2. Why does the presidential executive better suit Latin American legal culture than the parliamentary executive?

3. Professors Wiarda and Kline explain that the military may often be considered another branch of government. In fact the military generally sees itself as the defender of the constitution. Which legal institution serves that role in Europe?

4. Why is the judiciary relatively weak and the principle of judicial independence problematic in Latin America? Are these factors characteristic of a civil law system? Is this true for Europe?

5. Are social variables helpful in understanding Latin American legal structures? Consider the population and economic growth statistics in Tables 6.1 to 6.4, *supra*.

6. What functions does the legislature generally serve in Latin America?

7. Of the 20 or so Latin American nations, how many have adopted a federalist political structure? Of these, are they more like the strong federalist system in the United States or the quasi-federalist system in Germany?

8. In Chapter 1, Section C.10, where we first considered the idea of law and legal system used in this book, the concept of "legal penetration" was introduced. Is this similar to Wiarda and Kline's notions of "civilizing" and "centralization"?

9. What is the role of the Catholic church in a typical Latin American legal structure?

10. In what particulars do the examples of Argentina, Brazil, Colombia, and Mexico differ from the "typical" Latin American legal structure?

11. The popularly elected president in Mexico can only serve a single six-year term. Does this constitutional limitation help to counterbalance the enormous power of the executive branch in Mexico? What would be the advantages and disadvantages of transplanting a single six-year presidential term to the United States?

12. Is the Mexican court structure closer to that of the United States or more like one of its counterparts in Europe? What features seem to be influenced by the civil law tradition?

13. Autonomous state agencies have had great power in Latin American legal systems. A countertrend, however, has developed in some countries. For instance, the Mexican president in 1982 had the direct (or indirect through his ministers) authority to appoint the heads of 1,100 government entities, or to control their financing. By 1990 the de la Madrid (1982-1988) and Salinas (1988-1994) administrations had divested the federal government of 700 of these state-owned entities. In Argentina President Menem began to privatize many state businesses identified in the Administrative Reform Law of 23 August 1989. Those mentioned in the law include the national telephone, airline, mining, mail, telegraph, and railway companies and a number of state-owned television and radio stations.

14. For further reading on the issues discussed in this section, see (Argentina) William C. Banks & Alejandro D. Carrió, *Presidential Systems in Stress:*

Emergency Powers in Argentina and the United States, 15 Mich. J. Int'l L. 1 (1993); Alberto F. Garay, *Federalism, the Judiciary, and Constitutional Adjudication in Argentina: A Comparison With the U.S. Constitutional Model,* 22 U. Miami Inter-Am. L. Rev. 161 (1991); Alejandro M. Garro, *Nine Years of Transition to Democracy in Argentina: Partial Failure or Qualified Success?,* 31 Colum. J. Transnat'l L. 1 (1993); (Brazil) Fabio Konder Comparato, *The Economic Order in the Brazilian Constitution of 1988,* 38 Am. J. Comp. L. 753 (1990); Jacob Dolinger & Keith S. Rosenn, eds., A Panorama of Brazilian Law (1992); Jacob Dolinger, *The Influence of American Constitutional Law on the Brazilian Legal System,* 38 Am. J. Comp. L. 803 (1990); Augusto Nobre, *The Political Structure of the Federal Brazilian Republic Under the Constitution of 1988,* 21 U. Miami Inter-Am. L. Rev. 551 (1990); Keith S. Rosenn, *Brazil's New Constitution: An Exercise in Transient Constitutionalism for a Transitional Society,* 38 Am. J. Comp. L. 773 (1990); (Colombia) Roger W. Findley, *Presidential Intervention in the Economy and the Rule of Law in Colombia,* 28 Am. J. Comp. L. 423 (1980); Donald T. Fox & Anne Stetson, *The 1991 Constitutional Reform: Prospects for Democracy and the Rule of Law in Colombia,* 24 Case W. Res. J. Int'l L. 139 (1992).

7. SEPARATION OF POWERS

BUSTAMANTE, NATALIO

Supreme Court of Mexico (*en banc*)
Amparo 2026/51, November 19, 1970
23 S.J.F. pt. 1, at 41 (7th series 1970)

As a consequence of the concession of extraordinary powers bestowed upon the President of the Republic by the National Congress in the Decree of December 30, 1935, which created the Planning and Zoning Law and its regulations, and the Value-Added Tax, articles 14, 16, and 49 of the Federal Constitution are not contravened. This conclusion is appropriate because the National Congress may have conceded to the Executive certain opportunities to legislate, but two or more powers were not united in one person or one corporation with such delegation, nor was the legislative power placed in one individual. A situation arose in which the Executive enjoyed legislative opportunities delegated by the National Congress; however, the power of the Congress did not disappear with all of its attributes passing to the Executive, a situation specifically prohibited by article 49 of the Federal Constitution.... The Supreme Court of Justice has interpreted this constitutional provision to mean that the delegation of powers by the National Congress to the Federal Executive is not violative of individual guarantees, specifically in the theses of jurisprudence number 477 and 478 from the *Compilación de Jurisprudencia* 1917-1954. Interpreting these theses, it is concluded that what is prohibited by the Federal Constitution is the union of two or more powers in one person alone, that is, the fusion of powers in one branch of the government, which cannot happen without the destruction of the other governmental branch. In the present case the legislative branch continued to possess its own powers and function, only authorizing certain opportunities to the Executive Branch to expedite certain laws among which are those opposed here. The transmission of legislative function was thus partial and not total, and total delegation is what is prohibited by article 49 of the Federal Constitution.

Majority of 15 votes required
Majority opinion: MARIANO RAMÍREZ VÁZQUEZ
Dissenting: EZEQUIEL BURGUETE FARRERA

NOTES AND QUESTIONS

1. The Mexican Supreme Court decides whether an entire opinion should be published in *Semanario (Semanario Judicial de la Federación,* which is the official Mexican Supreme Court reporter). The *Bustamante* case is an example of a summary of the legal holding. Every case decided by the Supreme Court is published in at least this summary form and the Court has the discretion of ordering a portion or an entire opinion (including dissents) to be included in *Semanario* in addition to the summary. If a lawyer determines that he needs more than the summary of a prior decision to adequately argue his case, he can ask the Court for a photocopy of the full opinion as well as the lawyers' briefs.

2. Notice the style of this summary. What additional information would be helpful? Can we guess what article 49 of the Constitution states? Is the reasoning of the Court persuasive?

3. Would the decision in *Bustamante* provide much protection for the integrity of the legislature against a dominating president?

4. The reference to "theses of jurisprudence" in the summary is to propositions established as law by repeated holdings of the Court — so-called "consolidated jurisprudence," which is discussed in Chapter 9, Section A.

5. Striking a balance between ordinary and military jurisdiction has been a major problem, particularly in Latin America. Even in "normal" times, the ordinary courts have been reticent to interfere with military tribunals. Exacerbating the situation, there have been hundreds of declarations or extensions of a state of siege (*estado de sitio*) in the Latin American republics since World War II. The state of siege temporarily invests the executive branch with discretionary powers ordinarily pertaining to the legislative and judicial branches. Nevertheless, in some Latin American countries, the ordinary courts (and particularly the Supreme Court) have cautiously imposed some judicial limitations upon the powers vested in the executive (and the military tribunals within his command), even during the states of siege.

8. THE JUDICIARY AND THE MILITARY

CAICEDO VALENCIA, ARTURO

Supreme Court of Colombia (Penal Chamber)
Decision of December 7, 1970
136 G.J. 318 (1970)

DR. JUSTICE MARIO ALARIO DI FILIPPO delivered the opinion of the Court.

Having examined:

The Court proceeds to decide the petition filed by Arturo Caicedo Valencia against the March 11, 1970, decision of the Superior Military Tribunal, whereby the petitioner was condemned to four years in prison for the crime of military theft.

Facts

Miss María Virginia Gómez Herrera, employed by the Army's Rotating Fund, Melgar branch, filed a complaint on February 7, 1969 with the competent military authorities. On that day, upon opening warehouse No. 3 of the Fund and beginning the usual daily audit, she discovered that the cash register was empty and that money from the previous day's sales had disappeared. Upon informing Captain Valbuena, she noted that one of the roof tiles was not in place and that many tree leaves had fallen into the warehouse, thus deducing that a theft had occurred. The amount of money in the cash register was $2,553.90, in the form of two checks (one for $464.65 and another for $608.05) and the rest in cash.

An Army second corporal, Urbano Díaz Carvajal, in his statement on folio 39 stated that at approximately 12:30 a.m. on the night of February 18, 1969, while in his bedroom, he heard a noise in the Melgar Rotating Fund warehouse to which he paid little attention. But upon remembering that there had been a robbery therein a few days before, he began to think and sat down on his bed, smoking a cigarette so as not to go to sleep. Suddenly he heard some tiles being removed. He got up barefooted, put on his underwear, and armed himself with a piece of pipe and proceeded to see what was happening. Upon looking to the roof through which somebody had entered days before, he realized that the tile had been removed, but could not determine who was on the roof. Nevertheless he shouted: "Don't move or I will shoot." He then heard somebody say to him: "Don't shoot, I surrender." He shouted for help, and the person on the roof took advantage of the confusion, climbed down a tree near the warehouse, and ran. Officer Díaz went after him, beat him with the piece of pipe, and managed to overcome him completely. The captive then confessed in the presence of other officers to be the author of the theft which had been reported earlier by Miss Gómez Herrera. Officer Díaz also said that he afterwards climbed a tree and saw on the roof a few items and a cable hanging down with an adding machine and a package wrapped up in a black plastic material at the end....

Following the prescribed procedures, an ordinary Court Martial was held on October 14, 1969 (folio 167) in the Tolemaida barracks, with an unanimous guilty verdict against the accused. Based on this verdict, a sentence was issued on November 5 of the same year whereby Arturo Caicedo Valencia, retired Army officer, was condemned to four years in prison for the crime of military theft. This decision was appealed and confirmed by the Superior Military Tribunal by means of a resolution issued on March 11, 1970, which is now before this Court for review.

Petition for Review

The petitioner argues that the military trial was null and void because of lack of jurisdiction.

He points to article 170 of the Constitution, since this provision limits penal military jurisdiction to crimes "committed by military personnel on active duty and on matters related to such service."

Arturo Caicedo Valencia argues that he was a simple private citizen at the time of the incident. To consider him under military jurisdiction was to incur the above mentioned nullity, since the case *sub judice* occurred after the most recent state of siege had been lifted, when the nation was at peace (February 1969).

The state of siege through which our country has suffered, not only since Decree 1,288 (1965) was in force, but from before, ceased to be in force in December 1968. Another state of siege began to reign again in April of the current year, due to events we all know related to our last elections....

Considerations of the Court

A. Article 307 of the Military Code of Penal Justice (Legislative Decree 250, of July 11, 1958) states: "those who are under the military penal jurisdiction include: ... (6) private citizens, that is civilians not serving in the Armed Forces, who commit crimes set forth specifically for them in this Code."

B. This Court, in its decision of August 31 of this year, said:

> The Military Code of Penal Justice, in the part dealing with military and penal crimes, treats the embezzlement of public funds, larceny, theft and abuse of confidence in several chapters of Title X, under the heading "Crimes against State Property." Of these illicit acts, the statute requires that embezzlement of public funds and abuse of confidence involve an active member of the military or a civilian working for the Armed Forces, since the provisions in these chapters have a heading which states: "Military personnel or civilian employee of the Armed Forces who ..." (arts. 232-234 and 241). The same heading is not found for larceny or theft of movables, weapons, ammunition, or other items destined to be used by the Armed Forces. These penal categories, contained in articles 235 and 238, do not limit the potentially culpable agent....

C. The Court, as it has said on other occasions, does not see a manifest incompatibility between articles 238 and 307 of the Military Code of Penal Justice, on the one hand, and article 170 of the Constitution, on the other, which would force it to cease applying the former to protect the integrity of the Constitution....

Decision of the Court

From what has been said, the Supreme Court — Penal Cassation Chamber — in agreement with the Attorney General of the Armed Forces, and administering justice in the name of the Republic and by authority of law, rejects the petition filed by the accused Arturo Caicedo Valencia against the March 11, 1970 decision of the Superior Military Tribunal.

Copy, notify, and remand this opinion. Have it published.

JUSTICE JOSÉ MARIÁ VELASCO GUERRERO dissents....

1. The Supreme Court, and other lower courts established by law, administer justice....

If article 170 of the Constitution provides for Martial Courts and Military Tribunals to hear crimes "committed by military personnel on active duty and on matters related to such service," in agreement with the provisions of the Military Code of Penal Justice, it is possible, by extending this reasoning, to deprive private citizens committing crimes of the constitutional guarantee to be judged by the ordinary courts.

The reasoning of the Attorney General of the Armed Forces, arguing that article 13 of the Military Code of Penal Justice authorizes application of the Code to all persons violating its provisions, is faulty. This would encompass almost the totality of violations contemplated by the Penal Code; there would, thus, be no crime outside military jurisdiction....

2. I agree that certain crimes committed by private persons should qualify as "military crimes" when they relate to the fundamental mission of the military. For example, in the case of civilians dealing in weapons or taking them from arsenals, attacking guards, or obtaining military secrets and carrying out espionage activities, the safety of the institution itself is affected, and the superior interests of national defense are jeopardized. In these cases there is no obstacle for military jurisdiction, in times of war or civil disturbances, to hear the trials of such acts committed by civilians; its tribunals and judges are the best equipped to deal with them.

But it is unacceptable to give the Military Code of Penal Justice discretion *ad libitum* in deciding which cases it controls when acts are committed by civilians. The Constitution, article 170, is clear. The exceptional character of military jurisdiction has to be interpreted restrictively, without forgetting that all interpretations on penal matters should be equally restrictive....

5. [N]either the treatise writers nor Supreme Court doctrine [of Argentina] has ever admitted that military jurisdiction could hear crimes committed by civilians in time of peace. They have maintained repeatedly that except in time of war it is not appropriate to apply military laws to civilians....

The Italian Constitution authorizes, as does ours, some special jurisdictions ..., such as the military tribunals.... But in times of peace these jurisdictions are limited to better guard the freedom of citizens. [Thus, there must be a strictly "military crime" and the accused must be a member or agent of the armed forces.]

The same criteria are found in the doctrine and jurisprudence of constitutional systems founded on the principle, admitted by all democratic regimes, that citizens of a republic, without exclusion, have the right to be judged by the ordinary courts.

THE ARGENTINE MILITARY LEADERS CASE

National Appeals Court of Argentina
(Criminal Division, Buenos Aires)
Decision of 9 December 1985
309 Fallos 33 (1986)

[This case is described in an article by Enrique Dahl and Alejandro Garro in International Legal Materials, which is excerpted below.]

ENRIQUE DAHL & ALEJANDRO M. GARRO, ARGENTINA: NATIONAL APPEALS COURT (CRIMINAL DIVISION) JUDGMENT ON HUMAN RIGHTS VIOLATIONS BY FORMER MILITARY LEADERS, 26 International Legal Materials 317-19, 321-27 (1987)

[The Argentine National Appeals Court (Criminal Division) judgment of 9 December 1985, affirmed by the Supreme Court in its decision of 30 December 1986, concerned] the disappearance, torture, and murder of thousands of civilians between 1976 and 1983. The introductory note focuses on the factual background and some of the procedural and substantive issues of the judgment. It covers the period from the 1983 presidential order to investigate and prosecute former military leaders for human rights violations to the law of *punto final* or "full stop" of December 29, 1986 ....

This trial was the first of its kind in Latin American history. Never before had military leaders in Latin America been held responsible for actions committed under their governments. For the first time in the political history of Latin America, a democratic government decided to prosecute its military predecessors for human rights abuses in accordance with the rule of law. The judgment also represents the most comprehensive judicial review in Latin America of military responsibility for human rights violations....

Factual Background of the Judgment

Upon seizing power in 1976, the Argentine armed forces began an unprecedented attack aimed at left-wing terrorist groups. These gangs had killed and maimed not only government and police officials, but civilians as well. The military backlash affected a substantial sector of the population, who suffered unjust and indiscriminate punishment. Between 1976 and 1983, the military established an elaborate network of clandestine detention centers, where kidnapped victims or disappeared persons (*desaparecidos*) underwent interrogation and torture. The country was divided into a number of military zones, within which a regional commander was given complete autonomy over clandestine operations. Within each zone, middle-ranking officers of the three services of the armed forces cooperated in the abduction of suspected subversives. While some of the *desaparecidos* were eventually released, many others still remain unaccounted for.

During this period, Argentine courts were unable to secure justice. At the height of the campaign against subversion, the Supreme Court, whose members had been appointed by the military, repeatedly urged the commanders to clarify the fate of the *desaparecidos* in a consolidated action on some four hundred petitions for *habeas corpus* (*Perez de Smith,* 297 *Fallos de la Corte Suprema de Justicia de la Nación* [hereafter referred to as Fallos] 338 (1977); 300 Fallos 832, 1282 (1978)). Despite the many civilians kidnapped, murdered and tortured, not a single person was successfully prosecuted in either military or civilian courts. The military government at the time constantly denied that such crimes had ever taken place.

Political isolation, economic disaster, and the defeat over the Malvinas/Falkland Islands in 1982 gradually deteriorated the relative support enjoyed by the military immediately after the 1976 coup. Human rights leaders and a substantial sector of the Argentine people increasingly demanded the prosecution of the military. Elections were held in October 1983 and a civilian government took over two months later. Just before handing over power, the military junta enacted an amnesty law — the "Law of National Pacification." The purpose of this statute was to immunize every member of the military from prosecution for crimes committed during the so-called "dirty war" against subversion (Law No. 22,924, Sept. 22, 1983).... The self-amnesty law enacted by the military constituted a major obstacle for the government, because Article 18 of the Constitution prohibits the retroactive abrogation of penal laws, and Article 2 of the Criminal Code states that if the law changes after the criminal act, a judge should apply the law more beneficial to the defendant. Alfonsín's legal advisers offered three main arguments against the constitutionality of the self-amnesty law. First, that statutes enacted by a *de facto* government have only a precarious validity, outweighed by the offensiveness of their content, as was the case with the self-amnesty law. Second, that the statute violated Article 29 of the Constitution, prohibiting the concentration of all governmental power in one of the branches of government. Third, that the self-amnesty law violated Article 16 of the Constitution, which guarantees equal protection before the law ....

These arguments formed the basis for a government bill, later approved by Congress, nullifying *ab initio* the self-amnesty law (Law No. 23,040, Dec. 27, 1983). The National Appeals Court for the Federal District of Buenos Aires, Criminal Division (*Cámara Nacional de Apelaciones en lo Criminal y Correccional Federal,* hereinafter referred to as Federal Appeals Court), upheld the constitutionality of Law No. 23,040 and declared the self-amnesty law unconstitutional. The unconstitutionality of the self-amnesty law was based, in part, on the fact that the legislative powers exercised by the military government to enact that statute went beyond the legislative jurisdiction that the Supreme Court had been willing to recognize to *de facto* governments....

The Decision to Prosecute

President Raul Alfonsín took office on December 10, 1983. Three days later he enacted a decree ordering, as Commander-in-Chief of the Armed Forces, the arrest and prosecution of the nine military officers who formed the first three military *juntas* from 1976 to 1983 (Decree No. 158, promulgated Dec. 13, 1983 .... The decree was issued pursuant to the authority granted to the President by Article 86(15) of the National Constitution and Article 179 of the Code of Military Justice ....

Military Jurisdiction and Judicial Review

The Alfonsín government decided to confer initial jurisdiction over prosecutions of military personnel to the Supreme Council of the Armed Forces. This is the highest military tribunal and it has original jurisdiction to try senior officers (C.M.J., Art. 122(1)). At the same time, the government sought to open an avenue for review by civilian courts. To this effect, the Executive proposed to Congress a series of amendments to the Code of Military Justice

[C.M.J.]. Congress promptly acted upon the President's request by enacting Law No. 23,049 on February 14, 1984 ....

Under the jurisdictional framework devised by the amendments to the C.M.J., decisions of the Supreme Council of the Armed Forces are subject to a broad and automatic review by civilian federal courts of appeal. This procedure of plenary review is similar to the appeals process from other administrative courts, in which the appeals court may consider new evidence. Law 23,049 also authorizes the civilian federal courts to take over a trial at any stage if the military court unjustifiably delays it. Thus, if the Supreme Council fails to reach a decision within six months after the commencement of the proceedings, the reasons for the delay must be explained to the Federal Appeals Court of the place where the crime was allegedly committed. The court may return the case to the Supreme Council for a fixed period, requiring additional progress reports. However, unjustified delay or negligence by the military tribunal allows the appeals court to "assume the conduct of the proceedings at whatever stage they may be" (Art. 10, Law 23,049).

Constitutional Challenge to the Jurisdictional Framework

Under the federal rules of criminal procedure, victims of crimes, or their representatives, are entitled to initiate criminal complaints (*querellas*) involving serious felonies, or to join the public prosecutor (*fiscal*) as a party to the criminal proceedings (Federal Code of Criminal Procedure, Arts. 170-176). During the last months of the military government and the first months of civilian rule, many relatives of the disappeared demanded the prosecution of military officers in criminal courts. In many of those cases, public prosecutors, acting under the instructions of the Executive, moved to declare the criminal courts without jurisdiction and to transfer the cases to the Supreme Council of the Armed Forces, pursuant to the amendments introduced by Law No. 23,049 to the C.M.J.

The provisions of Law 23,049 vesting original jurisdiction on military tribunals presented a serious constitutional problem. Military tribunals are not constitutional courts within the meaning of Articles 94 and 100 of the Argentine Constitution, and Article 18 of the Constitution guarantees access to constitutional courts. Consequently, the establishment of a special military forum for the prosecution of common criminal offenses which do not amount to a violation of military discipline allegedly blocked the access to courts established by the Constitution. It was also argued that since the procedure established by the C.M.J. excludes any participation by the victims or their relatives in the criminal proceedings, the inaccessibility of a federal judicial forum guaranteed by Article 18 would constitute not only a denial of due process to those seeking the prosecution of the military, but also a violation of Article 16 of the Constitution, which incorporates both an equal protection clause (*principio de igualdad ante la ley*) and a prohibition of privileged judicial treatment for an identifiable group of persons (*fueros personales*).

When one of the many cases brought by the victims and their relatives against military officers reached the Supreme Court, the Court was confronted for the first time with the constitutional issues raised by Law 23,049.

In *Bignone, Reynaldo B.*, decided on June 21, 1984, a criminal action was brought by the relatives of three disappeared conscripts against the commanding officer of the military headquarters where the soldiers were stationed at the time of their disappearance.... Although the Supreme Court was ready to accept that the constitutional right of access to a judicial forum extends to both the accused and the victim, the majority concluded that both the appellate review provisions and the time limitations imposed on the jurisdiction of military tribunals sufficed for the law to withstand a constitutional attack....

Assumption of Jurisdiction by the Appeals Court

The Federal Appeals Court acted to take over the proceedings pursuant to Article 10 of Law 23,049. The court issued several indictments early in 1985 and placed five of the former military leaders under "rigorous preventive detention" (*prisión preventiva rigurosa*), requiring the other four to remain at the court's disposal. The public trial began on April 22, 1985.

The Trial

The trial of the former military leaders included 709 counts of murder, unlawful deprivation of freedom, torture, robbery, etc., selected by the prosecution to cover a specified number of victims from different sectors of Argentine society. The trial was held before a panel of six judges appointed by the government from a wide variety of backgrounds, who took turns presiding (Judges Andrés J. D'Alessio, Guillermo A.C. Ledesma, Ricardo R. Gil Lavedra, Jorge A. Valerga Araoz, Jorge Edwin Torlasco, and León Carlos Arslanian). The selection of cases made by the federal prosecutor covered crimes committed in different areas of the country and at different times, intending to prove the systematic and methodological criminal approach followed by the former commanders in the struggle against subversion. During the eight-month trial, the six-member panel of the appeals court heard 496 hours of testimony from more than 800 witnesses....

The defense attorneys formally denied that the disappearances had taken place and that the *juntas* had ordered them. At the same time, they argued that such a policy was justified on different grounds. First, it was contended that the alleged crimes were committed "in execution of a legal duty," pursuant to an executive decree enacted by the prior constitutional government which had delegated responsibility to the armed forces for the "elimination" (*aniquilación*) of terrorism. Second, the defense invoked the legal doctrine of "necessity" in the proposition that the campaign against subversion was necessary in order to save the country from imminent chaos. Third, the lawyers for the defendants contended that the armed forces had engaged in self-defense while protecting Argentine society from the violent attack of subversive elements. The court held that none of the alleged grounds of justification — execution of a legal duty, necessity, and self-defense — could be applied to the facts of the case.

The court also rejected the defense counsel's argument that the crimes were acts committed in excess by individual servicemen, for which their commanders could not be held responsible. According to the court, the sustained pattern of abduction, torture, and murder could not possibly be explained as the acts of a few deranged officers....

The Sentences

The court found five former military leaders guilty of specific crimes committed against identified individuals and received prison sentences ranging from four-and-a-half years to life. Four other members of the former military *junta* were acquitted....

Later Developments

On December 30, 1986, the Supreme Court upheld the judgment and the convictions handed down by the Federal Appeals Court. The sentences remained unchanged, except for a six-month reduction of former president Roberto Viola's 17 year sentence and 45 instead of 54 months for former Air Force Commander-in-Chief Orlando Agosti.

NOTES AND QUESTIONS

1. The leaders of authoritarian regimes often believe that the legitimacy of their rule is supported by maintaining the form of the classic tripartite division of government, including an independent judiciary. However, a powerful judiciary may prove disruptive to the plan of the executive branch. One solution to this dilemma is to enlarge the jurisdiction and use of special courts, such as military courts or labor courts, that are controlled by the executive. This drains off cases potentially conflictive for the executive branch and leaves the ordinary courts with routine matters that do not threaten the regime. The independence of these weakened ordinary courts is thus politically harmless. For the example of General Franco's Spain, see José Juan Toharia, *Judicial Independence in an Authoritarian Regime: The Case of Contemporary Spain,* 9 Law & Soc'y Rev. 475 (1975).

2. Do the facts in *Caicedo Valencia* concern more the structural issue of separation of governmental powers or the issue of individual rights? Are the two issues interrelated? Does the majority or the dissent provide the better view? The Colombian Supreme Court, in its decision of 5 March 1987, declared unconstitutional the practice of transferring all cases concerning public order to military courts during a state of siege.

3. Consider the form of the Colombian Supreme Court opinion in *Caicedo Valencia.* What similarities and differences does it have to a typical opinion from the U.S. Supreme Court?

4. Does *The Argentine Military Leaders Case* suggest that the military in Latin America should not be considered a separate branch of government? Does it help to know that the National Appeals Court took over the case in late 1984 after the Supreme Council of the Armed Forces declared that it was unable and unwilling to proceed?

5. For a provocative comparison of the legal structures in Latin America and the United States, see Keith S. Rosenn, *The Success of Constitutionalism* *in the United States and Its Failure in Latin America: An Explanation,* 22 U. Miami Inter-Am. L. Rev. 1 (1990).

C. EAST ASIA

1. JAPAN

HIDEO TANAKA, THE CONSTITUTIONAL SYSTEM OF JAPAN AND THE JUDICIAL SYSTEM, in LAW AND BUSINESS IN JAPAN 1-7, 18-21 (Akira Kawamura ed. 1982)

The Constitutional System

The Emperor

With the adoption of the present Constitution, which proclaims that sovereign power resides with the people, there has been a complete change. Not only does the Emperor now perform only ceremonial functions, but his position, according to Article 1 of the present Constitution, derives "from the will of the people with whom resides the sovereign power." His primary role now is in being "the symbol of the State and of the unity of the people." The Imperial Household Law is now a law enacted by the Diet which may be amended as the Diet wishes.

The Legislature

(a) The Diet (*Kokkai*) is a bicameral legislature, consisting of the House of Representatives (*Shūgi-in*) and the House of Councillors (*Sangi-in*).

The House of Representatives occupies a superior position under the Constitution in that it can override a decision of the House of Councillors with a two-thirds majority in the case of the passage of a bill, and with a simple majority in the case of the passage of a budget or approving a treaty. When both Houses disagree in their selection of the Prime Minister, the choice of the House of Representatives prevails.

(b) "The term of office of members of the House of Representatives shall be four years. However, the term shall be terminated before the full term is up in case the House of Representatives is dissolved [by the Cabinet]." [Const. art. 45.] The term of members of the House of Councillors is six years. The House of Councillors cannot be dissolved.

(c) In spite of the inequality in the powers of the respective Houses, "both Houses shall consist of elected members, representative of all the people." [Const. art. 43(1).]

The present electoral system is as follows:

(i) House of Representatives: The whole country is divided into 129 electoral districts, from each of which three to five members are elected, the total being 511.

One of the peculiarities about the Japanese election laws is that each voter votes for only one candidate regardless of the number to be elected from that district. This has the effect of improving the chances for minority parties to send their representatives to the Diet.

(ii) House of Councillors: Of the 252 members of this House, 100 are chosen at large, and the remaining 152 from each prefecture. Both types of members are elected by popular vote, each voter casting two votes, one for each. Since the terms of councillors are staggered, half the above number are elected every three years.

The very peculiar system whereby each voter votes for only one candidate in an election to choose 50 members at large from a total vote of over 50 million, was originally designed to create the possibility of electing leaders of various interest groups and nationally known figures such as news commentators. As a matter of practice, however, this system often requires a very expensive campaign with much difficulty in predicting the outcome.

(iii) Necessity for Re-apportionment: The basic form of the present distribution of electoral districts was fixed in 1947. Although the Election of Public Officials Act (*Kōshoku Senkyo Hō*) provides for a revision every five years on the basis of the preceding national census, the Diet has failed to observe this provision. This has resulted in a significant inequality in representation because of the rapid urbanization of Japan during the past quarter of a century. It is true that two statutes — one in 1964 and another in 1975 — were enacted to carry out re-apportionment, but each of them fell short of making an allocation in proportion to the population. Thus, in 1974 the most favored House of Representatives district elected one member per 80 thousand eligible voters, and the least favored district one member per 424 thousand (a ratio of 1 to 5.3). The 1975 Act only reduced this ratio to 1 to 3.71.

This is a natural source of dissatisfaction, but the members of the Diet have yet to find a workable compromise among the divergent systems of political mathematics. The conservative party in power favors the "small electoral district," *i.e.*, one-member-from-onc-district system under which it can have more of its candidates elected, but is reluctant to apportion the seats in proportion to the population, believing re-apportionment would give a stronger voice to the working class in big cities. On the other hand, the opposition parties propose either the adoption of a proportional representation system or the preservation of the present system of electing several members from each district while at the same time urging that the electoral districts be re-apportioned.

(d) It was originally expected that the House of Councillors would perform a role distinct from the other House, as is now expected of the British House of Lords. Such a role would be, for instance, to debate the technical points of law concerning a bill, or to give an opinion from a non-political standpoint. During the first years of its existence there were signs that the House of Councillors might go that way, the most notable of which was the formation of the *Ryokufū Kai* (Green Wind Association) by 73 of the first 250 members, who wished to remain independent. This turned out to be mere wishful thinking. As a result of keen efforts by political parties to entice more members into their folds, and the greater prospects of winning at the next election with the support of a party, one after another of these independents joined a political party until now the upper House to all intents and purposes is not too dissimilar to the lower House.

The Cabinet

(a) The Constitution of Japan adopts the parliamentary system for the national government, though it provides for the presidential system in relation to local government. Thus the "Prime Minister (*Naikaku Sōri-daijin*) shall be designated from among the members of the Diet by a resolution of the Diet," which is in reality that of the House of Representatives. In addition, a majority of the "ministers of state" (*kokumu-daijin*) must be chosen from among the members of the Diet. As a matter of practice, nearly all of them are so chosen.

The Cabinet (*Naikaku*) must command the support of the House of Representatives. "If the House of Representatives passes a no-confidence resolution, or rejects a confidence resolution, the Cabinet shall resign *en masse,* unless the House of Representatives is dissolved within ten days." [Const. art. 69(1).] According to the accepted constitutional practice, the Cabinet may dissolve the House of Representatives at its own convenience, *i.e.,* on grounds in addition to those provided in the above provision.

(b) Though the Prime Minister was merely a *primus inter pares* under the Meiji Constitution, he is now the head of the Cabinet with power to appoint and remove the ministers of state.

The Cabinet is a collective body, whose decisions have to be reached unanimously at a Cabinet meeting. The Prime Minister, however, can and does in fact exert strong influence over the other members of the Cabinet due to his power to hire and fire.

(c) The Cabinet consists of the Prime Minister and other ministers of state who shall be not more than twenty in number.

There are twelve ministries each headed by a minister of state. They are the ministries of Justice (*Hōmu Shō*), Foreign Affairs (*Gaimu Shō*), Finance (*Okura Shō),* Education (*Mombu Shō*), Health and Welfare (*Kōsei Shō*), Agriculture, Forestry [, and Fisheries (*Nōringyo*] *Shō*), International Trade and Industry (*Tsūshō Sangyō Shō*, commonly abbreviated as MITI in English and *Tsūsan Shō* in Japanese), Transport (*Un'yu Shō*), Posts and Telecommunications (*Yūsei Shō*), Labor (*Rōdō Shō*), Construction (*Kensetsu Shō*) and Home Affairs (*Jichi Shō*). Each ministry has several bureaus (*kyoku*).

In addition to these ministries, there are a number of offices which directly belong to the Prime Minister or to the Prime Minister's Office. Among these offices, the Prime Minister's Office (*Sōri Fu*), National Public Safety Commission (*Kokka Kōan linkai*), Administrative Management Agency (*Gyōsei Kanri Chō*), Hokkaido Development Agency (*Hokkaidō Kaihatsu Chō*), Self Defense Agency (*Bōei Chō*), Economic Planning Agency (*Keizai Kikaku Chō*), Science and Technology Agency (*Kagaku Gijutsu Chō*), Environment Agency (*Kankyō Chō*), Okinawa Development Agency (*Okinawa Kaihatsu Chō*) and National Land Agency (*Kokudo Chō*) are all headed by a minister of state.

The Chief Cabinet Secretary (*Naikaku Kambō Chōkan*) is also a minister of state. There are several ministers of state without portfolio.

Civil Service

Japan has a highly organized bureaucracy. It is headed by civil servants of high ability. Employees of the respective bureaus, especially those of the upper and middle ranks, are by and large tightly united by a highly developed *esprit de corps.* It seems that most of them feel that they are morally obligated to lead the Japanese people and believe that they are well qualified to perform this task.

One of the pillars supporting the Japanese bureaucracy is its system of handling personnel affairs.

Since 1885, the recruitment of civil servants has been based upon the merit system. The core of this system is the Examination for Upper Class National Employees (*Kokka Kōmuin Jōkyu Shiken*) which purports to select future leaders of the bureaucracy.

The Civil Service Commission (*Jinji-in*) sets standards of appointment, dismissal, wages, working hours and other conditions of employment for civil servants....

Local Government

(a) Local public entities are structured basically in two tiers in Japan. On the first tier are the prefectures, and on the second are the cities, towns and villages. In addition the eleven big cities are subdivided into wards (*ku*).

(b) There are 47 prefectures. One prefecture (Tokyo) is called a *to* (metropolitan area), one (Hokkaidō) a *dō,* two (Kyōto and Ōsaka) *fu* and 43 others *ken.* Though different in name, they are not different in nature, except that Tokyo *To* stands directly above the wards in the area which had been governed by Tokyo City (*Shi*) until 1944 when the city and the old Tokyo Prefecture (*Fu*) were amalgamated in Tokyo *To.* Tokyo *To* also stands above the other cities, towns and villages within the boundaries of the former Tokyo *Fu.*

Prefectures were divided into several administrative units called *gun* which comprised several towns and villages, but no cities. However, *gun* are no longer local public entities, though people still use that name to denote certain areas.

(c) Each local public entity, *i.e.,* prefecture, city, town or village, has its own assembly, whose members are elected by its inhabitants.

The chief executive officers of all local public entities, unlike the premier at the national level, are elected by direct popular vote within their respective communities.

(d) The Constitution of Japan has four articles on "local self-government." They were based upon the idea of doing away with the extreme centralization of authority under the Meiji Constitution, when the Home Ministry (*Naimu Shō*) controlled the entire police system and thereby supervised various phases of the daily life of the people.

It should be noted, however, that Japan is definitely a unitary state, and the status of prefectures in Japan is not comparable to the states in [federal systems], either constitutionally, legally or politically. Most of the important items of local government are regulated by national statutes. These local public entities have only limited financial autonomy — again a source of control by the central government through grants-in-aid....

The Judicial System

Organization of Courts

(a) Supreme Court (*Saikō Saibansho*): There are fifteen justices of the Supreme Court. (They divide themselves into three petty benches (*shō hōtei*) each consisting of five justices (three being the quorum), except in (i) cases on appeal involving a constitutional issue where there is no existing precedent of the Supreme Court, (ii) cases on appeal concerned with a non-constitutional point of law on which a petty bench has found it appropriate to overrule a precedent of the Supreme Court, (iii) other cases which petty benches have referred to the grand bench because they considered them of great importance, or (iv) cases where the opinions of the petty bench justices have ended in a tie. In these exceptional cases, all the justices of the Supreme Court sit together as the grand bench (*dai hōtei*).

Figure 6.5

Structure of the Japanese Court System

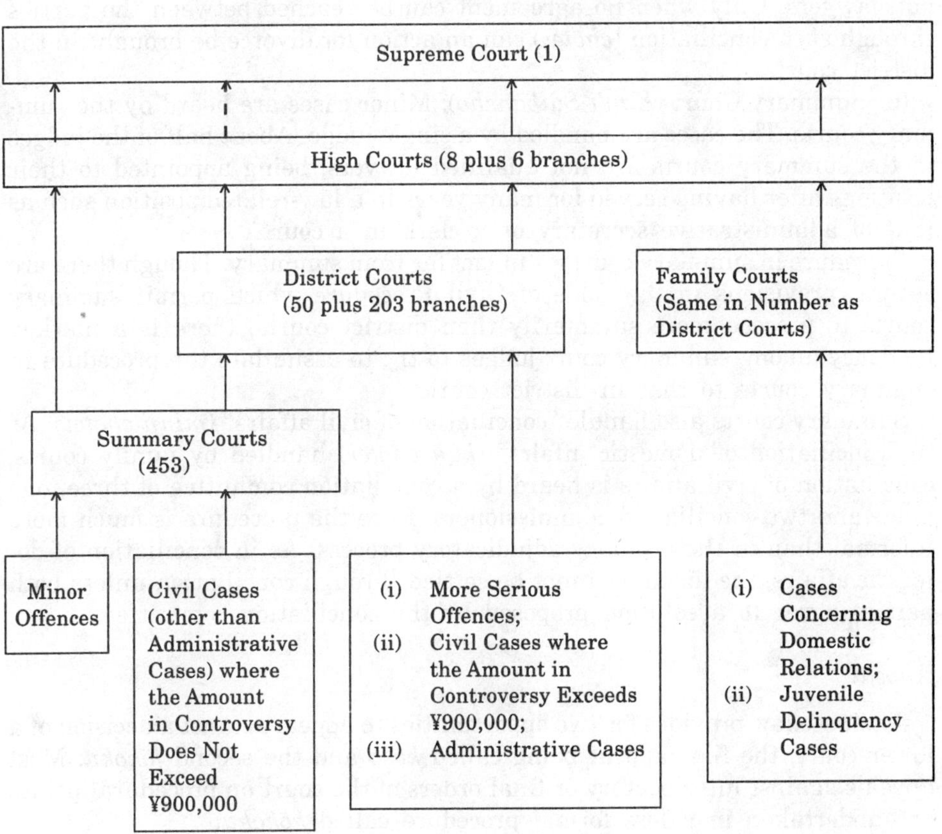

There are also twenty "research clerks" (*chōsakan*), almost all of whom have been judges for years, who carry out research for the purpose of furnishing the justices with data necessary for deciding cases.

(b) High Court (*Kōtō Saibansho*): High courts usually act as intermediate appellate courts, except that (i) they act as court of last resort in minor civil cases and (ii) they have original jurisdiction on insurrection cases as well as on certain types of administrative cases. They hear cases in a collegiate court of three judges.

(c) District Court (*Chihō Saibansho*): District courts are the courts of general original jurisdiction. They also have appellate jurisdiction over the decisions of the summary courts in civil matters. Cases are heard by a single judge or by a collegiate court of three judges, depending on the nature of the case.

(d) Family Court (*Katei Saibansho*): Civil cases involving matters concerning domestic relations and juvenile delinquency cases are handled by family courts. The more formal procedure in family courts, *shimpan,* is handled by a single judge. Most domestic proceedings such as divorce cases must first be heard by a conciliation committee (*chōtei iinkai*) of three, one judge and two conciliation commissioners (*chōtei iin*) who need not be, and in most cases are not, lawyers. Only when no agreement can be reached between the parties through such conciliation (*chōtei*) can an action for divorce be brought in the district court.

(e) Summary Court (*Kan'i Saibansho*): Minor cases are heard by the summary courts. The cases are handled by a single judge. About half of the judges in the summary courts are not qualified lawyers, being appointed to their positions after having served for many years in a law-related position such as that of administrative secretary or a clerk in a court.

Procedure in summary courts is in fact far from summary. Though there are several provisions in the Code of Civil Procedure which permit summary courts to proceed more summarily than district courts, there is a marked tendency among summary court judges to try to assimilate the procedure in summary courts to that in district courts.

Summary courts also handle "conciliation of civil affairs" (*minji chōtei*). As in "conciliation of domestic affairs" (*kaji chōtei*) handled by family courts, conciliation of civil affairs is heard by a conciliation committee of three, one judge and two conciliation commissioners. Here the procedure is much more informal than in the ordinary adjudicatory process. As in conciliation of domestic affairs, the dispute cannot be settled through conciliation unless both parties agree to a solution proposed by the conciliation committee.

Appeal

Japanese law provides for two opportunities to appeal against a decision of a lower court, the first appeal being called *kōso* and the second *jōkoku*. Most appeals against interlocutory or final orders of the court on procedural points are undertaken in a less formal procedure called *kōkoku*.

In civil cases, the party who lost in the final judgment of the court of first instance may file a *kōso* appeal for an alleged error in fact-finding as well as for an alleged error in law. In criminal cases, however, grounds for *kōso* appeal are limited to (i) an error in law which clearly affects the outcome of the case, (ii) an error in fact-finding which clearly affects the outcome, and (iii) an impropriety in fixing the penalty to be imposed. In the last two cases, the appellant must cite the facts as found by the court of first instance which prima facie show the alleged impropriety.

The grounds for *jōkoku* appeal in civil cases also differ from those in criminal cases. In civil cases, the grounds are (i) "an error in the interpretation of or other violation of the Constitution" and (ii) an error in law which clearly affects the outcome of the litigation. In criminal cases, a *jōkoku* appeal can be filed (i) for "an [alleged] violation of the Constitution or an [alleged] error in its interpretation," or (ii) for an alleged conflict with a precedent of the Supreme Court, the Great Court of Judicature (*Taishin-in*), *i.e.*, the highest court in the Japanese hierarchy between 1875 and 1947, or a high court. The Supreme Court may also hear on a *jōkoku* appeal any case which it considers to involve an important point of statutory interpretation. In this latter category, the Supreme Court has a discretion similar to that exercised by the Supreme Court of the United States in relation to a petition for the writ of *certiorari*. The grounds for reversal in criminal *jōkoku* appeals are somewhat wider than the grounds for appeal. Not only can the Supreme Court reverse the judgment below on constitutional grounds or on the ground of disregard of a precedent, it can do so if the Court finds it manifestly unjust not to do so, where there is (i) an error of law which may affect the outcome of the case, (ii) an extreme impropriety in fixing the penalty to be imposed, (iii) a significant error in fact-finding which may affect the outcome of the case, (iv) a ground which will justify a "reopening of the proceedings" (*saishin*), or (v) a change or abolition of the penal statute [which was the ground for conviction] or amnesty after the judgment was rendered.

Centralization in the Administration of the Judiciary

Japan has a tradition of centralization in regard to the "administration of the judiciary" (*shihō-gyōsei*).

Aside from those functions which are performed by the Department of Justice in the United States, the Supreme Court also manages all personnel business in relation to judges because of the structure of the "career judiciary" system.

Up to 1947, the "administration of the judiciary" (which then also included the administration of the public procurators' office) had been handled by the Ministry of Justice (*Shihō Shō*), where those who had served as public procurators had a very strong voice. In order to strengthen and secure the independence of the judiciary, this structure was changed in 1947. A huge General Secretariat (*Jimu Sōkyoku*) is now attached to the Supreme Court to manage affairs concerning the administration of courts. Its activities include all personnel business relating to the judges, court clerks and other staff of the court, as well as the duty to undertake or organize research on law and the administration of justice, to prepare statistics, and to furnish the inferior courts with necessary information.

The General Secretariat of the Supreme Court now has a staff of about 950, many of whom are qualified lawyers. It has seven bureaus — General Affairs, Personnel Affairs, Finance, Civil Matters, Criminal Matters, Administrative [Litigation] Matters and Family Matters — and 28 sections.

NOTES AND QUESTIONS

1. Classify the legal structure of Japan. Is its political structure unitary or federal? Is it a republic or a monarchy? Is its executive parliamentary or presidential? In these respects does Japan have a legal structure more like the United States or like a civil law European nation?

2. Consider the Japanese court system. What are its similarities to and differences from the French court system? The Spanish court system?

3. Japan's ruling Liberal Democratic Party (LDP) lost its majority in the July 1993 general election, which was held in the wake of successive political scandals and the defection of almost 20 percent of the LDP's lower house members. The subsequent formation of a coalition of opposition parties and election of Morihiro Hosokawa as prime minister thus ended 38 years of continuous LDP rule. The single issue uniting the new government is electoral reform. By early 1994 the Diet is expected to approve compromise legislation that would reduce the number of members of the lower house to 500, with 274 single-seat districts and 226 seats chosen by nationwide proportional representation. Major reforms of campaign financing are also included in proposed legislation.

4. For further information on the Japanese legal structure, see Hiroshi Oda, Japanese Law (1992).

NOTE ON LITIGATION IN JAPANESE COURTS

Table 6.12

Total Cases Filed in Japanese Courts in 1985, by Court and Type of Case

Court and Case Type		Cases Filed
Summary Courts		2,758,000
Civil cases		228,000
Criminal cases (defendants)		25,000
Summary criminal trials (including traffic)		2,417,000
Conciliation cases		88,000
Family Courts		389,000
Status and succession cases		304,000
Conciliation cases		85,000
District Courts		211,900
Civil cases		118,500
First instance	116,000	
Appeal	2,500	
Criminal cases (defendants)		91,000
Administrative litigation cases		800
Conciliation cases		1,600

Court and Case Type	Cases Filed
High Courts	17,800
Civil cases	11,300
Criminal cases (defendants)	6,200
Administrative litigation cases	300
Supreme Court	3,500
Civil cases	1,600
Criminal cases (defendants)	1,700
Administrative litigation cases	200

The statistics in Table 6.12 omit nonlitigation matters. For civil and administrative cases in the following courts, these include, e.g., requests for provisional attachment and execution:

Summary courts	1,445,000
District courts	626,000
High courts	7,400
Supreme Court	800

For criminal cases, nonlitigation matters include, e.g., claims for criminal indemnity, as follows:

Summary courts	319,000
District courts	179,000
High courts	2,500
Supreme Court	500

For family courts, nonlitigation matters include 13,800 actions insuring performance of a judicial decision or decisions implementing cooperation between courts.

Compare the Japanese court filings with similar data for Germany (Tables 6.5 and 6.6) and for Italy (Tables 6.7 and 6.8). What are your conclusions? Now consider the Note on the Comparison of Civil Litigation Rates Among Nations (*supra* Section A.5 of this chapter). Counting conciliation cases, 822,600 first instance civil (and family) cases were filed in 1985, for a litigation rate of 680 cases per 100,000 population. This rate is 18 percent of the level of civil filings in Germany and only 42 percent of the lower level in Italy. The Japanese rate is a mere 11 percent of the filings rate in the United States. Japanese attitudes toward civil litigation and possible explanations for the low propensity to sue are examined in Section E of this chapter.

The Japanese level of criminal litigation is also very low by European standards. See the Note on the Comparison of Criminal Litigation Rates Among Nations (*supra* Section A.5). Excluding Road Traffic Law violations handled in summary criminal trials (1,902,000), 631,000 criminal cases were filed in Japan in first instance. This provides a rate for Japan of 521 cases per 100,000 inhabitants compared to the German rate of 2,496 and the United States rate of 5,081.

Japan is even more notable as the only industrial country in the world that has experienced significant reductions in crime in all major categories, except those related to motor vehicle law violations, since the early 1950s. For example, between 1950 and 1990 the number of reported homicides decreased from 2,892 to 1,441. Reported robberies dropped from 7,821 to 1,771. The number of reported rapes similarly decreased from 3,558 to 1,741. The only significant increase in Criminal Code crimes was reported cases of larceny, which accounted for over half of Japan's non-traffic related offenses and which rose from 982,341 reported cases in 1950 to 1,422,355 in 1988.

For fuller treatment of crime control in Japan and the Japanese criminal justice system, see John Braithwaite, Crime, Shame, and Reintegration (1989); A. Didrick Castberg, Japanese Criminal Justice (1990); William Clifford, Crime Control in Japan (1976); Robert Y. Thornton & Katsuya Endo, Preventing Crime in America and Japan: A Comparative Study (1992); Daniel F. Foote, *The Benevolent Paternalism of Japanese Criminal Justice,* 80 Cal. L. Rev. 317 (1992). V. Lee Hamilton & Joseph Sanders, Everyday Justice: Responsibility and the Individual in Japan and the United States (1992) is an excellent comparative study of Japanese and American attitudes toward crime and punishment.

NOTE ON POLITICAL AND INSTITUTIONAL CHANGE IN EAST ASIA

During the half-century since the end of World War II in the pacific, Japan has enjoyed the greatest political and institutional stability of any country in East Asia. Throughout most of the region the emergence of nationalism and new states forged from dismantled European and Japanese colonial empires coupled with the communist revolutions in China and Vietnam produced violent upheaval, including protracted civil wars involving the United States, first in Korea and then in Vietnam. It is not surprising, therefore, that the political regimes that emerged in the midst of such conflict and changes tended to be dominated by the military with internal security and order an overriding concern. For much of the postwar era East Asia has thus been subject to a variety of authoritarian regimes, often ruling under emergency declarations or martial law. As order and increasing levels of prosperity have prevailed, however, progress has been made throughout the region, exemplified by the political reforms in the Philippines, South Korea, Taiwan, and most recently Thailand, to create or restore Western-style constitutional processes and institutions for civilian-controlled, democratic government.

Although to some the pace of reform may seem slow, the institutional changes that are gradually being implemented appear to have taken hold and promise to be enduring.

In this respect too Japan serves as a model. Emerging in 1952 from war, defeat, and occupation, Japan represents East Asia's most successful example of stable, democratic government. Its postwar Constitution has not been amended since promulgation in 1946. Except for a brief six-month interval in 1949, Japan has been governed continuously by a coalition of conservative political factions, represented since 1955 by the Liberal Democratic Party

(*Jiyu-Minshū tō),* but since the election of July 1993 by an array of newly formed political groupings. Moreover, despite extensive political and regulatory law reforms under the Allied Occupation, the basic structure of the Japanese legal system has remained largely unchanged for over a century.

Similarly, even radical political change in other countries in East Asia has not always extended to the basic structure of the legal system. As in the case of Japan, there has often been a significant degree of continuity. The Japanese institutional patterns also remain fairly representative of most of the civil law systems in the region, with South Korea the most similar and, at least institutionally, Taiwan among the most distinctive.

2. SOUTH KOREA

JAMES M. WEST & DAE-KYU YOON, THE CONSTITUTIONAL COURT OF THE REPUBLIC OF KOREA: TRANSFORMING THE JURISPRUDENCE OF THE VORTEX, 40 American Journal of Comparative Law 73-77, 88-90, 92-94 (1992)

[After the Korean War, America's attempt to build new cohesion around democratic institutions in Korea's First Republic of the 1950s failed and was overgrown by autocracy.]

The Second Republic, founded in the wake of the student revolution of April 19, 1960, was plagued by factionalism and survived barely a year before being overthrown by a military coup on May 16, 1961. After a period of martial law, the Third Republic was established in 1963 by Major General Park Chung Hee. In 1969 Park and his supporters amended the constitution to facilitate his retention of the presidency.

In 1972 Park again resorted to martial law and extensively modified the constitution — the repressive dictatorship known as the Fourth Republic or the *Yusin* system lasted until Park's assassination by the head of the Korean Central Intelligence Agency in October 1979. The Fifth Republic opened with a violent *coup d'état* in December 1979 and the bloody suppression of a popular revolt in the city of Kwangju in May 1980. It closed with President Chun Doo Hwan in disgrace, following large-scale civil disobedience in June 1987 which saw millions of Korean citizens demand a transition to a more democratic political system.

The Sixth Republic came into being in February 1988 with the implementation of the ninth amendment of the constitution of the Republic of Korea since the First Republic was founded in 1948. The direct presidential election in December 1987 resulted in the election of Roh Tae Woo, a close associate of Chun Doo Hwan, who obtained a plurality of the popular vote to prevail over disunited opposition parties....

After a period of legislative stalemate, the political scene was abruptly realigned on January 22, 1990, when Kim Young Sam and Kim Jong Pil announced the merger of their conservative opposition parties with the party of President Roh Tae Woo to form a new "Democratic Liberal Party." The new DLP, which through early 1992 held a secure majority in the National Assembly, was modelled after the Japanese Liberal Democratic Party not only in name but in expectations of factional dynamics....

Changes in electoral processes and in the structure and competence of political organs were central features of the transition from authoritarian rule to democracy projected in the June 29, 1987 Declaration of Roh Tae Woo. No less important were projected changes in the legal system, for outrage at chronic human rights abuses and widespread dissatisfaction with political manipulation of legal processes had aggravated the legitimacy crises of the Fifth Republic and of previous regimes.

Among the constitutional amendments intended to demonstrate the authenticity of the Sixth Republic's commitment to a more democratic order, one of the most far reaching in its potential implications was a revision establishing a Constitutional Court. Following a period of fifteen years during which judicial review of the constitutionality of legislation had been inoperative, the new organ was said to embody a new dedication to constitutionalism — a promise of effective legal protection of fundamental civil, political and economic rights....

The restoration of judicial review of the constitutionality of legislation was an implicit commitment of the 1987 June Declaration, although it spoke explicitly only of improving the independence of the judiciary and of guaranteeing more effective protection of civil and political rights. As the process of formulating constitutional amendments got underway, proposals were advanced to restore the power of constitutional review to the Supreme Court, which had exercised such a jurisdiction in the period of the Third Republic from 1962 to 1971.

This option was labeled "the American system" although the resulting judicial hierarchy would have been more similar to the Japanese than to the United States court system. The Republic of Korea is not a federal state and the ordinary Korean courts, like the Japanese, are organized in a unitary system of three levels:

(1) district courts and family courts of first instance (subdivided into single-judge and collegiate trial divisions, also containing appellate divisions which hear appeals of cases decided by single judges).

(2) high courts (hearing appeals *de novo* from administrative agency decisions and from collegiate divisions of district courts).

(3) Supreme Court (hearing appeals from high courts and appellate divisions of district and family courts, and exceptional appeals from courts of first instance).

In the Korea of the Third Republic (1963-1972) as in Japan the power of the Supreme Court to review the constitutionality of legislation had been exercised in an institutional setting predominantly influenced by Continental European antecedents of the civil law tradition. Korean conceptions of the role of the judge have been influenced far more by German than by American thinking.

Faced with the prospect of being called upon to resolve highly controversial constitutional questions, most of the sitting Justices of the Korean Supreme Court let it be known that they disfavored the proposed expansion of their jurisdiction to include constitutional review. This attitude comported with a general observation by Professor J.H. Merryman: "The tendency has been for the civil law judge to recoil from the responsibilities and opportunities of constitutional adjudication."

The disinclination of the Supreme Court to take a leading role in defining the content of "constitutionalism" was attributed to skepticism about "judicial activism," a phenomenon viewed by many Korean jurists as a distinctive — and objectionable — feature of the common law tradition. A number of influential Korean public law experts, notably Professor Kim Tscholsu of Seoul National University, had undertaken advanced studies in Europe, therefore structures of judicial review based on German and Austrian models had also been put forward as alternatives to the so-called American system.

Korea's own history, as well, furnished a precedent for a Continental European type of Constitutional Court, for the Second Republic Constitution of June 15, 1960 had established such an organ. This predecessor, however, had never had an opportunity to function because of the May 1961 military *coup*, thus the precedent was more of theoretical than of practical relevance.

The lineage of the Korean Constitutional Court as it was ultimately incorporated in the Sixth Republic Constitution can be traced back to the *Verfassungsgerichtshof* as reorganized under the Austrian Federal Constitution of 1920. Both directly and through the intermediation of Japanese commentaries, Korean jurists have long been familiar with German constitutional history, thus the Constitutional Court established in 1949 by Chapter IX of the *Grundgesetz* of the Federal Republic of Germany was also a highly significant reference for the draftsmen of Chapter VI of the revised Korean Constitution....

The core of the jurisdiction of the Constitutional Court is the power to adjudicate the constitutionality of statutes. As already noted, this competence conferred on the Constitutional Court coexists with the Supreme Court's power to adjudicate the constitutionality of presidential decrees, ministerial ordinances and other forms of administrative regulations. The Constitutional Court's power to review legislation is again basically similar to the jurisdiction of the German Federal Constitutional Court, although considerably narrower than that of the latter.

The Act provides that the Constitutional Court renders judgment on the constitutionality of a law only after receiving a request from the court with original jurisdiction over the case.[57] Procedurally, the request is channeled through the Supreme Court, however it may originate in a district court, a family court, a military tribunal, one of the four high courts, or at the level of the Supreme Court. Every court is constitutionally required to refer questions of the constitutionality of legislation to the Constitutional Court whenever resolution of such a question is a prerequisite to deciding a case.

Referral of constitutional questions may be made by trial courts at the request of a party or *sua sponte*. The decision whether to refer the constitutional question depends on preliminary determinations by the court that (1) the constitutionality of a particular law is doubtful, and (2) the final judgment

[57] CCA [Constitutional Court Act], art. 41(1). Judicial review of legislation is also possible in case of petitions under CCA, art. 68(2), as explained *infra*.

in the case will be predicated on an application of that law, or if only a portion of the law is of doubtful constitutionality, of the doubtful portion.

The frequency with which requests are referred to the Constitutional Court thus depends to a considerable extent on whether the regular courts are disposed to grant a strong presumption of constitutionality to legislation. A request for referral will be denied if the court preliminarily determines that the law is constitutional, even though a party urges to the contrary.

If a party raises a constitutional question in a civil or criminal trial, but the court declines to refer it to the Constitutional Court, there are two possibilities. The party may take a normal appeal of the case, and renew the constitutional argument in the appellate tribunal. Alternatively, the party may resort to a direct petition to the Constitutional Court under Art. 68(2) of the Act.[60] The latter route does not take the form of review of the court ruling rejecting the request for referral; rather, it involves a renewed presentation of the question whether a legislative act is unconstitutional.[61]

The Constitutional Court's jurisdiction in principle is mandatory like that of the German Constitutional Court and not discretionary like the *certiorari* jurisdiction of the United States Supreme Court. Its power to review the constitutionality of legislation is both passive and relatively narrow, however. When the Court's jurisdiction is invoked by the regular courts based on their preliminary assessment that unconstitutionality is arguable, it is "incidental" to the normal functions of the judiciary, in the sense that a concrete case or controversy must have arisen and be continuing....

[Another basis for Constitutional Court jurisdiction comes from Article § 8(1) of the Constitutional Court Act], which provides:

> Any person who alleges that his [or her] fundamental rights guaranteed by the Constitution have been infringed upon by the exercise or nonexercise of public power, except for dispositions by the courts, may petition for relief or remedy to the Constitutional Court through the procedure of Constitutional Petitions....

[T]he Article 68(1) petition jurisdiction as defined above is available in situations where existing laws do not afford remedies through ordinary court processes for unconstitutional state action. A petition of this type may be filed only if all available administrative and judicial remedies have been exhausted. If no ordinary judicial review is available then a direct petition is possible. An example would be a challenge of a discretionary prosecutorial decision not to indict an accused criminal, for in such cases the regular courts have no jurisdiction over the matter....

---

[60] CCA, art. 68(2) provides, in pertinent part: "Any party to a court proceeding whose request for referral to the Constitutional Court for judgment on the constitutionality of a law was rejected by the court of original jurisdiction may have recourse to the Constitutional Court to obtain a final and proper judgment."

[61] An art. 68(2) petition cannot be formulated as a request for review of the ruling declining to refer the question, given that art. 68(1) of the Act provides that petitions seeking relief against a "judgment of an ordinary court" are inadmissible. Art. 68(2) petitions therefore operate as an alternative party-initiated procedure for invoking the Constitutional Court's exclusive competence over questions of the constitutionality of statutes.

Thus, the two kinds of petition are quite distinct. An Article 68(1) petition, if granted, vindicates individual rights infringed by the state and involves fact-finding by the Constitutional Court itself. An Article 68(2) petition, if granted, stays ongoing litigation pending Constitutional Court judgment on the validity of a legislative act, but the finding of facts and the final disposition are made by the court of original jurisdiction, subject to the guidance of the Constitutional Court on the constitutional question.

Like others already discussed, the petition jurisdiction follows a German model, corresponding to the mechanism of *Verfassungsbeschwerde*, which was added to the original competence of the Federal Constitutional Court by a statutory enlargement of its review function. The scope of subject-matter reviewable through the Korean petition procedure is considerably narrower than under the German system, however, because the German system does not except regular court decisions from the scope of state action which may be the subject-matter of petitions for Constitutional Court review.

Under these circumstances, the constitutional petition procedure thus far has been invoked most often in certain circumstances in which ordinary judicial review is unavailable, although it has also occasionally been used to seek review of statutes. As of the end of 1990, more than one third of all constitutional petitions were filed by persons contesting decisions by public prosecutors not to institute (or to suspend) criminal indictments.

The process of screening petitions is important, given that the number of filings has been expanding, as follows:

Constitutional Petitions Filed

	1988	1989	1990	Total
Art. 68(1)	33	353	456	842
Art. 68(2)	1	16	69	86
Total	34	369	525	928

It is unclear whether or how rapidly the rate of filing will continue to expand, but Korean jurists have devoted considerable study to the experience in Germany, where by 1989 over 75,000 petitions had been filed with the Constitutional Court and between 2,500 and 3,700 petitions have been filed annually in recent years.

3. TAIWAN

HERBERT H.P. MA, THE SOURCES AND STRUCTURE OF MODERN CHINESE LAW AND THE CHINESE JUDICIAL SYSTEM, in TRADE AND INVESTMENT IN TAIWAN: THE LEGAL AND ECONOMIC ENVIRONMENT IN THE REPUBLIC OF CHINA 3-6, 27-34 (Herbert H.P. Ma ed., 2d ed. 1985)

Modern Chinese law is the result of judicial reform which began at the turn of the twentieth century when Western legal thought and institutions were imported into China. Basic laws were codified in the late 1920s and early 1930s, which in general followed the continental European system. A permanent constitution was finally promulgated in 1947 after several drafts had been made.

When the Communists overran the China mainland in 1949 the Constitution and the basic laws mentioned above were brought over to Taiwan by the central government of the Republic of China. They have since been in force in Taiwan.

The Constitution

The Chinese Constitution is unique in many respects. To begin with, it is based on the teachings of Sun Yat-sen, the father of the Republic, especially on his philosophy of *San Min Chu I*. Commonly translated as the Three Principles of the People, *San Min Chu I* consists of the Principle of Nationalism, the Principle of Democracy, and the Principle of People's Livelihood. Very briefly, the first principle is to achieve and maintain national unity and harmony against localism and particularism of race, class, or sect so that there will be a place for China in the world; the second principle is to uphold fundamental individual rights against the arbitrary exercise of governmental powers or infringements by officials or legislation; the third principle is to promote general services for the people and to reconcile the individual and society by a gradual process. In other words, the Three Principles of the People as formulated by Sun and adopted by the Chinese Constitution were based, on the one hand, upon the collective experience of Western democracies and, on the other hand, upon the best political, legal, and economic traditions of China....

Sun Yat-sen believed that government should be all-powerful but nevertheless controlled by the people. For this reason he distinguished the people's powers for controlling the government, which he called "political powers," from the government's powers, which he called "administrative powers." There are four people's political powers: election, recall, initiative, and referendum. There are five government powers: executive power, legislative power, judicial power, power of examination, and censorial or control power. According to Sun, his separation of five powers is an improvement of the Western doctrine of the separation of three powers and, therefore, accords with the main currents of political thought underlying any democratic form of government.

The four political powers of the people, according to Sun, are exercised in the central government by the National Assembly, which is composed of elected delegates of the whole body of citizens. On the local level, the four political powers are exercised by the people of the *hsien* (county) directly. However, under the present constitution, the four powers of the National Assembly have been much curtailed and the political powers of the people on the *hsien* level are not yet being exercised.... The five administrative powers of the government are vested in five independent departments called *yüan*; that is, the Executive *Yüan*, the Legislative *Yüan*, the Judicial *Yüan*, the

Figure 6.6

Governmental Organization of Taiwan

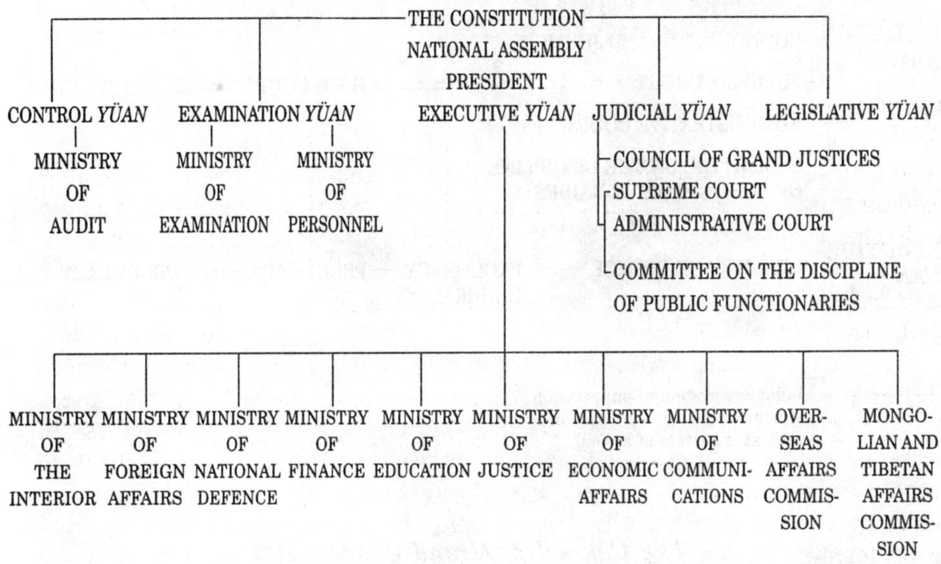

Examination *Yüan*,[a] and the Control *Yüan*.[b] For this reason, the Constitution is generally known as the "Five-power Constitution."...

The Judicial Yüan

The Chinese judicial system is unique in its organization and division of functions. First, there is the Judicial *Yüan*, one of the five constituents of the central government, which is established by the Constitution as the highest judicial organ of the state. According to the Constitution, the functions of the Judicial *Yüan* fall under two categories: (1) to have jurisdiction over civil, criminal, and administrative cases and over cases concerning disciplinary measures against public functionaries; and (2) to interpret the Constitution and to unify the interpretation of laws and ordinances. These functions are in fact executed by four distinct organs within the framework of the Judicial *Yüan*, namely, the Council of Grand Justices, the Supreme Court, the Administrative Court, and the Committee on the Discipline of Public Functionaries.

However, it is pertinent to note in this connection that the lower courts, that is the high courts and the district courts, which were administratively subjected to the executive branch of the central government, namely the Ministry of Justice of the Executive *Yüan*, have since 1980 been placed under the Judicial *Yüan*. A chart of the Chinese judicial organs is given in Figure 6.7.

[a] The Examination Yüan administers qualification examinations for professionals, technicians, and government officials as well as performance and retirement reviews of government officials.

[b] The Control Yüan passes on the appointment of certain officials, impeaches officials, rectifies inappropriate measures, and audits government agencies. It consists of members elected from provincial and city councils and from overseas Chinese groups.

Figure 6.7

Structure of the Taiwanese Judicial System

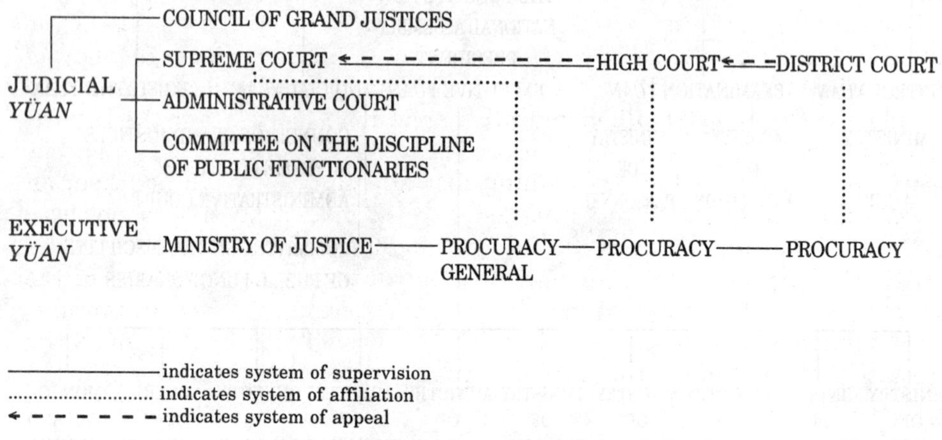

The Council of Grand Justices

The power to interpret the Constitution and the power to unify the interpretation of laws and ordinances are vested in the Council of Grand Justices of the Judicial *Yüan*. The council is composed of seventeen justices, with the President of the Judicial *Yüan* as chairman.

The scope of interpretation of the Constitution covers three areas: (1) when a doubt arises in applying the Constitution itself; (2) when a doubt arises as to whether or not a given law or ordinance is in conflict with the Constitution; and (3) when a doubt arises as to whether or not provincial or county self-government laws and provincial or county rules and regulations are in conflict with the Constitution.

However, an interpretation of the Constitution must be made upon receipt of written requests from government organizations or any individual. Any law or ordinance, local self-government law, or local government law or regulation that is found to be in contravention of the Constitution shall be null and void.

As regards uniform interpretation of laws and ordinances, a request may be made to the Council of Grand Justices through the Judicial *Yüan* only by a central or local government organization. As of May 1985, the Council of Grand Justices had handled 195 cases of interpretation of which 62 had to do with the Constitution.[c]

[c] By September 1988 the number of interpretations had reached 229, including 90 related to the Constitution. For a thorough study of the Council, see Lawrence Shao-Liang Liu, *Judicial Review and Emerging Constitutionalism: The Uneasy Case for the Republic of China on Taiwan,* 39 Am. J. Comp. L. 509 (1991).

The Ministry of Justice

The Ministry of Justice, first set up in 1912 when the Republic was founded, has undergone a number of changes hierarchically. However, since 1943, the Ministry of Justice has been a component part of the Executive *Yüan*.

Headed by a minister, the Ministry of Justice is composed mainly of the following departments: the Department of Legal Affairs, the Department of Prosecution Affairs, the Department of Prison and Detention House Administration, the Department of Rehabilitation and Civil Liberties, and the Department of General Affairs. To train judicial officials, the Ministry of Justice has operated a Judicial Officials Training Institute since 1955. In addition, an Investigation Bureau, which is charged with the investigation of crimes, was established in 1957 as an essential arm of the Ministry of Justice.

The Ministry of Justice is empowered to supervise the Procuracy of the Supreme Court. Inasmuch as the Procurator General supervises all procurators throughout the country, the minister through his control over the procuracy of the Supreme Court can actually direct the procurators in the performance of their duties at all levels.

Ordinary Courts

The ordinary court system in China is based, in general, on the principle of "trial" by three levels of courts; namely, the district courts, the high courts, and the Supreme Court, now all under the Judicial *Yüan*. As was stated earlier, the high courts and the district courts were until 1980 under the supervision of the Ministry of Justice of the Executive *Yüan*.

The District Courts

The district courts are set up in counties and municipalities. Each county or municipality ordinarily has one district court. In the Province of Taiwan, there are now fifteen district courts sitting in the cities and counties of Taipei, Taoyüan, Hsinchu, Taichung, Changhua, Yunling, Chiayi, Tainan, Kaohsiung, Pingtung, Taitung, Hualien, Yilan, Keelung, and Penghu. The Taipei District Court has two branch courts, one in Panchiao and one in Shihlin. On the Island of Kinmen (Quemoy), one of the two counties of Fukien Province under the control of the Republic of China, there is also a district court.

Headed by a president, a district court may set up civil and criminal divisions, if the total number of judges exceeds six. Except for cases of a serious nature, which require trials to be conducted jointly by three judges, all trials of the district court are handled by a single judge. The district court has jurisdiction over all civil and criminal cases of the first instance except those cases specifically excluded by law. It also handles nonlitigious matters.

In recent years, four kinds of special tribunals have been established as separate divisions at the district courts in major cities. First, there were the Financial Affairs Division and the Traffic Division. The former deals mainly with cases involving a fine and tax delinquency. The latter deals with the rapidly increasing number of traffic cases. Later, a Juvenile Delinquency Division and a Family Affairs Division were also established.

The High Courts

The high courts are established in the provinces, the capital of the Republic, and the special municipalities. Generally speaking, each province has one high court and may have a branch or branches if the size of the province so justifies. At present in the province of Taiwan, the high court is situated in the city of Taipei with branch courts in the cities of Taichung, Tainan, and Hualien. For the Fukien area, there is a branch court which sits in Kinmen (Quemoy).

Headed by a president, the high court may establish a number of civil and criminal divisions according to its actual needs. It sits with three judges on the bench. The high court mainly deals with appeals from judgments in civil and criminal cases rendered by the district courts as courts of the first instance, with certain serious criminal cases of the first instance, and with the cases of the first instance involving election matters.

The Supreme Court

Established in 1927 the Supreme Court is headed by a president and has at present five civil divisions and seven criminal divisions. Each division is composed of five judges, one of whom is a chief judge.

"Trials" in the Supreme Court are, in general, conducted by three or five judges sitting jointly. They only review the law and do not deal with matters of fact. The Supreme Court handles appeals from the judgments in civil and criminal cases rendered by the high courts as courts of the second instance, as well as appeals from the judgments in certain serious criminal cases rendered by the high courts as courts of the first instance.

The Office of the Procurators

The procurators form an integral part of the Chinese judicial system. They are assigned to different levels of courts and are charged with the responsibility to conduct investigations, to institute and conduct public prosecutions, to assist in or take charge of private prosecution, and to direct the execution of judgment in criminal cases.

A procurator functions independently of the court. In other words, whether or not to prosecute after investigation, whether or not to withdraw the prosecution after it is instituted, or whether or not to file an appeal against a court judgment, is decided by a procurator without being subject to the influence of the court. On the other hand, procurators must follow the orders and directions of their supervising officers.

The Administrative Court

The Administrative Court is charged with the adjudication of administrative suits. It is basically patterned after the European system found in France and Germany, but it varies from its archetypes in that it is more judicial. This is evidenced by the structure of the court.

Headed by a president, the Administrative Court has several divisions, each composed of five judges, of whom two must previously have sat on the bench of an ordinary court.

Access to the Administrative Court is obtained only after exhaustion of administrative remedies. Any person, on the ground that his rights or interests have been injured by an unlawful or improper administrative measure on the part of a central or local government agency, may file an administrative appeal with a competent organ of a higher administrative level. If he disagrees with the decision, he may then file an administrative reappeal with a competent organ of an even higher administrative level. In a case in which an individual's rights have been injured by an unlawful administrative measure, and if no decision concerning the reappeal has been given within three months or if the decision given does not satisfy him, the individual may institute administrative proceedings in the Administrative Court. A supplementary action may also be brought for compensatory damages. The judgment of the Administrative Court, which is final and not subject to appeal, may (1) revoke or change the original administrative measure or decision, or (2) dismiss the proceedings as groundless. Foreign traders or investors in their dealings with Chinese government agencies may, and in fact do, avail themselves of this remedy, especially in matters such as tax and trademark.

NOTES AND QUESTIONS

1. What political characteristics does South Korea share with many Latin American nations? Is the solution to irregular constitutional amendment in Korea to restrain the executive branch through a strong judiciary?

2. The Constitution of the Republic of China adopts five governmental powers, subject to the doctrine of separation of powers. Is this variation on European political theory a useful accommodation to Chinese legal culture in the same manner that a fourth branch of government (the military) exists in some Latin American legal cultures?

3. Japan's 1946 postwar Constitution, as noted, has yet to be amended despite its origins as keystone of the reforms imposed under the Allied Occupation. Nor, however, was the Meiji Constitution of 1889 ever amended. What factors help to explain this constitutional stability in Japan in contrast to other countries in East Asia? Is this an aspect of Japanese legal culture?

4. Both Japan under the Meiji Constitution and the Republic of China in its 1947 Constitution adapted the French *Conseil d'État* in the form of a single Administrative Court to adjudicate appeals from administrative or executive decisions. Reflecting American objections, Japan's postwar Constitution abolished the Administrative Court and prohibits any other special courts. What reasons support such objections? Do you agree?

5. One of the recurring issues related to judicial independence in most of the civil law systems in East Asia has been the determination of which governmental organ, such as a ministry, special agency, or the judiciary itself, should be responsible for the recruitment, training, and assignment of career judges. In Japan the occupation reforms gave the administrative arm of the Supreme Court this responsibility in lieu of the Ministry of Justice. A similar shift has taken place in Indonesia, South Korea, and Taiwan. In Thailand a special Judicial Service Commission of 12 members, all of whom are senior or retired judges, performs similar functions. How significant to judicial independence is this question of control? What are the advantages or disadvantages of each alternative?

D. LEGAL CULTURE AND LEGAL PENETRATION IN LATIN AMERICA

1. LEGAL PLURALISM AND WITCHCRAFT

DAVID S. CLARK, WITCHCRAFT AND LEGAL PLURALISM: THE CASE OF CÉLIMO MIQUIRUCAMA, 15 Tulsa Law Journal 679-83 (1980)

The idea of legal pluralism as a proper goal of national legal systems is in ascendancy today. This is true particularly in countries such as the United States with increasingly vocal indigenous minorities.[1] The courts in Canada, Australia, and New Zealand, similarly, are adjudicating claims of their native minorities to land rights and for recognition of their own laws.[2] And in much of Africa, Asia and Latin America, a significant — at times de facto — legal pluralism is encountered, involving one or more indigenous systems of customary law with the superimposition of a Western national legal system.[3]

Legal pluralism is one aspect of cultural pluralism in a society. Its emphasis generally reflects dissatisfaction with the more pernicious government policies aimed at assimilation of ethnic groups into the dominant culture. In the United States, for instance, the current interest in legal pluralism is a reaction against the nineteenth century notion of manifest destiny which justified geographical expansion across the American continent, subduing the Indians (and Mexicans) along the way. Americans exhibited the belief that they were carrying out the will of Providence, for example, in dismantling in 1898 the Cherokee tribal courts which had served their people exceedingly well for almost ninety years.

The belief in and use of witchcraft is a distinguishing characteristic of certain cultural groups. Witchcraft exists widely in human society, today as well as in the past. Records of witchcraft go back to the dawn of history, and some archaeological evidence suggests it even precedes written history. Faith in witchcraft provides a mystical medium through which important conflicts may be expressed and frequently resolved. For instance, the American Cherokee view law as the earthly representation of a divine spirit order. Consensus and harmony, rather than confrontation and dispute, are essential elements of

---

[1] *See, e.g., Santa Clara Pueblo v. Martinez,* 436 U.S. 49 (1978), where Justice Marshall states:

> Indian tribes are "distinct, independent political communities, retaining their original natural rights" in matters of local self-government. Although no longer "possessed of the full attributes of sovereignty," they remain a "separate people, with the power of regulating their internal and social relations." They have power to make their own substantive law in internal matters, and to enforce that law in their own forums.

Id. at 55-56 (citations omitted).

[2] M. Hooker, Legal Pluralism vii-viii (1975).

[3] *See generally* ... Law in Culture and Society (L. Nader ed. 1969).

the Cherokee world view. The inherent disharmonies in a social system, then, may be cloaked under an insistence that there is agreement about the values of society; those disturbances that do occur are attributed frequently to the wickedness of certain individuals.

The supernatural relates to law primarily as a support for primitive legal systems with their rudimentary mechanisms for resolving disputes. The supernatural is available as an instrument of judgment and execution where man's fallible devices to secure evidence are inadequate for the job of establishing the facts. Witch doctors or shamans have the mystical power to detect sorcerers and to combat their evil actions. The spirits know the truth. If properly requested, they will omnisciently judge and directly or indirectly punish a wrongdoer. On the other hand, witchcraft and sorcery frequently involve the misuse of supernatural powers. They may be regarded as a tort against the victim and his kinsmen, or as a criminal offense against society. In some cultures, the kinsmen of a witch's victim may kill the sorcerer after (or sometimes without) obtaining permission from the village or tribal authorities....

The formal network of Colombian legal norms reaches only certain elements of Colombian society. Because the distribution of legal resources (courts, lawyers, police, and bureaucrats) is allocated disproportionately to urban areas, the official Colombian legal system — along with its norms — has not penetrated into many rural parts of the nation. In addition to geographical distance, the social distance between the white elite, found mainly in the growing cities of the Colombian highlands, and the mestizo, Indian and black populations, with their separate ethnic heritages, would impede any attempt at cultural convergence.

The case reported here concerns the death of Francisco González, a witch among the Chocó Indians. The Chocó live in the dense tropical rain forest of northwest Colombia, which receives an average annual rainfall of 420 inches. They have their own distinct language and way of life, which includes minimal contact with the formal Colombian legal system. Since the time of the Spanish conquest, their relations with Spanish-speaking persons have most commonly been with missionaries. Beginning in the colonial period, the increasing black population of the savannas has pushed the Chocó upstream in their effort to avoid acculturation. Today, they number perhaps 10,000, still subsisting on slash-and-burn agriculture, supplemented by hunting with bow and arrow and with blowgun and poison darts. The Chocó Indians continue to avoid contact with outsiders, reserving special derogatory terms for the groups of blacks they encounter in the rain forests. In turn, the blacks, as Colombians and as Christians, look down on the Indians as uncivilized.

The *Miquirucama* case (the name of the Indian defendant) is a window by which to view Chocó society, although this perspective is distorted by the attitudes of the dominant Colombian legal culture. This distorted view is most clearly focused by the Court's use of expert medical testimony on the issue of Miquirucama's individual responsibility for the death of González.

There is, first, an implicit clash between the attitudes toward witchcraft of the Chocó who testify in this proceeding and those of the participating Colombian legal professionals. There is also a gap between the attitudes expressed by the Court's majority and dissent roughly reflecting outlooks reminiscent of the nineteenth versus the twentieth centuries. The majority approach, embodied in the legislation of 1890 and 1892, patronizes Indians in Colombia, and adopts the legal fiction used by the Spanish crown since the sixteenth century that Indians should be considered the juridical equivalent of minors. For the dissent, on the other hand, the Colombian Criminal Code of 1936 utilizes the modern territoriality principle for scope of coverage, along with the value of legal equality for all citizens. The Code thus implies that Indians, as citizens, are rational individuals capable of overcoming archaic institutions such as witchcraft.

CONSTITUTION OF COLOMBIA OF 1886

Articles 26, 58

Article 26

No one may be tried except ... by courts having competent jurisdiction.

Article 58

Justice is a public service for which the Nation is responsible.

MIQUIRUCAMA, CÉLIMO

Supreme Court of Colombia (Penal Chamber)
Decision of May 14, 1970
134 G.J. 303 (1970)

DR. JUSTICE JOSÉ MARÍA VELASCO GUERRERO delivered the opinion of the Court.

Having examined:

The Court proceeds to resolve the petition filed by the Superior Court of Villavicencio's public prosecutor against the July 1, 1969 decision of the lower court. By that decision, Célimo Miquirucama — an Indian from Mistradó (Chocó), son of Marco Miquirucama, thirty years old, a laborer, a resident of Mogotes (Granada), a widower, without documents for personal identification — was sentenced for the security of society to imprisonment in either a special farm colony or industrial establishment for a minimum of 48 months. He was found guilty of the September 29, 1967 homicide of Francisco Javier González U., which occurred in a neighborhood known as Mogotes within the police jurisdiction of Canaguaro, municipality of Granada.

Facts

The witch, Francisco González U., late at night on September 29, 1967, was in Luis Angel Cardona's house located in the neighborhood known as "Las Guayanas" or "Mogotes," State of Meta, preoccupied with praying for a sick child. It must have been about 2:00 a.m. when Francisco Javier González U. was praying for his patient. Soon the explosion of a firearm was heard and González fell mortally wounded. Those present were Abraham González Garcia, Luis Angel Cardona, Arvey González, Francisco Javier and Flora Javier, children of the victim, who minutes later confirmed the death of their father. When the Municipal Judge of Granada (Meta) initiated the investigation,[a] it originally focused on Bernardo Marcial Murillo, because of charges against him by José Arvey González, who asserted that the accused confided in him his guilt on the day of the burial. Marcial Murillo denied any guilt in the crime. Nevertheless, Arvey González categorically maintained his testimony in the confrontation with the accused on January 2, 1968. Before the confrontation with the accused on this date, however, Arvey González, without the least explanation, expanded his testimony at the inquest on December 20, 1967, changing his accusation toward Célimo Miquirucama as the murderer of Francisco González. On this occasion he cited Emma Marcial Murillo, wife or companion of Célimo, as the source of his testimony. Miquirucama then confessed being the author of Francisco Javier González' death in his testimony at the inquest, but discounted the significance of his act by reasoning that "he was a sorcerer," and had already killed his four children and wife, Matilde Dibaquieza, with a shotgun. However, while Miquirucama was elaborating on his testimony before the Superior Court, he stated that his children drowned in the Cingara River in Ansermavieja. At this latter hearing he did not know how Francisco Javier González' death occurred. He confessed at the previous inquest because of his fear of Luis Angel Cardona and José Arvey González, his supposed advisors. The court ordered that Miquirucama be examined by the Department of Forensic Medicine. With this done, the medical experts described the accused as "illiterate with an extremely limited command of the language in understanding questions or giving answers. He is a primitive person, in a semisavage state." (Signed: Dr. Antonio Segura Garzón, Chief of Forensic Medicine).

Concluding the investigative phase, the merits of the charge were evaluated and Miquirucama was called to answer in court for the crime of aggravated homicide. His conduct was regulated by the norms of article 29 of the Criminal Code. A procedural hearing terminated with the dismissal of charges against all others linked with the investigation. After the judgment and sentencing of Miquirucama, the Villavicencio Superior Court public prosecutor applied for a declaration of nullity based on article 37, section 1 of Decree 1358 (1964). The lower court pronounced sentence, ignoring the public prosecutor's petitions, confirming the judgment in all respects.

Considerations of the Court

The decision of the court of appeal, and the argument of the assistant attorney general for criminal matters, repeat an argument previously put forth by Dr. Luis Zafra, former assistant attorney general....

The criminal acts of the uncivilized Indian, argued Zafra, should be evaluated according to the general criminal rules, only taking into account that their status should not make them susceptible to ordinary sanctions....

Reputable Colombian scholars likewise share these ideas, affirming that articles 4 and 432 of the present Criminal Code are sufficiently clear and

[a] Criminal proceedings are split into two parts: an investigation, which is a series of hearings to gather evidence and compile a dossier, and the trial.

definitive, annulling the prior doctrine concerning the special application of the 1890 and 1892 laws. In addition, there are reasons of an anthropological and social nature which should impede the continuation of missionary practices. Their policy of paternalism is opposed to personality development in areas of material and spiritual endeavor. What is needed is to take advantage of the crime's occasion to make the criminal feel a compulsion to conform to general social norms. The Indian should be treated like any other man whose attitudes might not be in conformity with commonly accepted norms of conduct.

Certain crimes committed by Indians may result from unconquerable ignorance, according to article 23, section 2. This may be one of the few situations where the application of the stated precept constitutes an exception to the presumption of the knowledge of law. But this presumption cannot be extended to exceedingly special situations such as the one before us, without creating a serious threat against deficient intellects. And the fault is not the action of individuals, but the inaction of the State.

In our country coexist highly culturally evolved persons alongside others who maintain intact prohibited taboos and magic animism. The transformations of these people will not be affected by mere contact nor by osmosis. Instead, adequate penetration of these traditional forces will be a task of more than just a few years. It belongs to the anthropologist and politician, more than to the jurist and the doctor.

In this sense, various international conferences have expressed agreement in seeking special treatment for uncivilized peoples and groups. After many years of anticipation, our Law 89 (1890), article 1, juridically realized the constant hopes of anthropologists, psychiatrists and psychologists....

With this stated, it is now necessary to make clear that in the problem *sub iudice*, the essence of the question is rooted in finding out if article 1 of Law 89 (1890) is applicable, which excludes the uncivilized Indian populations from the principle of juridical equality. Article 26 of the Constitution, furthermore, does not allow application of criminal sanctions except in conformity with the rules of procedure, and then only by virtue of sentences decreed by competent judges.

The Court will consider the applicability of Law 89 (1890), article 1, in light of article 58 of the Constitution: "Justice is a public service for which the Nation is responsible."...

This norm becomes significant in light of article 2 of Law 72 (1892), authorizing the executive to delegate to missionaries the competence to judge Indians in matters of a civil or criminal nature....

[The assistant attorney general argues] that modern doctrine advocates the return to the concept of culpability as the foundation of all suppressive systems, and the return to a uniform system of punishment. But so long as our *rules* are not modified, these advocated reasons are valid for the legislator, but not for the judge who finds in the written law the exclusive source for his decisions.

The standard is erroneous which defines the minor, by the very fact of being a minor, as a person dangerous to society. This is also so when the standard defines the savage as psychologically deficient, for the simple fact that their existential environments have not risen to a degree of progress which distinguishes civilized peoples. In this manner it is forgotten that subintelligence is irreversible; the exquisite rustic character known in savages, which gives them the ability to adapt to agricultural labor, presupposes that they are capable of evolving and placing themselves in conditions of assimilating a farm culture, the original cement in the evolution of peoples and a permanent activity of the already civilized. The difference between savages and civilized, educated man is rooted in the different degrees of their evolution, which makes savages strangers in a world contemporary to theirs, a world whose values obey a complex conceptual hierarchy, slowly and patiently sculpted by history and processed with the interaction and experience of diverse cultures. A modern order of values demands the existence of an ethical personality, which is incompatible with the savage condition with its rudimentary social content and the "undifferentiated self" of its people, characterized by a diverse complexity in the peculiar and diffuse form of sensing intuitively....

Primitive peoples are ruled in their personalities by the law *pro toto*. Each part corresponds essentially to the whole and determines it. There are no accessory parts in the primitive "self." All parts of the corporeal and spiritual "self" represent to a certain point the psychic totality. The name is not part of the person, but is instead the person itself. Dress, arrows, hair, the shadow, a nose — these are not attributes or parts of the person. They are confused with the "self" from which they are projected, magically, without setting one against the other. This very thing occurs with the diffuse and undifferentiated "self" of the man and his surrounding world, in light of which his personality is strictly limited, for with it he is blended. The man, the jaguar, the goat, the fish — all are persons with different properties and aspects. The reason for this undifferentiated form of being in the primitive or savage "self" is derived from the non-existence of an ethical personality. Further, the Indian does not show a sense of the good or the bad. His concept of the individual is crude and is confused with the agreeable or prejudicial. His knowledge of the ideal or the moral do not form part of his conduct. (H. Wermer, Sociología Evolutiva.)

Existentially, the world of the savage does not coincide with the civilized world with which it is chronologically contemporaneous.... Sociologists would say that the modern and traditional coincide. Biologically, primitive man and civilized man coincide equally. But the former is not a social category. Because of this, although the two coexist in time within the ambit of nationality, they do not live together culturally and are governed by different rules.... Raúl Haya de la Torre notes with exceeding insight that to take a trip across time it is sufficient to journey from one corner of our American continent to the other. The distances widen when we think that in the last thirty years the civilized world has evolved geometrically, compared to preceding centuries. In the epoch of atomic fission, of genetic engineering, when molecular biology promises to revolutionize the behavior of animal groups, including man, the savage is our irreversible past — even more, the modern prehistoric. Our laws established for the contemporary world do not reach this past. The present Criminal Code does not contain juridical or mental categories to conform with the condition of these savages. Certainly it has categories for normal, civilized people....

Law 89 (1890) in article 1, is definitive in its provisions. It establishes a special regimen for savages who commit crimes and, in general, it divides them into three large categories: savages, semisavages, and civilized. Only for the last category of persons is general legislation considered applicable. Its text forms a complete juridical proposition, clear in its literal tenor.... The Commission of Redactors of the 1936 [Criminal] Code ignored [Law 89's] existence. Perhaps they considered it in force and simply did not amend it since tribes existed in the condition of life to which the provisions of the statute refer....

The Court insists that Indians, simply because they are Indians, are not deficient or retarded mentally. However, they may be equivalent to minors by the legal fiction established in article 40 of Law 89 (1890). Experts agree that psychopaths, the mentally retarded, and minors, psychologically speaking, show common characteristics. The three possess a special personality, the dominant trait of which is an undifferentiated "self" — labile, lacking concentration, and not distinct from the surrounding world, into which it blends.

This special "self" is encountered in each one of these three states, but for different reasons. In the child the "self" is incipient, but in a state of development. In the Indian the characteristic of the "self" depends on the conditions of its environment. The causes are exogenous. In neither of these cases is there abnormality. In the mentally retarded, on the other hand, the "self" is arrested in its development. Its condition is irreversible in character. The schizophrenic's condition is rooted in the dissolution of his personality, which in a normal state would be formally delimited. (Schilder, Storch.)...

Medrano Ossio believes that "the psychological state of today's Indian renders it impossible to make him a responsible person as demanded by the rules presently in force. The native does not, with his limited conscience, reach a true understanding of the act that he commits, even if it is an abominable crime.... The life of the contemporary Indian develops on the margin of the white and mestizo civilization. The principle of equality before the law in which he finds himself placed, therefore, is absurd." He sums up: "In view of these realities, the Indian should be considered nonculpable for his crimes; the punishment, being ineffective, should be replaced by psychopedagogical, psychiatric, and other measures which might make the Indian an innocuous person, a person definitively incorporated into present civilized society."

Some Latin American criminal legislation, doctrinally inspired by the principles which formed the basis of our 1936 reform in order to remedy the problems created in their territory by the existence of aboriginal peoples, promulgated specific provisions for the idiosyncrasy of primitive man. This is the case with Venezuela. In the draft Code of 1967, article 16 states: "The Court shall be able to declare nonculpable an Indian who commits an act classified as punishable, taking into account his inability to comprehend the illicit nature of his act or to conform with the legal standards of conduct."...

Conclusions of the Court

Célimo Miquirucama was described by medical experts as an "illiterate with an extremely limited command of the language in understanding questions or giving answers." This evidence, consequently, indicates with unquestionable precision that the accused is located in the second of three categories for Indians recognized by our legislation. He is a semisavage whose acts remain outside the control of the ordinary legislation of the Republic. Even so, the trial judge, and later the Superior Court of Villavicencio, subjected his conduct to the provisions of article 29 of the Criminal Code, and to the punishments dealt with in book I, title 2, chapter 2 of the same statute, condemning him to 48 months imprisonment in a farm colony. The lower courts relied upon medical testimony — folio 90 of the principal record — defining Miquirucama as a mental weakling, a victim, consequently of a serious psychiatric anomaly. By this application, they incurred a manifest error of fact in the evaluation of said evidence since the accused should be classified as what another medical expert called an illiterate semisavage.... In addition, the lower court judgment was vitiated by nullity — incompetence of jurisdiction — for failure to defer to article 1 of Law 89 (1890)....

This is not the first time the Court has considered operative provisions derived from laws prior to the promulgation of the present Criminal Code.... The Colombian criminal legislation is a complete whole. All of its provisions are not included in the same statute, or within special statutes. It is sufficient that the norms be considered operative in light of the correct juridical construction which determines their hierarchy and dominance....

Since article 1 of Law 89 (1890) excludes Indians found in a semisavage condition from the normative control of ordinary legislation, and article 2 of Law 72 (1892) gives the executive power to delegate competence in civil and criminal matters into the hands of missionaries, these norms clearly conflict with the Constitution [articles 26 and 58]. Jurisdiction is solely within the power of the government. It is a deplorable consequence that Indians, in a savage and semisavage condition whose acts are prohibited by the criminal law, lack the control of sanctioning norms and, for the same reason, competent judges.

It should not be too much to mention that jurisdiction must be clearly established by legislation. Judges are not permitted to enact or deduce it by analogy.

The petition is granted.

By merit of the expressed considerations, the Supreme Court — Chamber of Penal Cassation — administering justice in the name of the Republic and the Law,

Resolves:

First. The sentence announced by the Superior Court of Villavicencio, by which it imposed upon Célimo Miquirucama the punishment of imprisonment in a special farm colony or an industrial establishment for a minimum term of 48 months, because of his guilt for the crime of homicide perpetrated on the person of Francisco Javier González U., is invalidated.

Second. All that has occurred in the procedures against Célimo Miquirucama, from the hearing of October 3, 1967, the date when the Municipal Court of Granada (Meta) announced its finding, is declared null.

Third. The immediate release of the accused is ordered.

Publish, notify, copy, and insert this opinion in the *Gaceta Judicial*, and remand this case to the court of origin.

JUSTICES LUIS CARLOS PEREZ and LUIS ENRIQUE ROMERO SOTO dissent.

First. We agree with the majority of the Penal Chamber that the principal issue to determine with regard to Indians found in a state of savagery is whether (1) the provisions of the Criminal Code or (2) article 1 of Law 89 (1890), which excepted these Indians from the principle of juridical equality, govern. Also we agree that the criterion of dangerousness or mental sickness applied to Indians or minors, because they are Indians or minors, is not correct. This is an erroneous thesis, as the Chamber observes, since it revives ideological theories contrary to the advances of law and anthropology. The dangerous nature of Indians was argued by some South American professors at unfortunate moments of their careers; ... we have always believed in the adaptability of all human beings to overcome conditions of backwardness that are not precisely due to their caprice.

Second. We also agree with the majority of the Chamber on various appraisals of primitive mentality endorsed by foreign writers.... The savage, according to these studies, has great gusto for knowledge of things that surround him, a fact which presumes intellectual capacities. The universe for him, just as much as for the rest of mankind, is an object of thought and a means for satisfying needs.... If we were to strengthen this line of authority, we would refer to a constellation of North American scientists who unanimously agree with the brilliant and harmonious exposition of Claude Lévi-Strauss.

Third. For us, the key issue in the petition is resolved by affirming that articles 4 and 432 in the Criminal Code tacitly repeal Law 89 (1890) and Law 72 (1892). As a result, the criminal law should operate against all inhabitants of the Republic, whether they be citizens or foreigners, transients or domiciliaries, city dwellers or frontiersmen. There can be no other conclusion derived from the principle of national sovereignty, supported by the principle of territoriality consecrated in article 4. This public norm gives the State the right of authority over all who may be found in its territory.

DAVID S. CLARK, WITCHCRAFT AND LEGAL PLURALISM: THE CASE OF CÉLIMO MIQUIRUCAMA, 15 Tulsa Law Journal 679, 692-98 (1980)

There are several obvious sources of misunderstanding between the Chocó and the Colombian legal authorities. Language is one major problem. Significant cultural differences provide an even greater barrier to communication. But probably the greatest source of misunderstanding derives from the divergent Chocó and Colombian notions of what the criminal legal process is all about. On the one hand, the Colombian authorities, under the rules of criminal procedure, are concerned with ascertaining the truth regarding an accused's conduct, and thus his guilt or innocence. For the Chocó, on the other hand, it is likely that their perception of law is designed to produce a compromise. Verifiable facts are central to Colombian legal procedure, but probably secondary to Chocó purposes. The conflict between legal cultures is apparent.

The Colombian Supreme Court in *Miquirucama* appears aware of the undesirable result produced when the official legal system is used for Indian disputes. Steeped in the civil law tradition, the Colombian legal system has a long and notable history reaching back to the *Siete Partidas* of medieval Spain and ultimately to early Roman times. In contrast, many jurists trained in Colombian law schools see Indians as uncivilized savages, or at best, as individuals under the influence of primitive superstition.

The Indian perspective toward the Colombian legal system and its procedures, similarly, impedes rapprochement. Professor Collier, in her excellent study of Zinacantecos in southern Mexico,[20] implies that many Indian groups have only two explanations for homicide: the victim was a witch, as in this case, or the murderer was drunk. An Indian accused of murder, consequently, will give a predictable response. National authorities inevitably conclude that liquor and witchcraft superstitions are the principal causes of violence in Indian society. But Indian motives for violence are as complex as those in any community. The language for describing their behavior, especially to outsiders who are not familiar with Indian culture, appears simple. The local Indian dispute-resolution mechanisms, in seeking to understand the behavior of a murderer, delve deeper for the explanation. In the process these devices may ultimately provide a more satisfactory settlement for their community.

The moral dilemma presented by *Miquirucama* is primarily a problem of individual responsibility: How can a legal system prevent injustice when the criminal code presumes intent or at least criminal negligence in the commission of a crime, even though the accused believes his aims are legitimate because he is ridding the world of an evil witch? Is it not unjust to impose a harsh penalty on a superstitious Indian whose principal fault is lack of contact with a civilizing Western influence?[24]

In *Miquirucama*, the majority of the Colombian Supreme Court, through Justice Velasco, discusses feasible solutions to the problem of individual responsibility. First, the Court presents the argument of Luis Zafra, a former assistant attorney general, who believes that criminal acts of Indians should be evaluated according to the national criminal code, but that sanctions should vary for Indians, possibly based on the education or experience of the accused. This treatment might allow the use of doctrines analogous to provocation or diminished responsibility, where the circumstances reveal that the defendant could not be expected to control himself completely (according to national norms, although he might have acted consistently with tribal norms). Proof of these mitigating factors would then warrant classification to a lower degree of criminal homicide.

---

[20] J. Collier, Law and Social Change in Zinacantan (1973).

[24] J. Collier, *supra* note 20, at 43; *cf.* Fuller, *The Case of the Speluncean Explorers,* 62 Harv. L. Rev. 616, 621 (1949) (Justice Foster's reasoning for the Supreme Court of Newgarth absolves the cannibalistic spelunkers of murder on the ground that "a case may be removed morally from the force of a legal order, as well as geographically"). *But see Regina v. Machekequonabe,* 28 Ont. 309 (1898), where the Canadian court refused to acquit the defendant Indian who shot and killed a Wendigo (believed to be a cannibalistic evil spirit clothed in human flesh), but owing to mitigating circumstances permitted the verdict of manslaughter to stand. The threat of cannibalism was a matter of widespread concern to the Northern Ojibwa, and the Wendigo killings were considered acts of maintaining social order.

The standard of "adequate" provocation is obviously shaped by social convention, and a "reasonable person" test has been used in England and the United States. If this test were based on a subjective standard, as the Model Penal Code partially recommends, then a "reasonable Indian" inquiry might lead to a more just accommodation between the dominant and minority cultures. The doctrine of diminished capacity, likewise, recognizes that the impaired psychological condition of a defendant, though short of insanity, provides a mitigating rationale for classifying an intentional killing as manslaughter rather than murder.

Second, Justice Velasco appears to adopt the reasoning of the legal fiction in article 40, Law 89 (1890), treating Indians as minors for purposes of the criminal law. This fiction then justifies the application of article 1 from that statute, excluding semisavages from the normative control of ordinary national legislation. The nineteenth century plan for Indians foresaw missionary jurisdiction over uncivilized Indians under Law 72 (1892), but this statute is unconstitutional under articles 26 and 58 of the Colombian Constitution. Hence, no competent court — that is, a court with jurisdiction to apply the 1936 Criminal Code — is available to try Miquirucama. He is released, therefore, to face the dictates of his community.

Release of Miquirucama implies reliance upon the notion of excuse. The theory of excuse in criminal law concedes that an act is wrongful, but seeks to avoid attribution of the act to the defendant. The focus is thus on the actor's personal capacity to avoid either committing an intentional wrong or taking an undue risk. Insanity is the classic example of excuse. But here, the reasoning of the *Miquirucama* Court majority would appear to excuse an entire group of individuals.

Is the result of the majority tenable in the modern world? Should adults of ethnic minorities be treated as children or as "unconquerably ignorant"? Justices Perez and Romero, in dissent, say no. Citing recent anthropological research, they state their belief "in the adaptability of all human beings to overcome conditions of backwardness." Based on the desirability of the modern nation state and its territoriality principle, as well as the idea of juridical equality, Miquirucama should be treated as any other citizen and receive his punishment for the crime of homicide.

Does the majority or dissent present the better view? The equality principle has been expressed in the United States with growing frequency and even stridency throughout this century. But what would be the pragmatic consequence of "equal" treatment of Indians in national courts controlled by personnel schooled in the dominant legal culture? According to Bronislaw Malinowski:

> There is hardly anything more pernicious, therefore, in the many European ways of interference with savage peoples, than the bitter animosity with which Missionary, Planter, and Official alike pursue the sorcerer. The rash, haphazard, unscientific application of our morals, laws, and customs to native societies, and the destruction of native law, quasi-legal

> machinery and instruments of power leads only to anarchy and moral atrophy and in the long run to the extinction of culture and race.[37]

Providing formal equality to an Indian defendant within the context of the white legal system, therefore, without Indian participation at all levels of decisionmaking, is likely to be a sham.

A compromise between the majority and dissent might save something of Indian legal culture, bow to the ideology of equal justice under law, and reduce the dilemma of individual responsibility. This might most effectively be accomplished through a system of tribal courts which apply Indian law. Indian culture should be respected and accommodated where possible. When the national law must intrude, particularly in the penal area, a single code of norms should apply to all citizens. The special circumstances of tribal Indians, however, should be accommodated in these instances through the use of a mitigation doctrine, analogous to diminished responsibility, when imposing sanctions. This is preferable to totally waiving sanctions for serious crimes under the doctrine of excuse, or under the reasoning of the Court in *Miquirucama*. The problem with excusing groups of Indians is twofold. First, the tribal system of social control may be inadequate to handle serious criminal matters, thereby unjustly endangering the safety of its members. Second, and possibly more important, the potential for indigenous cultures to adapt and survive in a sometimes hostile Western environment demands partial acculturation toward that dominant culture.

NOTES AND QUESTIONS

1. Define the term "legal pluralism." Is current interest in legal pluralism directed more toward accommodation or assimilation of minorities? How does this interest relate to the concept of "legal penetration"?

Many Latin American nations, such as Bolivia, Brazil, Colombia, Guatemala, Ecuador, Mexico, and Peru, have substantial surviving indigenous populations. In all of these nations, the extent to which the official legal system of the state has penetrated and can be made to penetrate the lives of the people is a concern of those who are preoccupied with "development," "modernization," or "nation-building." More important for our purposes in this course is the question of how far one can propose to go in describing the law of, say, Peru by describing only the official legal system when, for millions of Peruvians, the law that counts for most purposes is the customary law. There is no satisfactory answer to that question. We can point to the obvious fact that, to the urban oligarchy (that part of the population that is cosmopolitan, participates in Western culture, owns or controls the bulk of private wealth, and fills positions of power and prestige in the public and private sectors), Western law is the significant law. The urban oligarchy are those who, in effect, replaced the Inca, and later the *conquistadores*, at the top of the pyramid. And for many others further down the socioeconomic pyramid (how far down is an interesting variable) the same is true. Still, in nations like Peru and Mexico, it is impossible to ignore the fact that those making up the base of the pyra-

[37] B. Malinowski, Crime and Custom in Savage Society 93 (1926).

mid are still wedded to customary law. The *Miquirucama* case from Colombia illustrates the situation.

2. *Miquirucama* reveals the kind of problem that can arise in a pluralistic environment. Several positions on the legal issues are discussed: that of the court of appeal (and former assistant attorney general Luis Zafra), that of the Supreme Court majority, and that of the Court's dissenting members. Which position seems to you to be the better policy? Why? Is total penetration, an absolute monopoly of state law, desirable?

3. Observe that the appeal from the conviction in *Miquirucama* was taken by the public prosecutor (*ministerio público*), a public official with duties roughly analogous to those of our district attorneys. In Chapter 10, Section B we will explain why such a prosecutor might appeal from a conviction.

4. Observe that there were still remnants of ecclesiastical jurisdiction in Colombia (the jurisdiction of missionaries over Indians) well into the 20th century.

5. For more on legal pluralism, see David S. Clark, *Legal Pluralism in Latin America,* 1 Ariz. J. Int'l & Comp. L. 27 (1982); Guillermo Floris Margadant, *Official Mexican Attitudes Toward the Indians: An Historical Essay,* 54 Tul. L. Rev. 964 (1980); Sally Engle Merry, *Legal Pluralism,* 22 Law & Soc'y Rev. 869 (1988). For an interesting United States case, in which the defendant — an undocumented Mexican — admitted killing his girlfriend in Chicago, but defended on the ground that she was a witch (*bruja*) who practiced *curanderismo* (a Mexican belief in folk healing and spirits) and that he was under a spell (*embrujada*), see Adrienne Drell, *Witchcraft Murder Defense Fails,* 79 A.B.A. J. 40 (May 1993).

The *Miquirucama* case is, of course, unusual, exotic. The following excerpts describe more ordinary ways in which problems of legal penetration and of legal culture affect the law in Latin America.

2. INDIAN COURTS IN RURAL MEXICO

LAURA NADER, HARMONY IDEOLOGY: JUSTICE AND CONTROL IN A ZAPOTEC MOUNTAIN VILLAGE 6-8, 10, 15-16, 29-31, 109, 120-122, 125, 127, 146-48, 162-63, 165-67, 169-71, 181 (1990)

Introduction

An examination of village social organization and the workings of village law courts among the mountain Zapotec of Talea reveals the heritage of penetration. The processes of internal and external forces appear in the interconnectedness of social organization and in the styles of disputing processes. The Rincón Zapotec villages have been organized as politically independent, self-reliant, endogamous places that remain free to determine their lives only to the extent to which they manage themselves successfully. Villages with divisive feuds or problems that escalate to the district seat in Villa Alta, to the state government, or beyond are vulnerable to state interference. For the Taleans, the ability to manage the wider world depends on their ability to manage their internal world. The illusion of peace is crucial to the maintenance of autonomy, or the ability to decide one's own destiny.

The state of Oaxaca is divided into districts. Each district is divided into a number of *municipios* (townships), which vary in area and population size. These townships administer their own affairs through elected town members and are also responsible for smaller villages and dispersed settlements (*rancherías*) located nearby and referred to collectively as *agencias*. In a political sense, several agencies lie within each township, several townships lie within each district, and all districts combine to form the state of Oaxaca. Geographically, however, these subdivisions do not lie within one another because agencies and townships have their own territories with established boundaries, which in some cases date from before the Spanish conquest. In regard to the case at hand, Talea lies in the district of Villa Alta and has jurisdiction over three agencies. In over a decade of fieldwork reported on here (1957-68), these communities had a combined population of approximately 2,400 people. The municipal building in Talea is the largest in the Rincón. In this building are located the three village courts of Talea.

Taleans have been hearing their own cases in village courts at least since the founding of the village in the sixteenth century. The local court hears all cases — family, land, slander, debt, and so forth. With the exception of cases where blood has been drawn, the village has the right under state law to conclude the case if the litigants so wish. The court deals mainly with cases involving individuals, but it also handles disputes between both intra- and inter-village groups if brought before the court by the litigants. In these small courts traditional ideas are formulated and expressed, and legal ideas introduced by the state are applied or challenged. It is a place where conformity is taught and rewarded, where local values are expressed, where images of the external world are built, and where village autonomy is declared. Like endogamy and the prohibition of the sale of land to nonvillagers, dispute-handling processes contribute to village self-determination.

The Talean court is both administrative (it manages the physical plant of the town, deals with life-cycle events such as birth, marriage, sickness, and death, and manages relations with the outside — *relaciones exteriores*), and judicial (it hears and handles disputes)....

In their presentation of self, Talean leaders are intent on believing and having outsiders believe that internal relations are harmonious and in equilibrium....

The political effectiveness of the Talean court depends on local participation, whereby it disperses power and reinforces community solidarity. In the name of harmony, the court can hold private power accountable for the general good of the village. In the name of autonomy, the court encourages decision-making that is accountable to the townspeople. In the name of solidarity, it makes decisions reflecting concerns about long-term consequences in order to avoid factionalism. It is through its legal processes that the court expresses and ranks social values important to the village and to its relationship with the outside world. The village court can compete effectively with the district court, for villagers generally opt for local dispute-handling processes. The courts are the vehicle through which political interest is pursued, using legal procedures grounded in the concepts of harmony and balance that permit conflicting interests to be accommodated. In terms of actual case handling, the harmony model pays attention less to the facts of a specific ease than to the language of disputing in the village court as opposed to the state courts. Villagers fend off the outside world by consciously differentiating their courts from those of the state....

I would argue that Talean Zapotec law will survive as a system separate from Mexican law only as long as village law rather than Mexican law is perceived as meeting village needs *and* only as long as the Mexican state (like the Spanish Crown previously) continues to regard local rule as in its best interests. As long as the Mexican state can continue to regulate the economy (labor, resources, consumption) and as long as local disorder does not threaten the state, local village law will continue in its present manner, fluctuating around changing issues but ever mindful of the connection between harmony and autonomy....

The Organization of Talean Courts

Early reports by Spanish friars describe the southern part of Mexico that is now the state of Oaxaca as a land of many different tribes, languages, and cultures. Maps made by these friars plot the distribution of at least fifteen language groups. The largest of these groups in area and in sheer number of speakers is the Zapotec, a people often described as intelligent, industrious, acquisitive, and progressive.

Zapotec, which today numbers approximately 425,000 speakers, is listed in the 1980 census as a single language, although the Zapotec dialects are in fact languages as distinct from one another as the Romance languages ....

The Zapotec have lived for more than 2,000 years in what is now the state of Oaxaca. The legacy of ancient Zapotec civilization remains in the ruins of Mitla and Monte Alban; the legacy of conquest remains in the language, which today is being replaced by Spanish, and in the social and political organization of the Zapotec peoples. According to the 1980 census, 338,276 Zapotec speakers are bilingual.

Colonization brought dramatic changes: the reorganization of labor, the heavy use of taxation, the use of Indian slaves in the mines and fields, which changed the traditional division of labor between men and women, and the concentration of Indians in larger compact settlements. It was only much later when new crops were brought in from Europe (wheat, sugarcane, and fruits of various kinds) and new tools (such as the wooden plow and the horizontal loom) and arms (the steel machete, axes) that economic changes benefited the Indian and the developing mestizo and creole classes....

The municipal building in Talea is the largest structure of its kind in the Rincón area. It has two rooms used by the elected town officials and a jail to hold difficult defendants. The first is a large room, the *presidencia*, where four of the town officials — the *presidente*, the *sindico* (responsible for the police and investigations), the town *secretario*, and the *tesorero* (treasurer) — conduct their official business. The presidente has a large desk, as does the sindico; litigants sit facing these officials. The *regidores* (aldermen) sit in the presidencia or in the corridor outside. The police sit and sleep in the corridors of the building. In the second room, called the *juzgado*, the *alcalde* (town judge) and his secretary carry out their responsibilities. The building itself was built over many years by *tequio* (communal work) and by the labor of defendants in lawsuits who could not pay their fines in cash and were required to contribute work instead. The municipio is the place of law and government; it is where citizens learn by performing the various offices of government and where citizens come for redress.

The most influential leaders in Talea, referred to as *principales*, are the only officials without space in the municipal building. These men are considered, and consider themselves, best qualified to advise elected officials in the municipal government. In actuality the principales decide town policies and are often successful in carrying them out. When they overstep their role, defined by the town as merely advisory, they are open to public criticism....

The municipal presidente (chosen from one of three candidates nominated by the principales) is elected at a town meeting. Only males can vote. Ideally, candidates for presidente are selected from town citizens known for their leadership abilities, for justness, and for the economic ability to serve without pay. Once elected, the presidente chooses the secretary and treasurer, who work in the same office with him. He has the authority and duty to call town meetings, to make town rulings, to resolve complaints and administer justice, to consider petitions, to perform marriages, and to take an active part in the nomination of other town government officials. The presidente is expected to represent his townsmen and to watch out for their welfare....

The sindico (also chosen from one of three candidates nominated by the principales) works in the presidente's office, and since much of the sindico's work involves close cooperation with the presidente, it is desirable that these two men be able to work as a team. The sindico manages the police force, investigates serious crimes, and administers the communal work program. He is the official legal representative of the village in its dealings with the state government. Both the sindico and the alcalde appeal cases to the *ministerio publico* (prosecutor) and the district judge in Villa Alta. Any case appealed beyond Villa Alta goes to the Tribunal Superior of Oaxaca....

The alcalde's duties entail the adjudication of all cases not resolved in the office of the presidente or the sindico. The alcalde is a man who may have an interest in and knowledge of legal affairs, a man whose abilities to arbitrate and reconcile conflicting interests among his fellow townsmen have already gained him renown....

Court Styles

One constant that runs through case materials from the Talean court may, for present purposes, briefly be described as the value placed on harmony and on achieving balance or agreement between the principals in a case. It is compromise arrived at by adjudication or, in some cases, adjudication arrived at by compromise. The *settlement* to a dispute may be designed to fine, jail, ridicule, or acquit the principals in a case, but the *outcome* desired is rectification. It is outcome rather than decision that is important to style. The outcome is the effect the decision has on the litigants and their dispute; outcome centers attention on desired results....

The Presidente's Court

The presidente's court has but few formalities: men take their hats off upon entering the court, the plaintiff sits to the right of the presidente; who is sitting, and the defendant is placed in front of the presidente; when a new case interrupts one that is being heard, the presidente stands up behind his desk to receive the case. In fact the proceedings are often interrupted by people who have administrative business. The presidente, upon being presented with a complaint, attempts to settle it immediately. The litigants may present their case quietly or vociferously. To Western eyes, the time spent in court seems interminably long and disproportionate to the amount of action that takes place there, but that is because the untutored eye sees very little of the "action." Many of these cases are linked to previous conflicts known to the presidente. Part of the "action" is giving the parties time to think, time for different points of view to take shape.

The presidente is a citizen, not a professional, giving his year of service to his fellow Taleans. Whether he spends most of his time hearing cases or doing other work depends on his reputation and his personal style. He decides cases without using written law, resolving conflict by minimizing the sense of injustice and outrage felt by the parties to a case. Ideally, his investigation of the facts is nondirective and flexible; there are no rigid rules of evidence. The presidente's stance, when patient, encourages litigants to decide what issues should be discussed and to present both real and abstract evidence to support their claims; there is no concept of objective truth. In family cases he is more likely to be directive and paternalistic and seeks to remind kinfolk of their responsibilities to the community. He is expected to use what he knows of town affairs and is theoretically selected for such knowledge. The presidente is expected to render a verbal and written agreement for each case — an agreement that town consensus would consider equitable. He is not expected to explain the basis of his decision. Legal documents do include the litigants' statements, the agreement, and/or a statement mentioning the fine, if any. It is what happens to the litigants that is central to the legal documents, not the reasoning of the judge in the case.

Although both parties have to agree on the decision, the "compromise" is not always a result of mutual concessions because it is the presidente who, after listening to the case, decides where the middle ground is or encourages the litigants to make their own agreement. And the decision is often the presidente's understanding of what is best for "making the balance" — which often means the restoration of relations to a former condition of harmony where conflict was absent....

The presidente's role is that of mediator, adjudicator, and group therapist, depending on case requirements. His principal function seems to be to listen, often asking questions to clear up contradictions and pointing the way to a more harmonious condition. He usually does not cross-examine, but rather allows the litigants to spell out their arguments. In this way he brings out the nature of the conflict, the basis of the points at issue....

The Sindico's Court

In the sindico's court, an air of privacy pervades the initial stages of the hearings. Many of the sindico's cases begin with *se presentaron*; that is, the disputants present themselves, singly, before the sindico for legal advice, much as they would go to a lawyer in the United States for advice on a will. The sindico usually speaks to the plaintiff first and alone and tries to see his or her degree of intransigency, and then does the same with the defendant. If necessary, he then uses *careo* (confrontation) as a fact-finding device, in order to find out what the truth or the lies are, as one sindico put it, and not in order to have the litigants mutually agree. I would not say that reconciliation is unimportant to the sindico, but it is not the only tool he has at his disposal; he can also investigate and establish facts. Certainly this would seem to create a different tone from that in the presidente's court, but it is a matter of degree. The sindico may make references to the *código penal*, and a reading of the cases provides instances in which a sindico has used coercive power. Still, he gives the litigants a chance to "make the balance," but if they do not wish to do so, he has at his disposal techniques that allow him to adjudicate a decision and force a compromise based on his fact-finding, and he is more likely to do so than the presidente....

The Alcalde's Court

Of the three court officials, the alcalde is the only one whose job is dedicated solely to judicial matters. For reasons I still do not fully understand, the man chosen for the post of alcalde often speaks only Zapotec or is weak in Spanish. A knowledge of Spanish is considered an important qualification for the offices of presidente and sindico, since these men in their administrative capacities so often need to communicate with the "outside." The alcalde does not have these "outside" responsibilities, but the style of his court is remarkably similar to the presidente's court even though the cases often take longer to hear, are often more complicated, and involve a greater number of witnesses and more lengthy testimony. The alcalde would also agree with the saying "A bad agreement is better than a good fight."...

Chief Causes of Complaint

The broad range of complaints in Talea indicates that the courts are not specialized but generalized institutions that handle the daily problems of a rural, mountain, agricultural community largely isolated from urban problems. Even though the ideal division of labor between the courts makes the sindico court the most specialized of the three, the users of the courts push to make them nonspecific. Villagers believe that courts should take care of the problems that come to them and should disregard central government attempts to give them specialized jurisdictions. The range of complaints and the overlap of complaints among the different users of the court indicate the range

Table 6.13
Categories of Complaints in Talea (1957-1968) by Type of Court

	Presidente	Alcalde	Sindico	
Type of complaint	Percent of total	Percent of total	Percent of total	Total complaints
Property (movable and immovable)	25%	32%	35%	158
Contract	8	8	14	50
Physical aggression	18	23	13	100
Verbal aggression	12	12	14	67
Conjugal or family duties	17	17	8	80
Drunk and disorderly	14	4	9	50
Administrative	2	1	5	11
Other	4	2	1	15
TOTAL	[n=221]	[n=204]	[n=106]	531

Note: "Administrative" complaints include the making of wills and the payment or nonpayment of taxes. "Other" complaints include contempt of court, perjury, and cases of health emergencies; the court sometimes figures in decision-making in life and death situations.

of rights and duties that citizens share, have serious conflicts about, and insist town officials address.

In the total sample of 409 cases, 531 formal complaints were presented to the Talean courts (see Table 6.13). In all three courts, complaints involving property form the largest category. Other common problems involve contracts, physical and verbal aggression, conjugal and family duties, and drunkenness. If we lump property and contract complaints together under the rubric of complaints dealing with movable and immovable property, and physical and verbal aggression together under the rubric of complaints dealing with persons, we do see some evidence of specialization. The case load of the presidente court was divided almost evenly between property complaints (33 percent) and person complaints (30 percent), as was that of the alcalde court (40 percent property and 35 percent person). The sindico court, on the other hand, heard almost twice as many property complaints (49 percent) as person complaints (27 percent). The sindico court dealt with fewer complaints having to do with conjugal or family duties (8 percent) compared with the presidente and alcalde courts (17 percent for each)....

The State District Court in Villa Alta

The district court is located in San Ildefonso de Villa Alta, a mestizo village between six and eight hours' walking distance from Talea. In traveling to Villa Alta, one has to cross a mountain called Matahombres (killer of men).

The name is apt, and I realized how motivated one would have to be to take a case to the district court after I had traveled the route myself....

Villa Alta is a village with a Spanish- and an Indian-speaking population. It has been an administrative center since 1529 and today administers 25 municipios and their agencies. Its population is characterized by a high degree of turnover — government officials and government workers come and go; the families of those imprisoned in its jail visit frequently to care for the prisoners or to plead for clemency; litigants come with their cases; and during its small Monday market commercial activity brings people together from the surrounding Mixe and Zapotec villages, and even from the more distant Chinantec communities....

As the district seat, Villa Alta maintains an archive of law cases from the sixteenth century to the present and houses the court (Juzgado Mixto de Primera Instancia) and other state offices. In Villa Alta one hears a mixture of unrelated languages and dialects of each that are only partly mutually intelligible; Spanish is the lingua franca. The permanent residents are farmers and small shop and cantina keepers, as well as teachers. Some of the teachers originate from villages in the region and act as interpreters for the monolingual peasant Indian peoples, who do not understand the state system of law or the language of that system, Spanish....

In Talea, local-level officials prefer to settle cases at home, but they may send a case to the district court if decision is difficult or if the presidente does not want to risk making an unpopular decision. Citizens themselves may take a case to the appeals court if they do not like local-level officials or if they feel that their chances of winning are better at the district level because state law can prevail in a conflict between Zapotec and state law. However, even after a case is appealed to Villa Alta, it may be rejected. Juquilans, for example, commonly appeal cases that are not accepted because district-level officials do not consider the act a crime, such as a mother taking something from her daughter or an accusation of witchcraft or comparable dealings with the supernatural. In order for local communities and their residents to use the district courts to advantage, they must have some knowledge of Mexican legal categories or, if not, the capability to use bribery ....

However, in cases of homicide or other violent acts in which blood is drawn, villagers usually turn to the district courts immediately because the state and state courts have made it clear since the colonial period that such cases are strictly their responsibility. I say usually because this rule, as we shall see, is not observed in some cases, although villagers know that the district court will intervene and that the village may be heavily fined if such cases go unreported. Otherwise, the district level does not for the most part interfere in local cases, although now and then district officials visit the villages to review hearing procedures....

Categories of Complaint Appealed

Over a ten-year period thirteen homicides were reported in the thirteen villages in the Rincón region .... The most used categories under personal offenses are acts that result in wounds (*lesiones*), homicides (*homicidio*), as-

Table 6.14

Cases from Talea Filed in the Villa Alta District Court (1953-1962), by Type

Type of offense	Number from Talea
Personal	
Amenazas (threats)	6
Estupro (rape)	5
Golpes (assault)	4
Homicidio (homicide)	2
Injurias (insults)	1
Lesiones (blood drawn)	5
Rapto (abduction, rape)	1
Violacion (violation)	3
SUBTOTAL	27
Property	
Daño en propiedad (property damage)	6
Despojo (vandalism)	7
Robo (robbery)	6
SUBTOTAL	19
Role-related	
Abuso de autoridad (abuse of authority)	4
Abuso de confianza (abuse of confidence)	1
Disobedencia (disobedience by a child of a parent)	1
Fraude (fraud)	1
SUBTOTAL	7
TOTAL	53

saults (*golpes*), and threats (*amenazas*). All categories under property cases show relatively high use, but under role-related offenses abuse of authority (*abuso de autoridad*) is the only category to appear regularly. The consistent reporting of the first three categories mentioned above corroborates the earlier observation that the appeals court in Villa Alta requires offenses involving bloodshed to be sent to it, although if all such cases were reported the category would be even more swollen. Threats are a high-use category because these acts usually accompany bloodshed.

Fewer villages use the district courts for role-related offenses. The lower incidence of such cases in the district court indicates that such conflicts may not escalate into violence. The one category that frequently appears is abuse of authority, which often involves conflicts with persons in positions of elected power in the village. As we shall see when we look at who uses the district courts and for what, this category may reflect their use as a power equalizer, as when a person with less power attempts to balance the power differential, or as a mechanism that increases the power of those with money and knowledge of the state system....

The single most important observation from this analysis of the district court docket, even correcting for nonrecording of cases, is how rarely that court is used. Taking a case to the district court is escalation, and Rinconeros do not escalate disputes both because escalation to an external system is linked to a loss of local autonomy and because village law is more elastic than the state system. The state system narrows disputes in a way that does not permit participants the possibility for creative harmony.

NOTES AND QUESTIONS

1. Zapotec Indians living in Talea theoretically have the option of using the Mexican federal district court, the Oaxacan state district court, or one of the Talean Indian courts. What are the advantages of using the Talean courts? Are there disadvantages?

2. What are the principal elements of style for the three types of Talean courts? How does a "judge" achieve harmony or "make the balance"? How does the Talean court setting and procedure differ from that of a typical American court?

3. In considering the Talean court caseloads (Table 6.13), why do you think property cases were more numerous than (or at least as numerous as) personal torts or crimes and other categories of complaints? Is it likely that the Talean courts more satisfactorily resolve Indian property cases than the Oaxacan state district court?

4. Why would a Talean official or litigant take a case to the state district court in Villa Alta? How does the district court caseload (from Talea) differ from the pattern of cases heard in Talean courts? Would the more Westernized population in Villa Alta have a distorted image of Talean disputes?

5. Why is it beneficial to the Mexican government to maintain the Talean and other Indian courts?

6. Useful material and insights on the topic of Indian law and courts in Latin America can be found in: Jane Fishburne Collier, Law and Social Change in Zinacantan (1973); Eva Hunt & Robert Hunt, *The Role of Courts in Rural Mexico,* in Peasants in the Modern World 109 (P. Bock ed. 1969); June Starr & Jane F. Collier, eds., History and Power in the Study of Law: New Directions in Legal Anthropology (1989).

3. THE LEGAL CULTURE OF BRAZIL

KEITH S. ROSENN, BRAZIL'S LEGAL CULTURE: THE *JEITO* REVISITED, 1 Fla. Int'l L.J. 1, 2-5, 14-15, 17-25, 29-30 (1984)

Introduction

The Brazilian way of coping with the formal legal system is typified in this story of a recent graduate of a European medical school who wished to immigrate to Brazil. At his visa appointment, the Brazilian consul in Paris immediately changed the applicant's profession from doctor to agronomist, explaining: "In that way I can issue you a visa immediately. You know how these things are? Professional quotas, confidential instructions from the department of immigration. Utter nonsense! ... In any event, this way will make it perfectly legal."

At first the European protested, thinking the consul was trying to trap him into making a false declaration. The consul, however, insisted that reclassifying the European doctor as an agronomist would solve rather than create problems. The consul explained that he was simply employing the *jeito*, a Brazilian word that has no precise translation but corresponds roughly to a knack, twist, way, or fix. Only after living in Brazil for some time did this "medical-agronomist" realize that he had immigrated to a country where laws and regulations are enacted upon the assumption that a substantial percentage will be disobeyed, and where "civil servants, be they small or powerful, create their own law. Although this law does not happen to correspond with the original law, it meets with general approbation, provided that it is dictated by common sense."

That Brazilian laws and regulations are regularly twisted to the demands of expediency does not make Brazil unique. The bending of legal norms to expediency occurs to some extent in all countries. It is especially common in Latin America, where the gap between the law on the books and actual practice is notoriously large. What is striking about Brazil is that the practice of bending legal rules to expediency has been elevated into a highly prized paralegal institution called the *jeito*. The *jeito* has become an integral part of Brazil's legal culture. In many areas of the law, the *jeito* is the norm and the formal legal rule is the exception....

For analytic purposes the *jeito* can be broken down into at least five different kinds of behavior:

(1) A government official fails to perform a legal duty because of private pecuniary or status gains; *i.e.*, the official awards a government contract to the highest briber.

(2) A private citizen employs a subterfuge to circumvent a legal obligation that is sensible and just (in an objective sense); *i.e.*, an exporter under-invoices a shipment, receiving part of the purchase price abroad in foreign currency in order to evade currency controls and taxes on part of his profits.

(3) A public servant performs his legal duty speedily only in exchange for private pecuniary or status gains; *i.e.*, an official refuses to process an application to renew an auto license unless he has received a tip or knows the applicant.

(4) A private citizen circumvents a legal obligation that is unrealistic, unjust, or economically inefficient; *i.e.*, loans are disguised as joint ventures or borrowers are required to maintain compensating balances at low interest in order to circumvent a usury law that limits lawful interest to a rate well below market rates.

(5) A public servant deviates from his legal duty because of his conviction that the law is unrealistic, unjust, or economically inefficient; *i.e.*, a labor inspector overlooks the failure of a marginal firm in an area of high unemployment to pay the official minimum wage on the theory that strict enforcement would be likely to throw many employees out of work and perhaps shut down the plant altogether.

The first two kinds of behavior fit the conventional definition of corruption — dishonest behavior benefiting an individual at the expense of the state. The third kind of behavior can also be labelled corruption by conventional standards, although most people would consider it less morally offensive than the first two forms of corruption. The fourth and fifth kinds of behavior are those in which public purposes are arguably served by evading legal obligations. These components of the *jeito* bear no stigma. On the contrary, they have made the *jeito* a highly prized Brazilian institution....

The Roots of the Jeito

The roots of the *jeito* run deep into the Iberian past. During the critical formative era, Portuguese attitudes toward law were fundamentally influenced by Roman law, legal pluralism, and Catholicism. As a result of Portuguese colonization, these same fundamental influences shaped Brazilian attitudes toward law. Brazilian attitudes toward the administration of law were also shaped by the peculiar character of Portuguese colonial rule, as well as five cultural characteristics bequeathed by the Portuguese: high tolerance for corruption, lack of civic responsibility, profound socio-economic inequality, sentimentalism, and a willingness to compromise. The *jeito* is firmly rooted in this Luso-Roman legacy....

Lack of Civic Responsibility and Personalismo

The Portuguese handed down to the Brazilians a weak sense of loyalty and obligation towards the society in which they lived, and a strong sense of loyalty and obligation towards family and friends. In comparing the Portuguese character with the Spanish, Marcus Cheke noted:

> [A] trait that is common to both peoples is their lack of what may be termed "civic sense." Even more than the Spaniard, the Portuguese is kind and charitable to five categories of persons: to his family, to his friends, to the friends of his family, to the friends of his friends, and lastly, to the beggar in his path. But to other fellow citizens he acknowledges little obligation.

The proposition that the law should be applied even-handedly and impersonally to all citizens conflicts with this Portuguese heritage. The dominant attitude is reflected in the familiar Brazilian adage: *Para os amigos tudo, para os indiferentes nada, e para os inimigos a lei* (For friends, everything; for strangers, nothing; and for enemies, the law). Family and friendship ties very frequently impose on Brazilian bureaucrats the duty to bend the law; the duty to execute the law in unbent form is usually relegated to a lesser plane. As a preeminent student of national character has explained: "[T]he basic Brazilian personality ... stresses direct personal relations, based upon liking rather than unconditioned, impersonal, practical relations. Personal liking is above the law."...

The Legal Culture: Paternalistic, Legalistic and Formalistic

Paternalism

The paternalism that stemmed from the Portuguese monarchy, the Catholic Church, and the extended patriarchal family still permeates Brazilian society. It is commonly expressed in the *patrão* (patron) complex of traditional Brazil. In return for fealty and service, the *patrão*, a member of the local elite, customarily looks after the interests of his employees, tenants, or debtors. The *patrão* plays the role of protector, interceding with the authorities when any of his flock is in trouble. This aspect of the *patrão* system serves to personalize and particularize legal relations for the lower class. The ultimate *patrão* is the state, from which the Brazilians seem to expect just about everything "from jobs, credit, high wages, health care, to economic stability, and subsidies for carnival masquerades."

Authority is tightly concentrated in Brazil, and is delegated most reluctantly. As with many developing countries, almost all decisions, even the most petty, must come from the top. A typical complaint is that of Jarbas Passarinho, former Minister of Education, that no sooner had he taken office than his subordinates began appearing with "urgent" documents that required his signature: permission to unload 156 pieces of paper and a lease of a home for an inspector of secondary education in the Northeast. Helio Beltrão, Planning Minister in the Costa e Silva regime and until recently Minister of Debureaucratization, has observed:

> The concentration of the power of decision at the highest levels was, and still is, the most serious ill of the country's administrative organism. The repugnancy for delegation has been responsible for the incredible delay in solving the most routine matters, ... for the interminable routing of processes for "higher consideration," and, in the final analysis, for the demoralization of those governing, who see themselves separated from the governed by a veritable bulwark of paper.

The long waiting period during which documents wend their way to the top encourages resort to the *jeito*.

Historically, elites have paternalistically bestowed constitutions and laws upon the Brazilian populace with little regard or awareness of the desires and capabilities of those governed. Instead of being the product of popular pressures, an objective fact-finding study, or a crystalization of custom, legislation is usually the product of what a small group imagines would be ideal for the people. Thus, the labor legislation that the Vargas regime enacted in the late 1930s and early 1940s paternalistically granted many benefits and protections to the worker that have been the object of extensive struggles by labor movements in other parts of the world. Paid vacations, maternity benefits, job security, minimum wages, special treatment for women and children, health and sanitary conditions on the job, were all granted to employees in the Consolidated Labor Laws. Instead of creating a strong, independent labor movement, this legislation turned the labor movement into a ward of the state. To this day labor has remained dependent on the Ministry of Labor and the labor courts to secure wage increases, better working conditions, and enforcement of the labor laws, many of which have been more breached than honored.

The disparity between the government's and the people's views of what is best has made Brazilians prone to act according to an old adage — *manda quem pode, obedece quem quer* (he who can, commands; he who wants to, obeys).

Legalism

Brazilian legal culture is highly legalistic; society places great emphasis upon seeing that all social relations are regulated by comprehensive legislation. Brazilians feel that new institutions or practices ought not be adopted without prior legal authorization. As has been said with reference to German legalism, Brazil has a "horror of a legal vacuum." The country has reams of laws and decrees regulating with great specificity every aspect of Brazilian life, as well as some aspects of life not found in Brazil. It often appears that if something is not prohibited by law, it must be obligatory.

Another facet of this legalistic mentality is the tendency to regard as done that which is enacted into law. Brazil inherited from Portugal the naive faith that almost any social or economic ill can be cured by legal prescription. Brazil has continually repeated the colonial pattern of Spain and Portugal by enacting laws with little regard for the prospects of enforcement. Unenforceable laws have typically been remedied by new laws, most of them equally unenforceable. The persistence up to the present of the assumption that all problems can be solved on a legal level is remarkable. Whether the society is willing and able to shoulder the costs of enforcement is seldom a suitable topic for discussion.

Lawmakers are generally not content to set forth desired conduct in general terms. They seem driven to try to anticipate and regulate all possible future occurrences with detailed, comprehensive, and occasionally incomprehensible legislation. Situations that should be left to judges or administrators in other countries to work out on a case-by-case basis under the rubric of "reasonableness" are preordained by statute. For example, the Law of Directives and Bases of National Education attempts to spell out the nature and structure of primary, secondary, and university education for all of Brazil. The statute establishes uniform curricula, schedules, and programs for the entire country. Article 92 states: "The Union shall apply annually for the maintenance and development [of education] 12 percent of its tax receipts, and a minimum of 20 percent for the States, Federal District and the Counties." With good reason, provisions of this type have seldom been honored. This legislative style reflects a deep-seated mistrust of those administering and interpreting the laws, as well as the entire legalistic and codifying tradition of the civil law, which exalts certainty as a supreme value.

Evidence of legalism can be found everywhere. Little stands on street corners sell copies of the latest laws. Questions such as whether a particular student was properly failed or which professor won a competition to be a chair professor are regularly litigated, even carried to the nation's highest court. A separate court system has been set up to resolve disputes growing out of sporting events, particularly soccer matches. Even when behaving arbitrarily and unconstitutionally, Brazilian governments feel compelled to go through a legalistic charade.

Legalism has contributed to the *jeito*'s popularity in two ways: it has led to an abundance of regulatory legislation, and a failure to build sufficient flexibility into that regulation. The *jeito* can be viewed as a legalistic response to both problems.

Formalism

Closely related to legalism is the exaggerated concern with legal formalities. Every nation has some formalistic behavior, but Brazilian concern with authenticity and verification is both impressive and oppressive....

Cashing a traveler's check at a government bank requires presentation of one's passport or identity card, supplying a local address and telephone number, signing numerous copies of a form, which is then typed up, stamped, and initialed by a regiment of bank clerks. Although the government has streamlined the process somewhat as part of an energetic campaign to stimulate exports, securing an export license in 1981 was reported to involve 1,470 separate legal actions with thirteen government ministries and fifty agencies. Even registering to vote may take weeks to secure the approvals of a dozen different governmental agencies. Then one must prove that one has been registered to vote in every previous place of residence. Moreover, ofttimes an approval from one government agency expires before all other necessary documentation is in order, requiring one to begin the process anew.

The presumption appears to be that every citizen is lying unless he produces written, documentary proof that he is telling the truth. The formal legal system, whether ascertaining criminal guilt or issuing employment benefits, displays a decided tendency to believe only documents and not people. Helio Beltrão's personal experience as Planning Minister bears this out well. A decree which he submitted to the President for consideration in 1968 was perceived as scandalous because it abolished the requirement that an official document certifying one is alive be presented by anyone personally appearing at the appropriate government department to collect his pension. The formalistic legal system was far more comfortable with documentary proof that the person at the window was indeed alive....

The failure to tailor laws to Brazilian needs is largely attributable to the legislative process. Most Brazilian legislation has been drafted by distinguished jurists or law professors in an atmosphere far removed from the clamor of special interest groups. The draftsmen have typically consulted the various solutions to the problem that have been enacted abroad and tried to select one that, as an abstract proposition, appears best, rather than seek a rule that crystallizes custom or practice. Seldom has there been a fact finding inquiry about the peculiarly Brazilian nature of the economic, social, political, or administrative problems involved. Disputes among jurists and professors about the rule being adopted are frequent, but these are typically technical, doctrinal disputes. The end product of this process has been the legislation of idealized standards of behavior, continuing a tradition that harks back to Portugal's adoption of Roman law....

There is more to formalism, however, than legal science and the superimposition of imported forms ill-suited to Brazilian needs. In certain instances formalism may be a conscious strategy for promoting social change. This thesis has been elaborated by Guerreiro Ramos, who argues that in the Brazilian historical context, formalism has been an important strategy adopted by the elite in order to forge a nation....

Many of the legal institutions that the elite imported had essentially hortatory and aspirational functions. Although Brazil may have lacked the social and political infrastructure that would allow the constitutional system imported from the United States to function in 1891, the hope was that Brazilian society would evolve sufficiently to convert the constitutional theory into practice....

Conversely, one can argue that there are cases where formalism has been adopted as a conscious strategy for averting social change. In Brazil, as in a great many developing nations, it is frequently easier and less socially divisive for opponents of legislation aimed at effecting fundamental changes in the society to prevent implementation rather than enactment. Proponents of basic reforms are accorded a symbolic victory, but in practice nothing changes because supporters of the status quo have sufficient political and economic power to defeat the reform at the administrative level....

Penetration of the Formal Legal System

Brazil's formal legal system has all the earmarks of a modern, developed institutional structure. At its heart are the Constitution and comprehensive basic codes of civil, criminal, and commercial law, as well as criminal and civil procedure. The Constitution is modeled after that of the United States, while the basic codes are largely drawn from European models. Disputes within the formal legal system are resolved by a hierarchical arrangement of courts on the basis of the wording and legislative history of the statutory rules, scholarly doctrine, opinions of distinguished jurists, and prior court decisions. This part of the legal system is administered by a specially trained, highly influential group of law professionals — lawyers, judges, and notaries.

The formal system has gradually begun to penetrate into the interior of Brazil, but this penetration is far from complete. Large areas of this huge country are still inaccessible, despite improvements in modern communications and transportation. Much of the rural interior still is only nominally under the control of the formal authorities. The great bulk of the rural population is still largely unaffected by the formal legal structure. Its disputes are resolved by *patrãoes, paterfamilias,* or large landowners in accordance with local custom. Although the situation is changing, especially since the military takeover in 1964, federal and even state law is little known or enforced in much of the interior. Continued tolerance of a system of local authority is a tacit compromise, with the local bosses delivering the rural vote to federal and state authorities in exchange for ample extralegal autonomy. The tradition is "to render justice to one's friends and to apply the law to one's adversaries."

Not only in rural regions has penetration of the legal system been limited. Millions of urban Brazilians live in *favelas*, squatter settlements that ring all major cities. Penetration of the formal legal structure in the *favela* is fragmentary and precarious, for the *favela*'s very existence is of doubtful legality. Instead, the *favela* is governed by a mixture of the formal legal system and an informal, customary system, as well as a curious set of laws and regulations designed to permit the formal authorities to deal with the *favelados* without having to acknowledge the lawfulness of the *favela*'s existence.

NOTES AND QUESTIONS

1. What is the *jeito*? Does it exist within the U.S. legal culture? How should one characterize a typical American lawyer's action in a criminal plea bargain, an uncontested divorce, or in inventing the minutes of fictitious shareholders' meetings for a small corporation?

2. What attitudes and social facts influence a Brazilian's view toward the administration of the law?

3. Brazilian legal culture is described as paternalistic, legalistic, and formalistic. Do these three characteristics appropriately describe important features of the legal culture in the United States?

4. Legal reform in Brazil may at times serve essentially a hortatory or aspirational function, which is an aspect of formalism. Can you think of any amendments to the U.S. Constitution that for a substantial time served primarily an aspirational function?

4. THE LEGAL CULTURE OF MEXICO

BELTRAN COLLANTES, MARTHA

Supreme Court of Mexico (3rd Civil Chamber)
Amparo 5670/69 of February 24, 1971
26 S.J.F. pt. 4, at 33 (7th series 1971)

The underlying liability of the state, according to article 1928 of the Baja California Civil Code, does not require fault on the part of the state. It is sufficient that state employees were derelict in exercising their functions and that they are insolvent. Doctrinally, this responsibility stems from a negligent choice, negligence in the action of an employee. Now, in an environment like the Mexican, with few economic resources, where the courts do not have safe deposit boxes or properly secured storage places, due to poor construction and to inadequate police services to protect them, the judge and his assistant cannot take responsibility for the theft of some items which they kept as unpaid trustees. [In this case, money and jewels valued at more than 100,000 pesos.] Thus, when judicial administrators received evidence related to a criminal matter heard before them, they are only liable for their own negligence or malice. They should not be liable if they act with diligence in keeping assets. There is a principle of law that says: "No one is obligated to do the impossible" ("*impossibilium nulla obligatio est*"). Therefore, the theft of objects under such circumstances as those described constitutes an act of God. The people of the city where the theft occurred, who could not or did not want to pay enough taxes to have tribunals secure in their construction or with safe deposit boxes, are in reality the only ones liable. At least the judge, his assistant, and the respective federal entity should be free of responsibility. To decide the contrary would be to put the justices of the Supreme Court and their assistants in jeopardy for the theft of documents and exhibits that on some occasions might contain titles of credit for large amounts or important contracts.

Majority of 5 votes required

Majority: Rafael Rojina Villegas
Mariano Ramírez Vázquez
Ernesto Solis López

Dissenting: Enrique Martinez Ulloa
Mariano Azuela

NOTES AND QUESTIONS

1. Notice the relationship between economic development and legal doctrine. The justices of the Mexican Supreme Court refuse to blind themselves to the economic realities of a provincial courthouse.

2. Does *Beltran Collantes* reflect the assertion that the judiciary in Mexico is a weak branch of government?

3. For commentary on the legal culture in Mexico, see Michael Wallace Gordon, *Mythical Stereotypes — Dealing With Mexico as a Lawyer,* 38 J. Legal Educ. 279 (1988); Boris Kozolchyk, *Mexico's Political Stability, Economic Growth and the Fairness of Its Legal System,* 18 Cal. W. Int'l L.J. 105 (1987); Keith S. Rosenn, *Corruption in Mexico: Implications for U.S. Foreign Policy,* 18 Cal. W. Int'l L.J. 95 (1987).

4. Consider the peculiar legal culture of Colombia, as described by Rachelle Marie Bin, *Drug Lords and the Colombian Judiciary: A Story of Threats, Bribes and Bullets,* 5 Pac. Basin L.J. 178, 179-80 (1986):

> Prior to the 1984 assassination of Minister of Justice Rodrigo Lara Bonilla, Colombian drug lords openly bribed Colombian public officials, including justices, and their actions were reluctantly tolerated by the government. The millions of dollars which the *trafficantes* reaped in profits transformed them into *narco-politicos*, drug lords wielding enormous political clout. Corruption was so commonplace that it was accepted as a way of life.
>
> The murder on April 30, 1984 of the Minister of Justice, Rodrigo Lara Bonilla, by *trafficante*-hired assassins, abruptly terminated the government's tolerance of the *trafficantes.* Minister [Lara] Bonilla had waged an almost solitary war against the drug trade, often upsetting his colleagues who preferred to maintain a less dangerous profile by ignoring the *trafficantes*....
>
> Immediately following [Lara] Bonilla's assassination, President Belisario Betancur declared a state of siege against all *trafficantes*....
>
> Betancur's promise to wage a war without quarter against the cocaine mafia and the government's subsequent crackdown on corrupt officials and drug lords did not quell the violence; instead, implementation of

those policies provoked violent retaliation. Shortly thereafter, Justice Manuel Castro Gil, who was in charge of investigating Minister [Lara] Bonilla's murder and who had ordered that charges be brought against sixteen persons, was shot and killed by *trafficante*-hired assassins. In November 1985, leftist guerrillas hired by the drug lords stormed the Palace of Justice in Bogotá, and killed more than forty people, including 10 associate justices and the Chief Justice [of the Supreme Court].

E. LEGAL CULTURE AND LEGAL PENETRATION IN EAST ASIA

No topic related to law and East Asia generates greater attention than the basic issue of how relevant Western law and legal institutions really are in East Asian societies. Central to most discussions is concern over what has been labeled a lack of "rights consciousness" in traditional East Asian societies — whether in the Confucianist or Hindu-Buddhist tradition — and the corollary restriction of the effectiveness of any system of legal rights enforced through the courts.

1. THE LEGAL CULTURE OF INDONESIA

DANIEL S. LEV, JUDICIAL INSTITUTIONS AND LEGAL CULTURE IN INDONESIA, in CULTURE AND POLITICS IN INDONESIA 283-87 (Claire Holt ed. 1972)

With a deep sense of relativism or, as Anderson has argued, tolerance, the Javanese are inclined to exceeding care in their personal relations, to caution, diplomacy, reserve, and respect for social status. Every effort is made to avoid personal conflict and, when it occurs, to cover it over by refined techniques of social intercourse, pending the least damaging and humiliating solution.

The style of conflict resolution which these values encourage is one that, in legal terms, pays more attention to procedure than substance. Legal rules and considerations of equity are not of course ignored. Rather they represent parameters which more or less broadly define the outside limits of justice. They are minimum requirements for maintaining the integrity of the social order. But within these limits considerable leeway exists for negotiation, and it is with the possibilities thus made available that conciliation and mediation (used interchangeably here) are concerned. What tends to be emphasized is not the application of given rules, but the elimination of a conflict which may cause social tension or disruption. Those who talk about rules as if they were absolute are likely to be considered obstructors, stubborn troublemakers, anti-social fools, or worse....

But the cultural penchant for compromise of personal conflicts remains strong and is not at all limited to villagers. A dispute in which this writer was involved illustrates how pervasive this value is at most levels of Javanese society, and how it contrasts with a legal culture that tends to be concerned with substance and "right."

In late 1960 I agreed to accompany an American visitor on a trip across Java. In Jogjakarta we registered at the city's largest hotel, where the events to be related took place. What follows is excerpted from my field notes, with a few grammatical and clarifying changes:

After registering, T and I went to our room. T went to the bathroom, where the toilet was an old-fashioned one with a wall tank and cord. When T pulled the cord the cover of the tank and the whole mechanism inside came down (though no water), nearly hit him and crashed onto the toilet bowl, knocking a huge chunk out of it. T was shaken. I told the servant about the matter, and the next morning a hotel repairman came to look over the damage.

During the afternoon, while I sat on the veranda writing and T slept, a servant came to the room and handed me a note which informed us that the hotel expected Rp. 5,000 for replacement of the toilet. I was astonished at this and without thinking everything over went directly to the hotel office and asked to see the manager.... For half an hour or more he and I argued about the bill. I told him that it was not T's fault the tank's insides had come down and that had T been hit by the falling metal, clearly the hotel would have been responsible for damages. [A hotel of this kind, classified as a "European" type enterprise, is subject to the civil code.] The manager would not accept this reasoning and said that T had not been hit by the metal and, since such a thing had never happened before, T must be responsible for the damage.... Finally I told him that we would not pay the bill, that it was best to take the matter to court, and that I would call Judge S [a friend] ... to talk the problem over.

[In the course of the next several hours the manager and I met at various times to establish our relative power positions by indicating which influential officials we knew, a game often played in this kind of conflict and one that involves a good deal of bluffing. As it happened, a new element was introduced into the affair when a friend from Djakarta stopped at the hotel and mentioned that not long ago another toilet tank had fallen from the wall in the hotel. When the manager was reminded of this, the situation changed somewhat.]

I finally called up Judge S, fully intending to take the case to court or at least to scare the manager into withdrawing his claim.... The judge came to the phone; I told him about the incident, referred to the law on the matter, and made it clear that I thought the hotel was to blame and that I was willing to take the issue to court. Judge S's reaction left me momentarily speechless. He agreed the civil code was on our side. Then he said, "Well, but of course you are willing to pay part of the expenses for replacing the toilet, aren't you? Offer the manager some money in payment of the damages, to show good will, and then come to a settlement somewhere between his demand and your offer." When I recovered my composure I said that T was convinced he was not wrong, and why should he pay anything? Judge S replied, "Yes, of course, but that is beside the point. What is important is that you show good will and settle by *damai* (peace, compromise) if at all possible. Only if the manager demands the full Rp. 5,000 and refuses the offer to *damai* should you take the case to court."

Later ... accepting Judge S's advice ... we offered the manager a thousand rupiah. He carried on a bit but finally accepted without demanding more, we had some tea and small talk together, and the issue was never raised again.

My own automatic strategy and that of Judge S were based on quite different appreciations of what the situation demanded, one of us insisting on legal vindication and the other on peace....

The greater than normal avoidance of government courts by commercial interests is due to considerations of efficiency, utility, and trust. The flight to informal underground procedures in the economy [is common]. In addition the courts themselves have often proved unable to meet demands of the private economy. Although there are exceptions, ethnic Indonesian judges tend to have little interest in commercial law. Few of the older men had an opportunity to work in commercial law in the colony. Most early Indonesian judges, moreover, came from an aristocratic class whose men have had little taste or respect for business; only recently have these values begun to change. After independence, businessmen found the courts inadequate and basically unsympathetic to or uninterested in their problems and needs. This condition grew worse during the period of Guided Democracy when anticommercial biases acquired ideological stature.

Judicial procedures have also discouraged businessmen from using courts. Civil trials are painfully time-consuming; frequently, as a result, financial disputes go to court only if one litigant seeks a delay sufficient to permit continued use of funds or an inflationary reduction of the real costs of settlement. Once pronounced, decisions in commercial cases offer little future legal guidance, partly because poorly paid and personally preoccupied judges have neither time nor inclination to write carefully reasoned conclusions, and also because public policy has been too uncertain to give the judges adequate direction. Finally, since judicial decisions do not always carry their own guarantee of execution, further administrative expense may be required under the table.

QUESTIONS

1. Does Daniel Lev imply that Civil Code rules are irrelevant in Indonesia?

2. How different is the style of Judge S in Indonesia from that of the judges in Talean courts in Oaxaca, Mexico? What seems to be their common aim? Is their approach more beneficial to society than the Western emphasis on fixed legal rights and remedies enforced by the state?

2. LITIGATION IN THAILAND

DAVID M. ENGEL, CODE AND CUSTOM IN A THAI PROVINCIAL COURT: THE INTERACTION OF FORMAL AND INFORMAL SYSTEMS OF JUSTICE 46-52 (1978)

As low as the modern Thai litigation rates are, ... they are approximately double the comparable rates of litigation for the period shortly after the founding of the modern Chiangmai court. During the year 1918, for example, ten years after the enactment of the original Law of the Courts of Justice and the Penal Code, there were only [177] criminal cases processed per [100,000] population in the "circle" of Chiangmai, and a mere [35] civil cases. The citizens of Chiangmai were initially hesitant to take their legal matters to the new courts, unlike the citizens of India and other nations, who responded immediately to the establishment of local courts as part of their newly centralized judiciary, producing an apparent "flood of litigation" at the local level.... Although the new courts served some purposes of the Thai people, there was — and still is — a tendency to avoid the entire process of formal litigation.

If we examine the four main streams of litigation in slightly more detail, we see, with regard first to criminal cases, that there are two important categories: public and private prosecutions (Table 6.15).... Public prosecutions are criminal suits brought by designated agents of the government acting in the name of the state. Private prosecutions, on the other hand, are criminal suits brought by private individuals who are vested by law with the power to sue in particular cases for alleged criminal violations. Not all private individuals have this right. The plaintiff must show that he or she is either the person injured by the alleged criminal act or a person entitled by law to proceed in the place of the injured person, either as: (1) the legal representative or custodian of a minor or incompetent person; (2) "the ascendant or descendant, the husband or wife, in respect only of criminal offenses in which the injured person is so injured that he died or is unable to act by himself"; or (3) "the manager or other representative of a juristic person" (Criminal Procedure Code, Sections 28 and 5). Table 6.15 shows that public prosecutions are far more numerous than private prosecutions. Many of the public prosecutions, however, represent the routine processing of minor misdemeanors resulting in fines of 50 or 100 *baht* (approximately $2.50 to $5). Among the ten most numerous public prosecutions, all are basically of this type. Many of the private criminal actions, on the other hand, are more serious matters, more time consuming, and more important to the parties involved.

The civil suits ... show a heavy preponderance of contract cases, many of which are brought by commercial enterprises. Second most numerous among the civil suits are cases arising from wrongful acts. Hidden among the wrongful acts, however, are a substantial number of disguised contract cases, for the Civil and Commercial Code defines "wrongful acts" to include unlawful injuries, either willful or negligent, to "the life, body, health, liberty, *property or any right* of another person" (Section 420, emphasis added). A number of cases classified as wrongful acts in fact arise from violations of contractual relationships between the litigants. Most of the remaining civil suits also involve the assertion of contract rights or property rights which give rise to the eviction of tenants or squatters, the collection of rent or damages involving real property, and actions to decide rights in and access to land and water. A final portion of the civil suits consists of uncontested petitions to the court regarding wills, the establishment of legal guardians, and other routine matters.

A different kind of overview is provided in Table 6.16, which classifies the litigation flow with reference to outcome. This form of classification reveals with some clarity three distinct functions that the Chiangmai court now per-

Table 6.15

Criminal Cases Litigated in Provincial and Magistrates' Courts of Chiangmai in 1965 and 1974, by Type

	Frequency of Cases		Aggregate [1965, 1968, 1971 & 1974]	
	1965	1974		
Subject Matter	% of Yearly Total	% of Yearly Total	Number	% of Total
A. Public Criminal Prosecutions				
1. Theft	17.8	10.1	1,810	13.8
2. Possession of firearms	10.6	13.8	1,626	12.4
3. Gambling	10.4	14.8	1,494	11.4
4. Prostitution	8.8	2.7	924	7.1
5. Bodily harm	5.9	6.3	909	7.0
6. Violations involving slaughter and distribution of livestock	7.3	4.1	858	6.6
7. Marijuana, opium, narcotics violations	0.1	14.7	822	6.3
8. Forestry violations	3.9	8.1	766	5.9
9. Illegal alcoholic beverages	8.9	0.2	558	4.3
10. Violations concerning workshops	11.9	0.2	422	3.2
11. Homicide	2.5	2.0	386	3.0
12. Traffic violations	0.5	2.6	299	2.3
13. Receiving stolen property	0.0	2.4	260	2.0
14. Sexual offenses	1.2	1.6	256	2.0
15. Misappropriation of property	2.4	1.4	245	1.9
16. Trespass	0.7	1.2	126	1.0
17. Robbery	0.8	0.9	113	0.9
18. Gang robbery	0.9	0.5	108	0.8
19. Offenses against officials	0.5	1.5	101	0.8
20. Violations involving protected lands	0.3	1.6	96	0.7
21. Others	4.7	9.3	898	6.9
Total	[n=3,336]	[n=3,714]	13,077	100.3
B. Private Criminal Prosecutions				
1. Violations involving checks	34.0	72.4	330	56.3
2. Offenses relating to justice	16.0	5.3	59	10.1
3. Cheating and fraud	6.6	4.6	32	5.5
4. Defamation	5.7	4.6	24	4.1
5. Misappropriation of property	5.7	2.0	20	3.4
6. Homicide	5.7	0.7	20	3.4
7. Trespass	6.6	0.7	19	3.2
8. Bodily harm	2.8	0.0	13	2.2
9. Theft	0.9	1.3	8	1.4
10. Malfeasance in public office	2.8	2.0	7	1.2
11. Others	13.2	6.6	54	9.2
Total	[n=106]	[n=152]	586	100.0

Table 6.16

Civil and Criminal Cases in Chiangmai Trial Courts, by Type of Result

	MODE I	MODE II		MODE III
		Lawsuits Alleging Private Wrongs		
	State Prosecutions for Criminal Offenses (N = 643) %	Private Criminal Prosecutions (N = 586) %	Civil Suits (N = 114) %	Enforcement of Contracts & Property Rights (N = 684) %
Completely favorable to plaintiff*	96.6	3.1	20.2	64.5
Completely favorable to defendant	2.3	11.3	1.8	2.3
Compromise verdict or settlement in court ...			50.0	11.1
Suit withdrawn	0.6	84.6	21.1	17.4
Outcomes unknown	0.5	1.0	7.0	4.7

Source: Court Registers for Provincial and Magistrates' Courts, Chiangmai Province, for 1965, 1968, 1971, and 1974.

*In criminal suits, a finding of guilt as charged; in civil suits, plaintiff wins full amount in controversy.

forms. All three functions, or "modes of justice," derive from the historical and social setting of the court.... The first "mode of justice" is the suppression of crime, a direct descendant of the traditional responsibility of the provincial ruler (who was also the highest judge) to use force and punishment to maintain order in the society.

Outcomes in these cases are overwhelmingly favorable to the state. The conviction rate in public criminal prosecutions is 96.6 percent. In the vast majority of these cases, the defendants formally confess guilt to the charges brought against them, knowing that they may thereby reduce their sentences by half because of their "repentance of wrongdoing and attempt to minimize the consequences thereof" (Penal Code, Section 78). Only 2.3 percent of the criminal defendants in public prosecutions succeed in establishing their innocence.

The second mode of justice involves the litigation of private wrongs. I include in this category all private criminal prosecutions and those civil suits grouped under "wrongful acts" and marital disputes.[a] The second mode of justice is characterized by negotiation rather than adjudication and punishment. Traditionally, private wrongs in Thai society were often mediated by *phuyai*, "big persons," who could exercise authority over the disputants to help them resolve their differences. In modern Thailand, ... mediation is still preferred by most people over litigation. When these disputes do come to

[a] Marital disputes are included with the other private wrongs because such lawsuits usually allege some form of wrongdoing or injury by one of the partners, comparable to the legal wrongs alleged in private criminal suits and civil "wrongful acts."

court, therefore, the court itself is likely to provide a forum where mediation takes place. Rather than a clear-cut decision on the merits, designating one side the winner and the other side the loser, the outcome is more likely to be some form of compromise. This pattern is clearly reflected in Table 6.16. In the private criminal cases, out-of-court compromises are reached between the parties in 84.6 percent of the cases. The defendant usually pays plaintiff a stipulated amount, and plaintiff then withdraws the prosecution. In the civil cases involving private wrongs, the result may be either an out-of-court compromise followed by plaintiff's withdrawal of the suit (21.1 percent) or, more typically, a compromise agreement formally announced in the court and recorded by the judge as a legally enforceable agreement for future performance (50.0 percent).

The third mode of justice involves the enforcement of contracts and property rights. The outcomes of these cases indicate a great judicial deference to written forms and to officially certified documents. The court tends to enforce such obligations strictly, ensuring that commercial transactions follow the letter of the contract and that official registration forms take priority over informal customary practices. Acting in this way, the court fulfills its original mandate to provide certainty for entrepreneurs and government officials in provincial Thailand. Defendants win only 2.3 percent of these cases; 64.5 percent result in verdicts wholly favorable to plaintiffs, while another 17.4 percent are withdrawn. Litigation in this third mode of justice produces results strongly favorable to persons who hold the relevant legal documents, as opposed to persons whose claims are based upon other less legalistic expectations and behavior. The outcomes of such cases reveal the power that the provincial courts have vested in those who understand and pattern their actions according to the norms of the Civil and Commercial Code and the administrative procedures of the central government.

QUESTION

Engel seems to view the withdrawal of 84.6 percent of private criminal actions as an indication of a cultural preference for mediation and compromise. Do you agree? Are there other, equally plausible explanations?

3. JAPANESE ATTITUDES TOWARD LITIGATION

JOHN O. HALEY, THE MYTH OF THE RELUCTANT LITIGANT, 4 Journal of Japanese Studies 359-70, 378-80 (1978)

The belief that the Japanese are an exceptionally nonlitigious people is remarkably pervasive. Commentators, both within and without Japan, are almost unanimous in attributing to the Japanese an unusual and deeply rooted cultural preference for informal, mediated settlement of private disputes and a corollary aversion to the formal mechanisms of judicial adjudication. As a result, they say, Japanese do not take advantage of the available mechanisms for formal dispute resolution. These attitudes, they commonly add, are bolstered by a peculiar Japanese penchant for compromise, distrust of clearcut "all or none" solutions and distaste for both public quarrels and their public resolution. As explained by Kawashima Takeyoshi, one of Japan's leading legal sociologists and most articulate exponents of this belief, the endurance of a traditional concern for preserving cooperative personal relationships makes unwanted any definitive delineation of rights and duties through litigation. Bringing a lawsuit has meant issuing a "public challenge and provoking a quarrel."

The importance of this notion is difficult to exaggerate. Most critical, upon it rests the conventional evaluation of the role of the judiciary within Japan's political and social order. The standard introductory works in English on Japanese government, for instance, uniformly dismiss the courts as politically insignificant on the basis of this perceived unwillingness of the Japanese to litigate. Without cases the courts cannot act. Unlike other arms of the state, the courts do not apply or enforce laws on their own initiative. They must wait passively for controversies to be brought before them for decision....

The dilemma posed by the institutional ideal of an active judiciary in a nonlitigious society is surmounted at least in part by those, such as Kawashima, who view Japanese aversion to litigation as a gradually fading, "traditional" response. Indeed, the literature is replete with observations on rising litigation rates in postwar Japan, which some take as a convenient index to measure Japan's progress toward a "modern" society....

The threshold problem is to define "litigiousness" in some meaningful fashion. There is little question that the Japanese generally use their courts less frequently than do Americans (although the contrast may not actually be as great as some have suggested)....

This relative lack of litigation is not, however, a uniquely Japanese phenomenon. In Austin Sarat's and Joel B. Grossman's study of litigation rates in a selection of ten countries, ... resort to court in civil cases in Japan appears to be modestly frequent.

The orthodox view of Japanese "litigiousness," however, relates to a reluctance to litigate, not simply the amount of litigation. Even assuming such a reluctance to exist, to be meaningful in terms of evaluating the role of the judiciary it must involve more than simply a desire to avoid lawsuits. While we might conceive of an individual or community as a whole that delights in engaging the complex litany of trial procedures or activating the public intervention of a magistrate, if such exist, they are rare. For most persons a lawsuit is a last resort. Litigation, is, after all, almost always a costly and cumbersome process for resolving disputes, and ordinarily an aggrieved party to a dispute will attempt to reach informal private settlement. The overwhelming majority of disputes in most societies are in fact resolved informally....

The paradigm process of dispute resolution for most societies, including Japan, is two or three-tiered. A dispute will typically move through several steps before reaching the courts — private negotiation between the immediate parties, perhaps mediation with the aid of a third party — but ultimately to the litigated solution only where there has been a failure to reach a settlement at each preceding stage. (These steps can be, and most often are, conducted concurrently with negotiation, mediation, and possibly both, taking place throughout trial proceedings, in some instances even after a judgment but before all appeals have been exhausted.)

The critical issue is whether the parties will settle only when neither believes he has more to gain by judicial intervention. If this is the case, a decision to settle necessarily involves an assessment of the outcome of the potential lawsuit, and the private settlement should reflect that outcome discounted by the costs (including time) and uncertainties of litigation. In this process, the judicial model operates in a manner similar to economic markets. And if the paradigm functions effectively, the legal norms that courts apply in these isolated cases become the standards used, albeit discounted, in resolving similar subsequent disputes.

Consequently, whether the Japanese are nonlitigious is in itself significant for our purposes here only if by "nonlitigious" we mean that Japanese involved in a dispute tend to reach negotiated or mediated settlements that do not reflect the litigated outcomes and one of the parties accepts a less favorable result because of an aversion to litigation in general. The frequency of litigation alone is not meaningful since the availability and successful utilization of alternative mechanisms for settlement may reduce litigation without impairing the efficacy of judicially-imposed norms. Also, a number of institutional factors can preclude litigation as a realistic option and thereby diminish substantially the influence of the courts. Indeed, resort to court would be rare to the extent that access is assured, the costs are minimal, judicial relief is effective, and the outcome is certain.

Litigation in particular types of disputes — for example, suits by children against their parents — should be distinguished. Inasmuch as in most instances litigation commonly involves a rupturing of relations as a result of public acknowledgement of the parties' inability to reach an amicable settlement between themselves in private, litigation is less likely where the parties wish to continue their relationship or where rupturing the relationship offends widely held social norms. Also, in many of these areas as a matter of public policy the courts may be given very limited jurisdiction to intervene (e.g., in disputes between husbands and wives). While we might want to isolate and investigate such specific areas where the judicial model may not be as effective, none involves the question of a general and peculiarly Japanese desire to avoid available mechanisms for formal resolution of disputes....

Is there, then, any evidence of an unusual Japanese aversion toward lawsuits that leads a party to accept a settlement less beneficial than one he anticipates he would gain by suing? The answer, I believe, is negative. What little evidence there is suggests the opposite — that most Japanese are willing to go to court in such circumstances....

The few direct surveys of Japanese attitudes that have been made provide further support for rejecting the orthodox view. For example, in the survey by Sasaki Yoshio cited by both Dan F. Henderson and Kawashima, when asked, "What would you do if a civil dispute arose and despite discussions with the opposite party you could not settle it?" 64% of the 2,098 respondents replied that they would willingly go to court.

Even more persuasive, however, is the pattern of litigation in Japan from 1890 to the present.... [L]itigation has been *less* frequent in absolute numbers in the postwar years than the period from 1890 to the outbreak of the Sino-Japanese War in 1937. Relative to population, the contrast is even more startling. In 1934, for example, 302 new civil cases involving formal trial proceedings were initiated in courts of first instance per 100,000 persons, while in 1974 there were 135 such cases per 100,000 persons — 2.2 times as many per capita in 1934 than there were in 1974.

By and large this pattern holds true for all categories of cases. While there is a slight variation in the frequencies of certain types of suits in some years, overall, over longer periods, there is a parallel rise or fall in the rate of litigation in each category. Nor do statistics reveal any aberration resulting from the prevalence of a particular type of suit during the prewar period, such as rural tenancy cases.

There was a greater frequency of litigation in absolute numbers in the prewar years in almost every category. (In the postwar period the increase in use of automobiles has led to a significant increase in personal injury actions.)... Again, in absolute numbers in 1926, several years prior to the prewar peak in 1934, there was far more litigation than in 1969. Since Japan's population increased by 40% during the interval, on a per capita basis there was only a slight increase in divorce actions and suits relating to land in 1969 and, if we discount traffic accidents as peculiar to the postwar environment, no significant increase in damage actions....

It is apparent that these patterns are inconsistent with conventional ideas about the reluctance of Japanese to litigate; moreover, they contradict the widely held belief that there has been a greater willingness to sue in the postwar period. In short, most of what is said or written about Japanese attitudes toward the legal process is a myth.

If the Japanese are not particularly averse to litigation, how then can we explain why they appear to use their courts far less frequently than do Americans and perhaps others? Why has litigation decreased since the war (and continues to do so)? Also, what accounts for the pervasive acceptance by the Japanese themselves that they are unusually "nonlitigious"? And how do such explanations relate to the efficacy of the judicial model in Japan? To answer these questions, we should first reconsider the paradigm process of dispute resolution.

Typically, the parties to a dispute will move through stages — from direct negotiation, to third party mediation and finally to litigation — as a result of failure in the preceding stage to agree to an acceptable resolution. In this process, a relative lack of litigation can be explained by several factors.

One is the effectiveness of third party intervention. The availability of suitable third parties who are willing and able to perform this role reduces the need to invoke formal judicial intervention. At the outset, mediation requires the presence of persons who, because of position or personal relationships, command respect and are able to exercise some measure of authority. In other words, to be effective, the mediator must be someone who can command the parties' trust and their obedience to the settlement.

One would thus anticipate that suitable third parties are more readily available in a stable, closely-integrated and hierarchical society like Japan, than in a more geographically mobile, less cohesive society like the United States in which individual autonomy and social equality are emphasized. Societal expectations and habits are equally relevant. The role of the mediator becomes increasingly legitimate for both the mediator and the parties to disputes where there is repeated reliance on third parties to settle disputes. A contrast in police attitudes in Japan and the United States pointed out by David H. Bayley is especially interesting in this respect. Japanese commonly rely on the police for assistance in settling disputes. But despite similar popular demand in the United States, "what is different," says Bayley, "is that American police organizations have not adapted willingly to perform this function." Another Japanese example is the mediating service some companies provide for employees involved in traffic accidents. In short, the Japanese may be more successful in avoiding litigation because of social organization and values more conducive to informal dispute resolution through mediation.

The tendency of the Japanese to mediate does not necessarily impair the effectiveness of the judiciary, however. As we have seen, the judicial model does not depend on the actual frequency of litigation, but rather the influence of the perceived outcome of the litigation on the mediated settlement.

Resort to court is, however, reduced by another set of factors that do inhibit or enhance the utility of the judicial model as a vehicle for social control and development.

First, for courts to have an impact through decisions in individual cases beyond those persons immediately affected in those cases, information about the courts and these decisions must be disseminated in order that parties to similar disputes are sufficiently aware of the legal norm for it to influence informal resolution of their disputes. This does not mean the judicial model cannot work unless people are fully aware of what the courts will do. But people must be generally cognizant that the courts do provide an available option, and they must have the means to become informed about what the probable outcome will be in the specific case. Thus in societies where illiteracy rates are high or little is communicated about the courts, the judicial model will be less successful. A lack of law trained persons and the absence of published reports of court decisions, for example, are serious barriers to the effectiveness of the judiciary.

There must also be meaningful access to the courts. Access can be denied directly by jurisdictional barriers that prevent the courts from adjudicating certain types of disputes altogether. Bondposting requirements that may place an intolerable burden on the parties seeking relief illustrate another form of conscious policy designed to prevent resort to courts. Limited institutional capacity also inhibits access. There must be a sufficient number of courts, of judges and lawyers, to insure that the costs and delays of litigation do not preclude lawsuits as a realistic option.

A third factor is the capacity of the courts to provide adequate relief. Courts must have available a range of remedial measures and forms of relief to suit the variety of controversies that arise. An award of monetary damages or declarations of the rights and duties of the parties will not always help the aggrieved party. In addition, especially in cases where the legal norm and thus the outcome is reasonably certain, filing suit may evidence a recalcitrant party against whom coercive measures have become necessary. Indeed, many of the cases courts handle each day do not involve any real controversy of fact or law, but simply a last resort to force the other party to perform an acknowledged legal duty. For relief to be adequate the courts must be able to provide a remedy that fits the case and have the capacity to enforce its judgments.

HIDEO TANAKA, THE ROLE OF LAW IN JAPANESE SOCIETY, COMPARISONS WITH THE WEST, 19 University of British Columbia Law Review 375-76 (1985)

In recent years interest in Japanese society and culture has markedly increased among Western people, along with the rapid development of political and economic relationships. People perceive Japan in many different ways. At one end there are those who tend to emphasize the traditional elements of Japanese culture. Some believe, or try to believe, that the Japanese still live a quiet and elegant life, as described in the *Tale of Genji*, a novel written by a female courtier in the eleventh century. Other Westerners have a slightly more modern view of Japan based upon Puccini's Madame Butterfly!

At the other end of the spectrum, there are those who insist that the Japanese are in no sense different from Westerners. They believe that people who produce a large number of automobiles should behave in the same manner as Americans. Some might add reservations to such a statement, saying that the Japanese have adopted the worst aspects of Western civilization while throwing away good old Japanese traditions.

There is a similar conflict of views on the role of law in Japanese society.... On this topic Japanese scholars join foreign observers to form various schools of thought. One of these schools says that Japanese people, by nature, do not like law and are reluctant to bring up their disputes to courts for resolution through a formal process. For instance, Professor René David, a world-famous French scholar of comparative law, wrote as follows:

> [T]he question is still very much open whether behind the facade of Westernization Japan really has undergone any kind of significant transformation and whether it has accepted the idea of justice and law such as is understood in the West.

Another school insists that such a view is a sheer myth. The reason why there are relatively few lawsuits in Japan, they argue, is to be found in a cold businessmanlike cost-benefit analysis by Japanese people which leads to a rejection of the litigation option.

I believe that neither of these schools of thought has given a satisfactory answer to the problem. As I see it, the right answer is to be found somewhere between these extremes. I think Japan has been, and still is, in a transitory stage from the period when a traditional concept of law prevailed, to a society where basic standards of conduct are essentially similar to those in Western nations. Therefore, if you over-emphasize traditional elements, you will be asked to explain a large number of phenomena which seem to contradict your statements. The same will be true if you say there is nothing peculiar about the Japanese attitude toward law.

SETSUO MIYAZAWA, TAKING KAWASHIMA SERIOUSLY: A REVIEW OF JAPANESE RESEARCH ON JAPANESE LEGAL CONSCIOUSNESS AND DISPUTING BEHAVIOR, 21 Law & Society Review 219, 231-35 (1987)

The first attempt to reconstruct individual dispute processes retrospectively did not occur in Japan until 1968, when [Professor Kahei] Rokumoto [of Tokyo University] conducted his dissertation research.

Rokumoto wanted to discover the factors that determined the degree of the legalization of social ordering in Japan. He defined legalization as the process through which society comes to rely increasingly on the formal legal system to maintain order. He first sent a card asking a representative sample of 2,013 residents of the Bunkyo ward of Tokyo if they had been involved in automobile accidents or housing disputes. He then interviewed 103 of the 226 respondents who answered affirmatively. Rokumoto reported data on forty-five accident cases and forty housing cases. Only three of the accident cases reached a court, while eleven of the housing cases went to litigation and another eleven went to mediation. Attorneys were used in only three accident cases but in thirty housing cases. Seemingly against the conventional view of the role of local officials in Japan, local politicians and police did not play any significant role in these cases. Instead, particularly in accident cases, nonattorneys who were nevertheless specialists in automobile accidents, such as insurance agents and accident managers of taxi companies, figured conspicuously as agents for parties, thus raising the possibility that these specialists sometimes engaged in the arbitrary manipulation of legal rules, exploitation of ignorant opponents, or deceit. The outcomes of these cases indicated that the parties who retained attorneys or specialists could expect favorable results.

Rokumoto's main argument is that the chance to obtain the assistance of attorneys and specialists and hence to mobilize the formal legal system to one's advantage is unevenly distributed in society. The people with the greatest advantage are those who are by occupation repeat users of legal specialists, most notably professional landlords .... Those with the second greatest advantage belong to natural networks that include legal specialists. For those outside these groups, it is difficult to obtain legal counsel in Japan. Even when one is able to retain legal representation, parties without a previous relationship with the specialists, however indirect, will often find it hard to receive full personal service.

As for legal consciousness, even mediation is a deliberate attempt to enforce one's legally protected interests. In some cases, mediation is used to block the use of litigation by the other party, whose legal basis may be much stronger. In contemporary Japan, at least in urban areas, parties use both mediation and litigation to pursue their own interests. These results apparently differ from a commonsensical version of the Kawashima thesis.

However, Rokumoto does not regard such interest-mindedness as the truly modern legal consciousness. Instead, he implies that this thinking lacks internalization of universalistic standards, acceptance of the reciprocity of right-duty relationships, and reliance on the court as an objective adjudicator. Indeed, the mobilization of law does not necessarily reflect legal consciousness, even in the sense of interest-mindedness. After all, if one happened to be in one of those networks mentioned above, the assistance of legal specialists would naturally be provided. In light of this argument, it seems logical that Rokumoto tries to resurrect Kawashima's conception of legal consciousness through his explication.[a]

J. MARK RAMSEYER & MINORU NAKAZATO, THE RATIONAL LITIGANT: SETTLEMENT AMOUNTS AND VERDICT RATES IN JAPAN, 18 Journal of Legal Studies 266-72, 285-90 (1989)

Most observers of Japanese disputes use two basic arguments to explain what they see. First, they claim that litigation threatens a fundamental Japanese concern for consensus and harmony. Japanese define themselves, they explain, by reference to the network of particularistic relationships within which they live and work. Accordingly, Japanese cultural norms place a premium on maintaining peace within those relations. By making disagreements public and compromise difficult, litigation threatens this social order. Out of deference to such considerations, Japanese potential plaintiffs avoid the courts. Second, these observers argue that law does not structure Japanese social relations. The universalistic principles embodied in modern law contradict the more particularistic and status-based principles of Japanese culture. Because modern law clashes with their cultural structures, Japanese ignore it. Instead, they live their lives according to indigenous communal values....

Over ten years ago, however, several revisionist scholars began to suggest that various institutional features of the Japanese legal system (primarily its alleged costs, ineffectiveness, and delays) explain the low Japanese litigation rates within standard rational choice models. If Japanese plaintiffs avoid litigation, they argue, they avoid it because it does not pay. Although these scholars offer a new explanation for Japanese litigation rates, many leave unchallenged the traditional account of the role that law plays in Japan. Because people cannot realistically invoke the courts to solve their disputes (so the revisionists argue), the law cannot be structuring the way they live their lives. Some revisionist scholars even characterize the legal system as a failure. After all, if the courts are slow, powerless, and expensive, then the system must be denying victims effective relief. After interviewing several such scholars, a *New York Times* reporter recently adopted what has almost become a new academic orthodoxy: the Japanese legal system is "bankrupt."...

There is a third alternative. Japanese disputants could also be settling such a high percentage of their disputes because they find it relatively easy to agree on how courts would adjudicate their disputes. That, in turn, would suggest that Japanese are settling their disputes in light of their expected

---

[a] Kawashima's celebrated book on the legal consciousness of the Japanese describes the Japanese reluctance to enforce rights and duties legitimately recognized by law; after describing the Japanese consciousness of law and rights in detail, he goes on to attribute this reluctance to the backwardness of the people and the society. Takeyoshi Kawashima, Nihonjin no Hoh Ishiki [The Legal Consciousness of the Japanese] (1967). Chapter 4 of Kawashima's book, which generally exemplifies his argument, has been translated into English. *See* Takeyoshi Kawashima, *The Legal Consciousness of Contract in Japan*, 7 Law in Japan: An Annual 1 (C. Stevens trans. 1974).

litigated outcomes. If so, then the traditional and revisionist theories are both wrong: wealth-maximizing models apply, plaintiffs recover damages, and law structures Japanese behavior.

To see why this third alternative might explain Japanese litigation rates, recall that high levels of agreement on expected outcomes will generate high settlement and low litigation rates. In Japan, as in other societies, litigation costs (C_{li}, i∈ (plaintiff, defendant)) generally exceed settlement costs (C_{si}). As a result, most rational parties try to settle out of court. Whether they are able to do so depends in part on how nearly their estimates of the litigated outcome ($E_i(V)$) converge. If their estimates are close, they usually settle to their mutual advantage. Thus, plaintiffs accept any amount that earns them at least their expected net gain from litigating the dispute (the plaintiff's reservation price $R_p = E_p(V) - C_{lp} + C_{sp}$; the expected recovery less the litigation costs saved but plus the settlement costs incurred). In turn, defendants pay any amount that costs less than their expected total burden from litigating it (the defendant's reservation price $R_d = E_d(V) + C_{ld} - C_{sd}$; the expected payout plus the litigation costs saved but less the settlement costs incurred). For example, a plaintiff who estimates recovery at 100, litigation costs at 25, and settlement costs of 5, will settle for any sum greater than 80. A defendant who estimates recovery at 90, litigation costs at 25, and settlement costs at 5, will settle for any sum under 110. At these numbers, the parties will have a settlement range of 80-110. If this defendant estimates the likely outcome of litigation at 50, however, then he or she will offer only 70. Because the plaintiff demands 80, litigation may ensue. The more nearly the parties' estimates of the outcome of litigation converge, in short, the greater the likelihood of settlement. More generally, if (i) the total net costs that the parties expect to save through settlement exceed (ii) the difference between the plaintiff's (greater) and defendant's (lower) estimates of the outcome of suit, then settlement is possible. If the costs they expect to save are less than the difference in their estimates, it is not. The settlement condition is thus $E_p(V) - E_d(V) < (C_{lp} + C_{ld}) - (C_{sp} + C_{sd})$.

At stake, therefore, is the ability of Japanese parties to agree on the litigated verdict. Reasons why they might agree more readily than American disputants are easy to find. First, the absence of juries decreases the uncertainty introduced by amateur fact finders. Attorneys can, instead, try their cases before professional judges who take pride in uniformity over time and whose past decisions lawyers can often discover. Second, the use of discontinuous trial sessions spaced over a long period gives Japanese judges a better chance to explain their views to the parties before the trial ends. Many judges even consider it their duty to offer such explanations. Once a judge has revealed his or her plans, few parties will have any reason to finish the trial. Third, as part of a program to standardize their decisions, Japanese judges use detailed, clear, and public formulae to calculate comparative negligence percentages and the victim's damages — whether for death, disability, or simple injury. Although judges need not follow the formulae, most apparently do. Attorneys can thus rely on the formulae when they negotiate settlements. Given the array of how-to books (including how-to comic books) on accident law in most Japanese bookstores, even lay people can use them. Last, Japan maintains only one national (as opposed to over fifty state and federal) body of law. Gone, as a result, are both the elaborate American conflicts-of-law questions and the confusion introduced by courts in one state interpreting the law of another.

Each of these aspects increases the predictability of the Japanese judicial system. In a world of rational and mathematically sophisticated parties, of course, unpredictability should not raise litigation rates. After all, if rational parties have the same information, they should settle by reference to the same expected mean, no matter how great the variance. In fact, however, information is rarely symmetrical, and seldom does either party possess enough calculating prowess to process correctly all the relevant information. In a world of asymmetric information and "bounded rationality," parties are far more likely to make similar estimates of the litigated outcome under the relatively clear and unified Japanese system than under the plastic and fragmented American one....

For disputes over traffic accidents, however, data close to the information required are available. Government statistics cover almost all serious automobile accidents. They disclose both the number of deaths from such accidents and the number and amounts of the claims that insurers pay. Other records detail the size of court judgments in litigated cases. As a result, one can accurately compare (i) the number of deaths from accidents with the number of wrongful death claims paid and (ii) the average amounts insurers pay in settlement with the amounts courts award in litigation.

True, one cannot generalize from traffic accident disputes to all others or from negotiations with insurance companies to those with neighbors or business partners. Liability insurers are generally more sophisticated than most disputants and do not deal with any particular claimants (the decedent's heirs) on a repeated basis. Yet these disputes may be less idiosyncratic than they initially seem. First, precisely because they are so extraordinarily common, they constitute as "typical" a kind of dispute as might be found. Second, they involve relatively simple legal issues. Third, because Japanese consumers insure against a wide variety of contingencies, negotiations with insurers occur in many different kinds of disputes. Finally, although a claimant may negotiate with the insurer, he or she can direct the negotiations only by threatening to sue the tort-feasor driver. The insurance dispute thus not only originates in a private dispute, it also remains private in at least this critical respect....

At least in fatal traffic accidents, models of actors who rationally use legal rules closely predict the way Japanese behave. In almost all such cases, the families of the victims assert their legal rights. When they settle their claims, they obtain average amounts that closely track the amounts for which the defendant's insurer would be liable in court. The traditionalists' assertions about the Japanese reluctance to press claims or about the irrelevance of law in Japanese society simply do not hold.

The evidence from traffic accidents also contradicts those revisionists who characterize the Japanese judicial system as one that does not work. The accident evidence suggests, quite to the contrary, that the system enforces legal rules amazingly well. In serious traffic accidents, everyone gets his or her just desserts: defendants pay and plaintiffs recover amounts close to the defendants' legal liability. Disputants seem to settle their quarrels rather than litigate them because legal rules are clear and predictable — because judges are doing their job well. In the process, almost everyone gains: plaintiffs and defendants save their litigation costs and taxpayers save their subsidy to the legal system. Litigation is scarce in Japan not because the system is bankrupt. It is scarce because the system works.

Through culture, people make sense of what they experience; through culture, they decide what it is that they most value. As a result, one cannot properly understand the empirical world without a sense of culture. But one also cannot understand the empirical world without a sense of the institutional means by which societies frame the financial incentives each person faces. The current emphasis on culture in comparative studies of Japanese law deflects attention from these mundane incentive structures. Yet the mundane matters critically.

NOTES AND QUESTIONS

1. Assess the descriptions of Indonesian and Thai attitudes toward litigation and the judicial enforcement of legal rights in light of the various views expressed with respect to Japan. Can arguments similar to those made by Haley or Ramseyer and Nakazato also be applied to Indonesia and Thailand? Review the statistics presented in the Note on the Comparison of Civil Litigation Rates Among Nations (*supra* Section A.5 of this chapter).

2. Similar observations regarding a lack of "legal consciousness" and the reluctance to sue are frequently made for Taiwan and South Korea. As in the case of Japan, concern for social harmony and compromise as a means of ending interpersonal conflict derived from Confucianist values is usually attributed as the cause. Given the apparent similarities with Indonesia and Thailand, neither of which is within the Confucianist tradition, what alternative explanations seem persuasive?

3. To what extent can all of the various views on "legal" or "rights" consciousness in East Asia be reconciled? Is the dichotomy between "cultural" and "institutional" factors analytically helpful or persuasive?

4. In both Taiwan and South Korea the criminal process is frequently used for the enforcement of contracts and other claims that would, from a Western perspective, seem to be more appropriately enforced in civil actions. American software manufacturers, for example, commonly resort to the criminal process in both countries as the most effective means for enforcing their copyrights. To what extent is such reliance on the criminal process explained by "cultural" or "institutional" factors? Is a similar pattern evident in the availability and use of private criminal actions in Thailand? Also, in Taiwan and South Korea a large number of criminal prosecutions include fraud for promissory notes and bad checks. In Japan, however, an essentially extralegal "consensual" mechanism for enforcement is used. As described by Ramseyer:

> The process works as follows. Should a customer default on two promissory notes within six months, Japanese banks automatically suspend all checking and discounting relations with that firm for two years. The rule

> is quick, hard, and fatal. After the fact, of course, a bank might find it profitable to relax the rules against a troubled firm. Although announcing a permissive strategy ex ante would not be advantageous, in other words, the bank still could find that relaxing the rules ex post pays. As a result, the benefit the bank could earn by saving troubled clients could often remove the credibility of its initial threat to suspend such firms. To eliminate this problem, Japanese banks enforce the suspension rule among themselves through their joint clearinghouse. By committing in advance to a third-party enforcement device, the banks protect the system against those of their peers that would otherwise cooperate with their troubled clients. In the process, they make credible their threat to suspend unreliable firms.

J. Mark Ramseyer, *Legal Rules in Repeated Deals: Banking in the Shadow of Defection in Japan,* 20 J. Legal Stud. 110-11 (1991).

Can this be construed as a feature of Japanese legal culture? Consider the following comment:

> Japanese banks have in effect substituted a purely contractual mechanism for enforcement for a legal one.... The clearing house rule itself is another "private" sanction. Any bank caught cheating by continuing to do business with a defaulting customer is itself subject to suspension.
>
> Such sanctions only work — that is to say, the community can exercise coercive power — only when each member has something to gain by belonging or to lose by withdrawal. Dependency on the group — in the case of banks and promissory notes, dependency on the clearing house — and the willingness of the group to exclude or expel are required. Weak law enforcement and legal controls limit alternative means of protection and thereby foster such dependence. In turn, the strength of the community as defined by both the degree of dependency of its constituents and its solidarity in defending community over individual interest make possible its alternative to state-directed legal controls.

John O. Haley, Authority Without Power: Law and the Japanese Paradox 182-83 (1991).

5. For further reading on legal culture in East Asia, see David M. Engel, Law and Kingship in Thailand During the Reign of King Chulalongkorn (1975); Hahm Pyong-Choon, Korean Jurisprudence, Politics and Culture (1986); *Id.,* The Korean Legal Tradition and Law (1967); M.B. Hooker, *Adat* Law in Indonesia (1978); Daniel S. Lev, Islamic Courts in Indonesia (1972); Frank K. Upham, Law and Social Change in Postwar Japan (1987); Dae-Kyu Yoon, Law and Political Authority in South Korea (1990).

10/18/05

1.) Did traditional "judges" head the Supreme Court of Cassation? If so wasn't there any concern that the judicial branch was acting on behalf of the legislature, which was in direct conflict with the aim of limiting French judicial power?

2.) On page 709 the book states that lower judges were not "in theory, required—or even allowed—to follow the higher court's decision in the French cassation system." I understand that the Supreme Court of Cassation is not a source of law, but what if there was overlap between the law and the Supreme Court of Cassation's use of that law in their decision—was the lower court "allowed"

I noticed that the German system uses peer evaluation reports for trial courts. How affective are these reports? Are they used by any other judges country to establish promotions or for any other reasons?

3.) Article 783 of the Civil Code of 1865 limited the civil liabilities of judges a great deal, namely malice, fraud, extortion & denial of justice. The text states that the scheme favored "internal responsibility" over "external liability." What did "internal responsibility" refer to? I'm sure there were many possible ways that a judge could commit misconduct that were not as extreme as those listed above—how were judges disciplined for those infractions.

Chapter 7
JUDICIAL REVIEW

This chapter is in some respects a continuation of Chapter 6 on the structure of legal systems. Here we examine in detail the third branch of government — the judiciary — and especially its role in maintaining the rule of law.

NOTE ON THE DIVISION OF JURISDICTION

It is analytically useful to think of the problems we in the United States usually subsume under the heading of "judicial review" in three categories: control of the legality of judicial action, of administrative action, and of legislative action. This way of looking at things corresponds both to the historical development of European civil law systems and to the common terminology of civil lawyers. In France and Italy the legality of judicial action is the primary concern of their respective supreme courts of cassation; in Germany it is the *Bundesgerichtshof*. The legality of administrative action is a major concern of the councils of state in France and Italy and of the administrative courts in Germany. The legality of legislative action is the primary concern of constitutional courts in Germany, Italy, and Spain and of the Constitutional Council in France. This "division of jurisdiction," a prominent feature of the civil law, is an expression of the distrust of judges.

Basically, the position was that judges should have no power to make law; that kind of power was reserved to the representative legislature. Making law in the guise of interpretation was as much to be feared as more direct forms of lawmaking. Thus in France the Law of the Constituent Assembly of August 16-24, 1790, reorganizing the judicial system, provided in article 12 that judges "shall have recourse to the legislative body whenever it appears desirable to interpret a law." Article 13 of the same law addressed a related problem — the troublesome practices of the *parlements* in interfering with the administration of the laws — providing: "The judicial function is distinct and shall always be separate from the administrative function. Judges shall not ... interfere in any way in the actions of administrative agencies or exercise jurisdiction over administrators."

The scheme thus contemplated that acts of the legislature and of the public administration would be immune from judicial control or interference. The law would be judge-proof. When statutes required interpretation, the judge should refer the question to the legislature — the so-called *référé législatif*. But since the number of such questions and the time it would take to deal with them were surprisingly large, a special body standing between the courts and the legislature, called the Tribunal (not "court") of Cassation, was given the power to act on behalf of the legislature. The gradual transformation of the *Tribunal* of Cassation into the *Supreme Court* of Cassation, standing at the head of the system of ordinary courts, is a matter of subsequent history. In the process the *référé législatif* was transformed into the power of the Court of Cassation to quash (*casser*) incorrect interpretations and applications of the law. Thus, the Court of Cassation became the institution charged with controlling the legality of judicial action. Observe, however, that it did not decide the case itself; it merely determined whether or not the interpretation and application of the law were correct. If they were correct, then the decision of the lower court stood; if not, then that decision was quashed and the case sent back to a different lower court for redecision. That is still the position in France. The Supreme Court of Cassation decides, stating its reasons, whether the law was or was not correctly interpreted and applied, but the case itself is decided by a lower court. If the court to which a case is returned incorrectly interprets or applies the law again, that decision is quashed. Since, in theory, the lower court is not bound by the reasoning of the Court of Cassation, this process could go on indefinitely. For practical reasons, however, the court to which the case is remanded after the second recourse in cassation is now required to employ the solution contemplated by the Supreme Court's reasoning.

Both the *référé législatif* and the Tribunal of Cassation were drawn from institutions existing in pre-Revolutionary France, where they had played a role in conflicts between the king and the *parlements*. Similarly, the power of *Revision* in the *Bundesgerichtshof* (the BGH), which is the highest in the hierarchy of ordinary courts in contemporary Germany, had its origins in the centuries before unification under Bismarck. Basically, it was the power of the emperor to "revise" (that is, to redecide correctly) a judicial decision incorrectly interpreting or applying imperial law. Thus the BGH need not, and ordinarily will not, remand the case, but will itself finally decide it, if the trial below was completed and if no further trial issues are raised by the BGH's consideration of the case.

With respect to the public administration, two major considerations applied: judges were to have no power to control or interfere in its activities, but some form of review of the legality of administrative action was clearly necessary in the interests of sound administration and of justice to the individuals affected by the acts of public officials and agencies. The *Conseil d'Etat* (Council of State, the descendant of the *Conseil du Roi*, another pre-Revolutionary institution), which stood at the head of the public administration in France and thus was not a part of the judiciary, was given this task. (A separate section of the Council is devoted to this kind of activity; other sections continue to perform administrative functions. When we refer to the Council of State here, we mean the section that decides cases challenging the legality of administrative actions: the *Section de contentieux administratif*.) A highly respected institution in France, the Council of State has, through its decisions, built the entire body of French administrative law with only minor legislative intervention. Since its jurisdiction is restricted to examining the legality of administrative acts, that jurisdiction was enormously expanded by the 1958 Constitution, which transferred a substantial portion of the legislative power to the Government, redefining it as the power to regulate (rather than legislate). It was decided in 1959 that review of the legality of decrees issued under this power fell within the jurisdiction of the Council of State.

The fact that the Council of State is part of the public administration whose acts it is supposed to control is a matter of concern to foreign observers, even though the institution has worked well in France. The alternative adopted in Germany was to establish a separate court at the federal level: the Administrative Court (*Bundesverwaltungsgericht*). As such, it is merely one of a number of separate judicial jurisdictions in Germany, together with the labor courts, the social courts, the tax courts, and the ordinary courts. Still, as in France, the basic separation is maintained: the ordinary courts have no power to review the legality of administrative action. That power is in a separate set of administrative courts.

The French model of division of jurisdiction has been more influential than the German one (which developed a good deal later). Accordingly it is not unusual to find courts of cassation and councils of state elsewhere in the civil law world, in nations whose own history provides nothing equivalent to the peculiar events and institutions that led to their emergence in France. Within Europe, Italy and Belgium closely follow the French model, although each has developed its own variations within the model. One such variation is in dealing with conflicts of jurisdiction, a problem that inevitably arises where there are multiple jurisdictions. Although it might appear that it would be easy to define matters so that one could tell clearly whether an action is properly brought before an ordinary court or an administrative court, in practice there are always doubtful cases. Accordingly, each nation has to provide a method of dealing with the problem. In Italy, the Supreme Court of Cassation has the final power of decision in such jurisdictional controversies. In France a special body, the Conflicts Tribunal, composed of the Minister of Justice (chairman), four members from the Court of Cassation and four from the Council of State, decides. In Germany the court to which the action is brought by a party decides, subject of course to appeal. This works well when the court accepts jurisdiction, but it is easy to see that a problem can arise if each of the courts to which an action is brought rejects it. The German solution is to require the court to which the action is taken after two rejections elsewhere to accept it.

Until this century the resistance in Europe to any sort of jurisdictional control of the legality of legislative action was very strong. Ideologically, the position was one of legislative supremacy. The popularly elected legislature enacted statutes, which it was the job of the public administration to execute and the job of the courts to apply to specific cases. There was little room in this ideology for any notion of control of the legality of legislative action, other than the obvious but impractical one of political control by an aroused electorate. This "deification of statutes" (a phrase used by European critics of their own systems) began to give way in the present century to the provision for judicial review in the Weimar Constitution in Germany and related experiments in Austria, Czechoslovakia, and Spain (most of which came to unhappy ends due to political events in Europe). After World War II, however, the trend toward judicial review became irresistible, leading to the establishment of constitutional courts in Germany, Italy, Spain, and elsewhere and the more limited but now evolving Constitutional Council in France. Thus again, for a variety of reasons related to the peculiarities of French history and Enlightenment political philosophy, it seemed essential that such power not be given to the (ordinary) courts. Hence their existence as another class of separate jurisdictions.

The division of jurisdiction just described is the pattern throughout most of Europe. It differs from the pattern in a typical common law country, such as the United States, which has a unified court system that might be represented as a pyramid with a single supreme court at the apex. In fact, in most Latin American nations, where the influence of the American Revolution and U.S. public law was particularly strong at the time of their wars of independence, they established unified judicial systems that control the legality of all branches of government. The United States also significantly influenced the unified judiciary in Japan. The supreme courts in these systems of unified jurisdictions, however, have never attained the prestige or exercised the power of the U.S. model.

A. JUDICIAL REVIEW OF JUDICIAL ACTS

NOTE

Previous materials have introduced the reader to the processes of recourse in *cassation* and *Revision,* which we briefly resummarize in the following excerpts. They demonstrate typical civil law approaches to review of judicial actions for conformity with "the law." With the rise of constitutionalism and constitutional review in post-World War II Europe came a new question. One way to phrase it is to ask whether the constitution is a "source of law." If it is, then presumably the ordinary judiciary will interpret and apply it in its work of deciding cases, and a losing party can complain on appeal that the lower court incorrectly interpreted or applied an applicable constitutional provision. Another way to put the question is this: in a nation with separate ordinary and constitutional jurisdictions, do ordinary courts interpret and apply constitutional provisions? We include materials here and in the remainder of the chapter showing different approaches to this question.

1. ORDINARY COURTS

JOHN HENRY MERRYMAN, THE CIVIL LAW TRADITION: AN INTRODUCTION TO THE LEGAL SYSTEMS OF WESTERN EUROPE AND LATIN AMERICA 40-41 (2d ed. 1985)

[T]he Tribunal of Cassation was not itself expected to provide authoritative interpretations of the statutes involved in the cases that came before it. On the contrary, its original function, consistent with its separate, nonjudicial nature, was merely to quash judicial decisions based on incorrect interpretations of statutes. Such cases would then go back to the judiciary for reconsideration and decision; that was, after all, a *judicial* function. Unlike the typical action of an appellate court in the United States, which not only quashes the incorrect decision of a question of law by the lower court, but also indicates the proper answer to the legal question incorrectly decided below and, when appropriate, applies that result to the case to produce a new decision, the French Tribunal of Cassation was created to perform only the first of these steps. However, by a gradual, but apparently inevitable, process of evolution, the tribunal came to perform the second step, as well as the first. Thus it not only indicated that the judicial decision was wrong; it also explained what the correct interpretation of the statute was. During this same period, the tribunal's nonjudicial origin dropped from view, and it came to be called the Court of Cassation; thus judicialized, it assumed a position at the apex of the system of ordinary courts. In France, as well as in Italy and other nations that have followed the French model, the full title is likely to be Supreme Court of Cassation. Thus the highest civil and criminal court in the jurisdiction — one that is manned by judges and that has primary responsibility for assuring the correct and uniform interpretation and application of the statutes by the lower civil and criminal courts — is the direct descendant of a legislative tribunal originally created to keep the power of interpretation out of the hands of judges.

The final step in the evolution of such bodies is illustrated by the German institution of "revision," as distinguished from the French cassation. The French system stopped at the second step: the Supreme Court of Cassation could quash a decision based on an incorrect interpretation, and it could instruct the lower court as to the correct interpretation. Still, the case had to be sent back to the lower court ("remanded") for decision. This was often a mere formality that unnecessarily took up valuable time; and occasionally more serious problems arose because lower judges were either unable or unwilling to understand and follow the interpretation announced by the Supreme Court of Cassation. Nor were they, in theory, required — or even allowed — to follow the higher court's decision. We have seen that a judge had to base his decision on the law, and the opinion of the Supreme Court of Cassation was not, and still today is not, a source of law. Thus the decision of the Court of Cassation is at most something that is persuasive for its reasoning and the eminence of its source. But if the judge on remand is convinced that the law is otherwise, he should so hold. Much of the history of the process of cassation since the court's creation is the chronicle of such problems and of the various devices that have been invented to solve them. By the time Germany was united under Bismarck, the defects of French cassation were clearly apparent. And by that time European legal thought had openly conceded that judges did, indeed, have to interpret statutes as part of their ordinary work. There was no reason to complicate matters unnecessarily, so the Germans did the rational thing: they created a supreme court with the power to review the decisions of lower courts for legal correctness, to quash incorrect decisions, to indicate the correct answer, and to "revise" the incorrect decision accordingly.

2. THE GERMAN SYSTEM OF MULTIPLE COURTS

DAVID S. CLARK, THE SELECTION AND ACCOUNTABILITY OF JUDGES IN WEST GERMANY: IMPLEMENTATION OF A *RECHTSSTAAT*, 61 Southern California Law Review 1797, 1837-40 (1988)

Appellate Review of Cases

The near universal method for maintaining legal accountability within a system of multiple courts is to provide for the appellate review of first instance decisions. German appellate practice is directed toward minimizing error in both findings of fact and rulings of law. Except in cases that are settled, first instance judges must write a thorough opinion reflecting their views on these two components of a decision. Good opinions reduce judges' reversal rates and guarantee high rankings in peer evaluation reports, which are determinative for promotions. From a litigant's standpoint, written opinions that include reasons guard against arbitrary or incompetent adjudication.

Appeal is commonly used in Germany. A dissatisfied party has the right of appeal de novo (*Berufung*) on both the facts and the law in most cases, followed by a discretionary appeal (*Revision*) limited to errors of law before a federal high court. Figures for 1984 illustrate the situation. In state district courts 101,159 fully contested civil judgments (*streitige Urteile*) — that is, cases that were not settled, withdrawn, defaulted, or decided in special judgments — formed the most likely group for the 53,487 civil appeals (*Berufungen*) filed in state courts of appeals. *Revisionen* taken to the Federal Supreme Court (3,696 civil and family cases) constituted a smaller ratio of the 26,668 civil *streitige Urteile* from the state courts of appeals.

A similar filtering pyramid exists in the hierarchy of labor courts. In 1984 plaintiffs filed 361,435 cases in state labor courts, while judges decided 36,315 with fully contested judgments. In the state courts of labor appeals, litigants filed 17,483 *Berufungen* and judges rendered 6,684 *streitige Urteile*. Finally, litigants took 674 *Revisionen* to the Federal Labor Court. These two examples demonstrate that roughly half of the dissatisfied first instance litigants file a *Berufung*, while about ten percent of those who are still disappointed after the second instance succeed in receiving a discretionary *Revision*.

Specialization of High Courts

The primary function of the six federal high courts is to maintain uniform interpretation of federal law within their respective subject matter jurisdictions. Thus, in addition to the Federal Constitutional Court, five distinct hierarchies of courts — processing ordinary civil and criminal, labor, administrative, tax, and social security cases — develop their own expertise in handling a specialty.

Within the system of ordinary courts, specialization begins at first instance, when cases are channeled to a criminal, civil, commercial, or family law division. In the state courts of appeals, which are sometimes staffed with more than a hundred judges, extensive specialization by chamber (four or five judges, with three sitting on a panel) begins. At the top, the Federal Supreme Court is divided into 23 subject matter chambers (*Senate*), each usually with seven judges. The *Präsidium* of the Supreme Court and of every appellate court annually prepares a public work allocation plan (*Geschäftsverteilungsplan*), which lists the categories of cases assigned to each *Senat* along with the names of that chamber's judges. From the standpoint of attorneys and their clients, this docket arrangement means that they can know in advance which judges will hear their case. Maritime cases, to illustrate, will always go to civil division II. Predictability of law is enhanced. John Langbein, in comparing this approach to our court structure in America, concludes:

> This system permits the judges to develop over the years just that sort of expertise in legal subspecialties that we expect of lawyers, particularly lawyers in large-firm practice, in the United States. The litigants get judges who know something about the field, in contradistinction to the calculated amateurism of our appellate tradition.

Supervision of Judges and Disciplinary Sanctions

... The principal reward for good performance is promotion. But supervision (*Dienstaufsicht*) can also lead to warnings and even disciplinary proceedings (*Disziplinarverfahren*). Supervision, moreover, entails more than assessing judicial activity (*richterliche Tätigkeit*) associated with the external perception of neutrality and legal accountability. It also covers general working obligations (*allgemeine Dienstpflichten*) common to all public office holders, as well as the control of certain outside conduct (*ausserdienstliches Verhalten*).

The purpose of supervision and discipline is to assure the just and efficient functioning of courts. This control, however, must not impair judicial independence and a judge's duty to apply the law. If a judge believes his independence is being affected, he can obtain a hearing before the appropriate judicial service court (*Dienstgericht*).

Oversight duties are generally shared between presidents of the various courts and the state or federal minister charged with responsibility for a particular type of court. There is no supervision of this sort for the Federal Constitutional Court. Supervision is limited to observation of judicial activity (*Beobachtungsfunktion*) and critical comments about actual breaches of duty (*Berichtigungsfunktion*). The strongest measures authorized under the German Judges Law are reproach (*Vorhalt*) and warning (*Ermahnung*). More serious measures and sanctions, including dismissal, can only be levied through a judicial disciplinary proceeding.

Oversight and disciplinary measures may be directed toward judicial activity outside the core (*Kernbereich*) decisional process protected by judicial independence. Thus, sanctions can be applied against a judge who fails to apply a well-known general statute, who applies a formally repealed statute, or who ignores a binding decision from the Federal Constitutional Court. Measures may also be used to warn or punish a judge who is too lax in his general administrative or procedural obligations. For example, a judge may be punished if he holds too few evidentiary hearings, if he works too slowly, or if he refuses to accept his assigned subject matter caseload. Furthermore, judges have a special obligation to instill trust in their own independence, especially independence from political forces. Sanctions have been enforced against those who engage in verbal excess (*verbale Exzesse*), by criticizing in a disparaging manner public prosecutors or another court's decision, or by including in a judicial opinion sweeping statements about the incompetence or corruption of a political party. This control extends to conduct by judges outside the courthouse. Judges must not impair the judiciary's prestige by their actions or words. Judges have been disciplined for assaulting a pursuing news photographer and for playing down a magazine report about Nazi concentration camps.

NOTES AND QUESTIONS

1. Are lower courts in the ordinary judicial hierarchy required to follow a legal interpretation of the high court? What forces, nevertheless, combine to produce uniformity of judicial decisionmaking?

2. Why is the supervision of judges and disciplinary sanctions almost nonexistent in the United States compared to Germany? Should there be more control of judicial activity in the United States?

3. The Italian case that follows raises the issue whether further safeguards should be built into the ordinary judiciary to maintain accountability to law. Like the German Basic Law, the Italian Constitution states (in article 101, paragraph 2): "Judges are subject only to the law."

3. THE ACCOUNTABILITY OF JUDGES

THE CIVIL LIABILITY OF JUDGES CASE

Constitutional Court of Italy
Decision No. 18 of 19 January 1989
39 Giust. Civ. I, 769 (1989)

(*Omissis.*) 1. The Court is asked to respond to questions concerning the civil liability of judges so similar in nature as to permit their resolution to be united in a single judgment.

2. The most general question, raised by the Regional Administrative Tribunal of Catania, Sicily [T.A.R.] involves a two-pronged argument concerning the entire Law of 13 April 1988 no. 117 which establishes the civil liability of judges for gross negligence (*colpa grave*) or malice (*dolo*).

According to the T.A.R. the prospect of such liability violates articles 101, 104, and 108 of the Constitution, compromising judicial impartiality by giving parties an instrument of pressure sufficient to influence judicial decisions. The possibility of a "counter-action for sanctions against the judge would give him, when deciding any controversy, a personal interest in prudence, in conformism, in the least risky choice in relation to the economic interests involved in the action," contrary to the principle that the judge is subject only to the law. From this would follow a loss of independence, which presupposes a condition of complete freedom from any external influence and intimidation. Further, the provision of an action for damages against the state, exposing the judge to eventual reimbursement [of the state], would impair his serenity, and therefore also his independence.... Judges would feel pressure to adhere to established judicial principles in order to limit their liability, with the consequent compromise of judicial independence and the evolution of case law.

In the [ruling suspending the trial and sending the question to the Constitutional Court] it is further suggested that the possibility of error is inherent in judicial procedure and the existence of appropriate means of attack aimed at the elimination of error [appeal, recourse in cassation, and Constitutional review] demonstrate the incompatibility between the procedural system and judicial liability for fault.

As another basis of unconstitutionality, the trial judge referred to the United Nations General Assembly Resolution of 29 November 1965, which stated the principle that judges must enjoy personal immunity from civil actions for damages for their improper actions or inactions in the exercise of their judicial functions. Since that resolution should be characterized as a norm of general international law, the statute in question would violate art. 10 of the Constitution, which establishes that the Italian legal order conforms to the generally recognized rules of international law.

3. The question [of unconstitutionality] is unfounded under both theories. It must be taken as a premise that the Law of 13 April 1988 no. 117 represents the final point of a long evolution that, on the subject of civil liability of judges, has seen significant changes in Italy.

In the 12th to 15th centuries, before the rise and establishment of supreme tribunals, the interpretation of the internal law of the various Italian states was the work of the "doctors," Glossators or Commentators. They did this in particular in their *consilia*, based on *communis opinio* and given to the judges of that era who frequently were inexpert in the law and subject to liability for ordinary fault. From this situation the normative path moved irregularly through a long arc of time in response to the varying configurations of the position of the judge.

The weakening of the idea of the state and of law as the will of the state brought on by the barbaric invasions also affected the idea of jurisdiction as a state function, that is, the function of interpreting and applying the legislative intention. With the establishment of feudal institutions and the increasing fractionization of sovereignty, jurisdiction became pulverized among the different judges (popular, royal, imperial, feudal, ecclesiastical, communal) and began to take on the aspect of a prerogative of the judge, with the characteristics of inheritable and alienable property, and the trial ceased to be considered a public function implicating of the law and appeared exclusively as a contest between litigants. The judge was no longer the public organ of a state function, but an arbiter charged with deciding the contest on the basis of the evidence.

Then, with the rise and consolidation of the figure of the judge-functionary, to whom was delegated the administration of justice, the way was opened to define with greater precision both his disciplinary responsibility and limitation of civil liability for wrongful acts.

This was the basis for the provisions of art. 783 of the Civil Code of 1865, which limited the civil liability of the judge to cases of "malice, fraud, or extortion" and "denial of justice," as did arts. 55, 56, and 74 of the 1940 Code of Civil Procedure.

This normative scheme favored internal responsibility of a disciplinary character over external liability, within a framework in which the progressive amplification of liability of the public administration, the fruit of a long evolution, was not yet established.

Even before the republican Constitution [of 1948], doctrine and jurisprudence agreed on the principle (most effectively resisted by the military and

railway administrations) that breach of the precept *neminem ledere* made the public agency liable.

This principle is expressed, with specific mention of those to whom it applies, in art. 28 of the Constitution, according to which functionaries and employees of the state and of public agencies are directly liable under criminal, civil, and administrative laws for acts performed in violation of rights. In such cases civil liability extends to the state and to public entities. This precept has been interpreted to mean that state liability can be claimed alone or together with that of state functionaries or employees and is not of a subsidiary character.

With respect to the reference to "criminal, civil, and administrative laws" [the Court cites several such statutes providing for personal liability of other — i.e. other than judges — state functionaries and employees and shows that if the state pays it can recover from the responsible functionary or employee.]...

5. While such laws were adopted for civil employees of the state, making them directly liable for injury caused by their intentional or grossly negligent acts in accordance with art. 28 of the Constitution, the previous special position of judges in Code of Civil Procedure arts. 55, 56, and 74 remained in effect.

On this basis the judge was civilly liable only when in the exercise of his functions he was "chargeable with malice, fraud, or extortion" or when without good reason he refused, failed, or delayed "responding to the claims or motions of parties or, in general, in performing his duty as a judge."...

The action for judicial liability also could not be brought without authorization by the Minister of Justice.

This system presented a kind of inversion of the normative situation prevailing before the Constitution came into force. At that time only judges were by law made directly liable — within the limits indicated — but with the ratification of the Constitution [and the implementing laws described above], other civil employees of the state were subjected to broader liability....

6. In this context this Court, in its decision of 14 March 1968 no. 2 — delivered when arts. 55, 56, and 74 of the Code of Civil Procedure were still in force — established certain principles relating to the civil liability of public employees in general, principles that it is proper to review in examining the constitutional question raised by the T.A.R.

First of all, the Court affirmed that art. 28 of the Constitution, with the expression "functionaries and dependents of the state" also refers to magistrates.

In the second place it held that the general principle of direct liability of public dependents, including judges, did not prevent that such "liability be differently regulated according to category and situation." Specifically, the peculiarity of the judicial function, the nature of judicial actions, and the position *super partes* of the magistrate justify limits and conditions on his liability without, however, permitting its total denial. That denial would be contrary to Const. art. 28 and also art. 3, for unjustified differential treatment of other public functionaries and dependents.

Finally, the Court held that under Const. art. 28 the state is liable for damage resulting from judicial action whenever the judge is liable, but that as to other violations of rights caused by the judge "the right to repayment by the state is not constitutionally guaranteed," but can be derived from general principles of the legal order or from specific statutes.

More recently the jurisprudence, strictly applying the principle of Civil Code art. 2043, which is generally applicable to the public administration on the basis of the organic relation between the judicial office and the state, has held the latter directly liable even in cases in which the judge would not be.

7. Against this background the Referendum of 1987 abrogated arts. 55, 56, and 74 of the Code of Civil Procedure. This was followed by enactment of the Law of 13 April 1988 no. 117, by which Parliament established a new regime of judicial liability sensitive to the peculiarity of the judicial function, which [responding to a decision of the Constitutional Court of 3 Feb. 1987 no. 26, permitting the Referendum], required setting conditions and limits on the liability of magistrates, in response to the constitutional guarantees of the independence and autonomy of the magistracy in arts. 101-113....

The Parliament, restricting judicial liability within the limits allowed by Const. art. 28, provided that judges are directly liable only for damage resulting from criminal conduct committed in the exercise of their functions. In other cases the injured party can act solely against the state, which has a limited action for indemnity against the judge.

8. The cases in which an action may be brought against the state — with a right of indemnity against the magistrate — are listed in arts. 2 and 3 of the Law. According to art. 2, "one who has suffered injury as a result of judicial conduct ... by a judge with malice or gross negligence in the exercise of his functions, or from denial of justice, may sue the state for compensatory and non-compensatory damages deriving from the deprivation of personal liberty." According to the express provisions of art. 2:

> the following constitute gross negligence: a) serious violation of law because of inexcusable negligence; b) finding a fact, because of inexcusable negligence, that is unarguably disproven by the record; c) failure, because of inexcusable negligence, to find a fact that is incontestably proved by the record; d) rulings affecting personal liberty other than in cases provided by law or without giving reasons.

Art. 2 also provides that "the activity of interpreting legal rules or evaluating evidence cannot give rise to liability."

The other hypothesis on which the action for liability may be based is "denial of justice," regulated by art. 3, according to which "the denial of justice consists of the refusal, failure, or delay of the magistrate in performing the duties of his office when, the statutory time for performance of the act having passed, the party has requested that it be performed and, without just reason, thirty days have passed without result since the request was filed."... Art. 7 provides that within one year of payment the state may bring an action for reimbursement against a magistrate. The amount of reimbursement (art. 8), except in cases of malice, may not exceed one-third of the judge's base annual salary or one-fifth of his total annual compensation.

9. The scheme contained in Law no. 117 of 1988 is characterized by constant care to protect the independence of magistrates, as well as their autonomy and the unimpaired exercise of the judicial function.

Starting from this general characterization it is necessary to examine the allegations of unconstitutionality of the statute under Constitution arts. 101, 104, and 108.

As this Court has held (decisions of 3 May 1974 no. 128; 27 March 1969 no. 60), the principle of independence seeks to guarantee judicial impartiality, assuring the judge a position *super partes* that excludes any direct or indirect influence on the case. To this end the statute must guarantee the absence of any expectation of advantage or fear of prejudice, providing whatever is appropriate to protect the objectivity of the decision. Regulation of the judge's actions must therefore be such as to render him immune from restraints that can subject him, in form or in substance, to other agencies [of government], attempting as far as is possible to make him "free of biases, fears, or influences that can lead the judge to decide in a way that is different from what learning and conscience dictate." Moreover (decision of 14 March 1968 no. 2), "the autonomy and independence of the magistracy and the judge do not put the first outside the state, as though *legibus soluta*, nor the other outside the state's organization." The judge must be independent of powers and interests extraneous to the judicial function, but he is "subject to the law": to the Constitution above all, which states on the one hand the principle of independence (arts. 101, 104, and 108) and [on the other hand] that of liability (art. 28), in order to insure that the position *super partes* of the magistrate is never divorced from the proper exercise of his high function.

10. The Court has already explained (nos. 3 and 4, above) that art. 28 establishes the rule — applicable to public functionaries and employees (and therefore also to judges) — of liability for "acts performed in violation of rights," according to "penal, civil, and administrative laws." The Law under attack — correctly applying the principles affirmed by this Court in the cited decisions of 14 March 1968 nos. 2 and 3 and February 1987 no. 26 — according to which, given the special nature of the judicial function, liability under art. 28 must be limited by providing conditions and limits that protect the independence and impartiality of the judge. The Law has made the judge directly liable solely for damage caused by criminal acts. Indirect liability to the state ... is in its turn limited to a few rigidly defined fact situations.

The limited and taxative nature of the fact situations in which the judge may be [indirectly] liable for gross negligence, related to "inexcusable negligence" in applying the law or determining the facts, or the issuance of orders restricting liberty other than in cases allowed by law or without giving reasons, as well as the specific and detailed limitation of liability for "denial of justice," do not permit the conclusion that these measures are likely to disturb the serenity and impartiality of the judge.... The judicial process, by definition and in fact, involves determination of the facts and application of the norms through an activity of valuation and interpretation, in which ample space is left to judges.

The constitutional guarantee of [the judge's] independence seeks to protect, *in primis*, autonomy in evaluating the facts and evidence and the impartial interpretation of legal norms. Such activity cannot lead to judicial liability (art. 2 no. 2 of Law no. 117), and the Parliament has increased the area of non-liability up to the point that the exercise of the judge's function in violation of his fundamental duties constitutes inexcusable violation of the law or inexcusable ignorance of the facts whose existence is not in controversy.

Nor can it be held — as did the trial judge — that the Law would press the judge to choose accommodative interpretations and safe decisions in relation to the interests of the parties. As already shown, art. 2 no. 2 of Law 117 expressly excludes liability for "the activity of interpreting legal norms" and that of evaluating the facts and the evidence.

This also disposes of the claim that the institution of an action for damages against the state, related to a specific case, could impair the impartiality of the judge in analogous cases or in those in which the person who brought the action for liability is a party. Where there genuinely are such difficulties, the remedy of abstention is available to deal with them. However, it should be emphasized that the provision for rejection of admissibility of the complaint (art. 51 of the Law) adequately protects the judge against the institution of "manifestly unfounded" actions that could impair his serenity or maliciously create the conditions for his abstention or recusal.

11. As to the claimed violation of Constitution art. 10 by way of a United Nations Resolution of 29 November 1985 — which stated the principle that judges should be immune from actions for civil liability "for improper acts and omissions in the exercise of their judicial functions," — the claim must be rejected. According to art. 10 of the Constitution "the Italian legal order shall conform to generally recognized rules of international law," and these do not include statements in United Nations resolutions, which according to international practice have no binding force.

They are not, in fact, sources of law, even if they have some influence on customs and agreements.

Further, this principle is one of a group of statements about guarantees of judicial independence and, in that context, it does not necessarily imply total freedom from liability so long as the independence of the magistracy is guaranteed by appropriate limitations and provisos, as this Court has held with reference to Constitution art. 28 and, as we have just shown, Law no. 117 provides....

For these reasons the Constitutional Court declares [the claims of unconstitutionality discussed above] unfounded. [Other less central provisions of the statute were found constitutionally invalid].

NOTES AND QUESTIONS

1. This report of the decision of the Constitutional Court, from which substantial portions were deleted, was published in *Giustizia Civile,* a private publication. Because of its importance and interest to the Italian legal community it was also published in *Il Foro Italiano,* the other major private publisher of Italian judicial decisions, as well as in the official reports of the Constitutional Court. The reports in *Giustizia Civile* and *Il Foro Italiano* were accompanied by signed "notes" written by academics in which the opinion (written by Judge Pescatore) was critically examined and the decision put into context by relating it to relevant legislation, jurisprudence, and doctrine. The note in *Giustizia Civile,* by Fabio del Castello, is entitled: "Attacks on judicial liability finally concluded" and begins:

> The annotated decision represents the final point of the political-legislative process concerning the civil liability of judges. As is well-known, the Law of 13 April 1988 no. 117 is the fruit of alternating political and institutional confrontations involving all (or almost all) actors in the Italian "political system." It began with the committee promoting the abrogative referendum on arts. 55, 56, and 74 of the Code of Civil Procedure; the referendarial route continued with the actions brought by the Central Referendum Office before the Court of Cassation and the Constitutional Court, which legitimated the call for a referendum; dissolution of the Parliament in 1987 suspended the referendum procedure, which was reinstituted by the Law of 7 August 1987 no. 332, which permitted reference to a popular vote only six months after the political elections; at this point the political parties entered the scene and were almost unanimous that the previous system should be abrogated but took diametrically opposing positions on solutions; the people voted for the abrogation by about eighty percent, and the abrogative effect of the referendum was then suspended by a Decree of the President of the Republic [for a specified time, in order to avoid a legislative vacuum while the Parliament considered new legislation on the topic].
>
> The Government presented its bill in the Parliament and many others were also introduced; in addition, strong positions were taken by the magistrates' organizations; Parliament, after various vicissitudes, and after several days of "normative vacuum," approved the present statute, which was then immediately attacked on constitutional grounds. Called on a second time, after having ruled on the admissibility of the referendum, the Court resolved questions of constitutionality with this ponderous pronouncement.

2. Does this history shock you? Is it significantly different from the history of controversial state or federal legislation in the U.S.?

3. How many ways can you identify in which this decision of the Italian Constitutional Court sharply deviates from the civil law model of a judicial decision?

4. How persuasive is the argument that subjecting judges to indirect civil liability would unduly interfere with their necessary independence?

5. Why might the issue of civil liability of judges be different from that of public employees in general? Should this distinction hold in the United States?

6. The Italian Law of 13 April 1988 no. 117 at issue in *The Civil Liability of Judges Case* is discussed in Michele Graziadei & Ugo Mattei, *Judicial Responsibility in Italy: A New Statute,* 38 Am. J. Comp. L. 103 (1990). For background on the 1987 referendum mentioned in section 7 of the Court's opinion see Giuseppe di Federico, *The Crisis of the Judicial System and the*

Referendum on the Judiciary, 3 Italian Politics: A Review 25 (Robert Leonardi & Piergiorgio Corbetta eds. 1989).

JAPAN v. ONDA

Supreme Court of Japan
Third Petty Bench
Decision of 3 July 1962
16 Minshū 1408 (1962)

Disposition (shubun)

The portions of the judgment of the court below decided against the jōkoku appellant are revoked and the entire case is remanded to the Matsue Branch of the Hiroshima High Court.

Reasons (riyū)

Concerning the arguments for *jōkoku* appeal by the appellant's designated representative, Nishimoto Toshiki:

Article 208(2) of the Criminal Code provides that for "unavoidable reasons," upon petition by a prosecutor, a judge may grant an extension of up to ten days of the period for detention of a suspect. The phrase "unavoidable reasons" can be properly construed to mean circumstances that make it difficult to decide whether or not to file an indictment without extending the period for detaining the suspect for additional questioning. Further interrogation may be necessary for a variety of reasons. The case could be quite complex (as in cases where there are multiple suspects or suspected facts, or where there is a considerable amount of conflicting evidence as a result of complicated financial records, conflicting statements by persons connected to the suspect, and the like, or where there are many items of evidence to obtain or material witnesses to be questioned). Or the case may involve significant delays or difficulties in collecting evidence (for example, additional time may be necessary to obtain expert testimony as a result of the possible illness, travel, or unknown address of an important consultant). (However, the proper limits of the decision as to whether "unavoidable reasons" exist or not must also be considered in terms of the relationship of the case in question to other similar cases.) Hence prosecutors who petition for an extension of the period of detention, as well as judges who receive such petitions, must ultimately make a legal value judgment in determining whether the prosecutor has to decide between filing an indictment without cause, should additional evidence and further questioning be necessary in addition to whatever materials have already been obtained. A mistake in this value judgment, we deem appropriate to conclude, would constitute a defect (*kashi*) under article 1, paragraph 1, of the National Compensation Law, entitling a petitioner to damages from the state.] However, such error would have to be obvious: for example, whether or not in determining under the circumstances either the need for further questioning of the suspect or the prosecutorial decision to seek an extension of detention, neither the ordinary prosecutor nor the ordinary judge would have petitioned for such extension or approved such petition on the basis of the materials supporting the petition for extension of the period of detention in question.

NOTES AND QUESTIONS

1. In applying the standard that the Court set out in the first part of the decision in *Japan v. Onda,* the five justices of the Third Petty Bench agreed that neither the prosecutor nor the judge in that particular instance had committed an "obvious" error. It thus revoked the portion of the Hiroshima High Court's judgment holding the state liable. In subsequent decisions the Supreme Court has defined further the limits of state liability for judicial error. In a 1968 case the Second Petty Bench confirmed that judges acting within the scope of their judicial authority, including their adjudication of facts and law, may subject the state to liability for error. *Yokoyama v. Japan,* 90 Saibanshū minji 655 (Sup. Ct., 2d P.B., March 15, 1968). As a result, the state may be held liable for damages in the event that on appeal a lower court judgment is revoked. Subsequently, in what is considered a landmark decision, the Second Petty Bench in 1982 dismissed an appeal from a high court decision rejecting the claim of a party who had sought damages for an error in a first instance decision without filing an appeal. *Takeda v. Japan,* 36 Minshū 329 (Sup. Ct., 2d P.B., March 12, 1982). The reasoning of that case, however, suggests a more restrictive standard for determining whether the state is liable for judicial error.

2. Is the potential liability of the state for judicial conduct more or less extensive in Japan than in Italy? In Japan does the state's liability depend upon liability of the individual judge? Would the Japanese approach satisfy Italian constitutional requirements? What effect, for example, could the Japanese approach have on judicial independence? Could potential state liability affect lower court adherence to precedent? Do the Japanese have more or less legal protection from judicial misconduct than Americans?

4. MAINTAINING THE UNIFORM INTERPRETATION OF LAW

HUSTON v. SOCIÉTÉ D'EXPLOITATION de la CINQUIÈME CHAINE

Court of Cassation of France
Civil Chamber, First Division
Decision of 28 May 1991
1991 J.C.P. II, 21731

English translation published in Jane C. Ginsburg & Pierre Sirinelli, *Authors and Exploitations in International Private Law: The French Supreme Court and the Huston Film Colorization Controversy,* 15 Colum.-VLA J.L. & Arts 135, 159 (1991)

Citing clause 2 of article 1 of law No. 64-689 of July 8, 1964 [the law concerning international reciprocity in copyright protection], together with article 6 of the law of March 11, 1957 [the copyright law];

Whereas, according to the first of these texts, in France, no violation may be made of the integrity of a literary or artistic work, whatever the territory on which the work was first disclosed; whereas the person who is the author of the work from the sole fact of the work's creation is invested with moral rights which are established for his benefit by the second of the texts cited above; whereas these rules are laws of imperative application;

Whereas the Huston plaintiffs are the heirs of John Huston, the co-director of the film "Asphalt Jungle," created in black and white, but of which the Turner Company, grantee of the producer, established a colored version; whereas, invoking their right to compel the respect of the integrity of John Huston's work, the Huston plaintiffs, joined by various entities [authors' rights societies], have requested the judges below to prohibit the television station "La Cinq" from broadcasting this new version; whereas the Court of Appeals dismissed their claim on the ground that the elements of fact and law found by the appellate court "prohibited the eviction of the American [copyright] law and the setting aside of the contracts" that had been concluded between the producer and the directors, contracts that denied the latter persons the status of authors of the film "Asphalt Jungle";

Whereas in so holding, the Court of Appeals has violated the above-cited texts by refusal to apply them;

For these reasons, and without need to hold on the other objections raised in the petition for this Court's review:

Reverse and annul, in all respects, the decision rendered by the Court of Appeals of Paris, July 6, 1989, reinstate therefore the case and the parties in the state in which they were before said decision and, for resolution of the case, send the parties before the Court of Appeals of Versailles.

JANE C. GINSBURG & PIERRE SIRINELLI, AUTHORS AND EXPLOITATIONS IN INTERNATIONAL PRIVATE LAW: THE FRENCH SUPREME COURT AND THE HUSTON FILM COLORIZATION CONTROVERSY, 15 Columbia-VLA Journal of Law & the Arts 135-38 (1991)

On May 28, 1991, France's Supreme Court, the *Cour de cassation*, rendered its long-awaited decision in *Huston v. la Cinq*, a controversy that opposed the heirs of film director John Huston against the French television station Channel 5 and its licensor, Turner Entertainment. Defendants sought to broadcast a colorized version of Huston's black and white film classic, *The Asphalt Jungle*. Plaintiffs, John Huston's children and Ben Maddow, who collaborated with Huston on the film's screenplay, asserted that broadcast of a colorized version violated Huston's and Maddow's moral right of integrity in the motion picture. The central question before the *Cour de cassation*, however, concerned not the substance of the integrity claim, but plaintiffs' entitlement to invoke it.

Under French law, the moral right to preserve a work's artistic integrity is an incident of authorship. Upon creating the work, authors are invested with exclusive moral and economic rights. While economic rights may be transferred, moral rights are both inalienable and perpetual. Thus, a film director who has granted all economic interests in her work nonetheless retains the moral rights to oppose violations of the work's integrity and to receive authorship credit for her work. Under U.S. law, by contrast, film directors do not enjoy rights tantamount to, or even approaching, their French counterparts. Most significantly, under U.S. copyright law's "works made for hire" doctrine, employees, or in most circumstances, commissioned creators who participate in the elaboration of a motion picture, are not considered "authors": the film's producer is deemed the "author."

The problem in the *Huston* case therefore was: Who is the "author" of the film? If the French courts applied the U.S. law concept of authorship, then John Huston would not have been ruled the "author," and accordingly, he and his heirs would lack any moral rights. If, however, the French courts applied the French concept of authorship, then John Huston's status as an "author" would have been recognized; accordingly, he and his heirs would have been the beneficiary of the moral right of integrity. Thus, first and foremost the *Huston* affair presented an international conflicts of laws controversy.

Although the lower courts, issuing preliminary relief, and the Paris first-level court had held for plaintiffs on a variety of grounds, the Paris Court of Appeals, on July 6, 1989, found for defendants. Declining to apply Article 14*bis* of the Berne Convention, which designates the competence of the law of the country where protection is sought to determine ownership rights in motion pictures, the appellate court announced a choice of law rule designating the law of the country of the work's origin to determine copyright ownership and authorship status. The court believed that application of U.S. law, under which the creative contributors to the film enjoyed no authorship rights, did not violate strongly held French public policy. The court found that the principles of moral rights lacked paramount importance even in internal French copyright law; therefore these principles could not command extraterritorial application. Finally, the Paris court stated that even if Huston had standing, his moral rights were not violated, because colorization constitutes an adaptation, and, in the court's reasoning, if the work is a licensed and well-executed adaptation, it cannot violate the moral rights of the author of the underlying work.

The Paris appellate decision provoked considerable discussion in French legal journals, almost all of it negative. Commentators criticized both the court's conflicts analysis, as well as its treatment of moral rights and their role in French jurisprudence. The *Cour de cassation* has now reversed the Paris Court of Appeals on the standing question. The High Court has held that French law directly governs all questions of authors' rights of integrity and attribution, without inquiry into the legislative competence of foreign laws that had significant points of attachment to the litigation. The Court has thus stressed the international applicability of the French concepts of authorship and of these moral rights, whatever the country of the work's origin, the nationality or domicile of the work's creators, or the law governing the contract between creators and grantees. The case was then remanded to the Court of Appeals of Versailles for a decision on the merits of the moral rights claim.

The *Cour de cassation*'s decision appears to strike a blow for artistic integrity, for the decision places in the hands of creators from all countries the power to oppose derogatory alterations of their works in France, even when these persons are not considered "authors" in their home countries or in the countries of the works' origin.

QUESTIONS

Does the French *Cour de cassation* fulfill its primary function of maintaining the uniform interpretation of the law? Is its job to protect the integrity of French law (i.e., on moral rights) at the expense of possible inroads by United States law? Is that what the Court means when it states that "these rules [relied upon] are laws of imperative application?" Should French law regulate the rights and obligations associated with American movies made in America? Does the Court leave any doubt that it disagrees with the Paris Court of Appeal decision ("reverse and annul, in all respects")?

CONSTITUTION OF SPAIN

Articles 18, 20

Article 18

1. The right of honor, to personal and family privacy, to one's own image (*imagen*) is guaranteed....

4. The law shall limit the use of information to guarantee honor, the personal and family privacy of citizens, and the full exercise of their rights.

Article 20

1. The following rights are recognized and protected:

(a) To freely express and disseminate thoughts, ideas, and opinions through words, writing, or any other means of reproduction; ...

(d) To freely communicate or receive true information by any means of diffusion. The law shall regulate the right to conscience and to business secrets in the exercise of these liberties....

4. These liberties have limits in respect to the rights recognized in this title [i.e., arts. 10-55], in the legal norms that develop them, and especially for the right of honor, to privacy, to one's own image, and for the protection of youth and infancy.

PANTOJA v. PROGRAPHIC CO.

Supreme Court of Spain
(Civil Chamber No. 1)
Decisions of 28 October 1986 and 25 April 1989
1987 La Ley no. 2, at 267 and 1989 La Ley no. 4, at 357

[This case is summarized by Luis Arechederra in an article appearing in the *International and Comparative Law Quarterly*, excerpted below.]

LUIS ARECHEDERRA, THE DEATH OF A BULLFIGHTER: SPANISH LAW ON PRIVACY AND THE RIGHT TO NAME AND LIKENESS, 40 International and Comparative Law Quarterly 442-45 (1991)

The Factual Circumstances

Francisco Rivera, popularly known as "Paquirri," a famous bullfighter, died as a result of injuries received in the bullring at Pozoblanco, near Córdoba, on 26 September 1984. In the full sight of the public he was gored by a bull, carried for a time on the animal's horns, dropped on the ground and eventually rescued by other bullfighters, who carried him across the arena to the bullring's infirmary. There he displayed great courage as he discussed his injuries with the doctor and with members of the public who, until they were expelled, had crowded into the infirmary. He died in the ambulance on the way to the hospital.

"Paquirri," as a gifted matador and a handsome man, was a popular figure. His second marriage, in Seville Cathedral, to a well-known actress and singer, Isabel Pantoja, had been a major social event, attracting the attention of the mass media. It is not surprising that there was a strong public reaction to the tragic ending of a life which had reached its zenith personally and professionally. Spanish television, skilfully combining archive film footage with shots of the goring and its sequel, including the scene in the infirmary, devoted part of a Saturday night news programme, *Informe Semanal*, to the bullfighter; and subsequently a commercial company, Prographic S.A., bought the tapes from Spanish television with the aim of putting together a video cassette, which they called *Paquirri: A Song of Love and Death*. Soon afterwards it was put on the market.

On 22 November 1984 the bullfighter's widow made a claim against the Public Prosecutor and Prographic S.A. in the Court of First Instance (No. 14) of Madrid. She asked for 40 million pesetas (approximately £225,000) in damages.

The Legal Background

It was not until 6 December 1912 that, by a decision of the Supreme Court of Spain, it became possible to obtain damages for a "moral" injury — that is, one neither of a pecuniary nor physical nature. It was, however, only by legislation that the moral domain was declared to include a constitutionally guaranteed "right to honour, personal and family privacy and to name and likeness." By Article 20.4 of the same law — which is much criticised by the mass media — even "the right," under Article 20, "freely to communicate or receive true information by any means of diffusion" is limited by — *inter alia* — "especially ... the right to honour, privacy and to name and likeness."

The right declared in Article 18.1 of the Constitution of 1978 has been implemented by Organic Law No. 1 of 5 May 1982, which lays down that where there is interference with a constitutional right the Penal Code is operative. This means in practice that such interference is prosecutable by the person affected, who — subject in some cases to the consent of the court — has the alternative of a civil remedy. The Supreme Court had tended to insist on criminal proceedings when the person whose right has been violated holds a high public position such as a judicial post....

Proceedings at First Instance and on Appeal

On 29 November 1984, seven days after proceedings were launched, the Court of First Instance (No. 14) of Madrid granted an interlocutory injunction against the sale of the video cassette prepared by Prographic S.A., which was taken off the market. In its judgment on the merits of 4 February 1985, the Court held that there had been "use of the name, voice or likeness of a person for advertising, commercial or similar reasons" in violation of Article 7.6 of Organic Law No. 1 of 5 May 1982, awarded the widow of the bullfighter 20 million pesetas (approximately £112,500) by way of damages and made the injunction permanent. In this connection the judgment referred in English to the "appropriation for the defendant's benefit of the plaintiff's name or likeness," the origin of which would appear to be Professor Prosser's description of one form of the right to privacy in the United States as "the unauthorised use of [a person's] name or picture in the defendant's advertising."

An appeal was made to Civil Court No. 2 of the District Court of Madrid, which on 16 July 1985 upheld the decision at first instance, emphasising however that the unauthorised publication in question related not only to pictures of the bullfighter's public appearances but also to "his being brought into the infirmary of the bullring, a place which, due to its characteristics and finality, necessarily confers the nature of privacy on whatever goes on inside."

A further appeal was made to the Supreme Court, which on 28 October 1986 overruled the Court of First Instance and the intermediate District Court. It was the first occasion on which it had pronounced on issues of the kind in question, and its decision therefore must be regarded only as an indication of the likely development rather than a firm statement of the law. So far as invasion of a person's privacy or unauthorised use of a person's name or likeness was concerned, the Supreme Court denied that there had been any breach of the law, agreeing with the appellants' contention that the lower courts had given insufficient weight to two provisions qualifying liability in Organic Law No. 1 of 5 May 1982. In the latter, Article 8, section 1 provides that interference with the rights protected by the law is not to be regarded as illegal if — *inter alia* — it has "a predominating historical, scientific or cultural relevance." And again, Article 8, section 2(a) of the same law provides that the right to one's name or likeness does not apply to a person exercising "some public function or profession having an obvious public projection, or when the likeness is made during a public event or in a place open to public access." In regard to the right of privacy, the Supreme Court drew particular attention to Article 2, section 1 of the 1982 Law, which states that privacy is to be construed "within the limitations set by law and social usage, having regard to the sphere which each person in his activities reserved to himself and to his family." The Supreme Court made use of this section to hold that the time which the bullfighter spent in the bullring's infirmary was not within his sphere of personal privacy, being protected neither by social usage and the nature of his professional activity nor by his own decision.

Incidentally, it may be observed that the very wide power of appreciation of the meaning of privacy which, in the interpretation of the 1982 Law, the Supreme Court gives to the courts has alarmed those in Spain concerned with the freedom to communicate or receive true information under Article 20.4 of the Spanish Constitution of 1978. This freedom, as has been pointed out above, is limited by the right to honour, personal and family privacy and to name and likeness given by Article 18.1 of the Constitution as implemented by Organic Law No. 1 of 5 May 1982.

In the result therefore the plaintiff widow of the bullfighter lost all the damages awarded to her in the lower courts and the injunction against the sale of the video cassette was terminated.

Appeal to the Constitutional Tribunal

Article 18.1 of the Spanish Constitution of 1978 is within a group of articles according rights which, if violated by a decision of a court, can be upheld by an appeal to the Constitutional Tribunal. Accordingly, within the prescribed time limit of 20 days from the challenged decision, the bullfighter's widow began proceedings in the Constitutional Tribunal. Court No. 2 of the Tribunal held by a majority of three to two that Article 18.1 of the Constitution had been violated. Its view was that what occurred to the bullfighter within the infirmary of the bullring belonged to the personal sphere of his life; the infirmary did not offer access to the public and the bullfighter was not "exercising a profession having an obvious public character" when he spoke about his injuries to the doctor and the public crowding into the infirmary. The filming of those scenes was an invasion of the "personal and family privacy" of the bullfighter and of his wife. The ruling of the Supreme Court of 28 October 1986 was therefore declared null and void, and the case was remitted to the Supreme Court to make a new decision recognising the right of the widow of the bullfighter to personal and family privacy.

However, the Constitutional Tribunal held that someone who was only the heir (in the present case, the widow) of a person with a right to his own name or likeness — and not the actual living person himself — could not use the constitutional appeal, as essentially property issues were involved for which ordinary civil procedures were available. This had the rather unfortunate result of enabling the Supreme Court, as will appear below, to reconsider the case remitted to it by the Constitutional Tribunal without regard to any violation of the right to name or likeness and the economic calculations (such as the profit made by the violator) which would be involved.

Reconsideration by the Supreme Court

The same Supreme Court judges (including the presiding judge who had meanwhile retired) who had given judgment on 28 October 1986 were convened to reconsider the case in the light of the decision of the Constitutional Tribunal. On 25 April 1989 they assessed the monetary compensation payable to the bullfighter's widow for the "pain and suffering" caused to her by the distribution in violation of her family privacy of the video cassette at 250,000 pesetas (approximately £1,400). This is in striking contrast to the 20 million pesetas (approximately £112,500) awarded to her by the Court of First Instance.

NOTES AND QUESTIONS

1. Are you surprised that the first instance court of Madrid cited as support the doctrine of a common law jurisdiction such as the United States (i.e., William L. Prosser's torts hornbook in its 1955 edition)? In fact, Spanish legal scholars have been actively writing about American law in such areas as freedom of expression and privacy. *See, e.g.*, Pablo Salvador Coderch, El Mercado de las Ideas (1990).

2. In France this case would have ended with the *Cour de cassation.* Have the Spanish added another level of appeal to review the decisions of ordinary courts by permitting access to the Constitutional Court? Will this promote uniformity in the interpretation of law or only generate jurisdictional conflicts with the Supreme Court?

3. What was the result of the Constitutional Court's decision? Note that the *Tribunal Constitucional* does not have jurisdiction to express a view on the private law issue of the transferability to an heir of a quasi-proprietorial right to one's own image (name and likeness) upon one's death. Why was the first instance court's 20 million peseta award to Isabel Pantoja not simply reinstated?

4. We saw in *Huston* that after the French *Cour de cassation* nullified the Paris *Cour d'appel* decision, it remanded the case to the Versailles Court of Appeal. Is it likely that this latter court will have less of a "personal stake" in the final outcome compared to the Paris court? Was this a problem with allowing the Spanish *Tribunal Supremo* (Supreme Court) to receive Pantoja for a second decision?

5. THE MEXICAN "CASSATION" *AMPARO*

HECTOR FIX ZAMUDIO, A BRIEF INTRODUCTION TO THE MEXICAN WRIT OF *AMPARO*, 9 California Western International Law Journal 306, 316, 323-25 (1979)

The Mexican *amparo* is a combination of procedural instruments or remedies, each with a specific protective function. It can be described as having five diverse functions: (1) protection of individual guarantees; (2) testing allegedly unconstitutional laws; (3) contesting judicial decisions; (4) petitioning against official administrative acts and resolutions; and (5) protection of the social rights of farmers subject to the agrarian reform laws....

The judicial or "cassation" *amparo* was imposed during the past century for social and political reasons. It is of major importance because in practice it accounts for more than eighty percent of *amparo* cases before the federal courts. The judicial *amparo* bears direct similarities to the French remedy of cassation (*casación*) in that it allows review and annulment of appellate decisions from all jurisdictions in the country that are inconsistent with the Constitution. The judicial *amparo* has its constitutional foundation in article 14 and may be brought against judicial and quasi-judicial judgments in criminal, civil — including all mercantile controversies — administrative, and labor cases. This form of the *amparo* is tried in original jurisdiction and single instance either with the appropriate chamber of the Supreme Court or with the collegiate tribunals, depending on some rather complex jurisdictional rules outlined in the 1967 reforms of the Law of *Amparo*. In general, however, the Supreme Court reviews only those cases considered to be of major social, economic, and political importance, with the remainder of cases reviewed by the collegiate courts.

The judicial *amparo*, following classic rules of cassation, may be directed against two classes of alleged violations: (1) those committed during the course of the trial which deprive the complainant of legally available defenses — procedural errors (*error en procedando*); and (2) substantive flaws in the judgments themselves (*error en judicando*). Procedural errors can be appealed only if the deprivation affects the final decision of the court (*sentencia definitiva*). Exceptions to this last requirement are few; for example, when judicial error, either at trial or in an ordinary appeal, is so highly prejudicial as to cause irreparable injury to the complainant or to an absent third party similarly affected. In this case, the *amparo* suit is tried in the first instance in the federal district court, from which an adverse ruling may be appealed in the second instance to the collegiate tribunals....

Classic rules of cassation also provide that *amparo* review of lower court decisions must be strictly limited to reviewing questions of law; that is, whether the trial court correctly applied the applicable law. Thus, in a judicial *amparo* proceeding, *de novo* review is disallowed.

Finally, the influence of liberal individualism in the 19th century persists in the *amparo* principle of "strict law" (*amparo de estricto derecho*) applicable to judgments of the civil courts. The Law of *Amparo* provides that the *amparo* court must confine its opinion to questions raised in the petition or brief; the court may not revise or amplify any point of law. It is the author's view that the principle of "strict law" constitutes an unacceptable formalism in modern jurisprudence.

NOTES AND QUESTIONS

1. Does the Mexican Supreme Court review of judicial decisions seem to owe more to European examples or to the United States example?

2. For information on judicial appeals, see Wallace R. Baker, *French Judgments Subject to Immediate Appeal*, 47 Law & Contemp. Probs. 17 (No. 3, Summer 1984); Herbert Bernstein, *The Finality of a Judgment as a Requirement for Civil Appeals in Germany, ibid.* 35; Richard B. Cappalli, *Comparative South American Civil Procedure: A Chilean Perspective,* 21 U. Miami Inter-Am. L. Rev. 239, 278-92 (1989-1990); Keith S. Rosenn, *Civil Procedure in Brazil,* 34 Am. J. Comp. L. 487, 504-11 (1986).

3. Chapter 10, Section A (civil procedure) and Section B (criminal procedure) discuss various aspects of the judicial review of court decisions, especially review in second instance.

B. JUDICIAL REVIEW OF EXECUTIVE AND ADMINISTRATIVE ACTS

1. ADMINISTRATIVE COURTS

JOHN HENRY MERRYMAN, THE CIVIL LAW TRADITION: AN INTRODUCTION TO THE LEGAL SYSTEMS OF WESTERN EUROPE AND LATIN AMERICA 87-88 (2d ed. 1985)

The notion that the legislature was to be the supreme source of law meant that there could be no inherent administrative power. The administration was to function only to the extent and within the limits of the authority granted it by the lawmaker. Accordingly, every administrative act was potentially subject to the test of legality, and some body other than the judiciary — which was excluded by the doctrine of separation of powers — was needed to rule on the legality of administrative action. In France this need was met by the Council of State, which began as a body of advisers to the King and gradually became the central organ of governmental administration. To its administrative functions was added that of hearing and deciding complaints concerning the legality of administrative action, and the section of the Council of State that regularly exercised this power soon developed judicial characteristics. It has its own procedure and its own catalogue of remedies, and it has built, on a slender statutory base, an immense body of case law that is regularly published and used by lawyers. The landmark decisions (*les grands arrêts*) of the Council of State are a principal source of French administrative law. A number of other nations, including Belgium and Italy, have followed the French model and allocated similar administrative jurisdiction to their own councils of state. In other nations, like Germany and Austria, administrative courts, as such, have been created.

The theory is that the ordinary and administrative jurisdictions are separate and exclusive, so that a case falls into one or the other, but never both. Occasionally, however, a doubtful case arises; if such a case is brought before the administrative court, for example, the defendant argues that it properly belongs in the ordinary jurisdiction. Despite the best efforts of scholars and legislators, no simple, infallible test has yet been devised, and accordingly the matter is settled by litigation. Three examples of the procedure for deciding this question in Europe are instructive. In Italy, the Supreme Court of Cassation is the ultimate authority on conflicts of jurisdiction between the ordinary and the administrative courts. In France the question is finally settled by a special court, called the Conflicts Tribunal. In Germany the court in which the action is brought decides whether or not it has jurisdiction. Its decision can be appealed within its jurisdiction, but it is not subject to further review.

2. THE FRENCH COUNCIL OF STATE AND CONFLICTS OF JURISDICTION

L. NEVILLE BROWN & J.F. GARNER, FRENCH ADMINISTRATIVE LAW 172-75 (3d ed. 1983)

The French administrative courts, with the Conseil d'Etat at their head, would claim to have been successful in subjecting the administration to the Rule of Law. This success may be attributed to a combination of the following factors:

(i) the composition and functions of the Conseil d'Etat itself;
(ii) the flexibility of its case-law;
(iii) the simplicity of the remedies available before the administrative courts;
(iv) the special procedure evolved by those courts; and
(v) the character of the substantive law which they apply.

(i) … [T]he "mixed" composition and multiple functions of the Conseil d'Etat ensure a proper awareness of the needs of public administration when it sits as the supreme administrative court; and from this position of eminence it can inculcate a like awareness in the inferior jurisdictions for which it serves as the ultimate court of appeal or cassation.

Confidence in the administrative courts is shared by administration and public alike; the members of the Conseil d'Etat are not only judges but they are also fully trained in the expertise of administration, and there is considerable movement between posts inside and outside the Palais-Royal. In its relations with the public the Conseil d'Etat commands surprisingly full press reporting of its activities and enjoys a general respect comparable with that shown to the High Court Bench in England.

This confidence in the administrative expertise of the Conseil d'Etat and (more recently) of the Tribunaux Administratifs has prevented the proliferation of … administrative tribunals: as new justiciable issues arise in the field of administration they pass quite naturally within the competence of the general administrative courts ….

(ii) In fashioning the principles of judicial review of administrative action the Conseil d'Etat has adopted a case-law technique which, whilst properly respectful of previous decisions, is not slavishly bound by them. Untrammelled by a strict doctrine of *stare decisis* or the strait jacket of a code, the Conseil d'Etat has proved itself agile in holding the scales even between, on the one hand, the shifting needs of public administration in an era of rapid economic and social change and, on the other, the rights of the individual in a free society. Nevertheless, the administrative judges have remained true to the cartesian tradition of French thought by seeking always a certain logic and coherence in their decisions. At the same time, the desire to systematise the *droit administratif* has had to be reconciled with the need for it to keep pace with events, including the ever-changing pattern of legislation itself….

(iii) Charged as they are with a general competence to review all administrative acts, the French administrative courts have utilised for this purpose three, and only three, simple forms of action, namely the *recours pour excès de*

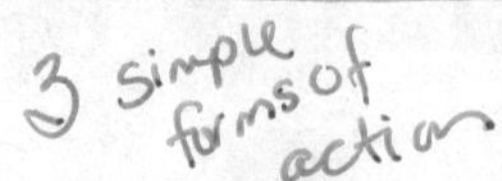

pouvoir and the *recours en cassation* in matters of legality, and the *recours de pleine juridiction* where damages or fuller relief are sought....

Moreover, in the *recours de pleine juridiction* the actual relief which the French administrative judge can give includes not only that available in England under the prerogative orders, the declaration and the common law action for damages, but stretches, for example in *recours électoral*, to quashing the invalid election, recalculating the total of votes and declaring the rightful candidate elected; or in the case of an administrative contract the court may review the whole financial relationship of the parties and, after a detailed survey of the accounts between them, may implement any contractual penalty or award damages, or may even make provision for the unexpected under the doctrine of *imprévision*.

Lastly, the appellate jurisdiction of the Conseil d'Etat over the Tribunaux Administratifs, together with the *recours en cassation*, is seen by the French as a guarantee that the law will be uniformly applied throughout the entire system of administrative courts, whether of general or special jurisdiction....

(iv) The administrative courts have evolved their own procedure.... Like the forms of action mentioned above, the procedure too is simple. It is also highly effective, for in the *instruction* of the *rapporteur* and the conclusions of the Commissaire du gouvernement the plaintiff has the aid both of an investigation into the facts and a survey of the law ....

(v) Most important of all, the substantive law which the Conseil d'Etat has fashioned over nearly two centuries of its existence has proved admirably adapted for its grand object — no less than the judicial control and review of all administrative action....

Thus, in proceedings for *excès de pouvoir*, as early as the middle of the nineteenth century the concept of *détournement de pouvoir* emerged as an inspired generalisation (still lacking in English law) whereby the administrative judge might penetrate beyond the outward semblance of legality to examine the motives of the administrator. More recently, *violation de la loi* has been perfected to permit review not simply of mistakes of law but also of fact; and since 1944 the doctrine of *les principes généraux du droit* has been evolved with great boldness by the Conseil as a kind of unwritten code of administrative right-conduct, a boldness all the more remarkable within a legal system commonly regarded as based upon written law.

By these means the administrative judge has been able to demarcate the boundary between what is legality and what is policy, but without trespassing upon the latter....

Again, in the development of the principle of administrative liability, as long ago as 1873 the [Council] set the stage for the emergence of a separate administrative law of obligations. [W]e described such striking illustrations as the delictual principle of liability for risk and the contractual doctrines of *imprévision* and *fait du prince*. Here the *droit administratif* has acted, albeit not designedly, as a pace-setter for the *droit civil* in the evolution of tort and contract, with the Cour de Cassation usually trailing a few laps behind the Conseil d'Etat.

The French find a justification for the distinct character of their *droit administratif* in its capacity to adapt the principles of administrative legality and administrative liability to the differing needs of the various public services, a capacity which could be found only in judges who are also trained administrators.

Yet the gap between *droit administratif* and *droit civil* must not be exaggerated. We have seen that since 1958 all litigation concerning accidents with motor vehicles has been entrusted to the exclusive jurisdiction of the ordinary courts, and this could hardly have been done if broadly similar principles of liability had not previously been applied to such accidents in both sets of courts. The tendency of the two bodies of tort law to move closer together is also evident in the more liberal approach which the Conseil d'Etat has recently adopted in allowing damages for mental anguish. In contract, however, the distinct character of the *droit administratif* is likely to remain ....

In this as in other respects the systematic and cohesive quality of the law constructed by the Conseil d'Etat is in sharp contrast with the piecemeal and disconnected character of the corresponding English law. This difference stems from the fact that the former is a special branch of French law, designed for its specific function by judges expert in both law and administration; whereas the latter has been a makeshift improvisation by the English Bench, often strangers to the administrative process and unsympathetic to its needs, and utilising and adapting as best they could such bits and pieces of the ordinary law as lay to hand and seemed most apt for the purpose. Small wonder that the French creation has an *elegantia iuris*, the study of which can yield much intellectual satisfaction.

NOTE ON THE FRENCH CONFLICTS TRIBUNAL

An inevitable consequence of establishing a separate system of administrative courts is that jurisdictional disputes will arise between the ordinary courts and the administrative courts. The French settled on the *Tribunal des conflits* to serve this function; it hears between 30 and 70 cases annually. *See* Chapter 6, Section A.1. The costs of resolving these disputes — delay and expense — should be balanced against the benefits described in the Brown and Garner excerpt.

In the case that follows, the French government was potentially liable for 216 million francs in a bankruptcy proceeding pending in a *tribunal de commerce,* a specialized court within the ordinary judiciary. *See* Note on the Structure of the French Court System, Chapter 6, Section A.1. An officer of the government, the *préfet,* can stop ordinary courts from acting in a case if it is necessary to protect the administration from encroachment by these courts, which are only subject to review by the Court of Cassation. The procedure, which implements the spirit of the *séparation des pouvoirs* as expressed in article 13 of the Law of 16-24 Aug. 1790, begins with a *déclinatoire de compétence.* The prefect presents the déclinatoire to the ordinary court. If the court rejects it, and the prefect does not agree, he takes the case to the Conflicts Tribunal. If the court accepts the déclinatoire and dismisses the case, that is the end of the matter subject to appeal to a higher court. The plaintiff must then file suit in the appropriate administrative court.

PREFECT OF LOIRE v. COMMERCE TRIBUNAL OF SAINT-ETIENNE

Conflicts Tribunal of France
Decision of 23 January 1989
1989 D.S. Jur. 367

[The Conflicts Tribunal's opinion is preceded by a longer opinion written by the commissaire du Gouvernement, Madame Flipo, who discusses the facts and legal issues in detail. This statement of the facts is taken from her opinion.

A lawsuit filed on 31 May 1977 put Manufrance Co. into temporary receivership, which resulted in judicial supervision on 7 Feb. 1979. The management took over the assets of New Manufrance Co., which itself declared bankruptcy on 22 Oct. 1980. Next the court on 22 June 1981 authorized management of the company under an employees production and distribution cooperative (SCOPD). This company lost the following sums: 44 million francs (1982), F 91 million (1983), and F 64 million (1984). On 4 Apr. 1985 the Saint-Etienne commerce tribunal accepted SCOPD Manufrance's petition of bankruptcy, which now had debts of F 216 million. Banks had uncollected loans of F 71 million and the French government had loaned F 206 million.

The commerce tribunal found that in financing SCOPD Manufrance, three protocols were involved. First, a "plan of development," dated 15 Mar. 1982, not signed by the government, with periodic reports due to the Ministry of Economy and Finance, provided a public subsidy of F 80 million. Second, a "plan of recovery," also unsigned, dated 4 Aug. 1983, provided a public subsidy of F 106 million and called for periodic meetings with and reports to public authorities. Third, in November 1984 the government directly intervened with a protocol signed by the Minister of Industrial Redeployment and Foreign Commerce. It provided F 20 million and put the goal of finding a partner for the enterprise under the ministry's explicit control. The tribunal determined that the government, directly and through its newly nationalized banks, acted as a company director in fact.

One of the interesting legal issues discussed by Mme. Flipo was whether the correct theory of the bankruptcy trustee's suit against the government was an action in contract or one in quasi-delict (the latter under Civil Code art. 1382). The Conflicts Tribunal's opinion as reported in *Recueil Dalloz Sirey* was followed by a note discussing the case written by two law professors, Paul Amselek and Fernand Derrida.

Article 99, Law of 13 July 1967, provides: "At the time of judicial accounting where the good faith liquidation of goods reveals there are insufficient assets, the tribunal can decide, at the trustee's or its own request, that the company debts will be paid, in whole or in part, with or without joint responsibility, by all the company directors, in law or in fact, apparent or secret, remunerated or not, or by certain of the directors."]

The Judicial Decision (Arrêt)

Considering that a letter from the Minister of Justice, registered with the Conflicts Tribunal secretary on 11 Oct. 1988, transmits a report by the procurator general of the Lyon court of appeal from the bankruptcy proceeding in which the trustee of the employees production and distribution cooperative (SCOPD) Manufrance sued the French Government, together with the report by the procurator that states that the Loire prefect has declined (*décliné*) the commerce tribunal's jurisdiction for the suit filed by the trustee on 29 Sept. 1987;

Considering the Loire prefect's decision of conflict dated 29 July 1988, together with the Saint-Etienne commerce tribunal's decision of 10 Aug. 1988 staying its proceedings while the Conflicts Tribunal hears the case;

Considering that the action taken in paying debts by the trustee, based on the provisions of art. 99, Law of 13 July 1967, against the government, which was so involved as a company director in fact, it assumed the behavior of a public power that went beyond the juridical limits of private law; that if the provisions of art. 99 of said Law gave jurisdiction to the judicial tribunals to decide — at the time of the judicial accounting where the good faith liquidation of goods revealed there were insufficient assets — the company debts, in whole or in part, would be paid by all the company directors, including directors in fact; the question of the government's knowledge, agreeing to aid an enterprise in difficulty, if it acted in fact as its director, is not unconnected with the determination that jurisdiction, if found to attach, is necessarily tied to determining if the government's responsibility was engaged by the intervention of the public authority at the time it gave assistance to the enterprise; that it follows that the provisions of art. 99, Law of 13 July 1967, do not permit the Saint-Etienne commerce tribunal — hearing the trustee's action in the SCOPD Manufrance bankruptcy, involving various parties, in which the government was condemned jointly to indemnify the mass of creditors — to declare itself competent to judge this action directed against the government, which was not found to be a director in law of the company; that the government's responsibility *vis-à-vis* said creditors could not find its source in a contract or quasi-contract in the absence of a tie between the government and said creditors; there is instead, consequently, the confirmation of the decision of conflict, under the regular conditions in regard to the demands of the Ordinance of 1 June 1828;

Art. 1: The Loire prefect's decision of conflict on 29 July 1988 is confirmed;

Art. 2: The proceeding filed by the bankruptcy trustee for SCOPD Manufrance against the government in the Saint-Etienne commerce tribunal and that tribunal's decision dated 20 July 1988 are declared null.

NOTES AND QUESTIONS

1. What are the beneficial features of the French network of separate courts for the review of the legality and constitutionality of executive action?

2. In *Prefect of Loire* was the Government either a director in law or a director in fact of SCOPD Manufrance? Was the Government's relationship with SCOPD that harmed its creditors more one in contract or in tort? What difference might a finding on the legal issues have for allocating this case to the ordinary courts versus the administrative courts? Why do you think the Government wanted this suit heard before an administrative court?

3. Statutes in France, once promulgated, cannot be reviewed for constitutionality. They must be applied by the ordinary courts even if incompatible with a principle in the Constitution. *Ordonnances* and regulations, however, can always be tested for conformity to the Constitution and to what is known as "general principles of law," which the Council of State has developed over the past 150 years. This jurisdiction was greatly expanded under the 1958 Constitution and was confirmed by the Council of State in its landmark decision, *Syndicat Général des Ingénieurs-Conseils* (26 June 1959), 1959 D. Jur. 541, 1959 S. Jur. 202. *See* Mauro Cappelletti & William Cohen, Comparative Constitutional Law: Cases and Materials 29-45 (1979). *See generally* L. Neville Brown & John S. Bell, French Administrative Law (1993).

3. COMPLEX ADMINISTRATIVE LAW ADJUDICATION IN GERMANY: THE WYHL ATOMIC ENERGY PLANT CASE

PETER ARENS, RECENT TRENDS IN GERMAN JURISDICTION: THE TRANSFER OF POLITICAL AND ADMINISTRATIVE DUTIES TO THE COURTS, in THE ROLE OF COURTS IN SOCIETY 97, 111-14, 117-22 (Shimon Shetreet ed. 1988)

Now we are concerned with ... courts performing tasks which originally belonged to the administration. In other words, we are dealing with the delimitation of judicial and administrative authority. Today, in the Federal Republic of Germany, large scale technical projects such as airports and atomic energy plants can be frozen, sometimes for up to ten years, due to court proceedings initiated by persons more or less directly affected. The licensing procedure for such projects, originally an administrative function, is being repeated by the courts, which sometimes hear fifty or more experts on the subject and claim to be able to decide the most difficult technical questions. In fact, the courts have made the standards stricter than those set by the experts, and do not follow their opinions. Thus the tendency evolved to transfer the decision of the administration to the courts. Moreover, the long duration of court proceedings have made the original project I mentioned useless. In view of this, the statement has been made that "permits for energy plants require judicial confirmation." This is not because of a legal provision, but due to empirical development....

[In] the Federal Republic of Germany there exist next to the ordinary courts, special administrative courts, having independent judges that are in all respects on an equal footing with civil and criminal judges. They have existed in this form since the end of the Second World War. Prior to this a very rudimentary system of administrative courts existed. The purpose of the system of administrative courts was differently interpreted in Prussia than in South Germany. In Prussia the purpose was to secure the objective legality of the administration, and in South Germany it was the protection of the individual rights of the citizens. After 1945 there was a dispute in jurisprudence concerning the functions of the newly-created jurisdiction of the administrative courts. The South German opinion prevailed. The purpose of the jurisdiction of the administrative courts was thus seen to be giving the individual the possibility of asserting his rights vis-à-vis the administration. Even though this indirectly serves also the legality of the administration, the main purpose decisively shaped the regulations governing administrative courts. The claims provided for always required some interference with individual rights. Thus claims for rescission or enforcement of an administrative decision may only be lodged if the petitioner claims that the administrative decision or its rejection of forbearance has infringed his rights (Section 42, Rules of the Administrative Courts). The petitioner may, if this is at issue, demand issuance or revocation of the administrative decision. (Besides these actions there also exist actions for performance and declaratory actions, Sections 43, 113, Rules of the Administrative Courts). In comparison, the action is inadmissible if it is not the petitioner's rights which are infringed by the administrative decision, its rejection or lack of decision, but instead the rights of a third party. An action based on a civil interest in maintaining the legal system would, therefore, be inadmissible....

The application of these principles often presents difficulties. This holds true for the question of how to distinguish rights from pure interests, as well as the question of when an administrative act exists. Both questions also play an important role for actions against large scale technical projects. Concerning the right of action, in other words the infringement of rights, the difference between a normal administrative decision as for instance an individual order addressed to the plaintiff to demolish his house due to its dilapidated condition, and the permit for a large scale project, such as an airport or an atomic energy plant, is obvious; the permit for such a large scale project is not directed against the individual citizen. Only the effect from such installations, such as the emissions from normal use, in addition to injury to life, health and property due to an emergency, can cause infringement of the rights to a third party and establish the right of action for violation of rights. From this, difficult problems of delimitation arise: does it depend upon the place of residence of the petitioner or upon the place where he exercises his profession? What distance is relevant — 10, 20, 50 or 100 km? The only certainty is that the neighbour may have injured his civil rights to life and health (Art. 2 sec. 2, Basic Law) and to property (Art. 14, Basic Law) and thus has a right of action. The greater the distance, the higher the requirement for the petitioner to demonstrate in detail how his rights have been violated. Thus, the Federal Administrative Court has dismissed the action of a petitioner living 25 km from an energy plant on the grounds that he had failed to demonstrate the infringement of his rights....

It is also generally acknowledged that, according to German law, the problem of the right of action cannot be solved by recognition of a representative claim ("Verbandsklage"), such as by regarding associations of citizens having a right to claim. For the "Verbandsklage" it has been stated this is necessary since the existing provisions on environmental protection were not sufficiently enforced by the authorities. Moreover, it was desirable to have the citizen participate more in the governmental making of decisions. Finally, a representative claim could summarize the objections often made by numerous individual persons. It can be left undecided here whether these arguments are generally or partially valid. The majority opinion keeps to the wording of the law (Sections 42 sec. 2, 113 sec. 1, Rules of the Administrative Courts), which requires an infringement of the rights of the subject which do not pertain to a group. . . .

In Germany, large scale projects begin with a decision of principle. The construction then occurs under a partial construction permit. Commencement of building occurs only upon the issuing of an operating licence. Fall-out emissions can only occur when the building becomes operational. If persons affected are to claim against the operating permit such a claim would come too late. The construction of an airport or an atomic energy plant would have produced a fait accompli, decisively diminishing the chance of success of any such actions. The courts, particularly the Federal Administrative Court, have therefore held, in licencing procedures in the field of atomic energy law, that even partial construction permits can infringe upon the rights of third parties and are thus contestable by rescissory action. Every permit for partial construction contains a preliminary positive overall verdict on the undertaking and must therefore take into account all the fall-out dangers from the operating of the installation. Moreover, permits for partial construction determine the location of the installation. Essential in this connection is the role of temporary judicial relief. In accordance with Section 80, Rules of Administrative Courts, rescissory action does have the power to suspend. However, the administrative agency may order immediate execution of the contested administrative decision.

First of all I shall give you a very typical example of the execution of safety rules by a court in reviewing the authorization of the building of an atomic energy plant. In 1977 the administrative court of Freiburg had to decide on a challenge of the first partial permit, issued on January 22nd 1975, for the erection of an atomic energy plant near Wyhl in the Kaiserstuhl.[82]

The petitioners lived in a region up to 7 km from the projected plant. In their action they claimed that the project would have a negative influence on the climate, environment and the health of the people. The administrative court assumed that a claim of violation of law was present since it was obviously not an impossible assumption. According to the Atomic Energy Act a permit in atomic energy law can only be issued if, due to the state of science and technology the necessary precautions against damages resulting from the installation have been undertaken (Section 7, sec. 2, number 3, Atomic Energy Act). If this has not occurred, it would be a violation of the law. According to the opinion of the court these requirements were not met by the authorized plan of the administrative board, because it had not provided protection against explosion out of steel concrete for the pressurized nuclear water reactor. The court admitted that an accident resulting from the reactor pressure-container was almost inconceivable. But due to the devastating consequences of such an accident, very far-reaching protection was necessary, even if the danger was very small. Economic considerations were not to play a role here. The court assumed that from the twin purposes of the atomic energy law, protection of life and material goods against the dangers of atomic energy and promotion of peaceful utilization of atomic energy, the former named purpose had preference.

[82] NJW 1977, 1645.

In order to be able to make a decision the court heard 53 experts. Moreover it was presented with 50 mostly quite extensive expert reports from the fields of safety technology, radioecology, hydrology, meteorology and seismology amongst others.

I have at this point to insert a remark on the ruling of expert evidence in German procedural law. In Germany the expert is not a witness. He is appointed by the court and considered its assistant.

He generally makes a written expert report and then explains it in an oral court hearing. The parties can reject him for the same reasons as they can reject a judge (Section 406, Code of Civil Procedure). The main problem for the relationship between court and expert for all procedural courts in Germany is the principle of free judicial evaluation of the evidence (Section 286, Code of Civil Procedure). This signifies that the judge has to evaluate freely the expert report just as any other form of evidence. He has to re-examine its logic and scientific argument. The method and result of this re-examination have to be stated in the grounds of the judgment, and are open to reviewable appeal. In case the court does not want to adhere to the expertise it has to make clear that its own knowledge suffices to render a decision which dissents from an expert's opinion.

The obvious consequences of this need to file supporting arguments of error by the courts is that according to most recent investigations, courts have in 95% of [their] cases complied either completely or in a major part with the expertise given ....

Let the number of experts ... in the Wyhl case serve as a reminder. Due to this flood of expertise, technical and scientific details, as well as conflicting experts' opinions, it must have been very difficult for the court to meet the requirements for evidence, such as determining the trustworthiness of the individual experts and evaluating the degree of scientific acceptance of their opinions. The court was able to base its actual decision on the necessity for a steel concrete protection against the reactor, only insofar as the statements of the experts had described the size of the disaster if the reactor pressure container blew up. The decision for protection against blowing up was therefore made by the court itself. The question here is whether the decision has any longer anything to do with consideration of evidence or is, much more than that, a political decision which does not belong to the functions of courts....

The decision of the administrative court of Freiburg was not of lasting duration, being reversed by the court of second instance.[90] The court of appeal assumed that protection against explosion believed necessary by the administrative court was unnecessary. The pressure container of the reactor of the atomic energy plant was so safe that no measures had to be undertaken against its failure. Absolute safety does not exist anyway since any safety measure can moreover fail. In the appeal on points of law by the petitioner, the Federal Administrative Court had finally to decide on the legality of the contested partial authorization by a judgment rendered on December 19th 1985, in other words ten years after it had been first issued.

---

[90] Judgment of the Administrative Appeals Court Mannheim of March 30th 1982. The judgment has not been published completely: the original encompasses not less than 548 pages.

Concerning the question of protection against explosion ... the Federal Administrative Court assumed that the relevant provision (Section 7, sec. 2, number 3, Atomic Energy Act) required precautions against damage. The requisite assessment has to accept the state of science and technology. The responsibility for investigation and evaluation of risks is incumbent upon the executive power, which shall take scientific counsel into account. In this sense the authorization board had also understood its task.

The Atomic Energy Act appoints the executive power with the task to consider the most recent findings in the field of radioactive protection and reactor safety, and to determine measures for precautions according to the present state of science and technology. It is not the task of the administrative courts to supplement, by way of further legal control, the evaluation of the executive power by its own appraisal and evaluation of risks. The judicial procedure is not a second procedure for licensing....

From this point of view the Federal Administrative Court has only to answer the question of whether the authorization board was able, due to the precautionary measures undertaken, to consider the risk of explosion so small that it did not have [to] be taken into account. The Federal Administrative Court believed it sufficient in this case that the board had made clear why it did not have any fear that the reactor pressure container might explode without prior notice. The authorization board had thus decided in proper form ... the question of safety. Thus, it was inadmissible for the administrative court of Freiburg to replace the evaluation of the authorization board with its own evaluation.

This decision of the Federal Administrative Court implies for the future a restriction of the power of review of the administrative courts as against authorization orders of administrative boards on the installation of atomic energy plants.... The readiness of the people to accept the installation of large scale projects will surely not be influenced by this. Problems will exist, therefore, also in the future. Whether they will be decided in less time than previously is doubtful. Also, the question of whether the authorization board has acted legally in issuing a permit can be hotly disputed. The delay which results from the implementation of large scale projects is unavoidable if one gives the individual every right of legal objection. The loss of efficiency is the result [and] is the price for the enlargement of legal protection for the individual. The knowledge of the probability of proceedings also increases the care of the administrative boards as they work. The primacy of legal protection should therefore be maintained despite all misgivings.

NOTES AND QUESTIONS

1. What view does the Federal Administrative Court take on the issues of standing and class action suits (*Verbandsklage*)? How does this compare to the U.S. Supreme Court's attitude toward federal court litigation of environmental suits (standing) or consumer class action cases?

2. The *Wyhl* case, as it worked its way up the administrative court hierarchy, illustrates divergent views about the appropriate degree of judicial deference to administrative decisionmaking. Did the Freiburg administrative court or the Federal Administrative Court have the better view? Is it accurate to call the Freiburg court's ruling a "political decision"?

How does the use of experts in litigation differ in Germany and the United States?

3. For further discussion of German administrative courts, see Dieter Lorenz, *The Constitutional Supervision of the Administrative Agencies in the Federal Republic of Germany,* 53 S. Cal. L. Rev. 543, 570-82 (1980).

4. THE MEXICAN *AMPARO*

HECTOR FIX ZAMUDIO, A BRIEF INTRODUCTION TO THE MEXICAN WRIT OF *AMPARO*, 9 California Western International Law Journal 306, 316-18, 325-27 (1979)

Protection of Individual Liberties

As a device to protect individual rights, the *amparo* performs functions similar to the English writ of *habeas corpus* as construed by statute and decisional law in the United States. For this reason the Mexican *amparo* differs from the *amparo* in other Latin American countries that have also adopted the *amparo* as a means of protecting individual freedoms.

Under the current Law of *Amparo*, any act which threatens deprivation of life, personal liberty, deportations, or banishment, as well as any official actions prohibited by article 22 of the federal Constitution,[44] may be suspended by way of the indirect *amparo*. The *amparo* petition is filed in the district court in first instance by the injured party, or in proxy by an individual in the name of any petitioner unable to file the petition personally, even though the petitioner's representative may be a juvenile or spouse. In such cases, the court is vested with the authority to investigate and direct the process of the petition, including any means necessary to respond to the proxy petition. This process may result in a decision to "suspend the act complained of" (*suspensión del acto reclamado*). If the petitioner or his representative has been threatened with loss of liberty, he must expressly solicit the court [about] such a danger. Initiation of the *amparo* proceeding is not subject to a specific time limit and may be initiated by the petitioner at any hour of the day or night.

The *amparo* petition may be brought orally (*comparecencia*) in urgent cases or even by telegram so long as the latter is verified by the petitioner within three days of its transmission. Moreover, the petition may be filed not only with the nearest federal district court — which is usually located in the state capital — but also with any local tribunal; absent both of these judicial authorities, the *amparo* petition may be delivered to any functionary of the local

[44] These rights protect against:

> Punishment by mutilation and infamy, branding, flogging, beating with sticks, torture of any kind, excessive fines, confiscation of property and any other unusual or extreme penalties. . . .
>
> Attachment proceedings covering the whole or part of the property of a person made under judicial authority to cover payment of civil liability arising out of the commission of an offense or for the payment of taxes or fines.

Mex. Const. art. 22.

or federal court. State judges are thus empowered to suspend acts threatening the freedom or physical well-being of the petitioner. At the earliest opportunity, the state judge must transmit the case to the appropriate federal court....

Administrative Amparo

Because there is no uniform system in Mexican law for challenging administrative actions and decisions, the position of those injured by administrative abuse is uncertain. Some hold that the injured party can find relief before an administrative tribunal, while others perceive his only recourse as being before the same administrative authority. In any case, the *amparo* is always available as a final remedy. It may be used to test administrative actions of both state and federal officials. This additional dimension of the *amparo* was inspired by the lack of an administrative tribunal with general jurisdiction, with the single exception of the Administrative Tribunal for the Federal District created in 1971. Thus, the *amparo* has assumed the role of an administrative review proceeding.

Judicial review of administrative acts in Mexican law has passed through various stages. The first — the long period from Independence to 1936 — developed from the influence of Spanish colonial traditions as well as from the public law of the United States. It mandated a system of questioning administrative acts and decisions before both federal and state courts. However, since 1936, elements of the French system have been introduced with the establishment of the Federal Fiscal Tribunal (*Tribunal Fiscal de la Federación*) which was created in the image of the French *Conseil d'Etat* (Council of State). The Fiscal Tribunal assumed review of financial decisions made by the federal bureaucracy. Its limited competency over strictly fiscal matters gradually expanded to the point where, with the Organic Law of 1967, it now reviews a much broader subject matter and possesses complete autonomy in rendering decisions. Thus, it must be considered as an agency of administrative justice much closer to the German system than to the French. In addition to the Fiscal Tribunal, the Administrative Court of the Federal District (1971), as well as some local tribunals fashioned after the Fiscal Tribunal, such as those in the states of Mexico, Veracruz, and Sinoloa, exist for airing complaints of administrative acts. *Amparo* review of decisions from these tribunals is similar to the procedures for the judicial, or "cassation," *amparo*; that is, it is tried in the first instance before the Supreme Court or collegiate tribunals, depending on the amount in controversy. In those instances where bureaucratic decisions are not reviewable by an administrative tribunal, the *amparo* will lie only after the complainant has exhausted ordinary administrative remedies. In the latter case, *amparo* is tried in the first instance in the district court with the opportunity to seek review of adverse judgments in either the Supreme Court or the collegiate tribunals, depending on the amount in controversy. In both direct and indirect *amparo* proceedings, Supreme Court jurisdiction extends to all cases in excess of $20,000 (U.S.). If the amount in controversy is indeterminable, or the issue is considered to be "of national importance," the Supreme Court may exercise jurisdiction. In this respect the

1968 legislative reforms which introduced this discretionary criterion followed the model of the writ of *certiorari* in the United States Supreme Court. Current opinion favors extending this discretionary power to other than administrative matters.

The Agrarian Amparo

The ... final function of the Mexican writ of *amparo* was authorized by the *amparo* law reform of February 5, 1963 and provides special protection to farmers subject to the agrarian reform laws. Culminating in the 1976 revision of the Law of *Amparo*, all protective provisions relative to the "agrarian *amparo*" were condensed into one section of the Law of *Amparo*.

These changes are based on the division of real property into two major categories in the Mexican legal system: (1) private holdings not exceeding a fixed acreage, with the excess expropriable to the benefit of farmers without land; and (2) social property divided into two subcategories: (i) communal lands of indigenous (Indian) villages stemming from pre-Hispanic claims which were reinstated after a showing of illegal dispossession; and (ii) "*ejidal*," or land granted to farmers previously lacking any landholdings and taken from private owners exceeding the aforementioned limits of farms classified as "small property" *(pequeña propiedad)*.[96] Title to the communal and *ejidal* lands belongs only to those villages and their inhabitants with claims to *usufruct* based on inheritance. Even when their titles are validated, however, the holders cannot sell or rent their lands, and all such holdings are regulated by the 1971 Federal Law of Agrarian Reform.

5. JUDICIAL PROTECTION IN BRAZIL AND COLOMBIA

KEITH S. ROSENN, A COMPARISON OF THE PROTECTION OF INDIVIDUAL RIGHTS IN THE NEW CONSTITUTIONS OF COLOMBIA AND BRAZIL, 23 University of Miami Inter-American Law Review 659, 680-86 (1992)

The drafters of both [the Brazilian Constitution of 1988 and the Colombian Constitution of 1991] determined that existing procedures were inadequate to protect constitutional rights. Therefore, they created or borrowed several intriguing procedural innovations designed to protect constitutional and legal rights....

---

[96] The concept of expropriating private land for the benefit of those not possessing land is based on the Law of Agrarian Reform of January 6, 1915, which has been incorporated into the Mexican Constitution.

> The Nation shall at all times have the right to impose on private property such limitations as the public interest may demand, as well as the right to regulate the utilization of natural resources which are susceptible of appropriation, in order to conserve them and to ensure a more equitable distribution of public wealth. With this view in mind, necessary measures shall be taken to divide up large landed estates.

Mex. Const. art. 27. Both the Agrarian Reform Law and article 27 must be viewed as expressing the fundamental social goal of the 1910 Mexican Revolution.

Habeas Corpus

Habeas corpus is now a constitutionalized remedy in both countries to protect against illegal deprivations of liberty.[110] The Colombian Constitution guarantees the right to bring an action of habeas corpus before any judge at any time if a detainee believes that he has been deprived of liberty illegally. The judge to whom the request for habeas is addressed has 36 hours in which to decide. The Brazilian guarantee of habeas corpus is significantly broader than the Colombian guarantee. Habeas corpus may be brought in Brazil not only when one has been detained, but also when one has been merely threatened with a constraint on his liberty by illegality or abuse of power. If the imprisonment is illegal, the judge must immediately relax the restraint. Moreover, illegality includes unconstitutionality; hence the writ of habeas corpus is frequently used in Brazil to challenge the constitutionality of statutes and executive acts.

The Collective Writ of Security

The Brazilian Constitution expands the writ of security to make it explicitly applicable to illegality or abuse of power committed not only by public authorities, but also by agents of private legal entities exercising public authority. More importantly, the new Constitution creates a collective writ of security to alleviate some of the problems stemming from the limited nature of class actions and the lack of a well-developed doctrine of *stare decisis*, which have generally required each person aggrieved by a particular law or regulation to bring an individual writ of security to obtain relief. Now any political party represented in Congress, or any union, business syndicate or association, legally constituted for more than one year, may bring a collective writ of security to defend the rights of its members or associates.

Habeas Data

The Brazilian Constitution imports from Portugal a new action called *habeas data*, which has also been adopted in the new Colombian Constitution, albeit without calling it by that name. This action allows anyone to discover information the government has about the plaintiff in its data banks and to rectify that data if it is incorrect. The draft of the Colombian Constitution, which used the terminology *habeas data*, contemplated excusing the government from releasing data for national security purposes, but this exception was eliminated by the Constituent Assembly.

The Brazilians adopted *habeas data* as a reaction to the abuses of the military governments that secretly gathered and stored information that was used against citizens without their having the opportunity to contest the accuracy of that information. *Habeas data* is a sensible reaction to the invasions of privacy produced by technological advancement in the area of data processing and storage. A number of *habeas data* actions have already been brought

[110] Habeas corpus has been a constitutional remedy in Brazil since the 1891 Constitution. Braz. Const. (1891) art. 72 § 22. Colombia's present Constitution is the first to make habeas corpus an explicit constitutional guarantee.

successfully in the Brazilian courts. These courts have taken the position that the action will be deemed appropriate only after the administrative authority has refused to act upon a specific request by the interested party.

Amparo or Tutela

Article 86 of the Colombian Constitution creates a *tutela* action to protect fundamental rights. Although denominated an action of *tutela* rather than *amparo*, its characteristics are that of *amparo*: a preferential and summary procedure that may be brought by the affected person or that person's representative that will result in immediate protection of the individual's fundamental constitutional rights when they are violated or threatened by an action or omission of any public authority. Whether a right is specifically enumerated in the constitutional text under Title II, Chapter 1 (Articles 11-41), which is denominated "Fundamental Rights," is not decisive as to whether a right is fundamental for the purposes of protecting it by an action of *tutela*....

The action of *tutela* makes Colombia an unusual hybrid, combining a decentralized form of judicial review with a constitutional court. Countries with constitutional courts generally prohibit any other courts from exercising the power of judicial review. In Colombia, however, an action of *tutela* can be brought in any court, which may then issue an order protecting the right. The judge has only 10 days in which to render a decision, which is to be carried out immediately. If the decision is challenged, its validity may ultimately be determined by the newly created Constitutional Court, which is thereby in a position to revise decisions of not only the intermediate appellate courts, but also those of the Supreme Court and the Council of State, which had hitherto been courts of last resort....

The action of *tutela* has been regulated by Decree 2591 of 1991, which expressly forbids its use to challenge judicial decisions because of erroneous interpretations of the law or to challenge the evidence. It also prohibits its use to challenge interlocutory judicial decisions. The initial decisions interpreting the reach of this statute have attempted to confine it narrowly to prevent the action of *tutela* from being used as a substitute for appeal. The action of *tutela* will not lie against judicial decisions that have become res judicata, against administrative acts, against striking judicial functionaries, or as a substitute for appeal....

Miscellaneous Actions

Article 87 of Colombia's Constitution permits every person to bring an action before the courts to enforce a law or administrative act. Article 88 states that the law shall regulate popular actions for the protection of collective rights and interests relating to public patrimony, space, security and health, administrative morals, the environment, free economic competition and others of similar nature. It also provides for a class action to deal with damages that are suffered by numerous persons, without prejudice to their bringing private actions.

Brazil has long had a popular action allowing any citizen to sue to nullify any act injurious to the public patrimony. The 1988 Constitution expands this popular action to include acts that injure administrative morality, the environment, and historic or cultural patrimony.

Article 89 of the Colombian Constitution permits the legislature to establish other types of actions, appeals, or procedures that may be brought for the protection of individual rights or collective interests when faced with an action or a mission by public authorities. Article 90 imposes liability upon the states for damages resulting from actions or omissions of public authorities. Article 91 imposes liability on a governmental agent that manifestly violates a constitutional precept to the detriment of an individual.

NOTES AND QUESTIONS

1. What is the advantage of the Mexican *amparo* compared to the writ of habeas corpus available in U.S. federal courts? Which methods of review of administrative action do you find noteworthy in Brazil and Colombia? Why does Mexico need a special "agrarian" *amparo*?

2. For an unusual example of judicial review of executive action in a criminal proceeding, see *The Argentine Military Leaders Case, supra* Chapter 6, Section B.8.

3. For further discussion of the Mexican *amparo*, see Richard D. Baker, Judicial Review in Mexico (1971); Carl E. Schwarz, *Rights and Remedies in the Federal District Courts of Mexico and the United States*, 4 Hastings Const. L.Q. 67 (1977); *id., Exceptions to the Exhaustion of Administrative Remedies Under the Mexican Writ of Amparo*, 7 Cal. W. L. Rev. 331 (1971).

6. LIMITS ON JUDICIAL PROTECTION IN JAPAN

JOHN O. HALEY, JAPANESE ADMINISTRATIVE LAW: INTRODUCTION, 19 Law in Japan 1, 4-14 (1986)

Occupation Reforms

The new constitutional order imposed on Japan under the Allied Occupation dismantled the principal institutional features of the Meiji administrative system. The cabinet became accountable to the Diet, special courts such as the Administrative Court were abolished, and a new American-styled, unified judiciary was established in which the "whole judicial power" was vested along with the power of judicial review.

Left to the Courts and Law Division in the Government Section of the Supreme Commander for the Allied Powers (SCAP) was the task of supervising the detailed review and reform of all basic statutes and codes as well as the court system ....

Three significant administrative law reforms were undertaken by the Division. The first and most successful was the expansion of state liability to compensate any person injured as a consequence of official misconduct. Although, as noted, Japanese courts had recognized a claim for damages against the state under the delict (*fuhōkōi*) provisions of the Civil Code where the causal activity of the state was managerial or economic and not governmental in nature, the state's liability remained narrowly confined.

A new National Compensation Law (State Redress Law) was enacted to effect the purposes of article 17 of the new Constitution, which reads in the English version:

> Every person may sue for redress as provided by law from the state or a public entity, in case he has suffered damage through illegal acts of any public official.

A more literal translation into English would be as follows:

> Any person who has been injured [damaged] by a delict [tortious act] of a public official is able to claim compensatory damages from the state or a public entity as provided by law.

Inserted during deliberations in the Diet over critical American objections, the provision became the basis for a new statute to expand state liability for damages, drafted with Jirō Tanaka as prime mover. The National Compensation Law thus reflected the purport of the Constitution in setting out a statutory basis for state liability in the case of negligent or willful conduct in the exercise of public authority as well as for any "defect" (*kashi*) in the management of public facilities, such as roads and rivers. The statute expressly abolished the state's immunity for governmental acts and thereby significantly broadened not only state liability in damage actions but also the scope of judicial oversight of official conduct.

The second area for reform was an attempt to deal with the procedural problems inherent in the shift to a system of direct review of administrative actions by the regular courts. Enacted for this purpose was the Administrative Litigation Special Measures Law. It provided first that administrative suits would be treated procedurally as ordinary civil actions, and then set out several special rules including the requirement for exhaustion of administrative appeals with provisos to protect against delay and emergency situations. Other provisions related to such technical issues as the appropriate agency as defendant, jurisdiction, the period for filing suit, concurrent claims (such as damages), intervention and joinder of other public authorities, and the taking of evidence by the court.

In addition, the statute included two major limitations on the courts' capacity to provide effective relief from illegal administrative actions. First, the courts were required to dismiss all suits if despite the illegality of the action at issue the relief sought would be against the public interest. Since the courts were left to define the "public interest" and to determine whether the situation of a particular case warranted dismissal, this provision on its face did not significantly impair judicial oversight. Under article 10, however, the capacity of the courts to provide effective relief was severely curtailed. In the technical language of article 11, filing an appeal to the courts did not automatically suspend the execution of the administrative actions at issue. As a result, challenged administrative measures could be carried out pending the outcome of the lawsuit regardless of the possibility that the courts would decide it was illegal. A special procedure for suspension of execution was provided for in article 10(2) but only in the case of "urgent necessity to prevent irreparable damage." However, even in this case the prime minister was granted the power to override such decision if delay in carrying out the administrative action was deemed to have a "material influence on the public interest." As detailed below, the provisions of both articles 11 and 10 as construed by the courts have significantly reduced the effectiveness of judicial review.

Such problems of commission were compounded by those of omission, the most serious of which was neglect of judicial remedies. Nowhere was the "judicial power" granted to the courts defined. The Special Measures Law lacked any provision delineating what relief the courts could give once an administrative action was found to be illegal. Nor did the statute define what actions could be reviewed. In contrast, the postwar legislation in the Federal Republic of Germany governing administrative procedure (*Verwaltungsverfahrensgesetz*) and administrative court proceedings (*Verwaltungsgerichtsordnung*) expressly broadened the ambit of administrative measures subject to review and the power of the courts to issue mandatory orders to administrative officials to take certain actions. For lack of new or broader definitions of judicial power, Japanese courts could only fall back on the restrictive concepts of the prewar system. The inadequacy of the Special Measures Law for a variety of other more technical reasons resulted finally in its repeal in 1962 and the enactment of the current Administrative Case Litigation Law.

Drafted within the government, the Administrative Case Litigation Law codified prevailing concepts and doctrines without, needless to say, expanding the notion of judicial power or the reviewability of less formal administrative measures.

The 1962 statute provides for four categories of suits. The first includes all *kōkoku* appeals, defined as "lawsuits of grievance relating to the exercise of public power by an administrative agency." Based on the German *Beschwerde*, *kōkoku* appeals include (1) actions for revocation of an administrative disposition (*gyōsei shobun no torikeshi no uttae*), (2) actions for revocation of administrative decisions (*gyōsei saiketsu no torikeshi no uttae*), (3) actions for declaratory affirmation of nullity (*muko kakunin no uttae*), and (4) declaratory actions for affirmation of the illegality of forbearance (*fusakui no ihō kakunin no uttae*).

The second category encompasses "party suits" (*tōjisha soshō*), in which administrative actions are attacked collaterally in ordinary civil suits, as in the prewar system. The third category are "public suits" (*minshū soshō*), which resemble taxpayer's suits in the United States. They are defined in the statute as actions that "seek correction of [administrative] acts that do not conform to the laws and regulations of the state or public entities and that are instituted by persons qualified to vote without having the qualifications of having any other legal interest." Such actions cannot be brought, however, unless under a statute that expressly allows such an action. Finally, the fourth category includes "agency suits" (*kikan soshō*), defined as suits between government organs or other public bodies to resolve conflicts over jurisdiction and authority.

An action that does not come within one of these categories is referred to as an "innominate" (*mumei*) action. Since the remedial actions provided for in the Administrative Case Litigation Law are limited to declaratory judgments for revocation and invalidity, some scholars have argued for recognition of nonstatutory, "innominate" actions for injunctive relief.

The third reform to have a major impact on postwar practice was at the time apparently viewed as only a minor change. Repealed in 1948 was the Administrative Enforcement Law of 1900 and enacted in its stead was the current Law for Administrative Execution by Proxy. Under the old law the police were empowered to enforce administrative regulations and thus to arrest and hold in custody persons suspected of violating administrative orders and regulations without the protection of the Code of Criminal Procedure. The Occupation authorities viewed the statute primarily as "an instrument for the suppression of civil liberties," and thus fatally inconsistent with the new Constitution. However, the Administrative Execution by Proxy Law did not provide an effective substitute. It was limited to situations where officials could themselves effect a legally required action. No means of coercion to force conformity with a regulation were included. Japanese courts were to continue to have little if any role in the enforcement of administrative actions, itself an important source of judicial supervision....

The Postwar Experience

The adequacy of judicial oversight of administrative conduct would perhaps be a relatively minor issue had a meaningful form of parliamentary supremacy been achieved in postwar Japan. The postwar settlement, however, assured the continuation for at least a decade of exceptional influence and control over national policies by the Japanese bureaucracies. Not only did the civilian bureaucracies emerge as the principal institutional beneficiaries of war, defeat and occupation, their position was buttressed by a national consensus as to both the priority of economic growth as a national goal and the predominant role of the economic bureaucracies in its realization. As a result, career government officials in Japan achieved a status of influence in the immediate postwar period unparalleled in any comparable industrial democracy.

The Japanese judiciary, however, also failed to assure administrative accountability. The legacy of continental notions, left intact by the Occupation, restricted access to the courts and, even where access was available, reduced their capacity to provide meaningful relief.

Access has been curtailed primarily by the confining concepts on the direct reviewability of administrative actions. The administrative acts doctrine that review is precluded unless the action is a disposition (*shobun*) that affects in some concrete fashion the rights and duties of the party seeking review continues to prevail. Focus on the *shobunsei* of the challenged action thus encompasses the question of what actions are subject to review, who is entitled to seek review and when review is appropriate. Excluded under the *shobunsei* test are most if not all informal actions by administrative agencies regardless of apparent illegality or actual injury. The landmark case under the Administrative Litigation Special Measures Law was the Supreme Court's *en banc* decision in *Hayashi Ken Zōsen K.K. v. Director of the Marine Accidents High Board of Inquiry*. The case involved a finding by the Board that the cause of an accident on the high seas between two Japanese ships was inadequate inspection and repair of a rudder by the plaintiff Hayashi Ken Zōsen K.K. Hayashi Ken had not been a party to the Board's hearing nor had it had an opportunity to present any evidence to the Board. After the findings were announced it brought suit to have them revoked. The Tokyo High Court held that the Board had illegally infringed the firm's rights by denying it an opportunity to be heard. On appeal by the Board the Supreme Court reversed and dismissed the action, stating:

> The decision [by the Board] is a decision clarifying the cause of the above maritime disaster. That it does not limit any duty on the part of the appellee or hinder any exercise of its rights is clear from the provisions of the law and the decision itself. As stated below, it does not have the effect of a binding determination of the appellee's negligence. This being the case, the decision does not have a direct effect on the appellee's rights and duties; thus it cannot be considered to be an administrative disposition and we must hold that the appellee is not allowed to file suit.

Two justices dissented. Justice Hachirō Fujita argued the law should be construed so that the plaintiff was in effect subject to an advisory decision (*kankoku shinketsu*) and thus permitted to file an exception. He also noted the negative influence the Board's finding would have on the reputation and business of the plaintiff — thus his rights and real interests. Justice Daisuke Kawamura echoed these concerns in an equally strong dissent.

The Court's reasoning in the *Hayashi Ken Zōsen* case has been followed consistently in subsequent decisions under both the Special Measures Law as well as the Administrative Case Litigation Law. In 1966, for example, in *Sakamoto v. Governor of Tokyo Prefecture,* another *en banc* decision, the Supreme Court applied the *shobunsei* requirement to deny the reviewability of a land planning measure. The Court held that formal publication of a plan was not a disposition that could be subject to an administrative suit even though publication meant that thereafter improvements and other modifications of land and buildings in the designated area would require governmental approval. Suit could only be brought against future denials of permits. More recently, on this basis the Tokyo District Court dismissed suit for revocation of formal approval by the Minister of Transportation of the plan to extend the *Shinkansen* (or "bullet train") from Tokyo to Narita. As illustrated by the *Narita Shinkansen* case, the doctrine has been especially inhibitive in environmental litigation.

The *shobunsei* restriction also limits who may seek review. Under the *Hayashi Ken Zōsen* precedent successful plaintiffs must show that challenged administrative actions have had concrete effect on their rights or legally protected interests. The specific provisions on standing of articles 9 and 36 of the Administrative Case Litigation Law — that only persons with "legal interest" in the revocation or invalidation of challenged actions may bring suit — have been construed to conform to the reasoning in the *Hayashi Ken Zōsen* case. Not only must the object of the suit be an action that creates a right or duty in an individual or legally determines their parameters, but also only the person so affected has the legal capacity to obtain review. Illustrative are two unsuccessful attempts to appeal from decisions by the Japanese Fair Trade Commission. Both involved recommendation decisions (*kankoku shinketsu*), by which the respondent agrees to take specified actions to eliminate an antitrust violation or unfair business practice recommended by the Commission and a decision is issued making the duty to do so legally mandatory pursuant to article 48 of the Antimonopoly and Fair Trade Law. In the first case the Commission issued a decision to the effect that the respondent Japanese pharmaceutical firm would not honor anticompetitive provisions in a license agreement with the Danish firm, Novo Industri A/S. The provisions benefited the Danish licensor and were correspondingly adverse to the Japanese licensee. Consequently, the respondent readily agreed to the Commission's recommendation. (Indeed, there is little doubt that the Japanese firm actively sought such action by the Commission.) Novo Industri responded by filing an administrative appeal with the Tokyo High Court to have the Commission's decision revoked. The Tokyo High Court dismissed the action and the Supreme Court upheld the dismissal on appeal. Both courts reasoned that Novo Industri lacked standing — that is, the requisite legal interest to sue — in that it was not a party to the Commission's decision.

The second case involved recommendation decisions against twelve of Japan's domestic oil producers and refiners for price-fixing in 1973. Six appealed and lost, two on further appeal to the Supreme Court. Again the Tokyo High Court and the Supreme Court dismissed the appeals on the grounds that since the findings of the violation in the recommendation decision were not the product of a formal, adjudicated hearing, nor were they binding (although the measures to be taken to eliminate the violation were mandatory), the firms could not appeal. The recommendation decisions could be used, however, as *prima facie* evidence of a violation in private damage actions as well as formal complaints by the Commission to the procuracy for criminal prosecution.

The consequence of restricted access to the courts for direct review of government actions has been to insulate most forms of official conduct from judicial correction, regardless of how illegal or potentially injurious to a party the conduct may be. Administrative guidance, for example, is generally beyond any direct review and injunctive relief by the courts. Only by means of indirect review in damage actions have the courts been able to fulfill their intended function under the Constitution. The first Supreme Court decision on the legality of MITI guidance was on an appeal by the Petroleum Federation from one of the few adjudicated decisions by the Fair Trade Commission. Had the federation accepted a recommendation decision as it and the oil companies did in subsequent cases, the issue would have come first to the Court in the context of the appeal from one of the 1980 decisions of the Tokyo High Court in the Oil Cartel criminal cases.

The National Compensation Law has therefore become a critical vehicle for judicial review. As under the prewar administrative court system, private damage actions serve as a mechanism for judicial scrutiny of official misconduct. One of the best early examples was the attempt to obtain judicial review of Prime Minister Yoshida's 1952 dissolution of the Diet without a Diet resolution. The attempt to bring an action directly to the Supreme Court failed in a well-known constitutional decision. Subsequently, the plaintiff, who lost his bid for reelection in the election that followed dissolution, sued for compensation for the salary he would have received as a member of the Diet had no election been held as a result of the allegedly illegal dissolution. The Tokyo District Court ruled in his favor, but he lost an appeal in both the Tokyo High Court and the Supreme Court on the basis of the "political question" doctrine.

The consequent role of damage actions is reflected in the statistics. The law was not used with great frequency until the mid-1960s. From 1947 to 1967, for example, only 1,524 actions were brought, and of these only 909 ended in a judicial decision. The other cases were either dropped or settled. Very few cases were brought under article 2. During this period only 107 article 2 cases were filed and only 27 reached judgment. The plaintiffs also fared badly in damage actions against the government and officials at least in comparison with damage actions against private parties: 78 percent had their claims completely denied, 10 percent won on their entire claim and 12 percent won only on a portion. Most striking for comparative purposes is the extent to which the police, procurators, and judicial officials have been sued. Indeed the plurality of all damage actions have been brought against judges and court clerks. Only since 1967 have plaintiffs begun to bring a substantial number of damage actions under article 2, for mismanagement of public facilities, primarily in environmental and disaster cases.... [D]amage actions have also provided a means for judicial review of administrative guidance.

In environmental protection cases, the provision for strict liability for "defects" in the management of public facilities has permitted plaintiffs to force officials to take positive action against environmental hazards in the management of rivers and other facilities. One example is the *Kochi Vinyl Pollution* case, in which the Kochi District Court held the state liable for not having rid the Ushiro River of waste vinyl sheets discarded in the river that became entangled in fishing nets.

In many cases damage actions are not appropriate, however, either because damages do not provide a useful remedy or because the amount is too uncertain or too difficult to calculate under the strict standards for proof in Japanese tort law. The lack of effective remedies remains a major limitation on the utility of seeking judicial redress. The limitations of existing definitions of judicial power have left the court powerless to compel the government to take corrective measures where on the merits the courts have determined the status quo to be illegal. Illustrative was the inability of the Supreme Court to provide any effective remedy in *Kurokawa v. Chiba Prefecture Election Commission*, in which Japan's electoral system was held to be unconstitutional as a denial of equality under article 14 of the Constitution. The *Osaka Airport* case is the best example, however, of how the Special Measures Law and the Administrative Case Litigation Law have restricted even further the limited remedial powers the courts do have.

In the *Osaka Airport* case, the Osaka District Court granted the plaintiffs injunctive relief to prevent flight landings and takeoffs. The Osaka High Court affirmed and went even further by extending the time period covered by injunction. Both courts attempted to avoid article 44 of the Administrative Case Litigation Law, which provides:

> No provisional dispositions [i.e., injunctive relief] as provided in the Code of Civil Procedure may be granted against dispositions of administrative agencies and acts involving the exercise of public power.

The two lower courts viewed article 44 as inapplicable in a suit for damages and injunctive relief brought under the National Compensation Law and the Civil Code, reasoning on the basis of prewar theory that the state's conduct in the management of the airport was governed by private law, not public law rules. The Supreme Court rejected the argument, however, in its *en banc* decision in December 1981. The management of the airport was held to be an exercise of administrative authority thus subject to the prohibition against injunctive relief.

A final example of statutory limitations on the courts' remedial powers is the *Naganuma* case. In order to build an air self-defense force base near the village of Naganuma in Hokkaido, a change in a national forest designation was obtained. A number of villagers filed suit in response, alleging injury because of the loss of their watershed, to have the change revoked and thus prevent building of the base. The Administrative Case Litigation Law kept intact the suspension of execution limitations of the Special Measures Law; consequently, they had to prove an "urgent necessity" to prevent the base from being built pending the outcome of judicial review of the merits (including the constitutionality of the self-defense forces). [Because the plaintiffs were unable] to do so, the base was built, other measures were taken to prevent harm from loss of the watershed, and the plaintiffs lost what standing they had by the time the Sapporo High Court and most recently the Supreme Court could reach the merits of the case.

7. JUDICIAL PROTECTION THROUGH COMPENSATION LAWS IN EAST ASIA

NATIONAL COMPENSATION LAW OF JAPAN

Articles 1, 2

Kokka baishō hō, Law No. 125 (1947)

Article 1

1. When a governmental official who is in a position to exercise governmental powers of the state or of a public body has, in the course of performing his duties, illegally inflicted losses upon another person either intentionally or negligently, the state or the public body concerned shall be liable to compensate for such losses.

2. If, in the case mentioned in the preceding paragraph, the government official involved was intentional or guilty of gross negligence, the state or the public body concerned shall have the right to obtain reimbursement from such official.

Article 2

1. When defects (*kashi*) in the establishment or management of roads, rivers and other public installations have caused losses on another person, the state or the public body concerned shall be liable to compensate such losses.

2. If, in the case mentioned in the preceding paragraph, there is some other person who is to be responsible for the cause of such losses, the state or the public body concerned shall have the right to obtain reimbursement from such person.

YAMAGATA PREFECTURE v. Y.K. TAIRA SHŌJI (THE TURKISH BATH CASE)

Supreme Court of Japan
Second Petty Bench
Decision of 26 May 1978
32 Minshū 689 (1978)

English translation published in David Blachman, *Case Comment*, 19 Law in Japan 188-90 (1986)

Facts

[The facts come from a comment on the case written by Professor Tsuyoshi Kodaka in 1979.]

Taira Corporation desired to operate a bathhouse business equipped with private rooms (the so-called Turkish bath) [*torukoburo*], and purchased some land in the town of Yomokucho in Yamagata Prefecture for that purpose. On May 23, 1968, Taira Corporation received construction certification and began construction, which was completed around the end of July of the same year. In addition, on May 11, 1968, Taira Corporation applied to the Governor of Yamagata Prefecture for the required permission under article 2(10) of the Public Bathhouse Law to operate a bathhouse equipped with private rooms. However, from the time construction commenced on the bathhouse, groups such as women's organizations undertook a campaign against the bathhouse. Because of these protests, the town and the Yamagata authorities were forced to map out a line of policy to prevent the bathhouse from opening for business.

Despite the fact that no real need existed, the city decided to establish a children's recreational center in [an existing facility] as a facility to promote children's welfare [see the Children's Welfare Law] approximately 134 meters from the area where the bathhouse was to open for business. On June 4, an application for authorization to establish the children's recreational center was hastily made to the Yamagata Prefectural Governor, and on June 10, in unprecedented speed, the city authorized the recreational center. Since permission to operate the public bathhouse was not given until July 31, 1968, Taira Corporation's commencement of operations fell behind the establishment of the recreational center. Since Taira Corporation insisted on opening for business, on February 25, 1969 the Yamagata Prefectural Standing Committee on Public Safety issued a 60-day restraining order against Taira Corporation prohibiting the operation of the bathhouse on grounds that the bathhouse violated article 4(4) (1) of the Law to Control Businesses Affecting the Public Morals.

In response, Taira Corporation demanded payment under article 1(10) of the National Compensation Law (State Redress Law) for damages incurred by the Yamagata prefecture's disposition restraining Taira Corporation's business operations. Taira Corporation claimed that the disposition authorizing the children's recreational center prevented the opening of the bathhouse and that the primary purpose of the disposition was to interfere in the operation of the bathhouse. In addition, Taira Corporation asserted that the authorization was illegal as an abuse of administrative authority [*gyōseiken*]. Taira Corporation first brought suit seeking rescission [*torikeshi*] of the restraining order on the business operations, but with the end of the 60 day restraining period, such a suit became moot. Taira Corporation then shifted to a suit demanding damages.

In the court of first instance, the Yamagata District Court rejected Taira Corporation's demands and found that although the disposition authorizing the recreational center was improper, the disposition could not be termed illegal. In the court of second instance, however, the Sendai High Court found that the authorization disposition was an abuse of administrative authority and approved Taira Corporation's claim. Yamagata prefecture then brought this *jōkoku* appeal.

The Decision

Title: A case of Demand for Damages

Topic: Case holding an exercise of administrative power to be a violation of the public power as stipulated in the National Compensation Law.

Summary

Based on the fact relationships found in the court below, the disposition of the prefectural governor authorizing the establishment of a children's recreational center, as a disposition with a primary purpose of preventing the opening of a bathhouse equipped with private rooms and as an extreme abuse of administrative authority, is an illegal exercise of the public power stipulated in article 1(1) of the National Compensation Law. The disposition was an abuse of authority even though it conformed with the standards for authorizing children's recreational centers.

References

1. National Compensation Law article 1(1):

When a public employee exercising the public power for the state or a public body and in the performance of his duties, intentionally or negligently inflicts injury on another, the state or the public body shall bear the burden of compensation.

2. Children's Welfare Law article 35(3):

A city, town, or village may, upon receiving permission from the prefectural governor, by order establish facilities to promote the welfare of children.

3. Law to Control Businesses Affecting the Public Morals article 4(4): Bathhouses equipped with private rooms which sponsor services for contact between customers of different sexes may not conduct business within an area of 200 meters of government offices, schools, libraries, facilities that promote the welfare of children, or other facilities in which, as determined by prefectural rules and regulations, there is a need to prevent activities which harm favorable morals.

4. In addition to the above, the prefecture, if there is a need to prevent injury to favorable public morals, may prohibit by regulation the operation of bathhouses with private rooms in specified areas.

5. The enforcement and application of the regulations in (1) and (4) above shall not apply to the operation of bathhouses receiving permission under article 2(1) of the Public Bathhouse Law and already in operation.

Decree

The *jōkoku* appeal is dismissed.
The cost of the *jōkoku* appeal shall be borne by the *jōkoku* appellant.

Reasons

In light of the evidence cited in the court below, this court can approve the fact-finding of the lower court. There is no illegality in the reasoning of the decision of the court below. Based on the fact relationships found in the court below, the disposition authorizing the establishment of the children's recreational center at issue in this case was illegal as an extreme abuse of administrative authority. In addition, since there is a sufficient causal relationship between the disposition authorizing the recreational center on the one hand, and the damages incurred by the *jōkoku* appellee from the restraining order on the operation of the bathhouse on the other hand, the *jōkoku* appellee's demand for payment of compensation should be approved. For this reason, this court approves as proper the decision of the court below reaching the identical conclusion. As for the *jōkoku* appellant's assertion of unconstitutionality in [the high court's] decision, we reject such a claim and find that this assertion requires an error in fact-finding and no such error exists. We cannot adopt the *jōkoku* appellant's argument.

NATIONAL COMPENSATION LAW OF SOUTH KOREA

Articles 1, 2

Kukka baesang pŏp, Law No. 1899 (1967)

Article 1 (Purpose)

The purpose of this Law is to provide for the liability assumed by the state or local autonomous governments for the redress of damages and the procedures for redress of damages.

Article 2 (Liability for Redress of Damages)

(1) When public officials inflict damages on other persons intentionally or negligently in the course of performing their official duties, in violation of laws or decrees or when they are liable for compensation damages under the provisions of the Automobile Accident Compensation Security Law, the state or local autonomous governments shall redress the damages. Provided, however, that when military personnel, employees in the armed forces, police officials or home land reserve forces are killed in action or in the performance of their duties or injured while on duty in connection with combat training or performance of other official duties, or in the facilities and automobiles, vessels, aircraft and other forms of transportation, all of which are used for national defense or the maintenance of public safety, they or their bereaved family shall not recover redress damages under this Law and the Civil Code if they can claim accident compensation, surviving family annuity, wound annuity, etc., pursuant to other laws and decrees.

(2) If, in the case of the main text of the foregoing paragraph, damage has been caused by bad faith or gross negligence of the public official involved, the state or a local autonomous government may demand from the public official subsequent reimbursement.

STATE COMPENSATION LAW OF TAIWAN

Articles 2, 3

Kuochia p'eich'ang fa, Law of 2 July 1980

Article 2

For the purposes of this law, "employee of the government" means any officer or employee acting in performance of his or her public duties under the law.

The state shall be liable for any damage arising from the intentional or negligent act of any employee of the government acting within the scope of his or her office or employment which infringes upon the freedom or right of any person.

The same shall be applied when the damage results from an omission by any employee of the government.

Should the damage referred to in the preceding paragraphs result from an act [or omission] committed with intent or gross negligence on the part of the employee of the government, the compensating authority shall have the right to reimbursement from the said employee of the government.

Article 3

The state shall be liable for damage to any person's life, body, or property resulting from a defect in the installation or management of any government-owned public facility.

The compensating authority shall have the right to reimbursement from the said third person who is liable for the damage referred to in the preceding paragraph.

NOTES AND QUESTIONS

1. What are the primary limitations on judicial review of administrative action in Japan? Are they likely the result of a German model, an American model, Japanese legal culture, or something else? Is the Japanese situation similar to that in Latin America, or something quite different?

2. The national or state compensation statutes in South Korea and Taiwan are both based on the Japanese statute. They also are used extensively as a vehicle for judicial review of administrative action.

3. Would *The Turkish Bath Case* have been decided differently under either the South Korean or Taiwanese statute? To what extent is the state liable for damages caused by police, prosecutorial, or judicial error? Review *Japan v. Onda, supra* Section A.3. Is the state potentially liable for damages caused by air or water pollution or by natural disasters, such as floods or earthquakes, under the statutes of any of these three civil law nations?

For a comparison of the Japanese response with that of China, New Zealand, Peru, the former Soviet Union, and the United States, see James Huffman, Government Liability and Disaster Mitigation: A Comparative Study (1986).

C. JUDICIAL REVIEW OF LEGISLATIVE ACTS

1. CONSTITUTIONALISM

JOHN HENRY MERRYMAN, THE CIVIL LAW TRADITION: AN INTRODUCTION TO THE LEGAL SYSTEMS OF WESTERN EUROPE AND LATIN AMERICA 136-40 (2d ed. 1985)

The movement toward constitutionalism in the civil law tradition can be seen as a logical reaction against the extremes of a secular, positivistic view of the state. During the period of the *jus commune* and prior to the Reformation, the authority of the Church and the writings of Roman Catholic natural lawyers about government and the individual provided a set of ideas and values that exerted some degree of restraining influence on the prince and on government officials. Many of these ideas were embedded deeply in the *jus commune* itself. But with the Reformation, the authority of the Church and of Roman Catholic natural law declined. With the growth of the nation-state the *jus commune* became a subsidiary system, inferior to the national law. At the same time the emphasis in secular natural law thinking on a popularly elected, representative legislature and on the separation of powers, combined with the revolutionary desire to limit the power of judges, produced an exaggerated emphasis on legislative autonomy. The old restraints on government were removed, and in the new positivistic state the representative legislature was given an inflated role and encouraged to be the sole judge of the legality (as opposed to the political acceptability) of its own action. In a sense the trend toward functionally rigid constitutions, with guarantees of individual rights against "unjust" legislative action, can be seen as a process of "codification of natural law" to fill the void left by rejection of Roman Catholic natural law and the *jus commune* on the one hand, and to deflate the bloated image of the legislature that emerged from the revolutionary period on the other.

A desire to review the constitutionality of legislative action does not necessarily lead to the institution of *judicial* review. On the contrary, fundamental notions about the separation of powers and about the nature and limits of the judicial function in the civil law tradition make constitutional review by the ordinary judiciary an unacceptable alternative. And the rejection of the principle of *stare decisis* further limits the attractiveness of (ordinary) judicial review. Constitutional questions are of such far-reaching importance that it seems necessary to have them decided authoritatively, with *erga omnes* effects, rather than accept the hazards of inconsistent decisions by different courts, or even by the same court, in similar cases. But civil law nations cannot accept the proposal that the decisions of ordinary courts be given authority as law. Consequently the system familiar to citizens of the United States, in which all courts at every level of jurisdiction have the power to decide constitutional issues with *erga omnes* effects, has generally been rejected in the civil law world. Even where, as in some Latin American nations, some power of judicial review has been given to ordinary courts, the tendency has been to concentrate that power in one supreme court [or, more recently, in one chamber of the supreme court or in a constitutional court] rather than diffuse it throughout the judicial system....

The ways in which demands for constitutional review of legislation have been gradually accommodated within the civil law tradition vary widely, although a trend toward the establishment of some form of constitutional review is evident. It is not surprising to find that France, the traditional source of the fundamentalist position on the separation of powers and the role of courts, has a system of nonjudicial review. The government organ that performs this function, established under the 1958 Constitution, is called the Constitutional Council. This body is composed of all former Presidents of France plus nine additional persons, three of whom are chosen by the President of France, three by the President of the Chamber of Deputies, and three by the President of the Senate. Before promulgation, certain kinds of laws must, and others may, be referred by the executive or the legislature to this council for a decision on their constitutionality. The council must respond within a certain time, after secret deliberations with no contentious procedure, no parties, no oral hearings, and no other marks of judicial proceedings. If the council finds the law in question unconstitutional, the law cannot be promulgated unless the Constitution is appropriately amended.

The original composition and procedure of the Constitutional Council made its nonjudicial nature clear. Its function seemed more like an additional step in the legislative process than a judicial proceeding, and it was common to characterize this sort of constitutional review as "political" rather than as "judicial." More recently, the work of the Constitutional Council has begun to take on judicial characteristics and to be more frequently perceived, by lawyers and the public alike, as a court-like institution. Meanwhile, the French Council of State (frequently) and even the Supreme Court of Cassation (very infrequently and narrowly) have become involved in constitutional litigation. Still, the theory remains that there is no judicial review of legislation in France....

The trend toward judicial review of the constitutionality of legislation in the civil law world has been strong, particularly in this century. In general it can be said that the experience with review by ordinary courts, even where concentrated in one supreme court, has not been encouraging. The tendency has been for the civil law judge to recoil from the responsibilities and opportunities of constitutional adjudication. The tradition is too strong, the orthodox view of the judicial function too deeply ingrained, the effects of traditional legal education and career training too limiting. Concentrated judicial review by the Supreme Court has existed in Chile for forty years, but only a few statutes have been found unconstitutional in that time, and those usually in cases of minor importance. [This function was transferred to the Constitutional Tribunal under the 1980 Chilean Constitution.]... This sort of experience, in addition to the traditional civil law distrust of ordinary judges, the force of the doctrine of separation of powers, and the desire to give decisions of unconstitutionality *erga omnes* effects, explains the decision in Austria, Germany, Italy, and Spain, among other civil law nations, to establish separate constitutional courts. The analogy with the 19th century decision to establish separate tribunals for judicial review of the legality of administrative acts is clear.

The German, Italian, and Spanish constitutional courts were established after World War II and represent the modern trend toward constitutional review in the civil law world. Although there are important differences between them, they share a number of significant characteristics. All are separate courts, distinct from all others in their respective jurisdictions. All have the exclusive power to decide on the constitutionality of legislation. In Germany, Italy, and Spain a decision by the constitutional court that a statute is unconstitutional is binding not only on the parties to the case but on all participants in the legal process. In all three instances the character of the proceedings and the rules governing the selection and tenure of judges give the constitutional court a definitely judicial character, in contrast to the political nature of the French Constitutional Council.

Generally, the procedure is this: in an action before a civil, criminal, administrative, or other court a party can raise a constitutional objection to a statute affecting the case. At this point the action is suspended, and the constitutional question is referred to the constitutional court for decision. When that decision is published, the original proceeding is resumed and conducted in accordance with it. If the constitutional court finds the statute constitutional, it can be applied in the proceeding; if the court rules it unconstitutional, the statute becomes invalid and cannot be applied in that specific proceeding or in any other. This procedure exemplifies the so-called "incidental" attack on constitutionality, in which the constitutional question is raised within the context of a specific judicial case or controversy in which the statute is applicable, but in which the case or controversy is the basis of jurisdiction and the constitutional question incidental to its resolution.

The incidental procedure, which permits a constitutional attack only within the context of a specific case or controversy, is the only one available in the system of constitutional review in the United States. In Germany, Italy, and Spain (and in other civil law countries, including Austria and Colombia), however, a "direct" attack is also possible. Certain designated official agencies of government (and, in Germany and Colombia, even individuals) can bring an action before the constitutional court to test the validity of a statute, even though there is no concrete dispute involving its application. In this way the limitations inherent in the restriction to incidental review in the United States are transcended, and a hearing can be had on the abstract question of constitutionality. Even though it has been limited by statute and decision, the direct review procedure expands the potential scope of constitutional review beyond that available in the United States.

2. THE FRENCH CONSTITUTIONAL COUNCIL

CONSTITUTION OF FRANCE
Articles 61, 62

Title VII: The Constitutional Council

Article 61

Organic laws,[a] before their promulgation, and regulations of the parliamentary assemblies, before they go into effect, must be submitted to the Constitutional Council, which rules on their conformity to the Constitution.

For the same purpose, laws may be submitted to the Constitutional Council, before their promulgation, by the President of the Republic, the Prime Minister, the President of the National Assembly, the President of the Senate, or by 60 deputies or 60 senators.

In cases arising under the preceding paragraphs, the Constitutional Council must rule within one month. Nevertheless, at the request of the Government, in case of emergency, this period is reduced to eight days.

In these same cases, referral (*saisine*) to the Constitutional Council suspends promulgation of the law.

Article 62

A provision declared unconstitutional may not be promulgated or put into effect.

The decisions of the Constitutional Council may not be appealed. They are binding on the public powers and on all administrative and judicial authorities.

F.L. MORTON, JUDICIAL REVIEW IN FRANCE: A COMPARATIVE ANALYSIS, 36 American Journal of Comparative Law 89-92, 94-96, 98-100 (1988)

The most striking characteristic of the *Conseil Constitutionnel* has been the rapid ascent of its political influence and prestige. The original role of the

[a] Organic laws, mentioned in article 46, are those laws that specify the organization or functions of public powers in developing the principles or rules enunciated in the Constitution. Within the hierarchy of the sources of law, organic laws come below the Constitution and above ordinary laws.

Conseil Constitutionnel was much more modest than the one it has recently assumed. It was intended to protect the new executive power, created by and for General de Gaulle, from parliamentary usurpations. It also was charged with the responsibility to investigate cases of alleged voting irregularities. From its creation in 1958 until the 1970s, the *Conseil Constitutionnel*'s work was limited to "separation of powers" issues and disputed elections. While both functions helped to stabilize French politics after the tumultuous experiences of the Fourth Republic, the *Conseil Constitutionnel* kept a low profile and was not considered an important institution.

In the 1970s, two events transformed the *Conseil Constitutionnel* from a secondary and relatively unimportant institution to a central agent in the governing process. Prior to 1971, the *Conseil Constitutionnel* had almost no role in protecting civil liberties and individual rights. Then in a 1971 decision dubbed by some as the "*Marbury vs. Madison* of France," it struck down a government bill that seriously restricted freedom of political association. To support their ruling, the *Conseil* interpreted the Preamble of the 1958 Constitution as incorporating all the rights enumerated in the 1789 Declaration of the Rights of Man and the Preamble of the Constitution of the Fourth Republic. While both these documents are mentioned in the 1958 Preamble, they had never been considered to have legal force. By this bold judicial stroke, *Parlement*'s freedom to legislate was suddenly fenced in by the full panoply of liberal rights and freedoms. Subsequent decisions incorporated additional rights declared in previous French laws and constitutions. By 1987, "fundamental rights" accounted for forty percent of the *Conseil*'s annullment of ordinary laws.

The second catalyst of the *Conseil*'s rise to political prominence was the 1974 reform that extended its authority to rule on the constitutionality of a law upon petition by any sixty members of the National Assembly or the Senate. Prior to this, a law could be referred to the *Conseil Constitutionnel* by only four officials: the President of the Republic, the Prime Minister, the President of the National Assembly, and the President of the Senate. Since all four were usually members of the governing majority party/coalition, they were unlikely to challenge the validity of their own legislation. The 1974 reform conferred this power of reference on opposition parties (providing they could muster sixty signatures), who immediately seized this opportunity as a way to obstruct, at least temporarily, new government policies. By 1987, parliamentary references accounted for eighty percent of all decisions dealing with ordinary laws. Even more striking — since 1979, forty-six of the forty-eight decisions nullifying laws have been initiated by members of *Parlement*.

The net effect of the two events described above has been a dramatic increase in the number and political significance of the laws brought before the *Conseil Constitutionnel*. From 1958 to 1974, there were only nine references to the *Conseil*. From 1974 to May 1981, the number leaped to 47. While they had originally opposed the 1974 reform, the Socialist opposition was now happy to use it against the Center-Right government of Giscard d'Estaing. After Mitterand and the Socialists swept to power in 1981, it was the Conservatives' turn. Notwithstanding their earlier criticisms of the Socialist "abuse" of the power of reference, the number of laws challenged between 1981 and 1986 rose to 66, almost all at the initiative of the Conservatives. The Socialists bitterly denounced the *Conseil Constitutionnel* for its decisions nullifying important social legislation in 1982 and 1983. But when they lost control of the *Parlement* in March of 1986, they quickly forgot their earlier criticisms, and referred nine different laws to the *Conseil Constitutionnel* during their first year in opposition.

It is now common practice for all major government bills to be challenged in this manner by the opposition. The more important the bill, the more likely the challenge. Combined with the vastly expanded scope of constitutional restrictions imposed by the Declaration of the Rights of Man and other implied liberties, this new procedure has thrust the *Conseil Constitutionnel* to the center of the policy-making process. It is now a "hurdle" that every major piece of legislation must clear before becoming law....

The most significant recent event in the development of the *Conseil Constitutionnel* was its 1982 confrontation with the then recently elected Socialist government of François Mitterand, a judicial-legislative confrontation that can be profitably compared to the American "New Deal court crisis" of the 1930s.

In 1981 the Right-wing (Gaullist) political coalition that had governed France since 1958 was swept from power by a coalition of the Left. Socialist leader François Mitterand was elected President, and his Socialist Party, with the support of the French Communists, gained a majority in the *Assemblée Nationale*. The *"alternance,"* as the French dubbed it, seemed at the time to mark a major political realignment in which a new political majority would be constituted by the Left.[20] The political ascendancy of the Left coincided with the *Conseil Constitutionnel*'s growing role as the protector of the constitutional rights of individuals. Some commentators predicted a collision between the new individualistic jurisprudence of the *Conseil Constitutionnel* and the collectivist, interventionist reforms of the new Leftist government.

Initial events supported the pessimists' scenario. Between May, 1981 and January 1982, the *Conseil Constitutionnel* ruled five of ten Socialist reforms partially unconstitutional. Of particular importance were the rulings of "*annulation partielle*" (invalid in part) in the *Nationalisations* case and the *Décentralisation* case. Both laws were centerpieces of Socialist Party policy, and both had been vehemently opposed by the Conservative opposition in *Parlement*, who referred them to the *Conseil* as a tactic of last resort. The Nationalization Law initiated the process of transferring certain financial and industrial institutions from private to public ownership. The second was the first attempt to decentralize the topheavy French state since the French Revolution. In both instances, it appeared that the Right was able to block through reference to the *Conseil Constitutionnel* what they had failed to achieve in Parliament.

The reaction from the governing Leftist coalition was predictably hostile. A chorus of condemnations filled the press. Most of the criticism focused on the anti-democratic character of the *Conseil*'s decisions. They were characterized

[20] The subsequent recapture of the *Assemblée Nationale* by Gaullist leader Jacques Chirac and a Rightist majority coalition in 1986 has undercut the position that the 1981 elections constituted an enduring realignment in favor of the Left.

as an assault on the "*volonté generale*," the sovereignty of the French people. Some criticism of the *Conseil* was also focussed on its members. They were, at various times, criticized for being too old, incompetent, and for belonging to the wrong political party. "We represent the people," declared one Socialist deputy. "*They* represent the majority of an earlier time." The Leftist journal *Libération* acidly referred to the entire *Conseil* as "*le gang du Palais Royale.*" There was considerable talk on the Left about the need to abolish the *Conseil*, but the extraordinary political majority required to amend the constitution, combined with the Socialists' fragile majority in *Parlement*, effectively precluded such drastic action.

Contrary to the rhetoric of the winter of 1982, a final confrontation between the Mitterand government and the *Conseil Constitutionnel* was averted. In the end, the *Conseil* was careful not to try to obstruct completely the government's reform agenda. More constitutional challenges were rejected than sustained. Even in those challenges that were accepted, the *Conseil* nullified the entire law only once. In the all important *Nationalisations* case, a refurbished version of the bill was adopted within a month of the *Conseil's* original declaration of unconstitutionality. The offending section, which dealt with procedures for reimbursing private stockholders, was rewritten to guarantee a fair market value for the stock. When this reformed version of the bill was again attacked by the Conservative opposition as unconstitutional, the *Conseil Constitutionnel* upheld it. The net effect of the *Conseil's* decisions was thus to slow the pace of reform, to force bills to be rewritten and presented to *Parlement* a second time. Perhaps these decisions also deterred more radical reforms from ever being tabled....

If the confrontation of the winter of 1982 was predictable, it was also predictable that it would not be as prolonged nor as severe as the American "New Deal" court crisis. The reason: the different modes of appointment and tenure of office in the American and French constitutional courts. The *Conseil Constitutionnel's* practice of a non-renewable nine year term, staggered so that one-third of its membership is replaced every third year, guarantees a constant flow of "new blood." By contrast, U.S. Supreme Court judges are appointed for life, and serve an average of fourteen years....

Because of these differences of appointment and tenure, the ideological disposition of the *Conseil Constitutionnel* is more responsive to changes in the public's electoral behavior than the U.S. Supreme Court. In this sense, the *Conseil* is more politically accountable, as an institution, than its American counterpart. Some commentators have reckoned this as a "fault," reflecting inadequate "judicial independence." But this criticism begs the prior and more fundamental question of *whether* the function of constitutional control should be vested in a normal court (i.e., with life tenure for judges) or a more political (i.e., accountable) body....

The advantage of the *Conseil Constitutionnel* has already been identified: confrontations with new governments are likely to be less prolonged and thus less critical because of the systematic infusion of new "political blood" every third year. It is, to put it simply, more democratic. From another perspective, however, this institutional pliability can be judged as a vice. A constitutional court is charged with guiding democracy not following it. What is the point in having a *written* constitution, our American colleagues might demand, if its meaning can be changed simply by changing the judges who interpret it?...

This is the paradox of constitutionalism. To be true to its purpose, its meaning must not change. But to survive more than a generation or two, it must change. A constitution must be simultaneously both rigid and supple. Since a written constitution is by definition rigid — a "parchment barrier" in the words of *The Federalist* — flexibility is introduced through the structure of the institution that interprets it.

THE FREEDOM OF ASSOCIATION CASE

Constitutional Council of France
Decision of 16 July 1971
1971 J.O. 7114

English translation published in Mauro Cappelletti & William Cohen, Comparative Constitutional Law: Cases and Materials 50-51 (1979)

[Facts: The *Conseil Constitutionnel* was summoned on July 1, 1971 at the request of the President of the Senate to decide upon the constitutionality of an unpromulgated bill. The bill, discussed by the National Assembly and the Senate, and then passed by the National Assembly, amended arts. 5 and 7 of the law of July 1, 1901 concerning the *contrat d'association* (freedom of association), placing prior restraints on that right. Passage of this bill was motivated by contemporary political controversy, since its provisions were essentially aimed against leftists (*gauchistes*).]

Opinion

Considering the Constitution and in particular its Preamble;

Considering the *ordonnance* of November 7, 1958 concerning the organic law on the *Conseil Constitutionnel* and in particular chapter II of Title II of the above-mentioned *ordonnance*; Considering the law of January 1, 1901 relating to the *contrat d'association*, as amended;...

Considering that the bill under examination before this *Conseil Constitutionnel* has been submitted to the vote of the two Assemblies, according to the procedure required by the Constitution during the parliamentary session that began on April 2, 1971;

Considering that among the fundamental principles recognized by the laws of the Republic and solemnly reaffirmed by the Preamble of the Constitution, we also find the principle of freedom of association; that this principle is at the basis of the general provisions of the law of July 1, 1901, concerning the *contrat d'association*; according to this principle, associations [including political, religious and commercial groups] can be created freely and they can be "incorporated" upon completion of the sole requirement that they make a preliminary declaration which is to be deposited with the competent authority [the *Préfet*]; that, therefore, except for provisions applying to special categories of associations, the creation of the associations cannot be challenged by the preliminary intervention of either the judicial or the administrative authority even if they seem defective or even if they have an illicit object for their purposes;...

The subject of the provisions of art. 3 of the bill under examination, which is coming under the scrutiny of this *Conseil Constitutionnel* before its promulgation, is the institution of a procedure according to which the acquisition of the legal capacity of "incorporated" associations will depend upon a preliminary check of the association's conformity to law, carried out by the judicial authority;

Considering, therefore, that there are grounds to declare the provisions of art. 3 of the bill under examination, which amends art. 7 of the law of July 1, 1901, unconstitutional; consequently, the last sentence of para. 2 of art. 1 of the bill under examination must also be declared unconstitutional because it makes reference to the above-mentioned art. 3;

Considering that it does not appear either from the text of the bill, as it was drafted and passed [by the Assembly], or from the parliamentary debate that the above-mentioned provisions are indivisible from the whole of the bill submitted to the *Conseil Constitutionnel*;

Considering, finally that the other provisions of this text do not violate the Constitution,

[This *Conseil* therefore decides]:

Those provisions of art. 3 of the bill submitted for the examination of the *Conseil Constitutionnel* amending the law of July 1, 1901, as well as the provisions of art. 1 of the bill under examination which made reference to those provisions of art. 3, are unconstitutional;

The other provisions of the above-mentioned bill are declared constitutional;

This decision will be published in the *Journal Officiel* of the French Republic.

CYNTHIA VROOM, CONSTITUTIONAL PROTECTION OF INDIVIDUAL LIBERTIES IN FRANCE: THE *CONSEIL CONSTITUTIONNEL* SINCE 1971, 63 Tulane Law Review 265, 266, 279-82, 295-97, 314-15 (1988)

Introduction

More than seventeen years have passed since France's *Conseil constitutionnel* (Constitutional Council) handed down its "revolutionary" decision of July 16, 1971, elevating individual freedom to the status of a constitutional right and establishing the *Conseil constitutionnel* as the protector of that freedom. That decision signaled the beginning of a transformation of the French legal system....

These developments are of particular interest to common-law observers for several reasons: (1) they demonstrate the increasing effectiveness of the French system of a priori constitutional control in protecting individual freedom; (2) they represent a fundamental shift in the French political structure, that is, the legislator's submission to constitutional norms; and (3) they symbolize the emergence of constitutional jurisprudence as an active force in French law....

Revolution/Evolution at the Conseil constitutionnel

Decision of January 12, 1977. This was one of the *Conseil constitutionnel*'s most influential and widely publicized decisions. The Government, in an attempt to fight rising crime, proposed a law giving the police very broad powers to search vehicles. The bill encountered stiff resistance in the legislature, where it was finally passed by the National Assembly after twice being rejected by the Senate. Its constitutionality was challenged immediately by over 200 senators and deputies.

The *Conseil* rejected the law on the ground that individual freedom is a principle of constitutional value whose protection is entrusted to judicial authorities (*l'autorité judiciaire*) by article 66 of the Constitution. The *Conseil* reasoned that judicial authorities can carry out this function only if the investigation of crimes (which may involve acts threatening individual liberty) is restricted to the judicial police, and only if the judicial police are restricted to the investigation of actual infractions. The proposed law gave the police the authority to take actions impinging on individual freedom (vehicle searches) without requiring that a crime have been committed or providing any precise conditions under which this authority could be exercised. By giving the judicial police virtually unlimited authority to search vehicles, and duties traditionally carried out by the administrative police, the law failed to provide adequate controls on police activity; thus, it was contrary to the Constitution.

The decision of January 12, 1977 had a significant impact on the development of constitutional jurisprudence because it affirmed the constitutional value of individual liberty in a broad sense, going beyond the immediate issue of vehicle searches. The *Conseil* found a general right to privacy (*la vie privée*) in the right to be free from arbitrary detention, the right to freedom of movement (*la liberté d'aller et de venir*), and the inviolability of the domicile (*l'inviolabilité de la domicile*). This expanded concept of individual freedom is not found in any of the texts comprising the "bloc of constitutionality." However, the *Conseil* found it in the "fundamental principles recognized by the laws of the Republic" and in article 66 of the Constitution.[73]

The second constitutional principle to emerge from this decision was the primacy of the judicial authority as guardian of individual freedom. Although this principle is expressed in article 66 of the Constitution, that article had apparently been added to the text at the last minute amid doubts about its precise meaning and value. The *Conseil constitutionnel*, however, affirmed it as a constitutional principle binding on the legislature. This principle would later prove instrumental in several important decisions of the *Conseil* and in the diffusion of its jurisprudence throughout the judicial order....

Decision of December 19, 1980. This decision, involving the reform of the laws on rape and public morals, focused on the principle of equality before the law, which had recently come into vogue as a means of constitutional challenge. The disputed provision provided that acts of indecent exposure committed or attempted (without violence, force, or surprise) against a minor of

[73] Article 66 of the Constitution reads as follows: "No one shall be arbitrarily detained. The judicial authority shall assure respect of this principle in the conditions provided by law."

fifteen years or under would be criminally punished. It also authorized criminal sanctions against anyone committing an "immodest or unnatural act" with a minor of the same sex who is eighteen years or under.

The law was challenged on two grounds: (1) that in differentiating between homosexual and nonhomosexual acts, it violated the principle of equality among offenders, and (2) that female minors would be unequally protected because indecent acts committed against them while between the ages of fifteen and eighteen would go unpunished.

The *Conseil constitutionnel* rejected both of these arguments and held that the legislature had the right to differentiate between offenses of a different nature (homosexual vs. heterosexual acts) without violating the principle of equality as long as the offender, whether male or female, incurred the same punishment. The *Conseil* avoided the issue of morality, since deciding the normality or abnormality of homosexuality was not necessary to decide the case....

Decision of September 3, 1986 (terrorism). In the first of four decisions handed down on the same day, the *Conseil constitutionnel* upheld one constitutional challenge and rejected three others to a law designed to facilitate the battle against terrorism.

In seeking more effective prosecution of terrorist crimes, the legislature created procedural rules designed to centralize and consolidate these prosecutions. It did not wish to create a new infraction because the crimes committed by terrorists already existed in the codes. The creation of a separate crime of "terrorist activity" would risk giving this infraction a political character that the Government wished to avoid.

The legislature instead defined two conditions under which certain existing infractions would be considered "terrorist" and therefore subject to the special rules of prosecution: (1) the facts at issue must constitute one of a designated (and limited) number of infractions, and (2) this infraction must be "related to an individual or collective enterprise having as its goal the serious disruption of public order by intimidation or terror."

The first challenge alleged that basing a different application of the law not on the elements of the infraction but on the subjective element of the actor's goal violated the principle of the legality of crimes and punishments (*la légalité des délits et des peines*). The *Conseil constitutionnel* rejected this challenge, finding that the first condition referred to infractions already defined by law, and that the second condition was set forth in terms sufficiently clear to conform to the principle of the legality of crimes and punishments.

The second challenge involved the most important procedural change in the proposed law: defendants accused of terrorist crimes were to be tried not before the traditional judge and jury, but before a special *Cour d'assises* (criminal court) composed of a presiding judge and six magistrates. This provision was considered necessary to ensure that trials would not be delayed or cancelled for lack of jurors willing to sit in judgment on suspected terrorists who frequently threatened them during the proceedings. The special court was challenged as violating the principle of equality before the law: whatever the motive, infractions defined by the same constituent elements must be judged according to the same rules and by the same judges.

The *Conseil constitutionnel* rejected this argument, and stated that the legislature may fix different rules according to the facts, persons, or situations to which they apply, as long as these differences do not arise from unjustified discrimination, and as long as the defendants are guaranteed their rights, especially the rights of the defense. In this case, the difference in treatment was justified by the need to avoid pressures or threats disrupting the trial court. In addition, the composition of the special court met the requisite criteria of independence and impartiality, so that the rights of the defense were adequately guaranteed....

The fourth and final challenge was to a provision which would make *all* crimes against the State subject to the special rules of procedure for terrorist crimes. The *Conseil constitutionnel* found this violated the principle of equality before the law: the difference in procedure justified by the nature of terrorist crimes was not justified in its extension to the general category of crimes against the State, not all of which are terrorist in nature....

Impact of Constitutional Jurisprudence on Judicial and Administrative Jurisdiction

Certain decisions [of the Court of Cassation and the Council of State] represent a significant increase in recognition of the *Conseil constitutionnel*, not only of its authority under article 62 but of its jurisprudential (interpretive) authority. According to Professor Favoreu, two factors point to the strengthening of this trend. One is the sheer number of decisions handed down by the *Conseil constitutionnel* since liberalization of the referral power in 1974. The increasingly frequent referral of laws to the *Conseil* has reinforced the idea of constitutional norms, and the jurisprudence of individual liberty has taken root in the judicial and administrative jurisdictions. As these authorities continue to apply constitutional jurisprudence, it will become less likely that countervailing decisions will be handed down.

The other factor is as yet unrealized on a large scale, although it is visible in the *Conseil d'Etat*'s *Ville de Paris* decree;[a] as more and more litigants become aware of the norms set forth by the *Conseil constitutionnel*, they will bring these issues before the lower courts, and judges will be obligated to adjudicate them. This will increase the application of constitutional norms in individual cases, and constitutional justice will be applied not just abstractly in a priori rulings, but concretely in the lower courts.

MARY ANN GLENDON, ABORTION AND DIVORCE IN WESTERN LAW 16-18 (1987)*

The first article of the 1975 [French statute on abortion] characterizes the factual situation upon which the law operates as involving human life, and

[a] The City of Paris had alleged a violation of article 66 as interpreted by the *Conseil constitutionnel* in its decision of December 29, 1983 on fiscal warrants. The *Conseil d'Etat* explicitly followed the *Conseil constitutionnel*'s interpretation of the judicial authority's role as protector of individual liberty in the inviolability of the domicile and followed its conditions for fiscal search warrants in nonpublic places. The *Conseil d'Etat* was not bound to follow this interpretation, but did so voluntarily.

sets forth the general principles that are to guide the interpretation of the new legislation: "The law guarantees the respect of every human being from the commencement of life. There shall be no derogation from this principle except in cases of necessity and under the conditions laid down by this law."...

After affirming the principle of respect for human life, the 1975 law then specifies the circumstances under which it will countenance derogation from that principle, calling these circumstances cases of "necessity." The law, imitating life in this respect, is not strictly logical in carrying out its basic principles. The first case of "necessity" it acknowledges is when, prior to the end of the tenth week of pregnancy, a woman finds herself in "distress" as a result of being pregnant. But while making abortion available in this case, the statute mandates several procedures designed to make the pregnant woman aware of, and able to choose, alternatives to abortion. First, the physician who receives the woman's initial request for termination of her pregnancy must furnish her with a brochure (supplied by the government) informing her that the law limits abortion to cases of distress. (There are no sanctions against the woman who pretends to be in distress. The idea seems to be simply to try to make sure everyone knows that abortion is considered to be a serious matter.) The brochure must contain information about the public benefits and programs that are guaranteed to mothers and children, and about the possibilities of adoption, as well as provide a list of organizations capable of giving assistance. Second, the pregnant woman is required to have a private interview, if possible with her partner, with a government-approved counseling service which, in principle, is not to be located in any facility where abortions are performed. This consultation, according to the statute, is supposed to furnish the woman with assistance and advice, "especially with a view toward enabling her to keep her child." Third, at least one week must elapse from the time of her initial request for an abortion, and at least two days from the time of the mandatory consultation, before the abortion can be performed. The waiting periods need not be observed if, in the physician's judgment, there is an emergency situation, or if they would cause the ten-week period to be exceeded.

After ten weeks the law in France permits only "therapeutic" abortions. In these cases, two physicians must certify that the "continuation of the pregnancy is seriously endangering the woman's health or that there is a strong possibility that the unborn child is suffering from a particularly serious disease or condition considered incurable at the time of diagnosis." To avoid bringing "abortion mills" into existence, the law provides that all abortions must be performed by physicians in approved facilities, and that the annual number of abortions in such establishments may not exceed 25 percent of all surgical and obstetrical operations carried out there. At present, in France, the state pays 70 percent of the cost of nontherapeutic abortions and the entire cost of those that are medically necessary.

Immediately upon its passage and before promulgation, the seventy-seven legislators who had opposed the 1975 law brought it to the French Constitutional Council for review, on grounds that it violated constitutional guarantees of human rights and protection of the health of children.[34] The council, which, unlike the United States Supreme Court, has rarely been inclined to differ with the parliamentary majority on a highly controversial question, upheld the law in a very short opinion. It began by noting that the Constitution "does not confer upon the Constitutional Council a general power of evaluation and decision identical with that of the Parliament, but gives it jurisdiction only to rule on the conformity to the Constitution of the laws submitted for its scrutiny."[35] The council ruled that the law did not violate any constitutional texts. The principle of respect for life was, in the council's view, satisfied by the fact that the statute permitted abortion only in case of necessity and under the conditions provided by law.

NOTES AND QUESTIONS

1. Compare the U.S. Supreme Court to the French Constitutional Council. Which is more responsive to popular political sentiment? What forces have pushed the French toward constitutionalism?

2. Is it persuasive to call *The Freedom of Association Case* the *Marbury v. Madison* (1803) of France? What are the similarities between the two cases? Although the Council cites the preamble to the 1958 Constitution, which "proclaims its attachment" to the 1789 Declaration of the Rights of Man and the preamble to the 1946 Constitution, none of these documents mention the freedom of association. Rather this freedom was implicitly connected to the 1946 preamble, which reaffirmed the "fundamental principles recognized by the laws of the Republic." Since 1901 the freedom of association had been recognized as a fundamental principle of the French republican tradition.

The Constitutional Council after 1971 recognized two distinct sources of individual rights: the Declaration of the Rights of Man and fundamental principles. The latter source refers to the "general principles of law," whose derivation from study of the concrete French legal order was an object of legal science.

3. Does the Constitutional Council's treatment of criminal law and procedure issues seem more like that of a political institution or a judicial institution? Do you understand Professor Favoreu's prediction that eventually lower ordinary and administrative law courts will be obligated to adjudicate constitutional law issues?

4. The Constitutional Council's abortion decision is about two pages long. Would you characterize it as more a political decision or a judicial decision?

5. A remarkable decision of January 1984 extends the notion of review for conformity with the "constitution" very far indeed in that it annuls legislation seeking to *repeal* an ordinary law of 1968 relative to the organisation of university faculties. The law is said to reflect a republican

[34] The constitutional texts appealed to were the Preamble to the 1958 Constitution, which states that "every human being ... possesses sacred and inalienable rights," and the Preamble to the 1946 Constitution, which states that the nation "guarantees protection of health to all, notably to children, and mothers."

[35] French Constitutional Council Decision of January 15, 1975 [1975] D.S. Jur. 529; *Journal officiel* Jan. 16, 1975, p. 671.

tradition respectful of academic freedom. Since the law proposed as a replacement did not contain what the court regarded as "equivalent guarantees" in that regard, the existing law could not constitutionally be repealed!

The Constitutional Council thus appears to have evolved in a few years towards a position without parallel in French legal history, towards the exercise of a supervision of the legislature which is more muscled than that exercised by the United States Supreme Court with regard to the United States Congress. Certainly United States jurisprudence offers no example of an ordinary law being held to have "constitutional value" protecting it from repeal.

Dallis Radamaker, *The Courts in France*, in The Political Role of Law Courts in Modern Democracies 129, 143 (Jerold L. Waltman & Kenneth M. Holland eds. 1988). *See* Note, *Resolving the Abortion Debate: Compromise Legislation, An Analysis of the Abortion Policies of the United States, France and Germany*, 16 Suffolk Transnat'l L. Rev. 513 (1993).

6. For further information on the French Constitutional Council, see Louis M. Aucoin, *Judicial Review in France: Access of the Individual Under French and European Community Law in the Aftermath of France's Rejection of Bicentennial Reform*, 15 B.C. Int'l & Comp. L. Rev. 443 (1992); Michael H. Davis, *The Law/Politics Distinction, the French Conseil Constitutionnel, and the U.S. Supreme Court*, 34 Am. J. Comp. L. 45 (1986); Burt Neuborne, *Judicial Review and Separation of Powers in France and the United States*, 57 N.Y.U. L. Rev. 363, 377-410 (1982); Martin M. Shapiro, *Judicial Review in France*, 6 J. L. & Pol. 531 (1990) (the Council is more like a third, specialized, legislative chamber than like a court); Alec Stone, the Birth of Judicial Politics in France: The Constitutional Council in Comparative Perspective (1992). *See also* John Bell, French Constitutional Law 9-56 (1992).

7. For an historical and comparative treatment of the expansion and legitimacy of judicial review, see Mauro Cappelletti, The Judicial Process in Comparative Perspective 115-211 (1989).

3. THE GERMAN FEDERAL CONSTITUTIONAL COURT

BASIC LAW OF GERMANY

Articles 93, 94, 100

IX. Administration of Justice

Article 93 (Federal Constitutional Court Jurisdiction)

(1) The Federal Constitutional Court shall decide:

1. on the interpretation of this Basic Law in the event of disputes concerning the extent of the rights and duties of a highest federal organ or of other parties concerned who have been vested with rights of their own by this Basic Law or by rules of procedure of a highest federal organ;
2. in case of differences of opinion or doubts on the formal and material compatibility of federal law or Land law with this Basic Law, or on the

compatibility of Land law with other federal law, at the request of the Federal Government, of a Land government, or of one third of the Bundestag members;

3. in case of differences of opinion on the rights and duties of the Federation and the Länder, particularly in the execution of federal law by the Länder and in the exercise of federal supervision;
4. on other disputes involving public law, between the Federation and the Länder, between different Länder or within a Land, unless recourse to another court exists:

4a. on complaints of unconstitutionality, which may be entered by any person who claims that one of his basic rights or one of his rights under paragraph (4) of Article 20, or under Article 33, 38, 101, 103, or 104 has been violated by public authority;

4b. on complaints of unconstitutionality, entered by communes or associations of communes on the ground that their right to self-government under Article 28 has been violated by a law other than a Land law open to complaint to the respective Land constitutional court;

5. in the other cases provided for in this Basic Law.

(2) The Federal Constitutional Court shall also act in such other cases as are assigned to it by federal legislation.

Article 94 (Federal Constitutional Court Composition)

(1) The Federal Constitutional Court shall consist of federal judges and other members. Half of the members of the Federal Constitutional Court shall be elected by the Bundestag and half by the Bundesrat. They may not be members of the Bundestag, the Bundesrat, the Federal Government, nor of any of the corresponding organs of a Land.

(2) The constitution and procedure of the Federal Constitutional Court shall be regulated by a federal law which shall specify in what cases its decisions shall have the force of law. Such law may require that all other legal remedies must have been exhausted before any such complaint of unconstitutionality can be entered, and may make provision for a special procedure as to admissibility.

Article 100 (Constitutionality of Statutes)

(1) If a court considers unconstitutional a law the validity of which is relevant to its decision, the proceedings shall be stayed, and a decision shall be obtained from the Land court competent for constitutional disputes if the constitution of a Land is held to be violated, or from the Federal Constitutional Court if this Basic Law is held to be violated. This shall also apply if this Basic Law is held to be violated by Land law or if a Land law is held to be incompatible with a federal law.

(2) If, in the course of litigation, doubt exists whether a rule of public international law is an integral part of federal law and whether such rule directly creates rights and duties for the individual (Article 25), the court shall obtain a decision from the Federal Constitutional Court.

(3) If the constitutional court of a Land, in interpreting this Basic Law, intends to deviate from a decision of the Federal Constitutional Court or of the constitutional court of another Land, it must obtain a decision from the Federal Constitutional Court.

DONALD P. KOMMERS, GERMAN CONSTITUTIONALISM: A PROLEGOMENON, 40 Emory Law Journal 837, 840-45, 848-52, 855-56, 858-61, 864-73 (1991)

The Role of the Federal Constitutional Court

The Constitutional Court's powers, set forth in ten different articles of the Basic Law, include the authority to examine, upon the request of a state (*Land*) or the federal government (*Bund*) or of one-third of the members of the federal parliament (*Bundestag*), the constitutionality of any federal statute or any state statute allegedly in conflict with the Basic Law or a federal law. Such proceedings fall within the Court's "abstract norm control" (*abstrakte Normenkontrolle*) jurisdiction, so called because they do not arise out of the normal course of litigation. Governments and legislators may petition the Court to review the constitutionality of a statute immediately after its enactment, a procedure that results in the instant judicialization of a constitutional dispute.

Three other proceedings underscore the Court's crucially important role in Germany's constitutional system. The first is the Court's "concrete norm control" (*konkrete Normenkontrolle*) jurisdiction. Judges presiding over the regular judiciary may not declare laws unconstitutional, but if they regard as "unconstitutional a law the validity of which is relevant to [their] decision," they "shall" refer the constitutional issue to the Federal Constitutional Court. (Once the latter decides the issue, the lower court may proceed with the case.) The second procedure authorizes the Court to declare political parties unconstitutional if they "seek to impair or abolish the free democratic basic order or ... endanger the existence of the Federal Republic of Germany."... Third, the Basic Law empowers "any person who claims that one of his basic rights ... has been violated by public authority" to file a constitutional complaint in the Federal Constitutional Court. The Court is constitutionally mandated to hear several other types of proceedings.... [A]ny decision of the Court on the constitutionality of a statute "shall have the force of law" and, as law, shall be published in the *Federal Gazette*, along with other federal statutes. As a consequence, the Court's decisions bind all organs of government, federal and state, and all courts and public officials. Finally, ... the Court's jurisdiction is compulsory; it may not avoid decision in a case properly before it by invoking a "political question" doctrine or the "passive virtues" of Bickelian jurisprudence. By the same token, conventional wisdom holds that the Court is powerless to exercise authority not rooted in the express language of the Basic Law. The German version of the *Rechtsstaat* leaves little doubt as to the nature of its jurisdiction or the effect of its decisions.

For all of these reasons, the source and authority of the Federal Constitutional Court are relatively undisputed. In the United States, by contrast, the main task of constitutional theory is to find the source and establish the limits of judicial review. *Marbury v. Madison* inaugurated this effort, but the glaring deficiencies of Marshall's reasoning have prompted a perennial search in the United States for a more convincing theory of when and why the judiciary should invalidate the acts of elected officials....

It would be misleading, however, to suggest that there is little or no controversy in Germany over the role of the Federal Constitutional Court. Judicial nullification of majoritarian policy draws as much fire in Germany as in the United States. What is different is that the fire in Germany is directed against government agencies or party leaders who would resort to constitutional litigation for essentially political ends. The Court itself catches the fire when it appears to cooperate in the achievement of these ends, one of the hazards, incidentally, of the abstract judicial review proceeding. Nevertheless, the so-called "counter-majoritarian difficulty," the term Alexander Bickel used to describe the root problem of judicial review in America, is not a major problem in Germany. The Basic Law itself resolves the difficulty, for no reliance on a theory of judicial review is necessary to justify the exercise of judicial power.

This picture of German constitutional decisionmaking, however, is only partially correct. The counter-majoritarian difficulty does arise in Germany to the extent that the Federal Constitutional Court decides cases on the basis of historical and functional considerations. In truth, as we shall see later on, the Court has invoked theories of its own creation, the most prominent being the notion of an "objective order of values," on the basis of which it has struck down a number of important statutes, including a liberal abortion law. Some of these decisions have invited the objection, so familiar to Americans, that the justices are doing little more than imposing their own personal values on the nation as a whole. What makes the Constitutional Court's "activism" less objectionable in terms of democratic theory, however, is that Parliament — not the executive — elects each justice by a two-thirds vote for a single nonrenewable term of twelve years, thereby averting the rise of an aging judicial oligarchy out of tune with major currents of modern life.

What also makes the exercise of judicial review in Germany somewhat less problematic — albeit no less predictable — than in the United States is a set of generally agreed-upon approaches to constitutional interpretation. These approaches might be brought together under the general heading of "constitutional textualism." The code law tradition, with its emphasis on specific norms and structures, leads to legal positivism in adjudication, and the Constitutional Court often talks as if it is adhering strictly to the constitutional text. But the Court also employs systematic and teleological modes of inquiry. The focus here is often on the unity of the text as a whole from whence judges are to ascertain the aims and objects — *i.e.*, the *telos* — of the Constitution, a style of reasoning that allows judges to incorporate broad value judgments into their decisions. These judgments are strikingly reminiscent of the Supreme Court's substantive due process decisions. Historical arguments, finally, are also legitimate, although German legal scholars agree that history ranks last in persuasive force among these modes.

History in the sense used here refers to the objective conditions out of which a constitutional value or provision arose. It helps to confirm judgments arrived at on the basis of purposive or teleological reasoning. Original intent, on the other hand, defined as the subjective understanding of the framers, plays no significant role in German constitutional interpretation. In the United States, by contrast, original intent and the weight it should be given in constitutional adjudication is a hotly contested issue, dividing both scholars and judges. It might seem that the "aims and objects" approach of teleological inquiry differs little from the determination of original intent, but the German judicial mind distinguishes sharply between these methods....

The New Constitutionalism of the Basic Law

Normativity of the Constitution

The Basic Law is an elaborate framework of rules and principles that define the nature of West Germany's constitutional state. Every provision of the Constitution is a legally binding norm requiring full and unambiguous implementation. In Kelsenian language, the Constitution may be said to represent the *Grundnorm* (basic norm) that governs and legitimates the entire legal order. It controls public law directly but it also influences, albeit indirectly, the interpretation of private law. In brief, any law, administrative regulation, legal relationship, or political practice that cannot be justified in terms of the Basic Law is by definition unconstitutional and, in the German variant of the constitutional state, it must be so declared if the order of legality and legal certainty — among the highest values of the German *Rechtsstaat* — is to be maintained.

The preservation of the constitutional state in *all* of its particulars is indeed the function of the Federal Constitutional Court. As already suggested, the Court's role is to *decide* constitutional issues, not to avoid them or to resolve them as a matter of last resort. When serious doubts arise over the validity of a law or practice having the force of law, the Court's function is to resolve the doubt in the interest of constitutional clarity and certainty. Gaps in the Constitution cry out for closure, for which reason all issues arising under the Basic Law and properly before the Court are justiciable. Even the Basic Law's provisions relating to the maintenance of peace and security appear to be justiciable.[35] Vague constitutional terms such as "human dignity," "democracy," and "social state" have also been found to possess a sharp set of teeth capable of killing legislation and even to compel certain forms of state action if public officials are to avoid its bite. In the United States, by contrast, major constitutional provisions like the republican form of government clause, the foreign relations powers clause, the privileges and immunities clause of the fourteenth amendment, and the clause on the ratification of amendments to the Constitution have been relegated to the limbo of nonjusticiability....

[35] German leaders invoked Article 24 of the Basic Law in defense of their position that the Federal Republic could not participate militarily in Desert Storm. Indeed, political parties in opposition to the government threatened to seek a temporary restraining order from the Constitutional Court in the event that the Kohl-Genscher government ordered German military forces into the Persian Gulf. Under the prevailing interpretation of Article 24, the Federal Republic may deploy its army and navy only within the framework of the North Atlantic Treaty Organization.

In short, and at the risk of over-simplification, the Anglo-American legal mind is content to let law evolve over time as reality unfolds, whereas the civilian public mind seeks to specify reality in comprehensive codes of law. These tendencies — and they are only tendencies — spill over into constitutional law. The discretionary authority of the American Supreme Court, for example, together with its various strategies for avoiding or postponing constitutional decisions, is perfectly compatible with this common law view of the world. The German Constitutional Court, on the other hand, is an organ explicitly entrusted with the perpetual guardianship of the Constitution, a stewardship that implies the continuous elaboration of the Constitution's meaning, its singular purpose being to close the gap between constitutional reality and constitutional normativity....

Unity of the Constitution

In German constitutional theory the Basic Law represents a unified structure of principles and values. As the Federal Constitutional Court remarked in one of its earliest decisions: "No single constitutional provision may be taken out of its context and interpreted by itself.... Every constitutional provision must always be interpreted so as to render it compatible with the fundamental principles of the Constitution and the intention of its authors." In other instances, the Court has alluded to "the unity of the Constitution as a logical-teleological entity," an interpretive principle that commands the assent of leading constitutional commentators in Germany. It is also a concept that seeks to fuse Germany's positivistic and natural law traditions of legality.

Closely related to the concept of the constitution as a structural unity is the principle of "practical concordance" (*praktische Konkordanz*). According to this principle, constitutionally protected legal values must be harmonized with one another in the event of their conflict. One may not be realized at the total expense of the other. Both are to be preserved in creative tension with one another. Thus, in adjudicating a concrete ease involving a conflict, say, between freedom of speech and the right to the "inviolability of [one's] personal honor" (Article 5, paragraph 1), the Court must seek to resolve the conflict so as to harmonize both values to the greatest possible extent. The Court may not prefer one value over another or perform a balancing act that would minimize the importance of a valid constitutional norm. To preserve the unity of the Constitution is to preserve the Constitution as a whole.

The German notion of an "unconstitutional constitutional amendment" also flows from the Constitution seen as a unity of values and structures. In the German constitutionalist view, accepted and propagated by the Constitutional Court itself, any constitutional amendment conflicting with the core values or spirit of the Basic Law as a whole would itself be unconstitutional. In the well-known *Klass Case*, for example, the Court considered the constitutionality of an amendment to Article 10 of the Basic Law limiting the "inviolable" right of "privacy of posts and telecommunications." Ratified along with the state-of-defense amendments of 1968, it replaced judicial with administrative recourse for any violation of this right. The Court sustained the validity of the amendment over the objection of three justices who felt that it did in fact contravene the principles of human dignity, separation of powers, and the rule of law....

The Structure of Rights and Values

The Primacy of Rights

The West German Basic Law takes rights seriously. It leads off by proclaiming that "[t]he dignity of man is inviolable" and then, in the very next sentence, commands the state to respect and protect it (Article 1[1]). All of the ensuing rights enumerated in the remaining eighteen articles of the Bill of Rights are designed to actualize this crowning principle of human dignity. Human dignity, as the Constitutional Court repeatedly emphasizes, is the highest value of the Basic Law, the ultimate basis of the constitutional order, and the foundation of guaranteed rights. All other rights proceed in logical succession, moving from the general to the particular. Article 2 secures to every person "the right to the free development of his [or her] personality" and the right to personal inviolability. Article 3 contains a general equality clause together with provisions forbidding discrimination based on gender, race, national origin, language, religion, and political affiliation. The remaining articles guarantee all the rights and liberties commonly associated with liberal constitutionalism. These include the freedoms of religion, speech, assembly, association, and movement as well as the rights to property, privacy, and petition. Conscientious objection to military service and the right to choose a trade or occupation round out this list of fundamental rights.[56]

The Bill of Rights, however, includes more than these personal liberties. It also protects communal interests such as marriage and the family and the right of parents to decide whether their children shall receive religious instruction in public schools. In sharp contrast to the United States Constitution, the German Bill of Rights speaks of duties and responsibilities as well as rights. Article 6, for example, tells parents that it is their "natural right" and "duty" to care for their children while simultaneously instructing the "national community" to "watch over their endeavors in this respect." Article 14 declares that the right to property "imposes duties" and should "serve the public weal." Under Article 12a, finally, all men eighteen years or older are subject to military service or, if a male citizen refuses induction because of conscience, he may be required to serve society in an alternative civilian capacity for a period equal to the time he would have spent in the military. While Article 20 is not part of the Bill of Rights it nevertheless incorporates the concept of the social welfare state in terms of which basic rights are often interpreted. German constitution-makers thus believed — and have always

[56]The Basic Law embraces rights other than those found in its first 19 articles (Bill of Rights). These include the ban on capital punishment (Article 102) and various procedural rights of criminal defendants (Articles 101, 103, and 104), the right to vote (Article 38 [2]), the right to resist any effort to abolish the constitutional order (Article 20 [4]), the right to form political parties (Article 21), the right of every German to equal treatment in seeking entry into the civil service or public office (Article 33), the right of any person to file a complaint with the Federal Constitutional Court in the event that his or her rights have been violated by the state (Article 93 (1) [4a]), and various provisions of the Weimar Constitution related to religious freedom (Article 140).

believed — that any realization of human dignity implies a fusion of individual rights and social responsibilities....

An Objective Order of Values

In its search for constitutional first principles, the Constitutional Court has seen fit, as noted earlier, to interpret the Basic Law in terms of its overall structural unity. Perhaps "ideological" unity would be the more accurate term here, for the Constitutional Court envisions the Basic Law as a unified structure of *substantive* values. The centerpiece of this interpretive strategy is the concept of an "objective order of values," a concept that derives from the gloss the Federal Constitutional Court has put on the text of the Basic Law. According to this concept, the Constitution incorporates the "basic value decisions" of the founding fathers, the most basic of which is their choice of a free democratic basic order — *i.e.*, a liberal, representative, federal, parliamentary democracy — buttressed and reinforced by basic rights and liberties. These basic values are objective because they are said to have an independent reality under the Constitution, imposing upon all organs of government an affirmative duty to see that they are realized in practice.

The notion of an objective value order may be stated in another way. Every basic right in the Constitution — *e.g.*, freedom of speech, press, religion, association, and the right to property or the right to choose one's profession or occupation — has a corresponding value. A basic "right" is a negative right against the state, but this right also represents a "value," and as a value it imposes an obligation on the state to insure that it becomes an integral part of the general legal order. One example may suffice: The *right* to freedom of the press protects a newspaper against any action of the state that would encroach upon its independence, but as an objective *value* applicable to society as a whole the state is duty-bound to create the conditions that make freedom of the press both possible and effective. In practice, this means that the state may have to regulate the press to promote the value of democracy; for example, by enacting legislation to prevent the press from becoming the captive of any dominant group or interest....

Not all of the justices — or constitutional scholars — are comfortable with the value theory of constitutional interpretation. For example, ... Wolfgang Zeidler, a former President of the Federal Constitutional Court, strongly criticized the Court's tendency "to superimpose 'a higher order of values' on the positive constitutional order." In his opinion, the notion of a basic value order — a "tyranny of values" according to some commentators — is often used as a tool to incorporate religious and philosophical views into the meaning of the Constitution. In any event, by advancing the notion of an objective value order, the Court seemed clearly to reject the legal positivism (*Rechtspositivismus*) and moral relativism presumed to have been at the basis of the Weimar constitutional order. That the Basic Law is a value-oriented — not a value-neutral — constitution is a familiar refrain in the Constitutional Court's case law. Early on in its jurisprudence the Court spoke of certain "unwritten" or "supra-positive" norms that presumably govern the entire constitutional order. Justices intellectually rooted in the Christian natural law tradition adhered to this view. Today the Court is more inclined to speak of the value system inherent in the Basic Law itself. The objective values of the Basic Law define a way of life to which the German people, as a nation, are committed. The task of the Court in adjudicating constitutional controversies is one of integrating these values into the common culture and common conscientiousness of the German people. The task is no less than creating and maintaining a nation of shared values....

Fundamental Rights: Some German-American Comparisons

Equality and the Welfare State

The Federal Constitutional Court's equal protection jurisprudence is substantial. It is also complex because of the Basic Law's numerous provisions relating to equality. These provisions are themselves arranged in a hierarchy, and they bear some resemblance to the high scrutiny jurisprudence of the United States Supreme Court. Article 3 contains a general equality clause and two additional clauses banning certain kinds of discrimination. It reads:

> (1) All persons shall be equal before the law.
> (2) Men and women shall have equal rights.
> (3) No one may be prejudiced or favored because of his [or her] sex, parentage, race, language, homeland and origin, faith, or religious or political opinions.

Paragraph 1 implicates what Americans would describe as "non-suspect" classifications; paragraphs 2 and 3, on the other hand, involve "suspect" classifications. With respect to these classifications, the standards of constitutional review are virtually identical in the United States and Germany, although judicial outcomes may differ. Article 3 (1), however, as informed by the social state principle (*Sozialstaatlichkeit*) has no equivalent in American constitutional law. The following discussion is limited to the *Numerus Clausus Case* because it illustrates the relationship between the general equality clause of Article 3 ("All persons shall be equal before the law") and the social state principle (*Sozialstaatlichkeit*) that the Constitutional Court has extracted from Article 20 (1) ("The Federal Republic of Germany is a democratic and social federal state.")...

Numerus Clausus challenged numerical limits imposed by two universities upon admission into their law and medical schools in order to relieve the pressure of overcrowding. The Constitutional Court struck down these limitations because they violated Article 12 when read in tandem with the general equality clause and the social state principle. Article 12 guarantees to "all Germans ... the right to choose their trade, occupation, or profession" while the social state principle, as interpreted, obligates the legislature to shape society and the economy in such a way as to maximize individual choice and minimize risks that threaten human dignity. No such constraints limit the state in the American constitutional order....

Thus, in *Numerus Clausus* the Court held that the principle of equality, when construed in the light of the *Sozialstaatsprinzip* against the backdrop of the constitutional right to choose one's occupation, requires the state to admit all qualified persons into their chosen fields of study.[79] The ruling required state governments to expand their facilities to permit the admission of such students or, alternatively, to prescribe *in law* new admission policies that would inform prospective students, exactly and precisely, what standards would be applied in admitting them to the university. The Court regarded this matter as too important to be left to the discretion of university authorities. After all, what is at stake here is the growth and development of the human personality. As an objective value of the constitutional order this principle of human dignity must be carved into the order of legality. This is part of what the Germans mean by the *Rechtsstaat* except that under the new dispensation of the Basic Law the traditional *Rechtsstaat* (*i.e.*, the state as formally conceived) has been indissolubly wedded to the modern *Sozialstaat* (*i.e.*, the state as materially conceived). There is no such marital bond in American constitutional law.

The constitutionalism of duty that one finds in the Basic Law, and which is conspicuous for its absence in the United States Constitution, reflects a deep theory of the human personality. In a nutshell, and at the risk of overdrawing the comparison, the United States Constitution incorporates a vision of personhood that is individualistic and self-regarding, whereas the Basic Law incorporates a vision of personhood that is both personalist and communal. In other words, the United States Constitution extols the ethic of individualism and, at the same time, exhibits a profound distrust of governmental power. The Basic Law, by contrast, while it surely vindicates the individual's personal search for happiness, sees the individual in terms of his social attachments and commitments. One vision is partial to the city perceived as a private realm in which the individual is alone, isolated, and in competition with his fellows, while the other vision is partial to the city perceived as a public realm where individual and community are bound together in some degree of reciprocity. Thus the authority of the community, as represented by the state, finds a more congenial abode in German than in American constitutionalism....

[I]n the German notion of the *Sozialstaat*, ... such things as homelessness, illiteracy, abject poverty, or some other grossly demeaning social inequity would be constitutionally suspect.... This constitutional view of the relationship between state and society — a relationship of mutual support and trust — is far removed from the theory underlying American constitutionalism, a point dramatically illustrated in *Deshaney v. Winnebago County*,[82] a case handed down by the Supreme Court in 1989. The case involved a father who over a two year period mercilessly beat his son of under five years of age into a condition of profound retardation even though state officials knew that the child was in danger and had arranged counseling sessions for the father. Later

[79] 33 BVerfGE 303 (1972). As a result of its increasing involvement in this field over the years the Constitutional Court "transformed itself into a veritable ministry of education. With each successive decision the Court seemed to narrow the discretion of university officials, forcing legislators to devise increasingly precise and nondiscriminatory standards governing university admissions."

[82] 489 U.S. 189 (1989).

the child's mother, who was divorced from the father, sued the state for not coming to the child's rescue and thus depriving him of the liberty protected by the fourteenth amendment. In any event, the facts of the case are less important than the Supreme Court's view of the person-state relationship. Chief Justice Rehnquist, speaking for the majority, rejected the mother's argument, saying in part:

> [There is] nothing in the language of the Due Process Clause [that] requires the State to protect the life, liberty, and property of its citizens against invasion by private actors. The Clause is phrased as a limitation on the State's power to act, not as a guarantee of certain minimal levels of safety and security.... [Its] language cannot fairly be extended to impose an affirmative obligation on the State to ensure that those interests do not come to harm through other means.

Whatever we may think of this doctrine, Chief Justice Rehnquist is surely right in suggesting, as he does late in the opinion, that American history does not support a theory of positive liberty, for the purpose of our Constitution was "to protect the people from the State, not to ensure that the State protected them from each other."

Church-State Relations

Church-state relations feature another major difference between the German and American Constitutions. For one thing, the boundary between church and state is drawn at different angles in the two documents. The first amendment simply bars Congress from making any law "respecting an establishment of religion or prohibiting the free exercise thereof." The rest is left to interpretation. By contrast, the Basic Law contains numerous provisions on church-state relations, leaving less to interpretation. Several of these provisions uphold religious liberty and vindicate the principle of nonestablishment. Other provisions, however, define churches as "religious bodies under public law" and clothe them with corporate privileges and rights, including the express power to levy taxes for the support of religious activities (Article 140). The Basic Law also provides for religious instruction in state schools (Article 9 [2]), although many German commentators see this practice as a manifestation of the free exercise of religion....

Both German and American constitutionalism require the state to be neutral with respect to religion, but neutrality means different things in the two systems. To Americans, neutrality means toleration and no public support; to Germans it means encouragement and at least some support. The American perspective reflects an essentially negative view of religion's role in the nation's public life, whereas the German perspective reflects a measurable degree of cooperation between cross and sword so long as each respects the autonomy of the other and the state favors no one religion over another....

Abortion

The constitutionalism of duty associated with the Basic Law's objective order of values is perhaps best illustrated in the *Abortion Case*. In 1975, two years after the decision in *Roe v. Wade*, the Federal Constitutional Court struck down a liberalized abortion statute because it violated the "right to life" as these terms are understood within the meaning of Article 2 (2).[89] Ruling that the right to life includes the unborn fetus, the Court said that fetal life is a value the state must protect throughout all stages of pregnancy, beginning with the fourteenth day after conception (*i.e.*, at the point of implantation), even against the wishes of the pregnant woman. Because the right to life is *the* preeminent value decision of the Basic Law, declared the Court, Parliament must not only proclaim *in law* that abortion is "an act of killing" but also it must punish any intentional destruction of the fetus in the absence of alternative non-criminal measures that would effectively protect fetal life.[90]

The American view, by contrast, holds that the state must refrain from influencing personal choices with respect to privacy. The individual's freedom of choice overrides all values rooted in community....

The *Abortion Case* also serves to illustrate the foregoing approach to interpretation. Two rights — or values — cried out for recognition here: the right to life (Article 2 [2]) and the countervailing right of pregnant women to the development of their personalities (Article 2 [1]). Both rights, in turn, were measured in the light of the principle of human dignity. The Court acknowledged that the right to personality is also an objective value that the state must respect, although it ranks lower on the scale of constitutional values than the right to life. While the right to life is cast in unqualified terms the right to personality may not "violate the rights of others or offend against the constitutional order or the moral code." In the end the Court sought to balance the value of unborn life against the woman's interest in her own well-being and ruled that in situations of extreme social hardship, the state has no right to impose upon the woman a burden that she cannot be expected to bear, and thus an abortion can legally be performed when, after counseling, the proper authorities decide that her pregnancy is indeed too heavy a burden for her to bear in the light of a set of given circumstances.

Conclusion

The American public mind is unlikely to share the Constitutional Court's enthusiasm for the notion of an objective value order, in part because of its pervasive skepticism in matters both moral and constitutional. The ethic of

---

89 Under the new version of the law a woman could procure an abortion during the first three months of pregnancy without penalty if she first submitted to a specified counseling procedure. The law permitted abortions after the third month only in the presence of medical, eugenic, or moral indications.

90 The two justices in dissent felt that the legislature's policy of decriminalizing abortion during the first three months of pregnancy, together with provisions for counseling prior to any decision to abort, was sufficient to protect the value of fetal life. All of the justices agreed that the right-to-life clause of Article 2 required the state to respect and safeguard the value of fetal life at all stages of pregnancy. They disagreed over whether the new abortion statute was enough to accomplish this result. In the minority's view Parliament had made an allowable legislative judgment on how best to protect unborn life and the interests of the pregnant woman. They argued that the implementation of an objective constitutional value is the primary responsibility of Parliament and not the judiciary. For a full translation of the majority and minority opinions, see 9 J. Marshall J. Prac. & Proc. 605-84 (1976).

individualism at the basis of the American Constitution celebrates negative not positive liberty. Ours is, moreover, a constitutionalism of rights not duties. As suggested, the two constitutions project different visions of personhood and social reality. The vision of the person in *Roe v. Wade* and its progeny is that of a woman alone, isolated and autonomous, unattached to any natural community, not even to the family, or to any ensemble of values that transcends her immediate interests. The person of American constitutional jurisprudence is a calculating person absorbed in self-vindication. The vision of the person in the German *Abortion Case* is that of a woman engulfed in a web of human relationships, one that sees the essence of personhood in communication, not separation, and views the individual as sheltered by a moral community or social structure larger than herself....

The Basic Law sees no necessary antagonism between individual rights and communitarian values. The German view, at bottom a Kantian moral perspective, finds the real meaning of liberty *in* community not apart from community.

THE LÜTH BOYCOTT CASE

Federal Constitutional Court of Germany
Judgment No. 28 of 15 January 1958
7 BVerfGE 198 (1958)

English translation published in Kommers, The Constitutional Jurisprudence of the Federal Republic of Germany 366, 368-75 (1989)

[Veit Harlan was a popular film director under the Nazi regime and the producer of the notoriously anti-Semitic film *Jud Süss*. In 1950, several years after his acquittal of having committed Nazi crimes, he directed a new movie entitled *Immortal Lover*. Erich Lüth, Hamburg's director of information and an active member of a group seeking to heal the wound between Christians and Jews, was outraged by Harlan's reemergence as a film director. Speaking before an audience of motion picture producers and distributors, he urged his listeners to boycott *Immortal Lover*. In his view, the boycott was necessary because of Harlan's Nazi past and the moral condemnation from inside and outside Germany that the film's showing would bring down on the German motion picture industry. Its producer and distributor secured an order from the Hamburg Superior Court enjoining Lüth to cease and desist from urging the German public not to see the film and asking theater owners and film distributors not to show it. The court regarded Lüth's action as an incitement in violation of Article 826 of the Civil Code. (It reads: "Whoever causes damage to another person intentionally and in a manner offensive to good morals is obligated to compensate the other person for the damage.") After the Hamburg Court of Appeals rejected his appeal, Lüth filed a constitutional complaint asserting a violation of his basic right to free speech under Article 5 (1). Article 5 provides that:

(1) Everyone has the right freely to express and disseminate his opinion orally, in writing, and in pictures, and to inform himself without hindrance from all generally accessible sources. The freedom of the press and

the freedom of reporting through radio and film are guaranteed. There is to be no censorship.

(2) These rights find their limits in the rules of the general laws, the statutory provisions for the protection of youth, and in the right to personal honor.

(3) Art and learning, research and teaching are free. The freedom of teaching does not release one from loyalty to the constitution.]

Judgment of the First Senate ....

B. II. The complainant claims that the superior court has violated his basic right to free speech as safeguarded by Article 5 (1) [1] of the Constitution.

1. The decision of the superior court is an act of public authority in the special form of a judicial decision. It can violate a basic right of the complainant only if the court was required to take the right in question into consideration when deciding the case.

The decision prohibits the complainant from making statements that could influence others to adhere to his opinion regarding Harlan's reappearance [as a film director].... Seen objectively, this limits the complainant's freedom of expression.... [But] such a ruling can violate the complainant's basic right under Article 5 (1) only if [a] provision of the Civil Code [Article 826] would be so affected by a basic right as to render it an impossible basis for a decision....

Whether and to what extent basic rights affect private law is controversial [citing legal literature]. The extreme positions in this dispute are, on the one hand, that basic rights are exclusively directed against the state and, on the other hand, that the basic rights as such, or at least some and in any case the more important of them, also apply in civil [i.e., private] law matters against everybody. Neither of these extremes finds support in the Constitutional Court's existing jurisprudence.... Nor is there any need here to resolve fully the dispute over the so-called effect of the basic rights on third persons [*Drittwirkung*]. The following discussion is sufficient to resolve this case.

... [T]he primary purpose of the basic rights is to safeguard the liberties of the individual against interferences by public authority. They are defensive rights of the individual against the state. This [purpose] follows from the historical development of the concept of basic rights and from historical developments leading to the inclusion of basic rights in the constitutions of various countries. This also corresponds to the meaning of the basic rights contained in the Basic Law and is underscored by the enumeration of basic rights in the first section of the Constitution, thereby stressing the primacy of the human being and his dignity over the power of the state. This is why the legislature allowed the extraordinary remedy ... of the constitutional complaint to be brought only against acts of public authority.

[An Objective Order of Values]

It is equally true, however, that the Basic Law is not a value-neutral document [citations from numerous decisions]. Its section on basic rights establishes an objective order of values, and this order strongly reinforces the effective power of basic rights. This value system, which centers upon dignity of the human personality developing freely within the social community, must be looked upon as a fundamental constitutional decision affecting all spheres of law [public and private]. It serves as a yardstick for measuring and assessing all actions in the areas of legislation, public administration, and adjudication. Thus it is clear that basic rights also influence [the development of] private law. Every provision of private law must be compatible with this system of values, and every such provision must be interpreted in its spirit.

The legal content of basic rights as objective norms is developed within private law through the medium of the legal provisions directly applicable to this area of the law. Newly enacted statutes must conform to the system of values of the basic rights. The content of existing law also must be brought into harmony with this system of values. This system infuses specific constitutional content into private law, which from that point on determines its interpretation. A dispute between private individuals concerning rights and duties emanating from provisions of private law — provisions influenced by the basic rights — remains substantively and procedurally a private-law dispute. [Courts] apply and interpret private law but the interpretation must conform to the Constitution.

The influence of the scale of values of the basic rights affects particularly those provisions of private law that contain mandatory rules of law and thus form part of the *ordre public* — in the broad sense of the term — that is, rules which for reasons of the general welfare also are binding on private legal relationships and are removed from the domination of private intent. Because of their purpose these provisions are closely related to the public law they supplement. Consequently, they are substantially exposed to the influence of constitutional law. In bringing this influence to bear, the courts may invoke the general clauses which, like Article 826 of the Civil Code, refer to standards outside private law. "Good morals" is one such standard. In order to determine what is required by social norms such as these, one has to consider first the ensemble of value concepts that a nation has developed at a certain point in its intellectual and cultural history and laid down in its constitution. That is why the general clauses have rightly been called the points where basic rights have breached the [domain of] private law [citation to Dürig, in Neumann, Nipperdey, and Scheuner, *Die Grundrechte*, 2:525].

[Function of Lower Courts]

The Constitution requires the judge to determine whether the basic rights have influenced the substantive rules of private law in the manner described. [If this influence is present] he must then, in interpreting and applying these provisions, heed the resulting modification of private law. This follows from Article 1 (3) of the Basic Law [requiring the legislature, judiciary, and executive to enforce basic rights "as directly applicable law"]. If he does not apply these standards and ignores the influence of constitutional law on the rules of private law, he violates objective constitutional law by misunderstanding the content of the basic right (as an objective norm); as a public official, he also violates the basic right whose observance by the courts the citizen can demand on the basis of the Constitution. Apart from remedies available under private law, [citizens] can bring such a judicial decision before the Federal Constitutional Court by means of a constitutional complaint.

The Constitutional Court must ascertain whether an ordinary court has properly evaluated the scope and impact of the basic rights in the field of private law. But this task is strictly limited: It is not up to the Constitutional Court to examine decisions of the private-law judge for any legal error that he might have committed. Rather, the Constitutional Court must confine its inquiry to the "radiating effect" of the basic rights on private law and make sure that the [judge below] has correctly understood the constitutional principle [involved] in the area of law under review....

[Freedom of Speech and General Laws]

2. With regard to the basic right of free speech (Article 5), the problem of the relationship between basic rights and private law is somewhat different. As under the Weimar Constitution (Article 118), this basic right is guaranteed only within the framework of the "general laws" (Article 5 (2)). [O]ne might take the view that the Constitution itself, by referring to limits imposed by the general laws, has restricted the legitimate scope of the basic right to that area left open to it by courts in their interpretation of these laws. Such an approach would mean that any general law restricting a basic right would never constitute a violation of that right.

However, this is not the meaning of the reference to "general laws." The basic right to freedom of opinion is the most immediate expression of the human personality [living] in society and, as such, one of the noblest of human rights.... It is absolutely basic to a liberal-democratic constitutional order because it alone makes possible the constant intellectual exchange and the contest among opinions that form the lifeblood of such an order; [indeed,] it is "the matrix, the indispensable condition of nearly every other form of freedom" [Cardozo, quoted in English].

Because of the fundamental importance of freedom of speech in the liberal-democratic state, it would be inconsistent to allow the substance of this basic right to be limited by an ordinary law (and thus necessarily by judicial decisions interpreting the law). Rather, the same principle applies here that was discussed above in general terms with regard to the relationship between the basic rights and private law. [Courts] must evaluate the effect of general laws which would limit the basic right in the light of the importance of the basic right. [They] must interpret these laws so as to preserve the significance of the basic right; in a free democracy this process [of interpretation] must assume the fundamentality of freedom of speech in all spheres, particularly in public life. [Courts] may not construe the mutual relationship between basic rights and "general laws" as a unilateral restriction on the applicability of the basic rights by the "general laws"; rather, there is a mutual effect. According to the wording of Article 5, the "general laws" set bounds to the basic right but, in turn, those laws must be interpreted in light of the value-establishing significance of this basic right in a free democratic state, and so any limiting effect on the basic right must itself be restricted.

The Federal Constitutional Court is the court of last resort for constitutional complaints relating to the preservation of basic rights. Therefore it must have the legal right to control the decisions of the courts where, in applying a general law, they enter the sphere shaped by basic rights.... The

Federal Constitutional Court must have the right to enforce a specific value found in the basic rights. [Its authority to exercise such control] extends to all organs of public authority, including the courts. It can thus create an equilibrium, as desired by the Constitution, between the mutually contradictory and restricted tendencies of the basic rights and the "general laws."

[Meaning of General Laws as Applied to Speech]

3. The concept of "general laws" was controversial from the very beginning.... In any event, ... the phrase was interpreted as referring not only to laws that "do not prohibit an opinion or the expression of an opinion as such" but also to those that "are directed toward the protection of legal rights which need such protection regardless of any specific opinion"; in other words, laws that are directed toward the protection of a community value that takes precedence over the exercise of free speech [citations to legal literature]....

If the term "general laws" is construed in this way, then we can say the following with regard to the purpose and scope of the protection of the basic right: [We] must reject the view that the basic right protects only the expression of an opinion but not the inherent or intended effect on other persons. It is precisely the purpose of an *opinion* to produce an "intellectual effect on the public, to help form an opinion and a conviction in the community" [citation to a commentary on the Basic Law]. Article 5 (1) of the Basic Law protects value judgments, which are always aimed at having an intellectual impact, namely, at convincing others. Indeed, the protection of the basic right is aimed primarily at the personal opinion of the speaker as expressed in the value judgment. To protect the expression itself but not its effect would make no sense.

If understood in this way, the expression of an opinion in its purely intellectual effect is free. However, if someone else's legal rights are violated [and] the protection of these rights should take precedence over the protection of freedom of opinion, then this violation does not become permissible simply because it was committed through the expression of an opinion. [Courts] must weigh the values to be protected against each other. [They] must deny the right to express an opinion if the exercise of this right would violate a more important interest protected [by private law]. [Courts] must decide whether such interests are present on the basis of the facts of each individual case.

[In the light of this discussion the court noted that "there is no reason why norms of private law should not also be recognized as "general laws" within the meaning of Article 5 (2)." The court thus rejected the prevailing view, cited in the literature, that "general laws" embrace only public laws regulating the relations between individuals and the state.]

4.... The complainant fears that any restriction upon freedom of speech might excessively limit a citizen's chance to influence public opinion and thus no longer guarantee the indispensable freedom to discuss important issues publicly.... This danger is indeed present.... To counter the danger, however, it is unnecessary to exclude private law from the category of "general laws." Rather, we must strictly adhere to the character of the basic right as a personal freedom. This is especially important when the speaker is exercising his basic right not within the framework of a private dispute but for the purpose of influencing public opinion. Thus his opinion may possibly have an impact upon another's private rights even though this is not his intention. Here the relationship between ends and means is important. The protection of speech is entitled to less protection where exercised to defend a private interest — particularly when the individual pursues a selfish goal within the economic sector — than speech that contributes to the intellectual struggle of opinions.... Here the assumption is in favor of free speech.

To conclude: Decisions of ordinary civil courts that restrict freedom of opinion on the basis of the "general laws" in the field of private law can violate the basic right of Article 5 (1). The private-law judge also is required to weigh the importance of the basic right against the value to the person allegedly injured by [the utterance of an opinion] of the interest protected by the "general laws." A decision in this respect requires the judge to consider all the circumstances of the individual case. An incorrect balancing of the factors can violate the basic right and provide the basis for a constitutional complaint to the Federal Constitutional Court.

[In section III of its opinion the Constitutional Court examined closely the facts of the case and the judgment of the lower court. In noting that the advocacy of a boycott is not always contrary to "good morals" within the meaning of Article 826 of the Civil Code, the court said: "'Good morals' are not unchangeable principles of pure morality; they are rather defined by the views of 'decent people' about what is 'proper' in social intercourse among legal partners." The court then proceeded on its own to weigh Lüth's interests against those of Harlan and the film companies, holding that the district court had given insufficient attention to the motives of the complainant and the historical context of his remarks. The court's concerns are captured in the following extracts.]

2. (b) ... The complainant's statements must be seen within the context of his general political and cultural efforts. He was moved by the apprehension that Harlan's reappearance might — especially in foreign countries — be interpreted to mean that nothing had changed in German cultural life since the National Socialist period.... These apprehensions concerned a very important issue for the German people.... Nothing has damaged the German reputation as much as the cruel Nazi persecution of the Jews. A crucial interest exists, therefore, in assuring the world that the German people have abandoned this attitude and condemn it not for reasons of political opportunism but because through an inner conversion they have come to realize its evil....

Because of his especially close personal relation to all that concerned the German-Jewish relationship, the complainant was within his rights to state his view in public. Even at that time he was already known for his efforts toward reestablishing a true inner peace with the Jewish people.... It is understandable that he feared all these efforts might be disturbed and thwarted by Harlan's reappearance....

The demand that under these circumstances the complainant should nevertheless have refrained from expressing his opinion out of regard for Harlan's professional interests and the economic interests of the film companies employing him ... is unjustified.... Where the formation of public opinion on a matter important to the general welfare is concerned, private and especially individual economic interests must, in principle, yield. This does not mean that these interests are without protection; after all, the basic right's value is underscored by the fact that it is enjoyed by *everyone*. Whoever feels injured by the public statements of someone else can make a public reply. Public opinion is formed, like the formation of a personal opinion, only through conflicts of opinion freely expressed....

IV. On the basis of these considerations, the Federal Constitutional Court holds that the superior court, in assessing the behavior of the complainant, has misjudged the special significance of the basic right to freedom of opinion. [Courts] must consider [the significance of this right] when it comes into conflict with the private interests of others. The decision below is thus based on an incorrect application of the standards applying to basic rights and violates the basic right of the complainant under Article 5 (1) of the Basic Law. It must therefore be quashed.

PETER E. QUINT, FREE SPEECH AND PRIVATE LAW IN GERMAN CONSTITUTIONAL THEORY, 48 Maryland Law Review 247, 339-42, 344-45, 347 (1989)

[T]here are important contrasts between German and American theories of the public and the private realm in constitutional law. Indeed, the German and American doctrines appear to reflect fundamentally differing views about the nature of the distinction between the public and the private realms.

The American doctrine posits a clear distinction between the state and society — an "essential dichotomy" between state and private action — and adheres to the position that only the state is bound by the fundamental law. Society enjoys a realm of freedom from constitutional restraint and, although individuals and private groups can be regulated to a substantial extent, that regulation must be undertaken by statutes or other measures of positive law which are subject to continuing contemporary adjustment unlike the more rigid rules of constitutional law. Although nongovernmental individuals or groups may sometimes be bound by the American Constitution, such a result occurs mainly when the members of society concerned have entered into some kind of partnership with the state — either through actual involvement with organs of the state or through the performance of traditional state functions....

The German position, in contrast, seems to rest on a different fundamental view. The underlying German theory appears to reject the problematic view that it is possible to separate the public from the private realm. At very least, the German view is skeptical of the position that the fundamental law should apply only to the "public" realm, even assuming that such a realm can be clearly delineated. The German doctrine rests on the position that certain constitutional values are so fundamental — for a decent life for all — that those values should permeate state and society, wherever the line between the two (if any) is to be drawn. This position may seem paradoxical in light of the clear traditional distinction between public and private law in German theory, but the doctrine that constitutional values should "influence" even private law indicates that, when constitutional values are at issue, the distinction between public and private realms cannot be absolute. That is a crucial difference between the American state action doctrine and the doctrine of the German cases first elaborated in *Lüth*. As a practical matter, this difference can be seen most clearly in the impact of the German Constitution on contractual relations (an area in which state action under American doctrine is rarely found) and in the recognition of constitutional causes of action by one private individual against another private individual — also ordinarily without an analogue in American doctrine.

Instead of attempting to exclude the application of constitutional values in the private realm, the German position recognizes that even in private law an accommodation of constitutional and private law values must be achieved. This accommodation is to be accomplished through a wide-ranging consideration of the specific circumstances of each case. In determining the strength of constitutional values in relations between individuals, a range of factors must be taken into consideration — the degree to which the asserted constitutional right has been impaired, the motive with which the constitutional values are asserted, the social and economic power of the person whose actions threaten those constitutional values, and any countervailing constitutional rights or other interests that such a person might have. Thus, under German doctrine, the status of an actor as a private person rather than the state is not dispositive — instead, it is just one factor to be taken into account in a broader determination of whether the constitutional values at issue are sufficiently weighty to require their imposition in a specific case....

Indeed the German view, in which all rules of private law are at least "influenced" by constitutional values, is more or less in accord with the perception of the American legal realists that there is no clear distinction between the public and private realms. According to the realists, even those realms of private law considered most private — such as tort, contract and property — actually represent the results of significant choices of public policy and applications of public power. If one accepts this position, there seems little reason to interrupt the impact of constitutional values — in what must seem to be an artificial manner — when the focus moves from the clearly identifiable realm of public power to another realm where public power is applied but in a somewhat less evident way.

In contrast to the German view, however, the American "state action" doctrine turns its back on these arguments of the realists when it posits a clear distinction between the public and private realms. In the American view, only the public realm — that is, governmental power — has sufficient danger to be subjected to constitutional limitations; the actions of private individuals do not possess that special measure of comprehensive danger unless they are closely aligned with the state....

Moreover, although the Constitutional Court did not pursue the point in *Lüth*, the impact of constitutional rights on private legal relationships might also have rendered plausible an argument that Harlan's article 5 rights of expression might — under some circumstances — have justified (or required) curtailment of Lüth's attack on Harlan's films. In this sense, the extension of the Constitution into the private realm may not necessarily be viewed with unreserved enthusiasm from the perspective of any given set of constitutional rights, because the result may be the elaboration of countervailing constitutional causes of action that may have the ultimate effect of restricting those rights....

In American defamation and privacy doctrine, the first amendment rights of the speaker extend up to a certain point, but after that point there are no countervailing constitutional rights but rather the discretionary power of the state. That is to say, within a certain area the speaker is protected by the first amendment, but outside that area the state can decide whether or not to impose penalties on the speech in question. As we have seen, there is no *requirement* that the state impose liability; consequently, there is room at this point for experimentation and legislative discretion. In a regime in which the Constitution influences individual legal relationships and in which (perhaps as a result) there are countervailing constitutional interests on each side — that is, for example, the speaker's constitutional right to speak and the defamed person's constitutional right of personality — there is less room for adjustment and legislative discretion. It may well be that in many instances in which the speaker is not constitutionally protected, the balance has fallen in favor of the constitutional right of the defamed person and, consequently, the state *must* under such circumstances vindicate the right of personality and provide a cause of action against the speaker. This may or may not be a disadvantage, but it is important to understand that the extension of the Constitution into private legal relations may have the effect of withdrawing legislative discretion and remitting all questions of private law in certain areas to judicial constitutional decisions that cannot be legislatively reconsidered....

An important underlying theme of American constitutional law is thus the withdrawal of the Constitution from society — both in its restriction of constitutional limitations to actions of the state and its exclusion of other types of constitutional provisions that might *require* the government to act in society. The broader German doctrine requiring that the Constitution influence private legal relations is in accordance with the Basic Law's more general acknowledgment of affirmative constitutional requirements affecting society — both through requirements that the government accord benefits to certain members of society and through requirements that the government impose burdens on certain members of society. This is accomplished not only by constitutional provisions which are interpreted directly to require such governmental action. The "influence" of the Constitution on private law also has this effect to the extent that it requires the state, as a constitutional matter that probably cannot be changed by legislation, to grant benefits to certain individuals whose constitutional rights may be violated and to impose burdens on other private individuals — those who have been found to have violated the constitutional rights in question.

NOTES AND QUESTIONS

1. Compare articles 93(1) and 100(1) of the German Basic Law and the German Federal Constitutional Court's abstract norm control and concrete norm control. Which method of control is closer to that used by the French Constitutional Council?

2. To what extent does the German approach to constitutional interpretation exemplify German legal science? Can some of the reasons for the worldwide influence of German legal theory be identified in Kommers's description of German constitutional theory? To what extent, for example, can the categories described by Kommers be applied in interpreting other constitutions?

3. Article 93(1)(4a) was added to the German Basic Law in 1969. This provision protects a person's jurisdictional avenue to the Federal Constitutional Court through a constitutional complaint. This procedure serves as an escape valve for litigants upset with judges who decide not to refer questions to the Court through concrete judicial review. It is also used in about five percent of the constitutional complaints to contest other official actions or to test laws and decrees for their constitutionality. In 1987 there were 3,476 filings with the Court: 6 were for abstract judicial review, 74 were for concrete judicial review, and 3,358 were constitutional complaints. The Court's caseload by 1992 exceeded 4,200 new filings, due partly to the new *Länder* that had joined the Republic.

4. Why is the counter-majoritarian difficulty of constitutional review less pronounced in Germany than in the United States? For one factor see article 94(1), German Basic Law. The Bundestag delegates the task of selecting its share of the justices for the Constitutional Court to a special Judicial Selection Committee, whose 12 members proportionately represent political party distribution in the Bundestag.

In 1989 nine of the 16 justices on the court were professors, while five others had earned doctoral degrees. Does this affect the democratic legitimacy of the Court's decisions?

5. Why does the German Constitutional Court not have justiciability doctrines to allow it to refuse to adjudicate certain constitutional issues, while the U.S. Supreme Court frequently relies on nonjusticiability to deny hearing a case?

6. Could the principle of "practical concordance" in constitutional decision-making be used to defeat an "unconstitutional" amendment to the Basic Law?

7. Is it possible to have an objective order of constitutional values? Can such an order be constructed for the U.S. Constitution? Would an objective order of values be consistent with efforts in the United States to promote multiculturalism?

8. What was the reasoning of the Federal Constitutional Court in the *Numerus Clausus Case* (1972) that led it to require state governments to expand their university facilities or to face voters with new preclusive admission policies? Would an argument of constitutional communal interests be successful in the United States to increase enrollment at a state university? What type of constitutional argument might be successful?

9. Both German and American constitutionalism require the state to be neutral with respect to religion. What are the distinctive meanings of neutrality in these two systems? Compare the situation in Italy and Spain: see Chapter 6, Section A, Subsections 3 and 4.

10. What are the differences in reasoning between the *Abortion Case* (1975) in Germany and the U.S. Supreme Court's decision in *Roe v. Wade*? Does the German Court impose a certain version of morality upon pregnant women, while the U.S. Court leaves the moral choice to a woman herself? Does the notion that abortion is an individual and private decision itself pose a moral question?

> In 1976 the West German parliament amended the criminal code to conform to the guidelines laid down in the 1975 decision.... Abortion is permitted in the first trimester if the pregnancy resulted from an illegal act against the woman or if it places the woman in a situation of serious hardship that cannot be averted any other way; abortion is permitted up to the twenty-second week if there are serious reasons for presuming the child will be born with such a severe defect that the woman cannot reasonably be required to continue with the pregnancy; and abortion is permitted at any time if there is a serious danger to the life or physical or mental health of the woman which cannot be averted any other way she can reasonably be required to bear. As in France, any woman seeking an abortion must first undergo counseling during which she is to be advised of services that would facilitate the continuation of the pregnancy. A three-day waiting period after such counseling is also required. As is typical in West European abortion legislation generally, the statute provides stricter penalties for the person who performs an illegal abortion than for the woman who consents to it.

Mary Ann Glendon, Abortion and Divorce in Western Law 31-32 (1987).

The *Abortion Case* dealt with a 1974 general reform of the German Penal Code, which liberalized abortion law to permit elective abortions in the first trimester. Five German Länder and several legislators who had unsuccessfully opposed the change in the Bundestag challenged the 1974 law in the Federal Constitutional Court. In a six-to-two decision the majority (with a 68-page opinion) ruled that the law, to the extent that it permitted abortion without good reasons, violated article 2(2) of the Basic Law. The Court explained that the priority given to the value of life is a reaction to the taking of innocent life during the years of Hitler's "final solution."

For further discussion see Kommers, *Liberty and Community in Constitutional Perspective,* 1985 B.Y.U. L. Rev. 371; *id., Abortion and the Constitution: U.S. and West Germany,* 25 Am. J. Comp. L. 255 (1977); Douglas G. Morris, *Abortion and Liberalism: A Comparison Between the Abortion Decisions of the Supreme Court of the United States and the Constitutional Court of West Germany,* 11 Hastings Int'l & Comp. L. Rev. 159 (1988).

11. The Federal Constitutional Court may hold statutes or regulations that it deems unconstitutional either null and void (*nichtig*) or incompatible (*unvereinbar*) with the Basic Law. A decision of *Nichtigkeit* means that the challenged norm ceases to operate. A decision of *Unvereinbarkeit,* alternatively, permits the unconstitutional provision to remain in force for a transitional period during which the parliament is expected to rectify the situation. Between 1951 and 1987 the Court declared 247 legal norms *nichtig* and 144 norms *unvereinbar*. Of these 391 legal provisions, 69 percent were federal norms and 31 percent were state norms.

12. Compare for style the *Lüth Boycott Case* (1958) from the German Constitutional Court with the *Freedom of Association Case* from the French Constitutional Council. What explains the great differences in opinion writing style between these two countries from the same legal tradition?

13. What does the Court in *Lüth* mean when it states that general clauses are the points at which constitutional rights breach the domain of private law? Does the basic right of free speech have a "radiating effect"? How does the Court avoid the limitation of "general laws" stated in article 5(2) of the Basic Law? Are some types of speech more protected by article 5(1) than others?

In *Lüth* the Court itself independently examined the particular facts and interests of the parties in balancing the conflicting values. After 1958, however, the Court lowered its level of scrutiny until dissatisfaction led it to reassert a heightened scrutiny of certain encroachments on speech justified in the name of personality rights protected by article 2(1) of the Basic Law. In the *Deutschland Magazin Case,* 42 BVerfGE 143 (1976), the Court set out its current standard of review:

> There are no rigid and invariable limits on the Court's intervention. We retain a degree of freedom to consider the particular facts of special situations. Important in this regard is the severity of the encroachment upon a basic right: The Constitutional Court may not disturb the judgment of a lower court simply because if it had decided the case it would have balanced the equities differently and therefore arrived at a different conclusion. The Constitutional Court may step in to defend an objective constitutional right at the point where the civil courts have erred in assessing the significance of a basic right.... The more a civil court's decision encroaches upon the sphere of protected rights, the more searching must be the Constitutional Court's scrutiny to determine whether the infringement is constitutionally valid; and where the infringement is extremely burdensome the Court may even substitute its judgment for that of the civil courts.

Kommers, The Constitutional Jurisprudence of the Federal Republic of Germany 388 (1989); *see* Peter E. Quint, *Free Speech and Private Law in German Constitutional Theory*, 48 Md. L. Rev. 247, 318-39 (1989).

14. What are the important contrasts between German and American theories of the public and the private realm in constitutional law? Is it ironic that the German theory undercuts a clear separation between the public and private realms? See Chapter 11, Section A on the distinction between public and private law. Why is there no appreciable influence of legal realism on the American doctrine of state action? *See* Donald P. Kommers, *The Jurisprudence of Free Speech in the United States and the Federal Republic of Germany*, 53 S. Cal. L. Rev. 657 (1980).

15. For further information on the German Federal Constitutional Court, see Ernst Benda, *Relationship of the Bundestag and the Federal Constitutional Court,* in The U.S. Congress and the German *Bundestag:* Comparisons of

Democratic Processes 225 (Uwe Thaysen, Roger H. Davidson & Robert Gerald Livingston eds. 1990); Erhard Denninger, *Judicial Review Revisited: The German Experience*, 59 Tul. L. Rev. 1013 (1985); Wolfgang Zeidler, *The Federal Constitutional Court of the Federal Republic of Germany: Decisions on the Constitutionality of Legal Norms*, 62 Notre Dame L. Rev. 504 (1987).

4. THE ITALIAN CONSTITUTIONAL COURT

CONSTITUTION OF ITALY

Articles 134, 136, 137

Title VI: Constitutional Guarantees
Section II: The Constitutional Court

Article 134

The Constitutional Court has jurisdiction over:

Disputes regarding the constitutional legality of laws, and of acts having the force of law, of the State and the Regions;

Conflicts of jurisdiction between State Authorities, or between the State and the Regions, or between Regions;

Charges made against the President of the Republic and the Ministers, in accordance with the provisions of the Constitution.

Article 136

When the Court declares a provision of a law or an act having the force of law unconstitutional, the norm ceases to have effect from the day following publication of the decision.

The Court's decision is published and communicated to the Chamber of Deputies and to interested regional councils so that legal norms may be revised in constitutional form where considered necessary.

Article 137

A constitutional law[a] establishes the conditions, form, and time limits for decisions on constitutional legality and guarantees the independence of the Court's justices.

Ordinary laws establish the other norms necessary for the constitution and functioning of the Court.

The decisions of the Constitutional Court may not be impugned.

ALESSANDRO PIZZORUSSO, THE ITALIAN CONSTITUTION: IMPLEMENTATION AND REFORM, 34 Jahrbuch des öffentlichen Rechts der Gegenwart 105, 114-16 (Peter Häberle ed. 1985)

The role of the Constitutional Court, like that of the President, has been outlined more clearly in the concrete exercise of the powers conferred on it than from the actual regulations written by the Constituent Assembly.

[a] Constitutional Law No. 1 of 9 Feb. 1948.

It must be said that of those who at that time debated the introduction of a constitutional review of legislation in Italy, very few had sufficient information on the legal bases for such an institution....

Ideas on this matter revolved around a general aspiration after a kind of control preventing violations of legality, such as had been accomplished in many countries in the period between the two world wars, and fitting into that "rationalization" of power which should have completed the process of subordinating the activities of public authorities to the law, begun during the 19th century under the banner of the *Rechtsstaat.*

How vague were such ideas is evident from a study of the proposals advanced (and even from some of the provisions put into the Constitution and its integrating laws), and even more so from an analysis of the serious lack of understanding often shown by technicians and politicians in their attitudes towards the work carried out by the Court, even after it finally began to operate in 1956.

Yet the system of *"incidentale"* control of the constitutionality of legislation effected in Italy — as in Austria, the Federal Republic of Germany and more recently in Spain, though without assuming the same importance, particularly from a quantitative point of view, in these countries — has come to represent a happy synthesis of the American model and the original Austrian one, so much so that today it can probably be considered as the true European model of constitutional justice.

By relating the constitutional judgement to an *a quo* judgement, that is to any procedure being carried out before a judicial authority, this model in fact links constitutional review to concrete situations, as does the American system in which judgement on the constitutionality of legislation is passed only in relation to specific controversies.

This characteristic allows constitutional review even of less recent legislation and of norms constructed through interpretations, and above all it permits a further review in cases where written law undergoes some tacit modification due to evolution in judicial interpretations or for other reasons.

Constitutional review, in spite of an unsystematic referral of matters to the Court, thus becomes a factor of constant and tendentially general adjustment of the law in force to conform with constitutional principles, and thus preserves the essential characteristics of the American system and particularly its dependence on specific controversy, without conferring on all judges the power to suspend legislation, a power inappropriate to the structures of European judiciaries and their traditions. The definitive suspension of legislation can only come about with decision from the Constitutional Court, which concentrates on matters of this kind and, moreover, is able to filter them from the point of view of the acceptability of their political repercussions.

Probably the most important aspect of this innovation lies in its freeing the judge, even if only partially, from his traditional dependence on the law. Any judge can now in fact suspend legislation while referring an issue to the Constitutional Court; his obligation towards the legislator is, likewise, no longer absolute and unconditional. The principle of the judge's subordination to the *legge (Gesetz)*, expressed in art. 101, para. 2 of the Constitution, should be read as his subordination to the *diritto (Recht)*, and that is to norms in force as a result of a whole series of operations, among which those accomplished by Parliament and by Government in their capacities as legislators constitute a prominent part but do not exclude any other contribution.

Another revolutionary aspect of this type of constitutional review of legislation lies in the unexpected importance it has lent to the grounds for the Court's decisions, bringing to Italian law the question of the rule of precedent of the *rationes decidendi*, previously considered exclusive to the common law systems.

A third consequence, still less acceptable in the eyes of many commentators, was the inclusion of the Constitutional Court's decisions granting referral in the catalogue of the sources of the law. Art. 136 of the Constitution seems to envisage, according to the famous Kelsenian formula, only a sort of *"legislazione negativa" (negative Gesetzgebung)* for the removal of norms from Italian law, and not the power to explicitly coin new ones. It was immediately clear, however, that removing certain regulations could but lead to the introduction of new ones, whether formulated from a discipline previously constitutionally repealed from legislation (restoring the valid part), or elaborated by interpretation from remaining regulatory material after the norm declared unconstitutional had been deleted.

Among this material, an important place came to be held by the actual judgements of the Court (as well as the legal reasonings from which these might derive); their force as *res judicata* consisted, in effect, of the transformation of the judgements themselves into rules of law, having the same legal force as statutes.

The precedents established by the Constitutional Court met with some resistance, and this stimulated its judges to invent new, more refined techniques, including "partial" judgements (invalidating only a part of the provision) and "manipulative" decisions (creating additional or substitutional norms to replace unconstitutional interpretations). It was thus increasingly evident that this "legislation" was not only "negative." ...

Contributing to these results were a series of circumstances, pertaining to the political and cultural situation in Italy in this period of its recent history, which the precursors of constitutional justice could certainly not have foreseen. These mainly derive from the considerable imbalance which had developed between constitutional principles on the one hand, and a legislation and administrative procedure at a standstill since the political stalemate caused by the cold war and its internal repercussions on the other.

Given that legislative immobility had prevented, for example, an adequate reform of the codes and of other very important legislation which needed bringing into line with new times and ideas, the Constitutional Court's activity, in close collaboration with the other judges, appeared as one of the few possible alternatives to the political stagnation, whence the particular fortune of the Court, which had its period of great success in and around the sixties.

The sudden success of the duo judiciary-Constitutional Court, however, provoked a reaction from the political class, which adopted some curbing measures, principally those contained in the constitutional law which in 1967 reduced the term of office of the constitutional judges and limited the Court's autonomy to some extent, and also a more careful selection of the candidates to the office of constitutional judge.

While this "reining in" of the Court by the political forces undoubtedly limited its influence, it could not halt it completely, even in the most recent phase. Moreover, the great re-evaluation of the role of the judiciary, deriving from the judges' power to suspend legislation, even if only temporarily, while awaiting a decision from the Court, has resulted in an unexpected political cultural maturing of the ordinary judges, much more important even than the practical effects of the actual sentences of unconstitutionality. The judges began to feel that they played a real part in the process of forming the will of the state, rather than being only executors of rules established by Parliament or Government.

BERTETT v. ITALY

Constitutional Court of Italy
Decision No. 190 of 10 December 1970
15 Giur. Cost. 2179 (1970); 94 Foro It. I, 8 (1971)

English translation published in Mauro Cappelletti & William Cohen, Comparative Constitutional Law: Cases and Materials 394-97 (1979)

Facts

In the course of a criminal proceeding pending before the Tribunal of Rome, the attorney for the defendant made a motion to be present, on an equal footing with the Public Prosecutor, at the interrogation of the defendant, one Luigi Bertett. After the denial of this motion, that attorney challenged the constitutionality of art. 303 of the Code of Criminal Procedure in light of art. 24 of the Constitution: according to the defense's argument, the principle of equality between prosecution and defense, implicit in the constitutional norm, clashes with art. 303 which allows the Public Prosecutor to assist in the acts of the *istruzione* (as well as to make observations and motions) while it does not provide for the presence or the assistance of the defense attorney.... [Article 24, in part, states: "The right of defense is an inalienable right at every stage and phase of the proceeding."] In considering the argument, this Court has extended its examination to include art. 304-*bis*, first para. which denies the defense attorney the right to assist in the interrogation of the defendant.... Thus ... the Court jointly considered the constitutionality of art. 303 and art. 304-*bis* in relation to art. 24 of the Constitution.

Opinion

As a preliminary matter, it is necessary to ascertain whether the role of the Public Prosecutor and that of the defense attorney are similar enough to allow a fair comparison of their respective authority.

It should be recognized immediately that the Public Prosecutor cannot, strictly speaking, be considered a party in the traditional sense. He is a member of the judiciary and, as such, independent from the other branches of government. In this position he seeks to safeguard the general observance of the law rather than any specific interests. The Public Prosecutor [does not necessarily act against the interest of the defendant; his duty also includes] ... examinations that may demonstrate the innocence of the defendant, ... requests that the charges be dropped (*decreto di archiviazione*), and requests for the acquittal of the defendant. The special position of the Public Prosecutor, however, does not allow us to conclude that he is on an equal footing with the judge.... In practice, when it is the criminal responsibility of the defendant that is in dispute ..., there are two opposing adversaries — the Public Prosecutor and the defendant. The clear contrast between the interests which they are each promoting justifies the conclusion that, before the judge, both must be considered parties....

It should be emphasized, however, that this conclusion does not mean that the powers of the Public Prosecutor must always be equal to those of the defense. The unique institutional position and the function assigned to the Public Prosecutor by the Constitution itself can justify disparate treatment, but can do so only when a reasonable justification can be found in the nature of the function or the institutional position of the Public Prosecutor.

Once it has been ascertained that the Public Prosecutor and the defendant are each adversaries, it is necessary to consider that ... the right of defense is assured only to the extent that the defendant has the opportunity to participate in an effective adversary debate, which opportunity he is not likely to have without the aid of an attorney....

One should bear in mind, however, that art. 24, second para. of the Constitution, in guaranteeing the right of defense in "every stage and phase of the proceeding" does not necessarily mean that the right to an attorney and the right to adversary debate must attach at every moment and in every step of the proceeding. On the other hand, at each step it is necessary to ascertain if the absence of the defense attorney and the consequently attenuated adversary debate, deprive the defendant of the constitutional right of defense. Therefore, in reference to the present problem we must determine whether the interrogation of the accused, seen in the light of the entire *istruzione*, is so important that the absence of the defense attorney and the presence of the Public Prosecutor cause a serious infringement of the right of defense.

The Court holds that it must give an affirmative response to this query. Indeed, the fundamental importance of the interrogation of the accused has already been recognized several times by this Court (see e.g., this Court's decision No. 109, 1970) ... [in that it is the basic tool] for the gathering of proof of innocence or guilt....

The fact that the defendant is exposed to the observations, accusations, and arguments of the Public Prosecutor at a critical act without being assisted by an attorney to advise him of the necessity for appropriate defensive explanations, cannot help but seriously infringe the right of defense. And this is true notwithstanding the privilege against self-incrimination reaffirmed by law No. 932, of Dec. 5, 1969. The legislature itself has provided for some defensive intervention during the interrogation; indeed ..., the transcripts of the interrogation must be filed with the clerk of the court within five days of its occurrence so that the defense attorney may view them and make motions; furthermore, art. 8 of the same law prohibits the use of statements given by the suspect before the appointment of the defense attorney. Nevertheless these legislative innovations, even if they demonstrate that the law has already pointed out the need for some protection, are clearly insufficient to afford effective protection. According to the rule still in force, the Public Prosecutor intervenes at the beginning of the interrogation while the defense attorney can intervene only after the interrogation has been completed, transcribed and filed. Moreover, art. 304-*quarter*, fifth para., of the Code of Criminal Procedure authorizes the judge, possibly even at the request of the Public Prosecutor, to order a delay in the filing of the transcripts; consequently, the intervention of the defense attorney can be delayed for a noteworthy period of time even beyond the completion of the interrogation. This gravely curtails the right of defense especially when the defense attorney, dealing with the matter of the defendant's detention, is constrained to ignore, in detail, both the charges brought against his client and the defenses already put forth by that client in the interrogation, in order to attempt to obtain the defendant's release from custody. Thus, the attorney is forced to make this attempt without being able to evaluate fully the defensive arguments that can be useful to get the defendant released.

The Court holds that such disparity of treatment between the Public Prosecutor and the defense of the accused — which, it bears repeating, can in some cases be extremely prejudicial — cannot be justified in light of the Constitution....

It appears from the government report accompanying the 1955 reform that the exclusion of defense attorneys from the interrogation was ... [justified] "in order to permit the defendant to respond to the questions with the greatest possible frankness — without the worry or the influence of a third party's presence." These reasons, in as much as they imply a complete distrust in the work of the defense attorney, conflict with the constitutional precepts implied by the right of defense. Rather than hindering or opposing justice, the presence of the attorney harmonizes perfectly with the ends sought by the judicial process. While it should be emphasized that the law authorizes the judge to repress any illegitimate interference, there is no reason to suppose that the motions and observations of the defense attorney will worry or influence the defendant any more than the activity and presence of the Public Prosecutor.

On the contrary it is reasonable to believe that equality of the disputants will not only guarantee the right of defense, but will also aid the judge in exercising his delicate function. Moreover, one should not underestimate the likelihood that the presence and the assistance of the defense attorney will confer greater reliability on the results of the interrogation, even for those results that are unfavorable to the defendant. Thus, it must be admitted that, in so far as it relates to the interrogation, adversary debate is useful to the administration of justice....

For all of these reasons, art. 304-*bis*, first para. of the Code of Criminal Procedure must be declared unconstitutional in that part in which it denies the right of the defendant to be assisted by an attorney at the interrogation.

NOTES AND QUESTIONS

1. From your reading of articles 136 and 137 of the Italian Constitution, which of the Constitutional Court's decisions regarding the constitutionality of statutes are binding *erga omnes*?

Does the Court have jurisdiction to decide the constitutionality of: (1) a legislative decree; (2) a regulation; or (3) an ordinary court or administrative tribunal decision?

2. The Italian Constitutional Court does not hear direct constitutional complaints from individuals concerned about infringement of their fundamental rights, as do the German and Spanish Constitutional Courts. Rather, the Italian Court relies on incidental concrete judicial review (art. 134, para. 2) to protect individual liberties. When a constitutional issue arises in an ordinary or administrative court, at any level, the judge (or judges) is required to decide whether it is (1) relevant and (2) not manifestly unfounded. If she finds the issue trivial and thus denies the validity of the constitutional issue, she so states in writing with reasons and the case proceeds. Alternatively, should the judge consider the question relevant and not manifestly unfounded, she must certify the issue to the Constitutional Court. This has the effect of suspending the case pending settlement of the issue by the Constitutional Court. After the constitutional decision the action in the referring court is resumed and conducted in accordance with the decision. *See* article 1, Constitutional Law No. 1 (1948); Law No. 87 of 11 Mar. 1953 (procedure for incidental judicial review).

For the first 15 years of the Court's experience (1956-1971), over 75 percent of its 4,000 filings concerned incidental review.

3. Suppose a party in a criminal action pleads that a statute involved in the action is unconstitutional and the judges rule that the constitutional objection is manifestly unfounded. What happens next? Is there any way to attack this ruling?

4. Suppose the trial judges find the constitutional objection not manifestly unfounded and the Constitutional Court decides that the statute is not unconstitutional. Is there any way to attack this decision? Who is bound by it?

5. Comment on the following proposition: "In the Italian legal system, only judges of the Constitutional Court interpret and apply the Constitution."

6. Luigi Bertett's lawyer was able to convince the first instance tribunal that his exclusion from a portion of the instruction stage of the criminal proceeding raised a serious constitutional issue. For more information on the civilian two-stage division in criminal cases between instruction (*istruzione*) and trial, see Chapter 10, Section B. For the role of the public prosecutor, see Chapter 8, Section B.

The Constitutional Court in *Bertett* interpreted very general language from article 24 of the Constitution. Is its decision persuasively justified? From a political standpoint, is it better for the Court or parliament to initiate criminal procedure reform?

7. The Italian Constitutional Court has had a substantial, some might say revolutionary, impact on the Italian judicial system. Its decisions in the areas of criminal procedure, preservation of the environment, and the economic, social, and political rights of individuals, among others, make it the principal judicial avenue for reform in Italy.

8. For further commentary on the Italian Constitutional Court, see Allan R. Brewer-Carías, Judicial Review in Comparative Law 215-24 (1989); John Henry Merryman & Vincenzo Vigoriti, *When Courts Collide: Constitution and Cassation in Italy*, 15 Am. J. Comp. L. 665 (1967); Alessandro Pizzorusso, Vincenzo Vigoriti & G.L. Certoma, *The Constitutional Review of Legislation in Italy*, 56 Temp. L.Q. 503 (1983); Mary Volcansek, *Judicial Review and Public Policy in Italy: American Roots and the Italian Hybrid*, in Comparative Judicial Review and Public Policy 89-105 (Donald W. Jackson & C. Neal Tate eds. 1992).

5. THE SPANISH CONSTITUTIONAL COURT

THE SPANISH ABORTION DECISION

Constitutional Court of Spain
Decision No. 53/1985 of 11 April 1985
49 Boletín de Jurisprudencia Constitucional 515 (1985)

[This case is summarized by Richard Stith in an article appearing in the *American Journal of Comparative Law*, excerpted below.]

RICHARD STITH, NEW CONSTITUTIONAL AND PENAL THEORY IN SPANISH ABORTION LAW, 35 American Journal of Comparative Law 513, 515-19 (1987)

Prior to the bill here at issue, the Spanish Penal Code did not explicitly exempt any abortions from punishment. However, the general defense of necessity includes an exemption for acts done to avoid harm equal to or greater than the harm caused, which would make non-punishable at least those abortions necessary to preserve maternal life.

Soon after the sweeping *Partido Socialista Obrero Español* (PSOE) electoral victory of 1982, which gave the party an absolute majority in the Spanish legislature, the new government proposed an addendum to prior abortion law, declaring abortion unpunishable in certain circumstances. As approved by the Congress of Deputies on 6 October 1983, and by the Senate on 30 November 1983, the bill read:

> Abortion will not be punishable if performed by a physician, with the consent of the woman, when any one of the following circumstances is present:
>
> 1. That it is necessary in order to avoid a serious danger to the life or health of the pregnant woman.
> 2. That the pregnancy is the consequence of an act constituting the crime of rape under art. 429, provided that the abortion is performed within the first twelve weeks of gestation and that the aforementioned act has been reported.
> 3. That it is probable that the fetus will be born with serious physical or mental defects, provided that the abortion is performed within the first twenty-two weeks of gestation and that the unfavorable prognosis is reg-

istered in an opinion issued by two medical specialists other than the one operating on the pregnant woman.

The post-Franco Spanish Constitution of 1978 established for the first time a Constitutional Court with the power of judicial review of statutes. Consistent with the Kelsenian European tradition, a petition alleging unconstitutionality may be interposed by certain authorized persons, without the need to await a concrete injury.[13] A 1979 sub-constitutional law, repealed in 1985, further established the right of these same persons to insist that the Court hear such a petition before certain allegedly unconstitutional bills could enter into effect.

On 2 December 1983, the latter sort of petition was filed in the name of fifty-four Deputies led by the conservative *Alianza Popular* party. After receiving a series of supplements and responses during the first half of 1984, the Constitutional Court finally announced its decision on 11 April 1985. The abortion reform bill was declared in certain details to be an unconstitutional violation of article 15 of the Constitution, which reads "All have the right to life and to physical and moral integrity ... " ("*todos tienen derecho a la vida y a la integridad fisica y moral* ... "). Although the twelve members of the Court were evenly divided for and against this declaration, Spanish practice in effect permitted a second and tie-breaking vote to be cast by the President of the Court, Dr. Manuel Garcia Pelayo y Alonso, an ex-soldier for the Spanish Republic who became an internationally-known scholar during his years outside of Spain.

After a lengthy development of the arguments presented by the petitioners and by the governmental respondent, the Court built its position on twelve "Legal Foundations" (*Fundamentos Juridicos*), concluding with the holding of unconstitutionality. Five dissenting opinions, one of which is co-authored, [were issued].

The Court's argument in brief paraphrase is this: Human life is a superior constitutional value (Legal Foundation, hereinafter L.F. 3) and a Social State such as Spain has an affirmative duty to secure it by law (L.F. 4). This life is a reality distinct from the mother from the beginning of gestation and, therefore, the "one to be born" (*nasciturus*) must be considered a "legal good" (*bien juridico*) accorded protection by the Constitution. Legislative history indicates that the framers of the Constitution intended this result (L.F. 5), even though neither Spanish nor international law requires the conclusion that the one to be born possesses a personal subjective right to this protection (LL.FF. 5, 6, and 7). Such protection must be effective and, if necessary, include penal sanctions, although it need not be absolute (L.F. 7).

The Constitution also guarantees personal dignity, which includes rights such as free development of one's personality, physical and moral integrity, and personal and family intimacy (L.F. 8). When constitutional values collide, the legislator must weigh them and try to harmonize them or, if necessary, to specify the conditions under which one may prevail. He must also not forget the limits to what is reasonably demandable by the penal law. In carrying out his judgments, he need not turn only to the generalized exemptions from

[13] Art. 162(1)(a) of the Constitution of 1978.

punishment found in article 8 of the Penal Code, but may use a different technique for certain crimes such as abortion (L.F. 9).

After disposing of statutory vagueness problems — by indicating, for example, that a "serious danger" is one which involves an important and permanent diminution of physical or mental health (L.F. 10) — the Court applies the foregoing principles to the bill in question. There is nothing unconstitutional in permitting the destruction of unborn life where the mother's life is at stake. Given a "serious danger" to her health, the mother's own right to life and to physical integrity is affected; not to punish abortion here is constitutional, especially in light of what is demandable by penal law. Rape violates personal dignity in the highest degree, and the law clearly cannot demand that the victim bear its consequences. As for the case of serious physical or mental fetal defects, recourse to penal sanctions against abortion would impose conduct beyond that which is normally demandable of a mother (L.F. 11).

The constitutionality of the non-punishment of abortion in such circumstances has thus been established, according to the Court. However, the State continues to have an obligation effectively to guarantee the life and health both of the woman and of the one to be born. It must, therefore, make sure that neither the former nor the latter is unprotected any more than may be required by those circumstances. For the protection of the woman, the State should provide that the abortion take place in public or private health centers authorized for this purpose. For the protection of the one to be born, in order to be certain that the first type of circumstance (serious maternal life or health danger) exists, the Constitution demands that the opinion of a medical specialist be obtained prior to the abortion. Similarly, the opinions of the two specialists regarding any fetal disabilities must be obtained in advance of any abortion. Such changes, without excluding other possible ones, would permit the bill finally to be enacted into law (L.F. 12).[17]

In the last two sections of its opinion, the Court declines to require paternal participation in the abortion decision (L.F. 13), or to enter into subsidiary civil law issues such as the relation of non-punishable abortion to social insurance. It does point out, though, that conscientious objection to abortion is protected by the Constitution (L.F. 14).

NOTES AND QUESTIONS

1. Since the Spanish Constitutional Court was established after the principal post-World War II European experiments with constitutional review, Spain in its 1978 Constitution (and Organic Law No. 2 of 3 Oct. 1979, as amended by Organic Law No. 6 of 9 June 1988) eclectically borrowed impor-

[17] The government did not delay in complying with the Court's demands. On 12 July 1985, a new enactment was published (Ley orgánica 9/1985, de 5 de julio, de reforma del articulo 417 bis del Codigo Penal). The significant changes are as follows: The new law contains a preliminary paragraph requiring abortions to be done in an accredited health center, and requires a prior second medical opinion confirming that an abortion is necessary to avoid a serious danger to the life or health (which now explicitly includes mental health) of the pregnant woman. The law, however, does not require the second opinion (nor the woman's express consent) in an emergency. A new section indicates, in accordance with a remark of the Court, that the pregnant woman will not be punished even when an (otherwise non-punishable) abortion occurs in violation of the requirements of a health center or of confirming medical opinions.

tant features from the German, Italian, and French systems. The Spanish Constitutional Court, to oversimplify, exercises: (1) abstract statutory norm control (inspired by the German model) in direct actions brought by certain governmental officials; (2) incidental concrete judicial review authorized by a judge (inspired by the Italian model); (3) preventive judicial review (inspired by the French model) brought by the same officials as in (1) to question the constitutionality of treaties, organic laws, and regional statutes of autonomy; and (4) review of constitutional complaints (closest to the German model, but perhaps with some Latin American influence), especially with *recursos de amparo* to protect fundamental rights. Of 967 filings with the Constitutional Court in 1987, about one-quarter were abstract norm control and one-third were incidental concrete judicial review, but only 13 involved preventive judicial review. Most of the remaining filings were constitutional complaints that only indirectly test the constitutionality of statutes (that is, by contesting an executive regulation based on a statute or by contesting a judicial interpretation of a statute).

2. Which method of constitutional review was used in the *Spanish Abortion Case*? What are the principal similarities and differences between that decision and the *German Abortion Case*?

3. Comment on the following statement made about the Spanish Constitutional Court, but perhaps applicable to other European constitutional courts. Does it also apply to the U.S. Supreme Court?

> Judicial review and the Social State should not be combined. Perhaps judicial review should not exist even for defense rights. Such review implies a hostility between the legislating community and the individual which ideally should be overcome by education and by more participatory forms of democracy, rather than accommodated. But in any event judicial review should not extend to the positive and programmatic social duties stated or implied in a constitution. Those principles should be the starting points for public reasoning by all citizens, not the privileged prerogative of a tiny group of jurists.

Richard Stith, *New Constitutional and Penal Theory in Spanish Abortion Law,* 35 Am. J. Comp. L. 513, 540 (1985).

4. For more information concerning the Spanish Constitutional Court, see Allan R. Brewer-Carías, Judicial Review in Comparative Law 225-35 (1989).

6. JUDICIAL REVIEW AND ITS INDEPENDENCE IN LATIN AMERICA

DAVID S. CLARK, JUDICIAL PROTECTION OF THE CONSTITUTION IN LATIN AMERICA, 2 Hastings Constitutional Law Quarterly 405, 416-22, 425-28, 431-42 (1975)

The Beginnings of Latin American Judicial Review

Every one of the Latin American nations has had since independence some period of explicit or implied authorization of judicial review of the constitutionality of legislative and executive action. Particularly in regard to judicial review of legislation, the United States' influence has been important. The framers of the American Constitution were divided on the issue of the supremacy of legislative versus judicial power. While Federalists were especially sensitive to the opportunities of arbitrary usurpations of power by a legislature, the Jeffersonian Republicans were more concerned about judicial improprieties. John Adams found Hamilton's discussion of judicial review in *The Federalist* most congenial and found comfort in Justice Marshall's opinion in *Marbury v. Madison*, convincingly asserting the Supreme Court's power in this area. In Europe, on the other hand, idealists were greatly concerned with securing bills of rights, but they gave little attention to securing sufficient legal guarantees for their enforcement. After the revolution in France, suspicion of the reactionary courts militated against efforts to give them the power of judicial review. State positivism, as expressed in the dogma of the absolute sovereignty of the state, coupled with Rousseau's formulation of the strict separation of powers, formed a matrix into which judicial review could not fit. Moreover, such review was believed not necessary, since the legislature, as the only directly elected branch of the government, alone could respond to the popular will. The European tradition of resolving fundamental issues, consequently, is by explicit legislative enactment. This has resulted in codification of such principles as freedom of expression and assembly. The European practice has not, accordingly, favored judicial development of broad constitutional rights. Only since World War I has a type of judicial review evolved, usually established in a special constitutional court.

Although both the United States' practice of judicial review and the European tradition of strict separation of powers influenced the authors of Latin American constitutions, the former seems to have had greater impact. The judicial institution, however, was not imported intact. Rather, the North American and European traditions stimulated the Latin American framers into thinking out the various alternatives confronting them in the years following independence.

The power to interpret the constitution was expressly or implicitly vested in the judiciary in most Latin American nations during the 19th century. Although such a provision was not immediately acted upon in some countries, it served as a basis for the evolution of judicial review, especially of the constitutionality of legislation, in the 20th century.

Table 7.1

Earliest Explicit or Implied Authorization of Judicial Review in Latin American Constitutions or Statutes by Country

Country	Review of Legislation	Habeas Corpus or Amparo Protection
Argentina	1853	1863
Bolivia	1851	1931
Brazil	1891	1830
Central American Federation	1824	—
Chile	1925	1925

Country	Review of Legislation	Habeas Corpus or Amparo Protection
Colombia	1886	1964
Costa Rica	1821	1847
Cuba	1901	1901
Dominican Republic	1844	1947
Ecuador	1845	1929
El Salvador	1886	1872
Guatemala	1839	1839
Haiti	1843	1964
Honduras	1894	1894
Mexico	1847	1847
Nicaragua	1838	1950
Panama	1904	1904
Paraguay	1940	1940
Peru	1856	1897
Uruguay	1934	1874
Venezuela	1811	1947

Table 7.1 details the earliest explicit or implied authorization of judicial review in Latin American constitutions or statutes. Most of the countries recognized the possibility of judicial review of legislation in the 19th century. About half, furthermore, adopted in this same period the writ of habeas corpus or something similar to protect freedom of movement. In some nations habeas corpus, as a writ used to protect one from unconstitutional executive action, was expanded to include the protection of other or all individual liberties, often under the name of *amparo* in Spanish America and *mandado de segurança* in Brazil. There were, however, some significant exceptions to this general trend. Chile, Paraguay and Uruguay, for instance, were strongly influenced by the French interpretation of the separation of powers which precluded judicial review. Guardianship of the constitution was left to the legislature until 1925 in Chile, until 1934 in Uruguay, and until 1940 in Paraguay....

The Reality of Latin American Judicial Review in the Twentieth Century

We have seen that all Latin American governments are required by their constitutions to respect the basic rights of man enumerated in the articles that define liberty, equality, justice and property. Courts, moreover, have generally been given the authority to declare legislative and executive action contrary to the constitution and thus invalid.

The extent to which judicial review is an effective restraint on unconstitutional government activity, nevertheless, is essentially an empirical question. It is, furthermore, inextricably intertwined with the concept of judicial independence. Paraphrasing Theodore Becker's interpretation, judicial independence is the *degree* to which judges believe they can decide, and do decide, disputes, consistent with their own conception of the judicial role in interpreting the law, in *opposition* to what those who have *political* power think about or desire in such matters. This definition, first, implies that there are degrees of judicial independence. There may be partial political control of judicial behavior; it is more than a simple dichotomous variable. Costa Rica may have a more independent supreme court than Mexico, for example, and they both may be more independent than the high court in Nicaragua. Second, independence denotes freedom from certain sources of influence — represented here as opposition from governmental power embodied in the legislative and executive branches.

Following this definition of judicial independence, it seems clear that a judiciary which is not independent to some degree cannot effectively undertake constitutional review. Independence, consequently, is a necessary, but not a sufficient, condition for effective judicial review. Independence of the judiciary, moreover, may occur without any provision for judicial review — as it has in England. In general, nevertheless, a judiciary's independence is related to the extent judicial review is exercised, and the power of judicial review is related to the actual degree of independence.

Effective judicial review, in Latin America as elsewhere, is a relative phenomenon. It may make little sense, as a result, to conclude that at a certain period in history, judicial review in the United States, or Chile, was a powerful or weak political force. Such a statement becomes meaningful only when it takes on the attribute of comparison. Was federal judicial review in the first half of the 19th century in the United States ineffective after *Marbury v. Madison* just because no federal law was declared void for another fifty years? Is it effective today if sixty-five percent of the federal public administrators *believe* judicial review is effective? In part the answer depends on how one measures judicial review. But equally important is the definition of "weak," "effective" or "powerful" judicial review. Terms such as these can be given meaning only by comparison — either across time, between political units at a given point in time, or by combining both dimensions. Thus, it may facilitate explanation to state that federal judicial review was more effective in the United States, returning to our example above, from the Civil War to World War II than from *Marbury v. Madison* until the Civil War because seventy-four statutes (or parts thereof) were declared unconstitutional by the Supreme Court after 1860. Similarly, a statement that Colombian judicial review is a powerful safeguard of individual constitutional liberties may be significant if seventy-five percent of the public officials believe judicial review is an effective deterrent to their action whereas an equivalent percentage in the United States is sixty-five percent.

By comparison, therefore, accurate assertions concerning the effectiveness of judicial review in various Latin American nations can be made. Inquiry, of course, need not end here. One might next ask what are the political and economic factors associated with judicial independence and effective judicial review: what causes a strong judiciary? For instance, the type of political system (whether democratic or authoritarian) might be an important variable explaining why some nations have strong court systems. Does a nondemocratic regime imply a dependent judiciary, largely submissive to the executive branch? Similarly, it might be hypothesized that effective judicial review correlates significantly with the national level of economic development. By investigating these kinds of questions, it is possible to speak more intelligently about judicial review in Latin America....

[An] even less reliable set of indicators is listed in Table 7.2. These are the structural variables normally found in the literature on judicial review. In fact, most assertions about effective judicial review are based on the conditions of tenure and the selection procedures for supreme court judges.

The principal shortcoming in using structural determinants to measure the effectiveness of judicial review is the propensity to confuse legal prerequisites with reality....

Table 7.2

Structural Determinants of Effective Judicial Review

Indicator	Code
Independence of supreme court judges	
I. Recruitment	
A. Appointment by judiciary	2 points
B. Appointment by executive with checks (by legislature or judiciary) or by legislature	1 point
C. Appointment by executive alone	0 points
II. Tenure	
A. Lifetime	3 points
B. De facto lifetime (automatic renewal with good behavior)	2 points
C. More than six years	1 point
D. Six years or less	0 points
III. Salary	
A. Equal or greater than executive minister	2 points
B. Equal or greater than full time law professor	1 point
C. Less than full time law professor	0 points
Restrictions in making constitutional complaint against government	
IV. Scope of competence	
A. Review of all jurisdictions	3 points
B. Excludes one important jurisdiction (administrative law, labor law, agrarian law)	2 points
C. Excludes two important jurisdictions	1 point
D. Excludes three or more important jurisdictions	0 points
V. Political questions	
A. Moderate political question exclusion	1 point
B. Substantial exclusion	0 points
VI. Case and controversy requirement	
A. Direct review of constitutional question	1 point
B. Incidental review with other issues	0 points
VII. Availability of review	
A. Diffused throughout lower courts	1 point
B. Concentrated in supreme court	0 points
Effects of constitutional ruling	
VIII. Efficiency of review	
A. Action or norm invalid for all (*erga omnes*)	2 points
B. Invalid only between parties (*inter partes*), but stare decisis can provide general invalidity	1 point
C. Invalid only *inter partes*	0 points
Effectiveness of judicial review	Total points

Table 7.3 ranks all twenty Latin American countries according to the present estimated effectiveness of their judicial review. It is based on four of the indicators in Table 7.2, and thus should be considered provisional. It was impossible to find current data on supreme court salaries as well as the political question exclusion for every Latin American nation. In addition, even though extensive information exists on the "case and controversy" requirement and the availability of review (concentrated in the supreme court or extended to lower courts), it was too confusing to be presented here. For instance, many countries have multiple procedures for deciding constitutional issues, depending on whether one lives in the capital, whether one is complaining about a law, about a decree by one ministry or by another, or about an official's discretionary action. For this reason, these two theoretically interesting variables may not be practical for measuring the effectiveness of judicial review.

Table 7.3

Effectiveness of Judicial Review in Latin America, by Country

	Recruitment	Tenure	Scope of Competence	Effects of Ruling	Effectiveness Score[1]
Argentina	1	3	3	0	7
Bolivia	1	1	2	0	4
Brazil	1	3	3	2	9
Chile	1	2	3	2	8
Colombia	1	3	3	2	9
Costa Rica	1	2	3	2	8
Cuba	0	3	0	2	5
Dominican Republic	1	0	2	0	3
Ecuador	0	0	2	0	2
El Salvador	1	0	2	2	5
Guatemala	1	0	2	2	5
Haiti	0	1	3	0	4
Honduras	1	0	2	0	3
Mexico	1	3	3	1	8
Nicaragua	1	3	3	0	7
Panama	0	1	2	2	5
Paraguay	0	0	2	0	2
Peru	0	3	1	0	4
Uruguay	1	1	3	0	5
Venezuela	1	1	3	2	7

[1] Based on the sum of four indicators from Table 7.2, calculated as of January 1, 1975. If the legislature normally participates in the selection of judges, but it was temporarily suspended in January 1975, "recruitment" would be coded "C" in Table 7.2 and listed with zero points in column one.

One additional warning should be made about using structural indicators to measure the effectiveness of judicial review. Since World War II, there have been hundreds of declarations or extensions of a state of siege in the Latin American countries. The state of siege is a constitutional measure — sometimes known as state of emergency or state of national defense — designed to provide for the security of the nation in times of emergency due to external attack or serious disturbances of the public order which the government is unable to control by normal action. What does a state of siege mean for judicial review? It temporarily grants extraordinary powers to the executive branch and permits the suspension or restriction of certain constitutional liberties. Even though the state of siege is a common occurrence in Latin America, it occurs in some nations with much less frequency than in others, and when it does occur, it is generally a temporary phenomenon. In this article, consequently, one should consider the "normal" situation when discussing the structural determinants of effective judicial review. During a state of siege, one could hypothesize that judges would tend to be much more circumspect in protecting individuals against unconstitutional norms and official action....

Table 7.3 may become clearer if we consider some examples. Argentina received a relatively high effectiveness score. The president there appoints, with the consent of the Senate, the magistrates of the Supreme Court and the lower federal courts. The justices hold office for life during their good behavior. There is a federal judicial system, and each province also maintains its own hierarchy of courts. The federal judiciary has jurisdiction over all cases dealing with the national constitution and laws, as well as cases that involve citizens of different provinces, even if only provincial laws are relied upon. Constitutional questions can be heard by the lower federal courts as well as by the Supreme Court. While certain military matters are not appealable before the Supreme Court, administrative, tax and labor cases are appealable, thus giving the Argentine high court a broad scope of competence. Since a constitutional ruling does not nullify an offensive statute or decree, however, the court's power only affects the parties in the particular case....

Colombia has a very high rating for effectiveness of judicial review in Table 7.3. Furthermore, there is some empirical evidence to support this rating. Colombia instituted in 1910 the "popular action" against statutes, which permits any person, regardless of any direct interest in the outcome, to bring an action directly to the Supreme Court challenging a statute. The Court's decision of unenforceability has the effect of annulling the statute. During the period 1910-1953, over fifty national statutes in whole or in part were invalidated under the popular action....

Mexican judicial review, of all the nations in Latin America, has been the most studied. It is possible, therefore, to assert with some confidence that the score assigned in Table 7.3 reflects the relatively high degree of effectiveness in constitutional review exercised by the Mexican federal judiciary. The practice of judicial review in Mexico today is associated exclusively with the *amparo* action. The writ of *amparo* lies against the actions of all types of officials, including judges, bureaucrats, police, legislators, and even the president and his cabinet. The writ takes three separate forms. First, the direct *amparo* may be used to reverse the final judgment of a state or federal court, a labor mediation board, or the federal tax court. A plaintiff takes his appeal "directly" to one of the chambers of the Supreme Court, or, since 1968, to the nearest collegiate circuit court, depending on the importance of the case.

A second form of the writ, an indirect *amparo*, is brought against all other types of illegal or fundamentally unfair acts of government authorities. The indirect *amparo* generally is utilized to enjoin or compel specific actions of nonjudicial authorities — the police, prosecutors and public administrators. Instead of proceeding directly to the appellate courts, the plaintiff must first bring his complaint before the nearest federal district court. From here, the case may be taken "indirectly" for consideration by the circuit or Supreme Court.

The third form of the writ is designed to attack the inherent constitutionality of an offending statute, decree or regulation. Called an *amparo contra leyes*, it permits an individual to enjoin enforcement, but only to protect himself, of an injurious self-executing law. Initiated in the federal district court, the *amparo contra leyes* may be ultimately decided by all the chambers of the Supreme Court sitting in plenary session. As in half the countries of Latin America, the Mexican constitutional ruling only has *inter partes* effects. There is, however, in Mexico a form of stare decisis, called *jurisprudencia*, which mitigates the inefficiency involved in having each aggrieved party take his own *amparo contra leyes* to the Supreme Court. *Jurisprudencia*, declaring a legal norm unconstitutional, is established by a two-thirds majority of the whole Supreme Court in five consecutive decisions on the same point. It is binding upon all lower courts, as well as military, labor and administrative tribunals. In spite of this, *jurisprudencia* is frequently ignored by administrative agencies. *Amparo contra leyes* judgments, as a result, can never have the effect of abrogating a law *erga omnes*.

Two excellent empirical investigations of judicial review in Mexico have concluded that the federal judiciary exhibits significant independence, especially from the executive.[111] One study sought to measure the number of *amparo* cases decided in favor of the complainant in which the president was named as at least one of the responsible authorities. During the period 1917 to 1960, 3,700 such cases were tallied — thirty-four percent were won by the plaintiff. In a similar examination of decisions before the United States Supreme Court in which the federal government was a party, thirty-six percent of the cases between 1900 and 1967 were decided in favor of the nongovernmental party. Even more impressive is the total output of the Mexican Supreme Court. Between 1963 and 1971, the high court decided 67,700 cases; almost ninety percent of these dealt with the writ of *amparo*, an annual average of 6,683 *amparos*. It is obvious that the Mexican citizenry is well aware of judicial remedies when aggrieved by official action. This is reflected even more in the case load of the lower federal judiciary. In 1971, the thirteen collegiate circuit courts disposed of 21,349 cases, most of which were *amparos*. Finally, the fifty-five district courts received in the same year some 58,000

[111] P. Gonzalez, Democracy in Mexico 21-24 (1970); Schwarz, *Judges Under the Shadow: Judicial Independence in the United States and Mexico*, 3 Cal. West. Int'l L.J. 314-15, 332 (1973).

filings; sixty-two percent of these were *amparo* petitions for relief from criminal proceedings. Fully 12.5 percent of the criminal *amparo* writs were granted; the analogous figure for federal habeas corpus in the United States is five percent.

Effective judicial review, of course, need not be a homogeneous phenomenon. In most nations, the judiciary will be more independent in protecting the constitution against some political agencies than against others. Table 7.4, considering only supreme court cases involving the government as a party, reflects this variability in Mexico compared to the United States for four subject matter areas: penal, administrative, labor and civil law.

Table 7.4

Percentage of Cases Decided in Favor of the Nongovernmental Party in Mexican and United States Supreme Courts, by Subject Matter[1]

Subject Matter	Mexico		United States	
Penal	49%	(49)	74%	(98)
Administrative	40%	(39)	39%	(48)
Labor	43%	(34)	0%	(0)[4]
Civil	40%	(69)	75%	(18)[5]
TOTAL	43%	(191)	55%	(164)

[1] This table represents a survey made of *amparo* cases decided by full written opinion as reported in the *Semanario Judicial* (Mexico) for a 33 month period during 1964-66, and 1968, compared with the United States Court's final dispositions with full written opinion during the three terms of 1966-68.

[4] National Labor Relations Board cases; 14 were decided in favor of the government.

[5] Private litigation with the government as a party.

In Mexico, the percentage of cases decided in favor of the nongovernmental party at the Supreme Court level is similar for all four subject matters, varying between forty and forty-nine percent. On the other hand, there is much more variability in the United States Supreme Court. Penal cases, representing two-thirds of the decisions in Table 7.4, are decided in favor of the nongovernmental party seventy-four percent of the time, reflecting a concern with this field on the part of the United States Court. The total percentage of cases decided in favor of nongovernmental parties, moreover, is higher in the United States compared to Mexico, fifty-five percent to forty-three percent. Nevertheless, the Mexican Supreme Court, viewing all the indicators discussed above, appears to be effective in serving as the guardian of the national constitution.

Economic Development, Democracy and the Effectiveness of Judicial Review

Comparison permits us to make meaningful statements about the effectiveness of judicial review in Latin America. This section will attempt a preliminary ordering of our understanding of a complex subject matter, one that is difficult to measure and about which little is empirically known. Once it is determined that constitutional review is more effective in some nations than in others, even with the imperfect indicators elaborated in Table 7.3, we may want to know why, or at least under what conditions, effective review seems to occur. After assessing the distribution of effective judicial review among Latin American nations, we shall compare the nations in terms of their level of economic development and their present type of political regime. In this way, one can determine whether or not effective judicial review in Latin America occurs randomly or under certain predictable circumstances.

A frequency breakdown for the scores on the effectiveness of judicial review from Table 7.3 reveals that there is a fairly even spread among levels two to nine, with the mode at level five.

Table 7.5

Degree of Effectiveness of Judicial Review in Latin America

2	3	4	5	7	8	9
Ecuador Paraguay	Dominican Republic Honduras	Bolivia Haiti Peru	Cuba El Salvador Guatemala Panama Uruguay	Argentina Nicaragua Venezuela	Chile Costa Rica Mexico	Brazil Colombia

Given the frequency distribution of scores in Table 7.5, one might wish to ascertain how widespread effective judicial review is with respect to population in Latin America.... Dividing the scores into three classes of approximately equal size — effective (7 to 9), somewhat effective (5), and ineffective (2 to 4) — it appears that out of a total Latin American population of 286 million, seventy-eight percent of the people live in countries with effective (scores 7 to 9) judicial review. Only fourteen percent live in the seven nations with a judiciary ineffective (scores 2 to 4) in protecting the constitution. Wild generalizations about Latin America as a region with ineffectual judiciaries, based upon occurrences in Bolivia, Haiti or the Dominican Republic, for instance, too often lead to misunderstanding and stereotyping.

Another manner of assessing judicial review is to consider its effectiveness in relation to the economic development of a nation.... The most widely accepted and commonly employed index to measure the production and resources of a country in terms of the size of its population is gross domestic product (GDP) per capita. GDP per capita is also frequently used as an indicator of relative comfort or well-being. A second indicator, male life expectancy at birth, has similarly been used as a measure of economic development, although it is obviously not an index of production. It also can be considered a rough measure of socioeconomic well-being....

Is effectiveness of judicial review associated with economic production per person in a Latin American country or with the average citizen's socioeconomic well-being? Figure 7.1 gives us a preliminary answer. It is a scatter-

Figure 7.1
Effectiveness of Judicial Review and Economic Development in Latin America

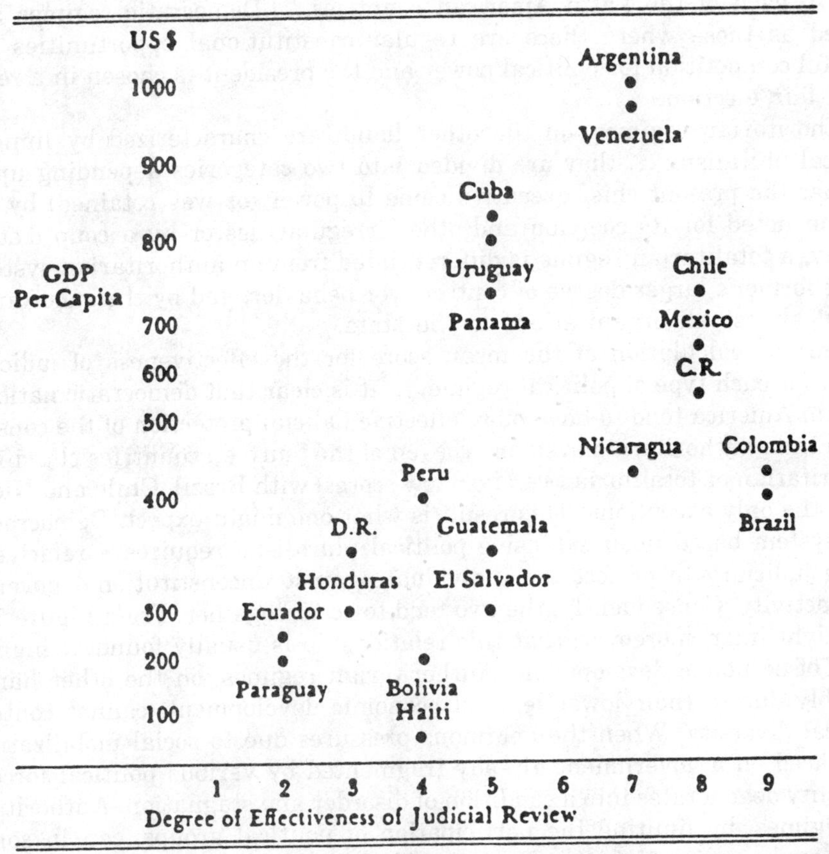

gram plotting the effectiveness score on the horizontal axis and GDP per capita on the vertical axis for all twenty Latin American nations.

There appears to be a positive association between the level of economic development and the degree of judicial effectiveness. Those nations where the court system is ineffective in protecting the constitution (scores 2 to 4) have a per capita GDP of $400 or below. Conversely, those Latin American countries with relatively effective judicial review (scores 7 to 9) all have per capita GDPs greater than $400. The strength of this apparent association between the level of economic development and judicial effectiveness can be determined by calculating the correlation coefficient for these two variables. The Pearson coefficient of correlation is 0.47, which is statistically significant at the 0.017 level. Accordingly, there is a moderate, positive correlation; as a Latin American nation's production per capita increases (and presumably the average level of socioeconomic well-being follows), we can expect the effectiveness of judicial review to also be greater. The 0.017 significance level means that the probability of finding this degree of correlation among these twenty countries if the variables were not associated is less than one in fifty....

Another avenue that may give us insight into the nature of judicial review is to consider its effectiveness in relation to the present type of political regime in each of the Latin American countries.... Democratic regimes are defined as those where there are regular constitutional opportunities for peaceful competition for political power and the president is chosen in a relatively fair election.

Authoritarian regimes, on the other hand, are characterized by limited political pluralism; ... they are divided into two categories depending upon whether the present chief executive came to power (or was retained) by an election noted for its coercion and other irregularities or by a coup d'état. Finally, a totalitarian regime is differentiated from an authoritarian system by the former's larger degree of control over behavior, and by the subordination of almost all organizations to the state.

From the calculation of the mean score for the effectiveness of judicial review for each type of political regime, ... it is clear that democratic nations in Latin America tend to have more effective judicial protection of the constitution than authoritarian systems. Eleven of the fourteen countries classified authoritarian or totalitarian received low scores, with Brazil, Chile and Nicaragua the only exceptions. This result is what one might expect. Democracy, as a system based upon extensive political pluralism, requires a relatively strong judiciary to protect the individual against unconstitutional government activity. Consequently, the two tend to occur together. From Figure 7.1 one might infer, moreover, that this relationship is usually found at higher levels of economic development. Authoritarian regimes, on the other hand, probably due to their lower level of economic development, cannot control political diversity. When the enormous pressures due to social mobilization are placed on a government already fragmented by various political forces, the polity degenerates into a condition of disorder and stagnation. Authoritarian regimes, by limiting the participation of political groups, can in some instances be more efficient in achieving desired national goals. Modernizing authoritarian governments frequently select economic growth as the primary goal, as in Brazil, or some notion of social justice, as in the case of Peru [in the 1970s]. On the other hand, conservative authoritarian regimes in Latin America, such as Paraguay or Haiti, may be characterized more as personal dictatorships, less interested in productively channeling the forces of modernization.

Restricting the effectiveness of the judiciary in protecting constitutional guarantees is one way authoritarian and totalitarian systems limit political pluralism. This need not, however, always be directed toward controlling the judiciary through recruitment and short tenure. Frequently, the political branches of government will simply reduce the jurisdiction of the supreme court so that it can review only certain types of disputes. Thus, all of the democracies in Latin America provide their supreme courts with wide competence over disputes in society. On the contrary, from Table 7.3 one observes that eight of the thirteen authoritarian nations restrict the jurisdiction of their supreme courts in one or two important subject matter areas. Cuba, moreover, receives the lowest score for breadth of jurisdiction since three important fields have been removed from supreme court review. It is a perfect example of an independent judiciary with no power.

KEITH S. ROSENN, THE PROTECTION OF JUDICIAL INDEPENDENCE IN LATIN AMERICA, 19 University of Miami Inter-American Law Review 1, 8, 12, 32 (1987)

How much judicial independence is desirable usually depends upon the extent to which one agrees or disagrees with the outcome of judicial decisions, particularly those involving constitutional interpretation. Judicial independence tends to be lauded by liberals and decried by conservatives when the decisions follow a liberal bent; conversely, judicial independence tends to be deplored by the liberals and praised by conservatives when the decisions take a conservative tack. In a universalistic legal system (i.e., where the same rules are meant to apply to all), judicial independence would be desirable if one were seriously committed to the ideal of equal justice under law for all persons. On the other hand, if one were committed to the maintenance of class privileges and the feudal notion of one law for the elites and another for the masses, an independent judiciary would be undesirable....

Judicial independence is both too complex and too subtle a concept to be measured by such crude and misleading techniques as calculating the percentage of *habeas corpus* or *amparo* cases decided against the government. If a country scrupulously observes the law and the constitution in the administration of criminal justice, *habeas corpus* should never be granted. Indeed, a low percentage of *habeas corpus* petitions decided against the government may signify a high degree of compliance with the law and with constitutional guarantees. On the other hand, it might also signify judicial impotence in the face of a regime that makes people disappear without any legal process and which refuses to acknowledge any information concerning the whereabouts of persons on whose behalf writs of *habeas corpus* are filed. Actually, in terms of sheer volume of cases, corruption is more likely to pose a greater threat to judicial independence than does political influence. The incentive to bribe is present in virtually every case, while the incentive for political authorities to apply pressure is present only when one of the parties is politically well-connected or the case is deemed to have some important political implication....

The lack of judicial independence is a chronic problem in Latin America. A recent assessment by two eminent Mexican jurists concluded that Costa Rica is the only Latin American country where the judiciary is truly independent. Argentina, Bolivia, Brazil, Colombia, Ecuador, Mexico, Peru and Venezuela were considered to have independent judiciaries but subject to interference by the executive, while Guatemala, Honduras, Panama, Paraguay and Uruguay were regarded as definitely lacking judicial independence. One can take issue with many of the conclusions in this incomplete impressionistic survey. Nevertheless, the underlying message — that Latin America as a region suffers from a judicial independence deficiency — seems undeniable. Yet this does not mean that Latin American judiciaries are corrupt, incompetent, or poorly trained. Nor does it mean that the majority of cases will not be resolved on the merits in accordance with the judge's proper application of the governing law. As a rule, Latin American judges are dedicated, scrupulous professionals. Indeed, many Latin American jurists deservedly enjoy high international esteem for their scholarship and dedicated work on international legal projects.

KEITH S. ROSENN, A COMPARISON OF THE PROTECTION OF INDIVIDUAL RIGHTS IN THE NEW CONSTITUTIONS OF COLOMBIA AND BRAZIL, 23 University of Miami Inter-American Law Review 659, 685 (1992)

Under the 1969 Brazilian Constitution, the Supreme Court had the power to determine the unconstitutionality of any law or normative act on its face, a decision with *erga omnes* effects, but standing to bring such an action, called a representation (*representação*), was the exclusive province of the Procurator General. In the current Constitution, representation has been renamed the direct action of unconstitutionality. Standing to bring the action has been expanded to include the President, the Directors (*Mesas*) of the Senate or House of Representatives, state governors, the Federal Council of the Brazilian Bar Association, any political party represented in Congress, and any national labor or business association. Brazil's direct action of unconstitutionality is still much more restricted than Colombia's popular action, which permits any citizen to challenge the constitutionality of any statute directly before the Constitutional Court. Brazil's modification of the representation action represents a very substantial increase in the ability of its Supreme Court to declare laws and statutes unconstitutional.

Both the popular action and the direct action of unconstitutionality have the unfortunate effect of depriving the highest constitutional courts of the benefit of the opinions of the lower courts, of seeing the actual effect of the statute on litigants, and of being able to duck untimely or too sensitive matters by imposing barriers to justiciability. Indeed, these direct actions involving abstract declarations of unconstitutionality may eventually embroil Colombia's Constitutional Court and Brazil's Supreme Court in an undue amount of conflict with the other branches of government.

NOTES AND QUESTIONS

1. Table 7.1 shows that judicial review of legislation for constitutionality often evolved at a different time than judicial review of executive action (e.g., with writs of habeas corpus or *amparo*) in most Latin American countries. In any case, the influence of the United States on the *structure* of judicial review dictated that the supreme court in virtually every country would have a unified jurisdiction over judicial review of both legislative and executive acts. Colombia (with a council of state) and Uruguay (with a court of administrative justice) are exceptions for review of executive acts, but even executive decrees with the force of law (i.e., as statutes) can be reviewed by the supreme court.

Of course, this history of judicial review is quite different from that of Europe. Another important difference is that many Latin American nations also adopted the diffuse system of judicial review used in the United States, which permits many or all courts to rule on the constitutionality of legislative or executive action. In Europe, alternatively, most countries have settled on concentrated judicial review of legislation by one authoritative court. However, some Latin American states only permit the supreme court to make constitutional rulings, and several countries have devised a mixed system that channels certain types of constitutional litigation to a high court but leaves other types of constitutional decisions to a range of courts.

2. The issues of judicial independence and effective judicial review are much more a matter of concern in Latin America than in contemporary Europe. Nevertheless, is it valid to say that judicial review in Latin America is a sham? How does one ascertain the reality of judicial review in a particular country (e.g., Mexico) at a particular time (e.g., the 1990s)? This question (for Mexico) was important in the early 1990s during negotiation over the North American Free Trade Agreement.

Does Professor Clark present a meaningful approach to these issues? What about Professor Rosenn's comment that one's view about the desirability of judicial independence depends on one's political orientation? Is judicial independence (or effective judicial review) too complex a concept to measure? If so, how do jurists from two countries have an intelligent conversation about the topic? Is economic development and political democracy ultimately the answer to effective judicial review rather than structural legal reform?

3. For further detail on Latin American judicial review, see Robert S. Barker, *Constitutional Adjudication in Costa Rica: A Latin American Model*, 17 U. Miami Inter-Am. L. Rev. 249 (1986): *id.*, *Taking Constitutionalism Seriously: Costa Rica's Sala Cuarta*, 6 Fla. J. Int'l L. 349 (1991); Allan R. Brewer-Carías, Judicial Review in Comparative Law 156-67, 243-50, 275-326 (1989); Hector Fix Zamudio, *A Brief Introduction to the Mexican Writ of Amparo*, 9 Cal. W. Int'l L.J. 306 (1979); *id.*, *The Writ of Amparo in La... America*, 13 Law. Americas 361 (1981); Alejandro M. Garro, *Nine Year... Transition to Democracy in Argentina: Partial Failure or Qualified Su...ss?*, 31 Colum. J. Transnat'l L. 1, 72-81 (1993); Keith S. Rosenn, *The S... of Constitutionalism in the United States and Its Failure in Latin A...: An Explanation*, 22 U. Miami Inter-Am. L. Rev. 1 (1990); Carl E. S...arz, *Rights and Remedies in the Federal District Courts of Mexico ... United States*, 4 Hastings Const. L.Q. 67 (1977).

7. THE JAPANESE SUPRE... ...URT

LAWRENCE W. BEER, THE CONSTITUTIONAL SYSTEM AND ITS JUDICIAL ...PRETATION, 17 Law in Japan 7, 20-21 (1984)

The Supreme ...okyo consists of fifteen justices, who are appointed by the cabi... ...mong people recommended by the Supreme Court. Whereas ...ment to the career judiciary is for ten-year renewable terms, ...ent compulsory at sixty-five, most justices are appointed whi... ...ixties; their mandatory retirement age is seventy.... ...reaching the Supreme Court are decided by three petty benches ...nto which the court divides, each containing five justices. At least three judges must be present to decide a petty bench case, while nine of the fifteen justices constitute a quorum of the full court, the grand bench (*daihōtei*)....

Lower courts as well as the Supreme Court have the power of judicial review, which extends to judging the validity of all laws, ordinances, and other official acts (article 81). Between 1947 and 1982, the Supreme Court accepted for adjudication 203,963 cases, of which 1,049 were referred to the Grand Bench. In 263 of these instances, a law, order, regulation, or other official act was held unconstitutional; but some foreign and domestic scholars have criticized the Supreme Court for not being more assertive in the cause of individual rights. Like judges in most democracies, the bench in Japan uses the judicial review power sparingly against other agencies of government. On balance, lower courts seem to have been more promotive of civil rights and liberties than the Supreme Court. The Supreme Court is not a "constitutional court," in the sense that it cannot decide issues except in the context of controversies between parties with standing to take legal action.

The technical legal effect of a judgment of unconstitutionality is debated. "A conclusion in a decision of a superior court shall bind courts below in respect of the case concerned," but not in general.[79] Consistency among judicial decisions is generally honored, but not a doctrine of *stare decisis*. If the Supreme Court holds a legal provision unconstitutional, the same or other courts may nevertheless rule differently on the same issue in other cases.... Since 1947, the judges of Japan have cautiously built a new, more visible, more independent, and more powerful judicial institution in the course of resolving millions of conflicts under the umbrella of the constitution; but the Supreme Court has chosen a markedly deferential role toward the Diet and administrators when dealing with some constitutional issues.

CONSTITUTION OF JAPAN

Articles 14, 15, 22, 29, 41, 44, 76, 81

Article 14

1. All of the people ar under the law and there shall be no discrimination in political, econom social relations because of race, creed, sex, social status, or family origi

2. Peers and peerage shall n recognized.

3. No privilege shall accompany ward of honor, decoration, or any distinction, nor shall any such awa alid beyond the lifetime of the individual who now holds or hereafte ceive it.

Article 15

1. The people have the inalienable right to ch ublic officials and to dismiss them.

2. All public officials are servants of the whole co nd not of any group thereof.

[79] Court Organization Law art. 4.

3. Universal adult suffrage is guaranteed with regard to the election of public officials.

4. In all elections, secrecy of the ballot shall not be violated. A voter shall not be answerable, publicly or privately, for the choice he has made.

Article 22

1. Every person shall have freedom to choose and change his residence and to choose his occupation to the extent that it does not interfere with the public welfare.

Article 29

1. The right to own or to hold property is inviolable.

2. Property rights shall be defined by law, in conformity with the public welfare.

3. Private property may be taken for public use upon just compensation therefor.

Article 41

The Diet shall be the highest organ of state power, and shall be the sole lawmaking organ of the State.

Article 44

The qualifications of members of both Houses and their electors shall be fixed by law. However, there shall be no discrimination because of race, creed, sex, social status, family origin, education, property, or income.

Article 76

1. The whole judicial process is vested in a Supreme Court ...d in such inferior courts as are established by law.

2. No extraordinary tribunal shall be established, nor any organ or agency of the Executive be given final judicial pow...

3. All judges shall be independent in the exercis... ...eir conscience and shall be bound only by this Constitution and ...

Article 81

The Supreme Court is the court of l... ...ith the power to determine the constitutionality of any law, o... ...tion, or official act.

...STIONS

NOTE

1. Considering articles ... of the Japanese Constitution, along with the Beer excerpt, ...at the Supreme Court can effectively nullify as well as d... ...tional acts of the Japanese legislature (Diet)?

2. Among the rights of citizens protected by the Japanese Constitution are rights of property, freedom of occupation, equality under the law, and participation without discrimination in the electoral process. Consider the following Supreme Court decisions involving these rights and assess the extent to which they are protected by the exercise of judicial power in Japan.

MUTSUO NAKAMURA, FREEDOM OF ECONOMIC ACTIVITIES AND THE RIGHT TO PROPERTY, 53 Law and Contemporary Problems 1, 4-9 (No. 2, 1990)

Freedom of Occupation

A. *Early Decisions*

In the early period after the 1947 Constitution went into effect, the Supreme Court applied the "public welfare" test to decide the constitutionality of statutes restricting the freedom to choose an occupation.

1. *Occupation Stability Act.* Among the early Supreme Court decisions, one of the leading cases that allowed limitations on the freedom to choose an occupation was the Grand Bench decision of June 21, 1950,[14] holding constitutional the challenged provision of the Occupation Stability Act (Shokugyō antei hō). This decision judged the purpose of the Act as "giving each person a certain occupation suitable for one's ability and planning a stable employment," and concluded that the purpose was reasonable. But legal scholars have criticized the Court's inadequate review of whether such a strict limitation was proper. In other words, in judging the constitutionality of statutes that limit the freedom to choose an occupation, the Court, it is argued, should first review the purpose of the limitation and, second, determine whether the means of limitation are proper. These scholars argue, however, that in its early decisions the Court did not adequately recognize the need to decide whether the means of the limitation itself were proper or improper, even if the limitation purpose was reasonable.

2. *Antiqu*[illegible]*aling Act.* The Supreme Court Grand Bench decision of March 18, 1953,[16] [illegible]ssed the constitutionality of the Antique Dealing Act (Kobutsu eigyō [illegible] which prohibited antique dealing without a license. The Court held that [illegible]atute was constitutional since Article 22 of the 1947 Constitution allow[illegible]ic welfare" limitations on the freedom to choose an occupation. As a ge[illegible]le, the Court noted that "if the Antique Dealing Act adopts the licens[illegible]m and if punishing non-licensed businesses is necessary to maintain [illegible]lfare, the limitation is constitutional." The Court then decided that [illegible]g system in antique dealing is "necessary to maintain the public wel[illegible]ect victims, to prevent crimes, to aid in the arrest of criminals, and[illegible]] national ... well-being." This decision adopted the "necessary re[illegible]ndard and operates as the leading case upholding statutes limitin[illegible] to choose an occupation. Other Supreme Court Grand Bench dec[illegible]pt the "necessary restriction" test are as follows: the decision up[illegible]nstitutionality of the Drug

14 4 Keishū 1049 (Sup. Ct., G.B., June 21, 195[illegible]

16 7 Keishū 577 (Sup. Ct., G.B., Mar. 18, 195[illegible]

3. Universal adult suffrage is guaranteed with regard to the election of public officials.

4. In all elections, secrecy of the ballot shall not be violated. A voter shall not be answerable, publicly or privately, for the choice he has made.

Article 22

1. Every person shall have freedom to choose and change his residence and to choose his occupation to the extent that it does not interfere with the public welfare.

Article 29

1. The right to own or to hold property is inviolable.

2. Property rights shall be defined by law, in conformity with the public welfare.

3. Private property may be taken for public use upon just compensation therefor.

Article 41

The Diet shall be the highest organ of state power, and shall be the sole lawmaking organ of the State.

Article 44

The qualifications of members of both Houses and their electors shall be fixed by law. However, there shall be no discrimination because of race, creed, sex, social status, family origin, education, property, or income.

Article 76

1. The whole judicial process is vested in a Supreme Court and in such inferior courts as are established by law.

2. No extraordinary tribunal shall be established, nor shall any organ or agency of the Executive be given final judicial power.

3. All judges shall be independent in the exercise of their conscience and shall be bound only by this Constitution and the laws.

Article 81

The Supreme Court is the court of last resort with the power to determine the constitutionality of any law, order, regulation, or official act.

NOTES AND QUESTIONS

1. Considering articles 41, 76, and 81 of the Japanese Constitution, along with the Beer excerpt, do you think that the Supreme Court can effectively nullify as well as declare unconstitutional acts of the Japanese legislature (Diet)?

2. Among the rights of citizens protected by the Japanese Constitution are rights of property, freedom of occupation, equality under the law, and participation without discrimination in the electoral process. Consider the following Supreme Court decisions involving these rights and assess the extent to which they are protected by the exercise of judicial power in Japan.

MUTSUO NAKAMURA, FREEDOM OF ECONOMIC ACTIVITIES AND THE RIGHT TO PROPERTY, 53 Law and Contemporary Problems 1, 4-9 (No. 2, 1990)

Freedom of Occupation

A. *Early Decisions*

In the early period after the 1947 Constitution went into effect, the Supreme Court applied the "public welfare" test to decide the constitutionality of statutes restricting the freedom to choose an occupation.

1. *Occupation Stability Act.* Among the early Supreme Court decisions, one of the leading cases that allowed limitations on the freedom to choose an occupation was the Grand Bench decision of June 21, 1950,[14] holding constitutional the challenged provision of the Occupation Stability Act (Shokugyō antei hō). This decision judged the purpose of the Act as "giving each person a certain occupation suitable for one's ability and planning a stable employment," and concluded that the purpose was reasonable. But legal scholars have criticized the Court's inadequate review of whether such a strict limitation was proper. In other words, in judging the constitutionality of statutes that limit the freedom to choose an occupation, the Court, it is argued, should first review the purpose of the limitation and, second, determine whether the means of limitation are proper. These scholars argue, however, that in its early decisions the Court did not adequately recognize the need to decide whether the means of the limitation itself were proper or improper, even if the limitation's purpose was reasonable.

2. *Antique Dealing Act.* The Supreme Court Grand Bench decision of March 18, 1953,[16] addressed the constitutionality of the Antique Dealing Act (Kobutsu eigyō hō), which prohibited antique dealing without a license. The Court held that the statute was constitutional since Article 22 of the 1947 Constitution allows "public welfare" limitations on the freedom to choose an occupation. As a general rule, the Court noted that "if the Antique Dealing Act adopts the licensing system and if punishing non-licensed businesses is necessary to maintain public welfare, the limitation is constitutional." The Court then decided that the licensing system in antique dealing is "necessary to maintain the public welfare, to protect victims, to prevent crimes, to aid in the arrest of criminals, and to [preserve] national ... well-being." This decision adopted the "necessary restriction" standard and operates as the leading case upholding statutes limiting the freedom to choose an occupation. Other Supreme Court Grand Bench decisions that adopt the "necessary restriction" test are as follows: the decision upholding the constitutionality of the Drug

[14] 4 Keishū 1049 (Sup. Ct., G.B., June 21, 1950).
[16] 7 Keishū 577 (Sup. Ct., G.B., Mar. 18, 1953).

which permits many or all courts to rule on the constitutionality of legislative or executive action. In Europe, alternatively, most countries have settled on concentrated judicial review of legislation by one authoritative court. However, some Latin American states only permit the supreme court to make constitutional rulings, and several countries have devised a mixed system that channels certain types of constitutional litigation to a high court but leaves other types of constitutional decisions to a range of courts.

2. The issues of judicial independence and effective judicial review are much more a matter of concern in Latin America than in contemporary Europe. Nevertheless, is it valid to say that judicial review in Latin America is a sham? How does one ascertain the reality of judicial review in a particular country (e.g., Mexico) at a particular time (e.g., the 1990s)? This question (for Mexico) was important in the early 1990s during negotiation over the North American Free Trade Agreement.

Does Professor Clark present a meaningful approach to these issues? What about Professor Rosenn's comment that one's view about the desirability of judicial independence depends on one's political orientation? Is judicial independence (or effective judicial review) too complex a concept to measure? If so, how do jurists from two countries have an intelligent conversation about the topic? Is economic development and political democracy ultimately the answer to effective judicial review rather than structural legal reform?

3. For further detail on Latin American judicial review, see Robert S. Barker, *Constitutional Adjudication in Costa Rica: A Latin American Model*, 17 U. Miami Inter-Am. L. Rev. 249 (1986): *id., Taking Constitutionalism Seriously: Costa Rica's Sala Cuarta*, 6 Fla. J. Int'l L. 349 (1991); Allan R. Brewer-Carías, Judicial Review in Comparative Law 156-67, 243-50, 275-326 (1989); Hector Fix Zamudio, *A Brief Introduction to the Mexican Writ of Amparo,* 9 Cal. W. Int'l L.J. 306 (1979); *id., The Writ of Amparo in Latin America*, 13 Law. Americas 361 (1981); Alejandro M. Garro, *Nine Years of Transition to Democracy in Argentina: Partial Failure or Qualified Success?,* 31 Colum. J. Transnat'l L. 1, 72-81 (1993); Keith S. Rosenn, *The Success of Constitutionalism in the United States and Its Failure in Latin America: An Explanation*, 22 U. Miami Inter-Am. L. Rev. 1 (1990); Carl E. Schwarz, *Rights and Remedies in the Federal District Courts of Mexico and the United States*, 4 Hastings Const. L.Q. 67 (1977).

7. THE JAPANESE SUPREME COURT

LAWRENCE W. BEER, JAPAN'S CONSTITUTIONAL SYSTEM AND ITS JUDICIAL INTERPRETATION, 17 Law in Japan 7, 20-21 (1984)

The Supreme Court in Tokyo consists of fifteen justices, who are appointed by the cabinet from among people recommended by the Supreme Court. Whereas an appointment to the career judiciary is for ten-year renewable terms, with retirement compulsory at sixty-five, most justices are appointed while in their sixties; their mandatory retirement age is seventy....

Most cases reaching the Supreme Court are decided by three petty benches (*shohōtei*) into which the court divides, each containing five justices. At least three judges must be present to decide a petty bench case, while nine of the fifteen justices constitute a quorum of the full court, the grand bench (*daihōtei*)....

Lower courts as well as the Supreme Court have the power of judicial review, which extends to judging the validity of all laws, ordinances, and other official acts (article 81). Between 1947 and 1982, the Supreme Court accepted for adjudication 203,963 cases, of which 1,049 were referred to the Grand Bench. In 263 of these instances, a law, order, regulation, or other official act was held unconstitutional; but some foreign and domestic scholars have criticized the Supreme Court for not being more assertive in the cause of individual rights. Like judges in most democracies, the bench in Japan uses the judicial review power sparingly against other agencies of government. On balance, lower courts seem to have been more promotive of civil rights and liberties than the Supreme Court. The Supreme Court is not a "constitutional court," in the sense that it cannot decide issues except in the context of controversies between parties with standing to take legal action.

The technical legal effect of a judgment of unconstitutionality is debated. "A conclusion in a decision of a superior court shall bind courts below in respect of the case concerned," but not in general.[79] Consistency among judicial decisions is generally honored, but not a doctrine of *stare decisis*. If the Supreme Court holds a legal provision unconstitutional, the same or other courts may nevertheless rule differently on the same issue in other cases.... Since 1947, the judges of Japan have cautiously built a new, more visible, more independent, and more powerful judicial institution in the course of resolving millions of conflicts under the umbrella of the constitution; but the Supreme Court has chosen a markedly deferential role toward the Diet and administrators when dealing with some constitutional issues.

CONSTITUTION OF JAPAN

Articles 14, 15, 22, 29, 41, 44, 76, 81

Article 14

1. All of the people are equal under the law and there shall be no discrimination in political, economic, or social relations because of race, creed, sex, social status, or family origin.

2. Peers and peerage shall not be recognized.

3. No privilege shall accompany any award of honor, decoration, or any distinction, nor shall any such award be valid beyond the lifetime of the individual who now holds or hereafter may receive it.

Article 15

1. The people have the inalienable right to choose their public officials and to dismiss them.

2. All public officials are servants of the whole community and not of any group thereof.

[79] Court Organization Law art. 4.

Control Act (Mayaku torishimari hō), which prohibits the delivery, receipt, and keeping of drugs;[18] the decision upholding the constitutionality of Article 17 of the Dentist Act (Shika ishi hō) and Article 20 of the Dental Technician Act (Shika gikōshi hō), which prohibit dental technicians from checking the line of teeth and from practicing orthodontics;[19] the decision upholding the constitutionality of the Massager Act (Anmashi, harishi, kyushi, oyobi jyudō-seihukushi hō), which prohibits certain businesses from providing services that are similar to medical treatment;[20] and the decision upholding the constitutionality of Article 5, item 2 of the Unfair Competition Protection Act [Fusei kyōsō bōshi hō], which prohibits all businesses from committing intentional acts of unfair competition.[21]

3. *Zoning*. In the Supreme Court Grand Bench decision of January 26, 1955,[22] the Court reviewed the constitutionality of a public bath zoning law, which required a certain distance between existing and newly planned public bathhouses before the state grants licenses for the new buildings. The purpose of the statute was to allocate public baths adequately. The Court characterized the public bath as "a sanitary accommodation that is a prerequisite in the daily lives of many nationals." The Supreme Court measured the necessity of public baths and concluded that "many nationals would suffer daily inconvenience with few public baths. And with too many public baths in competition, the bath business would become economically unstable. Consequently, the condition of sanitary accommodation would decline, adversely affecting national health and environmental sanitation." The point of the Supreme Court's analysis is that if there is no zoning on public baths, there would be more public baths in competition with one another. Consequently, the condition of sanitary equipment would decline. Many commentaries criticize the Supreme Court for failing to review adequately the legislative facts behind the zoning law and for simply ruling in accordance with legislative history.

B. *The Supreme Court Grand Bench Decision of November 22, 1972*

While the earlier cases uniformly applied the public welfare test, the first case to apply the "purpose" test to decide the constitutionality of a statute was the Grand Bench decision of November 22, 1972.[23] This decision was an important turning point in the development of the constitutional analysis of restrictions on the freedom to choose an occupation. The Court upheld the constitutionality of the Retail Business Adjustment Special Measure Act (Kouri shōgyō chosei tokubetsu sochi hō), Article 3, clause 1. This law zoned retail markets by requiring new markets to be licensed. For the first time, the Supreme Court classified the restrictions based on the purpose of the regulated economic activity.

Under this new test, the Supreme Court divides occupational restrictions into two categories based on their purposes. The first type of restriction is

[18] 10 Keishū 1746 (Sup. Ct., G.B., Dec. 26, 1956).
[19] 13 Keishū 1132 (Sup. Ct., G.B., July 8, 1959).
[20] 14 Keishū 33 (Sup. Ct., G.B., Jan. 27, 1960).
[21] 14 Keishū 525 (Sup. Ct., G.B., Apr. 6, 1960).
[22] *Shimizu v. Japan* (*The Fukuoka Bathhouse Case*), 9 Keishū 89 (Sup. Ct., G.B., Jan. 26, 1955).
[23] 26 Keishū 586.

negative, designed to keep public safety and order; the other is an affirmative restriction aimed at carrying out socioeconomic policy under the ideal of a welfare state. As to the affirmative restriction, the Supreme Court, respecting legislative discretion, adopted what is called the "clarity test." Under the clarity test, the restriction is deemed unconstitutional if the legislative branch abuses its discretion and the restriction is clearly unreasonable. In the case of the Retail Business Adjustment Special Measure Act, the Court recognized that an affirmative restriction protecting small or medium-sized enterprises has a reasonable purpose in protecting retailers from economic collapse caused by excess numbers of retail markets, and is, therefore, constitutional.

C. *The Supreme Court Grand Bench Decision of April 30, 1975*

In examining the constitutionality of zoning new pharmacies under the Pharmaceutical Business Act (Yakuji hō), the Supreme Court fundamentally adopted the reasoning of its 1972 decision,[24] classified the act as a negative purpose restriction, and held the Pharmaceutical Business Act unconstitutional by applying "the strict-reasonableness test," rather than the clarity test.

At first, the Supreme Court classified two types of measures: affirmative measures that promote socioeconomic policy and negative measures that protect the public from the harmful effects of free occupational activities. In the case of negative purpose restrictions, the Court required the legislative purpose (i) to be necessary and reasonable and (ii) to impose minimal restrictions on occupational activity. Next, the Supreme Court reviewed the necessity and reasonableness of zoning pharmacies and found that zoning a new pharmacy is a negative purpose measure, designed mainly to protect life and health from danger. The Court denied the necessity and reasonableness of distance restrictions in setting up new pharmacies and indicated that the "danger of supplying defective medicine caused by a sudden increase in competition or instability of business is not recognized as a reasonable decision, and is merely speculative." The Court held that the legislature's argument that business instability leads to a "supply of defective medicine is unreasonable." Thus, this decision refutes the legislature's logic of causation in adopting the distance restriction in its 1963 revision of the Pharmaceutical Business Act.

D. *The Relationship Between the Public Bathhouse Decision and the Pharmaceutical Business Act Decision*

On one hand, the Supreme Court decided that the zoning of public baths is constitutional, and thus affirmed the legislative findings in 1955 that, without zoning, too many public bathhouses would compete with one another and the condition of sanitary equipment would decline. On the other hand, in 1975, the Court decided that the zoning of pharmacies is unconstitutional, and thus denied the legislative findings that without zoning in this context, the competition among pharmacies would create instability and consequently de-

[24] 29 Minshū 572.

fective medicine would be supplied. Therefore, the question arises whether the decision in 1975 substantially overruled the decision of 1955.

There are two lines of commentary on the issue. On the one hand, there are three arguments denying the constitutionality of the public bathhouse restrictions. First, there is no causation between laissez-faire policy and the declining condition of sanitary equipment; rather, free competition increases sanitation standards. Second, administrative acts controlling public health and cancelling public bath permits should be done in response to decreasing sanitation. Third, free competition makes public baths geographically well apportioned.

On the other hand, the argument that the restrictions are constitutional is based on the special public character of public bathhouses. First, the public bath is public insofar as it is a prerequisite of daily life for persons not having a bath in their own house. Second, the bath charge is regulated and kept low by the Price Control Order (Bukka tōsei rei). Third, there is no strategic flexibility in the public bath business since the demand is regionally restricted. Fourth, although the cost of constructing baths is high, public bathhouse buildings cannot be converted to serve other industries.

The Supreme Court reaffirmed the decision of 1955 and held that the zoning of public baths is constitutional.[26] This decision mentioned the "public bath as a prerequisite public accommodation in the daily lives of citizens." The Court judged the purposes of zoning to be "maintaining the health of the citizens, protecting public bath managers from giving up or changing businesses because of difficulties, and encouraging a good and stable business for the 'public welfare.'"

The Court also classified zoning on public bathhouses as "an affirmative restriction." Citing the Supreme Court decision of November 22, 1972, the Court mentioned that "if the legislature's act deviates in its discretion and is clearly unreasonable, the act should be unconstitutional." The Court then applied the clarity test as a liberal standard of constitutional review. Since planning to ensure the stability of already existing public baths is an affirmative purpose restriction, the prevailing position among legal scholars is that zoning on public bathhouses is constitutional.

Property Rights

The Supreme Court distinguished between affirmative and negative restrictions in reviewing the constitutionality of statutes restricting freedom to choose an occupation. The Court then applied the clarity test to affirmative restrictions and the "strict reasonableness" test, which reviews the reasonableness of legislative discretion, to negative restrictions. The question arises whether this dichotomy between the affirmative and negative restrictions also applies to property rights cases. Scholars generally assert that the dichotomy applies to property rights as well.

The Supreme Court decision of April 22, 1987,[29] clarified the test for reviewing statutes restricting property rights. This decision, concerning the right to

[26] 1302 Hanrei Jihō 159 (Sup. Ct., 2d P.B., Jan. 20, 1989).

[29] *Hiraguchi v. Hiraguchi*, 41 Minshū 408 (Sup. Ct., G.B., Apr. 22, 1987).

claim division of joint ownership as prescribed by Civil Code (Minpō) Article 256, clause 1, dealt with the constitutionality of the Forest Act (Shinrin hō), which denied this right to persons owning less than half of a forest. The decision declared the Forest Act, Article 186, to be unconstitutional as a violation of Article 29, clause 2.

The majority opinion, citing the Pharmaceutical Business Act case of 1975, first stated that the purpose of regulating property rights varies from "affirmative restriction[s] on socioeconomic policy such as vindication for public accommodation or protection for [an] economically weak person" to "negative restriction[s] on behalf of security of social life or maintenance of public order." The question of whether the restriction fits the public welfare limitation in Article 29, clause 2, of the 1947 Constitution should be decided by balancing the purpose, necessity, and content of the restriction. The Supreme Court, however, decided that

> [t]he legislature's balancing should be respected. But, where it is clear that the restrictive purpose is not consistent with public welfare, or where, even if the restrictive purpose comports with public welfare, the measures of restriction are unnecessary or unreasonable in accomplishing its purpose, the restrictive statute should be construed as against Article 29, clause 2, of the 1947 Constitution. Thus, the decision of the legislature should be denied only when it exceeds the reasonable use of discretion.[31]

Next, the majority opinion, applying the test to Article 186 of the Forest Act, reviewed the constitutionality of both the Act's purpose and manner. First, the Supreme Court explained that the legislative purposes of Article 186 are "protecting the stability of forest management and consequently promoting the culture and the production capacity of the forest." The Court then decided that these legislative purposes were constitutional since it cannot be clearly argued that public welfare is not involved. Next, the Court examined the manner of the restriction from several angles and decided that the legislative decision to deny the right to claim division of joint ownership is beyond the legislature's reasonable discretion in relation to the legislative purpose of Article 186. Since the Court did not find both reasonableness and necessity, it held Article 186 to be unconstitutional.

In addition to the majority opinion of the twelve justices, a minority opinion of three justices clearly adopts the dichotomy between affirmative and negative restrictions. The minority applied the clarity test to the affirmative restriction but reached different results. Justice Obuchi decided that the restriction was unconstitutional, but Justice Kagawa held it to be constitutional.

Thus, the majority opinion did not necessarily decide that Article 186 was unconstitutional by defining which test would be applied to statutes restricting property rights. Consequently, legal scholars are divided over the interpretation of this case.

---

[31] 41 Minshū 408.

KUROKAWA v. CHIBA PREFECTURE ELECTION COMMISSION

Supreme Court of Japan
Grand Bench
Decision of 14 April 1976
30 Minshū 223 (1976)

[The background and holding in this case is discussed in an article in *Law in Japan*, excerpted below.]

RECENT DEVELOPMENTS, 9 Law in Japan 151-52 (1976)

Having experimented with several types of electoral districts for election of members to the lower house of the Diet, ranging from small single member districts to prefecture-wide, multi-member districts, Japan adopted in 1925 the present system of medium-sized, multi-member districts. Although 2 to 5 members are elected from each district (except for the Amami Islands, the only single member district), a voter can vote for only one candidate.

Among other effects, this system tends to give minority parties somewhat greater representation than they would have in a system of single member districts. Offsetting this advantage, however, has been the chronic malapportionment of the lower house as a result of sluggish Diet response to the growth of urban areas, particularly the once rural environs of the major cities, where the majority Liberal Democratic Party is generally weakest. Between 1950 and 1975, for example, there was a 30% population shift from rural to urban areas. Tokyo more than doubled in population. During this period the lower house was reapportioned only twice — once in 1964 and once in 1975. And by 1972 malapportionment had reached the point where there were five times as many voters per member elected from Osaka Prefecture's densely populated Third District than Hyōgō Prefecture's stable Fifth District.

It was in this context that Atsuo Kurokawa, a voter in Chiba's First District, brought a *kōkoku* appeal to the Tokyo High Court under article 204 of the Public Office Election Law challenging the validity of the December 10, 1972 general election. Despite the previous increase in members and districts in 1964, there were 381,217.25 voters per Diet member from the First District as compared with the median of about 149,869 voters per Diet member (the Wakayama First District) or the extreme of 79,172 voters per member in the Hyōgō Fifth District. This, argued Kurokawa, amounted to a denial of equality under the law in violation of article 14 of the postwar Constitution. The Tokyo High Court dismissed the action, relying on the Supreme Court's grand bench decision in *Ishiyama v. Tokyo Prefecture Election Commission*, in which the Supreme Court concluded the disparity of the political value of a vote among districts had not reached the point where it could be considered so unjust and unequal to be deemed an abuse of legislative discretion.

On *jōkoku* appeal the Supreme Court reversed in a grand bench decision of April 14, 1976. By a 14 to 1 vote, the Court held that the inequality in the political value of a voter's ballot and the apportionment of districts and representatives at the time of the 1972 election (thus prior to the 1975 apportionment) violated the provisions of the Constitution on equality under the law, universal suffrage and nondiscrimination among candidates. An 8 justice majority, however, refused to invalidate the election in the absence of an express constitutional provision to the effect that an election could be declared invalid for a constitutional violation, reasoning that such a decision would jeopardize the activities of the Diet and the validity of all legislative actions taken since 1972 (Chief Justice Murakami, and Associate Justices Sekine, Fujibayashi, Ogawa, Sakamoto, Kishigami, Takatsuji and Dandō).

Five justices (Okahara, Shimoda, Erikuchi, Ōtsuka and Yoshida) stated in a separate opinion that the Court should have gone further and invalidated the election even in the absence of express constitutional language. They reasoned that not only was such a decision logically unavoidable but also a failure to do so would render the judiciary powerless to remedy the existing violation.

Justice Kishi urged the Court to declare the Chiba election invalid.... The sole dissenter on the main issue, Justice Amano, argued that the case should have been dismissed inasmuch as the Chiba Election Commission was not responsible for apportionment and thus was not the proper party defendant.

Handed down in the midst of Japan's most serious parliamentary crisis in three decades, the decision, as predicted by the five justices, has been all but ignored. However, suits have already been filed challenging the December 1976 election and the 1975 attempt to reapportion the Diet. Since the Diet has reached the limits of expansion, an effort to make a substantial change in Japan's electoral system can be anticipated. But unless there is significant reform the Court will again face the dilemma of invalidating an election or exposing an inability to provide effective relief.

HIROYUKI HATA, MALAPPORTIONMENT OF REPRESENTATION IN THE NATIONAL DIET, 53 Law and Contemporary Problems 157-60, 170 (No. 2, 1990)

Malapportionment of Diet seats is one of the most serious problems confronting contemporary Japan. After World War II, there was a large-scale population shift from rural to urban areas in Japan, as in other industrialized countries. However, the postwar statutes for apportionment of Diet members have not been fully revised to reflect this shift. This situation exists because the conservative Liberal Democratic Party and its predecessors, which have received their main support in the rural areas, have been in power ever since the war's end, except for a short period during which the Japan Socialist Party led the government. In the early 1960s, many Japanese people began to question the degree of malapportionment, and some concluded that it had passed the bounds of tolerance....

Under the Constitution, apportionment and districting are expressly within the discretion of the National Diet, which consists of the House of Representatives and the House of Councillors. The Constitution provides that "[t]he number of the members of each House shall be fixed by law" and that "[e]lectoral districts, method of voting and other matters pertaining to the method of election of members of both Houses shall be fixed by law." The number of members of the House of Representatives and that of the House of

Councillors were first prescribed in 1947 by two statutes: the Revised Election Act for Members of the House of Representatives and the Election Act for Members of the House of Councillors. These two laws, however, were replaced in 1950 by the Public Officials Election Act, which provides in Schedule I for the number of Representatives and in Schedule II for the number of Councillors. The Public Officials Election Act made slight changes in the number of members of the House of Representatives because of demographic population shifts already evident at the time of enactment.

To determine apportionment of the House of Representatives, the nation was first divided into 117 electoral districts, each of which was allocated three to five seats. The computation was made on the basis of 150,000 electors per Representative in accordance with the National Census of April 26, 1946. The number of Representatives was fixed at 466, a number which had not changed since 1925. As to the apportionment of the House of Councillors, the total number of its members was fixed first at 250, then at 252 after the reversion of the Ryukyu Islands to Japan in 1972. Out of this number, 100 were elected at large, with the nation as a whole forming a single electoral district, and 150 (152 after 1972) were elected from all the prefectures, with each prefecture comprising a local electoral district. The original method of election for the members of the House of Councillors to be elected at large called for electors to cast their votes for the individual candidates of their choice. In 1982, however, this method was replaced by a form of proportional representation, according to which electors cast their votes for the list of candidates submitted by each political party. Seats are allocated to the candidates of the various parties in proportion to the votes they have acquired.

The apportionment of members of the House of Councillors to be elected from local electoral districts was made on the basis of 487,417 persons per Councillor, a number based on the population of Japan as of April 26, 1946, divided by 150. However, since the members of the House of Councillors were to serve six-year terms of office, and half the House was to stand for election every three years, every prefecture, however small in population, was allocated at least two seats. Therefore, there was from the beginning an imbalance of 1 to 2 in the ratio of population per Councillor between the most populated district and the least populated district.

Thus, the apportionment of both Houses was made on the basis of the population of the electorate derived from the National Census of April 26, 1946. Moreover, Schedule I of the Public Officials Election Act makes special provision for the apportionment of members of the House of Representatives and states that "[i]t is to be made a practice to correct this Schedule in accordance with the results of the most recent National Census every five years from the date of its enforcement."

After 1946, the rural population began to move, and still continues to move, to cities in large numbers as Japan's industry develops. For this reason, the relative difference in the ratio of voters per Diet member between the rural areas and the big cities has been growing, but the National Diet has failed to make an all-out effort to correct the situation. In the case of the House of Representatives, there have been only three reapportionment statutes. The first reapportionment was in July 1964, resulting in an increase of nineteen members, which barely reduced the disparity in the ratio of the number of the electorate per Representative to 1 to 2. This, however, proved to be nothing but a temporary solution. In fact, according to the 1970 National Census, the relative difference between the Third District of Osaka, which was the most populous district, and the Fifth District of Hyogo, the least populous one, had reached a ratio of 1 to 4.99.

The second reapportionment plan was put into effect in July 1975. It added twenty more seats in the House of Representatives, yet the disparity that existed between the Fourth District of Chiba and the Fifth District of Hyogo was still at 1 to 3.7. This disparity was the result of the Diet's long negligence in making a decisive move toward correcting the imbalance. What the Diet had done instead to that point was simply to create and allocate some seats to extremely disadvantaged districts. This approach avoided the true problem, however, because the Diet had not tried to deprive rural constituencies, which were overrepresented in the Diet, of their excessive seats.

On April 14, 1976, Japan's Supreme Court declared unconstitutional the rules of apportionment for the members of the House of Representatives at the time of the general election of 1972, when the maximum relative difference between electoral districts in the value of each vote was 1 to 4.99. Despite its ruling of unconstitutionality, however, the Court vacated the petition for invalidation of the election itself.[11] Again, on November 7, 1983, the Supreme Court hinted that, after a reasonable period of time (which the Court thought to be five years) had elapsed, it would declare unconstitutional the rules of apportionment revised according to the National Census of 1975, under which the maximum disparity had reached the level of 1 to 3.94.[12] Those decisions forced the Diet to revise the rules of apportionment a third time. The new apportionment plan was called the plan of "eight plus, seven minus," for it allocated one seat each to eight districts, which were intolerably under represented, and deprived seven districts, which were over represented, of one seat each. With this revision, the traditional electorate system, with three to five members allocated per constituency, underwent a partial change, and brought about four two-member districts and one six-member district.

With respect to the apportionment of the members of the House of Councillors to be elected from local districts, the relative difference in the value of a vote between electoral districts had exceeded constitutionally tolerable limits, just as in the case of the House of Representatives. On February 5, 1964, however, the Supreme Court upheld the constitutionality of Schedule II of the Public Officials Election Act at the time of the 1962 election, in which the maximum disparity between districts had reached a level of approximately 1 to 4.[15] Later, in April 1983, the Supreme Court again declared valid the rules of apportionment at the time of the 1977 election, in which the maximum difference had been 1 to 5.26.[16] The Court looked to the peculiari-

[11]*Kurokawa v. Chiba Prefecture Election Comm'n*, 30 Minshū 223 (Sup. Ct., G.B., Apr. 14, 1976).

[12]*Tokyo Metropolitan Election Comm'n v. Koshiyama*, 37 Minshū 1243 (Sup. Ct., G.B., Nov. 7, 1983) (reversing 984 Hanrei Jihō 26 (Tokyo H. Ct., Dec. 23, 1980)).

[15]*Koshiyama v. Tokyo Metropolitan Election Comm'n*, 18 Minshū 270 (Sup. Ct., G.B., Feb. 5, 1964).

[16]*Shimizu v. Osaka Election Comm'n*, 37 Minshū 345 (Sup. Ct., G.B., Apr. 27, 1983).

ties and uniquenesses of the House of Councillors to uphold the constitutionality of Schedule II, even though the disparity between districts was more than that which existed in Schedule I for the House of Representatives. The Diet has yet to make any attempt to correct electoral imbalances in the House of Councillors....

Even if the Court followed the suggestion of the concurring Justices and handed down a decision of prospective invalidation in the future, is there any guarantee that the Diet would respond favorably to the decision? On this point, the Japanese courts may obtain guidance by reviewing reapportionment decisions of the West German Federal Constitutional Court.

In West Germany, a suit was filed with the Federal Constitutional Court, challenging the validity of the 1961 election for members of the Bundestag on the ground that the election had been held based on an apportionment law that violated the Basic Law of West Germany. The Federal Constitutional Court handed down a decision of prospective invalidation that held that the election would be invalid unless the Bundestag reapportioned by the end of the 1965 legislative session.[48] Of course, had the Constitutional Court nullified the election at once, the Bundestag, which consisted of members elected under the election in question, would have ceased to exist, making it impossible to revise the apportionment law. That is why West Germany's Constitutional Court resorted to the technique of prospective invalidation instead of invalidating the election at once. The West German Federal Constitutional Court is vested with the means to ensure the enforcement of its own decisions; for example, it can draw up an apportionment plan under Article 35 of the Federal Constitutional Court Act.[49] Nevertheless, the Court hesitated to do more than make the decision discussed above because it did not want to be involved in the complex and burdensome problem of reapportionment, nor did it want to confront the legislature on this issue. The Bundestag, however, responding to the decision, corrected the imbalance in question by revising the apportionment law in February 1964.[50]

Yet, it remains questionable whether the Japanese Diet would respond like its German counterpart if the Supreme Court of Japan hands down a decision of prospective invalidation, giving the Diet time to revise the rules of apportionment. Nevertheless, it is possible that the Supreme Court may hand down a decision of prospective invalidation if the imbalance between districts in the ratio of the electoral population per Diet member reaches a constitutionally intolerable degree in the near future.

KAZUYUKI TAKAHASHI, COMMENT, 53 Law and Contemporary Problems 189, 190-92 (No. 2, 1990)

With regard to Professor Hata's article, please note that the constitutionality of apportionment is contested in a suit seeking to nullify the election only in the district at issue. It is not a suit against the whole election but only

[48] *See* BVerfGE 16, 130 (1963).

[49] "The Federal Constitutional Court may in its decision state who will execute it; it can also regulate the type and method of execution in each individual case." Federal Constitutional Court Act, art. 35.

[50] BGBl (Federal Gazette) I, 61 (1964).

against the election in a particular district. Also, these suits do not challenge the validity of any future election, but only affect an election held in the past. The plaintiff who is a voter in a disfavored district brings suit against the election commission governing that district and seeks to nullify the election by contending that the apportionment is unconstitutional. The remedy is limited to the nullification of the election only in the challenged district. The representatives elected in that district lose their seats and another election will be held in that district. Here we face a problem, however, because before we proceed to the new election, we have to reapportion, and this is the job of the Diet. The new election has to be held within forty days after the nullification, and the date of new election has to be announced at least fifteen days beforehand. This leaves only twenty-five days for the Diet to amend the apportionment, and this is almost impossible. If the Diet fails to amend the apportionment, however, its disregard of a judicial order may cause the court to lose face. Although I do not believe that the court will lose prestige in this situation, the court evidently does and is therefore reluctant to nullify elections.

One solution might be for the court to declare the election invalid as of a certain effective future date. This gives the Diet more time to agree on a redistricting plan. Our Supreme Court has not adopted this solution because no one thought of such a prospective ruling at the time that the Supreme Court handed down its 1976 decision declaring an apportionment unconstitutional.[5]

The Supreme Court believes that if an apportionment is declared unconstitutional, the elections in all the districts might possibly be annulled. That would be disastrous, for no Diet would exist that could alter the apportionment. However, this analysis is faulty because most of the districts (I would say at least three-fourths of them) are fairly apportioned. Of course, the number of legally apportioned districts depends on what measure is used to judge constitutionality. But even using as the maximum permissible deviance the ratio of two to one, which coheres with the prevailing opinion among constitutional scholars, more than 75 percent of the districts are constitutional and would not be challenged in court. The voters in those districts have no standing to challenge the malapportionment. Since the Constitution only requires a quorum of one-third of the Diet members to enact valid legislation, enough legally elected representatives would exist to alter the apportionment.

I will also say a few words on the availability of injunctive relief. An injunction is a commonly used remedy in the United States for malapportionment cases. It is a restriction on future elections that does not affect the validity of past elections. When the apportionment is found unconstitutional, an injunction could prevent future elections from being held without a change in the apportionment scheme. It is therefore a very effective remedy. If the legislature fails to alter the apportionment in due time, the judge can order the appropriate authorities to carry out the election at large. He or she can even reshape the apportionment. In Japan, however, judges have never enjoyed these sweeping powers. Politically speaking, I am not against our judges having that power, but the traditional mentality of our judges would prevent

[5] *Kurokawa v. Chiba Election Comm'n*, 30 Minshū 223 (Sup. Ct., G.B., Apr. 14, 1976).

them from wielding that power in practice. Our judges always seek justification for their actions in explicit provisions of law, and we do not have any provisions that would authorize injunctive relief. Therefore, so long as Japanese law does not grant judges wide discretion for remedies, no injunctions will be issued.

NOTES AND QUESTIONS

1. The Japanese Supreme Court prior to the *K.K. Sumiyoshi* (Pharmaceutical Affairs Law) case in 1975 had held legislation to be unconstitutional in only three cases. In the first — *Sakagami v. Japan*, 7 Keishū 1562 (Sup. Ct., G.B., 8 Oct. 1953) — the Court overturned a criminal conviction based on violation of an Occupation directive banning publication of *Akahata* (Red Flag), a Communist Party publication. The Court held that the freedom of expression guarantee of the postwar Constitution applied to post-Peace Treaty judgments and appeals despite contrary legislation (Sakagami was indicted prior to the signing of the 1952 Treaty). Nine years later in *Nakamura v. Japan*, 16 Keishū 1593 (Sup. Ct., G.B., 28 Nov. 1962), the Court ruled that confiscation under a customs statute of smuggled cargo without notice to the third party owner constituted a violation of the Constitution's property protection and due process clauses (arts. 29 and 31). Read narrowly, both cases can be construed to hold an administrative regulation or a judicial ruling rather than legislation to be unconstitutional. Moreover, neither case involved politically significant governmental policies. In both instances the legislation in question had either lapsed or been repealed by the time the Court announced its decision.

In a set of three cases decided in 1973, led by *Aizawa v. Japan*, 27 Keishū 256 (Sup. Ct., G.B., 14 April 1973), however, the Court faced a more sensitive issue: whether more severe penalties for crimes against lineal ascendants are constitutionally permissible under the equal protection provisions of the postwar Constitution (art. 14). In a 1952 decision — *Japan v. Yamato*, 4 Keishū 203 (Sup. Ct., G.B., 11 Oct. 1952) — the Court had upheld the constitutionality of article 205 of the Criminal Code, which mandated a harsher penalty for the crime of bodily injury resulting in the death of a lineal ascendant. Each of the 1973 cases involved the murder of a parent, which under article 200 of the Criminal Code, subjected the accused upon conviction to a minimum sentence of three and one-half years in prison in spite of circumstances that would in other cases have permitted the court to suspend sentence. Without overruling the *Yamato* decision, the Court held that the disparity in the severity of penalties under article 200 was too great to reconcile with the constitutional requirement of equality under the law. Although article 200 has not been repealed by the Diet, the procuracy has not sought its application in any subsequent case.

2. The Japanese Supreme Court has been described as conservative and cautious. Do the decisions in the cases noted above warrant such characterization? Would similar legislation have been invalidated under the U.S. Constitution?

3. What remedies were available in each of the noted cases? What forms of relief would have been available under U.S. law in the Japanese malapportionment cases? *See, e.g., Reynolds v. Sims*, 377 U.S. 533 (1964), and its companion cases. In light of Professor Takahashi's comment, do you agree with Professor Hata that the 1963 German Federal Constitutional Court decision may provide guidance for the Japanese Supreme Court?

4. For translations of major Japanese constitutional decisions, see John Maki, Court and Constitution in Japan: Selected Supreme Court Decisions 1948-1960 (1964); Hiroshi Itoh & Lawrence W. Beer, The Constitutional Case Law of Japan: Selected Court Decisions 1961-1970 (1978).

8. THE KOREAN CONSTITUTIONAL COURT

JAMES M. WEST & DAE-KYU YOON, THE CONSTITUTIONAL COURT OF THE REPUBLIC OF KOREA: TRANSFORMING THE JURISPRUDENCE OF THE VORTEX?, 40 American Journal of Comparative Law 73, 103-06, 111-15 (1992)

Judicial Review of Legislation, 1988-1991

As of July 31, 1991 the [Constitutional] Court had rendered 25 judgments on the merits in cases challenging the constitutionality of legislation. In only six of these cases was the constitutionality of the challenged law unconditionally upheld. The proportion of judgments resulting in invalidation or partial repudiation of legislative acts thus was relatively high.

Several judgments of the Constitutional Court, including rulings on constitutional petitions, briefly will be reviewed to afford a glimpse of how the Court has addressed controversial issues and also to note some ways in which the emerging process of constitutional review has departed from prior judicial practice in Korea. Thus far, the Court's decisions have focused on constitutional protections of economic interests as well as on the scope of civil and political rights of individuals.

In its decisions to date, the Court frequently has invoked the guarantee of equal rights of citizens established in Article 11 of the Constitution. This principle of nondiscrimination has been reinforced by references to Article 37(2), which provides that "Freedoms and rights of citizens may be restricted by law only when necessary for national security, the maintenance of public order or public welfare." The same article further states that even when compelling state interests warrant limitations on individual rights, the "essential content" of the freedom or right should be preserved.

Adopting a classic liberal stance, the Court has undertaken to balance individual rights against collective interests. In several cases legislation has been invalidated on the grounds that the legitimate public purpose of a statute could have been pursued by alternative measures with a less restrictive impact on individual rights.

Economic Rights Cases

The noteworthiness of several cases decided in the domain of economic rights consists in the Court's articulation of a constitutional principle to the effect that legal provisions bestowing exceptional privileges on the government or public institutions and overriding private economic interests are invalid when their effects are unjustifiably discriminatory.[112]

In a number of judgments the court rejected a simplistic "public/private" distinction which had been employed by past legislatures to impair contract and property rights of private persons relative to the state. In seven cases challenging the Special Act on Debt Moratorium for Financial Institutions, the Court invalidated statutory provisions subordinating the claims of private creditors to those of quasi-public or state-owned financial institutions.[113]

In another case, the Court voided a law which purported to immunize state property from a preliminary attachment remedy generally available against private defendants.[114] More recently, in May 1991 the Court held unconstitutional Article 5-2 of the National Property Act which purported to except state-owned land from the general Civil Code rules concerning acquisition of title through adverse possession.[115]...

Another example of the Court's elaboration of a principle of "equal protection" or nondiscrimination was presented in a judgment of October 1990 in which the Educational Civil Service Act was ruled invalid in so far as it accorded hiring preference for public school teaching jobs to graduates of public teachers' college over graduates of private universities.[117]

Civil and Political Rights Cases

The Constitutional Court has adjudicated a number of highly controversial challenges to criminal statutes under which political dissidents have been prosecuted in recent years. With political groups polarized over these issues, and the National Assembly stalemated in 1989, the Court faced a delicate, if not impossible, task in attempting to reach decisions acceptable to a broad spectrum of interests....

A. *The Private School Act Cases*

Restrictions on the rights of private school teachers to organize labor unions were upheld by the Constitutional Court in a recently decided case brought by members of the outlawed National Teachers' Union (*Chŏnkyojo*).[134] A majority of the Court rejected the contention, raised repeatedly in about 100 cases referred by the lower courts, that private school teachers were entitled to

[112] E.g., Art. 35(1)(iii) of the Basic National Tax Act was adjudicated unconstitutional because it accorded special priority to government tax liens over pre-existing private security interests. Judgment of September 3, 1990, 89-Hŏnka-95.

[113] Judgment of May 24, 1989, 89-Hŏnka-37 (Invalidating Art. 5-2 of Special Act on Debt Moratorium for Financial Institutions).

[114] Judgment of January 25, 1989, 89-Hŏnka-7 (Invalidating Art. 6 of Special Act for Expedited Litigation).

[115] Judgment of May 13, 1991, 89-Hŏnka-97.

[117] Judgment of Oct. 8, 1990, 89-Hŏnma-89.

[134] Judgment of July 22, 1991, 89-Hŏnka-106 (rejecting claims that Arts. 55 & 58(1)(iv) of the Private School Act were unconstitutional). As a result of this ruling some 1500 teachers who had been dismissed for unionizing lost their chance to be reinstated. "Teachers Union Loses Legal Grounds," *Korea Times*, July 24, 1991.

organize unions based on the freedom of association guaranteed by Article 33(1) of the Constitution.

It was held that the role of teachers is not the same as ordinary wage-laborers, and that the state may legitimately restrict organizational rights in view of the special responsibilities entrusted to teachers, as the Constitution by its terms permits in the case of public officials.[135]...

B. *Lawyers Act Cases*

Two judgments in cases challenging provisions of the Lawyers Act were significant not only for their vindication of personal liberties, but also for their potential impact on private attorneys' attitudes toward the Constitutional Court as an institution. In one case, the Court invalidated a provision which temporarily restricted the freedom of an attorney to open an office in the same territorial district where he or she had previously worked as a public official.[139]

The second case presented a challenge to Article 15 of the Lawyers Act, which conferred upon the Minister of Justice a discretionary power to suspend the license to practice law of any lawyer who has been indicted for a criminal offense. The Court ruled that this provision contravened the constitutional presumption of innocence, and that an attorney who had not been convicted of an offense should not be exposed to forfeiture of the capacity to earn a living by practicing his or her profession.[140]...

Conflict Over the Institutional Role of the Court

A petition case challenging the constitutionality of the Judicial Scrivener's Act Enforcement Regulation was important because it presented a situation in which the Constitutional Court adjudicated the constitutionality of a regulation which had been promulgated by the Supreme Court under the Judicial Scrivener's Act. The claim was that the Supreme Court, in its administration of licensure procedures for the legal paraprofessionals known as *sabŏbsŏsa* (judicial scriveners), gave discriminatory advantages to court clerks and employees of the public prosecutor's offices over individuals who had gained their experience working for private lawyers.

This led to controversy because ... the Constitutional Court's jurisdiction in cases referred by the ordinary courts is limited to situations where a decision on the constitutionality of a statute is a prerequisite to issuance of a trial court judgment. The constitutionality of decrees and administrative regulations, on the other hand, is within the jurisdiction of the Supreme Court rather than the Constitutional Court.[144]

[135] Art. 33(2) of the Constitution provides that the general rights of organizing unions and collective bargaining apply to "public officials," which has been statutorily defined to include school teachers, only if and to the extent authorized by law.

[139] Judgment of Nov. 20, 1989, 89-Hŏnka-102. The restriction in question, Art. 10(2) of the Lawyers Act, was purportedly designed to discourage exercise of undue influence by ex-officials for personal profit.

[140] Judgment of Nov. 9, 1990, 90-Hŏnma-48.

[144] Constitution Art. 107(2).

The threshold issue was whether the petition as filed was admissible. If the claim could have been properly pursued by ordinary judicial review of an administrative disposition, then the petition would have been dismissed for failure to exhaust available remedies. The petition was admitted, however, on the theory that no effective judicial remedy was available, and the administrative regulation in question was directly effective against the petitioners, immediately abridging their constitutional rights even without the intermediation of any otherwise reviewable administrative act.[146]

This approach to the question of *locus standi* was not novel within the larger comparative context of precedents of the German Constitutional Court, since a similar possibility of direct petition has there been recognized when the offensive norm has a direct impact on individual rights and no other effective means of judicial review is provided by law. The case attracted considerable attention among Korean legal professionals because the Constitutional Court invalidated an administrative regulation promulgated under the direct authority of the Supreme Court, which previously had been regarded as the sole arbiter of administrative matters within its statutory competence.

The Supreme Court proceeded to distribute to district and High Court judges a report asserting that "The Constitutional Court went beyond its domain in its overruling of an administrative regulation governing recruitment of judicial officials." One of the Justices of the Constitutional Court responded publicly by remarking that the Supreme Court in the past had very seldom exercised its constitutional power to invalidate administrative decrees or regulations.[148]

The Supreme Court's characterization of its own jurisdiction as exclusive thus diverged from the Constitutional Court's claim of a certain sphere of seemingly concurrent subject-matter jurisdiction, provided the standing requirements it had delineated were met. Strictly speaking, however, the jurisdiction exercised by the Constitutional Court was not concurrent, because in this realm the Supreme Court was functioning not as a court, but as an administrative agency with discretionary decision-making powers not subject to review under explicit legal norms.

The ultimate resolution of this stand-off presumably turns on an interpretation of the relevant constitutional provisions, a task entrusted to the Constitutional Court. However, that body's supremacy as expositor of the meaning of the Constitution can obtain practical recognition only if the Supreme Court forbears from presenting lower judges with a stark choice of allegiance between the two highest organs of the judiciary.

NOTES AND QUESTIONS

1. From 1988 to July 1991 the Korean Constitutional Court received 234 referrals from ordinary courts for rulings on the constitutionality of laws. Of these, 83 (concerning the Social Protection Act, which was amended in 1989)

[146] Judgment of Oct. 15, 1990, 89-Hŏnma-178.

[148] The intention of this remark was apparently to criticize some members of the Supreme Court for being overly deferential to the executive branch in cases presenting alleged violations of civil and political rights.

were withdrawn, 15 were dismissed in screening, and 111 were pending. That leaves 25 cases with judgments deciding that the challenged law was: constitutional (6), constitutional on condition of proper interpretation (3), unconstitutional (14), unconstitutional in part (1), and inconsistent with the Constitution (1). In addition, 11 other cases challenging the constitutionality of laws used an alternative Constitutional Court Act article 68(2) petition procedure available when an ordinary court denies referral to the Constitutional Court. In these 11 cases the Court invalidated two statutes.

2. What are the advantages of creating a Constitutional Court separate from the Supreme Court to review the constitutionality of laws? Do the different legal structures in South Korea and Japan explain the greater willingness of the Korean Constitutional Court than the Japanese Supreme Court to find a law unconstitutional? Are other factors relevant in explaining judicial boldness in South Korea?

3. Does the *Judicial Scriveners Case* in South Korea illustrate a disadvantage in creating a separate Constitutional Court? Between the Korean Constitutional Court and the Korean Supreme Court, which has the better argument for jurisdiction? How is this type of jurisdictional conflict resolved in other civil law nations?

4. For more on judicial review in South Korea, see Kun Yang, *Judicial Review and Social Change in the Korean Democratizing Process*, 41 Am. J. Comp. L. 1 (1993).

NOTE ON JUDICIAL REVIEW IN TAIWAN

In 1949 President Chiang Kai Shek issued an executive order declaring the Republic of China to be in a state of emergency, thereby largely suspending the 1947 Constitution and authorizing martial law. With the termination of this order in 1987 by Chiang's son and successor, President Chiang Ching Kuo, the Constitution became fully effective on Taiwan for the first time in four decades and an era of political reform began.

One consequence of reform is the potential for a more meaningful role by the Council of Grand Justices, described in Chapter 6, Section C.3, as Taiwan's constitutional court. This new direction is best evidenced in the Council's response to an application by the Executive Yüan for reexamination of a 1954 constitutional interpretation (No. 31), in which the Council had confirmed that the members of the National Assembly, Legislative Yüan, and Control Yüan, who had been elected in mainland elections held in 1947, could continue to hold office pending new nationwide elections (thus presupposing a return of republican rule to mainland China). On June 21, 1990, the Council modified its prior interpretation, thereby forcing the retirement of nearly 800 legislators who had held seats since 1947 as representatives of mainland constituencies:

> The terms of central representatives are provided in the Constitution [article 65, three year terms for the members of the Legislative Yüan; article 93, six year terms for members elected to the Control Yüan]. The first-term central representatives could not be elected because of the significant disaster faced by the country after their lawful inaugurations.

> Their continuing to hold office was therefore required for the maintenance of the constitutional system. However, periodic elections are necessary means to reflect the people's will and to carry out fully democratic constitutionalism. The Interpretation No. 31 of this Council ... [was] not intended either to change the terms of the central representatives or to allow them to continue in office indefinitely. In fact, the central government has, since 1969, held general elections for central representatives in free China [Taiwan] to supplement the central representative organ step by step. In the current situation, not only should first-term representatives, who have not been re-elected periodically and are not in fact able to exercise their duties or are often absent, be identified and immediately dismissed, but also all other such first-term representatives should cease to hold office as of 31 December 1991. In addition, the central government should hold a timely national election for second-term representatives in accordance with the spirit of the Constitution, the intent of this Interpretation, and the relevant statutes and ordinances, in order to ensure the functioning of this constitutional system. Interpretation No. 261, Council of Grand Justices, Judicial Yüan, June 21, 1990, in 32 (1) SSU-FA YUAN-PAO (Judicial Yüan Gazette) 1 (July 1990).

Pursuant to Interpretation No. 261, all "senior" members of Taiwan's National Assembly, Legislative Yüan, and Control Yüan had retired by the end of 1991, and in December of that year the first democratic election in the history of Taiwan for a majority of the seats of the national legislature was held. It should perhaps be noted that the *Kuomintang* (Nationalist Party), author of both repression and change, won 71 percent of the popular vote.

Chapter 8

LEGAL EDUCATION AND THE LEGAL PROFESSIONS

A. LEGAL EDUCATION

1. THE EDUCATION OF A CONTINENTAL LAWYER

MIRJAN DAMAŠKA, A CONTINENTAL LAWYER IN AN AMERICAN LAW SCHOOL: TRIALS AND TRIBULATIONS OF ADJUSTMENT, 116 University of Pennsylvania Law Review 1363, 1364-70, 1372-75 (1968)

A. *European Legal Education*

As in this country, so in European countries there is a great deal of controversy over the aims of legal education and the role universities should play in it. Traditional ideas on curricula as well as methods of instruction are increasingly questioned; new ideas are discussed and, in some countries, experimented with. Yet notwithstanding these winds of change and the considerable differences that exist among various European countries, fluctuation and diversity fade away when viewed from this side of the Atlantic. A distinctive Continental *mos iura docendi* still seems to exist. As I see it, one can distill the essential ingredients of Continental law school experience. This essence involves exposure to what I will call the grammar of law, a panoramic view of the most important fields of law, and some initiation into the patterns of legal reasoning. These three essential ingredients must be treated separately although they are imparted simultaneously.

1. *The Grammar of Law*

While it would be false to imply that grammar is completely absent from American law, the fact remains that there exists no real counterpart to the Continental grammar of law.[1] The difference is perhaps in the degree of refinement and importance of grammar in the two systems.

In order to gain an understanding of Continental legal grammar, Americans should imagine lawyers of an analytical turn of mind à la Hohfeld at work for a long time, studying the law as it emerged from legal practice. Americans should further imagine that both the analysts' dissection of law and their generalizations were generally accepted by the legal profession. Let

[1] The expression "grammar of law" has been borrowed from T. Holland, The Elements of Jurisprudence 7 (5th ed. 1895). This metaphoric term is not used on the Continent. Instead, labels such as "legal science" or "doctrine" are found. [However, Rudolf von Jhering (1818-1892) did use an analogous term, "alphabet of law" (*Rechtsalphabet*), in *Geist des römischen Rechts* 334-52 (5th ed. 1898, reprinted 1968)].

me pursue this hypothesis with specific examples and suggest what the consequences might be for American law.

Many rather amorphous American legal concepts would be subjected to rigorous analysis. An illustration is the concept of jurisdiction with its bewildering number of meanings. Words and phrases like "property," "standing to sue," "security," and "mens rea" also come to mind. In the process of analysis the twilight zone of the concepts would be somewhat reduced, sub-concepts isolated and separately labeled. A richer and more precise legal terminology would appear. Movement would also proceed in the opposite direction, that is, toward the creation of more general, sometimes almost cathedral-like concepts. For example, inquiry into what contracts, conveyances and wills have in common would probably result in something similar to the Continental concept of legal transaction (*Rechtsgeschäft, negozio giuridico*).[a] These newly created, broad concepts would become accepted as elements of standard legal terminology. Study would then proceed to the relationships between such legal concepts. Questions would be raised about the relationship of "jurisdictional" to "procedural" issues, of "mistake" to "mens rea." Inquiry into relationships between concepts would be linked to an investigation into the nature or essence of concepts. For example, what is the nature of "arbitration," or of "pleadings" and "stipulations" in criminal procedure? Pursuit of what is common to the decisional law of seemingly unrelated areas would be conducive to the creation of broader rules (*e.g.*, on misrepresentation in conveyances, contracts, and so forth) and even to the development of principles (*e.g.*, principles of procedure). Almost imperceptibly an urge to establish a rigid network of classification would develop; for example, the question whether we should separate real and personal property would arise. Thus, step by step, the conceptual digestion of the law would result in a network of precise interrelated concepts, broad principles and classificatory ideas. This network is the grammar of law.

Most American lawyers will be sceptical at best of the usefulness of this curious conceptual structure. Some, conversant with the latest trends in jurisprudential thinking abroad, will point out ... that the conceptualistic approach seems to be coming under increasing attack in Europe as well. It is my belief, however, that even those Continentals to whom conceptualistic jurisprudence is a bête noire would be taken aback at the paucity of conceptual digestion in most areas of American law.... Even anti-conceptualists would, I believe, concur in the traditional justifications advanced by Continentals in defense of their legal grammar.

Let me quickly sketch these often overlapping justifications. In the first place, it is claimed that a well developed legal grammar results in economy of thought. The concepts in such a grammar can be used independently of specific legal rules, just as elements in an algebraic system, and with all the advantages of algebra over arithmetic. Pursuing mathematical analogies, one can say that the urge to generalize results in factoring out common features,

---

[a] For the derivation of the concept of legal transaction or juridical act, see Chapter 5, Section B.5.

thus leading to simplification. A great many heretofore unrelated legal rules can be seen as offshoots of a single more general rule or principle.

A related advantage attributed to legal grammar is clarity of vision, sometimes expressed by the old Latin tag *praxis sine theoria caecus in via.* Broad interrelated concepts facilitate awareness of the ramifications of hypothetical legal situations, notably contemplated changes in the law. Thus law can more easily be tested by logic. It is further believed that profound analysis of the law sometimes fosters a sense of the proper order of analysis. This in turn goes a long way towards shielding the average legal mind from confusion. Finally, it is believed that legal grammar represents an essential prerequisite for the satisfactory drafting of comprehensive legislation[4] and the successful ordering of judge-made law.[5]

The importance attached to legal grammar explains why initiation into it represents one of the minimal requirements of legal education in Continental law schools. Even a casual glance at any student manual will immediately reveal the extent to which "grammatical" considerations dictate the organization and presentation of the body of law.

2. *The Panoramic View*

In addition to an initiation into the grammar of law, the Continental student is also offered what would, to an American lawyer, appear to be a panoramic presentation of the most important fields of law. This comprehensive view of the whole is considered to be of utmost importance. It is feared that if the young lawyer fails to perceive the great contours of private and public law in school, he will seldom acquire an overview later in practice. Entangled in the jungle of practical problems, he will be deprived of the guidance that comes from an awareness of the totality of law in his particular field.

The way in which the panoramic view is offered would be rather startling to an American lawyer. Even aside from discussion of the highly abstract legal issues closely connected with the Continental legal grammar, discourse proceeds most of the time on a level that seems much too abstract to the American legal mind. Statutory or code provisions are systematically presented on a level which seems to provide only vague guidelines for the solution of actual cases. Occasional references to actual cases will almost invariably be made in generalized form. The legal problems in a case will be treated in the abstract, as illustrations of how the court evolved legal rules, adapted to the solution of the case, from the more general ones found in the code or statute. When on a rare occasion the discussion does descend to the level of particular facts, it will be abruptly cut off by the remark that a *questio facti* is involved which does not merit further analysis.[7] The American lawyer would thus discover that,

[4] Legal grammar may offer a basis for logical rather than alphabetical arrangement of subject-matter. Further, it is possible that only legal grammar of some sophistication can provide a basis for avoiding antinomies and omissions in interrelated provisions. Finally, the wealth of long-range and intermediate concepts provides statutory language with the necessary breadth.

[5] For example, French administrative law, created by the *Conseil d'Etat,* has been very neatly ordered by French legal scholars.

[7] *"Questio facti"* is a misnomer and should not be confused with factual issues. It is a legal issue, but so closely intertwined with the factual circumstances of specific cases that it is of little

more often than not, where his interest really begins the law teacher's seems to end. A related and similar source of distress to an American would be the paucity of references to the meaning of legal rules in practical operation. He would be shocked to find that as much time is devoted to analysis of legal problems of only academic interest as to problems commonly confronting the courts. Almost never would he find discussion of the influence of procedural considerations on substantive issues. He would be positively annoyed by the method of instruction that still prevails in Continental law schools, with formal and not infrequently somewhat soporific lectures. Faced with professorial assertion on the basis of what to him seemed vague and inconclusive authorities, he would be tempted to think that the teacher was getting his law out of his head. I believe he would soon decide that he could make equally good (or bad) use of his time by reading lectures in the form of *scripta,* or by studying the professor's manual or treatise.

3. *Patterns of Legal Reasoning*

By American standards, Continental law schools give very little training in "how to think like a lawyer." Stimulation of students to participate in problem solving (on the Continental level of discourse), while not unknown, is comparatively insignificant. This is not to say that patterns of thinking are not implanted in students, if only through exposure to the style of thinking of the faculty. Let me present a very cursory sketch of this style, for it is important for my purposes. Very characteristic is an urge to relate particular problems to a whole array of rules, principles and "grammatical" ideas. Logical consistency within the array assumes a very great importance. Seldom does one find the feeling that discussion of rules apart from judicial application is somewhat vacuous. There is a significant lack of the argumentative approach towards the law which permeates the atmosphere of law schools in this country. The moving spirit of analysis is not the desire to find the best argument for a proposition, but rather the quest for the "right" answer to the problem at hand. Conspicuous by its absence is the intertwining of legal and nonlegal arguments so common here.

Comparatively speaking there is also very little preparation in Continental law schools for the practical problems awaiting the student (handling of sources, legal writing, and the like). But even though vocationally oriented education represents an inferior intellectual tradition to the Continental lawyer, I do not think that a typical Continental law professor is insensitive to the needs of practical training. He would agree that a full-fledged lawyer needs practical as well as theoretical preparation. *Theoria sine praxis rota sine axis*. However, he will probably argue that theoretical and practical preparation cannot both be offered in school, and that a choice of priorities must be made. Since in the Continental scheme of things theoretical preparation and a grasp of the whole must precede exposure to the complexities of practice, precedence is given to rendering instruction in the grammar of law and in the grand contours of most important fields of law. It is upon graduation and

academic interest to a civilian mind. For instance, what constitutes probable cause for arrest, being a mere *questio facti,* would not be discussed in class.

during the internship period preceding the bar and bench examinations that the student receives a rigorous practical training in how to find the law and write about it.

The three components may now be drawn together. If a Continental student has acquired some mastery of legal grammar, if he has learned the substantive rules as presented in the panoramic view, and if he has gained some grasp of the style of thinking described, he is a successful product of Continental legal education on the university level.

B. *The Expectations of a Continental Lawyer*

When the Continental law school graduate enters practice, the neatness, simplicity, and purity of the vision of the law imparted to him in school will be somewhat marred. Yet, even after extended legal practice most of the attitudes shaped in school, somewhat modified, will still influence his perception of law. Of course, if he is fresh from law school — as are many foreigners in American law schools — the impact of his legal education will be undiluted in its strength. Some features of the young lawyer's outlook should concern us here.

He will tend to associate at least modern domestic law with a more or less closed and orderly system. He will assume that precise terminology, conceptual specificity, and other elements of the Continental legal grammar are indispensable tools for mature legal analysis. Sensitivity toward logical consistency over relatively wide areas will appear to him to be an attribute of a good lawyer. It will seem natural to be able to gain a panoramic view of legal fields. He will believe that legal discourse of real importance proceeds on the level of rules he is familiar with, and that emphasis on factual questions and too much concern about justice in a given case betray a non-technical, layman's approach — what Max Weber called "khadi justice." For him the primary purpose of legal discussion — at least in the academic milieu — will be the quest for right answers rather than partisan arguments....

C. *The Clash Between Expectation and Reality*

If there is a measure of truth in the preceding description of expectations, the problems faced by a Continental lawyer attempting to adjust to a typical American law school are not too difficult to fathom. I cannot hope to discuss them all, so I shall limit myself to the most pressing.

There will be a stumbling block at the very first step. The foreigner will immediately discover that his specialty has no real counterpart in the American scheme of divisions of law. The student with an interest in property law will vainly seek "real actions" in American writing on property. On the other hand he will find matters inserted in the law of property that seem to be taken out of their natural habitat. Thus he will find the lease treated as a "real right" while its proper *situs*, to his mind, is in the law of obligations. To the possible chagrin of a privatist, taxation and zoning problems will also be incorporated into property books.

Some will say that there is nothing undesirable about this initial problem, for the student is just learning his first lesson in comparative legal studies, namely, to discard domestic boundaries of law. Many students, however, for all their orientation programs, spend a disproportionate amount of time chasing the topic of their interest all over the American legal landscape.

Sooner or later they will assemble what to them is comparable matter and select the right law school courses. Quite naturally they will attempt to gain the panoramic view described above. It is at this point that they will be in real trouble: courses will be of no help to them in this respect. Even if instruction is not limited to the Socratic discussion of cases, Continental students will still have the feeling of being offered an assembly of minuscule fragments when they want a synthesis. They will then resort to hornbooks and similar writings designed for those who, unencumbered by an alien legal training, seek basic information in an American branch of law. These books will seldom be of help. Their organization, unspoken assumptions, and general level of discussion will present to a Continental legal mind more questions than answers. Ever present will be the need for conversion formulae. If the students seek help from their instructor, he will explain that the view of the whole which they seek cannot be given even in a single jurisdiction, much less nationally. At least some instructors will be sceptical that such an instantaneous snapshot of the law can be offered at all, for law is living, constantly growing. To this the student will reply that he can see the twigs and branches of the system changing all the time, but that he would have expected the trees and the forest to be relatively stable. And, he will add, it is precisely the latter two that he is interested in at the moment. Not infrequently, in the absence of comparativists, there will be a difficulty in further communication at this point.

After exposure to the finely shaded rigidities of the Continental legal grammar, the student will discover that it has virtually no analogue in American law, and that very little importance is attached to the conceptual digestion of the law. He will find that definitions, so important to his mind, are viewed with a scepticism reminiscent of classical Roman lawyers.

In the meantime the Continental student will diligently go on reading cases and statutes in pursuit of the answers to problems that keep multiplying. Leaving aside the troubles he will experience with statutes and statutory compilations completely different from those with which he is accustomed,[15] let me quickly sketch what I think will be his typical attitude in reading cases. Many of his problems stem from this attitude. After reading a number of cases, he will feel an urge to rise above the bewildering richness of factual detail and distill legal propositions therefrom. He will then attempt to relate these propositions to newly distilled ones from an additional group of cases, and somehow peg all of them to a larger whole. Only in this fashion does he hope to come out with (what he would call) legal rules rather than mere

[15] Of these difficulties arising from differences in statutes, four seem to me to be most common. First, the Continental student feels a lack of vision resulting from frequent American classification in alphabetical sequence rather than in some kind of logical order. Second, the student is bewildered by regulation of minuscule detail, and by all the dangers such an approach entails. Third, he wonders whether the prolific use of near synonyms in the statutory language results in real or only apparent tautologies. For example, what is the difference between reversing and vacating a judgment? Last but not least, the Continental student approaches statutory interpretation in the civil law fashion.

answers to *questiones facti* or examples of the application of rules. More often than not, his structure collapses in the bewildering mass of cases seemingly or actually contradictory.

It is not improbable that at this point the Continental student will become so frustrated that he will seek solace in a discussion with his adviser on the openness of the system and on its fluidity. If his adviser happens to belong to the realist school of legal thought, he may attempt to help him with a little psychoanalysis à la Jerome Frank, and explain the student's longing for stability and certainty in terms of the immature child's need for infallible authority.

This brings me to problems of communication in legal discussion. Claiming no great discoveries, I can see at least four sources of difficulty. The first is produced by disparities in the level of discourse. As has been repeatedly intimated, the Continental tends to move on the level of abstract rules which to his American counterpart often seem to be only rather vague standards. In contrast, American legal discussion usually proceeds on the more concrete level of what a Continental would consider to be less significant *questiones facti*. Second, the strength of legal arguments differs substantially. Logical consistency over areas too wide for American taste is of very great importance to a Continental mind, which in turn remains closed to many specific arguments much higher on the American scale. In the third place, the Continental conceptual scheme imposes relatively rigid methods of analysis, while the non-grammatical American legal mind remains very flexible. Finally, the very goals of legal discussion frequently will not coincide. The Continental will seek the right solution; his counterpart will display a liberal agnosticism about "right" answers, coupled with a procedural outlook. He will be primarily concerned about good arguments for a case.

2. LEGAL EDUCATION THERE AND HERE

JOHN HENRY MERRYMAN, LEGAL EDUCATION THERE AND HERE: A COMPARISON, 27 Stanford Law Review 859, 861-66, 868-71, 874-76 (1975)

Higher Education: Three Fundamental Differences

There are certain fundamental differences between the systems of higher education in the United States and those in most civil law countries, and these differences strongly affect the two systems of legal education. I will discuss [two] such fundamental differences, the first of which might be summed up in the terms "democracy" and "meritocracy." In a sense this first difference results from two major inconsistent forces in higher education: on the one hand there is a desire to make higher education available to everyone without distinction; on the other there is the desire to make the university a place in which academic merit is recognized and rewarded. One ideal leads to the conception of the mass university; the other to the university in which admission and advancement are controlled on the basis of academic aptitude and performance. It is my observation that universities in the civil law world lean in the democratic direction, while meritocracy is the dominant ideal in

American universities. This is not to say that merit is totally ignored or devalued in the civil law world, nor that American universities ignore democratic considerations; it is only to suggest a significant difference in emphasis.

Thus, the Faculty of Law at the University of Rome has [in 1980 21,500] students, while the Stanford Law School has a student body of 450. The difference arises in part from the power of American law schools to exclude applicants on the basis of merit.... It is common for students to apply to several law schools, since they have no certainty of being accepted at any of them. Because of the competition among law schools for the best students, and the desire of the best students to go to the more eminent schools, a student who is denied admission at Harvard or Yale or Stanford may be admitted to some less highly regarded school. Thus, there is a tendency for the academic quality of student bodies to be stratified according to the national reputations of the schools. The cycle is, to some extent, self-perpetuating, since one of the important factors in the reputation of a law school is the quality of its student body. Thus, although there is likely to be a place in some law school for almost any student, the best students go to the best schools and get the best legal education and move more easily into the best careers.

The situation in many civil law universities is entirely different. There anyone who has completed certain formal prerequisites and has survived a certain number of years of prior education is automatically admitted to the university and to the faculty of law. In the post-World War II period of mounting affluence, rising expectations, the extension of public primary and secondary education to greater numbers of people, and the greater democratization of society in such nations, the old economic and social barriers to university education lost much of their effectiveness. Suddenly, great floods of students descended on universities with inadequate numbers of faculty and inadequate libraries, classrooms, and other physical facilities. This phenomenon provides a partial explanation of the student upheavals in Paris and other parts of Europe in 1968: too few universities with too few resources submerged by thousands of students. An adequate explanation of the situation of students in civil law universities would be extremely complex, but as this example shows, the democratic principle — the notion that the student is, at a certain stage of his education, entitled as of right to admission to the university — is an important component of it....

A second distinguishing feature of higher education in the civil law world is the minor role played by private universities. Indeed, in most civil law nations private universities do not exist. Instead, universities are maintained and are subject to control by the state, usually through the same ministry that has the responsibility for public elementary and secondary education. In the United States, on the contrary, both private and public universities compete with each other for faculty and students, as well as for gifts and grants from individuals, corporations, foundations, and government sources. In this competition, the private universities occupy a position of leadership and have done so throughout the history of the nation. There are excellent and influential public universities, but as a general proposition the private universities set the standard for higher education.

Because the private university is not subject to anything but the most limited form of governmental supervision, it has more freedom to experiment, to innovate, and in general to progress.... Since the major private universities provide the leadership for all of higher education, the other universities, including the public ones, tend to emulate them. Any attempt to establish rigid control over the policies, faculty, curricula, and operations of public universities is met with the objection that such controls will put them at a disadvantage in the competition with private universities and lead in the end to deterioration of the public university. In this way, the autonomy of the private university helps to maintain the autonomy of the public university....

In a number of civil law nations none but the most trivial reforms seems to be possible without ministerial, and sometimes legislative, action at the highest levels. Uniformity is the rule, so that policies adopted for one university extend to all. The notion of the dynamic university, constantly experimenting and progressing, does not exist. Nor does the notion of academic competition among universities, with each striving for leadership, for the best faculty and students, and for the most distinguished scholarship. Instead, one finds a relatively static and standardized university system....

The Goals of Legal Education

The objectives of legal education in the two systems are vastly different. This can be shown through a few generalizations that oversimplify but may be sufficiently instructive to justify the risk. First, legal education in the civil law world is, at bottom, general education, not professional education. It is true that many civil law faculties include some instruction of a technical or professional nature, but courses of this kind typically are recent minor additions to a corpus that is fundamentally liberal in character and outlook. It is not anticipated that all, or even most, of those who attend the faculty of law will become advocates or judges or notaries. Law is merely one of the curricula available to undergraduate students.

This is one reason why legal education in civil law universities seems to us to be comparatively "nonprofessional" or "nontechnical." Any movement in the direction of technical or professional education is a movement away from the paradigm. Thus, instruction in civil law faculties is more abstract, more concerned with questions of philosophic than immediate practical importance, more removed from the solution of social problems. University legal education in England shares these characteristics; in this respect it is more like the legal education in the typical European or Latin American university than that in most American law schools. In England and on the Continent the professional side is taken care of after the university: in the *Referendarzeit*, or in apprenticeship with a solicitor, advocate, or notary, or in special advanced professional schools for administrators or judges.

In the United States, legal education is primarily professional education, with some admixture of nonprofessional elements. In part this difference is structural: here legal education is *graduate* education, something undertaken *after* completion of the undergraduate degree requirement. Law is not regularly taught in the university as a liberal or humane subject, or as a social science. One obvious disadvantage of such a system is that the great mass of undergraduates leave the university without any organized exposure to the legal system. Virtually no courses are available for the student who wishes to learn about the legal system, but does not want to spend the additional years in law school....

Professors

One can also sharply contrast the role played by the law professor. The law professor in the United States generally spends his working time at the law school, in the classroom and in his office. His office there is his study; that is where he does his writing, prepares for class, and meets with students and colleagues. His presence there makes him more available to students and encourages faculty-student contact outside of class. The number of faculty, when compared to the number of students, produces a ratio that encourages small classes and a more personal relationship between professor and student than in the civil law counterpart.

The contrast with law faculties in civil law nations is striking. In most of them (Germany is a major exception), the concept of a full-time professor is relatively unfamiliar. The professor comes to the law school to deliver his lecture and leaves when it is finished. Outside of his actual time in class he is seldom seen at the school and he is not expected to be there. Confronted by an enormous number of students, it is almost impossible for the professor to become familiar with them, even if he had the time and the inclination. At the end of the class, both he and the student leave the university.

The American professor's continual presence at the law school deeply affects collegial life. It is easy to find a colleague to talk to about an interesting problem or to get an authoritative reaction to an idea. The situation permits spontaneity and informality, encourages collaboration in teaching and research, and offers easy accessibility to a wide range of interests and expertise. The result is a natural tendency toward "horizontal" or collegial scholarly and personal relationships that is lacking in many civil law universities. There one more typically finds a hierarchical or vertical pattern. At the top is the professor who occupies the chair. Arrayed beneath him are junior colleagues, assistants, and researchers. Communication habitually runs vertically within the *cathedra*.

The full-time nature of law teaching in America tends to produce a substantial number of professors who maintain little, if any, direct contact with the practice of law. In most civil law jurisdictions, however, professors carry on law practice or engage in other careers; teaching is viewed as an accessory activity. Stipends reflect this difference: in the United States law professors are paid enough to support themselves without the necessity for additional income. But in Chile and Italy, for example, the pay for university law teaching is low because it is anticipated that the professor will devote a major portion of his time to law practice or some other remunerative career. Indeed, in some civil law nations the position of professor in the faculty of law is more important for the prestige (and the additional business) it provides than for the professional stipend.

The organization of civil and common law law schools is another area of substantial difference. The typical civil law university is composed of a group of "faculties." Each faculty, in turn, is a collection of "chairs" or "*cathedra*" occupied by senior professors. Occupancy of a *cathedra* in a law faculty carries with it the direction of an institute, with its own budget, staff rooms and library, and the right to a certain number of younger assistants interested in academic careers. The assistants help the professor in his teaching and research. Where the professor maintains an active professional practice, his academic assistants are also likely to be his junior law associates. If he is engaged in a political career, his academic assistants will be part of his political staff. The professor is expected to promote the interests of his assistants, particularly to assist them in their academic careers. This system makes the senior professor lord of a substantial domain and gives him great power over the lives of his assistants and his staff. Indeed it is common to speak of the professor as a "baron" and to complain (if one is an impatient young scholar with unfulfilled academic aspirations) of the "baronial system."...

Curricula and Teaching Methods

The curricula of American law schools typically include a few prescribed courses and a large number of electives covering a broad range of subject matters. By comparison, the curricula at civil law universities tend to be much more limited, both in the number and in the scope of courses offered, and to include few electives. In part this difference may follow from the fact that the civil law faculty is less oriented toward professional training, and therefore less concerned with providing opportunities to study the nuances of various professional specializations. Another possible explanation is the greater freedom of American law schools to innovate and to experiment, unrestricted by an official policy of conformity or by the necessity for prior governmental approval of proposed reforms. Still another reason might be that the culture of the civil law takes a narrower, more restricted view of the nature of law and of the function of the lawyer in society, so that the conceptual limits on what seems appropriate for a law faculty curriculum are narrower.

There is yet another, more fundamental, basis for the difference. It is the belief, still widely held in the civil law world, that law is a science. From this it follows that the purpose of legal education is to instruct the students in the elements of the science. Such an approach tends to be dogmatic. The truth is known by the professor and is communicated to the students. There are, of course, disputes among scholars, and on some points one can find two or more theories that are sufficiently significant to deserve mention. But on the whole, the general structure, the broad outlines, are thought to be established. There are recognized categories. The law is divided into agreed subdivisions, which are taught as courses. The area of doubt is so narrow as to be imperceptible. Blessed with such certainty, the civil law feels less need for innovation and experimentation....

In the civil law world, the educational focus is primarily on substance; method is deemphasized. In the United States, we are of course concerned about what we teach; but the emphasis is less on what is taught and more on how it is taught. We are concerned about developing certain qualities in the student: skill in legal analysis, the ability to distinguish the relevant from the irrelevant, the ability to deal with a large mass of facts in an authoritative way, the ability to put together careful and persuasive arguments on any side of a legal question, the ability to think usefully and constructively about social problems and their solution. Of course the student needs to be familiar with the existing law before he can responsibly discuss its application to concrete social questions, but we see that as the easy part. Rather than devote valuable class time to discussing what the law is, we expect the students to be familiar with it through prior reading. We focus, instead, on how it does or does not work, on its implications, on the social reality out of which it grew, and so on.

Our objectives accordingly raise important questions of method. How can we prepare students to deal thoughtfully, responsibly, and usefully with the kinds of social problems that will come before them as they assume public and private positions of leadership? The traditional system of education in civil law universities obviously assumes a different function: The professor lectures; the students listen. That system is clearly designed to convey information to the student. The information is substantive knowledge. There is little concern with method of the sort that preoccupies American law teachers....

The fundamental differences between the traditions of teaching can be reduced to two. First, American legal education assumes that the student has studied assigned material before the class. In the civil law world, it is assumed that the student has not studied in advance of class; indeed, the main purpose of the lecture is to instruct him, to transfer basic knowledge to him. Second, in the United States the student is expected to participate actively in class discussion. Again, the contrast with law schools in the civil law world is clear. There the student does not participate; he is a passive, receiving object. The professor talks; the student listens....

The reasons our methods differ so sharply relate to differences in university context and to divergences in attitude toward the objectives of legal education, the nature of legal scholarship, and the roles and functions of lawyers in the two systems. It bears repeating, however, that our objectives and methodology are not tied to judicial decisions. Our case law provides a rich, fascinating, and relevant body of study material, but equivalents or alternatives are certainly conceivable, and probably exist, in civil law nations. The active method does not necessarily presuppose the doctrine of *stare decisis* or the study of judicial decisions.

Students

... [O]ur student bodies are, on the whole, much smaller. At the Stanford Law School we have a total of approximately 450 students. The Harvard Law School, which is considered large by our standards, has approximately 1,500 students. In the civil law world one typically finds much larger student bodies. The University of Rome, with [20,000] or more, is now the most extreme example. At some point (or points) on a continuum between 450 and [20,000] students, the human dynamics of the process of legal education drastically change. There are important qualitative differences between large and small law schools flowing from the simple fact of different student body size.

Another significant point is that American law students are expected to be full-time students; they are expected to devote their full energies to their studies and not to engage in any other significant enterprise for the 3 years of law school. In a number of civil law jurisdictions, attendance at the university faculty of law is very much a part-time undertaking. The difference can be exaggerated and is, in the end, one of degree, but the expectations of the two traditions are really quite different: in the United States, our expectation that the students will be full time makes it reasonable for us to make greater demands on, and to maintain higher expectations of, their performance. Students' lives are expected to center around the law school. They are expected to be there not only to attend classes but to prepare for them, to work in the law library, and to involve themselves in law review or the other paracurricular organizations that seem to grow up around our law schools. In civil law universities, there is no such assumption and consequently no basis for such expectation. Frequently, if only because of inadequate classroom facilities, it is not even anticipated that the students will regularly attend classes.

A third unique feature of our system is that it places great responsibility on the student. One sign of this greater responsibility is the student-run law review, a phenomenon that exists at over a hundred law schools in the United States.... The tradition is for such reviews to be independent, free of faculty authority....

Law review experience is still the most prestigious component of what has become, at many law schools, an extremely rich extracurriculum. The student may choose from a variety of activities: trial and appellate moot court, legal aid and civil rights organizations, environmental law societies, international law journals. Such institutions are also student-initiated and student-run. Professors help (when they are asked) and activities are subsidized by law school funds or by gifts or grants solicited by the students themselves from foundations or private donors. The extracurriculum is an extremely important part of legal education for a substantial number of students in American law schools. There is nothing remotely comparable to it in European law faculties.

NOTES AND QUESTIONS

1. Universities teaching national law are relatively recent in origin. In the medieval European universities, including the two in England, one studied Roman law, canon law, or both, but not the local or customary system of rules. The systematic study of national laws at university law faculties developed in the 18th century as an aspect of the intellectual revolution.

On the experience of bringing intellectual respectability to the teaching of law in the United States, see David S. Clark, *Tracing the Roots of American Legal Education — A Nineteenth Century German Connection,* 51 Rabels Zeitschrift 313 (1987).

2. Mirjan Damaška isolates three essential ingredients of continental law school experience. Taking the first one, the grammar of law — what advantages do civilians find in its development and use? To which of the five subtraditions of the civil law tradition is it most closely related? What would an American lawyer think about its utility?

3. Why do American law schools in the first semester not offer a panoramic view of the totality of U.S. law? Should they?

4. What is the fundamental difference between the civilian and American patterns of legal reasoning taught in law schools? Is this difference due more to philosophical disagreement about epistemology (the nature of knowledge) or more due to the structural disparity between civilian general education and American professional education?

5. Prepare a list of the dichotomies that John Merryman develops to compare legal education "there and here." Which seem most significant to you? Would you disagree with any of his characterizations of U.S. law schools?

The remaining excerpts in this section examine the experience of specific civil law countries in teaching law. Use your list of dichotomies as a preliminary device to analyze the situation in each country. At the end of Section A be prepared to present a revised list of dichotomies, supported by specific information, and to discuss major differences among civil law nations.

See Louis Vogel, *Dynamics of Legal Systems and Legal Education: Interactions in the United States and Continental Europe,* 15 Seton Hall L. Rev. 744 (1985).

3. FRANCE

THOMAS E. CARBONNEAU, THE FRENCH LEGAL STUDIES CURRICULUM: ITS HISTORY AND RELEVANCE AS A MODEL FOR REFORM, 25 McGill Law Journal 445, 463-74 (1980)

Prior to the May 1968 student riots, the French national government had been the chief architect of French educational policy. In matters relating to higher education, for example, the Ministry of National Education not only set university budgetary requirements and the procedures governing the recruitment of professors, but also established the substance of the university curricula for degree programs. Opposition to this rigid hierarchical system manifested itself in violence, which gave rise to an almost immediate legislative response. On November 12, 1968, the French Parliament unanimously enacted a statute, entitled the *Loi d'orientation de l'enseignement supérieur,* which provided for faculty and student participation in the administration and management of the universities. More importantly for purposes of the present analysis, the 1968 statute gave the universities some measure of autonomy vis-à-vis the national government in matters concerning the curriculum and pedagogical organization.

Under the provisions of the 1968 statute, the universities acquired the right to establish their teaching activities, their research programs, their pedagogical methods, their examination procedures, and the status of their teaching personnel. Moreover, by granting the universities the benefit of a moral personality and financial autonomy and by creating a network of elected university and regional advisory councils on educational matters, the statute further reduced the previously all-encompassing authority of the Ministry of National Education, and in effect made university curricula the fruit of a partnership between the Ministry and the individual universities. While the national government retained the discretion to set mandatory requirements for conferring nationally-recognized degrees, the universities were free to determine the distribution of these requirements and to supplement them with their own requirements and a broad range of electives. The administrative restructuring of the system of French higher education — its "decentralization" — did not alter, however, the basic pattern of French legal studies: the basic degree course remains a four-year program consisting of two principal "cycles" or stages of study.

The first two-year cycle essentially is a period of general orientation to the study of law; students achieve a limited concentration (or major) in an academic department only in the second year. Upon completing this first cycle, students are awarded a general studies degree, called the *Diplôme d'Études Universitaires Générales, mention Droit* (D.E.U.G.), which corresponds to an associate degree with specialization in law. During the second two-year cycle, students must concentrate in one of the departments providing instruction in law. For example, a senior law student may take the majority of his courses in the program designed by the departments of commercial law, political science, or economics. At the end of the third year, students receive a *licence en droit,* the equivalent of a B.A. in law; at the end of the fourth year, they are granted a *maîtrise en droit,* an M.A. in law, which, for all practical purposes, has become the basic French law degree. The weekly work load of French law students during each year of study normally amounts to twenty class hours, consisting approximately of fifteen hours of university lecture courses (*cours magistraux*), three hours of directed study classes (*travaux dirigés*), a one-hour introductory course to professional practices, and a weekly language seminar.

Although the basic pattern of legal studies in France is unchanged, the sharing of power instituted by the 1968 statute in matters of curriculum policy has accentuated the already marked tendency of French universities to teach law in an interdisciplinary fashion. As with the 1954 legal studies curriculum, the interdisciplinary perspective is present at the initial stage of study and continues, despite the specialization, into the final years of the program. Although the Ministry of National Education still determines nearly half of the substantive content of the legal studies curriculum, even these core courses foster the interdisciplinary objective. The remainder of the curriculum consists of university and departmental requirements as well as electives and it is here that the impact of the decentralization of educational policy is most pronounced. The French law student is confronted with a plethora of course packages and electives both within and without the area of chosen concentration. This allows the student to move from one social science perspective to another, from an initial introduction to a more advanced consideration, and provides for a well-rounded legal education with courses from allied or more remote academic disciplines. It also is worth noting that the required program includes courses in public or private international law as well as comparative law....

This study will focus upon the program that is being administered at the University of Paris I (Panthéon-Sorbonne), a university long recognized as one of the most distinguished centers for the study of law in France. Although its legal studies curriculum probably is more exemplary than it is representative of the programs offered at other French universities, Paris I provides a forceful illustration of the educational and intellectual advantages that can be derived from the interdisciplinary study of law.

At Paris I, five Teaching and Research Units (departments) provide instruction in law: the Departments of Public Administration and Domestic Public Law; Commercial Law; Development and International, European and Comparative Studies (Law Section); Political Science; and Labor and Social Studies. For both administrative and academic purposes, entering law students are required to select tentatively one Teaching and Research Unit as their major department. During the first two years of the program, the student's choice of a major area of academic concentration is of relatively minor importance and, in fact, can be changed from one year to the next; it does, however, become binding during the last two years of study when a final orientation in legal studies is chosen.

First year law students at Paris I are required to take three year-long university lecture courses, entitled Political Institutions and Constitutional Law, General Introduction to Civil Law, and Economics, and a one-semester ... History of Law and of Institutions. The program of elective courses also is administered on a departmental basis. Students registered in the Departments of Public Administration and Domestic Public Law, Commercial Law, and Labor and Social Studies may satisfy their elective requirements by taking three of the following courses: International Relations; Political Science: The Sociology of Politics; The History of Political Doctrines — 19th and 20th Centuries; or Sociology and Social Psychology. Students in these departments, however, also have the possibility of fulfilling their three credit elective requirement by taking certain specified courses in other university departments....

In addition to the foregoing program, first year law students at Paris I are required to take three hours of directed studies classes (the *travaux dirigés*) each week. These classes are intended to provide students with individual instruction on the subject matter covered in the basic curriculum....

By the second year of the D.E.U.G. program, law students at Paris I begin to work more closely within the framework of the program administered by their major department. Although the elective and inter-departmental offerings are reduced significantly during the second year, the curricula established by the individual departments, while promoting specialized study in a given social science discipline relating to the law, incorporate a sufficient diversity of courses to maintain a full-fledged interdisciplinary character. It is also during this final year of the D.E.U.G. program that law students at Paris I receive weekly instruction on the more practical aspects of professional life and work.

The table below summarizes the basic second year course requirements in two of the five departments. While one program is more traditional in character than the other, they both reflect an unfailing commitment to the interdisciplinary study of law.

	Department of Commercial Law	Department of Development and International, European and Comparative Studies
University Lectures:	Criminal Law Civil Law II	Contemporary Economic Problems, Political Organizations or Criminal Law
Professional Practices:	Corporate Accounting	Organizations and Relations (International Orientation)
Directed Studies Class:	Commercial Law Civil Law	Commercial Law Administrative Law and Institutions

The organization of the second year D.E.U.G. program around the departmental structure foreshadows the type of specialization law students engage in during the second cycle of the legal studies program. The candidates for the *licence* and the *maîtrise* have chosen a definite area of concentration; as a consequence, in their final two years of study, they are obliged to take the specialized program established by their major department. Specialization entails a drastic reduction in elective offerings and inter-departmental distribution requirements. These limitations, however, are counterbalanced by the interdisciplinary character of individual departmental programs. The tables on the following pages provide a description of both the *licence* and the *maîtrise* curricula in the Department of Commercial Law and the Department of Development and International, European and Comparative Studies. It should be noted that the *maîtrise* program is divided into two semesters in which special concentration is achieved in the second semester in the form of a certificate program....

LICENCE

	Department of Commercial Law	Department of Development and International, European and Comparative Studies
University Lectures:	Labor Law Civil Law Suretyship Family Law Commercial Law Negotiable Instruments Bankruptcy Public International Law I Private International Law Administrative Law I	Public International Law Private International Law Labor Law Administrative Law I Commercial Law Major Legal Systems and Anglo-American Law or German Law
Directed Studies Classes:	Three from among: Labor Law Suretyship Family Law Negotiable Instruments Bankruptcy	Three from among: Public International Law Private International Law Major Legal Systems and Anglo-American Law or German Law
Electives:	One from among: History of Business Company Organization and Financial Management Public Liberties Criminal Procedure Major Legal Systems Insurance Law Private Judicial Law	One from among: Public Liberties Economic Politics Administrative Law II Introduction to EEC Law Civil Law Suretyship or Family Law

MAÎTRISE

First Semester		
University Lectures:	Commercial Law Taxation Private International Law Civil Family Law	International Commercial Law Public International Economic Law Private International Law
Directed Studies Classes:	Commercial Law Taxation	International Commercial Law Public International Economic Law

Electives:	(None)	Two from among: The Sociology of International Relations Foreign Administrative Institutions Comparative Labor Law Seminar in German Law
Second Semester	*Certificate in International Business Matters*	*Certificate in the Law of International Life*
University Lectures:	International Commercial Law European Commercial Law European Organizations	European Organizations European Commercial Law
Directed Studies Classes:	International Commercial Law	European Organizations
Electives:	*	Two from among: Oil Law Middle East Oil Politics Maritime Law Computer Programming and International Relations International Law of Development
	Certificate in Domestic Business Matters	*Certificate in Anglo-American Law*
University Lectures:	Commercial Criminal Law Banking and the Stock Market European Commercial Law	U.S. Company Law Contract Law in Common Law Countries and Private International Law English Company Law Seminar in Anglo-American Law
Directed Studies Classes:	European Commercial Law	(None)
Electives:	*	(None)
	Certificate in Management	*Certificate in European Institutions and Law*
University Lectures:	Commercial Management Financial Management Banking and the Stock Market	EEC Institutional Law European Commercial Law EEC Economic Problems
Directed Studies Classes:	Financial Management	EEC Institutional Law European Commercial Law

Electives:	*	One from among: European Social Legislation (includes a directed studies class) European Tax and Finance Law

* In addition to the certificate program, all students in the Department of Commercial Law must take two electives from among Remedies, History of Private Law, English Company Law, European Social Legislation, Insurance Law, Industrial Property, Management Supervision, and Special Criminal Law.

In actual practice, the French legal studies curriculum suffers from a number of drawbacks which, although they do not undermine its status as a model of substantive legal instruction, call into serious question the pedagogical worth of some aspects of the French university system. On the one hand, these flaws are endemic to any educational system which places so much importance upon strictly academic values and establishes so clear a demarcation between the world of ideas and the realm of existing fact. Rightly or wrongly, the French university appears to function principally upon its own momentum. Academic inquiry becomes meaningful in itself; knowledge is prized exclusively for its own sake and perhaps at the expense of other human endeavors. Accordingly, despite statutory language and government policies proclaiming educational egalitarianism and the need to have the universities respond to the immediate needs of society, the French universities have held fast to an elitist tradition, envisioning themselves primarily as breeding grounds for academic vocations.

On the other hand, the deficiencies that attend the legal studies (or any other) curriculum within the setting of the French university system stem from the fact that higher education in France is "part of a nationally uniform system of free, secular, public education"[92] which is funded rather parsimoniously by the national government.... Admission to the French universities is open to any high school student who has obtained his *baccalauréat.* The exceedingly large numbers of students generated by this admissions policy, combined with inadequate government funding, leads to overcrowding and generally inadequate facilities for both students and professors, especially in the large metropolitan areas.

[92] Because of its public character, tuition and fees at the French university are minimal, rarely exceeding more than $50 a year; room and board costs are subsidized heavily by the State. The "open admissions" policy was instituted in France primarily for political reasons, to assuage critics who assailed selectivity as elitist and undemocratic; it is not a policy which reflects a purely pedagogical design. Although the open admission policy admittedly equalized access to higher education, it also created a more subtle form of post-admission selectivity, engendering, for example, a 50% attrition rate during the initial years of professional studies. A few years ago, the then Minister of National Education, Joseph Fontanet, recognized that the open admission policy had particularly brutal consequences, essentially eliminating after a few years of study many of those students whose expectations had been raised unjustifiably and whose investment of

As with other university programs, the university lecture courses in law may be attended by anywhere from five hundred to a thousand registered students. Professors deliver formal lectures, presenting a view of the law which is not only didactic, but also dogmatic in character. Clearly, the size of the courses discourages both formal and informal contacts between students and professors; the method of presentation prohibits any attempt to question the fundamental principles of the law, the memorization of which usually is the key to success in the final examination. Moreover, students often complain that the basic instruction is too erudite and theoretical to be of any value to them when they leave the university. For many French law professors, the lecture is an art form, the substance of which responds to a detached analytical imperative and is delivered in an elegant and impeccably articulated French. By his training and personal predilections, the French law professor avoids the practitioner's perspective; he weaves a web of theoretical abstractions that is destined to inspire those few members of his anonymous audience who aspire to follow in his footsteps.

The more individualized group instruction proffered by the directed studies classes was meant to remedy the impersonal and theoretical character of the lecture method of instruction. These weekly sessions were designed to provide students with an opportunity to apply the knowledge they acquired in lectures to existing legal problems. The actual operation of the directed studies classes, however, appears to deviate from this statement of purpose. In keeping with the training they have received and with the precedent set by the professors they wish to emulate, the graduate instructors, who conduct these sessions under the general supervision of a law professor, devote their teaching efforts to expounding upon fundamental legal principles rather than encouraging students to develop a critical perspective upon the law. Often, the analysis of the practical legal problem is relegated to a hurried treatment in the closing minutes of the sessions. Paradoxically, the professors, who have established themselves as educators, have the least amount of contact with students, while the graduate instructors, who have just begun to teach, have the most direct influence upon the students' education.

---

their time and effort in a program of study for which they were unsuited and unprepared went to naught. Most of the teaching personnel do not have offices or secretarial support. Libraries lack sufficient space to accommodate students, library hours are inconvenient, and it is difficult to get books and almost impossible to take them out. A sense of participation in the life of an academic community or a willingness to engage in extracurricular activities are unknown in the majority of French universities. These general conditions of university life promote an attitude of indifference and cynicism, not only among students, but also among the teaching staff. While students focus their attention almost exclusively upon getting a passing grade on examinations, professors, who usually can rely upon the job security guaranteed by their status as civil servants, minimize their pedagogical roles and devote their time and energy to research or other personal pursuits. Finally, in direct contradiction to the open admissions policy, the French university system remains hierarchical and elitist in character, catering primarily to the needs and interests of a small minority of academically-inclined students who aspire to enter the teaching profession.

NOTES AND QUESTIONS

1. Why do you think the French after 1968 moved toward decentralization between the Ministry of National Education and individual universities for curricular matters? Is the answer reflected in the curriculum at Paris I?

2. The French university offers three degrees on the path to becoming a lawyer: the D.E.U.G., *mention droit*; the *licence en droit*; and the *maîtrise en droit*. A student may terminate his university studies after earning a preliminary "general studies" degree and still make use of it for a career in business or government. Should American law schools offer a degree — for instance, a Master of Legal Studies — after one year of course work for those not interested in practicing law?

3. After a French student successfully completes the academic (university) phase of her legal training, she enters a distinct practical (apprenticeship) phase for one of certain legal careers: *avocat, notaire,* or judge or prosecutor, for example.

Consider the requirements to become an advocate. After receiving the university *maîtrise* diploma, the graduate applies to take the entrance examination (part oral, part written) to a one year program at a regional *centre de formation professionnelle*. Instruction consists of simulated clinical exercises and lectures on professional ethics. But the candidate also spends part of her time as an intern in an advocate's office, court, business firm, or government agency. The final examination covers practical problems (again with a written and oral portion) and includes the candidate's written report on her work (with employer assessments). Upon passing the examination, the candidate receives the *certificat d'aptitude à la profession d'avocat* (CAPA), which entitles her to use the *avocat* title, although she still must serve a two- to five-year probationary period working in the offices of other lawyers and enrolling in continuing legal education programs. After the probationary period is completed, the regional training *centre*, considering the local bar council's comments, issues the avocat a certificate that allows her to establish an independent office.

A judgeship or a prosecutor's position requires admission to the *École nationale de la magistrature*, while a prestigious job in the government requires admission to the *École nationale d'administration*.

4. For information on the recruitment of law professors in France, see C. Mouly & C. Atias, *Faculty Recruitment in France*, 41 Am. J. Comp. L. 401 (1993).

4. GERMANY

DAVID S. CLARK, THE SELECTION AND ACCOUNTABILITY OF JUDGES IN WEST GERMANY: IMPLEMENTATION OF A *RECHTSSTAAT*, 61 Southern California Law Review 1795, 1802-06 (1988)

An American viewing the German legal education system is struck by three of its features: (1) it is highly regulated by the federal and state governments; (2) it is primarily oriented toward the training of judges; and (3) except for the period from 1971 to 1985, it has had a striking degree of curricular uniformity among the university law schools.

At the top of what Alfred Rinken calls the "norm pyramid" for German legal education lies the federal German Judges Law (*Deutsches Richtergesetz*). It establishes certain minimum requirements for law study, particularly concerning the practical phase of training and the state testing of candidates. The federal government accomplished university reform in the 1970s through the *Hochschulrahmengesetz*. This reform reordered the relationships among professors, teaching and research assistants, staff, and students in all faculties, including law. Each of the eleven states have enacted for legal education a lengthy law (*Juristenausbildungsgesetz*), extensive regulations, or both. These rules regulate the periods of study, vacations, mandatory and elective courses, state examinations, grades, as well as other matters.[29] States have also promulgated detailed higher education laws that, within the framework set out in the federal *Hochschulrahmengesetz*, elaborate the rights and duties of university members along with the structure of the university itself.[30] In addition, each of the 30 state university law faculties — there are no private universities with law faculties or free standing law schools — has issued a specific student plan (*Studienplan*) to guide enrollees through the curriculum.

German law faculties have traditionally aimed at training standardized jurists (*Einheitsjuristen*), who can meet the qualifications to become a judge (*Befähigung zum Richteramt*). These qualifications are broadly established in the federal German Judges Law, which requires that one who desires to enter judicial service must pass two state examinations. The first test can be taken after seven semesters of law study, although most students wait until they complete five years in the university. Law is an undergraduate curriculum, for which enrollees need a certificate of maturity (*Reifezeugnis, Abitur*) from a secondary school. Once a candidate passes the first state examination, with its written and oral components, he may proceed to the stage of training known as preparatory service (*Vorbereitungsdienst*), which lasts two years.[a] The trainee, a *Referendar*, receives an allowance from the state as a temporary civil servant sufficient to support himself and his dependents. The German Judges Law sets out four mandatory work stations, followed by a list of elec-

[29] Bremen is illustrative of the detail involved in these rules for law study. The Bremen Law on Legal Education had 66 sections, supplemented by two regulations on law examinations, one with ten sections and the other with 36 sections.

[30] These statutes average over 90 pages in length for most German states.

[a] In 1992 the period of preparatory service was reduced from two and a half to two years. Law of 20 Nov. 1992, 1992 BGBl I 1926, art. 1.

tive stations from which a *Referendar* may select. Most trainees spend between three and nine months in each of the obligatory stations — a civil court, a criminal court or public prosecutor's office, an administrative agency, and an attorney's office — leaving six months for one elective experience that may be in one of these four mandatory stations or in another court. Under this pattern it is likely that a *Referendar* will spend about half his time in a judicial environment. He must also attend courses taught by judges and civil servants aimed toward the analysis of complex practical cases. After completing the preparatory service a *Referendar* is ready to take the written and oral parts of the second state examination, which is graded mainly by judges and senior civil servants who are concerned primarily about the application of theory to practice.

A *Referendar* who passes the second state examination becomes a *Volljurist* and is eligible to apply for a judgeship. In addition, these same qualifications for judicial service are required by statute or regulation in order to become a prosecutor or government lawyer, an attorney, or even a notary. By custom this standardized education promoting *Einheitsjuristen* also applies to lawyers who are permanently employed by business firms, banks, and insurance companies. Consequently, all *Volljuristen* share from their period of apprenticeship some degree of a judicial outlook and orientation toward the law. Dietrich Rueschemeyer believes that this system of education contributes to "a syndrome fostering civil service orientations and loyalty toward 'the State,'" which he also finds in the social backgrounds of university students in general.

The desire to create *Einheitsjuristen* in Germany has led to substantial uniformity in mostly mandatory university law school curricula. Traditional legal education in the late 1960s, however, came under serious attack amid student revolt at universities. Critics argued that training was too long (candidates for the second state exam averaged 29 years of age) and ineffective (law students spent substantial time and money in private cram courses with *Repetitoren*). The division between university study and preparatory service in the two-phase program created an artificial and harmful separation of theory and practice. Furthermore, the proper creation and application of law required more instruction in sociology, economics, and psychology.

After extensive national debate the social-liberal coalition in the Federal Legislative Assembly (*Bundestag*) in 1971 amended the German Judges Law to authorize states on an experimental basis to combine university law studies and practical training into one comprehensive unit (*einstufige Juristenausbildung*) and to replace the first state examination with either course grades or an intermediary examination. Eight such innovative programs were initiated in seven states, some with a significant infusion of social science theory and method. Certain reformers wanted to train judges who would act more aggressively as social engineers in creating law rather than act as mechanical servants to the existing corpus of codes and statutes. But the established law faculties, and a few new ones, opted to proceed with a modestly altered traditional two-stage program (*zweistufige Juristenausbildung*). To achieve some uniformity the Ministers of Justice Conference reached agreement in 1969 on law faculty curricula. In essence, the number of obligatory subjects to be studied and tested on the first state examination was reduced. Students had to add, however, one elective group of courses on which they would also be tested. The ministers further recommended that students come to the state examination not only with a technical knowledge of legal rules, but that they also understand the historical, social, economic, political, and philosophical context of law.

One-phase legal education had always been considered experimental. Whatever hopes its proponents had for fostering a new type of German jurist today lie smoldering in ashes. In 1984 the conservative coalition in the *Bundestag* eliminated the experimental clause from the German Judges Law, reconfirming its commitment to *Einheitsjuristen* and to traditional two-phase legal education. The last one-phase law students entered the university in 1985.

ERHARD BLANKENBURG & ULRIKE SCHULTZ, GERMAN ADVOCATES: A HIGHLY REGULATED PROFESSION, in 2 LAWYERS IN SOCIETY: THE CIVIL LAW WORLD 124, 131-32 (Richard L. Abel & Philip S.C. Lewis eds. 1988)[a]

To become a German jurist, one first must enroll in a university law faculty. People often do so without clear motives: most of those who qualify enter university because of the status it confers. Law students are more uncertain than others about their future careers. Legal training traditionally has been an all-purpose choice. In 1982 there were 74,756 law students and 14,105 apprentice lawyers. German universities are tuition-free, and, until the early 1980s, one-third of all students received grants to help finance their studies. [BAFÖG]. This made university study an attractive low-cost option for anybody who passed their secondary-school examinations. Now, however, loans have replaced grants.

There is widespread dissatisfaction with the quality of university legal studies, however. On average they take almost six years, although only three and a half years formally are required. University teaching consists mostly of lectures and concentrates on imparting knowledge of the legal codes and their application to hypothetical cases. Considerable pressure is exerted by rigid marking of tests and examinations. The drop-out rate is about 50 percent in the first phase of legal education and about 25 percent in the second; for other subjects, the average failure rate in 1980 was 10 percent. Final oral examinations have been described as a "conformity test" to see whether the candidate's thought processes fit the appropriate pattern of "perceiving, thinking and judging." To prepare for these examinations, many students attend courses with a private tutor (*Repetitor*). These offer a systematic, limited program oriented toward the examination and concentrate on case-solving techniques. Two types of tutor can be distinguished: the "impresario" who runs a one-person business and the large firms with employed tutors and branch offices in many university towns. Some tutors hand out course notes. About 70 percent of law students take part in these private courses and almost all students use some of their publications. Two out of three law students in 1980 used those of the largest establishment (*Alpmann* at Münster). Even private tutors

[a] Textual notes are omitted.

cannot guarantee a good result; to be successful, students must construct their own curriculum, and many form private study groups.

Students restrict their reading to legal dogmatics, and traditional legal training omits even a basic exposure to philosophy, sociology, economics, or political science. However, there also is no training in the skills needed by an advocate: there are no moot courts, legal clinics, or training in administrative skills in either the universities or the tutorial "crash courses." In the late 1960s both the neglect of social science and the perceived need for some skills training led to demands for reform. In 1971 educational programs were established combining university courses and in-service training. In 1982 approximately 12 percent of all graduating lawyers had completed these programs. In 1985, however, all legal training returned to the earlier model with its well-known deficiencies.

NOTES AND QUESTIONS

1. German legal education is the best financed among the European countries that we examine. The federal and state governments in 1988 spent DM 230 million for a national law teaching and research staff of 2,100, with average salaries of DM 110,000 (an amount comparable to that paid in the United States). Each law faculty has a relatively large corps of well-paid full-time professors; the student body size, although large (at some universities over 4,000), is usually manageable; the curriculum is a rich mixture of required and often interesting elective courses, seminars, and take-home written exercises; and the facilities and libraries (including seminar and institute libraries) are adequate.

2. What do you think of the German goal of *Einheitsjuristen* (standardized jurists)? Would such a goal be desirable in the United States, perhaps through tighter control over required courses by the ABA, which accredits American law schools?

3. In 1992 the German Judges Law was amended to promote the Europeanization of German legal education. Section 5a(2) now requires that testing for the first state exam include for the mandatory subjects an inquiry into "their European law dimensions." German states are now also allowed for the preparatory service to give credit for obligatory station training at supranational and international organizations and even for work with foreign lawyers. Law of 20 Nov. 1992, 1992 BGBl I 1926, art. 1.

4. How valuable is the German preparatory service (apprenticeship) to law students? Should this model, suitably modified, be imported to the U.S.? Who would pay for it? Compare the German apprenticeship system to that in France, *supra,* and Italy, *infra.*

5. European legal education presumes a drop-out rate exceeding 50 percent. This system permits almost open admission to study at a law faculty. Is this approach truly more democratic than the selective admissions used in the United States, or do other structural variables play a role in supporting a socially more elitist educational system?

6. For more on reform in German legal education, past and present, see Jutta Brunnée, *The Reform of Legal Education in Germany: The Never-End-*

ing Story of European Integration, 42 J. Legal Educ. 399 (1992); Wilhelm Karl Geck, *The Reform of Legal Education in the Federal Republic of Germany,* 25 Am. J. Comp. L. 86 (1977); Juergen R. Ostertag, *Legal Education in Germany and the United States — A Structural Comparison,* 26 Vand. J. Transnat'l L. 301 (1993). *See also* Jürgen Kohler, *Selecting Minds: The Recruitment of Law Professors in Germany,* 41 Am. J. Comp. L. 413 (1993).

5. ITALY

VITTORIO OLGIATI & VALERIO POCAR, THE ITALIAN LEGAL PROFESSION: AN INSTITUTIONAL DILEMMA, in 2 LAWYERS IN SOCIETY: THE CIVIL LAW WORLD 336, 344-46 (Richard L. Abel & Philip S.C. Lewis eds. 1988)[a]

A lawyer must obtain a university degree in *giurisprudenza* from one of the twenty-nine law faculties. Between 1938 and 1969 the *curriculum studiorum* in all Italian law faculties required examinations in eighteen compulsory and three optional subjects. Since then students have been able to choose twenty-one subjects out of all those offered, subject to the approval of the faculty council. In response to this liberalization, many *Ordini* [bar associations] have imposed their curricular requirements.

A century ago there were fewer than 3,000 students enrolled in Italian law faculties; as recently as 1969 there still were only [53,000]. That year saw the repeal of requiring a secondary school diploma in *Liceo Classico* or *Liceo Scientifico* for admission to the university. In 1977 there were 128,604 law students out of a total of 935,795 in all Italian universities, making law the third most popular subject after medicine and science....

Law courses traditionally have had three main objectives: research, training law teachers, and general legal education. Legal education still is formal, focused on the interpretation of doctrine, as is the Italian legal tradition itself. Consequently, it is not directed toward vocational preparation. Most instruction is through lectures; case studies and the seminars and practical exercises that have developed recently remain marginal. Because attendance is not compulsory and an increasing proportion of students are employed, the numbers at lectures are fairly low. A degree in giurisprudenza offers numerous occupational opportunities in government, banks, insurance companies, and so on. Only a small number of graduates actually enter the legal professions, and even fewer become lawyers.

Graduates who wish to be lawyers must enroll in the register of *praticanti procuratori* and begin a two-year apprenticeship in a lawyer's office. In fact, the apprenticeship rarely is less than three years, and because of the difficulty of the state exams the average period is between four and five years. The experience does not give the future lawyer the necessary technical and professional expertise. Rather, it is simply a means of reproducing traditional lawyers. The conditions are poor: little or no income, the exclusion of those who lack sufficient means, and acceptance by a studio on the basis of family relationship or friendship rather than merit....

[a] Textual notes are omitted.

Once the period of training is over, the praticante can take the state examination to become a *procuratore*. This consists of two written papers (one on civil and administrative law and the other on civil and criminal procedure) and six oral examinations (civil, criminal, administrative, and fiscal law and civil and criminal procedure). Two new substantive areas — industrial and international law — are not examined. The examinations are theoretical, and the pass rate varies from 13 percent to 70 percent across locales. The examination commissions, appointed annually by each court of appeal, are composed of three magistrates (one of whom is made the president), one law professor, and two lawyers. Those who pass can enroll in the professional Law List and, as members of the Ordine, start practicing law as procuratori. A procuratore becomes an *avvocato* after practicing for six years or passing another examination.

NOTE ON THE UNIVERSITY OF ROME LAW FACULTY'S REQUIRED COURSES

First Year

Political economy
Philosophy of law
Institutions of private law
Institutions of Roman law
History of Roman law

Second Year

Constitutional law
Commercial law
Tax law

Second and Third Year

Civil law I and II
Roman law I and II
Penal law I and II
History of Italian law I and II

Third Year

Civil procedure
Ecclesiastical law

Fourth Year

Administrative law
Labor law
International law
Penal procedure

NOTES AND QUESTIONS

1. The University of Rome's required law curriculum has changed very little since the 1960s. Does it seem directed more toward the past or toward the future in terms of a lawyer's practice in the 1990s?

2. For information on the recruitment of law professors in Italy, see Ugo Mattei & P.G. Monateri, *Faculty Recruitment in Italy: Two Sides of the Moon,* 41 Am. J. Comp. L. 427 (1993).

6. SPAIN

CARLOS VILADÁS JENE, THE LEGAL PROFESSION IN SPAIN: AN UNDERSTUDIED BUT BOOMING OCCUPATION, in 2 LAWYERS IN SOCIETY: THE CIVIL LAW WORLD 369, 371-73 (Richard L. Abel & Philip S.C. Lewis eds. 1988)[a]

There are twenty-eight universities in Spain, twenty-one of which contain law faculties (three of them are private). In 1978/79, nearly half of the 156,189 university students were enrolled in law faculties. The number of law students increased threefold in the seven years between 1971/72 and 1978/79. Students must be registered for a minimum of five years, but few manage to graduate in that short a period.

A recent study of the Faculty of Law at Barcelona confirms the failings of the educational system. Only about 10 percent of the students succeed in graduating within five years; another 7 percent take six years, and a further 7 percent require seven years. These failures of the system impose enormous costs not only on students but also on the state, which heavily subsidizes the public universities. Although a student who graduated in five years would have to spend only 2.5 million Pts [$18,000], the average expenditure actually is estimated at 8.3 million Pts [$60,000] because of the prolongation of study. Half or more of the students fail their examinations, but not because the academic standards are high. Rather, the level of secondary schooling is low, particularly in the private schools; and very few students really are interested in law — most simply want a credential that, until the mid-1970s, was useful in obtaining a job.

All students who complete their secondary education and pass a general university entrance examination are admitted to the law school closest to their secondary school. A student who wishes to move to another city usually has no difficulty in obtaining entrance to the law school there. Most students attend the nearest university because they live at home. Only those not situated near a law faculty choose among them on the basis of some factor other than geographic convenience. Even professors seek employment in a university primarily on the basis of the city in which they wish to live.

The creation of new universities during the late 1960s and early 1970s somewhat reduced the importance of those in Madrid and Barcelona, which most students attended in the past. Nevertheless, the incredible increase in law student enrollments did not allow those faculties to contract to the manageable sizes they had enjoyed earlier. Of the 74,117 law students in 1978/79,

---

[a] Textual notes are omitted.

14,476 were enrolled in the Universidad Complutense of Madrid and 11,559 in the Universidad Central of Barcelona — a third of all law students.

Private universities are operated by various orders within the Catholic Church: Deusto (the most prestigious) by the Jesuits; Navarra, by Opus Dei. Both are expensive compared to public institutions. Nevertheless, the quality of the education at Deusto attracts students with superior secondary-school records. Although some feel that private universities offer a better education because they are smaller and less "disorganized," the most prestigious professors in all fields teach at public universities. I also believe that private universities resemble secondary schools in being overprotective of their students.

Both public and private institutions receive state funds, although in different amounts. In the former, annual tuition is about 35,000 Pts (about $250), far below the actual cost. The real expense for the student, therefore, is maintenance. Since most students live with their parents, all those whose families can forego their wages for five years can attend university. Only those living far from the major cities are at a significant disadvantage. The very few scholarships are given to those who demonstrate both need and capacity, on the basis of earlier education and present performance.

Both the weight of tradition and the large number of students combine to lower the quality of legal education. It is conceptualistic, exegetic, and dogmatic. Although both Madrid and Barcelona attempted to encourage the discussion of alternative solutions to legal cases in the late 1970s, the rapid increase in enrollments forced a return to *ex cathedra* lectures. Indeed, the ratio of students to teachers worsened dramatically during the seven years between 1971/72 and 1978/79. Even these figures exaggerate the teaching resources available, for only young assistants teach full time; tenured professors maintain a heavy practice, arriving at the university just before their classes and leaving immediately afterward.

NOTE ON EUROPEAN LEGAL EDUCATION

Table 8.1

Total Number Law Students (in 000), by Country and Year

Country	1950	1960	1970	1980	1991
Germany	12	18	32	65	83[1]
Italy	37	50	59	148	142
Spain	17	14	21	80	160[2]
Private Universities			2	4	8[2]

[1] For unified Germany.
[2] In 1988.

Table 8.1 reveals the statistical history of legal education in Germany (West Germany before unification day: 3 October 1990), Italy, and Spain since World War II. Taking 1950 as our base year, we see that legal education was relatively more popular in Italy (36,635 students) than in Spain (16,853 students) or Germany (11,916 students). The number of law students per 100,000 population was respectively 79, 61, and 24. As societies in the postwar period developed, the number of students choosing to study law at the university steadily grew until 1970 (faster in Germany, but with some stagnation in Spain under General Franco). Then in the 1970s there was an absolute explosion in law student enrollment, as universities eased entrance requirements and students generally viewed law as a useful preparation for a number of careers. This growth continued in Spain during the 1980s, but slowed in Germany and actually declined slightly in Italy. The number of law students in 1991 stood at 159,692 for Spain (1988 figures), 142,332 for Italy, and 83,398 for Germany. Per 100,000 population the student differences were even greater: 410, 246, and 105, respectively. Perhaps the wealthier a nation, and the more elaborate its university system in terms of disciplines available, the smaller the ratio of law students to population.

Table 8.2

Percentage University Students in Law, by Country and Year

Country	1950	1960	1970	1980	1991
France	23	13	24	16	
Germany	10	9	9	7	6[1]
Italy	16	19	9	14	15
Spain	31	18	10	17	22[2]

[1] For unified Germany.
[2] In 1988.

Table 8.2 could support this last statement. Universities in general after World War II were expanding more rapidly than law studies, so that the percentage of university students in law declined until 1970 (until 1968 in France). Germany best illustrates this point, since the relative popularity of legal education has declined up to the present. In France, after a large surge in law enrollments in the late 1960s and in 1970, decline reappeared through the 1970s. On the other hand, the relative popularity of law studies today is stable in Italy and even growing in Spain.

In Europe law remains a popular course of study for careers outside the legal profession, even in Germany. The percentage of law students who actually graduate with a law degree is low. In Italy 13,657 graduated (in 1991) out of 142,332 studying law, in Spain 12,511 graduated (in 1988) out of 159,692 students, and in Germany 8,499 passed the first state exam (in 1989) out of 83,398 students studying law.

Table 8.3 illustrates the feminization of law study in the second half of the 20th century. In Germany the percentage of women studying law increased from six percent in 1950 to 42 percent in 1989. This trend appeared in other sectors of legal education, although more slowly. The percentage of women receiving doctorates (in 1989) or working on the professional staff of law faculties (in 1988) was 16 percent, while the full professorate remained essentially male (only two percent or 12 women in 1988). The percentage of women

Table 8.3

Percentage Women in Legal Education in Germany, by Position and Year

Position	1950	1960	1970	1980	1989[1]
Students	6	11	12	31	42
Passing First State Exam		10	11	28	39
Doctor Degree		4	4	8	16
Teaching & Research Staff		2		10	16
Full Professors				1	2

[1]Percentage students is for unified Germany in 1991; staff and professor data are for West Germany in 1988.

law graduates in France for 1980 was 50 percent and in Italy for 1991 was 49 percent.

Teaching (and research) staffs at European law faculties remain small relative to student body size. In Germany this component (with full professors in parentheses) rose from 750 (310) in 1960 to 1,444 (506) in 1972, to 2,013 (742) in 1980, leveling off at 2,102 (749) by 1988. This latter figure yielded a ratio of 40 to 1 law students to teaching and research staff. With 2,766 law teachers and researchers in Italy (860 full professors), the ratio was 51 to 1 in 1991. The ratio in Spain in 1988 for 3,099 law teachers and researchers was 52 to 1.

QUESTIONS

Ask your librarian to help you find statistical information about legal education in the United States since 1950. How has it developed in terms of the number of students, its place within higher education, the entrance of women and minorities, and the student-faculty ratio? What explains the major statistical similarities and differences between U.S. and European legal education?

7. COLOMBIA

RICHARD J. WILSON, THE NEW LEGAL EDUCATION IN NORTH AND SOUTH AMERICA, 25 Stanford Journal of International Law 375, 380-87, 402-03, 411 (1989)

Law School in South America: The Colombian Example

The *cátedra magistral* (formal lecture) is the overwhelmingly dominant law school pedagogy in Colombia and in Latin America generally. In this pedagogy, the law professor delivers a formal presentation of the material to be covered and only rarely takes student questions. The lecture focuses on law in codes and other statutory law adopted by the legislature, as interpreted both by great legal scholars in extensive theoretical exegeses and by the professor in class. In legal Spanish, *doctrina* has a different meaning than doctrine in legal English. *Doctrina* is legal doctrine revealed through the treatise, rather than law revealed through the case. In the *cátedra magistral* it is rare for students to read materials, even *doctrina*, in advance of class.

The most notable aspects of Colombian legal education, aside from its legal tradition and pedagogical style, are the large numbers of law schools and law graduates, the character of the law teaching profession, and the highly structured, government-controlled law school curriculum. These characteristics are not unique to Colombia, and have been noted in other Latin American legal systems.

Law graduates have traditionally accounted for the highest percentage of graduates from the eight higher education programs that generate the largest number of graduates in Colombia — law, accountancy, economics, business administration, political science, medicine, architecture and civil engineering (in descending order). In 1981, there were about 4,500 law graduates; accounting ran a distant second with less than 3,000 graduates. From 1960 to 1974, the size of the bar increased by more than 150%, demonstrating both the popularity of law as a career and the greater accessibility of higher education in general.

There were thirty-four law schools in Colombia in 1983, with a total enrollment of 27,405 students. Of the total number of students in Colombia, about forty-five percent (12,649) were women. About forty percent of all students (10,453) attended classes only at night. Bogotá, the capital, had twelve law schools, including La Universidad Libre, which led the country in total enrollment in 1983 with 2,538 students. Today, law schools are overwhelmingly private (twenty-nine of thirty-four), and tuition costs range from virtually nothing (thirty pesos a semester — less than a dollar — at the University of Antioquia, a public school) to relatively expensive, given average income levels of about 1,000 pesos per day (91,800 pesos — about 500 dollars — at the private University of the Andes). Highly competitive exams restrict admission to the inexpensive public schools. On the other hand, family money and status determine admission to private schools.

Teaching personnel are overwhelmingly *catedráticos* (adjuncts), who teach one or more courses while maintaining an active law practice to augment law school salaries. Only 804 of Colombia's 3,124 law professors are full-time employees, and only ten percent (314) are women.

Colombia's law schools, like those of much of the rest of Latin America, commence immediately after the U.S. equivalent of high school and continue through a five year program which combines many courses found in U.S. undergraduate liberal arts curricula with law-related requirements. The state has played a strong centralizing role regarding law school curricula, as it has in many other aspects of Latin American social and economic life. Legislative decrees frequently modify aspects of law school administration. This tendency most recently manifested itself in 1979 with the adoption of a decree governing in great detail both the establishment of new law schools and the requisites of law school curricula.

The 1979 decree expands the highly structured curriculum outlined by earlier legislation. As it now stands, the curriculum is divided into four conceptual groups: mandatory courses, optional courses, seminars, and *consultorio jurídico* (legal clinic). Mandatory courses are divided by statute into seven sub-groupings: 1) political law (constitutional theory, Colombian constitution, general and Colombian administrative law, international law and public housing); 2) private law (Roman law, general, personal and family civil law, goods, obligations, contracts, successions and commercial law); 3) criminal law (general and special criminal law, sociology and politics of criminal law and legal medicine); 4) labor law (substantive labor law and social security); 5) procedural law (theory of process, general and special civil procedure, criminal procedure, labor procedure, administrative procedure and evidence); 6) social studies (introduction to law, theories of knowledge and logic, history of philosophy and philosophy of law, political and Colombian economy, sociology and political science and professional ethics); and 7) seminars and clinics. Optional courses are left to the individual school; typical optional courses include, among others, mathematics, foreign languages and humanities. Seminars "preferably" are to be conducted within the topic areas of methodology of law, orientation to the exercise of the profession and the judiciary, methodology of legal research, legal pedagogy, legal technique, comparative law and jurisprudence.

The legal clinic program seeks to "familiarize the student with the exercise of professional skills before judicial functionaries, and will include attention to consultation, permitted powers and observation visits to *despachos* [the chambers of judges where records are kept]." Clinics became a mandatory part of the curriculum in 1971, pursuant to a decree which sets forth general organizational requirements for the clinics and identifies the proceedings at which students in their last two years may appear under faculty supervision:

> (a) in criminal proceedings before municipal judges and police authorities;
>
> (b) in non-appealable labor proceedings and in administrative settlement proceedings in the labor area;
>
> (c) in non-appealable civil proceedings heard by municipal judges; and
>
> (d) in criminal proceedings when appointed as spokespersons or defenders at trial.

A later resolution permits students to provide legal assistance to national prison inmates.

In order to graduate, the student must either pass a series of preparatory examinations, usually oral in most of the mandatory courses, or complete all such courses with a grade point average of not less than 4.25 on a five point scale. In addition to the legal clinic, the student must complete "directed research" as part of the seminar program and defend that research to a jury. Eligibility for licensure as an *abogado*, or attorney at law (the only category of practice in Colombia), occurs upon completion of these requirements. There is no bar examination.

A Profile of the Legal Profession in Colombia

The law graduate is in the upper two percent of all Colombians in terms of education. The incomes of law graduates interviewed by Lynch put them in the upper one percent of the Bogotá work force. Lawyers are considered members of the upper-middle class, and their family and educational backgrounds reflect this class status as well.[34]

A law degree has traditionally been a gateway to a number of fields in addition to law practice. Politics, government and business in particular attract many law graduates.[35] According to Lynch's 1973-74 survey, the majority (fifty-five percent) of practicing attorneys in Colombia were engaged in private practice, primarily in litigation. However, most obtained their first legal experience in a government legal position or as a judge or prosecutor. Lynch's data showed a highly stratified bar within the practitioner group. Graduates of elite schools tended toward long-term careers as legal advisors in the white collar context, while those who represented the middle and lower classes engaged heavily in litigation, usually in small firms or as sole practitioners. Within the practicing bar, the primary functions of the litigating attorney are, in descending order, meeting with clients, visiting the courts, preparing legal documents and conducting legal research....

Survey results suggest that most graduates of law schools are either satisfied or very satisfied with their legal educations. The reason most often given for dissatisfaction with law school was that school was "too theoretical and [did] not [provide] enough practical legal training," although only five percent responded that the lecture method was used too much. Eighty-five percent said that legal education needed reform, and most sought either to increase practical training or to reform the curriculum and add new courses.[44] ...

South America: Shortcomings of the Lecture Method

The lecture method has come under increasing criticism in Latin America. In 1975 and 1976, the National Autonomous University of Mexico's Institute of Juridical Research (*Instituto de Investigaciones Jurídicas*) published two significant books on law teaching prepared by the Chilean exile Jorge Witker. The first was his own work on law teaching, entitled *The Teaching of Law: A Methodological Critique*. The second, edited by him and published in the following year, was entitled *An Anthology of Studies on the Teaching of Law*. Witker's work has provided the basis for arguments for reform of law pedagogy in Colombia during the last ten years. Colombia's two leading critics of legal education and the legal profession both quote Witker extensively and rely on his arguments for reform of legal education.

[34] D. Lynch, Legal Roles in Colombia 43 (1981).

[35] One-fifth to one quarter of all law graduates pursue non-legal careers.

[44] However, respondents ranked the teaching of "first principles of law and all the codes" as the chief educational objective of law school, and ranked social and economic reform or the instrumental use of law as the lowest objectives of legal education.

Lynch suggests that one reason for the rejection of the instrumental view of law may lie in the bar's view of itself as an independent profession.

> An instrumental concept of legal education places more emphasis on the degree to which law can be manipulated to serve particular interests or goals as contrasted with legal science which views law as an autonomous body of thought governed by its own internal logic. The instrumental perspective makes a lawyer appear more as a technician using his skills to serve a client or the government rather than as an independent and neutral scientist applying law to arrive at a result determined by preexisting rules.

The principal pedagogical criticisms of the lecture method noted in these works are the passivity of the student; the focus on selection, organization and presentation of material by the teacher; the absence of any practical quality to the education; poor communication to the teacher of the level of student comprehension and retention; and the rote memorization and recitation of the material as the only means of student evaluation.

A defense of the lecture method was summarized and reported almost forty years ago at the Third International Congress of Comparative Law. Four points were noted in favor of the lecture method: 1) codified law is "most easily and effectively taught by means of systematic exposition"; 2) attentive students profit from the observation of careful arrangement and presentation by the lecturer, as a model for constructing a legal argument leading to a certain conclusion; 3) "[i]n many young students the auditory memory is better developed than the visual"; and 4) the lecturer benefits from the systematic study and research associated with preparing for lectures....

Active techniques are also advocated in several Colombian works. Edgar Saavedra Rojas, formerly a full-time legal academic and now a Magistrate of the Colombian Supreme Court, recently argued for the utilization of active styles in the teaching of criminal law based on the work of Witker and his colleagues.[131] Saavedra covers a range of active techniques including the active class, the seminar, the hypothetical case method, the use of *situaciones* (fact problems), the "jurisprudential casuistry" method (in which students examine the actual decisions of courts), the clinical method and the "axiological" method, in which the student and teacher critique the provisions of the Criminal Code. Witker's influence can also be seen in two recent general works on legal education and the profession of law in Colombia.

8. BRAZIL

JOAQUIM FALCÃO, LAWYERS IN BRAZIL, in 2 LAWYERS IN SOCIETY: THE CIVIL LAW WORLD 400-01, 403-11 (Richard L. Abel & Philip S.C. Lewis eds. 1988)[a]

One of the first challenges for the new country was to build a national elite capable of administering internal affairs, representing Brazil abroad, and defending it. Until then, this had been the task of the foreign Portuguese elite in both Lisbon and Rio de Janeiro. During the colonial period, the Brazilian elite had been educated in Coimbra (Portugal) or in England. In 1823, therefore, the first legislature discussed the creation of Brazilian universities. In 1827, however, the General Assembly and Emperor Pedro I decided instead to create two law schools: the Olinda Law School in the northeast and the São Paulo Law School in southern Brazil. Both sought not only to prepare lawyers, judges, prosecutors, or attorneys but also to train the political, bureaucratic, and administrative elite of the new country. Since then they have molded

[131] Despite his interest in active teaching, Saavedra, who taught as a *catedrático* at the University of the Andes, did not use the active method in his own teaching due to the preparation time the method requires and his responsibilities on the Supreme Court.

[a] Textual notes are omitted.

deputies, senators, civil servants, ministers, police officers, customs officers, and financiers, building the elite of a sovereign nation.

Brazilian law schools were modeled on the academic program, the readings, the teaching methods, and the subjects of Coimbra Law School. Although directed by the central government (even the required readings were established by the government) and entirely free, only the heirs of the economic and political elite could attend them. From 1827 until approximately 1920, law schools were the principal path toward a higher degree for students not attracted to the study of medicine or engineering or preparing for the church or the military. They offered a liberal education — the humanistic conception of politics, law, and social relations that an educated person would need to perform almost any role in the government of a traditional society....

The Law School

The bachelor of law degree is obtained by graduation from a law school. Public law schools are supported by the federal, state, and municipal governments. If they are directly and totally controlled by the government, they assume the legal form of autarchy; otherwise, they are public foundations, enjoying greater autonomy concerning staff recruitment and salary policies. Those who belong to the private sector may be either secular or religious, for in Brazil the Catholic Church maintains its own schools.

Both public and private law schools may be part of a university or a federation of schools, or they may be independent. In 1980, fifty-six law schools were part of the sixty-five universities (of which forty were public, fourteen religious, and six private but secular). Another ten law schools belonged to one of the fifty federations of schools (of which forty-seven were private and three were public). Finally, sixty-four law schools were independent. Public law schools generally are free or heavily subsidized, requiring students to pay much less than the monthly fees of $20 to $70 charged by private schools. Although educational institutions are not supposed to be profit-oriented, some of the independent law schools behave like business enterprises.... Private enterprise is responsible for most of this education: two-thirds of all law schools and three-fourths of all law students. Some schools place up to 120 students in a single room, indicating the thoroughly commercial character of private law schools.

Although Brazil is a federal republic, composed of twenty-three states and three territories, the regulation and inspection of university education is the responsibility of the federal government. The agency charged with this task is the Federal Council of Education (Conselho Federal de Educação [CFE]), connected to the Ministry of Education (Ministério de Educação e Cultura [MEC]). This Council issues standardized regulations for the entire country with respect to almost all aspects of legal education, such as enrollments, the courses and subjects to be taught, and the minimum requirements for the faculty. It also conducts (or at least should conduct) periodic inspections. Each diploma issued by a law school must be recognized by the Ministry of Education, independently of its registration by the Brazilian Bar Association. In fact, the Council's activities have been purely formal. It rarely reviews the quality of the teaching offered. Most students who have passed the entrance examination for law school will finish the course and receive the degree if they wish. Examinations within law school are not difficult. A few students will drop out for lack of interest or because they have come to prefer some other career. During the recession years of 1979 to 1984 a few dropped out for economic reasons.

In 1828, there were only two government-owned law schools and fewer than seventy students. In 1971 there were approximately ninety law schools, public and private, with some 53,000 students. By 1980, the economic boom of the 1970s had increased these numbers to 130 schools containing 135,026 students, representing 9.0 percent of all university students. Yet, this is far less than the 23.7 percent of all university students who were studying law in 1961.

The factors that stimulated this decrease are multiple and vary historically. They include the appearance of competing professions; the dwindling social and political prestige of lawyers; the poor quality, formalism, and conservatism of legal education; and the saturation of the job market, which directly affects legal fees and salaries.

The number of law students would have decreased more except for four other considerations: the historical and cultural role of law school in preparing not only lawyers but also *bachareis* (law graduates), through a humanistic and unspecialized education with little emphasis on professional skills; the slow expansion of schools of applied, biological, and agricultural sciences, which have been unable to meet the demand; the big gap between the salaries of those holding a university degree and those with only a technical degree; and the fact that the number of university students is below the international average....

In fact, the law schools play three competing, and sometimes conflicting, functions: a *residual* function — absorbing the university students who were not accepted for enrollment in the subjects they preferred; a *historical and cultural* function — providing humanistic and unspecialized training for many different professions; and, finally, a *legal-technical* function — preparing professionals to practice.

Curriculum and Degrees

Law schools may offer four degree programs: bachelor, specialization, master, and doctorate. The first satisfies the prerequisite for enrolling in the Brazilian Bar Association and practicing law. About 90 percent of the law schools offer only the bachelor's degree in morning, afternoon, or evening courses.

Since 1972, every bachelor's degree course must include at least 2,700 class hours during a period of four to seven years (Resolution 162/72, CFE-MEC). The minimum curriculum established by the Federal Council of Education is divided into two parts. The "basic cycle," lasting two semesters, includes introduction to the study of law, economics, sociology, and other subjects not directly related to law. The "professional cycle" includes constitutional, civil, criminal, commercial, and administrative law, civil procedure, practical legal training, and studies of Brazilian problems, plus two elective subjects. Of the nine subjects in the first curriculum in 1827, six remained in the curriculum of 1980. The law schools may add other subjects to complement the curriculum but rarely do so. Cross-registration in other faculties is rare, but allowed. Thus the minimum curriculum also is the maximum curriculum. It represents at least 90 percent of the curriculum adopted by almost all 130 schools. The curriculum of a law school in the Amazon is very similar to that of a school in southern São Paulo or in Caruaru, in the interior of Pernambuco in the Northeast. There is almost no regional, ideological, or market differentiation. This standardization is attributable not only to centralized regulation but also to the demand for unspecialized professional training (reflecting the residual and historical-cultural functions of the law school) and the profit orientation of those two out of three law schools that are private. The Brazilian Bar Association recently has been pressing the Federal Council of Education to disapprove new law schools and to make instruction more modern and practical. In response to these requests, the Council has frozen the number of places and law schools.

The OAB [Ordem dos Advogados do Brasil (Brazilian Bar Association)] battle against formalistic, rhetorical, conservative, and largely unspecialized instruction included a proposal to require practical legal training — an apprenticeship within the law school, the judiciary, or a law office. So far the OAB has failed to implement this reform. Most law schools deem the requirement an unacceptable interference by the bar and one that would increase the cost and administrative complexity of the course. Practical legal training, although required, paradoxically is taught in a "formal and rhetorical way."

The prominence of the residual and the historical-cultural functions over the legal-technical function of the law schools stimulated the development of an informal system of legal education for those who intend to be legal professionals if not necessarily private practitioners. Thus, we may say that the professional socialization of a lawyer results from the confluence of the formal diploma and unsystematic training within an informal system, during and after the law course. A major part of the latter occurs through apprenticeship in law offices for the students enrolled in the law courses. In the past the bar offered a scheme through which students could work as "solicitors" (*solicitadores*) in law firms. Nowadays, any apprenticeship depends solely on the efforts and personal connections of the students, and they are paid little or nothing. Only a small percentage of students, about a tenth, receive this training. Most of them work as secretaries, clerks, or librarians in urban law firms or associations. The nature and extent of training varies from one office to another.

Public agencies, bar associations, isolated professors, unions, and other groups also offer minicourses and seminars in legislation for lawyers. They deal with such fields as corporations, new economic legislation, accounting for lawyers, and tax law — specializations the law school did not cover adequately. The specialization programs require at least 360 hours of work, and they are not a permanent activity of the law schools.

The master's and doctorate programs are permanent activities and are strictly regulated by the Federal Council of Education, which adheres to a

North American model. In 1981 there were twenty master's courses and twelve doctorate courses, which together enrolled 2,183 students. Most are located in federal government law schools in Rio de Janeiro and São Paulo. Like the bachelor's degree courses, they also do not diverge by region or legal doctrine. The curricula are traditional, dividing their subjects into two: public and private law. In the last ten years, however, there have been some significant experiments with legal theory and instructional methodology.

Government educational policy directs graduate courses to integrate instruction with research, but this rarely occurs. In 1982 only 28 percent of the graduate professors were engaged in research. Legal research still is not institutionalized. On the contrary, traditional legal research, which tends to be dogmatic and doctrinal, is performed individually by jurists (important lawyers, law professors, ex-supreme court justices, and chief magistrates) in their law offices and generally is based on their professional experience and legal opinions. In addition, several federal agencies, such as the National Council of Scientific and Technological Development, the Coordinating Agency for the Preparation of Higher Education Personnel (CAPES) and the Financing Agency of Studies and Projects (FINEP), recently have funded juridical research groups, both within the law schools and outside, stimulating research based on social reality and empirical data.

The Law Faculty

Professors of law are not required to have any special training beyond a bachelor of law degree. Since the instruction is rhetorical, generalized, humanistic, and largely unspecialized, every graduate is a potential law professor. This results not only in the poor quality of teaching, which is condemned by all, but also in the debasement of law teacher salaries. Those who work in law schools owned by the federal government follow well-established patterns of recruitment and career progress. However, this is not necessarily true for those working in private law schools. The great majority of professors are paid by the class at the rate of $10 to $20 per hour. Even the privileged few who have part-time (twenty fixed hours per week) or full-time (forty fixed hours per week) positions receive a low monthly salary of $30 to $800. The majority of the latter work in federal government law schools. Therefore, we have the following typical profile of a law professor: a person with only a bachelor of law degree, who offers no individual assistance to his students, does not participate in the administration of the school, and performs his principal professional activities outside the school. Nine out of ten law professors in Rio de Janeiro and São Paulo fit this description. In 1969 there were 2,964 law professors in Brazil, and the law professor-student ratio was 1:26; in 1972 it was 1:23; for the university system as a whole, it was 1:7 and 1:10, respectively. This gap between law schools and the university system still persists.

At least three factors motivate a law graduate to become a law professor:

1. A vocation for instruction and research. These professors constitute a minority. Because of the low salaries, they are obliged to teach about seven class hours per day, in two or three different law schools, which is possible only in the larger cities.

2. The search for professional prestige, which is important to judges and lawyers. A lawyer gains prestige and clients from having the title of law professor. The more important law schools have no difficulty recruiting their professors from among prominent lawyers, judges, and prosecutors. For example, professors represent 11.7 percent of the lawyers heading legal departments in large corporations, who constitute the professional elite in the area of corporate and commercial law.

3. Failure to obtain a position in the job market or the need to supplement an inadequate salary. These generally constitute the faculty of smaller private law schools.

Normally a class takes the form of a lecture and is little different from a class in the University of Coimbra in the seventeenth century. It either concerns a theoretical-speculative issue of legal doctrine or attempts to present a logical-formal description of a statute or a section of a Code. Seminars, debates, case studies, and systematic analyses of legal sentences or contracts are extremely rare. Lectures are based on the text of a "manual," a handbook full of contradictory doctrinal quotations, taken mainly from the European jurists and full of fragmented and sometimes outdated legislation, all mixed up with one or two centuries of Portuguese and Brazilian legal history. It offers a "peculiar" synthesis of all the items required by the Federal Council of Education. Those teachers who have a legal occupation outside the school add unsystematic and generally critical observations on the basis of their professional experience. The dominant testing procedure consists of two or more written examinations per semester, in which the student regurgitates the legal contents of the "manual."

In 1982 there were 240 professors for 1,556 students in the master's and doctorate programs, a ratio of 1:6. According to the more rigorous standards of the Federal Council of Education, these professors should have a master's degree or its equivalent and should teach full time. In 1973 only 21 percent of them taught full time, but by 1982 the proportion had increased to 45 percent. This does not mean that they are exclusively law professors, much less that they devote themselves only to graduate programs. On the contrary, they generally teach on all levels and have another job besides teaching. The instructional methodology is fundamentally the same as for the bachelor's degree, with lectures predominating. However, a greater effort is made to go beyond doctrinal-speculative issues with the help of interdisciplinary perspectives and scientific methodology. A few innovative programs conduct sociojuridical or politicojuridical research.

The Students

We conducted a survey of 29,910 students at twelve law schools in Rio de Janeiro and São Paulo, asking them why they chose to attend law school. The principal motivation for two-thirds of the students was the fact that the law course would help them to pursue *other* professional activities; for another tenth, it was the social and economic prestige of the legal professional. In other words, most students only want to obtain the degree; they are not deeply interested in technical and specialized legal training. Because legal education is regulated by the federal government, these data reflect the situation throughout the nation, which probably has changed very little during the past ten years. If anything, there has been increased tension between those seeking only the degree (the residual and historical-cultural functions of the schools) and the future legal professionals who desire specialized training (the legal-technical function of the law schools)....

In 1968, 6,274 students obtained a bachelor of law degree; by 1973 the number had increased to 15,802. In 1984 the student: professor ratio in federal universities was 7.8:1, but it was 16.6:1 in private institutions. Private law schools flourished in Rio and São Paulo, offering low-quality evening courses and generating substantial profits for their owners.... Students managed to find places in the university but were unable to find employment after graduation. They attributed their plight to their own intellectual and cultural deficiencies (21 percent of Rio students and 26 percent of those in São Paulo) as well as the excessive number of students (31 percent and 37 percent, respectively). In 1961 there were 23,519 students enrolled in law school. In 1980 there were 135,026, most of them urban middle-class beneficiaries of the economic boom....

Since every law graduate (*bacharel*) is potentially a lawyer (free to enter and leave the job market), the excess supply has generated a destructive competition among lawyers. For this reason, the Brazilian Bar Association recently has pressed the Federal Council of Education to limit the opening of new schools and to "professionalize" the bachelor's course.

The social background of law students does not differ greatly from that of university students generally, both in Brazil and abroad. The first graduating class in 1832 included no women students; even in 1950 the proportion was only 3.3 percent; but in 1984, 24.6 percent of law graduates were women.... While 2.0 percent of law professionals were women in 1950, thirty years later this proportion had risen to 20.9 percent. Entry to university legal studies is by examination, which traditionally has included Latin, Portuguese, History, French, and English. Each law school prepared its own entrance examination, although some collaborate today.

As is the case everywhere, students from wealthier families have a better chance of entering a university. In the 1985 entrance examinations in Rio de Janeiro, while only 13.1 percent of the candidates from families with the lowest incomes passed, 26.5 percent of those from families with the highest incomes did so. Recent research shows that, paradoxically, candidates from the higher socioeconomic strata are more successful in obtaining places in the public law schools, which offer a free education of better quality, whereas those from lower strata are compelled to attend private law schools. Even so, the university plays an important role in social mobility. Thus, for example, only 35.3 percent of the parents of the law students in Rio de Janeiro and São Paulo were university graduates and only 32 percent of the parents of students at Recife Law School between 1930 and 1975 had a secondary school education. In less developed states this percentage is even smaller: in Espirito Santo only 18.4 percent of the parents of judges in the interior had a secondary school education.

Since the law schools require only class attendance (to take the examinations each semester, the student must have attended two-thirds of the classes), the majority of students work as well as study — 74.8 percent of those in Rio de Janeiro and São Paulo — in order to pay the tuition. Most work six to eight hours per day in the service sector of the economy in unspecialized administrative jobs. These jobs rarely lead to law jobs. Most students live with their parents. In the past century, by contrast, the few schools were regional and served the elite of the neighboring states. The law schools in Olinda (Recife), São Paulo, and Rio de Janeiro were favored.

In 1981 there were 2,076 law students enrolled in master's programs, of which 62 percent only attended classes and conducted no legal research. Of the 112 students who obtained a master's degree in 1980/81, 61 were teachers. This suggests that the course serves two functions. First, for the great majority of students who are practicing lawyers, the master's program allows specialization: less than 10 percent write the thesis required for the diploma. Second, more than half of the small minority who do write theses are seeking diplomas to advance their careers as law professors.

NOTE ON LATIN AMERICAN LEGAL EDUCATION

Colombia serves as an example of the trends in Latin American legal education.

Table 8.4

Total Number Law Students in Colombia, per 100,000 Population and as a Percentage of University Enrollment, by Year

	1950	1960	1970	1983
Law Students	1,985	4,106	7,998	27,405
Per 100K Population	18	27	38	102
As % of University Students	21	18	9	8

In Table 8.4 one can see that the growth in Colombian law student enrollment between 1950 and 1970 was strong, doubling in each decade. This was significantly moderated in per capita terms, however, since Colombia's population increase was very high. Nevertheless, the major expansion in legal education occurred between 1970 and 1983, when enrollment more than tripled. In 1983 women comprised 45 percent of the students in law schools.

The number of law students in Brazil increased from 24,000 to 53,000 to 135,000 between 1961, 1971, and 1980. As a percentage of all university students, however, they declined from 24 percent to nine percent between 1961 and 1980.

NOTES AND QUESTIONS

1. Is Colombian and Brazilian legal education clearly within the pattern found in continental Europe? What are the significant differences?

2. Should the lecture method — the predominant civil law teaching technique — be replaced or more fully supplemented? What are the arguments pro and con? Is the lecture method likely to be replaced by an alternative?

3. Joaquim Falcão states that Brazilian law schools serve three functions: (1) residual, (2) historical and cultural, and (3) legal-technical. Is this true of other civil law countries? What about law schools in the United States?

4. Since law professors in Italy, Spain, Colombia, and Brazil receive only a minimal salary, why do they make the effort required to teach? Is this structural factor of low salaries likely to support the dominance of the lecture method?

5. The National Autonomous University of Mexico (UNAM) law faculty enrolls about 13,000 students with a teaching staff in 1985 of 568. Of this latter number, only 61 were career professors: 10 emeriti, 25 full time, and 26 half time. Since the faculty is so large, it is divided into 21 colleges organized by subject, for instance social security law. The central law library contains 300,000 volumes, and each of 16 seminars (institutes) has its own library averaging about 3,500 books and periodicals.

See generally Richard C. Maxwell & Marvin S. Goldman, *Mexican Legal Education,* 16 J. Legal Educ. 155 (1963).

6. Compare the statistical profiles of European and Latin American legal education. What are the principal differences or similarities?

7. During a period of high interest in "law and development" in the 1960s and early 1970s a number of U.S. law schools and professors became involved in efforts to enrich and reform legal education in the developing nations. In Latin America the Ford Foundation, the International Legal Center (a Ford spin-off to operate in the field of law and development) and the Agency for International Development of the U.S. Department of State provided support for a variety of programs in Chile (with substantial Stanford Law School involvement), Brazil (Yale, with some Harvard participation), Colombia (Harvard and others), Peru (Wisconsin), and Costa Rica (Stanford and others). The premise of these programs was that reforms in the traditional patterns of legal education would contribute to modernization of the national legal systems and thus to national development. Two of the authors of this book were involved: Professor Merryman primarily in Chile and Professor Clark in Costa Rica. For a brief critical history and assessment of the law and development movement, see John Henry Merryman, *Comparative Law and Social Change: On the Origins, Style, Decline and Revival of the Law and Development Movement,* 25 Am. J. Comp. L. 457 (1977).

8. For an empirical study of legal education in Chile, see Steven Lowenstein, Lawyers, Legal Education, and Development 79-178 (1970).

9. EAST ASIA

NOTE ON EAST ASIAN LEGAL EDUCATION

As in Europe, Latin America and, indeed, every country except the United States and Canada, formal legal education in East Asia also generally begins and ends at the undergraduate level. Typically university law faculties are among the largest in terms of the number of students. Many include political science as well as law, but the basic curriculum usually emphasizes the codes, constitutional and administrative law, and international and comparative law. The content tends to be largely lectures on legal theory with little opportunity for problem-solving. Few law faculties teach the specialized professional courses that constitute the bulk of second- and third-year electives in most American law schools. Japanese law faculties, for example, rarely offer more than a single course or seminar on taxation, securities regulation, environmental protection, or government regulation of business. Based on actual transcripts, the following curricula illustrate the courses taken by representative graduates of leading law faculties in Indonesia, Japan, Taiwan, and Thailand. The greater influence of English and American models in Thailand is evident.

Faculty of Law
University of Indonesia

1. Required University Courses
   - Islamic Religion
   - Pancasira (national ideology)
   - National Resilience
2. Required Law Faculty Courses
   - Principles of Civil Law
   - Principles of Criminal Law
   - Principles of Constitutional Law
   - Principles of Administrative Law
   - Principles of Islamic Law
   - Principles of Adat Law
   - Introduction to the Science of Law
   - Introduction to the Indonesian Legal System
   - Theories of the State
   - Philosophy of Law
   - Man and Culture in Indonesia
   - Introduction to Sociology
   - Babasa Indonesia
   - English Language I and II
   - Dutch I and II
   - Legal Research and Methods I
   - Thesis

Faculty of Law
University of Tokyo

Constitutional Law I and II
Administrative Law I and II
International Law I and II
Civil Law I [General Principles]
Civil Law II [Property]
Civil Law III [Obligations]
Civil Law IV [Family and Succession]
Criminal Law I and II
Political Science
French Law
Science of Public Administration
Public Finance
Comparative Constitutional Law
Commercial Law I
Civil Procedure I
Judicial Administration
Political Process
Social Policy
History of Japanese Political Thought
History of International Politics
Seminar in Civil Law

College of Law, Department of Law
National Taiwan University

Year 1

The Thoughts of Dr. Sun Yat-sen
Chinese
English
Oral-Aural Training in English

Faculty of Law
Chulalongkorn University
(Thailand)

Year 1

Law of Persons
Criminal Law, General Principles
Introduction to Legal Principles
Introduction to Legal Research
Principles of Political Science

College of Law, Department of Law
National Taiwan University

Year 1 (Cont'd)
- General History of China
- Constitution of the Republic of China
- General Principles of Civil Law
- Sociology
- Introduction to the Study of Law

Year 2
- Contemporary History of China
- General Principles of Criminal Law
- Civil Law: Obligations, General
- Civil Law: Things
- Civil Law: Family
- Legal History of China
- International Law
- Seminar on Mainland Chinese Affairs
- Japanese
- Introduction to Anglo-American Law
- Native Plants
- Prisonology

Year 3
- Administrative Law
- Criminal Law: Specific Parts
- Code of Criminal Procedure
- Law of Civil Procedure
- Civil Law: Obligations, Specific Parts
- Company Law
- Law of Bills and Notes
- Insurance Law
- Maritime Law
- Law of Contracts
- Law of Torts
- I-Ching and Life
- Criminological Psychology
- Law of International Private Trade Law
- Taxation, General

Year 4
- Jurisprudence
- Conflict of Laws
- Administrative Law: Specific Parts
- Logic Principles of Criminal Law
- Case Study of Commercial Law
- Law of Patent
- Theory of Criminal Law Interpretation

Faculty of Law
Chulalongkorn University
(Thailand)

Year 1 (Cont'd)
- Thai Legal History
- Logic and Legal Reasoning
- Constitutional Law
- Introduction to Economics
- Property
- Contracts
- Criminal Law I
- Sociology
- Environmental Studies

Year 2
- Obligations I
- Sale, Exchange and Gift
- Loan and Deposit
- Insurance
- Criminal Law II
- Psychology
- Land Law
- Computer Data Processing
- Introduction to Accounting
- Torts and Undue Enrichment
- Obligations II
- Agency and Brokerage
- Family Law

Year 3
- Surety, Mortgage and Pledge
- Negotiable Instruments
- Law of Succession
- Criminal Law III
- Criminology and Penology
- Court Organization Law
- Civil Procedure I and II
- Administrative Law
- Corporations
- Evidence
- Criminal Procedure
- Bankruptcy
- Private International

Year 4
- Real Estate Business Law
- Seminar in Criminal Law
- Taxation Law
- Labor Law
- Copyright and Patents
- Public International Law
- International Economic Law

College of Law, Department of Law National Taiwan University	**Faculty of Law Chulalongkorn University (Thailand)**
Year 4 (Cont'd)	**Year 4 (Cont'd)**
Bankruptcy	Seminar on Civil Law
	Customs Law
	Law of Banking
	Seminar on Public Advocacy
	International Law of the Sea
	Maritime Law
	Law of International Trade

Legal training in most East Asian jurisdictions does not necessarily end, however, with university education. In Japan completion of a two-year apprenticeship program in the Legal Training and Research Institute (LTRI) administered by the Supreme Court is a prerequisite for admission to practice as well as for appointment as either a career judge or procurator. Since 1955 Taiwan has had a similar program for judges and procurators. Since 1951 Thailand, in contrast, has had an apprenticeship program under a bar association-administered Legal Institute, with judges and procurators appointed as in the United Kingdom and the United States from the practicing bar. These institutes and training programs usually include several months' apprenticeship with the courts and prosecutors' offices as well as law firms. They also tend to emphasize practical training in drafting documents related to court proceedings in both civil and criminal cases. In all five East Asian countries studied in this volume, admission to a legal training institute or directly to practice is based on an examination, generally administered by the Ministry of Justice. All tend to be restrictive, with increasing demand to allow more applicants to pass. Japan and South Korea appear to be the most restrictive. In 1991 the enrollment for the Japanese LTRI was increased to 600 for those entering in April 1992 and 700 for those entering in April 1993. The excerpt following this Note by Professor Yasuhei Taniguchi explains the background of this reform.

Table 8.5

Applicants Taking and Passing the Japanese National Legal Examination, by Year

Year	Applicants	Persons Passing Exam and Entering LTRI	Percent Successful Applicants
1949	2,512	265	10.5
1950	2,755	269	9.8
1960	8,302	345	4.2
1970	20,160	507	2.5
1980	28,656	486	1.7
1985	23,855	486	2.0
1990	22,900	499	2.2
1992	23,435	630	2.7

Table 8.6

Initial Positions Taken by Japanese LTRI Graduates, by Year[1]

Graduation Year	Assistant Judges[2]	Public Procurators	Attorneys	Other
1949	72 (1)	44 (1)	18	
1950	106 (1)	54 (1)	78	2
1960	81 (1)	44 (1)	166 (5)	
1970	64 (1)	38	405 (20)	5
1980	64 (5)	50 (5)	336 (21)	4 (1)
1985	52	49	343	3
1990	81	28	376	4
1992	65	50	381	12

[1]The number of women is shown in parentheses for the years 1949 through 1980.
[2]Includes summary court judges.

YASUHEI TANIGUCHI, *SHIHŌ KENSHŪ SHO NI OKERU HŌSŌ KYŌIKU* (LEGAL EDUCATION AT THE LEGAL TRAINING AND RESEARCH INSTITUTE), 25 *Jiyū to seigi* (Liberty and Justice) 7-12 (1974)

I. *Contemporary Problems: Has the Quality of the Institute Changed?*

While the Institute has taken institutional root in the legal culture of Japan in the space of a quarter of a century, the ideas on which the Institute stands and the means by which they are implemented have come into serious question....

What is the "crisis" of the Institute? And what has brought it about? A variety of views are possible by way of answer. The most common is the view that certain politically motivated forces have been behind the change in the quality of the Institute. For my part, I am of the opinion that certain changes surrounding the Institute are more primary. As I see it, the sense of crisis facing the Institute is rooted in the steady, uneventful development of the Institute. Certain contradictions finally surfaced between what made such progress possible and the manner in which the Institute had operated.

Over the years there have been both quantitative and qualitative changes in the Institute. In terms of quantity, there was an increase in enrollment. By the 1950s the number of trainees rose from the initial 250 to some 300, to 500 in the next ten years, reaching nearly 550 more recently. This increase, although not great in absolute terms, had a disproportionately large impact. This fact is significant because it indicates the limits of the legal professions as well as the Institute itself. In other words, it has become clear that further increase in numbers will create strains so long as the present mode of operating the training program is continued. The difficulty of obtaining appropriations for expansion of facilities or increase of the stipends for the trainees is understandable in view of the difficulty of convincing those in political power, who may not understand the problems of the legal professions. But what is more critical is a problem within the legal professions; it is thought that there is no way to expand the teaching staff to meet the increased numbers of trainees. With some 2,100 procurators, at full strength, throughout the nation, it has become quite difficult to provide instruction for nearly half that number of trainees. The difficulty of obtaining lawyer-instructors has been pointed out from inside the bar associations. Consequently, the assignment of two judges, one procurator and two attorneys for a group of about 50 trainees, as has been the characteristic practice at the Institute, could not be continued if there was any further increase in enrollment.

The Institute was designed to provide legal education for the legal professions. And since the number of trainees is necessarily restricted by the total number of legal professionals in the nation, the small professional population precludes any drastic increase in enrollment. Yet pressure to increase enrollment, emphasizing the need for more legal professionals, comes not only from among the legal professions, but also, it should be noted, from lay circles. If that is the case, the Institute is already in a state of crisis from the pressure of numbers. It was against this background that the improvident argument was advanced for a facile solution by separating trainees according to career objectives.

More significant even than the pressure of numbers would appear to be the pressure of "quality." Stated briefly, this relates to the increase in the number of highly qualified persons who seek careers as private attorneys. Around 1955, those who accepted government appointment [as career judges or procurators] and those who were destined to be private attorneys balanced out in number. By 1960 or thereabouts, the increased enrollment resulted in an increase of attorneys, with the absolute number of government appointees and others slightly above a one-to-three ratio. (Incidentally, more graduates accepted government appointments this year [1973] than in any recent year; further developments in this direction deserve attention.) This is a dramatic turnaround, one must say, when one considers that government appointees outnumbered attorneys during the formative years following the establishment of the Institute. In purely numerical terms, it is apparent that the training program turned out to be overwhelmingly for attorneys. The question, however, is not limited to numbers; changes in quality may matter even more. While in the past younger men with talent preferred government appointment, the situation has reversed itself. Many who would have before chosen government positions now aspire to be attorneys, with the courts and procurator offices having difficulty in recruiting....

II. *Background and Outcome*

Clearly, the role of litigation has recently expanded spectacularly. In cases involving labor, pollution, environment, sunlight, consumers and so forth, the courts have gone far beyond relief for individual cases, and indeed have exerted a significant influence on the formulation on national policies. No longer are lawyers the unsung heroes of yesteryear; they are in the foreground of the social scene. In executing the new functions of the courts, lawyers are rendering a vital, if secondary service.... For the first time in Japanese history, lawyers seem to have gained wide public recognition as a profession useful for society. In response to such change, applicants for the Institute too have changed. Lawyering has begun to attract the attention of young people with ambition and ability as a worthwhile occupation, quite apart from the lure of financial gain. These same people, decades earlier, would have streamed into the sector of the growth economy, fanning out to government agencies or private enterprise. Actually, there has been a great increase in the number of individuals taking government law examinations in blithe disregard of prosperity in private enterprise and [the government's] difficulty in recruiting staff; "examinations are all the craze at a time of recession" is now a thing of the past. Also, aspirations for self-employed professions are in part the result of a general revulsion against the advancing tendency toward a bureaucratic society. But what is important is the fact that becoming a lawyer has come to be seen as the most apt means to satisfy such aspirations. One does not have to compare the population of lawyers with that of other countries to see plainly that more lawyers are needed in Japan....

III. *Guiding Principles of Institute Education: From Practical to Theoretical*

As we have seen, the Institute has a near impossible task of having to train two different categories of legal professions by the same approach. They are, to use a somewhat inexact description, a small number of continental-type legal careerists and American-style lawyers many times that number. Any single approach in instruction is bound to favor one group to the neglect of the other; little wonder, then, that from its organization and tradition the Institute stresses the training of judges so that candidates for private practice should come out with a demand for less emphasis on judicial training. Suppose law students in the United States were required to draft decisions day in and day out. They would certainly complain. It is common knowledge that arguments on requisite facts and burden of proof conducted in relation to drafting of decisions in civil actions are useful for attorneys, and should be given proper emphasis (with the parties concerned taking the initiative). If one may be permitted to use the term "the right to education," candidates for private practice do have a right to an appropriate education for their needs. The real condition of training of attorneys not being fully what it should be, it is doubtful that the existing curriculum fully satisfies the need. But then, any overexpansion of training for lawyers would infringe on the rights of the candidates for government appointments, though they are small in number.

The fundamental solution will, of course, be division of the training program. One politician recently made a proposal along the same lines, but the impression is that the legal professions regard this proposal with utter distaste. The three professions must each have an axe to grind, but this is because they all recognize what the Institute has accomplished in its quarter of a century of existence, and hope to realize their own aspirations through the Institute. As a former trainee, I do not agree that the Institute has performed its mission and accordingly do not rule out the possibilities that might open up if the Institute rides out the present crisis — possibilities, in essence, for the unity of the legal profession. If the proposed separation materializes and is made permanent, opportunities for realizing unity would be lost for all time....

Under the Japanese system, legal education begins in the law faculty of the university. The completion of this phase of instruction is verified by the National Legal Examination, and then the student receives further education in the practical aspects of law at the Institute. Law students following this course, however, are very limited in number even in those universities that produce a greater number of successful candidates for the law examination. Accordingly, the issue of what principles should guide education in the law faculties troubled members of the faculty and has been a perennial source of debate. Some say it should basic education oriented toward jurisprudence; others claim it should be basic education leading to a career as a law specialist. In any case, legal education is not conceived as an education in legal professionalism itself. For this reason education in the law faculties of the universities is not directly related to education at the Institute. The National Legal Examination is sometimes viewed in terms of supplementing what university legal education has failed to deliver. Thus education in a law faculty alone is inadequate for moving directly into the Institute program, so the difficulty of the National Law Examination is supposed to provide the student with the opportunity to make up for inadequate grounding in the basics. Nevertheless, as is often pointed out, what happens is that the student, being so exclusively committed to preparing for the examination, still ends up with inadequate knowledge of the basics. As a result, the Institute has to make a fresh start providing an education more appropriate for being a law specialist. This gradually turns the Institute into a professional school along the lines of an American law school. Such observation was voiced as early as 1968. One can assume this trend is inevitable.

NOTES AND QUESTIONS

1. Compare the curricula at the four East Asian law faculties. Which seem most influenced by the pattern in continental Europe? Which most reflect indigenous concerns? Does it still make sense to refer to a civil law tradition that spans Europe, Latin America, and East Asia?

2. In 1986, 163,134 students were enrolled in law and law-and-politics faculties at Japanese colleges and universities. Of this total, 11 percent were women and 87 percent attended private institutions. For the approximately 41,000 new students admitted, there were almost 276,000 applicants. Also in 1986 there were 1,318 law students in master's courses and 856 in doctorate courses.

3. Do the statistics in Tables 8.5 and 8.6 support Professor Taniguchi's analysis of a continuing crisis at the Japanese Legal Training and Research Institute for the 1980s? Does he seem more influenced by the German or American model of legal education?

4. For more on Japanese law training, see Hakaru Abe, *Education of the Legal Profession in Japan,* in Law in Japan: The Legal Order in a Changing

Society 153 (Arthur T. von Mehren ed. 1963); Edward I. Chen, *The National Law Examination of Japan,* 39 J. Leg. Educ. 1 (1989); *id., The Legal Training and Research Institute of Japan,* 22 U. Tol. L. Rev. 975 (1991); Eric A. Feldman, *Mirroring Minds: Recruitment and Promotion in Japan's Law Faculties,* 41 Am. J. Comp. L. 465 (1993).

B. THE LEGAL PROFESSIONS

1. MULTIPLE PROFESSIONS

JOHN HENRY MERRYMAN, THE CIVIL LAW TRADITION: AN INTRODUCTION TO THE LEGAL SYSTEMS OF WESTERN EUROPE AND LATIN AMERICA 101-08 (2d ed. 1985)

Like the divisions of jurisdiction and of law, ... the division of labor among professional lawyers in the civil law world displays characteristics unfamiliar to the common law world, and particularly to those in the United States. Americans usually think of *the* legal profession, of a single entity. To Americans a lawyer, no matter what kind of legal work he happens to be doing at the moment, is still a lawyer. Although many young graduates start out as private attorneys, government lawyers, or members of the legal staffs of corporations, and stay in those positions for life, it is common for them to change from one branch of the profession to another. During his lifetime a lawyer may do a variety of legal jobs. He may spend a year or so as law clerk to a state or federal judge after graduation from law school. He may spend some time in the office of a district attorney or a city attorney, or in the legal office of a state or federal agency; or he may join a corporate law department. He may then move to private practice. If he has a successful career, he may ultimately secure an appointment as a state or federal judge. Americans think it normal for him to move easily from one position to another, and they do not think it necessary for him to have special training for any of these different kinds of work.

Things are different in civil law jurisdictions. There, a choice among a variety of distinct professional careers faces the young law graduate. He can embark on a career as a judge, a public prosecutor, a government lawyer, an advocate, or a notary. He must make this decision early and then live with it. Although it is theoretically possible to move from one of these professions to another, such moves are comparatively rare. The initial choice, once made, tends to be final in the majority of cases. The point of entry into any of these careers is almost always at the bottom, and advancement is frequently as much a function of seniority within the given career as it is of merit. Accumulated experience in another legal career does not give one a head start or any formal advantage in the process of advancement. Consequently the average young lawyer soon finds himself locked into a career from which escape is likely to be too costly to contemplate.

One predictable result is a tendency for the lines that divide one career from another to sharpen. Those involved in one branch of the legal profession come to think of themselves as different from the others. They develop their own expertise, their own career image, their own professional association. Rivalries, jurisdictional problems, and failures of communication between different kinds of lawyers are more likely to occur than they are in the United States, with its single, unified legal profession. England, with its division of the profession into barristers and solicitors, stands a step closer to the civil law model, but still is far from exhibiting the degree of compartmentalization and immobility one generally encounters in the civil law world. Bureaucratization, especially evident in the various governmental legal careers, is measurably greater than in the common law world, where easy lateral mobility among the different branches of the legal profession leads to a quite different mode of entry into and advancement within them.

The tendency of the initial choice of legal career to be final and the resulting sharp separation of each branch of the legal profession from the others combine to produce a number of effects considered undesirable by many civil lawyers. Frequently the career decision is made without an adequate basis for choice, before the young lawyer has been sufficiently exposed to the range of possible legal careers to decide wisely which is the best for him. And the isolation of those in one career from the others, the tendency to identify with only one set of professional interests and functions, encourages a limiting narrowness of attitude and a Balkanization of the legal professions. These are among the reasons why, in certain nations, law graduates are required to undergo a period of practical training, in which they must participate for designated periods in the work of the judiciary, of government lawyers, and of private practice before they can be admitted to any legal career. This institution is most fully developed in Germany, where the law graduate has to spend two ... years (called the *Referendarzeit*) in such a practical training program following his university legal education.

The judiciary provides an obvious and interesting example of the phenomena we are describing. On graduation from law school (or following the period of practical training, where required) the student who wishes to become a judge immediately applies for admission to the judiciary; if selected (often on the basis of a competitive examination), he enters at the bottom of the profession. In a few nations he will attend a special school for judges, but in most he will soon find himself assigned to the lowest in the hierarchy of courts in a remote part of the country. As the result of some combination of seniority and demonstrated merit, he will gradually rise in the judicial hierarchy to more desirable and prestigious judicial positions, and eventually retire. Normally he will compete for desirable positions only against other members of the judiciary. Although appointment to positions on the highest court — a supreme court of cassation or its equivalent — may in theory be open to distinguished practicing lawyers or professors, such appointments are rare. The highest courts, like the lower courts, are likely to be manned exclusively by those who have risen within the judicial career service. The typical judge will never have practiced law or have served in any other branch of the legal profession, except possibly during required practical training following graduation from the university. He will tend to restrict his professional and social contacts to other judges. He will see the law solely from the judge's point of view. He will be a specialist.

The public prosecutor is also a civil servant, and, typically, he has two principal functions. The first is to act as prosecutor in criminal actions, preparing and presenting the state's cases against the accused before a court. In this sense the public prosecutor is like a district attorney in a typical American state. His second principal function, however, is quite different; he is called on to represent the public interest in judicial proceedings between private individuals. Thus he may have the power to intervene, even at the trial level, in a variety of actions of the sort ordinarily considered to be private law matters, involving only the interests of the parties. He may also be required by law to intervene in other matters at the trial level, typically actions involving personal status and family relationships. Finally, in some nations, he may be required to appear and to present his own independent view of the proper interpretation and application of the law in actions before the highest ordinary courts. The theory is that a primary function of such courts is the correct interpretation and application of the law, that parties to cases cannot always be expected to present all the arguments, and that the judges need the assistance of a public prosecutor to assure that an impartial view, in the interest of the law, is presented.

The young university law graduate who wishes to become a public prosecutor ordinarily takes the state examination for this career shortly after he leaves the university or completes his practical training; if successful, he enters at the bottom of the service and begins a lifetime career in it. Recently there has been a tendency in civil law jurisdictions toward "judicialization" of the public prosecutor service, the idea being that since prosecutors perform quasi-judicial functions, they ought to have something of the independence and security of tenure that is given judges. This trend has reached an advanced stage in several nations, most prominently Italy, where the office of public prosecutor has been made a part of the judiciary. However, the career of judge and that of public prosecutor continue even in these nations to be separate careers within the judiciary; although the trend ultimately may be toward a merger of the two functions, this has not yet taken place. In particular, the relationship between the public prosecutor and the ministry of justice, which exercises authority over his work, continues to be quite different from the relationship of the judge to that ministry. Judicialization of the office of public prosecutor has, however, tended to encourage mobility between the judicial and prosecutorial professions.

In some civil law jurisdictions there is no general career of government lawyer; individual government offices and agencies have their own legal staffs, but appointment, advancement, salary, working conditions and benefits may vary widely from one agency to another. The lawyer works for a given agency or office and identifies with it, rather than, more generally, with a corps of government lawyers. In other countries, there is an office of government attorneys that provides legal services for all state agencies. Even in the former case, appointment and advancement are bureaucratized and regularized. And in either case the difficulty of lateral movement to another branch of the profession tends to fix the government lawyer in his career. As with the judicial service and the public prosecutor service, the student who wishes to become a government lawyer takes the state examination after he completes his legal education and practical training, and enters that service at the bottom. Normally he stays with it for life.

The advocate is the closest thing one finds in the civil law to the attorney-at-law in the United States. Divisions of this profession into subspecialties (e.g. the French *avocat* and *avoué*; the Italian *avvocato* and *procuratore*) still survive in a few nations, but are rapidly losing their significance. The advocate meets with and advises clients and represents them in court. He may also become involved in helping them plan their business and property affairs. He will be a product of a university law school and, typically, of a period of apprenticeship in the office of an experienced lawyer. He will normally practice in a law office in which he is the only senior lawyer, with one or two junior attorneys associated with him. Although law firms resembling those in the United States are beginning to appear more often in major cities in the civil law world, the general rule still is that of the individual law office; indeed, in some countries partnerships for the practice of law are still forbidden. Frequently there are similar restrictions on the development of corporate law departments or similar "house counsel" arrangements. This kind of restriction is the product of a traditional ideal of the lawyer as a totally independent person who is free to accept or reject clients and who makes his own decisions about how the client's affairs should be handled. However, there is a growing trend toward evasion of such restrictions, so it is not uncommon to find groups of lawyers practicing together in what look like partnerships or corporate law departments in a jurisdiction in which such arrangements appear to be forbidden by statute or by regulation of the bar association. Generally, all practicing advocates must be members of a bar association, which frequently is officially recognized and has the authority to establish rules governing the practice of the profession, including fee schedules. As in the United States and elsewhere, members of the practicing bar are likely to become involved in politics and to move into high public office. Although the matter varies from nation to nation, in many civil law countries the percentage of high public officials who began their careers as practicing lawyers is as high or higher than is the case in the United States.

If the civil law advocate closely resembles our practicing lawyer, any similarity between the civil law notary and the notary public in common law countries is only superficial. The historical origins of the civil law notary and the common law notary public are the same, but the two occupations have developed along very different lines. Our notary public is a person of very slight importance. The civil law notary is a person of considerable importance. The notary in the typical civil law country serves three principal functions. First, he drafts important legal instruments, such as wills, corporate charters, conveyances of land, and contracts. Although advocates sometimes get involved in drafting instruments, the notary continues to do most of this work in civil law nations. (In spite of the notary's established position in this field, however, there is some tension between advocates and notaries over jurisdictional matters.) Second, the notary authenticates instruments. An authenticated instrument (called everywhere in the civil law world a "public act") has special evidentiary effects: it conclusively establishes that the instrument itself is genuine and that what it recites accurately represents what the parties said and what the notary saw and heard. Evidence that contradicts statements in a public act is not admissible in an ordinary judicial proceeding. One who wishes to attack the authenticity of a public act must institute a special action for the purpose, and such an action is rarely brought. Third, the notary acts as a kind of public record office. He is required to retain the original of every instrument he prepares and furnish authenticated copies on request. An authenticated copy usually has the same evidentiary value as the original.

Notaries are usually given quasi-monopolies. A typical civil law nation will be divided into notarial districts, and in each district a limited number of notaries will have exclusive competence. Unlike advocates, who are free to refuse to serve a client, the notary must serve all comers. This, added to his functions as record office and his monopoly position, tends to make him a public as well as private functionary. Access to the profession of notary is difficult because the number of notarial offices is quite limited. Candidates for notarial positions must ordinarily be graduates of university law schools and must serve an apprenticeship in a notary's office. Typically, aspirants for such positions will take a national examination and, if successful, will be appointed to a vacancy when it occurs, although in some nations the successful aspirant still must purchase the "office" from the owner. Ordinarily there will be a national notaries organization that will serve the same sort of functions for notaries as the national bar association serves for advocates and other organizations for judges, prosecutors, and government lawyers.

We come finally to the academic lawyer, who teaches in the law schools and writes the doctrine that ... strongly influences all aspects of the legal process in the civil law tradition. He is the inheritor of the tradition of the Roman jurisconsult and of the medieval scholar, whose opinions, at some periods in the history of the civil law tradition, have had formal authority to bind judges. Formal authority aside, the academic lawyer is generally viewed as the person who does the fundamental thinking for the entire legal profession. His ideas, as expressed in books and articles, and his opinions on specific legal questions raised in litigation or lawmaking, particularly in the areas covered by the basic codes, are of substantially greater importance than the work of academic lawyers in the common law world.

It is not easy to become a professor in a civil law university. The road to appointment to a vacant chair is long, arduous, and full of hazards. The young aspirant to an academic career attaches himself to a professor as an assistant, sometimes with pay and sometimes without. Eventually, after meeting certain more or less formal requirements and publishing a book, he will take a state examination for admission to the category of "private-docent." If he receives this title, he is considered to be qualified for an academic post. When a chair becomes vacant, he will compete for it against other private-docents and, if the post is a desirable one, against professors who hold less prestigious chairs. Throughout this process his progress may depend as much on the influence of the professor to whom he has attached himself as on his demonstrated ability as a scholar. This system gives the professor great power over those who have attached themselves to him and makes them heavily dependent on him for their careers. The result is an academic world composed of professors surrounded by retinues of assistants. These assistants are expected to think and work along the same lines as the professor, and thus "schools of thought" are established and grow. Doctrinal, as well as personal, loyalty is expected by the professor, whose power over the assistant's career enables him to demand it.

The uncertainty of success in pursuit of a professorship is so great that few can afford to gamble exclusively on it. In addition, in many civil law nations professors are not expected to spend all, or even a major portion, of their time at the law school. In Latin America, in particular, their rates of compensation reflect this assumption; they are by any standard extremely low. The formal obligations of the professor are to lecture his classes a few hours a week and to give examinations (with the help of his assistants) two or three times a year. He is not paid enough for this to live well, and he consequently divides most of his time between another legal career — usually in practice, in the judiciary, or in public office — and his own and assistants' doctrinal writing. While professors are full-time teacher-scholars in some parts of the civil law world, such as Germany, these are exceptions to the general rule. The trend is in the direction of full time, but it is still only a trend.

Thus an aspirant to an academic position customarily embarks on an additional legal career, both as a hedge against possible failure in the academic world and as an additional source of income, even if he is successful in the competition for a chair. The professor is not full-time and is not expected to be. In the usual case he is also a practicing lawyer, and the prestige of his title as professor may be of most importance to him because of the business it will bring to his law office. An advocate with the title of professor will attract important clients and will be called upon to prepare opinions on legal questions by other lawyers (and also by judges) and be paid for them.

The tendency of the law professor also to be a practicing lawyer produces what appears to common lawyers to be a curious sort of professional schizophrenia. As a lawyer, he will be pragmatic, concrete, and result-oriented. He will follow the problem where it leads him, regardless of boundaries between fields of the law. He will be fact-conscious. He will seek and cite judicial decisions. He will be a tough, partisan advocate. As a professor, he will write and teach in the prevailing doctrinal style, working in the central tradition of legal science. Both his writing and his teaching will prominently display the academic characteristics typical of legal scholarship in the civil law world, and he may even exaggerate such characteristics to overcompensate because he is also a practicing lawyer. He becomes aggressively academic, as a kind of reaction against his practical work as advocate. His life is divided into separate halves, and he adopts a different professional personality for each.

2. AN INITIAL COMPARISON

DAVID S. CLARK, THE LEGAL PROFESSION IN COMPARATIVE PERSPECTIVE: GROWTH AND SPECIALIZATION, 30 American Journal of Comparative Law 163, 166-69 (Supp. 1982)

Merryman argues that the distinction between a unified legal profession in the United States and fragmented civil law legal professions both reflects and reinforces more fundamental differences between the two legal traditions, particularly in regard to the role of a judge. If the ideology of the French Revolution, and its reaction against the lawmaking excesses of the *parlementaires,* along with divisions traceable to the Roman legal professions, still influence modern civil law jurisdictions, what impact do external forces from the political and economic structure have on their legal professions? Table 8.7 presents information on the major divisions of the legal profession in the United States, Germany, Chile and Colombia.

Table 8.7

Percentage Distribution of Lawyers in the United States, Germany, Chile, and Colombia, by Position

	United States (1970)	Germany (1975)	Chile (1968)	Colombia (1974)
Private practice	73	33	23	42
Corporate counsel (or executive)	11	12	25	21
Government attorney (or administrator)	11	38	36	20
Judge (or staff)	3	17	15	16
TOTAL LAWYERS	355,242	85,000	3,911	
Per 100,000 population	174	137	42	

From Table 8.7, the relative size of a legal profession does not appear to be associated with whether it belongs to the civil law or common law tradition. Thus, the difference between the two civil law examples — Germany and Chile — is much greater (137 lawyers versus 42 lawyers per 100,000 inhabitants) than the difference between Germany and the United States (137 lawyers versus 174 lawyers per 100,000 inhabitants). The relative size of a nation's legal profession, on the other hand, correlates more closely with the level of economic development. This follows Weber's observation on the importance of law to industrial capitalism, and holds when we rank order our three nations according to the strength of their economy.

When we view the four occupational divisions in Table 8.7, Merryman's observation about a unified legal profession in the United States seems persuasive because 73 percent of the legal profession is found in one category: private practice. The comparable figure for the three civil law nations is less than half this in Germany and Chile, and only 42 percent in Colombia. In addition, there is irony in the fact that in the United States — where the judge is considered a protagonist in innovatively interpreting and developing the law — only three percent of the legal profession works in the judiciary. Alternatively, the civil law judge is relegated a minor role which excludes the creative formulation of policy. He applies rules made by others; his work is routine; and frequently the judicial task is given to young, inexperienced law graduates. What seems to be an unattractive career occupies from 15 to 17 percent of the legal profession in our civil law nations.

Does this mean that factors internal to the civil law and common law traditions tend to dictate the division of the legal profession? Perhaps partially. But societal forces are also significant. Germany, for instance, has the highest percentage of lawyers employed by the government (with 38 percent). In Dahrendorf's terminology, this would appear to reflect a preference for the plan as a legal mechanism to achieve social integration.[a] During the 1960s, in fact, approximately 70 percent of general administrative positions in the German government were filled by lawyers. Most government lawyers act in such an administrative capacity rather than as legal specialists. In the United States at the other extreme, only 11 percent of the legal profession works for the government in a nonjudicial capacity. The market model is dominant, as reflected by the high percentage of lawyers in private practice. The two Latin American nations are at intermediate positions in regard to the mix of attorneys in government service or private practice, with Colombia closer to the American situation. It is interesting to note that the dominance in Latin America of foreign corporate investment and the emergence of local corporate control over indigenous capital translates into the two highest percentages of lawyers in the business and corporate sector.

3. A CURRENT COMPARISON

DAVID S. CLARK, THE ORGANIZATION AND SOCIAL STATUS OF LAWYERS, in IXth WORLD CONFERENCE ON PROCEDURAL LAW: GENERAL REPORTS 254, 275, 277-79 (1991)

In 1990 the reporting countries had the following number of attorneys in private practice, listed in Table 8.8 as a total and then per 100,000 population to serve as a basis for comparison.

Table 8.8

Number of Lawyers in Private Practice (1990), per 100,000 Population and by Country

	Number of Attorneys	Attorneys per 100,000 Population
Common Law Countries		
United States[a]	460,200	185
New Zealand	4,700	138
Canada[b]	32,500	124
Civil Law Countries		
West Germany	54,000	89
Italy	45,600	79
Venezuela[c]	12,600	65
France[d]	27,700	49
Turkey	23,000	42
The Netherlands	6,000	41

a For 1985.
b For 1982, including Quebec notaries.
c About 40 percent of the 31,400 lawyers in all professions are in private practice.
d For 1983, including 7,000 notaries and 4,300 conseils juridiques.

a R. Dahrendorf, *Market and Plan: Two Types of Rationality,* in Essays in the Theory of Society 215 (1968).

The [nine] countries reporting statistics can be divided into [two] groups for analysis. First, the common law nations have the largest number of attorneys in private practice, ranging from 124 per 100,000 population in Canada and 138 in New Zealand to 185 in the United States. The United States is usually considered to have the most lawyers of any country in the world, in both absolute and relative terms. Several factors may account for the existence of a large bar in common law nations. One, the emphasis in sources of law on judge-made rules leads to a proliferation of legal materials that makes resolution of legal issues complex and time consuming. In civil law nations, by contrast, codes and scholarly treatises are efficient organizing tools for quick solution of most legal problems. Two, the common law system of procedure puts a heavy burden on attorneys to discover the facts in a case and even to brief legal issues for the judge. Civil law countries, alternatively, staff the judiciary and prosecutor offices more fully so that the ratio of judges to attorneys is much higher. In this sense, common law countries have a more privatized judicial procedure. Three, many common law nations (Canada and the United States here) are federal in political structure, further complicating legal analysis and stimulating demand for more attorneys.

Second, civil law countries have significantly fewer attorneys per 100,000 inhabitants, ranging from 41 in The Netherlands to 89 in former West Germany. This range in itself is substantial and is explained partly by the much greater propensity to litigate all types of disputes (private, administrative, and criminal) in West Germany compared to The Netherlands. It is interesting to note that, within the civil law group in Table 8.8, the level of national socioeconomic development does not appear to be a determinative factor explaining the number of attorneys....

Table 8.9 supports part of the analysis above, distinguishing between common law and civil law countries, by picking an important representative from each tradition. In the United States the entire legal profession is more highly privatized than in former West Germany, with only 13 percent of the profession in the U.S. serving as judges or working as government lawyers compared to 44 percent in West Germany. The ratio of judges to attorneys in the two countries also shows the much greater role in Germany that judges play to make the procedural system function properly: one judge for 2.8 attorneys in Germany compared to one judge for 18.5 attorneys in the United States.

Table 8.9

Number and Percentage of Lawyers in Germany and the United States (1985), by Type

	West Germany		United States	
	Number	Percent	Number	Percent
Judges	17,000	(15)	21,700	(4)
Government Lawyers	33,600	(29)	53,000	(9)
Attorneys (and Notaries)	48,300	(42)	460,200	(74)

	West Germany		United States	
	Number	Percent	Number	Percent
Corporate Lawyers	15,000	(13)	76,600	(12)
Law Teachers	2,000	(2)	7,300	(1)
TOTAL LAWYERS	115,900		618,800	
Per 100,000 Population	190		249	

New Zealand illustrates the common law pattern in an even more striking fashion. Of 5,214 members of the greater legal profession, 4,654 are barristers or solicitors (89 percent), while only 138 are judges (three percent). The remaining categories are 240 government lawyers (five percent), 149 corporate house counsel (three percent), and 33 law teachers (one percent).

NOTES AND QUESTIONS

1. Why is mobility among the various law jobs easier in the United States than in a civil law country?

2. How is a typical European judge likely to be different than an American judge?

3. What conception of law or legal process underlies the use of public prosecutors (state procurators or attorneys) to represent the public interest in judicial proceedings between private individuals?

4. The roles of advocate, corporate counsel, and government lawyer share many similarities between the United States and civil law nations. What is distinct, however, is the structural element of the American law firm. Why have large law firms been slow to develop in Europe, Latin America, and East Asia? Will the economics of global law practice stimulate the transplantation of American-style law firms?

5. Civil law notaries are quasi-governmental officials since they serve a number of public functions. Who serves the private and public functions of a notary in the United States?

6. Why do civilian law professors, successors to the Roman jurisconsults, typically teach only part time and receive low pay in some European countries and in most of Latin America? Is it possible to maintain the role of the scholar in the civil law tradition or does this simply shift the burden of maintaining doctrinal excellence to those countries with full-time, well-paid law professors?

7. How might a country's political and economic structure influence the size and major divisions of its legal profession? What role does the civil law tradition itself play? Are other historical or social factors likely to be relevant? We will consider the interesting case of Japan *infra* subsection B.9 of this chapter.

4. FRANCE

ANNE BOIGEOL, THE FRENCH BAR: THE DIFFICULTIES OF UNIFYING A DIVIDED PROFESSION, in 2 LAWYERS IN SOCIETY: THE CIVIL LAW WORLD 258, 259-60, 262-68 (Richard L. Abel & Philip S.C. Lewis eds. 1988)[a]

The Lawyer: A Jurist Among Others

The diversity observed among different legal professions pertains not only to different functions but also to different professional statuses. In this respect, one might distinguish among different legal professionals according to whether they receive a salary from an employer under the terms of a work contract. The first category of salaried professionals are those paid by the state — the magistrates (*magistrats*) — including both the judges (*juges*) who render decisions and the prosecutors (*procureurs*) who defend society and ask the judges to apply the law. Since 1965 the clerks of the court (*greffiers*), who assist the judge in administering the court, have been members of this salaried group. Salaried legal professionals in the private sector include those employed in offices of house counsel of corporations and insurance companies (*juristes d'entreprise*) and the notary clerks (*clercs de notaires*). Nonsalaried legal professionals practice as liberal professionals, the significance of which will be discussed below. Among them are the lawyers (*avocats*), the legal counselors who give advice, draft legal documents, and represent clients before administrative agencies and the commercial court (*conseils juridiques*), and a certain number of professionals who are also ministerial officers, which means that they enjoy a monopoly, in exchange for which they may not refuse their assistance to those who seek it. This last group includes the solicitors of the appeals court (*avoués*), who advise litigants before this court and draft the written documents, and the lawyers (*avocats*) of the Conseil d'Etat and the Cour de Cassation (French equivalents of the Supreme Court), whose role is to argue and to conduct the case before the high courts. Certain ministerial officers also are public officials in that they exercise state power. This is true of the notaries (*notaires*), whose special task is to authenticate documents that individuals either desire to submit to them or are required to do so, the bailiffs (*huissiers de justice*), who are responsible for notifying individuals of proceedings in which they are involved and for executing judicial decisions, and the clerks (*greffiers*) of the commercial courts.

Ministerial officers have a position inherited directly from the Old Regime. Prior to the French Revolution of 1789, the king sold offices responsible for public functions, including juridical and judicial duties (but excluding the position of avocat). These positions had become venal: they could be sold or bequeathed, like property. Notaries, bailiffs, clerks of the court, and magistrates bought their "position" or "office." The Revolution abolished venal offices, and magistrates were compensated for the loss. At first they were elected; after 1800, they were appointed by the government, which paid them. However, this hardly changed the situation of the other legal professions. In fact, bailiffs, clerks of the court, and notaries had the exclusive power to

[a] Textual notes are omitted.

perform certain legal procedures and therefore had a guaranteed clientele, which itself gave value to the position. After the Revolution, the titles of notary, bailiff, and clerk of the court were taken off the market, but the office-holder obtained the right to pass his title to his successor. Only the state could confer the title, but it generally conferred it on the person recommended by the former office-holder. The right to pass on one's title, therefore, acquired a value that replaced the price of the office. This system remains in effect today for notaries, bailiffs, and clerks of the commercial courts, solicitors of the appeals courts, and lawyers of the Conseil d'Etat and the Cour de Cassation.

This mode of operation makes these professions particularly inaccessible. The number of positions is restricted by a quota (numerus clausus). Only the state can decide to create or eliminate offices. As a rule, an office is abolished when there no longer is a candidate for the position. Thus, the decrease in the number of offices held by notaries and bailiffs corresponds to the elimination of offices located in rural areas or small towns. In contrast, the relatively small number of offices at the top of the legal pyramid (solicitors of the appeals courts, lawyers of the Conseil d'Etat and of the Cour de Cassation) or in particular sectors (clerks of the commercial courts) remains relatively stable. The most remarkable case is that of the lawyers of the Conseil d'Etat and the Cour de Cassation, whose number has remained at sixty since 1817! However, despite the restriction on the number of *posts*, a rise in the number of *professionals* is observed in all the legal professions. Whereas the office-holder once had to be a physical person, ministerial officers now may join together into a professional civil society, according to a law passed in 1966. Thus, it is the corporation which holds the office or title. This new form of responding to the demands of a more collective professional practice has permitted some expansion of recruitment. Nevertheless, access remains very difficult. Aside from the obvious financial requisites, the acquisition of a post is contingent on the completion of an assistantship, success in an examination, and, in most cases, a university degree....

Lawyers: An Activity in the Process of Being Redefined

Until 1971, when a litigant wished to initiate a legal proceeding (e.g., divorce), it was necessary to engage the services of two professionals: the solicitor (avoué), who would advise the client, and the lawyer, who would argue the case in court. The solicitor was responsible both for managing the different stages of the case and for informing the magistrates in writing of the client's claims; the solicitor acted in the name of the client. Lawyers, in contrast, spoke only in their own names, and what they said did not implicate their clients. Until the end of the nineteenth century, these two professions had exclusive rights of access to the judicial forum.

At the beginning of the twentieth century, the lawyers, who had a monopoly of rights of audience before the courts, allowed other occupations to intrude, which later were to become competitors in the areas of business and labor law. "The lawyers of the upper bourgeoisie considered that they could not appear before the inferior jurisdictions, such as the commercial court and the *conseil des prud'hommes* [a body that hears labor disputes] or justices of the peace [whose jurisdiction is petty disputes and misdemeanors].” Occupations emerged whose members filled the vacancy left by the bourgeois lawyers. The agréé of the commercial courts is an example.... This profession, which arose de facto, obtained legal status in 1941 and ultimately was integrated into the new profession of lawyer in 1971. In other instances, nonprofessionals acted in the absence of the auxiliaries of justice — an example is trade union delegates before the conseil des prud'hommes. Finally, the bar's hostility toward lawyers who engaged in counseling rather than advocacy and the fact that lawyers long had preferred to remain aloof from economic life created conditions favorable to the development of a new professional category, the legal advisors (conseils juridiques). This profession, which was barely regulated, catered to a market that turned out to be very important: advising the economic and financial world.

After World War II, this situation began to worry some lawyers, who found that the narrow judicial market did not offer sufficient scope for their energies and who decried the competition of an unregulated profession like the legal advisors. In 1952 five members of Parliament, who also were lawyers, drafted a bill to establish a monopoly of legal counseling for the benefit of the lawyers and several of the organized legal professions (law professors, notaries, and solicitors) but excluding legal advisors....

A decade later, when it had proved impossible to prevent legal advisors from giving consultations, the Association nationale des avocats (ANA) proposed to incorporate them, with certain conditions, into the "Great Profession" modeled after that of the American lawyer. The ANA aimed to regroup the entire body of legal and judicial professions: solicitors, lawyers, agréés of the commercial courts, and legal advisors. Notaries were excluded because they had been delegated "state authority which they enjoy in the authentication of legal documents, such delegation of state power being incompatible with the principle of absolute independence which the larger profession had to protect in its dealings with the state."

In place of the "excessive complexity" arising from the redistribution of tasks to several professions, the "anarchy of structures," the resulting "feeling of insecurity" on the part of the litigant, and the "artisanal" nature of work practices, a single "judicial and juridical" profession of a "liberal" nature was proposed, which would enjoy a broad monopoly....

This attempt to establish a great profession failed in part during the parliamentary debates. The outcome was the fruit of many compromises: the new profession of lawyer excluded the legal advisors but did not gain a monopoly on consultation, which was to remain completely open....

[T]he hostility of a large part of the organized bar toward the plan to incorporate legal advisors into the new profession certainly had something to do with the failure of the project.

In defining the new profession of lawyer, the reform of 1971 eliminated certain other professions — both the agréés of the commercial courts and the solicitors of the lower courts (*première instance*) — although the solicitors of the appeals courts were preserved. Since then, lawyers have had "a monopoly on representation before the courts in those areas formerly reserved to solicitors before the reform, the monopoly in principle on pleading, [and they] give legal consultations together with other professionals, notably the legal advisors and the notaries.... Finally, the lawyer draws up legal documents except for those within the monopoly of the notaries." Insofar as representation before the courts is concerned, the lawyer is subject to the rule of territoriality, as solicitors used to be: that is, lawyers may only represent clients before the court to which they are attached through membership in the bar. In contrast, the lawyer is not subject to any territorial limit whatsoever in pleading.... The "great profession," which was to control and oversee the totality of legal activities, was far from being realized.

Together with the traditional professions already mentioned (solicitors of the appeals courts, notaries, and bailiffs), the lawyers coexist with the legal advisors, whose title alone is regulated by the Law of 31 December 1971. In order to be included in the list of legal advisors, a candidate must meet certain standards of morality and hold university degrees, almost the same as the requirements for lawyers. Less burdened by the weight of tradition, this profession recognizes three fields of specialization: fiscal, social, and corporate law.

Unlike the legal advisor, the French lawyer does not officially have a legal specialty. In fact, however, specialization does exist and even structures the profession....

Sociography of Lawyers

With more than 15,000 members, lawyers constitute the largest group of legal professionals, not counting unorganized professionals such as house counsel for corporations and insurance companies (for whom no figures are available). The following numbers were recorded for 1983:

15,757	lawyers
80	lawyers at the Conseil d'Etat and the Cour de Cassation
4,264	legal advisors
7,001	notaries
288	solicitors at the courts of appeals
2,796	bailiffs
5,640	magistrates

Had the great profession envisioned in 1971 been realized, it would have included approximately 20,000 members.

The number of lawyers has grown considerably in the recent past, nearly doubling in ten years, from 8,307 in 1973 to 15,757 in 1983. This profession, like others, has been affected by the demographic upsurge of the postwar years and invaded, "as a result of the democratization of higher education, by a mass of young graduates." The rapid increase had two causes: entrance to the profession was relatively easy, and the profession was responding to the demands of greater judicial activity. In spite of this increase, the [number of lawyers per 100,000 population] remains relatively [low at 28] when compared to the ratios of neighboring countries having similar legal systems: [71] in Belgium, [77] in Italy, and [100] in Spain.

Lawyers may practice in a traditional individualist fashion or more collectively, sharing part or all of the means of production. This is where the notion of a liberal profession acts as a constraint. Lawyers have had to reconcile economic realities with the freedom required for professional practice. The difficult dialectic of these two imperatives has generated a broad spectrum of legal solutions that can be divided into two categories: logistical groups and associative groups. In the first, lawyers share common expenditures, which may be more or less substantial, but not fees. This participation may be limited to office-sharing arrangements (*cabinet groupé*) or extended to the collective management of offices and administration, known as a partnership of means. Associative groups, or partnerships, imply real professional cooperation. When this cooperation is limited, the group is an *association* in the strict sense of the term. Professional cooperation is loose enough to preserve the individuality of each participant (all participants retain their own fees) but strong enough to prevent members from representing opposing parties. When such cooperation is close, the group is considered a *civil professional society* or a corporation. The client no longer deals with a single lawyer but with a corporate body represented by one of its members. The lawyers share their fees according to their previous agreement. This last form of organization may contain the germ of the degeneration of liberal practice. This form of practice, which satisfies the demands of economic rationality and functional specialization, also has been favored by activist lawyers, for whom common ownership and profit-sharing have positive social and professional significance. On the whole, legal professionals remain attached to a mode of operation that preserves at least a minimum of liberal practice. In 1981, 84 percent of lawyers still practiced individually. Nonetheless, collective practice is on the increase.... [I]n Paris in 1981, there were:

135 office-sharing arrangements containing 338 lawyers
71 partnerships of means containing 262 lawyers
182 associations containing 534 lawyers
117 civil professional societies containing 367 lawyers

Thus, 30 percent of Parisian lawyers practice in some form of collectivity....

The distribution of lawyers throughout France is very uneven, since the city of Paris alone contains more than a third (about 36 percent, or 5,542 practitioners in 1983). Economic and political centralization, which are unusually pronounced in France, account for the relative overdevelopment of the Paris Bar.

NOTE ON THE NEW FRENCH *AVOCAT*

France up to 1971 certainly had one of the world's most complicated and fragmented legal professions, what Tang Lê accurately described as "a prisoner of its glorious past."[a] The Law of 31 December 1971, which merged the three professions of *avocat, agréé,* and *avoué près les tribunaux de grand instance,* was known as the small reform. It was a compromise between the

[a] Tang Thi Thanh Trai Lê, *The French Legal Profession: A Prisoner of Its Glorious Past?,* 15 Cornell Int'l L.J. 63 (1982).

great reform favored by the *Association nationale des avocats* — which would also have merged the *conseils juridiques* — and many members of the legal professions who rejected both the small and great reforms and instead preferred improvements in the court system. The small reform, however, did begin regulation of the *conseils juridiques.*

Since 1992 two Laws of 31 December 1990 (No. 90-1258 and No. 90-1259) have completed the great reform by eliminating the distinction between *avocats* and *conseils juridiques*. The "new" *avocat* is more broadly empowered to serve her client, including as house counsel, with a full range of advice, document services, and litigation support. The professions of notary and appellate *avoué* and *avocat,* however, remain intact. Support for the 1990 reform from *avocats* came from the visible success of foreign law firms in Paris and the imminence of the European single market in 1992. The new law is designed to encourage firms to grow larger, to become more specialized and competitive, and to aim at a wider clientele.

The two new statutes came into force in 1992. Law No. 1259 automatically admits all existing *avocats* and *conseils juridiques* to the new profession of *avocat.* Members of a European Union legal profession and those from a nation providing reciprocal access as of 1 January 1992 do not have to take the CAPA examination, but will be able to apply for French bar admission before 1 January 1994 if they practiced law (drafting documents and providing legal advice) continuously for three years, including 18 months in France. The statute for the first time recognizes *avocat* specialization, based on at least two years' practice and passage of a test from a regional professional training center.

Law No. 1258 permits *avocats* and *conseils juridiques* for the first time to establish a practice as a commercial company (*société d'exercise libéral*) under one of the following forms: *société à responsibilité limitée, société anonyme,* or *société de commandite par actions*. Advocates may also set up a true partnership (*société en participation*) or use the previously available *société civile professionnelle*. These firms are regulated by the Law of 24 July 1966 dealing with commercial companies, as amended in 1990.

Avocats are now permitted to serve as house counsel for commercial enterprises if they have practiced law for seven years, an inroad into the previous ideology of a free and independent profession (*profession libérale et indépendante*). Salaried lawyers currently speak of an "intellectual" independence. *Avocats* may also work as salaried employees of other *avocats*. The largest firms in the new profession will initially consist mostly of former *conseils juridiques,* who were closely tied to international practice and were better able to provide both legal and accounting services. The new firms of *avocats* will clearly have more flexibility in providing a fuller range of legal services, for instance by including lawyers from different local bars.

NOTES AND QUESTIONS

1. Consider all the categories of legal professionals that existed in France up to the 1960s. What explains the rise of the "new advocate" and the further development of law firms in the 1990s?

2. A litigant who wants to appeal to the *Cour de cassation* or the *Conseil d'Etat* must hire one of the 80 *avocats* affiliated with either of these two courts. What would be the advantages or disadvantages of such an elite bar appended to the U.S. Supreme Court? What about the right to pass on one's title?

3. For further information on the development of the French legal professions, see John M. Grimes, *"Une et Indivisible" — The Reform of the Legal Profession in France: The Effect on U.S. Attorneys,* 24 N.Y.U. J. Int'l L. & Pol. 1757 (1992); Peter Herzog & Brigitte Ecolivet Herzog, *The Reform of the Legal Professions and of Legal Aid in France,* 22 Int'l & Comp. L.Q. 462 (1973); Tang Thi Thanh Trai Le, *The French Legal Profession: A Prisoner of Its Glorious Past?,* 15 Cornell Int'l L.J. 63 (1982); Yves-Louis Sage, *The 1990 French Laws on the Legal Profession,* 41 Am. J. Comp. L. 649 (1993).

5. GERMANY

ERHARD BLANKENBURG & ULRIKE SCHULTZ, GERMAN ADVOCATES: A HIGHLY REGULATED PROFESSION, in 2 LAWYERS IN SOCIETY: THE CIVIL LAW WORLD 124, 132-38, 140-41 (Richard L. Abel & Philip S.C. Lewis eds. 1988)[a]

The Allocation of Graduates to Legal Occupations

Those who pass both examinations choose among the different legal occupations largely on the basis of their marks on the second state examination, supplemented by the evaluative report of the training judges. Very good grades on the second examinations (a *Prädikat,* which is achieved by one-sixth of examinees) open the door to a career in the judiciary or civil service. Legal job advertisements generally demand "a young jurist, possibly with professional experience and [two] Prädikat examinations." A Prädikat always was a prerequisite for employment in the judicial service and often was demanded in the civil service, except between 1965 and 1975, when graduates were in short supply. With the present oversupply of graduates and the contraction of all public service labor markets, not even a Prädikat can assure entry to the judicial or public service.

Work as an advocate has become an alternative. It rarely is a deliberate choice, except for those who "inherit" contacts with practicing advocates through family or friends or make contacts as a trainee. Advocates traditionally have been characterized by high self-recruitment and upper-middle-class backgrounds, but advocacy recently has become the occupation for all jurists unable to find government or civil service jobs....

1. *Judicial Careers*

Germany traditionally has had the highest ratio of judges to population of all countries with a developed formal legal system. This is due to a combination of high litigation rates, high appeal rates, and the inquisitorial system. Procedural law gives judges a dominant role in the proceedings, controlling

[a] Textual notes are omitted.

them, directing the inquiry, suggesting settlements, and passing judgment. Procedural law and ideology demand that judges give a detailed reasoned written judgment. Thus, German legal culture is thoroughly judge centered....

2. *Lawyers in the Civil Service*

Most higher civil servants with any sort of administrative responsibility traditionally have been recruited from qualified lawyers. A "judicial qualification" opens the door to higher positions in the civil service and local governments. Because of their employment status, civil servants cannot represent parties in most judicial proceedings.

Judicial qualification is particularly advantageous for public service careers. Jurists have a very strong position in both the executive and the ministerial bureaucracies. The judicial mode is deeply embedded in German administrative law: every public administrative decision is subject to judicial review on substantive as well as procedural grounds. Because public policy also relies heavily for its legitimation on a belief in legality, jurists play a central role in preparing new legislation.

Since jurists with a rather homogeneous background dominate the civil service, training in law has attained a central place in the idea of a "universal education" for public functions.

In spite of the uniform education, each legal occupation has its own career path, and interoccupational mobility is difficult after the early years. The relatively high incomes produced by seniority and promotion practices in both the judiciary and public administration render transfer to private practice after the age of thirty-five a financial sacrifice. Civil servants and judges rarely leave to become advocates. Most mobility is a one-way movement of younger advocates into permanent civil service jobs. Having obtained the status of a permanent civil servant, most lawyers are reluctant to return to advocacy. In contrast to the average advocate, civil servants enjoy extraordinary security: life tenure, health insurance, and generous pension schemes. Many lawyers who have graduated recently have enrolled as advocates simply to wait for a job in the civil service....

3. *Lawyers in Private Employment (Syndici)*

In Germany, larger companies tend to have their own in-house counsel. There are between 30,000 and 40,000 lawyers working in commerce and industry, banks, and insurance companies. Large corporations have legal departments with twenty or more fully qualified lawyers. Lawyers also work in personnel and administrative departments and exercise management functions. Professional associations, trade unions, and other organized interest groups employ lawyers as managers or legal advisers.

That so many lawyers work in salaried positions indicates a particular management style: rather than contracting with lawyers, consultants, or accountants for specific services, German business firms tend to incorporate these services within their permanent organizations. Company lawyers enter business firms at the beginning of their careers and tend to move up internal company ladders.

Some business lawyers are admitted as advocates. Official statistics estimate that 12 percent of all registered advocates are "Syndici," but we believe that the figure is more than twice as high. Income statistics for 1984 show that 30 percent of all registered advocates have no income from their practices. While a few are not practicing because of age or other reasons, the rest probably are employed. However, the dramatic increase in law graduates during the last two decades has not increased the proportion employed in business. Employed lawyers may not represent their employer in court (*Bundesrechtsanwaltsordnung* [BRAO], art. 46). Many become advocates just to have the privilege of using the title; they see themselves as employees bound by contract to their employer rather than as independent lawyers in private practice. Most are found in the big city bars.

4. *What Advocates Do*

Advocates traditionally have been regarded as "part of the system of justice." They have a monopoly not only of representation in court but also of legal advice (Legal Advice Act [*Rechtsberatungsgesetz*]). This "lawyer monopoly" has prevented any other type of advisor from penetrating the "legal market." It also has discouraged the development of any significant legal aid advocacy. Because legal education is oriented toward the judicial service, young advocates will see their role primarily as litigators. This consists mainly of preparing written statements; compared to common lawyers, civil lawyers play an insignificant role in collecting and presenting evidence. Once an action has been filed, the inquiry is in the hands of the court, which directs the proceedings, decides what evidence to take, and hears the witnesses.

Most advocates still work as solo practitioners or in small partnerships. If they are restricted to private clients with nonrepetitive needs, their incomes will derive largely from divorce cases. If they can routinize their litigation to increase volume, they may specialize in automobile accidents and traffic offenses, relying on continuing relations with legal-expense insurance companies. A very few advocates specialize in such administrative law matters as political asylum, admission to university, conscientious objection, and land development. Equally few manage to make a living doing social advocacy reimbursed by legal aid. Only those who have acquired additional skills in commercial, tax, and company law and have built up a regular business clientele establish larger more prosperous law firms. However, such specialists often are sought by companies for careers as in-house counsel or in management.

Legal advice outside court is not part of the lawyer's image, but it is lucrative. Solo practitioners generally concentrate on litigation, but in larger law firms the bulk of the work is advice. Here, lawyers face vigorous competition from tax consultants and chartered accountants, who combine advice on business strategies, tax strategies, and management. Tax consultants increasingly form their own partnerships offering comprehensive business advice, including the drafting of contracts and wills. By concentrating on the forensic areas in which they have a monopoly, advocates have lost much of the growing consultancy market.

5. *Notaries*

Advocates are not the only lawyers in private practice; there also are notaries. In most federal states, advocates can be admitted as notaries, a privilege dating back to a Prussian ordinance. In 1985 there were 7,171 advocates who could act as notaries. In the state of Württemberg and in parts of Baden, notaries are civil servants, although they also may collect private fees. In most of the states not previously ruled by Prussia, statute long has provided for a profession of notaries in private practice, with strict entry controls. There now are about 1,000 notaries who are not advocates (*nur-Notare*).

German law permits notarial certification and attestation in a wide range of matters, but it is required in only a few cases in order to validate legal documents: the purchase, sale, or mortgage of land; the decisions of company meetings; and the sale of shares in a private company. Some legal documents, such as a will (which is executed only if the testator wants to depart from the standard provisions of inheritance law), can be drafted by notaries.

Notaries hold public office and charge fees according to a fixed scale, but they are organized as an independent profession. They do their work under the supervision of their regional court of first instance, which controls admissions. Advocates who also wish to practice as notaries have to wait an average of six to ten years....

Regulation of the Practice of Advocates

If legal education in Germany seems highly regulated, so is the practice of advocates. While admission as an advocate is a pure formality, the regulation of how advocates must practice law has a distinctly restrictive effect. Advocates may not combine legal practice with other services, form law firms extending beyond the jurisdiction to which they are admitted, advertise their services, or freely announce that they specialize. Regulation not only affects the "product" advocates offer but also fixes the "price" of their forensic representation. Such regulation was justified as necessary to prevent unfair competition and maintain a high standard of professionalism, but it also restrained the innovations in legal services that would have followed the more aggressive marketing strategies of lawyers who could work on contingent fees or form partnerships with other professions. Much of this regulation, even of advocates' fees, is statutory; it is implemented by the "Chambers of Advocates" but under the supervision of the judicial authorities....

Divisions and Stratification Within the Profession

Preoccupation with preventing competition among practicing lawyers and defending the monopoly of legal advice has prevented German advocates from extending their services into innovative areas and exploring the possibility of cooperation with neighboring professions. At the same time, it also has avoided the sharp income differences and stratification that typify American lawyers. The social distance between solo practitioners (who still can make a decent living) and members of law firms (those with ten lawyers are among the biggest), although considerable, is far smaller than in the United States. There is not yet much "megalawyering" within the bar, nor are there "street-corner lawyers." German advocates still resemble a guild of craftsmen.

There are differences in the size of practice and the clientele, however. Senior practitioners in larger law firms prefer to serve a clientele of companies and associations and rarely go to court, while juniors in law firms and solo practitioners tend to do more litigation for a clientele of individuals, relying on divorce cases for a larger proportion of their income. Stratification among advocates may increase if the influx of young lawyers continues.

DAVID S. CLARK, THE SELECTION AND ACCOUNTABILITY OF JUDGES IN WEST GERMANY: IMPLEMENTATION OF A *RECHTSSTAAT*, 61 Southern California Law Review 1795, 1806-08 (1988)

Referendare who successfully pass the second state examination ... become *Volljuristen*. They are eligible to enter one of seven quite distinct legal professions available in Germany, including the judiciary. Table 8.10 sets out the number of jurists in the various professions.

Table 8.10

Number of German Jurists in 1985, by Profession

Profession	Number	Percentage of Total
Judges	17,031	14.7
Federal	(505)	
State	(16,526)	
Public prosecutors	3,646	3.1
Government lawyers	30,000	25.9
Law professors and researchers	2,038	1.8
Attorneys[a]	47,305	40.8
Notaries	990	0.9
Corporate or organization lawyers[b]	15,000	12.9
TOTAL (rounded)	116,000	100.1

[a] In some states attorneys may also be admitted as notaries. This includes 7,175 such *Anwaltsnotare*.

[b] Most of these lawyers work for business corporations, usually in the legal department. Others work for banks, insurance companies, labor unions, political parties, and interest group organizations.

In 1985 there were 17,031 judges in German state and federal courts, or approximately 15 percent of the legal profession broadly defined. By contrast, in the United States the judiciary represents about four percent of the lawyer population. The German legal profession is quite large — 190 jurists per 100,000 inhabitants — which is the same ratio of lawyers to population that the United States attained in 1972. What may be surprising, however, is the high percentage of judges employed within the German legal system. This is due primarily to the great number of cases litigated in German courts and to the active role that German judges take under their procedural rules.

FRANK WOOLDRIDGE, THE GERMAN RULES GOVERNING THE PROFESSIONAL CONDUCT OF *RECHTSANWÄLTE*, 39 International and Comparative Law Quarterly 683-88 (1990)

The *Rechtsanwälte* within the area of each regional court of appeal (*Oberlandesgericht*) form a professional association, namely the local association of *Rechtsanwälte* of which membership is compulsory. The *Anwaltskammern* participate in the Federal Association of Anwaltskammern (*Bundesrechtsanwaltskammern*) (BRAK) in Bonn. It is unfortunately the case that each local association is represented in the Federal Association by its president and, however many *Rechtsanwälte* belong to it, it has one vote therein. This appears rather absurd when one bears in mind that this leads to the result that one vote may be exercised both on behalf of the 6,000 members of the Munich *Anwaltskammer*, and on that of the 25 *Rechtsanwälte* who are elected to practise before the Supreme Court.

The rules governing the profession and practice of *Rechtsanwälte* are partly statutory, and partly a set of autonomous professional rules. Furthermore, the rules contained in genuine customary law in force before the adoption of the Basic Law in 1949 governing these matters are still operative. The statutory rules are contained in four principal enactments: the Federal Act on *Rechtsanwälte (Bundesrechtsanwaltsordnung)* (BRAO); the Federal Act on Fees *(Bundesrechtsanwaltsgebührenordnung)*; the Civil Procedure Act *(Zivilprozessordnung)*; and the Criminal Procedure Act *(Strafprozessordnung)*. The most important statutory provision governing the conduct and etiquette of *Rechtsanwälte* would seem to be paragraph 43 of the BRAO, which stipulates that a *Rechtsanwalt* must exercise his profession conscientiously and that, both within and without the scope of such exercise, he must show himself worthy of the respect and trust demanded of a *Rechtsanwalt*. Professional duties may be derived directly from paragraph 43 of the BRAO.

According to an enabling rule contained in paragraph 177(2) of the BRAO, the Federal Association of *Rechtsanwälte* is entitled to formulate rules expressing the general opinion concerning the exercise of the profession. These autonomous professional rules may be called the Principles of Professional Conduct and Etiquette *(Grundsätze des anwaltschaftlichen Standesrechts)*. Although the Constitutional Court stigmatised them as rigid in the two decisions of 14 July 1988,[1] they are in fact revised from time to time to take account of changes in the practices prevailing in the profession....

Disciplinary control is exerted by each local association over its members, but it does not possess exclusive jurisdiction. A *Rechtsanwalt* who breaks the rules can be reprimanded by the council of his association for minor offences, but more serious offences involve judicial proceedings. Disciplinary jurisdiction comprises three instances. First of all, there is the disciplinary court of

[1] For which, see Neue Juristische Wochenschrift ("NJW") 1988, 191, 196 and BVerfGE 76, 171 and 196.

first instance (*Ehrengericht*), which is made up of *Rechtsanwälte*, and which sits at the same place as the local association. Second, there is the disciplinary court of first instance appeals (*Ehrengerichtshof*), which consists of three *Rechtsanwälte* and two judges, and which hears appeals from the court of first instance. The disciplinary court of appeals also has competence at first instance in respect of certain matters. An appeal on a question of law only lies against a decision of the disciplinary court of appeals to the special division of the Federal Supreme Court, which deals with matters relating to *Rechtsanwälte*. It sits as a panel of four judges and three *Rechtsanwälte*. The severest disciplinary sanctions which may be imposed are suspension from the right of representation, and removal from the register....

One of the decisions of 14 July 1987 involved two joined cases, in both of which a *Rechtsanwalt* had made outspoken comments. In one case, a *Rechtsanwalt* made controversial comments before a medical committee concerning the death of the wife of his client from coronary thrombosis. In the other case a *Rechtsanwalt* made rather strong remarks concerning the conduct of a judge in bankruptcy proceedings in which he was appointed a receiver. The second decision concerned the press and television publicity given by a *Rechtsanwalt* to certain events which had happened to him during the course of his criminal practice and which may well have constituted oppressive conduct by State officials.

Disciplinary proceedings were taken against all three *Rechtsanwälte*; in the first two cases on the ground that they had infringed the obligation contained in the BRAO's rules to maintain an objective and impartial approach (*Sachlichkeitsgebot*), and in the last case on the ground that the *Rechtsanwalt* had been engaged in advertising contrary to the rules governing his professional conduct. All the *Rechtsanwälte* complained to the Constitutional Court about the adverse result of the proceedings which had been taken against them; all of them had been reprimanded. They claimed that the reprimands which they had received represented an infringement of their fundamental constitutional right to liberty of expression, which is guaranteed in paragraph 12 of the Basic Law (the Federal German Constitution).... In both decisions, the complaint was successful. The decisions will have a considerable impact.... The Constitutional Court pointed out that ... paragraph 177(2) of the BRAO permits the BRAK only to state the common opinion about questions of professional conduct and etiquette. It added that it would have been difficult to entrust more power to the BRAK, because it was not a democratically elected body, and there were objections to the method of representation of individual associations of *Rechtsanwälte*....

The Court's finding that the rules could not be used as a means of interpreting and supplementing paragraph 43 of the BRAO is of a more surprising character. The Court was clearly motivated by a number of different considerations in reaching this conclusion. It criticised the rules made by the BRAK on the ground that they do not comply with the requirements of clarity and legal certainty and were not in conformity with changing social needs. It also placed considerable emphasis upon the fact that the rules were not referred to in paragraph 3 of the BRAO, and hence could not be used to justify limitations upon the fundamental rights of citizens. Furthermore, the Constitutional

Court found that decisions and regulations arrived at by democratic processes, which pay regard to the future well-being of the community and the principle of proportionality are necessary before freedom to exercise a profession can be limited. The Court held that the latter limitation could not take place simply on the basis of the opinion of distinguished and learned *Rechtsanwälte*. The rules were also found to be objectionable by the Constitutional Court on the ground that they covered matters of status which should have been reserved for the legislature, and less important matters, which might properly be delegated to subordinate professional bodies....

The decisions at the Constitutional Court will certainly require the enactment of federal legislation (probably amending the BRAO) in this field; this legislation is likely to provide for the delegation of rule-making power in less important areas either to the local associations of *Rechtsanwälte*, or to a reformed *Bundesrechtsanwaltskammer*, which is given a greater degree of democratic legitimacy....

[T]he Court formulated principles which would be applicable during the transitional period before the enactment of such legislation. It held that the councils of the local associations of *Rechtsanwälte* and the disciplinary courts might continue to invoke the rules made by the BRAK to give substance to the provisions of paragraph 43 of the BRAO, in so far as this was indispensable to the administration of justice, and no breach of the rules governing fundamental rights was involved in such application. Furthermore, the Court also held that the disciplinary bodies might invoke professional duties which were derived directly from paragraph 43 of the BRAO, or from genuine customary law which predated the Constitution. Such rules might also be reflected in the rules made by the BRAK for the professional conduct and etiquette of *Rechtsanwälte*, such as those governing the maintenance of professional secrecy, or the prohibition on the furtherance of interests conflicting with those of the client....

The Court also held that the somewhat vague requirement of objectivity or impartiality (*Sachlichkeitsgebot*), which had not been clearly defined in the jurisprudence of the disciplinary courts, could be invoked only to a limited extent during the transitional period, in the first of its two decisions. It said that permissible critical remarks which were made by a *Rechtsanwalt* in the course of the exercise of his profession, and which were of a derogatory nature as far as other persons were concerned, could not give rise to intervention or the imposition of sanctions by the disciplinary bodies unless special circumstances existed. Such remarks would, however, be treated as a breach of professional duties if, by reason of their content or their form, they could properly be regarded as giving rise to criminal liability. The Constitutional Court held that otherwise, during the transitional period, sanctions could be imposed by the disciplinary bodies on *Rechtsanwälte* for infringements of the requirements of *Sachlichkeitsgebot* only in circumstances where the *Rechtsanwalt* had been guilty of unprofessional conduct involving the deliberate dissemination of untrue statements, or had made offensive remarks which hampered the search for the truth (*Kampf ums Recht*) and which were not justified by the conduct of other parties in the case, or by the development of the proceedings. The disputed conduct of the complainants in the two joined cases, which had involved the use of a few strong words, was not found by the Court to come within these exceptions, and was thus not held to merit the intervention of the disciplinary bodies.

In the second of the two decisions, the Court found that a provision of the rules made by the BRAK stipulating that a *Rechtsanwalt* should avoid giving the impression of sensationally advertising himself or his activities could be given only limited application during the transitional period. It found that the scope of the rule was uncertain, and that the complainant's conduct had not infringed it. The Court also noted that the disciplinary authorities had not considered whether they were entitled to issue their reprimand, against the background of the fundamental rights of the complainant. It found that the latter's conduct scarcely consisted of self-advertisement, but rather of the use of the complainant's constitutional right to inform the public of apparently oppressive conduct, which might be of interest to them, and which had caused him to breach his duty of confidentiality to a client. The Constitutional Court seems to have placed considerable emphasis on the freedom of expression enshrined in Article 10 of the European Convention on Human Rights in reaching its decision....

[I]t seems certain that the BRAO will have to be amended. Such amendment is made all the more necessary by reason of the fact that some of the rules governing *Rechtsanwälte* contained in the BRAO not only have a particularly restrictive effect which is scarcely consonant with the requirements of German lawyers or the needs of the modern business world, but also may be capable of operating in a manner which is contrary to Community law.

NOTES AND QUESTIONS

1. In Germany judgeships are preferred by law graduates with the best grades on the two state examinations. How is this likely to affect the self-image of the German judiciary? Are German judges likely to be more creative in participating in the lawmaking process than the poorly paid judges in Latin America?

2. The distribution of German judges by court is provided in Table 8.11.

Table 8.11

Number of State and Federal Judges in Germany (1985), by Court

State courts	
Ordinary courts	12,763
Labor courts	668
Administrative courts	1,680
Tax courts	457
Social security courts	962
Constitutional courts	82
Personnel and ethics courts	634
TOTAL STATE COURTS	16,526
Federal Courts	
Constitutional Court	16
Supreme Court	272

Labor Court	25
Administrative Court	52
Tax Court	52
Social Security Court	40
Personnel and discipline senates	49
TOTAL FEDERAL COURTS	505

About 15 percent of the state judges are women, while five percent of the federal judges are women. These percentages will grow, however, since one-third of the probationary judges are female.

3. Why are lawyers more common in the German executive branch (civil service) than in American government service? What impact might this have on the functioning of government departments and agencies?

4. Why have large law firms been slow to develop in Germany?

5. German rules of professional responsibility for attorneys are enforced through a three-tier court system. Is it accurate to say that these rules are being "constitutionalized," as with other areas of legal life? See Chapter 7, Section C. Or are these rules being "Europeanized" under the integrative pressure of European Union legal directives and economic realities? Is it important that attorney discipline rules have democratic legitimacy?

6. Is the German Constitutional Court acting like a legislature in formulating applicable principles for a "transitional" period? By the end of 1992 the German parliament still had not fully acted to implement the concerns in the two 1988 cases discussed by Wooldridge. The parliament did act to amend the BRAO, permitting German attorneys to avoid its territorial restriction on practice for those who establish an office in a foreign country (§ 29a). Section 206 now permits attorneys from European Union countries (and, subject to reciprocity, from nonmember countries) to practice their own national law and international law in Germany. Law of 13 Dec. 1989, BGBl. I, 2135.

7. For a valuable comparative analysis of the German and American legal professions, see Dietrich Rueschemeyer, Lawyers and Their Society: A Comparative Study of the Legal Profession in Germany and the United States (1973). *See also* Michael Hartmann, *Legal Data Banks, the Glut of Lawyers, and the German Legal Profession,* 27 Law & Soc'y Rev. 421 (1993) (the special situation of lawyers employed by insurance companies).

NOTE ON THE ITALIAN LEGAL PROFESSION

There are currently about 46,000 attorneys and procurators in Italy registered with 160 local bars. The classic distinction between *avvocato* and *procuratore* (*abogado* and *procurador* in Spain, *avocat* and *avoué* before 1971 in France) has evolved to a mere formality so that a young lawyer is first admitted as a *procuratore* (with territorial competence limited to a court of appeal district). If she so desires she may take an examination after two years to become an *avvocato,* but most lawyers wait six years when they are automatically eligible to become advocates. Procurators thus are in essence junior lawyers. There are proposals to end this division within the bar and to merge the two professions as the Germans did at the end of the 19th century. Admission to practice before the Italian high courts is similarly a matter of experience. For those *avvocati* who do not wish to take a special examination, enrollment occurs after eight years of practice as an advocate. Certain other legal professions, such as state attorney and law professor, are also provided the privilege of enrollment.

There are approximately 4,500 notaries in Italy. In addition, a substantial amount of law work in commerce and taxation is conducted by *commercialisti* (with degrees in economics or business) and *ragioneri* (accountants).

6. SPAIN

CARLOS VILADÁS JENE, THE LEGAL PROFESSION IN SPAIN: AN UNDERSTUDIED BUT BOOMING OCCUPATION, in 2 LAWYERS IN SOCIETY: THE CIVIL LAW WORLD 369-71, 375-76 (Richard L. Abel & Philip S.C. Lewis eds. 1988)[a]

Private Practitioners

The distinction between *abogado* and *procurador* does not correspond to that between the English categories of solicitor and barrister. The Spanish legal system requires each litigant to name a procurador as an official representative who will handle its relations with the court. Such representation tends to be merely formal: all pleadings, petitions, and briefs submitted to the court by the parties will be signed and presented by the procurador but prepared by the abogado. The procurador is lower in status than the abogado, although not necessarily in income.

Because this role increasingly is a mere formality (such as that of the "avoué," who has been eliminated in France, Belgium, and Switzerland), some people urge its suppression. However, one cannot ignore the fact that some procuradores possess such a thorough knowledge of the procedural rules that they are extraordinarily helpful to lawyers. This is why it is the abogado who chooses the procurador, even though it is the client who pays the latter (a fee that is determined partly by regulations and partly by the procurador).

There are very few procuradores in Spain today. In Barcelona, for instance, there are only 100, compared to approximately 5,000 lawyers. Given the limited functions they perform, it is very easy for procuradores to handle a vast number of cases, especially since the advent of photo-copying, computers, and word processors.

Since 1506 the Barcelona procuradores have had their own "Colegio" (association), to which anyone with a law degree can belong.... No special training is required, and practitioners may move freely between the categories of abogado and procurador, although they cannot practice both functions at the same time.

An abogado has exclusive rights of audience in all courts located within the territorial limits of the Colegios to which the abogado belongs. Until recently, therefore, only members of the Madrid Colegio could appear before the Tribunal Supremo located in the capital. Today, all lawyers appealing cases for

[a] Textual notes are omitted.

which they have had responsibility below can plead before the Supreme Court (Estatuto de la Abogacía, art. 22).

Although lawyers are entitled to practice all branches of law, they tend to specialize. They also encounter competition in certain areas — for instance, with economists and business consultants in advising and representing individuals and companies in tax matters (although lawyers retain their exclusive rights of audience in court). In labor matters, they also compete with social workers, who can appear before labor courts.

Public Lawyers

Abogados del estado must be distinguished from *fiscales* (prosecutors), although both represent the state and are civil servants. The duties of the latter are much broader, covering four areas. Fiscales issue opinions as to whether a court has jurisdiction in a particular case, are responsible for the discipline of judicial personnel, instruct the police, and represent the state and the government whenever those entities have an interest in litigation, unless legislation explicitly assigns such representation to an abogado del estado. In civil cases, they intervene in matters involving status, personality, or family law, represent minors and others who lack legal capacity, and appeal judicial decisions based on a misinterpretation or error of law.

Despite these formal responsibilities, fiscales commonly are perceived solely as prosecutors. Furthermore, their duties in criminal cases are so essential and have become so onerous that they have crowded out most other activities. In 1983, the 540 prosecutors and about 1,694 judges and magistrates in Spain handled 1,633,244 cases and participated in 99,660 trials ....

Abogados del estado often are asked by administrative bodies or government departments to give opinions about the legally appropriate forms through which goals may be pursued. They audit tax returns in order to ensure that the correct amount has been paid on the sale of goods, land, and shares in corporations. They represent the state when it has a financial interest in litigation (both civil and criminal) and represent civil servants who are sued for acts performed in the course of their official duties.

Numbers

At the end of 1982, there were about 32,000 practicing lawyers and about 10,000 non-practicing lawyers in Spain. In addition, many more people hold law degrees and have the right to enter practice at any time....

Law Firms

Very few lawyers practice in partnerships. Although most offices contain several lawyers, they share only the rent, secretarial expenses, and office equipment. Most offices also provide space and offer some training to recent graduates. The Estatuto General de la Abogacía distinguishes such loose associations from law firms (*despachos colectivos*), where lawyers share responsibility for clients, and it limits the number of partners in such firms to 20 (arts.

34-38). It also requires firms to obtain bar association approval of their bylaws and to register with the association.

Most law firms offer a wide variety of services to companies, to which they become "permanent counsel" in exchange for a fixed payment, supplemented for negotiating complicated contracts, advising on difficult issues, and conducting litigation. Individual lawyers also seek such agreements, since they offer security without the limits on independence associated with the status of house counsel. Larger companies tend to prefer to employ house counsel, although they continue to retain specialist practitioners when faced with a significant issue. Such specialists charge high fees, especially if they hold a chair in a university law faculty. Most large companies now employ a lawyer at least part time as house counsel. The practice began in banks and insurance companies, and some of the former are considered the best places to obtain legal training, since the heads of those departments used to be prestigious lawyers. Unlike house counsel in France, those in Spain retain their right to appear in court and can even practice privately, if their employer permits.

Lawyers may charge whatever they wish, although the bar associations publish recommended fee schedules (Estatuto General de la Abogacía, art. 56). Bar associations also mediate fee disputes. Madrid lawyers are known to charge the highest fees. Law professors and politicians temporarily out of office also are expensive.

7. BRAZIL

JOAQUIM FALCÃO, LAWYERS IN BRAZIL, in 2 LAWYERS IN SOCIETY: THE CIVIL LAW WORLD 400, 417-22, 427-30 (Richard L. Abel & Philip S.C. Lewis eds. 1988)[a]

With the creation of the Brazilian Bar Association in 1930 and the subsequent unification of civil procedure, the practice of law became the exclusive privilege of those citizens registered in the Brazilian Bar Association. Today, the requirements to obtain this registration are: (1) a diploma from a law school recognized by the government; (2) civil responsibility (which excludes minors, the insane, and Indians); (3) successful completion of either practical legal training or the bar examination; (4) qualification as a voter (eighteen years or older and registered) and satisfaction of the required military service; (5) freedom from any criminal convictions; (6) abstention from any professional activity incompatible with the function of a lawyer, such as being a judge or a secretary of state. Registration in the Brazilian Bar Association entitles the lawyer to practice in any state by satisfying a few formal supplementary requirements.

Legal Services

We may divide lawyers' activities into two categories: legal services and political-juridical activities. Legal services are directly related to the application of legislation and include those described in article 7 of the Statute of the

[a] Textual notes are omitted.

Brazilian Bar Association: representation in a court and before administrative agencies, extrajuridical representation and legal counseling, and the management of a legal department. The right to participate in judicial proceedings and to act in one's own name or that of one's client is the monopoly of the lawyer. In the labor court, however, the parties may defend themselves personally, although they cannot be represented by a layperson. Research indicates that only 33.6 percent of the complaints before the labor court are mediated by a lawyer. In the criminal court, the defendant also may appear without representation if there is no lawyer in the region. Finally, any person may apply for habeas corpus for oneself or for others. Besides pleading in court, only one other activity is the monopoly of lawyers: registering the contracts of commercial and civil entities with notaries public in order to make them enforceable against third parties. Notarial activities are state regulated and very profitable. The notary public does not need to hold a law degree — only a state license. Normally a son inherits this license from his father. Notaries public protest notes and bills, attest and certify certain classes of documents, and administer oaths. They also maintain the civil and the real estate registers....

Because of the slowness and inefficiency of some sectors of the Brazilian public administration, relationships with citizens are mediated by the "despachante," a specialist who lacks professional training but has enough information and personal connections to defend the interests of the citizen before the government agency. In the last ten years, lobbying has been growing as a professional activity, mainly at the federal level. So far, lawyer lobbyists have concentrated their efforts on government agencies in the financial and economic sectors of the public administration. However, there is increasing interest in Parliament as the redemocratization progresses. Lawyers are actively lobbying the drafters of the new Constitution.

Political-Juridical Activities

Political-juridical activities differ from legal services because the former are not devoted to the uncritical technical implementation of legislation. On the contrary, they normally take a highly critical stance toward legislation, the economic system, and the political regime. Legal justification for this activity is found in the Statute of the Brazilian Bar Association (OAB), which commit it to defending the legal order and the Federal Constitution, fighting for the proper application of the laws and the rapid administration of justice and helping to improve juridical institutions. Social and cultural support for this activity is found in the historical commitment of lawyers to liberal ideology, even when this ideology has been characterized by the permanent gap between the egalitarian ideals it defends and the hierarchical practice it obscures. Juridical-theoretical support is found in a concept of law that is not limited to legislation, regardless of whether it is denominated *jus naturalista* or linked to human rights. Justice is not simply government justice. Above all, the political-juridical activities of lawyers challenge official legality divorced from political legitimacy.

In contrast to legal services, which are individualized, these political-juridical activities are collective and pursued through professional associations. The lawyers generally receive no payment or only a nominal sum. In 1980, 52 percent of Rio de Janeiro's 36,000 lawyers believed that the struggle to improve the legal system should be the OAB's first priority. In other words, political-juridical activities are more important than legal-technical ones as far as the OAB is concerned. Lawyers may take political positions, issue manifestos, and make public statements in the press or in public debates. In contrast, legislative drafting is performed by individual lawyers and paid at market rates. These political-juridical activities have helped lawyers to perform their legal services less subordinated to governmental influence.

Lawyers in the Public Administration

Most lawyers hold two or more jobs, one of which may not be related to law. It is very difficult to find a lawyer who works only in a law firm or a public attorney who works only in government. This is due to at least two main factors: low salaries and the low level of regulation of legal activities. Although there is a trend toward specialization, "general advocacy" still is quite common. In São Paulo in 1984, 53.9 percent of the graduates of the two main law schools were practicing law, 41 percent of whom were generalists.

Brazilian public administration is divided into direct and indirect administration. The former is linked directly to the government and includes the state cabinets, city governments, state secretariats, and autarchies (units that enjoy unusual autonomy in accounting and personnel matters and in formulating policy). The legal professional responsible for providing legal advice, conducting negotiations, implementing the law, and appearing in court is called a "public attorney" or a "lawyer." The indirect administration — federal, state, or municipal — may assume very varied legal forms, such as foundations, state-owned corporations, and mixed-capital enterprises. The lawyers of these agencies may or may not be called "public attorneys." Their activities are not clearly differentiated. These professionals defend the public administration in court, offer legal advice, assist in negotiations, collaborate in the implementation and enforcement of administrative law, and participate in inspections. What distinguishes lawyers from public attorneys is more the way they are hired, paid, and employed. Attorneys in the direct administration must be hired through open public examinations, and the appointment generally is for life, since cause for dismissal rarely is found. Lawyers in the indirect administration may be hired through personal acquaintance rather than open public examination and are dismissed more easily. Public attorneys and lawyers working for the public administration previously enjoyed lifelong appointments but no longer do so. Most hold a second job or practice privately by themselves.

Lawyers in the public administration are hired either as public officials under the Statute for Civil Servants, which grants them special working conditions, salaries, and benefits, or under the Consolidation of Labor Laws (CLT), like most Brazilian laborers. The duties are the same for both; the main difference is the possibility of dismissal. A lawyer hired under the CLT may be dismissed at will. One hired under the Statute for Civil Servants may be dismissed only after proof of serious fault, through a complex administrative inquiry. The result is that the public attorneys of the direct public administration are lifelong employees, de facto.

The public sector definitely is expanding. The government accounted for 38.1 percent of the gross national product in 1964 but 43.7 percent in 1979. There were 14 public corporations in the federal government at the end of the 1950s but 560 in 1981. In 1984, 25 percent of the graduates of São Paulo Law School went to work for the public sector.

Lawyers in the Private Sector

Lawyers in the private sector are differentiated by the degree to which they specialize in legal planning, counseling, negotiation, mediation, and representation in court or outside. Law graduates usually begin general practice, accepting any case and job. Specialization is gradual and influenced by vocation, the type of clients, and success in an important lawsuit. It is greater in large cities. Approximately 50.2 percent of the lawyers active in Rio de Janeiro in 1980 specialized in only one subject. The main areas are labor law (30.1 percent), commercial law (27.3 percent), civil law (16.5 percent), and real estate law (10.3 percent).

A small group of important lawyers and well-known ex-judges stand out from the rest. Having acquired a reputation as full-time specialists in the course of a long career, these law graduates specialize in legal opinions, attempting to clarify an obscure issue in juridical doctrine and legislation on behalf of important clients. These lawyers generally are called "jurists," "jurisconsults," or "pareceristas" (legal opinion writers), honorific titles in Portuguese. Most also are law professors.

The importance of these opinions for the development of legal interpretation cannot be overestimated. In the common law system, the modernization of law occurs through innovative judicial decisions. In the civil law system, judges may play an innovative role but often hesitate to do so. In Espírito Santo, 15.8 percent of the judges from the interior said they never delivered opinions that disagreed with the prevailing law, and 76.3 percent did so only rarely. When innovations occur in the higher courts, these legal opinions are important points of reference, always inserted in a European doctrinal framework....

Types of Law Practice

There are three types of professional law practice: individual offices (solo practitioners), law firms, and legal departments. Solo practice is most consistent with the classic liberal tradition, which stresses autonomy, liberty, and individualism. In the past, the lawyers' offices were in their homes. Differentiation and specialization are minimal. For this reason, solo practice still is quite common in the interior of the country, which is less developed economically and socially. Solo practitioners accept any case and client. In the large- and medium-sized urban centers, these offices still are important, although some are specialized by subject. Very little capital is required to start an individual practice; at most, one needs the funds to rent a furnished room. In

1984, only 19.5 percent of recent young law graduates in São Paulo (less than 5 years since graduation) were solo practitioners.

When they first begin to practice, lawyers secure clients through personal contacts, relatives, and local networks; only later is professional performance significant. Advertising is forbidden by the Code of Ethics. There are no comprehensive directories.

Law firms can be divided into de facto and de jure. The former, far more numerous, are merely two or three lawyers sharing office space and common expenses, such as rent and secretarial services. They do not have any legal status, and their members are registered as individual practitioners. By contrast, de jure law firms are regulated by the OAB, must register, and enjoy their own legal status. They are defined by the Civil Code as partnerships and must divide work as well as profits. The assets belong to all the partners.

De jure law firms may include only partners or partners and salaried lawyers. The majority are based in Rio de Janeiro and São Paulo. The main services they render are legal planning, counseling, and representation before the public administration for a clientele composed primarily of multinational or large Brazilian corporations. A law partnership with twenty lawyers (partners and employees) is considered large. A few partnerships now have more than fifty lawyers. In Rio de Janeiro, only 8 percent of the law firms had more than five lawyers in 1980. In São Paulo in 1984, only 17 percent of lawyers who had graduated less than five years earlier worked in law firms with more than three partners.

Legal departments are divisions of public and private institutions, most of which are located in the large urban centers. They engage in counseling and negotiation with third parties. They also may represent their employer before the public administration or in court, as often happens with unions. These departments do not have independent legal status, nor must they register with the Brazilian Bar Association; those that do not register are not subject to inspection. Lawyers employed in these departments usually do not provide services for other clients. Most employed lawyers specialize in tax, commercial law, and labor law.

The legal departments of the largest national and international, public and private corporations in the states of São Paulo, Rio de Janeiro, Santa Catarina, Minas Gerais, Rio Grande do Sul, Bahia, Paraná, and Brasília D. F. were studied in 1979 by the Fundação Casa Rui Barbosa. Of the department heads interviewed, 74 percent entered the department through personal acquaintance and invitation, and 79.3 percent believed that a good knowledge of accounting and business administration was necessary in addition to legal knowledge. Almost all (96.1 percent) felt that the judiciary was not satisfying the expectations of large enterprises. These lawyers mobilized the judiciary primarily in labor disputes with individual employees (55.8 percent) or to collect debts and execute judgments (59.7 percent). Two-thirds of the corporations offered training and continuing education. Only 7 percent of these lawyers considered their professional practice to be identical to that of the prototypical liberal lawyer — the solo practitioner. Of these departments, 65.2 percent employ fewer than ten lawyers, and 38.2 percent occasionally hire outside legal services. Only 14 percent of these departments are registered with the Brazilian Bar Association.

[Another survey helps] us to visualize the three varieties of legal practice. [It] studied approximately 35,000 lawyers registered in the Rio de Janeiro regional division of the Brazilian Bar Association. This survey revealed that the majority of lawyers engage in two or more occupations. For instance, 44 percent held a full- or part-time job in the public administration, only some of which were related to law. Approximately 61 percent were solo practitioners, and 5 percent practiced alone and also were connected with law firms or legal departments. Twenty-four percent were employees of law firms, part-time or full-time....

This view of law practice would be incomplete if I failed to mention the emerging practice of lawyers who specialize in the defense of the legal interests of the lower-class urban populations and rural laborers. These "clients" cannot pay a lawyer, and the free legal services provided by the government are totally inadequate. These lawyers work through nonprofit nongovernmental institutions funded by religious groups from abroad, annual fees from their members (such as consumers, environmentalists, or activists within the Catholic Church), and government subventions. The best known are the lawyers of the Commission for Justice and Peace of the Catholic Church. They are engaged primarily in negotiating with the Public Administration and in judicial or extrajudicial representation before public or private third parties. The majority of cases deal with police violence and rural and urban land ownership. A major effort now is being made to integrate these groups into a national organization. A preliminary investigation has identified more than 150 groups throughout the country.

These groups rarely have their own legal personality. The lawyers within them usually have an ideological commitment to the clients they defend and receive a minimum fee or a salary below market value. Many of these lawyers originally worked for the defense of human rights in the period of greatest repression. Today, the battle for human rights is understood as a struggle for economic rights as well, such as the right to a dwelling place. In contrast to public interest law firms in more developed countries, however, the challenge is less defending minority rights than asserting the rights of the large majority. Recently, those groups defending the interests of the urban middle class against the National Housing Bank filed about 200,000 suits against the Bank and its agents.

8. GOVERNMENT LAWYERS

MAURO CAPPELLETTI, JOHN HENRY MERRYMAN & JOSEPH M. PERILLO, THE ITALIAN LEGAL SYSTEM: AN INTRODUCTION 98-99 (1967)

One agency (*Avvocatura dello Stato*) [in Italy] represents and provides legal advice to the state and most state organs, including governmental corporations such as IRI. It has no role in criminal prosecutions, and it does not intervene to represent the public interest in proceedings to which neither the state nor a state agency is a party. The centralization of government lawyers into one organ is the product of a long historical process during which various specialized bureaus, such as the attorneys' office of the state railways, were consolidated into a semiautonomous agency, responsible only to the Prime Minister. Agency personnel act as attorneys only; they have no power to compromise claims or otherwise dispose of the substantive rights in issue. This power belongs to the governmental organ that holds the substantive rights.

A district office of the agency is established in each of the twenty-three court of appeal districts. The office in Rome is headed by the *Avvocato Generale dello Stato*, who also exercises supervisory functions over the entire agency and determines its overall policy. The staff of the Avvocatura dello Stato is selected by competitive civil service examinations, which are partly oral and partly written.... Three years of service as *procuratore dello Stato* is the usual prerequisite to examination for the position of *avvocato dello Stato*....

A career in the Avvocatura dello Stato carries tenurial rights. [In 1979 a system of promotion similar to that of the magistracy (judges, state procurators) was adopted for state attorneys. Certain internal entities, such as the Council of State Attorneys and Procurators, promote democratic organization and decision making.]

The agency has developed a considerable amount of autonomy. Although the Prime Minister and the Cabinet have the authority to control its functioning through their powers to dismiss and appoint key personnel, these powers are not generally exercised for this purpose, and it is common to find statements that state's attorneys are accorded independence similar to that granted judges.

NOTE ON THE GOVERNMENT LAWYER

The Italian institution of *Avvocatura dello Stato*, a corps of lawyers that provides legal services to state agencies, representing them in civil and administrative proceedings, is unusual. In France, for example, state agencies hire private attorneys to represent them when they appear as parties in civil and administrative litigation. For legal advice French governmental agencies generally resort to their own "house counsel" — that is to lawyers who are part of the personnel of the agency itself. In Italy, however, the advising function is also served by the *Avvocatura dello Stato*, and the need of the agency for a lawyer familiar with its work is met by more or less permanent assignment of an *avvocato dello Stato* to deal with that agency, just as a specific member of a law firm will deal over time with the affairs of a specific client. The analogy is in many senses an apt one: the *Avvocatura dello Stato* is the law firm of the state. Spain has a similar profession: the *Abogados del Estado*. Germany, however, follows the French pattern, as do most other civil law nations.

NOTES AND QUESTIONS

1. What is the difference between the Italian and Spanish procurator? Which is likely to first disappear as a distinct legal profession?

2. Describe the varieties of high court advocate practice in France, Germany, Italy, and Spain. Why do you think Spain would have the most democratic access?

3. One of the least familiar to us of the legal professions in the civil law is the public prosecutor, who in France is an agent of the public ministry (*ministère public*), such as a procurator, procurator general, or advocate general, usually attached to a specific court. As a criminal prosecutor, the public prosecutor's resemblance to our district attorney is easy to see. But as a member of the judiciary, as one who participates ex officio in decisions of the Supreme Court of Cassation in noncriminal cases, and as intervenor on behalf of the public interest in a variety of civil actions, the public prosecutor seems strange to us.

In France the public prosecutor is in an executive branch department of the ministry of justice, but in Italy she is formally a part of the highly autonomous judiciary. Civil law culture generally prefers the Italian position, in part due to a long (and also recent) history of executive abuse of the prosecutorial power, and therefore desires to safeguard the prosecutor's independence with secure tenure and pay, putting assignment and advancement decisions in the hands of fellow magistrates on the *Consiglio superiore della magistratura* rather than in the discretion of the executive.

4. Identification of the public prosecutor with the judiciary does more than merely guarantee security and independence: it affects the psychology of the profession. Italian (and other civil law) public prosecutors identify with judges. They incline toward a nonpartisan perception of their primary functions. Thus, even in a criminal prosecution, the prosecutor may ask the court to acquit the accused and may appeal against a conviction. This is what happened in Colombia in the *Miquirucama* case, *supra* Chapter 6, Section D.1.

5. In Germany the public prosecutor has even less independence from the executive than in France and far fewer civil responsibilities, being almost exclusively a criminal prosecutor. The trend toward almost sole preoccupation with criminal cases is also evident in Italy and Spain (*fiscales*), although not in Brazil. The German position is that protection of the public interest can safely be left in the hands of the judges, who are specifically charged with the obligation to protect it. Still, even Germans consider the public prosecutor a part of the judiciary. The Italian-French model dominates other parts of the civil law world.

6. Compare the civil law public prosecutor with our district attorney. What are the important differences? Which model do you think preferable?

7. Joaquim Falcão divides lawyer activities in Brazil into two categories: legal services and political-juridical activities. Is this more appropriate in Brazil than in Germany? Why or why not?

8. Brazil in 1980 had approximately 86,000 attorneys, 4,600 judges, and 8,100 prosecutors. Are these proportions typical for a civil law country? Are the proportions more likely due to ideology, the political concerns of the governing regime, or the economic realities of a developing nation?

9. Judges in Brazil may not engage in any other professional activity except for law teaching. Why do you think this restraint also has not been placed on lawyers working for the government?

10. How do types of law practice (including the development of law firms) in Brazil compare to those in Europe? What might explain the differences?

11. For more detail on the Italian and Spanish legal professions, see G. Leroy Certoma, The Italian Legal System 43-75; Bernardo M. Cremades & Eduardo G. Cabiedes, Litigating in Spain 56-108 (1989). On the recruitment of judges, see Luis Muñiz-Argüelles & Migdalia Fraticelli-Torres, *Selection and Training of Judges in Spain, France, West Germany, and England,* 8 Boston College Int'l & Comp. L. Rev. 1 (1985). An excellent older study of the Chilean legal profession is Steven Lowenstein, Lawyers, Legal Education and Development: An Examination of the Process of Reform in Chile (1970).

The largest comparative study of the legal professions ever published is Richard L. Abel & Philip S.C. Lewis, eds., 1-3 Lawyers in Society (1988-1989). These three volumes include papers on comparative theories, civil law countries, and common law countries.

For further information on law professors, see Section A of this chapter and Chapter 5, Section B. More detail about judges and judicial activity is presented in Chapters 7 and 10.

9. JAPAN

JOHN O. HALEY, REDEFINING THE SCOPE OF PRACTICE UNDER JAPAN'S NEW REGIME FOR REGULATING FOREIGN LAWYERS, 21 Law in Japan 18, 19-21 (1988)

Japan first recognized professional representation in judicial proceedings in 1872 in regulations on judicial affairs. More detailed regulations, which defined members of the legal profession as trial advocates (*daigennin*) on behalf of parties in civil litigation, were issued in 1876. These regulations limited those permitted to act as advocates to specific districts or high courts based on examination. In 1880 the *daigennin* regulations were revised to institute a system of admission to practice before any court in Japan based upon an examination to be administered entirely by the Ministry of Justice. The new regulations also required the *daigennin* to organize bar associations established for each district court. The first real legislation on the legal profession, however, came with the 1893 Bengoshi Law, enacted after the establishment of Japan's political institutions under the 1889 Meiji constitution. The 1893 law, which coined the term *bengoshi*, a translation of the English title "barrister," to replace *daigennin*, remained in force until the enactment of a revised Bengoshi Law, enacted in 1933 but not effective until 1936. After the war, the 1933 Law was repealed with enactment of the currently effective 1949 Bengoshi Law.

The role of the *bengoshi* as a trial lawyer has been a constant premise in all prior legislation governing the profession. From the judicial regulations of 1872 through the 1949 Bengoshi Law, the practice of law in Japan was consistently defined in terms of legal assistance to the representation of parties in formal adjudicatory proceedings. The role of the *bengoshi* as trial lawyer was thus taken for granted both in practice and law. This is evident in the formal definitions of the scope of practice under current law — in articles 3 and 72 of the 1949 Bengoshi Law. They provide (emphasis added):

> Article 3. A lawyer shall, upon the request of a party and other persons concerned, or a government or public office, perform acts and other general legal business *related to* lawsuits, noncontentious cases, and appeals of dispositions by administration offices such as requests for investigation, objections, and petitions for review.
>
> Article 72. No person other than a lawyer shall, with the aim of obtaining compensation, engage in the presentation of legal opinions, representations, mediation or conciliation, and other legal business [*hōritsu jimu*] *in connection with* lawsuits or noncontentious cases, and such appeals filed with administrative offices as requests for investigation, objections, petitions for review, and *other general legal cases,* or act as agent therefore; provided that this shall not apply in such cases as otherwise provided for in this Law.

Both articles exclude counseling, drafting, negotiating, and other tasks performed by the lawyer unrelated to litigation and other "legal cases" (*hōritsu jiken*).

The limited scope of practice as defined in the 1949 Bengoshi Law is even more apparent in comparison with the 1933 statute. The 1933 reform was the result of an increase in the number of *bengoshi* and lawsuits that began in the early 1920s. With no restriction on admission to practice by graduates of Japan's imperial university law faculties [until the mid-1920s], the number of lawyers in Japan more than doubled between 1920 and 1930. One of several proposals put forward by the Japanese bar out of concern with both status and security was a redefinition of the scope of practice to cover legal counseling unrelated to representation in judicial and other proceedings — in other words, to expand the lawyers' monopoly to include the functions of solicitor as well as barrister. The 1933 statute as enacted, however, contained a relatively narrow definition of the *bengoshi*'s role.

Article 1 of the 1933 Bengoshi Law provided:

> Article 1: Lawyers perform the business of performing acts of litigation [*soshō ni kansuru kōi*] and other general legal matters pursuant to the request [*ishoku*] of a party or other interested persons or appointment by government office.

By separate statute enacted simultaneously with the new Bengoshi Law — the Law Concerning the Regulation of Legal Practice — persons not admitted to practice were prohibited from

> engaging regularly and for compensation in the business of providing expert opinions, representation, arbitration, or compromise related to litigation involving other persons or disputes involving noncontentious cases between other persons or other related acts; provided, however, this shall not apply to acts carried out pursuant to otherwise legitimate business activities.

The 1949 Bengoshi Law thus did not alter the fundamental definition of the *bengoshi* as a trial lawyer.

NOTE ON THE DISTRIBUTION OF JAPANESE JURISTS

The statistics in Table 8.12 show the trends over the past century in Japan for the numbers of judges, public procurators, and private attorneys (bengoshi).

Table 8.12

Number of Judges, Procurators, and Bengoshi in Japan, by Year

			Bengoshi	
Year	Judges[1]	Procurators	Number	Per 100,000 Population
1891	1,531	481	1,345	3.4
1900	1,244	473	1,590	3.6
1910	1,125	390	2,008	4.1
1920	1,134	570	3,082	5.6
1930	1,249	657	6,599	10.2
1940	1,541	734	5,498	7.6
1950	1,533 (2,261)	930 (1,673)	5,862	7.0
1960	1,687 (2,367)	1,044 (1,761)	6,439	6.9
1970	1,838 (2,605)	1,132 (1,983)	8,868	8.5
1980	1,956 (2,718)	1,173 (2,088)	11,759	10.1
1986	2,009 (2,740)	1,173 (2,092)	13,159	10.8

[1] The figures for judges and procurators beginning in 1950 do not include summary court judges or assistant procurators, who are nevertheless included in parentheses.

DAN FENNO HENDERSON, FOREIGN ENTERPRISE IN JAPAN: LAWS AND POLICIES 177-85 (1973)

Under postwar constitutionalism, Japanese lawyers are just now coming into their own. Such professional antecedents as they had before 1868 were concurrently innkeepers with little status in or out of court. Between 1886 and 1949, the Japanese lawyer's role was largely courtwork like a barrister, although in the context of the Japanese tradition and the consequently congenial German-style, inquisitorial trial procedure adopted for prewar Japan, their role in the courts and in society as well was a mere shadow of that of their British brethren.

Since the legal examination is very restrictive, a diminutive but generally very competent bar of [over 14,000], who are even now often essentially trial lawyers of a rather passive sort, now serves a nation of over 100 million people. Most of the Japanese lawyers practice in the three or four large cities and are still largely found in one-man offices. It stands to reason, then, that other types of experts must handle the vast volume of counseling, legal drafting, tax work, regulatory filings, and corporate documents and registration.

The Law-Trained Corporate Employee

Although the law-trained corporate employee is not a licensed or professionally trained lawyer, ... [m]uch of the law work handled in the U.S. by the corporate counsel or "office lawyer," or in England by a solicitor, is done in Japan by quasi-professionals of this sort. On the other hand, full-fledged and professionally licensed Japanese lawyers (two years of training after graduation from the law department and after passing the legal examination) almost never accept full-time employment with the government or a corporation as is common in the United States.

As mentioned above, these law-trained employees are the peculiar product of the law departments of Japanese universities. Those graduates who decide to go into government or corporate offices directly without taking the legal examination or those who fail the examination are the ones who perform the bulk of legal work, aside from litigation, in public offices and business. They lack the qualities of professionalism and the competence that come from intensive professional training, discipline, and organization, but in the specialized fields to which they are assigned, they often become skilled in technical legal matters. It is this type of quasi-professionals whom foreign investors will frequently encounter in joint-venture negotiations, contract drafting, tax filing, and corporate work....

Patent Agents (benrishi)

Rather like the situation in the U.S., patent work in Japan is done by separate specialists. However, unlike our practice, these specialists are ordinarily not lawyers but members of a separate profession called patent agents.... The professional work involved in filing, registering, and otherwise handling this large volume of patent work in Japan is ordinarily done by patent agents. Their association is regulated by the Ministry of International Trade and Industry, and their qualifications, scope of work, organization, and other affairs are governed by a separate law and regulations. However, any qualified Japanese lawyer (*bengoshi*) is also authorized to do patent work although patent agents need not be lawyers. Of all the other legal specialists in Japan, only the patent agent is qualified to handle litigation in his special area of competence.

The special status of the patent agent dates back to 1899, but the present organization of the profession dates from the Patent Agents' Law of 1921. All qualified patent agents must register and become members of the Patent Agents' Association (*Benrishikai*), which was organized in 1922. It had 1,536 members in 1967, almost two-thirds of whom (992) were in Tokyo. [Today there are slightly more than 3,000 patent agents in Japan.] Japanese citizenship is a requirement to become a patent agent, although foreigners may be authorized to handle specific matters on the basis of reciprocity. Otherwise, to qualify to become a patent agent, one must pass two examinations, the first of which is waived for graduates of Japanese universities. The final examination is given once a year in Tokyo and only roughly 4 percent are successful. No special training institute is provided to train successful candidates such as the Legal Training and Research Institute for lawyers.

The Patent Agents' Association provides a list of suggested fees to be charged for application registration, defense against objections, litigation opinions, and the like. The basic structure of the fee system is a commencement fee (*tesūryō*) and a success fee (*shakin*) at the end, although the latter is fixed and payable whether the work is successful or not....

Tax Agents (zeirishi)

As yet no sharp antagonism, such as we have had in the U.S., has developed in Japan between accountants and lawyers with respect to tax matters. One reason is that tax administration has just recently reached a point where controversies over tax liability are emerging as legal problems, as opposed to negotiating and fact-finding problems. Another reason is the legal structure governing the various practitioners in Japan. Japanese law recognizes the tax agent as a specialist separate from the lawyers and accountants in tax matters, but at the same time, both lawyers and certified public accountants (*kōnin kaikeishi*), including foreign C.P.A.s, are authorized to handle tax matters as an incidence of their respective professions. However, despite their recent aspirations, the tax agents have not been given a right corresponding to that of the patent agents to handle tax cases in the courts; such work is reserved to lawyers....

The first national legislation to organize and control tax agents dates from 1942, but it was not until Japan adopted the voluntary assessment system of tax returns of 1947 that the present basis for the tax agent's role was firmly laid. Soon followed the new Tax Agent Law (*Zeirishihō*) of 1951, which provided that the government tax office must notify the tax agent who had been retained whenever certain investigations were to be undertaken regarding a return.

The importance of the tax agent's work can be seen from the fact that as early as 1961, out of 976,020 individual proprietorships, 178,069 (18.2 percent) and, out of 578,241 corporate businesses, 398,072 (68.8 percent) filed their tax returns through tax agents. For this business the average tax agent made fees of 2,555,000 yen ($7,000) per year, which for that time was very high and probably considerably in excess of the average Japanese lawyer's earnings.

Control of the tax agents is under the Ministry of Finance, National Tax Agency. The agency director may fix the schedule of maximum (no minimum) fees, although since the new law was passed in 1951, no such schedule has been issued. The Tax Agents' Association has, however, established a maximum fee schedule.

To qualify, the tax agent must pass an examination supervised by a committee appointed by the minister of finance. In 1968 out of 35,516 candidates only 755 (2 percent) passed. Those qualified must register with the government and also join the Tax Agents' Association in the National Tax Bureau district where they are to practice. These local associations are then members of the national federation. [Today there are about 42,000 tax agents in Japan.]

Judicial Scriveners (shihō shoshi)

Judicial scriveners play an important role in drafting and registering legal documents for individuals and small enterprises, though they are less frequently used by larger corporations in Japan. Indeed, they may be characterized functionally as half lawyer and half legal secretary in our sense, as they perform many of the more menial of the legal services that our law offices or the English solicitor's offices provide. Nothing that they do could not be done also by a Japanese lawyer, but the scrivener's fees are lower, and they do a great deal of paper work of a legal nature which Japanese lawyers do not deign to do, notably documents for small incorporations. Judicial scriveners also draft pleadings and other documents for use in litigation, but they cannot appear in court for a client. However, since in about 75 percent of the cases in the Summary Courts of Japan one or both of the parties appear without lawyers, we can surmise that the scriveners may aid these litigants with their paper work but leave them on their own in court.

The foreigner will have little occasion to use the judicial scrivener's services, except indirectly, because the scrivener generally works only in Japanese and would under the circumstances most often render his services to a foreigner through a responsible lawyer. Although their work dates back to the early Meiji period, judicial scriveners were not given a legal status until 1919, and their present status is defined in the new Judicial Scrivener Law of 1950. At present, there are [over 15,000] active judicial scriveners in Japan who are serving as second-rate "lawyers," often in rural areas for people who cannot afford the barrister-like *bengoshi* and who, therefore, have the scrivener prepare the pleading and then let the judge try to work out the facts in court.

Judicial scriveners must be selected from persons who have served for five or more years as court secretaries, court clerks, assistant court clerks, secretaries to the minister of justice, or the like. These are, of course, all positions that are filled by special governmental examinations. The licensing of judicial scriveners is, however, done on a local level, and the judicial scriveners are supervised by the District Legal Affairs Bureau (*Chihō hōmukyoku*) of the Ministry of Justice. Thus, they do not have the independence from the executive branch that the bar enjoys. All judicial scriveners are required to maintain membership in the local Judicial Scriveners' Associations, which are federated at the national level.

Administrative Scrivener (gyōsei shoshi)

The administrative scriveners in Japan originated in modern Japanese law as early as 1873, but the modern system is based on the Administrative Scriveners Law of 1951....

To qualify as an administrative scrivener one must pass an examination given once a year by the governor of each prefecture in Japan. Then, it is necessary to register with the local Administrative Scriveners' Association. However, all persons qualified as lawyers, patent agents, C.P.A.s, or tax agents are also qualified as such to serve as administrative scriveners. Also, all employees of the local or national government who have handled administrative matters for eight years (or five years for those with a high school education) are qualified to become administrative scriveners.

The law of 1951 defines the function of the administrative scrivener very broadly to include the drafting for compensation of all "documents to be presented to governmental or public offices or other documents concerning rights, obligations or certification of facts." However, administrative scriveners may not do any drafting work that is restricted by other laws. This latter provision drastically narrows the work of the administrative scrivener because it is interpreted to mean that their work must not overlap with the work of the lawyer, legal scrivener, patent agent, tax agent, or C.P.A. So their work is considerably more constricted than it might appear on the face of the law. Also, unlike the lawyer, who may appear in any court in Japan, the administrative scrivener is only licensed to work within his prefecture and, of course, is not qualified to represent a client in any court.

The administrative scrivener must belong to the prefectural Administrative Scriveners' Association, which in turn must be affiliated with the Japan Administrative Scriveners' Federation. The prefectural association is regulated as to fees, discipline, and registration by the prefectural governor, and the national federation comes under the supervision of the Ministry of Domestic Affairs (*Jichishō*).... Because of their limited territorial license and their subordination to the various other nonlawyer specialists, the actual practice of the administrative scrivener tends to center around the problems of small operators. For example, they draft applications for restaurants and barber licenses and the like. Also, of the some [31,000] administrative scriveners registered as of [1983] about two-thirds of them are also qualified as legal scriveners or other professionals such as land and house investigators (*tochikaoku chōsashi*). Only about a third are exclusively engaged as administrative scriveners.

Japanese Notary (kōshōnin)

It would be better if another term other than "notary" were available to refer to the Japanese *kōshōnin*, because his function is very different from that of the notary public in the U.S. However, the usage has become so established that to select another term might be even more confusing now.

The foreign investor will most often encounter the notary in the incorporation procedure, but the notary's more important functions are: (1) making notarial deeds (*kōsei shōsho*); (2) attesting articles of incorporation; (3) and attesting all sorts of private documents. When he performs the above duties he authenticates the signatures or seals of the parties and keeps a copy of the document on file for a required period of thirty years. He is not paid a salary, but is paid by his clientele in accordance with a schedule of fees established by the Ministry of Justice. He is thus both a quasi-public official and in a sense a private practitioner.

Japanese notaries are assigned to a given district and supervised by the Ministry of Justice. They must not perform other duties. Frequently they are persons who have been appointed as notaries upon retiring from the bench or procuracy. There are [fewer than 500] notaries in Japan, organized into associations in each district of the Judicial Affairs Bureau of the Ministry of Justice. As noted, the foreigner's most common encounter with them is in establishing corporations, but foreigners should not overlook the efficacy of notarial deeds to express money obligations, because they can be executed on like a judgment in case of default.

NOTES AND QUESTIONS

1. Japan has a complicated and widely misunderstood pattern of legal professions. Should legally trained specialists in the legal departments of major Japanese companies (who have not been admitted to the Japanese bar as attorneys) be nevertheless considered lawyers? How useful are comparisons of the number or rate of lawyers between countries such as the United States and Japan?

2. Why has the number of bengoshi increased much more than the number of judges in Japan over the past century?

3. Most Japanese attorneys are trial lawyers. Few develop expertise in particular areas of the law, such as taxation, commercial transactions, and company law, unrelated to frequently litigated issues. Should this have any significant effect on the role of law in Japan or in other countries in which this is also the case? Who, for example, would individuals or small companies turn to for advice on issues in such areas of the law?

4. There are a number of excellent studies in English on the legal profession in Japan. They include Takaaki Hattori, *The Legal Profession in Japan: Its Historical Development and Present State,* in Law in Japan: The Legal Order in a Changing Society 111 (Arthur T. von Mehren ed. 1963); Zensuke Ishimura & Yuriko Kaminaga, *Attorneys and Cases Involving Automobile Accidents,* 9 Law in Japan 83 (1976); Richard W. Rabinowitz, *The Historical Development of the Japanese Bar,* 70 Harv. L. Rev. 61 (1956); Kahei Rokumoto, *The Present State of Japanese Practicing Attorneys: On the Way to Full Professionalization?,* in 2 Lawyers in Society: The Civil Law World 160 (Richard L. Abel & Philip S.C. Lewis eds. 1988); Tadao Tanase, *Urbanization of Lawyers and Its Functional Significance, Expansion in the Range of Work Activities, and Change in Social Role,* 13 Law in Japan 20 (1980). Comparative studies include: Masanobu Kato, *The Role of Law and Lawyers in Japan and the United States,* 1987 B.Y.U. L. Rev. 627; Richard S. Miller, *Apples vs. Persimmons: The Legal Profession in Japan and United States,* 39 J. Leg. Educ. 27 (1989).

11-3-05

(1) Generally, about how many opinions does it take to ~~constitute~~ set a custom in France and Italy?

(2) ~~In~~ Under the "dominating opinion" technique, ~~as~~ the text states that ~~of~~ the persuasiveness of the jurist is generally the deciding factor in the court's decision. However the text doesn't ~~mention~~ mention anything about evidentiary basis or scientific evidence. Do they simply play into the persuasiveness of the jurist's argument? ~~And if~~ What happens when the "dominant opinion" is clearly refuted by evidence?

(3) ~~On a little comp~~ ~~Could~~ The text states on page 947 that some ~~a~~ citations used in German courts that "refer to a "book or article that discusses a question the court raised, but explicitly refused to solve in any way". ~~On a little compare~~ In the United States, we're discouraged from using citations that don't further our argument — how can bringing up "secondary sources that refuse to solve any rule of law help an argument, other than drawing ~~a~~ attention to the fact that this question has been raised before?

Chapter 9

THE JUDICIAL PROCESS

Civil law and common law courts are involved in the same general kind of activity: they find the facts of the case, apply the law, and pronounce the result; but it is widely believed that they fundamentally differ in the materials they use and in the ways they perform their functions. We look more closely in this chapter at those differences and at a variety of judicial styles. We then turn to the closely related question of the scope of and limitations on judicial interpretation of "the law."

A. THE SOURCES OF LAW, JUDICIAL DECISIONS, AND SCHOLARLY DOCTRINE

NOTE

In all civil law nations judges are required to base their decisions on "the law." The judicial function involves the correct interpretation and application of the law. One of the principal obligations of supreme courts is to insure the uniform and correct interpretation of the laws. Access to the supreme courts is, on the whole, limited to challenging erroneous interpretations and applications of the law by lower courts. In each of these contexts "the law" has a peculiar and interesting technical meaning; it is one of the first things a law student in a civil law university studies, invariably under the heading "sources of law."

There is an important linguistic aspect to this topic. The languages of the civil law systems each contain two distinct terms that can be translated as "law." One such term (*droit, Recht, diritto, derecho*) is equivalent to "law" in the broad sense, as one might use the term in speaking of the science of law or in contrasting law with medicine or divinity as a profession. The other term (*loi, Gesetz, legge, ley*) is much narrower, and often means only legislation, as when we speak of "a law." There is a range of intermediate meanings in which one or the other of these terms will be employed in unpredictable ways, depending on the context, the language, and the culture. When speaking of the sources of law the practice is to use the broader term. Thus, in Spain and Latin America one speaks of the *fuentes del derecho*, not the *fuentes de la ley*. Still, it is not uncommon to hear the faculty of law in a university referred to as the *facultad de leyes*. The usage cannot be predicted, but must be learned.

The status of judicial decisions raises a special kind of question for civil lawyers because of the historical position of the judge in the Roman republic, the French doctrine of separation of powers, the dominant schools of legal thought in Europe in the 19th century, and related influences. One way to put the question is to ask whether judicial decisions are a "source of law" in civil law nations. Another way is to ask whether the doctrine of *stare decisis* applies, or whether civil law courts rely on precedent. These questions are inseparable from the theory of sources of law, as the following materials show.

1. THE INTERPLAY OF SOURCES OF LAW

ALAN WATSON, THE MAKING OF THE CIVIL LAW 168-78 (1981)

Codification profoundly affects the civil law tradition. For example, the sources of law undergo change, and they may now reasonably be categorized as primary, subordinate, and derivative. The previous tradition, though, where the *Corpus juris* was the organizing instrument, remains obliquely important.

With codification, law becomes basically and primarily statute law, and the code is the private law statute *par excellence*. The term "statute" is here used to include governmental and ministerial decrees. No other independent source of law need be recognized; if one is, it will be custom and custom alone and will be subordinate to statute, having only a minor role to play.

The systematic and comprehensive nature of the code with supporting legislation makes law statute-oriented to an extent that is otherwise impossible; and the code and supporting legislation provide the skeleton of the whole of private law. Lawmaking then, insofar as it is permitted, by interpretation whether of the code, other statute, contract, or will, or by filling gaps in the law, is in codified systems a making of derivative law, which raises the question of who has the authority to make this derivative law. The authority to interpret or to fill the gap may be attributed to legislators, to scholars, to judges, or to a combination, and the authority may be to settle the law for the instant case or also for the future.

No fixed pattern has emerged in the civil codes for the treatment of sources. Some, notably the German *BGB*, say nothing about sources at all. The French *Code civil* does not treat the sources except in a negative way: article 5 states that it is forbidden for judges to pronounce by way of general and regular disposition on the cases submitted to them. Articles 1-3 deal with statute in a way that shows, without any express statement to that effect, that it is at least the most important source of law. A valid law is not defined in the French code, but it is in some other codes, such as the *Código civil* of Chile, article 1. The Austrian *ABGB* also does not define statute, but it does explain the nature of "civil law" in § 1. The 1942 Italian *Codice civile* goes so far as to list in § 1 "regulations" (*regolamenti*) as a source of law and elaborates on these in § 3. Again, some but by no means all codes, such as the Austrian *ABGB* §§ 6-8 and the Chilean *Código civil* articles 19-26, set out principles and rules of interpretation. Many codes spell out the precise status of custom, which varies from place to place, and some, such as article 5 of the French *Code civil* and § 12 of the Austrian *ABGB*, deal with judicial decisions. Article 1 of the Swiss civil code has always been regarded as particularly noteworthy:

> The law regulates all matters to which the letter or the spirit of any of its provisions relates.

> In the absence of an applicable legal provision, the judge pronounces in accordance with customary law and, in the absence of a custom, according to the rules that he would establish if he had to act as legislator.
>
> He is guided by the solutions consecrated by juristic opinion and case law.

Custom may or may not be recognized as a source of law, and if it is, the scope given to it may be restricted. Thus, the *herrschende Lehre*, or dominant opinion, accepts only two sources of private law in Germany, statute and custom, and regards them as being of equal value. In fact, custom has a far smaller role than statute to play in legal growth....

But the particular nature of the modern civil law systems is to be seen in the treatment of the derivative sources relating to interpretation and the filling of gaps in the law....

The real contrast between common law and civil law systems, where the force of the old civil law tradition asserts itself, is in the weight to be attributed for lawmaking to judicial decision and to academic juristic opinion, in the judicial career structure and in the form of law reports....

In case law before codification, technically the opinions of the great doctors and other jurists were never binding; precedent might be, if it was from the Supreme Court of the state in question and formed a series establishing a judicial custom. But the weight of citation tended very much to be on the jurists. Although no individual jurist or group of jurists or even the majority cited was decisive, the prestige attributed to juristic opinion was enormous. The more the rules were Roman in descent and the more the *Corpus juris civilis* was used as the organizing instrument, the more highly was academic juristic opinion rated, however varied it might be, as the true interpreter of the law. Likewise the more Roman, the more international, and hence the greater the possibility of celebrity and influence. No civil law judge *qua* judge could ever hope to have the fame and influence of a Bartolus or Molinaeus. Juristic opinion was cited because of its supposed merit in a way significantly denied to judicial decisions from unrelated jurisdictions. Juristic opinion was treated as valuable in itself as an interpretation of the law and was timeless, whereas judicial decision was strictly tied to time and place. Whereas judges did not ignore jurists, jurists in their writings ignored the judges.

Further, in practice, precedent suffered from two other drawbacks. First, it was often, as in France and Italy, very local in character. In a jurisdiction which had no large population it would not be common to have a line of decisions long enough to establish a judicial custom on a precise point. Moreover, a great deal of doubt could exist as to what constituted a judicial custom. How many cases need there be with the same decision? How precisely on the issue need they be? How was one to find the determining factors? Were judicial statements made obiter to be relevant? Was one recent opposing decision fatal to the creation of the custom? And so on. In the absence of a statute on the matter there was no authoritative answer to these questions. And, of course, the jurists with their academic approach to law were little interested in suggesting answers....

Thus on the eve of codification the heroes of civil law systems were academic jurists, not judges. Logically this result of the emphasis on the *Corpus juris* need not have carried over to codified systems. A code is not usually a legal source remote in time, place, and language from the courts that enforce it.... But codification makes law much more accessible on a day-to-day level, if not necessarily at the most abstruse level, to law student and practicing lawyer alike. Confirmation for this can be found in the numerous civil law countries, particularly in Latin America, where in some states virtually all law teaching is conducted by part-time professors who are above all engaged in practice. In such countries the writing of law books or articles of any kind may be an exceptional activity; students may not be expected to read books or articles, or cases, apart from the code and some statutes but to concentrate for examinations on the lectures they have attended; and university law libraries may contain only a few hundred volumes....

Academic jurists nevertheless continue to have great influence in the civil law systems, though this influence seems to be waning. Unless some jurists are officially "licensed" to give particularly authoritative opinions, as seems to have happened in the early Roman Empire, no opinion of an individual jurist *qua* jurist can be binding. Nor can an unofficial system be devised that can technically give preference to the opinion of selected jurists. Of course, it can happen that in particular fields the reputation of one scholar is so high that his opinion is regularly given preference over others, but a less formal approach is usually adopted. A jurist's authority depends not on any specific position that he holds but on his persuasiveness both in general and on the particular point. This persuasiveness, to be effective, must be communicated to the judges, and this is most readily done if the jurist enjoys a generally high reputation among his fellows and if on the particular point his opinion is shared by his colleagues. Thus arises the doctrine in Germany and elsewhere of the "dominating opinion," the *herrschende Meinung* or *herrschende Lehre*. The prevailing opinion among the professors and also in precedent is usually followed by the courts. This approach is so accepted that authors of legal treatises usually give the *herrschende Lehre* as well as their own opinion. The importance of juristic doctrine in one country, Germany, is shown in four examples.

The first example is the doctrine known as *venire contra factum proprium*, or to act contrary to one's own past behavior. A person in whom a right is vested may not exercise that right if he has not done so in the past and if another person could and did fairly rely on his continued non-exercise of the right. This doctrine has come to be an accepted part of German law mainly as a result of a monograph, *Venire contra factum proprium, Studien im römischen, englischen und deutschen Civilrecht*, by Erwin Riezler, who at the time was an extraordinary professor at the University of Freiburg. Riezler's main aim in this comparative work is to demonstrate the usefulness of the English doctrine of estoppel for contemporary German law. He expressly states that the work will offer a modest contribution to the problem of legal decision *praeter legem*, namely filling gaps in the law by going beyond the existing statute.

In the second example, the German *BGB* deals with only two kinds of breach of contract: delay due to fault by § 286 and impossibility due to fault by § 280. But a third kind of breach of contract is accepted in German law, namely *positive Vertragsverletzungen,* or positive breaches of contractual duty. This gap in the *BGB*, which was uncovered by Herman Staub, has come to be filled thanks to the approval given to his *Die positiven Vertragsverletzungen,* despite considerable opposition expressed to his first version.

In the third example, by § 278 with regard to contract a person is liable for acts of persons in his service to the same extent as for his own acts, and by § 831 with regard to delict he is liable for the acts of persons in his service unless he exercised reasonable care in selecting his servants. By the doctrine of *culpa in contrahendo,* or fault in contracting, which in German law is due to Rudolph von Jhering, contractual liability now applies to cases where no contract was concluded, though the parties took preliminary steps toward entering a contract, and hence an employer cannot escape liability for a servant's act at that stage on the ground that he exercised due diligence in choosing his servant. The article of Jhering which was so influential was published almost forty years before the *BGB* came into force.

And fourth, in 1921 Paul Oertmann of Göttingen published his *Die Geschäftsgrundlage, ein neuer Begriff,* in which he argues that frequently a transaction has foundations which are vitally important but are not written into the contract because the parties mistakenly believe the foundations exist or will not cease to exist and further mistakenly believe that they have no reason to think the foundations do not exist or will cease to exist. The courts, following Oertmann, have held that in such circumstances either party to the agreement may terminate the contract, provided it would be very unfair for that person to be bound by the original agreement. This so-called *Geschäftsgrundlage,* or foundations of the transaction, doctrine proved extremely valuable during the period of hyperinflation in Germany.

In these and other instances of the development by juristic doctrine, the jurists were expressly putting forward new ideas with the deliberate aim of influencing the growth of the law. In such instances the acceptance of the doctrine may take years, and the author is not primarily interested in the immediate response of the courts. When the issue is not so much the filling of gaps in the law as interpretation, matters are a little different. The scholars cannot go too far away from the practice of the courts. Whatever the effect of judicial precedent may be, academic interpretation that is consistently at variance with the decisions of judges has little practical value: the judicial decisions settle the instant issue. The position of the civilian professor in this regard is worse after codification than before. Before codification his interpretations were not directed to the attention of judges in any particular jurisdiction; hence the failure of any local court to respond did not mean the academic's view was everywhere rejected. Consequently, in codified civil law systems judicial decisions are an important source of law for the future, provided at least that the courts consistently take the same line. This is true for France despite article 5 of the *Code civil*; hence a standard edition of the code contains not only the text but numerous references to decided cases.

In Germany a line of cases makes binding law and is treated as custom. Section 12 of the Austrian *ABGB* states:

> The decisions issued in individual cases and the judgments handed down in particular legal suits have never the force of a law; they cannot be extended to other cases or to other persons.

Thus the code; yet since 1853 there has been kept at the Supreme Court (Oberster Gerichtshof) a *Judikatenbuch,* or book of judgments, and also since 1872 a *Spruchrepertorium,* or collection of opinions. The following rule is applied through an instruction of July 8, 1872. At the order of a Senat, or bench of judges, the decisions on the legal issues of civil law and civil procedure which were the object of discussion are entered in the *Spruchrepertorium.* If a Senat wishes to depart from such a decision, the question is brought before a Senat of fifteen members. The decisions of this strengthened Senat are entered into the *Judikatenbuch* and are then binding on all the Senate of the Supreme Court. A legal rule set out in the *Judikatenbuch* can be departed from only on the decision of a Senat of twenty-one members, and the new decision is then inserted in the *Judikatenbuch* and published.

Thus, legal precedents have considerable force in civil law countries, a force that typically is greater than that enjoyed by precedent before codification and which, to generalize, continually strengthens relatively to academic opinion. Yet the old tradition asserts itself, and professors enjoy greater prestige and pay than do judges, except for those of supreme courts who themselves are frequently academics. Cause and effect here intertwine to account for two standard features of civil law systems. First there is usually a career judiciary. Judges are not chosen from among highly successful practitioners or professors. Instead, normally a young law graduate opts for a career as a judge. He starts in the lowest court and by a series of regular promotions rises to judgeships in more important courts. Second, the opinion of the court is issued as a combined judgment. The decision does not normally record any dissent among the judges, even if there should be only a bare majority, nor does the record reveal which points were made by which judge or the arguments that swayed individual judges.

The strong academic tradition, based on analyzing the *Corpus juris,* that existed before codification and the statutory basis of the law upon codification combine to make the law reports of civil law countries very different productions from those usual in common law countries. Naturally the reports vary greatly from system to system, but they have distinctive features. Thus, the facts of the case are generalized and are not set out in the detail usual in common law systems. An attempt is made to base the decision firmly on code or statutory provisions or on accepted rules of law. Above all, the decision is set out as expressing a legal rule or principle.

Thus, a reported Italian decision usually does not occupy more than two printed pages. The report begins with the name of the court, the date of the decision, and the members of the court. Then comes a bare list of the topics treated and the relevant statutory provisions, such as "Contract in general — formation of contract — presumption of knowledge of declaration that arrived at address of the person to whom sent — failure to observe postal rules in despatch of registered letter (*Codice civile,* art. 1335)." This is followed by a statement in a very few lines of the rules that are evinced by the decision. Then under the heading of "The Court" comes first the *Svolgimento del processo,* an extremely brief statement of the facts, plus the steps of the process in the lower court; then the *Motivi della decisione,* an examination and evaluation of the arguments produced on either side and of the reasons given in the lower court, and hence the higher court's own motivation and decision. To the statement of the legal rules evinced by the decision is attached a footnote which is usually much longer than the statement and which is written and usually signed by a jurist. This sets out the precedents with which the decision is or is not in harmony and the scholarly books and articles on which the decision is based or with which the decision agrees or disagrees.

French reports are very similar, although the members of the court are not named, and the jurist's note is written in a much more individual style, with the author freely expressing his own opinion on the adequacy or otherwise of the decision, of the court's reasoning, and even of the state of the law. German reports do not give juristic opinions and are written in an even more abstract form. First comes a statement of the legal rules that emerge from the case, then a list of relevant statutory provisions, and next the court that decided the case and the day of judgment. Then comes an account of the facts and of the proceedings in the lower court and finally of the grounds for the appellate decision.

These modern reports show that the legal tradition continues through them. They are very much the descendants of the reports for the civil law before codification.

NOTE ON SOURCES OF LAW

The first category mentioned as a source of law in all civil law discussions of the topic (leaving aside for the moment constitutions) is statutes or legislation. This category is not limited to laws enacted by the legislature. To these one must add legislative decrees and decree-laws. Legislative decrees are delegated exercises of the legislative power. In Italy, for example, Parliament may, under article 76 of the Constitution, delegate to the Government (that is, the executive) the power to issue decrees that have the force of statute, but the delegation must be for a limited time and for a definite object. When promulgated in proper form on the basis of proper delegation these legislative decrees have the same status in the hierarchy of laws as ordinary statutes. Article 77 of the Constitution specifically denies the Government the power to issue decrees with the force of statute without prior delegation *except* in "extraordinary cases of necessity and urgency." Such decree-laws are issued by the Government "on its own responsibility" and become void *ab initio* unless converted into law by Parliament within 60 days. Legislative decrees are issued quite frequently in Italy; decree-laws are unusual.

In other parts of the civil law world, particularly in Latin America, the legislative decree and the decree-law are heavily used, although the nomenclature sometimes varies. It is a notorious fact that "rule by decree" is far from uncommon in many Latin American nations. Franco made extensive use of decree-laws during his long tenure in Spain. It was a device employed to the full in the hands of the German Nazis and the Italian Fascists. Under the 1958 Constitution the President of France has extensive power to legislate by "regulation" (the French equivalent of decree-law) and may also issue "ordinances" under delegation from the parliament (the equivalent of legislative decrees).

Next in the hierarchical order come regulations, which themselves may be of various types and have their own subhierarchy.

Finally we come to custom or usage, which is routinely listed as a source of law in civil law nations. Although the concept of custom exerts an extraordinary fascination for civil law scholars and has provoked a substantial body of literature, its significance in practice is slight and is decreasing. The prevailing theory is that when persons act in accordance with custom under the assumption that it represents the law, their actions will be treated as law-based if there is no applicable statute or regulation. In practice the use of custom is limited to the few instances in which statutes expressly refer to custom.

NOTES AND QUESTIONS

1. Consider the following statement on the hierarchy of sources of law in Germany:

> The Grundgesetz (Federal Constitution) is dominant over all other legal sources, while the ordinary statute has precedence over the Verordnung (administrative regulation) and the Satzung (internal administrative regulation).
>
> The ordinary statute, regulation and internal administrative regulation must confine themselves to the scope of the Constitution. If they are contrary to the Constitution, they are void. The administrative regulation and internal administrative regulation require a statutory basis; if they lack this or if their content is irreconcilable with a statute, then they are in like manner void (so called Vorrang des Gesetzes — primacy of statute law).

Fritz Baur, *Einführung in das deutsche Recht,* in Gesellschaft für Rechtsvergleichung, Bibliography of German Law in English and German: A Selection 20 (Courtland H. Peterson trans. 1964).

2. Professor Watson divides sources of law into three types: primary, subordinate, and derivative. After determining what this means for civil law countries, construct the sources of law for the United States and then classify them. Does your analysis differ for the task of gap-filling compared to interpretation?

3. Watson points out that prior to codification the prestige and influence of juristic writing exceeded that of judicial precedent as a source of authority for deciding cases, especially when the *Corpus Juris Civilis* provided the relevant legal rule. The next excerpt explores the role of scholarly doctrine in contemporary France and Germany as well as in the United States.

2. THE ROLE OF SCHOLARLY DOCTRINE

HEIN KÖTZ, SCHOLARSHIP AND THE COURTS: A COMPARATIVE SURVEY, in COMPARATIVE AND PRIVATE INTERNATIONAL LAW: ESSAYS IN HONOR OF JOHN HENRY MERRYMAN ON HIS SEVENTIETH BIRTHDAY 183, 184-86, 190-91, 193-94 (David S. Clark ed. 1990)

In this study I will try to examine what use, if any, is made by courts in selected legal systems of *legal doctrine* as a source of arguments and ideas, as a restatement of the law as it stands, or as a mine of proposals about how the law should be....

Legal Scholarship in French Courts

Max Weber has pointed out that the climate of a society's legal system is ultimately determined by the kind of people who dominate it, that is, as Weber called them, the *honoratiores* of the law (*Rechtshonoratioren*). It would seem logical to conclude that the number of citations to legal authors, and the weight and influence granted them by the courts, are directly proportionate to the social prestige and public esteem of law professors and other legal writers. However, the opinions of the French *Cour de cassation* clearly demonstrate that this hypothesis is wrong. I am not sure whether French legal scholars are *Rechtshonoratioren* in the Weberian sense, but their influence on French legal culture is certainly not so marginal as to explain the fact that the highest French court does not cite them at all. While citations to legal writing and to previous decisions occasionally appear in the judgments of lower courts, the *Cour de cassation* will have none of it. This stems from its endeavour to make the text of its opinions as dense, terse, pungent, and compact as possible. Asides, divagations, and efflorescences are rigorously avoided, nor are there references to the background of the case, legal history, or legal policy. Its opinions shun the appearance of being the work of judges of flesh and blood who ever indulged in the luxury of doubt; it seems to be required by the *majesté de la loi* that a judgment should appear as a kind of surgical operation leading to the result by way of "a simple, clean-cut deduction from premises stated in the form of an abstract principle, normally drawn from statute." There is no question that the judges of the *Cour de cassation* take note of legal writings and of economic or social considerations. But they are always excluded from the text of the opinion and may be identified only in the rare cases in which a decision is published together with a fully referenced case note by the *juge rapporteur* or with the conclusions of the *ministère public.*

The reason for the French judicial style must be sought in history.... Nowdays French judges do not only interpret legislation, but are as bold and innovative in developing the law as other European appellate courts. Nevertheless, the old stylistic conventions survive:

> [T]he principal function of a high court opinion is to demonstrate to the world at large that the high court in exercising its exceptional powers has arrogated nothing to itself and is merely enforcing the law .... And so the

format of the 1790's continues unchanged. The majestic parade of whereas clauses is cast as an exercise in logic, working down inevitably from some provision of Code or statute. It is the law that speaks. The judges are merely its instrument although by now the whole process could better be described as extremely expert ventriloquism....

Legal Scholarship in American Courts

The courts in the United States have always had a more open attitude toward legal writers. One reason is that in the early post-colonial decades the use of English cases as primary authority was regarded as questionable. There had, after all, been a revolution in America, and while there was no choice but to continue the reception of English common law to the extent to which it was appropriate in the American environment, it seemed more acceptable to do so by relying on treatises by American authors who, like Story and Kent, discussed not only English materials but also principles drawn from civilian sources, and tended to stress the American character of the law they were expounding. Another reason for the courts' reliance on legal writing may be seen in the fact that the sheer number of reported cases in the United States makes it very difficult both for judges and practicing lawyers to keep up with the judicial output of their own jurisdictions, let alone handle the others. Courts may therefore be more inclined to consult and cite encyclopedias, textbooks, treatises, or other forms of "secondary authority," which help to canalize the endless stream of cases and to present them in a more orderly and accessible form. Finally, the growing prestige of American law professors in the twentieth century may have contributed to the increasing use of law review articles in judicial opinions....

One wonders therefore what the real impact of legal writing on judicial decision-making is. Some insight is provided by Merryman's seminal study of the citation practices of the California Supreme Court. He found that there were 2.2 citations to "secondary authority" per case in 1950, 1.7 citations in 1960, and 1.8 citations in 1970.[27] "Secondary authority" includes law review articles, restatements, encyclopedias, annotations, and "other" authority (mainly treatises)....

Legal Scholarship in German Courts

Choosing at random volume 95 of *Entscheidungen des Bundesgerichtshofes in Zivilsachen*, with 41 judgments rendered in 1985, I found 533 citations to "secondary authority," that is, 13 such citations per case. There were on an average 6.2 citations per case to what is called "commentaries,"[36] 3.5 citations

[27] John Henry Merryman, *Toward a Theory of Citations: An Empirical Study of the Citation Practice of the California Supreme Court in 1950, 1960 and 1970,* 50 S. Cal. L. Rev. 381, 405 (1977).

[36] "Commentaries" appear to be a type of legal literature found only in German-speaking countries. A "commentary" of a given statute (e.g., the Federal Constitution, the Civil Code, or the Act against Unfair Competition) follows the structure of the enactment by stating for each article or section the court decisions, legal writing, and other materials that are relevant to a proper interpretation of what the article or section says. Some commentaries will also discuss the cases

to law review articles, 2.5 citations to legal treatises, 0.4 citations to case notes, and 0.4 citations to other secondary material.

It admits of no doubt that doctrinal writing has a considerable influence on the decisions of German judges, but its precise nature and extent are hard to estimate. Many secondary source citations in the German cases are not authoritative in purpose, that is, their primary function is not to justify, or to give additional persuasive effect to, a given assertion of law. Sometimes the citation refers to a book or article that discusses a question the court raised, but explicitly refused to solve in any way. Sometimes the reference is made only to show the position of an identified person, and not put forth that position as correct or approved. Sometimes citations merely serve as a convenient guide to the further education of an interested reader by indicating where certain data, particularly further cases, can be found without implying that the data are conclusive or the consequences to be derived from them are accurate. Sometimes the citation is used as a shorthand reference to the state of the settled law from which the court then proceeds. Citing primary authority, while possible, may in this situation be rather tedious. However, citing a treatise or a commentary is not only quicker and easier, but may also show the settled law in a richer and fuller perspective.

On the other hand, there are many secondary source citations whose purpose is not simply to educate a reader, to save the court the trouble of referring to primary authority, or merely to "pad" the judgment by having a law clerk, in support of a fairly evident proposition, unearth all the authors who take the same view. The court may wish to demonstrate that its position, while controversial, is shared by a majority of the writers or by those with a special reputation in the relevant field. The court may go a step further by stating and discussing specific arguments advanced by a certain author for or against a rule laid down in an earlier case or urged upon the court by a party to the litigation. It is not at all rare that the court will in this way acknowledge the extent to which it feels indebted to ideas and arguments of legal writers regardless of whether the arguments are finally accepted or not.

It would not be difficult to point out a number of judgments of the Federal Supreme Court in which secondary authority has significantly enriched the Court's discussion of a particular point or has directly influenced its holding. Nor would it be difficult to cite a few cases in which the Court, in the present writer's view, instead of getting entangled in doctrinal niceties, should have had the courage to follow its own views of the matter.

3. MONTESQUIEU AND *STARE DECISIS*

NOTE

Before the Revolution, European courts regularly cited and relied on their own and other respected tribunals' decisions. *See* J.H. Baker, ed., Judicial Records, Law Reports, and the Growth of Case Law (1989). We saw an illustration of this use of judicial decisions in *Fabronis v. Marradi Ball Players*

---

and draw from them a body of coherent doctrine. They vary considerably in length, depth, and originality.

(1780), discussed by Gino Gorla in Chapter 3, Section G.2. For an analysis of the use of *stare decisis* for unanimous and well-known 14th century decisions of the Rota Romana, see G. Dolezalek, *Reports of the "Rota" (14th-19th Centuries)*, in Judicial Records, Law Reports, and the Growth of Case Law 69 (J.H. Baker ed. 1989).

After the Revolution, however, judicial decisions were rigorously, if artificially, excluded as formal sources of law in France, Germany, Italy, and most other European civil law nations. As we shall see below, Spain and Latin America took a different approach to the effect of prior judicial decisions. We shall also see that in contemporary Europe reliance on prior judicial decisions has come to be widely recognized and condoned. France, however, still denies formal source of law status to cases even though, in practice, they have great authority. The story is one of the interplay between Revolutionary dogma and the reality of legal practice. We begin at the beginning, with Montesquieu and the separation of powers.

ANDRÉ POUILLE, LE POUVOIR JUDICIARE ET LES TRIBUNAUX 11, 20 (1984)

Everything begins with Montesquieu where he wrote: "In every state there are three kinds of powers: the legislative power, the power that executes matters that relate to the law of nations, and the power that executes matters that depend on the civil law; ... the last of these is called the judicial power.... Liberty cannot survive unless the power to judge is separated from the legislative and executive powers...."

The judicial decision affects only the case under consideration. Judges do not have the right to issue general regulations.... That practice, which was common under the *Ancien Régime* ... is formally prohibited by art. 5 of the Civil Code: "Judges are forbidden to decide cases by issuing general regulatory provisions." ... It follows that judges are not bound by "precedents." ... The decision of the judge is effective only for the specific case in which it is given.

4. THE STYLE AND AUTHORITY OF FRENCH JUDICIAL DECISIONS

GINO GORLA, CIVILIAN JUDICIAL DECISIONS — AN HISTORICAL ACCOUNT OF ITALIAN STYLE, 44 Tulane Law Review 740, 748-49 (1970)

The historical development of the French judicial style shows no doctrinal influence, rather it is a pure product of the French courts, developed and molded within the judicial system. During the *Ancien régime*, French courts did not give *motifs* for their decisions, a practice which developed during the period between 1790 and the first years of the 19th century. This was a period of great change in which the ideology of a rigid separation of powers prevailed along with the notion of written law as the sole source of law. In accordance with these views, courts were simply charged with the application of the texts of the law (which was supposed to be clear and exhaustive) without any power of interpretation. Any employment of a "disputative" or "argumentative" style, the casting of the decision in the form of a dissertation or *consilium*, would certainly have run the risk of being considered interpretation.

Hence, the French *motifs*, especially those of the *Tribunal* (later *Cour*) *de cassation*, resemble the *prémisses* of an "act of will," *i.e.*, the will of the state represented by the court, rather than that of an official "opinion" or "legal advice." That "act of will" is the *dispositif* (the decree). The *motifs* in their capacity as premises of the *dispositif* are strictly tied with it, not only from the logical point of view, but also from the point of view of grammar and syntax. The *motifs* and the *dispositif* are molded into one sentence having only a single subject, the Court. Indeed, during the early years of the *Tribunal de cassation*, according to the technical language of the time, the term *dispositif* included the *motifs*.

It is important to note that during the early years of its life, the *Tribunal de cassation* in most instances simply quoted the text of the law without giving the *motifs*, and when *motifs* were given, it was in a very concise style. This style persisted even when, a short time later, it was admitted that courts had the power to interpret the law. Thus the peculiar feature of the *Cour de cassation's* style has been its conciseness and its seeming simplicity.

BARRY NICHOLAS, FRENCH LAW OF CONTRACT 14-16 (1982)

No one ... now disputes that the decisions of the courts (*la jurisprudence*) must play a large part in any attempt to state the law. To go no further, what we should call the law of torts, which is stated in the *Code civil* in only five articles, is very largely a creation of the courts, and the law of unjustified enrichment derives from a decision of the *Cour de cassation* in 1892 which did not even purport to be based on a text. The writers regularly, and increasingly, take account of *jurisprudence*; no practitioner would fail to deal with it in presenting a case; and though the judgments (with some exceptions in the lower courts) continue to make no reference to it, it is fully examined in the conclusions of the representative of the *ministère public* and in the *rapport*.

The constitutional theory that *jurisprudence* cannot be a legal source is, however, normally maintained. Theory and practice may be reconciled by drawing a distinction between a source (in law) and an authority (in fact). It is an obvious and important fact that courts do follow previous decisions, and statements of what the law is necessarily take account of this fact. But it is nevertheless a fact and not a rule; no court is legally required to follow any previous decision. There is no system of binding precedent, though there is a practice which produces similar results. This may look like splitting hairs to preserve a principle, but the distinction between rule and fact does have practical consequences, and the results, though similar, are not identical.

The practical consequences lie partly in the way in which judgments are formulated and partly in the attitude of judges. The former is indeed something of a technicality. A court may not cite as the justification for its decision a previous decision, or line of decisions, even of the *Cour de cassation*. If it does so, the decision will be quashed for lack of legal foundation. Conversely, if the *Cour de cassation* wishes to quash a decision as being in conflict with its own *jurisprudence,* and every lawyer knows that this is what it is doing, it will nonetheless state as the foundation for its decision not the *jurisprudence,* but the text or legal principle of which the *jurisprudence* is ostensibly an interpretation.

As far as the attitude of judges is concerned, the consequences of the distinction between rule and fact are not merely technical.... The French judges accept that they ought usually to follow decisions of the *Cour de cassation,* if only because stability and predictability are important in the law, but their legal duty is to apply the law and if they are convinced that a decision of the *Cour de cassation* does not represent the law, they will ignore it.... Resistance of this kind to decisions of the *Cour de cassation* is not very uncommon and may, if maintained, particularly by several *Cours d'appel,* presage a change (*revirement*). For what is true of the lower courts is true also of the *Cour de cassation,* and there has never been any suggestion that that court is bound by its own decisions....

There is, then, no rule of binding precedent, but there is a well-established practice that lower courts will normally follow the *jurisprudence* of the *Cour de cassation.* This leaves open, of course, the question of what constitutes a *jurisprudence.* It has often been said that the important difference in practice between the English and the French systems of precedent is that in England a simple decision is sufficient, whereas in France authority attaches to what is called a *jurisprudence constante,* i.e., to a concordant series of decisions. But it is easy to point to single decisions which marked a new departure and were immediately recognised as doing so. The significant distinction is rather between an *arrêt de principe* and an *arrêt d'espèce,* i.e., between a judgment which is intended to establish a principle (either because the case law has been uncertain or conflicting or because the court has decided to alter its previous *jurisprudence*) and one which, as an English lawyer might say, is to be confined to its own facts. This is not to suggest that all decisions are capable of being labelled as one or the other. The great majority of the vast number of *arrêts* rendered every year by the *Cour de cassation* are unremarkable decisions which merely augment an already well-established *jurisprudence constante* on the matter in issue. It is to the small residue of cases which do not fit into this category that the distinction applies. It is not, of course, a distinction which declares itself on the face of the *arrêt,* and its application is a matter of art as much as of science, but the reader of the French reports will acquire a part of the skill if he remembers that in a literary form as laconic as that of the French judgment, particularly as it is practised in the *Cour de cassation,* no word is wasted and none is unconsidered. For example, the formulation of the principle which constitutes the major premise of the judgment will often be repeated unaltered through dozens or hundreds of cases, while the critical reader wonders at the increasingly forced interpretation of either the principle or the facts which is necessary in order to complete the syllogism, until finally a small alteration is made which so adjusts the principle that the forced interpretation is no longer necessary. This is one example of an *arrêt de principe.*

There remains a very considerable difference in the methods by which in the two systems the principle established by a decision is identified. In the example just given the alert reader will notice the change in formulation, but may well be left in doubt as to what it portends. The judgment itself will give him no assistance. If he is fortunate, this may be one of the rare cases in which the *conclusions* or the *rapport* are published. Otherwise he must interpret the change in the light of the *doctrine* on the subject, which will have discussed the difficulties presented by the previous cases. An attempt at such an interpretation will often be appended as a *note* to the report.

5. THE AUTHORITY OF GERMAN JUDICIAL DECISIONS

FRITZ BAUR, EINFÜHRUNG IN DAS DEUTSCHE RECHT, in GESELLSCHAFT FÜR RECHTSVERGLEICHUNG, BIBLIOGRAPHY OF GERMAN LAW IN ENGLISH AND GERMAN: A SELECTION 12, 14 (Courtland H. Peterson trans. 1964)

Rules established by the opinions of the courts are *not* sources of law: A court which has expressed a particular legal viewpoint in one case is not prevented from giving up that view in another decision. No court is bound by the view of another court in a like case; precedents are not binding. A person subject to the law is not required to regulate his conduct according to an opinion expressed in a particular established line of judicial authority.

The principle just described, however, is subject to certain legal or *de facto* exceptions:

Decisions of the Federal Constitutional Court with respect to the compatability of a statute with the Constitution, or the compatability of a statute of one of the German Länder with a federal statute, have the force of a statute. This court is thus authorized to declare either a statute or a particular provision of a statute void.

An inferior court is bound by the view of the law taken by a higher court in the same legal proceeding. The impact of this rule is apparent when an upper court has reversed the judgment of the lower court upon appeal and has remanded the case to the lower court for decision.

Through various provisions, which will not be described in detail here, the law seeks to assure the greatest possible uniformity in the application and interpretation of statutes by the upper courts.

Example: The German Supreme Court (the highest German court in civil and criminal matters) decides cases through panels (departments of the Court). If one panel wishes to deviate in a civil or criminal case from a legal opinion already expressed by another panel, the legal question must be referred for decision to the "Great Senate" of the Court for either civil or criminal matters, as the case may be. The decision thus taken is then binding upon the panel which referred the question, as to that particular case. In this way a certain uniformity in the application of statutes by the upper courts is achieved. One may not on this account characterize rules laid down by the Great Senate as sources of law, however, since they bind neither the other courts nor private persons in general.

It cannot be doubted that the established opinions of the high courts exert a significant *de facto* influence upon the decisions of the lower courts. It is frequently possible that the legal controversy at the trial level will finally be decided by the same high court whose prior opinion is in question, in which case it is to be assumed that the upper court will adhere to its former opinion. In addition the opinions of the high courts acquire a persuasive effect by virtue of their position, because of the quality of their judges and often as a result of the correctness of the reasoning in the opinions. The observation must therefore be made that the lower courts usually do follow the views of the law taken by the upper courts with respect to a particular issue, whether because they are persuaded to do so or because there seems to be nothing to be gained by raising controversy to no avail. For the same reasons persons subject to the law abide by the judicially established rules. But this adherence to precedents is not legally binding; experience has shown that it is not uncommon for lower courts to depart from established lines of judicial authority, and in so doing even to persuade the upper courts of the correctness of *their* view.

NORBERT HORN, HEIN KÖTZ & HANS G. LESER, GERMAN PRIVATE AND COMMERCIAL LAW: AN INTRODUCTION 63-64 (Tony Weir trans. 1982)

The recognition of judge-made rules as proper law is rendered difficult by Montesquieu's theory of the separation of powers which we have already mentioned. Most authors incorporate judge-made law in customary law, whose hallmarks are common adoption and long and invarying habit; to find these characteristics in judge-made law, even with modifications such as some writers adopt, is far from convincing, however, since in fact even isolated decisions of the superior courts command respect, and do so immediately rather than after an interval. Nor does the notion of a special judicial customary law, which some have invoked, take us very much further.

The real question raised by the judges' power to make law is not how to classify it, but how to limit their power and increase their responsibility. Admittedly, judges are bound to decide in accordance with "statute and law" (art. 20 par. 3, Basic Law) but this is too unspecific a restraint; and attempts to use the principles of interpretation and the doctrine of legal sources as methods of limiting their room for play have been ineffective. A different consideration may perhaps prove helpful here. When the courts are developing the law, they follow the fundamental principle of the statute in question and thus seek ideally to maintain *consistency* with the law and its underlying principles. In so doing they have the support of scholars whose writings they regularly cite and discuss. This lively debate and reciprocal interplay between courts and writers can inhibit untoward developments and provide the best assurance of proper progress.

NOTES AND QUESTIONS

1. Consider the following two statements by French jurists about the place of judicial decisions in French sources of law:

> (a) Positive law ... is the ensemble of obligatory rules of law in a given time and place. Such law comes from two kinds of sources: the one direct (law and custom), the other indirect (judicial decisions [jurisprudence],

> legal scholarship [doctrine], and practice).... Jurisprudence has become a source of law of considerable importance in France even though judges are prohibited from issuing regulations, that is to say even though their decisions have authority only in the cases they decide.

Henri et Léon Mazeaud, Jean Mazeaud & François Chabas, Leçons de droit civil 102, 133 (François Chabas 9th ed. 1989).

> (b) [The formal sources of law] are two in number: statutes and jurisprudence.... Jurisprudence: the collection of solutions contained in judicial decisions; hence the existence of "precedents" to which reference is made in judging similar cases.

Michel de Juglart, Cours de droit civil 44-45 (13th ed. 1991).

2. Prepare a memorandum for an American lawyer about the proper use of judicial decisions and scholarly doctrine as legal authority to resolve French and German legal issues that have arisen through American choice of law rules that require a U.S. court to apply French and German law. *See* Michael Wells, *French and American Judicial Opinions,* 19 Yale J. Int'l L. 81 (1994).

3. The French hierarchy of sources of law presents an interesting issue for the force of the Constitution vis-à-vis a *loi,* a *règlement* (enacted by the Government on authority directly from the Constitution), or an *ordonnance.* An *ordonnance* is a legal rule enacted by the Government on authority delegated by the Parliament. It will have the force of a regulation until the Government presents Parliament with a ratification bill, which if passed gives the ordinance the force of a statute.

> Whereas statutes, once promulgated, cannot be subjected to any form of review as to their constitutionality and must accordingly be applied even if incompatible with one or more principles in the Constitution, regulations (including *ordonnances* until ratified) must always conform with the Constitution, with statute law and with what are known in French administrative law as the *principes généraux du droit* ("general principles of law"), and can accordingly be challenged in the administrative courts.

Martin Weston, An English Reader's Guide to the French Legal System 61 (1991).

4. For examples of the style of French and German judicial opinions, see the Table of Cases for this volume. Further examples of French and Italian cases, along with insightful commentary, are presented in David Pugsley, The Strange Case of the Exploding Motorbike, and Other Cases French and Italian (1991).

5. Does the French or the German style of opinion writing, and the use of judicial decisions in legal argument, provide a better method to promote the accountability of judges to law?

6. JUDICIAL LAWMAKING IN SPAIN

NOTE

In Spain, although there was a brief flirtation with the Revolution (described in Chapter 5, Section A), its influence was quickly suppressed. Revolutionary ideas about law and government, including the separation of powers and its corollary theory of sources of law, failed to survive south of the Pyrenees. As they had done before the events of 1776 and 1789, Spanish courts continued to apply case law when they found it useful as a supplement to the *jus commune* and to statutes and custom. Further developments are described in the following materials.

CIVIL CODE OF SPAIN

Article 1

1. The sources of the Spanish legal order are statutes (*leyes*), custom, and the general principles of law (*principios generales del derecho*).

2. Provisions that contradict those at a superior level lack validity.[a]

3. Custom only controls where there is no applicable statute, and then it must not be contrary to morals or public policy and it must be proven....

4. General principles of law are applicable where there is no statute or custom....

6. Case law (*jurisprudencia*) complements the legal order with *doctrina* that the Supreme Court establishes, by reiteration, to interpret and apply statutes, custom, and general principles of law.

7. Judges and courts have the absolute duty to decide the matters in issue in each case, abiding by the established system of sources [of law].[b]

L. NEVILLE BROWN, THE SOURCES OF SPANISH CIVIL LAW, 5 International and Comparative Law Quarterly 364, 366-69 (1956)

Los Principios Generales de Derecho

[I]t is generally accepted that the general principles of the law are not synonymous with the abstract rules of natural justice — those ideal principles to which the imperfect rules of every national law strive unsuccessfully to conform. The Code is not invoking natural justice to fill the lacunae in Spanish *ley* and *costumbre*: rather it is appealing to those principles which are implicit in Spanish law and of which the written law and the customs are the external and incomplete expression. One draws upon these principles to frame a statute or to establish a custom, but the principles remain still unexhausted and still incompletely expressed.

---

[a] The Organic Law of the Judiciary, article 5, states: 'The Constitution is the supreme norm of the legal order; it binds all judges and courts, which interpret and apply statutes and regulations according to constitutional precepts and principles in conformity with the interpretation given in the decisions rendered by the Constitutional Court in all types of cases."

[b] The Penal Code, article 357, states: "A judge who refuses to decide, on the pretext of the obscurity, insufficiency, or silence of the law (*ley*), will be punished by the penalty of suspension."

The most acute awareness of these underlying principles will be found in the judge. By reason of his training, by his experience of the practical problems of life which law seeks to resolve, and by his daily application and interpretation of the legislation entrusted to him to help in their solution, the judge is in a better position than politician or professor to become imbued with the spirit and awareness of those principles. We find therefore that the general principles of the law to which the Code refers are today largely, but not completely, identified with the case-law of the courts. Or, more precisely, a general principle of the law must be evidenced by a particular number of decisions in the same sense emanating from a particular court. The current of decisions bears the technical name of legal doctrine (*la doctrina legal*).

Case Law

The notion of legal doctrine was not new in 1889. A decree of November 4, 1838 had permitted appeal on cassation to the Supreme Court (*Tribunal Supremo*) for violation of *la doctrina legal*.[11] It did not, however, define this term: this definition was left to be worked out in subsequent decisions of the Supreme Court itself. What the French call *la doctrine*, that is, the opinions of learned commentators and academic writers, was distinguished from *la doctrina legal* in a decision of December 10, 1894: such opinions, however eminent their authors, could not found an appeal on cassation. Rather the law of 1838 intended what in France is described as *la jurisprudence*, the case-law of the courts.

At first, legal doctrine comprised the case-law of all the courts,... [b]ut the scope of legal doctrine was progressively narrowed down until it only applied to the case-law of the Supreme Court itself. Moreover, a single decision of the court was not sufficient to create a legal doctrine: it required at least two similar decisions to constitute a legal doctrine, any breach of which thereafter by an inferior court would give rise to recourse on cassation to the Supreme Court. The notion of legal doctrine has not been more precisely defined than this.... In general, two similar decisions suffice, but the Supreme Court is free to reject a would-be doctrine on no matter how many decisions it has been based. In practice, however, it rarely does so....

Where the judge has to create he may still create freely; but where a legal doctrine has already been formed, he is no longer free to disregard this doctrine: he must observe it or run the risk of his decision being upset on cassation. Legal doctrine in this way brings uniformity into the application of the general principles of the law, yet uniformity of error is avoided by the flexibility of the conception of legal doctrine. One mistaken application of the general principles of the law to a new set of facts does not bind future judges faced by the same facts. Nor, indeed, do two mistaken applications, although the likelihood of mistake is then less and so the Supreme Court is the more likely to accept the decisions as constituting a legal doctrine.

---

[11] The Spanish Supreme Court has adopted a technique of appeal different from the French *Cour de Cassation*. The latter is a true court of cassation, since it *breaks* the decision of the court below without substituting its own decision: instead there is a *renvoi*, not to the court first seized but to another court of like jurisdiction. The Supreme Court not only quashes the decision of the court below but also substitutes its own decision of the case.

CIC CO. v. SPAIN

Supreme Court of Spain
(Contentious-Administrative Chamber No. 3)
Case 9119 of 11 November 1988
55 R.J. 8927 (1988)

The CIC Company brought an action before the Provincial Economic-Administrative Tribunal of Madrid challenging an order of 7 June 1983 to pay a [film's] dubbing and importation tax of 22,465,000 pesetas. [After losing, the Company] appealed to the Central Economic-Administrative Tribunal, which rejected its claim on 3 May 1984. An appeal to the administrative jurisdiction of the Audiencia Nacional was rejected on 25 September 1986. On further appeal this Tribunal Supremo (Supreme Court) revokes the appealed decision and declares the disposition below void.

MR. JUSTICE D. RAFAEL DE MENDIZÁBAL Y ALLENDE delivered the opinion of the Court.

Legal Bases

FIRST. Even though the time when it first saw light is not known, "*doctrina legal* subsists as a source of normative production that makes the [legal] order self-sufficient and permits the judge to undertake and perform the weighty burden of deciding all matters brought before him," as required by art. 1 of the Civil Code, notwithstanding the obscurity or insufficiency of the statute.... *Doctrina legal* has been recognized in the regulatory norm governing administrative jurisdiction [citation omitted], whose art. 101 provides for an extraordinary appeal in the interest of the law.... Such *doctrina* grows out of judicial precedent or "case law," which we employ as a consequence of the principles of legal certainty and of equality of all before the law set out in arts. 9 and 14 of our Constitution. [Citation omitted.] Violation [of these principles] requires *revisión*, permitting and obliging us to quash decisions that conflict with dominant case-law criteria. On this point see our Decision of 30 November 1987.

The question raised by this case resembles in general and in detail earlier ones whose judicial response is found in a constellation of decisions of this chamber, beginning with those of 10 July and 3 October 1986 through various others including, among the most recent, those of 23 March and 13 April 1987 and 13 May 1988. [Citations omitted.] We are accordingly in the presence of a coherent body of *doctrina legal*, which reflects the way the Tribunal Supremo understands the Law (*Derecho*) and on that basis takes on normative value to complete the legal order and authoritatively state the *ius dicere*, which is the semantic and substantive essence of the judicial power. The concept, accepted in art. 1, paragraph 6 of the Civil Code, according to its 1974 version [citation omitted], appeared almost a century ago in the original version of art. 1692 of the Code of Civil Procedure (1881) that now — since its modification in 1984 [citation omitted] refers to *jurisprudencia*.

SECOND. Solution of the present dispute can only be found in the group of our decisions cited above. However, it will not be otiose here and now to restate the considerations on which they are based. The immediate object of this case is determination of the amount of the applicable fee for permission to dub, subtitle, and exhibit foreign films. However, the sole basis of appeal consists in the alleged invalidity of Decrees 4292/1964 of 11 December and 793/1973 of 26 April [citations omitted], which authorized a truncated procedure for determination of the applicable fees [citation omitted], by-passing the usual economic-administrative process as we set out in our Decision of 16 May 1986 [citation omitted].... We now once again face a claim of so-called indirect violation of general provisions by acts whose consequences are equivalent to those that we considered in the previous rejection of a direct attack, as set out in art. 39, 4th part, of the statute governing this jurisdiction. This requires us to issue another judgment and, at the same time, permits us to correct the earlier inchoate jurisprudential criterion, which did not rise to the character of *doctrina legal* and, consequently, lacked binding force as precedent in the strict sense. It must not be forgotten that such a judgment is an essential requisite of the prohibition contained in art. 6 of the governing Organic Law of the Judiciary.[a] ...

THIRD. The Law of 17 July 1958 [citation omitted] regulating the cinematographic fund, adopted by the Spanish Cortes (Parliament), alludes in the first part of art. 2 to "the rules concerning regulation, subtitling, and dubbing of foreign films" as one of the sources of income of the National Film Institute. That norm contained none of the elements that constitute a tax (dutiable event or act, obligor, basis, type, accrual) and consequently did not have a direct and immediate effect. It is clear to us, as it was to the legal advisors of the Budget Ministry, that the Law of 1958 did not create this parafiscal charge but merely provided for the possibility of its creation. Nor could it be interpreted as an "authorization" because of the vagueness of the limits it imposed. Lacking even the minimum structure, it is obvious that the announced charge created no liability then or during the next six years. The Law on Taxes and Parafiscal Exactions of 31 December 1958, promulgated a little later, did not affect the charge under consideration, because (the charge) did not exist as such and fell outside the ambit of a possible confirmation. Nor was it included in the report on existing taxes published by the Budget Ministry on 25 July 1960....

FOURTH. The Tax Reform Law of 11 June 1964 [citation omitted] explicitly revoked all legal provisions in force that could create parafiscal taxes (art. 225.1). That later specific norm caused the "authorization" contained in the Law on the Cinematographic Fund [of 17 July 1958] to evaporate and thus removed the essential support for a future and more problematic delegalization. It is accordingly precisely when Decree 4292/1964 of 11 December was published that there was established for the first time a tax on dubbing, subtitling, and exhibiting foreign films. This norm violated not only the Fundamental Laws then in force, which required that the Cortes vote on any kind of tax [citation omitted], but also [violated] ordinary legislation. In fact, art. 27 of the Law on the Legal Regime of State Administration [citation omitted] prohibited the imposition of exactions, taxes, and other similar charges by norms issuing from the regulatory power, unless they had been authorized by

[a] Article 6 reads: "Judges and courts will not apply regulations or any other provision contrary to the Constitution, a statute, or the principle of normative hierarchy."

statute. For its part, art. 10 of the General Revenue Law 230/1963 of 28 December [citation omitted] retained within the *reserva legal* [matters falling solely within legislative jurisdiction] decision on all elements directly determining the amount of tax owed. And finally, it [Decree 4292/1964] violates our Constitution, which proclaims the same principle in art. 133.

FIFTH. In brief, the Law of 1958 contemplated or announced a charge, in a way more prophetic than imperative. However, to the extent that it might have been an authorization, it disappeared in 1964, before the publication of Decree 4292 of the same year. Accordingly, [Decree 4292] imposed no obligation and was from its origin absolutely void under art. 28 of the Law on the Legal Regime because it established, created, and regulated a tax, the so-called dubbing tax or charge, a nullity that was carried over to Decree 793/1973 of 26 April in which specified earlier norms were modified. This initial invalidity could not be cured by inclusion of the tax in the General State Budget as an item of income because — first of all — such a document has the character of a simple forecast [citation omitted]. Further, art. 134.7 of the Constitution prohibits the Budget Law from implicitly or explicitly, directly or indirectly, creating taxes.... Finally, the conclusion that the Decrees regulating the dubbing tax are void inevitably nullifies actions to collect the tax based on their authority.

NOTES AND QUESTIONS

1. Construct the hierarchy of sources of law in Spain. Can we say that Spain recognizes the doctrine of *stare decisis*? For the Supreme Court? For the Constitutional Court?

2. What is going on in *CIC Co. v. Spain*, a Spanish example of judicial review of an administrative determination? Can you penetrate the style and terminology? Can you reconstruct the facts and the reasoning of the Court? Try.

3. Observe that the decision is by the Contentious-Administrative Chamber of Spain's highest court, the Supreme Court. Where would similar cases be finally decided in France? Germany? Italy?

4. What do the answers to the previous question suggest about the extent to which the Spanish legal system was affected by the Revolution?

5. The Court refers repeatedly to *doctrina legal*, uses the term *jurisprudencia*, and even "case law" as its equivalent, and expressly states that it is a source of law. Is this consistent with the Revolution's image of the legal process?

6. With the development of the European Community and now Union, many Europeans take a new view of their legal history. The Revolution is now seen as an interruption and the present trend toward a new European *jus commune* as a return to the proper order of things. This attitude deemphasizes the importance of the Revolutionary ideology and rejects its more obvious excesses. Consider the following excerpt from the German Constitutional Court:

> [There can be no] doubt that it was the intention of the member states to provide the Community with a court which would ascertain and apply the

law by methods developed over centuries of common European legal tradition and refinement of law. In Europe the judge was never merely "la bouche qui prononce les paroles de la loi." Roman law, the English common law, and the German *gemeines Recht* were to a large extent the creation of the judges in the same way as in more recent times in France, for instance, the development of general legal principles of administrative law by the Counseil d'Etat or, in Germany, general administrative law, large parts of the law of employment, or security rights in private-law business transactions. The Community treaties must also be construed in the light of a common European legal tradition and refinement of the law. In view of this it is mistaken to think that the Court of Justice of the Communities is prohibited from using the [judicial] method of developing the law.

In re Application of Frau Kloppenburg, German Constitutional Court, 3 Common Market L. Rep. 1, 19 (1988).

7. Most of the nations in Spanish America have unified judicial systems that deal with civil, penal, and administrative cases. In most of them some form of *jurisprudencia* is recognized as a source of law. Perhaps they inherited these features of their legal systems from the former colonial power, Spain. However, the American legal system also has unified jurisdiction and uses judicial decisions as a source of law. Does it seem likely that, on achieving victory in wars of independence, the former colonies would want their legal systems to emulate that of Spain? Was the legal system thought of as something apart from and unsullied by the politics and economics of colonialism? Or did the legal systems of the newly independent nations adopt such features out of a desire to emulate American law?

7. MEXICAN *JURISPRUDENCIA*

RICHARD D. BAKER, JUDICIAL REVIEW IN MEXICO: A STUDY OF THE *AMPARO* SUIT 252-54, 256, 259-60, 263 (1971)

The legal nature and permissible scope of *jurisprudencia* have always been subject to controversy. That this should be so is not surprising, given the rigid doctrinal separation of the legislative and adjudicative functions normally prevailing in civil law systems. Nonetheless, the mere fact that the Constitution, as amended in 1950-1951, declared it to be binding was enough to establish *jurisprudencia* as a true source of law. Even for purposes of doctrinaire argument it is improbable that the less explicit terminology of the present article 107 could raise a new question about this. The legislative characteristics of *jurisprudencia*, however, should not be taken to mean that the lawmaking powers exercised by the Supreme Court, and now by the collegial circuit tribunals as well, are equal in scope to those available to common-law courts through the rule of stare decisis. On the contrary, the majority of the commentators hold, and the Court itself has stated, that *jurisprudencia* should never intrude into the province of the legislative authority. In practical terms, this would mean that *jurisprudencia*, to be valid, must be confined to interpreting statutes, *reglamentos*, constitutional precepts, and other rules of law enacted by properly constituted legislative and constituent authorities. Consistent with this view, for the judiciary to enunciate new legal norms, that is, norms not founded directly upon pre-existing legislative enactments or constitutional provisions and limited to the clarification and necessary elaboration of their meaning, would mean an unconstitutional usurpation of power. As generally understood, therefore, *jurisprudencia* can be considered an auxiliary but not an autonomous source of law. That the Supreme Court has, in fact, acted in conformity with this proposition is well documented by the content of its collected *jurisprudencia.* Of the 1,122 theses contained in the compilation, published in 1955, almost all are concerned, partially or wholly, with technical points of statutory or constitutional interpretations, the majority of these relating to the Amparo Law itself. Nowhere does one find anything comparable to the dominance of the Constitution, political in its essence, which has marked the history of judicial review in the United States. Thus far, Mexican *jurisprudencia* affords nothing genuinely equivalent to the development by the Supreme Court of the United States of, for example, the commerce clause, the taxing power, or substantive due process. This is not to say that *jurisprudencia* is of no consequence, but that the Supreme Courts of Mexico and the United States are the heirs of substantially different legal and political traditions and, as a result, act within dissimilar environments and on different conceptions of the judicial role. From the practical point of view, *jurisprudencia* has been indisputably valuable as a device for clarifying the ambiguities and filling the gaps that neither statutory nor constitutional drafting can entirely avoid. In the doctrinal sense, it has defined the effective scope and limits of *amparo* and, consequently, determined the extent to which that institution can function as an effective constitutional defense....

The Formation of Jurisprudencia

Within their respective areas of jurisdictional competence, *jurisprudencia* is established by the Supreme Court *en banc,* by its chambers, and by the collegial circuit tribunals. In any case, five consecutive decisions to the same effect, uninterrupted by any incompatible rulings, must be rendered. When established by the full Supreme Court, each of the decisions contributing to the formation of *jurisprudencia* must be approved by a majority of at least fourteen ministers. In the chambers, a majority of four is required in each case. In the collegial circuit tribunals, the unanimous approval of all three magistrates is specified. In form, a jurisprudential thesis consists normally of a brief restatement of a single point of law abstracted and summarized from the conclusions of law (*considerandos*) expressed in the appropriate decisions. Consequently, none of the decisions involved is necessarily binding in its entirety, nor need the cases to which these decisions refer be entirely analogous....

The Obligations and Application of Jurisprudencia

Despite its obligatory character, *jurisprudencia* produces effects only partially equivalent to those resulting from the rule of stare decisis. In a purely technical sense, to be sure, neither *jurisprudencia* nor precedent, in the Anglo-

American usage, is binding upon any governmental agencies except courts of law and quasi-judicial administrative bodies that have been subsumed within this functional category. As a matter of practice, however, precedent in common-law systems tends to determine the behavior of the executive and legislative branches of government in much the same manner as that of the judiciary itself. As a result, if the Supreme Court of the United States determines that a given law is unconstitutional the practical effect is normally indistinguishable from abrogation of the offending statute, although technically it is nothing of the sort. Administrative agencies refrain customarily from any further attempts at enforcement, and legislative bodies, although they may attempt to achieve the same ends by different means, at least endeavor to avoid repeating their earlier constitutional errors. Further litigation on the same point is necessary only in extraordinary cases and, if it occurs, the result is usually predetermined. Somewhat differently expressed. precedent in the Anglo-American sense, whatever the nature of its content, is normally effective *erga omnes* when established by the highest court within the jurisdiction. This result cannot be claimed for *jurisprudencia*, although there is apparently a tendency on the part of administrative agencies and legislative bodies to respect those theses whose content is confined strictly to technical statutory interpretation and that have no bearing on questions of policy....

By way of illustration, the Supreme Court long ago declared unconstitutional those sections of the 1944 Law of Professions (*Ley reglamentaria de los artículos 4 y 5 constitucionales, relativos al ejercicio de las profesiones en el Distrito y Territorios Federales*) that discriminate against aliens. Nonetheless, in practice these provisions of the law remain fully in force and are regularly executed. When the executive branch chooses to ignore *jurisprudencia*, the only recourse available to persons adversely affected by this action is another *amparo* suit. This practice results necessarily in the multiplication of litigation and a decided inequality in applying the laws....

The Interruption and Modification of Jurisprudencia

The interruption of a jurisprudential thesis, to employ the terminology of the Amparo Law, is analogous to repealing a statute, that is, the thesis is totally divested of its obligatory effect. *jurisprudencia* established by the full Court is interrupted whenever that body pronounces a contradictory judgment supported by a majority of at least fourteen ministers. The requisite majority for overruling *jurisprudencia* established by the chambers is four, while in the collegial circuit tribunals unanimity is required. In conformity with the 1968 amendments, the reasons justifying the interruption of *jurisprudencia* should be stated and should be relevant to the justifications originally cited in support of the precedent in question. In any event, the overruling judgment itself does not acquire the status of *jurisprudencia* unless repeated five times....

The modification of a jurisprudential thesis, on the other hand, does not deprive it of its obligatory character but amends certain provisions of the thesis. Until these amendments take effect, the original text of the thesis remains in force. The procedures for modifying *jurisprudencia* are the same as those for establishing it originally.

NOTE

An illustration of a *jurisprudencia* headnote follows. *Ramírez Méndez* is the sixth similar decision of the criminal law chamber (the first chamber) of the Mexican Supreme Court. It was published in the *Semanario Judicial de la Federación,* which reports decisions of the federal collegial circuit tribunals and the Supreme Court.

RAMÍREZ MÉNDEZ, ENRIQUE

Supreme Court of Mexico (First Chamber)
Direct Amparo 3730/84
187-192 S.J.F. pt. 2, at 85 (7th series 1986)

PROHIBITED WEAPONS, CARRYING OF. VEHICLES. To comprise the crime of carrying a prohibited weapon, it is immaterial that it is transported on the seat or on the floor of an automobile, since it is not necessary for a person to confine it in his belt or pocket to constitute carrying a weapon, but only that he may reach for it at a certain moment.

Direct amparo 2283/78. Enrique López Gaxiola. 5 votes. Seventh series, vols. 115-120, pt. 2, at 35.

Direct amparo 2638/80. Marcos Rodríguez Zavala. 5 votes. Seventh series, vols. 139-144, pt. 2, at 11.

Direct amparo 6712/82. Emilio Equihua Zamora. Unanimity of 4 votes. Seventh series, vols. 169-174, pt. 2, at 20.

Direct amparo 2956/83. Hugo Luis García Madrid. 5 votes. Seventh series, vols. 175-180, pt. 2, at 13.

Direct amparo 8525/83. Domingo González Diáz. 5 votes. Seventh series, vols. 187-192, pt. 2, at 19.

Direct amparo 3730/84. Enrique Ramírez Méndez. 5 votes. Seventh series, vols. 187-192, pt. 2, at 85.

WOODFIN L. BUTTE, *STARE DECISIS,* DOCTRINE, AND JURISPRUDENCE IN MEXICO AND ELSEWHERE, in THE ROLE OF JUDICIAL DECISIONS & DOCTRINE IN CIVIL LAW & IN MIXED JURISDICTIONS 311, 323-28 (Joseph Dainow ed. 1974)

Our method was first to skim a few cases in Volume I of the *Semanario Judicial,*[18] then to read the first hundred civil cases decided by the Supreme Court in 1900, the first hundred decided in 1930, and the first hundred decided in 1968.

[18] The *Semanario Judicial de la Federación* is the officially established publication of all decisions of the Mexican Supreme Court. It has gone through six *épocas* and is in the middle of the seventh. In earlier *épocas* each volume contained the decisions for three or four months, all paged consecutively. Beginning with the sixth *época,* there has been a volume per month, with each volume divided into five "parts." The first part covers decisions of the full court; the second covers decisions of the First Chamber; the third, decisions of the Second Chamber; the fourth, decisions of the Third Chamber; and the fifth, decisions of the Fourth Chamber. The pages of each part of each volume are numbered separately. This makes citation pretty complicated, and the court has never worked out a satisfactory short form.

In Volume I, for 1871, we note, first, a practice of printing first of all as to each case the report and recommendations of the *promotor fiscal*, a government attorney who has, among other responsibilities, the right to comment on questions presented to the Supreme Court for decision. This report commonly contains a brief but complete narrative of the facts, a reference to pertinent legislation (which at that time in Mexico was quite likely to be a citation to the *Siete Partidas*) and a summary recommendation of what the *promotor* thinks the court's decision should be.

Then may come the decision of the trial court in an amparo action (a federal district court) and after that the decision of the Supreme Court, both generally adopting and confirming the report of the *promotor fiscal*. In an important case, there will be extracts from notes of the oral arguments of counsel.

Turning through a number of these cases, we found one in which the district court, in finding for a petitioner that a certain tax collected from him was unconstitutional, based its finding on a similar decision by the Supreme Court in an identical case two years earlier. We found another in which counsel quoted from a text written by a colleague; his adversary cited Carleval, Voet, Story, Wheaton, Calvo, "and many others"; and the Supreme Court cited 1.32, tit. 2°, Part 3ª [*Las Siete Partidas*] and a contemporary Mexican practice manual....

In another case, involving the right of a householder to continue to receive water from a town well, the *promotor fiscal* cites Justinian's *Institutes*, the *Digest*, and the *Partidas*, while the district court cites only the *Partidas* and the Supreme Court cites only a contemporaneous Executive Order.

In their brief for the petitioner for amparo in a capital case, counsel support their point that criminal laws are not to be applied retroactively by citing the whole chain of legal authority from the *Código de Legibus* 1.7, through the *Leyes de Estilo*, the *Fuero Real*, the *Partidas*, and the *Novísima Recopilación*. They cite a similar chain of laws and half a dozen commentators on the inadmissibility of the testimony of accomplices, and go back to the *Partidas* to support their argument that a witness who contradicts himself is not entitled to be believed! They won their case!

Here then, in 1871 in Mexico, was confirmation of the civil-law system as it has always been perceived — a heavy emphasis on statutes, going as far back as may be pertinent, enlightened by learned commentators, but with only casual reference to a recent Supreme Court decision which a district court judge happened to remember by name and date but not by citation.

Moving on thirty years, to the first hundred civil cases decided by the Mexican Supreme Court in 1900, we find substantial changes in the style and format of decisions. The *promotor fiscal* increasingly exercises the privilege the law gives him of not intervening in cases dealing with purely private rights. The lower-court decisions are no longer always printed in full, but sometimes show up only by being quoted either by the Supreme Court or in petitioner's brief (often, in the latter case, accompanied by counsel's references to it in terms we would find scandalous). The Supreme Court is developing the nonstop sentence as a hallmark of judicial writing.

Licenciado Rodriguez finds that of these first hundred decisions, ninety-seven are decided solely by the application to the facts of the case of a particular statutory provision which the court finds controlling. In all these cases, the court's decision is almost bare of reasoning or interpretation; the language is simply something to the effect that "This case is clearly controlled by Article 754 of the Code of Civil Procedure, which provides ...."

It is true that the cases tend to be simple ones: land-ownership cases, with a plaintiff suing for possession; *habeas corpus* cases, with a plaintiff either in jail or in the armed services without his consent and, in his opinion, in violation of his constitutional rights; or procedural cases. At any rate, the Supreme Court makes them *sound* simple; it reviews the facts and the proceedings below, briefly, then says, "It is plain that ...." And the reader wonders how so straightforward a case ever got to the Supreme Court.

Two of these hundred decisions of 1900 are cited by Licenciado Rodriguez as being based on "jurisprudence" of the Supreme Court. In one of these, the *promotor fiscal* observes that a complaint as to the weight given to evidence in the lower courts "cannot according to the jurisprudence of the Supreme Court of Justice be the basis for an amparo proceeding." In the other, the Supreme Court itself pronounces that "the jurisprudence of the courts of the Federation has established that no judicial proceeding can prejudice a third party who has been neither cited nor heard in proper form."...

Between 1900 and 1930 we must note the intervention of an important piece of legislation, the new *Ley de Amparo* of October 18, 1919. This law for the first time uses the word "*jurisprudencia*" in referring to decisions of the Supreme Court, and establishes the binding nature for inferior courts of "*jurisprudencia*" laid down by five consonant decisions of the Supreme Court. It is thus natural to expect more citation of jurisprudence as this reform works its way into the Mexican judicial process; and this is in fact what happened.

In studying the first hundred 1930 civil cases, Licenciado Rodriguez finds eighteen of them based on jurisprudence, seventy-one on the application of controlling statutes and eleven on citations of doctrinal writings.

The style and format of decision-writing in 1930 has not changed much from that of 1900. The Ministerio Público (the old *promotor fiscal*) hardly ever intervenes; the lower court's decision appears mostly in the form of quotations in petitioner's brief of those parts of it which he deems most objectionable; the Supreme Court feels the need for somewhat — but not much — more support for its decision than to say "It is clear that ...."

In the eleven cases out of the hundred in which doctrinal writings are cited, the citations are more specific than they were in 1871; but some of them are elucidating European code provisions different from the Mexican and contribute little to the court's reasoning. Even in the eighteen cases out of the hundred in which the court relies on its own jurisprudence, only in two or three of these does the court actually cite any cases by name. The court feels the pressure to support its decisions; but it usually does so by some such statement as "as this Supreme Court has decided in numerous cases ...."

We may note in passing that at this time it was still extremely difficult to *find* "jurisprudencia" in Mexico. At the end of each volume of the *Semanario Judicial* there was a listing, by alphabetical order of key words, of the headnotes of decisions in that volume; but it does not appear to have occurred to anybody to organize these into one publication anywhere.

By 1968 this had radically changed, and Mexico had various publications in which court or counsel could look for the rules of decision laid down in reported cases. The presiding justice in his annual report had initiated a section in which he referred to the more important rulings handed down during the year. And through the years 1932-1955, the *Semanario* published a series of appendices covering cumulatively all jurisprudence established since 1917. This series culminated with the publication, in 1955, of a three-volume *compilación* covering decisions of the court for the years 1917-1954. In this compilation are listed, alphabetically by key word, the headnotes of rules which had been enunciated in five decisions of the court (thus becoming *jurisprudencia* binding on all lower courts) and citations to those decisions. Under each heading the editors of the *Semanario* also, in a very interesting development, set out the headnotes and the citation of individual cases which lay down "related rules which establish precedent, but not jurisprudence." One notes in passing that, as might be expected, the "jurisprudence" tends to be one or two headnotes on each topic, citing five or more cases enunciating quite elementary rules of law, and that the "related rules" are much more interesting, varied, and useful.

In 1965 the editors of the *Semanario* published another of their appendices covering the years 1917-1965. This one is in five volumes, one for the full court and one for each of the chambers....

And in 1965 Licenciado Sergio Torres Eyras published the best and most ambitious compilation yet, in five volumes covering respectively the decisions of the full court and of each of the four chambers for the years 1955-1963. It is interesting to note that his index covers all decisions of the respective chambers, and that the ritual series of five decisions to constitute binding *jurisprudencia* are distinguished only by the word "*jurisprudencia*" in capital letters in the citation of each decision. In other words, *precedent* is becoming the more important concept; the formal binding character of *jurisprudencia* is frosting on the cake.

It is not surprising, therefore, that in his analysis of the first hundred civil cases decided by the Mexican Supreme Court, in 1968, Licenciado Rodriguez finds fifty-one in which the court cites its own jurisprudence, forty-two in which the decision is by application of a clearly controlling statute, and only two which contain any citation of doctrinal writings. Moreover, in turning through these cases, one finds that prior cases are no longer referred to only in general terms like "It has been decided in numerous cases by this Supreme Court that ...." They are now referred to by specific title, citation and more often than not by quotation of the applicable headnote.

We may summarize:

Table 9.1
Civil Cases of the Mexican Supreme Court, by Year and the Basis of Decision

First 100 cases in	Controlling statute	Doctrinal writings	Court's own "jurisprudencia"
1900	97	1	2
1930	71	11	18
1968	42	2	51

It is hard to know which is the chicken and which is the egg; but it is certainly true that in Mexico judicial precedent is much easier to find than in the past; and that in the decision-reaching process, precedent is now much more used and carries much more weight than doctrinal writings.

NOTES AND QUESTIONS

1. How would you explain the astounding growth in the citation of *jurisprudencia* in Mexican Supreme Court opinions during the 20th century and the relatively low rate of citation of scholarly writings?

2. Suppose a lawyer or notary, giving legal advice to a client in France or Germany, inadvertently fails to take into account a recent and relevant decision of the highest ordinary or administrative court. Should this provide the basis for an action for damages by the client? Why? Would your answer be different if the same facts occurred in Spain or Mexico? Why?

3. Suppose you were a young judge committed to a judicial career in Europe or Latin America. Counsel in a case at trial before you refers to one or more relevant decisions of your supreme court. Would you be inclined to follow such decisions, or would you feel free to adopt an independent approach to the legal questions at issue? Why? If you were an Italian judge whose future assignments and promotion were in the hands of the *Consiglio Superiore della Magistratura*, composed entirely of judges, but with the preponderance of power in judges of the Supreme Court of Cassation and the Courts of Appeal, what attitude would you be likely to take toward the decisions of those courts?

4. If judicial decisions have no value as precedents, there is little reason to publish (in the sense of print and disseminate) them (other than to subject the work of the courts to the discipline of public scrutiny, an objective that is at the bottom of the requirements that decisions be publicly announced and that they be rationally motivated). Conversely, a published decision invites use and citation. Accordingly, the extent to which and the manner in which judicial decisions are published and made available for use in research reflect their true position and function in the legal system. The enormous body of published full texts of appellate (and some trial) decisions in the U.S., together with the extensive (and expensive) system of digests, citators, encyclopedias, and annotations that facilitate access to and use of them, stand at one extreme. They indicate a legal process in which judicial decisions are a heavily used source of law. At the opposite extreme is the hypothetical situation in which judicial decisions are not published at all, but in no legal system in Europe or Latin America is this the practice. Even the most traditional of civil law jurisdictions publish some judicial decisions. The principal generalizations that one can make about the publication of judicial decisions in Europe and Latin America are:

a. Even the decisions of supreme courts are only selectively published. Those of lower courts are seldom published.
b. Sometimes only excerpts, summaries, or abstract headnote-type statements drawn from decisions are published.
c. Publication is often made in one part of a legal periodical that also includes parts devoted to doctrine, legislation, and executive acts.

d. There seldom exist research devices equivalent to the digest system or to the massive citations to cases in encyclopedias, treatises, and annotations of the sort familiar to us. Nor is there any equivalent to Shephard's to indicate the current value as authority of an earlier case.
e. However, one often does find published with the case, a note which criticises the decision and places it in doctrinal, and occasionally in jurisprudential, context.
f. The richness of case publication and its associated literature is affected by economics. In a small developing nation with few lawyers it is more difficult to marshal the economic and human resources needed to support an extensive system.
g. Computer technology may change some of the above stated generalizations. Today in Europe, for instance, cases from the high courts in some countries are available from online computer services or in the form of CD-ROM. As cost comes down one might expect more lawyers to use judicial decisions in legal argument.

5. Why do European and Latin American nations all seem to recognize an inherent power in the executive to legislate by decree, at least in times of emergency or during a "state of siege" (*estado de sitio*)? Is such a power recognized in domestic affairs under U.S. constitutional law? In fact the president does make law by decree (presidential orders and other directives). However, it is clear that in *most* cases (all cases?) there is at least a colorable legislative basis for the exercise of a presidential rule-making power. *Cf. Youngstown Sheet & Tube Co. v. Sawyer*, 343 U.S. 579 (1952).

NOTE ON SOURCES OF LAW IN EAST ASIA

The civil law jurisdictions in East Asia ostensibly adhere to prevailing continental European views on the formal sources of law. With the notable exception of Indonesia having, as mentioned previously, delineated spheres governed by Islamic or adat (customary) law, for most of the legal systems of East Asia the codes and other statutory law are accurately described as the primary source of legal rules and standards. All recognize a hierarchy of authority with statutory law at the apex. All thus in principle require that administrative regulations have a statutory basis. Only in cases of declared national emergency is any use of decrees having the force of a statute recognized, a situation that has been extraordinarily rare in Japan — e.g., under the Allied Occupation — but less so under military-dominated regimes in other East Asian states. Despite widespread resort to informal means to enforce administrative policy — such as "administrative guidance" — the necessity of at least minimal statutory authority is acknowledged. Less agreement exists with respect to whether custom, scholarly opinion, judicial decision, and, in the case of Japan, equitable principles (*jōri*) also constitute accepted sources of law, and, if so, which have priority. Aside from theoretical dispute, in practical terms, all serve as sources of law.

The legal orders of Northeast Asia share a reinforcing Confucianist tradition and history of legal reception in which scholars have played a major role in introducing the European codes and theory. Their views are frequently cited, at least in Japan, as authority by courts at all levels, especially in cases involving previously undecided issues of law or interpretations of code or statutory provisions. Scholars continue to facilitate the introduction of new ideas, often still from abroad. Custom too has decisive influence in the accommodation of socially accepted practices within the framework of transplanted legal rules. In several instances custom is explicitly recognized, as in the case of article 1 of the Japanese Commercial Code, which provides for commercial custom to prevail over the Civil Code in the absence of any applicable provision in the Commercial Code. Moreover, Japanese judges frequently ground interpretation of statutes and contracts on their understanding of the "general sense of the community" (*ippan shakai no tsūnen*).

Also reflecting tradition — particularly in Japan — as well as the influence of English and American practice, East Asian legal systems appear to give greater deference to judicial precedent than some European or Latin American systems. Although none recognizes a doctrine of *stare decisis*, the decisions and reasoning of the highest courts, particularly *en banc* judgments, are generally viewed as binding in practice. This acceptance of precedent combines with scholarly opinion and custom to form a significant wellspring for legal development and change often confirmed later by statute or code amendment.

8. THE AUTHORITY OF JAPANESE JUDICIAL DECISIONS

TAKEYOSHI KAWASHIMA, THE CONCEPT OF JUDICIAL PRECEDENT IN JAPANESE LAW, in 1 IUS PRIVATUM GENTIUM: FESTSCHRIFT FÜR MAX RHEINSTEIN ZUM 70. Geburtstag am 5. Juli 1969, at 85, 87-88, 91-95, 98-99 (Ernst von Caemmerer, Soia Mentschikoff & Konrad Zweigert eds. 1969)

The concept of judicial precedent, as differentiated from "examples of judicial decision," did not come into existence until 1917, when a young professor *Shigeto Hozumi* (1883-1957) at the Tokyo Imperial University published a challenging article soon after he returned from England where he had studied law. In that article he bluntly took issue with other scholars' criticisms of a decision of *Daishin-in*[a] on the ground that they were not based on the concept of judicial precedent and stated his own view on the study of judicial decisions from the viewpoint of precedent....

This pioneer was followed by another proponent of the same idea, *Izutaro Suehiro*, professor at the Tokyo Imperial University (1888 to 1951). In 1917 he went — correctly speaking, he had to go — to America for the study of law, because World War I made travel to Germany or France impossible. His stay in America at the University of Chicago had a profound effect upon him. For the first time in his life he learned that there existed an approach that was completely different from the one he had known.... In 1920 he came back from his Wanderjahre abroad to Japan, and in the next year he published a treatise

[a] The highest court in the hierarchy of courts, under the Court Organization Law prior to World War II. It was almost the counterpart of the *Cour de cassation* of France.

on the law of property and chattels (Sachenrecht), a really epoch-making and pioneering work which, for the first time in the history of jurisprudence in Japan, presented the law as it actually functions in the courts based on careful and exhaustive study of judicial precedents....

The influence of the works of *Hozumi* and *Suehiro* seems to have expanded gradually in the writings of scholars as well as in the practice of courts.... By and by, almost all the law journals regularly published studies of judicial decisions; in other words, the study of judicial decisions became a sort of fad among law scholars even before World War II. Although there is no material through which we could guess the extent to which judges felt themselves bound by judicial precedents of the *Daishin-in*, I would assume that the general atmosphere as stated above might have caused the courts to become more precedent-conscious and precedent-oriented....

Under the military occupation by Allied Powers after World War II, Japan underwent radical political and legal reforms which are rightly called a "revolution." With the start of the new court system and legal system there appeared two remarkable indications which suggest the basic attitude of the government and the Supreme Court.

First, the Court Law (Law No. 59 of 1947), which replaced the Court Organization Law (Law No. 6 of 1890), provides: "In case the opinion (of a Petty Bench of the Supreme Court) is incompatible with a previous decision of the Supreme Court concerning the interpretation or application of the Constitution or other laws or ordinances, the Grand Bench shall render a decision, and the Petty Bench may not" (art. 10). And the Enforcement Ordinance of the Court Law (Ord. No. 24 of 1947), article 5 provided that in so far as article 10, item 3 of the Court Law is concerned, a decision of the *Daishin-in* is regarded as a decision which the Supreme Court previously rendered....

Furthermore, the new Code of Criminal Procedure after World War II provides that a *jokoku* appeal, which is a counterpart of the Revisionsantrag in German law or the pourvoi en cassation in French law, may be lodged against a judgment in first or second instance rendered by a High Court, (i) on the ground that the judgment has been formed incompatible with a *hanrei* (judicial precedent) previously established by the Supreme Court, or (ii) in a case for which there exists no *hanrei* of the Supreme Court, on the ground that the judgment has been formed incompatible with a *hanrei* previously established by the *Daishin-in* or by a High Court as the Revisionsgericht, or after the new Code of Criminal Procedure came into effect, by a High Court as the *Koso*-court, which is a counterpart of the Berufungsgericht in Germany (art. 405, item 2 and 3) ....

[T]he Supreme Court started in 1948 to issue various kinds of reports of judicial decisions: the main publications are *Saiko-saibansho Hanrei Shu* (Collection of Judicial Precedents of the Supreme Court), *Saiko-saibansho Saiban Shu* (Collection of Judicial Decisions of the Supreme Court), *Koto-saibansho Hanrei Shu* (Collection of Judicial Precedents of the High Courts) and *Kakyu Saibansho Saibanrei Shu* (Collection of Examples of Judicial Decisions of the Lower Courts). In these titles various words are used to indicate judicial decisions, namely *hanrei, saiban,* and *saibanrei.* Categorization and designation of these reports of decisions were carefully done with a clear concept of judicial precedent....

What was the attitude or behavior of judges in their practice in the courts? Interesting is the fact that, prior to the reform of the court system in 1947, judges apparently felt themselves bound rather strictly by judicial precedents of the *Daishin-in* although the civil law doctrine of the sources of law prevailed, and on the contrary, after the reform there have appeared judges who dared to render decisions which conflicted with the precedents of the Supreme Court with the intention to have the Supreme Court eventually change the precedents. This fact was disclosed by Judge *Kishi* in a meeting of judges and law professors with Professor *Arthur von Mehren* in 1956. One might be rather surprised to learn this story, since it is to be expected that, under the clear official conception of judicial precedent after the war, judges would feel more strongly the binding effect of judicial precedents. I would, however, construe the fact differently: prior to the reform of the court system the disciplinary control of the bureaucratic organization of the judiciary was such that judges felt themselves bound rather strictly by the judicial precedents of the *Daishin-in*, which was definitely superior in its position in the hierarchy of courts, whereas after the reform of the court system, the bureaucratic atmosphere in the courts was more or less weakened due partly to the general ideological atmosphere and also due to the introduction of the Anglo-American institution of each justice of the Supreme Court stating his individual opinion in his decisions, which presumably encouraged judges to be more independent in judicial decision-making. Recruitment of judges from practicing lawyers, as a result of the judicial reform after the war, also might have contributed to some extent to the attitudinal or behavioural change stated above. In any event it is almost certain that judges generally feel themselves bound rather strongly by the precedents of the Supreme Court and probably to a lesser extent by the precedents of the higher courts under which their courts stand....

It is very difficult even to approximate the percentage of those who support the common law conception of judicial precedent and those who do not. If we take into consideration the fact that the official doctrine of the Supreme Court about judicial precedent is a variant of the civil law doctrine of sources of law rather than a Japanese adaptation of the common law conception of judicial precedent, the number of those who support the common law conception of judicial precedent is rather small.

I would summarize the attitude of the courts and the scholars as follows. The courts' attitude was rather flexible: the reactions of the courts to the doctrine and criticism of scholars who advocated the common law conception of judicial precedent, and probably also [recognition of] the actual needs in the society, have been always receptive. But at the same time they have adhered to the civil law doctrine concerning the sources of law so that their concept of judicial precedent is unique in that it views a judicial precedent as a decision which is recognized by the Supreme Court officially as a precedent; probably this was a merger of the concept of judicial precedent with the civil law doctrine which has been long taken for granted. On the contrary, the attitude of the majority of scholars has been strongly resistant. They have clung rather obstinately to the civil law doctrine, and have even denied the need for predictability of judicial decisions.

SUZUKI v. CITY OF TOKYO

Supreme Court of Japan
First Petty Bench
Decision of 18 October 1990
44 Minshū 1021 (1990)

Case Involving a Claim for Vacation of a Building

Question Presented: Inheritance of the Right to Use Public Housing by Successors upon the Death of a Resident of Public Housing.

Holding: The Heirs of a Decedent Resident of Public Housing Do Not Automatically Succeed to the Right to Use Such Public Housing.

Reasons

With respect to the first reason presented by the appellant on appeal:

The Public Housing Law [Law No. 193, 1951] is intended to promote social welfare and stabilize the lives of the people by providing housing at low rents to persons with low incomes who find it difficult to obtain housing (art. 1). Consequently, the statute restricts the determination of criteria for persons entitled to public housing (art. 17) by requiring the selection of residents by a fair process in accordance with regulations that comply with standards established by cabinet order (art. 18). The statute additionally provides in the event a resident's income exceeds the standard set by cabinet order, corresponding to the number of years of residence, that the resident must endeavor to vacate the public housing (art. 21-2[1]) and that the person in charge of the housing units in question may seek judicial action to have the premises vacated (art. 21-3[1]).

In view of the purport of these provisions of the Public Housing Law, there is no basis for holding that, upon the death of a resident, the successor automatically inherits the right to use public housing. Therefore, the decision to this effect of the court below can be confirmed as correct. The cases cited by the appellant do not adopt an interpretation contrary to that decision. The judgment of the court below is thus not contrary to law as argued. We cannot adopt the argument of the appellant, which is little more than a criticism of the judgment below based on an individual viewpoint.

NOTE ON PUBLIC REGISTRIES IN EAST ASIA

The public registries are perhaps more significant in East Asia, particularly in Japan, South Korea, and Taiwan, than in most other civil law jurisdictions. The three basic registries in Japan are the Family Registry (*Koseki*) administered by the Family Registry Bureau in local government offices (*shi* or *ku yakusho* or *yakuba*), the Immovable Registry (*Fudōsan tōki*) administered by local offices of the Ministry of Justice (*Hōmushō Chihō Hōmu kyoku Shutchōshō*), and the Commercial Registry (*Shōgyō tōki*) also administered by local Ministry of Justice offices. The Family Registry determines all familial relationships from birth through death, including parentage, adoption, marriage, and divorce, and thus any property rights derived from succession. For example, all that is required by a spouse or child to demand payment of the legally protected share of assets belonging to the deceased and held by a bank or other party is a certified copy of the appropriate family registration which is sufficient to show the death and the identity of the claimants. The Immovable Registry provides presumptive proof of all existing and contingent real rights (*bukken*) nationwide in immovables, such as ownership of and security interests in real estate. The Commercial Registry similarly is determinative of the status and authorized representatives of all companies and other juridical persons in Japan.

Detailed laws and regulations govern the procedures for each registry. Their most important function, however, is to substitute in large measure for fact-finding in that the registered information is for most practical purposes conclusive of the facts that establish legal relationships. The substantive rules governing family relationships, rights in property, and juridical persons are provided in the codes or in special statutes. Registration, however, is either constitutive of the legal relationship as in the case of the Family Registry, or gives public notice and thus presumptive proof of the facts shown, as in the case of the Immovable Registry. The special statutes and voluminous regulations that govern the procedures for registration are in practice as important as, if not more crucial than, the code provisions.

For example, the availability of provisional registration (*kari-tōki*) for contingent rights in immovables makes possible the creation of a variety of security interests by contract, such as a loan with related agreements for the sale, leaseback, and repurchase of real property (construed as a common law mortgage in the United States). Such arrangements are now governed by a special statute — the Law Concerning Provisional Registration of Security Contracts (*Kari-tōki tanpo keiyaku ni kansuru hōritsu*), Law No. 78, 1978.

In sum, the registries are crucial in the everyday affairs of all Japanese, and are an extremely important aspect of legal life in East Asia generally.

NOTES AND QUESTIONS

1. Review Questions 2 and 3 following the Butte excerpt, *supra* Section B.7, but now considering the case of Japan. How would you respond?

2. Should public registries in East Asia (or for that matter in Europe and Latin America, where they also serve an important function in the legal system) be considered a kind of source of law? Do registries in effect convert private law into regulatory law or at least provide an administrative as opposed to a judicial means for enforcement of legal rights?

3. The appellant in *Suzuki v. City of Tokyo* argued that a 1984 Supreme Court decision — *Hashimoto v. City of Tokyo, Hanrei jihō* (No. 1141) 58 (Sup. Ct., 1st P.B., 13 Dec. 1984) — established that use of public housing was basically the same as a private landlord-tenant relationship, governed in the absence of specific regulatory or statutory provisions to the contrary by Japan's Civil Code and House Lease Law [Law No. 50, 1921]. On the basis of this precedent, the appellant argued, the Civil Code right of succession applied to leaseholds under the Public Housing Law. Although the Supreme Court disagreed, did the court accept or reject the basic proposition that the 1984 decision was applicable and should be followed as binding judicial precedent? If judicial precedent was considered to be controlling, how do you explain the outcome of the case?

4. *Hashimoto v. City of Tokyo* involved a lawsuit brought by the Tokyo municipal authorities to have a public housing tenant evicted for enlarging the premises without permission and failure to pay a rental surcharge. The tenant argued that the municipality could not terminate the lease under the Civil Code principle of trust and provisions of Japan's House Lease Law. The Supreme Court upheld both lower court decisions rejecting the tenant's defense, finding that the municipality had not violated principles of trust. The Supreme Court acknowledged, however, that the Civil Code and the House Lease Law did apply to public housing arrangements in the absence of conflicting provisions of the Public Housing Law.

5. As in the French Supreme Court of Cassation decision in the *Scotch Whisky Association* case (*infra* Section B.3 of this chapter), the *Hashimoto v. City of Tokyo* case was published in a professional periodical *Hanrei jihō*, along with an explanatory comment by a Japanese legal scholar. Such comments typically include a description of the facts of the case, in addition to an analysis of the holding in relationship to prior court decisions and the views of leading scholars.

As for style, is a Japanese court decision more like a French or German judicial opinion?

6. Japanese Supreme Court decisions do not include statements of fact. Instead, the court gives reasons for its judgment in response to the arguments made on appeal. The official compilations of Supreme Court decisions — the *Saiko Saibansho Hanreishū* (Compilation of Supreme Court precedents) — in which *Suzuki v. City of Tokyo* was published under the volume of "civil precedents" (*Minji hanreishū*, abbreviated as "*Minshū*") ordinarily include the judgments of both the court of first instance as well as first appeal (*kōso*), which can involve a trial *de novo* of the facts. The facts found by the court of first appeal (*kōso*) are binding.

7. Japan's House Lease Law as well as the companion Land Lease Law [Law No. 49, 1921] and Buildings Protection Law [Law No. 40, 1909] were repealed in September 1991 by the new Land and House Lease Law [Law No. 90, 1991]. For a detailed discussion of these statutes and their historical background, see John O. Haley, *Japan's New Land and House Lease Law*, in Land Issues in Japan: A Policy Failure? 149 (Haley & Kozo Yamamura eds. 1992).

8. For further insight into many of the issues raised in this section, see Mauro Cappelletti, The Judicial Process in Comparative Perspective (1989).

9. THE IMPACT OF THE REGULATORY STATE

MARY ANN GLENDON, THE SOURCES OF LAW IN A CHANGING LEGAL ORDER, 17 Creighton Law Review 663, 682-84 (1984)

Civil and common law systems alike were fundamentally transformed in the transition from liberal laissez-faire governments to modern social welfare states with planned or regulated economies. In the process, the source of law that had distinctively characterized each legal system, and the legal methods associated with it, lost their centrality. First, case law in the common law and codes in the civil law lost ground to modern statutes; second, judicial decisions in the common law were increasingly detached from their moorings in precedent while civil law judges were becoming more conscious of and willing to exercise their law-making powers; finally, administrative law has encroached on *all* preexisting sources of law. We have entered the age of legislation triumphant, the judge militant, and bureaucracy rampant.

Taken together, the trends described above, the increase in regulatory and administrative law, the widening room for discretion, the transition from market to mixed economies, tend, as we have seen, to blur many of the usual distinctions made between the legal systems of civil law and common law countries, ... as are the great separations within legal systems between public and private law, courts and legislatures, and formal adjudication and administration.

In the new situation, the traditional mechanisms for maintaining reasonable predictability and continuity, while permitting flexibility and growth, have fallen out of equilibrium. Traditionally, in the common law, predictability and continuity were afforded by legal rules developed in cases and by the doctrine and practice of *stare decisis*, while flexibility and growth were furnished by the rules of equity and the techniques for limiting and distinguishing precedent. In the codified systems of the civil law tradition, predictability and stability were promoted by the "written law" of the codes, while flexibility and growth were permitted, internally, by general clauses tempering rigid rules and externally by interpretation, made more supple by the absence of a formal rule of *stare decisis*.

In both of these traditional systems, the present-day predominance of regulatory law has diminished the role of the traditional mechanisms — case law and the codes — for maintaining continuity and reckonability. In this new situation, it would seem at first that the civil law systems have the methodological advantage, in that techniques for statutory interpretation are now of more utility than are pure case law techniques. But in both systems, the use of traditional legal methods to gain relative predictability is of limited utility because modern statutory law, unlike the civil codes, generally is neither stable nor particularly rational (in the sense of being principled and systematic). The practitioners of law have had to struggle to deal with these changes, but legal theory has lagged behind. If one acknowledges how profoundly the sources of law have been transformed, one must also recognize how inadequate the tools currently used for legal analysis have become.

Judicial Process

B. THE INTERPRETATION OF THE LAW

The distribution of power between judge and legislator is a matter of basic importance in all legal systems, and the topic has stimulated a substantial body of thinking and writing in both the common law and the civil law traditions. In common law countries we speak of "the judicial process." In the civil law world the equivalent term is "interpretation of the law." As this term suggests, and as the preceding material on sources of law illustrates, the traditional civil law view diminishes the role of the judge and exalts that of the legislator. In this section we complete our examination of the relation between judge and legislator in the civil law tradition.

In civil law nations, as in the United States, there is a strong tendency for widely held beliefs about law, courts, and interpretation to constitute a sort of "folklore" that differs sharply from what actually goes on in practice. The situation in Italy, described in the following excerpt, is more or less typical.

1. ITALY: FOLKLORE AND PRACTICE

JOHN HENRY MERRYMAN, THE ITALIAN STYLE III: INTERPRETATION, 18 Stanford Law Review 583, 585-96 (1966)

The Folklore of Judicial Interpretation

Like the American, the Italian legal system operates in an atmosphere of assumptions which, although demonstrably unsound, tend stubbornly to persist because they are firmly rooted in the culture. This kind of folklore serves a variety of functions, some laudable and others regrettable. Although it exists in most exaggerated form in the lay mind, it tends, somewhat refined, to dominate the thinking of the profession itself. Alternately idealized and caricatured, it becomes the starting point of much scholarly discussion....

From the time of the Roman jurisconsults on, the history of continental law has been one in which the role of the judge is unfavorably contrasted with that of the scholar-jurist. Jurisprudence (in the continental sense: the reports of judicial decisions) follows and is dominated by the doctrine, just the reverse of what is generally thought to be the natural order of things in common law jurisdictions....

The scholar is the scientist, and the judge, at best, merely the engineer. The scholar provides the systematic, scientific legal structure that the judge accepts and applies. The work of the scholar is creative and exalted; that of the judge is, although important, on a lower plane....

The folklore of the strict separation of legislative and judicial power leads to an even more extreme oversimplification of the interpretive act and a further diminution of the stature of the judiciary. The attitude ... has at its base the dogma that only the legislature can make law. With its companion assumptions that the code is complete and that the legislature can enact laws whose meaning is clear and simple and whose application is certain, this premise makes the judge into a kind of expert clerk. Interpretation is not a problem because the meaning of the statute in application is obvious. While the doctrinal folklore admits that the judge must interpret and tells him how to do so, the legislative folklore, at the extreme, denies that there is any interpretive function....

The net image of the judicial process is one of something mechanical and automatic, of slot machine jurisprudence. Applying juridical logic — the way of legal thinking supplied by the folklore — the judge is driven inexorably to the proper decision. As a prominent Italian jurist has described it:

> There is everything in the statute: all is foreseen in advance. The legal order (it is said) does not have lacunae. The legal system is like an immense cabinet, in which each pigeonhole contains the provision for a certain fact situation: the work of the judge consists above all in the qualification of the facts found, that is, in finding which among the thousands of fact situations foreseen by the law is that to which the facts found correspond. Once having found this coincidence, the judge need do nothing except open the little box in the pigeonhole (which is the article of the code that applies to the case) and find inside, like a prescription, the ready solution. This is the famous logical mechanism according to which every decision can be schematized in a syllogism: the major premise is the statute, the minor premise is the facts: it is enough that the facts coincide with those contemplated by the statute for the conclusion to come out by itself....

The Practice of Interpretation

It is unlikely that Italian jurists have ever had much confidence in the extremes of the folklore.... It is too obvious that the practice is sharply different from the folklore. For one thing, the illusion of the self-applying statute, the legislative norm that is so clear its application is an automatic process, was long ago dispelled by the facts. The most obvious practical objection is that ever since 1865 the Italian courts have been busily engaged in hearing and deciding disputes whose resolution depends on the meaning to be given to a legislative norm. Such litigation is frequently appealed, and reversals of lower court decisions are far from uncommon. Hardly a norm in the civil code has escaped the need for judicial interpretation to supply a meaning that was unclear to the parties, to their counsel, and to the judges themselves.

Likewise, the dogma that the code is complete (no lacunae) and coherent (no conflicting provisions) fails to survive even a cursory glance at the jurisprudence. The books are full of decisions in which the court has had to fill gaps in the legislative scheme and reconcile apparently conflicting statutes. The claim of legislative prescience becomes nonsense in view of the constant appearance of new problems, clearly unforeseen by the legislature, demanding judicial solution. Although the text of the statute remains unchanged, its meaning in application often changes in response to new social pressures. The ideal of certainty in the law becomes an illusion in the face of the uncertainty that exists in fact, where determination of the rights of parties frequently must await the results of litigation....

The Tension Between Folklore and Practice

The greater the scope of judicial interpretation the greater the de facto power of the judge. And the greater his power the greater his responsibility. According to the folklore, judicial scope, power, and hence responsibility are all sharply limited. In practice they are substantial. The tension thus created is the source of serious problems for the Italian legal process.

Consider the judge who is persuaded by the folklore. He must decide hard cases; he must make law. But, unaware of what he is doing, he is liable to do it all wrong. Unconscious of his lawmaking power, he decides irresponsibly. Putting his faith in an omniscient legislature and the infallibility of judicial logic, he sets major and minor premise together and watches the decision trot forward, not recognizing it as his own. In this process of inadvertent lawmaking the product is bound to show the signs of its origin.

Consider the judge who is aware of his lawmaking power but unwilling to take the responsibility it entails. The folklore becomes his refuge. Faced with the opportunity to contribute to a better method of solving a social problem before him, he instead selects a more traditional interpretation, pleading that his hands are tied. It is not for him, a mere judge, to change the law, even if change is obviously desirable and the change is one that might more appropriately be made by evolutive interpretation than legislation. And so he adds judicial to legislative *immobilismo*, blocking the development of the law in the name of the separation of powers, certainty, and other traditional verities.

Consider the thoughtful judge, aware of his power and willing to accept the responsibility of its conscious exercise. He must clothe his work in the traditional costume, conceal what he is doing behind the camouflage of the folklore, or run the risks of reversal on appeal, of castigation by scholars, of injury to his career. The folklore tends to limit what the good judge can do....

The Problems of Interpretation

The debate about interpretation can be put in terms of three more or less classic problems: (1) The problem of interpretation in the strict sense — of the unclear norm, (2) the problem of lacunae — of the nonexistent norm, and (3) the problem of evolution — of the norm whose meaning changes while its text remains constant. To these a fourth, rationalization of the use of precedent, should be added. All of these draw attention to the variation that exists between folklore and practice, and all involve reexamination of the traditional distribution of power between legislator and judge.

The problem of interpretation in the strict sense assumes, as is abundantly clear, that it is not always obvious how a norm should be applied to a case. The judge is faced with a choice of possible interpretations and, by exercising that choice, runs the risk of making, rather than applying, law. Under a strict doctrine of separation of powers he should not decide, but it is settled law in Italy that he must. The judge is not permitted to say *non liquet*, the law is not clear, and dismiss the action. He must interpret the applicable norm.

The problem of lacunae is distinguished from that of interpretation in the strict sense by rather sharply (and, it would seem, sometimes artificially) contrasting the existence of an applicable unclear norm with the nonexistence of any applicable norm. Here again the judge should not decide, according to the orthodoxy of interpretation, but here again he must. The problem of interpretation is to supply meaning to the norm; that of lacunae is to supply the norm.

The range of points of view about these problems is very wide, from the simplistic discussion in the *manuali,* through various ingenious attempts to rationalize folklore and fact, to frontal assaults on traditional views. The serious contemporary discussion can be summed up as a polemic between those who seek to mediate between fact and tradition and those who attack tradition in the name of fact. But before turning to this current debate it is necessary to consider article 12, Provisions on the Laws in General, which states:

> *Interpretation of statutes.* In interpreting the statute no other meaning can be attributed to it than that made clear by the actual significance of the words according to the connection between them, and by the intention of the legislature.
>
> If a controversy cannot be decided by a precise provision, consideration is given to provisions that regulate similar cases or analogous matters; if the case still remains in doubt, it is decided according to general principles of the legal order of the State.

The first paragraph is the legislative instruction to the judge on interpretation in the strict sense; the second is a similar instruction on the problem of lacunae. The meaning of the first paragraph, in particular, seems to be clear enough: the judge applies the applicable statute according to its literal [or contextual] meaning and legislative intent; other approaches to interpretation are prohibited. However, this provision is a statute and, like other statutes, is itself subject to interpretation. This interpretation about interpretation has led to some interesting products....

Lacunae

The second paragraph of article 12 contains three important concepts: lacuna (no "precise provision"), analogy, and general principles of the legal order of the state. The first sums up the problem and the latter two the methods of solving it....

Once a lacuna is found to exist, the interpreter is told to try to decide the case first by recourse to analogic interpretation, by reference to "provisions that regulate similar cases or analogous matters." Theoretically this requires the judge to draw from the "similar cases or analogous matters" the legal principle inherent in the legislative norms that govern them and apply it to the case before him. The assumption that such broader principles are implicit in specific norms leads to the conclusion that the law, even though not complete, is self-sufficient. The process is called "logical expansion." Lacunae are filled from within the legislative scheme rather than from without. Analogic interpretation is a process of auto-, rather than hetero-integration, and so there is no need to resort to the creative power of the judge. This is on the whole the prevailing view.

If analogy fails, then the interpreter, according to article 12 of the Provisions on the Laws in General, decides the case according to "general principles of the legal order of the state." The principal dispute over the interpretation of this expression is between those who would find such general principles outside the positive legal order — in natural law or some other type of ideal system — and those who would stay within it. The terms of the statute are loaded in favor of the positivists — the judge is not to look to general principles of *law*, but to general principles of *the legal order of the state* — and theirs is the dominant view. Thus the process of drawing broader principles from specific legislative norms is merely a first step; such principles themselves contain equally valid but more general implicit principles, and so on up the scale.

This process of logical expansion is, of course, the fundamental method of the traditional legal science. The general principles of article 12 of the Provisions on the Laws in General and the conclusions of scholars as a result of their scientific study of the law consequently are identical under this view of the meaning of article 12. The scholar, by his work in bringing such principles to light, is engaging, at least indirectly, in the judicial process and hence making his contribution to the law in action. The judge, in the process of interpretation, is contributing to the science and hence performing a scholarly function. But since both are merely drawing forth principles that are implicit in the legislation, they are not making law. The dogma of strict separation of powers is preserved.

NOTES AND QUESTIONS

1. The Swiss Civil Code, article 1(2) provides: "If the Code does not furnish an applicable provision, the judge shall decide in accordance with customary law, and failing that, according to the rule which he would establish as legislator." This provision, enacted in 1912, caused a good deal of comment. Can you explain why? For a discussion of interpretation in Switzerland, see Alfred E. von Overbeck, *Some Observations on the Role of the Judge Under the Swiss Civil Code*, 37 La. L. Rev. 681 (1977).

2. The preceding excerpt fairly summarizes the orthodox civil law position. Similar views, though clearly in decline, are still commonly expressed in manuals (introductory textbooks) on private law and are still regularly taught to law students in the first year of law study in European, Latin American, and East Asian universities.

3. The most often cited German criticism of the folklore of interpretation appears in works of the legal philosopher Rudolph von Jehring: *Der Kampf ums Recht* (1873), *Der Zweck im Recht* (1877-1883) and *Der Geist des römischen Rechts* (1907). The leading French criticism is by François Gény, in his celebrated book *Méthodes d'interprétation et sources en droit privé positif: essai critique* (1899); an English translation of the second (1919) edition was published in 1963. Thoughtful jurists in other civil law nations also questioned and attacked the folklore, but with remarkably little effect on popular attitudes and beliefs. Even the common run of professional lawyers in much of the civil law world remains convinced that the folklore provides an accurate picture of how the legal system *ought* to work.

4. A little reflection suggests that the situation in the United States is not fundamentally different: we have our own folklore of the judicial process and of interpretation (of the Constitution, as well as of statutes). The general public, and many lawyers, still are attracted to legal formalism and are still swayed by simplistic appeals to "original intent" and "plain meaning" and "respect for precedent" even though the difficulties with such ideas have been exposed by sociological jurisprudence, legal realism, and linguistics in ways that many legal scholars have found convincing.

5. Is perpetuation of the judicial process folklore among the general public in Italy or the United States beneficial for society? Why or why not?

2. SPAIN

NOTE

The Spanish Civil Code, article 3(1) provides: "Norms shall be interpreted according to the proper meaning of their words, in relation to their context, to their historical and legislative antecedents, and to the social reality at the time they are to be applied, closely paying attention to their spirit and purpose." Does this article provide guidance on resolving the problem of evolution identified by Professor Merryman *supra* Section B.1? Consider the following case.

THE ORDER OF JESUITS v. SPAIN

Supreme Court of Spain (Civil Chamber)
Case 319 of January 24, 1970
37 R.J. 241 (1970)

The Order of Jesuits filed before the First District Court, number 4, in Seville, a petition for declaratory judgment against the State (represented by the Attorney General) for nullity of a property registration....

The trial judge decided for the plaintiff, ordering reinstitution of the Order of Jesuits as full owner of the land, without special imposition of costs. On appeal, the court of appeal (*audiencia*) reversed, without levying costs.

A cassation petition alleging infraction of law was filed for the reasons reflected below.

The Supreme Court denied the petition.

MR. JUSTICE FRANCISCO BONET REMÓN delivered the opinion of the Court.

HAVING CONSIDERED. Both parties recognize certain stipulated facts from which it is necessary to start in order to decide plaintiff's petition. First, the April 2, 1767 *Real Pragmática Sanción*, issued by Carlos III, which became Law III, Title XXVI of Book I in the *Novísima Recopilación*, ordered the expulsion of all regular members of the Order of Jesuits from all territories of Spain, the Americas, and the Philippines. This included dispossession from all their property, including both movables and immovables.... Second, among the things included in that dispossession was the Jesuits' *Casa Profesa* in Seville, which is the one object of the present action to revendicate. Third, His majesty Carlos III, by decree issued on August 22, 1769, established the *Literaria* University in the Jesuit *Casa Profesa* in Seville, with the desire to establish public schooling in that city as vigorously as possible....

Fourth, carrying out this mandate on December 31, 1776, the Royal University was moved to the *Casa Profesa* (also called Royal Building). To signify that possession of the building and its church was taken for said University, Mr. Juan Gutiérrez de Piñeres, First Lieutenant,... entered the outer door and walked around the main patio. One of the doctors, Father Fray Francisco Xavier González of the *Orden de Mínimos* and professor of theology, entered and took his professorship seat. He then went to the church, where there was a big group of the city's officials and nobles, including to the left of the main altar the very eminent and very excellent Mr. Cardenal de Solís, Archbishop of Seville. In view of all, ... several concertos were played until, with total silence, Mr. Pedro Manuel Prieto gave the prayer. All of this occurred peacefully and without problem.

Fifth, Fernando VII, by Royal Decree of May 29, 1815, ordered the reestablishment of the Jesuits in all Spanish cities and towns which had so requested. All laws and royal orders issued after the *Real Pragmática Sanción* were revoked and annulled so that the reestablishment of schools, charities, missions, and religious residences in the cities and towns which had requested them could be carried out.... In the preamble, it was recognized that the Jesuits "have been advantageous for the good education of the youth given to them because of great fervor displayed by their members in the study of ancient literature. Their efforts contributed much to the progress of good literature; they produced skillful teachers in the various sciences. They are able to boast of training a greater number of good writers than all the other religious communities combined. In the new world they exercised their talents with clarity and splendor, in a manner useful and beneficial for humanity."

Sixth, by the May 3, 1816 Royal Order of His Majesty and Royal Council, it is directed that the Royal Decree of May 29, 1815 ... be extended to all other territories of Spain and the West Indies in which the Order of Jesuits was established at the time of its exile. Fernando VII then stated that "in order to carry out the Order's restoration, with the brevity I desire and for the spiritual and temporal happiness of my kingdom, it is my royal will that the houses, schools, churches, hospitals, residences and other possessions occupied by Jesuits at the time of the expulsion and still existing today be returned to them, with the obligation to carry out the charges of teaching and other chores they should execute. I exempt from restitution lands and chattels sold or transferred with onerous cause and title in favor of groups or private persons, and those donated for public use or to public establishments which cannot be returned, without loss to the common good...."

Seventh, at the time of the Jesuits' reestablishment, and the restitution of their possessions, the *Literaria* University of Seville was still located in the old *Casa Profesa*, a situation which has existed until the time immediately prior to the filing of this suit. At that point, the University was moved to the old Tobacco Factory, today situated at 3 Larana St.

Eighth, when the University was moved, the State, using the Mortgage Law, registered the land in the Seville Real Property Registry in its name, even though it stated in the administrative certification "acquisition of title unknown."

Ninth, the Order of Jesuits, after filing a claim under administrative law, brought this suit for declaratory judgment, praying for the nullity of the State's property registration and that the administrative claim be considered in this revendication action. Further, plaintiff asks for return of the ownership and dominion of the land, with all its accessories, according to the terms established by the May 29, 1815 Royal Decree and the May 3, 1816 Royal Order of Fernando VII.

From the previous exposition, it appears that the principal issue consists of determining if the *Casa Profesa* ... was included in the restitution ordered by the May 29, 1815 Royal Decree, reiterated and extended by the Royal Order of 1816. The petitioner argues that the move of the Royal University to the *Casa Profesa* terminated its teaching responsibilities and it ceased to be a university. On the other side, the State argues that the *Casa Profesa*, as a public establishment which cannot be returned without public injury, was among those things excluded from restitution.

In regard to the interpretation of legal norms — as this chamber said in its decision of November 21, 1934 (Case 1833), even though it did not accept all the conclusions favored by the proponents of the so-called evolutive method of interpretation of juridical norms — it can be admitted today as common doctrine that to completely realize the interpretative function it is not enough to use literal or contextual interpretation. If Law is to be in contact with the exigencies of real life, which is its *raison d'être*, the results obtained from these two classic methods must be reinforced and controlled by what is usually called the sociological element, formed by a long series of factors — ideological, moral, and economic — which reveal and mold the needs and spirit of the community in each historical moment. It is true that the use of these factors — aside from the fact that they cannot authorize a judge to modify or not apply a norm, but only to soften it to a point permitted by the content of the text — require prudence because of the grave risk of arbitrariness involved. It leaves the judge with subjective criteria as subtle as the moral conscience of a people. Nevertheless, it must be recognized that the evolutive method of statutory interpretation is made more decisive when it refers, not to states of conscience still nascent or nebulous, but to tendencies or ideas which have already penetrated the system of positive legislation. [A discussion of case law follows.]

The application of the described *doctrina legal* to the case at hand requires us to reject the plaintiff's petition. A grammatical and contextual interpretation of the Royal Order of May 3, 1816 shows the existence of two classes of things taken from the Order of Jesuits. First, those objects immediately returned, even though the Order had the burden of certain procedures to follow, and second, those exempted from return because they were transferred under onerous cause or donated or given away to public establishments or for public use, which cannot be returned without injury to the public good. The petitioner argues [that by evolutive interpretation] a third *genus* exists. We are doubtful, however, that the *Casa Profesa,* where the *Literaria* University was established, was, as petitioner argues, not subject to a teaching burden. This is strengthened by the *Real Pragmática Sanción,* which ordered occupation of all possessions without prejudice to the function fulfilled. The use thereafter given by the State to said *Casa Profesa* falls fully within the exemption from return since it was a public establishment as a university....

The State has full ownership of the land in question. It is definitely excluded from restitution due to the solemn act of possession on the part of the university [in 1776] without any contradiction. In any case, it is evident that once title in the State is proclaimed, its possession as owner during the past 200 years cannot be denied....

The petition is dismissed.

3. FRANCE: RESPONSE TO THE FOLKLORE

NOTE

France, where the Intellectual Revolution first took hold, developed elaborate working methods to counterbalance the folklore of interpretation of the law. The following excerpt describes some of these developments.

JOHN P. DAWSON, THE ORACLES OF THE LAW 375-76, 379-81, 392, 397-405, 414-16, 431 (1968)

The Advent of the Reasoned Opinion

The leaders of the French Revolution soon undertook the urgent task of subjugating the judiciary. Debates began in the Constituent Assembly on March 24, 1790, and lasted nearly five months. The sale and inheritance of judicial offices were forbidden. The Assembly also voted among other things that all judges were to be elected by popular vote, judicial offices were to be for short terms, and juries both of accusation and trial were required in all criminal cases. Appellate courts were eliminated as potential centers of political resistance. Conciliation and arbitration were to be maximized. Courts were denied all power "to make regulations" (*règlements*) but were "to address themselves to the legislature whenever they think it necessary either to interpret a law or to make a new one." Judges were also forbidden to interfere with actions of the executive or to hold its officers accountable in any way; distrust of the judiciary played as large a part as the dictates of Montesquieu's logic in producing this strict separation of governmental powers, which was to remain a basic feature of French judicial organization. It was part of the same broad program of containing the judicial power for the Assembly to require that judicial decrees must not only disclose findings of fact but "express the motives that were decisive for the judge."...

Taken as a whole, the measures adopted by the revolutionary assemblies to subjugate the judiciary had a mixed success. In the comprehensive legislation of 1800 popular election of judges was abandoned and appointments by the government were supposed in principle to carry life tenure, though purges of the judiciary occurred periodically throughout the nineteenth century. The legislation of 1800 also provided for intermediate courts of appeal with full powers of appellate review and abolished the referral of cases to the legislature. But the prohibition of "regulatory decrees" by judges was carried into the Civil Code of 1804 and then reinforced by the criminal law. Likewise the requirement that judicial decrees be "motivated" was preserved and greatly generalized. It now applies to almost all courts in the judicial hierarchy; for most decrees absence of motives is in itself a ground for a declaration of nullity. Reasoned opinions, prepared by judges as one of the responsibilities of their office, are thus a lasting legacy of the Revolution and of its effort to control judicial power.

The style of the modern French reasoned opinion bears the marks of this origin. The style was set by the Court of Cassation in the early years of the Revolution. This was a time when the court was all too eager to prove beyond doubt its loyal submission to the Revolution and its acceptance of its own diminished role. Required to justify its actions in annual accountings to the legislature, it had also been ordered to publish all its decrees, so that it had to face in addition the scrutiny of a hostile and suspicious public.... The style it developed and projected on the future was as condensed and laconic as a style could be. Its overriding purpose was to demonstrate that the court in policing the lower courts was itself conforming to existing law. Its function could be equated with the flashing of a policeman's badge.

Not much invention was required. The court simply took over the formal language of the decrees currently issued by the legislature itself, with their recitals and whereas clauses leading up to rulings tersely stated. There were departures from this model in two respects: (1) any ruling that reached beyond the particular case was scrupulously omitted and (2) decrees of the 1790's were usually preceded by narrative statements of the facts (in later times the practice developed of mixing clusters of facts into the string of whereas clauses)....

The Declaration of Independence by the Authors

The so-called "exegetical school" of doctrinal writers was to dominate thought about law in France for fifty years, until very late in the nineteenth century....

It was after more than fifty years of experience under the Code that the two separate but parallel lines finally began to intersect. Communicating crossroads had been built in the meantime on the initiative, not of judges or law professors, but of the group of learned practitioners who had salvaged the case law of the earliest decades, organized the law-finding apparatus of the *répertoires* and also maintained current series of law reports, published in annual volumes. In the two major series of law reports named for Sirey and Dalloz, the editors from the outset had inserted occasional references to other reported cases and, more rarely, citations to text writers. In the 1830's these notes by the editors became more frequent and more ample. On important questions the analytical notes became small essays, placing the problem before the court in a larger setting, mobilizing the opinions of the doctrinal writers, and also bringing together past decisions to show trends, distinctions, or conflicts. To the audience of practitioners that was primarily addressed, these analytical notes must have been most serviceable. In re-editions of the chronological series these notes were expanded. The editors of other series, to meet the competition, hired notewriters from outside their own staffs. Until the late 1850's this work was done by practitioners, many of them men of talent....

The analytical note is a great invention. It is hard to imagine what French law would be without it. It is not a peculiarly French invention, for similar notes are appended to some of the reports in other European countries — Germany and Italy, for example. In France many of the notes are not written by law professors but by lawyers, even by judges. They appear as footnotes to reports of recent cases in several series that are published by private enterprise and commonly used by lawyers. They therefore have a far greater impact on the legal profession than do modern American law reviews, though they perform the same function as a forum for free criticism and exchange of views. Being comments on the cases reported, they address themselves to specific issues, to all the nuances in the facts, to the motives for decision whether expressed or veiled, and to the possibilities of reconciling results with those in earlier cases, by distinctions or otherwise. The analytical note is also expected to assemble all the resources of doctrine, to criticize and evaluate it in its bearing on the specific problem. It is an extremely flexible instrument, expressing the skill, learning, and insight of individual authors but requiring them to address themselves to the interests and needs of practitioners as well as to those of their academic colleagues....

To study court decisions was one thing, but to admit they made law was another. The problem that has tortured French lawyers ever since had emerged by 1900. The nature of the problem had been discerned by Gény, in his important work, published in 1899. His main object was to free interpreters of the Code from the limitations inherent in the exegetical method. In arguing for "free scientific research" he used as perhaps his most cogent arguments the great changes made through court decisions, changes that the older authors had ascribed to the legislator. Did this mean that courts had "a praetorian power," that their decisions had any of the attributes of law or could hamper the freedom of the interpreter? Emphatically not. Any such suggestions, however ingeniously or seductively made, would violate the principle of separation of powers and would confer on courts a legislative power which was clearly denied them by basic French legislation. The only way that judicial decisions could produce new law would be through translation into rules of custom....

The Working Methods of French Case Law

In discussing this topic it seems best to start with a simple affirmation: France has acquired case law in massive quantities. It is called *jurisprudence,* a term employed under the old regime to describe a similar phenomenon....

In estimating the contributions of French case law one does not need to rely on such startling feats of judicial creativity as the stringent rules of tort liability that have been manufactured in this century out of Code article 1384, the new law of unjust enrichment developed in the last 70 years with only the most tenuous connection with the Code, gross distortions of the Code restrictions on specific performance of obligations, the complete recasting of the law of contract, especially in its relation to the restrictions on gifts, not to speak of the whole system of administrative law evolved by the judicial decisions of the *Conseil d'Etat* with very little help from statute. The importance of French case law goes far beyond these particular instances of new creation or deliberate evasion. It would be hard to find a single article of the Civil Code to which there have not been added depths of meaning and major restrictions or extensions that could not possibly have been conceived in 1804.... Among twentieth century writers the immense contribution of judicial decisions is conceded by all. Many point to it now with pride as proving the capacity of the French codified system to respond to imperative demands in a changed and changing society....

The passage of time has thus altered perspectives toward the accomplishments of the courts, but the working habits of courts and lawyers have proved to be more durable.... Above all the principle that courts can never legislate is still a basic rule of almost constitutional dimensions. It continues to confuse all discussion of the work that courts have done....

During the 1830's reports of past decisions became available in abundance. The practice of citing them as instruments of persuasion was established then and is a standard feature in modern times. The arguments of counsel, when summarized in the law reports, are commonly studded with citations to past cases. I have never heard that anyone has considered this incongruous.

For similar reasons it was also soon established that it was proper and helpful for the court's own *rapporteur* to cite and analyze prior decisions. As in the practice inherited from medieval times the *rapporteur* is a member of the court itself, with important responsibilities in examining and sifting the record, identifying the issues as well as the means by which they might be resolved, and concluding with his own recommendation for final disposition. Legislation passed at the time of the Revolution requires that the *rapporteur*'s whole preliminary analysis, up to his own personal conclusion, be read in open court. Such documents are available to interested persons and are often published in the law reports. It is clear that by the early 1830's the practice was well established for *rapporteurs* to cite and analyze prior decisions, distinguishing them or relying on them as pointing to a particular result. In modern law reports likewise the analyses of the *rapporteurs* are often reproduced and are usually most illuminating. They reveal the careful attention that the *rapporteurs* give to consistency with past decisions and their great skill in drawing or excluding implications by resort to analogy or distinction....

It is more notable that lower courts too will sometimes cite and rely on the decisions of the Court of Cassation. It is notable because, as has been pointed out before, French legislation still reserves to lower courts a privilege to reject the version of the law that has been declared by the Court of Cassation. Since 1837 resistance must cease and the particular case must be decided according to the high court's version if the same case returns a second time and this version is then reaffirmed in plenary session. But this time-wasting and circuitous procedure merely decides the particular case and does not impose controls on lower courts in their decision of any other case. The tradition of independent judgment as to the meaning of the Code, so strongly asserted by doctrinal writers, also works at times on lower courts. There have been instances in which it has taken years for the resistance of lower courts on issues of legal doctrine to be finally overcome. Furthermore, purely as a matter of form, deviation by a lower court from the *jurisprudence* of the Court of Cassation cannot be urged as a ground for cassation, since *jurisprudence* is not part of the "law." Compliance by lower courts with doctrines previously announced by the Court of Cassation is thus thought of as voluntary. So it is a significant clue to attitudes that lower courts do cite and rely on prior decisions of the Court of Cassation....

A highly developed reporting system plus an experience in its use over a century and a half would seem to provide all the elements needed for an efficient system of case law.... A theory of precedent can thus limit power in a double sense: the court is constrained not only by the reasons expressed in earlier cases but by the need in the case before it to define with care the commitment it is making to the future. These constraints can become effective only if courts are conceived to have a duty to do more than decide the particular case by finding and applying an appropriate rule. They can be effective only if courts accept a responsibility to the legal system as a whole, to maintain its order and consistency while constantly engaged in new creations. So far as time and insight permit, we expect each individual court opinion to weave itself into the seamless web.

It is this sense of responsibility for the ordering of their own creations that seems to me to be missing in the opinions of French courts, especially the Court of Cassation. The initial handicap that the Court of Cassation has imposed on itself is its flat refusal to refer explicitly to its own past decisions, though this refusal is in itself symptomatic. Without explicit references it would be difficult even to make a good start on the task of reconciling the solution reached in any particular case with those of earlier cases. Also, the one-sentence format of the court's opinions, with its wearisome repetition of whereas clauses, is severely constricting, though its survival too is symptomatic. More basic is the extremely cryptic and laconic style with which the court expresses both facts and law. Propositions of law are drafted with utmost care and precision but they hang suspended in space, for no effort is made to reconcile them with very different propositions asserted in other, nearly related cases or to explain why they would not apply if the facts of the case were somewhat different....

The central *conviction,* which still lies deep, is that judges cannot be lawmakers; from this the conclusion seems to follow that they have no responsibility for shaping, restating and ordering the doctrine that they themselves produce. If the premise in this argument were more carefully defined, one could accept it, but however it may be phrased the conclusion does not follow.

Of the many *consequences* two are at this point most important:

(1) If one will grant, as some might not, that order is desirable and that codes alone cannot produce it, the reasoned opinion is a powerful instrument by which judges can help to organize the results of their own work. If they abstain from the effort to the degree that they have in France, the legal system as a whole is deprived of a key resource.

(2) An effective case-law technique employed by judges through the medium of the reasoned opinion, with the responsibilities that it should entail,

has the purpose and should have the effect of limiting the powers of judges. Its absence in France has resulted from a desire to limit the power of judges, but it has produced instead a much greater freedom for judges than we would consider tolerable.

The Enigma of Judge-Made Law

The account so far given suggests that the workload in organizing French case law has been distributed unevenly. Courts have been deterred from reasoned elaboration of their own grounds for decision by their cryptic and formalized modes of expression. These modes of expression merely symbolize the duty of extreme reticence that has been imposed by an inherited conviction that their role must be modest. The reticence persists despite the fact that French courts have laid over the codes a gloss of great depth; like the Accursian gloss to the *Corpus Juris*, it has in some areas almost the dimensions of a glacier. The result has been that the tasks both of analyzing specific accretions and of surveying new terrain are assigned to others, mostly to members of the academic profession. For long, almost a century, the academic authors displayed minimal interest in the task. This is certainly no longer true. Their principal media are analytical notes to reported cases, but their services take many other forms as well. The prestige of the academic profession is now deservedly high, for without its aid it is hard to imagine how French case law could be organized to the limited degree that it is....

The chief legacy of the Revolution was not judicial submission to the discipline of the codes but a deep-seated, widely-held conviction that judges lacked lawmaking power. The judges joined in this disclaimer and expressed it through a cryptic style of opinion writing whose main purpose was to prove their dutiful submission but which left them in fact more free. Their freedom was used for a hundred years to transform French law, with little guidance or aid from the academic profession. This freedom persists, though the interest of the academic profession is now fully aroused. It is strongly defended by French theorists since to them it appears that to organize self-restraint through theories of precedent would be to admit that judges by their own unaided action, merely through the process of deciding cases, inevitably have their own special form of lawmaking power. A principle directed toward restraining judicial power thus serves to enlarge it.

The working methods employed by the courts in their published opinions reflect and preserve this freedom. Much more is involved than the use or nonuse of specific case law techniques. For these techniques, administered by expert judges with candor, have the purpose of enlisting them in a common enterprise — that of maintaining continuity, coherence, and order in the inevitable process of new creation. Candor can be asked for if one is persuaded that the discoveries made in resolving conflict can be articulated best by those most directly exposed. To the extent that judges abstain from candid disclosure, the load is cast on others, outsiders; being outsiders, they must search out clues, speculate, surmise. This is the posture of French legal science, through the tradition that inhibits French courts in exploiting the modern resource of the reasoned opinion. It is here, it seems, that the effects of remembered history have been most lasting and destructive. Behind the cascades of whereas clauses one can still see stalking the ghostly magistrates of the Parlements, majestic in their moldy red robes.

QUESTIONS

1. Judges in all civil law jurisdictions are required, sometimes by constitutional provision (*e.g.*, Italy, Const. art. 111), to prepare written, motivated decisions. Why should a rule of this kind exist? Why should it have constitutional status? Are these objectives realized by decisions of the French Supreme Court of Cassation set out and described in the preceding excerpt?

2. In reading the following French Court of Cassation decisions, consider the extent to which the judges appear to have met their obligation to explain (motivate) their decisions. What error of law, if any, did the courts of appeal make? What sources of law were correctly or incorrectly interpreted or applied by the lower courts? What authority for its decisions did the high court cite?

SCOTCH WHISKY ASSOCIATION v. S.A. SUPREX

Court of Cassation of France
Commercial Chamber
Decision of 11 October 1988
63 J.C.P. II, 21297 (1989)

THE COURT: On the ground [submitted to the Cour de Cassation for review], considered in its first two parts:

Having seen ("vu") art. 1382 of the Civil Code; Considering that ("attendu que"), according to the decision attacked, the Scotch Whisky Association demanded judgment against the Suprex Company for unfair competition in selling two kinds of whiskies in ways that confused them with scotch whiskies; Considering that, in denying the claim the Court of Appeal gave as its reason that the indication of French origin of the whisky is all that is required to prevent the risk of confusion and that other elements have no importance; that, for the reasons given, after having conceded the resemblances between certain elements, examined separately, of the products in question, it rejected them as a source of possible confusion; Considering that in so acting when the origin of a product does not suffice in itself in all cases to eliminate the risk of confusion, and without investigating, as requested by the Scotch Whisky Association, what was the total impression given by the stated similarities, the Court of Appeal did not provide a legal basis for its decision in regard to the text indicated above;

For these reasons: reverses ("casse") and annuls in all of its provisions the decision rendered 21 October 1986 between the parties by the Court of Appeal of Paris and, so that right may be done ("pour être fait droit") remands to the Court of Appeal of Lyon.

Messrs. Baudoin, president, LeTallec, reporter, Montanier, attorney general.

NOTES AND QUESTIONS

1. Observe that the only authority cited by the Court is Civil Code article 1382, which reads: "Any human act that injures another obliges the person at fault to make reparation."

As is generally known in France and among comparative lawyers, the generality of this language provides little guidance to courts in deciding tort cases. The text of article 1382 is certainly unhelpful in deciding whether marketing French whiskey using bottles, labels, and trademarks that look like Scotch whisky bottles, labels, and trademarks constitutes unfair competition, even if it is stated somewhere that the whiskey is French. There is of course a large body of French case law (jurisprudence) and scholarly writing (doctrine) on the meaning and application of the provisions of article 1382. The jurisprudence and doctrine were certainly consulted by lawyers for the parties in preparing their briefs and arguments before the Court of Cassation. They were certainly considered and discussed by the Avocat-Général in preparing his "Conclusions" to assist the Court. But in the decision none of this appears; the only reference to any legal basis for reversal and remand of the decision of the Court of Appeals of Paris is to article 1382.

2. How about the facts? What were the alleged similarities between the defendant's products and those of the plaintiff? In what ways were they misleading? How prominently did the identification of the defendant's products as French whiskey appear, and where? What evidence was there that French consumers were or were not deceived by the defendant's packaging and marketing? The decision of the trial court may have included such facts, and some facts may have been described in the decision of the Court of Appeals of Paris. But in the decision of the Court of Cassation the facts have almost completely receded from view.

3. The report of this decision in *La Semaine Juridique*, a private publication, is accompanied by a "note" signed by Dr. Charley Hannoun, who is identified as "Chargé d'enseignement" (a teacher who does not hold the rank of professor) at the Universities of Paris. The decision occupies about one-third of a page in the *Semaine Juridique*; Dr. Hannoun's note fills about three and one-third pages. In it he discusses a variety of facts not mentioned by the Court, including the results of a consumer survey in which fewer than one-half of those interviewed said they believed Suprex whiskeys came from Scotland. (Stated another way, almost half of those questioned were fooled.) The note also cites and discusses more than 20 prior decisions and several books and articles. The reader, left mystified by the decision, is thus informed by the note, which puts the decision into factual, jurisprudential, and doctrinal context.

4. Since the Revolution, as we have seen, the decisions of French courts have to be explained ("motivée") and based on law (i.e., on a source of law in the formal sense). In what senses does this decision satisfy those requirements?

5. Suppose you were a judge on the Court of Appeals of Lyon, to which this case was remanded for decision. You are trained to read decisions of the Court of Cassation closely and know from experience that they contain few wasted words. Suppose further that you wish to decide consistently with this decision. Could you do so and still decide in favor of the French company Suprex?

CHARLES v. DESMARES

Court of Cassation of France
Civil Chamber, Second Division
Decision of 21 July 1982
1982 D.S. Jur. 449

English translation published in André Tunc, *Traffic Accidents: Fault or Risk?*, 15 Seton Hall Law Review 831, 838-39 (1985)

THE COURT: On the ground submitted to the *Cour de Cassation* for review, considered in its first four parts, as set forth in the amplifying submission:

Whereas, according to the judgment under review, at nightfall, in a built-up area, Mr. Desmares's motor vehicle struck and injured Mr. and Mrs. Charles as they were crossing the street on foot; Mr. and Mrs. Charles brought an action against Desmares and his insurer, La Mutualite Industrielle, seeking compensation for their injury; and the S.N.C.F., in its capacity as a Social Security fund, and the Ardennes Health Insurance Fund intervened in this action;

Whereas it is objected that the overruling judgment attributed liability to Desmares under Article 1384, paragraph 1 of the Civil Code;

Whereas, after determining the factual matter, that little credit could be given to the statements of a witness who had not seen the accident but only its consequences, the overruling judgment noted that Mr. and Mrs. Charles were thrust several meters from the pedestrian crossing, and found — on the basis of the skid marks on the road, taking account of the "reaction time" prior to braking and of the fact that Desmares did not see the pedestrians before the moment of impact — that the impact could only have occurred within the pedestrian crossing or in its immediate vicinity;

On the basis of these findings, the *Cour de Cassation* rules that the appellate court did not base its decision on hearsay or on conjectural grounds, and in properly rejecting such grounds, answered the relevant points of the submission, and thereby legally justified its judgment on this point submitted for review.

On the ground submitted to the *Cour de Cassation* for review, considered in its last two parts:

Whereas it is objected that the appellate court (i) failed to address the submissions holding that the victims failed to abide by Article R. 219 of the Traffic Code, which required them to refrain from crossing the street until they had made sure they could do so without any immediate danger; and (ii) failed to refute the findings of the court of first instance holding (a) that Mr. and Mrs. Charles had further been negligent in beginning to cross the street before making sure they could do so safely and in failing to take account of the speed and distance of the approaching vehicle, and (b) that Desmares automobile was too near for the pedestrians to cross the street safely and that therefore they should have refrained from beginning to cross the street in such circumstances, all the more given that the car to Desmares's right prevented Desmares from seeing them;

But whereas only in circumstances of *force majeure* can the custodian of property which causes injury be exonerated from his liability under Article 1384, paragraph 1 of the Civil Code; and accordingly the victim's behavior, unless unforeseeable and irresistable, cannot exonerate such custodian, not even in part;

And whereas after noting that the accident occurred at rush hour, in a pedestrian crossing or in its immediate vicinity on a four-lane avenue with street lights operating properly, the overruling judgment found that Desmares was driving in the left-hand lane when his automobile struck Mr. and Mrs. Charles, who were crossing from right to left with respect to the automobile's path;

On the basis of these findings, even assuming that the victims had committed the fault they are alleged to have committed, such fault would not constitute unforeseeable and irresistable circumstances; the *Cour de Cassation* rules that the appellate court consequently was not required to seek out the existence of such fault which, even if established, could not have exonerated the driver from his liability, and therefore legally justified its overruling judgment;

On the grounds set forth above, the *Cour de Cassation* dismisses the appeal against the overruling judgment handed down by the appellate court of Reims on January 15, 1981.

Messrs. Derenne, president, Liaras, reporter, Charbonnier, attorney general.

RUTH REDMOND-COOPER, THE RELEVANCE OF FAULT IN DETERMINING LIABILITY FOR ROAD ACCIDENTS: THE FRENCH EXPERIENCE, 38 International and Comparative Law Quarterly 502-09 (1989)

On 5 July 1985 the French Parliament passed Law no. 85-677, the expressed aim of which was to improve and accelerate the compensation procedures for the victims of road accidents. It was hoped that the new Law would help put an end to more than half a century of debate, both judicial and extrajudicial, as to the relevance of fault and causality in determining liability in road accident cases....

The Situation Before 5 July 1985

The principal provisions relating to tortious liability are contained in Articles 1382 *et seq.* of the Civil Code. While fault on the part of the defendant is clearly required by Articles 1382 and 1383, the position under Article 1384 was for many years less clear. Article 1384 provides:

> A person is liable not only for damage which he causes by his own action, but also for that which is caused by the action of persons for whom he is liable, or for things which he has in his custody.

During the nineteenth century the question of the extent to which fault on the part of the owner of an object which had caused damage constituted a prerequisite to a finding of liability under Article 1384 was fiercely debated in both France and Belgium. It was argued that the intention of the framers of the Napoleonic Code when drafting Article 1384 at the beginning of the nineteenth century was merely to introduce the specific provisions relating to liability of employers for the acts of their employees and apprentices (Article 1384, paragraphs 2 *et seq.*), of owners for animals (Article 1385) and of owners for ruined buildings (Article 1386).

Towards the end of the nineteenth century, with the rise in the number of accidents involving heavy machinery occurring in the workplace following the industrial revolution, it was felt by many that to oblige the victims of such accidents to establish fault on the part of the employer under either Article 1382 or 1383 was to place an almost insurmountable hurdle in the way of their obtaining compensation. In order to ensure compensation for as many of these victims as possible, first the Belgian and then the French[4] courts proceeded to a reassessment of their interpretation of Article 1384, declaring that the liability provided for in this Article was a general liability for all inanimate objects and not merely an introduction to the more specific forms of liability which follow. At first, liability was based on a presumption of fault,[5] thus enabling an employer whose defective machinery had caused injury to escape liability where he could show that he had committed no fault. The legislature was quick to react to this, and in 1898 the first of the French workers' compensation Acts was passed, providing workers with an automatic right to compensation without proof of fault in return for a lower level of damages than would ordinarily have been obtained.

Although the new interpretation of Article 1384 had initially been specifically aimed at ensuring compensation for workers, the enactment of the workers' compensation legislation did not prevent further widening of the scope of the Article. In 1919 it was established by the Cour de Cassation that absence of fault on the part of the owner or custodian of an object which had caused harm would no longer provide a defence in an action for damages.[6] Thus, where damage was caused by an inherent defect in the object, the owner would be liable notwithstanding the fact that the cause of the defect was unknown.

Once the principle of liability without fault had been established and accepted in the case of damage caused by defective objects, the question arose as to the extension of the principle to those cases where damage resulted, not from an inherent defect in the object itself, but from the way in which it was handled. The single most notable object which would be covered by such an extension was the motor vehicle, and legal opinion and the courts themselves were sharply divided on the issue. The proponents of the fault principle maintained that Article 1384 should be strictly limited to those cases where the damage resulted from an inherent defect in the object (for example, in the case of a motor vehicle, an unexplained failure of the brakes), and that where damage was caused by the manner in which the object was handled (for example a failure to stop in time to avoid hitting a pedestrian) Article 1382 or 1383

[4] Civ. 11 June 1896, S.1897.1.17.
[5] Req. 30 Mar. 1897, D.1897.1.433.
[6] Civ. 21 Jan. 1919, S.1922.1.265.

should be used, with the result that the driver would be liable only if he had committed a fault.

The Article 1382 versus Article 1384 debate was finally resolved in 1930 in the decision of the Chambres Réunies of the Cour de Cassation in the *Jand'heur* case, when, after nearly five years of appeals, it was held that accidents involving motor vehicles should be governed by Article 1384, and therefore proof of absence of fault on the part of the driver is irrelevant. The case concerned a young girl who was run over and seriously injured by one of the defendants' lorries. The action brought before the Tribunal Civil of Belfort relied almost exclusively on Article 1384(1). The court held that, where the object having caused the damage is of a dangerous nature, Article 1384 should apply even in the absence of an inherent defect. This decision was overturned by the Court of Appeal of Besancon (where it was held that Article 1384 could apply only in the case of an inherent defect, and therefore the action should have been brought under Article 1382), whose decision was in turn quashed by the Cour de Cassation. The Civil Chamber of the Cour de Cassation adopted a similar approach to the court of first instance and emphasised that the motor vehicle is an inherently dangerous object which therefore requires the person in control to pay special attention to the risks he is imposing on third parties by his use of the vehicle. No distinction should be drawn on the basis of whether or not the damage that occurred was caused by a defect in the vehicle or by the way in which it was handled.

Once the decision of the Besancon court had been quashed, the case was referred back for decision to the Court of Appeal of Lyon, which refused to follow the Cour de Cassation on the basis that Article 1384 should apply only to those cases where damage was caused directly by the object in question and cannot apply where human action has caused it. The refusal of the Lyon court to follow the Civil Chamber was in fact convenient, since it meant that the case was referred once more to the Supreme Court for definitive judgment of all the chambers sitting in plenary session, thus attaching far more judicial weight to the final decision.

Before the Chambres Réunies, Procureur général Matter argued that Article 1384 makes no distinction between objects causing damage by themselves and objects causing damage when controlled by man, and in any case, such a distinction would be extremely difficult to operate in practice and would result in arbitrary and unfair decisions. The conclusions of the Procureur général were followed by the Chambres Réunies, which held, first, that the presumption of liability contained in Article 1384 could be displaced only by a finding of "act of God, *force majeure* or an external cause for which he is not responsible" ("*cas fortuit, force majeure ou d'une cause étrangère qui ne lui soit pas imputable*") and, second, that liability under Article 1384 is founded solely on the question of custody (*garde*) of the object and therefore any attempt to distinguish on the basis of the origin of the damage (the object itself or the custodian's handling of it) is irrelevant.[11]

Thus was born the general principle of no-fault liability in relation to accidents involving motor vehicles. Under the *Jand'heur* decision the only possi-

[11] Ch. réun. D.1930.1.57; conclusions of Procureur général Matter D.1930.1.64.

bility of exoneration for the custodian of a vehicle which had caused damage lay in the establishment of some external, unforeseeable and unavoidable event (*cas fortuit or force majeure*). However, it was not long before proof of the contributory negligence of the victim was admitted as a basis for reducing the liability of the guardian.[12] By the 1960s, "fault" on the part of those injured in road accidents was an increasingly common cause for the reduction of damages, while "fault" on the part of the driver of the vehicle had ceased to be of any relevance.[13] However, a sense of the injustice and inconsistency of this approach led to its gradual abandonment, and in several cases the custodian of the vehicle was held to be responsible for the entire damage even where contributory negligence was established.[14]

The turning point with regard to contributory negligence came just over half a century after the decision in the *Jand'heur* case, when the Cour de Cassation once again emitted a strong pronouncement in favour of the victims of road accidents. The effect of the *Desmares* decision[15] was to exclude in any Article 1384 action the possibility of the plaintiff's damages being reduced on the basis of contributory negligence.

The facts of the case were by no means out of the ordinary: the plaintiffs were two pedestrians who were knocked over by the defendant's car when they were attempting to cross a busy four-lane road in the rush hour. Owing to the fact that they were either carried or thrown some small distance by the car it was not possible to establish whether or not they had been attempting to cross the road at the pedestrian crossing. The plaintiffs brought an action under Article 1384, but the court of first instance accepted the defendant's contention that the accident had been caused by the plaintiffs' imprudence in crossing the road at the place and time they did, behaviour which constituted a breach of the Highway Code. This finding was rejected by the Reims Court of Appeal, which awarded the plaintiffs full damages, without, however, fully explaining its reasoning. The second civil chamber of the Cour de Cassation confirmed this decision....

This decision of the second chamber of the Cour de Cassation, while restoring a certain logic to the interpretation of Article 1384 by placing the behaviour of the victim on the same basis as any other factor that is external to the defendant, was unpopular with many of the lower courts, some of which refused to follow it (it should be noted that the *Desmares* decision, unlike the *Jand'heur* decision, emanated from a single chamber of the Cour de Cassation and therefore lacked much of the persuasive authority of the latter). However, while some courts continued to apply the traditional rules of contributory negligence to injured pedestrians, others were prepared to widen the basis of the *Desmares* decision by extending it to cover contributorily negligent drivers of vehicles. The situation was further complicated by the fact that the new formula of non-apportionment of damages applied only to actions brought under Article 1384: in a traditional negligence action under Article 1382 (in which fault on the part of the defendant must be proved) apportionment of

[12] Req. 13 Apr. 1934, D.1934.1.41.
[13] Cass. 2e Civ. 15 Jan. 1960, S.1962.1.2.
[14] Cass. 2e Civ. 4 Mar. 1970.
[15] Cass. 2e Civ. 21 July 1982, D.1982.J.449.

damages on the basis of the plaintiff's contributory negligence is still permissible. In a French criminal action where the defendant has, as a result of his criminal act (for example dangerous driving), caused injury or loss, the victim may be joined to the criminal proceedings as a *partie civile* and will be entitled to damages in accordance with the civil law. However, in these circumstances the defendant's liability will always be assessed under Article 1382 on the basis of fault, rather than on the basis of mere custody. The question of the plaintiff's contributory negligence or fault will therefore continue to be relevant in such cases.

The notion of "fault" under Article 1382 has traditionally been interpreted in a very wide manner in order to help the victims, with insurance providing the implicit justification. The standard of care has therefore been totally objective and rather high. However, in cases of alleged contributory negligence, this wide interpretation of fault rebounds on the victim. Even where it is clear that the plaintiff whose contributory negligence is in question was too young to realise the danger, the court may not take this into account when assessing the total amount of damages to be paid by the defendant driver and his insurance company. In *Derguini v. Tidu*[21] the defendant was convicted of the manslaughter of a five-year-old girl who had started to cross the road on a pedestrian crossing, but upon becoming aware of the approach of the defendant's car had panicked and tried to run back to the pavement. It was agreed that the girl's sudden action had made it impossible for the defendant to avoid hitting her and the damages claimed by the parents were accordingly reduced by 50 per cent. However, it is important to stress that the girl was killed on a pedestrian crossing at a place where motorists were warned by road signs that there were likely to be children in the vicinity.

A huge and inequitable difference in treatment thus existed according to whether the victim of the road accident brought his action under Article 1384 against the driver as custodian of the vehicle that injured him, or under Article 1382 against the driver in respect of his personal negligence as an adjunct to criminal proceedings. In *Desmares* the victims were adults, presumably aware of the dangers of crossing a busy road, and it was never positively established that they were using the pedestrian crossing, yet damages were awarded in full. In *Derguini* the victim was probably too young to appreciate fully the dangers of road traffic, but she was at least crossing in the correct place, yet damages were reduced by 50 per cent (it is possible of course that, had the child survived the accident and sued in respect of her own injuries, the court might have been more lenient in assessing the extent of her contributory negligence).

At the end of 1984 this then was the situation confronting plaintiffs seeking damages in respect of personal injuries sustained in road accidents.

In the meantime, the French socialist government had been pushing through Parliament a bill designed to rationalise this confused and illogical situation by introducing a system of compensation which would no longer be entirely fault-based. The impetus for such reform was not new: in 1965 the Ministry of Justice had examined the "Tunc Project," which had proposed

[21] Cass. Ass. Plen. 9 May 1984, 1984.JCP.II.20256.

automatic compensation for the victims of road accidents with no account being taken of *force majeure* or of contributory negligence. This project was, however, rejected. The idea was then taken up once more by the socialist government in the early 1980s and, after much debate and opposition from the legal profession, was passed unanimously by Parliament on 5 July 1985.

"A Law Designed to Improve the Situation of the Victims of Road Traffic Accidents"

The Law's optimistic title described its aim: "A law designed to improve the situation of the victims of road traffic accidents and to accelerate compensation procedures." It was expected by Parliament, and indeed feared by many members of the French Bar Association, that the introduction of such a system would result in the majority of road traffic accident cases being decided not by the courts but by the insurance companies. This, however, has proved not to be the case. The combination of infelicitous drafting, an inability to agree on a uniform system applicable to all victims of road accidents and a certain hostility on the part of the legal profession has resulted in a far higher level of litigation than had been originally anticipated. A further factor explaining the huge number of cases coming before the courts on the new Law is that Articles 1-6 (relating to the principle of compensation) came into force immediately upon publication of the Law and applied not only to accidents which had occurred in the three years prior to the passing of the Law, but also to those cases where proceedings had already begun under the Articles 1382/1384 system, including those pending before the Cour de Cassation. In many instances, cases pending before the Cour de Cassation had deliberately been held in abeyance pending the publication of the new Law, and this therefore explains the very large number of cases on which the French Supreme Court has had to pronounce. All this is to the good, since the Law is both complicated and controversial, and academics and the courts alike have been divided in their opinions of the effect of certain provisions. Thus, although the Law has been in force for only a little over three years, it has already been the subject of numerous judicial interpretations at all levels.

By virtue of its Article 1 the Law applies to the victims of road accidents involving "terrestrial motorised vehicles" (including trailers), but not railway trains or trams running on their own tracks. The driver or custodian of such a vehicle may no longer raise the defence of *force majeure* or act of a third party as against any victim. In respect of a claim for personal injury, if the victim is anyone other than a driver of a terrestrial motorised vehicle, contributory negligence will be irrelevant unless it was such as to amount to an inexcusable fault which was the sole cause of the accident (although in the case of a "super-privileged victim" ... even an inexcusable fault will not result in an exclusion or reduction of damages). Any degree of fault on the part of the driver of a vehicle involved in an accident will reduce his claim for damages accordingly. Evidence of contributory negligence will continue to be relevant in respect of claims for property damage from all classes of victim.

NOTES AND QUESTIONS

1. The French Parliament, the Court of Cassation, inferior courts, and advocates and professors writing commentary following important cases or published separately in law journals have all contributed to the French law of responsibility for traffic accidents. Is it appropriate to view *Charles v. Desmares* as an example of the Court's evolutive interpretation of article 1384?

2. Which factors might be important in determining whether a judge should use an evolutive method of interpretation: (1) the age of a code or statute; (2) the level of a court in the judicial hierarchy; or (3) the subject matter of the legal controversy? Think of some examples.

3. In the 1980s about 100,000 lawsuits were filed annually in France concerning traffic accidents. Is it likely that Law 85-677 of 1985 will substantially reduce the business for lawyers in this area?

4. For more about this field of French law, see the articles by the author of the 1965 "Tunc Project": André Tunc, *Traffic Accidents: Fault or Risk?,* 15 Seton Hall L. Rev. 831 (1985); *id., The French Law of Traffic Victims Compensation: The Present and the Possible,* 31 Am. J. Comp. L. 489 (1983).

4. CERTAINTY AND EQUITY

NOTE

It is common to find traditional views of the judicial process bolstered with references to the primary value of certainty in the law. The unusual emphasis given to certainty, which in the hands of a traditional civil law jurist becomes an argument against *stare decisis*, and the special role of equity in judicial decisionmaking, is indicated in the following excerpt.

The Spanish Civil Code, article 3(2) provides: "Equity should be considered in applying [legal] norms, although court decisions can only be based exclusively on [equity] when a statute expressly so permits."

JOHN HENRY MERRYMAN, THE CIVIL LAW TRADITION: AN INTRODUCTION TO THE LEGAL SYSTEMS OF WESTERN EUROPE AND LATIN AMERICA 48-55 (2d ed. 1985)

There is a great emphasis in the literature of the civil law tradition on the importance of certainty in the law. Certainty is, of course, an objective in all legal systems, but in the civil law tradition it has come to be a kind of supreme value, an unquestioned dogma, a fundamental goal. Even though most civil lawyers would recognize that there are competing values whose preservation might require some sacrifice of certainty, the matter is usually not discussed in these terms. In the civil law world it is always a good argument against a proposed change in the legal process that it will impair the certainty of the law. In Italy under Mussolini, for example, some attempts of the Fascists to make the law into an instrument of the totalitarian state were successfully resisted by jurists in the name of certainty in the law. After the fall of Fascism and the establishment of the republic, many desirable reforms in the Italian legal system were resisted by other jurists, again in the interests of certainty. It is an abstract legal value. Like a queen in chess, it can move in any direction.

Although the ideal of certainty has been used for a variety of purposes, its most important application is a reflection of the distrust of judges. Judges are prohibited from making law in the interest of certainty. Legislation should be clear, complete, and coherent in the interest of certainty. The process of interpretation and application of the law should be as automatic as possible, again in the interest of certainty. In this sense the emphasis on certainty is an expression of a desire to make the law judge-proof....

The same general attitude exists toward equity. In its general sense, equity refers to the power of the judge to mitigate the harshness of strict application of a statute, or to allocate property or responsibility according to the facts of the individual case. Equity is, in other words, a limited grant of power to the court to apply principles of fairness in resolving a dispute being tried before it. It is a recognition that broad rules, such as those commonly encountered in statutes, occasionally work harshly or inadequately, and that some problems are so complex that it is not possible for the legislature to dictate the consequences of all possible permutations of the facts. Where problems like these are involved, it is thought better to leave the matter to the trier of the case for decision according to equitable principles. Equity thus is the justice of the individual case. It clearly implies a grant of discretionary power to the judge.

But in the civil law tradition, to give discretionary power to the judge threatens the certainty of the law.... [T]he dominant view is still that, in the interest of certainty, judges must be carefully restricted in the exercise of equity....

[C]ommon law judges traditionally have inherent equitable powers: they can mold the result in the case to the requirements of the facts, bend the rule where necessary to achieve substantial justice, and interpret and reinterpret in order to make the law respond to social change. These powers are not seen as threats to certainty in law; indeed certainty is to be achieved through the doctrine of *stare decisis*, itself a judicial doctrine. The difficulties of rationalizing the demand for certainty and the justice of the individual case thus become problems for solution by the judges themselves. There is no conflict on this question between the judicial and the legislative powers of government. In the common law the judge can exercise discretion, but he also must bear the major operational responsibility for certainty and stability in the law....

It is one thing to say that the civil law judge lacks inherent equitable power. That statement is true insofar as it is the prevailing theory. It is quite another matter to accuse the civil law of being less equitable than the common law. That statement is demonstrably false. Indeed, a good argument can be (and has been) made that the civil law has developed a better, because more equitable, body of substantive rules in some fields of law than has the Anglo-American system. Our concern here is not with relative fairness, but with the distribution of power between legislature and court. In the common law tradition the judge has inherent equitable power. In the civil law tradition that power is in the legislature. The way in which the legislature exercises that power, and the resulting effect on the judiciary, provides an excellent example of the contrast between the theory and the practice of the legal process in the civil law tradition.

The theory is that the legislature exercises its equitable power in either of two principal ways: it can specifically delegate that power, in carefully defined situations, to the judge, or it can itself enact rules of equity for the judge to apply like other rules. An example of the first type is found in Article 1226 of the Italian Civil Code, which tells the judge that if the precise amount of the damage to the plaintiff resulting from a breach of the defendant's obligation cannot be proved, the judge shall fix the amount according to equitable principles. An example of the second type is found in Article 1337 of the same Code, which provides that the parties to a contract shall act in good faith in the negotiation and formation of the contract. Any modern civil code anywhere in the civil law world will contain a number of such provisions.

It requires no great exercise of imagination to realize that the second type of statute transfers a large segment of undefined equitable power to the judge....

The practice of delegating power to courts through legislation that employs general clauses of this sort is a common one in the civil law world, although the extent to which judges have consciously exercised that power varies widely. Article 1382 of the Code Napoléon provides that one whose act injures another must compensate him for the injury. The French courts have built an entire body of tort law on the basis of that article. Article 242 of the German *Bürgerliches Gesetzbuch* (BGB) requires a person to perform his obligation in the manner required by good faith. The German courts have employed this statute to create an immense body of new law on the performance of obligations. Both sets of courts have, in the process, developed working attitudes toward case law that are much more like those of common law courts than the prevailing theory admits. The German courts have been particularly overt about it, and their reliance on Article 242 to deal with some of the problems arising out of Germany's disastrous post-World War I inflation provides an example of judicial activism that seems extreme even to hardened legal realists. The obligatory reference to a "source of law" in such decisions is an empty ritual that has little restraining effect on judges and, given the rejection of *stare decisis*, can hardly contribute much to certainty.

At the same time, the compliance of German judges with the wishes of the Nazi regime is often unfavorably compared with the more successful resistance of Italian judges to the Fascists. The German judges, so the argument goes, had aggressively opted for judicial discretion at the expense of certainty in the 1920's, both to justify their use of general clauses and to follow the theory advanced by the "free law" school of jurists. The Italian judges stayed with their traditional approach of emphasizing certainty and exercising only a very limited degree of discretion. When darkness fell, the German judges were unable to defend the legal order by calling on the importance of certainty. Unlike the Italians, they had openly abandoned that principle. Whether one is persuaded by this version of history or not is unimportant. The fact that many do believe it gives us some insight into the continuing vitality of the appeal to certainty and the continuing distrust of judicial discretion that one finds in even the most liberated of civil law nations....

There is no civil contempt power in the civil law tradition. A general power to address orders to specific persons and to punish them for failure to follow the orders is unknown. The French do have something they call the *astreinte*, which appears, in a limited way, to be a functional equivalent of the contempt power; and something like the *astreinte* can also be found in German law. The French *astreinte*, in particular, has recently been expanded by legislation, but it is still only a pale imitation of the broad power of the common law judge.

The very idea of giving a court the general power to compel individuals in civil actions to do or to refrain from doing certain acts under penalty of imprisonment or fine or both is repugnant to the civil law tradition. For one thing, it is inconsistent with the demand for certainty; it gives the judge a great deal more power than civil lawyers think judges ought to have....

The different kind of emphasis on certainty, and the presence or absence of inherent judicial discretion and the contempt power, thus exemplify the fundamental differences in the roles of the judiciary in the two legal traditions. They reveal the extent to which the civil law judge is still limited by a variety of historical influences, most prominently by the image of the judicial process that emerged in the period of the French Revolution.

5. GERMANY AND THE FLIGHT INTO THE GENERAL CLAUSES

NOTE

In 1933 the German scholar J.W. Hedemann published a study entitled *Die Flucht in die Generalklauseln*. Both the thesis of the study and its title have since become widely known. "The flight into the general clauses" refers to an important period in modern German legal history. There is an excellent discussion in John P. Dawson, The Oracles of the Law 461-79 (1968). As Professor Dawson relates it, economic catastrophe following Germany's defeat in World War I produced a rate of inflation of incredible proportions: in November of 1923 the mark had been reduced to one *trillionth* of its prewar value. Inflation on this scale created enormous dislocations and intolerable injustices, and the courts eventually intervened. One of the means used was article 242 of the BGB, which provides: "The obligor is bound to carry out his performance in the manner required by good faith and in accordance with prevailing usage." Beginning in 1920 this "general clause" became the basis for a series of major creative decisions by the *Reichsgericht* (Supreme Court) to relieve debtors from the performance of contract provisions that inflation had made grotesquely burdensome and to protect creditors of fixed sums against payments made in worthless money. In the process the court developed theories justifying its actions and adopted attitudes concerning its powers that magnified its own independence and reduced nearly to the vanishing point its reliance on statutes as the basis of its decision. The notion that the court merely carried out the legislative will in applying the statute, always largely a fiction, became an obvious hypocrisy and was abandoned in favor of the view that the court had the obligation to interpret and apply the law creatively, as required by the social situation in Germany.

An additional step was taken in 1923 when, in a decision interpreting recent legal tender legislation, the court suggested that legislation (even *subsequent* legislation) in conflict with article 242 would have to give way. This suggestion was soon repeated in stronger terms, although in neither case was there a direct holding to that effect. Still, the mere statement of such a position in an opinion of the German Supreme Court was, as Professor Dawson described it, a revolution.

JOHN P. DAWSON, THE ORACLES OF THE LAW 475-77 (1968)

It was on April 1, 1933, that Hedemann published his well-known tract: "The Flight into the General Clauses, A Danger for Law and State." He saw the flight as something more than a magnifying of judicial power, though he opposed this too. Its great danger in his view was that it had begun to obliterate legal rules as restraints on power, leaving discretion uncontrolled. He linked this movement in private law with the disintegration of Germany's public order, the conflict between great power groups that had brought government close to paralysis; he found a parallel also in the solution adopted — to entrust political authority to supposed "neutrals" and dilute the restraints on their discretion through new forms of general clause. He solemnly warned that Rome had followed a similar path to the dictatorship of Byzantium, in which "the absolute emperor proclaims in the name of equity the authority of the imperial will, unrestrained by law." One phase of this gloomy prophecy had in fact already been realized. One week before Hedemann's book was published, Hitler had acquired command of the state; thereafter the public law of Germany was to be subject to one overriding general clause, the will of the *Führer*. It is of some interest to note that Hedemann himself adjusted to Nazism cheerfully, was loaded with honors, and became a leading exhibit among jurists serving the Nazis.

The predictions of Hedemann were realized also in another way: the advent of the Nazis on the whole promoted, it certainly did not arrest, the flight into the general clauses. This is not the place to describe in detail the ambivalence of the Nazis toward the established judiciary. For judicial activities which they considered important, they set up special courts, or else simply stacked up their victims without pretending to follow judicial procedure. Where the will of the Führer had been manifested, whether by legislation or executive order, disobedience or critique by judges was of course foreclosed. Yet it was hoped that the established judiciary, when sufficiently purged and "coordinated," would be a useful instrument for realizing the party's aims. Judges were to promote the "togetherness" of the *Volk*, its racial purity, common good above private good, the world view of National Socialism, and so on. The general clauses — especially "good faith" and "good morals" — were to be main ports of entry for these principles of the new order. On the whole, therefore, the Nazi leadership was cordial toward the general clauses and willing to have their use expanded. This meant some expansion of judicial power in ways that did not hamper but might promote the purposes of the regime.

The *Reichsgericht* too was cordial. Perhaps its most impressive declaration on the subject was an opinion of the Great Senate for Civil Matters in 1936. In response to a question certified by one of the Senates, this plenary body declared that a contract could be void as offensive to "good morals" if the values exchanged were unequal and "in its content, motive and object it offends the sound sense of the people."

> The concept of an "offense against good morals" as contained in articles 138 and 826, Civil Code, includes in essence the content of the National Socialist world outlook, which has become since the revolution the prevailing sense of the people (*Volksempfinden*). Filled with this content, article 138 is to be applied also to transactions of the period preceding that have not yet been performed. When a transaction offends good morals according to the views that now prevail no legal protection can be accorded it by any German court.

The court then resorted to the spray technique that had been so freely used in the inflation cases — all the circumstances, elements, and motives of the parties must be examined; no single formula would suffice. But judges were reminded that their task was to apply the "sound sense of the people," newly redefined. In the particular instance of the unequal exchange all the resources of the legal order, including both civil and criminal law, must be mobilized to prevent the pursuit of private self-interest to the injury of others and to further the needs of the community of the *Volk*.

NOTES AND QUESTIONS

1. Which of the following permits the greatest inroad on the civilian interest in certainty of law: (1) equity, (2) general clauses, or (3) evolutive interpretation? Are any of these instruments *a priori* good or bad for a system of justice? Is the experience of Italy and Germany during the 1930s instructive?

2. Consider the following view of history. After the French Revolution in Europe and the Wars of Independence in Latin America, the basic problem in the 19th century was one of order, stability, and certainty. Society was in chaos and required a body of authoritative norms that would appear to be rational, neutral, logically related, and certain. The codes provided such instruments of reason and order. In the latter part of the 20th century, as society becomes increasingly complex and future societal relationships are difficult to predict, there is a need for flexibility and adaptability to change within the structure of society's legal rules.

What method of flexibility best fits the logic of the civil law tradition?

3. Should equity be considered a true source of law within the civil law, or only a form for mitigating the strict application of a particular statute in a particular case?

4. Prior to the enactment of the German Civil Code (the *Bürgerliches Gesetzbuch* or BGB) in 1896, to go into effect in 1900, German decisions were fuller and looser than the French, more discursive and scholarly in style. It was not unusual for them to cite prior decisions, although there was a much stronger tendency to cite (and to adopt the intellectual style of) the doctrine. Enactment of the BGB, which embodied the results of German legal science, began a new spirit of deference to legislation and a consequent diminution of the creative role of judges. The subsequent flight into the general clauses can be seen as a reaction against the view of the judicial process inherent in conceptual jurisprudence, embodied in German legal science and the BGB — a restoration, perhaps an exaggeration, of the former German judicial style. In contemporary Germany, the courts approach their functions in a manner consistent with German historical development and with the tradition of the courts themselves. Thus the ordinary courts, and particularly the *Bundesgerichtshof*, or Supreme Court, perceive themselves as participants in an old European judicial tradition. They bear a greater weight of history and are inclined to be more logically rigorous, more formal, more deferential to the legislature, than the Constitutional Court. The latter, newly formed and invested with the power to void legislation as unconstitutional, understandably adopted a different style. Thus, for example, the rule of unanimity, with no disclosure of dissenting votes and no publication of dissenting opinions, still applies in the ordinary courts but not in the Constitutional Court. Although the ordinary courts cite and discuss prior decisions, the doctrine of *stare decisis* is still rejected by them. Judicial decisions are not a source of law. Decisions of unconstitutionality by the Constitutional Court, however, *do* have the force of law. And so on. Still, even the decisions of the German ordinary courts seem much more American than French in style.

6. THE LATIN AMERICAN VARIANT: ARGENTINA

ENRIQUE ZULETA-PUCEIRO, STATUTORY INTERPRETATION IN ARGENTINA, in INTERPRETING STATUTES: A COMPARATIVE STUDY 29, 33, 60-62, 65, 69-71 (D. Neil MacCormick & Robert S. Summers eds. 1991)

General Origins of Interpretational Issues

Interpretational issues do not grow from sources very different from those in any other statutory-based legal system. As has been said, the early Argentine experience integrated a complex tradition, in which the ancient Spanish colonial law, valid even 20 years after the 1853 Constitution and until the time of adoption of the new private law codes, co-existed with the new imported legal traditions, represented by the American constitutional model and the French codes. Some scholars underline the idea that the Argentine legal system evolved out of the replacement of ancient customary law by new scientific ideas about systematization, codification and drafting, and out of the displacement of the original normative disorder by the coherent order of codes.

Nevertheless this idea must be discussed from a strictly historical point of view. In fact, Spanish and colonial law recognized a relatively high degree of stability, in an integrated and hierarchical relationship between different positive sources: the *Recopilación de Leyes de los Reynos de Indias,* the *Ordenamiento de Alcalá,* the *Fueros Municipales,* the *Fuero Real* and the *Partidas.* In addition, there was a complex regulation of public matters. A very casuistic judicial doctrine, inspired in the Spanish law tradition, evolved without significant conflicts.

The new Constitution of 1853 reshaped the entire structure of institutional power, redefining the scheme of legal sources. The idea of a systematic legal order, unique and complete, presided by statutory law and subsidiarily completed by other traditional sources as a result of a mechanism of normative habilitation, became central. The rule of law, considered by Arts. 18 and 19 of the Constitution as a basic leading principle, established the premise that whatever is not prohibited is permitted....

Style and Structure of Opinions

The style and structure of the Supreme Court decisions reflect not only the highly doctrinal approach to the judicial function of the tribunal, but also a deep awareness about the public role of its decisions. Decisions are written to be known not only by the parties, but also by the specialized and general public. In Argentina there are two legal newspapers and some more weekly legal magazines, that reproduce in full decisions and publish doctrinal articles, bibliographical notes and professional news. The Supreme Court publishes all its decisions, whatever the relevance in a special collection (*Fallos*). Any decision of the lower tribunals and judges may be published, depending on the editorial decision of the newspapers and magazines, and a substantial part of the higher tribunals' decisions is finally published — sometimes even with comments by scholars.

This possibility of an almost universal knowledge about opinion leads to very careful argumentation, foundation of arguments, footnotes, and comparative and doctrinal references. This external circumstance has influenced the structure and style of opinions and decisions. The idea of not only objective but also public control of the argumentation pervades the intellectual tasks of judges and courts. The presupposed addressees of the reasoning processes are the parties, lower courts and, especially, public opinion. Justices are deeply aware of the creative role of the Court and of the objective and general impact of their opinions on the general legal order. The opinion not only indicates the results of the conflict to the parties and the general public, but it is also an attempt to justify the decision.

Regarding the minimum content, opinions vary, depending on the level of the tribunal. There are no explicit rules about structure, but there is a minimum content specified by law. Art. 163 of the Nat. Civ. and Comm. Procedural Code says that the first instance definitive sentence must contain: (1) place and date; (2) name of the parties; (3) a brief account of the issues; (4) a separate consideration of every question considered in the case; (5) the grounds and the applicable law; (6) the express, positive and precise resolution, and its relation to the contentions of the parties, considering the facts and the law; (7) the term of the sentence; and (8) express decision about costs and [attorney fees].

Regarding the form, in general, every decision has four parts: firstly the "vistas" — "vistos" — that summarize the content of the different steps of judicial proceedings, describing the factual situation and the problem under consideration; secondly, the "considerandos," devoted to the tribunal's account of positions and arguments of the parties, the results of evidence production and also the norms that ought to be considered for a decision; thirdly, the "resultandos" where the tribunal analyses the facts, the evidence, the reasons and motivations argued by the parties, and, after all that, the tribunal's own view about the case; and fourthly, the final decision, written in a very concise way and expressed in numbered paragraphs. Every decision means an exhaustive delimitation of relevant facts, a legal qualification, and explicit mention of the norms applied to the case, solving all the interpretative or integrative problems, and the foundations and grounding of the resolution. The opinion contains references to the law to support every step of the decisional process.

The decisions of the Supreme Court have a different structure because of its activity at the final highest level. A brief section of "vistos" only mentions the name of the parties and the nature of the issue. Then the "considerandos" describes, in numbered paragraphs, the different positions and arguments of the parties. It identifies the arguments and questions, giving explicit arguments about them. The argumentation is always supported by doctrinal references about the Supreme Court's traditional doctrine on every point of the debate. In a final paragraph, the Court fixes its position, deciding the case. The decision is signed by the justices, with an express mention of dissents, that are also published. The general mode of decisions is very flexible. The weighing model is the most common, but an attempt is always made to establish a rightly reasoned conclusion.

Decisions usually contain substantive reasons, besides a formal consideration of applicable law. The former are the most important and there are now limits to explanation and illustration. Opinions also try to link the partial and final conclusions to established interpretative patterns, quoting extensively prior judicial doctrine of the Court. There is nothing like an official ideology of the Court. The majority opinion only decides a case, without any formally binding consequence in terms of generality. This could be, of course, the natural consequence of the institutional weight of a Supreme Court decision....

The Institutional Role of the Courts

Only in very recent times, again under the influence of American ideas about the activist role of judicial review, have some very well known decisions expressed the idea of progressive judicial activity of a legislative kind. But the acceptance of creative powers of the judge has more to do with the possibility of everyday law application, searching for basic values, related to just solution of concrete cases, than with the more progressive idea of a legislative function of the Court. Some recent decisions may have changed this basic position. The most remarkable has been the invalidation of the prohibition of divorce after almost a century under the Civil Marriage Act. The decision was based on the argument that the Court can act subsidiary to the legislative power whenever there are political obstacles to social change. Over many decades, the doctrine of *political questions* protected the courts from conflicts with the political power. Every question belonging to the realm of what the courts defined as "political" was outside the field of judicial decision and reserved to the authority of the political power. Recent changes in this doctrine, mainly after the recent restoration of democracy, seem to offer a new institutional landscape, in which the courts tend to exercise plainly their constitutional political role....

Interpretation and Legal Culture

Some basic features must be underlined.

1. Two main aspects of legal culture coexist. One is derived from the continental codified systems and the other from the American tradition. This gives rise to a rather tense coexistence of interpretational approaches: one close to the exegetic movement, derived from the influence of European codifications, and the other from more functional and pragmatic approaches that start from the American influence. This also explains why the American doctrines about constitutional interpretation and judicial review have displaced the influence of European doctrines, traditionally deriving from private law. Within this broad process of change, substantive approaches tend to displace formal views about interpretation and gap-filling activity.

2. Rapid social change and economic crisis must be considered as an outstanding factor of legal change. One can even distinguish between general stages in the development of interpretative judicial doctrine, related to the changing role of law in society. First, after national organization (1853-63) and until the beginning of this century the exegetical view was influential within a framework of liberal individualistic law, courts and society; second, between 1900 and the 1930s, the influence of scientific positivism was quite clear, especially in terms of systematic interpretation; third, after the 1930s and until the middle of the 1940s, interventionistic economic ideas were received within an intellectual framework that included Keynesianism. During this period, judicial theory began to receive American realistic ideas and a more functional approach to interpretation; fourth, between 1945 and 1955, during the first Peronist government, natural law theories were influential in the Supreme Court doctrine, specially through the leading intellectual influence of the president, T.D. Casares. Functionalism and anti-formalism also had an important role in this stage; fifth, after 1955 and during part of the 1960s, realistic and functionalistic approaches continued to be important, but, between 1966 and 1983, institutional interruptions generated a complex doctrinal picture in which liberal economic individualism coexisted with realistic and natural law theories about interpretation; sixth, since 1983, there has been a great change in doctrinal influences, with significant reception of American doctrines about a very activistic role of the judiciary: this has been very clear in the Supreme Court interpretative doctrine.

3. Argentine legal culture is the result of a complex process of reception, where the original factors remain strong and active. The importance and prestige of French, Spanish and Italian civil and commercial law doctrine, Italian constitutional and administrative law doctrine, American constitutional and judicial doctrine are complemented by a rich set of theoretical trends, in which natural law, analytical philosophy and critical legal theories exert real influence on judicial doctrines about interpretation. In the light of interpretative doctrine, we deny the existence of any unique interpretive ap-

proach. What we see is a tension between coexisting and even contradictory models. Political turmoil, institutional interruptions and economic crises are factors contributing to this complex and dynamic situation.

QUESTION

What makes judicial interpretation significantly different in Argentina compared to the folklore of France and Italy? Is it because Argentina has a different theory of sources of law? If not, what are the reasons?

7. THE ABUSE OF RIGHT DOCTRINE IN JAPAN

KAZUAKI SONO & YASUHIRO FUJIOKA, THE ROLE OF THE ABUSE OF RIGHT DOCTRINE IN JAPAN, 35 Louisiana Law Review 1037-40, 1043-46 (1975)

In a recent case, *Mitamura v. Suzuki*,[1] the plaintiff sought compensation for loss of enjoyment of sunshine and obstruction of ventilation resulting from defendant's addition of a second floor to his one-story house southern to the plaintiff's in a residential section. Deciding in favor of the plaintiff, the Japanese Supreme Court stated:

> In all cases a right must be exercised in such a fashion that the result of the exercise remains within a scope judged reasonable in the light of the prevailing social conscience. When a conduct by one who purports to have a right to do so fails to show social reasonableness and when the consequential damages to others exceed the limit which is generally supposed to be borne in the social life, we must say that the exercise of the right is no longer within its permissible scope. Thus, the person who exercises his right in such a fashion shall be held liable because his conduct constitutes *an abuse of right....*

The Development of the "Abuse of Right" Doctrine

The abuse of right doctrine emerged from reflection on the absoluteness of a right whose exercise is left entirely for individuals: *Qui iure suo utitur, nemini facit iniuriam.* The doctrine emphasizes that exercise of a right cannot be considered in isolation of the interest of others who might be affected thereby, because the notion of a "right" serves only as a tool for regulating individual relationships in the society. The doctrine is now expressly prescribed in article 1(3) of the Japanese Civil Code, which was incorporated at the time of the revision of the Code in 1947. Article 1 reads: "(1) A private right shall conform to the public welfare; (2) The exercise of right and performance of duties shall be conducted in good faith and sincerity; (3) No abuse of rights shall be permitted." It is important to note that the doctrine constitutes only a part of article 1. No direct answer has yet been given in the Japanese jurisprudence as to whether the other provisions in article 1, particularly paragraph (1) concerning the public welfare, have independent roles or are only subsidiary

[1] 26 Saiko Saibansho minji hanreishū. 1067 (Sup. Ct., June 27, 1972) [hereinafter cited as Minshū].

in support of the abuse of right doctrine. Nevertheless the public welfare notion, which is provided as inherently restrictive of a private right, might influence some judges in evaluating the meaning of the abuse of right doctrine in article 1(3), since the abuse of right doctrine is directed toward the adjustment of conflicting private interests in the light of the *social* life.

The abuse of right doctrine, however, was not new to the Japanese jurisprudence even before it was expressly incorporated into the Civil Code in 1947. The Great Court of Cassation, a former body of the present Japanese Supreme Court, was already providing room for the emergence of the doctrine through its decisions. The influence of other civil law countries, especially France, which favorably treated the doctrine of abuse of right as a means to solve the question of nuisance, provided grounds for the development of this doctrine in Japan in the early 1900's....

Development After the Incorporation of the Doctrine in the Civil Code

The generality in provision of the doctrine in article 1(3) of the Civil Code would permit judges flexible approaches to concrete disputes. The rigidity of other legal rules would no longer be a barrier for a judge where he wished to avoid an undesirable result arising from the strict application of such other rules of law. On the other hand, the free hand given to courts through this general provision might make a judge a sole arbiter of disputes according to his own standards. The difficult question in applying such a general provision is how to achieve some flexibility in the resolution of individual disputes while retaining a desired legal stability or predictability.[19] So far the Japanese courts refrained from an unduly extensive use of article 1(3). The Japanese judiciary has proved conservative regarding use of this general provision, as contrasted to a relatively progressive attitude of academia. The judge's attitude is, of course, partly due to their understandable reluctance to resort to a general provision where a dispute, however complicated, could be handled by maneuvering within the realm of interpretation of concrete rules provided elsewhere in the Code. The number of cases wherein the abuse of right doctrine is applied did not notably increase after incorporation of the doctrine into the Code. The courts have relied on the abuse of right doctrine only in exceptional cases where no other alternative could bring about a fair solution of a dispute. This attitude is a sound one.

The recent *Mitamura* case, involving an exercise of the right of ownership which disturbed another landowner's enjoyment of sunshine has already been noted. A similar approach was used in solving a dispute where digging for the purpose of obtaining a hot spring on one person's land affected another's enjoyment of a hot spring already in use in a nearby area.[22] ...

---

[19] The function of general clauses in formulating new rules of law to fill the lack of specific rules in the Code is closely connected with the relationship between judiciary and legislature. As to how scholars treat this question, see M. Ishida, *Seiteihō no kōsokuryoku* (Binding force of statutes), 550 Juristo 18 (1973); M. Ishida, *Hōkaishaku hōhō no kiso riron* 1 (Fundamental theory concerning methodology on the interpretation of law), 92 Hōgaku kyōkai zasshi 65 (1975); Kurusu, *Hō no kaishaku ni okeru seiteihō no igi* (The place of a statute in the application of law by the judiciary), 73 Hōgaku kyōkai zasshi 1 (no. 2) (1956).

[22] *Daimaru Bessō Co. v. Takeishi,* 12 Minshū 1640 (Sup. Ct., July 1, 1958).

According to article 612(2) of the Civil Code, subletting of a leasehold by a tenant without the landlord's permission constitutes a ground for rescission by the landlord. However, several lower courts have refused in certain cases to give effect to such a rescission, basing their refusal on article 1(3). The Japanese Supreme Court, while exhibiting some reluctance to rely on this general provision, sustained those decisions.[25] In doing so, the Court stated in *Uchino v. Kobayashi*[26] that termination of a landlord-tenant relationship was not justified merely because conduct of the tenant formerly constituted ground for rescission under article 612(2), unless the relationship became such that the landlord could no longer have faith in leaving his property to the tenant. The Court thus avoided a rigid application of article 612(2). In a series of decisions where the occupancy of a leasehold tenant was protected even after the title for the subject property had been transferred by the landlord to another party, the courts refused the new owner's request that the tenant evacuate the leased property because the transferee lacked legitimate practical interests.[27] It is important to note, however, that the period when these decisions were rendered was after World War II when the shortage of houses was very keen, and that the legislature had been active to strengthen the tenants' position through the enactment of a landlord-tenant statute.

Matsumoto v. Japan,[28] the so-called *Itatsuke Air Base* case, illustrates another type of dispute where the doctrine becomes applicable. In that case the Japanese Government had a lease of land from a citizen for use by the American Air Force in accordance with an administrative arrangement between the two governments. The government rejected the landlord's claim for return of the land on expiration of the lease. The court sustained the government's contention that the citizen's assertion of reclamation constituted an abuse of right. The court stressed that the basis of the protection of a private right by law lies in its social and public utility. The repossession sought by the landlord would have created a serious problem for the maintenance of the air base, and the court felt that repossession would not give the landowner greater protection of his right. In passing, it may be noted that the motive of the plaintiff in bringing this suit was rather political.

Obonai v. Orizume Sangyō Co.[29] exemplifies still another type of dispute. Performance of a contract declared null and void because it contradicted an administrative regulation was to be regarded as retroactively illegal where the performance had taken place before the nullity became known to the parties. In such a case, a party to that invalid contract might wish to take advantage of its nullity, asserting that the execution under the contract constituted a tortious wrong. This case, however, denied a claim for damages based on this theory. The court said that such a claim for damages could constitute an abuse of right.

---

[25] *See, e.g.*, *Kawaguchi v. Mizunoya*, 24 Minshū 2015 (Sup. Ct., Dec. 11, 1970).
[26] 7 Minshū 979 (Sup. Ct., Sept. 25, 1953).
[27] *Maruyama v. Ikejima*, 22 Minshū 1767, 1817 (Sup. Ct., Sept. 3, 1968); *Sunahata Seikan Kōgyōsho Co. v. Tominaga*, 17 Minshū 639 (Sup. Ct., May 24, 1963).
[28] 19 Minshū 233 (Sup. Ct., Mar. 9, 1965).
[29] 19 Minshū 2212 (Sup. Ct., Dec. 21, 1965).

NOTES AND QUESTIONS

1. Does judicial development of the abuse of right doctrine in Japan and its consideration of the "prevailing social conscience" reflect evolutive interpretation, the use of equity, or interpretation of a general clause? Can such a development involve two or all three of these methods?

2. For more on the general theme of judicial interpretation, see Julio C. Cueto-Rua, Judicial Methods of Interpretation of the Law (1981); D. Neil MacCormick & Robert S. Summers, eds., Interpreting Statutes: A Comparative Study (1991); Jaro Mayda, François Gény and Modern Jurisprudence (1978).

Chapter 10

PROCEDURE

"In the law, all questions of procedure are at bottom questions of substance, and vice versa." Where rights depend on the outcome of litigation, and where the outcome of litigation is affected by procedure, the truth of this legal realist observation seems unchallengeable. Systems of procedure guide and control the process of litigation and necessarily affect the result.

Of all the areas of the law, civil and common law traditions diverge most dramatically in matters of procedure. Substantive rules often appear similar but they are brought to bear in such a strikingly different manner that contrary results in otherwise similar cases are a constant possibility. The substantial differences in civil and criminal procedure in the common law and the civil law are accordingly matters of the deepest interest to the student of foreign and comparative law.

In America, the 1970s and 1980s were a golden age of comparative scholarship in the law of procedure, marked by a high level of study and exposition (exemplified by the Kaplan, von Mehren & Schaefer articles on German civil procedure), provocative evaluative comparison (e.g., Langbein's German Advantage and plea-bargaining articles), erudition in pursuit of grand theory (all of Damaška's work, culminating in his imposing book: *The Faces of Justice and State Authority* (1986)), and scholarly bickering (largely in reaction to Langbein). All are represented in the following materials.

A. CIVIL PROCEDURE

1. AN OVERVIEW OF CIVIL PROCEDURE

JOHN HENRY MERRYMAN, THE CIVIL LAW TRADITION: AN INTRODUCTION TO THE LEGAL SYSTEMS OF WESTERN EUROPE AND LATIN AMERICA 111-23 (2d ed. 1985)

Just as civil law is the heart of the substantive law in the civil law tradition, so civil procedure is the heart of procedural law. Strictly speaking, the law of civil procedure applies only to the process of judicial enforcement of rights and duties arising under the civil law part of private law. The distinct nature and purposes of criminal proceedings and the existence of separate sets of courts, such as administrative courts, have produced separate bodies of criminal procedure and administrative procedure. But all systems of procedure in the civil law tradition have a common origin in Roman, canon, and medieval Italic law. All have tended to follow the lead of civil proceduralists in molding and developing procedural law. Civil procedure is central and basic, and special procedural systems — even criminal procedure — have tended to develop as variations on the civil procedure model.

At the same time, there are important differences between civil and criminal proceedings, and criminal procedure has, particularly since the period of revolutions, been an essentially independent field of regulation and study. Most civil law systems include separate codes of civil procedure and criminal procedure. The subjects are separately taught in the law schools, and a separate literature has grown up around each of them. At a very fundamental level, however, they are based on common notions, and the development of such notions — general theories and general principles of procedure — is traditionally assumed to be the job of the civil proceduralist, just as the development of general theories and principles of law ... is primarily the task of the civil lawyer.

A typical civil proceeding in a civil law jurisdiction is divided into three separate stages. There is a brief preliminary stage, in which the pleadings are submitted and a hearing judge (usually called the instructing judge) appointed; an evidence-taking stage, in which the hearing judge takes the evidence and prepares a summary written record; and a decision-making stage, in which the judges who will decide the case consider the record transmitted to them by the hearing judge, receive counsel's briefs, hear their arguments, and render decisions. The reader will observe that the word "trial" is missing from this description. In a very general way it can be said that what common lawyers think of as a trial in civil proceedings does not exist in the civil law world. The reason is that the right to a jury in civil actions, traditional in the common law world, has never taken hold in the civil law world. This tradition continues most strongly in the United States today, where in most jurisdictions there is a constitutional right to a civil jury. (Elsewhere in the common law world the civil jury has been abolished.)

The existence of a jury has profoundly affected the form of civil proceedings in the common law tradition. The necessity to bring together a number of ordinary citizens to hear the testimony of witnesses and observe the evidence, to find the facts, and to apply the facts to the law under instructions from a judge, has pushed the trial into the shape of an event. The lay jury cannot easily be convened, adjourned, and reconvened several times in the course of a single action without causing a great deal of inconvenience and expense. It seems much more natural and efficient for the parties, their counsel, the judge, and the jury to be brought together at a certain time and place in order to perform, once and for all, that part of the civil proceeding that requires their joint participation. Such an event is a trial as we know it.

In the civil law nations, where there is no tradition of civil trial by jury, an entirely different approach has developed. There is no such thing as a trial in our sense; there is no single, concentrated event. The typical civil proceeding in a civil law country is actually a series of isolated meetings of and written communications between counsel and the judge, in which evidence is introduced, testimony is given, procedural motions and rulings are made, and so on. Matters of the sort that would ordinarily be concentrated into a single event in a common law jurisdiction will be spread over a large number of discrete appearances and written acts before the judge who is taking the evidence. Comparative lawyers, in remarking on this phenomenon, speak of the "concentration" of the trial in common law countries and the lack of such concentration in civil law countries. In general it can be said that civil lawyers favor the more concentrated system and that the trend in civil law jurisdictions has been toward greater concentration, with the rate of development varying widely. (Austria and Germany seem to be moving most rapidly in this direction.) The tradition, however, continues to be one of relative lack of concentration.

Lack of concentration has some interesting secondary consequences. For one thing, pleading is very general, and the issues are defined as the proceeding goes on; this practice differs considerably from that found in common law jurisdictions, where precise formulation of the issues in pleading and pretrial proceedings is seen as necessary preparation for the concentrated event of the trial. For somewhat similar reasons, the civil law attorney typically spends less time in preparing for an appearance before the court during the evidence-taking part of the civil proceeding. The appearance is usually for the purpose of examining only one witness or of introducing only one or two pieces of material evidence. The pressure to prepare the entire case at the very beginning, felt by the common lawyer preparing for trial, does not exist. The element of surprise is reduced to a minimum, since each appearance is relatively brief and involves a fairly small part of the total case. There will be plenty of time to prepare some sort of response before the next appearance. The lack of concentration also explains the lesser importance of discovery (advance information about the opponent's witnesses and evidence) and pretrial procedures (preliminary discussions with opposing counsel and the judge to reach agreement on matters not really at issue and so on). Discovery is less necessary because there is little, if any, tactical or strategic advantage to be gained from the element of surprise. There is no necessity for pretrial proceedings because there is no trial; in a sense every appearance in the first two stages of a civil law proceeding has both trial and pretrial characteristics.

A second characteristic of the traditional civil law proceeding is that evidence is received and the summary record prepared by someone other than the judge who will decide the case.... [C]ontemporary procedural institutions in the civil law world have been strongly influenced by medieval canonic procedures. In the canon law proceeding, evidence was taken by a clerk, and it was the clerk's written record that the judge used in making his decision. This procedure eventually was modified to place the evidence-taking part of the proceeding under the guidance of a judge, but quite often the case would still be decided by other judges, or by a panel of judges that included the judge who took the evidence. Comparative lawyers customarily contrast this form of proceeding with the custom in the common law system by which the evidence is heard and seen directly and immediately by the judge and jury who are to decide the case. Accordingly, it has become common to speak of the "immediacy" of the common law trial, as distinguished from the "mediacy" of the civil law proceeding. Here again, comparative commentators tend to think of the common law system as preferable, and there is a steady evolution in civil law jurisdictions toward greater immediacy. The "documentary curtain" that separated the judge from the parties during the medieval period and that was then thought to produce a greater likelihood of fair proceedings, unaffected by influence brought to bear on the judges by interested persons, no longer seems necessary. On the contrary, preparation of the record by someone other than the judge who is to decide the case is now seen to be a defect because it deprives the judge of the opportunity to see and hear the parties, to observe their demeanor, and to evaluate their statements directly.

In a mediate system, procedure tends to become primarily a written matter. Those in common law countries think of a trial as an event during which witnesses are sworn and orally examined and cross-examined in the presence of the judge and jury. Motions and objections are often made orally by counsel, and the judge rules orally on them. In the civil law, on the contrary, even the questions asked a witness during the civil proceedings are often asked by the judge on the basis of questions submitted in writing by counsel for the parties. Where the practice persists of having one person receive the evidence and make the record and another decide the case, a written rather than oral proceeding is obviously necessary. A trend toward immediacy in civil proceedings carries with it a trend toward orality, and orality is promoted also by the trend toward concentration. Civil law proceduralists think of the three matters as related to one another, and one frequently encounters discussions in which concentration, immediacy, and orality are advanced as interrelated components of proposals for reform in the law of civil procedure.

Foreign observers are sometimes confused by the fact that, in most civil law nations, questions are put to witnesses by the judge rather than by counsel for the parties. This leads some to the conclusion that the civil law judge determines what questions to ask and, unlike the common law judge, in effect determines the scope and extent of the inquiry. People talk about an "inquisitorial" system of proof-taking, as contrasted with the "adversary" system of the common law. The characterization is quite misleading. In fact, the prevailing system in both the civil law and the common law world is the "dispositive" system, according to which the determination of what issues to raise, what evidence to introduce, and what arguments to make is left almost entirely to the parties. Judges in both traditions have some power to undertake inquiries on their own, and in Germany the law and the judicial tradition encourage the judge to play an active role in the proceedings. Elsewhere, however, civil law judges are more passive. The common law judge is occasionally inclined to intervene, but usually does so only when juveniles or other incapacitated persons are involved in a case, or where there appears to be a clear public interest that the parties are not adequately representing. In similar cases in civil law jurisdictions, a public prosecutor or similar official is required by law to participate in the proceeding as a representative of the public interest. But these are exceptional occurrences, and in the great mass of civil litigation in both traditions the rule is that the parties have considerable power to determine what will take place in the proceedings. Where the civil law judge puts questions to the witness, he does so at the request of counsel, and he ordinarily limits his questions to those submitted by the lawyers.

The practice of putting the judge between the lawyer and the witness does, however, further illustrate the traditional lack of orality in the civil law. Ordinarily the lawyer who wishes to put questions to a witness must first prepare a written statement of "articles of proof," which describes the matters on which he wishes to question the witness. These articles go to both the judge and the opposing counsel in advance of the hearing at which the witness is to be examined. In this way the opposing counsel (and possibly also the witness himself) has advance written knowledge of what will go on at the hearing and can prepare for it. This profoundly affects the psychological positions of questioning lawyer and responding witness at the hearing, and the fact that any questions the lawyer asks must pass through the judge at the hearing reinforces this effect. The familiar pattern of immediate, oral, rapid examination and cross-examination of witnesses in a common law trial is not present in the civil law proceeding.

Cross-examination, in particular, seems foreign to the civil law proceeding. There has never been a jury to influence. There is little effort to discredit witnesses (in part, perhaps, because parties, their relatives, and interested third persons have been — and in many jurisdictions still are — disqualified from appearing as witnesses). The hearing judge is professionally and impartially interested in getting the relevant facts, and all questions are filtered through the judge. The "offer of proof" determines the scope of the witness's testimony and diminishes the possibility of surprise. Opposing counsel's principal activity in the process often consists only in making suggestions to the judge about the precise wording of the summary of the witness's testimony that goes into the record.

The contrast between common law and civil law procedure, in terms of the interrelated criteria of concentration, immediacy, and orality, can be illustrated by example. Plaintiff's lawyer may propose (in writing) to the hearing judge that a witness be called to testify. A copy of this "offer of proof" will go to the defendant's lawyer. The defendant's lawyer may object, perhaps because he believes that the proposed witness is disqualified by a family or business relationship with the plaintiff. The hearing judge will then set a hearing, usually a few weeks later, when the lawyers will submit written briefs and orally argue the question. The hearing judge will then take the question under consideration, and eventually, after a few more weeks, will issue his ruling in writing. If the ruling is in favor of the proposed "offer of proof," a date will be set for a further hearing at which the witness's testimony will be taken. In a typical civil action in a common law court, this entire sequence of events — stretching over several weeks or months in a civil law court — would be telescoped into less than a minute of oral colloquy between judge and counsel. Plaintiff's lawyer asks the court to call a witness; defendant's counsel objects and briefly states his reason; plaintiff's counsel replies; the judge rules; and the witness, who is waiting in the courtroom, is called and takes the stand.

Suppose the witness in the previous example is called and testifies. The hearing judge will make notes (there is no verbatim record) of testimony and dictate a summary to the clerk. After the witness and lawyers agree about the accuracy of the summary, the summary will enter the record that goes to the deciding panel of judges. They in turn must base their findings of fact (and justify those findings in writing) on the record. Even if the deciding panel includes the hearing judge, as it does in Italy, the written record strictly limits the determination of facts. The hearing judge's recollection of the witness's hesitancy, furtive demeanor, or patent insincerity — unless reflected in the written summary of his testimony in the record — cannot affect the findings of fact. In the common law, a jury's verdict is summary and requires no specific findings of fact. The witness's demeanor, as well as a variety of other circumstantial factors, can and often will significantly affect the jury's verdict. Where a case is tried in our courts by a judge without a jury, the judge who decides the case is the judge who sees and hears the witnesses. Our procedure permits, indeed requires, him to base his findings on his observations as well as on the witness's words.

A number of factors explain the substantial differences in the law of evidence between the civil law and the common law tradition. One of the most important of these, again, is the matter of the jury. In civil actions in common law jurisdictions, a variety of exclusionary rules, rules determining the admissibility or inadmissibility of offered evidence, have as their prime historical explanation the desire to prevent the jury from being misled by untrustworthy evidence. An alternative policy, one providing that the common law jury be warned of the unreliability of the evidence but then be allowed to evaluate it on the basis of the warning, has uniformly been rejected. The evidence is totally excluded.

The most obvious example is the "hearsay rule."... Such rules do not exist in civil law jurisdictions because of the absence of a jury in civil actions. This does not mean, however, that evidence can be freely introduced without restriction in civil law proceedings. On the contrary, there are a number of restricting and excluding devices. However, the origin of, and the functions served by, these rules are different from those of exclusionary rules in the common law. To understand these rules we must first go back to the medieval system of "legal proof."

Introduction of the system of legal proof in judicial proceedings was an important civilizing development in European law. It replaced trial by battle and trial by ordeal, the standard methods of deciding litigation in the turbulent feudal world of early medieval Europe. Even though it seems arbitrary, crude, and unjust to us today, this system of legal proof, when it was introduced, exerted a great humanizing influence on the administration of justice and was a long step forward in the attempt to turn judicial proceedings into rational investigations of the truth of conflicting allegations. The civil law judge then, as now, was not a very powerful person. However honest he might wish to be, he could not easily withstand persuasion, bribery, or threats — particularly threats made by the wealthy and powerful. To be workable at all, the system of legal proof had to provide some means of protecting judges from such pressures. The means that were developed included a set of formal rules for weighing testimony, a set of exclusionary rules, and the institution of the decisory oath (i.e. an oath that would decide a fact at issue).

The rules governing the weight to be given to certain kinds of testimony were mechanical in operation. The court was required to give predetermined weight to testimony based on the number, status, age, and sex of the witnesses. To prove a fact, a given number of witnesses was required. The testimony of nobles, clerics, and property owners prevailed over that of commoners, laymen, and those without property. The testimony of an older man prevailed over that of a younger. The testimony of women was either barred or given a fraction of the weight of a man's testimony. These and similar rules for evaluating evidence, in which all evidence was given an *a priori* arithmetical value (full proof, half proof, quarter proof, and the like), were based on what was believed to be common experience.

The exclusionary rules disqualified certain kinds of people from testifying at all. The principal groups of such people were the parties, relatives of the parties, and interested third persons. Their testimony was considered basically untrustworthy, and hence was entirely excluded. This rule protected the party's conscience against perjury, which he might be tempted to commit to win his case. It may also have reduced the vulnerability of the judge to coercion or bribery.

The decisory oath worked in the following way: Party *A* could put Party *B* on his oath as to a fact at issue that was within Party *B*'s knowledge. If Party *B* refused to swear, the fact was taken as conclusively proved against him. If Party *B* swore, the fact was taken as conclusively proved in his favor. The compulsion on Party *B* against swearing falsely lay not only in the religious consequences of a false oath, but also in his criminal liability for perjury and his civil liability for damages.

The early institution of the civil jury in England inhibited the development of some of these restrictions (and led to others) on the introduction and evaluation of evidence in the common law. A group of laymen was less vulnerable to threats of violence or other forms of influence than was a single judge, particularly if the jurors were the "peers" of the parties, as the common law required. Consequently the need for protection provided to the civil law judge by the system of formal proof was not so strongly felt. The need to protect the jury against unreliable testimony led not only to the disqualification of interested persons as witnesses, but also to a set of restrictions on the admissibility of certain kinds of testimony by qualified witnesses. The jury as finder of fact fulfilled the function served by the decisory oath in two ways: It was an effective method of fact-finding, and it relieved the vulnerable judge of the dangers of party influence in deciding the facts. In this way, although the institution of the civil jury developed its own formalistic characteristics, the system of formal proof and the decisory oath failed to develop the importance in the common law that they acquired on the Continent.

Traces of these medieval devices still exist in the civil law world. The mechanical rules of legal proof have evolved into the irrebuttable presumptions of modern civil law. In some civil law jurisdictions, parties are still disqualified from testifying. The decisory oath remains in effect today in many countries (among them France, Italy, and Spain), although its use is primarily tactical. In general, however, the movement for procedural reform has had as its objective what is called "free evaluation of the evidence" by the judge. Such a movement was given great impetus by the rationalist spirit of the revolutionary period, but its thrust has been limited by the general weakness of the civil law judge and by the widespread mistrust of judges among civil lawyers. Nevertheless, proceduralists in civil law jurisdictions generally regard free evaluation of the evidence as the ideal toward which reform should point.

In the United States, if *A* sues someone, he usually must pay his own lawyer, whether he wins or loses. In civil law countries, as in England, the loser usually pays the winner's counsel fees. Although this "loser pays" rule seems fairer at first glance, and may in practice be preferable, it has one significant secondary consequence. To avoid imposing unreasonable counsel fees on the loser, the court uses an official schedule of fees for legal services. The lawyer for the winning party presents his account of services performed, and the court determines the fee that the loser must pay him according to the schedule. The lawyer may, of course, have stipulated with his client for a higher fee, but the client is responsible for the excess. It is considered unethical for the lawyer to have a financial interest in the outcome of a case, and contingent fee arrangements are accordingly prohibited in [most] civil law jurisdictions. The common use of contingent fees in the United States is considered by many civil lawyers to be a shocking practice, although some acknowledge its value as a form of legal aid.

As a general rule there is a right to an appeal in civil law jurisdictions. "Appeal" has a special meaning here that is unfamiliar in the United States, where it is thought of as primarily a method of correcting mistakes of law made by the trial court. In the civil law tradition, the right of appeal includes the right to reconsideration of factual, as well as legal issues. Although the tendency commonly is to rely on the record prepared below as the factual basis for reconsideration of the case, in many jurisdictions the parties have the right to introduce new evidence at the appellate level. The appellate bench is expected to consider all of the evidence itself and to arrive at an independent determination of what the facts are and what their significance is. It is also required to prepare its own fully reasoned opinion, in which it discusses both factual and legal issues.

The use of a jury in civil actions at the common law obviously forestalls review of the factual issues by an appellate court. The jury does not make specific findings of fact; it may, and often does, consider demeanor and other circumstantial factors; it need not justify (i.e. explain) its verdict; and its proceedings are not written. If the appellate court could independently decide factual questions, the jury's role would, in effect, be nullified. As long as there is *some* factual basis in the record to support the jury's (or the trial judge's) verdict, the appellate court in a common law jurisdiction will honor it.

In addition to the technical appeal, the dissatisfied party typically has the right to a further hearing before a higher court. In some jurisdictions (e.g. France and Italy) this procedure is called recourse in cassation; in others (e.g. Germany) it is called revision. The function, in either case, is similar: to provide an authoritative, final determination of any questions of law involved in the case. Recourse in cassation and revision, in other words, approximate the typical functions of common law appellate courts, which ordinarily restrict their consideration on appeal to questions of law....

In general, there are no separate concurring or dissenting opinions, even at the appellate level, in civil law jurisdictions. Although exceptions do exist, the general rule is one of unanimity and anonymity. Even dissenting votes are not noted, and it is considered unethical for a judge to indicate that he has taken a position at variance with that announced in the decision of the court.

A recent tendency toward noting dissents and separate concurrences, and even toward the publication of separate opinions, has developed in the constitutional courts of some civil law jurisdictions. But the standard attitude is that the law is certain and should appear so, and that this certainty would be impaired by noting dissents and by publishing separate opinions....

Another fundamental difference between the civil law and common law traditions occurs in enforcement proceedings. Civil law jurisdictions have nothing comparable to the common law notion of civil contempt of court.... [I]n the common law a person can be compelled to act or to refrain from acting by the threat of imprisonment or fine for contempt of court — that is, for refusing to obey a court order addressed to him as a person. There is, it is commonly said, a wide range of effective action *in personam* in the common law. The civil law, by way of contrast, knows no civil contempt of court and tends to operate solely *in rem*. This means that regardless of the type of claim one has against another person, the only way one can collect the claim is by obtaining a money judgment against him. The reverberations of this difference reach well back into the legal process, affecting, for example, the very legal definition of a contract. According to the civil law tradition, a promise that cannot be converted into money does not create a legal obligation; if the promise is not enforceable in money terms, it is not enforceable at all. The lack of a power to act *in personam* also affects every aspect of the civil proceeding in the civil law tradition. The power to compel the production of documents, business records, and other evidence or to subject a party or his property to inspection is much weaker than it is in common law jurisdictions. Judicial remedies in civil proceedings are restricted almost entirely to remedies that can be enforced against the property of the defendant (e.g. attachment and sale of his property, delivery of specific property to the claimant, or eviction from the property) or acts that can be performed by a third person and charged to the defendant (e.g. destruction of a structure unlawfully built). In the civil law, a person who disobeys a lawful order of the court in a civil action may thus be liable to a party for damages (e.g. the French *astreinte*), but he cannot be *punished* by the judge. The most the judge can do is ask that he be criminally prosecuted. By contrast, the common law judge in a civil proceeding can punish for contempt.

If one stands back and looks at the two systems of civil procedure, the outlines of two somewhat different ideologies begin to emerge. In the common law world the judge is an authority figure who administers a merged system of law and of equity. (It must be remembered that the court of equity originated as a court of conscience.) Actions are traditionally tried in the presence of a jury composed of a group of neighbors of the plaintiff and defendant who bring to bear throughout the proceeding the prevailing attitudes and values of the community. The judge has a civil contempt power, enabling him to order people to act or refrain from acting and to punish them if they refuse. The whole proceeding is permeated by a moralistic flavor. The parties play out their roles before the father-judge and the neighbor-jury. In the civil law tradition, by way of contrast, a judge is an important public servant, but he lacks anything like the measure of authority and paternal character possessed by the common law judge. Parties and witnesses can disobey his orders with less fear of serious reprisal. There is no jury of neighbors to look on, approving or disapproving. The civil law tradition is more thoroughly secularized, less moralistic, and more immune to the ethic of the time and place.

This basic difference in general outlook is dramatically illustrated by the law of damages. In the common law world we see nothing extraordinary in the awarding of penal damages, multiple damages, and so-called general damages (that is, damages over and above those proved) in civil actions against defendants whose conduct appears to be malicious or grossly negligent. In the civil law tradition, however, such damages are rarely available to a plaintiff in a civil proceeding. The line between the civil and the criminal is more sharply drawn, and morally reprehensible (i.e. malicious or grossly negligent) actions are matters for the criminal law rather than for the civil law. In the civil trial, as a general rule, the plaintiff's recovery is limited to compensation for the loss he suffered. If the judgment of the community is going to be brought to bear on a defendant because of the moral character of his action, it must be done through the processes of the criminal law, where the defendant is protected from arbitrary or exaggerated imposition of penalties by the principle of the criminal law that no penalty be assessed for something that was not legally defined as a crime at the time the action took place. And, as is generally true of criminal law in Western nations, the penalties in such cases are limited to those established in the statute.

NOTES AND QUESTIONS

1. What are the traditional civil law analogues to the common law's commitment in civil procedure to concentration, immediacy, and orality? How do the three civil law elements reinforce each other?

2. The completely different pace and style of the civil proceeding and the absence of a hearsay rule and other "jury-protecting" exclusionary rules strongly affect the functions of counsel. There are few, if any, occasions for objections to the introduction of evidence or the admissibility of testimony. There is little opportunity for the display of skill in direct and cross-examination. There are fewer opportunities to gain tactical advantage by procedural moves or through surprise. Can you see how these differences would affect "trial practice" in civil law nations?

3. It might appear that a procedure that places so little emphasis on skill of the kind we associate with successful trial practice is less of a game, less likely to cause the outcome of the trial to depend on the choice of counsel-champion, the press of time, and the hazards of trial procedure. Still, the civil law doctrinal opinion in favor of more concentration, orality, and immediacy in civil proceedings is almost unanimous. Why?

4. The law of evidence is merely a part of the law of procedure in the civil law. Rules of evidence in civil cases are typically found in the code of civil procedure (and in the civil code); rules of evidence in criminal cases are found in the code of criminal procedure. Discussions of evidence form chapters of treatises on procedure. Evidence is studied in courses in civil and criminal procedure in the law schools. Can you think of any reasons for the much slighter emphasis on evidence as a special topic or field for teaching and scholarship in civil law nations than in the United States?

5. Do civil and common lawyers bring fundamentally different attitudes to the process of introducing and evaluating facts in litigation? Consider the following excerpt.

> Western legal tradition displays two contrasting schemata for ascertaining facts in adjudication. According to an "atomistic" view, mental processes employed in "finding" facts can be decomposed into independent parts. Probative force is attributed to distinct items of evidence and discrete inferential sequences, and the final determination is made by aggregating these separate probative values through some sort of additive process. Because such mental operations are heavily propositional, the factfinder's state of mind produced by this atomistic process is relatively free of volitional components. The proof sufficiency standard for finding a particular fact can be expressed in graded probability terms.
>
> Under a second view, sometimes termed "holistic," the probative force of any item of information arises from interaction among elements of the total informational input. In this vision, separate weights of individual items of evidence cannot be disentangled from global judgments. Factfinding thus depends on schemes of thought not yet articulated and on volitional factors; and a proof sufficiency standard defies expression in probability terms.
>
> The implications of these two models of cognition for the law of evidence are clear and immediate. It stands to reason that a law of evidence undergirded by atomistic assumptions interferes with the factfinder's processes of belief formation much more than a law of evidence resting on holistic premises. For example, under an atomistic approach, it makes sense to require of a factfinder that he pay no attention to a specified informational item, or attribute to it a designated weight, while under a holistic view these demands imply asking the factfinder to do the impossible. The two models of cognition also are reflected in divergent criteria that justify the factfinder in taking a factual proposition as proven: holistic proof systems tend to invoke inner persuasion, or similar mental states, while atomistic systems usually refer to external yardsticks, such as the viewpoint of a reasonable person exposed to the same information.
>
> It would be transparently naive to expect that Anglo-American and Continental evidentiary arrangements are pure versions of either an atomistic or holistic approach. Yet, at the trial stage, Anglo-American adjudicative systems intrude in the factfinder's processes of belief formation more than is the case on the Continent. Anglo-American jurisdictions also use a different rhetoric in describing standards of proof sufficiency. And as the comparativist surveys these differences, he begins to suspect that the divergencies in the treatment of evidence in the two Western legal traditions reflect somewhat discrepant assumptions about the mental processes used to make factual inquiries.

Mirjan Damaška, Atomistic and Holistic Evaluation of Evidence: A Comparative View, in Comparative and Private International Law: Essays in Honor of

John Henry Merryman on His Seventieth Birthday 91-92 (David S. Clark ed. 1990).

For further insights on comparative evidence law by Professor Damaška, see *Of Hearsay and Its Analogues,* 76 Minn. L. Rev. 425 (1992); *Presentation of Evidence and Factfinding Precision,* 123 U. Pa. L. Rev. 1083 (1975).

6. What are the principal purposes behind a civil system of appeal? Are they better promoted by the civilian division between appeal (*appel, Berufung*) and cassation (*cassation, Revision*) and by their general rule of a single, anonymous appellate opinion than by the American structure and practice of appeal?

7. The contrast between the common law father-judge and neighbor-jury and the civil law functionary is made by Alexander Pekelis, *Legal Techniques and Political Ideologies: A Comparative Study,* in Law and Social Action: Selected Essays of Alexander Pekelis 42 (Milton R. Konvitz ed. 1970). Does this contrast seem to you to be valid? Is it significant? How?

8. Professor Damaška contrasts "hierarchical" and "coordinate" judicial organizations and processes:

> Systematic study of features impressed on the legal process by state officialdom requires a scheme to identify and describe different modes of organizing procedural authority.... [O]ur theme permits selection of only two composite structures of authority from a larger number of possibilities. The first structure essentially corresponds to conceptions of classical bureaucracy. It is characterized by a professional corps of officials, organized into a hierarchy which makes decisions according to technical standards. The other structure has no readily recognizable analogue in established theory. It is defined by a body of nonprofessional decision makers, organized into a single level of authority which makes decisions by applying undifferentiated community standards. The first structure I shall call the *hierarchical* ideal or vision of officialdom, and the second I shall term the *coordinate* ideal.
>
> The reason for this narrow selection has been suggested: the two ideals of officialdom can be used to organize into new configurations many scattered but widely shared observations about salient differences between two important judicial organizations developed in the West and disseminated through the world — the traditional judicial apparatus on the European continent, and the traditional machinery of justice in England. To the extent to which the organization of judicial authority influences the design of the legal process, the hierarchical and the coordinate ideals thus offer a convenient perspective upon the always intriguing, never fully grasped contrast between Continental and Anglo-American styles of administering justice.
>
> It hardly needs saying that actually extant features that distinguish the Continental and English judicial organizations will not be fully captured in these two constructs. This is because tendencies observed in actual organizations — for example, the tendency toward professional decision making in one and the tendency toward lay decision making in the other — become constitutive elements of these two ideals even if these

tendencies were never fully realized on the Continent and in the British Isles. It is precisely this relationship between reality and these two constructs that permits the use of the hierarchical and the coordinate ideals to illuminate reciprocities between procedural authority and procedural form on a scale broader than the conventional opposition between common-law and civil-law systems....

The special emphasis here on traditional organizations of authority may come as a surprise. It is often said that broadly similar circumstances in contemporary states have brought the judicial organizations of various countries closer together than they were in the past. Pronounced trends toward professionalization, centralization, and organized expertise have been reported everywhere, so that some have even predicted that centralized bureaucracies will inherit the earth. Is it anachronistic, then, to dwell on the recessive contrast between bureaucratic and non-bureaucratic authority rather than on internal variations of modern bureaucracies? The short answer is that modern pressures toward bureaucratization of the machinery of justice interact with inherited structures in complex ways and produce hybrids that can hardly be analyzed without regard to their historical antecedents. Nor have traditional structures become totally obsolescent, or surrendered to modern trends in equal measure. The American machinery of justice, for example, while increasingly professionalized and centralized in this century, continues to be more deeply permeated by features embodied in the coordinate ideal than are judicial administrations of any other industrial state in the West. These perduring features not only account for some perplexing tensions in the modern American administration of justice but may also illuminate, in part, the widening gap between American and British legal sensibilities.

Mirjan R. Damaška, The Faces of Justice and State Authority: A Comparative Approach to the Legal Process 16-18 (1986). What is your initial (i.e., without reading Damaška's full development of it) reaction to this comparative idea? Is it consistent with the comparison in Question 7? Complementary to it? Is it valid? Do you see value in comparisons of this kind, at this level of abstraction? Might it be possible to derive a group of such generalizations that would accurately and efficiently characterize and compare the two procedural traditions?

9. There is a completely annotated record of a civil action in Italy, setting out all the pleadings, briefs, minutes, orders, rulings and decisions from the original citation through trial, appeal, review in the Supreme Court of Cassation, and proceedings on remand in Mauro Cappelletti, John Henry Merryman & Joseph M. Perillo, The Italian Legal System: An Introduction 315-438 (1967). One can acquire a much more concrete feel for the nature of civil proceedings in a typical continental system by browsing through this "history of a civil action."

10. There is a substantial literature on comparative civil procedure. In addition to the works cited elsewhere in this section, one might profitably begin by reading Mauro Cappelletti, chief ed., *Civil Procedure,* 16 International Encyclopedia of Comparative Law (1973-present) and proceed to Cappelletti, The Judicial Process in Comparative Perspective (1989); Konstantinos D. Kerameus, *A Civilian Lawyer Looks at Common Law Procedure,* 47 La. L. Rev. 493 (1987); Courtland H. Peterson, *An Introduction to the History of Continental Civil Procedure,* 41 U. Colo. L. Rev. 61 (1969); and Charles Platto, ed., Trial and Court Procedures Worldwide (1991).

NOTE ON ATTORNEY FEES AND COURT COSTS

Contingent fee contracts (*pacta de quota litis*) in the litigation context have been disfavored in both the civil law tradition and the common law tradition, and today are illegal or unethical in most — but not all — countries outside the United States. The historic rationale for this prohibition aimed to limit a lawsuit to those parties immediately affected by it and to discourage strangers from stirring up litigation.

Among the countries surveyed in this volume, most prohibit contingent attorney fee agreements for litigation as either illegal (e.g., France) or unethical under the rules of professional responsibility (e.g., Germany). The exceptions are Japan, Indonesia, and Thailand. In Japan, as in the United States, these agreements are permitted as part of the freedom of contract existing between an attorney and his client. They are not as commonly used by *bengoshi* in Japan, however, as by lawyers in the United States. Even in countries that historically have prohibited contingent fee contracts, there may be some softening of the ban. In France, for instance, although the simple contingent fee contract remains illegal, since 1991 an agreement that adds a fixed charge for the services performed to a supplemental payment based on the result reached is permitted. Law No. 91-647 of July 1991, art. 72.

In civil law nations, as in the United States, litigation costs are usually assigned to the losing party. The position on attorney fees, however, is strikingly different. In most of Europe and Latin America, and much of the rest of the world, including England and Canada, the rule is that the loser pays the winner's attorney fees (according to judicially administered schedules of permitted charges). A lawyer and client may contract for higher fees, but the loser is not liable for the excess. Among the nations surveyed, only in the United States and in Brazil, Indonesia, Japan, Taiwan, and Thailand does the winner, as a general rule, pay her own lawyer. The American rule, as it is called, has been modified, usually by statute, in a variety of specific instances in order to encourage plaintiffs to institute meritorious litigation or, less frequently, to penalize undesirable lawsuits or defenses. As of 1984 there were reported to be 130 federal and over 1,900 state statutes of this kind, prompting one author to wonder whether the American rule of each side bearing its own attorney fees will continue to be the rule in America.

Three examples will illustrate the variety in civil law nations. The general rule for litigation costs in Germany is that the losing party bears the responsibility for paying his own as well as his adversary's necessary litigation expenses, including attorney fees. Statutory costs also include loss of time to travel to and participate in hearings. The rationale for this rule is that a winning party should not be deprived of his full success by having to pay part of his own costs. The winning party applies for taxation of costs (*Kostenfestsetzung*) at a special department in the court (*Geschäftsstelle*). Court fees depend primarily on the amount in controversy (*Streitwert*) and how many stages are involved in the proceeding. Other fees must be paid to witnesses and experts. Attorney fees depend mainly on the amount in controversy and how many steps the case proceeds through in the court system: filing and initial advice (*Prozessgebühr*); oral hearing (*Verhandlungsgebühr*); evidence taking (*Beweisgebühr*); and termination by settlement (*Vergleichsgebühr*). An agreement to pay more than the fee prescribed by statute must be in writing. A judge may, however, reduce an excessive fee. It is considered unethical to charge a fee lower than the statutory amount. Nevertheless, a fixed fraction of the statutory fee may be charged where the attorney only consults with his client.

The general rule for allocating litigation costs in Mexico is that the loser must reimburse the other party for the legal costs (*gastos procesales*) he has incurred, including attorney fees (*costas procesales*). The states follow this federal rule. Reimbursable lawyer fees are determined by official tariffs related to the amount in controversy and the procedural steps pursued in the lawsuit. Most lawyers find these amounts inadequate for their services, so they negotiate a fee contract with their clients, which is enforceable.

In Japan, the basic structure of the fee system for litigation and other contentious matters consists of a commencement fee (*chakushu-kin*) which is paid before beginning work, and a success fee (*shakin*), which is based on a percentage of the award, if any, for the plaintiff's attorney and of the difference between the amount claimed and the amount won for the defendant's attorney. The Japan Federation of Bar Associations has adopted an attorney fee schedule to guide local bar associations in setting their own schedules. Where the amount in controversy is less than one million yen, they recommend a commencement fee between ten and 30 percent. Where the amount exceeds one million yen, the recommended percentage drops to between seven and 20 percent. The Federation suggests that the combined commencement and success fees should not exceed 50 percent of the amount in controversy. The fees actually charged tend to be less than these suggested rates. The attorney fees charged for noncontentious matters — such as drafting contracts and other documents, filing documents with the government, or negotiations — and for conciliation are determined by several factors: the monetary value at stake, complexity of the matter, and time involved. A flat hourly rate is not commonly used.

In assessing costs after litigation, Japanese courts follow the rule that a losing party is required to compensate the prevailing party for litigation expenses. These include those costs directly and necessarily incurred by the parties and the court in processing an action, such as filing fees, expert fees, and certain preparatory expenses in drafting the complaint and other documents, in collecting evidence, and in interviewing indispensable witnesses. Attorney fees, however, as mentioned above, usually are not included in reimbursable litigation expenses. There is an exception for counsel fees paid to a lawyer who was ordered by a judge to attend oral proceedings with a party. In addition, a person injured by a tortious act who must sue to recover may collect reasonable counsel fees as part of his tort damages, but not as costs. The typical amount allowed by a judge in these circumstances is ten percent of the other damages.

Another manner in which to compare court costs and attorney fees is to ask major law firms in various countries how much the costs and fees would total in the following hypothetical case. A foreign merchant sells goods for $100,000 to a buyer in your country, who does not pay his bill. The seller retains your law firm and commences a law suit against the buyer, who does not actively contest the claim. How much would the firm charge and the court costs be for the following services that are successful in recovering most or all of the amount due?: (1) a lawyer's letter demanding payment from the debtor; (2) filing the claim in court and proceeding to judgment; and (3) attaching movable goods for sale to execute on the judgment. See Table 10.1 and Ivo Greiter, How to Get Your Money in Foreign Countries: A Survey of Court Costs and Lawyer's Fees in 151 Countries (1988).

Table 10.1

Court Costs and Attorney Fees for a $100,000 Claim, by Country and Level of Service Performed

Country	Letter	Judgment	Execution
France	$1,200	$2,900	$2,900
Germany	700	1,300	500
Italy	400	2,100	400
Spain	100	9,000	2,900
Argentina	500	13,000	4,500
Brazil	1,000	10,000	500
Colombia	500	1,500	3,000
Mexico	400	2,100	400
Indonesia	100	1,500 + 10%	—
Japan	3,000	8,900	4,500
South Korea	250	4,500	1,900
Taiwan	100	24,000	500
Thailand	—	1,900 + 13%	—

NOTES AND QUESTIONS

1. Defend the American contingent fee contract on policy grounds. Is its popularity tied to other features of the U.S. system of civil procedure or of American culture?

2. Which is the preferable way of allocating attorney fees? Does the "loser pays" rule discourage frivolous or otherwise unjustified litigation? Does it encourage meritorious litigation? Does it lead to more out-of-court settlements? Does it reduce delay in litigation? Does it shift the population of litigants in the direction of risk-takers? Is it fairer to victorious plaintiffs? To victorious defendants? Don't be too quick to commit yourself; although the answers to such questions may seem obvious to you, there is a large and disputatious literature on the topic, and the more one reads the less certain one becomes.

3. For more on attorney fees, see John J. Donohue III, *Opting for the British Rule, or If Posner and Shavell Can't Remember the Coase Theorem, Who Can?*,

104 Harv. L. Rev. 1093 (1991); F.B. MacKinnon, Contingent Fees for Legal Services: A Study of Professional Economics and Responsibilities (1964); and the symposium issue edited by Thomas D. Rowe, Jr., *Attorney Fee Shifting,* 47 Law & Contemp. Probs. 1 (Winter 1984), including Werner Pfennigstorf, *The European Experience with Attorney Fee Shifting,* at 37, and Note, *State Attorney Fee Shifting Statutes: Are We Quietly Repealing the American Rule,* at 321.

2. CHARACTERISTICS OF GERMAN CIVIL PROCEDURE AND ITS "ADVANTAGE"

NOTE

German civil procedure is atypical. It has progressed further in the directions of concentration, orality, immediacy, and free evaluation of the evidence than in France, Italy, Spain, and much of Latin America and East Asia. An important aspect of that development is the more active role of the judge, described in the following excerpts.

CIVIL PROCEDURE CODE OF GERMANY

Section 139

Section 139 [Judicial Duty to Clarify]

(1) The presiding judge shall see to it that the parties make full statements about all material facts and make appropriate motions, especially to elaborate on insufficient statements regarding the facts alleged and to indicate the means of proof. For this purpose, so far as necessary, he shall discuss with the parties the case and issues, in their factual and legal aspects, and ask questions.

(2) The presiding judge shall bring to the parties' attention doubts that the court has because of its duty to take certain points into account on its own motion.

(3) He shall permit each member of the court to ask such questions as that member requests.

HEIN KÖTZ, CIVIL LITIGATION AND THE PUBLIC INTEREST, 1 Civil Justice Quarterly 237, 241-43 (1982)

English procedure is generally based on the premise that the court has no independent knowledge of the law and must therefore be informed about it by argument. German procedure, on the other hand, basically leaves it to the judge to determine and to apply the law in each case irrespective of the extent to which counsel have drawn his attention to points of law. In many cases, particularly where a large amount of money is at stake, the attorneys will submit a full legal argument. Even then the judge will engage in independent legal research, and he will by no means do so only in matters which touch upon public policy or are likely to affect the public interest. In many other cases, however, the attorney will rely on the principle of *jura novit curia* and will simply place the facts before the judge without worrying too much about the law.

Not only is the court supposed to know and apply the law without waiting for counsel to deploy it, but more importantly, section 139 of the Code of Civil Procedure imposes a duty on the judge to clarify the issues and help the parties to develop their respective positions fully. Accordingly, the court asks questions and makes suggestions with the aim of inducing the parties to improve, modify or amplify their allegations, to submit more documents, to offer further proof, to correct misunderstandings and to throw light upon what may be obscure. The extent to which a court will do this depends on a number of factors. Of course, the court must not take over the litigation. It is the parties, not the court, who fix the factual basis of the action by their allegations and admissions of fact, and it is not for the court to insist that issues not raised by the parties should be investigated. All the court can do under section 139 is to ask questions, to raise doubts, to make suggestions, to recommend taking certain steps. However, as the parties are likely to follow the court's suggestions, there is a significant potential in the court of shaping the course of the proceedings in its attempt to arrive at the right solution of the controversy regardless of faults of advocacy, inadvertence or thoughtlessness.

It is very difficult to describe how far courts lead the parties in practice. On the one hand, the judge must at all events avoid the appearance of partiality, and if he goes too far in exercising his corrective and advisory duties the disadvantaged party may ask the higher court for an order disqualifying the judge from further handling the case. On the other hand, a judge's failure to discharge his duties under section 139 constitutes a procedural error on which an appeal may be based.... Much depends also on whether or not the parties are represented by counsel and on the judge's evaluation of their professional capacity and energy in the case before the court. Some writers have argued that regard must be had also to whether the applicable rules of substantive law are based on a policy of protecting certain groups of litigants, such as tenants or instalment buyers. According to these authors the advisory duties of the court must be given a wider scope if that is necessary to carry the policy of the law into effect.

For these reasons it is difficult to state with precision where the borderline lies between giving too much or too little advice and assistance. Clearly the judge must tell the parties that their factual allegations, even if true, do not in his view constitute a cause of action or a valid defence. Incompleteness or inconsistency of factual statements and indefinite or self-contradictory demands are also clearly within the scope of section 139. If a party has alleged certain facts but has failed to indicate means of proof the judge must notify the party of the situation if he believes the alleged facts to be relevant to the disposition of the case. There is no doubt either that the judge must not spring a surprise on the parties by basing his decision on a point of law of which they were not aware and which, if it had been ventilated with them in time, might have caused them in some way to change their positions.[20] On the other hand, the court will not lead a defendant to raise a defence which under the applica-

[20] See § 278 par. 3 ZPO.

ble rules of substantive law he has the option to raise or forego. For instance, if the facts already at hand show that the defendant has a counterclaim which he might use as the basis for a set-off or that the defendant might successfully rely on the defence of limitation the court will not normally prompt the defendant to raise that defence. However, if it can be implied from what the defendant has said or written that some sort of defence is in his mind the judge is under a duty to indicate the correct procedural device to be used for that purpose.

WILLIAM B. FISCH, RECENT DEVELOPMENTS IN WEST GERMAN CIVIL PROCEDURE, 6 Hastings International and Comparative Law Review 221, 254-57, 279-82 (1983)

The Principal Hearing and the Role of the Judge

The effort to overcome the traditional diffusion of the lawsuit into multiple hearings by concentrating as much as possible into a single, comprehensively prepared hearing required a broad statutory blueprint for the principal hearing. This is provided by [the 1977 reforms to the Code of Civil Procedure (*Zivilprozeßordung*)] ZPO section 278, which, in combination with section 137, presents the following model:

(a) call of the case and identification of participants present;
(b) introduction and statement of the case by the judge or presiding judge;
(c) response of the parties, if any, to that statement;
(d) discussion of the case among court and parties and/or attorneys;
(e) proof-taking;
(f) further discussion and argument with reference to the results of the proof-taking;
(g) deliberation by the court; and
(h) announcement of the judgment, or fixing of a subsequent date for the announcement, possibly with an interim deadline for written statements by the parties.

This model corresponds roughly to that followed by the Stuttgart Model. The role of judicial proposals for settlement, central to the Stuttgart Model, was also formally strengthened by the 1977 reform. This was accomplished largely by transforming a technically permissive provision into a duty to consider settlement possibilities at every stage of the lawsuit.

Other than the fact that a model for a single hearing is now set forth in the statute, perhaps the only new item in the list is the required statement of the case by the judge at the outset, although even this was already standard practice in many courts before 1977. This provision has been viewed with scorn by some writers, on the basis that, at least in cases with counsel, the parties are already informed about the matter. It is clear, however, that what was intended is a statement from the court's point of view, including indications of how the court views the questions of law, probable outcome, and so forth. This is often the most important missing link in settlement discussions, and of course, it gives the parties something to focus on during argument. The extent to which this device is used for the purpose of disclosing the court's thought varies from judge to judge and from case to ease. So used, however, it is a powerful instrument for guiding the hearing directly to the disputed points. In current terminology, this is often referred to as "legal dialogue" (*Rechtsgespräch*). There are arguments to the effect that open disclosure by the court of its views soon enough to allow the parties to respond and direct their factual statements accordingly is not merely a good idea, but an obligation. This form of disclosure, of course, can occur already prior to the hearing, in the form of directions to the parties to clarify specified points. The ZPO now also contains an express requirement that the court give the parties an opportunity to speak before ruling on a legal basis which one or both parties have obviously overlooked or thought unimportant.

The obligation of the court, embodied in ZPO section 139, to assure that the parties make full statements concerning the relevant facts and make appropriate demands for relief, has remained formally unchanged since 1924. While it is difficult to point to a universal trend, the new emphasis on expedition by the parties, enforced with deadlines and preclusion, brings a corresponding focus of attention on the role of the court in assuring that the case is as fully developed as possible. Moreover, at least one decision of the Federal Constitutional Court gives this judicial duty another dimension: a violation of section 139 caused by obtaining the consent of a non-represented spouse to accept the other spouse's low bid at an execution sale without first ascertaining that she understood the consequences was held to be a denial of equal treatment under Article 3 of the Basic Law.[230]

Some recent decisions have dealt with the question of whether section 139 permits a court to bring previously overlooked claims or defenses to a party's attention. There is a split of authority on the propriety of court initiative regarding the defense of prescription (statute of limitations). No doubt the traditional conception of the judicial role supports disapproval of such initiative, and would limit the role of the court to pointing out the burdens and risks of the parties regarding issues over which they hold the power of disposition. Contemporary notions of the welfare state (*Sozialstaat*) pull in the opposite direction, demanding that public authorities compensate for differences in resources among social combatants. It is certainly difficult to distinguish judicial questions designed to raise new issues from those designed to clarify those issues imperfectly stated. Likewise, it is difficult for the court to separate its obligation of assuring awareness of the necessity for offers of proof on disputed propositions, from its duty to assure that appropriate demands for relief are made concerning facts already fully alleged and proven. The specific issue of the defense of prescription fits within the latter category if the passage of the crucial period of time is proven by the plaintiff's own allegations. Moreover, it has been held that the defense of prescription can be raised at any time, even for the first time on appeal, and cannot be waived by mere silence nor be precluded as a late offering under section 296, because it can only work to shorten the proceedings. The public interest in efficient judicial administration therefore supports judicial initiative. Otherwise, a silent defendant can

[230] Judgment of Mar. 24, 1976, BVerfG, 41 BVerfGE 64 (2d Sen.).

strike at any time, nullifying the court's preparation for other disposition of the case. Finally, critics have noted the irony of correcting the error by disqualifying the judge, when the newly educated defendant will surely present the defense to a new judge. The result may well be a rule, purporting to limit judicial activity, which can be relatively easily evaded by judges so disposed, just as the command of section 139 to stimulate the parties to clarify was apparently ignored by more passive judges....

Points of Contrast with American Procedure

1. *Episodic Proof-Taking Disapproved*

The West German reforms of the 1970's have gone a long way to discourage that feature ... thought to be the German lawsuit's distinguishing characteristic: the fragmentation of the prooftaking process into multiple hearings, with freedom of the parties to raise new issues at virtually any time before judgment. Century-long criticism of the delays inherent in this practice finally gained favor, and the reformers' stated goal of concentrating the trial into a single principal session has been backed up by real commitment. The use of deadlines and preclusion generate considerable pressure to disclose claims and defenses, supported by offers of proof, in the pre-hearing procedure. Even where prooftaking is done separately, there is now typically only one such session.

2. *The Dominant Role of the Judge*

The "grand discriminant" between West German and American procedure today is the division of labor between judge and lawyers. German civil procedure is a judge-driven system, and, if anything, the reforms of the 1970's have reinforced that tendency. A number of functions which are performed principally by the lawyers or a court reporter in the United States are allocated to the judge in West Germany. The most important of these functions are: (a) determination of the trial agenda, including an order of proof directing appearance of the parties and witnesses, and the presentation of documents; (b) examination of parties and witnesses, with lawyers performing only an interstitial role; (c) production of the record of witnesses' testimony, excluding questions and frequently rephrasing or reorganizing answers; and (d) direct communication with the parties, not only for factual assertions, but also to explore settlement possibilities. While West German procedural theory continues to adhere to the principle of party control (*Verhandlungsmaxime*) in civil cases, it seems clear that this guarantees only the judge's ultimate dependence on the raw material which the parties present. The opportunity of the judge, as fact finder, to influence the form and organization of the material on which he must base his findings, and even to stimulate production of more material, is so much greater in the West German than in the American system that it must be regarded as a distinguishing feature — however varied its exploitation by different judicial personalities.

3. *Evidence and Its Production*

Kaplan's observation that "the search for facts is neither broad nor vigorous"[368] in West Germany is essentially valid today. There is some possibility that the pressures of malpractice claims for failure to meet deadlines, resulting in preclusion of otherwise dispositive material, will infuse the legal profession with greater investigative desire. Increases in the statutory fee scale may also help, but the scheme of attorneys' fees remains virtually free of rewards for extra effort.

Moreover, the German system remains relatively indifferent to possibilities for pretrial exchange of information and evidence between the parties. The reform discussions contain some expressions of concern over this issue, and some references to United States or English discovery procedures occasionally appear in the literature. At this point, however, no fundamental change seems likely. What has changed in this respect, perhaps, is the United States attitude toward discovery. Given the current obsession in the United States' with the abuses, costs and delays of discovery, and our efforts to bring its use under control, it can hardly be expected that other systems will follow the United States example.

With the disapproval of "episodic proof-taking" as the principal means of self-correction available to the German judge, appeal now bears the major burden of factual correction. Here, too, the trap of preclusion may seriously limit the opportunities for new evidence or defenses, and the corrective measure may often consist simply of renewed examination of the evidence by a different set of minds.

4. *Quick Access to a Judge*

Whether it results from these differing attitudes toward judges and evidence or from some other cause, the West German system retains and perhaps has strengthened its single greatest advantage over the typical United States lawsuit, namely, its comparative ease of access to a judge for consideration of the merits at a relatively early stage in the litigation. Judges are sufficiently numerous that backlogs are at bearable levels in most places. Hearings can be scheduled within a few months, at least. Despite the long standing and recently intensified interest in settlement, the continued high proportion of contested judgments suggests that decision is what litigants most frequently desire after all. This impression is now being reinforced in the United States by the experience of at least some compulsory arbitration plans, in which it appears that the overall settlement rate declines as processing time is shortened. Certainly, the West German system is especially well suited to the average dispute, flexible and still relatively inexpensive.

---

[368] Kaplan, *Civil Procedure: Reflections on the Comparison of Systems*, 9 Buffalo L. Rev. 409, 420 (1960).

JOHN C. REITZ, WHY WE PROBABLY CANNOT ADOPT THE GERMAN ADVANTAGE IN CIVIL PROCEDURE, 75 Iowa Law Review 987-90, 1001-03, 1007-09 (1990)

In 1985, Professor John Langbein published an article entitled "The German Advantage in Civil Procedure,"[1] in which he claimed that certain aspects of the modern German (formerly "West German") system of civil procedure make it superior to American civil procedure. This provocative article sought to acquaint American lawyers with the German system of trial, in which the judges, not the parties' attorneys, have chief responsibility to (1) determine the order of proof, (2) examine the witnesses, (3) create a compact record of the witnesses' testimony by dictating summaries of their testimony, and (4) secure the testimony of experts, if needed. German lawyers and their clients, like their counterparts in our system, are responsible for producing documents in support of the client's claims and identifying for the court the fact witnesses whose testimony they believe will support those claims. The German system differs from ours, however, by making the judge responsible for and in control of the process of examining both fact and expert witnesses and creating the record based on those examinations. Furthermore, the German system strongly discourages attorneys from having any contact with nonparty witnesses out of court.

Langbein argues that the German system secures two significant procedural advantages: (1) it reduces the cost of litigation, and (2) it enhances the quality of the testimony by reducing the opportunity for an lawyers, intentionally or unintentionally, to influence that testimony. According to Langbein, we should, therefore, modify our system of procedure to incorporate these advantages. He notes the recent trend in the United States for judges to become more involved in the pretrial phase in order to prevent discovery abuse, expedite the proceedings, and promote settlement — a trend that has been christened "managerial judging." Langbein views the development toward "managerial judging" critically because the American judicial system lacks most of the control mechanisms placed upon German judges to prevent abuse of judicial power. But he also views the trend toward "managerial judging" as "telling evidence for the proposition that judicial fact-gathering could work well in a system that preserved much of the rest of what we now have in civil procedure."...

Langbein points out that the German system of judicial control over witness examination permits judges to eliminate unnecessary testimony. For example, if there is one disputed factual contention that would bar the plaintiff's claim if established, the court can concentrate the initial proof taking on that issue. If the contention is proved, all further expense of trial can be spared. In the same manner, if the court is satisfied that a particular point is proved after two witnesses have testified, the court need not hear the other three witnesses a party has nominated to prove that point.

Moreover, such a system avoids the typical three rounds of testimony to which we subject many witnesses: initial interviews of "friendly" witnesses, discovery depositions (with direct and cross-examination), and testimony at

[1]52 U. Chi. L. Rev. 823 (1985) [hereinafter Langbein].

trial (again with direct and cross-examination). Indeed, the entire proof process is so economical that the first level of appeal in German courts is de novo and routinely includes rehearing of witnesses with regard to the crucial factual issues still in dispute....

Even more significant, however, is the potential gain in accuracy that may result from the German system of proof-taking. Langbein argues that the German system is free of the pressures for truth-defeating distortions that inhere in our system of partisan preparation and production of witnesses. Partisan preparation may result in witness coaching, intentional or otherwise, and because expert witnesses are usually called by one of the parties, they are generally vulnerable to impeachment on the grounds of bias. In the German system, expert witnesses are neutral third parties called by the court and paid by the losing party after the trial. German attorneys can protect their clients' interests by suggesting witnesses to be called, asking follow-up questions of the witnesses after the judges have finished their interrogation, objecting to the judges' summation of the witness' testimony, commenting on the court-appointed expert's report, and offering other experts to challenge the opinion of the court-appointed expert. Judicial control of the evidentiary process greatly reduces, if not eliminates, the attorneys' opportunities to coach witnesses prior to trial or bully or confuse them during their testimony. Finally, de novo review gives every party the opportunity for a rehearing of all crucial, disputed testimony.

For Langbein, long-standing complaints on this side of the Atlantic about the expense and complexity of discovery and trial, as well as the opportunities and incentives for lawyers to influence witnesses' testimony are inevitable in a system of adversarial fact production. Langbein notes that the German system is also an adversarial system of procedure — the lawyers advance their clients' positions throughout the proceedings — but the important difference is that in Germany, the judge plays the central role in building the record of the witnesses' testimony, and the parties' attorneys are quite restricted in what they can do to influence the shape of that record....

The strongest objections to the introduction of German-style judicial domination of witness examination are based on our rules of discovery. While there is still much criticism of discovery within our own legal culture, no one today seriously proposes to eliminate it. Yet essential features of the "German advantage" are in conflict with this institution, whether one tries to implement the German system through judges or through parajudicial personnel like magistrates or masters.

In order to understand the force of these objections, one must first understand how strongly the German judge-led search for evidence differs from our institution of discovery. The German system thus far described may appear to collapse into one phase our two phases of pretrial discovery and trial production of evidence....

It is true that German civil procedure provides some analogues to our discovery. German procedure protects the litigants from surprise by requiring each party to identify the evidence upon which it relies, including the witnesses and what they are expected to say, in advance of any evidentiary hearing. But our institution of discovery goes far beyond the prevention of surprise by allowing a party to search for evidence in opponents' and nonparties' hands to support its own claims and defenses or to challenge opponents' claims and defenses. Germany simply does not provide any general rights to discovery evidence.

The scope of witness interrogation in Germany is much more limited than in the United States. In the United States, a very liberal standard of relevancy applies in the discovery phase according to Federal Rule of Civil Procedure 26(b)(1): "reasonably calculated to lead to the discovery of admissible evidence." In Germany, by contrast, parties cannot be forced to testify, and the court will refuse to take the testimony of any witnesses who are nominated solely to find out what they might know about the facts in dispute. Moreover, the taking of evidence in German trials is governed by a strict standard of relevancy. This standard includes a requirement of "substantiation," pursuant to which the court may "order testimony only where a party can generally describe the facts that the evidence is intended to prove." The "substantiation" requirement is intended to prevent a party from using the courts to "probe" or "fish" for evidence of which the party has no concrete knowledge. The traditional principle was that "no party is required to provide for his opponent's victory in court material which the opponent did not already have at his disposal."[38] While there is considerable debate today in Germany concerning how concrete a party's suspicions have to be to justify taking a witness's testimony, and while some situations give rise to a duty to disclose certain information,[39] the "substantiation" requirement evidences a much more restrictive attitude toward discovery than our rules.

A German party also has only limited rights to see specifically identifiable documents in the possession of the other party or nonparties, relating to specific legal, generally contractual, relationships.[40] Outside of these limited rights, a party cannot force the opposing party or any nonparty to provide documents, which might support its case or cast doubt on its opponent's case. There has been some discussion in Germany over whether the courts have fashioned a duty to cooperate, at least for parties, by shifting the burden of proof or drawing unfavorable inferences against parties who fail to come forward with certain types of evidence. This limited duty remains highly contro-

[38] Judgment of May 4, 1964, BGHZ, W. Ger., 1964 *Neue Juristische Wochenschrift* 1414, 1414 (author's translation). This case involves a sole heir seeking to share in the value of gifts made by her father to the defendant, allegedly in violation of the plaintiff's right to a forced share of her fathers estate. The defendant alleged that the father also had made substantial gifts to the plaintiff during his lifetime which should be taken into account in determining whether the gifts to the defendant had deprived plaintiff of her forced share. The court held that the defendant's unsubstantiated allegations provided no basis for examining the plaintiff on that subject.

[39] For example, in the case cited in the previous note, the *Bundesgerichtshof* held that, despite the general requirement of substantiation, the defendant transferee had, under § 2314 of the German Civil Code requiring heirs and legatees to give information about the estate to those parties entitled to a forced share, a substantive law right to information about an inter vivos gift to the heir.

[40] The most expansive right is provided by § 810 of the German Civil Code. It provides a right to see a document in the hands of others if it was made for the benefit of the party seeking to see it or if it documents a legal relationship between the party and another or describes negotiations relating to such a relationship. The "substantiation" requirement would, however, appear to prevent examination of persons to determine if they had any such documents in their possession unless the party seeking disclosure has some justifiable basis for believing that they do and can describe the documents with some specificity.

versial, but it still does not confer the broad power that litigants in the United States have to search for admissible evidence.

Finally, expansive testimonial privileges complement these limits against the general discovery of evidence in German civil cases. These privileges protect confidential relationships and private spheres of interest, most notably business secrets, to a much greater extent than in the United States.

Perhaps as important as the differences in the standards for obtaining information from parties and nonparties is the difference in the mechanisms. Under the United States federal and most state discovery rules, discovery proceeds without the participation of the court until someone complains. This system, coupled with the breadth of our discovery rules, tends to put the burden on the party opposing discovery to justify why specific discovery should not be had. Judicial hostility toward discovery disputes and the fact that too much discovery has virtually never been cause for reversal have led many counsel to a policy of tolerating as much discovery as possible in order to save their efforts and credibility with the judge for the matters they deem most important. In Germany, judicial control over all witness examination, coupled with the rules requiring substantiation and identification, puts the burden on the party seeking disclosure. As a result, Germany does not know the wholesale exchange of documents nor the extensive grilling of large numbers of potential witnesses that characterize our discovery practice.

The differences on this point reflect a fundamental difference in value choices. Both systems recognize the importance of truth for the fact-finding process and both recognize the importance of protecting areas of personal or business privacy from unreasonable invasion, but the two systems strike very different balances between the two goals. Our expansive system of discovery appears to make truth on the whole more important than privacy in civil litigation. The Germans' system of specific disclosure duties and expansive privileges shows greater concern for protecting privacy interests and less concern for finding the truth....

A consideration of Langbein's challenge leads us to appreciate how integrated apparently independent aspects of our legal culture are. Our method of witness examination is bound up in cultural definitions of the respective jobs of judge and attorney. Many other aspects of our legal culture — including the use of juries, the way we choose and control judges, and attorneys' fee structures — have interacted with the development of these cultural role definitions, as well as newly developing institutions, like discovery. The German legal system is also an organically whole legal culture in which the disparate institutions and rules are interdependent. Borrowing among legal cultures is certainly possible, but clearly problematic when the rule or institution to be borrowed is closely related to other important institutions or rules that the culture does not wish to change....

Professors Fisch and Langbein are correct in viewing the division of witness examination functions between judge and attorney as a "grand discriminant" among legal systems, at least among Western legal systems. Professor Kaplan originally identified the single-episode trial of the English and United States systems, in contradistinction to the "continuous or staggered proof-taking" of the civil law family of legal systems as the "grand discriminant, the watershed feature, so to speak, which shows the English and American systems to be consanguine," and that "determines in considerable part the attitudes and characters of lawyers and judges." Fisch and Langbein nominate the witness examination roles as the "grand discriminant" in light of the recent German trend toward concentration of evidentiary proceedings, which has tended to eliminate continuity of proof-taking as a discriminant.

The arguments advanced in this article demonstrate the centrality of the judge's role in characterizing a legal system. The procedurally passive judge who does not participate in the presentation of evidence has long been seen as a product of the jury system; judicial passivity in the presentation of evidence avoids infringing on questions of fact committed to the jury. The procedural passivity of the United States judge also enables us to get by with sufficiently few judges that their appointment or election may be thought to have the prominence necessary to make democratic control over their selection meaningful. Effective democratic control appears to be vital for making the judges' power of constitutional review acceptable. Moreover, the passivity of the judge appears to be the key to satisfactory control of delay, which is endemic to our institution of pretrial discovery; and it is the passivity of the judge that appears to make the relatively unrestricted search for evidence through discovery much more acceptable than it would be in a culture with procedurally active judges.

Of course, human institutions have a remarkable capacity for change, and the problem of delay, which in the German system has led to the trend toward concentration and which in the United States system has led to the rise of the "managerial judge," seems to be pushing both systems toward convergence. Nevertheless, if the activity or passivity of the judge is truly a "grand discriminant" among legal systems, it should be expected to set limits to convergence. Indeed, it is strange that Langbein would identify something as the "grand discriminant" while at the same time suggesting that it could be eliminated without significant impact on the rest of the legal system. Our current "managerial judge" is still a long way from the procedurally active German judge. To the extent the "managerial judge" departs from the passive model for judges in the common-law tradition, that style of judging attracts strong criticism from within our culture. Rather than eliminating the "grand discriminant" among Western legal families, I expect further procedural innovations designed to minimize delay and other abuses by attorneys to stay within the common-law tradition of the neutral and passive judge, for instance, by formalizing the supervision of discovery by magistrates along the lines of the English use of masters, who conduct all pretrial proceedings as umpires, not as parties charged with carrying the ball.

NOTES AND QUESTIONS

1. Is the active role of the judge in Germany, as described in these excerpts, consistent with the restricted image of the civil law judge and of the judicial function described in previous chapters? Is it consistent with the "dispositive system" of procedure, or would it be more accurate to call the German system "inquisitorial"? Is this the direction in which the concern for concentration, orality, and immediacy in civil law nations inevitably leads?

2. Does the principle of *jura novit curia* as it is interpreted in Germany, together with the judge's duty to clarify the issues, lead to an improved system of justice? Under what set of assumptions? Compared to what?

3. Professor John Langbein identified other characteristics of the German system of civil procedure. Which of these do you believe provide an advantage over the analogous characteristics in the American system of civil procedure? Which provide a disadvantage?

Langbein has made a more general argument for the superiority of European (not merely German) civil procedure in *Comparative Civil Procedure and the Style of Complex Contracts,* 35 Am. J. Comp. L. 381 (1987). He asked why American contracts are longer and more detailed than European contracts and found the answer in "the efficiency and predictability of the procedural system.... If the procedural system .... is reasonably efficient, you have less to fear from litigation than if it is not.... American civil procedure is inefficient. It is expensive, protracted, and unpredictable, and it does a poor job of discouraging frivolous suits (or frivolous defenses). The European systems are markedly more efficient and more predictable (some, to be sure, more than others)." Do you agree or disagree? Why?

4. Even if we agree that the German procedural system offers certain important advantages, could we actually import them successfully into the American procedural system, or would the foreign plant wither in American soil? *See* Ernst C. Stiefel & James R. Maxeiner, *Civil Justice Reform in the United States — Opportunity for Learning from "Civilized" European Procedure Instead of Continued Isolation?*, 42 Am. J. Comp. L. 147 (1994), and the excerpt by Ramseyer & Nakazato in Chapter 6, Section E.3.

A system of civil procedure *is* a system, a complex of interrelated elements, so that changing any element requires compensatory changes in the others. If we import the German active judge, then we have to change everything else: police, prosecutors, defense lawyers, the law of procedure, the law of evidence, the civil jury, and so on. These cultural and systemic concerns invariably (and properly) arise whenever someone proposes that we import a foreign legal institution. Should the same concerns arise when someone proposes to export some aspect of our law to a developing nation or to the newly emerging nations in eastern Europe or in the former Soviet Union? See John Henry Merryman, *Comparative Law and Social Change: On the Origins, Style, Decline and Revival of the Law and Development Movement,* 25 Am. J. Comp. L. 457 (1977).

5. Is there a tendency toward convergence of the German and American civil procedure systems? Is "managerial judging" in complex litigation in the United States similar to the active role of the judge in Germany? Are recent developments in American discovery and pretrial practice moving our system away from concentration toward something like the episodic procedure typical of civil law countries?

6. Interest in German civil procedure has spawned a substantial literature (besides Langbein's article and the three excerpted articles), including: Ronald J. Allen, Stefan Köch, Kurt Reichenbach & D. Toby Rosen, *The German*

Advantage in Civil Procedure: A Plea for More Details and Fewer Generalities in Comparative Scholarship, 82 Nw. U. L. Rev. 763 (1988); Allen, *Idealization and Caricature in Comparative Scholarship, ibid.* 785; Herbert L. Bernstein, *Whose Advantage After All?: A Comment on the Comparison of Civil Justice Systems,* 21 U.C. Davis L. Rev. 587 (1988); David J. Gerber, *Extraterritorial Discovery and the Conflict of Procedural Systems: Germany and the United States,* 34 Am. J. Comp. L. 745 (1986); Peter Gottwald, *Simplified Judicial Procedure in West Germany,* 31 Am. J. Comp. L. 687 (1983); Samuel R. Gross, *The American Advantage: The Value of Inefficient Litigation,* 85 Mich. L. Rev. 734 (1987); Benjamin Kaplan, Arthur T. von Mehren & Rudolf Schaefer, *Phases of German Civil Procedure I, II,* 71 Harv. L. Rev. 1193, 1443 (1958); John H. Langbein, *Trashing The German Advantage,* 82 Nw. U. L. Rev. 763 (1988); John Ratliff, *Civil Procedure in Germany,* 2 Civ. Just Q. 257 (1983); Arthur T. von Mehren, *Some Comparative Reflections on First Instance Civil Procedure: Recent Reforms in German Civil Procedure and in the Federal Rules,* 63 Notre Dame L. Rev. 609 (1988).

7. Although much admired in principle, the "active" German judge is not widely emulated in practice in other civil law nations, as illustrated by the following excerpt on the French civil procedure system.

3. FRANCE AND THE NEW CODE OF CIVIL PROCEDURE

JAMES BEARDSLEY, PROOF OF FACT IN FRENCH CIVIL PROCEDURE, 34 American Journal of Comparative Law 459, 466-69, 475, 485-86 (1986)

French civil procedure is marked by a strong preference for written proof and by the tendency of French judges to avoid factual determinations that must be based on evidence which is complex or otherwise difficult to evaluate. Confronted with evidence of this kind the French judge will normally appoint a lay *expert* to carry out the fact-finding task. When an *expert* is appointed, he will often pursue his investigations in a manner which attenuates the traditional distrust of oral evidence and which is functionally similar to the common law trial. The court may also delegate one of its own members to take oral evidence in the *enquête* procedure, but this is rarely done.

The distrust of oral evidence and the unwillingness of the judge to compel the parties to produce evidence under their control is an attitude that has not much changed even under the impact of a New Code of Civil Procedure which, on its face, gives the judge broad powers to require the production of evidence. In some measure this attitude means that the much-praised civil law solution (in the French version, at any rate) to the perceived evils of common law, and particularly American, styles of litigation is obtained by refusing to hear, or at least by refusing to require the production of, evidence that might be thought vital to the court's perception of historical truth....

The party faced with the requirements of proof described in this essay faces a task that he is ill-equipped to discharge. Notwithstanding the seemingly generous fact-oriented proof provisions contained in the New Code of Civil Procedure, a system that claims to be an "accusatorial" system in which it is for the parties to make and prove their case reserves the principal mechanisms for the discovery and production of evidence to the judge. The parties may call for the application of investigative measures, but they have no power to require the judge to carry them out.[28] As a rule, the judge will only act — if he acts at all — to require the production of evidence when he is satisfied of the existence and relevance of the proof which is sought, and, though here matters are rather less clear, when he is convinced that by doing so he is not relieving the requesting party of its duty to go forward with the proof of facts relevant to its claims. There is plainly no room for "fishing expeditions."[30] The discretionary character of the judge's powers with respect to production of evidence marks the entire process and has been emphasized repeatedly by the courts.[31]...

[T]he New Code of Civil Procedure allows considerable power in the pre-hearing stages to be delegated to a member of the deciding court who is known as the *juge de la mise en état*.[34] For present purposes we shall call him the "investigating magistrate" (or sometimes just the "magistrate") although he rarely investigates for the reasons indicated in this essay and is normally more concerned with supervising the exchange of documents between the parties, the submission of pleadings (*conclusions*), the fixing of deadlines and, in general, with the preparation of the case, as presented by the parties, for public hearing. In those cases in which there is to be a serious investigation of the facts by the court, it is usually, but not necessarily, the investigating magistrate who carries out the measures decided upon and reports back to the collegial body, normally a court of three judges, which decides the case. In reading the provisions of the New Code of Civil Procedure, one gains the impression that the judge (either the court or the investigating magistrate) can do practically anything that can be done in American proceedings. As a matter of practice, again for the reasons already mentioned, those powers are not often exercised....

[T]he investigating magistrate may call the parties themselves, who may be invited in the presence of their lawyers to give their versions of the facts.[41] As has already been pointed out, they do not do so under oath. The parties may be heard in chambers, for there is no requirement that the parties' declarations be made publicly.[42] The parties' statements — other than admissions — are not in any event treated as proof.[44] They merely "enlighten" the judge in reaching his conclusions but, taken alone, cannot resolve issues of fact. Similarly, third persons may address matters of fact either by way of written attestation or may be invited by the magistrate to give oral testimony within the framework of an *enquête*.[45] ...

[28] E.g., Syndicat des Habitants des Couronneries c. Société Montenay, 1980 *D.* 365 (Cass. civ., 14 Nov. 1979).

[30] E.g., Trib. de Gd. Inst. de Marseilles, 20 Feb. 1974, *Gazette du Palais* (hereafter "*Gaz. Pal.*"), 2d Sem., 544.

[31] E.g., Cass. civ., 4 Dec. 1973, 1973 *Bull. Civ.* I, No. 336.

[34] Arts. 762-63, NCPC.

[41] Arts. 184-98, NCPC.

[42] Arts. 188, NCPC.

[44] Art. 198, NCPC.

[45] See arts. 232-84, NCPC.

[M]ost cases proceed on the basis of the documents that each party gives to his *avocat* and which the *avocats* then exchange in the process known as *communication de pièces*, a process which is sanctioned principally by rules which prevent a party from relying on documents which are not included in its pleading file (and therefore available to the other party) and which permit the court to draw adverse conclusions from failure to produce any document to the other side upon which reliance is placed (or, for that matter, failure to produce any document shown to be relevant and to be within the possession of the party requested to produce).[73] Under the New Code of Civil Procedure, the *avocat* does have the right to require production of documents cited by the other party.[75] He can also require the production of documents that he can show to be in the possession of the other party, but is frequently reluctant to do so unless he is certain of their contents.[75] The court does not usually see the documents exchanged between the *avocats* until their respective files are laid before the court at the end of the oral pleading at the public audience. Nothing is more delicious than to be able to prove one's case on the facts out of documents that are voluntarily communicated by the other side. Argument before the court on the facts therefore often tends to focus almost entirely on the interpretation of the papers relied on by each side. Again, this becomes an intellectual and rhetorical game rather than a fact-oriented investigative process. It is argued by practitioners that the purpose of *communication de pièces* is above all to insure the contradictory character, the adversarial nature, of the exercise. Each party knows that it must disclose to its adversary the documents upon which it proposes to rely. Unfavorable evidence may remain undisclosed and there will be little reason to fear that the opposing party will learn of its content or, even, of its existence....

The application in France of fact-finding methods which are strikingly different from those employed in common law countries is most troublesome to the outside observer for what appears to be an attitude of fact-avoidance on the part of the courts and for the considerable difficulty which the parties encounter in obtaining evidence to support their claims.

The *expertise* offers a limited response to this problem by providing a procedure in which there is a greater exchange and criticism of information. While it is important to keep in mind that this procedure may produce a satisfactory result — there is, of course, no way of knowing whether it comes closer to finding the "truth" than some other mechanism — it is equally important to recognize that it is operated by laymen and not by the judges who are charged by law with the ultimate determination of facts in civil litigation. What occurs within the framework of the *expertise* has the merit of permitting all concerned to be heard in an environment which encourages free expression before a person who has or can obtain the relevant technical knowledge, can pursue other evidence and doesn't speak on behalf of any party.

Notwithstanding the existence of this important palliative — one that it is difficult finally to evaluate — the French procedural system remains one in which broad, but largely unexercised, powers are reserved to the judge, while

[73] Arts. 132-37, NCPC.
[75] Art. 142, NCPC.

the parties have little in the way of evidence gathering measures available to them without the intervention of the judge. This may be changing. Some *avocats* express the view that judges are more willing than they have been in the past to exercise their investigative powers. It is clear, however, that neither judge nor lawyer, nor for that matter, anyone else intimately involved with the system wants anything like party-directed discovery of evidence.

Present attitudes reflect the conflict between the desire for better and more effective fact-finding methods — those that the judge could apply if he wished to do so are not skimpy — and constraints that derive essentially from notions about the nature of civil proceedings, the product of long tradition rather than the fruit of a rigorous reading of the New Code of Civil Procedure. From these traditional ideas, the Frenchman — judge, lawyer or party — has acquired a concept of civil procedure which is primarily focused on putting an end to the dispute on the basis of what, in common law perspective, may seem like a mere approximation of the truth. Nonparties are to be disturbed as little as possible and even parties may find it more important to plead well than to have the facts on their side.

The great merit of the French approach is that it does not impose the costs associated with common law procedure and appears to satisfy those who operate it and those whose claims are decided by it. The disadvantage, apart from whatever reservations one may have about the system's ability to found its decisions on a satisfactory vision of the "truth," is in the profound inconsistency between the provisions of law and the duties assigned to the courts by law, on the one hand, and the way the system really works, on the other.

NOTE ON TYPES OF CIVIL PROCEEDINGS

Civil lawyers distinguish "contentious" from "voluntary" civil proceedings. The latter category is the rough equivalent of our *ex parte* procedure: resort to courts for judicial action in which there is ordinarily no dispute between plaintiffs and defendants. Familiar examples in our own system are probate proceedings, change of name, adoptions, and the approval of certain kinds of actions by trustees. Contentious proceedings, as the name suggests, ordinarily involve adjudication of a dispute between the parties.

Civil law jurists also distinguish "ordinary" and "summary" (and sometimes "executory") procedure. A very substantial amount of civil litigation takes the form of a summary proceeding for the collection of a matured, defined obligation. The following excerpt describes this procedure in Italy. *See also* Mauro Cappelletti, John Henry Merryman & Joseph M. Perillo, The Italian Legal System: An Introduction 120-24 (1967). For descriptions of comparable procedures in France, Germany, Spain, and Japan, see Peter Herzog, Civil Procedure in France 491-94 (1967); Benjamin Kaplan, Arthur T. von Mehren & Rudolf Schaefer, *Phases of German Civil Procedure I,* 71 Harv. L. Rev. 1193, 1265-67 (1958); Bernardo M. Cremades & Eduardo G. Cabiedes, Litigating in Spain 213-17, 295-331 (1989); Takaaki Hattori & Dan Fenno Henderson, Civil Procedure in Japan §§ 9.02-9.09 (1985).

4. ITALY: SUMMARY PROCEEDINGS AND OTHER MECHANISMS TO REDUCE DELAY

OSCAR G. CHASE, CIVIL LITIGATION DELAY IN ITALY AND THE UNITED STATES, 36 American Journal of Comparative Law 41, 70-74, 76-77 (1988)

[*Summary Proceedings*]

Italian procedure, even apart from recent reforms, has long made available provisional remedies and other short-cutting devices. Among the most important of these, "as well as the most frequently resorted to," is the summary *ex parte* proceeding. Available to a claimant seeking liquidated monetary relief or specific chattels, this procedure allows the plaintiff to apply to the court for a judgment without notice to the defendant. The application must include supporting documentary evidence, except when made by certain licensed professionals, including attorneys. If convinced of the validity of the claim the court issues an enforceable order directing the defendant to pay the claim. The latter, upon receipt of the notice, may file an opposition which automatically negates the decree and requires the commencement of an ordinary civil proceeding, with the burden of proof on the plaintiff. Spurious defenses are discouraged by the threat that an unsuccessful defendant will have to bear costs and attorneys fees. It is estimated that 90 percent of the decrees are not challenged.

The importance of the *ex parte* summary proceeding to the Italian system is due in part to the rule that a default in an ordinary proceeding does not constitute an admission of the validity of the claim; rather the court must hear the plaintiff's evidence and adjudicate the merits....

A similar function [of reducing delay] is performed by Italian rules which allow the enforcement, without prior adjudication on the merits, of negotiable instruments, of contracts of defined formality of execution and of some governmental obligations, including tax assessments. Again, the debtor learns of the proceeding only after an enforceable decree has been issued, and again he has an opportunity to force the creditor to an ordinary proceeding by entering an opposition. The court does have the power to deny the debtor's application however, or to require him to post a bond as a condition of suspending the enforcement proceeding. Commentators note that most of the instruments which may be so enforced are available to "entrepreneurs ... and agencies of public administration."...

The Italian Code also establishes some proceedings which are summary but not *ex parte*. An important instance — although it is something of an amalgam — is the eviction proceeding for residential premises. The defendant is entitled to service of process but the court may schedule an appearance in as little as three days. The procedure will take the form of an ordinary civil action only if the tenant appears and raises a defense based on written evidence. If he does not appear, an enforceable eviction order may be entered (although the court can order that he be re-served). If he does appear, but presents no written evidence, the court may order an immediate eviction, while requiring the plaintiff to post a bond. Thereafter, the tenant can continue to defend on the merits as in an ordinary proceeding.

[*Provisional Remedies*]

Another source of relief from the delay of ordinary litigation in Italy, as in the United States, are provisional remedies.

While the American and Italian systems share an understanding of the purpose of provisional remedies — a means of protecting the plaintiff from harm during the pendency of an otherwise predictably long proceeding — they are available in Italy in far more circumstances and under procedures which are somewhat relaxed when compared with those prevalent in the U.S....

It is true in Italy, as in the U.S., that a provisional remedy may be granted only by a judge. In both countries it may be granted *ex parte,* subject to the right of the defendant to be heard subsequently on the merits of the application. A party who has obtained provisional relief from an Italian court but who loses the action is, however, liable for damages only if he acted without "normal prudence," whereas in some American jurisdictions liability results simply if the attachment is improperly obtained or the plaintiff fails to prevail on the merits.

Among the various interests which may be protected by provisional remedies under the Italian Code are those of creditors seeking to prevent a dissipation of assets needed for the enforcement of judgments. Sequestration is available when the plaintiff has reasonable grounds to believe that this will occur....

Although there are numerous other specific situations in which provisional relief is available, the Italian Code also includes a catchall article which allows a court to grant "urgent relief" when there is a danger of immediate and irreparable injury and no specific remedy is available. This provision, redolent of an American court's powers to grant temporary or preliminary injunctions, has been used in Italy to protect, among other things, political and civil rights, employment rights and freedom from unfair competition. The judiciary has reportedly been of late increasingly open to applications to it to exercise this power, and "the trend is now firmly towards its broad interpretation," particularly when the right at stake is not predominantly economic....

The Reforms

"[T]he most important procedural reform enacted in recent years," the Law of 11 August 1973, No. 533, reformed the procedure relating to certain disputes arising under labor, employment benefits and pension laws: "[I]n this kind of proceeding the plaintiff is normally a worker suing his employer for payment of wages, pensions, welfare benefits, etc...."

In order to reduce the time and expense to the parties of resolving such claims, the 1973 law vested mandatory jurisdiction in the Preture; imposed statutory deadlines for key procedural steps; obliged the parties to reveal the facts on which their claims are based in their first pleadings; expanded the court's power to control the flow of proof; and required the parties to appear personally (this is intended to facilitate conciliation, which the court is required to attempt). Rather than contemplating the series of hearings and submissions which we have seen to be typical of the ordinary Italian proceeding, "The labor proceeding, and this is its distinguishing characteristic and primary value, is focused on the hearing."

The goal is a single hearing at which all of the evidence may be heard. Other provisions of the statute increase the court's power to grant relief as a practical matter: back pay may be awarded provisionally and a judgment in favor of the worker is immediately enforceable regardless of the taking of an appeal. Neither new claims nor new defenses may be added while the case is on appeal, and new evidence may be introduced only if the appellate court, on its own motion, seeks it.

A driving force behind the 1973 reform of labor proceedings was the desire to change the balance of power in employer-employee litigation.... [A]part from its political effects, the 1973 reform was important "because it embodied the principles expounded for decades by the progressive wing of Italian procedural scholarship, and aspired to serve as a model for further reforms."...

Since 1970 condensed proceedings similar to (though not identical with) those enacted in the law of 1973 have been provided for a number of other grievances such as the enjoining of anti-union activities (a right of action of labor unions); the enforcement of laws prohibiting employment discrimination on the basis of sex; the enforcement of child support obligations; and controversies relating to a "fair rent" statute.

Perhaps the most far-reaching effect of the 1973 summary proceeding law has been its invocation as a model for a proposed thorough-going reform of civil procedure. After substantial committee work along this line (at the request of the Ministry of Justice) a bill designed to simplify and accelerate the ordinary civil proceeding was submitted to Parliament in 1981. The bill has, however, not been enacted and its fate remains uncertain.

In any event, piecemeal reform has continued, adopting the model of the provisional remedy in addition to or in combination with the new model of concentration and orality. We have already noted the power of the judge to grant provisional relief under the labor dispute procedure and its companion reforms. Just as interesting (and rather remarkable from an American perspective) is a provision of the Italian compulsory auto insurance law which authorizes the court to make an interim award of damages to a claimant who has demonstrated a need for it and a likelihood of success on the merits.

NOTES AND QUESTIONS

1. Do the French New Code of Civil Procedure (1975) and the Italian reforms in civil procedure tend to confirm or refute the views presented by Professor Merryman in Section A.1? In which particulars?

2. Professor Chase mentions the Italian rule that authorizes a judge to make an interim damage award to an automobile accident plaintiff if he demonstrates a need for it and a likelihood of success on the merits. What impact would such a rule have on American tort litigation? Would the insurance industry support it? See N.Y. Ins. Law § 5102 (a), (b), which entitles the injured victim to prompt compensation from the insurer for medical expenses and some lost earnings under New York's no-fault insurance program.

3. Even though civil law courts have no inherent contempt power, the French *astreinte* is in many ways its functional equivalent in compelling specific performance of obligation. The basic notion of the *astreinte* is that the judgment debtor is liable to the judgment creditor for damages suffered as a result of delay in performance. A comparable procedure is available in Germany under § 890 of the Code of Civil Procedure. Most civil law systems, however, contain no equivalents of the *astreinte.*

4. One measure of procedural justice ("justice delayed is justice denied") is the speed at which the system produces results. Would you expect civil trials in the United States to be faster or slower than those in, say, Italy or Germany? Why? *See* Chase, *Civil Litigation Delay in Italy and the United States,* 36 Am. J. Comp. L. 41 (1988). There has been relatively little scholarly effort to compile the sort of data that would make such comparisons possible (Professor Chase cites the relevant literature). A major exception, in which the authors and their collaborators set out to provide the basis for "quantitative comparative law," is John Henry Merryman, David S. Clark & Lawrence M. Friedman, Law and Social Change in Mediterranean Europe and Latin America: A Handbook of Social and Legal Indicators for Comparative Study (1979). *See* David S. Clark & John Henry Merryman, *Measuring the Duration of Judicial and Administrative Proceedings,* 75 Mich. L. Rev. 89 (1976).

5. Is there a relation between wealth and litigation? Would you expect to see higher rates of litigation in wealthier countries? Consider the following statement:

> The amount of litigation has decreased enormously in Italy in the last seventy years. Taking only ordinary proceedings in courts of first instance, there was an average of 72.3 proceedings begun each year for every 1,000 inhabitants in the last five years of the nineteenth century. The average dropped to 62.7, 47.8, 45.2, and 22.3 in the next four five-year periods. Despite an enormous increase in population, there were only 438,000 ordinary cases begun in 1962; at the end of the nineteenth century, however, there were 2,316,000 cases begun in one year. This extraordinary reduction involves primarily small claims.... In the last five years of the nineteenth century and the first five years of the twentieth century, an average of 1,300,000 such cases were begun yearly, whereas in 1962 there were but 65,000 (85,000 in 1961; 113,000 in 1960; 126,000 in 1959). It is interesting to note that by far the largest decrease has been in the most economically developed areas. Apparently, litigiousness is a reflection of poverty and economic underdevelopment.

Cappelletti, Merryman & Perillo, The Italian Legal System: An Introduction 126-27, n.71 (1967). Do you agree with this conclusion? See the discussion of litigation rates in Chapter 6, Section A.5.

5. BRAZIL: BETWEEN TRADITION AND REFORM

NOTE

The Latin American law of civil procedure is highly derivative of the European model. The codes are based on European codes, and continental authors (particularly Italians) are regularly cited as authorities. This reflects a broader generalization: the traditional civil law view of the role of the judge and of the nature of the proceeding dominates Latin American trial courts. The ordinary courts play out the 19th century model of the judicial process and are comfortable with a 19th century civil (and, to a lesser extent, criminal) procedure. The Latin American supreme courts, which typically have much broader jurisdiction and powers than the trial courts, also act, when sitting in cassation or revision of the work of the lower courts, much like their European equivalents. The U.S. influence on judicial structure, although substantial, has not generally affected procedure.

KEITH S. ROSENN, CIVIL PROCEDURE IN BRAZIL, 34 American Journal of Comparative Law 487-90, 523-25 (1986)

Introduction

Brazil inherited from Portugal an entirely written system of civil procedure based largely upon Roman and canon law. That system has been colorfully characterized by one Brazilian writer as "developing in successive phases, interrupted at each step by appeals of interlocutory decisions — dragging itself slowly, far from the sight of the judge, growing fat within the belly of its tiresome record." This system of Roman-canonical procedure survived long after Brazil achieved independence in 1822. Although the 1850 Commercial Code simplified and improved the procedure governing commercial disputes, civil cases continued to be governed by the rules of civil procedure established in the *Ordenações Filipinas*, promulgated for the Portuguese in 1603 by Phillip III of Spain (Phillip II of Portugal). The 1891 Constitution, which adopted a federalist, republican form of government, authorized each state to promulgate its own procedural laws. With few exceptions, the resulting state legislation adhered to the Romano-canonical system of civil procedure. Despite numerous calls for reform, little was done until the 1934 Constitution bestowed legislative authority over civil procedure on the federal government. Five years later this resulted in the adoption of the first national Code of Civil Procedure. The 1939 Code substantially reformed Brazilian civil procedure, introducing oral proceedings, concentrating many proceedings, and giving the judge a much more active role. Nevertheless, it contained numerous defects, and it was widely blamed for long delays that have chronically plagued the Brazilian court system. Thirty-four years later, it was replaced by a new code.

The Brazilian Code of Civil Procedure of 1973 [hereinafter CPC], which presently governs civil cases in both federal and state courts, is widely regarded as one of the best codes in Latin America. Drafted originally by Alfredo Buzaid, a distinguished jurist who served as dean of the University of São Paulo's Law School, Minister of Justice, and a Minister of the Supreme Federal Tribunal, the draft code was revised in 1969 and 1972 by two distinguished commissions of jurists before receiving numerous amendments on the floor of Congress. The 1973 CPC was designed to minimize the defects commonly criticized in Latin American codes, such as excessive emphasis on written documents and pleadings, lack of a trial or focused hearing, severe circumscription of the powers of the judge, and a plethora of opportunities for creating seemingly interminable delays.

The CPC made a number of desirable reforms. It permits the parties, albeit in limited fashion, to present evidence, objections, and arguments orally in a single concentrated hearing (*audiência*),[8] a reform that has saved considerable litigation time. Brazil has also departed from traditional civil law practice by giving judges greater powers in all phases of judicial proceedings. Most Latin American codes reduce judicial activity to the final stage of the proceedings, the judgment stage, giving judges few powers to intervene at prior stages. Brazil, on the other hand, grants its judges the power to dismiss a complaint for failure to state a cause of action, to dismiss a party for lack of standing, to make evidentiary rulings, to order discovery, to raise procedural defects during the proceedings *sua sponte*, to grant summary judgment at an early stage, and even to make personal inspections of places, persons, or things *sua sponte*.[10]

Nevertheless, Brazilian civil procedure remains well within the civil law tradition. All determinations of law and fact are made by judges; juries are not used in civil proceedings. The common law lawyer will search in vain for rules of evidence, direct lawyer-to-witness cross-examination, or even a trial as he knows it. Instead, evidence is introduced piecemeal in the pleadings, in a series of written submissions to the clerk, and in a public hearing held before a judge prior to final judgment. Brazilian courts still have a decided tendency to give undue weight to documents and to be highly suspicious of oral testimony.

The CPC grants extensive powers to Brazilian judges, but these powers are frequently not exercised to any significant extent. The typical Brazilian judge does not view his role as an activist. Brazil still adheres to the principle that the parties control the issues, evidence and arguments presented. A party must demand action from the court to secure relief. Even though the CPC contains numerous provisions permitting judges to act *sua sponte*, Brazilian judges normally take no action unless requested to do so by the parties.[11] Moreover, in comparison with judges in the United States, the powers of Brazilian judges are still somewhat limited. For example, Brazilian judges have no civil contempt power, nor do they have inherent equitable powers. Lack of these powers limits the ability of Brazilian judges to direct litigation and tends to make them less creative in finding solutions to legal problems. Moreover, virtually any court order, whether final or interlocutory, is appealable.[12] This not only limits judicial power but also ensures that a party bent on delay can keep litigation moving at a snail's pace.

[8] CPC, arts. 444-57.

[10] CPC, arts. 295; 295 (II) and (III); 130, 331, and 395; 342, 355 and 381; 301, para. 4, 327, and 267, para. 3; 330; and 440.

[11] CPC, art. 2. But see CPC, art. 262.

[12] CPC, arts. 513, 522, and 464. The only unappealable orders are those that are merely ministerial.

Brazil is currently undergoing a serious crisis in the administration of justice, marked by a widespread dissatisfaction with the operation of the courts. The causes are numerous and complex, but the existing procedural system appears to have been an important contributor to the crisis. A recent empirical study of the Rio de Janeiro bar revealed that most of the practicing lawyers attribute the crisis in the administration of justice to the long delays, excessive procedural formalism, routine disregard of procedural time limits, and corruption.

Types of Basic Proceedings

Brazilian doctrine and the structure of the CPC divide civil proceedings into three basic types: cognitive, executory, and provisional. Cognitive proceedings, which are the most common, are designed to produce a determination of which litigant should prevail on the merits. Cognitive proceedings are, in turn, subdivided into three types of actions: declaratory, condemnatory, and constitutive. A declaratory action corresponds to the Anglo-American declaratory judgment action, where the plaintiff seeks a judicial declaration of his or her rights but no specific relief beyond that declaration. A condemnatory action, on the other hand, seeks specific relief, such as damages, from the defendant. A constitutive action seeks to create, modify, or extinguish a status or legal relationship, such as a suit for divorce or to terminate a contract.

The second basic type of proceeding is the executory proceeding, which seeks execution of a judgment or an executory title that is given the force of a judgment. Although in some ways resembling the Anglo-American writ of execution, the Brazilian executory action is considerably broader. It is often brought as a summary proceeding to collect liquid and certain debts without first obtaining a judgment....

The third general type of proceeding is the provisional proceeding which is designed to aid or to protect the outcome of cognitive and executory proceedings.[16] It covers ancillary proceedings and provisional remedies incident to a cognitive or executory action. The successful provisional proceeding usually results in attachment of the defendant's property or an order requiring that he post a bond.

Cognitive proceedings are further divided into two basic categories: ordinary and summary. Ordinary proceedings are usually lengthy affairs. In major cities, even without appeals, delays of several years between filing the suit and securing a final judgment are common. In theory, the summary proceeding requires only 90 days between filing suit and final judgment in the trial court,[17] but such litigation is seldom completed in that time frame.[18]

---

[16] CPC, art. 796.

[17] CPC, art. 281.

[18] In some Brazilian courts, summary proceedings take longer than ordinary proceedings.... Typical is Civil Appeal No. 92.390 (1983) before the Tribunal de Alçada of the State of Rio de Janeiro, involving a summary proceeding to prevent a private nuisance in the form of a neighbor's piano playing. No hearing was held until nine months after the action had been filed. The trial court handed down its decision eleven-and-one-half months after the action had been filed. Four months later the trial court's decision was reversed on appeal. Further appeals were attempted, including one to the Supreme Federal Tribunal. The dispute did not become *res judicata* until two years and three months following the filing of the action.

Executory proceedings are often completed within a few months,[19] but such proceedings begin with a judgment or its functional equivalent....

Conclusion

Brazil has a sophisticated and well-developed system of civil procedure that applies uniformly throughout the country. In many respects, it has the most modern system of civil procedure in Latin America, displaying much greater emphasis on orality and concentrating much of the evidence-gathering function into a single hearing resembling an Anglo-American trial. Brazil has also granted more powers to the judge to control the proceedings and to obtain evidence than one normally finds in civil law countries....

Nonetheless, Brazil's system of civil procedure has not functioned well. Its biggest defect is that it generally moves at a snail's pace. There is much truth to the maxim that justice delayed is justice denied. One can readily identify several defects in the Brazilian system of civil procedure that are largely responsible for the mammoth delays. First, the system permits such a multiplicity of appeals, particularly interlocutory appeals, that a litigant, if so inclined, can delay proceedings for lengthy periods. Second, collateral attacks on final judgments are permitted in too many circumstances. Third, the system constantly attempts to deal with the problem of delay by prescribing rigid time periods during which judges must perform certain tasks and render decisions. Such time constraints are flagrantly disrespected, for they are unrealistic for complex litigation and for judges in urban areas with congested dockets. The principle that time limits for judges can be disregarded is not easily cabined, however, and once established for complex litigation, it quickly spreads to simple litigation. The precedent of the judiciary disregarding the law is not a felicitous one, and it feeds back into the serious and more generalized problem of disrespect for law in Brazil. The problem would be better handled by differentiating cases on the basis of complexity and setting up an incentive system to reward judges who churn out certain quantities of high quality work. One also needs substantial increases in the number of judges in urban centers, and a judicial supervisory committee or ombudsman with power to transfer cases from judges unable or unwilling to decide them within a reasonable time.

Another defect is that the CPC provides for myriad special actions, with a bewildering multiplicity of special procedures. Book IV of the CPC sets out special procedures for a number of specific actions.[234] These actions are treated specially for a variety of reasons, mainly historical. The detailed pleading requirements for these special actions are reminiscent of the forms of action at common law. A failure to plead correctly, however, does not under Brazilian

[19] The time needed to complete an executory proceeding varies from place to place in Brazil. In Rio de Janeiro, for example, six to seven months is common. In cities with less congested dockets, two or three months will suffice.

[234] Some of the more significant actions with special procedures contained in Book IV of the CPC are: payment into court (art. 890); deposit (arts. 901-06); cancellation of bearer instruments (arts. 907-13); an accounting (arts. 914-19); ejectment (arts. 926-31); trespass (arts. 932-33); to block construction (arts. 934-940); adverse possession (arts. 941-45); partition (arts. 946 et seq.); inventory and distribution of a decedent's estate (arts. 982 et seq.).

law result in an outright dismissal. So long as no prejudice to the defendant occurs, pleading defects can be cured.[236] Nevertheless, Brazil would be much better off eliminating most of the special procedures.

Excessive formalism is still one of the biggest problems with Brazil's civil procedure. Complaints should not have to be prescreened by judges before they can be served, and service by registered mail should be extended to individual litigants. Plaintiffs should be able to amend freely the amount of damages they seek, and the unfair practice of charging costs as a percentage of the damages alleged should be abandoned.

Litigation needs to be made less costly for the litigants. Presently all but the very rich and the very poor are effectively precluded from litigating. Even then, indigents are often effectively precluded from litigating by the sporadic and often non-existent legal aid system....

More resources need to be allocated generally to the judicial system. The federal government allocates much less than one percent of its budget to the judiciary, and the percentage has been declining steadily. All but a few Brazilian states spend less than one percent of their budgets on their judiciaries. Perhaps the biggest problem in the administration of justice in Brazil today is directly linked to the insufficiency of governmental resources devoted to the judiciary. The clerks are badly underpaid and supplement their salaries with payments from litigants. This petty corruption undermines the integrity of the judicial system and substantially delays the litigation process. Eradication of this corruption is never easy, but payment of adequate salaries, prosecution and dismissal of offenders, and computerizing the distribution and progress of cases would help significantly.

NOTES AND QUESTIONS

1. Reform for civil procedure in Latin American nations tends to lag behind the pace of reform in Europe. Professor Rosenn describes the current Brazilian Civil Procedure Code as one of the "best" and "most modern" in Latin America. Nevertheless, Brazilian lawyers complain of a crisis in the administration of justice and criticize the system of civil procedure. Is the central problem one of defects in the Code, the Brazilian legal culture, or lack of economic resources committed to the judicial system?

The typology of civil proceedings discussed by Rosenn is typical of the pattern found in Spain and much of Latin America.

2. The Brazilian Constitution of 1988 expressly includes a number of procedural principles that earlier constitutions ignored or applied solely to criminal matters. These guarantees for civil cases include rights to a "regular" judge, a "court of law," adversary proceedings and an opportunity for an ample defense, exclusion of evidence obtained by illegal means, a public trial, a reasoned judicial decision, and due process. Arts. 5, 93. The Constitution also: broadens certain proceedings, such as the *mandado de segurança* (writ of security), popular action, and direct action for the declaration of unconstitutionality; elevates the public civil action, a restricted form of class action, from solely the level of statute; and introduces new remedies, such as the *mandado*

[236] CPC, art. 250.

de injunçao (injunction), habeas data, and the special appeal. Arts. 5, 103, 105, 129. *See* José Carlos Barbosa Moreira, *Brazilian Civil Procedure: An Overview,* in A Panorama of Brazilian Law 183 (Jacob Dolinger & Keith S. Rosenn eds. 1992).

3. For more on Latin America, see Richard B. Cappalli, *Comparative South American Civil Procedure: A Chilean Perspective,* 21 U. Miami Inter-Am. L. Rev. 239 (1989-90).

6. JAPAN: ORDINARY LITIGATION AND OTHER TYPES OF PROCEEDINGS

JOHN O. HALEY & DAN F. HENDERSON, LAW AND THE LEGAL PROCESS IN JAPAN 814-16, 897-902 (1988)

The Japanese civil suit [as in most civil law systems] ... is conducted through a series of discontinuous, piecemeal court hearings rather than a concentrated, uninterrupted trial. Despite the greater emphasis on adversarial elements under postwar reforms, Japanese judges continue to play a more dominant role than their American counterparts in the development of a case, [particularly under postwar decisions on] the judicial duty to clarify (*shakumeiken*).

Formal proceedings in open court or the "oral proceedings" (*kōtō benron*) usually begin within a few weeks after the complaint is filed, commencing the action. There also may be preliminary or "preparatory proceedings" (*jumbi tetsuzuki*) if the case is complex in which the judge and the parties meet to clarify issues, narrow the points in contention and otherwise attempt to expedite the trial.

In a typical case, there will be a series of preliminary hearings on the pleadings during which the issues — factual and legal — in contention are defined, lists of witnesses and experts are drawn up for the court to call, and any public documents, such as police reports, are requested for the court to obtain. The evidentiary hearings follow during which the parties, witnesses and possible experts testify. As in American practice, they are questioned and then cross-examined by the attorneys, but the judges, too, will ask questions.

In the event of a three-judge panel (required in criminal cases for capital crimes or crimes punishable by a year or more imprisonment and in [most] civil cases [other than small claims]) ..., one judge who can be identified since he or she will dominate the questioning from the bench will be in charge of the case. Ordinarily the judge in charge drafts the decision and will also meet with the parties in the formal compromise session.

There are two court sessions a day, from 10:00 a.m. to 12:00 noon and from 1:00 p.m. to 5:00 p.m. A number of cases at different stages may be called up at the beginning of each session with what time remains used for testimony in a single case. At the end of each hearing the attorneys and the judge (the presiding judge in the case of a three-judge panel) will set a mutually convenient time for the next hearing, typically two weeks to a month or more later. Consequently, court delays in Japan represent the time between the first trial session and the final judgment (which may not be handed down for several months and sometimes not for years or more after the last trial session), instead of the time between filing the complaint and the commencement of the trial.

The following [outline illustrates] the course of [an actual] trial in a wrongful death action involving a child hit by a private kindergarten school bus in Osaka on April 20, 1970.

From: Park v. Fukuoka, Shōwa 45 [1970] (wa) No. 3785: Case of Claim for Damages, Osaka District Court, Civil Department No. 15.

Complaint filed .... July 14, 1970

Oral Proceedings

Answer filed with first Request for Evidence (for police report of accident) .... September 22, 1970

Plaintiff's first brief and first Request for Evidence (witness to be called) .... November 17, 1970

Defendant's second Request for Evidence (witnesses) .. June 7, 1971

Defendant's third Request for Evidence (witnesses) .... November 9, 1971

Plaintiff's second brief (with exhibits and police report of accident) .... November 15, 1971

Testimony by defendant bus driver (Fukuoka), by bus attendant and by plaintiff mother of deceased child ... November 15, 1971

Testimony by bus driver (continued), by defendant principal and owner of kindergarten and by father of deceased child .... March 14, 1972

Hearing for clarification of damages claimed (one member of three judge panel transferred and replaced by new judge) .... May 2, 1972

Compromise (*wakai*) session .... June 1, 1972

Supplementary Brief filed by plaintiff and final argument .... June 20, 1972

Final argument .... August 22, 1972

Decision .... Jan. 22, 1973

....

The remedial and enforcement powers of the courts in Japan are considerably weaker than those in common law and most other civil law jurisdictions. As defined in Japanese legal theory and practice the judicial power [of the courts under the postwar constitution] does not encompass ... powers [taken for granted by common law courts] .... Japanese judges lack authority to fashion remedies to assure adequate relief or to retain jurisdiction over a case once they render a final judgment. Unable to monitor or to police compliance over time, they do not exercise authority to grant prospective or on-going relief, such as permanent injunctions. A court's formal involvement with an action in effect ceases once its judgment becomes irrevocable. Enforcement actions and even retrials are in form and effect new, separate actions usually adjudicated by different judges. As in other civil law jurisdictions, the courts in Japan do not have contempt power. Nor does Japanese criminal law provide for analogous penalties as in most continental systems. The maximum penalty for most violations of a judicial order is a non-penal fine recently raised from 5 to 100 thousand yen, still less than [1,000] U.S. dollars [at prevailing exchange rates]. In terms of formal sanctions, at least, many parties can ignore judicial orders with impunity. Compliance is thus more a result of self-help and social constraints than effective legal controls.

Even the topic of remedies receives scant attention in Japan or, for that matter, in other civil law jurisdictions. No Japanese commentary or treatise on remedies appears to have been written. Nor is there much positive law. The Civil Code, for example, contains only eight articles that deal directly with damages (Civil Code arts. 417-422), and only one to the measure of damages (Civil Code art. 416). As general provisions of the law of obligations (*saiken*), these articles ostensibly cover the entire law of damages for all contract, tort and other actions involving *in personam* rights. The Code of Civil Procedure is similarly bereft in defining available judicial relief, other than the provisions for temporary attachment and injunctive relief in anticipation of a suit. Generally plaintiffs are limited to remedies provided either by special statute, as in the case of *kōkoku* appeals from reviewable administrative actions under the Administration Case Litigation Law, or as encompassed by the specific substantive rights being enforced. In a contract action, for example, Japanese legal theory recognizes a general right to claim specific performance or "coercive performance" (*kyōsei rikō*) or, if specific performance is impossible or inappropriate, substitute damages. In addition the parties have broad latitude in setting out by agreement remedial schemes of their own, including, for example, liquidated damages. In the absence of such contracted remedies, as a rule, the particular remedy available to a party is bound to the substantive right being enforced.

In final judgments Japanese law does recognize three basic *modes* of judicial relief. The first is the declaratory judgment of a "confirmation action" (*kakunin no uttae*, from the German *Feststellungsklage*) in which the court confirms the rights or duties of a party or the validity of a particular legal relationship. The second is a "constitutive" judgment, which is also declaratory in form but itself creates or dissolves a legal relationship, as in the case of a divorce judgment. The third and most common mode is a judgment embodying a judicial order for performance of some sort, such as payment of money, delivery of personal property or conveyance of land.

Neither confirmation nor constitutive judgments usually require further judicial process, insofar as public authorities, such as registry officials, honor them as determinative statements of the rights of a party. Judgments ordering performance, like other judicial orders, on the other hand, are often only [effective through civil execution. This is available against real property or other property registered in the debtor's name and against contractual or other obligation rights of the debtor in relation to a cooperative third party.] Otherwise, however, the legal process in Japan may offer a claimant little help.

Two types of temporary or provisional relief in anticipation of a civil suit are available, however: provisional attachment (*kari-sashiosae*) and provisional dispositions (*kari-shobun*). Both are protective measures designed primarily to protect the claimant from prejudicial harm in the status quo before a suit is filed or pending its outcome. Consequently, both are temporary devices incidental to the principal action to be brought by the petitioners and are predicated on the validity of the petitioner's claim. Both are also widely used. As indicated in the table below, a petition for "provisional" remedy is filed for every two ordinary civil actions.

Table 10.2

Civil Proceedings Filed in Japanese District Courts, by Type and Year[a]

Type	1975	1980	1984
Ordinary civil litigation actions	74,907	105,559	107,677
Civil conciliation	2,828	2,118	1,693
Summary actions for bills & notes	17,507	21,513	13,942
Provisional remedies	37,920	50,315	53,997
Execution on immovables	7,435	10,306	17,828
Execution on contracts & other obligations	43,560	54,370	66,979

A provisional disposition is in effect a form of injunctive relief designed first to secure execution by preventing threats to the "realization" of the rights of the claimant in a dispute (Code of Civil Procedure art. 755). In this form, it is referred to as "provisional disposition with respect to the subject matter in dispute" (*keisobutsu ni kansuru kari-shobun*). As a "provisional disposition temporarily fixing the affairs with respect to the legal relations in dispute" (*kari no chii o sadameru kari-shobun*), it is also used to establish a temporary relationship that effectively grants the claimant all or part of the relief sought in the principal action (see Code of Civil Procedure art. 760). For example, a court may grant a provisional disposition enjoining a firm from using a patent pending the outcome of an infringement action or a manufacturer from discharging an employee pending the outcome of an employment contract action. Provisional disposition may also be used to protect the claimant from coercion and threats of violence (Code of Civil Procedure art. 760).

Petitions for both provisional remedies are predicated on a credible claim and reasonable concern that the relief is necessary to ensure the effectiveness of a judgment for the petitioner (see Code of Civil Procedure arts. 338, 755, 760). Such concern can be based solely on the subjective fears of the petitioner.

Provisional attachment, but only if urgent, provisional dispositions, may be issued (and often are) *ex parte* without prior notice to the respondent. However, the respondent may file an objection (*igi*) (Code of Civil Procedure arts. 744[1], 756), which, while not operating to stay the effectiveness of the order, does obligate the court to institute oral proceedings (Code of Civil Procedure art. 745), after which the attachment or disposition is to be confirmed, modified, or annulled in a final judgment (Code of Civil Procedure arts. 745[2], 756).

[a] This table is a simplified version of the original.

ABE v. CHIBA

Supreme Court of Japan
Second Petty Bench
Decision of 26 June 1964
18 Minshū 954 (1964)

English translation published in Henderson & Haley, Law and the Legal Process in Japan 647-48 (1979)

Title: Case concerning Petition for Payment of Damages and Declaration of Ownership in Land.

Topic: Instance in which non-exercise of the clarification right in connection with proof was held to be illegal.

Summary

In judging the propriety of a petition for payment of damages premising ownership of certain lands and on the grounds that standing timber growing on these lands has been unlawfully cut down, when it is the court's conviction that only part of the lands concerned are owned by the petitioner, and further, it is natural that the court should further inquire into such matters as the quantity and value of what was cut down of the standing timber growing on that part and it is necessary to have new evidence in addition to prior evidence regarding these points when making this inquiry, it is properly considered that the court must urge the parties to submit evidence regarding these points, unless it is clear that there is no other evidence regarding them; to simply dismiss a petition without resort to such measures, on the grounds that there is no evidence, we must say, is to neglect the exercise of the clarification right and to commit the illegality of inexhaustive examination of facts.

Reasons

Code of Civil Procedure article 127:

> The presiding judge may, in order to clarify the relations involved in the suit concerned, put questions to the parties or urge them to produce evidence on matters of fact and law.
>
> An assistant judge may take such measures as provided in the preceding paragraph after informing the presiding judge (of his intention to do so).
>
> The parties may ask the presiding judge to put necessary questions.

Concerning Point 3 of the [*jōkoku* appeal]: It is clear from the text of the decision below that upon finding that because lands A and C were a part of the [uncultivated] wilderness area owned by the *kōso* appellee (*jōkoku* appellant), [for the *kōso* appellant] to cut down standing timber growing thereon obviously constituted an unlawful act based on negligence at the very least, the court held that proof of the amount of damages arising from the cutting on lands A and C was insufficient because it could only know, from the evidence submitted, what the total amount cut on lands B and C was and what its value was, but it was impossible to calculate the value of the timber cut on the lands individually and there was no evidence to clarify this; the court thus dismissed appellant's petition in this regard. But in judging the propriety of a petition for payment of damages premising ownership of certain lands and on the grounds that standing timber growing on these lands has been unlawfully cut down, when it is the court's conviction that only part of the lands concerned are owned by the petitioner, and further, it is natural that the court should further inquire into such matters as the quantity and value of what was cut down of the standing timber growing on that part and it is necessary to have new evidence in addition to prior evidence regarding these points when making this inquiry, *it is properly considered that the court must urge the parties concerned to submit evidence regarding these points*, unless it is clear that there is no other evidence regarding them; to simply dismiss a petition without resort to such measures, on the grounds that there is no evidence, we must say, is to *neglect the exercise of the clarification right and to commit the illegality of inexhaustive examination of facts*. [T]he parties cannot anticipate what the conviction of the court will be, and cannot know whether there will be need of proof regarding these points. Consequently, in the present case, having reached the judgment that of the lands B and C only the latter is owned by the *kōso* appellee, the court below ought to have urged proof by the *kōso* appellee concerning the quantity cut of the standing timber on these lands. Given this, we can only conclude that for the court below to have not resorted to such measures and to have simply refused the *kōso* appellee's petition on the grounds that there was no evidence, was to have neglected the exercise of the clarification right and to have committed the illegality of inexhaustive examination of facts; the part of the decision below that dismissed appellant's petition for payment of damages must be quashed. Accordingly, we hold that the *jōkoku* appeal concerning points other than the above part which must be quashed, should be dismissed; we decide as in the decree by the unanimous agreement of all justices, applying Code of Civil Procedure articles 407, 396, 384, 95 and 89.

Presiding Justice Ken'ichi Okuno, Justices Sakunosuke Yamada, Yoshihiko Kido, and Kazuto Ishida.

NOTES AND QUESTIONS

1. Does Japanese civil procedure seem more like the German, French, or American system? In what ways?

2. The ratio of provisional remedies to ordinary civil litigation actions in Table 10.2 is about one to two. Why do you think provisional remedies are so popular in Japan? Does the ratio of execution actions to ordinary civil litigation actions seem high, given what we know about the Japanese legal system? Why do you think the ratio increased between 1975 and 1984?

3. The first appeal in Japan is known as the *kōso* appeal and the second appeal on questions of law is called the *jōkoku* appeal. In *Abe v. Chiba* what should the lower court judge have done to fulfill his duty to clarify the issues?

4. Consider the problem of delay in Japan:

> The average delay between filing and judgment for cases that require at least a minimum level of proof-taking or an evidentiary hearing is 27 months. Far longer delays are experienced before final judgment if an appeal is made.
>
> The typical civil case proceeding through litigation will be heard before a career judge without a jury. On average, each case will have seven oral hearings, two settlement hearings, and four party or witness examination sessions. In the average case, little more than 3 witnesses are examined for a total of 4 hours. The average time spent between sessions is 40 days. However, evidentiary hearings can be scheduled only once every 75 days. Moreover, in half of all cases the judge is moved to another jurisdiction and replaced due to Japan's system of rotating judges to serve in different jurisdictions.
>
> This deplorable reality has recently led to renewed efforts to tackle the problem of delay in Japan. Two groups that have been particularly important in this effort are two local bar associations and the Tokyo and Osaka district courts. The First Tokyo Bar Association and the Second Tokyo Bar Association have each separately published their own recommendations as to how to remedy the situation.

Takeshi Kojima, *Civil Procedure Reform in Japan,* 11 Mich. J. Int'l L. 1218-19 (1990).

5. For an excellent treatise on Japanese civil procedure, see Takaaki Hattori & Dan Fenno Henderson, Civil Procedure in Japan (1985).

B. CRIMINAL PROCEDURE

1. AN OVERVIEW OF CRIMINAL PROCEDURE

JOHN HENRY MERRYMAN, THE CIVIL LAW TRADITION: AN INTRODUCTION TO THE LEGAL SYSTEMS OF WESTERN EUROPE AND LATIN AMERICA 124-32 (2d ed. 1985)

Although the revolution profoundly affected every part of the civil law tradition, its effects are most clearly observable in public law. And, within the field of public law, much of the criticism of the *ancien régime* and much of the call for reform tended to be concentrated in the field of criminal procedure. Among the writers and philosophers of the eighteenth century who contributed to the ideology of revolution, most had something to say about the sorry state of criminal law and criminal procedure. The most important commentator in this field was Cesare Beccaria, whose book *Of Crimes and Punishments* exploded on the European scene in 1764 and became the most influential work on criminal procedure in Western history.

Substantive criminal law in Western, capitalist civil law countries does not differ greatly from that of common law countries. The same kinds of actions are considered criminal, and the same general approaches to punishment are discussed and debated throughout Western culture. There are, however, significant operational differences in criminal procedure, and it is striking to observe the extent to which the revolutionary reform of criminal procedure reflects the causes and effects of the revolutionary period in the civil law tradition. We can illustrate this point by examining the principal thesis and the organization of Beccaria's book.

He begins by establishing the principle of *nullum crimen sine lege* and *nulla poena sine lege*. As Beccaria states it: "Only the laws can determine the punishment of crimes; and the authority of making penal laws can reside only with the legislator, who represents the whole society united by the social compact." Thus, according to Beccaria, crimes and punishments can be established only by law, and by law he means statute. Beccaria then proceeds to discuss the interpretation of laws. His position is that "judges in criminal cases have no right to interpret the penal laws, because they are not legislators." And further, "the disorders that may arise from a rigorous observance of the letter of penal laws are not to be compared to those produced by the interpretation of them.... When the code of laws is once fixed, it should be observed in the literal sense, and nothing more is left to the judge than to determine whether an action be or be not conformable to the written law." In the same paragraph, speaking of judges, he refers to "the despotism of this multitude of tyrants." Later, in the chapter on obscurity in the law, he says: "If the power of interpreting laws be an evil, obscurity in them must be another, as the former is the consequence of the latter. This evil will be still greater if the laws be written in a language unknown to the people; who, being ignorant of the consequences of their own actions, become necessarily dependent on a few, who are interpreters of the laws, which, instead of being public and general, are thus rendered private and particular." Beccaria then goes on to establish two basic principles. The first is that there should be a proportion between crimes and punishments, so that the more serious crimes are more severely punished. The second is that punishments should apply impartially to criminals, regardless of their social station, position, or wealth.

The reader will observe the similarity of these observations to the general characteristics of the revolutionary legal tradition.... They are permeated with state positivism, rationalism, and a concern for the rights of man as enunciated by the school of secular natural law. Principles similar to those stated by Beccaria were, at the same time, affecting the evolution of criminal procedure in the common law world. One difference, however, was the emphasis on, perhaps the exaggeration of, these principles in Europe as a result of the French Revolution and the effect of that revolution on the thinking about law and the state in the civil law world. Hence even today one finds a sharper emphasis in civil law jurisdictions on the principle that every crime and every penalty shall be embodied in a statute enacted by the legislature. To a civil lawyer, common law courts seem to violate this principle every day when they award penal damages, multiple damages, or general damages in civil actions, when they convict people of "common law" crimes, and when they summarily punish people for contempt. Another significant difference between the two traditions is the earlier movement toward reform of penology in the civil law world. Under the influence of Beccaria and his successors, the death penalty was abolished in Tuscany in the eighteenth century, and fundamental reforms leading to less drastic penalties for minor offenses took place throughout Europe well in advance of similar reforms in Great Britain and the United States.

It is obvious that an emphasis on the principle of legality (no crime or penalty without a statute enacted by the legislature), together with a desire to have such statutes written down as part of a rational scheme in a language that could be read by the citizen, should lead to codification of the criminal law. In fact, the first object of codification in revolutionary France was the criminal law, and a criminal code was actually written during the Revolution. If a case for codification exists, it exists most clearly in the fields of criminal law and procedure. But once the case is made for criminal law, it is easily extended to other fields, particularly in a legal tradition in which judges are distrusted and a representative legislature is a hero. This, as we have seen, was the case throughout the revolutionary period in the civil law world.

One of the commonest comparisons one hears made about criminal procedure in the two traditions is that the criminal procedure in the civil law tradition is "inquisitorial," while that in the common law tradition is "accusatorial." Although this generalization is inaccurate and misleading as applied to contemporary systems of criminal procedure, it has some validity when put into historical context. In a sense it can be said that the evolution of criminal procedure in the last two centuries in the civil law world has been away from the extremes and abuses of the inquisitorial system, and that the evolution in the common law world during the same period has been away from the abuses and excesses of the accusatorial system. The two systems, in other words, are converging from different directions toward roughly equivalent mixed systems of criminal procedure.

Let us first consider the accusatorial system, which is generally thought by anthropologists to be the first substitute an evolving society develops for private vengeance. In such a system the power to institute the action resides in the wronged person, who is the accuser. This same right of accusation is soon extended to his relatives, and as the conception of social solidarity and the need for group protection develops, the right of accusation extends to all members of the group. A presiding officer is selected to hear the evidence, decide, and sentence; he does not, however, have the power to institute the action or to determine the questions to be raised or the evidence to be introduced, and he has no inherent investigative powers. These matters are in the hands of the accuser and the accused. The criminal trial is a contest between the accuser and the accused, with the judge as a referee. Typically the proceeding takes place publicly and orally and is not preceded by any official (i.e. judicial or police) investigation or preparation of evidence.

The inquisitorial system typically represents an additional step along the path of social evolution from the system of private vengeance. Its principal features include first, attenuation or elimination of the figure of the private accuser and appropriation of that role by public officials; and second, the conversion of the judge from an impartial referee into an active inquisitor who is free to seek evidence and to control the nature and objectives of the inquiry. In addition, the relative equality of the parties that is an attribute of the accusatorial system, in which two individuals contest before an impartial arbiter, has been drastically altered. Now the contest is between an individual (the accused) and the state. Historically, inquisitorial proceedings have tended to be secret and written rather than public and oral. The resulting imbalance of power, combined with the secrecy of the written procedure, creates the danger of an oppressive system, in which the rights of the accused can easily be abused. The most infamous analogue familiar to us in the common law world is the Star Chamber, which was basically an inquisitorial tribunal.

The Star Chamber was, however, exceptional in the common law tradition. Historically the system was basically accusatorial in nature, and the early development of the jury as a necessary participant in the criminal proceeding in England tended to prevent any strong movement toward excesses like those of the Continental inquisitorial system. If a jury was to have the power to determine guilt or innocence of the accused, the proceedings would necessarily have to be oral and be conducted in the presence of the jury. Although it became the rule early in the development of the English criminal trial that the accuser need not employ and compensate the prosecuting attorney, the public prosecutor came very late to the common law. Even today, in England, a member of the practicing bar will be retained to represent the public interest in a criminal proceeding, and will be compensated from public funds. The creation of a professional police force and of a public prosecutor, to investigate the commission of crimes, compile evidence, seek authority to prosecute, and actually conduct the criminal proceeding on behalf of the state, are comparatively recent developments in the common law world. In effect, they represent a shift away from the accusatorial and toward the inquisitorial system. But the public nature of the trial, the orality of the proceedings in the trial, the existence of a jury, and the limitations on the power of the judge, all combine to perpetuate some of the more desirable features of the accusatory system. The result is a kind of mixed system of criminal procedure.

In the civil law world, the movement toward the extremes of the inquisitorial model was impelled by the revival of Roman law, the influence of canonic procedure, and, most important, the rise of statism. The criminal action was an action by the state against the accused individual. The proceedings were written and secret. The accused had no right to counsel. He could be required to testify under oath, and torture was a common device for compelling testimony and eliciting proof. The judge was not limited to the role of impartial arbiter, but played an active part in the proceedings and determined their scope and nature. The prince, as the personification of the state, had the power to punish and to pardon, unrestricted by rules against ex post facto laws, by principles of equal treatment of individuals, or by what we would now call considerations of ordinary humanity and justice.

As a result of the work of Beccaria and others in the eighteenth century, public sentiment against the abuses of criminal procedure became very strong, and reform of criminal procedure became one of the principal objectives of the European revolutions. Reformers of the time pointed to the criminal procedure of England as an example of a just, democratic system, and called for reform of their own criminal procedure along common law lines. Prominent among the demands made were (1) institution of the jury, (2)

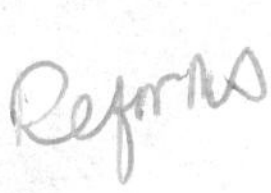

substitution of the oral public procedure in place of secret written procedure, (3) the establishment of the accused's right to counsel, (4) restriction of the judge's inquisitorial powers, (5) abolition of the requirement that the accused testify under oath, and (6) abolition of arbitrary intervention by the sovereign in the criminal process, by way of either penalty or pardon.

In the fervor of the French Revolution an attempt was made to abolish the criminal procedure of the old regime wholesale and substitute an entirely new procedure based on the English model. The failure of that effort soon became apparent, and a counterrevolution took place. The result is a mixed system, in France, composed in part of elements from prerevolutionary times and in part of reforms imposed after the Revolution.

The typical criminal proceeding in the civil law world can be thought of as divided into three basic parts: the investigative phase, the examining phase (the *instruction*), and the trial. The investigative phase comes under the direction of the public prosecutor, who also participates actively in the examining phase, which is supervised by the examining judge. The examining phase is primarily written and is not public. The examining judge controls the nature and scope of this phase of the proceeding. He is expected to investigate the matter thoroughly and to prepare a complete written record, so that by the time the examining stage is complete, all the relevant evidence is in the record. If the examining judge concludes that a crime was committed and that the accused is the perpetrator, the case then goes to trial. If he decides that no crime was committed or that the crime was not committed by the accused, the matter does not go to trial. (In 1975, Germany abolished the examining phase. The entire pretrial process is now in the hands of the prosecutor and the police, as it is with us. In the great majority of civil law nations, however, the examining phase continues to be the heart of the system of criminal procedure.)

In a very general way it can be said that the principal progress toward a more just and humane criminal proceeding in Europe in the last century and a half has come through reforms in the investigative and examining phases of the criminal proceeding. These reforms have been of two principal kinds. First, every effort has been made to develop a core of prosecuting attorneys who act impartially and objectively. In Italy, for example, prosecuting attorneys are now members of the judiciary, having a security of tenure and consequent freedom from influence similar to that enjoyed by judges. Second, a number of procedural safeguards have been developed to assist the accused in protecting his own interests during the examining phase. Principal among these is the right of the accused to representation by counsel throughout this phase of the proceeding. This does not mean that counsel for the accused has unrestricted freedom to cross-examine witnesses or to introduce evidence on behalf of his client. The examining phase is still conducted by a judge. Counsel for the accused can, however, participate in the proceedings in such a way as to protect his client's interests, calling certain matters to the attention of the court and advising his client on how he should respond as the proceeding unfolds. The dossier compiled by the examining magistrate is open to inspection by the defense, routinely providing information about the prosecution's case that in an American proceeding would be unavailable to the defense until its production was compelled by a motion for discovery or it was revealed at the trial.

As a rule the defendant can be questioned during the examining phase and at the trial. He cannot, however, be sworn, and he may refuse to answer. His refusal to answer, as well as his answers, will be taken into account in deciding questions of guilt or in fixing the penalty. As in civil proceedings, there is no developed system of cross-examination comparable to ours, although the prosecutor may suggest questions to be put to the defendant by the judges. In our criminal justice system, the defendant need not take the stand, and inferences from his failure to testify are prohibited. If he does testify, however, he must be sworn and is subject to cross-examination by the prosecutor. An eminent comparative lawyer has characterized our system as one that puts the defendant to a "cruel choice" between testifying under oath, subject to cross-examination, and not testifying at all. He suggests that the civil law, by not subjecting the accused to so drastic a choice, is more humane.

As a consequence of the nature of the examining phase of the criminal proceeding, the trial itself is different in character from the common law trial. The evidence has already been taken and the record made, and this record is available to the accused and his counsel, as well as to the prosecution. The function of the trial is to present the case to the trial judge and jury and to allow the prosecutor and the defendant's counsel to argue their cases. It is also, of course, a public event, which by its very publicity tends to limit the possibility of arbitrary governmental action.

Civil lawyers criticize the common American practice of plea bargaining (giving the prosecutor discretion to charge a lesser offense or call for a lighter sentence if the defendant agrees to plead guilty). This practice seems to them to frustrate legislative intent and the legitimate expectations of victims, and to compromise the rule of law. Their law and their prosecutorial traditions both sharply limit prosecutorial discretion. Where discretion is permitted, it is controlled by law and, perhaps more importantly, by hierarchical review procedures within the prosecutorial bureaucracy. In most civil law nations the victim of the crime also has standing to object to the abuse of prosecutorial discretion. Most significant of all is the different effect of the guilty plea, which is an essential component of the plea-bargaining system. With us, the defendant who pleads guilty forgoes a trial. In the civil law world, a trial cannot be averted by a guilty plea. The accused's confession can be admitted as evidence, but the trial must go on. The court determines guilt, it is said, not the defendant or the prosecutor.

One frequently encounters two common misapprehensions about criminal procedure in the civil law world. One is to the effect that there is no presumption of innocence; the other is that there is no right to a jury trial. As stated, these are demonstrably false. Although the precise nature of the presumption and the degree to which it serves to protect the accused vary within the civil law world, it can be said that a legal presumption of innocence does exist in many civil law jurisdictions. In those in which it does not exist as a formal rule of law, something very much like it emerges from the examining phase of the criminal proceeding, where the character of the examining judge and judicialization of the function of the prosecuting attorney tend to prevent the trial of persons who are not probably guilty. The common supposition that there is no right to a jury trial in the civil law world is simply contrary to the facts. The jury or its functional equivalent is an established institution since the reforms of the revolutionary period. It may not be available for as wide a range of offenses (even in some American states a jury trial is not granted in misdemeanor cases), it may not consist of twelve persons, it may frequently take the form of lay advisers who sit on the bench with the judge, and even where it looks like ours, it may not have to render a unanimous verdict of guilty in order for the accused to be convicted. These are, particularly when they accumulate, important differences between our conception of a jury and theirs. But the fact remains that the jury is a well established institution in the criminal proceedings of civil law jurisdictions. It is indicative that the new constitution of Spain, adopted in 1978, [provides for trial by jury in criminal cases, although implementing legislation has not yet been enacted.] Continental lawyers also have an aversion to single-judge courts, summed up in the aphorism *juge unique, juge inique.* Recently the French Constitutional Council held unconstitutional an attempt to establish single-judge courts for cases involving less than major crimes. The usual provision is for three judges at the trial level. Even where there is no jury, the requirement of three judges reduces the danger of an arbitrary decision.

For those readers who wonder which is the more just system, the answer must be that opinion is divided. Recently a Harvard professor wrote a book charging American criminal procedure with "denial of justice" and advocating reforms along French lines. Other Americans have sought to prove that our system is fairer to the accused. The debate is clouded by ignorance of the law and practice in civil law nations and by preconceptions that are difficult to dispel. In the end, a statement made by an eminent comparative scholar after long and careful study is instructive: he said that if he were innocent, he would prefer to be tried by a civil law court, but that if he were guilty, he would prefer to be tried by a common law court. This is, in effect, a judgment that criminal proceedings in the civil law world are more likely to distinguish accurately between the guilty and the innocent.

2. THE COURSE OF A CRIMINAL PROCEEDING FROM ARREST TO APPEAL, AND THE SEARCH FOR TRUTH

RUDOLF B. SCHLESINGER, COMPARING CRIMINAL PROCEDURE: A PLEA FOR UTILIZING FOREIGN EXPERIENCE, 26 Buffalo Law Review 361, 364-72, 337-81 (1977)

Outline of the Course of a Criminal Proceeding in a Continental Country

In the civilian systems, as in our own, the policeman normally is the first public official to arrive at the scene of an alleged crime, or to receive a report concerning it. He may conduct an informal investigation; but his power to arrest the suspect without a judicial warrant, or to proceed to warrantless searches and seizures, generally is more limited than here. Thus, at least as a rule, it becomes necessary at a very early stage of the investigation to involve the prosecutor and the court.

There is no grand jury. The official phase of the pretrial investigation is in the hands of a judge — whom the French call *juge d'instruction* — or of the prosecutor. Both the judge and the prosecutor are essentially civil servants. The judge enjoys the usual guarantees of judicial independence. The prosecutor does not; he may be a link in a hierarchical chain of command, often leading up to the Minister of Justice. Nevertheless, except perhaps in cases having strong political overtones, the civil-servant prosecutor operating in a continental system can be expected to be reasonably impartial. He does not have to run for re-election; and his promotion within the civil service hierarchy may depend as much on his efficiency in sorting out and dropping investigations mistakenly commenced against innocent suspects as it does on his record of procuring convictions of the guilty.

The magistrate or prosecutor conducting the investigation will build up an impressive dossier by interrogating all available witnesses, including those named by the suspect, and collecting other relevant evidence. The suspect himself will be interrogated, and in the most progressive continental countries such interrogation will take place in the presence of his counsel. In many civil law countries the law expressly provides that the suspect has a right to remain silent and that he must be informed of this right. Of course, there is no physical compulsion to make him talk. Experience in continental countries shows, nevertheless, that in the preliminary investigation as well as at the trial itself the defendant usually does talk. The reasons for this will be explored below.

At the conclusion of the official investigation, the prosecutor (or, in some countries, the investigating magistrate) must decide whether in his judgment the evidence is strong enough to warrant the bringing of formal charges against the suspect. If charges are brought, the accused still does not necessarily have to stand trial. Under the traditional civil law practice, the dossier now goes to a three-judge panel — on a higher level of the judicial hierarchy. Only if this panel, having studied the dossier and having given defense counsel an opportunity to submit arguments and to suggest the taking of additional evidence, determines that there exists what we would call "reasonable cause," will the accused have to stand trial. (It should be noted here how misleading it can be to call the continental procedure "inquisitorial" and to contrast it with our allegedly "adversary" process. Under continental procedure, the accused has a twofold opportunity to be heard — first in the course of the preliminary investigation, and again when the three-judge panel examines the dossier — *before* any decision is made whether he has to stand trial. This should be compared with the completely nonadversary grand jury proceeding by which a prosecutor under our system can obtain an indictment.)

In every civil law country, counsel for the accused has the absolute right to inspect the whole dossier. This will be discussed later.

At the trial, the bench normally (though not uniformly) will consist of one or three professional judges and a number of lay assessors. The jury system, which was introduced in continental Europe in the wake of the French Revolution, more recently was replaced in most continental countries by the system of the mixed bench. Under this system, the professional judges and the lay assessors together form the court, which as a single body passes on issues of law as well as fact, and determines both guilt and sentence. Thus, the trial does not have to be bifurcated into a first hearing devoted solely to the issue of guilt, and a subsequent second hearing dealing with the sentence. The issue of guilt and the measure of punishment are determined simultaneously and by the same body of adjudicators.

The dossier, reflecting the pretrial investigation, plays a role during the trial as well. Three of the *dramatis personae* at this point are thoroughly conversant with its contents: the prosecutor, the defendant's counsel, and the Presiding Justice. The Presiding Justice has the dossier in front of him during the trial. On the other hand, the lay judges, and often the professional judges other than the Presiding Justice of the court, are unfamiliar with the dossier. Consequently, only the evidence received in open court (as distinguished from the contents of the dossier) may be considered in reaching a decision.

After a reading of the charges, the Presiding Justice normally will call upon the defendant to give his name and occupation and to make a statement concerning his general background. Then, after a warning that he has the right, at his option, to remain silent concerning the charges against him, the defendant will be asked what (if anything) he wishes to say about the charges.[28] The defendant, who is not put under oath, at this point has the opportunity to tell his side of the story by way of a coherent statement. This will be followed by questions addressed to the defendant. In practice most of the questioning will be done by the Presiding Justice, who is well prepared for this task by previous study of the dossier in his hands. Prosecution and defense counsel may suggest, or be permitted to ask, additional questions.

After this interrogation of the defendant, the witnesses will be examined in similar fashion. Normally, the witnesses will be the same individuals whose preliminary testimony is recorded in the dossier, but additional witnesses, not discovered in the course of the pretrial investigation, may be subpoenaed by the defense or may appear voluntarily at the trial. Nontestimonial evidence, especially physical evidence, also may be produced, and the court may inspect the place of the crime....

After closing arguments by prosecution and defense, and after the defendant has been accorded the last word, the court retires to deliberate. The lay judges, whose vote in most (but not all) continental countries carries the same weight as that of their professional colleagues, may outnumber the latter. In the great majority of civil law countries, the judgment does not have to be unanimous; and the fact that it is not unanimous will not be disclosed. Unless the judgment is one of acquittal, it will pronounce conviction and sentence. It will say, for example, that defendant is found guilty of armed robbery and for such crime is sentenced to four years in the reformatory.

As a rule, the judgment of the court of first instance is subject to an appeal on both the law and the facts. New evidence may be presented to the appellate court, and the proceedings before that court, which has power to review the

[28] The trial described in this and the following three paragraphs of the text reflects the applicable code provisions. In practice, many of the steps outlined in the text can be omitted or condensed in cases where a confession has been obtained, that is, in the great majority of routine cases.

sentence as well as the determination of guilt or innocence, may amount to a trial de novo. The decision of the appellate court normally can be attacked by a second appeal to a court of last resort, but in this last court only questions of law will be reviewed. The right to appeal is given not only to the defendant but to the prosecutor as well....

Arrest and Pretrial Detention in Civil-Law Countries

In this country, it is still the general rule that criminal proceedings routinely "start with the harsh, and in itself degrading, measure of physical arrest." In the federal courts, and in less than one-half of the states, this brutal and (as a rule) unnecessary routine has been modified by statutory provisions that in certain situations authorize the issuance of a summons in lieu of arrest. But these modifications are halfhearted; frequently they are limited to cases of minor violations, and most of the relevant provisions leave it to the discretion of the police or the prosecutor whether a summons should take the place of physical arrest.

The civil law countries, on the other hand, unanimously recognize that the initiation of a judicial proceeding, whether civil or criminal, never requires the defendant's physical arrest. It follows, according to civilian thinking, that the necessary notification of the defendant is to be effected by a summons, in criminal as well as civil proceedings, and that it is unthinkable to use physical arrest as a routine measure against a suspect who has not yet been tried and who, consequently, must be presumed innocent.

The question whether a suspect should be detained pending trial is, in the civilians' view, completely separate and distinct from the routine of initiating the proceeding. Such detention is regarded as the exception rather than the rule. Except in carefully defined emergency situations, a judicial order is required to detain the suspect before trial. The requirements for the issuance of such an order are strict. In West Germany, for instance, it can be issued only if the court, by definite findings of fact, determines that the following three elements exist: First, there must be strong reasons for believing that the suspect has committed the crime. Second, the evidence before the court must show a specific, rational ground for pretrial detention, such as danger of flight or danger of tampering with the evidence. Third, such detention must meet the requirement of proportionality; that is, it will not be ordered if the hardship caused by it is disproportionate to the gravity of the offense. The order, which must state the grounds on which each of these requirements is thought to be met, is subject to immediate appeal....

The Prosecutor's and the Defendant's Contribution to the Search for Truth

A. *Discovery*

The first of these two related topics comes under the heading of "discovery." The continental systems invariably provide that at an early stage of the proceedings, and in any event well before the trial, the defendant and his counsel acquire an absolute and unlimited right to inspect the entire dossier, that is, all of the evidence collected by the prosecution and the investigating magistrate. Thus it is simply impossible to obtain a conviction by a strategy of surprise. It must be remembered, moreover, that in most cases there can be a trial de novo on appeal, which, of course, acts as a second barrier against the successful use of surprise evidence.

To facilitate inspection of the dossier by defense counsel, German law provides that upon his request he should normally be allowed to take the dossier to his office or home for thorough and unhurried study....

B. *The Accused as a Source of Information*

The role of the accused as a source of information in the truth-finding process is an important and thorny topic in any system of criminal procedure. It is also the topic concerning which — upon superficial inspection — the gap between common law and civil law appears most unbridgeable.

Closer analysis, however, shows that the rock-bottom principle that is the foundation of all specific rules in this area of the law today is shared by virtually all civilized legal systems: no physical compulsion may be used to make the suspect talk. In this sense, almost all civilized legal systems give the suspect, even before he becomes the defendant, the right to remain silent. The more enlightened legal systems, whether of the common law or the civil law variety, also are in agreement today on the principle that from the very beginning of the investigation the accused is entitled to the assistance of counsel. It follows that when the suspect, at any stage of the proceedings, is called upon to exercise his all-important option — to talk or not to talk — at least the more enlightened legal systems will make it possible for him to be guided by counsel's advice.

Up to this point, I repeat, there is a large measure of agreement among civilized and enlightened legal systems, regardless of whether they belong to the common law or the civil law orbit. Crucial differences, however, come to light when we ask the next question: Which course will counsel advise the defendant to take? Under our system, "any lawyer worth his salt will tell the suspect in no uncertain terms to make no statement to police under any circumstances." Quite often, counsel will keep his client equally silent at the trial; indeed, in the many cases where the client has a criminal record, our rule permitting the prosecution to unearth such record on cross-examination makes it almost impossible for counsel to let the defendant take the stand. In its perverse striving to keep the defendant silent, our law, furthermore, seeks to assure the defendant and his counsel that legal rules can repeal the laws of logic, and that by legal rules the jury can be induced not to draw the natural inferences from defendant's silence....

In thus encouraging the accused to remain silent, our legal system stands virtually alone. In England, defendants rarely opt for silence, because English law differs from ours in two crucial respects. If the accused takes the stand, the English rule is to the effect that he cannot by reason of that alone be cross-examined as to previous convictions. And if he remains silent, the judge is authorized by English law to "suggest to the jury that it draw an adverse inference from the defendant's failure to explain away the evidence against him."

Implementing a similar policy by partly different techniques, the continental systems likewise discourage the accused from standing mute. In many (though not all) of those systems the defendant's silence may serve as corroborating evidence of guilt. Even where, as in West Germany, this traditional rule has been modified, a defendant generally is not well advised to remain silent. At the very outset of the trial, he has to stand in front of the judges, to be questioned by the Presiding Justice of the court. True, he may refuse to answer any questions relating to the charges against him; but he must announce such refusal in open court and cannot simply, as he might under a common law system, remove himself from the questioning process by deciding not to take the stand. Moreover, only in the event of a total refusal by the defendant to answer any questions relating to the charges does German law prohibit the drawing of inferences from his silence. If he answers any of such questions, but then refuses to answer others, the court may draw logical inferences from his refusal. Thus, selective silence is strongly discouraged. Total silence of the defendant (although in theory under the present German rule it does not support adverse inferences) will occur only rarely in a German court because it carries with it a grave disadvantage for the defendant: since there will be no separate hearing regarding the sentence, a totally silent defendant may forfeit the opportunity to present facts tending to mitigate his punishment.[86]

The continental systems, moreover, reject our dysfunctional rule that previous convictions of the defendant can be proved if, but only if, he takes the stand. The rules developed in those systems regarding admissibility of previous convictions are neither simple nor uniform, but they exhibit unanimity on the crucial point: the admissibility of previous convictions *never* hinges on whether or not the defendant testifies. Thus he will never be dissuaded from testifying by the fear that his decision to do so will open the door to evidence of his criminal record.

---

[86] Under German law the questioning of the defendant at the trial is divided into two phases. *See* STPO § 243. The first deals with his personal history and general circumstances, while the second phase centers on the charges against him. His right to remain silent comes into play only when the second phase is reached. It follows that those mitigating facts that relate to defendant's personal history and general circumstances (for example, poverty or lack of education) can always be mentioned by him during the first phase. But mitigating facts connected with the crime itself (for example, that he was only a minor participant; that he tried to persuade his accomplices not to hurt the victim; that he is remorseful) cannot be brought out by his testimony if he decides to remain completely silent during the second phase of the questioning, the phase dealing with the charges against him.

Defendant's right to have the "last word," STPO § 258, furnishes no substitute for such testimony. Section 258 makes it clear that whatever the defendant says by way of his "last word" is not evidence; it is part of the parties' argumentative summing-up, which according to that provision occurs "after the end of the proof-taking phase of the trial."

The disadvantage thus suffered by a silent defendant is further accentuated in those legal systems where a confession in itself would he treated as a mitigating circumstance. *See, e.g.*, Huston, *A Preliminary Survey of the Criminal Procedure in Thailand,* 16 Syracuse L. Rev. 505, 524-25 (1965).

Nor does a defendant who decides to testify before a continental court have to dread that a prosecution for perjury might arise out of such testimony. What he says in his defense is not under oath.

Thus the inducement to speak, and not to stand mute, is very strong in the civil law systems. Experience shows that "almost all continental defendants choose to testify" at the trial. This being so, the accused normally has little to lose and much to gain by presenting his side of the story not only at the trial, but also in the earlier phases of the proceeding. If the accused is innocent, this may lead to an early dismissal of the charges. In any event, the combination of a talking defendant and unlimited discovery will clarify the issues well before trial and make the trial both shorter and more informative — much to the benefit of an innocent defendant.

In cases where the accused is clearly guilty, the same combination of factors will prove equally potent. Through active colloquies between the accused and the investigator, combined with inspection of the dossier, such an accused and his counsel are apt to become persuaded that a denial of guilt simply will not stand up. The usual result is a confession, followed by an attempt to present evidence of mitigating circumstances.

Thus, by combining unlimited discovery for the benefit of the defense with rules making it advantageous for the accused to talk, the continental systems have fashioned a highly efficient vehicle for the ascertainment of truth. If the accused is in fact innocent, unlimited pretrial discovery will give him the best possible chance — a much better chance than he would have under a system of trial by surprise — to meet whatever evidence there may be against him. And if he is guilty, the unavailability of silence as a viable strategy will make his conviction more probable and less time consuming.

NOTES AND QUESTIONS

1. Do you agree that the "natural" evolution of criminal justice systems for a substantial part of Western civilization has been from private vengeance to the accusatorial system and, finally, to the inquisitorial system? Why or why not?

2. Do modern common law and civil law countries today have roughly equivalent mixed accusatorial-inquisitorial systems of criminal procedure? In what ways? In what respects is the U.S. system unusual?

3. Explain the reasoning behind the statement: "If I were innocent, I would prefer to be tried by a civil law court. But if I were guilty, I would prefer to be tried by a common law (U.S.) court." Would one's preference change if one were rich rather than poor?

4. The criminal defendant is questioned and his testimony taken both in the instruction and at the trial. He is not placed under oath, however, and he may refuse to answer questions, although his refusal to answer will be taken into account by the judges. Is this procedure fair, when compared to the criminal defendant's privilege not to take the stand in the United States? Does the fact that the defendant will have seen the full dossier before he is questioned at the public trial affect your opinion on this question? Recall that the defendant is questioned first, before other evidence is adduced at the trial. Does that affect your opinion? *See* Mirjan Damaška, *Evidentiary Barriers to Conviction and Two Models of Criminal Procedure: A Comparative Study,* 121 U. Pa. L. Rev. 506, 526-30 (1973); *United States v. Grunewald,* 233 F.2d 556 (appendix to dissenting opinion of Jerome Frank, 587-92) (2d Cir. 1956).

5. Coaching of witnesses (who are sworn) in either civil or criminal proceedings is unethical conduct in the civil law and may expose the attorney to criminal penalties. How significant is this difference?

6. In civil law nations appeals from the decision at the criminal trial can be taken by the prosecution. The rule in the United States is *contra* under decisions based on the double jeopardy clause of the U.S. Constitution. Professor Damaška relates this difference to the nature of appeal in the civil law world, where one has a right (constitutionally protected in some nations) to review of the facts, law, judgment, and sentence. This makes the appeal, in his words, "part and parcel of one single proceeding." Thus original jeopardy continues, and appeal by the prosecutor does not constitute double jeopardy. Mirjan Damaška, *Structures of Authority and Comparative Criminal Procedure,* 84 Yale L.J. 480, 491 (1975). Is this suggestion convincing? Which rule promotes a truth-finding policy? Which is the preferable rule?

7. There is a large literature on civil law criminal procedure, much of it directed toward reform of inadequacies in the American system. In addition to materials already cited or referred to later dealing primarily with a single jurisdiction or a special topic, see George F. Cole et al., eds., Major Criminal Justice Systems: A Comparative Survey (2d ed. 1987); Mirjan R. Damaška, The Faces of Justice and State Authority: A Comparative Approach to the Legal Process (1986); Gordon Van Kessel, *Adversary Excesses in the American Criminal Trial,* 67 Notre Dame L. Rev. 403 (1992); Thomas Volkmann-Schluck, *Continental European Criminal Procedures: True or Illusive Model?,* 9 Am. J. Crim. L. 1 (1981); Thomas Weigend, *Continental Cures for American Ailments: European Criminal Procedure as a Model for Law Reform,* 2 Crime and Justice: An Annual Review of Research 381 (1980).

NOTE ON THE JOINDER OF A CIVIL PLAINTIFF

France is like most civil law nations in permitting a civil plaintiff to join in the criminal proceeding. Germany is an exception, since its joinder procedure (*Adhäsionsverfahren*) has fallen into disuse. The civil party, ordinarily the victim, will be represented by his own lawyer, but the main burden of the proceeding will fall on the public prosecutor. If the defendant's guilt is established by the prosecution, the civil party need only prove causation and damages. The court deals with guilt and liability and sentence and remedy in the same action. As in France, the victim in many civil law nations has the power to institute the penal proceeding, thus compelling the public prosecutor who might otherwise not have pursued the matter to prosecute. One reason why the civil plaintiff might wish to compel prosecution is that in some jurisdictions "moral damages" (i.e., damages for pain and suffering) are awarded only if the defendant's act constituted a crime. Another obvious reason is that the state, rather than the plaintiff, undertakes the burden of proving commission of the illegal act. A further important consideration is that in civil law nations most cases of negligent infliction of injury (including automobile accident cases) are treated as crimes. Civil parties of course are not required to join in penal actions, and many do not, preferring for a variety of reasons to bring their own separate civil actions.

Consider the following excerpt:

> In describing the victim's role in presenting civil claims in the criminal process, two terms are commonly used. The victim who raises the civil claims may be termed a *partie civile* or the proceedings may be designated "adhesive." The former term has traditionally been used in Belgium, Italy, and France and the latter term in those jurisdictions with a German legal tradition. However, both descriptions reflect the same phenomenon. In each case, the main proceeding is criminal and the victim is allowed to present his civil claim at the discretion of the court. In both types of jurisdictions, the court may decide the criminal and civil issues simultaneously or may divert the civil claim to a separate civil proceeding.
>
> In all jurisdictions in which civil claims are considered in the criminal process, the civil claims must be based on the criminal act with which the defendant is charged. In most jurisdictions, the civil action may include all physical and emotional damages flowing from the criminal act. The civil action must generally be for damages in the form of monetary compensation or restitution of property. For example, in jurisdictions in which adultery is an offence, an action for divorce will generally not be considered ancillary to the criminal prosecution.
>
> Several arguments can be made in favor of permitting the presentation of civil claims in the criminal process. Presenting all claims in one proceeding is judicially and administratively economic and assures that the penal and civil decisions will be consistent. For the victim, the use of the criminal process is frequently quicker, simpler, and cheaper than a civil proceeding. The prosecutor proves the guilt of the offender, thereby relieving the victim of the obligation. In some jurisdictions, the prosecutor may also present the civil claim. Furthermore, some important criminal investigatory means are not permitted in civil actions. A general criminal policy that considers civil liability together with criminal liability also promotes a preventive philosophy that crime does not pay. This philosophy is enhanced by publicly demonstrating that the offender is liable to both the victim and the state for the crime.

Matti Joutsen, *Listening to the Victim: The Victim's Role in European Criminal Justice Systems,* 34 Wayne L. Rev. 95, 115-16 (1987).

Would such a system work in the United States? See Patrick Campbell, A Comparative Study of Victim Compensation Procedures in France and the United States: A Modest Proposal, 3 Hastings Int'l & Comp. L. Rev. 321 (1980); J.A. Jolowicz, Procedural Questions 4-15, in Torts, 11 Int'l Ency. Comp. L. chap. 13 (André Tunc ed. 1972).

3. FRANCE: THE INVESTIGATION OF OFFENSES

EDWARD A. TOMLINSON, THE SAGA OF WIRETAPPING IN FRANCE: WHAT IT TELLS US ABOUT THE FRENCH CRIMINAL JUSTICE SYSTEM, 53 Louisiana Law Review 1091, 1103-09 (1993)

The French are no more satisfied with their criminal justice system than Americans are with theirs. High on the list of complaints are the slowness and complexity of the process, problems which are no doubt aggravated by the limited (and often decrepit) means at the system's disposal. Another frequent complaint is that the system is too politicized and the judges are not sufficiently independent. These familiar themes reappear in the report recently submitted by the prestigious Delmas-Marty Commission to the Minister of Justice.[44] That report, however, focused on a quite different complaint about the system: the inadequate protection afforded individual liberty....

To understand the scope and allocation of investigatory powers under French law, it is first necessary to know a bit of history. Modern history in France begins with the Revolution of 1789 and Napoleon, and it was before the latter's Council of State in 1808 that drafters of the original Code of Criminal Procedure (then called the Code of Criminal Investigation or *Code d'instruction criminelle*) adopted the basic principle of separating the prosecution of an offense from its investigation. The new Code thus assigned to the imperial prosecutor the authority to initiate a prosecution — normally by requesting the opening of a judicial investigation, or *instruction préparatoire*, of facts believed to constitute an offense; but it entrusted to a judge (or judges) the actual gathering of proofs and the determination of their sufficiency to put a named defendant on trial. Thus was born the examining magistrate, or *juge d'instruction*, soon dubbed by Balzac the most powerful man in France. The magistrate's investigation, triggered by a prosecutor's petition charging named persons or, more likely, persons unknown, was to be secret, written and nonadversarial — a purely inquisitorial process which did not recognize suspects as having any rights.

Today, the examining magistrate's investigatory authority remains quite broad, but the judicial investigation is no longer purely inquisitorial due to the recognition of certain rights of the defense. The rights of the defense derive primarily from an 1897 statutory reform which drew a distinction between ordinary witnesses and an accused. As presently codified, these provisions require the magistrate to notify formally an accused of his right to counsel and to grant that counsel access to the investigatory file at least forty-eight hours before an interrogation. The interrogation then takes place in counsel's presence. The term "accused" has a functional definition covering all "persons against whom there exist grave and concordant indications of guilt." Once suspicion of guilt so focuses on an individual, the magistrate must for-

---

[44] The Committee's official name is *La Commission justice pénale et droits de l'homme* (The Commission on Criminal Justice and the Rights of Man). Its chair, from whom it takes its name, is a well-known law professor named Mireille Delmas-Marty. The Minister of Justice, Pierre Arpaillange, appointed the Committee in 1988, and it submitted its final report in June 1990. Commission justice pénale et droits de l'homme, La mise en état des affaires pénales 1991 [hereinafter La Mise en état]. That report focuses on the pretrial phase (*la mise en état*) of criminal cases. In France, the pretrial phase is considerably more important than it is here.

mally accuse that person and may no longer interrogate the person incommunicado without recognizing any right to counsel, as magistrates may do in the case of other witnesses summoned by them to their chambers.

Under the present Code, the magistrate's investigatory authority broadly includes "all acts of investigation he deems useful to the manifestation of the truth." In particular, the Code authorizes the magistrate to search for and seize evidence (articles 92 to 97), to summon and question witnesses (articles 101 to 113), to interrogate and confront with witnesses the accused, subject to the rights of the defense (articles 114 to 121), to detain an accused pending trial (articles 137 to 150), and to designate experts for the resolution of technical questions (articles 156 to 169-1). The magistrate's discretion to designate experts and summon witnesses is total. More surprisingly, the magistrate's authority is similar with respect to searches and seizures because there are no probable cause or particularity requirements limiting the scope of the magistrate's search or what may be seized.[53]

In addition, the magistrate need not perform these investigatory acts personally but, except for interrogating an accused or confronting an accused with witnesses, may delegate them to the police by issuing a rogatory commission (articles 151 to 154). The commission must designate the offenses which the police are to investigate, but may leave to their discretion what investigatory acts to perform, i.e., what places to search or what proofs to seize. Such a general rogatory commission, authorizing the police[55] to investigate in any fashion they wish a designated offense or offenses, gives them the same broad discretionary powers enjoyed by the examining magistrate. However, the rights of the defense apply to protect an "accused," and the term "accused" has the same functional definition to bar the police from interrogating any person (and not just one formally accused) against whom there exist "grave and concordant indications of guilt."[57] Needless to say, this focus test is often the subject of manipulation by police officers who simply close their eyes to evidence which incriminates the person whom they wish to interrogate.

The justification advanced in 1808 for separating prosecuting from investigating was the fear of executive authority. Those functions had melded considerably during the revolutionary period. There was much sentiment, provoked by recent bad experiences with demagogic prosecutors and with the popular juries introduced by the revolutionaries, for a return to Louis XIV's Ordinance of 1670, which had recognized the predominant role of professional judges. Ironically, the chief spokesperson for this point of view was the Archchancellor Cambacérès, a former member of the Convention who had voted for the death of Louis XVI in 1793 but who was then happily ensconced as Napoleon's right-hand man charged with administering on a daily basis the affairs of the Empire. According to Cambacérès, if the imperial procurator was able to investigate offenses, he "would be a little tyrant who would make

[53] Special regulations apply to dwelling searches — sometimes referred to in France as the "common law" (*droit commun*) of search and seizure — but these provisions only restrict nighttime searches and mandate the presence during the search of homeowners or other observers. Proc. Code arts. 57, 59, and 95.

[55] Police here means judicial police.

[57] Proc. Code art. 104.

the city tremble.... All the citizens would shudder if they saw in the same official the power of accusing them and that of bringing together proofs that might justify his accusation." Later, Cambacérès asked rhetorically: "Who would not shudder to see a single official, invested with such inquisitorial power, invade his home?"

This distrust of prosecutors, or at least of prosecutors with too much power, explains the origins of the judicial investigation. This distrust motivated the drafters of the 1808 Code even though French prosecutors were then (and still are) judicial officers of sorts, called *magistrats debout* (standing judges) to distinguish them from the *magistrats du siège* (sitting judges) who do not stand when they speak in court. The judicial label attached to prosecutors may confer a certain dignity on the office, but it does not confer independence because French prosecutors remain hierarchically subordinate to their superiors, up to and including the politically appointed Minister of Justice.

Conferring on examining magistrates a monopoly of investigatory powers proved to be an unworkable idea. The drafters themselves recognized that the urgency of certain situations might justify the gathering of proof by prosecutors or by members of the judicial police acting under their supervision.[62] According to Cambacérès, there was no "disadvantage" to the imperial procurator gathering the proofs if there were "a capture in the act" of the offender. This criterion of flagrance, of capturing an offender red-handed, justified in his opinion an immediate reaction, but the 1808 Code explicitly authorized the judicial police to investigate, prior to the opening of a judicial investigation, only for offenses that were infamous ones.

This police authority to investigate flagrant offenses has gradually expanded over time; the 1958 Code explicitly extends it — under the rubric of *enquête de flagrance* — to cover all but the least serious category of offenses, the equivalent of petty misdemeanors in America. During the investigation of a flagrant offense, an officer of the judicial police may seize any means, instrumentalities, or evidentiary items found at the scene of the offense (article 54), detain persons found there until fully securing the site (article 61), search dwellings and other places for evidence (articles 56-59), seize any papers or other incriminating evidence found (article 56), question any person (article 62), and detain persons for up to twenty-four hours, renewable for an additional twenty-four hours by the prosecutor (article 63 — the notorious *garde à vue*). As in the case of the examining magistrate, the judicial police have total discretion as to whom to question, where to search, and what to seize. In particular, the only standard restricting their detention power (the *garde à vue*) is "the exigency of the inquiry."[65] The rights of the defense do not apply, and they may even question as a witness (i.e., incommunicado and without counsel) a person against whom there exists grave and concordant indications of guilt.

[62] Traditionally, French prosecutors have been more directly involved in the work of the police than have their American counterparts, but the Delmas-Marty Commission found wanting the supervision actually exercised today.... That supervision primarily affects those police officers formally recognized as having "judicial" or law enforcement responsibilities, i.e., officers of the judicial police.

[65] Proc. Code art. 63.

The time span during which the judicial police may exercise these coercive powers, supposedly limited by the criterion of urgency, has received a liberal interpretation. The police may open an investigation of a flagrant offense not only if they catch an offender red-handed, but also if they discover an offense within several hours after its commission. More importantly, the investigation may continue indefinitely; termination does not occur with the passage of any particular period of time but only when there has been a "notable break" in the investigatory process or when the prosecutor requests an examining magistrate to investigate.[67] Plainly, urgency is no longer the justifying criterion for this variety of police investigation. What justifies police action is the discovery of external signs of a recent offense. Such an offense is "flagrant" in the sense of "glaringly evident."[68] What the police discover in plain view thus normally authorizes them to initiate their own investigation.

The drafters of the 1808 Code, in addition to recognizing the need for the nonjudicial investigation of flagrant offenses, also recognized that some offenses might not need to be investigated at all, or at least not need to be the subject of a protracted judicial investigation. The Code therefore gave the prosecutor, except for the most serious offenses, the authority to charge defendants directly before the trial courts. The exercise of this power has always caused knotty problems in France. It is uniformly accepted that not all offenses require the formality of a judicial investigation. Often the facts are either clear and not readily disputable, or so simple and straightforward as not to warrant the delay of an intermediate investigatory phase between the prosecutor's initial charging decision and trial. But in those cases, who was to perform whatever limited investigation was necessary and how could the system assure the defendant's presence at trial, since only an examining magistrate had the authority under the Code to order a person's arrest or pretrial detention?

On the latter question, the French have tried a great variety of solutions; the most recent one, found in 1983 amendments to the Code, permits prosecutors to bring defendants charged by them promptly before the trial court (*la comparution immédiate*) and authorizes, for the first time, trial judges to detain defendants pending trial if an immediate trial is not possible and if some form of pretrial detention is appropriate. On the former question, the police responded by informally investigating offenses even though they did not satisfy the criterion of flagrancy. This practice found no explicit support in the 1808 Code, which had separated the prosecution from the investigation of offenses, but the evident necessity of some mechanism by which prosecutors could inform themselves to determine whether to bring charges before either a trial court or an examining magistrate encouraged its development as an "extralegal" practice, i.e., one neither authorized nor explicitly condemned by the Code. These advantages convinced the French Parliament to legitimatize the preliminary police investigation (now called the *enquête préliminaire*) in the 1958 Code of Criminal Procedure. This infringement on the separation

[67] The opening of a judicial investigation automatically terminates any police investigation and subjects the judicial police to the examining magistrate's control. Proc. Code. art. 14(2).

[68] This justification for the police investigation of flagrant offenses has been advanced, but found wanting, by the Delmas-Marty Commission.

principle was justified in part by the absence of coercive powers given the police during a preliminary investigation. But this justification suffered one striking exception: Article 78 of the new Code gave officers of the judicial police conducting a preliminary investigation the same authority to detain persons (the *garde à vue*) previously authorized only for the investigation of flagrant offenses....

The above described infringements on the examining magistrate's former near monopoly of investigatory powers have certainly contributed to a decline in that figure's importance. But one should not exaggerate the decline. There remain six hundred examining magistrates in France who conduct approximately 70,000 judicial investigations annually. The latter figure has remained relatively constant over recent decades, but there is little question that the percentage of criminal prosecutions that include a judicial investigation has dropped sharply, perhaps as sharply as from twenty to ten percent of all prosecuted cases, according to the Delmas-Marty Commission.[75] Those statistics, however, only tell part of the story because those offenses which are the subject of a judicial investigation are the most serious ones (homicides, armed robberies, etc.) or the most difficult ones to investigate (white collar offenses and cases of political corruption). The examining magistrate therefore still plays an important role in the French criminal justice system.

NOTES AND QUESTIONS

1. Have the French reached a better balance between the public's interest in investigating crime and the individual's right to privacy than that found in the United States? Which aspects of the French system might serve to improve the American system of criminal justice and which aspects should be rejected?

Professor Richard Frase argues that American police powers are in practice almost as broad as those enjoyed by French investigating authorities. U.S. constitutional rights seldom apply or are easily avoided by the police so that the exclusionary remedy is rarely granted. Studies show that prosecutors decline to prosecute for constitutional reasons in fewer than one percent of their cases in the federal system and from one to nine percent of their cases in state systems. Motions to suppress physical evidence, identifications, or confessions occur in five to seven percent of state cases (depending on the category), are granted in one-tenth to seven-tenths of one percent of all cases, and result in no conviction in about half of the motions granted. Richard S. Frase, *Comparative Criminal Justice as a Guide to American Law Reform: How Do the French Do It, How Can We Find Out, and Why Should We Care?*, 78 Cal. L. Rev. 539, 573-94 (1990).

2. Another study shows that the *juge d'instruction* is involved in only eight percent of French criminal cases. The investigation is normally conducted by young, inexperienced judges fresh out of the *École nationale de la magistrature* and on the average adds nine months to the duration of a crimi-

[75] In the 1830s, by contrast, nearly one-half of all criminal cases were the subject of a judicial investigation.

nal process. *See* Basil S. Markesinis, *The Destructive and Constructive Role of the Comparative Lawyer,* 57 Rabels Zeitschrift 438, 442 (1993).

3. French investigatory detention (*garde à vue*) permits officers of the judicial police (OJPs) to seize, detain, and interrogate suspects for up to 24 hours (extended to 48 hours with a prosecutor's approval) without probable cause, judicial approval, or a mandatory court appearance. French citizens, watching American criminal shows on TV, recently have complained to judges, much to their chagrin, that during the *garde à vue* they were not read or permitted their *Miranda* rights.

4. French criminal procedure has been widely influential throughout the civil law world, including Germany. France's most recent (1958) Code of Criminal Procedure and subsequent amendments retain the basic pattern established in the original Code of 1808. For a translation of the 1958 Code, see Gerald L. Kock & Richard S. Frase, trans., The French Code of Criminal Procedure (rev. ed. 1988), which also contains Professor Frase's lucid 40-page summary of French criminal procedure.

5. For an extensive evaluative comparison of French and American criminal procedure, see Frase's 140 page article cited in note 1. An earlier proposal for reform of American criminal procedure along French lines is Lloyd L. Weinreb, Denial of Justice (1977). *See also* Joseph J. Darby, *Lessons of Comparative Criminal Procedure: France and the United States,* 19 San Diego L. Rev. 277 (1982); Barton L. Ingraham, The Structure of Criminal Procedure: Laws and Practice of France, the Soviet Union, China, and the United States (1987); Edward A. Tomlinson, *Nonadversarial Justice: The French Experience,* 42 Md. L. Rev. 131 (1983).

6. For an extraordinary criminal process and trial, *France v. Klaus Barbie,* which raised myriad issues under French criminal procedure (e.g., validity of arrest, double jeopardy, statute of limitations, joinder of civil parties) as well as under European human rights law and customary international law, see Guyora Binder, *Representing Nazism: Advocacy and Identity at the Trial of Klaus Barbie,* 98 Yale L.J. 1321 (1989); Nicholas R. Doman, *Aftermath of Nuremberg: The Trial of Klaus Barbie,* 60 U. Colo. L. Rev. 449 (1989).

NOTE ON THE GUILTY PLEA, PROSECUTORIAL DISCRETION, AND PLEA BARGAINING

Until the late 1970s it was still possible to state with some confidence that, although defendants might and often did confess and their confessions were taken into account by the court, there was no true equivalent of the guilty plea in criminal proceedings in the civil law world. Guilt, it was said, is for the court, not the defendant, to decide. Thus, even though the defendant might wish to plead guilty and avoid the inconvenience and exposure of a trial, the trial had to take place. Coupled with the absence of the guilty plea was an alleged absence of prosecutorial and judicial discretion in prosecuting, charging, and sentencing. The prosecutor was required to prosecute whenever the evidence so indicated (the "rule of compulsory prosecution," a rule indirectly supported by the victim's right to require initiation of the prosecution if the public prosecutor failed to act on his own) and, unlike American prosecutors, had no discretion to drop a prosecution once begun. The charge had to be the maximum permitted by the facts and, in the event of a guilty verdict, the sentence should equate with that charge. All of these conclusions followed from the "principle of legality": that public officials are bound by the law (i.e., statutes and other sources of law) and can vary from the law only when expressly granted discretion to do so by the lawmaker. This "principled" view of criminal procedure was advanced for Germany in John H. Langbein, *Controlling Prosecutorial Discretion in Germany,* 41 U. Chi. L. Rev. 439 (1974); see Joachim Herrmann, *The Rule of Compulsory Prosecution and the Scope of Prosecutorial Discretion in Germany,* 41 U. Chi. L. Rev. 468 (1974).

Since the guilty plea, prosecutorial discretion, and judicial compliance are necessary components of the familiar American practice of plea bargaining, civil lawyers and American comparatists commonly concluded that there was no plea bargaining in the civil law world. And since plea bargaining seems to many Americans to raise serious right-to-trial and due process questions, it was easy to conclude that, in this respect, the civil law model of criminal procedure was superior to ours. One scholar compared our plea bargaining system to the use of torture to produce confessions in medieval European criminal proceedings. John H. Langbein, *Torture and Plea Bargaining,* 46 U. Chi. L. Rev. 3 (1978).

Some Americans, however, wondered how civil law prosecutors and judges could cope with the flow of criminal litigation typical of most modern Western nations. Plea bargaining is institutionalized in the United States; it is the process by which the vast majority of criminal proceedings (estimates run from 90 percent to 99 percent, depending on the jurisdiction) are terminated, a way of disposing of criminal cases without the time, trouble and expense of trial. *See* Albert W. Alschuler, *The Changing Plea Bargaining Debate,* 69 Cal. L. Rev. 652 (1981). American judges, prosecutors, and police generally believe that without plea bargaining our criminal justice system would be swamped. There has accordingly been intense interest in the question whether civil law systems can really function without some form of covert, if not overt, plea bargaining. If they do not plea bargain, how do they deal with the tide of criminal prosecution?

That was the central question in Abraham S. Goldstein & Martin Marcus, *The Myth of Judicial Supervision in Three "Inquisitorial" Systems: France, Italy, and Germany,* 87 Yale L.J. 240 (1977). After interviewing prosecutors, judges, defense lawyers, and professors in the three nations, the authors claimed to have identified a variety of ways in which criminal proceedings in the three nations varied from the theoretical model. On the centrally important question of prosecutorial discretion they stated (at 280):

> Claims that prosecutorial discretion has been eliminated, or is supervised closely, are exaggerated. Discretion is exercised in each of the systems for reasons similar to those supporting it in the United States. However much Continental writers describe their criminal statutes as narrowly drawn, the codes are sufficiently general to make it necessary for prosecutors to interpret fact and law.... Decisions must be made, and when the Code — or the prevailing ideology — prevents them from being

made openly, each system finds ways to mask them.... The principle of compulsory prosecution, which formally permeates the German and Italian systems, and informally the French, demands the impossible: full enforcement of the law in a time of rising crime and fierce competition for resources.

There was a spirited response by John H. Langbein & Lloyd L. Weinreb, *Continental Criminal Procedure: "Myth" and Reality,* 87 Yale L.J. 1549 (1978), to which Goldstein and Marcus replied in *Comment on Continental Criminal Procedure,* 87 Yale L.J. 1570 (1978). Then, in 1979, Langbein went on the offensive with *Land Without Plea Bargaining: How the Germans Do It,* 78 Mich. L. Rev. 204 (1979) (observe that France and Italy are no longer involved: the debate now centers on Germany, which comparatists considered to adhere most closely, in practice, to the principled model of criminal procedure). This may have been the last serious attempt by a comparative scholar to convince Americans that the principled model worked to prevent plea bargaining, even in Germany.

4. GERMANY: BARGAINING JUSTICE

NOTE

Meanwhile, in Germany and elsewhere in the civil law world, a change was quietly but rapidly taking place: there was a growing tendency to notice that criminal justice practice covertly diverged in significant particulars from the principled model, and there were many who argued that some form of open, officially sanctioned plea bargaining, properly supervised and controlled, was preferable to the existing informal, covert, and unsupervised practice. Consider the following excerpt by a prominent German law professor.

JOACHIM HERRMANN, BARGAINING JUSTICE — A BARGAIN FOR GERMAN CRIMINAL JUSTICE?, 53 University of Pittsburgh Law Review 755-65, 767-69 (1992)

Introduction

The administration of criminal justice in Germany has undergone dramatic changes in recent years. Bargaining over charges and sentences and settling cases have become common practice, even though they previously were considered repugnant to the principles and tradition of German criminal justice.

German-type bargaining does not fully conform to plea bargaining in the United States, since there is no equivalent to the guilty plea in German criminal procedure. Nonetheless, the new German practice displays interesting similarities with American plea bargaining. It operates to avoid or mitigate the potentially harsh sanctions of the criminal law. Like American plea bargaining, it is mainly a consequence of the over-burdened criminal justice system....

The origin of bargaining in the German criminal justice system can be traced back to the early 1970s. At first, it was practiced on a relatively small scale and was restricted to exceptional cases, mainly involving petty crimes. Because it lacked legal foundation, however, it was not discussed in public.

Over time, bargaining became more and more common, even in serious cases. As it became widely accepted in the early 1980s, German practitioners felt justified in revealing its existence. As could be expected, this has given rise to much criticism and heated controversy in German legal publications and in the media.

Today, bargaining is practiced in Germany on a large scale. Estimates indicate that some kind of bargaining takes place in roughly twenty to thirty percent of all cases....

Major Instances and Features of Bargaining

In German practice, the type of case determines the likelihood that bargaining will occur. In large and complex cases involving white-collar crimes, tax evasion, drug offenses and crimes against the environment, bargaining seems to have become almost inevitable when there are difficult evidentiary or legal problems. Likewise, bargaining occurs in cases of less serious crimes, which are processed summarily with imposition of only a fine or no criminal sanction at all. Bargaining is the exception in cases involving violent and other very serious crimes.

Since bargaining and settlement of cases has been developed by German practitioners, there are no legal provisions to structure or to restrict their activities. Some informal rules of practice have been established, however, which are quite different from the rules governing American plea bargaining. In Germany, negotiations are conducted at all stages of the proceedings: during pretrial stages, at trial, and even during appeal if there is a trial *de novo*. In addition to the prosecutor and defense counsel, the judge may actively participate in the negotiations. In fact, it will surprise the American observer that negotiations may occur with only the judge and defense counsel present. It may actually be the judge who takes the initiative by intimating to defense counsel that he would be ready for some kind of bargaining.

The parties who engage in negotiations generally do not attempt to reach a definite agreement. They generally limit themselves to pointing out what their preferences are. Thus, a judge would never state exactly what sentence the accused could expect in exchange for a confession. He instead would indicate an upper limit beyond which he would not go. This practice of leaving decisive questions open requires mutual trust and a good working relationship among participants in the negotiations.

Bargaining is ordinarily kept confidential; the accused almost never participates. It is generally accepted, however, that defense counsel should have the accused's general consent before he engages in negotiations. Defense counsel is also required to inform his client about what the other side has offered.

In German criminal practice, there are three main types of bargaining.

A. *Bargaining as to Petty — and Not so Petty — Crimes*

One common form of bargaining has developed as a consequence of the prosecutor's power not to prosecute even though there would be sufficient evidence to press a charge. Section 153a, which was added in 1975 to the German Code of Criminal Procedure, authorizes the prosecutor, in misdemeanor cases, to offer to terminate proceedings on the condition that the accused, for example, agrees to pay a sum of money to a charitable organization or to the state. After the accused has complied with such a condition, the case against him will be closed.

Because German misdemeanors include a number of crimes that would be considered felonies under American law, such as larceny, embezzlement, fraud, most drug offenses and most crimes against the environment, section 153a seems to provide the German prosecutor with quite broad discretionary power. However, section 153a explicitly limits the prosecutor's discretion: he is authorized to end proceedings only in cases where the offender's guilt is minor and where the public interest does not require a trial and a criminal conviction. In addition, when section 153a was enacted, there was general agreement that the idea of compulsory prosecution — one of the overriding principles of German criminal justice administration — should operate to restrain the exercise of the prosecutor's new powers. It was assumed that the new provision might give rise to some kind of bargaining between the prosecutor and defense counsel as to the conditions under which a case could be dropped. There was no doubt, however, that bargaining would remain the exception and that it would be strictly limited to trivial cases.

This expectation has turned out to be wrong. It did not take long before prosecutors and defense counsel began to use section 153a as a ground for large-scale bargaining. The requirement of minor guilt was not taken seriously. Upon the defense counsel's suggestion, prosecutors have, for example, dropped white-collar crime cases involving up to 100,000 German Marks after the accused paid a great sum of money to a charitable organization or to the state. Had the accused in such cases decided to go to trial, he would most likely have been fined, since fines are the common sanction in Germany.[14] By accepting the settlement, the accused could avoid the emotional burden and publicity of a trial, as well as the negative effect of having a criminal record.

According to section 153a the prosecutor can often terminate a case only with the judge's consent. This requirement, however, does not serve to restrict the prosecutor's discretion since in practice the judge consents as a matter of course....

According to section 153a, proceedings may not be terminated if a felony is involved. Even this barrier has not remained inviolate. In cases where the offender's guilt is obviously minor, prosecutors and defense counsel have agreed that a misdemeanor charge be substituted for a felony charge. For example, a charge for attempted manslaughter has been downgraded to a charge of committing dangerous bodily harm, which is a misdemeanor under German law. In another case, the accused was charged with assisting in perjury, a felony under German law. The judge, prosecutor, and defense counsel met during a break in the trial and agreed that a felony sentence would be too harsh. They concluded that the defendant had perhaps intended to render assistance only to an unsworn false statement — a misdemeanor under Ger-

[14] Fines are imposed in more than 80 percent of all criminal convictions.

man law. With the help of this maneuver, the case was then prepared for settlement.

B. *Bargaining and Penal Orders*

A second common form of bargaining has originated from the German penal order procedure. This is an entirely written, summary procedure designed to handle the great bulk of routine misdemeanor cases where there is sufficient evidence of the accused's guilt and where he is expected not to object. In such cases, the prosecutor may apply to the judge for a penal order rather than moving for a trial. The prosecutor prepares a draft of the penal order which states the details of the case and which requests a specific fine. No sanction other than a fine, or in traffic cases, suspension of a driver's license, may be imposed by a penal order. The prosecutor's draft is, together with the official file of the case, submitted to the judge who routinely signs it without examining the merits of the case. The penal order is then sent to the accused by registered mail.

To the accused, the penal order is an offer to pay the fine and, thereby, admit his guilt. To that extent the penal order may be compared to the guilty plea or, rather, to a plea of *nolo contendere* in American criminal procedure. By paying the fine, the accused avoids the embarrassment, publicity, and costs of a trial. To the prosecutor and the judge, the penal order is an efficient means of docket control.

These mutual interests have given rise to a great variety of negotiations between defense counsel and prosecutor. In a considerable number of cases, defense counsel with a client ready to admit his guilt contacts the prosecutor and offers that the accused would be willing to accept a penal order as long as the fine does not exceed certain limits. Fines in Germany may be rather high; they depend on the accused's income and may go up to 360,000 German Marks for each individual crime. As a consequence, fines have become the common sanction even for serious misdemeanors. One can easily imagine that this leaves defense counsel and prosecutor with much freedom to bargain....

An accused who rejects a penal order and is subsequently convicted at trial runs the risk of being punished more harshly than was suggested by the penal order. He might even be sentenced to a prison term. A higher sentence at trial is, however, not an automatic consequence of the rejection of a penal order. It is also considered advisable that judges give reasons for any increased sentence in the written judgment. These reasons may be subject to review by an appellate court....

C. *Bargaining Over Confessions*

A third type of bargaining is centered around the accused's confession. Since there is no guilty plea in German criminal procedure, bargaining over confessions plays a decisive role. Unlike a guilty plea, a confession does not replace a trial but rather causes a shorter trial. At a German trial, the accused is examined by the judge before the witnesses are heard and the other evidence is taken. Whenever the accused confesses in the course of this examination, the judge will take only some of the evidence to make sure there is a sufficient factual basis for the confession....

When bargaining over a confession, German defense counsel ordinarily has a better position than his American counterpart engaging in plea bargaining. German defense counsel has a right prior to the trial to inspect and copy the official file. Thus, defense counsel can inform his client about the evidence the prosecutor has amassed. Since defense counsel and the accused know what the accused will have to expect if he does not make a confession, bargaining is a game the other side has to play with open cards.

As long as the prosecutor has not brought a formal charge, negotiations regarding a confession are conducted between defense counsel and the prosecutor. The outcome of such negotiations is usually the promise of a confession in exchange for the prosecutor's offer to limit the charge to one of the several offenses the accused has allegedly committed. The prosecutor may also offer to move at the trial for a lenient sentence. Unlike American procedure, the German trial combines the two phases of guilt determination and sentencing.

There may also be an opportunity for bargaining after the prosecutor has proffered the formal charge and while the judge is preparing the trial. At this stage it is mainly defense counsel and the judge who engage in negotiations. If a judge finds out that a trial is likely to take a long time, or if he is under time pressure because of a backlog on his docket, he may contact defense counsel and inquire whether there may be a chance the accused will make a confession at the beginning of the trial. Defense counsel will then ask what sentence his client could expect if a confession is offered. The judge may indicate an upper limit but, as has already been pointed out, no definite settlement will be worked out. If the accused agrees with the outcome of the bargaining, he will make a confession, the sentence will most likely be below the indicated upper limit, and the trial will be finished within a few hours rather than taking days or weeks.

Often, there is bargaining during trial as well. In a large and complex case, the accused may, for technical reasons, decide not to make a confession when he is examined at the beginning of the trial. He may rather contest the charge and see how the evidence develops. Time will be ripe for bargaining only after the trial has been dragging on for a while. In such situations, the first step is often taken by the judge during a break in the trial. The judge typically will talk about the possibility of a sentencing concession or will offer the dismissal of one of several charges in exchange for a confession. Defense counsel may promise to withdraw his motions to take additional evidence or agree not to bring motions previously announced, or promise not to bring an appeal. In this kind of bargaining the prosecutor usually plays only a limited role...

Legality and Constitutionality of Bargaining

In 1987 [the Federal Constitutional Court] had to decide whether or not to admit a constitutional complaint invoked by someone convicted after a settlement.[50] The chamber found that the complaint asking that the conviction be overturned was without merit. The chamber held that bargaining and settle-

[50] Judgment of Jan. 27, 1987 which was published in 1987 Neue Zeitschrift für Strafrecht 419.

ments are not unconstitutional as long as they comply with the requirements of a fair trial and the main principles governing German criminal procedure. These principles have a constitutional dimension since they are considered to be included in the German constitutional concept of *Rechtsstaat*, which may be compared to due process in American law.

The principles the chamber of the Constitutional Court referred to were compulsory prosecution, the duty of the judge at the trial to conduct his own investigation in order to ascertain the facts of the case, and the requirement that the level of punishment correspond to the accused's guilt. One could add to that list the presumption of innocence, the principle that the accused is entitled to a public trial, and the principles of orality and immediacy, which require that a conviction be based not on the evidence contained in the official file but rather solely on the testimony of the witnesses and other evidence taken at the trial....

The chamber of the Constitutional Court further emphasized that negotiations leading to a settlement should never replace the court's independent decision as to guilt and punishment. Since no judge would ever admit that he felt bound by an agreement, this holding provides little guidance.

The principles and criteria the chamber of the Constitutional Court listed in deciding the constitutionality of bargaining have turned out to be rather vague and susceptible to differing interpretations. This provides an opportunity for developing the law of criminal procedure and adapting it to the changes that can be witnessed in German practice.

GERMANY v. D and Y

Federal Supreme Court of Germany
Judgment of 30 October 1991
45 NJW 519 (1992)

Facts

In June 1987 the defendant Y promised his compatriot D upon his request to deliver 25 grams of heroin for 5,000 German marks. Shortly thereafter he delivered 21 grams of ten percent purity based on D's promise to pay him later.

The district court sentenced the defendant Y, on account of his illegal commerce with restricted narcotics, to an individual punishment of seven years and to an aggregate punishment of seven years and nine months, but on other charges acquitted him. The court acquitted the defendant D on charges of illegal commerce with restricted narcotics, but sentenced him to an aggregate punishment of five years and four months for violation of the weapons law. In addition, it seized the narcotics, a weapon and ammunition, as well as an automobile. Against D's sentence, the state prosecutor filed an appeal to the detriment of the defendant aimed at altering the court's judgment. She complained that the court on the basis of a procedural error had fixed the penalty too low.

Y's appeal was unsuccessful; the prosecutor's appeal was partly successful.

Reasons

B

The prosecutor's appeal to the detriment of the defendant D attacking his criminal sentence is successful.

1.a). The petitioner validly states that there has been a misapplication of section 33[a] and 261 of the Code of Criminal Procedure. She maintains that during the course of the proceedings the court reached an agreement (*Absprache*) with the defense in case the defendant determined he would confess to the two criminal acts to levy a punishment between five years and five years and 11 months. The defendant agreed as to the narcotics offense. The prosecutor obtained knowledge of this agreement for the first time at the oral presentation of the presiding judge's grounds for judgment. It cannot be foreclosed that the determination of the individual punishment and the aggregate punishment were influenced by the agreement.

b). On the basis of official explanations from the office of state attorneys and career judges, this panel (*Senat*) is assured about the following circumstances with respect to the proceedings prior to the pronouncement of judgment.

Upon the defense counsel's inquiry about what penalty the defendant could count on in case he might confess to both criminal acts, the judicial panel including the lay judges made a preliminary determination. The defense counsel was informed about the result of this determination. The defendant, if he confessed and on condition that the evidence did not change, could count on a punishment between five years and five years and 11 months. The court clerk and — in substantial accord — the presiding judge have officially explained:

> "We took the evidence existing at that time as our basis. The process began with both defendants," although it was later separated between the co-defendants. The judge did not revise his sentence "in reference to D's narcotics trafficking with about two kilograms of heroin since he felt D could not be regarded as a manipulator due to the decisive influence of his narcotics use. It was also clear that the above mentioned preliminary determination in so far as it was in effect did not substantively change the state of the evidence. This determination was finally communicated to the defense counsel."

Later the defendant D made a confession. Nevertheless, the judicial panel held a full evidence-taking session. It fixed the sentence for each individual act at five years for the narcotics offense and at seven months for the weapons charge as well as for an aggregate punishment of five years and four months.

The prosecutor did not participate in the mentioned understanding between the defense counsel and the court and was also not later informed of it. The

[a] Section 33.

(1) A decision of the court rendered during the main proceeding shall be issued after hearing the parties involved.

(2) A decision of the court rendered outside the main proceeding shall be issued after a written or oral statement by the prosecutor.

(3) In case of a decision under paragraph 2, another party shall also be heard if, to his detriment, facts or evidentiary conclusions are to be used for which he has not had a hearing.

session judge drew up the mode of conducting the final meeting in which the promises were made. Thus the prosecutor first saw a probable basis for a notice of appeal due to the reported agreement at the oral presentation by the presiding judge of his grounds for judgment.

2. This practice is objectionable.

The appellate panel, however, does not see the error as inherent in the practice whereby a judicial panel makes a preliminary determination involving judicial questions outside of the main proceeding (*Hauptverhandlung*) with the defense counsel and presiding judge or clerk present, but without informing the prosecutor. But it is obvious that the court should secure a preliminary deliberation after pursuing the possibility of knowing the views of all interested parties. Nevertheless, a mode of procedure, such as that selected here, under appropriate circumstances, may be completely necessary. This applies first of all, perhaps, if the court wants to obtain clarification in this manner for either a question or suggestion with which it is confronted, especially when it will continue to follow up on a point.

This practice becomes legally incorrect, however, when the court informs a party of a significant preliminary judicial determination, without first giving the other parties notice of questions under discussion so that they will have an opportunity to make a statement. Indeed neither this notice nor one from the defendant's confession file can produce an obligation on the court in the sense that the final judicial judgment must be expected to be in accordance with the stated determination. This is obvious for cases concerned with the admission of guilt under notorious circumstances or where another judgment demands attention as to its amount or the measure of liability. This is also clear for cases after a stay of proceedings, in a second instance appeal, or after remand from a third instance appeal or the granting of a new hearing where another judge must handle the matter. A court shall not relinquish its freedom in evaluating a communicated representation to reach a different judgment on the basis of better knowledge of a determining factor. A filed confession in such cases is admissible. Its use would not violate the requirement of a fair procedure. The applicable law does not leave the procedural risks with the judicial panel; when interested parties are hindered in finding out about judicial communications, they may easily bring a motion to hear evidence or they may file an appeal.

Nevertheless, such judicial communications to the recipient create a statement of fact in trust. In each case the recipient has a right to notice from the court, before it would indicate its plan to deviate from the promised sentence to his detriment (BGHSt 36, 210 = NJW 1989, 2270).

For this reason the court's announcement of a determination of its preliminary decision to an interested party is a direct, procedurally serious occurrence. It requires application of the fundamentals of section 33 of the Code of Criminal Procedure, that the court should meet with other concerned parties on these occasions and permit them to make their comments.

Since this did not happen here, an error is established. It is not foreclosed that the prosecutor with a proper hearing might have influenced the defendant's sentence to his detriment.

NOTES AND QUESTIONS

1. "But it is not ... self-evident that the French *procureur* and German *Staatsanwalt* are simply district attorneys who speak a foreign language; that the French *police judiciaire* and the German *Polizei* are just the homicide squad of an American city dressed in different uniforms; that the *juge d'instruction*, the *Richter*, and the American trial judge are, beneath the robe, one and the same." John H. Langbein & Lloyd L. Weinreb, *Continental Criminal Procedure: "Myth" and Reality,* 87 Yale L.J. 1549, 1550 (1978). Should we expect differences in the selection, training, professional ideologies, and institutional structures of civil law police, prosecutors, and judges to make a significant difference in the way plea bargaining works in civil law nations? *See* Mirjan R. Damaška, *Structures of Authority and Comparative Criminal Procedure,* 84 Yale L.J. 480, 502 (1975).

2. Prepare a list of the significant similarities and differences between plea bargaining in the United States and Germany. What role does the prosecutor, judge, and defense counsel play in each system? Which system has reached a better balance between justice and efficiency?

3. In civil law jurisdictions defendant and her counsel have access to the dossier during the investigation and the instruction. The trial is based on the dossier. Thus the defendant can be fully informed about the prosecution's case, including the evidence against her, before the trial. Does this affect the criminal defendant's bargaining position? More generally, is this fairer to the defendant than discovery rules in U.S. criminal proceedings?

4. Do you agree with the German Supreme Court in *D and Y* that a judge who plans to offer a defendant a sentencing concession in exchange for his confession should inform all parties to the trial and give them an opportunity to comment? Should this opportunity be given to a civil party? Who is better situated to protect the public interest in a plea bargaining situation — the judge or the prosecutor?

5. Should a judge who has actively participated in negotiations for a plea bargain — with either the defense counsel or the prosecutor — be forced to recuse himself from the trial?

6. For more on plea bargaining and prosecutorial discretion in Germany, see Mirjan Damaška, *The Reality of Prosecutorial Discretion: Comments on a German Monograph,* 29 Am. J. Comp. L. 119 (1981); William L.F. Felstiner, *Plea Contracts in West Germany,* 13 Law & Soc'y Rev. 309 (1979); Comment, *The West German Day-Fine System: A Possibility for the United States?,* 50 U. Chi. L. Rev. 281 (1983). Plea bargaining is spreading in the civil law world. For example, Italy's new Code of Criminal Procedure, which became effective in 1989, provides for guilty pleas and expressly contemplates plea bargaining. Bargaining also became possible in the Spanish criminal justice system after a reform in 1989.

7. Useful materials on German criminal procedure have been compiled in John H. Langbein, Comparative Criminal Procedure: Germany (1977). *See also* Craig M. Bradley, *The Exclusionary Rule in Germany,* 96 Harv. L. Rev. 1032 (1983); Joachim Herrmann, *The Federal Republic of Germany,* in Major Criminal Justice Systems: A Comparative Survey 106 (George F. Cole et al. eds., 2d ed. 1987); Hans-Heinrich Jescheck, *Principles of German Criminal Procedure in Comparison with American Law,* 56 Va. L. Rev. 239 (1970); Thomas Weigend, *Sentencing in West Germany,* 42 Md. L. Rev. 37 (1983).

5. JURIES AND LAY JUDGES

NOTE

In the 19th century there was a strong European movement to adopt the English jury in criminal proceedings. In the present century an equally strong reaction set in, leading to the abolition of juries, replaced in some nations by mixed panels of professional and lay judges. Other major civil law nations have preserved the continental tradition of professional judges in penal actions, though usually requiring a panel of three or more judges for serious offenses. Most of Latin America uses a panel of professional judges. Brazil's jury is the outstanding exception, although in the 19th century Mexico experimented with the jury. Generally on the origin and use of lay judges *see* John P. Dawson, A History of Lay Judges (1960). The reasons for the decline of the jury in Europe are explained in Hermann Mannheim, *Trial by Jury in Modern Continental Criminal Law,* 53 Law Q. Rev. 99, 388 (1937). Jury trials existed on a limited scale in Japan from 1923 to 1943. For recent interest and proposals, see Richard Lempert, *A Jury for Japan?,* 40 Am. J. Comp. L. 37 (1992). There has never been a serious effort to introduce the *civil* jury in Europe, Latin America, or East Asia.

What difference does it make whether questions of guilt and punishment are made by professional judges alone, by mixed panels of professional and lay judges, or by judge and jury? The following materials describe the role of lay judges in Germany.

DAVID S. CLARK, THE SELECTION AND ACCOUNTABILITY OF JUDGES IN WEST GERMANY: IMPLEMENTATION OF A *RECHTSSTAAT,* 61 Southern California Law Review 1795, 1829-32 (1988)

In a system so deeply committed to professional competence in the application of law to disputes, it may appear ironic that Germany has the most extensive use of lay judges of any country in continental Western Europe. As illustrated in Figure 6.2 (*supra* Chapter 6, Section A.2), citizens may participate in deciding certain types of cases in all first instance state courts, controlling the majority of votes on commercial, criminal, labor, and social security three judge panels. Furthermore, in agricultural cases, and in most disciplinary and personnel disputes involving civil servants, soldiers, and non-governmental professionals, lay judges hold the majority of votes at the first instance level. Even in tax and administrative matters, as well as in the most serious criminal cases, lay judges take part in the decisions, although they are in the minority on these five judge panels. By the time cases reach federal high courts on appeal, lay participation (as a minority) continues only at the Federal Labor Court, the Federal Social Security Court, and in certain agricultural cases and disciplinary and personnel matters. Overall an aura of substantial citizen involvement pervades the German justice system, as Table 10.3 illustrates.

Table 10.3

Number of Lay Judges in the 1980s, by Jurisdiction

Jurisdiction	Number
Criminal	27,200
Juvenile	10,400
Commercial	1,200
Agricultural	6,200
Labor	12,500
Administrative	11,100
Tax	2,300
Social security	11,100
TOTAL	82,000

Several grounds have been advanced to justify lay participation in the judicial process: it fosters democracy by checking executive despotism and ensuring independent decisionmaking; it contributes to citizenship training; and it legitimates the decisions made. In addition, since lay judges help to resolve both factual and legal issues, they can act to guarantee the basic fairness of the judicial process and, more importantly, can bring special insight from their own backgrounds to bear on factual issues.

Lay judges are subject to the same professional obligations as career judges and have the same right to judicial independence, which means they can be removed from the bench only after a court hearing. They take an oath of office, serve fixed terms (four years in criminal and juvenile courts), and are usually assigned to 12 sessions per year, for which they receive a stipend. They are required to remain impartial, maintain secrecy about the proceedings, and decide cases according to the law. This latter obligation makes it difficult for lay judges to thwart unpopular laws, since on appeal to the federal courts there are either no lay judges on a panel or they are in the minority.

Although the independence of lay judges is guaranteed by law, it may be affected by the politicization of their recruitment or the dominating influence exercised by the career judge or judges sitting on a mixed court's panel. Lay judges are either selected from the general population — for criminal, juvenile, and administrative cases — or from special interest groups for other jurisdictions. For instance, on labor courts one lay judge represents employer groups and the second lay judge represents labor unions and other employee groups. On social security court panels specializing in health insurance, doctor and patient groups nominate persons who serve as lay judges. Merchants sit on commercial cases, farmers on agricultural cases, attorneys on lawyer disciplinary cases, and so forth.

Where the general citizenry is eligible to serve, as for criminal and juvenile cases, local political party officials control the selection process and tend to allocate positions according to party strength in the community. According to the Judicial Organization Law (*Gerichtsverfassungsgesetz*), within each local court (*Amtsgericht*) district the authority (*Gemeinde, Gemeindevertretung*) or authorities should compile a list of nominees for lay judging, representative of all groups in the population, once every four years. In the second phase of the selection process, a commission meets at the *Amtsgericht* to choose (by two-thirds vote) the estimated number of lay judges needed over the next four years from the lists of nominees. The commission is chaired by an *Amtsgericht* judge, who oversees the work of one state administrative officer and ten "trustworthy" citizens usually chosen by the local municipal council. John Richert, in his study of criminal and juvenile lay judges, found: "The ideal lay judge emerges as a middle-aged man, possessing a solid education, hailing from the middle class, and preferably supporting the political party in power."

Richert's conclusion that reliance on representatives from select and homogeneous groups unduly reinforces the biases of a career judiciary may be unduly harsh, especially when one looks at the full breadth of jurisdictions. Research by Gerhard Casper and Hans Zeisel on lay judges in criminal courts, as reinterpreted by John Langbein, implies that once easy cases are removed from the sample (for example, where an accused confesses), citizens exert significant impact on the question of guilt or innocence, and even more influence regarding the severity of a sentence. Ekkehard Klausa believes, in addition, that lay judges in juvenile, commercial, labor, social security, and disciplinary cases exert significant influence. The great majority of lay judges, except in tax and administrative courts, felt that they were a positive factor in the judicial process, although career judges were less enthusiastic.

JOHN H. LANGBEIN, MIXED COURT AND JURY COURT: COULD THE CONTINENTAL ALTERNATIVE FILL THE AMERICAN NEED?, 1981 American Bar Foundation Research Journal 195, 197-205 (1981)

Although the notion of lay participation in criminal adjudication traces back to Germanic antiquity, its only important survival in the late medieval world was the English jury. For cases of serious crime the courts of the early modern absolutist states of Europe were staffed exclusively with professional judges. At a time well before the independence of the judiciary had been established, these courts were subjected to political interference in cases that interested the rulers.

Court structure was one of the major interests of legal reform efforts in the eighteenth century. Reform writers were certain that they wanted judicial independence, in order to eliminate executive interference in adjudication, but they were nonetheless distrustful of a judiciary that had for so long been under the heel of political authority. Accordingly, Beccaria and others popularized the English jury as a safeguard against judicial subservience.

French experimentation with jury-like bodies commenced immediately after the Revolution. The form that ultimately emerged was a jury meant to decide all matters of "fact" but with questions of "law" reserved to the bench. This impossibly conceptual distinction was supposed to be implemented by having the jury render what amounted to a detailed special verdict in response to interrogatories framed by the bench. Napoleon planted this institution in parts of Germany, especially on the Rhine where the French ruled until 1814. When the Revolution of 1848 forced rulers in the German states to acquiesce in demands for the criminal jury, the French model was widely instituted in a somewhat modified form; a special verdict system was retained, but jurors were also asked to express their view on guilt or innocence.

During the 1850s and 1860s the practical difficulties in operating this style of jury gave rise to considerable complaint in Germany, which ultimately led to experimentation with another mode of lay participation, the mixed court. Several of the German states developed versions of this so-called *Schöffengericht,* especially Hanover and Saxony; the Prussians embraced the mixed court after conquering Hanover. By the 1870s when unified national codes of procedure and court structure were being drafted, the Prussians sought to eliminate the jury court entirely in favor of the mixed court. The politics of the moment resulted in a compromise for the 1877 code that lasted until 1924: The jury court was retained for the most serious crimes, the mixed court tried the least offenses, and a wholly professional court exercised jurisdiction over a middle band of offenses. Dissatisfaction with the jury court never abated; it was abolished in favor of the mixed court in 1924....

The System in Outline: Mixed Courts

In current practice mixed courts come in two basic varieties. A court of five judges — two lay and three professional — tries cases of more serious crime; this court is ordinarily known as the *Grosse Strafkammer* but is called the *Schwurgericht* when sitting for certain very serious offenses including homicides. Less serious crimes are tried to a court of three judges — two lay and one professional — still called the *Schöffengericht.* (Petty offenses are tried to a single professional judge, but from him there is a right of appeal de novo to a three-judge court, the *Kleine Strafkammer,* staffed with two lay judges and one professional.) For simplicity's sake and despite the inelegance, we shall speak of the two types of mixed courts by their composition figures, lay-judge figures first, as the Two-Three and Two-One courts....

A single statutory formula governs the voting arrangements in both the Two-Three and Two-One courts. Section 263(1) of the Code of Criminal Procedure provides that any decision that disadvantages the accused (meaning both verdict and sentence) must be taken with a two-thirds majority. In the Two-Three court this voting rule requires that a minimum four of the five judges agree upon a verdict of conviction. The two laymen have, therefore, a veto power if they act together; they can acquit over the opposition of the three professionals, but they cannot convict without the votes of two professionals. In the Two-One court that tries the lesser cases, the two-thirds voting rule allows the two laymen either to convict and sentence or to acquit over the opposition of the professional. In either court the outcome of a trial is conviction or acquittal; there is no provision for stalemate comparable to the Anglo-American hung jury....

The professional judge or judges are responsible for preparing a written opinion to explain the court's findings of fact and law. In the event of conviction this opinion must also supply the reasoning for the court's sentence. This expansive document has, of course, no counterpart in the one- or two-word general verdict of the Anglo-American jury.

The requirement of a reasoned opinion supports a system of appellate review that departs markedly from Anglo-American expectations. The appellate system has a major effect on the operation of the mixed-court system. From any decision of the Two-One court there is a full appeal de novo (*Berufung*) to the Two-Three court. That is, no presumption of correctness attaches to the first-instance proceeding, and the case is fully retried. From the Two-Three court, whether sitting as a first-instance court in cases of serious crime or as a de novo trial court in cases once tried in the Two-One court, appeal lies only for error (*Revision*) and is heard by a court of five professional judges.

Prosecution and defense have equal rights of appeal, on issues both of culpability and of sentence. German law adheres to the Continental tradition that appeal lies against acquittal as well as conviction ....

The mixed court retires at the conclusion of the oral public trial for deliberations in order to formulate its judgment. The presiding judge (the only professional in the Two-One court, the senior professional in the Two-Three court) "leads" these *in camera* proceedings and also, in the words of the statute, "puts the questions and takes the votes." By convention the presiding judge (or, in the Two-Three court, another of the professionals) opens the deliberations by summarizing the evidence that has just been adduced at the trial.

Modern German mixed courts discharge their caseloads with enviable dispatch. The study by Gerhard Casper and Hans Zeisel established that an average trial for a serious offense in a Two-Three court lasts one day; trial in the Two-One court requires about two hours. The mixed-court structure accelerates German procedure by comparison with our own because it dispenses with the time-consuming features of the jury system that are so prominent in common law jury trials, especially the rules of evidence, jury instructions, and the other elements of jury control. (The extended voir dire of prospective jurors common in American jury practice is another source of delay that, we shall see, lacks any counterpart in the German mixed-court procedure.)...

No modern system can delegate unrestrained powers of criminal adjudication to laymen — that is, to people who lack legal training and experience and who do not bear professional responsibility for their work. The Anglo-American jury, system, by isolating the laymen, complicates the task of safeguarding against the dangers of ignorance and bias that inhere in any attempt to use laymen in adjudication. Because the jury deliberates without professional participation and decides without giving reasons, there is virtually no opportunity to provide learned guidance to the jurors during deliberations, and the means of detecting and relieving against errors after verdict are quite limited. Accordingly, our system of jury control has been designed to work anticipatorily. Voir dire is supposed to discover and reject for service potential jurors who would not be fair-minded, notwithstanding the difficulty of making such predictions and the amount of time that the process can require. We conceive of potential error, and we try to prevent it. The law of evidence is meant to exclude from jurors information whose relevance they might misapprehend, but the cost of this exclusionary system in time and complexity is immense. The trial judge's instructions ostensibly identify and resolve for the jurors in advance of their deliberations the legal problems that may arise, although the format of multiple contingent instructions protracts the trial and probably bewilders the jurors.

The mixed court relies upon three quite different safeguards against lay inexperience: the presence of professional judges in deliberations, the requirement of reasoned opinion, and liberal appellate review. Professional judges discuss the rules of law and caution against unfounded uses of evidence *in camera* when and if the need arises. Since these deliberations occur out of the presence of counsel, the requirement of written opinion is a central protection. Important findings of fact and rulings of law are meant to show up in the judgment and be subject to appeal. Collegiality serves as another protection against judicial arbitrariness or error in the deliberations, because three professionals sit in the Two-Three trial court (and in the Two-Three court that proceeds by trial de novo in appeals from the Two-One court).

Influence of the Laymen

By comparison with the Anglo-American jury system, the German mixed court enhances lay authority in certain significant respects. In the mixed court the lay judges participate in determining sentence as well as verdict, whereas at common law the work of the criminal jury ceases with the verdict, and only relatively minor statutory intrusions into sentencing have been made. German lay judges also participate in all rulings of law; and, accordingly, no exclusionary rules can be employed to limit their view of the evidence.

In other respects, however, the mixed court diminishes lay authority. Laymen are much fewer in number, and they do not act independently of the professionals. They have the power to force acquittal, but only in the Two-One court for lesser offenses can they convict without professional assent. The requirement of reasoned opinion exposes the judgments of the mixed courts to deep-reaching appellate review at the behest of either the defendant or the prosecution.

One serious attempt has been made to measure the influence of the laymen in the German mixed courts. In their landmark empirical study undertaken a decade ago, Casper and Zeisel compiled a careful sample of about six hundred cases from both types of mixed courts.[28] Following to some extent the methodology of the earlier *American Jury*[29] project, the investigators had professional judges reply anonymously to a standardized questionnaire about the mixed-court trials in which they presided. One object of the study was to

[28] For detail on the study design, including the weighting of certain data, see Gerhard Casper & Hans Zeisel, *Lay Judges in the German Criminal Courts,* 1 J. Legal Stud. 135, 143-46 (1972).

[29] Harry Kalven, Jr., & Hans Zeisel, The American Jury (Boston: Little, Brown & Co., 1966).

identify the proportion of cases in which lay and professional judges found themselves in initial disagreement and then to see how frequently the laymen persisted in their views.

The main findings of this aspect of the Casper and Zeisel study may be summarized as follows:

1. On the question of guilt (verdict), some lay and professional judges in the mixed courts found themselves in some disagreement at the outset of their deliberations in 6.5 percent of all cases.

2. On the question of sentence, where the range of permissible outcomes is much broader than on verdict, some initial disagreement between lay and professional judges occurred in 20.1 percent of all cases.

3. In the 6.5 percent of the cases in which there was initial disagreement on guilt, one or more of the lay judges persisted in voting against the professionals in 30 percent of the cases; in 21 percent (mostly in the Two-One court) the lay votes affected the verdict. These cases in which lay voting altered the outcome constituted 1.4 percent of the entire sample of cases.

4. Lay influence on sentencing was greater, in part because sentencing disagreements were often resolved by compromise. The lay votes affected 32 percent of the cases in which there was initial disagreement, or 6.2 percent of the entire sample of cases.

Commenting on their findings, Casper and Zeisel remarked that the "traceable overall effect of the lay judges on the verdicts of the German criminal courts is indeed small.... Compared to the American jury, the difference is marked. American juries arrive at a verdict that is different from that of the presiding judge in 22 percent of all cases [according to the *American Jury* data]."

The contrast between a 1.4 percent figure for lay influence on verdict in the German mixed court and a 22 percent figure in the American jury court needs to be probed with care. If the contrast were a fair one, it would indicate that the laymen in the German procedure are far less influential than American jurors, and it might incline us to suspect that the purposes attributed to the jury system are not being served at adequate levels in the German mixed courts. In my view, however, the contrast is seriously misleading for several reasons:

1. It does not correct for the marked disparity between the two groups of cases. In Germany every case of serious crime goes to trial before one of the mixed courts. In the United States only the tiny fraction of cases that have resisted negotiated diversion (primarily plea bargaining) go to trial. Most of the easy cases, where disagreement between judge and jury would be least likely, have been filtered out of the American trial statistics. Indeed, in calculating their 1.4 percent figure for Germany, Casper and Zeisel did not exclude the 41 percent of their case sample in which the accused confessed at trial, making disagreement about guilt a practical impossibility.

2. The 1.4 to 22 contrast overlooks the import of the relatively substantial 6.2 percent figure for lay influence on sentencing in the German mixed court. In the American system where the jury is excluded from direct participation in sentencing, it is by the manipulation of degrees and counts that the jury brings what are in truth sentencing considerations to bear on the outcome.

The 22 percent American figure for judge/jury disagreement on guilt includes disagreements over offense characterization and the number of counts that are mostly sentencing disputes in function.

3. The assumption that the measure of lay influence is persistence in disagreement with the professionals is misleading if it implies that laymen yield because they are intimidated rather than persuaded. The Casper and Zeisel study describes the circumstances in a number of the deliberations in which the laymen yielded after initial disagreement. These were in general cases in which the professional judges were unmistakably correct on rational, legal, and humanitarian grounds. Judicial persuasion prevented lay intolerance or misunderstanding from resulting in injustice.

4. Lay participation has a predominantly preventive purpose.... [T]he presence of laymen is meant to deter professional judges from political subservience and from arbitrariness. A system of lay participation that serves these goals quite fully need leave no trace in lay/professional disagreement. The methodology of the Casper and Zeisel study simply does not address this realm of lay influence.

To conclude: There are some respects in which it is fair to say that two laymen who are merged with one or three professional judges lack the authority of a dozen laymen who possess the exclusive verdict power. But the laymen on the mixed court are fully informed; no law of evidence has concealed probative matter from them, no system of jury control has been employed to cordon them off from the totality of criminal adjudication. Rather, their votes extend to matters of law and of sentence.

NOTES AND QUESTIONS

1. What are the principal arguments for and against lay participation in judicial decisionmaking? Is the position for lay participation stronger in criminal cases or civil cases? Why?

2. Does an American criminal judge, through jury instructions, have greater control over the verdicts of juries than that exercised by German professional judges over the verdicts of lay judges? Why or why not?

3. In the Casper and Zeisel study, it is reported that American criminal juries arrive at a verdict different from that of the presiding judge in 22 percent of all cases. In 19 percent the juries acquit the defendant where the judge would have convicted, and in three percent of the cases they convict the defendant where the judge would have acquitted. What do these statistics tell us about the American criminal justice system?

4. Does the German system of lay participation in criminal cases serve most of the purposes of the American criminal jury system? If the Sixth Amendment constitutional issues could be set aside, would it make sense to use the more efficient German lay judge system for most serious crimes processed in U.S. federal courts instead of the complex and expensive jury system that is actually used in only about ten percent of the criminal cases?

5. If you were a German judge or prosecutor, would you be inclined to favor the use of lay judges? Why?

6. ITALY: THE 1989 CODE OF CRIMINAL PROCEDURE

NOTE ON THE ITALIAN REVOLUTION IN CRIMINAL PROCEDURE

Until 1989 Italian criminal procedure followed the traditional civil law model. Its Code of Criminal Procedure, enacted under the Fascist government in 1930, also included repressive features that could not be totally removed after 1945 by amendment, interpretation, and Constitutional Court decisions. Adoption of a new Code had accordingly been a prominent objective of Italian scholars and reformers for decades.

A dramatic rupture in the civil law tradition occurred in 1989 with the adoption of Italy's new Code of Criminal Procedure (*Codice di procedura penale*). For the first time in any major modern civil law nation a systematic effort, based on extensive comparative research and years of scholarly and legislative study, was made to replace the traditional civil law "inquisitorial" model with American-style "adversary" criminal procedure. Some of the new Code's more prominent features are: abolition of the instruction and the instructing judge; public prosecutor and defense counsel control over evidence-gathering; abandonment of the episodic procedure in favor of a concentrated trial; introduction of evidence by the parties at the trial; oral direct and cross-examination of witnesses by counsel at the trial; and the opportunity for avoidance of the trial by the equivalent of guilty pleas and a statutory form of plea bargaining.

The traditional civil law scholarly concerns for procedural concentration, immediacy, and orality clearly supported the introduction of evidence in a concentrated trial and oral direct and cross-examination of witnesses by counsel in the presence of the deciding judges "*alla Perry Mason*" (as it is popularly called in Italy and elsewhere in Europe). The acceptance of guilty pleas and the institution of plea bargaining were driven by the usual practical concerns: a heavy backlog of pending cases, discomfort with the growth of informal practices that seemed increasingly inconsistent with the reigning principled model of criminal procedure, and a desire to deal explicitly with the necessity to move the process more expeditiously.

While opting for important features of the American model, the new Code did not directly affect the recruitment, selection, career patterns, and bureaucratic organization of police, public prosecutors, and judges. Nor does it appear to opt for substantially broadened prosecutorial or judicial discretion. Instead, the Italians seem to have sought to establish an otherwise innovative procedural model that retains the traditional principles of compulsory prosecution and legality (both of which are embodied in the Italian Constitution).

So drastic a reform has of course raised a number of problems for Italian prosecutors, judges, defense counsel, and judicial staff. At the most banal level, courtrooms designed for the traditional procedure provide awkward, sometimes inadequate arenas for the new procedure. Actors trained for the old way of doing things have to be retrained. For example, a lawyer unaccustomed to the demands of a concentrated, oral procedure has to acquire a new set of skills and adopt an entirely different way of preparing for trial. The instructing judge no longer exists, and the trial judge is involved in a dramatically different role in a dramatically different kind of process.

There are, in addition, important legal issues of two predictable kinds. One kind occurs in the process of supplying meaning to the terms of a novel and complicated statute through the normal process of judicial and scholarly interpretation and application of its provisions. Second, the provisions of the new Code must be tested for their conformity to the Italian Constitution. In fact, a number of such questions have come before the Constitutional Court.

Although Italy is the first major civil law nation to opt for this style of criminal proceeding, others may not be far behind. In France, a Commission on Criminal Justice and Human Rights of the Ministry of Justice, in a 1989 report, expressed interest in establishing a criminal procédure *similaire à la procédure anglo-saxonne*. The *Avocat Général* at the *Cour de Cassation* predictably opposed the proposal and characterized the effect of the Italian reform as a *triste expérience*. Other civil law nations will certainly be intrigued by the Italian experiment.

WILLIAM T. PIZZI & LUCA MARAFIOTI, THE NEW ITALIAN CODE OF CRIMINAL PROCEDURE: THE DIFFICULTIES OF BUILDING AN ADVERSARIAL TRIAL SYSTEM ON A CIVIL LAW FOUNDATION, 17 Yale Journal of International Law 1, 10-15, 17, 19-26, 33-35 (1992)

An Introduction to the New Italian Code of Criminal Procedure[44]

A victim's report of a crime places the police under a tight deadline: within forty-eight hours they must inform the public prosecutor of the crime and send him all the information they have gathered. Upon learning of the crime, the public prosecutor must record the crime in the crime register. This act is more than simple record-keeping. Recording the crime triggers certain time limits within which investigation of the crime must be completed, creating in effect a speedy trial provision.[47] The Italian Code places the public prosecutor, rather than the police, in control of the pretrial investigation of a crime, although the police are at the prosecutor's disposal. The public prosecutor functions to some extent as an advocate, but the Code also places on him an obligation of fairness that requires him to investigate exculpatory as well as inculpatory evidence. Arrested suspects are not accorded *Miranda* protections, primarily because statements obtained through police questioning are not admissible at trial unless defense counsel was present.

[44] The Code of Criminal Procedure [C.P.P.] comprises 11 books and 746 sections. The first four books constitute the "static" part of the Code, so called because they deal with the structure in which trials and other procedures take place. The remaining seven books constitute the "dynamic" part of the Code, dealing with the actual steps in the process from the preliminary investigation through execution of the sentence.

[47] Normally, the preliminary investigation must be completed within six months of the date that the crime was entered in the crime register. C.P.P. art. 405, para. 2. In complex cases, however, the judge in charge of the preliminary investigation may grant a six-month extension, up to a maximum of 18 months. *Id.* arts. 406, 407. Any evidence obtained after expiration of the time limits in the Code may not be used by the public prosecutor. *Id.* art. 407, para. 3.

Italy, like other civil law countries, is wary of broad prosecutorial discretion in deciding whether or not to charge a suspect. The Italian Constitution reflects this distrust by mandating compulsory prosecution.[54] Nevertheless, the Code provides a method for disposing of weak cases. A prosecutor may ask the judge for a judgment of dismissal (*decreto di archiviazione*) whenever the evidence is insufficient to prove that a crime was committed or that it was committed by a particular defendant.[56]

The *incidente probatorio*, a deposition-like procedure, is an important investigatory device that can occur at any time before trial. This procedure allows either the prosecutor or defense to request the hearing of testimony from a witness if there is a compelling reason for the request, such as the need to protect a witness from physical harm or the need to obtain the testimony of a witness who may die before trial. The *incidente probatorio* thus serves to "freeze" the testimony of a witness, as evidence so obtained is included in the file the judge receives at the start of trial. A judge is assigned specifically to supervise all preliminary investigations. The judge determines such matters as bail and preserves the impartiality of the investigation. While control of the investigation is largely in the hands of the public prosecutor, the judge serves as a check on his power.

The Italian Code also provides for a preliminary hearing (*udienza preliminare*), which unlike its U.S. equivalent is essentially a document review by the judge. A public prosecutor requesting a preliminary hearing sends the judge a file containing all documents and reports collected during the investigation. At the hearing (held *in camera*), the public prosecutor presents no witnesses, but instead outlines the investigation and its results using the documents developed in the investigation. The defense, also working from the investigation file, has the opportunity in turn to argue against setting the case for trial. In addition, the defendant may ask to be examined by the judge, and he may not be cross-examined. The judge may ask the parties for any additional evidence he considers necessary. The judge then must decide whether or not to set the matter for a trial at the conclusion of the preliminary hearing.

The preliminary hearing is largely a formality, however, because the judge applies an extremely lenient standard to the prosecutor's case. A weak case against the accused is not a basis for dismissal. Rather, a judge may dismiss the case only if he concludes that no crime actually took place, that the events described in the charges do not constitute a crime, or that the defendant clearly did not commit the crime. In short, the decision to dismiss the charges against a suspect after the preliminary hearing amounts to a declaration that the defendant must be acquitted immediately without a trial.

Italy's preference for a preliminary hearing based on documents is consistent with the civil law tradition, which places a premium on the careful assembly of a complete dossier on the case. This dossier usually serves as the basis of the judge's questioning at trial. But while the preliminary hearing permits the judge to make use of the entire investigative file, the new Code

[54] COST. art. 112.

[56] It appears that the standards for a motion to dismiss are now broad enough to give the prosecutor considerable responsibility in deciding whether a case merits prosecution.

parts company with civil law tradition by limiting the written materials a court may consider at trial. Article 431 limits the file sent to the trial judges to the charging documents, physical evidence connected with the crime, and evidence gathered using the *incidente probatorio*.[67] The rest of the evidence must be presented at the trial by the parties. For trial judges educated and trained in the civil law tradition, these innovations are significant. Given the civil law's distaste for excluding probative evidence, judges will probably feel pressure to read broadly the exceptions contained in Article 431....

The trial itself begins with opening statements by the public prosecutor, the lawyers representing any civil parties, and the defense attorney, in that order. Parties bring witnesses in the same order, and each party is granted an opportunity to cross-examine the others' witnesses. Closing statements then follow in the same order. After closing statements, each of the advocates is entitled to present a rebuttal to the other summations. Unlike U.S. trials, in which the prosecution is allowed the last word, the defense always has the opportunity to speak last in an Italian trial.

The defendant traditionally plays an active role in a civil law trial. The new Code continues the tradition by permitting the defendant to speak at any point in the trial to challenge a witness's testimony. While a defendant may remain silent, a defendant who wishes to present mitigating facts relevant to sentencing must do so at trial. It is unclear whether adversarial trial procedures will encourage more defendants to exercise the right to remain silent.

Following trial, the court must explain its decision in an opinion that reviews the evidence and explains in detail the grounds (*motivazione*) for the decision. If the court cannot draft its opinion immediately after the trial, it must do so within thirty to ninety days, depending on the complexity and seriousness of the case.

The new Code retains the broad appellate review characteristic of civil law systems; in fact, the 1988 reform left the Code provisions concerning appeal virtually untouched....

Coping With Judicial Backlog: Italian Attempts to Solve the Problem

The new Code was, in significant part, intended to provide the Italian criminal justice system with new, efficient procedures to combat its perennial case backlog. The Italian approach to prosecution differs substantially from U.S. methods. In the United States, essentially one rigid system of trial applies to all non-petty offenses, whether the evidence is overwhelming or doubtful, or whether conviction entails a sentence of years or only a few days. The selection of the jury, the rules of evidence, the principles of examination and cross-examination, and so on, remain the same. Italy takes a more flexible approach. Instead of requiring all cases to proceed down a single highway, Italy sets up a number of different avenues along which a case may proceed to resolution, governed by factors such as the seriousness of the crime and the strength of the evidence. The new Code offers defendants significant sentencing reductions in exchange for selecting simplified procedures.

[67] Evidence obtained by the police or the public prosecutor through procedures that cannot be repeated, such as evidence from wiretaps, is included in the file.

The special procedures in the new Code can be broken down into two general categories: procedures that eliminate the preliminary hearing in the interest of expediting the case, and procedures that offer an alternative to trial (see Table 10.4)....

Table 10.4

Special Procedures of the New Italian Code of Criminal Procedure

Procedure	When Available	Preliminary Hearing	Trial	Finding of Guilt	Limitations on Appeal
giudizio direttissimo	Defendant caught in act or offers full confession	No, direct trial	Yes, full adversary trial	Normal verdict and written judgment	None
giudizio immediato	Cases where evidence is overwhelming	No, direct trial	Yes, full adversary trial	Normal verdict and written judgement	None
procedimento per decreto penale ("penal decree")	Minor cases where fine is the punishment	No, case disposed of by immediate fine	No	Defendant receives only the proposed fine (which is fifty percent of what would otherwise be imposed)	No appeal; defendant is free to reject penal decree and go to trial
Applicazione della pena su richiesta delle parti ("plea bargaining")	Relatively minor crimes because final sentence, after one-third discount, may not exceed two years	Possibly, depending on when the plea bargain is reached	No	No, but judge must review the plea bargain to see that the bargained punishment fits the crime	Agreed-upon plea bargain disposes of case
giudizio abbreviato	Any criminal case, except those which impose a life sentence	Yes, judge decides the case based on the dossier, but the judge may not ask for additional evidence as would be permitted at normal preliminary hearing	No	Normal verdict and written judgment, with sentence reduced by one-third	Yes, severely limited appellate rights

Three Alternatives to Trial

1. *Proceeding by Penal Decree*

The second category of special procedures in the new Code of Criminal Procedure includes alternatives to trial. The first of these is the *procedimento per decreto penale*, which translates roughly as "a proceeding by penal decree." A penal decree is, in essence, a unilateral offer by the public prosecutor to resolve the case by a discounted fine. The defendant is free to accept or reject the offer. It is available only for minor crimes where the public prosecutor believes that a fine would be sufficient punishment. In such cases, the public prosecutor can ask the judge to sentence the defendant directly, resulting in a fifty percent fine reduction. There is no preliminary hearing and no trial — simply the direct imposition of the fine. The large discount in the fine is obviously intended to encourage defendants charged with minor crimes to accept the penal decree. But if the defendant is dissatisfied with the fine or desires a trial for other reasons, he is entitled to demand a trial any time within fifteen days after the judge imposes the fine.

A conviction by penal decree is not a new procedure in Italy. Even under the old Code, lower courts trying minor crimes punishable by fines used a form of the penal decree. The new Code's innovations include the requirement that the prosecutor initiate the penal decree, and the fixed fifty percent discount in the fine....

2. *Italian Plea Bargaining*

The United States does not need a procedure such as the penal decree, in part because large numbers of minor cases are handled through plea bargaining. Italy, too, has adopted a mild form of plea bargaining in the new Code: the *applicazione della pena su richiesta delle parti*, the second of the three alternatives to trial. The phrase roughly translates as "the application of punishment upon the request of the parties." Under this procedure, before the trial begins the public prosecutor and the defense attorney may agree on a sentence to be imposed and ask the judge to impose it. The normal sentence can be reduced by as much as one-third, so long as the final negotiated sentence is not more than two years.[115] Prosecutors can bargain to defer the sentence, since any sentence up to two years can be deferred.

Although Italian-style plea bargaining may appear similar to U.S. plea bargaining — and is even referred to by Italian lawyers as a *patteggiamento*, which is the Italian word for "bargain" — certain limitations differentiate it from what occurs in U.S. courts. First, in the Italian system the public prosecutor and the defendant do not bargain over the nature of the crime to which the defendant will plead guilty. If a defendant is charged with assault and the charge fits the facts of the case, the Code does not provide for a plea to a lesser

[115] The statute provides, ambiguously, that a sentence reduction *fino ad un terzo* is possible. The courts initially interpreted the provision to hold that a plea bargain could reduce the final sentence to a third of the normal sentence or, in other words, by two-thirds. However, the *Corte di cassazione* has now rejected that argument, ruling that the maximum possible sentence reduction through plea bargaining is one-third of the normal sentence. *See* Judgment of Mar. 24, 1990, Cass. Sez. Un., 1990 Cass. pen. 118.

included offense, such as menacing, to lower the defendant's sentencing exposure. Second, the fixed maximum reduction of one-third of the normal sentence, coupled with the restriction that the final sentence may not exceed two years, considerably limits the range of cases that qualify for plea bargaining. A defendant subject to a sentence of more than three years cannot plea bargain because the resulting sentence would exceed the two-year limitation. Third, the defense may ask the judge for the one-third reduction in sentencing under the statute even if the prosecutor refuses to join in such a request. In such cases, the prosecutor must state his reasons for refusing the proposed disposition.[119] The intent of the Italian Code is to make sentence reduction available to all defendants who wish to plea bargain, whether or not the prosecutor agrees. This arrangement reflects the traditional civil law distrust of prosecutorial discretion and commitment to uniform treatment of defendants — that defendants would receive different sentences simply because of a prosecutor's whim is anathema to civil law....

3. *Giudizio Abbreviato*

The third alternative to a trial is the *giudizio abbreviato* or "summary trial." This procedure grants a defendant quick resolution of his case based solely on the investigative file, in return for a substantial sentencing reduction should he be found guilty. It is not a U.S.-style plea bargain, because the issue of guilt remains open, nor is it a trial, because the evidence is limited to the materials in the investigative file. Only the defendant may appear as a witness, and he may request interrogation by the judge. Thus, the *giudizio abbreviato* has aspects of both plea bargain and trial — it is like a plea bargain in that the defendant gets a sentence reduction in exchange for choosing an expedited resolution of the case, and it is like a trial in that the issue of guilt must still be decided by the judge. The *giudizio abbreviato* is the most important of the special procedures in the new Italian Code, because it is designed to resolve a substantial percentage of the system's criminal cases without a full adversarial trial.

A defendant may request a *giudizio abbreviato*; the public prosecutor must join in this request.[127]...

Once he receives a request for a *giudizio abbreviato*, the judge must decide whether the case can be resolved definitively on the basis of the preliminary hearing documents.... The hearing is based on the complete case file, which

---

[119] C.P.P. art. 446, para. 6, art. 448, para. 1. For a decision in which a court granted the defendant a reduction despite the prosecutor's refusal to join in the request, see Judgment of Feb. 1, 1990, Trib. Perugia, 1990 Giur. It. 276 & note (Paola Sechi, *Sul dissenso del pubblico ministero dall' applicazione della pena su richiesta* [*Dissent of the Prosecutor in Plea-Bargaining*]).

If the judge grants the defendant's requested disposition, the prosecutor may appeal that decision. *See* C.P.P. art. 448, para. 2. That is the only case in which the sentence is appealable by *appello*. The *ricorso per cassazione* is always permitted under Article 111 of the Italian Constitution.

[127] Injured parties do not have to consent to the use of the summary trial. The *parte civile* does not have the power to veto a summary trial and need not consent for one to occur. C.P.P. art. 441. But if the *parte civile* chooses to participate after the court has agreed that the case is appropriate for summary trial, this amounts to acceptance of the summary trial by the *parte civile*. *Id.* para. 2. If the *parte civile* does not appear after that point, he then can pursue his civil remedy independently of the summary trial. *Id.* para. 3.

includes all documents and reports produced through the investigation, as well as statements made in front of a judge during the investigation....

The *giudizio abbreviato*, by sparing the state a full adversarial trial, offers tremendous savings of judicial resources. The procedure is also designed to save resources at the other end of the process, by tightly restricting appellate review of the judgment.

The *giudizio abbreviato* procedure may be very attractive for certain classes of defendants. For example, a defendant caught red-handed committing a robbery or other serious crime would not otherwise be permitted to plea bargain under the new Code, because even with the one-third reduction the sentence would exceed the two-year statutory maximum. The one-third discount of the *giudizio abbreviato*, however, remains available. The *giudizio abbreviato* is thus expected to supplant plea bargaining in cases involving more serious crimes....

The Difficulties of Implementing the Code: A New System Caught Between Two Traditions

Italy's bold reforms demand a great deal of the participants in its criminal justice system. The judge must withdraw from the role of the dominant inquiring figure and assume a more passive role. The defense lawyer must bear greater responsibility for investigating exculpatory and mitigating evidence and must be prepared to cross-examine witnesses in court, a new experience for most Italian attorneys. The public prosecutor must come down from the bench and face the defense attorney in the courtroom. These changes are so significant that, under the best of circumstances, the adjustment to the new adversarial system would take time.

Both the *giudizio abbreviato* procedure and the Italian version of plea bargaining require a philosophical reexamination of the system. The heart of a civil law trial has always been the decision of the court — that document which blends verdict and sentence into an opinion that weaves together fact and law. The civil law system places a high value on the accuracy of that document and protects that accuracy by allowing full appellate review of every aspect of the decision, including the sentence. The judge, as the central figure in a system that places paramount importance on truth, plays a more active role in the search for truth than a common law judge, and consequently bears more personal responsibility for the accuracy of the decision and verdict. Responsibility cannot be shifted to the advocates if the outcome is not accurate. Since plea bargaining so challenges traditional concepts of justice, the reluctance of civil law systems to embrace it is hardly surprising.

The Code's *giudizio abbreviato* and plea bargaining provisions thus present a serious challenge to the way the Italian courts treat a case. Both procedures require a judge to determine exactly the sentence that the defendant would receive for his crime. Presumably, the judge considers all the mitigating factors and then cuts that sentence by one-third. In the U.S. system, where plea bargaining is common and where a jury always adds an element of uncertainty, one grows accustomed to negotiated sentences. But the sentencing discount is more difficult for a judge in a civil law system, because the judge must give the defendant a sentence he believes inappropriate for the crime.

A recent decision of the Constitutional Court demonstrates this philosophical difficulty facing the Italian system.[171] In this decision, the Court held the plea bargaining provisions of the Code unconstitutional as a violation of the constitutional presumption of innocence, to the extent that they do not provide judicial review of the bargain to ensure proper balance between the crime and the bargained punishment.[172] The judge who would otherwise preside at the trial and possibly sentence the defendant must review the offered plea bargain to assure an appropriate sentence....

The traditional civil law emphasis on the accuracy of adjudication and the correctness of the sentence is further challenged by the *giudizio abbreviato* provisions. These provisions encompass more serious crimes, and the occasions for reliance on the procedure that will be most attractive to defendants are precisely those occasions when the evidence is overwhelming. But even if the public prosecutor consents to a *giudizio abbreviato*, will the defendant actually receive the one-third discount? Will judges have a tendency to give such defendants a heavier initial sentence before the one-third reduction, so that the final sentence is closer to what the judge feels appropriate?

NOTES AND QUESTIONS

1. The 1989 Italian Code has been called "revolutionary." Is the shift in ideology found in this code comparable in extent to the changes attempted in French codes after the Revolution of 1789?

2. What differences or similarities do you find between the new Italian criminal procedure and recent developments in France and Germany? Is it plausible that the European Court of Human Rights is creating a pan-European legal culture that promotes unification of national rules in this field?

3. What problems do you see in implementing these procedural reforms in Italy? For instance, the public prosecutor (*pubblico ministero*) retains much of his judicial outlook as a member of the *magistratura* along with judges. Does this matter?

4. In the 1980s the Italian legal system made a more vigorous effort to bring the mafia to justice, including the creation of the crime of mafiosa association. What impediments will the 1989 Code bring to this effort as the role of investigative judge is eliminated and the power of decision shifts from the inquisitorial pretrial to the adversarial trial stage? Consider the following excerpt:

> [A] special law of 1982 (issued ten days after the assassination of Palermo's *Prefetto*, General Carlo Alberto Della Chiesa) created the specific crime of *mafiosa association* which is defined as follows:
>
>> An association is *mafiosa* if members and associates use the force of intimidation by the association itself and the rules of *omerta* and duress in order to commit crimes, to acquire directly or indirectly management

[171] Judgment No. 313 of July 3, 1990, Corte cost., 35 Giur. cost. 1981 (1990).

[172] The basis of the decision was Article 27 of the Italian Constitution.

or control of economic activities, special administrative concessions, licenses, public contracts and services, or in order to gain unfair profits or advantages in favor of themselves or other parties....

In the last several years, law enforcement against organized crime has improved substantially because of the new 1982 law and because some members of organized crime decided to cooperate with judicial police, *carabinieri*, prosecutors, and investigative judges. Among them, the most famous is without doubt Tommaso Buscetta, who became a cooperating witness in the United States and a cooperating accomplice in Italy. Others, frightened by the bloody fight among organized crime families, looked for protection and safety by making deals with law enforcement personnel. In Sicily alone, about one thousand organized crime members are now on trial. At the end of 1987 the biggest trial — that of Palermo involving 454 defendants — ended with more than 300 convictions.

Nevertheless, serious difficulties are created by the requirement of mandatory prosecution coupled with the broad coverage of the crime of *mafiosa association*, which together compel joint prosecution of hundreds of defendants. The real problem in case management in Italy is not how to handle preliminary investigations, but rather how to be able to bring to trial simultaneously and successfully hundreds of defendants, which under the broadly defined crime of *mafiosa association* includes all the known members and associates of organized crime families against whom judiciary police and prosecutors have collected evidence.

Louis F. Del Duca, *An Historic Convergence of Civil and Common Law Systems — Italy's New "Adversarial" Criminal Procedure System*, 10 Dick. J. Int'l L. 73, 87-88 (1991). The 1989 Code was amended in 1992 to better carry out the campaign against the mafia. These changes increased police powers and expanded the grounds on which out-of-court statements could be used as evidence. Law No. 356 of 7 August 1992.

5. For more on the Italian experiment, see Ennio Amodio & Eugenio Selvaggi, *An Accusatorial System in a Civil Law Country: The 1988 Italian Code of Criminal Procedure,* 62 Temp. L. Rev. 1211 (1989); Stephen P. Freccero, *An Introduction to the New Italian Criminal Procedure,* 21 Am. J. Crim. L. 345 (1994); Note, *The Italian Penal Procedure Code: An Adversarial System of Criminal Procedure in Continental Europe,* 29 Colum. J. Transnat'l L. 245 (1991); Note, *Plea Bargaining and Its Analogues Under the New Italian Criminal Procedure Code and in the United States: Towards a New Understanding of Comparative Criminal Procedure,* 22 N.Y.U. J. Int'l L. & Pol. 215 (1990).

6. Spain adopted in 1989 a summary procedure (*procedimiento abreviado*) that permits a judge to determine a defendant's guilt or innocence on the basis of investigation records. Both the defendant and the prosecutor must consent to the procedure, the defendant must confess, and the judge must believe that a sentence of no more than six years is appropriate. The statute (Ley Orgánica No. 7 of 28 Dec. 1988) does not provide for sentence reductions, but the prosecutor may request a reduced sentence.

For other features of Spanish criminal procedure, see Henry W. McGee, Jr., *Counsel for the Accused: Metamorphosis in Spanish Constitutional Rights*, 25 Colum. J. Transnat'l L. 253 (1987).

7. LATIN AMERICA: DELAY, SOCIAL INEQUALITY, AND POLITICAL REPRESSION

NOTE

Criminal procedure in Latin American nations is derived from and closely resembles in form the traditional European model. We have seen that some European nations are altering elements in their system to improve procedural justice or to achieve greater efficiency. To a lesser extent the same trend is occurring in Latin America. For instance, Colombia has recently abandoned the investigative judge and shifted his duties to the office of the prosecutor general (*fiscalía*). Real change in Latin America, however, is more problematic due to a lack of the official system's legal penetration and to attitudes of distrust and despair in the general legal culture. One major difference with Europe is that most Latin American nations have incorporated the writ of habeas corpus, or its equivalent, into their constitutional systems. The utility of the great writ to defendants varies from time to time and place to place, depending on the relative strength and independence of the judiciary vis-à-vis the executive and the military and on whether constitutional guarantees have been suspended during a state of siege. The following materials illuminate what is distinctive about criminal procedure in Latin America.

ROGELIO PÉREZ PERDOMO, LA JUSTICIA PENAL EN LA INVESTIGACIÓN SOCIO-JURÍDICA DE AMÉRICA LATINA, in COMPARATIVE AND PRIVATE INTERNATIONAL LAW: ESSAYS IN HONOR OF JOHN HENRY MERRYMAN ON HIS SEVENTIETH BIRTHDAY 257, 272-74 (1990)

The first area to consider deals with the excessive duration and other dysfunctions characteristic of the criminal process. In Latin America the process, growing out of an inquisitorial tradition, emphasizes written communications that distances the judge from the parties and promotes bureaucratization. The first studies to actually measure excessive delay in criminal cases were published in the 1970s. Most cases in first instance took between one and three years and in second instance took between three and six months. Few of the accused were released from preventive detention pending a final judicial decision. Therefore for some crimes — theft, fraud, and felonious homicide — the punishment actually levied was less than or about equal to the time served, leaving aside those found to be innocent.

Muñoz Gómez found that the criminal process in Bogotá lasted an average of 836 days, even though the legal maximum was 276 days. Factors promoting delay were the request for a jury trial, release of the accused, and use of a superior jurisdiction court with more complicated procedures. Studies in Mexico show that even a constitutional limit of one year to process major crimes was violated in 26% of the cases.

A principal cause of delay is the high number of penal cases filed compared to the smaller number decided. This has resulted in a huge number of prisoners without sentences waiting in Latin American prisons. An influential study by Carranza et al. of 30 countries in the region reveals that for civil law nations the percentage of non-sentenced prisoners ranges between 50% (Costa Rica, Netherlands Antilles) and 90% (Bolivia, Paraguay), with a mean of 69%. For common law nations, alternatively, the percentage is between 2% (Cayman Islands) and 38% (Guyana), with an average of 23%. Much could be learned from a comparative study of these data using sociolegal analysis.

The second area to survey relates to criminal justice and social inequality. A significant feature of Latin American societies is severe inequality, both economic and social. Studies show that the clientele for criminal courts are primarily poor young single men with limited educational backgrounds. Van Groningen examined Venezuelan court files of convicts from the lower class and those few of upper class convicts. She found that the quality of defense counsel and their arguments for poor persons were abysmal. Public defenders were overwhelmed with a large number of cases, were poorly motivated, and had a negative attitude toward their clients, a majority of whom had been brutalized by the police. All poor defendants in the sample were convicted, with an average sentence of 17 years, while 30% of the upper class defendants were absolved and the remainder received average sentences of five years. The same pattern was discovered in Colombia, reflecting the proverb: "La ley es para los de ruana."

The third area concerns criminal justice and political repression. In Latin America most regimes are reluctant to use the ordinary penal courts for the goal of repressing political dissent. They find military courts more satisfactory, with their summary procedure, limits on defendants' rights, military judges, and dependence on the executive branch.

Nevertheless, the limited sociolegal research finds that military courts suffer delay similar to that of ordinary penal courts, for example more than two years in Colombia and almost five years in El Salvador. Authorities must prefer military courts for their other features. They may also use non-judicial procedures, some involving the armed forces, including unofficial detention, torture, and murder. In countries that have had military regimes, such as Argentina and Chile, the supreme courts have been reluctant to interfere with the operation of military courts.

Overall criminal justice in Latin America suffers from inefficiency, delay, discriminatory procedures, undue deference to executive branch abuses, and failure to protect human rights. But Latin America is diverse, and not all countries live with the problems of the others. State terrorism as used in the southern cone, for instance, is not as severe in Venezuela or in Mexico.

8. ARGENTINA: THE NEED FOR PROCEDURAL FAIRNESS

ALEJANDRO M. GARRO, NINE YEARS OF TRANSITION TO DEMOCRACY IN ARGENTINA: PARTIAL FAILURE OR QUALIFIED SUCCESS?, 31 Columbia Journal of Transnational Law 1, 29-34, 37-46 (1993)

Protecting the Integrity of the Criminal Process

A fair and efficient administration of criminal justice, with the capacity to prosecute the powerful and to protect the individual rights of both the weak and the powerful evenhandedly, is an essential component of the rule of law. Military dictatorships and their powerful supporters had little incentive to develop an efficient and fair criminal justice system as they often resorted to illegitimate violence to coerce compliance. However, the failure to control both political violence and street crime is a central factor in the instability of a new democracy.

Much has been written about the tendency of the inquisitorial features of the civil law tradition to contaminate the criminal process with its penchant for truth-seeking and finding the culprits, even at the cost of individual liberties. In continental civil law systems, the towering figure of an investigative magistrate or judge, calling witnesses and seeking objective truth through questions formulated with the aid of an extensive pretrial dossier, applies an inquisitorial approach to the criminal process that appears somewhat inimical to the protection of the individual rights of the accused. In contrast, the Anglo-American pattern of criminal justice, generally portrayed as an adversarial match between the prosecutor and defense counsel with a judge acting as an impartial referee, seems to reflect a fear and mistrust of the judge and the government that is consistent with "classic English liberalism" and hence more conducive to procedural fairness. Indeed, it is true that some structural aspects of the old inquisitorial procedure, characterized mainly by secret and written proceedings and a limited role for defense counsel during the pretrial investigation, remain influential in the present-day practice of Latin American criminal procedure. However, more than the inquisitorial, as opposed to the adversarial structure of the criminal process, there are other elements in need of readjustment. Those are the factors that are likely to determine the adequate balance between the finding of the truth and the speedy conviction of the guilty on the one hand, and the preservation of privacy and human dignity of the accused on the other.

One of the problems in need of recalibration involves the working relationships between the police, judges, and prosecutors. Judges and prosecutors should be able to rely on a police body directly responsible to them, with the technical capacity to investigate, but under close supervision or control of the judiciary. This has not been possible in Argentina and most of Latin America, where police forces dependent on the administrative sphere of the executive have become the main protagonist of the pre-trial investigatory stage of the criminal process. The police are meant to be merely auxiliary to the judge empowered to investigate crimes, without the power to try or dismiss on their own authority cases that do not warrant the intervention of the judicial machinery. However, expanded police activity with very little judicial control is tolerated by overworked investigative magistrates. This expanded role of the police is advantageous in operating as a filter that prevents all criminal cases from clogging even more an overburdened judicial machinery. It also makes possible a more complete police report, to the benefit of the judicial inquiry. These practical advantages, however, are more than offset by the fact that the preliminary inquiries conducted by the police more often than not leave an individual accused of crime completely unprotected from abuses of state power. Whereas some legal systems may find it possible to compel the police to conform to standards of fair play, in Argentina it is difficult to enforce constitutional standards protecting individual rights in a way that achieves adherence in daily police practice.

Another important problem that gravely affects effective law enforcement in the administration of criminal justice is the fear of intimidation. Investigations into allegations of abuse of authority and government corruption are frequently hindered by intimidation of those whose cooperation is crucial for the success of the investigation. Judges, lawyers, victims, and witnesses are not encouraged to cooperate in a criminal investigation when their lives, and those of their family members, are threatened. This problem of intimidation must also take into consideration a basic apathy on the part of the population at large, whose attitude towards law enforcement is bred of cynicism, despair, a long history of bad experiences with police abuses, and an inefficient judiciary.

Aside from the foregoing factors hindering the efficacy and fairness of the criminal process, what truly reflects the commitment of the criminal justice system to individual rights is the actual operation of basic procedural safeguards guaranteed by the constitution. Standards of criminal due process vary from country to country, but one could plausibly argue in favor of a "minimalist" conception of procedural safeguards whose effective implementation appears relevant for the consolidation of democratic values. Procedural efficiency in law enforcement against the guilty is extremely important, but procedural fairness to both the innocent and the guilty contributes even more to place the criminal process at the service of democratic consolidation. A government committed to serve the liberty of all cannot justify prosecutorial or criminal encroachment upon the rights of an individual unless it complies with those minimum standards of procedural fairness. Procedural fairness includes effective protection against arbitrary arrests, insuring the right to counsel as of the time of the arrest, exclusionary rules precluding the use of evidence obtained in violation of the right to counsel, privilege against self-incrimination, and constitutional requirements for searches and seizures. A closer look at these problems in Argentina reveals some recent and significant jurisprudential developments, many of which were accomplished after the return to civilian rule; it also shows that these noble goals have a long, thorny way to go for their full realization.

Arbitrary Arrests

One way to prevent recurrent arbitrary detention is to establish prompt and effective mechanisms for reviewing the legality of a detention. A corollary of this mechanism is the elaboration of clear judicial standards as to what should be accepted as reasonable grounds for a warrantless arrest. Under Argentine law, police officers may carry out an arrest only for crimes committed in their presence or whenever there are "strong indications that a crime has been committed by a particular person," a requirement which may be functionally compared to requirements such as "probable cause" or "reasonable suspicion." One of the main problems in this area remains that the notion of "reasonable initial suspicion" has never been tested by the Argentine Supreme Court.[98] Another problem is that at least two procedural mechanisms have provided a legal cloak for arbitrary and warrantless arrests — the authority conferred on the police to adjudicate misdemeanor cases and to detain persons for purposes of identification....

Timely Right to Counsel

A constitutional right to counsel has been traditionally recognized in Argentina for all kinds of offenses and to all defendants.[108] Article 18 of the Constitution provides in this regard that "no inhabitant of the nation shall be punished without a previous trial ... and the right of defense shall not be violated." However, under Argentine law a person accused of a crime does not become a "defendant" (*procesado*) until he or she is interrogated by the investigating judge, and the courts have been reluctant to extend the scope of the constitutional right to counsel to investigatory proceedings that take place prior to the judicial interrogation of the accused. Thus, the Supreme Court has repeatedly held that as long as persons charged with crimes are provided with counsel as soon as they obtain the status of defendants, no constitutional error derives from limiting the assistance of counsel during the preliminary stages of the investigation.[111] The rationale underlying this restrictive view can be grasped in light of antiquated rules of criminal procedure that conceive of no meaningful participation of counsel during the preliminary phase of the investigation.[112] This conception derives in turn from a widely held perception,

---

[98] In those cases where this issue was submitted to the Supreme Court, it was held the questions concerning whether the arrest was supported on reasonable grounds of suspicion does not involve a constitutional or federal question but a procedural issue subject to the exclusive jurisdiction of the lower courts and beyond the scope of Supreme Court appellate jurisdiction through the writ of error (*recurso extraordinario*). Altini, CSJN, 68 Fallos 316 (1897).

[108] Argentine law provides public defenders for indigents, although caseloads exceed the system's capacity to provide adequate legal counseling in a significant number of cases.

[111] *See, e.g.*, Chamudis, CSJN, 235 Fallos 332 (1956) (finding that the alleged vices and shortcomings of the investigatory process as claimed by the defendant do not amount to a direct violation of the Constitution as long as the appellant was afforded enough opportunities to defend himself at later stages of the proceedings).

[112] Under Argentine law, the criminal proceedings are secret during the first ten days of the investigation in order to allow the magistrate broad powers of discovery. Although the public prosecutor is allowed to examine the record, neither the defense counsel nor the lawyer representing the victim has access to the record. Article 180 of the Federal Code of Criminal Procedure allows the investigating judge, in his unreviewable discretion, to extend the secrecy for running periods of ten days, or to reimpose it at any later moment. C.P.P. art. 180. Moreover, under the

still very much alive, that early attorney-client contact in the criminal process is somewhat inimical to the paramount goal of the criminal justice system, i.e., the discovery of the truth.

Any discussion of the limited role assigned to defense counsel during the preliminary stage of the criminal process must address the weight given by the legal system to extrajudicial confessions. Under Argentine law, the defendant's confession cannot be accepted as the basis for an entry of a plea of guilty; there is no plea bargaining and the proceedings go forward regardless of a full admission of guilt.[113] Paradoxically, the "real" criminal justice system places a high reliance on confessions, which have been and continue to be the easiest and most persuasive foundation upon which to support a conviction. Admissions of guilt before the investigative judge are surrounded by procedural safeguards concerning the giving of proper warnings, the place of interrogation, and the impartiality of the interrogator. The real challenge to the Argentine criminal justice system has been whether to admit in evidence extrajudicial confessions made before the police, when the interrogation is more likely than not to be psychologically coercive.

Privilege Against Self-Incrimination

Article 18 of the Constitution of Argentina provides for the privilege against self-incrimination in stating that "no one shall be compelled to testify against himself." For a long time the defendant had the burden of proving that confessions obtained at the police station were not given as freely and spontaneously as it appeared from the police records. However, during the last decade Argentine courts have significantly enhanced the rights of the accused under police questioning. During the early 1980's, the Argentine Supreme Court started to develop exclusionary rules with regard to coerced confessions, not because such confessions are unreliable, but because they are illegally obtained.[116] A few years later an amendment was introduced into the Federal Code of Criminal Procedure precluding the admissibility in evidence of extrajudicial confessions. Although the inadmissibility in evidence of incriminating statements given to the police has decreased the likelihood of police abuses, some courts have continued to hold that the exclusion of admissions of guilt does not necessarily lead to the exclusion of other evidentiary leads obtained through statements given under police custody. Obviously, this judicial posture weakens the framework of restraint that is necessary to eradicate the habit of abuses at the police station. The strong potential for abuse of individual rights in the use of extrajudicial confessions given without advice of coun-

---

federal rules of criminal procedure a defendant may be held incommunicado for five days, which may be extended for another three. C.P.P. arts. 184(10), 256-57. A suspect held incommunicado cannot talk to a lawyer or anybody else without permission of the investigating judge....

For recent amendments introduced by a new code of criminal procedure that came into force in September 1992, see *infra* note 135.

[113] Argentine law adheres to the "principle of legality" (*Legalitätsprinzip*), according to which prosecutors are legally bound to prosecute all crimes, no matter how insignificant, that come to their attention. Cód. Proc. Pen. arts. 71, 274; Cód. Proc. Pen. art. 460.... It is questionable, however, the extent to which the idea of mandatory prosecution is reflected in actual practice.

[116] Montenegro, CSJN, 303 Fallos 1938 (1981), [1982-IV] J.A. 368 (1982) (holding that coerced confessions cannot be admitted in evidence irrespective of the question of their reliability).

sel points to the need for a minimalist conception of due process requiring the total exclusion of extrajudicial confessions and any evidence obtained from unrepresented defendants after the arrest. This approach will, however, throw a heavy burden to the administration of criminal justice in Argentina, where modern techniques of crime detection and the judicial apparatus to support them have been traditionally nonexistent as a result of stagnant or declining judicial resources.... Under a recently enacted Federal Code of Criminal Procedure, the interrogation of suspects by the police is expressly prohibited, except for identification purposes.[120] It remains to be seen, however, whether the interrogation will actually be conducted by the judge and not by lower level judicial officers.

Search and Seizure

Article 18 of the Argentine Constitution further provides that "dwelling, written communications, and private papers shall not be violated or trespassed, and a law is to determine in what cases and under what circumstances their search and occupation shall be permitted." The regulation of this constitutional guarantee is found in the Federal Code of Criminal Procedure and similar codes adopted by the provinces. Thus, a judicial warrant is required for entry in a private dwelling, except under "exigent circumstances" defined by the codes.[123] However, searches and seizures have been traditionally conducted in Argentina without much judicial control, mainly on the ground that the flaw of searching the premises without a warrant was cured by the implicit consent of the dweller, inferred from the absence in the police record of an express objection to the entrance. For almost a century of constitutional jurisprudence, the Supreme Court perceived the acquisition of evidence through warrantless searches not within the statutory exceptions provided by the codes of criminal procedure as an issue involving the application of procedural rules to the facts of the case, left to the sovereign decision of state courts and not involving federal or constitutional questions subject to the appellate jurisdiction of the Supreme Court. This judicial approach has been changing, noticeably since Argentina's return to civilian rule.

During the early 1980's, some criminal courts of appeal began to rule that evidence obtained through the illegal search of a dwelling could not be used against a defendant. In 1984, the Supreme Court held for the first time, on constitutional grounds, that evidence obtained through illegal searches of private dwellings could not be used at trial.[127] This ruling was later expanded, through split majorities of the Supreme Court, to invalidate the evidentiary

---

[120] Cód. Proc. Pen. Law No. 23984, Boletín Informativo de Anales de Legislación Argentina, No. 24, art. 184(a) (1991).

[123] Exigent circumstances that permit dispensing with a judicial warrant include situations where the police are in hot pursuit of a criminal or when voices are heard crying for help. *See* Cód. Proc. Pen. arts. 188-89, 399-410.

[127] Fiorentino, CSJN, 306 Fallos 1752, 1754, [1985-A] L.L. 160 (1985) (holding that once the illegality of the search is established, subsequent seizures are also illegal, as they are no more than the fruit of a proceeding condemned by law and any use of such evidence for conviction would amount to the judicial process condoning the use of evidence secured in violation of the constitutional rights of the defendant which would not only be inconsistent with the rule of law, but also impair the fair administration of justice).

fruits derived from warrantless searches of private dwellings.[128] However, the exclusionary rule developed by the Supreme Court was made subject to the caveat that a warrantless search may be validated if the beneficiary of such a rule is found to have waived his constitutional right to object to the entrance of law-enforcement officers. Recent pronouncements of the Court cast some doubt about the guidelines that will determine who and how one gives a valid consent, as well as what can be considered "exigent circumstances" enabling the authorities to dispense with the requirement of a judicial warrant. Moreover, this exclusionary rule has been established only in the context of evidence obtained through illegal searches of a private dwelling, and it is not clear whether it will be expanded to exclude evidence gathered through illegal arrests or as a result of violations of other constitutional rights.[130] Admittedly, the development of exclusionary rules calls for a careful weighing of the public's interest in effective prosecution against the interest in fair treatment of those who benefit from a presumption of innocence. However, in a country like Argentina where the balance of interests has traditionally weighed in favor of governmental power at the expense of individual rights, affirming the sanctity of the judicial process at this juncture of a transition to democracy, even at the cost of suppressing unquestionable evidence that could serve to convict a wrongdoer, would further the rule of law and foster a legal culture tied to procedural fairness.

Transparency of the Criminal Justice System

A final point which emphasizes the relevance of the criminal justice system to the consolidation of democratic institutions relates to the need to replace a slow and arcane criminal process with a relatively speedy and open system of administration of justice. The establishment of open, oral, and concentrated trials, to be held with relative speed after the commission of a crime, is crucial for providing transparency to the administration of justice.

1. *Oral Form of Criminal Trials*

Criminal proceedings are in written form in most Argentine jurisdictions, and although the public is theoretically free to attend the interrogation of witnesses, in practice those hearings are carried out solely in the presence of the interested parties. In this sense, the Argentine criminal process cannot be considered truly public. The codes of criminal procedure of some Argentine provinces introduced oral trials for some major criminal offenses, but trials on written files without public hearings have survived in the federal rules of criminal procedure which have been in force since the nineteenth century. However, recent developments in Argentina show a renewed effort to implant once and for all a criminal process that is both open and expedient. Since the return to civilian rule, both transitional governments worked on the elabora-

[128] Rayford, CSJN, [1986-C] L.L. 396 (holding that the defendant may benefit from the suppression of evidence obtained in violation of the constitutional rights of a third person).

[130] Police officers in Argentina have long had undisputed authority to conduct searches incidental to arrests, and no constitutional limits have been established as to the discretion of the investigating magistrate to issue a warrant for an arrest or a search of a private dwelling.

tion of a new code of criminal procedure that would introduce oral trials and other changes to the criminal process. Whereas the draft procedural code sponsored by the first transitional government failed to obtain the approval of Congress, a second draft supported by the second transitional government was finally adopted as the new Federal Code of Criminal Procedure. This new code entered into force on September 5, 1992, and it is too early yet to assess the impact of this initiative.[134] Significantly, in addition to providing for oral and public trials, the revamped code includes significant changes intended to enhance the right of suspects detained by the police.[135]

2. *Jury Trials*

The ingredient of fairness in being judged by one's peers, so closely connected to the development of the common law tradition, is not necessarily related to the need for instilling the degree of transparency desirable for the administration of criminal justice. Nevertheless, it is significant that in the common law countries where jury trials have been established, the involvement of lay jurors remains closely connected with open, public, and concentrated trials. The general benefits that come from public involvement and awareness of the administration of criminal justice cannot be obtained in jurisdictions where the written proceedings, developed during the course of isolated procedural stages, escape more easily from public observation. The framers of the Argentine Constitution tied the benefits of transparency, furthered by oral and concentrated trials, with the democratic values associated with the involvement of the citizenry in the administration of justice through jury trials. Articles 24, 67(11), and 102 of the Constitution contemplate the involvement of jurors in criminal cases pursuant to a law that Congress was to pass. However, the law implementing the organization and functioning of jury criminal trials was never enacted, and when the Federal Code of Criminal Procedure was passed, some thirty years after the adoption of the Constitution, the drafters thought that the country was not ready for trials by jury as it might lead to political clashes if leaders of one faction were tried by members of another. Thus, although the founding fathers anticipated that Congress would provide for jury trials in criminal cases, in over 150 years Congress never instituted anything even remotely resembling a jury trial,[138] and the Supreme Court has repeatedly held as beyond its jurisdiction rulings which could remedy this omission of the legislature.... It is also noteworthy

[134] *See* Cód. Proc. Pen. Law No. 23984, *supra* note 120.

[135] The new code clearly spells out the duty of the police to adequately inform the defendant of his rights, such as the right to remain silent and the right to be represented by counsel. Cód. Proc. Pen. arts. 295-98. The police must make a detainee available for questioning by a judge within six hours of the arrest, Cód. Proc Pen. art. 286, and police officers are expressly precluded from questioning a suspect unless for the purpose of establishing their identity, Cód. Proc. Pen. art. 184. For the first time in Argentine legal history, the new code of criminal procedure authorizes the defense counsel to speak to and assist a detainee held incommunicado *before* the detainee appears at a hearing to be interrogated by the judge. Cód. Proc. Pen. arts. 184, 197, 205(3), 294.... One legal scholar criticized this amendment as inimical to societal interests in seeking the truth and punishing the guilty.

[138] Argentine law also failed to establish mixed tribunals in the continental fashion, in which professional judges sit with lay jurors (*escabinos*) to decide a case.

that jury criminal trials have not met with much success in those few Latin American countries where they have been introduced.[143]

NOTES AND QUESTIONS

1. Prepare a list of the major problems facing Latin American criminal justice systems. How many of your items are associated with elements of an inquisitorial procedure and how many are basically tied to lack of economic resources? Or to something else?

2. In the United States about one-third of all state felony defendants are not released from jail prior to trial. Thus, about two-thirds of U.S. accused are free before a determination is made concerning their guilt or innocence. During this period 18 percent of the released defendants are re-arrested for a felony. In Latin American civil law countries, as Professor Pérez reports, the incidence of pretrial release is much lower. What values do the two systems reflect and which approach do you believe is better for society?

3. Criminal procedure reform in Argentina was a joint effort of the federal Supreme Court in the 1980s and the federal Congress through passage of a new Code of Criminal Procedure that went into effect in 1992. Does the Court's role, in particular, belie its place within the civil law tradition? How important do you think the influence of the U.S. Supreme Court and its criminal procedure jurisprudence has been for the Argentine Court?

4. For additional information on Latin American criminal procedure, see Weber Martins Batista, *An Overview of Brazilian Criminal Procedure,* in A Panorama of Brazilian Law 207 (Jacob Dolinger & Keith S. Rosenn eds. 1992); Alejandro D. Carrió, The Criminal Justice System of Argentina (1989); John P. Mandler, *Habeas Corpus and the Protection of Human Rights in Argentina,*

---

[143] Jury criminal trials were introduced in Brazil, Colombia, El Salvador, Mexico, Nicaragua, and Panama. Jury trials in Brazil were first instituted in 1822 and are currently mandated for felonies against life. C.F. art. 5(38); C.P.P. arts. 394-408 (providing for the "Tribunal of the Jury," which is composed of one professional presiding judge and seven lay jurors chosen by lot from a list of 21 citizens).... Under Article 483 the role of the trial judge is largely restricted to posing the questions which the jury will answer in deciding the case. C.P.P. art. 483. The jury's verdict can only be appealed if it is against all material evidence in the case or in case of procedural irregularities. Although Article 28 of the Brazilian Criminal Code provides that "emotion or passion does not exclude criminal responsibility," juries have traditionally found that a man could legitimately kill his adulterous wife caught in the act of adultery, thus equating a so-called "honor defense" with legitimate self-defense in order to justify "crimes of passion.".... Although Brazilian appellate courts have repeatedly reversed such verdicts on the ground that they were not supported by the law, trial judges conducting the retrial of those cases on remand tend to ignore the higher court's ruling on the ground that they are constitutionally bound to defer to the sovereignty of the jury. The second jury's decision is final and cannot be appealed again, unless on other grounds. Human rights organizations have criticized this social prejudice, stressing that the jury's sovereignty does not extend to deciding contrary to law and that to hold otherwise makes a mockery of the appellate process and the administration of justice.... Articles 20(VI), 111, and 130 of the Mexican Constitution of 1917 refer to the possibility of establishing jury trials for certain criminal offenses, but as a matter of practice jury trials are rarely resorted to in Mexico.... The jury system (*jurado de conciencia*) was abolished in Colombia in 1989, a decision whose constitutionality was upheld by the Supreme Court.... Jury trials were contemplated by the Nicaraguan Code of Criminal Procedure, ... but they were abolished in 1988. The reasons given for the abolition of juries were the time and costs involved, the lack of sufficient training and understanding of lay persons, and the perception that juries were too lenient.... It is noteworthy that Article 125 of the Spanish Constitution of 1978 calls for a jury to try criminal cases, but more than 15 years after its adoption the regulating legislation is yet to be enacted.

16 Yale J. Int'l L. 1 (1991); Michael R. Pahl, *Wanted: Criminal Justice — Colombia's Adoption of a Prosecutorial System of Criminal Procedure,* 16 Fordham Int'l L.J. 608 (1992-1993); Keith S. Rosenn, *A Comparison of the New Constitutions of Colombia and Brazil,* 23 U. Miami Inter-Am. L. Rev. 659 (1992).

9. JAPAN: EFFICIENT LENIENCY

JOHN OWEN HALEY, AUTHORITY WITHOUT POWER: LAW AND THE JAPANESE PARADOX 125-33, 135-38 (1991)

[*The Formal and Informal Tracks*]

The criminal process in Japan in effect moves along two parallel tracks. The first involves a formal institutional process similar to most contemporary legal systems derived from continental European models. Detailed substantive and procedural rules set out in the Constitution, codes, and statutes govern each stage of the formal process from the investigation and apprehension of offenders by the police to formal sentencing and appeals by judges. Few if any of Japan's institutions reflect adaptations of traditional practices and procedures. Even the most exceptional often turn out to be innovations derived indirectly from Western models. Japan's system of discretionary prosecution, for example, is a notable departure from German practice. However, Japan's apparently unique system for citizen review of exercises of prosecutorial discretion through an "inquest of prosecution" or prosecution review commission [*kensatsu shinsakai*] was in fact designed ... as a compromise to fend off [U.S. government officials] who wished to include an American-styled grand jury system as a component of the criminal procedure reforms.

Japan's formal system of criminal justice is therefore somewhat of a hybrid. It combines basic features of continental European, especially German, law and practice with elements of American law, particularly the procedural protections included in provisions of the postwar Constitution and the revised Code of Criminal Procedure. The most striking departure from German and other European practice, which dates to Japan's earliest regulations on criminal procedure in the mid-nineteenth century, is the extent of discretion enjoyed by police, prosecutor, and judge alike.

The process begins with investigation of a reported crime and the identification of a suspect as the offender by the police, who exercise considerable discretion in reporting to the procuracy cases involving "minor crimes." For example, in 1978, Japanese police identified suspects in 599,302 cases out of 1,136,448 reported offenses. In these cases they identified 231,403 suspects, many apparently responsible for several offenses, who could be subjected to prosecution. However, only 168,646 suspects were actually reported to the procuracy; 62,727 (21.12 percent) were instead released without further process pursuant to article 246 of the Code of Criminal Procedure authorizing the police to close "simple" cases [*bizai shobun*]. In this manner, between 1975 and 1980 the police disposed of nearly 18 percent of all Criminal Code offenses (not involving violations of motor vehicle traffic laws and other special statutes). An even higher figure is given for the Tokyo Metropolitan District. It is estimated that the police fail to report about 40 percent of all referable cases.

For cases reported to the local procurator's office, several avenues are open. After a second investigation, the procurators may transfer the case to another procurator's office on jurisdictional grounds, close the case for lack of sufficient evidence or other reasons, prosecute in either summary or ordinary trial proceedings, or suspend prosecution. For example, as indicated in Table 10.5, in 1987 Japanese procurators had a total caseload of 3,441,024 cases, of which 1,169,185 represented Criminal Code offenses (including certain traffic-accident related offenses like bodily injury or death resulting from professional negligence), 2,084,152 criminal motor vehicle and traffic violations under special statutes, and 187,687 other offenses under special statutes, such as possession of illicit drugs, violation of Japan's gun control law, and electoral law violations. Of the total caseload, only about 50 percent were prosecuted. Twenty-seven percent were transferred to other procurator offices or to family courts (cases involving juvenile offenders, constituting 14.5 percent of the total caseload). Less than 2 percent were closed for lack of sufficient evidence or other reasons. Prosecution was suspended in the remaining 10 percent....

Table 10.5

Disposition of Criminal Cases Processed by Japanese Public Prosecutors in 1987, by Type and Disposition

	Caseload	Prosecuted Cases	Formal Trial	Summary Proceedings
Total Offenses	3,441,024	1,742,508	125,421	1,617,087
Criminal Code	1,169,185	377,407	79,732	297,675
Homicide (art. 199)	2,989	1,060	1,060	—
Bodily injury	39,722	15,607	4,604	11,003
Larceny (art. 235)	220,434	37,513	37,513	—
Indecency through compulsion (art. 176) & rape (art. 177)	2,382	771	771	—
Rape or death in course of robbery (art. 241)	930	423	423	—
Robbery (art. 236)	874	449	449	—
Fraud (art. 246)	19,462	10,095	10,095	—
Motor vehicle violations	2,084,152	1,282,320	10,725	1,271,595
Other offenses under special statutes	187,687	82,781	34,964	47,817

[T]here is no guilty plea in Japanese criminal procedure. In all prosecuted cases — including those subject to simplified procedures — the procurators must provide the court with sufficient evidence of guilt to convict. However, the vast majority of all prosecuted cases (93 percent) are adjudicated with only documentary evidence in uncontested summary proceedings [*ryakushiki tetsuzuki*] in which the maximum penalty is 200,000 yen ([about U.S. $2,000] at prevailing exchange rates). Formal trial proceedings — with or without a defense — were used in 1987 in only 7 percent of all prosecuted cases and less than 4 percent of the total caseload. Summary proceedings are an available alternative for any offense for which the penalty of a fine is an available statutory option. Serious offenses punishable by mandatory jail terms must be tried in ordinary proceedings. These include such offenses as homicide, rape, larceny, robbery, fraud, and extortion. Thus a far greater proportion of ordinary proceedings — 63 percent — involve these and other Criminal Code offenses.

The police report very few suspects who are not convictable.... [I]n 1987, out of 3,441,024 reported offenses, only 37,631 or 1 percent were dismissed by the procurator's office for lack of sufficient evidence. This percentage has been constant for over a decade. Those who are prosecuted are almost always convicted. Prevailing conviction rates hover at about 99.5 percent. Since guilt is not contested in the vast majority of cases, the conviction rate in cases where guilt is at issue is probably closer to 90 percent.

Few offenders, however, are punished with more than a minor penalty. As noted, in summary proceedings the maximum penalty is a fine of 200,000 yen.... Most offenders pay considerably less. For example, in 1987 over 70 percent of all defendants convicted in summary proceedings were fined less than 50,000 yen (about U.S. $[500] at prevailing exchange rates). Nearly 43 percent were fined less than 30,000 yen (about U.S. $[300]). Only 0.5 percent received the maximum 200,000 yen fine.

Defendants subject to more stringent penalties than those allowed in summary proceedings are treated upon conviction with similar leniency. With hardly any variation for over a quarter-century, Japanese first instance trial courts annually sentenced between 60,000 to 65,000 defendants to prison terms or detention a year. In slightly more than 50 percent of all cases, the court suspends the sentence. About 5 percent of all convicted defendants are sentenced without suspension to prison terms of less than six months; 12 percent to terms of six months to a year, 12 percent to terms of one to two years; 5 percent to terms of two to three years, and only 2 percent to terms of 3 years. Less than 2 percent of those convicted are sentenced to prison terms of more than five years.

Even in cases involving violent crime the courts suspend sentences in a relatively large number of cases. In 1977 and 1987, for example, sentences were suspended in 25 percent (1977) or 20 percent (1987) of all homicide cases, 46 percent (1977) or 35 percent (1987) for all arson convictions, 47 percent (1977) or 37 percent (1987) of all rape cases, 32 percent (1977) or 26 percent of all robbery cases, and in 55 percent (1977) or 52 percent (1987) of all convictions for bodily injury. Moreover, lenient parole requirements have meant that more than half of the relatively few offenders Japan imprisons are paroled before the expiration of their terms.

Even pretrial detention is rarely used except in cases involving violent crimes. More than "four-fifths of all suspects," observes David Bayley, "are handled without arrest on an 'at home' basis."[25] He continues, "[I]n 1972 88 percent of all suspects were examined by prosecutors without detention; only 12 percent were actually arrested." (Bayley's estimate may be somewhat low,

[25] David H. Bayley, Forces of Order: Police Behavior in Japan & the United States (Berkeley: University of California Press, 1976), at p. 146.

at least for the present. Ministry of Justice figures for 1989 show that about 22 percent of suspects were arrested.) Of those suspects actually indicted, Bayley notes, fewer than 10 percent were detained in 1972 (most of whom were subject to summary proceedings).

In other words, by almost any standard criminal justice in Japan is extraordinarily lenient. Large numbers of offenders identified by the police are never reported as suspects to the procuracy. Of those reported, most are convictable. Yet the vast majority are allowed to take advantage of summary proceedings that result in minor fines equivalent to a few hundred dollars. For many others prosecution is routinely suspended. Even though prosecution of those that remain seems tantamount to conviction in ordinary trials, sentences are generally suspended in more than half of all cases. Except for detention during police interrogation, few offenders, it appears, ever see the inside of a jail. This is the outcome of the informal "second track" of Japanese criminal justice.

Confession, Repentance, and Absolution

The police, procurators, and judges take a variety of factors into account in their decisions on how to treat a particular suspect or defendant. They include considerations common to most criminal justice systems: the gravity of the offense relative to the stigma for the offender of a criminal conviction, the circumstances and nature of the crime, the age and prior record by the offender. Added to this matrix in Japan, however, are additional factors that appear to be missing elsewhere — at least in the West. First, the attitude of the offender in acknowledging guilt, expressing remorse, and compensating any victims, but also the victims' response in expressing willingness to pardon, are determinative elements in the decision whether to report, to prosecute, or to sentence the offender.

Minoru Shikita, former director of the United Nations Asia and Far East Institute for the Prevention of Crime and Treatment of Offenders (UNAFEI), describes the role of the police:

> [T]he police, with the general accord of the chief public prosecutor of a district, need not refer all cases formally to the prosecution, but may report cases in consolidated form monthly, provided the offenses are minor property offenses, the suspects have shown repentance, restitution has been made, and victims forgive the suspects.

Even in the cases referred to public prosecutors, Shikita notes, "the police invariably recommend a lenient disposition if a suspect has shown sincere repentance about his or her alleged crime and the transgression against a social norm is not particularly serious."

Similar considerations motivate prosecutors in deciding whether to suspend prosecution. The critical factors include "the existence of a confession, sincere repentance by the suspect and the forgiveness of the victim."...

Japanese judges also uniformly confirm that a defendant's acknowledgment of guilt and sincerity in displaying remorse, evidenced in part by compensation of the victim and the victim's forgiving response, are pivotal in their decision on whether to suspend sentence. One senior Japanese judge is said to have refused even after conviction and sentencing to allow defendants to leave the courtroom until they confessed and expressed remorse.

Typically, the suspect not only confesses, but through family and friends also seeks letters from any victims addressed to the prosecutor or judge that acknowledge restitution and express the victim's sentiment that no further penalty need be imposed. So customary are such letters that most Japanese attorneys have some sense of the amounts usually required.

The victim thus participates in the process. Restitution is ordinarily made and the victim has a voice in the authorities' decisions whether to report, to prosecute, or to sentence the offender....

In this way the victims participate in the process but do not control it. Ultimately they must defer to the authorities' decision.... The process, however, does give the offender an incentive to make amends and the victim an opportunity to forgive. The victim does not assume the role of adversary or prosecutor nor is the victim enabled to use the formal process as a means of retribution and revenge.

Most studies of the criminal process in Japan note the evidentiary importance of confession but seldom proceed further either to analyze its implications or to note the victims' role in the process....

The focus on the evidentiary importance of confessions to the exclusion of its rehabilitative effect, whether or not elaborated by charges of abusive coercion, is generally premised on Western-derived notions of the primacy of the formal process and the exclusivity of its function to ascertain guilt. Prior to sentencing, the criminal justice system is conceived to have a single overall objective — to identify accurately the offender. This premise inexorably leads to a predominant emphasis on the credibility of evidence of guilt as well as procedural controls to prevent error in the investigatory and trial process. American observers tend to be particularly sensitive to such concerns because confessions and plea bargaining play so significant a role in reducing the burdens on the criminal process in the United States. While Japanese judges also display great concern with the probative value of coerced or induced confessions, they do not neglect their correctional value.

No person in Japan is convicted solely by confession. As noted previously, unlike the United States, the United Kingdom, and other common law jurisdictions, there is no guilty plea in Japan, eliminating the need for a trial on guilt. In all cases, even summary proceedings, an evidentiary hearing to determine that a crime has been committed and the guilt of the accused is necessary. Even where there is a confession, the prosecutor has the burden to prove it was made voluntarily and proffer at least collaborative evidence of the crime.... Moreover, the judge in the trial has the duty to clarify evidence and, as the finder of fact, be convinced of guilt and thus the reliability of any confession. Although prosecutorial and judicial scrutiny of collaborative evidence is not likely to be as vigorous if the accused has confessed and offers no defense, nevertheless, such procedural protections may not be as relevant to accuracy as the concern of judges as well as police and prosecutors over the "sincerity" and truthfulness of the confession and demonstrated remorse. The second track includes telling tests of credibility.

A fundamental aim of the criminal process in Japan is correction, not just determination of guilt or punishment of the offender. Law enforcement officials at all levels tend to share this objective.... Thus, their roles are not confined to the formal tasks of apprehending, prosecuting, and adjudicating. Rather once personally convinced that a suspect is an offender, their concern for evidentiary proof of guilt shifts to a concern over the suspect's attitude and prospects for rehabilitation and reintegration into society, including acceptance of authority. Leniency is considered an appropriate response if the correctional process has begun. The sincerity of confession and remorse therefore becomes a significant factor in deciding whether correction is likely. Since confession and repentance provoke leniency — and most do confess — law enforcement authorities also generally expect offenders to confess and to behave with remorseful submission. For a suspect the authorities believe to be guilty not to confess thus poses a dilemma. Either they have erred and the suspect is not guilty or he is unrepentant and less correctable. Under these circumstances, it is not surprising — nor, one hastens to add, excusable — that police, prosecutors, and judges are tempted to induce or coerce acknowledgment of guilt. The more convinced the authorities become that the suspect is guilty, the more likely they are to resort to harsh and abusive measures. Yet there is also an incentive for them to reexamine more carefully the evidence of guilt before attempting to coerce the suspect....

Cultural explanations tend to be equally, albeit more subtly, ethnocentric by quarantining the Japanese experience and denying its relevance outside of Japan's peculiar cultural setting. There is no question that history and societal values underpin the pattern of confession, repentance, and absolution in Japan. East Asian legal orders all place extraordinary emphasis on confession. At least as early as the T'ang dynasty, codified Chinese law provided for more lenient treatment to those who confessed voluntarily. If the commission of the crime itself was unknown to the authorities, confession resulted in pardon, and for all categories of crime voluntary confession gained a reduction in penalty. Similar patterns are observed in contemporary China....

Prevailing societal values in Japan, whatever the historical origin, do encourage the use of confession and, more important, permit a lenient response. In this respect perhaps the West, not Japan, should be considered peculiar. The moral imperative of forgiveness as a response to repentance is surely as much a part of the Judeo-Christian heritage as the East Asian tradition. For whatever reason, Western societies failed to develop institutional props for implementing such moral commands. Instead the legal institutions and processes of Western law reflect and reinforce societal demands for retribution and revenge. Indeed as one recent comparative study shows, American and Japanese attitudes toward punishment differ considerably. In the United States punishment is favored as the primary response to crime. In Japan, compensation is considered far more important. Such studies, like most cultural explanations, however, depict reality in static terms; they offer rationalizations for what exists and miss the critical contrasts between the reinforcement and disintegration of similar values in different societies. The Japanese may well prefer compensation because their system works. Americans, on the other hand, may seek punishment because theirs does not....

The Japanese experience also confirms a growing literature on the importance of acknowledgment of guilt and restitution of victims to the psychological rehabilitation of offenders and attitudes of victims toward the offender and the criminal justice system. Studies have found that offenders attempt to relieve distress experienced after committing a crime involving harm to others by justification, derogating the victim and denying responsibility, or restitution. Consequently, there is considerable empirical support for the notion that encouraging remorse and restitution reduces recidivism....

Thus it is at least arguable that the Japanese second track contributes to a process of positive reinforcement in which rehabilitation is both more likely to succeed and, in turn, to be ethically or socially a more acceptable objective. The second track of confession, repentance, and absolution of the Japanese criminal process may provide insights for other industrial societies seeking to establish a more humane and effective system of criminal justice, one free from the human and economic costs of overcrowded prisons, increasing crime, and victim alienation....

Behind the trappings of ubiquitous authority is a state far less powerful and far more dependent than most Western observers have fathomed. Although norms articulated as law in constitution or code may thereby gain greater legitimacy and societal acceptance, the reliance by the state and its instrumentalities for their enforcement on informal, social mechanisms of control represents a transfer of power. Inasmuch as the efficacy of legal norms ultimately rests with those who control their enforcement, by depending upon informal social mechanisms for crime control, the Japanese state has in effect abandoned the most coercive of all legitimate instruments of state control. In contemporary Japan these powers thus reside with the society at large and its constituent, lesser communities of family, firm, and friends.

In effect, state institutional incapacity and the successful emphasis on reintegration of repentant offenders into society and corollary reliance on informal social means of crime control have reinforced the capacity of social groups to exercise coercive controls usually reserved in the West as an exclusive prerogative of the state. The consequence is a weaker state and stronger, more autonomous and cohesive society.

NOTES AND QUESTIONS

1. Professor Daniel Foote refers to the Japanese criminal justice system as "benevolent paternalism," which he describes as follows:

> Japan's clearance rate — the percentage of reported crimes that are solved — is among the highest in the world, and its conviction rate stands at over 99.8%. Yet fewer than 5% of the adult suspects considered by police to have committed Penal Code offenses are sentenced to prison; those who are sentenced to prison serve a median sentence of under two years. In the United States, by contrast, over 30% of arrestees are sentenced to prison where they spend an average of nearly four and one-half years.

Daniel H. Foote, The Benevolent Paternalism of Japanese Criminal Justice, 80 Cal. L. Rev. 317, 318 (1992). Are the statistics he describes the cause or effect of benevolent paternalism?

2. The formal track of Japanese criminal procedure resembles in many ways the German system. What is fascinating about Japan — besides revealing the diversity that exists within the civil law tradition — is its informal track, with the acknowledgment of guilt, the expression of remorse, including direct negotiation with the victim for restitution and pardon as a precondition for lenient treatment, and the sparing resort to long-term imprisonment. Would the Japanese "second track" be workable in the United States?

3. What does Professor Haley mean when he writes that the consequence of the Japanese criminal justice system "is a weaker state and stronger, more autonomous and cohesive society"?

4. As indicated by Haley, the Japanese did not adopt the principle of mandatory prosecution, opting instead to allow broad prosecutorial discretion. In an attempt to provide oversight in lieu of an American-styled grand jury, the Allied Occupation authorities introduced a system of citizen review boards or, more formally, prosecution review commissions (*kensatsu shinsakai*). For more on prosecutorial discretion in Japan and on the review commissions, see B.J. George, *Discretionary Authority of Public Prosecutors in Japan,* 17 Law in Japan 42 (1984); Marcia E. Goodman, *The Exercise and Control of Prosecutorial Discretion in Japan,* 5 UCLA Pac. Basin L.J. 16 (1986); Daniel F. Foote, *Prosecutorial Discretion in Japan: A Response, ibid.* 96; Note, *Prosecution Review Commissions: Japan's Answer to the Problem of Prosecutorial Discretion,* 92 Colum. L. Rev. 684 (1992).

5. Various aspects of the Japanese criminal justice system are further analyzed in A. Didrick Castberg, Japanese Criminal Justice (1990); V. Lee Hamilton & Joseph Sanders, Everyday Justice (1992); Frank Bennet, Jr., *Pretrial Detention in Japan: Overview and Introductory Note,* 23 Law in Japan 67 (1990); Daniel H. Foote, *Confessions and the Right to Silence in Japan,* 21 Ga. J. Int'l & Comp. L. 415 (1991); *id., "The Door that Never Opens"? Capital Punishment and Post-Conviction Review of Death Sentences in the United States and Japan,* 19 Brooklyn J. Int'l L. 367 (1993).

Chapter 11

SUBSTANTIVE RULES AND THE PRIVATE LAW CODES

We come at last to the substantive rules of law. Earlier chapters have emphasized the intellectual, institutional, and procedural context within which the substantive rules are formed and applied. In this chapter we look more closely at the rules themselves.

Most introductory manuals on law of the sort used in the first year of legal education in civil law universities begin with a discussion of "the juridical norm," which can be translated as "the legal rule." This initial emphasis on rules is consistent with traditional legal science, which as we have seen in Chapter 5 is a science of rules. Accordingly, the nature and qualities of the legal rule itself are prominent and early objects of attention. In our own system of legal education such an examination, if it takes place at all, is likely to occur as part of a course in jurisprudence which examines the work of analytical jurists like John Austin, Wesley N. Hohfeld, and H.L.A. Hart. Some of the flavor of the discussion of legal rules in civil law introductory manuals can be evoked by rereading the Merryman excerpt in Chapter 5, Section B.5 and the Damaška excerpt in Chapter 8, Section A.1, *supra*, which will not be extended here.

Many rules of law in civil law systems — particularly those systematically organized and stated in codes — are easy to find and to read, but it soon becomes clear that, even in English translation, one is reading a foreign language. The words are often familiar enough but the organizing ideas, the working categories, the concepts used are unfamiliar. One needs a new conceptual vocabulary — the vocabulary of the foreign legal system — to read its rules with any degree of comprehension. Thus, to take examples with which we are already familiar, such terms as "law," "court," "judge," "appeal," "law school," "supreme court," "trial," and others mean something different in civil law systems than in our own. There are, in addition, peculiar unfamiliar terms: "cassation," "revision," "state of siege," "decree laws" are examples that we have already seen. Even when put in English form these terms are obviously foreign in content.

One purpose of this chapter is to introduce you to the principal organizing concepts — the vocabulary — of the rules of law in the civil law tradition, with particular emphasis on private law. We will also examine the structure of the major civil codes and look briefly at the controlling concepts in property law and examples of the use of general principles in tort and contract law in Japan.

A. HOW THE LAW IS DIVIDED

1. LEGAL CATEGORIES

JOHN HENRY MERRYMAN, THE CIVIL LAW TRADITION: AN INTRODUCTION TO THE LEGAL SYSTEMS OF WESTERN EUROPE AND LATIN AMERICA 90-100 (2d ed. 1985)

It is obvious enough that the law can be divided in various ways to serve a variety of functions. It is equally obvious, although more difficult to demonstrate, that any division of the law is bound to shape the legal system. The conventional way of dividing the law becomes a part of the law itself, affecting the way that law is formulated and applied. Thus the manner in which the law is divided and classified will affect such activities as characterization (how shall a problem be characterized for legal treatment), teaching (what courses will make up the law school curriculum), scholarship (what are the typical fields of specialization among legal scholars), organization of law libraries (how shall books be classified), codification (what constitutes an appropriate area of the law for codification), legal writing and publishing (what will be the area of concern of a book or a legal periodical), and ordinary communication among lawyers. The generally accepted way of dividing and classifying the law in the civil law world is quite different from that to which the common lawyer has been accustomed.

One of the most characteristic aspects of the traditional civil law way of dividing law is the measurably greater degree of emphasis on, and confidence in, the validity and utility of formal definitions and distinctions. While common lawyers tend to think of the division of the law as conventional, i.e., as the product of some mixture of history, convenience, and habit, the influence of scholars, and particularly of legal science, has led civil lawyers to treat the matter of division of the law in more normative terms. As we have seen in Chapter [5, Section B], definitions and categories are thought to be scientifically derivable from objective legal reality. Once scientifically found and refined, they are incorporated into the systematic reconstruction of the law that is the subject matter of legal science. Thus the descriptive merges into the prescriptive. The emphasis of legal scholars on system, abstraction, formalism, and purity further amplifies the apparently authoritative impact of the distinctions and definitions of legal science. The definitions and categories become part of the systematic legal structure that is employed by legal scholars, is taught to law students, and is thereby built into the law. Their methodological utility is considered incidental to their essential validity.

The main division of law in the civil law tradition is into public law and private law. This distinction seems to most civil lawyers to be fundamental, necessary, and, on the whole, evident. Treatises, monographs, and student manuals all contain discussions of the dichotomy, often in confidently dogmatic terms that put to rest incipient doubts. The European or Latin American law student, who encounters this sweeping division at the outset of his career, tends uncritically to absorb it. It quickly becomes basic to his legal outlook. Some legal scholars attack the dichotomy (which the English jurist T. E. Holland termed "the mighty cleavage") as being neither fundamental nor necessary, and certainly not clear; but such doubts seldom occur to the average civil lawyer. He knows that public law and private law are essentially different. Where classification as one or the other seems difficult, he is encouraged to blame the positive legal order for not yet adequately comprehending and articulating the true nature of the underlying reality. Fortunately, legal scholars continue to work on such problems, and eventually, he believes, legal science will make it all clear. Meanwhile statutes, decisions, and doctrine that either assume or attempt to clarify the dichotomy continue to appear, embedding it ever deeper in the law. Examining the origins and the current "crisis" of the distinction is an interesting way to learn more about the civil law tradition.

The distinction between public law and private law has a long history in the civil law tradition. There is some uncertainty about whether it first appeared in classical Roman law or only later, in the *Corpus Juris Civilis* of Justinian, but there is no doubt that the Glossators and the Commentators made the distinction in their writing and teaching. It became a part of the common store of assumptions of the *jus commune*, and was actively employed during the process of codification and reform in the nineteenth century. When, later in the same century, the law was subjected to the scrutiny of legal scientists, the division between public and private law became basic to their systematic reconstruction of the legal order. The continuous history of the cleavage gave it authority and built it into the culture. Concepts that had been used by legal scholars for many centuries seemed fundamental, necessary, and evident.

Much of the force behind the public law-private law cleavage in modern European legal thought is ideological, the expression of those currents of economic, social, and political thought dominant in the seventeenth and eighteenth centuries that found expression in the civil codes of France, Austria, Italy, and Germany in the nineteenth century. This codified civil law was the heart of private law, and the dominant concepts of the codes were individual private property and individual freedom of contract. This individualistic emphasis was an expression in forensic terms of the rationalism and secular natural law of the age. The emphasis on rights of property and contract in the codes guaranteed individual rights against intrusion by the state. The civil codes were thought of as serving something like a constitutional function. Private law was that area of the law in which the sole function of government was the recognition and enforcement of private rights.

Accompanying this basic attitude were various corollary assumptions. Among these were a rather primitive view of the economy, in which the principal actors were private individuals, and an extremely limited view of the appropriate sphere of government activity. Neither associations of individuals engaged in concerted activity, such as corporations and labor unions, nor broad participation by government in the economic and social life of the nation — both familiar to us in the twentieth century — was contemplated. The only actors in the legal universe were the private individual and the state, and each had its domain: private law for one and public law for the other.

In the legal scholarship of the nineteenth century this ideology was accepted, at times perhaps without question. Indeed, much of the effort of legal science went into the construction of theories that embodied, but did not directly express, the essentials of what is commonly called nineteenth-century liberalism. One of the major achievements of the German Pandectists was to raise this ideology to a highly systematic and abstract level in the name of legal science; they did it so well that these essentially nineteenth-century attitudes have been preserved in much of the European legal scholarship of the twentieth century. The fundamental concepts of the German doctrine are juridical formulations of the role of individual autonomy in the law, and they operate in an area coterminous with that of private law.

It was a kind of negative implication of this private law ideology that an entirely different attitude was appropriate in public law matters. There the role of government was not limited to the protection of private rights; on the contrary, the driving consideration was the effectuation of the public interest by state action. Public law had, from this point of view, two major components: constitutional law in the classic sense — the law by which the governmental structure is constituted — and administrative law — the law governing the public administration and its relations with private individuals. In private legal relations the parties were equals and the state the referee. In public legal relations the state was a party, and as representative of the public interest (and successor to the prince) it was a party superior to the private individual. The development of these two quite different ideologies of private law and public law further embedded the distinction in the legal order.

It has been shown in Chapter [5, Section A] that the separation of powers doctrine necessitated the existence of two sets of courts — the administrative courts and the ordinary courts. There has been a good deal of discussion, legislation, and litigation in civil law countries about the division of jurisdiction between the two. In no country is the distinction between public law and private law entirely congruent with that between administrative and ordinary jurisdiction. (For one thing, criminal law, invariably classified as public law by Europeans, is uniformly kept in the ordinary jurisdiction.) There remains, however, a rough correspondence between private law and ordinary jurisdiction, since in Europe the ordinary courts have traditionally been the ones in which controversies about private rights have been decided. This does not mean that all public law questions (other than criminal matters) are exclusively in the administrative jurisdiction and that all private law questions (in addition to criminal matters) are in the ordinary jurisdiction. The matter is much more complicated than that, but the public law-private law distinction is closely related to the phenomenon of the separate system of administrative courts on the Continent and elsewhere in the civil law world.

Thus a variety of influences combine to give the distinction a special importance in the civil law tradition: (1) scholars, particularly legal scientists, with their emphasis on systematic conceptual structures and their ability to convert the descriptive to the prescriptive; (2) tradition, since the distinction figures importantly for at least fourteen centuries; (3) ideology, deeply embedded in the ostensibly value-free concepts of legal science; and (4) the division of jurisdiction between ordinary courts and administrative courts. Meanwhile there have been great changes in government and in economic and social institutions; and consequently a substantial disparity between the bases of legal theory and the facts of contemporary life is now apparent. The distinction is in crisis, and this crisis is the subject of a good deal of lively discussion in European juridical circles. It may be useful to examine briefly some of the reasons.

First, civil lawyers have learned a great deal about the common law. It might have been possible for a parochial Continental jurist of the nineteenth century to believe that the common law was crude and barbarous by comparison with the civil law. But increased cultural interaction between the civil and common law worlds, and in particular the flowering of comparative legal studies on the Continent, have revealed to the civil lawyer that Anglo-American common law is not measurably less sensitive, efficient, or just than his own legal system. He is aware that other Western, democratic, capitalist societies than his own have been able to reach an advanced state of legal development without making a technical distinction between public law and private law. This need not lead him to conclude that his own legal system should discard the dichotomy, but it does suggest that it is not a necessary part of every developed legal order.

Second, the Nazi regime in Germany, the Fascist period in Italy, a variety of totalitarian governments in Latin America, and the development of socialist legality in Cuba, Eastern Europe, and the Soviet Union in this century have all tended to dispel the comfortable illusion that the traditional civil law conceptions of public law and private law expressed ideologically neutral scientific truth. As civil law Europe became ideologically heterogeneous, familiar legal terms took on unfamiliar meanings. The contrasting assertions of social reformers that "all law is public law" and of Lenin that "all bourgeois law is private law" illustrate the point. Astute civil lawyers have always been aware that these conceptions had, at bottom, an ideological basis, but the political history of this century has broadened and intensified that awareness. Such terms as public law and private law do not import any given meaning; their meaning is supplied by the culture of a given time and place. This truism has been underlined by both those who attack and those who defend traditional conceptions.

Third, governments have changed; today it is common for the state to become involved in the society and the economy. The individualistic state of the nineteenth century has been replaced by the social state of the twentieth. The expanded role of government has often been viewed as leading to a contraction of the area set off for private autonomy. According to one view, fundamental private law concepts have consequently been modified by the addition of social or public elements; such terms as the "socialization" or "publicization" of private law are frequently encountered in the literature. Modern constitutions, starting with the [Mexican Constitution of 1917 and the] Weimar Constitution of 1919, explicitly limit private rights in the public interest, producing what civil lawyers commonly refer to as the "social function" of property and other private rights. Although a more traditional doctrinal writer may insist that the legal, as distinguished from the social and economic, content of private rights remains unchanged under the new governments, such a distinction is unconvincing. In fact, the content of private rights has been substantially altered.

Fourth, the involvement of the state in the economic life of the nation has, to a growing extent, been carried on by the direct participation of state entities or state-controlled corporations engaged in commercial or industrial enterprise and using the legal forms of private law. In this way the private law exerts a growing force on public activity carried on not through the traditional medium of the administration but through the conduct of industrial and commercial enterprise by state organs or by companies controlled by the state. This has been summed up by some administrative law scholars as tending toward a "privatization" of public law, an expansion of the role of private law at the expense of administrative law.

Fifth, this century has seen the growth in importance and legal recognition of so-called "intermediate groups" — associations of persons engaged in concerted activity. The earlier image of a legal universe populated solely by the individual and the state, each with its own clearly defined role, is clearly inadequate. In its place is a much more complicated universe, peopled not only by the individual and the state, but also by a wide variety of organizations such as trade unions, cooperatives, foundations, commercial and industrial companies, consortiums, and religious societies. Many of these — one need only mention political parties, trade unions, and commercial and industrial corporations — exercise great economic and social power, particularly in post-war democratic societies. They constitute a kind of "private" government, which frequently has greater impact on the lives of large numbers of individuals than do formally constituted "public" governments. In so complicated a legal universe, simple dichotomies like public law and private law seem to lose their utility.

Sixth, European and Latin American constitutions have come to be the medium for the statement of fundamental individual rights, including property rights, guarantees of the right to engage in economic activity, and the like. Thus the civil codes have been deprived of their constitutional function. That function has been transferred from the most private of private law to the most public of public law sources. In a sense this might be described as a "deconstitutionalization" or "depublicization" of private law. This development tends to reduce the significance of the public law-private law distinction in the eyes of those who see the distinction primarily as a means of protecting individual rights.

Seventh, rigid constitutions and judicial review of the constitutionality of legislation have been established in Austria, Italy, Germany, and other nations in Europe and Latin America. Special constitutional courts exist in some countries, but in others the ordinary judiciary performs this function. This necessarily reduces the significance of rigorous theories about the separation of powers, and tends to blur the public law-private law distinction in the minds of those who see a close relation between that distinction and the separation of powers.

Eighth, the substantive differences between public law and private law have been reduced by the action of two separate but related forces. For one, the growth of administrative law has produced progressively greater restrictions on the power of the state to disregard or violate the claims of private persons. Pursuit of the *Rechtsstaat* — insistence on the applicability of the rule of law to the state itself — leads ultimately to a homogeneous legal system in which the state is merely one kind, although still a very important kind, of subject of the law. This trend has been reinforced by the efforts of scholars to apply the conceptual structure of traditional legal science, originally developed out of the private law, to public law fields. Together the two trends have produced a strong movement toward "privatization" of public law.

Ninth, the traditional aims and methods of legal science and the general theory of law as taught in the law schools, both largely derived from the work of the Pandectists in the nineteenth century, have come under attack during this century by a small but growing scholarly avant-garde. Others, who see the traditional legal science as valid but spent, seek new directions for the fundamental work of legal scholarship. One result is that the scholar's field of interest has expanded beyond the law itself. He is now concerned about how the law relates to the cultural context from which it draws life, and to the society whose problems it must seek to resolve. Another result is a relaxation of emphasis on the validity and usefulness of conceptual structures and logical-formal thinking. The tendency clearly is toward a more "open" jurisprudence and a less technical methodology. In the course of this development, a primarily methodological emphasis on the public law-private law distinction inevitably loses some of its force.

Finally, civil law nations have seen the growth of fields that defy classification as either public or private law. For example, labor law and agrarian law are a mixture of public and private elements, and are incompatible with the traditional classification. Professorial chairs, courses, and institutes in these fields exist in the universities, and journals devoted to them are regularly published. Their existence tends further to blur the distinction between public and private law.

One can say, then, that a rather drastic reshaping of the traditional conceptions of private and public law is under way in the civil law world. The distinction continues, for the reasons mentioned earlier, to have great practical importance. Even under the impact of the forces tending toward newer definitions, substantial areas remain clear, and the great majority of problems and interests remain easily classifiable into one category or the other. But at the frontier between them there is great flux, and few sophisticated civil lawyers today would attempt any functional definition of private law or public law.

The prescriptive effect of the distinction between public and private law tends to overshadow its descriptive utility, but the distinction does also serve a descriptive function. It serves to sum up a division of labor, a separation of the law into smaller parts to facilitate teaching, scholarship, and discussion. But the prescriptive overtones tend to make the distinction a fairly emphatic one, even when used in a descriptive sense. A teacher of private law does not, as a rule, attempt to teach or study the public aspects of his subject. Although he teaches about property, for example, he will not discuss property taxation, regulation of urban land use, or the constitutional protection of property rights. These are all parts of public law, and he leaves them to specialists in that area.

He also tends to make very sharp distinctions, even within private and public law, between procedure and substance and between one substantive field and another. On the whole such distinctions seem to be considerably more emphatic in the civil law world than in the common law world. It is unusual for the scholar to follow a problem where it leads him, regardless of boundaries; and the notion that one should keep within one's own territory has gradually become an important assumption of the doctrine, and hence part of the law itself. Indeed, in extreme cases, distinctions of this sort are conceived of as embodying reality, as indicating a classification that is not merely conventional but is based on the nature of the material itself. Hence one occasionally finds doctrinal discussion about the autonomy of certain subjects, even where the field under discussion would seem to have been the result more of historical accident than of any inherent qualities. In an aggravated case a writer may insist that only one of various proposed arrangements of the law is correct.

The civil lawyer thus divides the law into public and private law and a group of hybrids (such as labor law and agrarian law) that have elements of both. Public law itself is further divided into constitutional law, administrative law, and criminal law. Criminal procedure is generally similarly classified, in part because of its close relation to criminal law. The proper classification of civil procedure has been the subject of considerable scholarly discussion. At present, the dominant view favors considering it as part of public law.

Private law is composed of civil law and commercial law. Of these, civil law is much the more important. It is the modern manifestation of the oldest component of the civil law tradition: Roman civil law. Until the general decline of the temporal jurisdiction of ecclesiastical tribunals set in, the civil law lived in a state of symbiosis with the canon law. When systems of justice were secularized, following the Reformation, the civil law survived, greatly enriched by canon law, and the latter lost most of its temporal significance. Today there is a comparable trend toward the absorption of commercial law by civil law.

Commercial law, it will be recalled from Chapter [3, Section F], began as a separate system of justice created by merchants to govern their own affairs. It had its own rules and customs, its own system of tribunals and judges, its own procedures for adjudication and enforcement, and its own constituency. It was not a part of the official systems of civil, criminal, or ecclesiastical justice. These independent features of commercial law have gradually been lost. Commercial justice was nationalized with the rise of the nation-state. The law of civil procedure was extended to proceedings in commercial courts. Gradually the notion of a separate commercial jurisdiction began to disappear. Today, in some nations, separate commercial courts no longer exist, even in name. In others they have a nominal separate existence at the trial level, but are distinguishable from ordinary civil courts only by the presence of a merchant who sits on the bench together with the civil judges. At the appellate level no distinction exists: the same court that decides civil appeals hears and decides commercial appeals. The commercial court in such a system is no longer a separate court; it is a special sub-jurisdiction of the civil court.

The commercial law continues to be the object of a separate commercial code in most civil law nations. This, however, is also passing. Both Switzerland and Italy have abolished their separate commercial codes and have combined the matters previously included in them with their civil codes. Those charged with a revision of the French Civil Code have recommended that France take a similar course. Others will surely follow.

Separate chairs in commercial law continue to exist in the universities, and the law libraries of the civil law world contain a substantial literature on commercial law. More and more, however, the trend is toward dominance by the civil lawyers. They are the ones who do the basic theoretical work for the whole of private law (and much of public law). Commercial law doctrine accepts the work of the civil law jurists and builds on it. By a gradual but apparently inexorable process, commercial law has become less a parallel field within the private law area and more a division of, or specialization within, civil law. Civil law is becoming synonymous with private law; commercial law is being "civilized."

As civil law takes over, and as commercial law gradually loses its separate identity, a process analogous to the enrichment of civil law by canon law is taking place. As a general proposition, the civil law has traditionally viewed transactions between individuals as isolated juridical events. The commercial law, by way of contrast, has viewed transactions involving merchants as a part of the normal flow of commercial activity. The difference in attitude has, through the centuries, produced differences in rules and practices. Not surprisingly, the tendency in modern industrial-commercial nations has been to favor the commercial law approach over that of the civil law. This process, predictably, has been described as the "commercialization" of private law.

Private law thus consists of two major fields existing in symbiosis with each other. Civil law is enriched by "commercialization"; commercial law is diminished by "civilization," and is in decline. The tendency is toward a unified private law that is synonymous with civil law. The oldest subtradition in the civil law tradition lives on.

NOTES AND QUESTIONS

1. The principal dichotomy in the civil law system of legal rules is between public law and private law. How would you explain this distinction, and what it is supposed to cover, to an American lawyer?

2. Why is the public law-private law division in crisis today among legal scholars?

3. Be prepared to explain the following phrases often used to describe the changing nature of legal rules in the civil law world:

(a) all law is public law;
(b) publicization of private law;
(c) depublicization of private law;
(d) privatization of public law;
(e) intermediate groups;
(f) civilization of commercial law; and
(g) commercialization of civil law.

4. The next excerpt by the late René David describes the major divisions in French law. The French pattern has been very influential in Belgium, Italy, Luxembourg, Portugal, and Spain within Europe as well as in Algeria, Egypt, Lebanon, Morocco, Syria, Tunisia, francophonic Africa and Asia, and in most of Latin America.

2. FRENCH LEGAL CATEGORIES

RENÉ DAVID, FRENCH LAW: ITS STRUCTURE, SOURCES AND METHODOLOGY 95-97, 108-22, 127-30, 132-35, 137-42, 144-46 (Michael Kindred trans. 1972)

In many countries a fundamental task of legal science, often its most important one, is to divide the law into branches and to analyze and classify legal rules according to these divisions. In today's complex societies, it is only possible to know the law where legal categories and distinctions give order to the variegated mass of rules that bind us. Although legal classification is often the work of scholars, its use is not limited to the academic and pedagogic. It is important in the area of conflict of laws, where characterization is essential. But most important, in domestic law an established structure is a necessary prerequisite for any legal research.

When a jurist has a legal problem, whether practical or theoretical, his first step is to determine the branch of law to which the problem belongs. Does the question call into play rules and principles of civil law, administrative law, or procedure? And further, is it a problem of personal capacity, succession, or marriage arrangements concerning property? Consciously or unconsciously, the jurist must put the problem in context. He will not understand the problem, much less know where to begin research to solve it, until he has situated it within the divisions and categories that form his legal system.

But contrary to what one might suppose, this categorization is not just a simple preliminary operation which then allows the jurist to do his research and discover the legal rules applicable to the question at hand. No doubt this is its most important function; it imparts an organization to the law and facilitates research. Nevertheless, as we shall see, the problem is more subtle than this. Legal classification, aside from this technical aspect, has its own value....

In each branch of the law, special importance is given to fundamental policies related to the function of the rules in question. For example, in commercial law one stresses the practical needs of commerce, in administrative law one emphasizes the necessity for public services to function regularly, and in labor law special importance is (or at least was) given to stability of employment. These are considerations particular to a specific area of the law and must receive primary attention when one is dealing with rules in that area, but they have little importance in other places. The preoccupation of all lawyers to achieve just results is implemented in different ways by civil, penal, and tax law specialists. They do not see problems from the same vantage point. For this reason, the difference between various branches of the law is not simply one of subject matter. Sometimes the rules are conceived, interpreted, and applied in a special way....

When the lawyer determines that his problem requires the application of rules from a particular branch of the law, and then from a particular subcategory of that branch, he is not just trying to situate the question in order to find the particular legal rule that will finally permit him to answer it. His whole attitude toward the problem and his method of investigation will be influenced by the categorization upon which he settles....

Civil Law

A description of the various branches of French law must begin with that branch whose age and technical perfection have made it preeminent: civil law.... Civil law today is the law that is applicable between individuals, whether or not they are citizens; it is contrasted only with the legal rules that affect the state. Civil law is thus distinguished from public law and criminal law; it constitutes all of private law, except for a very few areas which tradition or the circumstances of modern life have kept somewhat independent of it. The distinction between civil law and canon law fell into disuse with the secularization in 1792 of the law of civil status and of marriage, when civil law absorbed those matters dealing with affairs between individuals that had formerly been in the exclusive jurisdiction of canon law. There still is, to be sure, a canon law regulating these matters, and many Frenchmen continue to attach great weight to it. But there is now, in addition to the rules of canon law, an increasingly divergent set of civil law rules in the same areas, so that French national law never makes reference to canon law. Individuals are invited and obliged by the church to observe two sets of rules concurrently. As Frenchmen they obey civil law rules; as Christians, canon law rules.

Nevertheless, commercial law, which was traditionally distinguished from civil law, must still be treated as a separate category for some purposes. Parallel to the Civil Code, France has a commercial code; the rules of French private law are still different in certain respects depending on whether one envisages relations between businessmen or those between nonbusinessmen, and "commercial acts" and acts which are not termed "commercial acts." For the last fifty years, there has also been a tendency for labor law to become as distinct as commercial law. Rural law, too, tends to take on a certain particularity within civil law. And civil procedure is not included in the French concept of civil law.

The best way to understand the meaning and scope of the French concept of civil law is to study the recent commercial editions of the Civil Code or the treatises and elementary manuals on French civil law. According to these manuals, the broad divisions of civil law seem to be the following:

1. Law of persons: physical and moral persons, attributes of personality (name, domicile, acts of civil status), capacity of minors and the insane and the protection of their interests.

2. Family law: marriage, divorce, separation, filiation, obligations of maintenance.

3. Property law: movables and immovables, contents and transmission of real rights.

4. Law of obligations: contract in general and particular contracts, delicts, unjust enrichment.
5. Law of matrimonial property relations: the statutory community, conventional systems established by marriage contract.
6. Law of succession: intestate and testamentary.

These divisions are made by writers for teaching purposes on the basis of the Civil Code. They are not, however, fully satisfactory and do not exhaust the contents of the Civil Code.

The attention of the foreign lawyer ought to be called to the following points. For various reasons, certain questions are not studied at the point where it would logically seem they ought to be. Suretyship is studied at the end of contracts, although its source need not be a contract. Donations are studied with succession rather than as a special type of contract. Various questions which do not, properly speaking, belong to civil law, on the other hand, are studied in books on civil law because for one reason or another they have been regulated in the Civil Code. Examples are questions concerning promulgation, publication, and nonretroactivity of laws, and regulations concerning the registers of civil status, as well as many questions of evidence, the distinction between authentic acts and acts under private signature, organization of the notaries, *res judicata*, and procedure (the procedure in actions for divorce and concerning status and purge of mortgages). All of private international law, including the law relating to nationality, on the other hand, is treated in special works, even though the general principles governing this area were originally and still partly are, dealt with in the Civil Code.

In addition to the subjects dealt with in the Civil Code, civil law includes various other matters, such as copyright law. These questions, however, are ordinarily omitted from, or dealt with in a fairly summary way in, general civil law treatises, so that it is better to consult special treatises concerned with them....

Civil law is the center, the very heart, of French law. What we have said above concerning the distinction between public law and private law explains this. Public law is more recently formed than private law, and it is less pure than civil law, since it includes questions of administrative practice and general policy goals. Also, civil law, based on the Roman tradition and developed through the ages, has attained greater technical perfection and stability than has public law, which is subject to the vicissitudes of political crises. Lawyers rejoice in this stability. French privatists are proud of their Civil Code, which has celebrated its 150th anniversary and becomes ever more firmly established, as contrasted with the many constitutions that France has had during the same period. To them the Civil Code seems to be the most lasting and the only true constitution of France....

Commercial Law

Commercial law has a history that makes it distinct from civil law. It was developed originally by international tribunals that existed at markets and fairs and in port cities. It grew from the custom of merchants and maritime customs, i.e., from international customs. In prerevolutionary France, these unique sources made commercial law very different from civil law, which traced its origins to either Roman law or regional customs.... Since then, commercial law has increasingly become a branch of the national civil law, and its autonomy as a special branch has become increasingly difficult to understand and defend. The organization of commercial activity in guilds, however, allowed commercial law to retain some autonomy until the Revolution. Another reason for this continued autonomy was that prerevolutionary legal scholars neglected commercial law completely. To them commercial law seemed like little more than the daily practices of men of little social importance, merchants. Such practices were obviously of little interest or worth compared to the glorious principles of Roman law and the customary law of land and succession, the very bases of stable fortunes and family position.

Because the Revolution aspired to rid France of all class distinctions, it abolished the commercial guilds and thus took away the strongest support for a separate commercial law. Still, commercial law was not merged with the rest of the civil law. Probably the principal reason was that few lawyers were competent in both kinds of law; there were civil and commercial lawyers. Thus the separation between civil and commercial law continued and, along with the Civil Code, the Commercial Code was drafted. This code went into effect in 1807, but has never had the prestige of the Civil Code. It was not supported by a tradition of the same value, and in addition, had the misfortune of being drafted between two crucial periods. It came after the guilds, but before the industrial revolution, the machine age, and the development of transport, all of which were to revolutionize both regular and maritime commerce.... For many it seems like nothing more than a heterogeneous grouping of rules concerning various contracts and activities which may be carried on by anyone who so desires. Now one is governed by commercial law as soon as he does something that falls in the new legal category of "acts of commerce," but not because he is in a particular profession. Still, this principle is difficult to maintain against an opposite tradition, and the code itself has distorted it in various ways. Sometimes an act is an act of commerce just because it is performed by a person in the interest of, or in connection with, his profession (commercial undertakings, theory of the accessory act). In addition, certain special institutions are established for those who perform acts of commerce regularly or as their profession (bankruptcy, commercial registers).

Thus, since the enactment of the Commercial Code, the basic rationale for commercial law has been unclear, and the whole organization of the subject reflects this weakness. After the code even more than before, the area has lacked general principles; it is a mixture of rules that cannot be dealt with as a logical whole. And its basic principles have to be found in the Civil Code.

The industrial revolution of the nineteenth and twentieth centuries has only accentuated the problem. Increasingly, commercial law has become the legislative regulation of business and business institutions. It is less and less the product of an international, or even national, custom of merchants. Merchants have lost even their name and are now called businessmen. The new name is a sign of the change.

What does modern commercial law contain? For the most part, it is made up of legal rules governing institutions that are particularly important to business: for example, all kinds of business organizations, checks, bills of exchange, industrial and commercial property, banking, stock exchange transactions, and bankruptcy.

With the tendency toward a planned economy and regulated professions, commercial law increasingly resembles administrative law. This appearance is strengthened by the tendencies of recent commercial law treatises, which have been adapted to new curricula and include a discussion of business taxes. Nevertheless, the jurist who studies French private law must bear in mind that some parts of private law are split in two: civil law and commercial law. Ordinarily, civil law furnishes the principles; exceptions to these principles, some more justified than others, will be found when the relationship in question is one of business. This split exists with respect to numerous contracts: for example, transport, insurance, sale, lease, pledge, and compromise. The formation of such contracts, their proof, and their effects may differ according to whether or not they are subject to commercial law rules. Similarly, problems of capacity are seen differently by civil law and commercial law. There are other problems of maritime commercial law and of recent formation in internal commercial law that are regulated principally by commercial law, with civil law seldom having any role at all: banking and stock exchange transactions, business organizations, and negotiable instruments. Finally, one should note that France has special commercial courts, the judges of which are elected by the businessmen of the district and need not be lawyers....

Criminal Law

Criminal law, also called penal law, occupies a special position in the French legal system. It is now incontestably a branch of public law. Theft, murder, assault, and battery are not just private matters between perpetrator and victim or his representatives. There is a violation of public order with which penal law is concerned. Independently of any civil compensation that civil law may require him to pay, the criminal must also account to society for his actions, even though it is not the direct interest of the state which he has injured as would have been the case if there were counterfeiting or trespassing on public property.

Although criminal law is part of public law, it is nevertheless traditionally considered in France the concern of privatists.... The main reason for this apparent anomaly is that the courts with jurisdiction to administer criminal law and pronounce convictions and sentences are always the regular private law courts and never, except for certain very minor offenses, the administrative courts. This is the case even where the accused is a government employee accused of an offense committed in the exercise of his duties. Here, the desire to insure individuals the guaranties offered by the regular courts and their procedures has prevailed over the fear of court interference in the activity of government administrators that might hamper their actions.... At the present time, there is, however, considerable concern over the power given to the executive under a variety of circumstances to apply clearly repressive sanctions, outside of the classical type of penalty. Examples of such sanctions are closure of a business establishment, prohibition from exercising a profession, and denial of a passport. The Council of State of course does have a power of review of such sanctions, but many persons deplore the refusal to grant jurisdiction over them to the regular courts....

Failing a Roman tradition, criminal law developed in prerevolutionary France on the basis of customary notions, which evolved in important ways under the influence of canon law. As soon as criminal law became a matter of public concern and ceased to be simply a squaring of accounts between the criminal and the victim under the supervision of the state, the repression of criminal activity came to be thought of in France as posing a problem for the public rather than legal problems. Of course it was up to the courts to fix penalties, but they did not consider it to be the highest of their functions. Lawyers so ignored criminal law that no important criminal law treatise existed in France until the eighteenth century. It was only when, at this time, the natural rights of man became a matter of concern, that the importance, and even the possible existence, of criminal law was noticed. Only then did the idea develop that one might limit, in this area as well as others, the possible abuses of police power by creating a penal code and a code of criminal procedure. After some preliminary work during the revolutionary period, these two codes were produced in the First Empire. This work has not preserved the same degree of prestige today as has the Civil Code. Nevertheless, it is quite possible that it is in this area that codification constituted the greatest advance.

Because there was no solid Roman criminal law tradition, the study of criminal law has been relatively neglected in France. There have been few "criminalists," and the important works on criminal law have been written by judges, who are the practitioners in the area, rather than by legal scholars. A professor of law who devoted himself to something so unexalted would ordinarily leave aside the purely legal side of the question and become, rather than a criminalist, a criminologist, concerned with the sociological aspects of criminal behavior and its suppression rather than with the formal rules of criminal law and procedure. He would ordinarily write in the area of "general" penal law. Special penal law never has been a required subject for French law students; it is regarded as a subject for practitioners.

The fact that, on the one hand, criminal law is a part of public law and, on the other, is administered by the regular courts, provides a key to understanding certain attitudes and contradictions that can be observed in the area. The magistrate who makes a career of criminal law administration will have received in law school, and will keep, the education of a privatist.... The criminalist retains the attitudes of a privatist in another respect. He feels uncomfortable and not fully justified when he is called upon to supervise the activities of the agents of the executive branch, i.e., police officers. Criminal procedure in France is hamstrung by this approach.

On the other hand, the French attitude toward criminal law can be understood only if one remembers that it is, in the final analysis, a branch of public law. Criminal law may be administered by the regular courts and thus in some ways be similar to private law. But basically it is public law and when one says public law, a Frenchman knows that it is not and cannot be law in the strict sense.

Law in the strict sense can only develop in the area of relations between individuals, where the state is an impartial arbiter. In criminal as in administrative law, the government is required to play a more active role. Society's interest is obviously and directly involved....

French criminal law is codified. During the Napoleonic period, a penal code and a code of criminal procedure were enacted. The Penal Code of 1810 [was replaced in 1994 with the New Penal Code and] in 1959 a new criminal procedure code replaced the original code of procedures ....

Administrative Law

To define administrative law imposes a real strain on French writers, and their attempts in this direction often fail. First, administrative law is hard to keep distinct from constitutional law, which provides its structure and basic principles. And, like constitutional law, it tends to fuse with political science, and particularly with the subcategory called public administration.

Defining administrative law is further complicated by the existence of administrative courts and the resulting natural tendency to define in terms of court jurisdiction....

[M]uch of administrative law deals with its case law, that is, with the results of litigation arising from administrative action, both between the government and private individuals and between independent government departments. Let us begin our discussion of this case law by noting a basic principle of administrative law which illustrates clearly the French view of the special position held by public law. This is the so-called principle of the preliminary decision (*décision préalable*). The procedure in a dispute between the government and an individual is not, as in private law, to go to court and ask the court for a settlement of the dispute. First, the government, by virtue of its privileged position, decides the matter as it considers proper. It imposes the tax, dismisses the civil servant, or closes the establishment that it considers illegal or unhealthy. It does not go to court for a determination that X is its debtor, that Y deserves dismissal, or that Z's business has been operated in violation of the law. Before administrative courts, the individual is always the plaintiff. The government first judges its own case; the individual is limited to contesting the government's conception of the law and having the courts adjudicate it. In private law, the situation is naturally very different. Any procedure that allows parties to solve their disputes by judging their own case without going to court (such as a penalty clause, a right of unilateral termination, or a clause providing for automatic cancellation in case of nonpayment of the price) is regarded with hostility.

Administrative litigation, as we have said, is ordinarily handled by a special hierarchy of courts, called administrative courts, at the apex of which is the Council of State. The principle, which has a historical explanation, is, however, not absolute. A variety of clearly administrative litigation is placed by special legislation within the jurisdiction of the regular courts. For example, the regular courts handle litigation on indirect taxes, expropriation for public use, municipal liability in case of riots, and automobile accidents. And all penal cases automatically come to them.

More important than the dual court structure is no doubt the French acceptance of the principle that administrative law differs from private law. Different rules govern relations between private individuals, on the one hand, and relations between government departments or between a department and an individual on tne other. The civil and commercial codes contain private law; they do not govern administrative law relations.

Where can we find the rules of administrative law? For many years, they were far from precise, but throughout the nineteenth and twentieth centuries things have changed gradually. Courts and legal scholars have developed French administrative law, and arbitrariness has largely disappeared, as prevailing democratic ideals require....

We should note another aspect of modern French administrative law: it is uncodified. There are statutes dealing with many aspects of administrative law, but the principles of administrative law that have been developed by the Council of State and scholarly writers have never been codified. And there is no movement favoring codification of this area. [However, the publisher Dalloz has organized many administrative law decrees and statutes in alphabetical order in its publication called *Code administratif.*]

Some of the fundamental principles of administrative law are inspired entirely by public law considerations and derive from the basic notions of French constitutional order that have prevailed since the Revolution of 1789. Since the difficulties of the German occupation, the Council of State has articulated these principles carefully and denominated them expressly as general principles of administrative law. Except for these, the French administrative courts have generally found in the Civil Code the rational principles upon which they have based their decisions. It is understood of course that these principles must be adapted somewhat when incorporated into administrative law....

Without minimizing the great progress in administrative law, one must recognize that technically it remains less advanced and less perfect than private law and less able than the latter to insure justice. Its doctrines are not so well established; its principles and particular rules are more flexible. In short, administrative law is less certain in France than private law, so that it is still too early to consider the drafting of a true administrative code. The fact that this uncertainty allows the equitable aspects of particular cases to be given greater attention in administrative law is sometimes advantageous. Nevertheless uncertainty in legal rules is generally undesirable, and the equity of the Council of State conceals a certain arbitrariness and is just as objectionable as the equity of the prerevolutionary supreme courts....

Tax Law

Tax law is clearly a most important branch of administrative law, as taxation is one of the most essential and manifest relationships between individuals and the state. In today's society tax law is so important, however, that we tend to treat it as an independent branch of the law, particularly because it is too broad and complex to be dealt with in a general administrative law course. The truth is that it is one of the few specialized subdivisions of administrative law studied in law schools.

Tax law has two unusual characteristics which distinguish it from the rest of administrative law. The first is that some tax litigation is left to the regular courts. All litigation as to direct taxes is in the jurisdiction of the administrative courts. But most indirect taxes, and in particular those collected on specified transactions (stamp tax, registration tax) are within the jurisdiction of the regular courts. This fact does not remove the subject from the area of administrative law, but writers frequently forget this and confuse the distinction between public and private law with the division of jurisdiction between the administrative and regular courts. For this reason, the privatists who deal with legal problems of registration frequently speak of the "particularity of tax law" when they see that private law principles are not always applied to these problems....

One thing that shows clearly the particularity of tax law even within public law is the power that tax authorities have to compromise with individuals on the penalty to be paid for tax law violations. The authorities responsible for indirect taxes and those responsible for customs can, before bringing suit or even after a judgment has been given setting the taxpayer's penalty, compromise with him. In other words, they can agree not to prosecute if the individual will pay a particular fine, or they can agree to a reduction of the fine fixed by the court. "Tax fines" are considered to be both penalties and compensation, and in French law are subject to rules completely different from "penal fines," which are imposed for other penal offenses.

The second important distinctive characteristic of tax law, when compared to administrative law in general, is that there are two codes of tax law in France: the general tax code (which was published in 1934 to replace five earlier codes: the codes of direct taxes, indirect taxes, transfer taxes, stocks and bonds, and business turnover taxes) and the customs code.[a]

But one should not be deceived. In spite of a nominal similarity, the tax codes are very different from the traditional civil law codes, particularly because the same stability cannot be achieved in so rapidly changing an area as tax law. The executive is required by law to incorporate annually into the tax codes by decree new provisions required to keep the codes up-to-date. The simple fact that the tax codes are thus supplemented and changed by simple executive decree makes evident the difference between them and the traditional codes....

Labor Law and Social Security Law

Labor law is a subject that arouses particular interest among lawyers at the present time in France, as in many other countries. The very expression *labor law* is new to France. When the Civil Code was drafted, no one thought about "labor law." There were workers and employees bound to their employers by contracts of employment. Other citizens worked independently and entered into contracts to sell their products and merchandise. It seemed sufficient if the law regulated ownership and a few essential kinds of contracts, such as sale and employment. This had been the position of Roman law and of the

[a] The current *Code général des impôts* dates from a decree of 6 Apr. 1950, as amended, while the *Code des douanes* was enacted by a decree of 8 Dec. 1948.

French Revolution. The Revolution had abolished the class structure of prerevolutionary France and intended to guarantee the triumph of individualism and exalt humanity by creating a classless society. For the future, there would be simple citizens; to set apart a class called laborers and give them a special legal status would be to continue the mistakes of the past. Thus, the law refused to recognize such a class or give it a special status. The demands of workers at the time were for legal equality through the suppression of guild-inspired restrictions of all kinds; this seemed enough.

The development of large-scale industry during the nineteenth century changed the fundamental problem. With industrialization and urbanization, a working class developed. Supported by a new class-consciousness, they attempted to organize themselves to secure an economic equality that did not follow automatically from the legal equality obtained earlier. Thanks to universal male suffrage, adopted in France in 1848, they were able to have legislation enacted gradually to satisfy their demands: recognition of the fact that legal equality was insufficient, abolition of prohibitions against workers compensating for their economic inferiority by organizing and taking collective action, establishment of a whole new body of legislation for the protection of workers. In this way a new area of law developed during the nineteenth century in response to the demands of the labor movement. It was law especially for industrial workers and was thus called industrial, or workers', legislation.

Subsequently, measures similar to those enacted for industrial workers were extended to other labor groups: commercial employees, agricultural workers, commercial representatives, artisans....

Now even the term *labor law* has become insufficient. The protective legislation originally developed in favor of salaried laborers has been extended to all who are, according to a current phrase, "economically weak" and has finally even gone beyond this group. Under the heading *labor law*, we now study measures that are increasingly independent of one's being salaried or even being a "worker." These measures are principally inspired by a preoccupation with social equality and the battle against poverty; they provide the citizen with some guarantees against various risks to which they are exposed and insure them compensation in particular cases. *Social law* has been proposed as a term to replace *labor law*, but the present tendency is more toward a division, so that labor law and social security law would be separately studied....

Aside from the inclusion in labor law of numerous rules of public law origin, it seems clear that labor law has a very real and considerable originality with respect to civil law, so that one can speak of the autonomy of this branch of law, or if one wishes to avoid so sharp a break, of its particularity. All labor law specialists now insist on this particularity....

From the middle of the nineteenth century, Marxist criticism, the validity of which is indisputable on this point, denounced the theoretical nature of the political equality achieved by the French Revolution. It showed that this equality was but a trap unless it was accompanied by some economic equality. In addition, the development of industry and commerce, due to the capitalist impetus, had upset the economic and social conditions in which the working world had to live. As mass production became necessary, it introduced, along with industrial concentration and urbanization, the growth of the proletariat. As in prerevolutionary France, although for different reasons, it is essential today that the special context of labor law be recognized....

French civil law, incorporated into a code more than 150 years ago, is based on individualistic principles from which all judicial efforts have been unable to free it. But labor law requires that legal relationships be viewed from a collective point of view; in this way it appears as a product of the socialist spirit. The civilist thinks in terms of individuals' rights and obligations, while the labor law specialist considers more the status of particular classes of persons. The very idea of status is repugnant to the individualist spirit of the Civil Code. This tension is accentuated by the fact that laborers often regard the Civil Code as a bourgeois code, interested primarily in established fortunes. Such persons are little inclined to share the admiration of lawyers for this code, in which the contract of employment is sandwiched into three articles between lease and bailment. They ask if the dignity of labor and the laborer can be insured in a code that speaks disdainfully of "working men," as they are called in article 1799, which refuses to give the same credence to the word of one who sells his services as they do to his master....

Another, related aspect of labor law that distinguishes it from civil law is its very birth and growth processes. The civil law was formed so long ago that one no longer thinks of its formation. Although it is actively and constantly evolving, this evolution is concealed by fictions. The courts pretend that they are always interpreting the law, and legal writers speak of finding the true meaning of legal rules. Labor law is still too underdeveloped to allow such pious fictions. It is clear that here one must create, make something new. One cannot rest on a tradition that is either inexistent or rejected today. For this reason, decrees, judicial decisions, even contracts take on a different appearance. The rule set forth by article 5 of the Civil Code, forbidding judges to decide cases submitted to them as if they were stating regulations, is sometimes set aside in labor law. Collective agreements are very much like regulations issued by public authorities and sometimes look almost like legislation. Decrees and regulations of the public authorities are proclaimed within a framework of very broad powers conferred by law.

The civilist is thus shocked by various accepted labor law rules. He does not regard labor law as a branch of civil law; rather he considers it a new branch of the law that has been developed in opposition to the principles of civil law....

Today it is only at the lower level that there are labor courts, bearing various names, sometimes supervised by the regular courts, sometimes by the administrative courts: for example, labor boards (*conseils de prud'hommes*) and the social security court of first instance....

Law of Evidence and Procedure

Procedural rules were of first importance in the development of Roman law. The history of Roman law is the history first of the actions, then of the formula with all the improvements and subtleties that were gradually incorporated in it by legal technique. Slowly, however, things changed, with the progress of legal science in the late Roman empire and in the modern legal systems of Roman inspiration. From the actions, interdicts, injunctions, and various other procedural remedies of Roman law, lawyers inferred the existence of rights and on the basis of these established new outlines for their system. The court action is no longer regarded as the most essential aspect of the problem; the possibility of going to court has come to be regarded as just one of the consequences normally attached to legal rights....

In the law schools, civil procedure is studied in a single one-semester third-year course; criminal procedure is dealt with in another one-semester course; and administrative procedure is almost totally ignored. Law students do not really expect to learn procedure in the university. It is implicitly agreed that the subject can only be learned in practice. Efforts are seldom made to present legal questions from the procedural point of view.

In this area, practitioners do not use the works written by theoreticians, which are few and always out of date. Rather there are compilations especially prepared for them: repertories, formularies, *jurisclasseurs*, and practice manuals written by legal practitioners. These works are little known in the law schools, where it is even unusual for the libraries to purchase them. Procedure is an area where there is a clear divorce in France between the law schools and practice.

This divorce is clearly undesirable. The specific disposition of a case is often explained by its procedural context, and one cannot properly evaluate judicial decisions without understanding this context. Thus scholars sometimes express surprise that a court, in a particular case, did not invoke a particular theory or argue in a particular way that would have led to a better solution to the case than was given by the court. In such criticism, they often forget that the court is not free to consider the case just as it likes. It is bound by the positions of the parties and cannot give a remedy not requested by them, even though it may think this would be a better solution. Much criticism of the courts is misplaced; it should be addressed rather to the representatives or advocates of the parties. The judge does his best, but he is not free to consider a case as teachers and scholars often do.

The law of evidence is probably even more neglected in France than that of procedure. Whereas procedure maintains a certain independence with respect to civil law and is dealt with especially within the framework of criminal and administrative law, evidence is never given more than a chapter in each area. The expression *law of evidence* does not even exist in France, and one must go back a hundred years to find a book that deals with the subject as a whole.

NOTES AND QUESTIONS

1. René David, one of this century's great comparatists, states that a civil lawyer's "whole attitude toward the legal problem and his method of investigation will be influenced by the categorization" of the problem. Why is this so important for the civilian? Is it equally true of common lawyers? How does this relate to the "particularity" of a branch of the law?

2. Professor Walter Weyrauch has remarked that some legal systems are "table of contents" systems and others are "index" systems. Which type does Professor David describe? *See* Walter Otto Weyrauch, *Book Review*, 38 Am. J. Comp. L. 389 (1990).

3. "Civil law is the center, the very heart, of French law." Why? Does the law in the United States have a comparable center or heart? Where is it?

4. David states that although criminal law is part of public law, it is nevertheless traditionally considered in France the concern of privatists. Why does this anomaly exist?

5. What does David mean when he says that "public law ... is not and cannot be law in the strict sense"? Do you agree?

6. French administrative law has the principle of the preliminary decision. What purpose does such a principle serve? Do we have a similar principle in U.S. administrative law?

7. Observe Professor David's objection to the "equity" and "uncertainty" of the Council of State. What does he mean? Does the certainty of which he speaks exist in greater measure in the ordinary courts?

8. Labor law was and is included in the French Civil Code. Why, then, did labor law in France (and in most civil law jurisdictions) develop apart from the civil code? Should it be classified as private law or public law?

9. Compare the importance of procedure and evidence in French and American law. Why is evidence, in particular, of such minor significance in French law? Why is the whole field of procedure of secondary rank at French university law faculties?

10. Hans Leser lists the following division of law for Germany:

(a) private law and related areas;
(b) commercial law;
(c) company law;
(d) judicature and civil procedure;
(e) labor and social security law;
(f) criminal law, criminal procedure, criminology, and juvenile law;
(g) public and constitutional law, including international law and the law of supranational bodies [e.g., the E.U.]; and
(h) administrative law [including tax law] and procedure.

Norbert Horn, Hein Kötz & Hans G. Leser, German Private and Commercial Law: An Introduction 52-56 (Tony Weir trans. 1982).

11. The Japanese use similar categories but classify labor, social security, consumer protection, and similar legislation as "social law," and antitrust, trade controls, and other economic regulatory statutes as "economic law."

BIBLIOGRAPHIC NOTE

The *International Encyclopedia of Comparative Law* treats many areas of private law in comparative perspective: family law (vol. 4); succession (vol. 5); property and trust (vol. 6); contracts (vols. 7 & 8); commercial transactions (vol. 9); restitution (vol. 10); torts (vol. 11); transportation law (vol. 12); business enterprises (vol. 13); copyright and intellectual property (vol. 14); and labor law (vol. 15).

In addition, many fine books in English are being published about civilian substantive law, often in response to the growing internationalization of law practice within the European Union. Among them are: G. Leroy Certoma, The Italian Legal System (1985); E. J. Cohn, 1-2 Manual of German Law (2d ed. 1968, 1971); Giovanni Criscuoli & David Pugsley, Italian Law of Contract (1991); Mary Ann Glendon, Abortion and Divorce in Western Law (1987); Donald Harris & Denis Tallon, Contract Law Today: Anglo-French Comparisons (1989); Norbert Horn, Hein Kötz & Hans G. Leser, German Private and Commercial Law: An Introduction (Tony Weir trans. 1982); B.S. Markesinis, A Comparative Introduction to the German Law of Torts (3d ed. 1994); Barry Nicholas, French Law of Contract (1982); Konrad Zweigert & Hein Kötz, 2 Introduction to Comparative Law: The Institutions of Private Law (Tony Weir trans., 2d ed. 1987).

For Brazil, see Jacob Dolinger & Keith S. Rosenn, eds., A Panorama of Brazilian Law (1992). For Japan, see Zentaro Kitagawa, ed., 1-10 Doing Business in Japan (1984-present); Hiroshi Oda, Japanese Law (1992); Kazuo Sugeno, Japanese Labor Law (L. Kanowitz trans. 1992).

B. CODIFICATION AND THE CODES

The five codes enacted in the 19th century in France and elsewhere in the civil law world were the civil code, code of civil procedure, commercial code, penal code, and code of criminal procedure. Observe that all of them are interpreted and applied in the ordinary courts (except where separate commercial courts still exist, and even there only at the trial level). This jurisdictional fact, plus the dominance of civil law scholars and the consequent tendency of their ideas to affect the other fields, gives a certain coherence to the five codes and to the areas of law they regulate. Of the five codes, the civil code is traditionally regarded as the most fundamental, and one often encounters references to its "constitutional" character. In this section we examine the general character of codification and then look at the contents and arrangement of the French, German, Italian, Mexican, and Japanese civil codes.

1. CODIFICATION AS A CONTINUING PROCESS

DENIS TALLON, REFORMING THE CODES IN A CIVIL LAW COUNTRY, 15 Journal of the Society of Public Teachers of Law 33-41 (1980)

The traditional image of codification has changed since Napoleon's time, in Civil Law as well as in Common Law countries. On the Continent, the 19th century was the golden age of codification with, at either end, the Napoleonic codes and the German codes. Codes were considered as the natural means of issuing legal rules. And as the prevailing opinion was that the only source of the law was statute law, it could be asserted that the codes represented the totality of the legal system....

The works of Saleilles and Gény, at the end of the century, convinced French legal opinion that written law was not all the law and, at the same time, obsolescence hit the French codification in various degrees....

In France, the word "code" covers now very different situations. After a period of partial reforms and patching-up, the time has come to consider the global reform of the traditional codes; and this was achieved in different ways. Moreover, the scope of legislation has greatly increased, as new branches of the law have appeared or old ones grown considerably. In these new fields, codification has been used, but not always. And when it was, the growth of the "pouvoir réglementaire" — that is to say, of the rules left to the normative competence of the Executive — now sanctioned by the present French Constitution, has made more intricate the process of codification, for instance when the "general principles" of an institution are to be laid down by Parliament and the applications left to the Executive. The proliferation of administrative regulations has increased the need for a "codification" of these rules. Thus codification appears to be much more diversified than a century ago. In order to account for this phenomenon, we are led to look first at what has become of the five primitive codes of the Napoleonic period and then to examine the new fields of codification.

I. *The Fate of the Napoleonic Codification*

The general codification of French law was an idea of the Revolution and it was decided by the Assemblée Constituante as early as 1790. But it needed the vigorous impulse of Napoleon Bonaparte, as First Consul and afterwards as Emperor, to bring it to a successful issue, between 1804 and 1810. Five codes were completed in what were, at the time, the major branches of the law: the Civil Code (1804); the Code of Civil Procedure (1807); the Code of Commerce (1808); the Code of Criminal Procedure (1808); the Penal Code (1810). And for decades, the "five codes" remained unchanged. When, in the second half of the century, the movement for legal reforms began, some were introduced in the codes, some were left outside, so that the whole of the law was not any more codified. And, with the passing of time, proposals were made here and there to make new codes. For instance, at the time of the centennial celebration of the Civil Code, it was strongly suggested that the preparation of a new Civil Code should begin, and a Commission was even appointed. But in the end, various policies were adopted according to the different subject-matters. The Code of Commerce was condemned to a slow death (A); the Penal Code, the Code of Criminal Procedure and the Code of Civil Procedure have been ... remade (B); and for the Civil Code, a cure of rejuvenation has been decided upon (C).

A. *The Slow Death of the Code of Commerce*

Nearly all the major reforms of commercial law up till now were accomplished by statutes which were not integrated in the Code of Commerce — for instance, the well-known Company Act of 1867 as well as the Company Act of 1966 which superseded it. The Code of Commerce was no longer the place where this matter was to be found. And in 1945, the Government decided to prepare a new Code of Commerce as well as a new Civil Code and a Commission was appointed. Its work was important and was used for some separate reforms of Commercial Law but it never achieved its aims and it was suppressed in 1958. The result is that the initial Code of Commerce still exists but it is reduced to less than 200 sections (out of 648), many of them obsolete. They concern a few general dispositions on the definition and status of traders, some rules on a few commercial transactions and on negotiable instruments (as introduced in 1935 after the Uniform Law of Geneva) but not on cheques. Most of the Commercial Law of today is constituted by important statutes, which are in fact small codes, many of them part of the vast law reform movement of the Fifth Republic. This is the case of Maritime Law (now constituted essentially by five statutes), Company Law, Patents and Trade Marks, Commercial Establishment (fonds de commerce), Commercial Leases, Cheques, etc.

The Code of Commerce is now but an empty shell. Why is this so? The first reason is certainly that it was too much inspired by the past, on which were grafted a few ideas of the Revolution. It did not contrive — as the Civil Code did — to merge the old law and the new ideas. Thus its conceptual basis remained uncertain, torn between the subjective approach (which was that of the Old Commercial Law, the law of traders) and an objective approach (favoured by the revolutionary conception, according to which Commercial Law ought to be the law of business transactions — actes de commerce). The consequence was that it could not provide an adequate conceptual framework for the new institutions which arose from the industrial revolution of the 19th century. The other reason — which may explain the failure of a new codification — is that in most countries, the distinction between Civil and Commercial Law is tending to disappear.

The result of this evolution is that we still have a Code of Commerce but that Commercial Law is no longer to be found in it.

B. *The Replacement of the Penal Code, the Code of Criminal Procedure and the Code of Civil Procedure*

Three of the five Napoleonic codes have been ... replaced by new ones. Thus, a new Code of Penal Procedure superseded in 1958 the old "Code d'Instruction Criminelle" of 1808. The fundamental principles of the matter have not been deeply modified but the whole of criminal procedure has been reviewed (and even its title) and brought up-to-date. And a new concern appears, that of comprehensiveness. The code from now on will include not only the statutory rules but also all kinds of delegated legislation. The result is that it is divided in five parts: legislation; general regulations (réglements d'administration publique); ordinary regulations (décrets); ministerial regulations (arrêtés); ministerial instruction (instruction générale).[8]

[8] The "réglements d'Administration publique" are the most solemn kind of executive orders. They must be submitted for advice to the Conseil d'Etat. Under them, we find the ordinary "Décrets." Both are signed by the President of the Republic and/or by the Prime Minister. The "arrêtés ministériels" are issued by the different ministers. The "Instruction générale" (or "circulaire") is the official commentary (compulsory for the Administration but with no binding effect for the general public) on the legal rules.

The reform of the Code of Civil Procedure is [complete]. The matter has undergone many reforms since 1807, but recently complete overhauling was decided upon and various committees appointed. Civil procedure belongs to the sphere of "pouvoir réglementaire," which makes things easier. Five "Décrets" were successively promulgated and a regulation of 5th December 1975 codified these five texts in a code of 972 sections.... The changes brought about by the new code are important (for instance in relation to the respective part played by the court and the litigants in the trial); yet it does not include [rules on the enforcement of judgments, which were enacted by statute (Law No. 91-650 of 9 July 1991), nor rules on] the organisation of the courts, which is now regulated by a code of the new category (*infra*, II), the "Code de l'Organisation Judiciaire" of 1978. And as to form, special attention was given to the language of the code, in order to clarify and simplify it.

The Penal Code of 1810 [was replaced by the Nouveau code pénal, which went into force on 1 March 1994].

Some common conclusions may be drawn from this recent experience of codification. First, the three new codes are codes in the full meaning of the term and not only a patching-up of the old ones or the consolidation of previous texts. The whole of the matter has been considered and organised on the basis of general principles. For instance, the New Code of Civil Procedure opens with a series of general rules which govern the various dispositions of the code and ought to direct its interpretation and fill its lacunae. And these codes have in common the other characteristic of a true code, that is to supersede all previous law, even if many of its dispositions have been reenacted by the new code. As regards now the technique of these reforms, the important part played by the Ministry of Justice ought to be stressed. It does not only provide for the material working of various groups and commissions (secretarial staff; preliminary studies; collecting of statistics; etc.) but it gives a permanent impulse to the work and, of course, "nurses" the project through the various phases of its promulgation (consultation with other ministries; review by the Conseil d'Etat; and, if the reform is of a legislative nature, Parliamentary proceedings).

C. *The Renovation of the Civil Code*

Quite a different technique has been adopted for the Civil Code, after the major change of policy decided in 1958. As already mentioned, a Commission was appointed in 1945 with the mission to make an entirely new code, at the same time as the Commission for the reform of the Code of Commerce. Its work was considerable, too, and inspired many limited reforms of civil law, as well as the later ones, but it could not achieve its major aim. And the change of policy which was decided involved the object as well as the method of the reform of Civil Law.

The idea of a new code was abandoned. The old one — the Code of 1804 — was to be kept. The experience of the 1945 attempt had shown that it was too difficult to find a consensus on new general principles on which the code was to be built. And after all, the general principles and the framework of the old one (despite its rather unscientific general scheme) were still satisfactory.

And a renovation from the inside of all the parts which had become unadapted to the present time was undertaken according to a general programme. This deliberate decision to keep the old code as the basis of the reform, is illustrated by the way the new sections were to be numbered. The major texts — those which are known by all jurists and even by the students — were to keep their original numbers and additional sections were to be inserted with an additional number. For instance, section 311 still gives the so-called scientific presumption of paternity (even though the content has been modified), and eighteen sections, numbered 311-1 to 311-18, have been inserted between section 311 and section 312 — another well known text on the presumption of paternity of the husband. Vacant numbers were also used; for instance sections 9 and 10, which initially concerned nationality, a matter which was taken out of the code in 1927 and is now codified in the "Code de la Nationalité," are now devoted to privacy (since an Act of 14th July 1970) and to the duty to help justice (since an Act of 5th July 1972).

This renovation has concerned mainly Family Law (including matrimonial property). It may be said that nearly all this branch of the law has been thoroughly reformed since 1964. But other matters have also been the subject of important reforms: "absence," joint ownership, civil corporations, possession and building contracts for instance. At the end, over a thousand sections (out of the original 2,281)[15] have been reenacted since 1804.

The method too was new. Instead of a Commission, nearly all the reforms were entrusted to a single draftsman, Professor Jean Carbonnier. This has given a unity of conception and of style to the reform. Professor Carbonnier has contrived to keep the original style of code — which was excellent — but stripped of its archaism.

The process of renovation is now nearly over. The last item of the programme, the law of succession, has been delayed. There will of course be minor reforms and, for sure, they will be included in the code. But this method cannot be used indefinitely. There will be a time when the code, instead of being a coherent and orderly statement of the law, will have become a jumble of provisions with an intricate numbering and once more the problem of preparing a new code will have to be faced. But in the meanwhile, we shall keep the 1804 Code and one can but wonder at the vitality of this 175-year-old document which has survived the changes of society and successfully undergone a cure of rejuvenation. The contrast with the Code of Commerce is complete.

This short survey of the fate of the various Napoleonic codes shows that, with the exception of the Code of Commerce, codification in the traditional sense is still very much alive in France. The matters which were chosen for codification at the beginning of the nineteenth century are still codified today, and codified in the old way. But the five codes are no longer the only codes known to French Law. New fields have been opened to codification. But the question is: is it the same kind of codification?

[15] There are now 2,283 sections in the code, two sections on the protection of possession having been added in 1975.

II. *The New Fields of Codification*

A great number of so-called codes have been added to the five major ones. They correspond to various functions of codification and they have not gained the same prestige as the Napoleonic codes. Yet codification does not cover all of French law, so that we shall have to look first at codification and then at its limits.

A. *Codification Since the Beginning of the 19th Century*

Few codes were made in the 19th century. We can only mention the Code of Forestry and the Rural Code (which absorbed the Code of Forestry) published part by part between 1881 and 1898. Since then and before the Second World War, a Code of Labour was begun between 1912 and 1927 but was never completed; there were also the Code of Military Justice and various codes in fiscal matters. Some texts of more limited scope were even christened codes in order to stress their importance: Code of Wine, Code of Cereals and even a so-called Family Code, which took various measures in favour of family and natality but did not include the essential parts of family law.

But the real boom in codification began with what has been called — not without ambiguity — the "administrative codification," even if this type of codification is not the only one to be found in this period. Such a codification aims primarily at simplification and rationalisation of a branch of law and mainly (but not exclusively) concerns administrative law. It was decided upon in this field in 1948 and a Superior Commission of Codification installed, with the task of supervising the codifications laid down by statutes and drawing a programme of such codification for Administrative and Welfare Law. As a rule, the preparation of such a code is entrusted to the interested ministerial department. A preliminary draft is prepared and examined by the Commission, then by the Conseil d'Etat. And the code is promulgated by an Executive Order (and not by Parliament, hence the term "administrative codification"). This procedure means that no change may be brought to the rules to be codified — at least when they are of legislative origin.

The general idea is to collect in the same document all the scattered texts, whether acts of Parliament or delegated legislation, and to distribute them according to a coherent schedule. And these codes are to be brought up to date every year.

The list of new codes is very long and we shall mention only the more important ones: Code of Pensions, Code of Social Security, Code of Urban Planning and Habitation, Code of National Health, Code of Taxes (Code Général des Impôts — which has brought together the previous codes for each kind of tax), Code of Insurance, Code of Labour (superseding the previous one without major change), Code of Court Organisation.[20]

[20] The more recent ones, such as the Code of Insurance or the Code of Labour have adopted a new kind of numbering, as already used by modern codes such as the Uniform Commercial Code of the U.S. or the new Civil Code of the Netherlands. The first number indicates the book, the second the title, the third the chapter and the last one (or two) the number of the section. And of course, before the number, the letter indicates the nature — statutory or regulatory — of the text. Thus article L. 442.8 C.Trav. means section 8 of chapter 2, Title 4, Book 4 of the legislative part of the Code of Labour.

The result of this movement is not as impressive as the reformation of the major codes. Compared with them, the new codes appear as poor relations. Yet their usefulness is certain at a time of legislative inflation. They give the public and Administration an easier access to a mass of complex regulations, frequently difficult to find (as some are not published in the Journal Officiel, but only in the Bulletin of various ministries).

They have in common with the major codes the function of simplification and rationalisation of the law. But they are not by themselves an instrument of reform of the law (except in a few cases such as the Code of Nationality). They provide the frame for all future reforms. As a rule, they have a more limited scope, sometimes very narrow indeed (the Code of Decorations and Medals...); on the other hand, they include all the rules related to their subject-matter, legislative as well as regulatory — which was not the case for the traditional codes. As to form, the rules are generally much more detailed; for it is not possible, in such matters, to legislate by way of general principles in the way prescribed by Portalis in the famous "Discours Préliminaire au Code Civil."

B. *The Limits of Codification*

Law reform does not always take the form of codification, at least avowedly. There are still important statutes which have neither been inserted in pre-existing codes nor been officially called "codes." This is the case for instance for the Act of 1st July 1901 on "Associations" (non-profit corporations), for the Decree on Land Registration (4th January 1955), for Copyright (Act of 11th March 1957), for Patents (Act of 2nd January 1958), and for most commercial institutions, as mentioned before (*supra* I.A). For instance, the new Company Act (L.24 July 1966) has 509 sections and is implemented by a "Décret" of some 309 sections. These statutes are neither traditional codes, because of their limited scope, nor new codes, as the legislative and administrative rules are kept separate. But it is not impossible to imagine their codification. It has just been done for Insurance. The new code includes now all the legislative rules and all regulations on insurance (including maritime insurance, which was till 1967 in the Code of Commerce). It is mainly a question of opportunity whether such a codification is undertaken or not. And this means that there is no blind tendency in favour of codification. As a matter of fact, it is difficult to assess the proportion of codified and un-codified legislation. But isolated statutes or rules do cover a respectable part of the field.

A more interesting phenomenon is that codification has failed in some important branches of the law such as Private International Law and Administrative Law.

There have been many attempts to codify Private International Law — which is mainly case-law. They were all unsuccessful. In the last few years, rules of conflicts have been introduced in some reforms of family law such as filiation and divorce. This new policy has been criticised as tending to disintegrate Private International Law as such. But it appears that the failure of a general codification is due to a lack of consensus among the authors and to the technical difficulty of codifying case-law.

Case-law is also mainly involved in Administrative Law, as all the major rules have been elaborated by the Conseil d'Etat. And it has been a long-standing project to codify this general part of Administrative Law. But here again, we find a lack of doctrinal consensus and, of course, a fierce opposition from the Conseil d'Etat, because a codification would deprive the Supreme Administrative Court of its almost unlimited power to create and reform the general principles of Administrative Law. French Administrative Law has sometimes been compared to English Common Law. And there is a similarity in the argumentation against codification of the one and the other. As regards French law, the academic debate between the flexibility of case-law as opposed to the rigidity of codification remains open. But it cannot be said that codification has been as such an obstacle to law reform.

Conclusion

Codification is still very much alive in France. Not only has it survived the reform of the traditional branches of the law (with the exception of Commercial Law), but in the new fields of legislation, it has developed under new aspects. This does not mean that French Law is completely codified. Some of its branches are still largely ruled by case-law and there are many texts which are left outside the codes. And codified law has no special nature, no greater value (except, in some cases, in prestige) than uncodified texts.

Far from being a hindrance to law reform, codification has been one of its instruments. In its full meaning, codification requires of the law reformer a general review of a whole branch of law and, as such, is an incentive for a global reform. And it provides the frame for further limited reforms. And this latter function is assumed by codification by way of consolidation. And between these two extreme forms of codification, there are many intermediate degrees, so that the law reformer may choose the form best adapted to the subject-matter and to the range of the proposed reform.

2. THE STRUCTURE OF A CIVIL CODE

ALAIN LEVASSEUR, ON THE STRUCTURE OF A CIVIL CODE, 44 Tulane Law Review 693, 694-97, 699-703 (1970)

There is no doubt that in our civil law systems of today the meaning of the word "civil" has undergone a considerable limitation, since it refers only to that part of the law that governs the relations of men with one another. This limitation of the scope of the word finds its explanation in the history of Rome, the fall of the Roman Empire, and the second revival of Roman law in Europe in the late sixteenth century.

> Of the Roman laws which became the written reason of Europe, only those laws dealing with family, successions and contracts were selected. All that was concerned with the government, the police, administration and the military had become too foreign to what then existed to be adopted. The habit developed of giving the name of civil law exclusively to that part of Roman law that governed the personal interests of the citizens. As a consequence the words "civil law" no longer had so exten-

sive a meaning as they had in the past. Thus there resulted in our modern days this division between different codes of the different kinds of laws according to the various things they deal with.

It is this last meaning of the word "civil" that prevailed in the days when the French Civil Code, and later the Louisiana Civil Code, were drafted. The scope of the civil code was thus limited to those matters having to do with the relations between men. Yet these matters were so numerous as to impose the necessity of organizing them into a coherent frame. In their search for such a frame, the drafters of the code could rely heavily on the teachings and experience of the past before they decided on one alternative or another.

Teachings and Experience of the Past

How many Louisiana lawyers have asked themselves the question: why three books in the civil code? Nothing, *a priori*, seems to justify such a distribution, and it is well known that when the four drafters of the *Code Civil* started working on their code, there had been no previous discussion as to the division of the code into three books. There is no doubt that the weight of Roman law forced the hazard of the choice, if hazard there was. In fact, the plan can be traced back to Gaius and his Institutes.

The plan of these Institutes is built around three titles, and all the rules of civil law are gathered under them. "*Omne autem jus quo utimur vel ad personas pertinet, vel ad res, vel ad actiones.*" Thus, according to Gaius, all the law that we use belongs either to persons or to things or to actions. There seems to be no earlier legal work with such a division into three parts, and one can think that Gaius fathered it and that Justinian simply borrowed it. However, until the end of the sixteenth century, the plan of Justinian's Institutes had very little influence, and Domat ignored it completely in his famous treatise. In Domat's opinion, the most natural division is that which consists in distinguishing the legal ties that men create in their everyday lives from those they inherit from their fathers by succession. This division by Domat illustrates a collective approach to private law, whereas the essence of the latter is to be individualistic, and for that reason, it is believed that Domat's classification has had no influence at all on jurists. Among the other works which were written from the time of the second revival of Roman law until the late 1870's and which show a strong influence on the plan of the Institutes, we must mention Pothier's treatise of 1670, which reproduced the division between persons, things and actions, and Bourjon's work of 1747.

Organization of a Code

One could say that there is no book, either in the Louisiana Civil Code or in the *Code Civil*, on the matter of actions, but rather a third book on the modes of acquiring the ownership of things. There lies, indeed, a very important difference between our modern works and those of Gaius and Justinian. One half of what was encompassed in the third book of the Institutes has been transferred, in our codes, to the book on "persons" and the other half has been included in the Code of Civil Procedure. In the law of the Institutes, obligations were inserted between "things" and "actions" and belonged to both categories. It was so because at Roman law obligations were considered not as a mode of acquiring ownership, but simply as a preliminary step towards acquisition, which was completed only by *traditio* or actual transfer of the thing. This has changed since the courts and tribunals of the Ancien Régime which effected a drastic change in the consequences of the obligation "to give" by holding it to be sufficient of its own accord to achieve the transfer and acquisition of ownership.... Obligations, therefore, had to be separated from *res* and *actiones* to become part of a new third book, due to take the place of the then disrupted book on "actions." This tripartite division was adopted by the drafters of the French Code as a natural heritage of a juridical tradition. Maleville tells us that such a division was agreed upon without any adverse opinion, although he admits that it is far from being the best. This division into three parts was thus not rested upon fully convincing justifications.

Subsidiary to the main question of tripartite division is that of setting in order the topics of the three books. Why have "persons" been placed before "things," and why have the latter been placed before the modes of acquiring them? Such an order is often taken for granted and does not appeal to the curiosity of the reader. There is, however, a logic and an explanation behind this taken-for-granted presentation. There would not be any law in the absence of a human being to create it, a human being to benefit from it or to suffer under it. Natural sense and logic command that persons be considered before the things they will own, or benefit from, or suffer from. And things should be dealt with before the modes of acquiring them — establishing the kind of legal ties men can create with things requires that the latter be defined first. Lastly, things becoming the objects of transactions between men, the third book should logically define these various transactions and enumerate the rights they generate.

This problem of organizing the code, putting it into order, was the least difficult that the drafters of the civil code had to face in their immense work. In fact, this was done as the last matter and did not raise many difficulties. The hard core of the work was the actual writing of the articles themselves. There, indeed, lay the mammoth work. "A code is not the arbitrary and spontaneous product of legislative thought in the process of enacting. A code sums up in its provisions the results achieved by the labor of reason in the past centuries." The redactors of codes "adopt what has been given to us by the general legal culture. But not everything can be adopted, adapted to the needs of the State that expects this 'important codification.' It is necessary to create many new legal rules: codification cannot be a compilation." Codification is an art that obeys some stringent rules....

The Institutions

Within the broad field hedged by the imprecise contours of the captions of the books, the drafters of the code intended to fit a group of well-defined institutions linked together by the simple thread of the necessity of a total organization. These institutions have been identified by one word or one short heading that corresponds to the captions of the different titles. Each single institution has been analyzed as a whole within the title of which it forms the substance (*e.g.*, Of Domicile, Of Absentees, Of Husband and Wife). The analysis of the institution leads to a listing of its elements either in chapters (whenever the title consists of one institution only) or in sections (whenever several institutions are grouped within one title, each institution subsequently becoming the caption of a chapter). The purpose of such systematic construction in the titles, chapters and sections was to create an intellectual mechanism that would inevitably and necessarily guide the lawyer toward an awareness of the existence of a fixed rapport between all the elements of each institution. The intended result is that, for example, whenever the word "sale" is mentioned, it brings to one's mind not only the definition of sale but also all the elements of "a sale," such as risk of the thing, or obligations of the parties. All these elements are necessary parts of a coherent and solidary whole, which is the institution. Such a "whole" could easily be compared to a chemical product that could not be achieved if any one of its components were missing. Furthermore, any extraneous element would spoil the product wanted, ruin it or result in something else. Thus, a judge or any interpreter of the law must necessarily distinguish between those elements required by the law and those that would be outside its scope. In a codified system of law, whatever is not explicitly laid down in the articles will of necessity lie in the domain of uncertainty and controversy....

Interdependence

Although we have insisted on the fact that each institution must be considered as a whole and each title as an entity, we are by no means saying that the code consists of a simple juxtaposition of institutions foreign to one another. It is there that the concept of "code" and the spirit that pervades it emerge to provide the intellectual mechanism that is like the framework of a building, the weakness of which would cause the building to fall. This mechanism consists mainly in the methods of reasoning ... and, secondarily, in the notions of interdependence between the articles. This interdependence exists on two levels: between the code articles as such and between the articles that define an institution and those defining another institution.

The demonstration of the close interdependence between two or more consecutive articles need not be long to be convincing. Broadly speaking, a code article is composed of two elements. The first could be dubbed the "hypothesis;" the second would then be the "solution." For example, in article 57 the hypothesis is, "[w]hen a person shall not have appeared at the place of his domicile or habitual residence, and when such person shall not have been heard of, for five years...." When such a situation exists, the solution is that "his presumptive heirs may...." In article 1893 the hypothesis laid down consists in "[a]n obligation without a cause, or with a false or unlawful cause," and the solution is that it "can have no effect." Furthermore, an article may have as its hypothesis another article. For example, article 223 is the hypothesis of the solution given in article 224.... These examples show that the rules of law cannot be separated one from the other, that they are linked and interwoven so as to support one another.

1st Level of Interdependence

… level of interdependence appears with the institutions contained …e. A careful reading of the preparatory works for the French Civil …ll convince the reader that the drafters meant to organize the different …tutions strictly and at the same time to reach a precise correspondence …tween the headings and the provisions they encompass. However, the use of these separate headings did not carry with it the partitioning of the institutions. They cannot be relied on so as to exclude one another or oppose one another.… [A]rticle 2438 also provides clear illustration of this interdependence between two institutions. But there is, in this case and in several others, another reason for this interdependence: it is the existence of a rapport between the "general" and the "particular." The contract of sale is but a particular kind of "conventional obligation." Some less conspicuous rapport exists in the code between institutions, and it can even happen that the "particular" precedes the "general." This may sound aberrant at first hand, but when one thinks about it, it simply testifies that the civil code is but "one law" with so many articles which had to be organized one way or another. One example is that of Titles II and III of Book III. Title II reads "Of Donations *Inter Vivos* and *Mortis Causa*;" article 1468 reads, "A donation *inter vivos* (between living persons) is an act by which the donor divests himself, at present and irrevocably, of the thing given, in favor of the donee who accepts it." Bringing this article together with article 1761 of Title III will necessarily lead one to the conclusion that a donation *inter vivos* is a "particular" element of the general category of "conventional obligations." The reason is that donation *inter vivos* is also a "particular" item in another general category which is defined by article 1467 as being a "gratuitous transfer of property." These examples are simple evidence of the fact that the heading should not be given a decisive legal authority, excluding any provision which pertains to another institution. The headings help the lawyer to find his way through the code, but the interpreter that he is should not be misled. "One must admit that the provisions that each [heading] encompasses are mainly related to the subject defined by such heading. But, one must not forget that law is not a theoretical manual, that every legal provision must be considered in itself as well as in its relations with those that precede it or that follow it."

Conclusion

The civil code appears through these short remarks as the work of real architects. Quite understandably, its look and its shape have not attracted the jurists so much as has the substance of its provisions. Nevertheless, the drafters of the civil codes have proved themselves to be "legal" technicians to the point of paying the utmost attention to the problems of organization and composition of the articles. The civil code presents itself as an *a priori* impossible combination of two diametrically opposed trends: one is systematization, the other is parcelling out. Indeed, any one of the code articles can be taken out with its number, which is like a name to identify and individualize it, to serve as the basis for a court's decision. An article will be the basis of a lawyer's brief and may be challenged by another article that will serve as the cornerstone of the opponent's brief. It will be up to the judge to gather the pieces together and reconcile the code articles in order to achieve the systematization that was the goal of the drafters of the code. The civil code is one and only one law; it is a whole built on "n" articles, each essential to the whole. "The civil code is a well ordered monument, whose design and outlooks have a meaning. Beyond this apparent arrangement, there exist implicit and changing coordinations, a deep life, hidden feelings and conceptions which are the true cement of the legal provisions."

3. THE FRENCH CIVIL CODE

FRENCH CIVIL CODE
Principal Headings

[The numbers in parentheses are the numbers of the articles of the code falling under each heading.]

PRELIMINARY TITLE. Publication, effects, and application of laws in general (1-6).

BOOK ONE. Persons [and family] (7-514).

Title	I.	Civil rights: enjoyment and loss (7-33).
Title	II.	Civil status: records (34-101).
Title	III.	Domicile (102-111).
Title	IV.	Absent persons (112-143).
Title	V.	Marriage (144-228).
Title	VI.	Divorce (229-310).
Title	VII.	Filiation (311-342).
Title	VIII.	Adoption (343-370).
Title	IX.	Paternal authority (371-387).
Title	X.	Minority, tutelage, and emancipation (388-487).
Title	XI.	Majority, interdiction and curatorship [guardianship of incompetent adults] (488-514).

BOOK TWO. Property and property rights (516-710)

Title	I.	Types of things (516-543).
Title	II.	Ownership (544-577).
Title	III.	Usufruct, use, and habitation (578-636).
Title	IV.	Servitudes (637-710).

BOOK THREE. Modes of acquiring property rights (711-2283).

General provisions (711-717).		
Title	I.	Successions (718-892).
Title	II.	Donations: *inter vivos* and *mortis causa* [testamentary] (893-1100).
Title	III.	Contracts and conventional obligations (1101-1369).
Title	IV.	Extra-contractual obligations [quasi-contracts and torts] (1370-1386).
Title	V.	Marriage contracts and rights of spouses [matrimonial regimes] (1387-1581).
Title	VI.	Sales (1582-1701).

Title VII.	Exchange agreements [barter] (1702-1707).
Title VIII.	Hiring and leasing agreements (1708-1831).
Title VIII[bis].	Land development agreements (1831-1 to 1831-5).
Title IX.	Partnership agreements (1832-1873).
Title IX[bis].	Agreements about rights in undivided property (1873-1 to 1873-18).
Title X.	Loans (1874-1914).
Title XI.	Bailment and sequestration (1915-1963).
Title XII.	Aleatory contracts (1964-1983).
Title XIII.	Mandate [type of agency] (1984-2010).
Title XIV.	Suretyship (2011-2043).
Title XV.	Compromise (2044-2058).
Title XVI.	Arbitration (2059-2061).
Title XVII.	Pledge (2071-2091).
Title XVIII.	Liens and mortgages (2092-2203).
Title XIX.	Forced sale and ranking of creditors (2204-2218).
Title XX.	Prescription [statute of limitations] and possession (2219-2283).

NOTES AND QUESTIONS

1. California has a large number of codes, including a civil code. Does that make California a civil law jurisdiction? If there is a difference between a code as a form and as an ideology, what elements identify the latter? Would Denis Tallon and Alain Levasseur agree on what is a "true" code?

2. Professor Tallon speaks of the diversification of codification. What seems to determine whether an older code enters the process of slow death, replacement, or renovation? Why are there so many new fields of codification in France today? Why has French administrative law not been codified?

3. What is the origin of the French *Code civil*'s tripartite structure? Professor Levasseur argues that logic dictates the *order* of the tripartite division. Do you agree or is another order equally plausible?

4. The French Civil Code, enacted in 1804, was the first of its type and is still in force. It has been widely emulated in Europe and Latin America — much more so than the German Civil Code (BGB). For example, only the Brazilian Civil Code, among all the civil codes of Latin America, employs the BGB as its principal model. Its age and prestige make the Code Napoléon a monument of French legal culture and give a special international influence to French civil law, legal education, and legal scholarship.

5. There have been ambitious attempts at revision of the French Civil Code, even on an international level. After World War I a joint French-Italian commission drafted a proposed Code of Obligations that, if adopted, would have removed the entire topic of obligations from the *Code Civil* (much as Switzerland has a separate civil code and code of obligations). This effort at massive amendment of the French and Italian civil codes, which was published in 1928, failed to achieve adoption in either nation.

6. The French face a problem: what should be done with an antiquated civil code that is also a cultural monument? Although the historical position of the

Code Napoléon is secure and would certainly survive, even if it were taken out of service, the influence of contemporary French civil law and scholarship outside France, which is to some extent dependent on continuance in force of the Code itself, might decline. But to keep the Code in service poses other difficulties. Can you identify some of them? What should the French do?

7. The issues raised in the preceding excerpts are further discussed in Bernard Audit, *Recent Revisions of the French Civil Code*, 38 La. L. Rev. 747 (1978); Mirjan Damaška, *On Circumstances Favoring Codification*, 52 Rev. Jur. U. Puerto Rico 355 (1983); Hein Kötz, *Civil Code Revision in Continental Europe: The Experience in the Fields of Contract and Tort, ibid.* 235; *id., Taking Civil Codes Less Seriously*, 50 Mod. L. Rev. 1 (1987). *See also* Frederick H. Lawson, A Common Lawyer Looks at the Civil Law 47-61 (1955).

For an English language translation of the *Code civil*, see John H. Crabb, The French Civil Code (1977). *See also* Françoise Grivart de Kerstrat & William E. Crawford, New Code of Civil Procedure in France: Book 1 (1978).

4. THE GERMAN CIVIL CODE

E.J. COHN, I MANUAL OF GERMAN LAW 56-57, 62-63, 94-96, 170-71, 221-22, 257-60, 282-83 (2d ed. 1968)

The Civil Law and the Civil Code

The term "civil law" (*bürgerliches Recht*) is a German translation of the Roman term *jus civile*. It designates that part of private law which is contained in the Civil Code (*Bürgerliches Gesetzbuch*, abbreviated *BGB*) and in those laws which have been enacted in order either to carry out the principles laid down in the Civil Code or to amend its provisions. The Civil Code deals with the law of contracts and quasi-contracts, the law of torts, the law of property (excluding the law of patents, copyrights and designs) the law of domestic relations and the law of succession. In addition to these topics, each of which forms the subject-matter of one of books 2-5 of the *BGB*, the Code deals in its first book with a number of topics which are of general importance in connection with all the topics dealt with in books 2-5 and with all other relations of private law. This book is therefore described as the "general part" (*allgemeiner Teil*)....

There are a number of private law topics which are outside the scope of civil law. Commercial agencies, commercial partnerships, maritime law and a number of other topics are dealt with in the Commercial Code (*Handelsgesetzbuch*, abbreviated *HGB*) and the many laws enacted for the purpose of supplementing and implementing it. This part of private law is commonly referred to as commercial law (*Handelsrecht*). Similarly the law relating to patents, copyrights and designs is contained in a number of separate codifications. This part of private law is commonly referred to as the law relating to the protection of industrial rights (*Recht des gewerblichen Rechtsschutzes*). Finally, the relationship between workman and employer has been the subject-matter of a considerable number of modern statutes. This legislation contains elements of both private and public law. It is commonly referred to as the law of labour (*Arbeitsrecht*).

At the time when the Civil Code came into force each of the individual *Länder* of the *Reich* had its own particular civil law. In most of the *Länder* this was codified. In Prussia the codification enacted under Frederick the Great was in force, the *Allgemeine Landrecht* of 1794. In the Rhine Province French Law, *i.e.*, the French Civil Code, introduced during the time of the Napoleonic wars, was in force, amended by subsequent German legislation. The relation between the Civil Code and the laws of the *Länder* is the subject-matter of articles 55-152 of the Introductory Law of the Civil Code (*Einführungsgesetz zum Bürgerlichen Gesetzbuch*, abbreviated *EGBGB*), which was enacted at the same time as the *BGB*. In most editions of the *BGB* the *EGBGB* is printed after the text of the *BGB*. The principle, stated in art. 55, is that the rules of the *Länder* laws relating to private law cease to be in force with the exception of those rules which are upheld by either the *BGB* or the *EGBGB*. A large number of exceptions are made from this principle in art. 56 *et seq.* *EGBGB*. These are sometimes called the "casualty list" of legal uniformity. However, many of the topics with regard to which the *EGBGB* upheld the existing *Länder* laws have meanwhile been covered by separate laws with a consequent strengthening of legal uniformity within Germany. The most important topics of private law still governed by the law of the *Länder* are the law of mining (*Bergrecht*, art. 67) and the law relating to water courses (*Wasserrecht*, art. 65).

On the other hand the *Länder* had power to enact new rules of private law on topics not covered by the *BGB* or by any other *Reich* law and to enact rules for the carrying-out of the *BGB, i.e.*, laws dealing with questions of detail not mentioned by the *BGB* or assigned by a special provision of the *BGB* to the law of the *Länder*. These carrying-out laws of the *Länder* are styled *Ausführungsgesetze* (abbr.: *AGBGB*). They differ not inconsiderably from one another.

The *BGB*, which came into force on January 1, 1900, and was at the time widely hailed as the most scientific law ever drafted, savours in many respects more of the nineteenth century than of the twentieth. Roman law contributed to much of its contents. The systematic arrangement follows the example of the textbooks of the German pandectist school of the nineteenth century known to many English lawyers from Ledlie's translation of Sohm's *Institutions of Roman Law*. The inclination of that school towards conceptionalism and abstractness has left deep traces on the work. Its language is highly technical. Many of its technical terms convey little meaning to the average German layman. The influence of Roman law is most clearly discernible in the first and second books. The law of property, the law of domestic relations and the law of succession incorporate a number of Germanic legal ideas. The same applies to the law of landlord and tenant in the second book. Modern social developments and contemporary social thought have on the whole found little support in the Code. The attitude of the legislator to social problems is patriarchal rather than influenced by social tendencies. The law of workmen and employers has been developed by special legislation outside the Code. Similarly the law of landlord and tenant is now largely governed by complex legislation supplementing and amending the rules of the Civil Code....

There have been comparatively few inroads into the sphere of the Civil Code by the federal legislation since 1949, but some of them go very deep....

The Function of the General Part of the Civil Code

From the point of view of an English-speaking lawyer the most astounding feature of the legislative technique of the *BGB* is the sharp distinction that is made between "general" and "special" rules and the great emphasis laid on swelling the number of "general" rules. The first book of the Code contains rules which are "general" to all legal relations governed by the civil law. In nearly all cases in which the rules of the Civil Code have to be applied, it is consequently necessary to apply both the rules of the "general part" in addition to those of one of the special books.

> EXAMPLE: A and B have concluded a contract of sale. The question of their capacity to enter into such a contract is governed by the rules of the first book. So is the question as to the influence of fraud or mistake upon their contractual declarations. On the other hand the second book (law of obligations) deals with the liabilities incurred by the parties and the consequences of a breach of contract.

The chief practical purpose of this arrangement is to avoid repetition. Rules which are common to all legal relations need to be stated only once. On the other hand books 2-5 contain a considerable number of exceptions to numerous general rules contained in the first book. Thus the rules on nullity of contracts, contained in the first book, do not apply to the contract of marriage. The rules on the influence of mistake on contracts are modified by the special rules applicable to the contract of sale.

The legislator's tendency of distinguishing between the "general" and the "special" or particular rules makes itself strongly felt in the second and third books of the Code. Thus the second book contains seven chapters, of which the first six form what is commonly referred to as the "general part of the law of obligations," while the seventh chapter deals with individual types of obligations, such as sale, donation, civil delicts, unjust enrichment, etc. The rules of the first six chapters apply to all these individual relations, except in those cases where a rule in the seventh chapter expressly excludes them or where the circumstances of the individual case render them for some special reason inapplicable.

The rules of the general part apply also to those legal relations which are governed by rules of private law, not contained in the Civil Code, such as those to which the Commercial Code or one of the modern supplementary laws of the *BGB* are applicable. The general part deals therefore very largely with topics which English lawyers are accustomed to find dealt with in textbooks on analytical jurisprudence.

The arrangement of the first book is as follows: The Code deals first with the law of persons (holders of rights, sections 1-89); this is followed by a chapter on corporeal things (sections 90-103), which in the standard textbooks is usually elaborated into a full treatment of all possible objects of rights. The next three chapters deal with legally relevant events. The first of these chapters treats legal transactions (sections 104-185) including the law of agency; the second and third chapters deal with the influence of the effluxion of time on legal relations, *i.e.*, with periods, dates and the statutes of limitation (sections 186-225). The last two chapters are devoted to the treatment of two questions connected with the enforcement of rights, other than by way of civil proceedings, *i.e.*, with self-defence and self-help (sections 226-231) and the giving of security (sections 232-240). This last topic was considered fit for inclusion in the general part of the Code, because the exercise of a number of private rights is conditioned by the giving of security....

The Law of Obligations

The second book of the Civil Code, entitled *Recht der Schuldverhältnisse* (law of obligations), contains much, if not most, of the material which an English lawyer is accustomed to find in books on the law of contracts, the law of torts, and in books on special types of legal relations such as sale of goods, landlord and tenant, etc. Contracts (*Schuldverträge*) are, however, merely one type of the wider species of *Verträge* (agreements) on which the first book of the Code contains many rules. Consequently the rules relating to the formation of agreements are to be found in the first book of the *BGB* ... where also the doctrine of nullity and voidability (form, mistake, fraud) is dealt with.... The same applies to the rules relating to ability to conclude legal transactions, to conditions and to the institution of agency.... The interpretation of contracts is partly dealt with in the first book ... and partly in the second. To obtain a complete picture of the German law relating to contracts it is therefore necessary to remember that the second book must be read in conjunction with the first, which as a "general" part of the Code is applicable to all legal relations in regard to which "special" rules are not provided.

What the English-speaking lawyer calls a contract is in German law styled *Schuldvertrag*. The relation which arises from a contract or a tort is called *Schuldverhältnis*; the title of the second book itself hints therefore at the fact that this part of the Code deals not so much with the contract, its validity and formation as with the relation which arises from a contract or from a tort. The contractual or tort relation itself forms the basis for the relative rights which each party has against the other.

> EXAMPLES: The purchaser can demand transfer of the property in Redacre which he has bought from the vendor. The vendor can demand payment of the price.

Such rights, arising out of *Schuldverhältnisse*, are called *Forderungen*, while the corresponding liability on the part of the debtor is called *Schuld*. Because the *Schuld* is the most important aspect of this part of the civil law, this branch of German law is often briefly referred to as *Schuldrecht*. A debtor is, of course, as a rule, responsible for his debts to the extent of his entire property. There are, however, in German law a number of cases where he is responsible only to the extent of certain parts of his property. These cases are relatively more important than the corresponding cases in English law. They are referred to as cases of limited responsibility (*beschränkte Haftung*).

> EXAMPLES: In a limited liability partnership (*Kommanditgesellschaft*) the responsibility of some of the partners is limited. The responsibility of the heir for the debts of the deceased may be restricted to what he has acquired by way of succession. The *Gesellschaft mit beschränkter Haftung* on the other hand constitutes — like the English limited liability company — a misnomer, because the company is a separate legal entity and as such responsible to the extent of its entire property, while its individual member of the company is not responsible at all.

In the preceding paragraphs the term "tort" has been used in place of the German expression "*unerlaubte Handlung*" or as German legal terminology, following the precedent of Roman law, frequently calls it "delict." This rendering is inaccurate and will not be used hereafter. German law, following in this respect the example of Roman law, allots to the conception of "delict" a much less important function than does English law. It understands by "delict" certain unlawful actions, which as a rule must be either intentional or negligent. The owner of a corporeal thing ... can, however, and as a rule will, assert his ownership without resorting to the law of delicts. He can make use of other remedies. These are provided for him by the third book of the *BGB*. These remedies do not require that the defendant has committed a delict. They are additional to those dealt with in the second book.... In English law, on the other hand, the owner is confined to asserting his ownership through the law of torts, a fact which partly — though by no means wholly — explains why German law can comprise most of the law of *unerlaubte Handlungen* within not more than thirty sections of the Code.

> EXAMPLE: A detains a purse belonging to B. In English law B asserts his right by bringing an action for the tort of detinue. In German law on the other hand, B will in the first instance bring an action for the recovery of his property under section 985 (3rd book of the Civil Code). Only if he wants to demand damages in addition to recovering possession need he resort to the law of delict, in which case he has as a rule to prove that the possessor acted intentionally or negligently in acquiring or retaining possession.

The German term "*unerlaubte Handlungen*" will in the following pages always be translated as "delicts."

As has already been stated ... the German legislator has distinguished between general and special rules not only in the arrangement of the first book of the *BGB*, but also of the second book. While the first book contains all the rules which the legislator considered to be of general application throughout the entire sphere of private law, other rules which were intended to be of general application within the entire sphere of the law of obligations — but not further — are separated from the rest of the law of obligations and contained in sections 241-432 *BGB*. This first part, though not officially described as such, is usually referred to by German lawyers as the general part of the law of obligations. Unfortunately the arrangement is logically not as sound as it should be. Though many of the rules contained in sections 241-432 really do apply to both contractual and delictual obligations, a great number of them apply to the former only. Furthermore, some of the rules apply in rather "special" situations only and might just as well have formed part of the special part, *e.g.*, the rules on penalties.

The categories of contract and tort are as little able to exhaust the whole field of obligations in German law, as they would be in English law. There are a considerable number of obligations which arise neither from contract nor from delict — one more reason why the German legislature was right in heading the second book "Law of Obligations" instead of Law of Contracts and Delicts. There are a number of obligations which result directly from a unilateral declaration by one party. Public promises of rewards form the most significant example of these. Others arise directly from a legal provision. The best-known example of the latter are the obligations resulting from unjust enrichment, which play a most important part within the structure of the German legal system — much more so than their namesakes in English law. The terms "quasi-contract" and "quasi-delict" for obligations of this kind, have for some time past become unfashionable in Germany, the fiction that such obligations can in any way either be based on a supposed intention of the party or parties or be considered as possessing some similarity to delicts having been discarded. It is usual to refer to such obligations as to "obligations *ex lege*" (*gesetzliche Schuldverhältnisse*)....

The Law of Things

The third book of the Civil Code, entitled *Sachenrecht*, deals with the law of movable and immovable property. This part of the Code must, therefore, in the first instance be read in conjunction with that part of the first book of the Code which deals with "things," seeing that only these can be the object of property and other absolute rights. Section 90 *et seq. BGB* form therefore a necessary supplement of the third book of the Code....

The third book deals with absolute rights in respect of things, not with relative rights. Contracts and delicts are, therefore, outside the scope of this book. The special rules relating to property which originate in the relation of husband and wife and parent and child and in succession are also not dealt with here. Contracts and delicts are treated in the second book, domestic relations in the fourth and succession in the fifth book of the Code.

More than any other book of the Code the third shows peculiarities distinguishing German law sharply from other legal systems — not only from the English but also from the Roman and cognate systems. The following general features of this part of German law deserve special mention.

(*a*) The principle of the protection of good faith: absolute rights (including ownership) in respect of things are extinguished under certain circumstances if the objects are transferred to a person who is in ignorance of the existence of such rights. The transferee acquires in these cases full and unencumbered ownership.

(*b*) The principle of publicity: great care is taken to ensure that absolute rights in respect of things are as often as possible clearly ascertainable by the public at large, in order that cases in which the transferee must and can rely on the principle of good faith (see (*a*), above) may be reduced to the least possible minimum.

(*c*) The principle of speciality: contrary to English law which recognises absolute rights in respect of a totality of things, *e.g.*, in respect of the entire property of a company, German law recognises the existence of such rights only in respect of defined things....

> EXAMPLE: A can grant to B a mortgage in respect of the houses X, Y and Z, but not "on all my immovable property."

(*d*) The principle of distinguishing between movable and immovable property. While Roman law treated movable and immovable property well-nigh alike, Germanic law made a sharp distinction between the two types of property. The Civil Code is based on the Germanic rule but not inconsiderable concessions have been made to the Roman principle. The consequence is that the third book is not divided into a section dealing with the law of immovable and another dealing with movable property, but that several of its sections deal with both kinds of property, while others deal with only one of them....

The Law of Domestic Relations

The fourth book of the Civil Code under the title of *Familienrecht* contained originally the entire law of domestic relations, *i.e.*, not only the law relating to husband and wife, to divorce, nullity and voidability of marriages, but also the law relating to parent and child, adoption, relationship and guardianship, including guardianship over persons other than minors....

[S]ome rules laid down in the Basic Law are of considerable importance for the law of domestic relations and have strongly influenced both the legislation of the Federal Parliament and the practice of the German courts in this field.

(*a*) Article 6 (1) *GG* grants to the marriage and family the special protection of the Constitution. This principle is not merely a programme for future legislation, but a rule of constitutional law and, also, a binding line of guidance for the interpretation of all legal provisions in the field of private and public law relating to marriage and family.

(*b*) Articles 3 (2) and 117 (1) *GG* provide that men and women shall have equal rights. In order to comply with this constitutional principle the Law on Equal Rights of Men and Women in the Field of Civil Law (*Gesetz über die Gleichberechtigung von Mann und Frau auf dem Gebiet des bürgerlichen Rechts*) of June 18, 1957 (*BGBl* I 609) has been enacted. Under this law the rules of the Civil Code on the relationship between husband and wife during matrimony have been replaced by new provisions which were subsequently inserted into the text of the *BGB*....

(*c*) Article 6 (5) *GG* provides that illegitimate children are to be given the same conditions of physical and spiritual development and of acquiring a position in society as legitimate children enjoy....

The Law of Succession

Art. 14 (1) of the Basic Law guarantees "the right of succession," *i.e.*, the freedom to dispose by last will and the fundamental institution of intestate succession by next-of-kin. The details are, however, of course, not covered by this constitutional guarantee. The law of succession, both testate and intestate, is treated at great length in the fifth book of the Civil Code entitled *Erbrecht*, which at one time was considered to be technically the best part of the Code. This view is completely abandoned today. Many rules contained in this part are obsolete as they deal with contingencies which rarely, if ever, arise and introduce rules of interpretation for clauses in wills which are today no longer usual. As in other countries, succession duty plays an important part in Germany....

The German law on intestate succession contains a number of rules inherited from Germanic law, but very much fewer than does English law. The bulk of this part of German law is due to Roman influence. For this reason many of the main principles of German law differ most strongly from those rules of law to which English lawyers are accustomed.

Perhaps the most important principle of German law is the principle of *Universalsukzession* laid down in section 1922 *BGB*. This principle, which is unknown to English law, means that on the death of a person, his or her entire property passes immediately and automatically to his or her heirs. The death of a person is in this connection referred to as the *Erbfall*. No distinction is made between movable and immovable property; on the death of the deceased person both types of property are automatically and without any interval in time or any further outward action of any kind vested in the heirs, whoever they may be, no matter whether they are known or whether it is necessary to take steps to ascertain their identity. Such persons are the owners of the deceased person's property, even though they do not know of the *Erbfall* or of the property and its whereabouts. The consequence is that by the death of a person the contents of the land register, in which the deceased person still appears as the owner of the land registered in his or her name, become inaccurate. They require an adjustment to the effect that in the place of the registered owner his heirs are now owners. The heirs obtain the adjustment upon production of proof that they have succeeded to the estate of the deceased person. This is as a rule done by obtaining from the *Amtsgericht* a certificate, called the *Erbschein* (certificate of inheritance), which to a certain extent fulfils the same functions in German law as letters of administration in English law, though its legal character is different. Under German law possession, too, passes — by a legal fiction — over to the heirs at the time of the *Erbfall* (see section 857 *BGB*). This applies even though the latter do not know of either the death or the fact that they are succeeding to the estate.

It follows that there is in German law no interval between the death of the deceased and the succession to the title by his successors. The space which in Roman law had to be filled by the well-known conception of the *hereditas jacens*, is therefore non-existent in German law and the many theories concerning the nature of such an inheritance, developed in Roman law and in some of the contemporary systems based upon Roman law, have no place in modern German law. There is also, of course, no need for any vesting of title in the successors of the deceased. The death itself vests title, even though nobody at the time when it occurs knows in whom the title is vested.

All rights and all liabilities pass over at the same time to the heirs. The heir is a successor to both the assets and the debts of the deceased person. This, too, is included in the conception of the *Universalsukzession*. It follows that there is no room for the institution of trustees, executors and administrators of an estate in the sense of English law. German law recognises, however, that a person, other than the heir, may be entitled or bound to administer an estate. Such a person is called a *Testamentsvollstrecker*. His legal position differs from that of an executor or administrator under English law, in that neither rights nor liabilities pass over to him. The latter remain vested in the heirs. The *Testamentsvollstrecker* is merely a person entitled to act for and on behalf of the heirs, to dispose of the estate within the limits set by the law and the will, by which he has been appointed, and to exercise those other powers which have been granted to him by the will. He has powers and duties, but not rights or liabilities. In certain cases administrators (*Nachlassverwalter*) may also be appointed by the court, but these administrators too, are merely exercising powers and not rights legally vested in them.

Those persons to whom the title to the estate or to part of it immediately and automatically passes over on the death of the testator are called *Erben* (heirs). No estate can be without an *Erbe*. If no *Erbe* has been appointed by a will, intestate succession takes place. If there are no relatives, the *Land* inherits by way of intestate succession (section 1936). Even the most distant relatives may inherit *ab intestato*.

Persons who have not been granted the right to an immediate share in the estate of the testator, but who are entitled to demand from the heir the delivery of specified movable or immovable property or the payment of a sum of money are called *Vermächtnisnehmer* (legatees). They may be granted the right to claim specified items of property (*e.g.*, the horse in the stable, the *Encyclopaedia Britannica* from the testator's library). The heirs on the other hand can only be granted a right to either the entire estate of the deceased or to a fraction of it, but never to a specified item forming part of the estate (so-called *heres ex re certa*). Under German law — unlike Roman law — it is impossible for any person to acquire directly on the death of a testator ownership in any item or specified items of the testator's estate. A person may receive either ownership of the entire estate or ownership of a fraction of the undivided estate: in this case he is an heir. Or a person may be entitled to demand from the heir or heirs the delivery of specified items from the estate, in which case he is a legatee. The legatee has merely an *Anspruch* ... which is directed against the heir or heirs.

If there is no valid will or if the will merely provides for legacies, but not for the appointment of heirs, certain persons succeed as statutory heirs (*gesetzliche Erben*). The persons so succeeding are the next-of-kin of the deceased, his spouse and, in default of others, the *Land*. German law makes provision for certain near relatives of the testator even in those cases in which the testator has left a will, but without providing for these relatives. Such relatives, who have been passed over by the testator may be entitled to claim from the heirs, an amount of money fixed by law (section 2303). This is called the compulsory portion (*Pflichtteilsrecht*)....

German law permits the making of dispositions *mortis causa* not only by will (*Testament*), *i.e.*, by a unilateral and revocable declaration on the part of the testator, but also by an agreement made between the testator and a third party (*Erbvertrag*). Many of the provisions in the Civil Code refer to both *Testamente* and *Erbverträge*. In the following sketch the word "will" will be used for the sake of brevity. It should, however, be understood that what is stated here of a will, is in most cases true of *Erbverträge* as well — though in practice the latter are not too frequent.

German law provides that the testator may impose upon both heirs and legatees certain burdens without at the same time giving to those persons who are favoured by the burdens thus created a right which they could enforce against the persons who have been thus burdened (section 1940). Such burdens (*Auflagen*) are usually created in favour of a large circle of vaguely defined persons (*e.g.*, where scholarships have been created) or even in favour of the public (opening of a park or a picture gallery to the public). The testator will in such cases frequently appoint an executor in his will to carry out the *Auflage*. The Code provides, however, also certain other ways and means by which the *Auflage* may be enforced (*e.g.*, an administrative authority may be entitled to bring an action, if the *Auflage* is in the public interest.)...

Like other Continental laws, German law provides that certain near relatives of the testator are entitled to receive from the heirs certain benefits, if they have not been appointed as heirs themselves. German law has, however, adopted a different course from many other Continental laws in that the relatives passed over in the testator's will do not themselves become heirs against the will of the testator. Unlike French, Swiss and other Continental laws, German law does not prevent the testator from disposing by will of his entire estate. Descendants of the testator, his parents and his spouse, provided they would be intestate successors, but for the fact that the testator has made a will excluding them from succession, are entitled to what is called a *Pflichtteil* (compulsory portion), if in consequence of the testator's will they are excluded from participating in the succession. The *Pflichtteil* is a right to demand from the heir or heirs the payment of a sum of money equal to one-half of what would have been the intestate share of the excluded relative if there had been intestate succession to the testator (section 2303 (1) *BGB*). The *Pflichtteil* thus gives no direct participation in any of the assets forming part of the estate. These remain always vested in the heirs. The person entitled to the *Pflichtteil* can merely demand that the heirs pay him or her a sum of money. The *Pflichtteil* is consequently one of the debts which the heir has to meet.

EXAMPLE: A dies leaving a wife and two children. The value of the estate is *DM* 100,000. By his last will A has appointed the wife as his sole successor. In this case each child is entitled to a compulsory portion of three-sixteenths of *DM* 100,000, because the intestate share of each child would have been three-eighths. Each child is therefore entitled to claim from the mother the amount of *DM* 18,750 as his compulsory portion. If A had left the entire estate to his two children, the wife would have been entitled to a payment of one-eighth of the value of the estate, *i.e.*, of *DM* 12,500, as her intestate share is one-quarter of the estate.

It should be noted that descendants have a right to a compulsory portion to the extent only to which they would have been entitled to succeed *ab intestato* to the estate. Where there is no such title there is no right to a compulsory portion.

> EXAMPLE: If in the above example one of the children has issue, there would have been no right on the part of any issue of the child to receive a compulsory portion, because of the principle that the son while living excludes the grandson from succeeding to the estate of the father....

A party entitled to a compulsory portion who has been appointed as heir, but to a portion which is smaller than one half of his or her intestate share, is entitled to a compulsory portion of an amount sufficient to make up for the difference between the amount left to him and that of his compulsory portion (see section 2305). Similarly the Code protects a person entitled to a compulsory portion who has been appointed as heir but whose share is burdened with restrictions; (for details see section 2306).

GERMAN CIVIL CODE
Principal Headings

[The numbers in parentheses are the numbers of the sections of the code falling under each heading.]

BOOK ONE. General part (1-240).
- Part One. Persons (1-89).
- Part Two. Things and animals (90-103).
- Part Three. Juridical acts (104-185).
- Part Four. Limitations and terms (186-193).
- Part Five. Prescription (194-225).
- Part Six. Exercise of rights, self-defense and self-help (226-231).
- Part Seven. Security (232-240).

BOOK TWO. Obligations (241-853).
- Part One. Content of obligations (241-304).
- Part Two. Contract obligations (305-361).
- Part Three. Termination of obligations (362-397).
- Part Four. Assignment of claims (398-413).
- Part Five. Assumption of debt (414-419).
- Part Six. Multiple debtors and creditors (420-432).
- Part Seven. Particular obligations (433-853).
    - Title 1. Sale (433-515).
    - Title 2. Donation (516-534).
    - Title 3. Lease (535-597).
    - Title 4. Gratuitous loan (598-606).
    - Title 5. Loan (607-610).

Title 6. Service contract (611-630).
Title 7. Artisan and travel contract (631-651k).
Title 8. Brokerage contract (652-656).
Title 9. Reward (657-661).
Title 10. Mandate (662-676).
Title 11. Management without mandate [*negotiorum gestio*] (677-687).
Title 12. Gratuitous bailment (688-700).
Title 13. Bailment to a hotel (701-704).
Title 14. Partnership (705-740).
Title 15. Joint ownership (741-758).
Title 16. Annuity (759-761).
Title 17. Gaming and betting (762-764).
Title 18. Guaranty (765-778).
Title 19. Compromise (779).
Title 20. Promise or acknowledgment of debt (780-782).
Title 21. Order (783-792).
Title 22. Bearer bonds (793-808).
Title 23. Production of things (809-811).
Title 24. Unjust enrichment [quasi-contract] (812-822).
Title 25. Delicts (823-853).

BOOK THREE. Property (854-1296).[a]
Part One. Possession (854-872).
Part Two. General provisions on rights in land (873-902).
Part Three. Ownership (903-1011).
Part Five. Servitudes [and usufruct] (1018-1093).
Part Six. Preemptive rights (1094-1104).
Part Seven. Charges on land (1105-1112).
Part Eight. Mortgage (1113-1203).
Part Nine. Security interests in movable things and rights (1204-1296).

BOOK FOUR. Family law (1297-1921).
Part One. Civil marriage [and marital property rights] (1297-1588).
Part Two. Relationships [parent and child] (1589-1772).
Part Three. Guardianship (1773-1921).

BOOK FIVE. Succession (1922-2385).
Part One. Order of succession (1922-1941).
Part Two. Heirship (1942-2063).
Part Three. Wills (2064-2273).
Part Four. Inheritance contract (2274-2302).
Part Five. Compulsory shares (2303-2338a).
Part Six. Unworthiness to inherit (2339-2345).
Part Seven. Renunciation of inheritance (2346-2352).
Part Eight. Certificate of inheritance (2353-2370).
Part Nine. Purchase of inheritance (2371-2385).

[a] Part Four was repealed in 1919, but certain hereditary building rights in effect prior to that time are preserved.

NOTES AND QUESTIONS

1. Leaving aside differences in style and in the content of specific rules, and focusing on structure, what are the major differences between the French and German civil codes?

2. Why did the Germans add a general part (Book 1) to their Civil Code? How wide is its influence within the total German system of legal rules?

3. What would a contract and a tort have in common so that civilians have ordered them under the same branch of law (obligations)?

4. Why has the German Basic Law had more influence on Book 4 (family law) than on the code's other books?

5. Explain the concept of compulsory share (*Pflichtteil*) in German inheritance law. What are its Roman and canonic roots? What is universal succession (*Universalsukzession*)? Why is there no decedent's estate to probate? Is a *Testamentsvollstrecker* the same as a common law executor or administrator?

6. The BGB is divided into books, parts, titles (occasionally two levels of subtitles), and sections. Every level, including each section of the code, has a descriptive heading. Consider book 2, part 7, title 23 — named production of things. Under German civil procedure there is no general procedural duty similar to the American discovery rule that requires a party to produce documents and things for his adversary to inspect and copy. However, a German litigant can discover information about documents or things if the discoveree is under a *substantive* duty from title 23 (§§ 809-811) to produce such an item.

7. The BGB (sometimes called "Big German Book") is available in English translation: Ian S. Forrester, Simon L. Goren & Hans-Michael Ilgen, The German Civil Code (1975) and Goren, 1981 Supplement to the German Civil Code ... (1982).

See also Simon L. Goren & Ian S. Forrester, The German Commercial Code (1979); Goren, The Code of Civil Procedure Rules of the Federal Republic of Germany ... (1990).

5. THE ITALIAN CIVIL CODE

MAURO CAPPELLETTI, JOHN HENRY MERRYMAN & JOSEPH M. PERILLO, THE ITALIAN LEGAL SYSTEM: AN INTRODUCTION 229-39 (1967)

The Geography of the Code: Book I. The internal arrangement of anything as comprehensive and systematic as a contemporary civil code is affected by the substantive view taken of the materials arranged. The topography of such a code is a product of its geology. The purpose of the remaining part of this chapter is to conduct a rough survey of some of the most important of these relationships within the Italian Civil Code of 1942. Such a "geography of the code," while it cannot go very far in explaining the substantive content of Italian civil law, offers additional perspective on the way Italians think about their law, and hence on the Italian style.

Following the thirty-one articles of Provisions on the Law in General, which are generally treated as a part of the code, but technically are not, there are six "books" or main divisions, containing 2,969 articles. The contents of the first four books, taken together, reflect the traditional European concept of the civil law,[122] books five and six are innovations.

The first book, on persons and family, contains few surprises for the common lawyer. Although specific institutions appear to differ in nature and effect from their common law analogues, the area of concern is roughly the same. The principal exceptions are: title II, containing general provisions dealing with legal persons and some fairly detailed rules concerning the internal affairs of nonbusiness organizations, matters which common lawyers generally consider more closely related to business associations than to persons and the family; and title III, on domicile and residence, matters which common lawyers would ordinarily assign to conflict of laws. From the titles of the various parts of this book, with the exceptions noted above, one can conclude that both its subject matter and its principal institutions are quite similar to those with which the common lawyer is familiar.

The Geography of the Code: Book II. The second book is quite a different matter. The Italian law of inheritance is fundamentally different from that of the common law, primarily because of the existence of two institutions: forced inheritance and universal succession. Forced inheritance, or *legittima*, is common in continental law and consists of the right of certain relatives of a property owner to inherit from him on his death. In Italy, for example, one-half of the decedent's property is reserved for his child, if he has only one, and two-thirds, if he has two or more. This obligation cannot be avoided by making inter vivos gifts; such gifts are considered to be part of the decedent's property for purposes of the *legittima*, and may be reclaimed from the donee if needed to satisfy the claim of the legitimate heir. This interrelation between gifts and forced inheritance helps to explain why gifts (*donazioni*) are included in this book, rather than in the third book, on property, or in the fourth book, on contracts; and it also provides a partial key to the importance and difficulty of distinguishing between gifts and nondonative transactions in Italian law. Only donative transactions are subject to the *legittima*; the typical business or exchange transaction, even one so imprudent as to diminish the owner's total wealth (his patrimony, in Italian law) substantially, cannot be revoked in the interest of the legitimate heir.

The institution of universal succession has at its base the concept of succession to the obligations, as well as to the wealth, of the deceased. Subject

---

[122] The French Civil Code contains 2,281 articles, divided into a brief introductory section (6 articles) and three books: I. Of Persons (509 articles); II. Of Property (195 articles); and III. Of the Different Ways in Which Property Rights Can Be Acquired (1,571 articles). The third book actually contains the provisions governing intestate succession, wills, inter vivos gifts, torts, unjust enrichment, marital property, contracts, landlord and tenant, agency and partnership, bailments, pledges, liens, mortgages, creditors' rights, and the limitation of actions.

The German Civil Code contains 2,385 articles in five books: I. General Part (240 articles); II. Obligations (613 articles); III. Things (443 articles); IV. Family Law (625 articles); and V. Inheritance (464 articles). While the organization of this code is substantially different from the French, the subject matter is similar. The principal difference is that the general part (Book I) of the German Code has no equivalent in the French Code.

The first four books of the Italian Civil Code of 1942 (Persons and the Family, Succession, Property, Obligations) are broader in scope than the French and German Civil Codes to the extent that material on commercial obligations formerly found in a separate commercial code is now incorporated into the fourth book (Obligations). Similar subject matter is still found in separate commercial codes in France and Germany.

always to the *legittima*, the heir may be designated by the will or by the rules of intestate succession, but this designation is not binding on the heir; he may either accept the status of heir, with its concomitant obligation to pay debts and legacies, or reject it. The concept of a decedent's estate as a legal entity which pays debts, taxes, and legacies and which is subsequently distributed after administration under the supervision of a court is unknown in Italian law. The heir can, however, limit his liability to the extent of the decedent's property by qualifying his acceptance "with benefit of inventory." Without such a qualification the property of the accepting heir also becomes available to pay the obligations of the deceased. The theory is that the heir literally "succeeds," or occupies the place of, the deceased.

The Geography of the Code: Book III. The subject of the third book is property. Both this book and the Italian law of property are dominated by the concept of ownership, a concept foreign to the common law. The principal relevant characteristics of this concept as employed in Italian law are its absoluteness, in contrast to the relative nature of the common law concept of better title, and its resistance to fragmentation, in contrast to the common law propensity for dividing up property interests into estates, into legal and equitable title, into beneficial and security title, and the like. Both of these characteristics resound throughout the Italian law of property and cannot be fully explored here, but some of the more obvious implications bear directly on the content and arrangement of the code.

For one thing, nothing remotely comparable to the common law concept of the estate exists in Italian law. Indeed, except for certain limited property interests which historically have been considered to be real rights, as distinguished from personal rights, the concept of an "interest in property" hardly exists. One either owns a thing or he does not; there is no middle ground, and this theory is maintained even in the face of the limited group of real rights just mentioned. These real rights are the various servitudes, more or less equivalent to common law easements and profits; the *superficie*, which has no exact equivalent in the common law; the *emphyteusis*, likewise unknown in the common law but similar in effect to a perpetual lease; and the usufruct, which approximates in general effect a life estate. None of these is conceived of as affecting the ownership of the property. The owner of land subject to a usufruct for life is no less owner of it according to Italian law. Whereas common lawyers would say that there are two estates, a life estate and a reversion, an Italian conceives of the situation as one of ownership subject to a real right.

Other interests that common lawyers would consider estates do not even have the status of real rights. Most prominent among these is the lease. In Italian law the lease is not a conveyance of an estate or interest in the land; it is merely a contract, creating personal rights. Hence the code provisions concerning leases are not found in this book but in the next one, on obligations.

Finally, the great range of what common lawyers call future interests: reversions, remainders, executory interests, and the like, simply do not exist in Italian law. Nor does the trust, or anything like a division between equitable and legal title, appear. Security interests exist but are included in the fourth book, on obligations, or in the sixth book, on protection of rights, rather than in this one. Gifts, as already mentioned, are included in the second book, on succession.

It is also interesting to note that title II, chapter III of this book, on the methods of acquiring ownership, deals only with the so-called original titles. Transfer of ownership is not included, and the reason is again one of fundamental difference in outlook. In Italian law the concept of a conveyance, such as the deed, does not exist. The device for effectuating a transfer of real rights or of ownership is the contract, whether the transaction is one for value or is a gift. Thus the provisions governing the typical transfer of land are found in the fourth book, on obligations.

The Geography of the Code: Book IV. This is the largest of the six books of the code by a substantial margin. It includes material we would ordinarily classify into contracts, torts, sales, bills and notes, agency, landlord and tenant, bailments, banking, insurance, suretyship, creditors' rights, unjust enrichment, and conveyances. The first question a common lawyer asks when confronted by so heterogeneous (to him) a collection of provisions is what unifying concept, if any, operates to bring them together in this place. The answer is the generalized conception of obligation.

The idea is that a party to a contract, a tortfeasor, and one who ought to perform under principles of what common lawyers generally call unjust enrichment all owe an obligation, and that such obligations, whether deriving from contract, tort, or unjust enrichment, are legally more or less the same in nature. This concept is not peculiar to Italian law, but is found also in French and German law and is based, according to a distinguished commentator, on a misunderstanding of Roman law, although, he adds: "a place must be found for the tendency to ruthless analysis which is often encountered among academic thinkers." Whatever the source, the idea of obligation or, perhaps better, of the obligatory relation, seems firmly rooted in Italian law and doctrine.

Given the conception of the obligation, the content and arrangement of the fourth book begin to seem more logical. First, there are certain provisions on obligations in general, provisions presumably applicable to all obligations, regardless of source. Then come provisions on contracts, then those on unjust enrichment, and then those on torts.

Confusion reappears, however, when one notes that of the 887 articles in this book, only 17 deal with torts and 15 with unjust enrichment, while 148 concern obligations in general, and a massive 707 govern contracts. It is difficult to avoid the impression that the fourth book is primarily a contracts book, with unjust enrichment and torts constituting rather undeveloped appendages. The fact is that the law of contract is much more fully elaborated in the code than either of the other sources of obligation, but it is also true that parts of what common lawyers consider tort law appear elsewhere in the code. In particular, some property torts, or rather their equivalents, are treated in Book III; there, what common lawyers would think of as trespass, nuisance, and conversion are governed by provisions on the protection of ownership, the protection of real rights, and the protection of possession. The protection of the right of privacy in the first book is another example. In addition, there are private remedies in damages for many penal offenses against persons and things, and an investigation of the applicable provisions of the Penal Code and

Code of Criminal Procedure amplifies the more general provisions of the Civil Code.

The fact remains, however, that the elaboration of contract norms in the fourth book seems considerably out of proportion to a common lawyer. This is partly due to the broader scope of contracts in Italian law, including matters common lawyers would put into property (leases, bailments) or commercial law (sales, negotiable instruments, banking). Further, it is due to the importance in Italian law, and indeed in the civil law generally, of the so-called "typical" contracts, or rather the "typicality" of certain contractual transactions. The conception goes back to the formative period of the Roman law, to a time when it, like the early common law of England, was primarily a law of actions rather than of rights. Only certain kinds of promises were enforced in this Roman law; there was no generalized conception of contract and no comprehensive contract remedy. Rather, certain kinds of promises could be enforced through the appropriate actions.

Although this historical foundation has undergone twenty centuries of evolution, it has left its mark on the civil law, and in Italy today one distinguishes between the typical or "nominate" contracts, on the one hand, and the remaining undifferentiated scheme of enforceable contracts classified as "innominate," on the other. Of these, the former are by far the more important, including in their scope the great majority of normal promissory relations. Each of these has its own group of applicable rules, and the classification of a transaction as of one "type" rather than another has significant legal consequences. Although there are provisions on "contracts in general," provisions that might lead one to think of the specific types as mere elucidations of fundamental contract principles, in fact they are more post hoc in nature, embodying the result of attempts to draw general principles from the variety of typical contracts.

Finally, the law of typical commercial contractual relations is largely contract law. With the merger of civil and commercial law in the codification of 1942, commercial contracts were added to the typical civil contracts, substantially increasing the bulk of the contract provisions of the new code.

The Geography of the Code: Book V. The fifth book, with the somewhat misleading title "Labor," contains matter common lawyers would include in business associations, corporate finance, securities regulation, unfair competition, trademarks and trade names, copyright, patents, government regulation of business and property, as well as labor law in a very broad sense, taken to include regulation of professional activity. Here again the common lawyer faces the initial problem of trying to discover the organizing concept that has led to the inclusion of such apparently disparate matters within the same book of the code.

The answer can be found in the confluence of a number of factors. First, the decision to abandon the Commercial Code and combine its contents with those of the Civil Code raised obvious problems of arrangement. Certain parts of the Commercial Code had substantial analogies in the Civil Code and hence could be merged with them. Thus, as we have seen, much of the law of commercial obligations was eventually incorporated with the law of civil obligations in book four of the code. Other parts of the Commercial Code could not be fitted so easily into the traditional structure of the Civil Code, however, so new categories became necessary if a genuine merger was to be carried out.

Second, labor law in the traditional sense was very slow in developing in Italy, and the earlier codes said very little about it. By the time of the 1942 codification, the pressure for a more detailed codified labor law, aided by the program of the government in power and its professed regard for labor, was very great. This body of law was viewed as primarily private rather than public in nature, and hence a place had to be found for it in the new Civil Code, which was to be a unified code of private law.

Third, the legal concepts of the entrepreneur and the enterprise (*imprenditore* and *impresa*) were adopted as fundamental institutions under the new code. According to the formulation ultimately adopted, the entrepreneur is "one who professionally carries on economic activity organized for the production or exchange of goods or services." The enterprise is not defined as such, but as used in the code refers to the activity of the entrepreneur. These two new legal concepts were enthusiastically received and used by a government interested in increasing national productivity.

Fourth, in the early decades of this century Italy experienced a great deal of governmental intervention in agriculture, and in the process a great deal of law specifically concerned with agriculture was developed. These laws were, however, scattered among the codes and in special legislation. Pressure from the specialists in agrarian law and the interest of the government in increased agricultural production combined to support an integrated, codified statement of agrarian law.

Fifth, under the Charter of Labor and other programmatic documents the government sought to establish a conception of the economy in which employers, employees, and government worked together. From the governmental and also from the fascist doctrinal point of view, labor, on the one hand, and capital and management, on the other, were simply parts of the same process: the production and exchange of goods and services. One of the more prominent features of the corporative state was an attempt to create rule-making bodies that represented both employers and the employed. Thus it was not at all unusual at the time to conceive of labor and enterprise as closely related not only in the economy, but also in law.

These factors converge in Book V. Labor and the enterprise are the dominant institutions, and everything else is somehow related to either one or the other. Professional activity and the work of artisans are included and regulated because such activities are a form of labor. Competition is regulated because it relates to the conduct of the enterprise. Agrarian law is included by treating agriculture as agrarian enterprise. Business associations are included because they concern the form of the enterprise. Little imagination is needed to understand how such broad and flexible rubrics could also include such matters as securities regulation, patents, copyright, and trademarks and trade names. In this way what remained of the Commercial Code was combined with the "private" law parts of labor law and agrarian law to produce a novel synthesis.

The Geography of the Code: Book VI. The organization of Book VI, on the protection of rights, is understandable only in historical and practical terms.

This book contains provisions on recording land and some other property transactions, on evidence in civil actions, on the enforcement of judgments, on pledges and mortgages, and on prescription and decadence (expiration) of rights. In the 1865 Code the equivalent provisions were more or less appended to Book III, which bore the title "On the Ways of Acquiring and Transferring Ownership and Other Rights in Things," and included all of the law of obligations, much of the law of inheritance, and a large part of the law of property. The drafters of the 1942 Code wished to group these institutions together in some more organic way. Neither that wish nor the assertion that these were "institutions of a prevalently instrumental character, having the function of protecting and preserving subjective rights" can conceal the fact that this book is a kind of receptacle for miscellaneous provisions that were not, for one reason or another, put elsewhere in the code. They were included in the Civil Code because of their suitability or because traditionally they had been so included in the past. They were put into this book because they had to be put someplace, and the criticisms made of it by Italian jurists seem justified.

ITALIAN CIVIL CODE
Principal Headings[a]

[The numbers in parentheses are the numbers of the articles of the code falling under each heading, as updated.]

Provisions on the Law in General (1-31).

FIRST BOOK. Persons and the family (1-455).

Title	I.	Physical persons (1-10).
Title	II.	Legal persons (11-42).
Title	III.	Domicile and residence (43-47).
Title	IV.	Absence and declaration of presumed death (48-73).
Title	V.	Consanguinity and affinity (74-78).
Title	VI.	Marriage (79-230).
Title	VII.	Filiation (231-90).
Title	VIII.	Adoption (291-314).
Title	IX.	Parental authority (315-42).
Title	X.	Guardianship and emancipation (343-97).
Title	XI.	Minors entrusted to public or private care and affiliation [affiliation is an institution similar to but short of adoption] (400-03).
Title	XII.	Infirmity of mind, interdiction [a proceeding to declare a person incapable of performing legal acts], and disability [a proceeding to declare a person incapable of performing some legal acts, but not all] (414-32).
Title	XIII.	Maintenance (433-48).
Title	XIV.	Public record concerning civil status (449-55).

[a] From Mauro Cappelletti, John Henry Merryman & Joseph M. Perillo, The Italian Legal System: An Introduction 439-52 (1967).

SECOND BOOK. Succession (456-809).
- Title I. General provisions concerning succession (456-564).
- Title II. Intestate succession (565-86).
- Title III. Testamentary succession (587-712).
- Title IV. Partition (713-68).
- Title V. Donations (769-809).

THIRD BOOK. Property (810-1172).
- Title I. Things (810-31).
- Title II. Ownership (832-951).
- Title III. *Superficie* [the right to build and the right in a building on or over another's land] (952-56).
- Title IV. *Emphyteusis* (957-77).
- Title V. Usufruct, use, and habitation (978-1026).
- Title VI. Predial servitudes (1027-99).
- Title VII. Common property (1100-39).
- Title VIII. Possession (1140-70).
- Title IX. Action concerning new work and feared damage (1171-72).

FOURTH BOOK. Obligations (1173-2059)
- Title I. Obligations in general (1173-1320).
- Title II. Contracts in general (1321-1469).
- Title III. Individual contracts (1470-1986).
  - Chapter 1. Sale (1470-1547).
  - Chapter 2. *Riporto* [a sale of documents for cash and a promise to sell documents of the same kind back to the vendor at a future time and stated price] (1548-51).
  - Chapter 3. Barter (1552-55).
  - Chapter 4. Sale on approval (1556-58).
  - Chapter 5. *Somministrazione* [contract to supply goods continuously to purchaser] (1559-70)
  - Chapter 6. Lease (1571-1654).
  - Chapter 7. *Appalto* [something like our independent contractor] (1655-77).
  - Chapter 8. Transportation (1678-1702).
  - Chapter 9. Mandate [one kind of contract of agency] (1703-41).
  - Chapter 10. Contract of agency [in narrow sense, as an automobile agency] (1742-53).
  - Chapter 11. Brokerage (1754-65).
  - Chapter 12. Bailment (1766-97).
  - Chapter 13. Sequestration by agreement (1798-1802).
  - Chapter 14. Gratuitous bailment (1803-12).
  - Chapter 15. *Mutuo* [deposit of fungible goods against promise to redeliver goods of same kind and quality] (1813-22).
  - Chapter 16. Running account (1823-33).
  - Chapter 17. Banking contracts (1834-60).
  - Chapter 18. Perpetual rent (1861-71).
  - Chapter 19. Life annuity (1872-81).
  - Chapter 20. Insurance (1882-1932).

Chapter 21. Gambling and wagering (1933-35).
Chapter 22. Suretyship (1936-57).
Chapter 23. Guarantee of credit (1958-59).
Chapter 24. *Anticresis* [a form of security in which the creditor receives possession of immovable property and applies income from it first to interest and then to principal] (1960-64).
Chapter 25. Compromise (1965-76).
Chapter 26. Composition for the benefit of creditors (1977-86).
Title IV. Unilateral promises (1987-91).
Title V. Commercial paper (1992-2027).
Title VI. *Negotiorum gestio* (2028-32).
Title VII. Payment of an obligation not owed (2033-40).
Title VIII. Unjust enrichment (2041-42).
Title IX. Torts (2043-59).

FIFTH BOOK. Labor (2060-2642).
Title I. Regulation of professional activity (2060-80).
Title II. Labor and enterprise (2082-2221).
Title III. Autonomous labor (2222-38).
Title IV. Subordinate labor in particular situations (2239-46).
Title V. Companies (2247-2510).
Title VI. Cooperative enterprise and mutual insurance companies (2511-48).
Title VII. Partnership (2549-54).
Title VIII. *Azienda* [a business or enterprise in the descriptive sense; the physical properties, contracts, accounts, debts and credits, etc., that make up the business or enterprise] (2555-74).
Title IX. Rights in works of industrial ingenuity or invention (2575-94).
Title X. Regulation of competition and consortiums (2595-2620).
Title XI. Penal provisions concerning companies and consortiums (2621-42).

SIXTH BOOK. Protection of Rights (2643-2969).
Title I. Transcription (2643-96).
Title II. Evidence (2697-2739).
Title III. Property subject to execution, preferences, and preservation of security (2740-2906).
Title IV. Judicial protection of rights (2907-33).
Title V. Prescription and decadence (2934-69).

NOTES AND QUESTIONS

1. Return again to the structure of the civil codes we have seen. Can the structural differences in the French, German, and Italian codes be attributed to the period in which they were adopted? How does that affect the length of the codes?

2. Return also to the concepts of forced inheritance (compulsory share), universal succession, and obligations. The discussion of Italian law should help you to better understand these civilian ideas.

Is it clear now why donations are studied with successions rather than with obligations? Why might an heir reject his designation? In cases where a decedent's debts exceed his assets, why might an heir nevertheless accept the designation? Can a man escape the *legittima* by giving away to a favored child or to a mistress most of his property before he dies?

3. What seem to be the basic differences between American and Italian property law?

4. What is the difference between a general or innominate contract and a typical or nominate contract in terms of the applicable legal rules?

Review the headings for the French, German, and Italian civil codes. Make a list of the nominate contracts in each system and then compare the similarities and differences.

5. Consider Book 5 in the Italian Civil Code, which combines commercial law and labor law. This joinder was partly due to the corporative ideology of Benito Mussolini. Should this innovation continue in postwar Italian democratic society? Are legal rules sufficiently neutral or flexible that they can accommodate both fascist and democratic political systems? In this regard consider the German BGB, created during the Second German Empire (Reich), used during democratic (Weimar 1920s) and fascist (Nazi) periods, and still alive and well in a reunified Germany in the 1990s.

6. The Italian Civil Code of 1942 exists in two English translations. The first, prepared by the U.S. occupation forces, was unpublished (it was, incredibly, "classified" as a potentially dangerous or subversive document), and the second is Mario Beltramo, Giovanni E. Longo & John Henry Merryman, trans., The Italian Civil Code and Complementary Legislation (Beltramo rev. ed. 1991).

See also Edward M. Wise, The Italian Penal Code (1978).

6. THE MEXICAN CIVIL CODE

HELEN L. CLAGETT & DAVID M. VALDERRAMA, A REVISED GUIDE TO THE LAW & LEGAL LITERATURE OF MEXICO 69-70 (1973)

The Mexican Civil Code as adopted in 1928 followed the example of its predecessors by limiting its jurisdiction to the borders of the Federal District and Federal Territories and again leaving the autonomous States to enact their own codes. And again, the autonomous States either adopted the new code or retained the earlier code with revisions in statutory form.... In keeping with the liberal and revolutionary principles embodied in the 1917 Constitution and in the Carranza Family Law of 1917, the new code required changes in depth. The rugged and laissez-faire doctrines adopted from the Code Napoleon now commenced to give way to those with more concern for the individual within the context of the good of the social community as a whole. It also afforded protection to persons from what was defined as the "greed and power of vested interests," of large and, particularly, foreign corporations. In the language of Ignacio García Téllez, a member of the revisory commission on the code, "It was an inescapable obligation to work for the amelioration of the Mexican proletariat and to crystallize in the new civil code the social justice that had consistently clamored to be recognized, and yet had always remained in the margin of the law. It was also necessary that our civil legislation not remain aloof from the transcendental reforms that other countries had already carried into fruition in their private legislation, made imperative for the activities of daily life by scientific discoveries and economic interdependence."

In its form, the new civil code followed that of its predecessors, but its contents were reduced to 3,044 [now 3,074] articles as contrasted to the 3,823 of the 1884 text. Although adopted legislatively in 1928, this code did not actually go into effect until 1932. Referring to this new body of civil law, President Plutarco Calles remarked that "The principal doctrine formulated by the new Civil Code may be briefly expressed in the following terms: to harmonize individual interests with those of society, thus correcting the excess individualism permitted by the Civil Code of 1884."

MEXICAN CIVIL CODE
Principal Headings

[The numbers in parentheses are the numbers of the articles of the code falling under each heading.]

Preliminary provisions (1-21).

FIRST BOOK. Persons (22-746).

Title	I.	Physical persons (22-24).
Title	II.	Artificial persons (25-28*bis*).
Title	III.	Domicile (29-34).
Title	IV.	Civil registry (35-138*bis*).
Title	V.	Marriage (139-291).
Title	VI.	Family relationships and support (292-323).
Title	VII.	Paternity and filiation (324-410).
Title	VIII.	Parental authority (411-448).
Title	IX.	Guardianship (449-640).
Title	X.	Emancipation and majority (641-647).
Title	XI.	Absent and missing persons (648-722).
Title	XII.	Homestead (723-746).

SECOND BOOK. Property (747-1180).

Title	I.	Preliminary provisions (747-749).
Title	II.	Classification of property (750-789).
Title	III.	Possession (790-829).
Title	IV.	Ownership (830-979).
Title	V.	Usufruct, use, and habitation (980-1056).
Title	VI.	Servitudes (1057-1134).
Title	VII.	Prescription (1135-1180).

THIRD BOOK. Successions (1281-1791).

Title	I.	Preliminary provisions (1281-1294).
Title	II.	Testamentary succession (1295-1498).
Title	III.	Types of wills (1499-1598).
Title	IV.	Intestate succession (1599-1637).
Title	V.	Common provisions for testamentary and intestate succession (1638-1791).

FOURTH BOOK. Obligations (1792-3074).

First Part.		Obligations in general (1792-2242).
Title	I.	Sources of obligations (1792-1937).
Title	II.	Types of obligations (1938-2028).
Title	III.	Transmission of obligations (2029-2061).
Title	IV.	Effects of obligations (2062-2184).
Title	V.	Termination of obligations (2185-2223).
Title	VI.	Non-existence and nullity (2224-2242).
Second Part.		Types of contracts (2243-2963).
Title	I.	Preparatory contracts (promise) (2243-2247).
Title	II.	Sale (2248-2326).
Title	III.	Barter (2327-2331).
Title	IV.	Donation (2332-2383).
Title	V.	Loan [*mutuo*] (2384-2397).
Title	VI.	Lease (2398-2496).
Title	VII.	Gratuitous bailment (2497-2515).
Title	VIII.	Deposit [bailment] and sequestration (2516-2545).
Title	IX.	Mandate (2546-2604).
Title	X.	Service contract (2605-2669).
Title	XI.	Associations and companies (2670-2763).
Title	XII.	Gaming and betting (2764-2793).
Title	XIII.	Guaranty (2794-2855).
Title	XIV.	Pledge (2856-2892).
Title	XV.	Mortgage (2893-2943).
Title	XVI.	Compromise (2944-2963).
Third Part.		[No heading] (2964-3074).
Title	I.	Bankruptcy and creditor preferences (2964-2998).
Title	II.	Public registry (2999-3074).

NOTES AND QUESTIONS

1. Consider the structure of the Mexican Civil Code. Is it closest to the code of France, Germany, or Italy?

2. The Mexican Revolution and the subsequent Constitution of 1917 flavored the code drafters' attitudes toward laissez-faire capitalism and socialism, which appear in some places in the 1932 Civil Code. Article 17 is an important example:

> When someone, taking advantage of the total ignorance, notorious inexperience, or extreme misery of another, obtains an excessive profit that is evidently disproportionate to the obligation he assumed, the person

harmed has the right to elect either rescission of the contract or an equitable reduction of his obligation, plus demand the payment of corresponding damages.

The right granted by this article continues for one year.

3. The Mexican Civil Code is applicable only in the Federal District, but it has served as the model for the state civil codes in the remainder of Mexico. The Mexican Commercial Code, on the other hand, is applicable throughout Mexico.

For an English translation, see Michael Wallace Gordon, The Mexican Civil Code (1980).

4. For an example of the impact of social welfare legislation on 20th century Latin American civil codes, see Juan Matus Valencia, *The Centenary of the Chilean Civil Code,* 7 Am. J. Comp. L. 71 (1958).

7. THE JAPANESE CIVIL CODE

NOTE

The Japanese Civil Code, as noted in Chapter 5, Section C, was the product of drafting efforts that took over two decades to complete. In 1890 the Japanese Diet passed one version, drafted with the help of the French jurist Gustave Emile Boissonade. The government postponed its promulgation, however, in an ensuing controversy. A second code, based largely on the first draft of the German Civil Code and enacted in two stages in 1896 (Law No. 89, 1896: Books One through Three) and 1898 (Law No. 9, 1898: Books Four and Five), did not become fully effective until 1898. It has rarely been amended. The most significant changes were enacted in 1947 (Law No. 222) under the Allied Occupation in an effort to "democratize" the Japanese family system and to remove legal impediments to the equality of women. More recent amendments have included the 1971 (Law No. 99) addition of "base-hypothecs" (*neteito*), a form of floating lien long recognized by judicial decision, as a real right (*bukken*) in Book Two (arts. 398.2-398.22). Provisions were also added in 1987 (Law No. 101; arts. 817.2-817.11) in Book Four for special adoption (*tokubetsu yoshi*) based on petition to a family court by persons seeking to adopt. Except in the area of family law, the institutions and categories of the Japanese Civil Code reflect their German and French origins.

JAPANESE CIVIL CODE
Principal Headings

[The numbers in parentheses are the numbers of the articles of the code falling under each heading.]

BOOK ONE. General Provisions (1-174).

Chapter One. Persons (1.3-32).

Section One. Enjoyment of Private Rights (1.3-2).

Section Two. Capacity (3-20).

Section Three. Domicile (21-24).

Section Four. Disappearance (25-32).

Section Five.	Presumption of Simultaneous Death (32.2)
Chapter Two.	Juridical Persons (33-84.2).
Section One.	Formation of Juridical Persons (33-51).
Section Two.	Management of Juridical Persons (52-67).
Section Three.	Dissolution of Juridical Persons (68-83).
Section Four.	Delegation of Authority to the Competent Government Office (83.2).
Section Five.	Penal Provisions (84-84.2).
Chapter Three.	Things (85-89).
Chapter Four.	Juridical Acts (90-137).
Section One.	General Provisions (90-92).
Section Two.	Declarations of Intent (93-98).
Section Three.	Agency (99-118).
Section Four.	Voidness and Avoidability (119-126).
Section Five.	Conditions and Term (127-137).
Chapter Five.	Periods of Time (138-143).
Chapter Six.	Prescription (144-174.2).
Section One.	General Provisions (144-161).
Section Two.	Acquisitive Prescription (162-165).
Section Three.	Extinctive Prescription (166-174.2).

BOOK TWO. Real Rights (175-398.22).

Chapter One.	General Provisions (175-179).
Chapter Two.	Possession (180-205).
Section One.	Acquisition of Possession (180-187).
Section Two.	Effect of Possession (188-202).
Section Three.	Extinction of Possession (203-204).
Section Four.	Quasi-Possession (205).
Chapter Three.	Ownership (206-264).
Section One.	Limits of Ownership (206-238).
Section Two.	Acquisition of Ownership (239-248).
Section Three.	Co-ownership (249-264).
Chapter Four.	*Superficies* (265-269).
Chapter Five.	*Emphyteusis* (270-279).
Chapter Six.	Servitudes (280-294).
Chapter Seven.	Right of Retention (295-302).
Chapter Eight.	Preferential Rights (303-341).
Section One.	General Provisions (303-305).
Section Two.	Classes of Preferential Rights [General, Movable Property, and Immovable Property] (306-328).
Section Three.	Priority Among Preferential Rights (329-332).
Section Four.	Effect of Preferential Rights (333-341).
Chapter Nine.	Pledges (342-368).
Section One.	General Provisions (342-351).
Section Two.	Movable Property Pledges (352-355).
Section Three.	Immovable Property Pledges (356-361).
Section Four.	Obligation Pledges (362-368).

Chapter Ten. Hypothecs (369-398.22).
Section One. General Provisions (369-372).
Section Two. Effect of Hypothecs (373-395).
Section Three. Extinction of Hypothecs (396-398).
Section Four. Base-Hypothecs (398.1-398.22).

BOOK THREE. Obligations (399-724).
Chapter One. General Provisions (399-520).
Section One. Subject of Obligations (399-411).
Section Two. Effect of Obligations [including Remedies] (412-426).
Section Three. Multiple Party Obligations [including Suretyship] (427-465).
Section Four. Assignment of Obligations (466-473).
Section Five. Extinction of Obligations [Performance, Setoff, Novation, Release, and Merger] (474-520).
Chapter Two. Contracts (521-696).
Section One. General Provisions [Formation, Effect, and Rescission] (521-548).
Section Two. Donations (549-554).
Section Three. Sales (555-585).
Section Four. Exchange (586).
Section Five. Loans for Consumption (587-592).
Section Six. Loans for Use (593-600).
Section Seven. Leases (601-622).
Section Eight. Employment (623-631).
Section Nine. Contracts for Work (632-642).
Section Ten. Mandates (643-656).
Section Eleven. Deposits [Gratuitous Bailments] (657-666).
Section Twelve. Partnerships (667-688).
Section Thirteen. Annuities (689-694).
Section Fourteen. Compromises (695-696).
Chapter Three. Management Without Mandate (697-702).
Chapter Four. Unjust Enrichment (703-708).
Chapter Five. Delicts (709-724).

BOOK FOUR. Relatives (725-881).
Chapter One. General Provisions (725-730).
Chapter Two. Marriage (731-771).
Section One. Formation of Marriage [Requirements, Invalidity, and Annulment] (731-749).
Section Two. Effect of Marriage (750-754).
Section Three. Spousal Property System (755-762).
Section Four. Divorce [by Consent and by Judicial Decree] (763-771).
Chapter Three. Children (772-817.11).
Section One. Children by Birth (772-781).
Section Two. Children by Adoption (782-817.11).

Chapter Four. Parental Authority (818-837).
Section One. General Provisions (818-819).
Section Two. Effect of Parental Authority (820-833).
Section Three. Loss of Parental Authority (834-837).
Chapter Five. Guardianship (838-876).
Section One. Commencement of Guardianship (838).
Section Two. Agencies of Guardianship [Guardians and Guardian Superintendents] (839-852).
Section Three. Functions of Guardianship (853-869).
Section Four. Termination of Guardianship (870-876).
Chapter Six. Support (877-881).

BOOK FIVE. Succession (882-1044).
Chapter One. General Provisions (882-885).
Chapter Two. Successors (886-895).
Chapter Three. Effect of Succession (896-914).
Section One. General Provisions (896-899).
Section Two. Compulsory Shares (900-905).
Section Three. Division of Assets (906-914).
Chapter Four. Confirmation and Renunciation of Succession (915-940).
Section One. General Provisions (915-919).
Section Two. Confirmation [Full and Restricted] (920-921).
Section Three. Renunciation (922-940).
Chapter Five. Separation of Assets (941-950).
Chapter Six. Missing Successors (951-959).
Chapter Seven. Wills (960-1027).
Section One. General Provisions (960-966).
Section Two. Form of Wills [Ordinary and Special] (967-984).
Section Three. Effect of Wills (985-1003).
Section Four. Enforcement of Wills (1004-1021).
Section Five. Extinction of Wills (1022-1027).
Chapter Eight. Remaining Portions (1028-1044).

NOTES AND QUESTIONS

1. Compare the Japanese Civil Code with the preceding examples. Which code does it resemble most in organization and categories? How does it differ from each of the previous examples?

2. How do Japanese lawyers use the structure of the code to find answers to legal problems? For example, where might a Japanese attorney look to determine the contractual liability of principals for the acts of agents? Liability in tort? What articles are most likely to deal with mistake, fraud, and duress? Where would one look to find provisions related to common law notions of restitution as a contractual remedy?

3. The Japanese Commercial Code provides for two forms of incorporated partnerships. How would a common law partnership be characterized under Japanese law?

4. Except for family law and succession, the South Korean Civil Code is nearly identical to the Japanese code, which was applied to Korea under Japanese rule. For similar reasons what European code would the Indonesian Civil Code be most likely to resemble? The Thai and Taiwan codes also share certain features with the Japanese code because of the use of the Japanese code as a model and because of a common German influence.

C. A BRIEF LOOK AT SUBSTANTIVE LAW: PROPERTY

Section B provided an overview of some of the major areas of private law. Of all the fields of private law, property is the one that is most dramatically different between the civil law and the common law traditions. The next excerpt illustrates these differences for Italian law, but they are generally applicable to the civil law world. An astonishing judicial decision follows, around which an entire course in comparative law could be built.

1. ITALIAN PROPERTY LAW

JOHN HENRY MERRYMAN, OWNERSHIP AND ESTATE (VARIATIONS ON A THEME BY LAWSON), 48 Tulane Law Review 916, 924-45 (1974)

Basic Legal Concepts

Ownership is, as concepts go, a very powerful one, and those who employ it pay its price. The land law of Italy and other civil law nations, based firmly on Roman law, is a law of individual ownership. It is part of the tyranny of the concept of ownership that it strongly resists fragmentation. To say that I own a thing is to imply that you do not, for if it is yours how can it be mine? Such thinking thus tends to eliminate all intermediate possibilities between ownership and non-ownership. Consequently, when it becomes desirable to equate power over land with more than one person it seems preferable to do so by a device which, at least apparently, avoids dividing ownership. In every transaction ownership must be transferred *in toto* or not at all.

This, although simplified, gives some of the flavor of ownership in the Italian land law. Although its non-legal composition may vary from time to time with social and economic change, legal ownership remains exclusive, single, and indivisible. Only one person can own the same thing at the same time. But, since the requirements of society are such that power over land must frequently be divided between individuals, it becomes necessary to rationalize the dictates of theory and the requirements of practice. If the theory is a powerful one it will resist, and in this way the achievement of practical ends will be retarded.

The inconsistency between ownership and fragmentation can, of course, be exaggerated. Even in the civil law, land can be "owned" simultaneously by two or more persons *in comune*, a form of co-ownership much like our tenancy in common. But a functional division between beneficial and security title, or between legal and equitable title, or a temporal division into present and future estates, simply does not exist. Ownership is, in theory, indivisible in function and time. Consider:

Illustration 1. *A*, owner of land in Italy, creates an *usufrutto* in *B*, a natural person, for *B*'s life.

The practical consequences of this transaction are that *B* now has, and will have until his death, extensive powers of use and enjoyment of the land. *A*, during the same period, is deprived of its use. True, he retains the power of disposition, but even this is limited; he cannot convey the present right to use and enjoyment. If ownership includes the power to dispose and the power to enjoy, it is obvious that these powers are now divided between *A* and *B*, and it would seem natural to conclude that the ownership of the land is now shared by them. But such a conclusion is unacceptable. Under Italian law, *A* is still the owner of the land. *B* is not owner in any sense; he has certain rights as a result of the transaction, and indeed they are called real rights, but no part of the ownership was conveyed to him.

To treat one who has neither the right of present enjoyment of land nor the power to dispose of that right as "owner" is inconsistent with the common meaning of the term. It is also inconsistent with the definition of an "owner" in the Italian Civil Code, which provides in article 832:

> The owner has the right to enjoy and dispose of things fully and exclusively, within the limits and with observance of the duties established by the legal order....

These inconsistencies are recognized on all sides. We are told that the *common* meaning of a term is often different from its legal meaning. As to the conflict between a legal meaning that will call *A* owner and the definition of owner in the Civil Code, we are told that *A* has a special class of ownership called "naked." Thus *A* is *nudo proprietario*, but he is still *proprietario*.

Consequently, even in the simplest possible situation — the creation of a usufruct for life — ownership turns out to be a slippery concept. It becomes even more difficult to grasp if we look at a more complex situation. Consider:

Illustration 2. *A*, owner of land in Italy, creates an *usufrutto* in *B*, a natural person, for life. *A* then dies, devising the land, subject to the usufruct, to his son *C*, and provides that on *C*'s death it shall go to *C*'s children.

In this case we are told that *C* is the owner of the land. Let us look for a moment at the content of his ownership. *C* cannot possess or take the fruits or otherwise benefit from the land during *B*'s life, nor can he convey such rights to anyone else. It is already provided, through what civil lawyers call a "fiduciary substitution" (*sostituzione fedecommessaria*, Italian Civil Code art. 692), that on *C*'s death the land will pass to *C*'s children, and *C* has no power to affect that provision. So what is left to *C* is the possibility that, if *B* predeceases him, *C* may enjoy the land for the remaining part of his life. To a common lawyer this looks like a remainder for life after a life estate, an interest that hardly qualifies as "ownership," either in the common meaning of the term or as it is legally defined in Civil Code article 832 quoted above.

What we are really facing is this: the Romanic concept of ownership is a product of the age of reason applied to Roman legal materials and has been worked out with the kind of legal precision that is typical of the period in European history that saw the introduction of decimal currency and the adoption of the metric system of weights and measures. The principal axioms, for present purposes, are two:

1. Where land is the object of rights (*i.e.*, so-called "vacant" land does not count), one of those rights is "ownership." For every piece of land, in other words, there is an owner.

2. There are a number of real rights in land, but the distribution of such real rights among a number of different persons does not affect the "ownership" of the land. No matter how widely such rights are disseminated, there is still an identifiable person who has the "ownership."

Such a concept has its uses and its common law analogy: it is most convenient to have a legal system in which every piece of land is identified with some responsible natural or legal person, who is its owner. In this sense the right of ownership in Romanic systems is like seisin in the early English land law; someone always had it — "the seisin could not be in abeyance" — and the ability to identify the person who had the seisin was a significant administrative convenience. The person seised owed certain feudal obligations to his lord and was entitled to certain rights associated with his tenure of the land. In modern Romanic systems, the "owner" may be responsible for the performance of certain civic duties (including the payment of property taxes), and has historically had certain public rights to vote and to hold office. These attributes of ownership have, of course, taken new forms after the defeudalization of property law and the democratization of government and society that took place in the West in the eighteenth and nineteenth centuries. But the convenience of the legal concept of ownership makes it a continuing device for the specification of civic rights and obligations of a different kind.

The contrast with English theory is remarkable. In England, ownership resided in the king, and the distribution and retention of lands throughout the kingdom was carried out according to the theory of tenure. Those who actually occupied and used the great mass of English land were not owners of it but holders of derivative rights from the king or from the king's tenants, and hence English land law was concerned not with ownership and the rights and duties of owners but with tenure and the rights and duties of tenants. The concept of ownership simply did not come into play.

This basic difference between Romanic ownership and the Anglo-American "estate" or "interest" in land can be illustrated by a simple metaphor. Romanic ownership can be thought of as a box, with the word "ownership" written on it. Whoever has the box is the "owner." In the case of complete, unencumbered ownership, the box contains certain rights, including that of use and occupancy, that to the fruits or income, and the power of alienation. The owner can, however, open the box and remove one or more such rights and transfer them to others. But, as long as he keeps the box, he still has the ownership, even if the box is empty. The contrast with the Anglo-American law of property is simple. There is no box. There are merely various sets of legal interests. One who has the fee simple absolute has the largest possible bundle of such sets of legal interests. When he conveys one or more of them to another person, a part of his bundle is gone.

This basic difference has several possible theoretical consequences. First, tenure seems to be a more flexible concept than ownership. Consequently, it might be expected that the number and variety of institutionalized interests in land will be greater in a tenure than in an ownership property system. In short, improvisation is likely to be inhibited by the theory of ownership and encouraged by that of tenure.

The much greater variety of permissible future interests (vested and contingent remainders, executory interests, powers of appointment, reversions, rights of entry, possibilities of reverter) in the common law than in the civil law (where they really do not exist) supports this prediction. It is further supported by the existence of the trust and the concept of separate legal and equitable interests and by the distinction between security interests and beneficial interests in land, both found in the common law but not in the civil law.

The second consequence is somewhat more subtle, but tends to produce the same effect. The analytical jurist has little difficulty in establishing that, in a certain sense, both ownership and tenure are simply methods by which the law allocates interests among persons with respect to the land. Whatever their source, these interests have legal effect only as they are recognized and enforced by the legal system. To say that one owns land is merely to say he has certain legal relations with respect to it, and analytically this is equally true of tenure. But in less analytical times ownership was not so understood. One said of *A* that he owned the land, not that the law had fixed certain legal relations between him and others with respect to it.

In England, during the formative period of its property law, the dominance of the tenure concept necessarily made this distinction more obvious. Lawyer and layman alike were compelled to deal with tenure — legal relations having their source in the legal system — and to realize that they were doing so. Thus, the English law began as law about rights with respect to land rather than about ownership of it. The nature and extent of these rights could vary widely, depending in part on the agreement of the parties, in part on custom, and to a large extent on the will of the dominant party — the lord. Eventually, these conventional arrangements became fixed and limited and were given distinctive names. As a group they were called estates, and each kind of estate became to some extent reified — it became a thing that could be "owned." But the initial distinction between ownership and tenure prevented the oversimplification of the relationship between man and land that came so easily to the Roman law. The most that could be said of the Englishman was that he "owned" or "held" or was "seised of" an estate in the land, so that the estate was a legal concept interposed between the tenant and the land.

The estate is a relatively pure legal device. Although Englishmen would fight and romanticize about their estates, still it was not as easy to become concerned in a theoretical way about their nature and origins as was the case with ownership. "Estate" offered no aspect of indivisibility, nor did it hint of divine or natural or socio-economic justification. It was a tool, not a weapon. Ownership, on the contrary, even as employed by Romanists and Civilists, has always seemed to have a life and vigor of its own. It is easy to speculate about its source and its functions. Speculation of this kind may easily become debate about private property, and this opens the door to the full range of questions about man and the state, man and his nature, and man and God. No culture has successfully freed ownership of such associations. It is a loaded concept.

Thus, the working theoretical unit of the English land law was, in its critical period, a legal abstraction free of the extra-legal associations and the inhibitions imposed by the Roman concept of ownership. This does not, of course, imply any superiority of one to the other; it merely illustrates a fundamental and highly important theoretical difference in legal theory during the formative period of the common law. In later centuries this distinction became, in a sense, less real as power over land moved from the king and the lord to the tenant in possession under an estate. Eventually the practical difference between a tenant in fee simple in England and an owner in Italy became, for some purposes, insignificant. Indeed, it might be said that, in England, a point was reached in which he who was in theory merely a tenant had all the practical advantages of ownership and he who was technically owner had none.

Variations

These historical and theoretical differences are impressive. The separate development of the English common law, freer in the land law than in any other private law area from Roman and civil law influence, with its own quite different institutions and terminology, has resulted in what would appear to be a uniquely different system. In Italy, as in other civil law nations, unification, codification, the rejection of "undemocratic" feudal property institutions, and the reliance on Roman principles all emphasize the contrast with the feudal concepts and institutions of the English land law. Consequently, one can expect to find that there will be significant variations in the practical workings of the Italian and American land law — in the beneficial interests created and the processes for their creation and transfer. We turn now to a brief exposition of the most significant of these variations.

Estates

The apparent differences between Italian ownership and the Anglo-American estate in fee simple are very slight. The tenant in fee simple is no longer a tenant in anything like the feudal sense; for all practical purposes his powers and duties with respect to land are indistinguishable from those of the owner under Italian law. Indeed, if one assumes that "ownership" implies greater freedom to deal with land than "estate," he can find evidence that the tenant in fee simple of today is more of an "owner" than his Italian counterpart. Neither in England nor in the majority of American jurisdictions is forced heirship the rule,[20] and the Englishman or American has far greater opportu-

[20] Forced heirship is, of course, the rule in Italy. The governing provisions are found in articles 536-64 of the Italian Civil Code. In general, if the decedent leaves only one child, one-half of the patrimony is reserved for him. If he leaves more than one child, the reservation is of two-thirds. C. Civ. art. 537 (M. Beltramo, G. Longo & J. Merryman transl. [rev. ed. 1991]). Such rights, of

nity for the exercise of dead hand control over his land through the creation of legal future estates or use of the trust than the Italian owner. When an American court or legislature today refers to a person as "owner," rather than in the technically more correct terms of "tenant in fee simple," it is recognizing a fact; in the nine centuries since the Norman conquest of England, derivative tenure has gradually been transformed into allodial ownership.

The most obvious practical consequence of the separate development of the two property systems is that the Italian land law contains no equivalent of the estates that are so characteristic a feature of the Anglo-American law. The *usufrutto* is in some ways similar to the life estate, and the owner who grants it to another has an interest that is in some ways very much like our reversion, it is true. Indeed, to carry the example further, it is possible for an owner to convey the *usufrutto* to one person and the ownership to another in simultaneous transactions so as to produce what might appear to be a life estate followed by a vested remainder. But the theory of each such transaction is entirely different from our own. Unlike his Italian counterpart, our reversioner is not the owner of the land; he "owns" an estate, a future interest, in it. Our life tenant has, as the result of the conveyance to him, a present estate; the *usufruttario* has, as the result of contract, real rights in land belonging to another. Centuries of legal development according to such different premises are bound to result in variations of detail. Thus, the *usufrutto* can be made inalienable by the terms of the gift or contract creating it but the life estate cannot, as a general rule, be so restricted. The *usufruttario* has a substantially greater right than the life tenant to remove improvements or to be reimbursed for them, and in general there are variations in detail concerning what acts constitute waste (or its Italian equivalent) and the remedies that are available when it has been committed.

On the whole, however, substantial similarities exist in the situations just given that are enough to justify the generalization that the simple creation of an *usufrutto* for life is not greatly different in practical result from simple creation of an estate for life. More significant differences begin to appear when one considers slightly less elementary situations.

> *Illustration 3. A*, owner of land in Italy, creates an *usufrutto* in *B* for *B*'s life, and, on *B*'s death, in *C* for *C*'s life.

It is obvious enough that the use of successive *usufrutti* in this manner could, if extended to permit gifts to unborn persons, become a device for entailing land, making it both indivisible and inalienable in the same manner as a strictly enforced fee tail in England might have done. Indeed, it seems to have been put to such use both in the later Roman law and in Italy in the Middle Ages, although perhaps not as extensively as the *sostituzione fedecommessaria*, or fiduciary substitution, discussed below. It is equally obvious that, if a single *usufrutto* strains the concept of ownership, entailment through successive *usufrutti* makes it quite meaningless.

---

course, are distinct from the rights of the widow, who is basically entitled to an *usufrutto* in two-thirds of the patrimony. *Id.* art. 540.

Accordingly, it is not surprising to discover that successive *usufrutti* are carefully limited in the Italian law, particularly when created by will. Article 698 of the Civil Code specifically provides that a gift of this kind is valid only in favor of the person who, at the death of the testator, is first entitled to enjoyment. Thus if, at *A*'s death, *B* is alive, has the capacity to take the gift, and does not renounce, *C* takes nothing. If *B* predeceases the testator, lacks the capacity to take, or renounces, then *C* may take in his place. The same rule applies if the successive *usufrutti* are created *inter vivos* by gift, but if they are created by contract and *C* is a person to whom the obligation of the contract extends, he may take on *B*'s death. In no case, however, is the gift to *C* effective if he is not an ascertainable person at the time of the gift; there are no contingent remainders in Italian law.

Thus, in Italian law, the equivalent of our vested remainder for life following a life estate can be created only in narrowly described situations, and contingent remainders cannot be created in unascertained persons at all. There are, of course, substantial policy reasons to support this position, but they are reinforced by theory and history of the sort described above and are consistent with the present Italian view with respect to the *sostituzione fedecommessaria*.

The essence of the *sostituzione fedecommessaria* or, as it is often called, *fedecommesso*, is the transfer of ownership to *B* with the obligation to retain the property and transfer it to *C* on his death. This institution, which has its roots firmly in Roman soil, flourished in Italy in the Middle Ages as a device for the strict entailment of family estates, and, by the end of the seventeenth century, the greater part of landed property in Italy was held in this form. In the eighteenth and nineteenth centuries, the *fedecommesso* came under strong attack, both as a relic of feudalism and as an impediment to economic and social progress, and the Civil Code of 1865, "... obedient to economic interests and the principle of equality, abolished it in every possible form."

The present Civil Code, in response to the desire for some measure of dead hand control, has reinstituted the *fedecommesso* in narrowly described situations and prohibited it in all others. A testator can leave the residue of his estate to his child, his brother, or his sister, with the provision that he retain and conserve the property and that on his death it go to that person's children (or to a public corporation). Thus,

> *Illustration 4.* *A* devises the residue of his estate to his son *B*, directs *B* to retain and conserve the property, and provides that, on *B*'s death, it shall go to *B*'s children.

The analogies to common law estates are obvious. Illustration 4 has an effect similar to creation of a life estate followed by a remainder to a class (contingent if *B* has no children at the time of *A*'s death, vested subject to open if he does). However, under Italian law, *B* gets neither a life estate nor its Italian analogue, an *usufrutto*; he gets ownership. As we have already remarked above, this ownership is hardly recognizable to an eye unaccustomed to Italian theory, since the "owner" can neither consume the property nor convey it. When *B* dies, his children become owners.

This completes the catalog of Italian interests in lands that are comparable to common law "estates," with the exception of the lease, discussed below. It is, by common law standards, a slender catalog. The range of devices open to the Italian owner planning disposition of his property is quite narrow. With minor qualifications, he is unable to create: a) powers of appointment, b) contingent remainders, c) springing or shifting interests, d) estates subject to total or partial defeasance, e) determinable estates, f) possibilities of reverter, or g) powers of termination. He has no rule against remoteness of vesting; certain interests can be created and others cannot. His rule against perpetuities is built in. Estate planning is easy, both from a property and from a tax point of view. A large part of our law of property simply does not exist for the Italian lawyer.

The relative simplicity of the Italian scheme of estates is, to some extent, an incidental consideration, a by-product of the operation of other factors rather than a value sought for itself. One such factor is historical. The modern Italian land law is the product of reform and codification undertaken, in part, for the purpose of abolishing feudal property. Greater freedom in creating estate-like interests is, within the Italian legal system, likely to occur only through relaxation of these reforms. Anti-feudalism may not be as powerful a battle-cry as it once was, but it still has emotional force.

Another obstacle to freer innovation is the infrangibility of the concept of ownership. The existence of such simple institutions as the *usufrutto* and the *fedecommesso* put a heavy strain on the dogma that ownership is indivisible in the dimension of time. To permit the creation of additional interests would stretch it further, perhaps beyond the breaking point. Even though he thought some alternative system superior, one would hesitate long before recommending that so ancient and so fundamental a concept as unfragmented ownership be torn from the fabric of Italian law.

In any event, it is difficult to make a strong case against the existing Italian scheme of interests in land. An Italian lawyer could argue that his is, when compared to our own, more likely to keep land freely alienable, to promote its development, to deal fairly with creditors and to give later generations more of the satisfactions that come with the power to alienate *inter vivos* or by will. These are worthy socio-economic objectives, which we also profess, and conceivably the balance between variety and flexibility of property arrangements over time, on the one side, and limitation of dead hand control on the other, has been more properly struck in Italy than in the United States.

Leases

It is an interesting historical paradox that the lease of land, which had its common law origin in commercial transactions, sometimes as a method of avoiding the prohibition against usury and at others as a kind of security device, has become the only surviving example of the tenurial relationship between lord and tenant in our land law. Interests of the kind that formed the very foundation of feudal property — the freehold estates in land — have gradually been converted into independent forms of ownership. But the lease, which only at a comparatively late date became a property institution, retains a part of its feudal character in our law, and the common term applied to the relationship — "landlord and tenant" — is still to some extent descriptive. The lease, even when it pertains to commercial premises in an urban area, is considered to be an instrument of conveyance of an estate in the land, like the deed. It is not a contract. Promises may be contained in the lease, but they are not treated in the same way as promises in contracts. Instead they retain the characteristics of an earlier age, aptly conveyed by the name "covenants." The law governing leases is a part of the law of property, and in this way it was, by definition, excluded from the great creative development of commercial law in England.

In Italian law, the lease is a contract. With the exception of the peculiar institution called *enfiteusi,* which is no longer of substantial importance, transactions that have purposes analogous to our leases of land create only personal rights in the lessee. No real rights — no part of the ownership of the land — are conveyed to him. The law governing leases is found in that part of the Civil Code dealing with obligations, rather than in the part dealing with property. As a consequence, the two systems start with quite different premises. The Italian law adopts contract principles and modifies them when necessary in order to deal appropriately with the peculiar nature and subject-matter of the lease. The common law struggles to overcome the remaining traces of feudalism and to bring contract principles to bear on a property transaction that frequently is primarily commercial in purpose and significance.

Several interesting consequences flow from this difference in theory. Since no interest in land is involved in the *locazione*, it is unnecessary to classify the interest created as real or personal property for any purpose, and the concept of the chattel real of the common law is thus avoided by definition. Distinctions between leases of personal property and of land are made on a more functional basis and not on some supposed difference between real property and personal property. The problem of surrender simply does not arise; since the Italian lessee has no estate, the arrangement can terminate without an actual or fictional reconveyance to the lessor of the unexpired term. The obligation to pay rent, in the absence of a provision in the contract, arises from the law of unjust enrichment in Italy, rather than out of the supposed tenurial relationship of lord and tenant we have inherited from the Middle Ages. The extent to which remote parties are bound by or entitled to the benefit of promises in the lease again depends on contract principles in Italy, and privity of estate, as a concept, is alien to their law. The Italian lease is not complicated by our dogma that the rent issues from the land. The independence of covenants in our lease, which either prevents the appropriate solution of disputes that the parties might reasonably expect to be settled according to contract principles, or that requires the use of peculiar fictions, like "constructive eviction," in order to reach desired results, does not exist in Italian law. Ordinary contract principles apply to matters of performance and breach, and the theory of the unity of the transaction prevails. Frustration of commercial purpose is, in the civil law, an adequate excuse for non-performance by the tenant. The lessor is under a duty to mitigate damages if the lessee abandons the premises. In these and many other ways the Italian law of leases more closely resembles our law of contracts than our law of landlord and tenant.

The complications retained in our law through insistence that the lease be treated as a conveyance of an estate are thus entirely avoided in Italy. Theirs is much the more rational system. Ours is best described as an expensive and cumbersome form of antiquarianism. The estate theory is, in terms of utility, dead. Modern life goes on in spite of it. Every one thinks and acts as if a lease were a purely commercial transaction, which it usually is. The estate theory, based on feudal tenure, merely makes leases more complicated than they need to be and incurs unnecessary social costs.

The Italian system has complications of its own, however. There are general provisions applicable to all kinds of leases, but typically applicable primarily to leases of movables. Other provisions apply to leases of urban premises for the purpose of habitation; to leases of non-agricultural productive enterprises; to leases of productive agricultural enterprises of some size; and to leases dealing primarily with the family farm. Consequently, a good deal of learning is spent on borderline cases, in deciding whether a lease is properly classified as a *locazione di cose mobile*, an *affitto*, an *affitto per fondi rustici*, and so on. Such distinctions are frequently very difficult to make, even though they are, in the main, functional.

Trusts

Maitland called the trust "the greatest and most distinctive achievement performed by Englishmen in the field of jurisprudence" and an institution "as elastic, as general as contract." The first of these observations has not been lost on comparative lawyers. Of all property devices, the trust is the only one to have been the subject of a substantial literature in comparative common law-civil law scholarship. And it is, and perhaps will remain, the only common law property device that has been successfully exported to other systems.[55]

There is no civil law property institution quite like the trust. Its generality and flexibility as a device for disposing of property, together with its peculiar juridical nature, combine to make it unique. A civil lawyer who sets out to do so can demonstrate that many of the functions served by the trust can be achieved in his legal system by using indigenous institutions, but each such arrangement would be significantly different in legal structure and in legal consequences from the trust.[57] No single analogous concept exists in the civil law, and no combination of different legal devices to achieve substantially similar ends quite adds up to the same thing. The trust, like the contract, is a

[55] The principal examples usually cited are Louisiana, Quebec, Mexico, Puerto Rico, Panama, the Philippines, Japan, and Liechtenstein. The success of the attempt to incorporate the trust into these foreign systems appears to have varied from place to place.

[57] Devices commonly mentioned as possibly analogous to the trust are the *treuhand* of German, Austrian, and Swiss law, the *prête-nom* of French law, and such generally recognized originally Roman institutions as the *enfiteusis*, the *fiducia*, and the *fideicommissum*.... [T]here is little real similarity between these and the trust. Nor is the fiduciary position of an executor or administrator of the property of a deceased, incompetent, or bankrupt person evidence of trust similarity, since the same institution exists in our law independent of the trust.

fundamental legal institution of great generality and flexibility; unlike the contract, it has no counterpart in the civil law.

Something like the separate jurisdictions of law and equity in England can be found in the classical Roman law, and indeed for a time "quiritary" and "bonitary" ownership existed side by side, with the legal (quiritary) owner holding title subject to the rights of the equitable (bonitary) owner. Although the analogy was never an exact one, the seeds of the kind of development that ultimately took place in England can be said to have existed in Rome. Under Justinian, however, quiritary ownership disappeared and the more flexible bonitary ownership occupied the field. Since then, ownership in the civil law has been indivisible in function as well as in time.

Our express private trust typically involves both kinds of division of ownership. In the simplest case, three interests are created: that of the trustee, who temporarily has what we call legal title, that of the beneficiary, who temporarily has what we call equitable title, and that of the person who will, on termination of the trust, become our equivalent of owner. Our rules against the indefinite duration of private trusts thus require in every case a division of ownership over time, and in this sense the statement of an Italian writer that "the concept of the estate is the principal obstacle to possible acceptance of the trust in the civil law" is in part understandable. If Italian legal theory rejects most of the typical common law estates, it must find the formation of analogous interests by trust equally unacceptable.

But the matter goes deeper than that. The conditions that led to the growth of the estate concept in England, including royal ownership and the concept of universal tenure, removed the ownership problem from the area of private property law and theory. Habits of thinking were formed among lawyers and judges that were different from those on the Continent. One cannot understand why it is an "improper question" to ask who owns the thing subject to the trust unless he can understand why it is equally improper to ask who owns land subject to a life estate followed by alternative contingent remainders in fee. In Lawson's words: "The freedom of invention developed in handling estates has proved particularly useful in enabling the distinction between management and enjoyment of property to be expressed in terms of law."

Viewed in this way, the trust is another example of what appears to the Italian lawyer to be the fragmentation of ownership, the division into parts of something that is, or ought to be, indivisible. The phenomenon of the trust is similar to that of the estate; each is "an alien concept." Writers on the subject generally give this as a principal reason for the nonexistence and unacceptability of trusts in the civil law. To this can be added the "principle of publicity construed as requiring a *numerus clausus* or taxative enumeration of real rights." According to this view, the codes enumerate all possibly permissible rights *in rem*, and no others are permitted. Since the interests of the parties to the trust are not included in the list of permitted interests, they receive no legal recognition.

A final reason given for the nonexistence of trusts in the civil law is related to those just described: since the trust is an alien institution outside the *numerus clausus*, indigenous legal institutions would naturally be favored. To the extent that a jurisdiction has its own legal devices for achieving the results achievable under our trust, it will naturally tend to rely on them. The more adequately such devices serve desired social and economic functions, the less need exists for the introduction of new legal institutions.

Thus, it can be argued that trusts do not exist in the civil law because they are not needed. The principal use of our private trust is in family property settlements, and that matter is greatly reduced in importance in civil law countries by the institution of forced heirship. Where succession to as much as two-thirds of one's wealth is dictated by the legal system, and cannot be evaded by will or by *inter vivos* gift, the incentive toward complex family settlements of the Anglo-American type is drastically reduced. It is reduced even further when the forced heirs are the same people one would normally consider in developing his estate plan. For the bulk of his wealth, therefore, the typical person contemplating the devolution of that wealth in a civil law nation is supplied with a statutory, non-derogable estate plan. He retains greater power over the so-called "disposable portion," but the kind of social pressure needed to force the legal system to expand property concepts in the interest of estate planning simply does not arise.

The European civil law jurisdictions differ widely in the degree to which trust equivalents have been developed, with the spectrum substantially broader in Switzerland, Germany, and France than in Italy. In each of them, it is possible to do through indigenous legal arrangements some of the things that are commonly done by us through use of the generality and flexibility of the trust. But in none of them does anything exist that can approach serving the purposes most commonly served by the trust in our law, as the most frequently employed vehicle for the transmission and distribution of wealth over generations.

Thus, under Italian law, property may be conveyed to a *fondazione* for charitable or cultural purposes, and the estate of a spendthrift, like that of any other incompetent person, may be made subject to legal supervision for his protection and that of his family. But only in the common law, under the broad rubric of trust, could these and other objectives be achieved as parts of one integrated plan for the care and distribution of wealth over a substantial period of time after the owner's death, with a variety of alternative provisions for a variety of alternative circumstances, with broad discretionary powers of management in a responsible and competent corporate trustee, and with a view toward minimizing the incidence of taxes. This is the most typical and, in many ways, the most important kind of trust in our law.

In this way, the trust, viewed primarily as a mechanism for effectuating estate plans, combines the concept of the estate and that of fiduciary ownership in a manner unique to the common law. The resulting flexibility in planning property dispositions is, by comparison, very great. The range of opportunities for dead hand control is broader in the common law, and the period during which such control may be exercised is greater. This flexibility is achieved, however, at the cost of a higher degree of legal complexity, burdening the American legal system with a large and extremely difficult body of law not only on future interests and trusts but in such allied fields as taxation and creditors' rights.

Conclusion

Several conclusions emerge from this brief comparison of ownership and estate. The first is that they are different in application as well as in theory; they are not alternate names for the same or similar things. A legal system in which ownership is a basic legal concept might conceivably have developed institutions and interests paralleling those of the common law, and perhaps during the Middle Ages substantial similarities existed, but the emphasis on a Napoleonic version of Roman ownership since codification and reform has led to a quite different body of property law in the civil law nations.

Second, the attitude that ownership is indivisible has played an important role in this development; occasionally, it may even have become an end in itself, without reference to discoverable social or economic functions. It has the lure of certainty, the attraction of simplicity, the ease of generality. The commitment to it in Italy and a number of other civil law nations seems to be unshakeable at the present time. This both inhibits improvisation in the system of property interests and requires the use of fictions to explain how those that are allowed can be made consistent with theory.

Third, the Italian land law has been reformed and defeudalized. It is consequently a good deal simpler to understand, at least on first acquaintance, than our own land law. Many of our legal terms and institutions can only be comprehended in the light of a very complex historical development, beginning with the establishment of Norman feudalism in England in the eleventh century. History is not, of course, irrelevant to a proper understanding of Italian property law, but the process of reform and defeudalization has greatly simplified the task of the Italian student by removing many feudal, and some Roman and Germanic, terms, notions, and institutions from the area of contemporary significance.

Fourth, the Italian law of property in land is codified. Hence, it is more systematic than ours is. There is a uniform terminology. Basic concepts are defined, and relationships are described in these terms. Rules are based on these concepts and relationships. The code was drafted with simplicity, inner consistency, and comprehensiveness as accepted values, and, although these can never be fully realized in practice, the resulting Italian law comes far closer to their realization than our own highly diffuse "system."

Fifth, the variety and flexibility of devices for preserving and disposing of property interests are much greater in the common law jurisdictions than in Italy. There are historical (the anti-feudal, democratic spirit in which reform and codification were undertaken) and formal (the dogma of indivisible ownership and the concept of the *numerus clausus*) explanations for the extremely limited range of opportunities given the Italian man of property in planning his estate. But we would greatly underestimate the quality of European legal scholarship were we to assume that a balanced social and economical judgment did not play an important role in arriving at the present juridical scheme. The remarkable thing is that their judgment has been so different from our own.

In part, the distance between their system and ours is attributable to the extremes of rationalism and anti-feudalism that colored property law reform in nineteenth century Europe. Extreme positions were rigorously taken with respect to fiduciary substitutions, successive usufructs, and so on, though there has been a noticeable tendency toward relaxation of these positions in more recent times. Still, the greater reason for the lack of similarity in the two property systems lies on the common law side, in the peculiarity — better, the idiosyncracy — of our law of property. Much of the complexity that we tolerate, and even glorify, is fun for the antiquarian and profitable for the lawyer versed in the black arts of property, but society pays a high price for these dubious benefits. Unlike civil law nations, the United States had no property revolution. The process has been evolutionary, and the pace has been unconscionably slow. Fifty years ago, when the British abolished all legal estates except the fee simple absolute and the term of years (while leaving unaffected equitable interests and estates), an important step was taken that American jurisdictions have, inexplicably, failed to emulate. That, and a few other measures of comparable scope and audacity, would make our property law a good deal simpler and more efficient without any loss of sensitivity.

Whether the notion of "estate" would or should survive fundamental reform in the law of property is not likely to be a very important question. Some central concept is necessary, and it is not clear that "ownership," at least as it is employed in modern civil law systems, is a particularly good one for the purpose. The meanings attributed to "estate" in our law, when contrasted with the meanings attributed to "ownership" in theirs, seem more sophisticated, more richly and variously useful, and freer from extra-legal cultural baggage. If these values could be retained while ridding our property law of the useless antiquarianism and arcane complexity that now characterize it, then it might be preferable to stay with "estate."

NOTES AND QUESTIONS

1. John Merryman uses two metaphors to stand for important differences between the Romanic notion of property "ownership" and the Anglo-American concept of "estate" or "interest" in land. Catalog how these metaphors — a box and a bundle (of sticks) — represent distinct historical backgrounds and today serve to distinguish civilian property law from American property law.

2. Professor Merryman states that "conceivably the balance between variety and flexibility of property arrangements over time, on the one side, and limitation of dead hand control on the other, has been more properly struck in Italy than in the United States." Do you agree? Does the greater "dead hand" control in the United States promote values of individualism or communitarianism?

3. Why is the American lease a part of property law and not a part of contract law? What difference does it make?

In Japan one of the differences between the French-based code of 1890 and the German-influenced code of 1898 was the classification of leaseholds as a contract under the category of obligations in Book Three (see German Civil Code, arts. 535-597) instead of a real right under Book Two (see French Civil Code, arts. 578-636). What difference in effect did this change have? By special statute, leaseholds could be registered. What effect would this have? (See Note on the Registration of Rights, at the end of this section.)

4. "Trusts do not exist in the civil law because they are not needed." Construct an argument *pro* and *contra*.

5. Professor Merryman concludes: "Much of the complexity that we tolerate, and even glorify, is fun for the antiquarian and profitable for the lawyer versed in the black arts of property, but society pays a high price for these dubious benefits." Do you agree?

6. Review the civil code headings in Section B of this chapter and attempt to list the common law equivalents to each of the following civil law terms: usufruct, *superficie, emphytheusis,* servitude, *anticresis,* and ownership. Determine which common law property institutions are not found in civil law property systems.

7. For more information on the civilian view of property law, see Norbert Horn, Hein Kötz & Hans G. Leser, German Private and Commercial Law: An Introduction 169-88 (Tony Weir trans. 1982); Athanassios N. Yiannopoulos ed., *Property and Trust,* 6 International Encyclopedia of Comparative Law (1973-present).

For an interesting discussion of the Roman *fideicommissum,* see David Johnston, The Roman Law of Trusts (1988).

2. AN ITALIAN CASE: *PIERCY v. E.T.F.A.S.*

NOTE

The following case pits an English family — the Piercys — against the Italian government agency — E.T.F.A.S. (Ente per la trasformazione fondiaria e agraria di Sardegna) — responsible for planning and executing in Sardinia a program of land and agrarian reform, including breaking up and redistributing large estates. The central issue in the case turns on the Italian judge's treatment of Major Piercy's attempt to impose a testamentary trust on Italian land, but in doing so the judge finds it necessary to decide questions of conflict of laws and Italian constitutional law and to deal with the division of jurisdiction between ordinary and administrative courts. The case is thus a sort of compendium of comparative law, in which we find an opportunity to review some of the major distinguishing features of civil law systems.

ITALIAN CIVIL CODE

Articles 692, 698

Article 692

Limits. A provision by which the testator imposes on his child the obligation to conserve and on his death to transfer in whole or in part the property constituting the disposable portion (556) in favor of all the children born or to be born of the instituted heir or to a public body is valid.

A provision that charges a brother or sister with the obligation to conserve and transfer the property left to him or her in favor of all children born and to be born of him or her or to a public body is also valid.

In every other case a substitution is void.

Any provision by which the testator prohibits the heir from disposing *inter vivos* or by will of inherited property is likewise void.

Article 698

Successive usufruct. A disposition by which a usufruct, annuity, or annual income is left successively to several persons has effect only in favor of those who, at the death of the testator, are the first entitled to enjoy it.

VERA NORINA MAMELI née PIERCY IN HER OWN RIGHT AND FOR MARIA LUISA BASHFIELDS PIERCY AND ANTONY FITZIVIAN PIERCY v. AGENCY FOR SARDINIAN AGRICULTURAL AND LAND REFORM (E.T.F.A.S.)

Tribunal of Oristano, Italy, Section One (1955)
(Unpublished)

Facts

The plaintiffs allege that they are owners *pro indiviso* — by succession from the erstwhile Major B. H. Piercy under his will of Dec. 10, 1939, deposited in Oristano with the notary Pippio, July 12, 1949, duly registered and transcribed, and by the wills of his successors, his children Benjamin James and Vivian Henry (deceased, with the same registration as above, who died May 18, 1943, and February 2, 1944) — of the following immovable property situated in the territory of the *Comune di Bolotona* and constituting part of the well-known estate of "Piercy di Padru Mannu e badde Salighes," which has been constituted for over 50 years by: ... [A detailed description of the property is omitted]; that until October 1953, E.T.F.A.S. was, under the Decree of the President of the Republic n. 4156 of Dec. 18, 1952 ... issued against testator's widow, Mrs. Daphne Hardwick Piercy, in possession of the above described immovables, notwithstanding the protests of the legitimate owners, appropriating the income and causing damage to the established agricultural and animal husbandry business; that they called the aforesaid E.T.F.A.S. before this Tribunal with a summons of April 5, 1954, in order to demand the following remedy, every other argument and exception being rejected: 1) that the Tribunal declare the plaintiffs absolute owners of the above described immovables ... and, therefore, require E.T.F.A.S. to immediately render them up; 2) that the Tribunal require E.T.F.A.S. to reimburse the fruits wrongfully received through illegitimate possession and to pay damages to be ascertained and liquidated in a separate proceeding; 3) with the award of their expenses and fees and with immediate execution of the judgment pending any appeal.

At the preliminary investigation were produced: the proper land registration certificates for the disputed property, its certificate of historical background and of correspondence with the old land register, an authentic copy of the will of Major B. H. Piercy with the proper notation of transcription, authentic copies of the wills of the children of the testator, Benjamin and Vivian, with respective notations of transcription, the summonses all dated by hand, a copy of the original deed of acquisition from the *Comune di Bolotona* dated

May 11, 1880, and strictly subordinate testimonial proof tending to show possession of the immovables *de quibus* by the plaintiffs for over thirty years.

The defendant E.T.F.A.S. contested the allegations of the plaintiffs, alleging that ownership of the land in question legitimately passed to it under a decree of expropriation issued following the regular procedure provided by the current legislative provisions, and placed in evidence that the widow, Daphne Hardwick Piercy, the owner from whom the property was expropriated, had taken a partial appeal from the judgment of the Tribunal of Oristano of February 10, 1954 (no. 3) with the result that her demands and those of the present plaintiffs for an award for expropriation corresponding to the actual value of the lands *de quibus* in current money freely transferable abroad were rejected. The defendant requested absolution from all the adverse claims.

Then the aforementioned Daphne Hardwick intervened voluntarily. She declared that she had never claimed and did not claim any right of ownership over the immovables here in question. After some postponements the Investigative Judge ordered the admission of the testimonial proof offered by the plaintiffs and, his duties completed, the case was assigned to the Tribunal. Plaintiffs persisted in their arguments outlined above, while Daphne Hardwick, the party subjected to the decree of expropriation, asked that the action be dismissed, with the award of her expenses. E.T.F.A.S. persisted in its arguments given above.

Law

It is uncontested between the parties, and seems clear from the contents of the complaint, that the plaintiffs — asking to be declared owners of the contested immovables and that E.T.F.A.S. be consequently bound to immediately abandon the land and to reimburse profits wrongfully received from the unjust possession — have brought *an action for recovery of the property* and have also brought an action for damages caused by defendant's possession of the land.

Both these demands, considered *per se*, are in the jurisdiction of the court of general jurisdiction and, specifically, within the competence of this Tribunal. The contested immovables are located in its jurisdiction, and the acts injurious to the plaintiffs (if true), on which they base their claim to damages, occurred here.

Neither does the fact that the contested immovables came into the possession of the defendant E.T.F.A.S. by virtue of a decree of expropriation issued under the ancillary law on land reform of Oct. 21, 1950, n. 841, and of the Presidential Decrees which have extended the rules contained in that law to all the territory of Sardinia, defeat the jurisdiction of this Tribunal. In fact, since the only party subjected to the decree of expropriation (Decree of the President of the Republic, Dec. 18, 1952, n. 4156) was Piercy's widow, Daphne Hardwick, who has intervened in this case only to declare that she asserts no right over the immovables in question, while the plaintiffs Vera Norina Piercy and Maria Luisa, widow of a Piercy, and Antony Fitzivian Piercy were not such parties, it cannot be argued that their possible right of ownership and the transformation of such rights into legitimate interests would be weakened by the decree of expropriation. On the contrary it is certain that the issue is one of perfect subjective rights, which are not affected by the expropriative rules contained in the decree, which was aimed at a person other than the present plaintiffs.

Moreover, as the Supreme Court has held in numerous recent decisions, decrees of expropriation issued by the government pursuant to the ancillary statute do not constitute acts or provisions of an administrative authority or an administrative tribunal, which continue in administrative jurisdiction. Decrees of expropriation actually cannot be considered subjectively and objectively administrative, because they are delegated legislative provisions, by definition of the legislature itself.

Nor can we accept the position of those who argue: that since decrees of expropriation lack the character of generality and of abstractness in effect they are administrative acts; that this means that Parliament's legislative delegation to the Government to provide for individual expropriation is unconstitutional and that since the delegation fails because of unconstitutionality, only an administrative act remains. On one hand, it has been held that the characteristics of generality and abstractness are not absolutely essential to a statute since even traditional doctrine recognized and allowed the category of *leges in privas latæ*.[a] On the other hand, nothing prevents the Parliament, with its sovereign power, from incorporating (if only exceptionally and for established specific purposes) individual and concrete activities of an essentially administrative nature into the ambit of the legislative function, or from carrying out these activities with statutes, as happens, for example, in the approval of budgets. And nothing prohibits the legislature, after such an incorporation, from delegating the issuance of the specific provisions of law to the Government, under art. 76 of the Constitution.

Even conceding *arguendo* that decrees of expropriation or the acts of execution which follow them could in some way be considered administrative acts, nevertheless this Tribunal would have jurisdiction deriving from the fact that the plaintiffs base their claim on the conflict of a perfect subjective right (their right of ownership over the land, expropriated against another party) with the operation of the so-called administrative acts. If the plaintiffs' right of ownership is recognized it will only be necessary to see which of their demands can be accepted under the limitations posed by art. 24 of the Law on Administrative Adjudication, Mar. 20, 1865, n. 2248, on the power of the ordinary judge, in controversies over rights which are allegedly violated by an act of administrative authority.

Nor can this court be found to lack jurisdiction because of the argument that, since the Government by expropriating land has exceeded the limits of the parliamentary delegation of power by issuing a decree of expropriation in the absence of the subjective and objective conditions required by the Ancillary Law of Reform, that is, against the wrong person, there arises a question of the constitutionality of the legislative decree of expropriation.

It is now unanimously recognized that the transitional provision VII of the Constitution establishes that, until the Constitutional Court begins to oper-

[a] Laws of a private, particular scope.

ate, decision of the controversies indicated in art. 134 of the Constitution is to take place within the forms and limits existing at the time the Constitution itself becomes effective. It has provisionally given the ordinary judge (or the administrative judge, according to the nature of the controversy) jurisdiction over questions of constitutionality until the Constitutional Court begins to function. This jurisdiction is not only over extrinsic and formal questions, but also over those which are intrinsic and substantive, to ascertain whether a law conforms to the precepts of the new Constitution, which, unlike the Albertine Constitution, has a rigid character and therefore cannot be modified by ordinary laws. The only difference from the power which the Constitutional Court will exercise over questions of constitutionality is that the ordinary (or administrative) court must decide *incider tantum*, with effect only *inter partes*.

And it is also commonly agreed that an agency which exceeds the power delegated by a legislative act does so without power and therefore without constitutional character; therefore it falls, temporarily, within the jurisdiction of the ordinary or administrative court for the reasons outlined above.

Having established its jurisdiction, this Court must proceed to an examination of the merits. Regarding the merits, the plaintiffs have not proved that, by themselves, they possessed the lands in question for the period necessary to acquire them by prescription. But, availing themselves of the principle of *accessio possessionis*, they have demonstrated by means of the documents produced and testimonial proof that the contested immovables comprise part of the complex of goods constituting the farm of "*Padru Mannu e badde Salighes*" which was possessed for over thirty years by Major Benjamin Herbert Piercy, who died Dec. 15, 1941, and which became part of his patrimony. The plaintiffs assert themselves to be the only owners by virtue of the will of Dec. 10, 1939, notwithstanding the will of April 8, 1939, of the Major's son, Benjamin James Ernest Piercy, who died May 18, 1943, and the will of August 18, 1929, of the other child, Vivian Henry Piercy, deceased Feb. 2, 1944. All the wills were produced in court.

It is evident, therefore, that in deciding whether the plaintiffs have become owners of the lands by derivative title after the death of Major Piercy and his two male children, an examination must be made of the alleged title of acquisition, that is of the above mentioned wills, in order to establish whether they validly transferred ownership of the contested property to the plaintiffs.

From examination of the will of Major Benjamin Piercy it appears that, after stating his intention that the will be interpreted and operate "as far as possible" as if he had remained in England until his death, the testator first of all named as "trustees" or fiduciaries of his will: his wife, Daphne Beatrice Hardwick, his daughter, Vera Norina Mameli, and his son, Benjamin James Ernest. Then he gave to his wife: 1) the *right to use, occupy and enjoy during her life* (or until sale of the property) the house and ancillary structures and the gardens and lands used in connection with it, together termed *Villa Piercy*, which, subject to the right of the wife, *should comprise part of his remaining patrimony and pass accordingly*; 2) a gift of all movables, of the silverware and of the objects of personal, domestic and ornamental use. He then provided for his son Benjamin James: 3) a gift of £4,100 sterling, but until that sum should be entirely paid over, an annual income of £150 sterling.

It is clear that these testamentary dispositions cannot be considered to be anything but legacies (and so they are termed by the testator further on in clause 10). More precisely, the first is a legacy of usufruct, the second a legacy of a sum of money, and the third a legacy of a sum of money together with an income.

But with these dispositions the wife is given no right of ownership over the land possessed by the testator in Italy and more particularly over the land in controversy, which is distinct and different from the Villa Piercy and its immediate environs.

In subsequent clauses (9-12) Major Piercy provided that all his *remaining movable and immovable property be placed in "trust"* and that the trustees before nominated: a) in their absolute discretion could consolidate it or convert it into money by selling it, but with the most ample power, in their discretion, to postpone the conversion, consolidation, and sale of the property constituting the patrimony and to maintain it in its then form of utilization for as long as they felt it convenient; b) would pay, with the proceeds of sale or otherwise (with income from the property), the expenses of death and succession, and the legal debts of the testator; c) would invest the sum recovered from conversion of the property into money in those funds, shares, loans, and investments, guaranteed or not, which they in their discretion find appropriate; d) *would hold possession of the sums so invested and of those sums not invested and of the part of the property not yet converted into money, in order to divide the whole into three equal parts* which were destined for the testator's three children in the following manner: 1) one-third *held in trust to pay the income* to the son, Vivian Henry, *during his life*, with prohibition against encumbering or anticipating the interest, and after his death (or in case of encumbrance or anticipation of the interest) *to pay the income* to his grandson, Antony Fitzivian, and after the latter's death (or in case of encumbrance or anticipation of the interest) *to reunite the third with the remainder of the trust patrimony.* 2) Another third, both capital and income, held in trust for the daughter, Vera Norina, on the condition that she add to the hotchpot of remaining assets the ownership of the movable and immovable property assigned to her in a 1939 gift; otherwise this third should also be reunited with the remainder of the trust patrimony. 3) The last third, *both capital and income,* held in trust in an absolute manner (that is, unconditionally) for the son, Benjamin James.

The testator expressly provided that if any of these trusts created in favor of his children *were to fail*, the parts which failed (that is, their objects) should go to augment in equal amounts the trust or trusts remaining (i.e., the shares assigned to the others).

Now the whole question which is contested between the parties and which constitutes the center of the present action is whether, under the will, the heirs and owners of the generality of Major Piercy's patrimony placed in trust as put forth above are to be considered in Italy to be the three fiduciaries of the trust or "trustees" nominated by the testator, i.e., the wife, Daphne Hardwick, and the children, Vera Norina, and Benjamin James Piercy, or the three beneficiaries of the trust, i.e., the two above children and the third, Vivian Henry Piercy, excluding the widow Daphne Hardwick, against whom the decree of expropriation was issued on the initiative of E.T.F.A.S. And thus if, as the defendant proposes in its first argument, Daphne Piercy should be considered in whole or in part as heir to the patrimony of her deceased husband together with the two children, Vera and Benjamin, and therefore a co-owner of the property expropriated by E.T.F.A.S., E.T.F.A.S. would have properly expropriated the lands in question under art. 8 of the Law of May 18, 1951, n. 33.

This statute provides that in the case of ownership in common the expropriating Agency may provide expropriation of lands held in common up to the value of the share belonging to the co-owner on whom expropriation is imposed, and that the expropriated portion continues to be imputed to the share of that co-owner.

Therefore, since it has not been proved or even argued by the plaintiffs that the portion expropriated from Daphne Beatrice Hardwick exceeds the third which would belong to her if, as co-trustee with the two children, she should be considered co-heir, and since on the contrary it must be held that the opposite is true, because it appears from the land registration certificates that other lands were registered to the deceased Major Piercy and still others to his daughter Norina under the 1939 gift, signifying a complex of several thousands of hectares, it is rightly argued by the defendant that the expropriation was, under the cited provision, truly against Daphne Beatrice Hardwick within the limits of her share, if she can be recognized as co-heir and co-owner of the lands.

In order to resolve this fundamental issue it is first necessary to examine closely the institution of trust, which is conceived and utilized in Anglo-Saxon legislation, in order to establish what value it can be given by the Italian legal system.

We are in fact dealing with an institution which is absolutely peculiar to the law of England and North America, where it finds vast application in various fields, from family relations to rights *in rem* to relations after bankruptcy, etc.

We are dealing with a legal relation which belongs to a category of fiduciary relations (in a broad sense) which can arise through the intent of a private party, denominated "settlor," or by law, and by virtue of which the legal or nominal ownership (legal estate) of a given thing, or the titular right, is attributed to one party, denominated "trustee," and the beneficial ownership of the same (equitable estate) is attributed to another party, denominated "cestui que trust" (beneficiary), and the former party is required to protect, administer, and use the thing in trust exclusively for the benefit of the second (or for a given purpose).

The fundamental characteristic of the institution, almost inconceivable in those legal orders, such as ours, which in the wake of the Romanistic tradition conceive the right of ownership as something absolute, unlimited and exclusive, is a splitting of the original right of ownership into two new rights of ownership, belonging contemporaneously to two different parties, over the same object, investing one with formal or outward ownership and the other with substantial ownership. More precisely the powers of disposition contained in the right of ownership are attributed to the trustee and the right to enjoyment is attributed to the *cestui que trust.*

This phenomenon finds its explanation in procedural history. Originally in the most ancient English law full and absolute dominion over immovables belonged to the King, while other persons could have only subordinate legal positions (estates) — and from this it has followed that there is no repugnance to conceiving ownership as limited in England. And such splitting of ownership is nothing but the reflection of the twofold nature of the sources of English law, Common Law and Equity, and of the twofold nature of the means of legal protection corresponding to the subjective rights created by one or the other source — that is, the Common Law Courts to defend legal rights and the Courts of Chancery to defend equitable rights. The latter were created by the Chancellor to respond to new social needs, to certain imperatives of conscience which did not find recognition in the pre-existing body of common law. Among these was the defense accorded by the Chancellor to the interests of the beneficiary of a relation founded on the good faith of a fiduciary to execute the relation in conformity with the true scope established by the creator at the time of creation, interests which under the common law were without legal protection and confided solely to the honor and conscience of the fiduciary. The defense was created by detaching the power of enjoyment from the "legal estate" of the fiduciary and attributing it to the beneficiary under the form of a right which opposes the legal estate and which constitutes the "equitable estate." The other principal characteristics of the institution are the following:

1) The splitting of the right of ownership distinguishes the trust from every other legal relation: where there is such splitting there is necessarily a trust; where such splitting is not found there is no trust.

2) A trust is normally based on an act of transfer *inter vivos* or *mortis causa.*

3) He who creates the trust (settlor) is considered only in the moment of creation. Afterwards he vanishes, no longer having any participation in the life of the trust, which continues to be regulated by the intent he expressed and the scope he intended at the moment of creation, but these are understood as something from that moment as autonomous and objective, cut off from the settlor, as law regulative of the trust crystallized in the act of establishment.

4) The trustee as formal holder of the right held in trust has all the rights and powers necessary to fulfill the purposes of the trust that an absolute owner would have, *but he must utilize such rights and powers only for the purposes of the trust established in the act of establishment, and in the exclusive interests of the cestui que trust.*

In relation to such ends he may carry out not only acts of ordinary administration but also acts of extraordinary administration, when these are expressly conceded to him in the act of establishment or are authorized by judicial authority.

He must, normally, hold the thing in trust in his possession and protect it, conserve it whole and put it to profit, pay over any element of the fiduciary thing to whomever has a right to it and finally give any information, particularly to the beneficiaries, that is requested of him regarding the state of the fiduciary thing.

In the exercise of these powers and duties the trustee is held to the diligence that a man of average prudence displays in the administration of his affairs. The trustee is a party to proceedings having the fiduciary thing as object.

5) *The trustee must not and cannot himself derive any profit or advantage, direct or indirect, from the thing in trust.* This is a cardinal principle which does not permit exceptions, and the trustee is liable for every violation or abuse of the trust and for every deviation from the duties imposed by law, by the act of establishment and by the courts. When the trustee sues for the trust he sues in his own name and his own account. He is therefore liable for obligations contracted on behalf of the trust, not only with the fiduciary patrimony, but also personally. But conversely, for his personal obligations he is liable only with his own patrimony, and if this is insufficient, property held in trust for others cannot be used to make up the difference.

6) The *cestui que trust*, owner of the equitable estate or interest, has above all the *right of enjoyment of the benefits derived* from the thing in trust in the measure and in the manner determined by the act of establishment and, normally, the *right to alienate the equitable estate* or beneficial interest and *to dispose of it by act mortis causa or inter vivos*; he has all the rights corresponding to the duties of the trustee regarding the administration of the trust and *the right to put an end to the relation of trust*, even *against the letter of the act of establishment* and the intent of the settlor or of the trustee, any time that in relation to the purposes of the trust the presence and participation of the trustee appears superfluous. In any case, *on termination of the trust the legal estate reunites with the equitable estate, and the owner of the latter then becomes the full owner*. The *cestui que trust* has the right to be a party in proceedings concerning the equitable estate. This is the general protection of his creditors.

7) There are different types of trust which are variations on the basis of the fundamental elements. One of these is the "trust for sale," created for the purpose of selling the thing in trust (especially ownership of immovables) and converting it into money, and then of holding both the income produced by the trust property before sale and the price recovered for its sale for the purposes and for the benefit of the persons established in the founding act. The trustee in "trusts for sale" has the power within his discretion to delay the sale of the property until he believes it convenient. The *cestui que trust sui juris* in the trust for sale *has the right to have the trust maintained in the state in which it is found* (that is, without sale) or *to have the trust terminate*, with the effects discussed above.

8) In a trust there may be trustees who are beneficiaries and trustees who are not beneficiaries.

In the light of these principles it is easy to see that the trust created by Major Benjamin Herbert Piercy is a trust for sale, in which were named one trustee not a beneficiary, the wife Daphne Hardwick, two trustee beneficiaries, the children, Benjamin James and Vera Norina, and one beneficiary not a trustee, the son Vivian Henry.

The point which must now be examined is whether the creation of the trust may be recognized as valid in Italy. With regard to this proposition this Court observes that were the trust given all the effects which it produces in the English legal system it would undoubtedly violate fundamental principles of public order in the Italian legal system.

It is true, indeed, that according to the rule of art. 23 of the preliminary provisions to the Civil Code, succession on death is regulated, wherever the property may be found, by the law of the state to which the deceased in question belonged at the time of death. This means that in the present case the law regulating the succession of Major Piercy is the English law, since it is undisputed that the Major was a citizen of England at the time of his death. But not only the rules on succession, but also and above all those on *in rem* rights and especially on ownership are relevant to the resolution of this question. Therefore with regard to the validity of the trust as such it is necessary to refer to art. 22 of the preliminary laws rather than to art. 23. Under art. 22, possession, ownership and the other rights over movable and immovable things are regulated by the law of the place where they are found. Moreover, defense counsel rightly observes that art. 23 is limited by art. 31, according to which, notwithstanding the preceding provisions, in no case can the laws and orderings of a foreign state have effect in Italy when they are contrary to the public order.

The whole question is reduced, therefore, to seeing whether the testamentary dispositions of Major Piercy, with which the property was put in trust in the manner discussed earlier, or the English law which regulates the trust, are contrary to the norms which regulate the right of ownership in Italy or with those of the public order, by which is meant the international public order with regard to private persons, distinct from the internal public order binding only on Italian citizens. Now, even on superficial examination it is quickly clear that the institution of trust defined as the English define it, with its essential characteristic of splitting the right of ownership between two parties, who nevertheless both continue to be considered parties by means of the attribution of formal and apparent ownership and the power of disposition to one, and substantial ownership and the power of enjoyment to the other, does not find the slightest counterpart in our system.... There governs in Italy, with regard to rights *in rem*, the fundamental principle that such rights constitute a *numerus clausus* and are of typical structure, which structures are preordained and recognized by the Civil Code. The free formation of relations of an *in rem* character is not allowed, as it is in relations of obligation.

And if, for whatever purpose, legal effect in Italy could be given to a trust created over property located in England, it is not possible to recognize purely and simply the validity of trusts over property located in Italy with all the legal effects they have in England, especially with regard to the splitting of the right of ownership, without subverting and confusing our legal ordering of ownership. And precisely because the trust, so defined, is in conflict with absolutely fundamental principles of Italian law it seems evident that these principles are of public order, inderogable by foreign legal norms and acts. The public international order is constituted by those fundamental principles of our order whose violation by means of the insertion of foreign legal institutions would produce grave turbulence in public conscience and opinion and in the Italian economy. The ordering of property by trust cannot be accorded full validity in Italy without need for recourse to other principles of public order, such as the prohibition of substitution *fedecommissaria* established by art. 692 C.C. It is in fact incorrect to assert that a trust always contains a *fedecommesso*: it may contain one or it may not, but usually it does not, and in particular the one with which the Court is occupied does not. It has been correctly observed that in the *fedecommesso* the beneficiary's ownership begins where that of the fiduciary ends, while in the trust both coexist contemporaneously.

In the trust *mortis causa*, however, there is neither duplication of testamentary vocation nor successive order: according to English law there is only one heir, the beneficiary, who is also the sole appointee to the inheritance. Nor does the property remain not freely saleable, as in the *fedecommesso*, since the object of the trust can be sold, and even must be in the case of trust for sale.

Nevertheless, once having admitted *the invalidity of the trust as such in Italy*, we do not draw the conclusions which the defendant Reform Agency urges. *There are* in fact *three hypotheses* which may be proposed following disallowance of the trust.

The first is that since the creation of heirs contained in the will of Major Piercy was done in a form and with a content that cannot find application in Italy, such creation and the testamentary intent of the *de cuius* must fail totally and must therefore give way to the rules of intestate succession. If this solution is adopted no advantage would be derived by the defendant Agency and the plaintiffs would be entirely victorious, since, if the rules on succession *ab intestato* of the English law are applied, it is incontestable that the intestate heirs to the lands in question would be the three children and not the wife, Daphne Beatrice Hardwick.

Indeed in England, in intestate succession, a surviving wife with descendants is given full ownership only over "personal chattels," that is, those movables necessary to the domestic *menage*, and £1000 sterling. Over the rest of the patrimony she has only the right to usufruct for half, while the children and their descendants inherit all the patrimony in full ownership, except for the said rights of the wife. It is therefore evident that Daphne Hardwick can claim no right of ownership over the immovables of her husband's succession and therefore none over the lands expropriated by E.T.F.A.S.

But this Court holds that such a solution would not be correct because it would completely ignore the intent of the testator and disapply the trust more than is necessary to salvage the fundamental principles of public order discussed above. It is instead more correct, and on this, moreover, all the parties agree, to inquire, on the basis of the principle of "*utile per inutile non vitiatur*"[b] and that of honoring the intent of the testator, what may remain of Major Piercy's will and the creation of the trust that does not conflict with the inderogable rules of our system.

The defendant argues that even though the trust failed there was an attribution of ownership to those designated as trustees. He places emphasis on the ample powers of the trustee, particularly on the fact that in contracting with third parties it is his action and intent which counts, on the fact that the trustee is a party to proceedings having the thing held in trust as object and that he has the power and the right, particularly in the trust for sale, to alienate the thing. Defense counsel minimizes the powers and rights of the beneficiaries, and asserts forthrightly that the trust for sale created by Major Piercy should be treated as a non-obligatory mandate to pay over an income, a relation to which doctrine and case law both accord all the effects of transfer of ownership.

The plaintiffs, on the other hand, emphasizing the substantial and not merely formal nature of the rights of the *cestui que trust*, the fact that in England the thing in trust, for all substantial purposes, is considered to be part of the patrimony of the beneficiary, and the testator's ultimate purpose of securing his ownership of the lands to his children in three equal parts, argue that the three beneficiaries appointed by the testator (his three children) must be considered heirs and owners in Italy.

It seems to the Court that an Italian interpreter — required, because of the disallowance of the splitting of ownership essential to the trust, to decide who are the heirs and owners of a thing held in a trust created by a will — could not hesitate to prefer the substantial, effective, and real right of the *cestui que trust*, for whose benefit the trust was created, to the merely legal, formal and in point of fact solely apparent ownership of the trustee. To refer to the ample powers of the trustee in support of the opposite conclusion is to forget that these powers, although ample, are attributed to the trustee solely to serve the purposes of the trust and always in the interest and for the benefit of the *cestui que trust*. And if to fulfill such trust purposes he is also established as representative party in controversies relating to the legal estate, this is done for the purposes of administration of the trust. The *cestui que trust*, moreover, is accorded the status of party in controversies relating to the equitable estate. Finally, even the fact that the trustee can, in the trust for sale, sell the object of the trust, this is in relation to the testator's intent to pass on to his heirs — that is, the beneficiaries of the trust — its equivalent in money or securities rather than the property in its original state.

Nor is it correct to liken the trust for sale to an agency without obligation to render an account. If ample discretion with regard to the administration of the trust, together with exoneration from liability for losses, is accorded to the trustee for sale in general, and to those named by Major Piercy in particular, such discretion refers only to the *time and manner of sale and appropriate reinvestment, and particularly to the power to postpone, for the period he thinks proper, the sale, consolidation and conversion of the patrimony held in trust.* It suffices to reread provisions 9, 11, and 13 of the will to convince one of this.

[b] The useful is not vitiated by the useless.

But this does not mean that trustees for sale are not required, according to the general rules on trust, to use the diligence of a man of average prudence in the administration of the trust, nor that they are exonerated from liability for wrongful acts according to the rules established for "breach of trust," nor even less that they are authorized to refuse to render up the property held in trust for sale in cases in which the trust may be terminated, or the equivalent of such property in money or securities when the trust terminates through fulfilling its purpose, nor, moreover, that the trustees are exonerated from rendering an account to the *cestui que trust* of their administration and of how much remains on termination of the trust.

In order to attribute ownership of the property in trust to the beneficiaries, diverse elements already stressed are essential: 1) that the formal ownership of the trust is temporary and destined to be united with the substantial ownership of the *cestui que trust* which is perpetual; 2) that the trustee of the legal ownership cannot serve his own interests and that he is unable to derive any personal advantage or benefit from his position; 3) that there is no confusion between the trustee's own patrimony and that of the trust — which serves as a guarantee to the creditors of the beneficiary; 4) that the trustee is unable to alienate the legal ownership of the thing in trust as his own thing but only as the thing in trust, while the beneficiary can alienate the equitable estate and substantial ownership as his own; 5) that the trustee cannot transmit the legal estate, even *mortis causa*, to his heirs, while the *cestui que trust* can transmit the equitable estate to his heirs; 6) that the *cestui que trust* can terminate a trust for sale when he wishes and take full ownership of its object.

We add that the trustee may in determined cases be exonerated and replaced, even *ex officio*, by decree of court, which is not conceivable with regard to the *cestui que trust*; that often one of the numerous fiduciary firms or companies (trust companies) which have as the object of their social and commercial activity the administration of trusts, for which they are particularly equipped and specialized, is named trustee (and we have an example in the will of Benjamin James Piercy which nominates as trustee Midland Bank, Ltd., Company for Fiduciary Administration and Management); that there even exists a preestablished public body or functionary (public trustee) to act as trustee for those who prefer to turn to it because of its public, official nature; that in English succession even where there is no trustee (executor) named by the *de cuius* and even in intestate succession there is, *ope legis*, a phenomenon — analogous to that of the trust — of splitting of ownership involving the "personal representative" who must be named in all successions *mortis causa* as intermediary in the passage of the hereditary patrimony from deceased to heir, so that he receives the decedent's estate and administers it, winding up all its active or passive pending affairs, in order to transmit it to the testamentary or intestate heirs; that like the trustee the "personal representative" acquires the "legal estate" over the hereditary patrimony while the "beneficial estate" belongs to the heirs, in whom both estates unite at the end of the personal representative's term of office, so that in point of fact the personal representative is none other than a trustee and the heirs *cestuis que trust*, and it cannot be doubted that, according to our law, the true heirs are the latter. There is an imposing complex of reasons operating to remove ever farther from the figure of the trustee the concept and qualification of owner as defined by the tradition, mentality and ordering of our national law, and to cause it to vest in the opposite pole of the mechanism of the trust, in the beneficiary.

In the trustee under our law may be recognized, if anything, the figure of an administrator *sui generis* furnished with the broadest powers — composed a little of the agent, the representative, the commission agent, the depositary and the fiduciary administrator, and when he has charge of a trust constituted *mortis causa*, such as the present one, the *testamentary executor*. Nor are the broad powers of the trustee a hindrance to such an interpretation, since they have their origin in the intent of the settlor, which the trustee is held to follow exactly in the same way as is, for example, the testamentary executor under art. 703 C.C., last paragraph; nor is the power to sell the thing in a trust for sale (a hindrance to such an interpretation) — this is allowed the testamentary executor even independently of the wishes of the testator and the heirs under the next to last paragraph of the above article.

Therefore, *excepting the splitting of ownership*, nothing prohibits the trust from having its other effects in Italy: in particular, the trustee as fiduciary administrator and as testamentary executor well may follow the testamentary provisions regarding the property located in Italy, either by administering it or by selling it and employing the proceeds in the ways and within the terms established by the testator. In all this nothing can be found which is contrary to the laws in any way concerning the public order in Italy.

Moreover, the principle of respecting the testamentary intent of the *de cuius* where possible cannot permit considering as heirs the trustees named by the settlor rather than the *cestui que trust*. It is certain, because it appears from the will, that the intent of Major Piercy was to cause his patrimony to be enjoyed and received by his children, and to leave his wife only a usufruct over Villa Piercy and a legacy of money. The absurdity of the contrary opinion, which attributes appointment as heirs to the trustees, is evident when one considers that if this were so then Benjamin James in naming the Bank of Midland trustee in his will intended to benefit the bank and to leave his patrimony to it rather than to his siblings named *cestuis que trust*.

It must not be forgotten that *the effects of Major Piercy's will* and the trust established by him *are discussed in order to establish who should be considered owner* with regard to the law on agrarian land reform, and that is to establish who is the party subject to expropriation. One cannot forget that the laws of reform have a fundamentally socio-economic character seeking to limit private ownership if, beyond certain limits of scope, it is found economically and socially harmful. Now it is undoubted that in the trust the innermost socio-economic content of the right of ownership is constituted by the equitable estate, which is the complex of the powers of enjoyment, which are part of the patrimony of the *cestui que trust*, while the trustee has as his patrimony only the merely legal powers, external and formal, constituting the legal estate. Therefore, for our purpose in this case of attributing the right of ownership either to the trustee or the *cestui que trust*, it is to the equitable estate that we must look.

The consequences at which we would arrive following the thesis of E.T.F.A.S. would be strange and contrary to every reason of equity and of law, with regard to the application of the law of reform. Persons named *cestuis que trust* over reaches of land enormously beyond the minimum necessary would not be subject to expropriation, even though they enjoy such lands as owners and even though such lands, or their equivalent, are ineluctably destined sooner or later to wind up absolutely and without limitations in their patrimony; and on the contrary, persons in their own right owners of small pieces of land not subject to expropriation could be deprived of their entire holdings only because, temporarily and in the interests of another person, they as trustees are considered by a foreign legal order mere formal owners of lands in substance composing part of the patrimony of others and even the formal ownership of which is destined to vest entirely in the others, so that at a given point when the trust ceases, such trustees would be completely deprived of ownership of any land at all.

For all the reasons discussed, it must be concluded that Daphne Beatrice Hardwick is not an heir of her deceased husband, Major Piercy, and that therefore she can claim no right of ownership, on the basis of his will, over the lands in question. *The daughter, Vera Norina, however*, to whom the testator (willed) a third of his patrimony, *with regard to both capital and income, is undoubtedly an heir and co-owner* of the property, *as is the deceased son, Benjamin James Ernest*, to whom a third was also attributed in an absolute manner *with regard to both capital and income*. The position of the third child, Vivian Henry, also deceased, is otherwise, since the remaining third of his father's patrimony was attributed to him only "*to pay him the income during his life*," without power in any way to subject his interest or equitable estate to encumbrances or to anticipation, that is prohibiting him from entering into acts of disposition regarding the share allotted him. This means that according to the intent of the testator, Vivian Henry was nothing more than the beneficiary of a right of usufruct or income over a third of the patrimony, i.e., a simple legatee, and that Vera Norina and Benjamin James (or their heirs) were heirs to this third as well, as bare owners until the deaths of their brother and his son, Antony Fitzivian, and then as full owners. In fact the testator specified in provision n. 12 that "then," that is on the deaths of Vivian Henry and his son, "*the aforesaid share is to be added to the remainder of my property*" held in trust in the way discussed previously, and this provision was confirmed by the affirmation that on the lapsing of any of the one-third trusts (and therefore on the lapsing of the one created in favor of Vivian and Antony Fitzivian because of their deaths) its contents should go to augment the remaining one-third trusts, in equal proportions.

From this conclusion it may be inferred that on the basis of Major Piercy's will the plaintiff Antony Fitzivian can claim no right of any sort, neither of ownership nor of usufruct nor of income over the contested property. It is true that the will provides that on the death of the son, Vivian, entitled to the income from the third of the patrimony held in trust in his favor, such share should likewise be used "*to pay the income to my grandson Antony Fitzivian*"; but it has been correctly argued by the defendant E.T.F.A.S. that such a testamentary clause is without legal validity in Italy, since it conflicts with the provision of art. 698 C.C. It is in fact a testamentary disposition with which a usufruct or an income was left to more than one person successively, which under the cited article is valid only with regard to the first appointed on death of the testator — that is, in the present case, with regard to Vivian Henry, who was living at the time of his father's death, and not valid with regard to the second appointee, Vivian Henry's son. *The cited rule in fact has the character of public order, inderogable even by acts executed by foreigners*, since it derives from essential principles in our law regarding the free commerciability of goods. The *ratio legis* of the prohibition against successive usufruct is in fact analogous to that of the prohibition of substitution *fedecommissaria*, inasmuch as a chain of usufructs which could last many years would also practically annul the value of the ownership, constitute an obstacle to the improvement of landed holdings, and render such ownership in fact non-commerciable.

Given therefore the nullity of Major Piercy's testamentary disposition in favor of Antony Fitzivian, it follows that on the death of Vivian Henry, which is said to have occurred February 2, 1944, the usufruct or income of the third of the patrimony put in trust in his favor by his father did not pass to his son, but would have to have reunited with the bare ownership, which over that third belonged to the beneficiaries of the other two-thirds (or to their successors on these last two-thirds).

It is necessary, however, in order to determine the final destination of the trusts created in favor of Vivian and Benjamin James, to consider their wills also.

Benjamin James, who died before Vivian, after leaving in a legacy to his mother, Daphne Beatrice Piercy, his books, papers, furniture, wardrobe, and his other objects of personal (use) and ornament, and to his sister, also in a legacy, his letters and manuscripts and his cinematographic and photographic equipment and film, and finally a legacy of £30 to his cousin, Eva Margherita Omrod, left all the remainder of his movables and immovables, both those which he actually possessed and those reversionary to him in trust "*to pay the income to my mother, Daphne Beatrice Piercy, during her natural life*" and after her death "*to hold both the capital and the income on behalf of my brother, Vivian, and sister, Vera, in equal shares*" (and in case they predecease her, on behalf of their children respectively, Antony Fitzivian Piercy, and Georgina Eva Elena Paolina Mameli).

In virtue of this will, therefore, Daphne Beatrice has not acquired any right of ownership or co-ownership over property left by her son, Benjamin, at his death, and therefore no share of ownership over the original patrimony left by her deceased husband, but only a right of usufruct over a share of the part of such patrimony belonging to Benjamin, in the measure in which Benjamin intended to give her such right, while the ownership, in part bare and in part full, of the patrimony of Major Piercy and therefore of the lands in question remained, after the death of Benjamin, attributed to Vera Norina Piercy and Vivian Henry Piercy in the measure of the respective shares resulting from the two wills considered up to now.

Vivian, who died after Benjamin, named as his trustees his wife, Maria Bashfields Piercy, and Alban Ludovich Grant Chavasse, a lawyer, and disposed of his belongings in the following way: 1) he left to his wife *during her natural life and after her death to the child* or children who survived her and reached the age of 21 years *all the interest and annual sums of money which might be owed to him in virtue of the contractual act of July 22, 1916*, stipulated between himself and his father, "*and also all the interest and annual sums of money, and ownership, which might be owed to him in virtue of the same act*, on the death of his father," and all the *capital and interest* owed to him in "*consequence of a loan*" made to his father around the aforesaid date; 2) he left all the remainder of his property, of whatever kind, in trust *to his wife* and "*for her use and benefit in an absolute manner*."

From an examination of these dispositions it is clear that Henry Vivian Piercy's son, Antony Fitzivian, cannot claim, even on the basis of his father's will, any right of ownership over the immovables in question.

In fact, the first testamentary disposition gives him, after the death of the testator's wife, only: a) a *usufruct or an income in money*, that is, the annual sums owed to Vivian by his father until the latter's death, by virtue of a contractual act (the object and content of which do not appear), to which nullity under art. 698 C.C. again applies; b) a *usufruct or an income*, not of money, of the *ownership* owed to him on the death of his father, in virtue of the same act — but it does not appear (and the burden is on the plaintiffs) that it involved the immovables in question, and at any rate this attribution incurs the same nullity as the above; c) all the *capital* and *interest* of a *loan* made to his father (and therefore concerning a sum of money) to which the nullity threatened by art. 698 applies with regard to the interest and that threatened by art. 692, 2nd para., applies with regard to the capital.

Consequently, on the basis of the subsequent disposition (number 2) of Vivian Henry's will, which attributed all the remainder of his property of any kind (and therefore including immovables) to his wife "in an *absolute manner*," the rights of ownership over the immovables in question which were part of his patrimony under Benjamin James' will passed by succession to *Maria Bashfields Piercy*, who thus succeeded her husband in co-ownership with Vera Norina Piercy of the complex of the deceased Major Piercy's patrimony. But no share of ownership, full or bare, passed to Daphne Hardwick by effect of Vivian Henry's will and death. Since Vivian attributed no such right over his property to his mother, it only remains to see whether, on the basis of Benjamin James' will, which gave the mother a usufruct over all his property "*both actually possessed by him and reversionary to him*," the usufruct attributed to Vivian Henry over one-third of Major Piercy's patrimony by the paternal will is wholly reunited to the bare ownership (after Benjamin's death such third going half to Vera Norina and half to Vivian Henry and then to his heir, Maria Luisa Bashfields) or whether instead only that half destined to go to Vera Norina is then reunited with ownership, while Benjamin James' share goes to increase Daphne Beatrice Hardwick's usufruct over the property whose bare ownership is already in Benjamin.

But this problem is not important for the purposes of the present decision on recovery of the lands. In any case Daphne Beatrice Piercy cannot, on the basis of the three wills here examined, claim any right other than a greater or smaller usufruct over the immovables in question. Conversely, it is firmly established that the ownership of these immovables, burdened with the usufruct, belongs in common to the two said plaintiffs, in the proportion of their respective rights resulting from the three wills. It therefore follows that while Antony Fitzivian's action for recovery is without merit, the demand of Vera Norina Piercy and Maria Luisa Bashfields is well founded. They rightly complain that E.T.F.A.S. proceeded against Daphne Hardwick to expropriate lands belonging to them, and that as legatee of a usufruct over a share of these lands, Daphne was not holder of the right of ownership which was subjected to expropriation by the defendant Agency.

The proper objects of expropriation under art. 4 of the Law of October 21, 1950, n. 841 and subsequent provisions, by which the Government has been delegated authority to order individual expropriations with decrees having the force of law under art. 5 of the same law, are the *private owners of the land* comprising the territory affected by such expropriation, not the holders of possible *in rem* rights burdening the ownership of the land. Such rights are shifted to the person indemnified (art. 1020 C.C. and art. 9, Law of May 12, 1950, n. 230).

Therefore, we accept the first argument of the plaintiffs, Vera Norina Piercy Mameli, and Maria Luisa Bashfields Piercy, that the decree expropriating the lands in question is unconstitutional because it exceeded the limits of the legislative delegation in bringing expropriation against improper parties, injuring these plaintiffs' perfect right of ownership, and that consequently the decree of expropriation must be set aside and held of no validity and these plaintiffs must be declared owners of the lands in question, *pro indiviso*, each in the manner and within the limits indicated *supra*, subject to the widow Daphne Beatrice Hardwick Piercy's usufruct. As a consequence of the disapplication of the decree of expropriation the rights of the plaintiffs and the corresponding obligations of the defendant to restore the expropriated lands must be declared with a merely declarative judgment.

Art. 4 of the Law of March 20, 1865, which prohibits an ordinary judge from revoking or modifying the provision of an administrative act, which can be revoked or modified only by the competent administrative authorities, does not prevent a complete judgment in this case. This prohibition does, it is true, prevent an ordinary judge from pronouncing such a judgment against the public administration, and E.T.F.A.S. must be held to be such a legal entity of public law (art. 3 Decree of the President of the Republic, April 27, 1951, n. 215), because of the activities it conducts (arranging programs of detailed mapping and of expropriation, land reclamation, transfer and assignment of land to peasants, related material activities necessary to its functions, such as taking possession of lands), the ends for which it was created (actuation of the agrarian and land reform in Sardinia), its obligation to sue for the realization of these ends, the position of supremacy the law attributes to the Reform Agency over private persons in various aspects of their activity, the controls of public character to which E.T.F.A.S. is subject, etc. But, as is undisputed in doctrine and case law, the rule does not prevent declarative judgments from being rendered against the public administration, which, within the limits of the object of the proceeding, ascertain the existence of a citizen's perfect right and its injury by the public administration and the consequent obligation of the latter (which must conform to the judgment of the tribunals) to eliminate the injury to the subjective right by restoring the proper situation. Although recognition of the right of the plaintiffs to the lands in question also requires the recognition of their right to occupy such lands, this latter right and the Agency's consequent obligation of redelivery cannot be declared specifically (to cover the contingency that the Agency might refuse to redeliver), for which purpose the plaintiffs may have recourse to the Council of State....

Since we have recognized the plaintiffs' right of ownership over the lands in question and their right to possession and enjoyment of the lands, which were illegally possessed by the defendant Agency under an unconstitutional decree of expropriation, it follows that the Agency has the obligation to reimburse these plaintiffs for the income wrongfully received through the wrongful possession, i.e., from Oct. 1953 to the time of redelivery.

The demand for damages from the interruption of the normal functioning of the farming business and the economic hardship and financial difficulties created for the plaintiffs by the occupation of the expropriated lands by the defendant Agency, the Court also finds justified, and therefore E.T.F.A.S. is condemned to the proper indemnification, subject to concrete and effective proof of the injury by the plaintiffs in a prompt liquidation hearing.

The defendant Agency's liability is based, other than on the very general principle of *neminem ledere*, on art. 28 of the Constitution, according to which civil liability for acts in violation of law committed by the functionaries and employees of the public agencies extends to the public entities, without distinction or limits of any kind regarding the nature of the act from which the violation of law derives, and therefore without excluding acts committed in the execution of a law vitiated by unconstitutionality. It cannot be objected that once a decree of expropriation having the force of law is issued the Reform Agency is bound to execute it and that therefore the consequences of an act of the legislature cannot fall on the Agency. It is easy to counter that if the judge has been given the power to declare a claim based on an unconstitutional law void because of the unconstitutionality of the law itself, then no one, not even the public administration, has the legal power to apply the unconstitutional law and to litigate in conformity with its precepts and that, in substance, even the public administration has the power, in order to determine its course of action, to challenge the constitutionality of the law.

Thus nothing prohibited E.T.F.A.S. from refusing to put the impugned decree of expropriation into operation once the plaintiffs had notified it of the unconstitutionality of the decree in exceeding the delegation. And if, instead, it wished to follow a different path of behavior, the damage produced to the plaintiffs is a consequence not only of the unconstitutional decree, but also of the voluntary act of the defendant E.T.F.A.S. in executing it — even leaving out of consideration the fact that it was the same E.T.F.A.S. which proposed that the Government expropriate lands from Daphne Hardwick which did not belong to her.

Nor would the contrary, as has been argued by some, follow from the provision of art. 136, para. 1 of the Constitution, according to which laws or acts having the force of law declared unconstitutional by the Constitutional Court cease to have effect the day after publication of the decision. This pertains to the beginning of the cessation of effect *erga omnes* of the unconstitutional law rather than to the effect of the Court's decision, and is not relevant, in the opinion of this Court, to the civil liability for damages caused *medio tempore* by those who, though knowing of the possible or likely unconstitutionality of the law, decided to execute it or to set up an excuse on the basis of the unfounded right.

Nor could the demand for damages be rejected because of the lack of demonstration of the element of fault in E.T.F.A.S.'s act which produced the damages. Even omitting the fact that the element of fault does not have to be proved directly in administrative law, and must be presumed from the violation of any rule which the administrative organs are required to observe, including constitutional provisions, it is easy to deduce the existence of fault from the fact, asserted by the plaintiffs in their pleadings and not contested by the defendant, that E.T.F.A.S. took possession of the immovables notwithstanding the protests of the legitimate owners, and above all from E.T.F.A.S. unfounded resistance in this case despite the production of documents by the plaintiffs demonstrating their right, together with its continuing possession of the lands in question at the present time.

Therefore we also accept plaintiffs' requests with regard to damages.

With regard to Daphne Hardwick's strange request for absolution from further compliance with the judgment in which she voluntarily intervened, we observe that this kind of pronouncement is allowed, especially under the authority of the repealed Code, when the case cannot be decided on its merits or the procedure was not proper, or the decision is extinguished by renunciation or other cause, or else when the plaintiff fails to appear and the defendant asks absolution from observance of the judgment. None of these has occurred in the present case. Because Daphne Hardwick entered the proceeding without opposition as third party plaintiff, did not renounce the proceedings, and the trial terminated with a decision on the merits, she cannot now, at the final hearing, without the consent of her co-parties, who have an interest in her permanence in the proceeding (i.e., E.T.F.A.S.), ask *sic et simpliciter* to be excluded from the judgment and absolved from its observance.

Therefore this request is not accepted.

The costs and fees as between the two victorious plaintiffs and the defendant E.T.F.A.S. follow the defeat.

In the relations between the defendant and the plaintiff, Antony Fitzivian, and the defendant and the intervenor, each will bear his own expenses, since with regard to the relations between the first two, Antony Fitzivian's unfounded claim did not appreciably aggravate E.T.F.A.S.'s expenses, and with regard to the relation of the latter, considering that the intervenor did not put forward any substantive claims against E.T.F.A.S., the latter was not truly defeated by her, and vice versa, and on the other hand her intervention did not cause the defendant any noticeable aggravation of expense.

Finally, since the judgment on the principal claims of the plaintiffs is declarative and not susceptible to forced execution against the defendant public agency, the request for provisional execution must be denied.

NOTES AND QUESTIONS

1. It may be helpful to diagram the cast of characters in *Piercy v. E.T.F.A.S.*

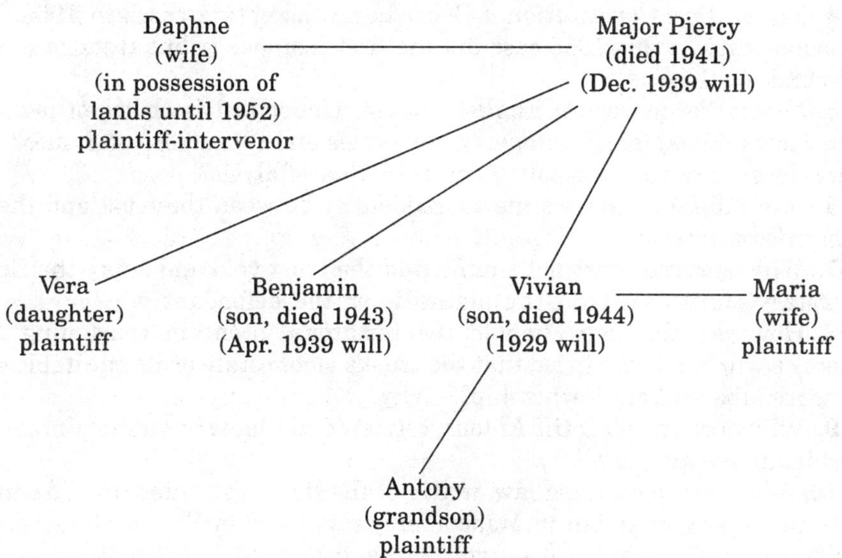

The three wills resulted in the following:

Piercy's will

Trustees: Daphne (W), Vera (D), and Benjamin (S).
Beneficiaries to income (usufructs): Vera (D), Benjamin (S), and Vivian (S), with Antony (GS) as contingent beneficiary.
Beneficiaries to corpus (ownership): Vera (D) and Benjamin (S).
Legacy usufruct to the villa: Daphne (W).

Benjamin's will

Corpus interest: passed to Vivian and Vera.
Income interest: passed to Daphne.

Vivian's will

Corpus interest (via Benjamin): passed to his wife Maria.
Income interest: passed to Vera and Benjamin's successors (due to failure of successive usufruct).

2. Why would Major Piercy and his family have executed wills of this kind? Surely any Italian lawyer could have told them that Italian law did not recognize a number of the interests these wills sought to create. The wills read as though they were drafted by a London solicitor. Is it possible that they were so drafted? Was Major Piercy one of those wonderful people one thought existed only in fiction, who believed that "God is an Englishman"?

3. What is the central underlying issue in this case for the court to decide? Why was it useful for Daphne Hardwick to intervene? What role does Major Piercy's will play in resolving this issue?

4. The Italian Constitutional Court began accepting cases in 1956. What responsibility in this 1955 case did the first instance tribunal judge have for constitutional issues?

5. Major Piercy was an English citizen. Under Italy's choice of law rules, what law applied for: (1) property law issues and (2) succession issues? What part does Italy's public policy serve in this analysis?

6. What differences does the court identify between the trust and the Italian *fedecommesso*?

7. Why does the court not simply find the trust void and apply the English intestacy statute? Would the plaintiffs or the defendant win?

8. How can the court uphold the testator's intent in construing Major Piercy's will? Is it convinced that the trust's legal estate or its equitable estate is more like Italian "ownership?" Why?

9. Why does the plaintiff Antony Fitzivian not have a valid claim for ownership in the property?

10. What is the common law analog of the Italian statutes invalidating the gifts to Antony Fitzivian in Major Piercy's will and in Vivian Henry Piercy's will? *See* Italian Civil Code arts. 692 and 698.

11. What difference does it make, in the present action, whether or not Antony Fitzivian acquired part ownership of the land in question?

12. Why does the court declare the expropriation decree unconstitutional? Do you follow the explanation of why the court had power to issue a declaratory judgment and to award damages but lacked power to declare the action of E.T.F.A.S. void?

13. Does this decision advance or retard the policy of agrarian reform in Italy? Would a contrary decision have made it easier or more difficult to evade the statutory intention to break up large holdings?

NOTE ON THE REGISTRATION OF RIGHTS

In most civil law jurisdictions registration supplements the civil codes as a mechanism for the creation of legal relationships (constitutive registration) and for proof (notice-giving registration). The Japanese, for example, like some other civil law jurisdictions, have three registries: immovable property, family, and commercial. The registration of rights in immovables gives notice and establishes priority in the event of transfers. Registration thus in effect "creates" property rights in that registered rights are effective against unregistered claimants and those in subordinate priority. Provisions in the Japanese Immovable Property Registration Law that permit the registration of contingent contractual rights in real property in effect allow the creation by contract of new forms of security interests that are today recognized and regulated by statute. The registration of rights under lease contracts similarly had the effect of converting a contractual lease into a usufruct.

Family registration in Japan is constitutive. Thus the legal relationships of marriage, divorce, and adoption are actually formed by registration. As a result, no judicial acts are necessary, and, under current law, each of these familial relationships can be formed with the voluntary consent of the parties involved. For an insightful description of family registration and some of the contemporary issues it poses, see Taimie L. Bryant, *For the Sake of the Country, For the Sake of the Family: The Oppressive Impact of Family Registration on Women and Minorities in Japan*, 39 UCLA L. Rev. 109 (1991). On adoption, see *id., Sons and Lovers, Adoption in Japan*, 38 Am. J. Comp. L. 299 (1990).

D. THE USE OF CIVIL LAW GENERAL PRINCIPLES: TORT AND CONTRACT IN JAPAN

1. PRECONTRACTUAL LIABILITY

SHOJI KAWAKAMI, PRECONTRACTUAL LIABILITY: JAPAN, in PRECONTRACTUAL LIABILITY: REPORTS TO THE XIIIth CONGRESS OF THE INTERNATIONAL ACADEMY OF COMPARATIVE LAW 205-21 (E.H. Hondius ed. 1990)

"Freedom of contract" is one of the basic principles of contract law in Japan like in other western countries. According to this principle, parties should be able to negotiate freely, at their own risk, and to use diplomacy in order to effect the most profitable transaction. Of course, the negotiations must be fair, but, in the business world, beating the competition by means of one's power of discernment, as well as one's power to bargain and to make decisions, and using relatively accurate and superior information is proof of one's ability, rather than something to be blamed for. Also, properly speaking, parties should be free to break off or discontinue their preliminary negotiations at any time until the contract has been concluded, without being held liable. In other words, until the moment when the contract is actually concluded, parties should be free to "vacillate" between the various possibilities to invest their goods in order to guarantee maximization of their respective commodities. So, generally speaking, the precontractual stage between starting negotiations and concluding the contract has been a legally neutral zone for a long time.

In the 1960s, some district courts started to impose several duties based on good faith between the parties negotiating a contract. They allowed plaintiffs a claim for damages caused by precontractual misconduct of the other party. At first, most cases concerned contracts which had somehow or other been concluded, so the litigants did not object to the contract itself. Notwithstanding the conclusion of a contract, some of the conditions the court had declared indispensable in order to prevent the other party to suffer damages, had not been fulfilled properly due to the misconduct of one of the parties. These conditions are clearly indicated in one judgment.[a]

> If, during the preparations of the contract, one of the contracting parties makes illegitimate statements contrary to good faith about facts which are important and significant for the decision-making of the other party

[a]*Arima v. Den'en Chōfu Sky Mansion Y.K.*, Hanrei Times (No. 307) 246 (Tokyo Dist. Ct., January 25, 1974).

(and these facts need not necessarily relate to the contents of the contract itself), and if these statements lead the second party to enter into a contractual relation which causes him to suffer damages, or if one of the contracting parties deliberately or negligently fails in his duty to inquire, notify or explain matters as obliged by good faith, causing the second party to enter into contractual relations and to suffer damages, the first party will be liable for compensation of these damages, even though the contract was effectively concluded....

The number of cases in which parties could eventually not reach an agreement for one reason or another, but one of the parties suffered damages caused by the other and consequently sued him, has increased gradually since 1975.

Some 30 cases have been reported, including 2 cases of the Supreme Court,[b] and now the duty to bargain in good faith during the precontractual phase has secured a firm foothold. Among academics as well, there has been a growing interest and the subject is discussed eagerly in several treatises and papers.

Thus, a rather opaque area between a concluded contract and no contract at all has been created.

Usually, most cases concerning precontractual liability have been dealt with under the heading of "Good faith during the preparatory stage of the contract" (*Keiyaku junbi dankai nu okeru shingisoku*) in the case reports, treatises and textbooks. Of course, with reference to comparative law, these articles sometimes discuss this subject using the traditional framework of *Culpa in contrahendo* (*Keiyaku teiketsu jo no kashitsu*), and recently some have been indicating the intimate relationship with "promissory estoppel" (*Yakusoku teki kinhangen*).

Legislation

Except for fraud and duress (§ 96), the Japanese Civil Code has no regulation which specifically extends to precontractual negotiations. The conclusion of a contract is based on the traditional theory of demand and supply/offer and acceptance, and is regulated by only a few provisions concerning pre-engagement (§§ 556, 557). However, there are some special laws which, according to the nature of the object of the contract and/or the parties (e.g. real estate transactions, travel agencies, consumer trading/retail etc.), oblige traders to give their customers regular information in writing during the negotiations and which prohibit misrepresentation, unfair invitation, unjust means of sale and so on. The number of this special type of legal regulations is increasing.

Judicial Development

It is remarkable that the judiciary has been imposing new duties on precontractual bargaining despite the absence of specific legislation in the Civil Code.

---

[b] *Ikeda v. Kadoya*, Hanrei Times (No. 542) 200 (Sup. Ct., September 18, 1984); *Tahira K.K. v. Tahara*, Hanrei Jihō (No. 1082) 47 (Sup. Ct., April 19, 1983).

The cases concerning a breach of duties during the preparatory stages can be grouped into two classes. First, there are the cases when a contract has been concluded. Second, the cases in which the negotiations reached a deadlock and parties did not come to an agreement.

Cases in Which a Contract Was Concluded

In some of the cases, the parties' duty to inquire, notify or explain, as obliged by good faith, and the requirements of fair dealing were taken into consideration, especially if after the concluding of the contract some conditions or formal requirements were clarified or proven unfulfilled, or in case the acts performed did not correspond with one party's expectations as shaped by the inadequate information given by the other. A breach of these duties leads to liability for compensation of damages based on "*Culpa in Contrahendo.*"

For example, cases admitting the claim for damages include[1] Tokyo Dist. Court, 22 June 1959 (concerning the sale of a building on rented ground, when the vendor negligently failed to get the legally required consent of the landowner, and thus, the contract was not fulfilled),[2] Fukuoka High Court, 17 January 1972 (concerning the sale of farmland when the buyer immoderately drove the vendor to prepare the performance without the legally required permission of the prefectural governor).

In some cases the plaintiff's claim was rejected, but in general, rules of good judgment acknowledged the existence of duties during the preparatory stage of the contract. Some examples are[3] Tokyo Dist. Court, 25 January 1974 (concerning the aggravation of daylight and ventilation circumstances after the purchase, due to a tall building to the south),[4] Tokyo Dist. Court, 19 May 1975 (concerning the purchase of land which became unusable under a new land regulation).

In the cases [1] and [2], when liability was accepted, the damages suffered were caused by reliance on the maintenance of a valid contract, so-called "reliance interest." Although usually the compensation for reliance interest damages requires that the plaintiff is innocent without negligence, the court did not necessarily adhere to this theory in each case and furthermore, there was a tendency to take "contributory negligence" (*Kashitsu sosai*) into account.

The nature of this liability is not clear, but some cases mentioned "*Culpa in Contrahendo,*" especially in case [4], this liability was declared contractual. This interpretation expands the time range covered by contractual liability which could be based on the completed contract.

Case [1]: *Fuji Kenchiku K.K. v. Kikuchi*, 10(6) Kakyū minshū 1318 (Tokyo Dist. Ct., June 22, 1959).

Case [2]: *Kiyota v. Yoshiyama*, Hanrei Jihō (No. 671) 49 (Fukuoka High Ct., January 17, 1972).

Case [3]: *Arima v. Den'en Chōfu Y.K.*, Hanrei Times (No. 307) 246 (Tokyo Dist. Ct., January 25, 1974).

Case [4]: *K.K. Tōto Kigyō*, Hanrei Jihō (No. 806) 62 (Tokyo Dist. Ct., May 19, 1975).

Failed Negotiation

In case of failed negotiation, the duties to inquire, notify or explain as obliged by good faith, are acknowledged and parties must take care (especially when notifying or warning) not to damage the property of the other because of reliance interest. In addition, in accordance with some cases, "a duty to negotiate faithfully towards a conclusion of contract" was imposed upon the negotiating parties once the negotiations had proceeded in earnest, and when negotiations had reached a serious stage close to the conclusion of the contract, parties have "a duty to commit themselves in good faith to complete the contract."...

The nature of the claim was explained in various ways, perhaps influenced by the reasoning of the claim, but roughly as follows: a few cases mention contractual liability ... (in [one case] the breach of duty to negotiate faithfully based on a provisional contract was interpreted as a breach of contract), but most cases relied on tort.... There are also cases which indicate the existence of "special liability based on good faith, neither on contract nor on tort" ... or "liability based on reliance interest which is analogous to contract."... In general, it can be said that courts tend to treat precontractual liability like tort liability....

The damages suffered in these cases were mainly caused by "reliance interest," by believing the deal would be completed in the future, but the courts did not necessarily require the plaintiff to be innocent and without negligence. Although in no case yet have damages for expectation interest been admitted, it is noteworthy that some of the cases included additional consolation money (*solatium: isharyo*), ... and some cases took contributory negligence into account.... These tendencies may be the result of the difficulties, not only in assessing the damages, but also in establishing whether or not the reliance was reasonable. This kind of decision should be possible on the basis of careful consideration of many factors and interests including the behaviour of each party, financial affairs, etc. Therefore, the requirement of innocence without negligence should be abandoned and "absence of serious negligence" will probably prove to be the practical requirement.

2. INFORMED CONSENT

CIVIL CODE OF JAPAN

Articles 1, 415, 643-645, 656, 709

Enjoyment of Private Rights[a]

Article 1. 1. Private rights shall be exercised in conformity with the public welfare.

2. The exercise of rights and the performance of duties shall be carried out in conformity with the principles of good faith and trust.

3. No abuse of rights shall be permitted.

---

[a] Book I (General Provisions), chapter I (Persons), section I.

Effect of Obligations[b]

Article 415. If an obligor does not perform according to the true intents and purposes of his obligation the obligee may demand damages. The same applies where it has become impossible to effect performance for a cause imputable to the obligor.

Mandates[c]

Article 643. A mandate takes effect when one party commissions the other party to perform a juristic act and such other party accepts the commission.

Article 644. A mandatory is bound to deal with the matter(s) entrusted according to the true purport of the mandate and with the care of a good manager.

Article 645. A mandatory must report on the matter(s) entrusted at any time upon demand of the mandator, and after the termination of the mandate he must, without delay, give a report of its particulars.

Article 656. The provisions of this Section apply *mutatis mutandis* to the commissioning of matters other than juristic acts.

Delicts[d]

Article 709. A person who intentionally or negligently has infringed upon the rights of another person is liable for the resulting damages.

HIROYUKI HATTORI ET AL., THE PATIENT'S RIGHT TO INFORMATION IN JAPAN: LEGAL RULES AND DOCTORS' OPINIONS, 32 Social Science & Medicine 1007-10 (1991)

The Japanese approach to ethical issues in health care has been characterized by the Japanese cultural values of consensus and deference to authority. For example, the late Japanese Emperor Hirohito passed away in early 1989 apparently without ever realizing he had intestinal cancer, thus vividly illustrating the extent to which patients in Japan are deliberately left ignorant of their health condition. Whether the patient be royalty or an ordinary citizen, Japanese doctors still believe disclosure of terminal cancer will cause unnecessary grief.

However, with the remarkable development of medical science and technology, philosophical and moral attitudes toward what is considered appropriate medical care or conduct have changed considerably. Issues in medical law and ethics, such as informed consent, have become topics of heated discussion among medical and legal specialists, as well as among the general public. Physicians and lawyers tend to hold widely divergent views on medico-legal issues, and this has contributed to making medical malpractice suits difficult to settle....

[T]he traditional relationship between physician and patient, which is closely akin to the teacher-student relationship in Japan and involves great

---

[b] Book III (Obligations), chapter I (General Provisions), section II.

[c] Book III (Obligations), chapter II (Contracts), section X.

[d] Book III (Obligations), chapter V.

deference to the physician's advice and decisions, has thus been rapidly vanishing. For example, even when a physician has conducted a proper medical examination and dispensed appropriate treatment, his patient may complain of less than satisfactory medical service due to the lack of personal rapport between physician and patient. This has led to an increasing number of medical malpractice suits ....

Heavily influenced by German civil law theory, the concept of informed consent in Japan appears in bifurcated form as "Aufklärungspflicht" (physician's duty of disclosure) and "Einstimmung" (patient's consent). As far as legal theory is concerned in Japan, a number of possible sources of the legal duties regarding informed consent with respect to the physician-patient relationship have been identified and discussed by scholars. First, in general, any touching of a person can constitute battery in criminal law unless there has been consent. In the context of medical treatment, the consent of the patient justifies the invasion of his physical integrity, provided that the patient is given a full explanation by his physician. Secondly, the failure to use reasonable care in the conduct of one's activities, resulting in harm to others, constitutes negligence. In an informed consent case, negligence involves not the manner in which the physician performs a medical procedure, diagnoses illness or prescribes medication, etc., but in his making a deficient disclosure to the patient. Third, the arrangement between physician and patient is viewed as a special type of contractual relationship. The contract is usually implied from the actions of the parties and is not expressed in written contractual terms *per se*. The relationship has been interpreted as a kind of "quasi-mandate," which is one of the enumerated contract types in the Japanese Civil Code concerning an affair other than a juristic act (Art. 656, Japanese Civil Code). Article 645 of the Japanese Civil Code states that on demand of the mandator (in this case, the patient), the mandatory (the physician) must at any time report the condition of business under his management. The mandatory must also report full particulars upon termination of the mandate. Hence, Article 645, which sets forth the "quasi-mandate" relationship, could thus be considered as one of the legal sources of informed consent.

In most medical malpractice suits, the physician's duty to inform is derived, however, from Article 23 of the Medical Practitioner Act. Article 23 reads:

> A physician who diagnoses a patient must prescribe the necessary treatment, and give any other instruction needed for promoting health, either to the patient himself/herself or his/her guardian.

This article is closely related to the physician's duty to give proper instructions for treatment and addresses the physician's advice regarding such matters as drug administration, drinking and exercise, and contraindications for treatment purposes....

In the past, most medical malpractice trials involved malpractice with respect to the actual performance of medical examination and treatment. However, ever since Professor Koichi Bai introduced the West German legal concept of informed consent into Japanese academic legal theory in 1970, the number of medical malpractice suits alleging the physician's breach of duty to obtain informed consent has increased steadily. According to the Yamashita report, the ratio of the number of suits alleging breach of the duty to obtain informed consent to the total number of malpractice suits exceeded 10%.

In one celebrated case, a young lady was informed by her physician that she had mammary cancer of her right breast and she consented to an operation to remove the breast. However, during the operation, mastopathy was found in the left breast. The physician performed a mastectomy without the patient's consent, believing that the mastopathy had carcinogenic potential. In this case, a Japanese court held for the first time that the operation without consent constituted an illegal physical injury to the patient.

Then, in 1981, the Japanese Supreme Court finally discussed informed consent in the context of medical malpractice.... A 10 year old boy by chance fell down on the pavement while riding a bicycle and injured his head in the temporal area. A depressed bone fracture was observed. Although an operation was performed to remove the suspected bone fragment from the brain, the boy died of heart failure due to massive brain hemorrhage. The court held that the content of the operation and the risk involved must be explained to the patient or to his or her legal proxy by the attending surgeon. Furthermore, if there exist indefinite factors such as the present symptoms and their etiology, the level of improvement expected by the operation, as well as the exact prognosis and risks if the operation is not performed, then, the physician need not explain the level of assessment in the causative symptom and the preparation to cope with the situation. The medical act taken by the physician includes a series of procedures involving objective assessment and medical judgment of the symptoms and selection of the best available medical treatment. The court also noted that there is always some variability between the appearance of the symptoms and progression of the disease. In light of these facts, this ruling has been interpreted as meaning that the duty of a physician to inform a patient of his condition should be confined to those situations in which the factors involved in a particular condition are to a considerable extent clearly understood, and in which the course and prognosis of the disease are definite.

Generally speaking, a physician's civil liability arises when an obligation to the patient is not fulfilled. In most cases, the same fault may constitute both a breach of contract and the commission of a tort, assuming that the fault is a breach of duty owed to the patient. In Japan, a physician's liability has traditionally been perceived and pursued under the rubric of tort. Under Article 709 of the Japanese Civil Code governing tort liability and jurisprudence thereunder, the plaintiff must prove the requisite factors to establish liability, namely, proof of negligence and causation that the damage resulted from the negligence alleged. However, because medical knowledge is very specialized, it is often very difficult for patients to know in detail the state of their illness and the kind of treatment prescribed by the physicians. It is therefore very onerous for a patient to prove a negligent medical act and the existence of a causal relationship between the act and the alleged injury. In Japan, for reasons related to the patient's limited access to information discussed below, the traditional burden of proof is almost impossible for a patient-plaintiff to meet.

Legal theoreticians have proposed a number of ways to circumvent this difficulty. It has been proposed, for instance, that a physician's liability should be viewed as contractual. According to the Japanese Civil Code (Art. 415), the patient has only to prove a breach of contract to establish the liability of the physician. The courts have also held physicians liable in cases which distinguish between the physician's obligation to produce a particular result as fulfillment of the contract (result obligation), and the physician's obligation to use his best efforts to attain a certain goal (effort obligation). According to the concept of effort obligation, the physician is not liable for unsuccessful results by reason that he followed established medical standards, and, therefore, he used his best efforts.

Ultimately, due to the difficulty of determining the terms of the contract between physician and patient, the burden of proving a breach of contract has proven just as difficult as that needed to prove a tortious medical act.

Another approach would shift the burden of proof to the physician or hospital. One possible method for shifting the burden of proof in favor of the patient is to impose a rebuttable presumption of causation, when a "prima facie case" has been made ... by the plaintiff. This view states that a causal relationship could be inferred by indirect facts and experiential presumption on this point. In judicial context, as seen in "prima facie case" or presumptive evidence, a fact is presumed to be true and sufficient to sustain a judgment unless the fact is contradicted or rebutted by other evidence. Therefore, the physician must make it clear that what happened did not form an unlawful act [tort] on his/her part, but resulted from another cause. Otherwise, the physician should be blamed for a negative medical treatment.

However, if a causal relationship cannot be established, the concept of informed consent has been used as one method to surmount, or at least circumvent the proof problem inherent in a claim, whether in tort or contract, alleging faulty performance of a medical act *per se*. An informed consent approach shifts the focus from the physician's act *per se* to the physician's level of disclosure and failure to attain informed consent.

3. NEGLIGENCE

WATANABE v. CHISSO K.K. (THE KUMAMOTO MINAMATA DISEASE CASE)

Kumamoto District Court
Decision of 20 March 1973
Hanrei Jihō (no. 696) 15, Hanrei Kōgaihō 1641

English translation published in Julian Gresser, Koichiro Fujikura & Akio Morishima, Environmental Law in Japan 86, 91-96 (1981).

III. *The Defendant's Liability (Negligence)*

(A) As noted above, the defendant's factory began the production of acetaldehyde for use in the manufacture of an acetic acid compound in 1932. As the demand increased, the defendant gradually increased production. Production particularly increased each postwar year after 1946. The amount of wastewater discharged from the factory consequently also increased markedly after this year. It has been clearly demonstrated that the plaintiffs, as is noted for each individual in part VI, were stricken with Minamata disease from 1953 to 1961 as a result of exposure to discharged wastewater containing dimethyl mercury compounds.

The plaintiffs' contentions, set forth as follows, assume that a discharge of contaminated wastewater is permitted only when its safety is assured. As long as it is foreseeable that discharges of contaminated water could result in injury to another's legally protected interests, there is a duty to ascertain beforehand whether such discharges are poisonous in content and to assure that the wastewater is harmless. Since the defendant was able to foresee the risk and failed to take precautions, it cannot escape liability for negligence. The defendant answers that until the middle of 1962, when it was detected and confirmed at the medical school of Kumamoto University, the fact that methyl mercury chloride, CH_3HgCl, the causal substance of the disease, would be produced in the production process of acetaldehyde was totally unknown by the chemical industry and academicians. The defendant contends that it therefore follows that it could not have known of the existence of a dimethyl mercury compound in its wastewater, the process of its accumulation in fish and shellfish, or that residents who consumed these fish would contract Minamata disease. The defendant argues that there should be no liability for negligence where there was no foreseeability of the consequences.

(B) Since the production process of the chemical industry generally utilizes large quantities of dangerous substances such as raw materials and catalysts, there is an extremely high probability that unpredictably harmful by-products such as unreacted materials, catalytic agents, intermediate products, or the finished product itself will be in the factory's wastewater. When these dangerous materials are discharged into the rivers and seas, harm to plants, animals, or people can be easily anticipated. Therefore when a chemical plant discharges wastewater, it must always use the best knowledge and technology to determine whether harmful substances are present and what effect there might be on plants, animals, and humans. In addition to assuring the safety of its wastewater, if by any chance harm becomes apparent or there arises doubt about its safety, the factory should immediately suspend operations and adopt the necessary maximum preventive measures. Especially with regard to the life and health of area residents, the factory must exercise a high degree of care to prevent harm before it happens. It must bear alone the obligation of guaranteeing the safety of the lives and health of residents since there is no way for residents to know what or how things are produced or what kind of wastewater is being discharged. Certainly the factory did not tell them. After all, no factory of whatever kind should pollute or destroy the environment through its operation; even less should it infringe on the health and lives of the residents or allow them to be sacrificed.

The defendant claims that foreseeability is limited to the foreseeability of the production of the specific causal agent and contends that it did not violate any duty since it could not possibly have foreseen this specific outcome. But if one were to proceed along these lines, the degree of danger could only be proven after the environment was polluted and destroyed and lives and health of people harmed. Until that point, the discharge of dangerous wastewater would have to be tolerated. The inevitable consequence would be that the encroachment on the lives and health of residents could not be stopped. Since this would be tantamount to allowing the residents to be human experiments, it is clearly unjust.

[The court notes that the amount of production of acetaldehyde and vinyl chloride increased greatly during the 1950s, and that the defendant's factory became one of the leading chemical plants in Japan by its use of the most advanced technology in the field. As the defendant's facilities were enlarged and its production expanded, so also did the risk of dangerous substances forming in the production process and mixing in the discharged wastewater increase every year.]

In order to comply with the high degree of care expected of one of the nation's leading chemical synthesis plants, the defendant should have conducted continuous research and investigation. At the same time that it should have frequently analyzed and investigated the quality of its wastewater to ensure its safety, it should have studied the topography, tides, etc., of Minamata Bay into which the wastewater was being discharged and noted any changes therein. It cannot be denied that the defendant was expected to assure the complete safety of its wastewater.

[From the submitted evidence and testimony of witnesses, the court found that, had the defendant researched available technical literature carefully, it could have learned even before 1955 that a methyl mercury compound soluble in water might be formed in the production process of acetaldehyde. The court found that the defendant should have known from its own experience that unexpected by-products were often formed by chemical reactions in the production process. The court found no evidence that the defendant researched available literature on the catalytic function of mercury before 1959. Occasionally, the defendant had analyzed wastewater discharged from its factory for the purpose of improving the efficiency of the production process or of ascertaining whether it complied with administrative regulations for pH, suspended solids, biochemical oxygen demand (BOD), chemical oxygen demand (COD), and dissolved oxygen. The court emphasized that the defendant had failed to undertake the necessary measures to ensure public health and safety.]

Despite the fact that the defendant's factory had some of the best equipment and technology in the nation, it had failed to comply with the required standard of care before heedlessly discharging its wastewater. It can be held liable for negligence on this point alone.

(C) We will now examine how the defendant reacted to events like the observable changes in the environment, disputes over compensation for the fishing industry, research into the cause of Minamata disease, treatment of factory wastewater, and animal (cat) experiments. We examine the defendant's behavior concerning these matters as factors in our decision on the issue of negligence.

1. *Unusual Changes in the Environment.* The amount of fish caught drastically decreased in and around Minamata Bay between 1953 and 1954. Fish such as snapper, gray mullet, and scabbard were often observed floating dead in the bay. From 1954 to 1956 many cats in the villages around the bay

[names omitted] died with symptoms of nerve damage. In those three years more than fifty cats died, some pigs and dogs displaying similar symptoms died, and in some areas birds became unable to fly or walk and dropped dead. These unusual and strange phenomena became almost common occurrences....

2. *Disputes over Compensation for Damages to Fisheries....*

3. *Efforts to Determine the Cause of the Disease.* As we have already mentioned, after 1956 the defendant's plant came under strong suspicion because its discharge water was viewed as connected with the occurrence of the disease. The defendant, therefore, before anyone else, should have made every effort to investigate and to identify the cause of the disease.... However, the defendant did not undertake any investigation worth noting, and in no instance did it make the results of its investigations public....

Even after Kumamoto University developed the organic mercury theory, there is no indication that the defendant, whose factory used mercury in its production process, made any effort to investigate or to analyze its wastewater [that is, the acetaldehyde and vinyl chloridate wastewater] for the presence of organic mercury compounds.

Moreover, the defendant prolonged the university's efforts to identify the cause of the disease by its unwillingness to disclose an overall picture of its production layout, the processes of the factory, and other relevant information such as materials used, catalytic agents, by-products in the production processes, and the method of wastewater treatment. It is no exaggeration to say that the defendant contributed largely to the growth of the number of Minamata patients. The defendant failed to cooperate with the university teams and failed utterly to take proper independent action to determine the cause of the disease.

4. *The Treatment of Wastewater and the Amount of Mercury Discharged.* According to the testimony of the plant manager, Nishida Eiichi, a total of 60 tons of mercury was estimated to have been lost by an account made in July, 1959. The basis of this estimate is unclear, but the daily production records reveal that more mercury may have been lost from the factory production process. [During 1954, 38,058 tons of mercury were used in the production process; of this, 28,069 tons were retrieved, meaning that 9,939 tons were lost in the process. During 1955, 51,716 tons were used, 39,701 tons retrieved, and 12,015 tons lost.] In October 1969, Professor Namba of Kumamoto University Medical School estimated that a total of 600 tons of mercury had been discharged in wastewater from the defendant's factory. The total amount of mercury discharged, if 600 tons is exaggerated, clearly exceeded by far the 60 tons estimated by the defendant. The defendant cannot escape criticism that in order to protect itself it made a too conservative, and even misleading, estimate of mercury used and lost.

5. *Experiments on Cats, Especially Cat Number 400.* [As noted above, some factory hospital doctors with the cooperation of the factory's engineering department undertook an experiment of feeding cats with fish caught in the bay. In the middle of 1959 they adopted a direct feeding method where cats were fed with food soaked with water discharged from different production processes such as acetaldehyde and vinyl chloride. The experiment continued

until December 1962, and the number of cats experimented on reached 900. The condition of the cats was observed daily and recorded in detail. Every cat was classified and registered in the so-called cat registry.]

In mid-July 1959 Hosokawa himself took a sample of wastewater from the mouth of the acetaldehyde plant's discharge pipe and starting on the 21st, poured 20 cc's of it daily on the food for cat number 400. By October 6th or 7th the cat had developed a light paralysis in its hind legs and thereafter Minamata disease symptoms such as spasms, salivation, shivering, dancing, and running in circles appeared. Its weight decreased from 3 kg at the beginning of the experiment to 1.8 kg and it became weaker every day. On October 24, the doctor killed the cat, performed an autopsy, and sent the samples to Kyūshū University for pathological analysis....

[The court notes that Hosokawa testified that he had informed the engineering department of the results of the experiment on cat number 400, and that he was subsequently ordered to terminate direct feeding experiments. Witnesses for the defendant, including personnel employed at the time in the engineering department, strongly denied these allegations. The court noted that the journal of the cat experiments corroborated the termination of direct feeding.]

It is reasonable to assume that the officials of the engineering section were aware of the fact that cat number 400 was directly fed food soaked with the discharged water from the acetaldehyde plant and that it had developed symptoms almost identical to those of Minamata disease....

We find that at least those who were in the engineering section of the defendant's factory knew the results of the experiment on cat number 400 by October 1959. On November 30 the chief of the section ordered the termination of that experiment. Since the results of the experiment on cat number 400 were not made public, the researchers of Kumamoto University Medical School were misled as to the direction of their research. The termination of Hosokawa's experiment clearly delayed the identification of the cause of Minamata disease. The defendant's responsibility on this point is extremely grave. Even if those in the engineering section did not in fact know the result of the experiment on cat number 400 and did not order the experiment terminated, if they regarded the experiments as important and were following their progress, they could have known about cat number 400. In fact they should have directed and promoted such experiments themselves and by doing so made every effort to find and identify the cause. By failing to do so, the defendant cannot escape liability.

(D) We summarize here what we stated under headings B and C. The defendant's factory was a leading chemical plant with the most advanced technology and facilities. As such, the defendant should have diligently researched the relevant literature and should have assured the safety of its wastewater before discharge by analyzing it for the presence of hazardous substances. Also the defendant should have cast a watchful eye on the environmental conditions of the area into which the discharged water flowed and noted any changes therein. Defendants should have made sure that no harm whatsoever came to the residents in the area from the discharged water. Had the defendant not failed to exercise this duty, it would have been possible to foresee the risk from the discharged water to humans and other living things. The defendant could have prevented the occurrence of Minamata disease or at least have kept it at a minimum. We cannot find that the defendant took any of the precautionary measures called for in this situation whatsoever. There were many signs, such as strange environmental phenomena, the fishery disputes over compensation, the investigation into the disease's cause, concern over the waste treatment facilities, and experiments with cats. We cannot find even one measure taken by the defendant that was either adequate or satisfactory. We find absolutely unsupportable the defendant's contentions that factory officials gave full cooperation to the investigation team of Kumamoto University, that management of wastewater was adequate, or that the defendant completely treated these wastes.

Judging from the above, the presumption that the defendant had been negligent from beginning to end in discharging wastewater from its acetaldehyde plant is amply supported. Even if the quality of wastewater was within legal and administrative standards and the facilities and methods of treatment at the defendant's plant were superior to those of other factories in the same industry, it is not enough to overcome this presumption. The discharge of wastewater occurred as a result of the defendant's industrial activity, and the defendant cannot escape liability for negligence in that context.

Therefore the defendant, by the discharge of a dimethyl mercury compound in wastewater from its plant, inflicted Minamata disease on the plaintiffs, thereby imposing on the plaintiffs, victims and their families, the damage described in sec. VI of this opinion. Furthermore, the discharge of wastewater was part of the defendant's industrial activities. This is not a case of vicarious liability of a corporation where a representative agent (art. 44(1)) or employee (art. 715(1)) in the course of performing his duty causes damage to a third person. The defendant company, while engaged in its enterprise, discharged wastewater and thereby became directly liable for damages under art. 709 of the Civil Code.

NOTES AND QUESTIONS

1. To what extent does Professor Kawakami's description of the Japanese courts' use of the "good faith" principle indicate that civil codes are adaptable to changing social conditions and concerns? (Review Chapter 9, Section B.7 for a description of the Japanese courts' use of the "abuse of rights" principle.)

2. Why do Japanese courts construe the physician-patient relationship as a "quasi-mandate" contract to establish a right to informed consent? Why is not article 23 of the Medical Practitioner Law sufficient? What other possible sources for a right to informed consent might be pursued?

3. Article 709 is the basic tort provision of the Japanese Civil Code. Does it allow for strict liability? If not, what alternatives might be possible to establish liability in the absence of proof of negligent or willful conduct? Consider the court's finding of negligence in *Watanabe v. Chisso K.K.* How helpful is this approach in other contexts? What are its limitations?

4. What problems does reliance on general provisions pose for civil law jurisdictions? Are there particular features of the Japanese legal system that make it easier or more appropriate for courts to adapt general code provisions to current circumstances?

Chapter 12

THE FUTURE OF THE CIVIL LAW TRADITION

JOHN HENRY MERRYMAN, THE CIVIL LAW TRADITION: AN INTRODUCTION TO THE LEGAL SYSTEMS OF WESTERN EUROPE AND LATIN AMERICA 151-58 (2d ed. 1985)

We have seen the image of a legal system that emerged from the revolution and legal science: one that contemplated such things as a legal universe inhabited only by the individual and the state; legislative supremacy; a rigorous separation of the judicial from the legislative and administrative powers; a narrowly defined and uncreative judicial role; the denial of *stare decisis*; the primacy of the civil code and of civil law scholarship; a highly developed and coherent conceptual structure; and a constant preoccupation with certainty. We have also seen a number of the ways in which this nineteenth-century model has been subjected to criticism and erosion in modern civil law nations. In this chapter we look further at the process of erosion and describe what appears to be a fundamental transformation now taking place in the civil law tradition. That transformation is symbolized in part by the decline of civil codes, in part by the rise of constitutions, and in part by the growth of European federalism. These associated tendencies toward the "decodification," "constitutionalization," and "federalization" of the civil law tradition seem to be irreversible. They also seem to have substantial momentum, indicating that they will continue to affect the development of the civil law tradition in the foreseeable future. We begin with decodification.

"Special legislation," in the civil law world, refers to laws that grow up around the codes and regulate topics that articles of the codes themselves treat. That there are large bodies of special legislation supplementing the civil codes is easily verified by a look at any major civil law jurisdiction. Some of this legislation merely elucidates matters governed by code provisions, completing and clarifying the original code design. But the great bulk of it does something quite different: it sets up special legal regimes, "microsystems of law," that differ ideologically from the code and in this sense are incompatible with it. Labor law provides a familiar and significant example. In the classic civil codes, the "labor relation" is treated as merely one variety of contract between individuals exercising liberty of contract; labor contracts are not greatly different from other contracts, except that here money is exchanged for labor, rather than for goods or for real estate. But in modern civil law nations, just as in the United States, the central players are big labor and management, not private individuals. Labor legislation has a variety of objectives quite unfamiliar to the regime of the civil codes: the welfare and safety of workers; industrial peace and productivity; regulation of the internal affairs and public accountability of labor unions and employers' associations;

and so forth. Whereas the traditional civil codes left it to private individuals to pursue their own interests, with the state acting largely in the restricted role of a referee, enforcing the rules of the game, the new provisions embody policy choices and are designed to further specific social objectives. The microsystem of labor law is thus fundamentally different in approach and technique from the code provisions for labor contracts.

The labor law example illustrates another aspect of special laws. They are not the agreed products of tranquil reflection by legislators expressing a substantial consensus; they are instead compromises worked out between special interests (here labor and management) in the legislative arena. Legislators of course affect the outcome, but the political and economic power of the partisan interests and the quality of the expertise and advocacy that these interests bring to bear give them a dominant voice. (According to an Italian scholar, the classic civil code provision that "the contract is law for the parties" has been reversed in the case of special legislation to "the law is the contract of the parties.") Since special interests are special, they tend to be interested in their own problems and to have divergent concerns. One result is that special legislation is heterogeneous, diverse, and pluralistic, in contrast to the formal and ideological coherence of the civil code.

Important microsystems of statutory law have grown up on a variety of civil code topics: urban leases, agrarian leases, intellectual property, the formation and conduct of companies, and the marketing and trading of company securities, to name just a few. Such laws are not mere supplements to the code; they are successful competitors to it. (Indeed, it has become common to call such microsystems "codes" — e.g. the French *Code de Travail* — and thus to formalize their rival status.) Cases are decided according to the provisions of the special legislation, not the civil code provisions. As the amount of special legislation grows, the code becomes more and more a body of residual law to be turned to only if some more specific provision of special legislation cannot be found. If we recall that one function of a carefully drafted, substantively coherent civil code was to provide certainty in the law (see Chapter 5), it is apparent that much special legislation impairs the quest for that kind of certainty.

Parallel to the growth of statutory microsystems is the growth of equally important systems of judge-made law. The law of torts under French-style codes is a prominent example, to which we have previously referred. The code provisions are so rudimentary and so empty of substance that judges have had to create the applicable law on a case-by-case basis. The effective law of torts is accordingly not found in the code but outside it, in the widely published, consulted, and cited decisions of the courts. Unlike the legislative process, which proceeds sporadically and in substantial increments, the judicial process is gradual and accretive. Over time, the significance attached to facts and the attitude of judges toward proper outcomes imperceptibly change, and the law also changes. No French or German judge deciding an automobile accident case today can truly ignore the mass phenomenon of the automobile, the inevitability of automobile accidents, or the existence of public liability insurance. As such considerations creep into judicial decisions, the law changes in ways that are analogous to the changes introduced by much special legislation. The new law is fundamentally different in outlook from the premises and objectives of the code.

The number and importance of the microsystems created by special legislation and by judges help us to understand something that often puzzles common lawyers: why civil law jurisdictions — in particular France, with the oldest civil code still in force — retain their old civil codes, rather than replace them with modern ones. In the case of France, one partial answer is that the French are proud of and sentimentally attached to the Code Napoléon. It is a cultural monument. There is bound to be some resistance to proposals to replace it. Even so, there have been two attempts at wholesale revision in this century. The first almost literally came to nothing. The second began bravely, in 1945, with a distinguished commission headed by a respected scholar, and with lots of fanfare, confident speeches, periodic published reports, and partial drafts. Gradually, however, the commission subsided and dropped from public view. Eventually it stopped work entirely and was quietly abolished. Since then the effort has been to amend the code piecemeal, and by now more than a third of the original provisions have been revised, replaced, or simply repealed. The process is done in such a way as to preserve, rather than replace, the monument. The original numbering of articles in the code has been retained, so that the new matter follows the old organization. Even this process has, after a period of fairly rapid activity, begun to slow. Meanwhile the large body of legislative and judicial microsystems of law outside the code remains substantially unaffected by the code revision process.

The reason for this is that the civil code is a coherent expression of a particular ideology.... The microsystems of special legislation outside the code, however, express their own attitudes and values, which are often inconsistent with those of the code. The piecemeal process of revision just described has dealt with the easy parts, with those aspects of the code that can be adapted without undue difficulty to contemporary life. Any attempt to incorporate the body of special legislation into the code faces insuperable problems, of which the most significant may be that the microsystems themselves are often incompatible in outlook. They are also voluminous, and to incorporate them into a civil code would blow the code up to an unmanageable size. The practical solution is to abandon the project for a new civil code and to leave the old one, with its historical dignity and utility as residual law, in place. It is significant that the new civil codes of this century have been adopted in the U.S.S.R. and other socialist nations, where socialist ideology and authoritarian regimes provided the necessary unifying and propelling force; in Fascist Italy, where a quite different authoritarian regime and ideology were at work; and in Greece, where something was badly needed to replace the ninth-century *Basilica* as the primary civil law source.

The decline in legislative supremacy ... has recently taken on an important additional dimension. The reader will recall that legislatures can delegate lawmaking power to the executive, who then, by "legislative decree," actually legislates. This practice has accelerated at an extraordinary rate throughout the civil law world in recent decades, for reasons that seem to reflect a growing inability of representative parliaments to fulfill the roles assigned to them by nineteenth-century ideology. Much contemporary legislation is thus the product not of a popularly elected parliament, but of a less public process conducted within the offices of the executive. What some observers consider to be the next logical step occurred in France with adoption of the Constitution of the Fifth Republic, in 1958. The legislative jurisdiction of parliament, previously unlimited, was sharply reduced by transferring a substantial portion of it to the executive, and a special organ, the Constitutional Council, was provided to ensure that parliament did not exceed its now restricted jurisdiction. The executive exercises his legislative jurisdiction simply by issuing "regulations." To give some idea of the effect of this constitutional alteration, a new French code of civil procedure was adopted by such a regulation. It was not necessary for the parliament to repeal the old code or consent to the new one. The executive regulation alone had the necessary repealing and enacting effect.

A further aspect of the decline of legislatures (and of legislation, including the codes) is found in the growth of public administrations. The people who hold positions in the public administrations interpret laws, issue rules, and make decisions. They form the largest branch of government, which far exceeds in personnel and in volume of business the combined judicial and legislative branches. It is true that administrative officials are in theory subject to the law and cannot legally exceed or misuse the authority given to them. But the same is true of judges, and we have seen how ineffective legislative control is over judicial interpretation. In interpreting and applying laws, issuing regulations, and deciding disputes, administrative officials have an irreducible space for incremental lawmaking. In France and in nations following the French model, alleged excesses and misuses of administrative power are judged not by the legislature or by ordinary judges, but by members of the public administration itself, sitting in a council of state. The council has developed its own body of law, largely independent of legislation, to guide it. In this way administrative law has become detached from its legislative source. It is a rival law that often affects the lives of citizens more directly and profoundly than legislation or litigation.

The outcome of the process of decodification and the decline of legislative authority has been compared by some civil lawyers to the situation in Europe before the revolution .... The law, they say, is once again uncertain, complex, and particular, and thus at odds with the needs for certainty, simplicity, and uniformity. Others see the movement in less alarming terms: the evolution from a monocentric to a polycentric legal system is seen by them as a normal result of the movement toward a more complex, pluralistic, and polycentric society. If laws have a shorter half-life and become more quickly antiquated, this is simply a normal reflection of the increasing pace of social change. In a consumer-oriented, "disposable" society, individual laws, or prevailing interpretations of them, also become disposable.

While legislatures and codes have declined throughout the civil law world, the practice of treating constitutions as the supreme sources of law has grown, as has the range of opportunities to challenge the constitutionality of legislative or other official acts. In Europe the phenomenon has taken the form of new constitutions that provide for the establishment of special tribunals with the power of judicial review — e.g. the Austrian, German, and Italian constitutional "courts," the Spanish constitutional "tribunal," and the French Constitutional Council. In Latin America and Japan, influenced by the United States example, the power of review is generally lodged in national supreme courts, which have long been theoretically capable of a form of judicial review. What is new is the growing extent to which that power is exercised.

In no civil law nation is constitutional review exactly like the review familiar to us (nor are any two review procedures within the civil law world identical). Through the Colombian "popular action" and the German "constitutional complaint," for example, people in those nations have a direct access to judicial review that we do not enjoy. Latin American supreme courts can refuse to apply an unconstitutional statute or can set aside an administrative or judicial action, but they cannot declare an unconstitutional statute void; their decisions are not binding *erga omnes*. The French Constitutional Council, preserving the appearance of a separation of powers, is a nonjudicial body that can prevent the promulgation of an unconstitutional law, but can do nothing about one that has already been promulgated....

Despite these variations, the movement toward constitutionalism displays a number of common features. For one thing, the new constitutionalism has prominently sought to guarantee and to expand individual rights: rights to civil and criminal due process of law; to equality; to freedom of association, movement, expression, and belief; and to education, work, health care, and economic security. The "old" individual rights that were an objective of the revolution and that received their "constitutional" protection in the civil codes — rights of personality, property, and liberty of contract — have to a large extent been achieved and solidified in the work of ordinary courts quietly applying the traditional sources and methods of law. The constitutions are the situs of the new individual rights, and the clash of constitutional litigation is the medium of their definition and enforcement. The rise of constitutionalism is in this sense an additional form of decodification: the civil codes no longer serve a constitutional function. As we have previously remarked, that function has moved from the most private of private law sources — the civil code — to the most public of public law sources — the constitution.

It is clear that the new constitutionalism involves a significant transfer of power and prestige to judges. Admittedly, these judges are not those who staff the ordinary courts (although ordinary judges have also received a portion of this new power), but the very distinction has lost most of its importance. To the ordinary citizen, and to a growing number of scholars, constitutional court decisions are the work of judges who have the power to declare legislation void. There is only a limited and rapidly decreasing nostalgia for legislative supremacy, for the separation of powers, and for a limited judicial role in the legal process. Constitutional decisions are often glamorous, attracting the attention of the public and the media in a way that the decisions of ordinary courts seldom do. Indeed, the tradition is for ordinary judges to avoid excitement, to act as anonymous functionaries obediently applying the legislative will. Constitutional judges, by contrast, are often personalities; their votes and opinions are news, the subject of public debate. Their decisions exhibit a drift away from the conceptual structure and the style of traditional civil law scholarship, employing terms and ideas unfamiliar to legal science (hence they are said to be unscientific, which, in this sense, they are). The loss of "certainty" that follows from decodification is thus magnified by the loss of the logical structure of legal science. In short, every aspect of the traditional image of the legal process ... is impaired by the growth of constitutionalism.

The development of the European Communities and the legal apparatus of the European Human Rights Convention add exponentially to the breakdown of the old system. The Court of Justice of the EC can set aside national laws that conflict with Community law; Community law in the EC, like federal law under the U.S. Constitution, is supreme. National courts are required to refuse to apply national laws that conflict with Community law. They must refer questions of interpretation of Community law to the EC Court. National laws in violation of the European Human Rights Convention can be challenged before the European Commission and Court of Human Rights. Both the internal and the external sovereignty of the state have been decisively reduced. Internally, the growth of human rights and the recognition of group and class interests transfer sovereignty from the state to individuals, groups, and classes; externally, the growing authority of the EC and the European Human Rights Convention transfers sovereignty from the state to international bodies.

Contemplating these events, some observers draw an analogy with the medieval period, when Europe was united by the Roman civil law-canon law *jus commune*. They see the law of the EC and the European Human Rights Convention as the foundation of a new European *jus commune*, based on common culture and common interests, after centuries of exaggerated glorification of the nation-state. The fact that Great Britain, the mother country of the common law tradition, is a member of the EC and a party to the Convention suggests to them the possibility, indeed the necessity, of a rapprochement of the civil law and common law traditions. Although there have been difficulties and disappointments, European federalism is a lively and significant force with important consequences for contemporary civil law (and common law) systems.

Despite the apparently dramatic impact of movements toward decodification, constitutionalism, and federalism, it would be inaccurate to assume that the civil law tradition is losing its vitality. On the contrary, it may be more alive than ever. Just as it has been necessary in this book to speak of earlier major developments — the different lives and ages of Roman law; the vicissitudes of canon law; the independent rise, evolution, and eventual absorption of commercial law; the earthshaking events of the revolution; and the extraordinary intellectual structure achieved by legal science — so one day it will be necessary to add a sixth to the catalog of civil law subtraditions. We do not know what it will be called or how it will be described by future observers. We can, however, be reasonably confident that this oldest and most influential of the Western legal traditions has entered a new and dynamic stage of its development.

QUESTIONS

1. Of the three tendencies described by John Merryman — decodification, constitutionalization, and federalization — which do you believe is the most important in fundamentally changing the civil law tradition?

2. Can you think of any other tendencies that will significantly affect the civil law world?

3. Professor Merryman speaks of the sixth subtradition. What should it be called?

Table of Cases

References are to pages.

Argentina

Altini, 1113, n. 98
Argentine Military Leaders Case, 629
Chamudis, 1113, n. 111
Fiorentino, 1115, n. 127
Montenegro, 1114, n. 116
Rayford, 1116, n. 128

Canada

Regina v. Machekequonabe, 665, n. 24

Colombia

Caicedo Valencia, Arturo, 626
Miquirucama, Célimo, 664

France

Charles v. Desmares, 991
Decentralisation Case, 762
Decision of 3 September 1986, 767
Decision of 4 December 1973, 1042, n. 31
Decision of 4 March 1970, 995, n. 14
Decision of 11 June 1896, 993, n. 4
Decision of 12 January 1977, 766
Decision of 13 April 1934, 995, n. 12
Decision of 15 January 1960, 995, n. 13
Decision of 19 December 1980, 766
Decision of 20 February 1974, 1042, n. 30
Decision of 21 January 1919, 993, n. 6
Decision of 30 March 1897, 993, n. 5
Derguini v. Tidu, 996
France v. Klaus Barbie, 1080
Freedom of Association Case, 764
French Abortion Decision, 768
Huston v. Société d'Exploitation de la Cinquième Chaine, 720
Jand'heur, 994
Nationalisations Case, 762
Prefect of Loire v. Commerce Tribunal of Saint-Etienne, 733
Scotch Whisky Association v. S.A. Suprex, 989
Syndicat des Habitants des Couronneries v. Société Montenay, 1042, n. 28
Syndicat Général des Ingénieurs-Conseils, 735

Germany

Abortion Case, 782, 793
Application of Frau Kloppenburg, In re, 959
Atomic Weapons Referenda Case, 562
Deutschland Magazin Case, 794
Germany v. D and Y, 1087
Judgment of 4 June 1992, 101, n. 20
Judgment of 4 May 1964, 1037, n. 38
Judgments of 14 July 1988, 913
Judgment of 24 March 1976, 1032, n. 230
Judgment of 27 January 1987, 1086, n. 50
Klass Case, 776
Lüth Boycott Case, 783, 794
Numerus Clausus Case, 779
Siemens Aktiengesellschaft v. Bavaria, 141
Wyhl Atomic Energy Plant Case, 737
X Company v. Bavaria, 97

Italy

Bertett v. Italy, 797
Civil Liability of Judges Case, 712
Judgment of 1 February 1990, 1105, n. 119

Judgment of 3 July 1990, 1107, n. 171
Judgment of 24 March 1990, 1104, n. 115
Vera Norina Mameli Née Piercy v. Agency for Sardinian Agri. & Land Reform (E.T.F.A.S.), 1206

Japan

Abe v. Chiba, 1058
Aizawa v. Japan, 833
Arima v. Den'en Chofu Sky Mansion Y.K., 1227
Arima v. Den'en Chōfu Y.K., 1229
Daimaru Bessō Co. v. Takeishi, 1009
Decision of 18 March 1953, 822, n. 16
Decision of 20 January 1989, 825, n. 26
Decision of 21 June 1950, 822, n. 14
Decision of 22 November 1972, 823, n. 23
Fuji Kenchiku K.K. v. Kikuchi, 1229
H. Saeki, Inc. v. Osake, 96
Hashimoto v. City of Tokyo, 972
Hiraguchi v. Hiraguchi, 825, n. 29
Ikeda v. Kadoya, 1228
Japan v. Onda, 719
Japan v. Yamato, 833
K.K. Tōto Kigyō, 1229
Kiyota v. Yoshiyama, 1229
Kurokawa v. Chiba Prefecture Election Comm'n, 827
Lemme v. Wine of Japan, Inc., 96
Maruyama v. Ikejima, 1010
Matsumoto v. Japan (Itatsuke Air Base Case), 1010
Mitamura v. Suzuki, 1008
Nakamura v. Japan, 833
North Con I v. Katayama, 101
Obonai v. Orizume Sangyō Co., 1010
Park v. Fukuoka, 1055
Sakagami v. Japan, 833
Shimizu v. Japan (Fukuoka Bathhouse Case), 823, n. 22
Shimizu v. Osaka Election Comm'n, 830, n. 16
Suzuki v. City of Tokyo, 971
Takeda v. Japan, 720
Tokyo Metro. Election Comm'n v. Koshiyama, 830, n. 12
Uchino v. Kobayashi, 1010
United States v. Matsumura, 135
Watanabe v. Chisso K.K. [Kumamoto Minamata Disease Case], 1234
Yamagata Prefecture v. Y.K. Taira Shōji (Turkish Bath Case), 753
Yokoyama v. Japan, 720

Korea

Judgment of 8 October 1990, 835, n. 117
Judgment of 9 November 1990, 836, n. 140
Judgment of 13 May 1991, 835, n. 115
Judgment of 15 October 1990, 837, n. 146
Judgment of 20 November 1989, 836, n. 139
Judgment of 22 July 1991, 835, n. 134
Judgment of 24 May 1989, 835, n. 113
Judgment of 25 January 1989, 835, n. 114

Mexico

Beltran Collantes, Martha, 684
Bustamante, Natalio, 625
Ramírez Méndez, Enrique, 962

New Spain

Texcocan Villages v. Hacienda La Blanca, 390

Rome

Caecina v. Aebutius, 242

Spain

CIC Co. v. Spain, 956
Decision of 12 September 1988, 27
M v. E, 313

Order of Jesuits v. Spain, 980
Pantoja v. Prographic Co., 722
Spanish Abortion Decision, 802
Vizcaya v. Diputación Foral de Vizcaya, 597

Switzerland

Swiss Federal Attorney General v. A, 129

Tuscany

Fabronis v. Marradi Ball Players, 327

USA

Ackerman v. Levine, 199
Avianca, Inc. v. Corriea, 75
Bankston v. Toyota Motor Corporation, 93
Commerical Ins. Co. of Newark v. Pacific-Peru Constr. Corp., 117
Corporacion Salvadorena de Calzado (Corsal), S.A. v. Injection Footwear Corp., 184
Deshaney v. Winnebago County, 780
Diaz v. Southeastern Drilling Co. of Argentina, S.A., 164
Doan Thi Hoang Anh v. Nelson, 117
Dresdner Bank AG v. Edelmann, 117
Eastern Airlines, Inc. v. Floyd, 171
Farmland & Dev. Co. v. Toho Co., 179
Franklin v. Smalldridge, 105
Hilton v. Guyot, 198
Karaszewski v. Honda Motor Co., 92
Marbury v. Madison, 770
Marriage of Osborn, In re, 117
Nippon Emo-Trans Co. v. Emo-Trans, Inc., 193
Panama Processes, S.A. v. Cities Serv. Co., 206
Philp v. Macri, 104
Roberts v. Heim, 127
Roe v. Wade, 793
Ruff v. St. Paul Mercury Ins. Co., 110, n. 89
Santa Clara Pueblo v. Martinez, 656, n. 1
Société Nationale Industrielle Aérospatiale v. United States District Court, 149
Swiss Credit Bank v. Balink, 170
Teknekron Mgt. v. Quante Fernmeldetechnik, 92
United States v. Daneza, 80
Volkswagenwerk Aktiengesellschaft v. Schlunk, 85
Walpex Trading Co. v. Yacimientos Petroliferos Fiscales Bolivianos, 119
Williams v. Employers Liability Assur. Corp., 54

List of Foreign Abbreviations

Argentina	
Fallos	Fallos de la Corte Suprema de Justica de la Nación [the official Supreme Court reporter].
Colombia	
G.J.	Gaceta Judicial [the official source of Colombian court cases].
France	
Bull. Civ.	Bulletin des arrêts de la Cour de cassation, chambres civiles [the official Court of Cassation reporter for civil cases].
D. Jur. or D.	Recueil Dalloz [a predecessor to D.S. Jur.].
D.S. Jur.	Recueil Dalloz Sirey [a major unofficial source of French court cases].
Gaz. Pal.	Gazette du Palais [a major unofficial source of French court cases].
J.C.P. II	La Semaine Juridique, Juris-Classeur Periodique, Part II (Jurisprudence) [a major unofficial source of French court cases].
J.O.	Journal Officiel de la République Fran/Ccaise [an official source of French legal materials].
S. Jur. or S.	Recueil Sirey [a predecessor to D.S. Jur.].
Germany	
BVerfGE	Entscheidungen des Bundesverfassungsgerichts [the official reporter for the Constitutional Court].
NJW	Neue Juristische Wochenschrift [a major unofficial source of German court cases].
RiW	Recht der Internationalen Wirtschaft [a source of court cases affecting international business].
Italy	
Giur. Cost.	Giurisprudenza Costituzionale [a major unofficial source of constitutional court cases].
Giur. Ital.	Giurisprudenza Italiana [a major unofficial source of Italian court cases].
Giust. Civ.	Giustizia Civile [a major unofficial source of non-penal cases].

Japan

Hanji	Hanrei Jihō [a major unofficial source of Japanese court cases].
Kakyū Minshū	Kakyū Saibansho Minji Saibanreishū [the official reporter for lower court civil cases].
Keishū	Saikō Saibansho Keiji Hanreishū [the official reporter for Supreme Court criminal cases].
Minshū	Saikō Saibansho Minji Hanreishū [the official reporter for Supreme Court civil cases].

Mexico

S.J.F.	Semanario Judicial de la Federación [the official Supreme Court reporter].

Spain

R.J.	Repertorio de Jurisprudencia [a major unofficial source of Spanish court cases].

Switzerland

BGE IV	Entscheidungen des Schweizerischen Bundesgerichts, Part IV (Criminal) [the official source of Swiss court cases].

USA

I.L.M.	International Legal Materials [the principal U.S. source for foreign and international primary legal materials in translation].

Table of Tables

Table No.	Title	Page
4.1	Population of Latin America in 1830, by Country	372
4.2	Kinds of Cases Before the General Indian Court, Declarations of August-September 1784	394
4.3	Characteristics of the Adjudicative and Disciplinary Systems	408
6.1	Total Population (000,000), by Region and Year	535
6.2	Total Population (000,000), by Country and Year	535
6.3	World's Largest Metropolitan Areas in 1990, by Rank and Population (000,000)	536
6.4	Gross National Product Per Capita (in Constant 1989 US $), by Country and Year	536
6.5	Total Cases Filed in German Ordinary Courts in 1984, by Court and Type of Case	566
6.6	Total Cases Filed in German Specialized Courts in 1984, by Subject Matter and Court	567
6.7	Total Cases Filed in Italian Ordinary Courts in 1987, by Court and Type of Case	581
6.8	Total Cases Filed in Italian Administrative Courts in 1987, by Court	582
6.9	Total Civil Cases Filed in First Instance Courts in Europe, by Country and per 100,000 Population	599
6.10	Crime Rates (per 100,000 Population) in a German and an American State in 1981, by Type of Crime	601
6.11	The Mexican Chamber of Deputies (1988-1991), by Party Representation	619
6.12	Total Cases Filed in Japanese Courts in 1985, by Court and Type of Case	642
6.13	Categories of Complaints in Talea (1957-1968) by Type of Court	674
6.14	Cases from Talea Filed in the Villa Alta District Court (1953-1962), by Type	676
6.15	Criminal Cases Litigated in Provincial and Magistrates' Courts of Chiangmai in 1965 and 1974, by Type	690
6.16	Civil and Criminal Cases in Chiangmai Trial Courts, by Type of Result	691
7.1	Earliest Explicit or Implied Authorization of Judicial Review in Latin American Constitutions or Statutes by Country	806
7.2	Structural Determinants of Effective Judicial Review	809
7.3	Effectiveness of Judicial Review in Latin America, by Country	810

Table No.	*Title*	*Page*
7.4	Percentage of Cases Decided in Favor of the Nongovernmental Party in Mexican and United States Supreme Courts, by Subject Matter	813
7.5	Degree of Effectiveness of Judicial Review in Latin America	814
8.1	Total Number Law Students (in 000), by Country and Year	870
8.2	Percentage University Students in Law, by Country and Year	871
8.3	Percentage Women in Legal Education in Germany, by Position and Year	872
8.4	Total Number Law Students in Colombia, per 100,000 Population and as a Percentage of University Enrollment, by Year	883
8.5	Applicants Taking and Passing the Japanese National Legal Examination, by Year	887
8.6	Initial Positions Taken by Japanese LTRI Graduates, by Year	888
8.7	Percentage Distribution of Lawyers in the United States, Germany, Chile, and Colombia, by Position	898
8.8	Number of Lawyers in Private Practice (1990), per 100,000 Population and by Country	899
8.9	Number and Percentage of Lawyers in Germany and the United States (1985), by Type	900
8.10	Number of German Jurists in 1985, by Profession	912
8.11	Number of State and Federal Judges in Germany (1985), by Court	916
8.12	Number of Judges, Procurators, and Bengoshi in Japan, by Year	930
9.1	Civil Cases of the Mexican Supreme Court, by Year and the Basis of Decision	965
10.1	Court Costs and Attorney Fees for a $100,000 Claim, by Country and Level of Service Performed	1028
10.2	Civil Proceedings Filed in Japanese District Courts, by Type and Year	1057
10.3	Number of Lay Judges in the 1980s, by Jurisdiction	1092
10.4	Special Procedures of the New Italian Code of Criminal Procedure	1103
10.5	Disposition of Criminal Cases Processed by Japanese Public Prosecutors in 1987, by Type and Disposition	1120

Table of Figures

Figure No.	*Title*	*Page*
3.1	Map of Western Europe circa 1050	269
4.1	The Hierarchy of Legal Control in Inca Peru	353
4.2	Legal Organization of the Spanish Empire in America	367
4.3	Extension of the Spanish Viceroyalty System in America in 1800	368
6.1	Structure of the French Court System	550
6.2	Structure of the German Court System	565
6.3	Structure of the Spanish Court System	594
6.4	Total Civil Cases Filed in Europe and Latin America, 1945-1980s, by Country and per 100,000 Population	600
6.5	Structure of the Japanese Court System	639
6.6	Governmental Organization of Taiwan	651
6.7	Structure of the Taiwanese Judicial System	652
7.1	Effectiveness of Judicial Review and Economic Development in Latin America	815

Index

A

ACCOUNTABILITY OF JUDGES, pp. 712 to 720.

AFRICA.
Further reading, pp. 11, 12.
Religious legal traditions, p. 9.

AMERICAN INDIANS.
Accommodation of Spanish and Indian law, pp. 382 to 386.
Aztec legal system, pp. 360 to 362.
Inca legal system, pp. 352 to 360.
Mexico.
  General Indian court, pp. 393 to 398.
  Indian cases in the royal courts, pp. 386 to 393.
  Indian courts in rural Mexico, pp. 668 to 677.
Precolonial Latin America, pp. 351 to 363.
Witchcraft and legal pluralism in Latin America, pp. 656 to 668.

AMERICAS.
Latin America.
  See LATIN AMERICA.
United States.
  See UNITED STATES.

AMPARO.
Mexico, pp. 727, 728, 740 to 742.

APPEALS.
See JUDICIAL REVIEW.

ARGENTINA.
Criminal procedure, pp. 1111 to 1119.
Interpretation of the law, pp. 1004 to 1008.
Structure of legal system, pp. 614, 615.

ARREST.
Argentina, p. 1113.
Criminal procedure, p. 1069.

ASIA, EAST, pp. 399 to 433.
See EAST ASIA.

ATTORNEYS AT LAW.
Education.
  Generally, pp. 841 to 892.
    See LEGAL EDUCATION.
Generally, pp. 892 to 935.
  See LEGAL PROFESSIONS.
Jus commune.
  Demand for academic lawyers, pp. 326, 327.
  Learned lawyers in Castile, pp. 342, 343.

ATTORNEYS' FEES, pp. 1026 to 1029.

AZTEC LEGAL SYSTEM, pp. 360 to 362.

B

BRAZIL.
Civil procedure, pp. 1049 to 1054.
Intellectual revolution, pp. 467 to 470.
Judicial review, pp. 742 to 745.
Judiciary's development, pp. 379 to 381.
Legal culture, pp. 677 to 684.
Legal education, pp. 876 to 883.
Legal professions, pp. 920 to 925.
Portuguese settlement and legal system, p. 366.
Structure of legal system, pp. 615 to 617.

C

CAECINA CASE.
Roman civil law, pp. 242 to 244.

CANON LAW, pp. 294 to 316.
Case of M v. E, pp. 313 to 316.
Church and, pp. 294, 295.
Codex iuris canonici, pp. 310 to 313.
Contracts, pp. 303, 304.
Inheritance, pp. 300 to 302.
Introduction, pp. 217, 218.
Jurisdiction, pp. 298 to 308.
Marriage, pp. 299, 300.
  Codex iuris canonici, pp. 312, 313.
Papal government, pp. 308 to 310.
Procedure, pp. 305 to 307.
Property, pp. 302, 303.
Studies of, pp. 296, 297.

CHILE.
Codification, pp. 470 to 473.

CHINA.
Imperial Chinese tradition, pp. 405 to 416.
Taiwan.
  See TAIWAN.
Traditional Siam and China, pp. 400 to 405.

CIVIL CODE STRUCTURE, pp. 1156 to 1161.

CIVIL PROCEDURE, pp. 1013 to 1060.
Brazil, pp. 1049 to 1054.
France, pp. 1041 to 1044.
Germany, pp. 1029 to 1041.
Italy.
  Summary proceedings and other mechanisms to reduce delay, pp. 1045 to 1048.
Japan.
  Ordinary litigation and other types of proceedings, pp. 1054 to 1060.
Overview, pp. 1013 to 1029.
Types of civil proceedings, p. 1044.

CODEX IURIS CANONICI, pp. 310 to 313.

CODIFICATION AS A CONTINUING PROCESS, pp. 1149 to 1156.

COLOMBIA.
Codification, pp. 473 to 475.
Judicial review.
  Protection of constitutional and legal rights, pp. 742 to 745.
Legal education, pp. 872 to 876.
Structure of legal system, p. 617.

COMMERCIAL LAW, pp. 316 to 324.
Introduction, pp. 218, 219.
Partnerships and contracts, pp. 322 to 324.
The law merchant, pp. 316 to 322.

COMMON LAW.
Academic lawyers, demand for, pp. 326, 327.
"Ballgame" case, pp. 327 to 333.
Blackstone's comparative studies, p. 14.
Convergence and divergence with civil law, pp. 16 to 27.
European reception, pp. 325 to 349.
French reception, pp. 333 to 335.
German reception, pp. 335 to 338.
Italy.
  Note on Italy and the jus commune, pp. 325, 326.
Learned lawyers in Castile, pp. 342, 343.
Patria potestas, pp. 343 to 347.
Portuguese reception, p. 341.
Spanish reception, pp. 340, 341.
U. S. comparative study of law, pp. 15, 16.

COMPARATIVE LAW, pp. 1 to 69.
Common and civil law compared, pp. 14 to 27.
First look at the civil law tradition, pp. 54 to 66.
Functionalism in, p. 44.
Hortatory comparative law, pp. 48 to 50.
Japanese law, pp. 37 to 40.
Laboratories of comparative analysis, pp. 44 to 46.
Legal transplants, pp. 46, 47.
Major legal traditions, pp. 3 to 13.
Note on law and development, pp. 36, 37.
Note on "law" as legal rules and as legal systems, pp. 50 to 53.
Objectives, pp. 29 to 32.
Origins, pp. 28, 29.
Practice of transnational law, pp. 32 to 34.
Research in, pp. 66 to 69.
Scientific explanation, pp. 34 to 36.
What is, p. 1.
Why study, pp. 1, 2.

COMPENSATION LAWS IN EAST ASIA.
Judicial protection against government action, pp. 752 to 757.

CONFUCIANIST TRADITION IN YI KOREA, pp. 416 to 418.

CONSTITUTIONALISM.
Judicial review of legislative acts, pp. 757 to 760.

CONTRACTS.
Canon law, pp. 303, 304.
Commercial law, pp. 322 to 324.
Japan.
  Precontractual liability, pp. 1227 to 1230.

CORPUS JURIS CIVILIS.
Roman civil law, pp. 246 to 249.

COURT COSTS, pp. 1026 to 1029.

CREOLES.
Intellectual revolution in Latin America, pp. 458 to 462.

CRIME RATES.
Comparison among nations, pp. 601, 602.

CRIMINAL PROCEDURE, pp. 1060 to 1126.
Argentina, pp. 1111 to 1119.
Arrest, p. 1069.
Course of criminal proceeding from arrest to appeal, pp. 1066 to 1074.
Discovery, pp. 1069, 1070.
France.
  Investigation of offenses, pp. 1075 to 1080.
Germany.
  Lay judges, pp. 1091 to 1093.
  Plea bargaining, pp. 1082 to 1091.
Italy.
  Code of criminal procedure, pp. 1099 to 1109.
Japan, pp. 1119 to 1126.
Joinder of a civil plaintiff, pp. 1073, 1074.
Judges.
  Lay judges, pp. 1091 to 1098.
Juries, pp. 1091 to 1098.
Latin America, pp. 1109, 1110.
Overview, pp. 1060 to 1066.
Plea bargaining.
  Generally, pp. 1080 to 1082.
  Germany, pp. 1082 to 1091.
Pretrial detention, p. 1069.
Silence of defendant, pp. 1070 to 1072.

D

DEFENSES TO FOREIGN JUDGMENTS, pp. 199 to 212.

DEFENSOR DEL PUEBLO.
Spain, pp. 588, 589.

DISCOVERY, pp. 125 to 162.
Criminal procedure, pp. 1069, 1070.
Discovery in Japan for U. S. use, pp. 132 to 136.
Hague convention in France, pp. 149 to 162.
Hague convention in Germany, pp. 141 to 149.
Hague evidence convention, pp. 137 to 141.
Sensibilities and extraterritorial discovery, pp. 125 to 132.

DOCUMENTARY EVIDENCE OF FOREIGN LAW, pp. 164 to 170.

DOMINATE.
Roman civil law, pp. 225, 226.

E

EAST ASIA, pp. 399 to 433.
China.
  Imperial Chinese tradition, pp. 405 to 416.
  Traditional Siam and China, pp. 400 to 405.
Compensation laws, pp. 752 to 757.
Confucianist Yi Korea, pp. 416 to 418.
Economic data, pp. 536, 537.

EAST ASIA—Cont'd
Hindu-Buddhist tradition, pp. 399, 400.
Imperial Chinese tradition, pp. 405 to 416.
Indonesia.
  See INDONESIA.
Japan.
  See JAPAN.
Korea.
  See KOREA.
Legal culture and legal penetration, pp. 686 to 703.
Legal education, pp. 884 to 892.
Note on civil law tradition, pp. 6, 7.
Population data, pp. 535, 536.
Reception of European law in East Asia, pp. 507 to 534.
Siam.
  See THAILAND.
Sources of law, pp. 967, 968.
South Korea.
  See KOREA.
Structure of legal systems, pp. 635 to 656.
Taiwan.
  See TAIWAN.
Thailand.
  See THAILAND.

ECONOMIC DATA, pp. 536, 537.

EMANCIPATIO.
Roman civil law, pp. 261, 262.

EMOTIONAL DISTRESS.
French law, pp. 171 to 179.

ENCOMIENDA IN AMERICA, pp. 369, 370.

ENGLAND.
Resistance to Roman law, pp. 347 to 349.

EUROPE.
Canon law, pp. 294 to 316.
Civil law traditions before the revolution, pp. 213 to 350.
Commercial law, pp. 316 to 324.
Common law, pp. 325 to 349.
  See COMMON LAW.
Crime rates.
  Comparison among nations, pp. 601, 602.
England.
  Resistance to Roman law, pp. 347 to 349.
France.
  See FRANCE.
Germany.
  See GERMANY.
Italy.
  See ITALY.
Legal systems, pp. 535 to 602.
Litigation rates.
  Comparison among nations, pp. 599 to 602.
Medieval Europe, pp. 265 to 281.
Portugal.
  Reception of the jus commune, pp. 340, 341.
Roman civil law, pp. 213 to 265.
  See ROMAN CIVIL LAW.

EUROPE—Cont'd
Spain.
See SPAIN.

EVIDENCE.
Discovery within civil law countries, pp. 125 to 162.
Documentary evidence of foreign law, pp. 164 to 170.
Expert witnesses.
See EXPERT WITNESSES.

EXPERT WITNESSES, pp. 162 to 171.
Court-appointed experts, pp. 182 to 188.
Shubun in Japanese law, pp. 179 to 182.

F

FAMILY LAW.
Canon law of marriage, pp. 299, 300.
Codex iuris canonici, pp. 312, 313.
Jus commune, pp. 343 to 347.
Legal science.
Patria potestas, pp. 505 to 507.
Roman civil law, pp. 238 to 242.
Code of Justinian.
Concerning paternal control, pp. 257 to 259.
Digest of Justinian, pp. 259 to 261.
Justinian's institutes, pp. 255 to 257.
Society in legal change, pp. 261 to 265.

FEUDALISM, pp. 277 to 281.

FOREIGN COUNTRY JUDGMENTS.
Domestic enforcement, pp. 191 to 212.
Public policy defense and other defenses, pp. 199 to 212.
Uniform recognition act, pp. 192 to 199.

FOREIGN DEFENDANTS, SERVICE ON, pp. 73 to 103.
German defendants, pp. 97 to 103.
Hague service convention, pp. 81 to 93.
Interplay of service and jurisdiction, pp. 73 to 81.
Japanese defendants, pp. 93 to 96.

FOREIGN LAW.
Appellate resolution of issues, pp. 188 to 191.
Discovery within civil law countries, pp. 125 to 162.
See DISCOVERY.
Judicial notice statutes, pp. 108 to 118.
Judicial review.
Standards of review, pp. 190, 191.
Pleading.
Fact approach, pp. 103 to 107.
Failure to plead, pp. 107, 108.
Proving, pp. 162 to 188.
Summary judgment hearing, pp. 119 to 124.

FRANCE.
Administrative organization.
Structure of legal system, pp. 544 to 546.
Civil code, pp. 1161 to 1163.
Drafting, pp. 447 to 449.
Ideology, pp. 449 to 454.

FRANCE—Cont'd
Civil code—Cont'd
Influence of the French codes, pp. 453, 454.
Civil procedure, pp. 1041 to 1044.
Common law.
French reception, pp. 333 to 335.
Constitution.
Structure of legal system, pp. 537 to 544.
Constitutional council.
Judicial review of legislative acts, pp. 760 to 771.
Council of state.
Judicial review of executive and administrative acts, pp. 730 to 735.
Criminal procedure.
Investigation of offenses, pp. 1075 to 1080.
Drafting the civil code, pp. 447 to 449.
Hague evidence convention, pp. 149 to 162.
Ideology of the civil code, pp. 449 to 454.
Influence of the French codes, pp. 453, 454.
Interpretation of the law, pp. 983 to 998.
Judicial decisions.
Style and authority, pp. 948 to 951.
Judicial organization.
Structure of legal system, pp. 546 to 551.
Judicial review of executive and administrative acts.
French council of state and conflicts of jurisdiction, pp. 730 to 735.
Judicial review of legislative acts.
Constitutional council, pp. 760 to 771.
Jurisdictional conflicts.
Judicial review of executive and administrative acts, pp. 730 to 735.
Jus commune.
Reception in France, pp. 333 to 335.
Legal education, pp. 854 to 862.
Legal professions, pp. 902 to 908.
Legal scholarship in French courts, pp. 945, 946.
Lesion corporelle, pp. 171 to 179.
Parlements, pp. 436 to 440.
Structure of legal system, pp. 537 to 553.
Substantive categories of law, pp. 1136 to 1148.

FRENCH CIVIL CODE, pp. 1161 to 1163.
Drafting, pp. 447 to 449.
Ideology, pp. 449 to 454.
Influence of, pp. 453, 454.

FUNCTIONALISM IN COMPARATIVE LAW, p. 44.

FUTURE OF THE CIVIL LAW TRADITION, pp. 1241 to 1247.

G

GAIUS, INSTITUTES OF.
Roman civil law, p. 227.

GERMAN CIVIL CODE, pp. 1163 to 1175.

GERMANY.
Basic Law.
Structure of legal system, pp. 554 to 564.
Civil code, pp. 1163 to 1175.

GERMANY—Cont'd
Civil procedure, pp. 1029 to 1041.
Common law.
  German reception, pp. 335 to 338.
Constitution.
  Structure of legal system, pp. 554 to 564.
Constitutional rights and values.
  Judicial review of legislative acts, pp. 777 to 791.
Crime rates.
  Comparison among nations, pp. 601, 602.
Declaration of intention.
  Civil code, pp. 502, 503.
Federal constitutional court.
  Judicial review of legislative acts, pp. 771 to 795.
Hague evidence convention, pp. 141 to 149.
Ideology of the civil code, pp. 477 to 479.
Influence of German law in the United States, pp. 503, 504.
Interpretation of the law.
  "Flight into the general clauses," pp. 1001 to 1004.
Judges.
  Lay judges, pp. 1091 to 1093.
  Selection and accountability, pp. 912, 913.
Judicial decisions.
  Authority of decisions, pp. 951 to 953.
Judicial organization.
  Structure of legal system, pp. 564 to 568.
Judicial review of complex administrative decisions, pp. 735 to 740.
Judicial review of judicial acts.
  Multiple courts system, pp. 709 to 712.
Judicial review of legislative acts.
  Federal constitutional court, pp. 771 to 795.
Jus commune.
  Reception in Germany, pp. 335 to 338.
Lay judges, pp. 1091 to 1093.
Legal education, pp. 863 to 867.
Legal professions, pp. 908 to 912.
  Professional conduct rules, pp. 913 to 916.
Legal scholarship in German courts, pp. 946, 947.
Legal science, pp. 476 to 507.
  Elements, pp. 480 to 485.
  Ideology of the German civil code, pp. 477 to 479.
  Influence, pp. 493, 494.
    German law in the United States, pp. 503, 504.
  Introduction to law courses, pp. 494 to 502.
  Origins, pp. 485 to 492.
  Patria potestas, pp. 505 to 507.
  Scholars, pp. 480 to 485.
  Thibaut-Savigny debate, pp. 476, 477.
Multiple courts system.
  Judicial review of judicial acts, pp. 709 to 712.
Pandectist system, pp. 488 to 492.
Plea bargaining, pp. 1082 to 1091.
Reunification.
  Structure of legal system, pp. 553, 554.
Roman empire and the Roman church, pp. 273 to 277.
Romanticism, p. 477.
Service of process in, pp. 97 to 103.
Structure of legal system, pp. 553 to 569.

H

HAGUE EVIDENCE CONVENTION, pp. 137 to 141.
French evidence-taking, pp. 149 to 162.
German evidence-taking, pp. 141 to 149.

HAGUE SERVICE CONVENTION, pp. 81 to 93.

HINDU LAW, p. 8.
Further reading, p. 12.
Siam.
  Hindu-Buddhist tradition, pp. 399, 400.

HORTATORY COMPARATIVE LAW, pp. 48 to 50.

I

IBERIAN LAW.
Spread of law to Latin America, pp. 370 to 373.

INCA LEGAL SYSTEM, pp. 352 to 360.

INDIANS.
See AMERICAN INDIANS.

INDONESIA.
Dutch colonial rule.
  Reception of European law in East Asia, pp. 528 to 533.
Legal culture, pp. 686 to 688.
Legal education, p. 885.

INFORMED CONSENT.
Japan, pp. 1230 to 1234.

INHERITANCE.
Canon law, pp. 300 to 302.
Roman civil law, pp. 251 to 255.

INTELLECTUAL REVOLUTION, pp. 436 to 476.
Brazil, pp. 467 to 470.
Chile.
  Codification, pp. 470 to 473.
Colombia.
  Codification, pp. 473 to 475.
Elements, pp. 441 to 444.
European civil law traditions before the revolution, pp. 213 to 350.
France.
  Drafting the civil code, pp. 447 to 449.
  Ideology of the civil code, pp. 449 to 454.
  Influence of the French codes, pp. 453, 454.
  Intermediate law, pp. 447 to 449.
  Parlements, pp. 436 to 440.
Italy, pp. 454 to 457.
  Legislation of the Restoration, p. 456.
  Legislative policy before the French revolution, pp. 454, 455.
  Legislative unification, pp. 456, 457.
  Revolutionary and Napoleonic legislation, pp. 455, 456.
Latin America, pp. 458 to 463.
Mexico, pp. 463 to 467.
Natural law, pp. 444 to 447.
Spain, pp. 457, 458.

INTERPRETATION OF THE LAW, pp. 975 to 1011.
Argentina, pp. 1004 to 1008.

INTERPRETATION OF THE LAW—Cont'd
Certainty and equity, pp. 998 to 1001.
France, pp. 983 to 998.
Germany.
"Flight into the general clauses," pp. 1001 to 1004.
Italy, pp. 975 to 980.
Japan.
Abuse of right doctrine, pp. 1008 to 1011.
Judicial review of judicial acts, pp. 720 to 727.
Shubun in Japanese law, pp. 179 to 182.
Spain, pp. 980 to 983.

ISLAMIC LAW, p. 8.
Further reading, pp. 12, 13.

ITALIAN CIVIL CODE, pp. 1175 to 1184.

ITALY.
Case of Piercy v. E.T.F.A.S., pp. 1205 to 1226.
Civil code, pp. 1175 to 1184.
Civil procedure.
Summary proceedings and other mechanisms to reduce delay, pp. 1045 to 1048.
Common law.
Note on Italy and the jus commune, pp. 325, 326.
Constitutional court.
Judicial review of legislative acts, pp. 795 to 802.
Criminal procedure.
Code of criminal procedure, pp. 1099 to 1109.
Intellectual revolution, pp. 454 to 457.
Interpretation of the law, pp. 975 to 980.
Judicial review of legislative acts.
Constitutional court, pp. 795 to 802.
Legal education, pp. 867 to 869.
Legal professions, pp. 917, 918.
Government lawyers, pp. 925 to 928.
Property law, pp. 1191 to 1205.
Structure of legal system, pp. 569 to 585.

J

JAPAN.
Adaptability of Western law, pp. 518 to 520.
Ambivalent legal tradition, pp. 418 to 433.
Attitudes toward litigation, pp. 692 to 702.
Authority without power, pp. 420, 421, pp. 429 to 433.
Civil code, pp. 1187 to 1191.
Civil procedure.
Ordinary litigation and other types of proceedings, pp. 1054 to 1060.
Codification in Meiji Japan, pp. 509 to 515.
Comparison of law, pp. 37 to 40.
Compensation law, pp. 752 to 755.
Constitutional system, pp. 635 to 638.
Contracts.
Precontractual liability, pp. 1227 to 1230.
Criminal procedure, pp. 1119 to 1126.
Discovery in Japan for use in U. S., pp. 132 to 136.
Foreign enterprise in, pp. 930 to 935.
Foreign lawyers in practice, pp. 928 to 930.
Informed consent, pp. 1230 to 1234.

JAPAN—Cont'd
Institutional history.
  Note, pp. 418 to 420.
Interpretation of the law.
  Abuse of right doctrine, pp. 1008 to 1011.
Judicial decisions.
  Authority of decisions, pp. 968 to 973.
Judicial review.
  Limits on protection against administrative acts, pp. 745 to 752.
  Review of legislative acts.
    Supreme court, pp. 819 to 834.
Judicial system, pp. 639 to 642.
Legal education, pp. 885, 887 to 892.
Legal profession, pp. 928 to 935.
  Distribution of Japanese jurists, p. 930.
Legal science in Meiji Japan, pp. 509 to 515.
Litigation in Japanese courts, pp. 642 to 644.
Meiji constitution, pp. 515 to 518.
Negligence, pp. 1234 to 1239.
Service of process in, pp. 93 to 96.
Shubun, pp. 179 to 182.
Structure of legal system, pp. 635 to 645.
Substantive rules of law.
  Tort and contract law, pp. 1227 to 1240.
Supreme court.
  Judicial review of legislative acts, pp. 819 to 834.
Tokugawa law, pp. 422 to 428.

JAPANESE CIVIL CODE, pp. 1187 to 1191.

JEWISH LAW, pp. 8, 9.
Further reading, p. 13.

JOINDER OF CIVIL PLAINTIFF.
Criminal procedure, pp. 1073, 1074.

JUDGES.
Accountability of judges, pp. 712 to 720.
Germany.
  Lay judges, pp. 1091 to 1093.
  Selection and accountability, pp. 912, 913.
Independence of judiciary.
  Latin America, pp. 805 to 819.
Interpretation of the law, pp. 975 to 1011.
  See INTERPRETATION OF THE LAW.
Lay judges.
  Criminal procedure, pp. 1091 to 1098.

JUDGMENTS OF FOREIGN COUNTRIES.
Domestic enforcement, pp. 191 to 212.
Public policy defense and other defenses, pp. 199 to 212.
Uniform recognition act, pp. 192 to 199.

JUDICIAL DECISIONS.
France.
  Style and authority, pp. 948 to 951.
Germany.
  Authority of decisions, pp. 951 to 953.
Japan.
  Authority of decisions, pp. 968 to 973.
Mexico.
  Jurisprudencia, pp. 959 to 967.

JUDICIAL DECISIONS—Cont'd
Review generally.
See JUDICIAL REVIEW.
Spain.
Judicial lawmaking, pp. 954 to 959.
Stare decisis, pp. 947, 948.

JUDICIAL NOTICE OF FOREIGN LAW, pp. 108 to 118.

JUDICIAL PROCESS.
Interpretation of the law, pp. 975 to 1011.
See INTERPRETATION OF THE LAW.
Sources of law, judicial decisions and scholarly doctrine, pp. 937 to 974.

JUDICIAL REVIEW, pp. 705 to 839.
Accountability of judges, pp. 712 to 720.
Administrative and executive acts, pp. 729 to 757.
Brazil.
Judicial protection of constitutional and legal rights, pp. 742 to 745.
Colombia.
Judicial protection of constitutional and legal rights, pp. 742 to 745.
Constitutionalism.
Review of legislative acts, pp. 757 to 760.
East Asia.
Judicial protection against government action through compensation laws, pp. 752 to 757.
Executive and administrative acts, pp. 729 to 757.
Foreign law on appeal, pp. 189, 190.
France.
Conflicts of jurisdiction, pp. 730 to 735.
Constitutional council, pp. 760 to 771.
Council of state, pp. 730 to 735.
Germany.
Complex administrative law adjudication, pp. 735 to 740.
Federal constitutional court, pp. 771 to 795.
System of multiple courts, pp. 709 to 712.
Italy.
Constitutional court, pp. 795 to 802.
Japan.
Limits on protection against administrative acts, pp. 745 to 752.
Supreme court, pp. 819 to 834.
Judicial acts, pp. 708 to 729.
Korea.
Constitutional court, pp. 834 to 838.
Latin America.
Judicial review and its independence, pp. 805 to 819.
Legislative acts, pp. 757 to 839.
Maintaining the uniform interpretation of law, pp. 720 to 727.
Mexican amparo, pp. 740 to 742.
"Cassation" amparo, pp. 727, 728.
Resolution of foreign law issues on appeal, pp. 188 to 191.
Spain.
Constitutional court, pp. 802 to 805.
Standards of review of foreign law, pp. 190, 191.
Taiwan, pp. 838, 839.
Uniform interpretation of law, pp. 720 to 727.

JURIES.
Criminal procedure, pp. 1091 to 1098.

JUS COMMUNE.
See COMMON LAW.

JUSTINIAN, DIGEST OF, pp. 228, 246 to 249.
Family law, pp. 259 to 261.
Inheritance law, pp. 252, 253.

K

KOREA.
Compensation law in South Korea, pp. 755, 756.
Confucianist tradition in Yi Korea, pp. 416 to 418.
Constitutional court.
  Judicial review of legislative acts, pp. 834 to 838.
Japanese colonial rule.
  Reception of European law in East Asia, pp. 520 to 522.
Structure of legal system in South Korea, pp. 645 to 649.

L

LATIN AMERICA.
Accommodation of Spanish and Indian law, pp. 382 to 386.
Argentina.
  See ARGENTINA.
Aztec legal system, pp. 360 to 362.
Brazil.
  See BRAZIL.
Chile.
  Codification, pp. 470 to 473.
Colombia.
  See COLOMBIA.
Colonial times, pp. 364 to 399.
Constitutions.
  First Latin American constitutions, pp. 602 to 604.
Criminal procedure, pp. 1109, 1110.
Economic data, pp. 536, 537.
Executive dominance, pp. 604 to 613.
Iberian law, spread of, pp. 370 to 373.
Inca legal system, pp. 352 to 360.
Independence of nations, pp. 602 to 604.
Indian courts in rural Mexico, pp. 668 to 677.
Intellectual revolution, pp. 458 to 463.
Judicial review of legislative acts, pp. 805 to 819.
Judiciary and the military, pp. 626 to 635.
Judiciary's independence, pp. 805 to 819.
Legal culture and legal penetration, pp. 656 to 686.
Legal education, pp. 872 to 884.
Legal pluralism and witchcraft, pp. 656 to 668.
Litigation rates.
  Comparison among nations, pp. 599 to 601.
Mexico.
  See MEXICO.
Military and the judiciary, pp. 626 to 635.
Note on original American inhabitants, pp. 351, 352.
Peru.
  Judiciary's development, pp. 377 to 379.
  Spanish conquest, pp. 365, 366.
Population data, pp. 535, 536.

LATIN AMERICA—Cont'd
Precolonial times, pp. 351 to 363.
Separation of powers, pp. 625, 626.
Spanish legal system in America, pp. 366 to 368.
Structure of legal systems, pp. 602 to 635.
Witchcraft and legal pluralism, pp. 656 to 668.

LAW MERCHANT, pp. 316 to 322.

LAY JUDGES.
Criminal procedure, pp. 1091 to 1098.

LEGAL CULTURE AND LEGAL PENETRATION.
East Asia, pp. 686 to 703.
Latin America, pp. 656 to 686.

LEGAL EDUCATION, pp. 841 to 892.
Brazil, pp. 876 to 883.
Colombia, pp. 872 to 876.
Continental lawyers, pp. 841 to 847.
East Asia, pp. 884 to 892.
France, pp. 854 to 862.
Germany, pp. 863 to 867.
Indonesia, p. 885.
Italy, pp. 867 to 869.
Japan, pp. 885, 887 to 892.
Latin America, pp. 872 to 884.
Spain, pp. 869 to 872.
Taiwan, pp. 885, 886.
Thailand, pp. 885, 886.
U. S. compared with civil law countries, pp. 847 to 854.

LEGAL HUMANISM.
Roman civil law, pp. 291 to 294.

LEGAL PLURALISM AND WITCHCRAFT IN LATIN AMERICA, pp. 656 to 668.

LEGAL PROFESSIONS, pp. 892 to 935.
Brazil, pp. 920 to 925.
Common law countries compared with civil law countries, pp. 899 to 901.
France, pp. 902 to 908.
Germany, pp. 908 to 912.
  Professional conduct rules, pp. 913 to 916.
Government lawyers, pp. 925 to 928.
Italy, pp. 917, 918.
  Government lawyers, pp. 925 to 928.
Japan, pp. 928 to 935.
Legal education, pp. 841 to 892.
  See LEGAL EDUCATION.
Multiple professions, pp. 892 to 897.
Spain, pp. 918 to 920.
U. S. and civil law countries compared, pp. 897 to 899.

LEGAL SCHOLARSHIP, pp. 945 to 947.

LEGAL SCIENCE.
Germany, pp. 476 to 507.
  See GERMANY.
Meiji Japan, pp. 509 to 515.

LEGAL TRANSPLANTS, pp. 46, 47.

LEGITIM.
Roman civil law, pp. 251 to 255.

LESION CORPORELLE.
France, pp. 171 to 179.

LEX AQUILIA.
Roman civil law, pp. 249 to 251.

LITIGATING INTERNATIONAL CASES IN AMERICAN COURTS, pp. 71 to 212.

LITIGATION RATES.
Comparison among nations, pp. 599 to 601.
Thailand, pp. 688 to 692.

M

MARRIAGE.
Canon law, pp. 299, 300.
  Codex iuris canonici, pp. 312, 313.
Family law generally.
  See FAMILY LAW.

MASTERS.
Special masters, pp. 182 to 188.

MEDIEVAL EUROPE, pp. 265 to 281.
Complexity within the civil law tradition, p. 350.
Customary local law, pp. 268 to 273.
Decay of Roman law, pp. 265 to 268.
Feudalism, pp. 277 to 281.
Germanic Roman empire and the Roman church, pp. 273 to 277.

MENTAL DISTRESS.
French law, pp. 171 to 179.

MEXICAN CIVIL CODE, pp. 1184 to 1187.

MEXICO.
Amparo, pp. 727, 728, 740 to 742.
Civil code, pp. 1184 to 1187.
Codification, p. 467.
General Indian court, pp. 393 to 398.
Indian cases in the royal courts, pp. 386 to 393.
Indian courts in rural Mexico, pp. 668 to 677.
Intellectual revolution, pp. 463 to 467.
Judicial amparo, pp. 727, 728.
Judicial decisions.
  Jurisprudencia, pp. 959 to 967.
Judiciary, pp. 620, 622, 623.
  Evolution, pp. 374 to 377.
Legal culture, pp. 684 to 686.
Legislature, pp. 618 to 620.
Presidential power, pp. 620, 621.
Separation of powers, pp. 625, 626.
Spanish conquest, pp. 364, 365.
State and local government, pp. 621, 622.
Structure of legal system, pp. 618 to 625.

N

NATIVE-AMERICANS.
See AMERICAN INDIANS.

NATURAL LAW, pp. 444 to 447.

NEGLIGENCE.
Japan, pp. 1234 to 1239.
Roman civil law torts, pp. 249 to 251.

P

PANDECTIST SYSTEM.
German legal science, pp. 488 to 492.

PAPAL GOVERNMENT.
Canon law, pp. 308 to 310.

PARLEMENTS.
French judicary before the revolution, pp. 436 to 440.

PARTNERSHIPS.
Commercial law, pp 322 to 324.

PATRIA POTESTAS.
Jus commune, pp. 343 to 347.
Legal science, pp. 505 to 507.
Roman civil law, pp. 238 to 242, 255 to 265.

PECULIUM.
Roman civil law, pp. 262 to 265.

PERU.
Judiciary's development, pp. 377 to 379.
Spanish conquest, pp. 365, 366.

PLEA BARGAINING.
Generally, pp. 1080 to 1082.
Germany, pp. 1082 to 1091.

PLEADING OF FOREIGN LAW.
Fact approach, pp. 103 to 107.
Failure to plead, pp. 107, 108.

POPULATION DATA, pp. 535, 536.

PORTUGAL.
Reception of jus commune, pp. 340, 341.
Settlement and legal system in Brazil, p. 366.

PRETRIAL DETENTION.
Criminal procedure, p. 1069.

PRINCIPATE.
Roman civil law, pp. 224, 225.

PROCEDURE.
Canon law, pp. 305 to 307.
Civil procedure, pp. 1013 to 1060.
  See CIVIL PROCEDURE.
Criminal procedure, pp. 1060 to 1126.
  See CRIMINAL PROCEDURE.

PROPERTY LAW.
Canon law, pp. 302, 303.
Substantive rules of law, pp. 1191 to 1226.

PSYCHIC INJURIES.
French law, pp. 171 to 179.

PUBLIC POLICY DEFENSE TO FOREIGN JUDGMENTS, pp. 199 to 212.

R

RELIGIOUS LEGAL TRADITIONS.
Canon law.
See CANON LAW.
Note on, pp. 7 to 9.

ROMAN CIVIL LAW, pp. 213 to 265.
Caecina case, pp. 242 to 244.
Constitutional history, pp. 221 to 227.
Corpus juris civilis, pp. 246 to 249.
Dates in Roman legal history, pp. 220, 221.
Decay in medieval Europe, pp. 265 to 268.
Dominate, pp. 225, 226.
Edicts as sources of law, pp. 230 to 233.
Emancipatio, pp. 261, 262.
England's resistance, pp. 347 to 349.
Family law, pp. 238 to 242.
Code of Justinian.
Concerning paternal control, pp. 257 to 259.
Digest of Justinian, pp. 259 to 261.
Justinian's institutes, pp. 255 to 257.
Society in legal change, pp. 261 to 265.
Gaius, institutes of, p. 227.
Germanic Roman empire and the Roman church, pp. 273 to 277.
Inheritance law, pp. 251 to 255.
Introduction, pp. 213 to 217.
Juristic interpretations as sources of law, pp. 233 to 237.
Justinian, digest of, pp. 228, 246 to 249.
Family law, pp. 259 to 261.
Inheritance law, pp. 252, 253.
Legal humanism, pp. 291 to 294.
Legitim, pp. 251 to 255.
Lex aquilia, pp. 249 to 251.
Patria potestas, pp. 238 to 242, 255 to 265.
Peculium, pp. 262 to 265.
Principate, pp. 224, 225.
Republic, pp. 221 to 224.
Revival, pp. 281 to 294.
Sources of law, pp. 227 to 238.
Torts, pp. 249 to 251.
Trusts, pp. 254, 255.
Universities as the centers for the revival of Roman law, pp. 281 to 291.
Wealthy bias, pp. 245, 246.

S

SCHOLARLY DOCTRINE, pp. 945 to 947.

SERVICE OF PROCESS ON FOREIGN DEFENDANTS, pp. 73 to 103.
German defendants, pp. 97 to 103.
Hague service convention, pp. 81 to 93.
Interplay of service and jurisdiction, pp. 73 to 81.
Japanese defendants, pp. 93 to 96.

SHUBUN IN JAPANESE LAW, pp. 179 to 182.

SIAM.
See THAILAND.

SILENCE OF DEFENDANT.
Criminal procedure, pp. 1070 to 1072.

SOURCES OF LAW.
East Asia, pp. 967, 968.
Generally, pp. 937 to 944.
Impact of the regulatory state, p. 974.
Judicial decisions, pp. 947 to 973.
Roman civil law, pp. 227 to 238.
Scholarly doctrine, pp. 945 to 947.
Stare decisis, pp. 947, 948.

SOUTH KOREA.
See KOREA.

SPAIN.
Conquest of Mexico, pp. 364, 365.
Conquest of Peru, pp. 365, 366.
Constitutional court, pp. 587, 588.
  Judicial review of legislative acts, pp. 802 to 805.
Constitution of 1978, pp. 585 to 587.
Defensor del Pueblo, pp. 588, 589.
Intellectual revolution, pp. 457, 458.
Interpretation of the law, pp. 980 to 983.
Judicial lawmaking, pp. 954 to 959.
Judicial organization, pp. 592 to 595.
Judicial review of legislative acts.
  Constitutional court, pp. 802 to 805.
Jus commune.
  Reception, pp. 340, 341.
Languages, pp. 597, 598.
Legal education, pp. 869 to 872.
Legal professions, pp. 918 to 920.
Legal system in America, pp. 366 to 368.
Ombudsman, pp. 588, 589.
Regional government, pp. 589 to 592.
Structure of legal system, pp. 585 to 598.

SPECIAL MASTERS, pp. 182 to 188.

STARE DECISIS, pp. 947, 948.

STRUCTURE OF LEGAL SYSTEMS, pp. 535 to 703.
Argentina, pp. 614, 615.
Brazil, pp. 615 to 617.
Colombia, p. 617.
East Asia, pp. 635 to 656.
Europe, pp. 537 to 602.
France, pp. 537 to 553.
Germany, pp. 553 to 569.
Italy, pp. 569 to 585.
Japan, pp. 635 to 645.
Latin America, pp. 602 to 635.
Litigation rates.
  Comparison among nations, pp. 599 to 602.
Mexico, pp. 618 to 625.
South Korea, pp. 645 to 649.
Spain, pp. 585 to 598.
Taiwan, pp. 649 to 655.

SUBSTANTIVE RULES OF LAW, pp. 1127 to 1240.
Categories, pp. 1128 to 1136.
French legal categories, pp. 1136 to 1148.
Codification and the codes, pp. 1149 to 1191.
French legal categories, pp. 1136 to 1148.
Introduction, p. 1127.
Japanese tort and contract law, pp. 1227 to 1240.
Note on the registration of rights, pp. 1226, 1227.
Property law, pp. 1191 to 1226.

SUMMARY JUDGMENT HEARING.
Pleading or judicial notice of foreign law, pp. 119 to 124.

SUMMARY PROCEEDINGS IN ITALY, pp. 1045 to 1048.

T

TAIWAN.
Compensation law, p. 756.
Japanese colonial rule.
Reception of European law in East Asia, pp. 520 to 522.
Judicial review, pp. 838, 839.
Legal education, pp. 885, 886.
Structure of legal system, pp. 649 to 655.

THAILAND.
Law and tradition of Siam, pp. 400 to 405.
Legal education, pp. 885, 886.
Litigation rates, pp. 688 to 692.
Westernization and judicial reform, pp. 522 to 528.

THIBAUT-SAVIGNY DEBATE, pp. 476, 477.

TOKUGAWA LAW, pp. 422 to 429.

TORTS.
Japanese negligence, pp. 1234 to 1239.
Roman civil law, pp. 249 to 251.

TRUSTS.
Roman civil law, pp. 254, 255.

U

UNIFORM FOREIGN MONEY-JUDGMENTS RECOGNITION ACT, pp. 192 to 199.

UNIFORM INTERPRETATION OF LAW.
Judicial review of judicial acts, pp. 720 to 727.

UNITED STATES.
Crime rates.
Comparison among nations, pp. 601, 602.
Economic data, pp. 536, 537.
Encomienda in America, pp. 369, 370.
German law.
Influence in the United States, pp. 503, 504.
Legal education compared with civil law countries, pp. 847 to 854.
Legal professions.
Compared with civil law countries, pp. 897 to 899.
Legal scholarship in American courts, p. 946.
Litigating cases with foreign parties or foreign law issues, pp. 71 to 212.
Population data, pp. 535, 536.

UNITED STATES—Cont'd
Spanish legal system in America, pp. 366 to 368.

W

WITCHCRAFT AND LEGAL PLURALISM IN LATIN AMERICA, pp. 656 to 668.

WITNESSES, EXPERT.
See EXPERT WITNESSES.

① I know that there was a lot of emphasis on limiting judic[ial] power in France. How were ~~elected~~ judges procured in Fran[ce]? Were they all appointed to try and limit ~~[illegible]~~ the judiciary or were they elected, where any qualified person could run, or was there a mixture of both? 10/20

According to the text
② Court proceedings in Germany can ~~[illegible]~~ have an extremely long duration during which "large scale technical projects" can be frozen for up to ten years. ~~In the~~ Can that project then, if victorious, sue for money lost due to that freeze, like you can in the U.S.?

③ How often are expert witnesses rejected in German administrat[ive] law cases?

10/25/05

① How much of the German law is written? The book states that some judicial decisions are published ~~[illegible]~~ in the Federal Gazette ~~and other~~ ~~[illegible]~~ but I've noticed that many civil law ~~[illegible]~~ nations prefer customary, unwritten law and I wondered if German law held to that.

② Can you ~~[illegible]~~ ellaborate on the "objective order of values" that is mentioned on page 774? The text states that a liberal abortion law was struck down due to this "objective order of values" – what else has been struck down due to this order?

③ The German Bill of Rights ~~[illegible]~~ ~~[illegible]~~ not only outlines basic rights of German citizens but also impo[ses] duties upon those citizens. It seems that German law [has] taken on the task to affirmatively impose ~~duties~~ (mo[ral]) duties unto ~~[illegible]~~ their citizens. Is there a historical b[asis/] genesis of this high concern with moral obligations?

10/27/05

① The text states on page 781 that ~~[illegible]~~ may political commentato[rs] see the practice of religious instruction in schools as a "manifestation of free exercise of religion" and that the state must not favor one re[ligion] over another. How can ~~you~~ the German government refrain from ~~[illegible]~~ appearing to show favoritism for one religion over another without includi[ng] study of every religion in their curriculum?

② In the Luth Boycott case, it is stated that Luth violated Ar[t.] 826 of the Civil Code, namely that ~~his~~ ~~[illegible]~~ action offended "good m[orals]"